P9-BZW-552

CANNOT BE CHECKED OUT

DEMCO

# II CORINTHIANS

VOLUME 32A

THE ANCHOR BIBLE is a fresh approach to the world's greatest classic. Its object is to make the Bible accessible to the modern reader; its method is to arrive at the meaning of biblical literature through exact translation and extended exposition, and to reconstruct the ancient setting of the biblical story, as well as the circumstances of its transcription and the characteristics of its transcribers.

THE ANCHOR BIBLE is a project of international and interfaith scope: Protestant, Catholic, and Jewish scholars from many countries contribute individual volumes. The project is not sponsored by any ecclesiastical organization and is not intended to reflect any particular theological doctrine. Prepared under our joint supervision, THE ANCHOR BIBLE is an effort to make available all the significant historical and linguistic knowledge which bears on the interpretation of the biblical record.

THE ANCHOR BIBLE is aimed at the general reader with no special formal training in biblical studies; yet, it is written with most exacting standards of scholarship, reflecting the highest technical accomplishment.

This project marks the beginning of a new era of co-operation among scholars in biblical research, thus forming a common body of knowledge to be shared by all.

*William Foxwell Albright*
*David Noel Freedman*
GENERAL EDITORS

Adaptation of a tenth-century fresco in the St. Patroklus Church,
Naturns, Switzerland: "Paul's Flight from Damascus" (2 Cor 11:32–33).

THE ANCHOR BIBLE

# II CORINTHIANS

Translated with Introduction,
Notes, and Commentary by

VICTOR PAUL FURNISH

DOUBLEDAY & COMPANY, INC.
GARDEN CITY, NEW YORK
1984

Unless otherwise noted, ancient Greek and Latin authors are cited and quoted according to the Loeb Classical Library editions (Cambridge, Mass.: Harvard University Press, various dates and editors).

Quotations from *The Dead Sea Scrolls in English* by G. Vermes. Pelican Books, Second edition 1975. Copyright © 1962, 1965, 1968, 1975 by G. Vermes. Used by permission of Penguin Books Ltd.

Most texts from the Bible other than from II Corinthians are taken from the Revised Standard Version of the Bible, copyrighted 1946, 1952 © 1971, 1973. Used by permission of the National Council of Churches of Christ.

Quotations from *The Apocrypha and Pseudepigrapha of the Old Testament,* R. H. Charles, ed., 2 vols., Oxford University Press, copyright 1913. Used by permission of Oxford University Press.

Library of Congress Cataloging in Publication Data

Bible. N.T. Corinthians, 2nd. English. Furnish.
1984.
II Corinthians

(The Anchor Bible : v. 32A)
Bibliography: p. 58.
Includes index.
1. Bible. N.T. Corinthians, 2nd—Commentaries.
I. Furnish, Victor Paul.  II. Title.  III. Series:
Bible. English. Anchor Bible. 1964 ; v. 32A.
BS192.2.A11964.G3   vol. 32A 220.7′7s [227′.3077]
[BS2675.3]
ISBN: 0-385-11199-1

Library of Congress Catalog Card Number 83-2056
Copyright © 1984 by Doubleday & Company, Inc.
All Rights Reserved
Printed in the United States of America
First Edition

*In Memoriam*

**PAUL SCHUBERT (1900–69)**
**ERICH DINKLER (1909–81)**

Bookstore

1/60

26 Nov 84

69673

# PREFACE

My objective in this commentary has been to identify and discuss the major points and issues with which any serious reader of 2 Corinthians needs to be acquainted. The NOTES seek to clarify and explain the TRANSLATION by providing textual, lexical, and grammatical information. In addition, important parallels are cited and various geographical and historical data are presented. Many readers, however, will wish to turn first to the COMMENT, which is usually divided into two sections. In the first (COMMENT: GENERAL) the structure and theme(s) of the passage are identified, and in the second (COMMENT: DETAILED) they are analyzed and explicated.

The lengthy Select Bibliography and the numerous references throughout to the work of other scholars will show how much I am indebted to those who have engaged themselves with 2 Corinthians and with Paul's thought generally. Among the commentaries, that of Hans Windisch deserves special mention, for no other scholar, before or since, has probed 2 Corinthians so deeply and helpfully. Even though many of his judgments need to be revised in the light of more recent research, his commentary remains valuable for the questions it raises and for the materials it draws into the discussion. Among the more recent commentaries, that of C. K. Barrett is undoubtedly the most important. It is instructive even when it is not fully persuasive.

The publication of this commentary comes at the conclusion of my twenty-fifth year on the faculty of the Perkins School of Theology, Southern Methodist University. During this quarter century my understanding of the New Testament and, especially, of the Pauline letters has been enlarged and enriched by my students and colleagues. Among the latter, it is a pleasure to mention specifically Professors Harold Attridge, William Babcock, Phyllis Bird, John Deschner, Schubert Ogden, and James Ward—who, in various specific ways, have been of help to me as I have worked on 2 Corinthians. The excellent resources of Bridwell Library and the generous assistance of its staff—above all Page Thomas and Mary Lou Williams—have also been indispensable. In addition, Professor Kenneth Shields of SMU's Department of English offered helpful suggestions as I polished my translation of 2 Corinthians.

A major portion of the work on this commentary was accomplished during a research leave in 1979–80, supported jointly by the Perkins School of Theology and the Association of Theological Schools. I am also indebted to the American Council of Learned Societies for a grant that allowed me a month of intensive research on Roman Corinth at the American School of Classical Studies in Athens and at the site of Corinth itself. Drs. Charles K. Williams II and Nancy Bookidis, of the Corinth Excavations staff, and Professor James Wiseman, of Boston University, have kindly assisted me in understanding the site and its history.

Through Professor Edwin A. Judge of Macquarie University (Australia) I have been introduced to a number of ancient sources that help to illumine the sociocultural context of 2 Corinthians. He also introduced me to two other Australian scholars, Peter Marshall and Christopher Forbes, who graciously made their work available to me even before it was completely ready for publication.

The constant encouragement and help of Professor David Noel Freedman, the general editor of this series, have been invaluable, as have the interest shown in the project and the help provided for it by Eve F. Roshevsky of Doubleday & Company, Inc., and in the later stages also by her assistant, Jill Grundfest. Without the stenographic skills of Bonnie Jordan and Mary Ann Marshall the completion of this commentary would have taken much longer, and without the patient endurance exhibited by Jody, Brianna, and Rebecca, it could not have been completed at all.

Finally, the dedication page of this book will suggest how deeply I am indebted to two of my teachers at Yale. Paul Schubert, whose enthusiasm for Paul and commitment to thorough, critical exegesis has left a lasting imprint on my own career, was my *Doktorvater* in more than one sense. Erich Dinkler, in whose seminar on New Testament theology I gained my first real understanding of Rudolf Bultmann's contributions to New Testament study, helped me learn the importance of rigorous theological analysis. Each, in his own way, experienced the profound truth of the Lord's word to the apostle (2 Cor 12:9a): *arkei soi hē charis mou, hē gar dynamis en astheneia teleitai.*

VICTOR PAUL FURNISH
*Perkins School of Theology*
*Southern Methodist University*
*Dallas, Texas*

# CONTENTS

# LIST OF ILLUSTRATIONS

*Figure 1* (page 5): The Isthmus, Corinth, and Environs. Adapted from a map published in James R. Wiseman, *The Land of the Ancient Corinthians,* Studies in Mediterranean Archaeology 50 (Göteborg: Åströms, 1978), p. 44, and used here by permission of the author. (The map was originally drawn by G. v. Peschke and revised by Richard Trimble on the basis of notes by Professor Wiseman.)

*Figure 2* (page 11): Corinth, Central Area, ca. 50 C.E.

*Figure 3* (page 23): Rome's Aegean Provinces.

I. Corinth, Central Area, ca. 50 C.E.

II. Lechaeum Road (Fig. 2, No. 8), looking south toward the monumental arch (Fig. 2, No. 12) and the Forum, with Acrocorinth in the background. *Photo: I. Ioannidou and L. Bartziotou; courtesy American School of Classical Studies, Corinth Excavations.*

III. Corinth, central area, looking north toward Lechaeum and the Gulf of Corinth. The *Bouleutērion* (council chamber) is in the foreground (see Fig. 2, No. 29), and the Archaic Temple (see Fig. 2, No. 3) is in the background. *Photo: I. Ioannidou and L. Bartziotou; courtesy American School of Classical Studies, Corinth Excavations.*

IV. Archaic Temple (sixth century B.C.E.), viewed from the southeast, with the Northwest Stoa in the foreground (Fig. 2, Nos. 3 and 6). *Photo: I. Ioannidou and L. Bartziotou; courtesy American School of Classical Studies, Corinth Excavations.*

V. Cenchreae (Kenchreai): the harbor viewed from the south mole (see Fig. 1), with remains of the Isis sanctuary/Christian basilica in the foreground. *Photo: Victor Paul Furnish.*

VIa. Erastus inscription ("Erastus in return for his aedileship laid [the pavement] at his own expense") in situ in the pavement east of the scene building of the theater (Fig. 2, No. 1); second half of the first century C.E. *Photo: I. Ioannidou and L. Bartziotou; courtesy American School of Classical Studies, Corinth Excavations.*

VIb. Synagogue inscription ("Synagogue of the Hebrews"), perhaps as late as the fourth century C.E. *Photo: I. Ioannidou and L. Bartziotou; courtesy American School of Classical Studies, Corinth Excavations.*

# PRINCIPAL ABBREVIATIONS

[*Note:* Abbreviations for the books of the Bible, the Apocrypha, and the Apostolic Fathers have not been included, since these are generally known.]

| | |
|---|---|
| AB | The Anchor Bible (Garden City: Doubleday) |
| ᶜ*Abod. Zar.* | ᶜ*Aboda Zara* |
| ᵓ*Abot R. Nat.* | ᵓ*Abot de Rabbi Nathan* |
| AER | *American Ecclesiastical Review* |
| AF | *The Apostolic Fathers: A New Translation and Commentary,* ed. Robert M. Grant, 6 vols. (New York: Nelson, 1964–68) |
| AGJU | Arbeiten zur Geschichte des antiken Judentums und des Urchristentums (Leiden: Brill) |
| AGRL | Aspects of Greek and Roman Life (Ithaca, N.Y.: Cornell Univ. Press) |
| *AJP* | *American Journal of Philology* |
| AnBib | Analecta Biblica (Rome: Pontifical Biblical Institute) |
| *ANF* | *The Ante-Nicene Fathers,* eds. A. Roberts and J. Donaldson, 10 vols. (repr. New York: Scribner's, 1925) |
| *ANRW* | *Aufstieg und Niedergang der römischen Welt. Geschichte und Kultur Roms im Spiegel der neueren Forschung,* eds. H. Temporini and W. Haase (Berlin and New York: de Gruyter, 1972–) |
| Apoc Abr | Apocalypse of Abraham |
| 2–3 Apoc Bar | Syriac, Greek Apocalypse of Baruch |
| Apoc Mos | Apocalypse of Moses |
| Apoc Paul | Apocalypse of Paul |
| *APOT* | *Apocrypha and Pseudepigrapha of the Old Testament,* ed. R. H. Charles, 2 vols. (Oxford: Clarendon, 1913) |
| *Arch* | *Archaeology* |
| ASCSA | American School of Classical Studies in Athens |
| As Mos | Assumption of Moses |
| ASNU | Acta Seminarii neotestamentici upsaliensis (Uppsala: Almqvist & Wiksells) |
| *ASV* | *The Holy Bible,* newly edited by the American Revision Committee A.D. 1901, standard ed. (New York: Nelson, 1901) |
| *AT* | *The New Testament in the Language of Today,* translated by W. F. Beck (St. Louis, Mo.: Concordia, 1963) |
| ATANT | Abhandlungen zur Theologie des Alten und Neuen Testaments (Zürich: Zwingli) |
| *AusBR* | *Australian Biblical Review* |

| | |
|---|---|
| *AUSS* | *Andrews University Seminary Studies* |
| *b.* | Prefixed to a rabbinic tractate; indicates the Babylonian Talmud |
| *BA* | *Biblical Archaeologist* |
| BAG | Walter Bauer, *A Greek-English Lexicon of the New Testament and Other Early Christian Literature,* translated and adapted by W. F. Arndt and F. W. Gingrich; 2nd ed. revised and augmented by F. W. Gingrich and F. W. Danker (Chicago: Univ. of Chicago Press, 1979) |
| BBB | Bonner Biblische Beiträge (Bonn: Hanstein) |
| *BC* | *The Beginnings of Christianity,* eds. F. J. Foakes-Jackson and Kirsopp Lake, 5 vols. (repr. Grand Rapids, Mich.: Baker, 1979) |
| BDF | Friedrich Blass and Albert Debrunner, *A Greek Grammar of the New Testament and Other Early Christian Literature,* translated and revised by R. W. Funk (Chicago: Univ. of Chicago Press, 1961) |
| BEvT | Beiträge zur evangelischen Theologie (München: Evangelischer Verlag) |
| BFCT | Beiträge zur Förderung christlicher Theologie (Gütersloh: Bertelsmann) |
| BGBE | Beiträge zur Geschichte der biblischen Exegese (Tübingen: Mohr) |
| BGU | *Ägyptische Urkunden aus den Museen zu Berlin: Griechische Urkunden I–VIII* (Berlin: Königliche [Staatliche] Museen, 1895–1933) |
| BHT | Beiträge zur historischen Theologie (Tübingen: Mohr) |
| *Bib* | *Biblica* |
| BibS(N) | Biblische Studien (Neukirchen-Vluyn: Neukirchener Verlag) |
| *BT* | *The Bible Translator* |
| *BTS* | *Bible et terre sainte* |
| BU | Biblische Untersuchungen (Regensburg: Pustet) |
| *BZ* | *Biblische Zeitschrift* |
| BZNW | Beihefte zur Zeitschrift für die neutestamentliche Wissenschaft (Giessen/Berlin: Töpelmann) |
| CBC | The Cambridge Bible Commentary (Cambridge: Cambridge Univ. Press) |
| *CBQ* | *Catholic Biblical Quarterly* |
| CD | Cairo (Genizah) text of the Damascus Document |
| CG | Coptic Gnostic library from Nag Hammadi |
| CGNTC | Cambridge Greek New Testament Commentary (Cambridge: Cambridge Univ. Press) |
| *CIG* | *Corpus Inscriptionum Graecarum* (Berlin: Deutsche Akademie der Wissenschaften, 1828–77) |
| ConB | Coniectanea Biblica (Lund: Gleerup) |
| *ConNT* | *Coniectanea neotestamentica* |
| Corinth | Corinth (published by the American School of Classical Studies in Athens, 1929–; 1929–43, Cambridge, Mass.; thereafter, Princeton, N.J.) |
| *CRINT* | *Compendia Rerum Iudaicarum ad Novum Testamentum,* eds. S. Safrai and M. Stern, 2 vols. (Assen: Van Gorcum, 1974–76) |

| | |
|---|---|
| *CTM* | *Concordia Theological Monthly* |
| *CurTM* | *Currents in Theology and Mission* |
| DM | H. E. Dana and Julius R. Mantey, *A Manual Grammar of the Greek New Testament* (New York: Macmillan, 1927) |
| ÉBib | Études bibliques (Paris: Gabalda) |
| 1-2-3 Enoch | Ethiopic, Slavonic, Hebrew Enoch |
| Ep Arist | Epistle of Aristeas |
| ÉPRO | Études préliminaires aux religions orientales dans l'Empire romain, ed. M. J. Vermaseren (Leiden: Brill) |
| *ETL* | *Ephemerides theologicae lovanienses* |
| *ÉTR* | *Études théologiques et religieuses* |
| *EvQ* | *Evangelical Quarterly* |
| *EvT* | *Evangelische Theologie* |
| *ExpTim* | *Expository Times* |
| FRLANT | Forschungen zur Religion und Literatur des Alten und Neuen Testaments (Göttingen: Vandenhoeck & Ruprecht) |
| FTS | Freiburger theologische Studien (Freiburg: Herder) |
| Gdspd. | *The Bible: An American Translation;* the Old Testament translated by various scholars under the editorship of J. M. Powis Smith; the New Testament translated by Edgar J. Goodspeed (Chicago: Univ. of Chicago Press, 1935) |
| *GAGNT* | *A Grammatical Analysis of the Greek New Testament;* Vol. II: *Epistles—Apocalypse,* by Max Zerwick and Mary Grosvenor (Rome: Biblical Institute, 1979) |
| *GNT* | *The Greek New Testament,* 3rd ed., eds. K. Aland et al. (New York: United Bible Societies, 1975) |
| *GNTG* | *Grammar of New Testament Greek,* by James H. Moulton, Wilbert F. Howard, and Nigel Turner, 4 vols. (Edinburgh: Clark; vol. I [3rd ed.], 1908; vol. II, 1919–29; vol. III, 1963; vol. IV, 1976) |
| *GRBS* | *Greek, Roman and Byzantine Studies* |
| GTA | Göttingen theologische Arbeiten (Göttingen: Vandenhoeck & Ruprecht) |
| GTS | Gettysburg Theological Studies (Leiden: Brill) |
| *Hag* | *Hagiga* |
| HDB | James Hastings, ed., *A Dictionary of the Bible,* 5 vols. (New York: Scribner's, 1902) |
| Hermeneia | Hermeneia—A Critical and Historical Commentary on the Bible (Philadelphia: Fortress) |
| *Hesp* | *Hesperia* |
| HespSup | Supplementary volumes to *Hesp* (Princeton, N.J.: ASCSA) |
| HNT | Handbuch zum Neuen Testament (Tübingen: Mohr) |
| HNTC | Harper's New Testament Commentary (New York: Harper & Row) |
| HSW | Edgar Hennecke, *New Testament Apocrypha,* ed. W. Schneemelcher, 2 vols.; English tr. edited by R. McL. Wilson (Philadelphia: Westminster, 1963–64) |

| | |
|---|---|
| HTKNT | Herder's theologischer Kommentar zum Neuen Testament (Freiburg-Basel-Wien: Herder) |
| *HTR* | *Harvard Theological Review* |
| HUT | Hermeneutische Untersuchungen zur Theologie (Tübingen: Mohr) |
| *IBS* | *Irish Biblical Studies* |
| ICC | The International Critical Commentary on the Holy Scriptures of the Old and New Testaments (Edinburgh: Clark) |
| *IDB, IDBSup* | *The Interpreter's Dictionary of the Bible,* eds. G. A. Buttrick et al., 4 vols. (Nashville, Tenn.: Abingdon, 1962; supplementary vol. edited by K. Crim et al., 1976) |
| *Int* | *Interpretation* |
| *ISBE* | *The International Standard Bible Encyclopedia,* eds. Geoffrey W. Bromiley et al., 4 vols. (Grand Rapids, Mich.: Eerdmans, 1979–) |
| Isthmia | Isthmia (Princeton: ASCSA) |
| *ITQ* | *Irish Theological Quarterly* |
| *JAAR, JAARSup* | *Journal of the American Academy of Religion,* and Supplements |
| JAC | Jahrbuch für Antike und Christentum (Münster: Aschendorff) |
| JB | *The Jerusalem Bible* (London: Darton, Longman & Todd, 1966) |
| *JBL* | *Journal of Biblical Literature* |
| *JBR* | *Journal of Bible and Religion* |
| *JRH* | *Journal of Religious History* |
| *JRS* | *Journal of Roman Studies* |
| *JSNT* | *Journal for the Study of the New Testament* |
| JSNTSup | Supplementary volumes to *JSNT* (Sheffield: Journal for the Study of the Old Testament) |
| *JSS* | *Journal of Semitic Studies* |
| *JTC* | *Journal for Theology and the Church* |
| *JTS* | *Journal of Theological Studies* |
| Jub | Jubilees |
| *KD* | *Kerygma und Dogma* |
| KEK | Kritisch-Exegetischer Kommentar über das Neue Testament (Göttingen: Vandenhoeck & Ruprecht) |
| Kenchreai | Kenchreai: Eastern Port of Corinth (Leiden: Brill) |
| *KJV* | King James Version |
| LSJ | Henry G. Liddell and Robert Scott, *A Greek-English Lexicon,* revised and augmented by H. S. Jones, with the assistance of R. McKenzie (Oxford: Clarendon, 1940) |
| LXX | Alfred Rahlfs, ed., *Septuaginta,* 5th ed., 2 vols. (Stuttgart: Privileg. Württ., 1952) |
| MM | James H. Moulton and George Milligan, *The Vocabulary of the Greek Testament Illustrated from the Papyri and Other Non-Literary Sources* (London: Hodder & Stoughton, 1930) |
| MNTC | The Moffatt New Testament Commentary (New York and London: Harper) |
| Mof. | James Moffatt, *The New Testament in the Moffatt Translation* (repr. of the revised ed.; London: Hodder & Stoughton, 1953) |

| | |
|---|---|
| MTS | Münchener theologische Studien (München: Kommissionsverlag Karl Zink) |
| *NAB* | *The New American Bible* (New York: Kenedy, 1970) |
| NCB | New Century Bible Commentary (Grand Rapids, Mich.: Eerdmans) |
| *NEASB* | *Near Eastern Archaeological Society Bulletin* |
| *NEB* | *The New English Bible with the Apocrypha* (Oxford and Cambridge: Univ. Presses, 1970) |
| Nestle | *Novum Testamentum Graece,* succeeding E. and E. Nestle; 26th ed. unless otherwise specified; eds. K. Aland et al. (Stuttgart: Deutsche Bibelstiftung, 1979) |
| *NHLE* | *The Nag Hammadi Library in English,* translated by various scholars under the direction of James Robinson (San Francisco: Harper & Row, 1977) |
| NICNT | New International Commentary on the New Testament (Grand Rapids, Mich.: Eerdmans) |
| *NIV* | *The Holy Bible. New International Version* (Grand Rapids, Mich.: Zondervan, 1978) |
| *NKZ* | *Neue Kirchliche Zeitschrift* |
| *NovT* | *Novum Testamentum* |
| NovTSup | Supplementary volumes to *NovT* (Leiden: Brill) |
| *NPNF* | *A Select Library of Nicene and Post-Nicene Fathers of the Christian Church,* eds. P. Schaff [and H. Wace], 24 vols. (New York: Christian Literature Co. [and Scribner's], 1886–1900) |
| NT | New Testament |
| NTAbh | Neutestamentliche Abhandlungen (Münster: Aschendorff) |
| NTD | Das Neue Testament Deutsch (Göttingen: Vandenhoeck & Ruprecht) |
| *NTS* | *New Testament Studies* |
| *NTT* | *Norsk Teologisk Tidsskrift* |
| NTTS | New Testament Tools and Studies (Grand Rapids, Mich.: Eerdmans) |
| NumenSup | Supplementary volumes to *Numen* (Leiden: Brill) |
| *OCD* | *Oxford Classical Dictionary,* 2nd ed., eds. N. G. L. Hammond and H. Scullard (Oxford: Clarendon, 1970) |
| Odes Sol | Odes of Solomon |
| *OGI* | *Orientis Graeci Inscriptiones Selectae,* ed. W. Dittenberger (Leipzig: 1903–5) |
| OT | Old Testament |
| *Pesiq. Rab Kah.* | *Pesiqta de Rab Kahana* |
| POxy | Oxyrhynchus Papyrus (cited according to the enumeration and quoted in the translations in *The Oxyrhynchus Papyri,* published under the direction of various editors by the Egypt Exploration Fund [Society]; London, 1899–) |
| Ps. | Pseudo |
| Pss Sol | Psalms of Solomon |

| | |
|---|---|
| PTMS | Pittsburgh Theological Monograph Series (Pittsburgh: Pickwick) |
| PW, PWSup | *Paulys Real-Encyclopädie der classischen Altertumswissenschaft,* and supplementary volumes, ed. G. Wissowa (Stuttgart: Metzler, 1894–) |
| 1Q, 2Q, etc. | Numbered caves of Qumran, followed by abbreviation of ms. cited |
| *Rab.* | *Rabbah* |
| *RAC* | *Reallexikon für Antike und Christentum,* ed. T. Klauser (Leipzig: Hiersemann, 1941–) |
| *RB* | *Revue biblique* |
| RechBib | Recherches bibliques (Louvain: Desclée de Brouwer) |
| *RefThRev* | *Reformed Theological Review* |
| *RestQ* | *Restoration Quarterly* |
| *RevQ* | *Revue de Qumran* |
| *RevScRel* | *Revue des sciences religieuses* |
| *RGG* | *Die Religion in Geschichte und Gegenwart,* 3rd ed., ed. K. Galling, 7 vols. (Tübingen: Mohr, 1957–65) |
| *RHPR* | *Revue d'histoire et de philosophie religieuses* |
| *RHR* | *Revue de l'histoire des religions* |
| *RSV* | *Revised Standard Version Bible* (copyrighted 1973 by the Division of Christian Education of the National Council of Churches) |
| *RTP* | *Revue de théologie et de philosophie* |
| *Šabb.* | *Šabbat* |
| *Sanh.* | *Sanhedrin* |
| SANT | Studien zum Alten und Neuen Testament (München: Kösel-Verlag) |
| SBLDS | Society of Biblical Literature Dissertation Series (Missoula, Mont./Chico, Calif.: Scholars Press) |
| SBLSBS | Society of Biblical Literature Sources for Biblical Study (Missoula, Mont./Chico, Calif.: Scholars Press) |
| SBLTT | Society of Biblical Literature Texts and Translations (Missoula, Mont./Chico, Calif.: Scholars Press) |
| SBT | Studies in Biblical Theology (Naperville, Ill.: Allenson) |
| SCHNT | Studia ad Corpus Hellenisticum Novi Testamenti (Leiden: Brill) |
| SD | Studies and Documents (Grand Rapids, Mich.: Eerdmans, 1977–; various places and publishers 1934–) |
| SEÅSup | Supplementary volumes to *Svensk Exegetisk Årsbok* (Uppsala: Wretmans) |
| *Semeia* | *Semeia: An Experimental Journal for Biblical Criticism* |
| SJLA | Studies in Judaism in Late Antiquity (Leiden: Brill) |
| SNT | Studien zum Neuen Testament (Gütersloh: Gütersloher Verlagshaus) |
| SNTSMS | Society for New Testament Studies Monograph Series (Cambridge: Cambridge Univ. Press) |
| SO | Symbolae osloenses (Oslo: Societatis graeco-latinae) |
| SPB | Studia post-biblica (Leiden: Brill) |
| S.P.C.K. | Society for the Promotion of Christian Knowledge |

| | |
|---|---|
| *ST* | *Studia theologica* |
| Str-B | [H. L. Strack and] P. Billerbeck, *Kommentar zum Neuen Testament aus Talmud und Midrasch*, 6 vols. (München: Beck, 1922–56) |
| *StudCath* | *Studia Catholica* |
| Studia | Studia: Travaux de recherche (Bruxelles-Paris-Montreal: Brouwer/Bellarmin) |
| SUNT | Studien zur Umwelt des Neuen Testaments (Göttingen: Vandenhoeck & Ruprecht) |
| T 12 Patr | Testaments of the Twelve Patriarchs |
| T Abr | Testament of Abraham |
| T Job | Testament of Job |
| T Judah | Testament of Judah |
| T Levi | Testament of Levi |
| T Zeb | Testament of Zebulon |
| *TBl* | *Theologische Blätter* |
| TBü | Theologische Bücherei (München: Kaiser) |
| *TDNT* | Gerhard Kittel and Gerhard Friedrich, eds., *Theological Dictionary of the New Testament* (translated and edited by G. W. Bromiley), 10 vols. (Grand Rapids, Mich.: Eerdmans, 1964–76) |
| *TEV* | *Good News Bible. The Bible in Today's English Version* (New York: American Bible Society, 1976) |
| TF | Theologische Forschung (Hamburg-Bergstedt: Evangelischer Verlag) |
| Theophaneia | Theophaneia (Bonn: Hanstein) |
| *TLZ* | *Theologische Literaturzeitung* |
| TNTC | The Tyndale New Testament Commentaries (Grand Rapids, Mich.: Eerdmans) |
| *TQ* | *Theologische Quartalschrift* |
| *TS* | *Theological Studies* |
| *TSK* | *Theologische Studien und Kritiken* |
| TU | Texte und Untersuchungen (Berlin: Akademie-Verlag) |
| *TyndB* | *Tyndale Bulletin* |
| *TZ* | *Theologische Zeitschrift* |
| UNT | Untersuchungen zum Neuen Testament (Leipzig: Hinrichs) |
| Wey. | Richard Francis Weymouth, *The New Testament in Modern Speech*, 6th ed. (London: Clarke, n.d.) |
| WH | B. F. Westcott and F. J. A. Hort, *The New Testament in the Original Greek* (London: Macmillan, 1900) |
| WMANT | Wissenschaftliche Monographien zum Alten und Neuen Testament (Neukirchen-Vluyn: Neukirchener Verlag) |
| WUNT | Wissenschaftliche Untersuchungen zum Neuen Testament (Tübingen: Mohr) |
| *Yebam.* | *Yebamot* |
| *ZDPV* | *Zeitschrift des deutschen Palästina-Vereins* |
| *ZNW* | *Zeitschrift für die neutestamentliche Wissenschaft* |
| *ZTK* | *Zeitschrift für Theologie und Kirche* |

## OTHER ABBREVIATIONS

| | |
|---|---|
| B.C.E. | Before the Common Era ( = B.C.) |
| bibliog. | bibliography |
| ca. | circa |
| C.E. | Common Era ( = A.D.) |
| cf. | compare |
| ed., eds. | editor, editors; edition, editions |
| et al. | *et alii* (and others) |
| mg. | marginal reading, usually given in a footnote |
| ms., mss. | manuscript, manuscripts |
| n., nn. | note, notes |
| par. | parallel(s) |
| repr. | reprint, reprinted |
| sc. | *scilicet* (to wit) |
| ser. | series |
| s.v. | *sub voce* (under the word) |
| tr., trs. | translator, translators; translation, translations |
| v., vv. | verse, verses |
| v.l. | *varia lectio* (variant reading) |

# INTRODUCTION

# INTRODUCTION

No Pauline letter requires more of its readers or offers more of a reward to those who apply themselves carefully to its interpretation than 2 Cor. Here one sees the apostle Paul in spirited and sometimes anguished dialogue with his congregation in Corinth, with a group of rival apostles who have intruded themselves into the congregation there, and even with himself. Here one finds Paul writing quite candidly of his sorrows and joys, of his fears and hopes, of his uncertainties and convictions, of his weaknesses and strengths. Here one catches a glimpse of him in Corinth on a short, painful visit; of a tearful letter written soon thereafter; of the dispatch of Titus to the congregation and of Titus' return; of a financial contribution solicited and pledged but not yet made; and of the apostle's expectations about his own impending third visit. Here, more than in any other letter, Paul offers specific comments on the meaning of apostleship and reflects on its distinctive character and responsibilities. Yet his remarks on this and related topics are not those of a person who has drawn apart for a time of unhurried self-evaluation. Rather, they are the remarks of one who, even as he writes, feels the pressure of his responsibility for "all the churches."

One gains from 2 Cor, therefore, an unusually vivid picture of Paul the apostle, and especially of his dealings with the Corinthian congregation. But this picture does not emerge without a considerable amount of exegetical midwifery. While the apostle's anxious involvement with the issues he addresses means that 2 Cor is written with an intensity and urgency no reader can miss, it also means that the issues themselves are nowhere systematically set forth within it. To understand them—and thus to understand why Paul writes as he does—much more is required of the modern reader than of those Corinthian Christians who, like the apostle, were directly involved in the situation. Indeed, the student of 2 Cor quickly discovers that, particularly in this instance, biblical interpretation involves in virtually equal measure historical reconstruction, literary analysis, and a sensitivity to theological concerns. Because Paul writes as one who has been called to preach the gospel of Jesus Christ, the interpreter must reckon with the apostle's fundamental theological convictions. Because Paul writes as one who understands the gospel to require important behavioral as well as attitudinal changes in the lives of those who accept it, one must also reckon with the social and historical realities the apostle and his first readers are facing. And, finally, one must be alert to the writing itself, to its overall literary form and structure, and also to the lexical and grammatical details which help to clarify Paul's meaning. Especially in the case of 2 Cor, no one of these tasks can be carried on in isolation. Why and how this is so will become clear in the course of this INTRODUCTION and in the NOTES and COMMENT on the translation of 2 Cor which follows.

## I. ROMAN CORINTH

### The Greek City and Its Destruction in 146 B.C.E.

Paul's Corinthian letters are written to a congregation resident in a Roman colony situated at the southwest end of the narrow isthmus connecting mainland Greece and Macedonia with the Peloponnesus. The isthmus is about ten miles long and at its narrowest point about four miles wide (see Figures 1 and 3). Although this colony had been founded scarcely more than a century before the apostle's first visit there (see below), a large Greek city, renowned and envied for its prosperity (commonly referred to as "wealthy Corinth" [e.g., Pindar, *Eulogies* 122]) had occupied the same site for many centuries. The geographer Strabo, writing not long after the founding of the Roman colony, still looked back with admiration on the Greek city "called 'wealthy' because of its commerce" (VIII.vi.20). Due to its strategic location, Corinth served both as the gateway to the Peloponnesus, commanding trade with the rest of Greece, and as the chief protector and overseer of the safest and most direct trade route from Asia to Italy, across the isthmus (ibid.; cf. Lenschau in PWSup IV:991–97).

During the late third and early second centuries B.C.E., Corinth and the other Greek states which belonged to the Achaean League found themselves increasingly dependent on Macedonia to the north and increasingly threatened by Rome to the west (see Wiseman 1979:450–60). In order to weaken the several Hellenic confederations, Rome sought to deal, insofar as possible, only with the individual member states, and by the middle of the second century B.C.E. this policy was enabling Rome to exert ever more power in Greece. For the Achaean League the crisis came in 147 B.C.E. at a convocation held in Corinth to settle a dispute between Sparta and the other members. When a delegation from the Roman senate proposed that Corinth and several other members, including Sparta, withdraw from the league, thus effectively dissolving it, the Achaeans stormed out. A second meeting, scheduled later the same year for Tegea, was attended only by the Romans and the Spartans, and early in 146 B.C.E. the other members of the Achaean League declared war on Sparta. This at once precipitated a war between the league and Rome, a war which began when Metellus, advancing from the north, scored important

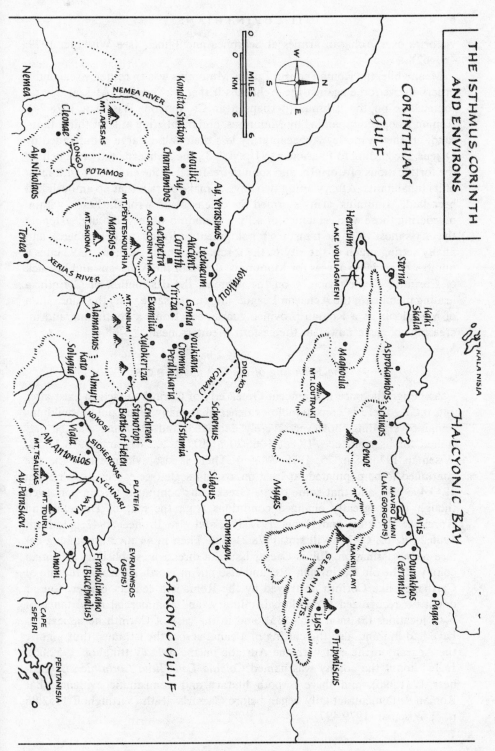

Figure 1: The Isthmus, Corinth, and Environs.

victories over Achaean armies at Scarphea and Phocis (see Wiseman 1979: 460–62).

Meanwhile, the Roman consul Lucius Mummius was en route by sea, under orders to use force against the Achaeans if that was needed. At Leucopetra, somewhere on the isthmus (perhaps near Crommyon; Wiseman 1978:74), Roman troops commanded by Mummius, and numbering at least thirty thousand, crushed a motley Achaean army less than half as large commanded by Diaeus. According to Pausanias (VII.xvi.7–8), the Achaeans retreated behind the fortifications of Corinth, and soon thereafter fled the city along with most of its inhabitants. After waiting two days to make certain that no ambush had been laid, Mummius' army stormed the defenses and wrought havoc within, murdering those who remained or selling them into slavery, looting, stripping the city's most valuable treasures for shipment to Rome (and elsewhere), and finally setting much of the city to the torch. (Wiseman 1979:462 n. 92 cites a number of ancient sources for Mummius' defeat of the Achaeans and his sack of Corinth.) Rome's victory on the isthmus, the destruction of Corinth, a leading member of the Achaean League, and (in the same year) the annexation of Macedonia as a Roman province guaranteed Rome a continuing and increasing role as a power in the eastern Mediterranean.

### The Founding of the Colony, 44 B.C.E.

Although the once magnificent Greek city of Corinth ceased to exist after 146 B.C.E., there is considerable evidence that many of its public buildings remained standing, however severely damaged, and the same may be presumed for its residences (Kent 1966:20 n. 10; C. K. Williams 1978:21–23; Wiseman 1978:15 n. 25; 1979:494–96). There is also evidence that the site continued to be populated, at least on a small scale (see especially Wiseman 1979:493–94), and that some of the Greek cults continued to function, even though under greatly changed conditions (e.g., the cult of Demeter and Kore; see Bookidis and Fisher 1972:316, and also Broneer 1942:161; Kent 1966;20 n. 10; C. K. Williams 1978:21–22). Then in 44 B.C.E., not long before his assassination, Julius Caesar issued a directive establishing a Roman colony at the old Corinthian site, and also one in North Africa, at the site of Carthage—like Corinth destroyed by the Romans a century earlier. Caesar doubtless recognized the political, military, and commercial importance of both locations (Salmon 1969:135), and in the case of Corinth he appears to have had in mind also the cutting of a canal across the isthmus, thus joining the Aegean on the east with the Adriatic on the west (Vittinghoff 1952:86). In his honor the colony was named *Colonia Laus Iulia Corinthiensis* (Broneer 1941:390), and there is both literary and numismatic evidence that Roman settlement actually began before Caesar's death (Vittinghoff 1952:86 n. 5; Wiseman 1979:497).

While most Roman colonies were founded for—and thus settled by—army veterans, this was not the case with Corinth. Rather, the colonists sent out from Rome to Corinth were drawn from the poor (Appian, *Roman History* VIII.xx.136), most of them *libertini,* freed slaves (Strabo, *Geography* VIII. vi.23). This means, in turn, that the first settlers were not in fact "Romans" but persons from the eastern Mediterranean, probably for the most part Syrians, Egyptians, and Jews (cf. Gordon 1924:94–95), men and women "of no nationality and of a civilization not their own" (ibid.:110). The contemporary poet Crinagoras lamented the fate of Corinth:

> What inhabitants, O luckless city, hast thou received, and in place of whom? Alas for the great calamity to Greece! Would, Corinth, thou didst lie lower than the ground and more desert than the Libyan sands, rather than that wholly abandoned to such a crowd of scoundrelly slaves, thou shouldst vex the bones of the ancient Bacchiadae! (*Greek Anthology* ix.284)

According to Appian (*Roman History* VIII.xx.136), about three thousand settlers were sent out to Carthage, but there is no report and no evidence as to whether a comparable number of people may have been dispatched to Corinth. Corinth, which was a one- to two-week journey from Rome (Casson 1974:152; cf. Broneer 1939:185), would, like other colonies, have been modeled on the mother city. (Aulus Gellius, writing in the second century C.E., notes that the colonies "have the appearance of miniatures, and are reproductions of Rome herself" [XVI.xiii.9; cited by Salmon 1969:18].) Latin was the official language (see, e.g., Kent 1966:18–19). There is evidence that a Roman gridpattern of roadways was laid out over the old Greek city (Williams and Zervos 1982:118, 128). A forum, which probably served less as a marketplace than as the administrative center of the colony (H. Robinson 1965:23), took shape not on the site of the Greek *agora* but to the south of the old city's most prominent temple (Figure 2, No. 3). Local government was in the hands of a city council (*decurio;* Greek *boulē*), on which (in the case of Caesar's colonies) *libertini* were eligible to serve (Duff 1928:66 n. 3) and which was presided over by two chief magistrates *(duoviri iure dicundo)* elected annually. (Wiseman 1979: 497–502 summarizes the whole administrative structure of Roman Corinth.)

## Political and Commercial Importance

From the beginning of its existence as a colony of Rome, the importance of Corinth was primarily commercial (Salmon 1969:135). Its location at the site of the old Greek city made this inevitable. By commanding the isthmus it automatically commanded the premier sea route from Rome to the eastern Mediterranean. Julius Caesar, and later the emperor Gaius Caligula (37–41 C.E.), had hoped to be able to join the Saronic Gulf (to the east) and the Gulf of Corinth (to the west) by means of a canal across the isthmus, and Nero

(54–68 C.E.) actually inaugurated the project, with considerable fanfare, on 28 November in the year 66 or 67 (Suetonius, *Julius* XLIV, 3; *Caligula* XXI; *Nero* XIX, 2; XXXVII, 3; cf. Gebhard 1973:86–87; Wiseman, 1978:48, 74–75 n. 21). Work was barely started, however, before it was abandoned, and the canal which presently bisects the isthmus (Figure 1) was cut through only in the late nineteenth century (1881–93, under the direction of French engineers; Wiseman 1978:50). From the sixth century B.C.E. and into Roman times, smaller vessels were loaded onto wheeled, wooden vehicles and pulled overland across a grooved pavement (the *diolkos;* see Wiseman 1978:45–48), while the larger ships had to be emptied of their cargoes, which were then transported to the other side of the isthmus and reloaded on ships waiting there. Roman Corinth naturally benefited from these operations, as host city to sailors and travelers (cf. Strabo's remarks about the Greek city, VIII.vi.20) and as a financial center of no less importance than Patras and Athens (Plutarch, *That We Ought Not to Borrow* 831 A; Larsen 1938:491–92). The resulting cosmopolitan character of life in Roman Corinth has been documented archaeologically by the excavation of the "Cellar Building," which was damaged by an earthquake in 22 or 23 C.E., and subsequently repaired. Located in the southwest corner of the forum (Figure 2, No. 23), it was probably a public restaurant or tavern. The establishment not only used pottery of Corinthian manufacture but also pottery made in Syria, Asia Minor, the Aegean islands, southern Italy (or Sicily), and Rome (Wright 1980:174–75).

Corinth's western port of Lechaeum (Lechaion), some two miles distant (Figure 1), provided an inner harborage of about sixty-two square miles (Scranton, Shaw, and Ibrahim 1978:14 n. 2). From the early fourth century B.C.E. long walls linked the port with Corinth, and in Roman times the road between Lechaeum and Corinth was lined with buildings (Wiseman 1978:87). Strabo (VIII.vi.22) says that there were few residences there in his day. Shortly after the middle of the fifth century C.E. a Christian basilica, the largest yet discovered in Greece (Wiseman 1978:87), was dedicated to the memory of the third-century martyr Leonides and his friends, who—because they publicly mourned his death—were themselves martyred by drowning (Scranton 1957:4).

Corinth's eastern port was Cenchreae (Kenchreai), six miles east of the forum on the Saronic Gulf (Figure 1). After the resettlement of Corinth in 44 B.C.E., Cenchreae regained its previous status as a major port (Wiseman 1978:75 n. 43), although its harbor area (Plate V) was less than one third the size of Lechaeum's (Scranton, Shaw, and Ibrahim 1978:14) and larger ships probably could not have pulled up to the quay (ibid.:15). In the Augustan period extensive warehouses and other facilities were built on the southwest side of the harbor and a long stoa was constructed on the north side (ibid.:51). In contrast to Lechaeum, there was at least a small town at Cenchreae (Strabo, VIII.vi.22, refers to it as a "village" [*kōmē*]), and in Paul's day there was a

Christian congregation there sponsored by a woman named Phoebe, whom Paul commends in Rom 16:1–2. According to Acts 18:18, prior to boarding a ship for Syria the apostle "cut his hair" at Cenchreae, presumably having completed a Nazirite vow (see Num 6:5, 18).

Roman Corinth's fame and fortune did not arise only from its mercantile activity as a shipping and business center. Like the earlier Greek city, it was also known for its production of bronze and for its manufacture of various small decorative and utilitarian articles. Corinthian bronze was valued throughout the empire, "before silver and almost before gold," wrote Pliny (*Natural History* XXXIV.i.1; cf. iii.6–8; xviii.48; XXXVII.xii.49; Strabo VIII. vi.23; Petronius, *Satyricon* 31, 50, 119; Josephus, e.g., *Life* 68; Pausanias II. iii.3). Excavators have identified several bronze foundries which were in operation from the first century C.E., two near the forum and another to the north near the gymnasium (Wiseman 1969a:222; 1969b:67–69; 1978:13, 15 n. 40; Mattusch 1977:380, 389; cf. Davidson 1952:64). There was also an active terra-cotta industry in the early colonial period (Davidson 1952:21–22), the manufacture of various small bone implements (ibid.:174), the production of pigments (Wiseman 1978:13; note Petronius, *Satyricon* 119: "bright colours dug from the earth"), and perhaps the manufacture of glass (Davidson 1952:5). From the late first or early second century C.E., Corinth was exporting lamps of exceedingly fine quality (see H. Williams 1981:35–48).

Finally, Roman Corinth was important as a political center. In 27 B.C.E., Achaia (which included the Peloponnesus, Epirus, Akarnania, Aetolia, and perhaps Thessaly; Finegan *IDB* A–D:25) was organized into a senatorial province, of which Corinth was a leading city—if not, indeed, the capital. In 15 C.E., however, Tiberius deprived Achaia of this status and combined it with Macedonia into one imperial province attached to Moesia (Tacitus, *Annals* I.lvi.4; lxxx.1), an arrangement which continued until 44 C.E. In that year Claudius returned both provinces to the control of the senate (Suetonius, *Claudius* XXXV, 3; Dio Cassius LX.xxxiv.1; see Larsen 1938:438; Wiseman 1979:503). That Corinth rather than Athens seems to have been established as the capital of this reconstituted province (the evidence for this is only circumstantial; see Wiseman 1979:501–2) is in keeping with Rome's respect for the traditional independence of Athens—just as Ephesus, not traditionally independent Pergamum, was made the capital of the province of Asia (Hammond 1972:289). Until the time of Hadrian (117–38 C.E.) Corinth paid taxes directly to Rome (Larsen 1938:459–60), and as a senatorial province Achaia was governed by a proconsul sent out annually from Rome. Proconsular terms —certainly under Tiberius and probably still under Claudius—ran from July through June, and there is substantial evidence that Lucius Junius Gallio, before whom Paul was brought during the apostle's first period of residency in Corinth (see below), had assumed his office in the city on 1 July in the year 51 (evidence and arguments for this dating are cited in Jewett 1979:38–40;

Murphy-O'Connor 1983:141–50). According to the philosopher Seneca, one of Gallio's two younger brothers (on the family see *OCD* under Gallio, Mela [2], and Seneca [1 and 2]), the proconsul regarded the climate in Achaia as detrimental to his health (*Moral Epistles* CIV, 1), so it is probable that he did not remain there beyond the normal one-year term, and perhaps not even for its duration (Murphy-O'Connor 1983:147).

Favorinus, in an address to the Corinthians (falsely attributed to Dio Chrysostom, XXXVII, 36), aptly described the status which Roman Corinth had already attained by the end of the first century C.E.:

> For you are now, as the saying goes, both prow and stern of Hellas, having been called prosperous and wealthy and the like by poets and gods from olden days, days when some of the others too had wealth and might; but now, since wealth has deserted both Orchomenos and Delphi, though they may surpass you in exciting pity, none can do so in exciting envy.

## Civic and Cultural Life

Just as it is impossible to know how many settlers had been sent out to Corinth at the foundation of the colony, or how many squatters they would have found living among the ruins of the old city, so it is impossible to know how large the population had grown by the time of Paul's arrival slightly more than a century later. Wiseman (1978:11–12) estimates a population for Corinthia as a whole of as much as 130,000 during the classical and Hellenistic periods, and believes the number must have soared even higher during Roman times, until the area was overrun by Alaric in 395 C.E. That Roman Corinth grew rapidly, especially under Tiberius (14–37 C.E.) and Claudius (41–54 C.E.), is well attested by the many public buildings which were constructed or restored during these years, as well as by what is known of the political and commercial importance of the city in the second quarter of the first century. One may safely conclude, then, that Paul came to a thriving urban center which was already the home of tens of thousands of people.

Who were these Corinthians, and what was life like in the Roman city? It is important to remember that the colonists were a very diverse group, few of them Italian and most of them with ethnic and cultural roots in the lands of the eastern Mediterranean. Some, indeed, may have been descendants of the original Greek population (Broneer 1942:161), and one can be sure that the common language of the colony would have been Greek (Broneer 1951:82), despite the use of Latin for official business and in many public inscriptions. Since 70 percent of the names of slaves and freed slaves known from inscriptions in Rome itself in the last two centuries B.C.E. are Greek (Duff 1928:1–11), it is not surprising to find that one of the most prominent citizens of Roman Corinth in the first half of the first century C.E. bears the mixed Latin-Greek name Gnaeus Babbius Philenus. As a slave he would have been known by the

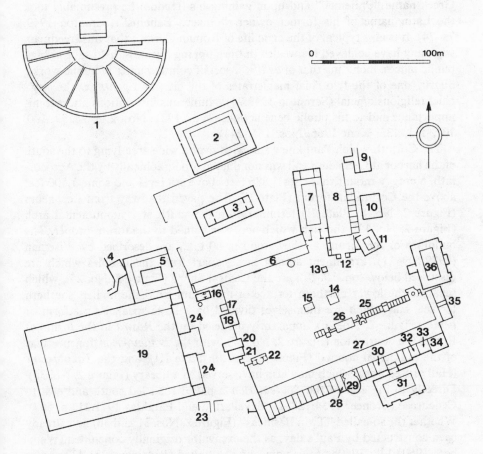

Figure 2:
1. Theater   2. North Market   3. Archaic Temple, sixth century B.C.E.   4. Fountain of Glauke, sixth century B.C.E.   5. Temple C (unidentified)   6. Northwest Stoa   7. North Basilica   8. Lechaeum Road (see Plate II)   9. Bath (of Eurycles?)   10. Peribolos of Apollo   11. Fountain of Peirene   12. Propylaea (see Plate II)   13. Tripod   14. Statue of Athena   15. Altar (unidentified)   16. Temple D (*Tychē;* see Plate VIII)   17. Babbius Monument   18. Fountain of Poseidon (Neptune)   19. Temple of the Imperial Cult   20. Temple G (Pantheon?)   21. Temple F (Aphrodite)   22. Unidentified Building (temple or civic structure)   23. "Cellar Building" (public restaurant or tavern)   24. West Shops   25. Central Shops   26. *Bēma*   27. South Stoa   28. Room XX (Sarapis shrine; see Plate VII)   29. *Bouleutērion* (see Plate III)   30. "Fountain House"   31. South Basilica   32. Room C (*Agonotheteion*)   33. Room B   34. Room A   35. Southeast Building (*Tabularium* and library?)   36. Julian Basilica

Greek name "Philenus," and upon gaining his freedom he presumably took the Latin name of his former owner, "Gnaeus Babbius" (Scranton 1949: 73–74). It is also typical of the civic life of Roman Corinth that this freedman, who may have achieved his wealth in the shipping business, held several high public offices, including that of *aedile,* a sort of commissioner of public works; *duovir,* one of the two chief magistrates of the city; and *pontifex,* the city's chief religious official (Scranton 1949:74). Numerous inscriptions attest to his importance and to his public benefactions (West 1931: Nos. 2, 3, 98, 99, 100, 101, 131, 132; Kent 1966: Nos. 155, 241).

The Corinth which Paul knew sprawled over a wide area lying to the south of the harbor at Lechaeum and was dominated topographically by the Acrocorinth, a craggy mount that rises 1,886 feet above sea level and some 1,500 feet above the Corinthian forum (Plate II). The paved roadway from Lechaeum (Figure 2, No. 8; Plate II) terminates on the south at a monumental arch (Figure 2, No. 12), through which access is gained to the forum proper. The buildings of the forum, as they stood in 50 C.E., are described by Wiseman (1979:509–21). Prominent among these, apart from the temples which are discussed below (pp. 15–20), are the Central Shops (Figure 2, No. 25), which separate the lower northern terrace of the forum from the higher, southern terrace, and which are themselves divided by a large speaker's platform or *bēma* (Figure 2, No. 26), apparently modeled on the *Rostra* in the forum at Rome; the South Stoa (Figure 2, No. 27), with the *Bouleutērion* for meetings of the municipal council (Figure 2, No. 29; Plate III); and the *Tabularium* (Hall of Records), which may also have served as a library (Figure 2, No. 35). Directly to the east of the *Bouleutērion* a paved road led south and east to Cenchreae (Broneer 1954:128–29; Sakellariou and Faraklas 1971:213 n. 597). Whether the so-called "Twin Basilicas" (Figure 2, Nos. 31 and 36) had already been constructed by Paul's day, as the excavator originally concluded (Weinberg 1960a:137; 1960b:56), is now being restudied (Ridgway 1981:432 and n. 40), but there is no doubt that the long, narrow basilica to the north (Figure 2, No. 7) was in existence by that time. The theater was located to the north and west of the forum, and a large market complex stood directly to the east of that (Figure 2, Nos. 1 and 2). Apart from some outlying villas, no domestic buildings have been excavated at Corinth; but the most extensive residential quarters in the first century C.E. seem to have been located north and east of the forum (C. K. Williams 1979; Sakellariou and Faraklas 1971:137).

In his address to Corinth (first century C.E.), the rhetor Favorinus refers to the city as thoroughly Hellenized despite its status as a colony of Rome (Dio Chrysostom XXXVII, 26). This was true in many important respects: its common language was Greek, not Latin (as Paul's letters to the Corinthians themselves attest); the greater portion of its art and architecture was deliberately archaistic, imitating that of the older Greek city (Ridgway 1981:430–31); and the Greek cults, never entirely abandoned after 146 B.C.E., continued to operate in the new colony (see below). At the same time, however, the influence of Rome on the cultural life of Corinth was unmistakable, thus illustrating Roman policy in the provinces: to encourage conformity to its own ideas and practices, even while preserving as much as possible of what was indigenous and traditional to the area (Larsen 1958:123). In the case of public entertainment, at least, Rome prevailed, for in the late Augustan period—or early in the reign of Tiberius—Corinth's theater was remodeled to meet the needs of Roman productions (Stillwell 1952:135); and by the end of the first century gladiatorial shows, to which Greeks had a strong aversion (see Dio Chrysostom XXXI, 121; Sakellariou and Faraklas 1971:136), were delighting the inhabitants of the city and, doubtless, many of those who regularly passed through. The popularity of these spectacles is a good indication of the generally superficial cultural life of Roman Corinth. Its values were essentially material (Hammond 1972:184; Elliger 1978:246), and while the city was a flourishing commercial center it was, as one scholar has described it, "spiritually and intellectually empty" (H. Robinson 1965:21). Ancient writers, too, regarded Roman Corinth as the epitome of crass materialism—and, along with that, of moral decadence. Thus, in his *Metamorphoses,* Apuleius (second century C.E.) switches the penultimate scene of Lucius' story from Thessalonica to Corinth, apparently regarding the latter as a more appropriate setting than the former for the tale of sexual debauchery he recounts (X, 19–23, 29–35; see Mason 1971). And Alciphron, writing at about the same time, complains that among all the luxuries of Corinth he found nothing to enjoy, since the people were so ungracious and uncultured and since the poor of the city were so grossly exploited by the rich (*Letters* 15 and 24 [iii.51 and iii.60]).

No survey of the civic and cultural life of Corinth, Greek or Roman, is complete which does not emphasize the importance for the city of the Isthmian Games, held biennially at a place about ten miles east on the isthmus (Figure 1). Dedicated to the sea god Poseidon (see below), in 582 or 580 B.C.E. they were reorganized into a Panhellenic festival which attracted throngs of people (Broneer 1962:17). There were not only athletic contests but also competitions in music, oratory, and drama. The festival was administered by Corinth until the city's destruction in 146 B.C.E., at which time it was moved to Sicyon (Broneer 1973:4), remaining under Sicyonian management until sometime between 7 B.C.E. and 3 C.E. (ibid.:67; Wiseman 1979:496). The first Corinthian president *(agōnothetēs)* of the festival in the Roman period was a certain L. Castricius Regulus (Kent 1966: No. 153), who served as one of the city's chief magistrates sometime during the reign of Tiberius, and who was buried in one of the Roman tombs at Cenchreae (Cummer 1971). This Isthmian festival flourished during Roman imperial times until it was terminated late in the fourth century, along with other pagan festivals, by Theodosius (Broneer 1971a:103). The administrative headquarters of the festival were located, evidently, at the east end of the South Stoa (Figure 2, Nos. 32, 33, 34; see Broneer

1954:110–11; on the administration of the games in general, see Geagen 1968).

The facilities at Isthmia included, in addition to the sanctuaries mentioned below, a theater and a stadium. The theater, built about 400 B.C.E., was extensively repaired and altered after a fire in 390 B.C.E., and was altered once more just before Nero's visit in 66–67 C.E. (Gebhard 1973:26, 53, 60, 63, 70). The stadium in use in Paul's day, which remains largely unexcavated, is also dated to the fourth century B.C.E. (Broneer 1962:10–11; 1973:55–63). Two passages from Dio Chrysostom (VIII, 6–14; IX, 10–22; both cited by Broneer 1962:17–19), purportedly describe the scene at the games in the fourth century B.C.E. when Diogenes, the Cynic philosopher, attended them. The details of the account, however, are truer to Dio's own time (the late first century C.E.): "crowds of wretched sophists around Poseidon's temple shouting and reviling one another . . . ; writers reading aloud their stupid works, many poets reciting their poems . . . , jugglers . . . , fortune-tellers . . . , lawyers innumerable perverting judgment, and peddlers not a few huckstering whatever they happened to have" (VIII, 9). This is precisely the kind of setting in which an itinerant philosopher, healer, and fortune-teller like Apollonius of Tyana could have drawn a crowd. Indeed, he is reported to have visited Corinth on at least one occasion (Philostratus, *Life of Apollonius* VII.x), and to have been acquainted with one of its wealthy citizens, a certain Bassus, described as "a philosopher and president of the Isthmian games" (*Epistles of Apollonius* XXXVI; for comments on this Corinthian family, see West 1931:61, 78, and Kent 1966:25, No. 8; 31, No. 13, both of whom date Bassus' presidency of the games to the year 61 C.E.). If, as claimed, it was common knowledge that Bassus had poisoned his father (Philostratus, *Life* IV.xxvi; *Epistles* XXXVII), and that he had offered the sexual favors of his wife to a man named Praxiteles on condition that the latter would murder Apollonius (*Epistles* XXXVI), then one has further evidence of social attitudes and moral standards in the Corinth of Paul's day.

As for the apostle himself, one can imagine Paul, too, making his way through the jostling, boisterous crowds at Isthmia, perhaps even trying to find a hearing for his gospel there. In comparison with the noisy claims and shrill accusations of the sophistic philosophers, however, his style would have seemed as strange as his message. One may note 2 Cor 2:17, where he, like Dio, refers disparagingly to those who huckster ideas as if they were so much cheap merchandise (cf. 4:2a), and 2 Cor 10:10; 11:6, where he takes cognizance of those who think his own speaking bland and unpersuasive. Moreover, it is conceivable that when, in an earlier letter to the Corinthians, he contrasts the "imperishable" wreath for which the Christian runs with the "perishable" one for which an athlete strives (1 Cor 9:25) he wants his readers to think of the distinctive crown bestowed on Isthmian victors—not fresh and green like those awarded at the Olympian, Pythian, and Nemean games, but a wreath made of withered celery (Broneer 1962:16–17; 1971b:185–86).

## Religious Life

It is impossible to abstract the "religious life" of an ancient city like Corinth from its political, commercial, and cultural activities, and no meaningful distinction can be made between its "sacred" and "secular" institutions. However little their religious beliefs and affiliations may have influenced what people did and how they did it, they perceived their public and private lives to be in some measure dependent upon the favor of the gods. In Roman Corinth, as elsewhere, the evidence of these beliefs—however superficial they may have been —is present on every side: in the temples and religious sanctuaries of the city, in its sculpture, on its coinage, in the inscriptions, and in its major civic institutions—not least, in the case of Corinth, in the Isthmian Games dedicated to the god Poseidon.

During the Claudian period (41–54 C.E.), even as traditional Roman religious rites were being revived, it was imperial policy to be broadly tolerant of foreign religions (Momigliano 1961:28; cf. Scramuzza 1940:151–52). The effect of such a policy on the religious life of a burgeoning and cosmopolitan city like Corinth is totally predictable; its religious life was as diverse as the cultural backgrounds of the first colonists and of those who subsequently were attracted to the city because of its growing importance as a center of trade and commerce. The literary evidence for the religions of first-century Corinth is rather meager apart from the Book of Acts and Paul's Corinthian letters themselves (where the evidence is very indirect). But the archaeological evidence is fairly abundant, and amply documents the religious diversity of the Roman city in the first century C.E.

1. *The deities and cults of Greece.* It has already been remarked that, even during the century between the destruction of the Greek city and the founding of the Roman colony, a number of the old Greek cults remained active at the site. The Greek temples and sacred precincts, although damaged, were not completely destroyed, and many of them were repaired or rebuilt by the colonists. This was true, for example, of the grandest temple of the old city, to the south of which the colonists laid out the forum of the new city. Probably built in the third quarter of the sixth century B.C.E. (Weinberg 1939:198–99), its Doric columns were twenty-four feet high and almost six feet in diameter. It had a double-chambered cella (Figure 2, No. 3; Plates IV and IX; see Fowler and Stillwell 1932:115–34). Within its peristyle court there would have been an altar to the god of the temple (H. Robinson 1965:27), but which god that was remains uncertain. The majority of scholars identify it with the temple of Apollo, which Pausanias saw along the road to Sicyon (II.iii.6), but some (e.g., Wiseman 1979:530) think it may be the temple of Athena, which, according to the same writer, was nearby (II.iv.1).

It is clear that both Apollo and Athena were worshiped in the city to which

Paul came preaching. A bronze statue of Athena stood in the middle of the forum (Figure 2, No. 14; see Pausanias II.iii.1 and Scranton 1951:150), her likeness appeared on coins minted in the colony (e.g., Edwards 1933:16, No. 18), and she is one of the three deities portrayed in relief on a pier, perhaps from a building in the forum, which was found in 1979 (C. K. Williams 1982:178). Statues of Apollo also adorned the Roman city (see F. Johnson 1931: Nos. 12, 17–19; Stillwell et al. 1941:221–22, No. 17, and note Pausanias II.ii.8), and from the Augustan period a courtyard dedicated to Apollo was situated to the east of the road coming up from Lechaeum (Figure 2, No. 10; Stillwell et al. 1941:1–54).

Other temples dedicated to Greek deities stood at the west end of the forum, facing east. Two of these, both dating from the reign of Augustus, can be identified with some confidence as temples of Tyche (Temple D; Figure 2, No. 16) and of Aphrodite (Temple F; Figure 2, No. 21), respectively. (On these identifications see Wiseman 1979:528–29.) Tyche, goddess of good fortune (the Roman goddess Fortuna), and traditionally the protector of cities (see Ferguson 1970:77–87), is represented among the archaeological finds at Corinth by, for example, a head of fine Pentelic marble (Plate VIII; discussed by Freeman in Stillwell et al. 1941:215, 216; see also F. Johnson 1931: Nos. 6, 54), on a coin minted in the colony in the year 51–52 C.E. (Edwards 1933:22, No. 54), and by several inscriptions (the most important is given by Kent 1966: No. 128). Evidence abounds from Roman Corinth for the popularity there of Aphrodite (the Roman goddess Venus), the goddess of love, fertility, and beauty. She was honored by statues (F. Johnson 1931: Nos. 36, 39, 42, 44–50, 53) and on coins (Edwards 1933:17, Nos. 25, 26); in the first century C.E. she was a favorite subject for the terra-cotta figurines manufactured in the city (Davidson 1952:20 and Nos. 378–81). Moreover, at the northeast end of the Roman harbor of Cenchreae excavations have disclosed a building complex dating from the first century B.C.E. which has been identified as an Aphrodision, a modest shrine established for the worship of the goddess (Scranton, Shaw, and Ibrahim 1978:88–90; cf. Pausanias II.ii.3). However, the claim cited by Strabo (VIII.vi.20) that Aphrodite's temple in Corinth owned one thousand prostitutes, on account of whom "the city was crowded with people and grew rich," was little more than a sailor's fantasy, and was said, in any event, of the old Greek city, not of the Roman colony (see Conzelmann 1974; 1975:12 and n. 97).

Two further precincts at the west end of the Corinthian forum deserve mention. Temple G (Figure 2, No. 20) may be the Pantheon, the "sanctuary for all the gods" seen by Pausanias in the second century C.E. (II.ii.8). This is a tentative identification (C. K. Williams 1979, 1982:179) based on the possibility that two piers found in the vicinity, portraying a total of six Greek deities, may be from that structure. Each pier has four sides, three of which contain a relief, while the fourth is smooth. On one of the piers the reliefs are of Demeter, Zeus Chthonios (cf. Pausanias II.ii.8), and Kore (C. K. Williams and Fisher 1975:23–24, No. 28; also C. K. Williams 1982:174–78), while on the second are the likenesses of Athena, Ge Cthonius, and Dionysus (C. K. Williams 1982:178, and Plates 31–32). Also located in front of the west terrace of the forum in Paul's day (Figure 2, No. 18) was an ornamental fountain dedicated to the sea god Neptune (the Greek god Poseidon). This featured a statue of Aphrodite, cascading waters, dolphins, and a bronze statue of the sea god himself. According to an inscription, the fountain was a gift to the city by Gnaeus Babbius Philenus (Scranton 1951:32–36, and Plates 13–14; H. Robinson 1965:24).

One of the most important religious establishments of Roman Corinth, situated about half a mile north of the forum, was the Asclepieium, a sanctuary of Asclepius, the god of healing (Roebuck 1951; Wiseman 1979:487–88, 510). This impressive complex, most of which had been constructed in the fourth century B.C.E., was repaired by the Roman colonists and continued to attract large numbers of people seeking cures for their infirmities. It consisted of a temple, facing east, with an altar before it; an *abaton* (sleeping quarters) for those awaiting directions from the god on how to be cured; and a large fountain house with facilities for bathing, dining, and open-air exercise. As at the more famous shrines of Asclepius at Epidauros, Cos, and Pergamum, treatment here involved the offering of sacrifices, placing cult images of Asclepius (and Hygeia) in the temple, lustral baths, spending at least one night in the *abaton* awaiting some direction from the god in a dream, and a regimen of exercise and special meals. A fascinating account of such procedures from the second century C.E. is provided in the *Hieroi Logoi (Sacred Teachings)* of Aelius Aristides (on which see Festugière 1954:85–104; also Edelstein and Edelstein 1945, especially II:181–213; cf. Ferguson 1970:110–11). It would appear that this Corinthian sanctuary was used primarily by local people, since there were few facilities for visitors from afar (Roebuck 1951:159). But its importance locally is well attested, not only by the building complex itself but also by the large number of terra-cotta votive offerings, representing afflicted parts of the body (ears, arms, legs, breasts, hands, feet, fingers, genitalia, etc.; see, e.g., Roebuck 1951: Plates 32–46), which have been excavated there. It may be that Paul's imagery of the body and its parts (1 Cor 12) would have had special meaning for the Corinthians, who were familiar with the practices at their local Asclepieium (A. Hill 1980); but it is unfair to suggest that the emphasis there was on "the individual dismembered parts of the body, rather than on the whole, newly healed person" (ibid.:438). The facilities provided at this and similar establishments elsewhere suggest that diet, exercise, and relaxation were, along with worship of the god, a normal part of the procedure.

The cult of Demeter and Kore was also established at Corinth. The sanctuary that Pausanias saw on Acrocorinth above the city (II.iv.7) has been located on the north slope and partly excavated (Stroud 1965, 1968; Bookidis 1969;

Bookidis and Fisher 1972, 1974). In use from the seventh century B.C.E., the sanctuary was rebuilt in the fourth century, then largely but probably not completely abandoned between 146 B.C.E. and the founding of the Roman colony. There is some evidence that the cult was in operation between 44 B.C.E. and the middle of the first century C.E., but on a greatly reduced scale, concentrated on the middle and upper terraces of the complex (Bookidis 1981). In the second half of the first century C.E., however, activity increased at the site, and at least three new buildings were constructed (Bookidis and Fisher 1974:280–85; Bookidis 1981). This cult was based on the myth of the rape of Persephone (Kore) by the god of the underworld, and the search for her by Demeter, her mother (see, e.g., Mylonas 1961:3–22; Ferguson 1970:99–101). It was the most ancient of the Greek Mysteries, having been imported to Eleusis, its most important sanctuary, by 1300 B.C.E. at the latest. The cultic practices at Corinth, however, seem to have been substantially different from those at Eleusis (Bookidis 1979).

Demeter also had a shrine at Isthmia (Figure 1), at least prior to the Mummian destruction, after which the Isthmian Games were transferred to Sicyon (Wiseman 1979:491). But it was the worship of the sea god Poseidon that was dominant on the isthmus. According to a Greek myth, the dispute between Poseidon and Helios for control of the isthmus was settled by an agreement that it would belong to Poseidon, and Acrocorinth to Helios (Broneer 1971b:171). The temple of Poseidon had been built in the fourth century B.C.E. and was still standing in Roman times, although it had to be repaired by the colonists (Broneer 1971a:1–2). A statue of the god, three times larger than life, stood in the temple, as did one of his wife Amphitrite, who was also worshiped there (Broneer 1971a:103; 1971b:173). By the time of Paul's visit in the middle of the first century C.E., the cult, including its traditional animal sacrifice (Broneer 1971b:174–75), was again being practiced.

From Augustan times the cult of Palaimon ("Wrestler") was also important at Isthmia (see Broneer 1971b:174–78; 1973:67–98). It was based on the myth of Melicertes, son of King Athamus of Orchomenos and his wife Ino. As a baby, Melicertes drowned in the Saronic Gulf, but his body was returned to the isthmus on the back of a dolphin. According to the Corinthian version of the myth, the body was found by King Sisyphus of Corinth, who instituted the Isthmian Games in honor of the boy, now named Palaimon. This cult was flourishing by the middle of the first century C.E., and it seems eventually to have eclipsed even the worship of Poseidon in popularity (Broneer 1977:92). While the Palaimonion, the god's sanctuary, was not built until the second century, the enclosure walls were built before 50 C.E., as were the earliest sacrificial pits—where, to climax the cult's nocturnal rites, a black bull was ceremoniously incinerated (Broneer 1973:68–69, 100–1; 1971b:177–78).

2. *The Roman imperial cult.* The reigning monarchs in Egypt had accepted divine titles for several centuries (Ferguson 1970:89), and Augustus was hailed

there from the first as a divinity (ibid.:90). To the Greeks, however, he presented himself, more cautiously, as *divi filius,* "son of the Divine," referring
to Julius Caesar, who had been deified by vote of the Roman senate two years
after his death (cf. Ferguson 1970:90; Larsen 1958:130). Augustus wanted the
Greeks to regard him not as their conqueror but as their patron, as a statesman
under the special protection of their god Apollo (Larsen 1958:130). After
Augustus' death, however, he too was accorded divine honors, and this continued as the general pattern for his successors (Ferguson 1970:91–92).

In Corinth the cult of the imperial family was represented by a temple,
probably built during the time of Claudius, at the west end of the forum beyond
the west shops and overlooking the temples already standing (see Figure 2, No.
19). After an earthquake damaged it in 77 C.E., it was replaced by another
(probably during Domitian's reign), which has been identified as the temple
of Octavia (sister of Augustus and sometime wife of Marc Antony) that
Pausanias saw in the second century (II.iii.1; Stillwell et al. 1941:168–79;
Wiseman 1979:522; C. K. Williams 1979). The imperial cult also played a role
in the Isthmian festival, at least by Paul's day. Early in the first century C.E.
it was extended to include, every four years, a series of contests in honor of
the deified Julius Caesar (the "Caesarea"). Then, when the cult in Achaia was
being reorganized under the direction of P. Memmius Regulus (governor of
Moesia-Macedonia-Achaia from 35 to 44 C.E.), a third series of competitions
was added to honor the reigning emperor (the "Imperial games"; see Broneer
1971b:184–85; West 1931:29–31).

3. *Egyptian cults.* There is substantial evidence (assembled and assessed by
Smith 1977) that Egyptian cults were also present and active in Roman Corinth. On his ascent of Acrocorinth, Pausanias saw two precincts dedicated to
Isis and two dedicated to Sarapis (II.iv.6). While neither of these has been
located, an inscription from the middle of the first century C.E. records the
dedication of a column to the two divinities by a certain Gaius Julius Syrus
(Kent 1966:33, No. 57; Smith 1977:218), and another inscription mentioning
them shows that they were already being honored in the old Greek city (Smith
ibid.:217–18, citing an inscription of the third or second century B.C.E.).

Isis seems to have been especially popular at Corinth in her aspect as
goddess of the sea (Smith 1977:228–31); her cult flourished there, particularly
in the second century C.E. (ibid.:227). Indeed, Corinth's port at Cenchreae is
the place where Lucius, in Apuleius' famous tale, is finally initiated into the
cult of Isis (*Metamorphoses* X, 35–XI, 24; see Griffiths 1975), and it appears
that the sanctuary excavated at the southwest end of the Cenchrean harbor (see
Plate V), dating at least from the time of Augustus but with subsequent
construction and repair, is to be identified with this cult (Scranton, Shaw, and
Ibrahim 1978:39–78). In view of the fact that a temple had been dedicated to
Isis in Rome itself as early as 43 B.C.E. (Duff 1928:205 n. 3), it is not surprising
that the cult of this Egyptian goddess found many adherents among the

ethnically and culturally diverse inhabitants of Roman Corinth. (On the importance of the cult in the Roman world generally, see Festugière 1954:68–84; Ferguson 1970:23–26, 106–8; Witt 1971; Dunand 1973; Heyob 1975.)

Sarapis, like the rather more popular Isis, had also been imported into the Greek world from Egypt (see, e.g., Hornbostel 1973; Ferguson 1970:36–37). Often portrayed as Zeus-like, he was regularly credited with healing powers like those of Asclepius. Although the Sarapis sanctuaries Pausanias saw on Acrocorinth have not been found, there is archaeological evidence, other than inscriptional data, that the cult was functioning in Roman Corinth. A head of the god, belonging to a marble statuette of the Roman period, was found along the Lechaeum Road north of the basilica (Smith 1977:224), and a life-size head of the bearded Sarapis was found in one of the rooms of the South Stoa (Figure 2, No. 28; Plate VII). If the object atop the latter head is a calathus (so Hornbostel 1973:2 n. 2, followed by Smith 1977:214 n. 34), a basket used for carrying fruit, then Sarapis is being represented as the provider of the fruits of the earth. The head was found in front of what the excavators judge to have been a shrine, placed along the back wall of a two-room complex which had undergone extensive renovation in the late second century C.E. (Broneer 1954:132–35; Smith 1977:212–16). The head itself, which may have stood originally on a wooden torso, has been dated to the middle of the same century (Smith ibid.:215).

4. *Judaism.* Clearly, one cannot expect the same kind of archaeological evidence for the presence of Jews in Roman Corinth as one has for the activity there of the Greek, Roman imperial, and Egyptian cults. Although the Roman policy of tolerance for foreign religions was extended also to the Jews, the radical monotheism of Judaism and the Jews' sense of being the chosen people of God precluded the kind of accommodation to popular religious ideas which might have made this religion attractive to significant numbers of Gentiles. The chief evidence for the presence of Judaism in Roman Corinth is, therefore, literary.

First, it may be safely presumed that there were Jews among the *libertini* who were sent out to colonize the site for Rome in the first century B.C.E. There had been a Jewish presence in Rome itself as early as the second century B.C.E. (Leon 1960:2–4; Wiefel 1977:101–2), and this was substantially increased in the first century B.C.E. (Leon 1960:4), especially in the year 61, when Pompey brought back a number of Jewish captives from Jerusalem (ibid.; Wiefel 1977: 101–3). When civil war broke out in 49 B.C.E., the Jewish community supported Julius Caesar against Pompey (Leon 1960:9–10), and it is reasonable to suppose that one of the favors subsequently bestowed on the Jews by Caesar was the opportunity to help colonize Corinth. Indeed, when Philo pleaded the case for the Alexandrian Jews before the emperor Gaius Caligula in 39 C.E., he listed Corinth as one of the cities of Greece where there was a Jewish settlement (*Embassy to Gaius* 281).

However small the contingent of Jewish colonists may have been, it is possible that the Jewish community was significantly enlarged when, in 19 c.e., Tiberius expelled many Jews and Egyptians from Rome (Tacitus, *Annals* II.xcv.4; Josephus, *Antiquities* XVIII.iii.4–5; see Leon 1960:17–20; Wiefel 1977:104–5; Duff 1928:10). Then again under Claudius (41–54 c.e.) many Jews were forced to leave Rome, this time because of an imperial edict which was evidently prompted by strife between the Jewish community as a whole and those of its members who had become Christians (Suetonius, *Claudius* XXV, 4). According to Acts 18:2, it was this edict, most likely issued in 41 c.e. (Murphy-O'Connor 1983:130–39, with the relevant literature), which caused Aquila and his wife Priscilla eventually to flee Italy for Corinth, where, shortly thereafter, they met the apostle Paul. In fact, Acts attests to the existence of a sizable Jewish community in Corinth in Paul's day (Acts 18: 4–17) and identifies two of its leaders as Crispus (Acts 18:8; cf. 1 Cor 1:14) and Sosthenes (Acts 18:17, probably not to be identified with the Sosthenes of 1 Cor 1:1).

Archaeological evidence of Judaism in Roman Corinth consists of two main items. One is a piece of white marble, broken off at each end and bearing the remnants of an inscription (in Greek) which can be restored with confidence as *SYNAGŌGĒ HEBRAIŌN*, "Synagogue of the Hebrews" (see Plate VIb; only the last four letters of the first word and the first three letters of the second word are preserved). This evidently served as the lintel over a doorway (West 1931:78–79, citing Powell), but it is extremely unlikely that the synagogue it identified was the one in which Paul preached. On the basis of the crude lettering and the fact that the lintel was fashioned from what was originally the cornice block of some other building (there is finely worked ornamentation on the underside), the inscription could be as late as the fourth century c.e. (C. K. Williams 1979; cf. West 1931:79). The other item is a marble impost decorated with three seven-branched candlesticks separated by palm branches (Lulab) and citron (Etrog) (Scranton 1957:116, No. 130 and Plate 30). This, too, must come from a synagogue (Cecil Roth, quoted ibid.:116), but the execution of the piece points to a date in the fifth century c.e. (Scranton 1957:26).

Since the synagogue inscription was found along the Lechaeum Road (Figure 2, No. 8), it is commonly presumed that the building itself stood there, perhaps even near or on the site of the synagogue known to Paul (e.g., West 1931:79). Over the centuries, however, Corinth has experienced numerous earthquakes and invasions, not to mention constant looting, and these repeated calamities have resulted in much disturbance of the site (e.g., the marble impost was found in the theater). Also, given the pervasive anti-Semitism in the Hellenistic-Roman period (see J. Daniel 1979), it is not likely that the Jewish synagogue would have been situated on such an elegant street and adjacent to some of Corinth's most important buildings. More probably it would have been located in a specifically Jewish quarter, perhaps on the periphery of the city (thus Dinkler 1967:131–32).

## II. CHRISTIANITY IN CORINTH:
## THE EARLIEST YEARS

Christianity was first brought to Corinth by the apostle Paul. On this point all the primary sources for Christianity in first-century Corinth (the apostle's Corinthian letters, the Book of Acts, and 1 Clem) are agreed. Dionysius, a second-century bishop of Corinth, is quoted as referring to Peter and Paul as co-founders of the congregation there (Eusebius, *Ecclesiastical History* II.xxv.8), but that tradition cannot be taken seriously. One can see how it might have arisen on the basis of the reference to Cephas (Peter) in 1 Cor 1:12, combined with the tradition that Peter and Paul were both later martyred in Rome (e.g., 1 Clem 5:2–7).

### Paul's First Visit to the City, 50–51 C.E.

According to Acts, Paul brought his gospel to Corinth after having spent some time in Macedonia, where he established congregations in Philippi (16: 11–40), Thessalonica (17:1–9), and probably also in Beroea (17:10–14; cf. 20:4) and a shorter period of time in Athens (17:14–34). This itinerary is in general confirmed by Paul's own remarks to the Thessalonians (1 Thess 2:1–2, 17–18; 3:1) and the Philippians (Phil 4:15–16). If, as Acts also reports, Paul's initial residence in Corinth came to an end when, after some eighteen months there, he was taken before Gallio, the Roman governor of Achaia (18:11–18), then the date of his arrival in Corinth for the first time can be fixed with some certainty. Gallio's term of office ran from 1 July 51 through June of 52 (see above, pp. 9–10), so Paul's hearing before him would have occurred at some point during that twelve-month period. This means, in turn, that Paul himself could have arrived in Corinth any time from early in the year 50 (if he was taken before Gallio shortly after the latter assumed office) through early in the year 51 (if the hearing took place only toward the end of Gallio's term). The former is more likely since, as many have observed, Paul's accusers might well have thought that a new proconsul would be more willing to hear and act on their complaints. Thus, early 50 C.E. is the most probable date for the inception of Paul's mission in Corinth (cf. Murphy-O'Connor 1983:139–50).

Shortly after his arrival Paul was joined by Silvanus (in Acts called Silas) and Timothy; the apostle himself associates them closely with his missionary activity in Corinth (2 Cor 1:19; cf. Acts 18:5). Upon their arrival Paul wrote to the recently founded congregation in Thessalonica, for he mentions both of them in the salutation of that letter (1 Thess 1:1) and then refers specifically

Figure 3: Rome's Aegean Provinces.

to Timothy's coming from Thessalonica (1 Thess 3:2, 6). Corinth, therefore, has the distinction of being the city in which the earliest of Paul's surviving letters was written.

When Paul arrived in Corinth he would have found the city much as it has been described above (pp. 7–22): a fast-growing urban center, buildings under construction everywhere, a diverse and generally prosperous population— swollen every second year with throngs of people coming to the Isthmian Games. The latter were held, along with the Imperial Games and the quadren- nial Caesarean Games, in the spring of 51 (Broneer 1971b:184–85), before Paul's departure. Who Gallio's predecessor was as Achaian proconsul in 50–51 C.E. is not known, but it is possible that the *duoviri* of Corinth (the city's two chief magistrates) were L. Paconius Flam. and Cn. Publicus Regulus, succeeded for the 51–52 term by T. Claudius Anaxilaus and P. Ventidius Fronto (Edwards 1933:7). There is some evidence that food supplies were short in Achaia during these years, as they were in many other parts of the empire (West 1931:73 [cf. Nos. 86–90]; Kent 1966: Nos. 158–63). Of this particular famine, however, there is no direct mention in Acts or in Paul's Corinthian letters.

According to his own later testimony, the apostle's preaching of Jesus Christ crucified (1 Cor 2:1–2), the Son of God (2 Cor 1:19; cf. 11:4; Acts 18:5), had been accompanied in Corinth by a "demonstration of the Spirit and of power" (1 Cor 2:4, *RSV;* cf. 2 Cor 12:12). He himself had not baptized very many of his Corinthian converts (1 Cor 1:14–17); but he had taught them the basic articles of faith (1 Cor 15:1–11) and the basic traditions and customs of Christian behavior (1 Cor 3:1–2a; 11:2). During those eighteen months in Corinth he had sought to be self-supporting, working at his craft (1 Cor 9:3–17), but he was evidently not completely so, because he expresses gratitude to the Philippians for having sent aid to him there, as they had also in Thes- salonica (Phil 4:14–16).

A number of the apostle's converts in Corinth are known to us by name. Stephanas and his household are identified as the first converts in Achaia (1 Cor 1:16; 16:15). Other members of the earliest congregation were Crispus (1 Cor 1:14; Acts 18:8), Gaius (1 Cor 1:14; apparently host to a house-church, Rom 16:23a), Prisca (Acts: Priscilla) and Aquila (1 Cor 16:19; Rom 16:3; Acts 18:2, 18, 26), and perhaps Chloe with her household (1 Cor 1:11). If, as most interpreters agree, Rom 16 was written from Corinth (the mention of Cen- chreae in v. 1 is strong support for this view), then a number of other names may be added to the roster of Paul's Corinthian congregation: Lucius (unless this is Luke, Phlm 24) and Jason (Rom 16:21; Sopater was perhaps from Beroea, Acts 20:4), Erastus (Rom 16:23b; Acts 19:22; 2 Tim 4:20), Quartus (Rom 16:23b), and probably Tertius the scribe (Rom 16:22). Phoebe, a leading member of the congregation in the port town of Cenchreae (Rom 16:1–2), may also be listed here. And finally, from Acts, one may add the name of Titius

Justus (18:7). Despite Paul's remark about there being "not many" Christians in Corinth who were "powerful" or "of noble birth" (1 Cor 1:26, *RSV*), it is apparent that those who are specifically named are persons of some means and standing in the city (see Theissen 1982, especially 94–96).

One of these, Erastus, deserves special notice. He is probably to be identified with a person of the same name memorialized in an inscription found at Corinth in 1929, to which pieces discovered in 1928 and 1947 also belong (see Plate VIa and Kent 1966:99–100, No. 232). It remains in place in a public square (to the east of the stage building of the theater; see Figure 2, No. 1) which was paved sometime in the second half of the first century C.E. (Kent 1966:99). Except for two punctuation marks, excavators found no trace of the metal letters which were originally affixed to the limestone blocks. But the cuttings into which the letters were set allow the text on the surviving blocks to be restored.

> [missing] ERASTVS PRO AEDILITATE
> S P STRAVIT

The donor's praenomen and nomen are missing, but the rest of the inscription (part of which uses standard abbreviations) reads: "Erastus in return for his aedileship laid (the pavement) at his own expense" (tr. in Kent 1966:99). An *aedile* was in effect a commissioner of public works, and two prominent citizens were elected to the position each year (ibid.:27). Although the Erastus to whom Paul refers in Rom 16:23 is identified by the Greek phrase *oikonomos tēs poleōs* (*RSV:* "city treasurer") rather than as *agoranomos* (the usual Greek term for an *aedile*), it is highly improbable that there would have been two prominent citizens named Erastus living in Corinth at the same time. The cognomen is not common, and the name "Erastus" appears in Corinth only in this inscription (Kent 1966:99). Since a person was elected to the prestigious office of *aedile* only after having served the city in other ways, one may readily suppose that Paul's Erastus, specifically associated with Corinth in 2 Tim 4:20, was elected *aedile* after having previously been an *oikonomos* (perhaps = *quaestor;* so Theissen 1982:75–83; cf. Harrison 1964, especially 105, and Elliger 1978, especially 229–30). If this identification is correct, then the Erastus inscription provides further evidence not only that some of Paul's Corinthian converts were people of means and status but also that membership in a Christian congregation did not necessarily preclude their election to—or willingness to serve in—important municipal offices.

Paul's first hosts in Corinth, according to Acts 18:2–3, were Priscilla (Paul refers to her as Prisca) and Aquila, recently come from Rome because of a Claudian edict expelling Jews (on which see above, p. 21). Whether they were already Christians is not indicated; Paul's association with them is explained, rather, by their common craft of tent-making. That the apostle made it a point to be self-supporting in Corinth is attested by his own letters, especially 1 Cor

9:3–18 (cf. 2 Cor 11:7–11, with NOTES and COMMENT). It may be that Prisca and Aquila were among those Paul converted to the gospel in Corinth. They later moved to Ephesus (see Acts 18:18, 24, 26), and in 1 Cor, written from that Asian city, Paul sends the Corinthian congregation greetings from the couple and from "the church [that meets] in their house" (1 Cor 16:19; cf. Rom 16:3—written to Ephesus?).

Among the first of Paul's converts in Corinth was a certain Crispus, identified by Acts (18:8)—but not by Paul (1 Cor 1:14)—as a leader of the Corinthian synagogue. That Paul's initial preaching was to the Jews of the city is attested by Acts 18:4–5—but, again, not by the apostle himself. Similarly, only Acts reports the hostility of most of the Jewish community toward Paul (18:6), which culminated in their bringing him before the provincial governor, Lucius Junius Gallio (Acts 18:12–17). Gallio, however, refused to get involved in what he must have regarded as only a dispute between two factions of the Jewish community (vv. 14–15), and he dismissed complainants and defendant(s) alike (v. 16).

Many scholars (e.g., Elliger 1978:225–27) have argued that a likely place for this hearing would have been at the *bēma,* the elaborate podium which overlooked the lower terrace of the Corinthian forum (Figure 2, No. 26); indeed, the word *bēma* is used in Acts 18:12–16 (*RSV:* "tribunal"). However, this ornate complex, modeled after the imperial *Rostra* in Rome (Scranton 1951: 51–110), was probably used only for the most important official proceedings and ceremonial occasions. One can hardly conceive of its being the site for hearing such minor cases as the complaints against Paul (cf. Dinkler 1967, whose discussion of this topic remains the most thorough). It is far more likely that the hearing (and subsequent scuffle; Acts 18:17) took place in one of the colony's administrative buildings. The so-called "Twin Basilicas" (Figure 2, Nos. 31 and 36) may well have served judicial purposes (C. K. Williams 1979), but whether they had been constructed by the time of Paul's first visit to Corinth is no longer regarded as certain. The North Basilica, however (Figure 2, No. 7; Plate II), was one of the first public buildings constructed by the colonists (Fowler and Stillwell 1932:211), and it was doubtless used for judicial business. (Its *bēma* would have stood at the north end of the central hall of the building; ibid.:198.) If one must choose the single most probable location for Paul's appearance before Gallio, this basilica on the Lechaeum Road would be it (so also, e.g., Meinardus 1973:68–69). Shortly after this, according to Acts 18:18–19, Paul left the city, sailing from Cenchreae to Ephesus with Prisca and Aquila.

## Paul's First Two Letters to Corinth

1. *Letter A.* Between the time of Paul's departure from Corinth, probably in the summer of 51, and the writing of the letter known as 1 Cor, written

perhaps in the fall of 54 (see below), the apostle wrote another letter to his church in the Achaian capital. We know about this letter because Paul himself refers to it in 1 Cor 5:9. From this brief reference one learns that it included a warning to tolerate no immorality within the congregation; it may be presumed that the apostle had even counseled the expulsion of errant members. The Corinthian Christians had misunderstood these instructions, however, thinking that they were being admonished to sever their relationships with all non-believers, in effect withdrawing themselves from pagan society. It is to correct this false impression that Paul writes as he does in 1 Cor 5:9–13.

The proposal that part of this letter is preserved in 2 Cor 6:14–7:1 (so, e.g., Strachan, xv, 3–6; Schmithals 1971:94–95; and especially Hurd 1965:225–37) is not persuasive. First, there are serious reasons to doubt whether 2 Cor 6:14–7:1 is of Pauline composition (see NOTES and COMMENT on 6:14–7:1, especially pp. 375–83). Second, even if the passage is Pauline in a primary sense, it so emphatically urges separation from non-Christians (2 Cor 6:14–15) that 1 Cor 5:9–13 could represent only a fundamental reversal of position on Paul's part, not his correction of a misunderstanding on the part of the congregation. And, finally, it would be all but impossible to explain how just this one (subsequently repudiated) paragraph came to be preserved in yet another letter to Corinth. One must simply acknowledge that little more can be said about this letter than Paul himself says in 1 Cor 5:9. What else it may have contained, where it was written, and by whom it was carried must remain unanswered. One can say only that it was written sometime between the summer of 51 and the fall of 54. As such, it is the earliest Pauline letter to Corinth of which we have knowledge, and is best identified as Letter A in order to distinguish it from canonical 1 Cor.

2. *Letter B.* Unlike canonical 2 Cor (on which see below), canonical 1 Cor presupposes no other Pauline residency in Corinth than the initial eighteen-month mission of 50–51. It does, however, presuppose an earlier letter to the congregation (Letter A); thus, within the whole series of known Pauline letters to the Corinthians, canonical 1 Cor stands as Letter B. On the basis of 1 Cor 16:8 it may be assigned to the long period of Paul's Ephesian residency (cf. Acts 19:1–22). One also learns that Timothy has been sent out to Corinth (presumably from Ephesus, 1 Cor 16:10–11) in order to remind the Corinthian Christians of Paul's "ways in Christ" as the apostle has taught them "everywhere in every church" (1 Cor 4:17, *RSV*). Since Paul anticipates that this present letter will be received before Timothy's arrival in Corinth (1 Cor 16:10), one may suppose that Timothy is en route by way of Macedonia (perhaps accompanied by Erastus, Acts 19:22), while this letter is being carried straight to Corinth (see Figure 3), perhaps by Stephanas, Fortunatus, and Achaicus (1 Cor 16:17).

Paul's reference to Pentecost (1 Cor 16:8) has led most interpreters to suppose that he must be writing in the preceding winter or very early in the spring. However, except for the emergency transport of troops or food, ships did not sail from November through April (Casson 1974:150). It is therefore more likely that Letter B was written in the preceding fall, while passage could still be arranged for the person(s) by whom it was to be carried from Ephesus to Corinth. This means that Timothy would have left for Macedonia some time before, probably intending to spend the winter there and to proceed on to Achaia in the spring (see Figure 3). Because Paul knows his present letter will arrive in Corinth ahead of Timothy, he uses the opportunity to commend Timothy to the congregation and to urge a warm welcome for him (1 Cor 16:10–11; cf. 4:17).

The chief purpose of Letter B is not, however, to support Timothy's mission. The apostle's principal concern in it is to deal with a number of specific problems in the Corinthian congregation. He has learned about these from at least two sources. First, from "Chloe's people" he has received reports of dissension and factions, perhaps stemming in part from the sometime residency of Apollos in Corinth (1 Cor 1:11–12; cf. 3:5–9; 4:6; 16:12; Acts 18: 27–19:1). Perhaps from the same persons he has heard also about the flagrantly immoral conduct of one of the men of the congregation, and that the other members have been quite willing to tolerate it (1 Cor 5:1). Obviously disturbed by these reports, Paul now writes to chastise the Corinthians for their arrogance, spiritual elitism, and indifference to immorality in their midst (1 Cor 1–6).

Paul's second source of information about the current state of affairs is a letter he has received from the congregation (1 Cor 7:1). In it, the apostle has been asked to give his counsel on several controversial matters. Is it proper for Christians to marry? to remain sexually active if they already are married? to remarry? to divorce a non-believing spouse (chap. 7)? Should Christians eat meat which has been ritually slaughtered in a pagan temple (chap. 8)? What about conduct in public worship (11:2–34) and, in particular, the value of spiritual gifts, like speaking in tongues (chaps. 12–14)? And what, in fact, does Paul expect them to do about that collection for the Jerusalem church for which he has solicited them, if not already on his first visit then perhaps in Letter A or by some representative (16:1–4)? On all these points, and also on some others (notably the resurrection of the dead, 15:12–58), Paul here offers his earnest counsel and admonitions. It is apparent that he is profoundly uncertain about the future of the Christian movement in Corinth (see, e.g., 1 Cor 3:1–3; 4:8–21; 5:6a; 6:6a, 8; 15:2b, 34).

Scholars differ considerably on their dating of 1 Cor. Lüdemann, who argues that Paul first preached in Corinth in 41, would date 1 Cor in either 49 or 52 (1980:181–206, 272–73); Barrett (1968:3–5) and Koester (1982 II:121) think the winter of 53–54 is the most probable; Kümmel (1975:278–79) opts for early in 54 or 55; Conzelmann (1975:4 n. 31) and Jewett (1979:104) propose early 55; and Orr (Orr and Walther 1976:120) dates it "about 56." Assuming, against Lüdemann, that Paul had first visited Corinth in 50–51, 1 Cor could not have been written earlier than the fall-winter of 53–54, since he had in the interim visited Judea and Syria (Acts 18:18a, 22), worked among the Christians of Galatia and Phrygia (Acts 18:23), and established his ministry firmly in Ephesus (Acts 19:1–22), from where he now writes. On the other hand, a date as late as 56 for 1 Cor hardly allows enough time for all the events which must have taken place between the writing of this letter and Paul's arrival in Rome, probably in 59 or 60 (see, e.g., Jewett 1979, especially 40–46, 49–50, 100–4). It is likely, therefore, that Letter B was written in the fall (October?) of 53 or 54, more likely in the latter year.

## III. CANONICAL 2 CORINTHIANS

### External Attestation

The "strong and early attestation" to 1 Cor (e.g., in 1 Clem and in the letters of Ignatius and Polycarp [Moffatt 1918:114]) does not obtain in the case of canonical 2 Cor. The earliest certain attestation to 2 Cor is its inclusion in Marcion's canon (ca. 140–150) as that is known from Tertullian (*Against Marcion* V.xi–xii). Later it appears as well in the Muratorian Canon (usually dated as late second century, but perhaps no earlier than the fourth century; see Sundberg 1973), and is known and used, e.g., by Theophilus (Westcott 1896:232), by the author of the Epistle to Diognetus (5:12–13; cf. 2 Cor 6:9–10), and not least by the Gnostics (e.g., Apoc Paul [CG V, 2], *NHLE*, 239–41; see also Pagels 1975:95–99), the Ophites (Westcott 1896:289 n. 4; Gregory 1907:201), and the Sethians (Westcott 1896:290 n. 2). Although Polycarp may be quoting 2 Cor 6:7 in Phil 4:1 (so, e.g., Kümmel, 1975:292 n. 30; Schoedel in *AF* V:16—but questioned by Moffatt 1918:129, 148; see also 2:2 [ = 2 Cor 4:14?] and 6:2 [ = 2 Cor 5:10?], cited by Westcott 1896:49 n. 5; Oxford 1905:91; Gregory 1907:201; Barnett 1941:173, 176–77), Polycarp's letter cannot be much earlier than Marcion's canon— and may even be later.

Evidence that 2 Cor was known in the church in the late first or early second century is by no means so clear. While it is just conceivable that the author of 1 Tim 2:13–15 was familiar with 2 Cor 11:1–3 (so Barnett 1941:258; Hanson 1968:71–72), one can hardly say more than this—and 1 Tim itself may be no earlier than ca. 125. It is even less plausible (despite Oxford 1905:70; Barnett 1941:152–70) that 2 Cor is echoed in Ign Eph 15:3 (cf. 2 Cor 6:16); Ign Trall 9:2 (cf. 2 Cor 4:14); Ign Phld 6:3 (cf. 2 Cor 1:12; 11:9–10; 12:16; cf. 2:5), and (see Barnett 1941:203–7) in Barn 4:11–13 (cf. 2 Cor 5:10); 6:11–12 (cf. 2 Cor 5:17); see Moffatt 1918:129. What is genuinely surprising, however, is the lack of any certain knowledge of 2 Cor displayed by the author of 1 Clem. This late first-century letter from the Roman church to the Corinthian church (on which see below) makes full and frequent use of 1 Cor (see, e.g., 1 Clem 47:1–5), although the situation being addressed in Corinth (viz., rebellion against authority) more nearly matches that of 2 Cor (see especially J. H. Kennedy 1900:142–53). Of the various alleged allusions to 2 Cor in 1 Clem (systematically examined by Oxford 1905:51–52; Barnett 1941:88–104; Hagner 1973:209–13), the two most plausible instances occur in 1 Clem 5:5–6 and 38:2. The first of these is a reference to Paul's endurance of great difficulties —including imprisonments, exile, and stoning—and could echo the hardship catalogs in 2 Cor, especially 6:5 (on which see COMMENT) and 11:23ff. But there is only one point of contact between the vocabulary of 1 Clem 5 and the catalogs in 2 Cor (*lithastheis*, "he was stoned," 1 Clem 5:6; *elithasthēn*, "I was stoned," 2 Cor 11:25), hardly enough on which to base a secure conclusion. The second passage, 1 Clem 38:2, might possibly contain an echo of 2 Cor 9:12 (on which see COMMENT), although the two authors could be commonly dependent on a liturgical formulation (note Hagner 1973:210, who thinks 1 Cor 16:17 is the more likely background of the wording in 1 Clem). Thus, even 1 Clem 5:5–6 and 38:2 provide no clear evidence that the author of 1 Clem knew 2 Cor. Although Hagner is willing, finally, to conclude that there is "a strong possibility" that 2 Cor was known to him (1973:213), he too must acknowledge that the evidence is not really conclusive (ibid.:212).

To summarize: from about the middle of the second century there is clear and certain evidence that 2 Cor was part of the Pauline Corpus. Prior to this time, however, there is no clear and certain evidence that 2 Cor was known to the church at large. This fact is not sufficient to raise a question about the authenticity of 2 Cor, for it is in general thoroughly Pauline in form, style, and content. Rather, the question with which one is left is whether 2 Cor was *circulated* as early as other Pauline letters, including 1 Cor, and if not, why not.

## The Question of Literary Integrity

Any thoughtful reader of canonical 2 Cor will be struck at once by the abrupt shift—not only in subject matter but also in tone and style—between chaps. 9 and 10. In chap. 9, Paul makes reference to the Corinthians' eagerness to contribute to a collection for Jerusalem, and he seems optimistic about their following through on a previous commitment to that. In chap. 10, however, the subject is suddenly Paul's own status and authority as their apostle, and he is clearly troubled about the state of affairs in the congregation. This impression of a discrepancy is only increased when one compares the whole of chaps. 1–9 with the whole of chaps. 10–13. The following points are especially noteworthy.

1. The issue in chaps. 10–13 is, above all, whether the Corinthians will reject

the lure of false apostles and reaffirm their commitment to the Pauline apostolate and gospel. Here the tone is sharply polemic and passionately apologetic (see especially Drescher 1897:59–66). In chaps. 1–9, on the other hand, Paul expresses his confidence in the congregation's fidelity, and the style is by and large expository. These differences are exhibited most clearly when chap. 7 is set over against chaps. 10–13. In chap. 7 the apostle writes of the "pride" (7:4), "comfort" (7:4, 6–7, 13), and "joy" (7:4, 7, 9, 13*b*) he experiences because of what he knows about the state of affairs in the Corinthian church, including his readers' "zeal" and "earnestness" for him (7:7, 11, 12). Here he affirms the "obedience" of the Corinthians (7:15) and rejoices that he can have complete "confidence" in them (7:16). In chaps. 10–13, however, there are no such expressions of confidence. Paul is concerned that the obedience of the Corinthian Christians is not complete (10:6); he writes not of their zeal for him but of how little they love him (12:15*b*), of their suspicion that he does not love them (11:11; cf. 12:13), and of their temptation to espouse a different gospel (11:2–4). Here he writes not of his confidence in them but of his "fear" that when he comes he will find "general disorder" (12:20) and a need for repentance (12:20; contrast, e.g., 7:8–12). Similarly, one may contrast 1:24, where Paul has no doubt that the Corinthians "stand firm in faith," with 13:5, where he urges them to "find out whether [they] are in the faith" and worries lest they should fail the test.

2. The statement in 13:10—namely, that Paul writes as he does so that he will "not have to deal harshly" with the Corinthians on his forthcoming visit —is fully appropriate as a description of the function of chaps. 10–13, with its sharp warnings and admonitions; but it is not at all appropriate with reference to chaps. 1–9. As a matter of fact, the prospect of an impending visit, which so pervades chaps. 10–13, is nowhere apparent in chaps. 1–9.

3. It is extraordinary that the appeal issued in chaps. 8–9 on behalf of the collection for Jerusalem should be followed by the sharp polemic of chaps. 10–13 (see, e.g., Windisch, 288–89). This incongruity is especially striking when one recognizes how carefully the appeal of chaps. 8–9 has been prepared for by the assurances of confidence in chap. 7. And, again, the statement in 13:10 takes no account whatever of the concern for the collection, so eloquently expressed in chaps. 8–9.

4. On the basis of chaps. 1–9 alone one must conclude that Titus has so far made just one trip to Corinth (see COMMENT on 7:14), and there is no hint in these chapters that he had been accompanied by any other official representative of Paul. In 12:18*a*, however, reference is made to a brother whom Paul had sent with Titus, so it is probable that Titus' *second* mission to Corinth (see 8:6, 17–24) is now in view (see NOTES and COMMENT on 12:17–18). Moreover, one wonders how Paul can be so optimistic about Titus' prospects for completing the collection for Jerusalem on this second trip (chaps. 8–9) when he knows that some in Corinth suspect, or have even specifically charged,

that money is being raised under false pretenses (12:14–18, on which see COMMENT).

5. Finally, while the first person plural predominates in chaps. 1–9, the first person singular predominates in chaps. 10–13 (emphatically introduced in 10:1). While alternation between the first person singular and plural is common in Paul's letters—and notoriously difficult to assess (see, e.g., Dick 1900; Windisch, 33–34; Lofthouse 1947; Prümm II/1, 31–35; Kijne 1966; Baumert 1973:25–36; Carrez 1980; Cranfield 1982)—the kind of shift apparent here in 2 Cor occurs in no other Pauline letter.

These and other apparent discrepancies between chaps. 1–9 and 10–13 have led many interpreters to the conclusion that canonical 2 Cor is a composite of parts of at least two originally separate letters. This hypothesis was first proposed by Semler in 1776, who suggested that perhaps chaps. 1–9 were from an earlier letter, and chaps. 10–13 from a later one. He was supported in this judgment by Weber (1798) and—a century later—by, among others, Krenkel (1895:308–78) and Drescher (1897). This view is essentially continued in several twentieth-century commentaries (e.g., those of Windisch, Bruce, and Barrett). Meanwhile, however, Hausrath (1870, 1875:302–14) had argued that chaps. 10–13 must have been written prior to chaps. 1–9 and are, in fact, to be identified as the letter to which Paul refers in 2 Cor 2:3–4, 9; 7:8, 12 ( = the "tearful letter," 2:4). This hypothesis, with various modifications and supporting arguments, was widely adopted, not only in Germany (a number of the early proponents there are listed by Moffatt 1918:109, 121) but also in England (ibid.)—especially as a result of the independent work of J. H. Kennedy (1900; see, e.g., Plummer, xxii–xxxvi; Lake 1927:144–73; Strachan, xvi–xx)—and in the United States (e.g., Enslin 1938:254–61; Filson, 269–71).

More complex partition hypotheses have also been proposed, involving not only the separation of 6:14–7:1 as alien to the argument of 2 Cor (fully discussed in the NOTES and COMMENT on these verses) but also the identification of another letter fragment in 2:14ff. Indeed, Halmel (1904) argued that three letters are not only combined but significantly rearranged in 2 Cor. These he identified (in chronological order) as ("A") 1:1–2; 1:8–2:13; 7:5–8:24; 13:13; ("B") 10:1–13:10; and ("C") 1:3–7; 2:14–7:4; 9:1–15; 13:11–12. Moreover, from the last of these Halmel excluded 3:12–18; 4:3–4, 6; 6:14–7:1 as later interpolations. Subsequently, Weiss (1959:323–57) proposed that 2:14–6:13 plus 7:2–4 were, along with chaps. 10–13, part of the "tearful letter," that 2 Cor 6:14–7:1 plus several sections of 1 Cor had constituted Paul's earliest letter to the Corinthians (the one referred to in 5:9), and that chaps. 8 and 9 were sent on two separate occasions—chap. 8 on the occasion of Titus' first visit to the city (thus prior to all of 2 Cor except for 6:14–7:1), and chap. 9 along with 2 Cor 1:1–2:13 and 7:4–16 as part of the apostle's last letter to Corinth. A similar reconstruction of the correspondence was adopted by Goguel (1926: 72–86)—who, however, regarded 2:14–6:13; 7:2–4 as integral to chaps. 1–8, and identified chap. 9 as a separate letter, chronologically the last in the sequence. Other variations of the Weiss hypothesis were offered by Preisker (1926) and Dean (1947:40–94).

Bornkamm (1971) does not follow Weiss and Goguel in their partitioning of 1 Cor, and unlike them he regards 2 Cor 6:14–7:1 as non-Pauline. In other ways, however, his analysis of 2 Cor in effect combines elements from each of the earlier hypotheses. With Weiss, he identifies 2:14–6:13 plus 7:2–4 as a discrete entity within chaps. 1–9, but unlike Weiss he does not take it along with chaps. 10–13 as part of the "tearful letter." Rather—and in this respect he is closer to Halmel—he regards it as part of yet another letter, sent subsequent to 1 Cor but (in distinction from Halmel) prior to 2 Cor 10–13. Then, with Goguel, Bornkamm proposes that chap. 9 was originally an independent letter, Paul's last to Corinth (or Achaia). The placement of chap. 8 he regards as uncertain. Bornkamm's reconstruction has been adopted, with little or no alteration, by a number of recent scholars, including Marxsen (1968:77–82), Georgi (1964:25–29; cf. his article on 2 Cor in *IDBSup:* 183–86), Perrin (1974: 104–5) and Koester (1982 II:126–30). Others, however (e.g., Bultmann, 22–23; Vielhauer 1975:150–55), have continued to follow Weiss in associating 2: 14–7:4 (excluding 6:14–7:1) with chaps. 10–13 as part of the "tearful letter," and Vielhauer (ibid.) would date chap. 9 earlier than chap. 8. Finally, in another slight variation of this general scheme, Schmithals (1973:275–88) discovers parts of six authentically Pauline letters in 2 Cor, which he arranges in the chronological sequence (1) 6:14–7:1; (2) 2:14–6:2; (3) 6:3–13 + 7:2–4; (4) chaps. 10–13 ( = the "tearful letter"); (5) chap. 9; and (6) 1:1–2:13; 7:5–8:24.

Despite the difficulties these various partition hypotheses have been formulated to resolve, there are many who believe that there are insufficient grounds for questioning the literary integrity of 2 Cor and that, indeed, there are certain features which guarantee its unity (see, e.g., Allo, L–LVI; Tasker, 23–35; Hughes, xxi–xxxv; Stephenson 1964, 1965; Bates 1965; J. L. Price 1967; Hyldahl 1973; Kümmel 1975:287–93). The arguments most commonly marshaled in defense of the literary unity of 2 Cor may be summarized as follows:

First, it is noted that there is no manuscript or patristic warrant for thinking that any section of canonical 2 Cor ever circulated independently or as part of a separate letter (e.g., Stephenson 1965:92; Bates 1965:62–63). This includes 2 Cor 6:14–7:1, a passage whose authenticity, as well as whose place in 2 Cor, is frequently questioned.

Second, it is often held that the alleged discrepancies within 2 Cor have been overdrawn and, insofar as they may exist, can be explained without resorting to partition hypotheses. It is pointed out, for example, that there are certain apologetic and polemical features in chaps. 1–7, not only within 2:14–7:4 (sometimes associated with chaps. 10–13 or taken as an independent unit) but also in 1:1–2:13 (see, e.g., Kümmel 1975:290; Stephenson 1965:87–89; Bates

1965:63–65, 67, and Notes and Comment on 1:12–14; 1:15–2:2; 2:12–13, as well as on 2:14–6:13; 7:2–4). Again, it has been urged that the change in tone between chaps. 9 and 10 is no more difficult than that between Rom 8:38–39 and 9:1 (de Boor, 197) or between Gal 5:1 and 5:2 (Bates 1965:66), and that there are, in any case, various reasonable explanations for such a shift as may be acknowledged. Among the explanations suggested, the following are most frequently mentioned:

(a) There could well have been a "lapse of time" between Paul's dictation of chaps. 1–9 and 10–13 (e.g., Kümmel 1975:290–91), or at least "a sleepless night" (Lietzmann, 139).

(b) In chaps. 1–9, Paul's remarks concern the congregation as such, whereas in chaps. 10–13 he is specifically confronting certain "false apostles" who have intruded themselves into the congregation (Lietzmann, 139; Hughes, xxiii–xxiv, 343; cf. Kümmel 1975:290).

(c) It is possible that chaps. 1–9 are the work of Paul's scribe, taking down (and perhaps moderating?) the apostle's dictation, and that, beginning in 10:1, Paul is writing with his own hand (e.g., Deissmann 1927:167 n. 7; Bates 1965:67; Bahr 1968:37–38). Holtzmann (1926 II:717) even suggests that Timothy (see 1:1) could have been the author of the first nine chapters, but in this case one could hardly explain such passages as 1:19, 1:23–2:13, and 7:4–13.

In the third place, the literary integrity of 2 Cor has been defended on the grounds of a perceived thematic, structural, and functional coherence binding the thirteen chapters together. There is no doubt that apostleship—specifically Paul's authority as the apostle to and for Corinth—is the pervasive underlying theme of canonical 2 Cor, and several commentators argue that certain points made in chaps. 10–13 specifically presuppose or develop points made in chaps. 1–9 (e.g., Lietzmann, 140; Hughes, xxxi–xxxiii; cf. Bates 1965:67 and Kümmel 1975:292–93). Hughes, xxii (following Zahn), perceives a structural coherence as well—chaps. 1–7 focusing on Paul's experiences from Troas to Macedonia, chaps. 8–9 on the churches of Macedonia, and chaps. 10–13 on conditions in the Corinthian church. And, finally, numerous interpreters have argued that chaps. 10–13 are a meaningful sequel to chaps. 1–9, for in the latter section of the letter the apostle turns, logically, to speak of his forthcoming visit to Corinth and to prepare his congregation for that (e.g., Hughes, xxii, 344; Bates 1965:67; de Boor, 196; Kümmel 1975:291; Olson 1976:224 n. 3, 225, 239).

Anyone who reads carefully through the literature on the question of the literary integrity of 2 Cor is bound to be impressed with the complexity of the problem, with the ambiguity of much of the data, and with the many different, reasonable interpretations of the data that are possible. One thing, at least, remains clear throughout: the problems which have led to the various partition hypotheses cannot be dismissed as imaginary, even though one may think they can be surmounted. The literary integrity of 2 Cor cannot just be presupposed.

Indeed, partitionists are not the only ones who must employ hypotheses. Those who would defend the integrity of the canonical letter must regularly resort to their own hypotheses in order to explain the phenomena others regard as evidence for its composite character (cf. Vielhauer 1975:155).

### A Two-Letter Hypothesis

The hypothesis with which the present commentary operates is that canonical 2 Cor is a composite of parts—probably the major parts—of two originally distinct letters, chaps. 1–9 being from the earlier and chaps. 10–13 from the later of these. This hypothesis, as noted above, originated with Semler in the eighteenth century, and has been supported by such twentieth-century commentators as Windisch, Bruce, and Barrett. Their impressive arguments will not be repeated here in detail. Only the following major points need to be made in response to other partition hypotheses and to those who defend the integrity of the letter:

1. While it is apparent that the material in 2:14ff. is functionally distinct from that in 1:1–2:13, the break between 2:13 and 2:14 is not so severe as to require the hypothesis that 2:14ff. is drawn from a separate letter (see NOTES and COMMENT on 2:12–13 and 2:14). It is also the case that the formal and material affinity between 2:12–13 and 7:5ff. is not so pronounced as is often claimed (see NOTES and COMMENT on 2:12–13 and 7:4, 5). Moreover, if, with Bornkamm and others, one regards 2:14–7:4 as part of a letter sent subsequent to 1 Cor and prior to 2 Cor 10–13, then one is required to postulate a letter to which there is no clear reference in later correspondence; one could only suggest a possible allusion to it in 2 Cor 10:10, as Bornkamm does (1971: 177–78). The alternative—namely, to regard 2:14–7:4 as belonging to the "tearful letter" (chaps. 10–13) itself (Weiss, et al.)—is even less satisfactory, because the theme of apostleship is handled in utterly different ways in 2:14ff. and chaps. 10–13 (so, e.g., Schmithals 1971:98–99; Bornkamm 1971:176–77; Barrett, 243–44). It is, moreover, impossible to conceive of 7:4 as standing in the same letter with chaps. 10–13 (e.g., 12:20–21).

2. The case for separating 6:14–7:1 from 2 Cor is much stronger, primarily because there are so many decidedly non-Pauline features in the passage (detailed in the NOTES and COMMENT). But if, for this reason, the passage is to be excluded from 2 Cor, then it is impossible to reassign it (as some have) to the earliest letter in the Corinthian correspondence. The two likeliest possibilities would seem to be (a) that 6:14–7:1 is non-Pauline material which the apostle has himself incorporated into his letter, and (b) that it is non-Pauline material which a later redactor has seen fit to insert into the letter. The issues involved are fully examined in the NOTES and COMMENT; see also above, p. 27.

3. The case for separating chap. 8 from chap. 7 is not persuasive, because

Paul's expressions of confidence in the Corinthians which pervade 7:4(5)–16 are best understood as preliminary to the appeal for the collection in chap. 8 (see COMMENT: GENERAL on 7:4–16 and 8:1–15). Even Goguel and Schmithals, two of the more venturesome partitionists, decline to separate chap. 8 from 7:5ff., and Bornkamm, too, thinks that chap. 8 probably stands in the same letter, at least as an appendix (1971:186). A decision about the original place of chap. 9 in the Corinthian correspondence is, however, more difficult. The arguments for and against the hypothesis that chap. 9 is to be identified as an independent letter are examined in the COMMENT: GENERAL on 8:16–9:5. The conclusion reached there is that, while the hypothesis is plausible, there is no insuperable difficulty in regarding chaps. 8 and 9 as part of one letter; and they are so treated in this commentary.

4. The arguments in favor of regarding chaps. 1–9 and 10–13 as parts of separate letters are generally more convincing than the counter-arguments advanced by those who defend the literary integrity of 2 Cor. The latter commentators may be answered, in general, as follows:

(a) While it is true that there is neither manuscript nor patristic support for partitioning 2 Cor into even two independent letters, this constitutes no decisive argument against a partition hypothesis. It suggests only that 2 Cor never circulated except in its canonical form, and that any redactional combination of originally separate letters must have taken place before the circulation of any one of them.

(b) One may grant that some of the discrepancies and incongruities between chaps. 1–9 and 10–13 have at times been overdrawn (e.g., there is indeed a polemical and apologetic dimension to the argument of chaps. 1–9). But the points of tension between the two parts of 2 Cor remain serious enough that even those who defend the integrity of the letter have been constrained to propose explanations for them. Many of these explanations are, however, quite farfetched. Is it plausible that the apostle (or his secretary) would allow a long dictation pause or a sleepless night to alter so completely the tone and intent of a letter which up to that point (i.e., through chap. 9) had been composed so thoughtfully and carefully? Is it possible to believe that the visit about which Titus reported to Paul in Macedonia (7:5ff.) is the same one—referred to in 12:17–18—on which he was accompanied by at least one "brother"? Or, alternatively, that the visit reported in chap. 7 had *not* been Titus' first to Corinth? Can one believe (with, e.g., Hyldahl) that 1 Cor is the "tearful letter," that the offender mentioned in 2 Cor 2:5–11 and 7:12 is to be identified with the immoral brother of 1 Cor 5:1–5, and that 2 Cor 12:14; 13:1–2 do not require us to posit two previous visits to Corinth by Paul? (Such matters are taken up at the appropriate points in the NOTES and COMMENT.) And is it really the case that the discrepancies are resolved by regarding chaps. 1–9 as concerned with the congregation itself and chaps. 10–13 with the false apostles? Paul's rivals are also in view in chaps. 1–9 (notably in 2:17; 3:1; 5:12, on which see NOTES and COMMENT), and the congregation as such is also in view in chaps. 10–12 (e.g., 10:6; 11:1–4; 12:11, 14–16, 19–21). As 11:20 shows especially well, these two concerns are in any case closely connected.

(c) Finally, one may also grant that there is an underlying thematic coherence between 2 Cor 1–9 and 10–13. In both sections of the canonical letter the fundamental theme is apostleship, and the specific issue is the nature and authority of the Pauline apostolate. However, the basic thematic coherence of these two sections is no guarantee of their literary unity. An underlying thematic coherence may also obtain in the case of two (or more) separate letters dispatched over a period of time, especially when they are addressed to the same congregation. A two-letter hypothesis does not deny that there is an important continuity of theme between chaps. 1–9 and 10–13. It suggests only that this theme and the issues related to it are approached and developed in such significantly different ways in these two sections that it is reasonable to conclude they were written on different occasions and under somewhat different circumstances. The alleged structural and functional coherence of canonical 2 Cor is another matter, however. It is certainly true that chaps. 10–13 consist, essentially, of appeals issued in prospect of a forthcoming visit of Paul to Corinth. In itself this would be appropriate for the closing section of a letter. However, there is also a long section of appeals in the preceding chapters (5:20–9:15), and these are not only formulated in a very different way but are issued in conjunction with a visit by Paul's *representatives,* who are *preceding* him to Corinth (9:3–5). It is extremely difficult to conceive how these two sections of appeals (5:20ff. and 10:1ff.), so utterly different in their intention and formulation, could stand in the same letter.

5. The hypothesis that chaps. 10–13 are to be identified with the "tearful letter" mentioned in 2:3–4 (cf. 2:9; 7:8, 12) cannot be sustained. The case for such an identification rests primarily on the collection of several passages in chaps. 10–13 which supposedly correspond to the remarks made about the "tearful letter" in chaps. 2 and 7 (see, e.g., J. H. Kennedy 1900:81–85; also Bruce, 167, and Barrett, 13—both of whom, however, reject the hypothesis). Thus, 10:6 is compared with 2:9; 11:11 and 12:15 with 2:4; and 13:2, 10 with 2:3 (cf. 1:23). If one looks closely enough, however, similar parallels can be identified in 1 Cor, or even in 2 Cor 1–7 (Buck 1950:6; Barrett, 168); and it is easier to think of chaps. 10–13 as written in anger than in sorrow. But the most important reasons for rejecting the hypothesis that chaps. 10–13 represent the "tearful letter" are:

(a) One, or perhaps even *the* major topic of the "tearful letter" was the case of the brother who had wronged Paul (2 Cor 2:3–11; 7:8–12); but to this case there is not the slightest allusion in chaps. 10–13. To counter that chaps. 10–13 represent only part of the "tearful letter" is, like any argument from silence, an admission that one lacks substantial evidence for the hypothesis.

(b) The "tearful letter" had informed the Corinthians of a change in itinerary (see COMMENT on 1:15–17 and 2:3–4), but chaps. 10–13 make no reference to this.

(c) The "tearful letter" had been written in place of a visit, to spare the Corinthians Paul's coming (1:23–2:4); but chaps. 10–13 are written in anticipation of an impending visit by the apostle (10:2; 12:14, 20–21; 13:1–2, 10).

(d) Paul's references to the salutary effect of the "tearful letter" (see especially 7:5ff.) completely ignore the concern which dominates chaps. 10–13: namely, that the Corinthian congregation give no quarter to the "false apostles."

(e) There are good reasons for concluding that chaps. 10–13 represent a letter written after rather than before the letter of chaps. 1–9. But with this, one moves on to another point.

6. There is important evidence, even if it is not quite decisive, that chaps. 10–13 must have been written and sent some time after the dispatch of chaps. 1–9.

(a) As argued in the NOTES and COMMENT on the respective passages, the mission of Titus (and a brother) to Corinth referred to in 12:18 is most probably to be identified with the mission of Titus (and two brothers) to Corinth which is in view in 8:16–24; 9:3–5. But the context of 12:18 requires that the aorist-tense verbs in that verse be interpreted as real aorists—"I urged . . . , I sent," etc. (referring to a past occasion)—while those in 8:17, 18, 22 are to be interpreted as epistolary aorists: "is going . . . are sending" (referring to present action). The only way to avoid the conclusion that 12:18 is part of a letter written later than chaps. 1–9 is to identify the mission of Titus referred to in 12:18 with some still earlier visit. But it could not have been the visit about which Titus reported to Paul in Macedonia (7:5ff.), for there is no indication that any other official representative(s) accompanied Titus on that one. And the wording of 7:14 (on which see COMMENT) strongly suggests that Titus had been in Corinth on no previous occasion.

(b) Paul is aware, as he writes chaps. 10–13, that some in Corinth suspect him of collecting money for the Jerusalem church under false pretenses (12: 14–18), that there are rumors about "deceit" and "fraud" (vv. 16, 17). However, in his discussion of the collection project in chaps. 8 and 9 there is no indication that he is aware of any such suspicions circulating about his motives and aims. Indeed, he seems confident that the procedures he is following will prevent any suspicions of that sort from arising (8:20). This kind of confidence about the collection is as inconceivable in a letter which postdates chaps. 10–13 as it would be in the same letter with the remarks of 12:14–18.

7. Any proponent of a partition hypothesis is under an obligation to offer some plausible explanation(s) of how originally independent units could have come to be combined into a literary whole. Unfortunately this responsibility is often overlooked, perhaps because it almost inevitably involves conjecture. But what is required of partition theories is not that they provide evidence of

why and how the editing (redaction) actually took place, but only that there
would have been opportunity for redaction and some conceivable motive(s) for
it. In the case of the Pauline letters it is clear enough that there was opportunity
for redactional work, since letters which had been sent to and were the possession of congregations in such widely separated places as Rome, Corinth, and
Galatia came at last to be assembled and circulated as a group. And there is
textual evidence (e.g., in the case of the letter to the Roman church) that a
certain amount of redaction was carried out in the process.

Naturally, the more elaborate a partition hypothesis is, the more difficult it
becomes to establish a credible motive for the redactor's work. Thus, in the
case of 2 Cor the matter is especially complex for those who suggest that
several—perhaps as many as six—originally separate units have been combined redactionally into one. Bornkamm, who identifies five independent units
(1:1–2:13 plus 7:5–16 and chap. 8; 2:14–6:13 plus 7:2–4; 6:14–7:1; chap. 9;
chaps. 10–13) and allows for a sixth if chap. 8 was a separate letter, is one of
the few to have struggled with the question of how, when, and where these
disparate units (at least the three major ones) could have come to be put
together in just this way (1971:179–90, 192–94; the most elaborate earlier
attempt was by Halmel 1904:112–35). He suggests that the redaction took
place in Corinth about the same time the Book of Acts and the Pastoral
Epistles were being written, presumably (although Bornkamm does not specifically say this) in order to circulate in suitable fashion Pauline materials which
had survived to that point only as fragments. Bornkamm conceives of the
redactor using the so-called "letter of reconciliation" ( = 1:1–2:13; 7:5–16;
chap. 8?) as the foundational document, because it shows that earlier difficulties had been resolved. Into this he inserted an earlier letter ( = 2:14–6:13;
7:2–4), positioning it between 2:13 and 7:5 in order to present Paul's journey
from Ephesus to Troas to Macedonia as an instance of the "triumphal procession" of the apostle's gospel throughout the Gentile world. Finally, according
to Bornkamm the redactor added chaps. 10–13. Although in Bornkamm's
view these chapters were part of the "tearful letter" and hence chronologically
prior to the "letter of reconciliation," they were placed at the end of the newly
fashioned "letter" in order to present Paul's opponents as "false prophets of
the end-time" and to enhance the apostle's own image by providing a sort of
apocalyptic climax.

Bornkamm's explanation for the location of 2:14ff. after 2:13 requires that
one interpret *thriambeuonti hēmas* in 2:14 as a metaphor of triumph—an
interpretation for which there is no lexical support (see NOTES and COM-
MENT); it therefore fails to convince. Hardly more persuasive is the explanation offered for the placement of chaps. 10–13 at the end. As Barrett, 24,
observes, Bornkamm himself must acknowledge that these chapters are not in
any sense apocalyptic, and it is difficult to see how anyone, even fifty years after
Paul's death, could read them—or expect them to be read—as anything other

than straightforward polemic against the apostle's rivals. Bornkamm has not attempted to explain how 6:14ff. came to be interpolated between 6:13 and 7:2 or how chap. 9 came to be added to chap. 8. With the latter, however, there is no real problem, for one can easily imagine a redactor joining a short, independent letter about the collection (chap. 9, according to Bornkamm) to chap. 8, which is devoted to the same topic. As for 6:14–7:1, the puzzle remains whether one regards it as integral to its present context or as an interpolation (see NOTES and COMMENT for details).

A distinct advantage of the simpler partition hypothesis employed in this commentary is the relative ease in imagining how just two originally independent letters came to be combined. One possibility is that an editor, finding two letters of unequal length but responsive to the same (or related) issues, or close in date, simply joined them by adding the shorter to the longer, or the later to the earlier. In either case the result would be what one finds in 2 Cor: the letter of chaps. 1–9 followed by that of chaps. 10–13. The editor would have needed only to remove the letter closing of the first and the letter opening of the second. A similar kind of redactional procedure was followed by the editors of the letters of Isocrates and Apollonius of Tyana, respectively (Vielhauer 1975:154–55), by Pliny the Elder in compiling his own letters (Thraede 1970: 77), and by the editors of the ancient copybooks (Deissmann 1927:236). A second possibility is that an editor found one letter with either its opening or concluding section(s) seriously damaged or missing entirely—probably not an uncommon fate of manuscripts which were kept and consulted in the archives of local congregations over many decades (cf. Deissmann, ibid.). One can imagine how, if there were a second letter associated with it by virtue of theme or date (or both), the editor might decide to combine the two by merely removing what the combination would render superfluous in the complete text —either its opening or closing. (One need not suppose, with J. H. Kennedy 1900:154, 159, that the redactor was confronted with the coincidence that one manuscript was missing an ending and a second manuscript its opening.)

On the basis of external evidence (see above, pp. 29–30), it would appear that 2 Cor was given its present form sometime during the period 96–125 C.E., since it was probably not known to the author(s) of 1 Clem but was certainly being circulated with other Pauline letters by the time of Marcion. It is not unreasonable to suppose that the editing of 2 Cor occurred shortly after 1 Clem, a letter from the Roman Christians to the troubled Corinthian congregation, had been received in Corinth about the year 96. As J. H. Kennedy suggested (1900:158), the exhortation of 1 Clem 47:1 to "take up the epistle of the blessed Paul the apostle," although it seems to confirm a knowledge only of 1 Cor, might well have spurred an interest among the Corinthians in recovering other Pauline letters which had been addressed to their church. Kennedy's own proposal (ibid.:157–62) was that the Roman representatives to Corinth (Claudius Ephebus, Valerius Bito, and Fortunatus—1 Clem 65:1) had found two neglected letters of Paul at Corinth, previously uncirculated because neither was complete, and that they had edited them for use locally and in Rome. Another possibility is that the Corinthian presbyters themselves, finding their authority over the congregation seriously threatened (see, e.g., 1 Clem 3:3; 44:1–6; 47:5–6; 54:1–2), retrieved from the congregational archives two letters, or parts thereof, in which the founding apostle had responded to similar threats, and edited them for use against the present insurgents (cf. Clayton 1977: 10–12).

In summary, the most plausible hypothesis is that canonical 2 Cor is a composite of parts (probably the major portions) of two originally independent letters. Internal evidence suggests that chaps. 1–9 represent the earlier of these, and chaps. 10–13 the later.

## Chapters 1–9 (Letter D)

Chapters 1–9 of 2 Cor must be later than 1 Cor, since 1 Cor presupposes that Paul had been in Corinth only once—the visit of 50–51 C.E., when he founded a congregation there—whereas 2 Cor 1–9 presupposes an additional visit, on which the apostle looks back with considerable pain (1:23–2:1, on which see NOTES and COMMENT). Moreover, chaps. 1–9 also presuppose that, subsequent to the painful visit, Paul had written a "tearful letter" to Corinth. This letter, which seems not to have survived, is referred to in 2 Cor 2:3–4, 9 and 7:8, 12; and its salutary effects in persuading the congregation to act responsibly in the case of an errant brother were subsequently reported to Paul by Titus (2 Cor 7:5–16). It may be designated as Letter C, since it is the third known to have been written to the Corinthian Christians by Paul. Thus, chaps. 1–9 of 2 Cor, the next in the sequence, would be Letter D.

1. *Occasion and purpose.* This letter was written from Macedonia, probably not long after Titus had brought Paul news about the state of affairs in the Corinthian congregation (7:5–6; cf. 9:4). Titus had not taken part in the original Pauline mission to Corinth (2 Cor 1:19), and it would appear that the visit from which he has just returned was his very first to the church there (see discussion on 7:14). While Paul, in writing now, emphasizes the encouraging parts of the report Titus has brought (see especially 7:4–16), the apostle is also aware that there are at least some among the Corinthians who are not certain he is being fully candid in his dealings with them (see, e.g., 1:12). They may harbor some resentment about the tone of his previous ("tearful") letter (see 2:4), and they have perhaps criticized him for trying so hard to please that he commits himself to things he does not seriously intend to do (see discussion on 1:15–2:2). He is also aware, as he writes, that there are "some" who have intruded themselves into the congregation on the basis of letters of recommendation (3:1), and who, in the process of their self-confident boasting (5:12), have insinuated that Paul's credentials are not "adequate" for one who claims

apostolic status (e.g., 2:14–3:6; 4:1–15, 16; 5:11; 6:4–10). Primarily, though, Paul has been heartened by Titus' report, and he is now generally confident of the congregation's loyalty to the gospel and to his apostolate. He is so confident, in fact, that Titus is being asked to return to Corinth, along with two Christian brothers, to help the Corinthians complete the pledge they had made to Paul's collection for the Jerusalem church (chaps. 8, 9; cf. 1 Cor 16:1–4).

From 2 Cor 1:8–11 one learns that Paul has been delivered, probably recently, from some mortal threat in Asia. As indicated in the COMMENT on the passage, it is reasonable to suppose that the incident was associated with an Ephesian imprisonment. If Phil 1 and 2 (at least) were written during that imprisonment, then the imprisonment must be dated after Timothy's return to Ephesus from the Corinthian visit mentioned in 1 Cor 4:17; 16:10–11, because Timothy is now again with Paul (Phil 2:19–23). The imprisonment must also have been subsequent to Letter C and to Titus' departure from Ephesus for Corinth on his first visit, since Paul appears to be informing the Corinthians about it for the first time here in Letter D (see discussion on 1:8). Thus, working forward from the likely date of Letter B (fall of 54), one may reasonably suppose that Paul was imprisoned in Ephesus in the summer of 55 —Timothy's return from Corinth, the "sorrowful visit," the "tearful letter," and Titus' dispatch to Corinth having occurred after the sea-lanes were opened in the spring of the same year. Upon his release from prison, Paul went first to Troas (2:12), and then, after but a short stay, on to Macedonia (2 Cor 2:13), perhaps Philippi (see Figure 3). He was probably accompanied on this trip by Timothy, for Timothy is named as the co-sender of Letter D (2 Cor 1:1), written after the reunion with Titus in Macedonia. The date of this letter can be tentatively fixed as late summer or early fall in the year 55. It is clear that events, especially his imprisonment in Ephesus, have delayed the apostle's long-planned visit to the churches of Macedonia. They have also rendered it impossible for him to spend the winter of 55–56 in Corinth as he had once hoped (see 1 Cor 16:5–7).

In view of the events which occasioned its writing, Paul's objectives in Letter D may be summarized as follows: (a) to assure his Corinthian congregation that he is genuinely concerned for them despite the severity of the "tearful letter" and despite his cancellation of a projected double visit to their city; (b) to clarify what he understands his apostolic commission to require in general, and to mean for the Corinthians in particular; and (c) to appeal to the Corinthian Christians to strengthen and confirm their commitment to the gospel and to his apostolate, not least by co-operating with Titus, who is returning to Corinth (along with two others) on behalf of the collection for Jerusalem. Indeed, one may even say that the underlying *practical* purpose of Letter D is to appeal to the Corinthians to make good on their long-standing commitment to contribute to the collection. It is within the context of this appeal (chaps. 8, 9) that those who are to supervise the collection in Corinth are commended (8:16–24; 9:3–5). Since they are, at the same time, the bearers of this letter, it seems clear that Paul's assurances of concern and his comments on the meaning of his apostleship are intended, finally, to support their specific mission, as well as to clear up certain points about his ministry which the Corinthians continue to misunderstand.

2. *Structure and style.* There is no compelling reason to assign the address of canonical 2 Cor to a second-century redactor (see COMMENT on 1:1–2), nor to suppose that it was transposed to its present position from some other letter in the Corinthian collection. It is most reasonable to presume, barring evidence to the contrary, that it was left in place when Letter D (chaps. 1–9) was joined with Letter E (chaps. 10–13). The closing paragraph(s) of Letter D must be lost, however, for the final verses of canonical 2 Cor are best taken with Letter E (see COMMENT on 13:11–13). The lost verses would have included, one may suppose, the apostle's usual closing greetings and benediction. But it is not necessary to presume that any more than this has been removed (or lost) from the end of the letter, because the appeal on behalf of the collection in chaps. 8 and 9 forms an appropriate climax to what has gone before. Thus, what is left of the original may be analyzed as follows:

  I. Letter Opening, 1:1–11
     A. Address, 1:1–2
     B. Blessing, 1:3–11
 II. Letter Body, 1:12–9:15
     A. Assurances of Concern, 1:12–2:13
     B. Comments on Apostolic Service, 2:14–5:19
     C. Appeals, 5:20–9:15

That the address is followed by a paragraph formulated as a blessing rather than as a thanksgiving (which is more usual for Paul) is probably due in part to Paul's remaining somewhat unsure of his relationship to the readers, and in part to his gratitude for having been delivered from a recent peril in Asia (see further discussion on 1:3–11). The three major sections of the letter body correspond to the main reasons Paul is writing, as summarized above: to assure his congregation he is still concerned for them despite apparent evidence to the contrary; to help them understand why his apostleship takes the form it does; and to appeal for their loyalty to his gospel and, in particular, for their co-operation in the matter of the collection.

The first person plural predominates in Letter D, interrupted by the first person singular only in 1:13*b*, 15–17, 23; 2:1–13; 5:11*b*; 6:13*b*; 7:3, 4, 7*b*–12, 14*a*, 16; 8:3, 8, 10*a*[–15], 23*b*; 9:1–4. The dominance of the first person plural is not adequately explained by the fact that the address mentions Timothy as co-sender of the letter (1:1), for co-senders are also mentioned in 1 Cor (1:1, Sosthenes) and Phil (1:1, again Timothy), but with no corresponding use of the first person plural. (See, however, 1 Thess.) More important, the use of the first person plural in 2 Cor 1–9, whether calculated or not, lends to the whole an aspect of solemn purposefulness and authority—one that is appropriate in a letter intended above all to assure the readers (a) that their confidence in the Pauline apostolate has not been misplaced, and (b) that this should now be demonstrated by the payment of their pledge to the collection for Jerusalem. In most of the places where the first person singular does intrude, its appearance can be explained by the apostle's sense of personal involvement with or responsibility for the matter in question (see, e.g., 1:15–17).

The overall tone of Letter D is earnest, and Paul's mood as he writes is guardedly optimistic. His expressions of confidence in the congregation (especially in 7:4–16), while doubtless influenced by his concern that it should heed his appeal on behalf of the collection, seem genuinely based on the generally encouraging report he has just received from Titus. Thus, insofar as he deals at all with the specific situation in the Corinthian church or with certain lingering suspicions about his ministry (primarily in 1:12–2:13), he does so tactfully, even gently. The same kind of tactfulness is evident in the appeals, especially those of 6:11–7:3 (to be fully reconciled with his apostolate) and 7:4–9:15 (to fulfill their commitment to the collection). Finally, Paul's exposition of the meaning of apostleship, and of his in particular (2:14–5:19), is formulated more didactically than polemically, even though it has an apologetic aspect and, on occasion, a polemical edge. He gives the impression here of being fully in control of the scriptural (e.g., 3:7–18), rhetorical (e.g., 4:8–9; 6:4c–5), and creedal (e.g., 5:14–15) traditions on which he relies and which he is able, with impressive skill, to adapt for his own purposes.

### Chapters 10–13 (Letter E)

The arguments against identifying 2 Cor 10–13 with the so-called "tearful letter" referred to in 2:3–4, and for dating it after 2 Cor 1–9, have been summarized above (pp. 37–38). Thus, chaps. 10–13 represent the last in the sequence of letters Paul is known to have written to the Corinthian Christians, and may be designated Letter E.

1. *Occasion and purpose.* The purpose of the letter is stated by Paul himself in 13:10—"This is why I am writing these things while I am absent, so that when I am present I shall not have to deal harshly . . ." The presuppositions of this statement are (a) that at present the Corinthians need some stern warnings and admonitions, and (b) that Paul expects to be visiting them in the near future. Both points are borne out by the actual content of chaps. 10–13: the principal intention here is to appeal to the readers to be obedient to the gospel they have received from Paul (see especially 10:1–18; 12:14–13:10), and the warnings and admonitions are issued in advance of and in preparation for the apostle's forthcoming third visit to the congregation (12:14; 13:1–2; cf. 10:1–2, 10–11).

Even though the presupposition of these exhortations must be that the Corinthians may yet amend their ways and demonstrate their loyalty to Paul and his gospel, the fundamental optimism of Letter D has all but disappeared. Only in 13:5–9—and there very tentatively—does the apostle actually express some hope for the Corinthians' improvement. Elsewhere the letter expresses primarily his anxiety, his frustration, even his sense of outrage at the way things seem to be going in the Corinthian congregation. It is clear that the situation has substantially deteriorated since Titus and the two accompanying brothers had been dispatched with Letter D; or else Titus' earlier report (2 Cor 7:4–16) had been overly optimistic, or Paul had over-interpreted its encouraging aspects. Whatever the case, Letter E must have been written following receipt of new and profoundly disturbing reports, perhaps again from Titus, although Paul gives no indication of the source.

Now Paul has learned, or has come to realize for the first time, that certain rival apostles who have intruded themselves into his congregation are having some success. He had been aware of the presence of such people when he wrote Letter D (e.g., 2:17; 3:1; 5:11), but seems not to have considered them a serious threat at that time. Now, however, he recognizes that the interlopers are actually trying to establish themselves as the apostolic authorities in Corinth (10:12–18), and that in the process they have raised serious questions about his apostolic credentials, authority, and even integrity (see, e.g., 10:1–10; 11:5–11; 12:14–18). Indeed, Paul has come to believe that the congregation is in imminent danger of being won over to a gospel which is in important respects different from his own (11:2–4). Who these rival apostles were and what, in particular, their charges against Paul included are considered below (pp. 48–54).

There are no specific references in Letter E to the collection for Jerusalem, on behalf of which Titus had been sent for a second time to Corinth (2 Cor 8:6). It is clear, however, that the collection is in mind when, in 12:14–18, Paul responds to charges that he has been guilty of deceit and fraud in his dealings with the congregation. From this paragraph, in which there is specific mention of Titus' second visit to Corinth (vv. 17–18), one may infer that the Corinthians have become so suspicious of Paul's motives that they are refusing to fulfill their commitment to the collection. It is likely that Paul's rivals have planted the seeds of this suspicion by pointing out an apparent contradiction in his behavior: on the one hand, he has declined to accept any financial support from the Corinthians for himself, claiming that he wants to spare them any such burden (11:5–11); on the other hand, he has solicited them by letter (1 Cor 16:1–4; 2 Cor 8, 9) and through Titus for a contribution to the fund for Jerusalem. One can imagine that Paul's opponents have encouraged his congregation to think not only that the apostle's actions are contradictory but also that Paul himself is planning to use for his own purposes the money he says he is raising for Jerusalem. Thus one immediate, practical result of the activity of rival apostles in Corinth was probably the failure of Titus' second mission, which was to ensure that the collection would be completed by the time of Paul's arrival, en route to Jerusalem. If so, the sense of urgency and frustration which permeates the whole of Letter E may be due to more than the deterioration of his relationship with the Corinthians. It may be due, as well, to Paul's fear of what this could mean for his collection project as a whole, and thus for his planned trip to Jerusalem and meeting with the apostles there.

This letter, like Letter D, must have been written from Macedonia (this is by no means precluded by 10:16, on which see the NOTES), and conceivably from the same city. But just as it is likely that Letter D had been written shortly after Paul's entry into Macedonia from Troas (thus, perhaps from Philippi), so it is likely that Letter E was written shortly before his departure from Macedonia, because he seems to anticipate seeing the Corinthians soon. For this reason one might conjecture either Thessalonica or Beroea as the place of writing. There were Pauline congregations in both places (for Beroea see Acts 17:10–12; cf. 20:4) which the apostle would doubtless have visited before leaving Macedonia, and either of these cities could have served as his last stop before proceeding to Corinth (see Figure 3). A date in the summer of 56, somewhat less than one year after Letter D, would allow time for Paul's itinerating among the Macedonian churches (winter and spring of 56), and also for a winter to be spent in Corinth (56–57) before sailing for Jerusalem in the spring of 57 (from Philippi; see Acts 20:3–6 and cf. Jewett 1979:49–50, 100–4). There are enough similarities between 2 Cor 10–13 and Gal (even when many of those identified by Borse 1972:84–119 are discounted) to make it likely that Paul wrote his letter to the churches of Galatia at approximately this time.

There is no way of knowing precisely what effect Letter E had upon the Corinthian congregation. It is highly probable, however, that Rom was written from Corinth on the occasion of the visit which Paul had anticipated in 2 Cor 12:14; 13:1–2, etc., and from Rom 15:26–27 one may surmise that the Corinthians finally made a contribution to the collection for Jerusalem. Moreover, as P. Marshall (1980:481–82) has suggested, Paul may have provided us (unintentionally) with a "cameo" of the Corinthian situation in Rom 16:17–20, probably also written in Corinth (see Rom 16:1–2), even if it was not originally part of Rom. There the apostle appeals to his readers to be watchful of those who oppose true Christian teaching (Rom 16:17) and who "by fair speech and flattery [dia tēs chrēstologias kai eulogias] . . . deceive the hearts of the innocent" (Rom 16:18). It is not difficult to imagine this kind of general warning being formulated by Paul in the light of what he had encountered in Corinth, where the intruders have sought by wily deceits to replace his gospel and to take over his congregation (note especially 11:2–4, 12–15, cited by P. Marshall 1980:482 n. 1). Although they pass themselves off as "apostles of Christ" and "ministers of righteousness," Paul decries them as "false apostles" and ministers of Satan (2 Cor 11:13, 15).

2. *Structure and style.* The opening of Letter E is missing, as may already have been the case when an editor decided to join Letter E to Letter D. It would have had to be omitted anyway in the process of redaction. One may suppose that the address identified Paul as the only sender, since the mention of a co-sender (e.g., Timothy in Letter D, 2 Cor 1:1) would have fit poorly with the emphatic first person singular with which chap. 10 opens (10:1–2a) and which predominates throughout chaps. 10–13 (cf. Rom 1:1 with Rom 1:8, 16, and Gal 1:1 with Gal 1:6, 10, 11, etc.; in Phlm, however, the first person singular is used throughout despite the mention of Timothy as co-sender— Phlm 1). The first person plural is used only in 10:2b–8, 11–18; 12:18b–19; 13:4b, 6b–9; and momentarily in 11:4, 6, 12, 21. It would appear that the letter closing of canonical 2 Cor was, in fact, the original closing of Letter E (see COMMENT: GENERAL and DETAILED on 13:11–13), and that nothing between that and the letter body has dropped out.

Whether a paragraph of thanksgiving (comparable to those of Rom 1:8ff.; 1 Cor 1:4ff., etc.) or of blessing (comparable to the one in Letter D, 2 Cor 1:3ff.) originally stood between the address and the body of Letter E cannot be decided. Given the urgency with which Paul writes, and his evident frustration with affairs in the congregation, it is possible that such a paragraph was omitted by Paul himself (cf. Barrett, 245), as under comparable circumstances in Gal (cf. Gal 1:6). But it is also understandable how an editor might have decided to omit the thanksgiving (blessing) paragraph—found only at the beginning of letters—when Letter E was appended as the last part of Letter D. If a thanksgiving (or blessing) was a part of Letter E, then the original structure of the letter would have corresponded to that of 1 Cor and Phlm— where, following the address (1 Cor 1:1–3; Phlm 1–3) and thanksgiving (1 Cor 1:4–9; Phlm 4–7), the letter body is opened with an appeal (1 Cor 1:10; Phlm 8–9; 2 Cor 10:1). In broad outline, then, Letter E, as it has survived, may be analyzed as follows:

    I. Letter Body, 10:1–13:10
        A. An Appeal for Obedience, 10:1–18
        B. A Fool's Speech, 11:1–12:13
        C. Renewal and Conclusion of the Appeal, 12:14–13:10
    II. Letter Closing, 13:11–13[14]

What Paul introduces in 11:1 as "a little bit of foolishness" ends up constituting substantially more than half of the body of Letter E. This "foolishness" consists of a series of boasts about himself, a tactic to which he feels he has been forced by the circumstances in Corinth (note, especially, the prologue and the epilogue to the boasting proper in 11:1–21a and 12:11–13, respectively). Despite Paul's description of himself as "an amateur in public speaking" (11:5), throughout this central section he makes effective use of a number of the rhetorical conventions of his day, among which *synkrisis* ("comparison"), self-display, irony, and parody are especially prominent. These are employed both polemically, against the rival apostles, and apologetically, as he defends himself against their insinuations and charges.

The rhetorical device of *comparison,* already present in 10:12–16, is further evident in 11:5–6, 21*b*–23*a;* 12:11*b,* and is implicit throughout 11:23*b*–12:10. The catalog of hardships in 11:23*b*–29 and the escape narrative in 11:32–33 have formal parallels in the ancient literature of *self-display. Irony* is extensively employed, as in 11:19–21*a,* but especially when the apostle insists that he will boast only of his weaknesses (11:30; 12:5, 9*b*–10). And there is also an element of *parody* involved in all of this—as suggested in 11:18, where Paul says he will match the boasts of his rivals with boasting of his own. Do others boast of their personal courage and valor in overcoming hardships? Paul's hardships display only his weakness. Do others claim to have gained special religious knowledge by virtue of uncommon religious experiences? Even Paul's journey to Paradise had only limited value. Do others claim the ability to call upon divine power for help in time of need? Paul's repeated prayer to be delivered from "a thorn in the flesh" brought him no relief. Even in the midst of this strange boasting, the apostle makes it clear that he is boasting only of his weaknesses (11:30; 12:5); the theological basis of that is provided in 12:9, where the Lord's response to Paul's call for help is reported: "My grace is enough for you; for power is made fully present in weakness."

The length and rhetorical distinctiveness of the "fool's speech" should not, however, be allowed to obscure the overall hortatory character of Letter E. The explicit appeals and admonitions come primarily at the beginning and end of the letter body (verbs of entreaty: 10:1, 2; imperative forms: 10:7 [two], 11, 17; 13:5 [two], 11 [five], 12). Within the long middle section the few direct appeals are not for any change of behavior on the part of the readers but rather, in two instances, for indulging Paul in his foolish boasting (11:1, 16), and in one instance, fraught with irony, for excusing his refusal to lay any (financial) burden upon them (12:13). Nevertheless, even this "fool's speech" is implicitly hortatory. Both the sharp attacks on his rivals and the numerous points he seeks to register in his own defense support the appeal which dominates this letter: that the Corinthians should pay no more attention to the "false apostles" and should make their obedience to the Pauline gospel complete by the time of Paul's arrival.

## The "False Apostles"

The polemic of Letter E is directed at a group (see 10:2, 12; 11:12–13, 15, 18, 19, 21*b*, 23*a*), although there is no way to judge how many persons were involved; there need have been no more than two or three. Because the Corinthian congregation could have been in no doubt as to the identity of these opponents, it is understandable that Paul nowhere provides a systematic description of them—not of their background, their claims, their methods of operation, or their teachings. Such evidence as bears on these points is incidental and, of course, partisan, since Paul is concerned only to expose these persons as "false apostles" (11:13) and to defend his own apostolic authority against the charges and suspicions they are raising in Corinth. Apart from the derogatory expressions he applies to them ("super-apostles," 11:5; 12:11; "false apostles, deceitful workers," 11:13; ministers of Satan in disguise, 11:14–15; "fools," 11:19), Paul refers to them only obliquely, thereby following the ancient rhetorical convention of denying one's enemies even such status as the use of their names could accord them (see P. Marshall 1980:528–38). Thus, he uses instead the expressions *tis, tines* ("some," "someone," "certain persons"—3:1; 10:2, 7, 12; 11:20, 21*b*); [*hoi*] *polloi* ("so many," "many"—2:17; 11:18); and *ho toioutos, hoi toioutoi* ("such a person," "such people"—10:11; 11:13); or else substantive participles which describe their actions, as in 5:12; 10:18; 11:4, 12.

In addition to general studies of Paul's opponents (e.g., Gunther 1973), there have been numerous books and articles specifically on his Corinthian opponents (e.g., Schmithals 1971; Bieder 1961; Friedrich 1963b; Georgi 1964; Oostendorp 1967; Barrett 1971; Machalet 1973; Thrall 1980), a survey of which discloses what varied conclusions can be drawn from the limited evidence that is available. The history of the research on this topic has been often reviewed (see, e.g., Hughes, 356–58; Barrett, 28–30, and 1971:233–36; Friedrich 1963b:192–96; Georgi 1964:7–16; Machalet 1973:183–90; G. Barth 1980:257–59), and need not be repeated here. One may simply note that most proposals about the identity of Paul's opponents in 2 Cor can be listed under one or another of three broad headings: (1) those which identify them as some kind of Judaizers (e.g., Windisch, 23–26; Oostendorp 1967; Gunther 1973, especially 299–303), perhaps official representatives of the Palestinian church (e.g., Käsemann 1942; Barrett, 28–32, and 1971); (2) those which identify them as some kind of Gnostics (e.g., Lütgert 1908; Bultmann, especially 132–41, and 1947; Schmithals 1971); and (3) those which identify them as Christian propagandists from a Hellenistic-Jewish background (e.g., Friedrich 1963b; Georgi 1964; Bornkamm 1971:169–71). In addition, there is the important question of whether the "super-apostles" mentioned in 11:5 and 12:11 are to be identified with the "false apostles" (11:13) who were active in Corinth (so most interpreters), or whether they are to be distinguished from those itinerant preachers and identified with the leaders of the Palestinian church (so, e.g., Käsemann 1942:41–48 and Barrett 1971).

As indicated in the NOTES and COMMENT on 11:5–6, the arguments which have been advanced in favor of distinguishing the "super-apostles" from the "false apostles" are not convincing. The evidence strongly suggests that Paul has just one group in mind—namely, those persons who from his point of view, at least, have set themselves up in Corinth as his competitors. Where do they come from, what do they stand for, and what are they doing in Corinth?

Insofar as answers to these questions are possible at all, they must be based on a careful survey of the evidence present in the Corinthian correspondence. In gathering and assessing the data from these letters, several important methodological principles must be observed (compare the remarks on method by Dahl 1967:317–18; Machalet 1973:190; Hanson 1980:23; Berger 1980).

(a) The evidence from Letter D (2 Cor 1–9) and Letter E (2 Cor 10–13) must be examined independently, and without presuming anything on the basis of the situation being addressed in Letter B (1 Cor).

(b) Specific references to opponents must be given absolute priority in the attempt to discover who they are and why they are in Corinth. Since these are far more numerous in Letter E than in Letter D, the former rather than the latter is the proper starting point for any investigation.

(c) Allusions to the opponents, their activities, and their teachings should be sought out and evaluated only on the basis of the profile of them which can be developed from the explicit references. One must not presume that every point made by Paul is designed to counter a point made by his rivals.

(d) Data from other Pauline letters, and from other canonical and non-canonical sources, can be allowed only insofar as they confirm or clarify what the data from the primary texts already suggest.

(e) Due account must be taken of the partisan standpoint from which Paul writes, and of the possibility that he himself may have been inadequately or even erroneously informed about the opponents.

In accordance with these principles, the chief data pertinent to the identification of the "false apostles" who are opposed in 2 Cor may be summarized (1, 2) and synthesized (3) as follows.

1. *Explicit references.* (a) Letter E (2 Cor 10–13): 10:2, 7, 10–11, 12; 11:5–6, 12–15, 18–20, 21b–23a; 12:11. From these references (on which see NOTES and COMMENT) it is clear, first, that Paul has been accused of lacking any special relationship with Christ (10:7), of being inferior with respect to his religious knowledge (11:6), of being ineffectual in public speaking and in carrying out the apostolic claims he makes in his letters (10:10–11; 11:5–6), and of conducting himself "according to worldly standards" (10:2). Second, it is also evident that Paul, for his part, views his opponents as intruders who have brought "another gospel" to Corinth, and who have sought—with some success—to seduce the congregation from its devotion to the Christ he himself had preached there (11:3–4). Presumptuously boasting of their superior apostolic credentials (10:12; 11:18; cf. 11:5 and 12:11), they have, in fact, misrepresented themselves as true apostles (11:12–15) in order to exploit the hospitality of their Corinthian hosts (11:19–20). Finally, from these passages one may surmise that the intruders were skilled in the art of Hellenistic rhetoric (11:6; cf. 10:10), and that they boasted specifically about being of Jewish stock (11:21b–22).

(b) Letter D (2 Cor 1–9): 2:17; 3:1; 5:12. From these passages (on which see

NOTES and COMMENT) one learns that the Corinthians are familiar with "some" who have come to their city with letters of recommendation and who, Paul presumes, would expect such letters from the Corinthians (3:1); that these people "are boasting of what is outward and not of what is within"; and that in so doing they have sought to diminish Paul's stature in the eyes of the congregation (5:12). These points correspond closely enough with the profile of the opponents which emerges from the explicit references to them in Letter E (e.g., 10:12; 11:18 and 10:7, 10–11) that one may safely conclude that Paul is thinking of the same people in both letters. Once this is recognized, the reference in 2:17 to "so many huckstering the word of God" is readily seen as a further description of those who have come to Corinth preaching "another gospel" (11:4), and Paul's comment about his own "pure motives" in preaching (2:17) can be understood as an allusion to the impure motives of his rivals (cf. 11:12–15, 20).

2. *Apparent allusions.* (a) Letter E. In 10:13–18, Paul undoubtedly intends to contrast his own practice with that of the "certain persons" to whom he has just referred in 10:12. Thus, it is clear that he regards them as having invaded his mission field and having attempted to take credit for what he has done there. One can be equally confident of allusions to the rival apostles throughout the "fool's speech" (11:1–12:13), even where there are no specific references to them; for Paul emphasizes that his "boasting" is prompted by the preposterous claims of those whom he opposes (11:18). His insistence that he boasts only of his weaknesses (11:30; 12:5, 9b–10) suggests that they have boasted of their extraordinary powers and experiences, and is reasonably taken as a response to the charge that he is a spiritual weakling (10:10; cf. 11:21a). This suggests, in turn, that the reference in 12:12 to the performance of "apostolic signs" has been prompted by charges that Paul has not exhibited these, and that the references in 12:19 and 13:3 to Paul's "speaking in Christ" and to Christ's speaking through Paul are also responsive to charges that he lacks spiritual power (cf. 13:4). Again, the apostle's defense of his refusal to accept financial support from the Corinthians (11:7–11) is so closely associated with a reference to the "super-apostles" (11:5–6) that one may suppose this was another point on which they had attacked him (cf. 12:11, 13). And the remarks in 12:14–18 are especially significant if, as it would appear, the opponents have also raised suspicions about Paul's solicitation of a collection for Jerusalem. (See NOTES and COMMENT on each of these passages.)

(b) Letter D. It is probable that Paul's comment about ecstatic experiences in 5:13a (on which see NOTES and COMMENT) is prompted by his specific reference in the preceding sentence to "those who are boasting of what is outward . . ." (5:12). One may suppose that ecstatic experiences were among those things of which his rivals were boasting. Similarly, the specific reference in 3:1 to those who employ letters of recommendation prompts the apostle to write about his own credentials (3:2–3) and, in particular, to affirm his own apostolic "boldness" (3:4, 12; cf. 10:1–6). Therefore, while 3:7–18 is more expository than polemical (see COMMENT), there is unquestionably a polemical and apologetic aspect to the argument. This becomes clear when, in 4:1–2, Paul reaffirms his apostolic boldness (4:1) and, doubtless with an eye on his opponents, declares that his manner of preaching and commendation is very different from theirs (4:2; cf. 2:17). Again, in the hardship lists of 4:8–9; 6:4c–5, and their wider contexts (4:7–5:10; 5:20–6:10), it is likely that Paul is at least in part responding to the charges of opponents that his career manifests only weakness (cf. 10:1, 10; 11:21a, 21b–29, 30–33, etc.).

3. *Synthesis of the data.* For all the differences of form, function, and tone between Letters D and E, it is apparent that the opposition of which Paul is aware as he writes the earlier letter (chaps. 1–9) is essentially the same as that which he sharply condemns in the later letter (chaps. 10–13). The persons in question are not, like Paul's opponents in Letter B (1 Cor), resident Corinthians and members of the congregation there; rather, they are outsiders (11:4) who by means of commendatory letters from elsewhere (3:1) have sought to establish themselves as apostolic authorities in territory evangelized by Paul (10:12–18). They had probably not yet arrived in Corinth—or at least the apostle was not aware of their arrival—when Letter B (1 Cor) was written (fall of 54), but they had become active in the city by the time of Letter D (chaps. 1–9, fall of 55). There is no way of knowing whether they were already on the scene when, in the spring of 55, Paul made a short emergency visit to the congregation. If they were, it is conceivable that they were somehow involved in the unpleasant confrontation Paul had with one of the members of the congregation (see discussion on 2:5–11).

One can be reasonably certain that these intruders claimed a relationship with Christ and an apostolic authority superior to Paul's, and that they sought, with some success, to win the Corinthian Christians over to their version of the gospel and to assume leadership of the congregation. They supported their claims not only by letters of recommendation but also by extravagant self-recommendation, pretentiously boasting about their being of Jewish stock and about special "signs" of their apostleship: their rhetorical eloquence and impressive personal bearing, their boldness and missionary achievements, their ecstatic experiences, their special religious knowledge derived from extraordinary visions and revelations, and their ability to perform miracles.

In accordance with their high estimation of external signs of apostleship, they were critical of Paul for being weak and ineffectual: unmannered in his speech; manifesting only weakness in his physical appearance; his energies constantly depleted by various sufferings and hardships; demeaning himself by refusing financial support from the Corinthians and, instead, remaining active at his craft. They seem to have charged him, as well, with acting duplicitously in his dealings with the congregation: making strong demands in his letters which he was too weak to enforce when he was present, and soliciting a collection for Jerusalem while ostensibly refusing to accept aid for himself lest a burden be placed on the Corinthians. It may be, too—although this is less clear—that Paul's rivals had encouraged the congregation to interpret the apostle's several changes in travel plans as evidence that he was a mere flatterer whose word could not be trusted (see discussion on 1:15–2:2).

For his part, Paul opposes these people as intruders and deceivers. They have intruded themselves into a church he has founded and for which he alone should have apostolic responsibility. They are deceivers who, misrepresenting themselves and preaching an aberrant gospel, have seduced the Corinthians from the faith to which, through Paul's preaching, they had been committed.

It is clear that the opponents were of Jewish background, but this does not mean that they were Judaizers (see COMMENT on 11:22). The kind of polemic against Judaizers one finds in Gal is absent from 2 Cor, despite the similarities otherwise between Gal and 2 Cor 10–13. The proposal that they were Jewish-Christian Gnostics is no more persuasive, since every reference to "knowledge" in 2 Cor is unqualifiedly affirmative (2:14; 4:6; 6:6; 8:7; 10:5; 11:6). The kind of polemic against gnosticizing ideas found in 1 Cor is not present in 2 Cor, not even in 5:1–10 (on which see COMMENT). Insofar as the opponents exhibit some traits typical of Gnostics (e.g., an interest in visions and revelations), these are common as well to Hellenistic thought in general, including Hellenistic Judaism. Indeed, the evidence as a whole strongly favors the view that Paul was confronting Christian missionaries whose background was, like his own, Hellenistic-Jewish.

Looking back at the evidence overall, one is struck in particular by the fact that there is no direct information about the "doctrinal" stance of the opponents, not even in 11:4 (on which see the COMMENT). Whatever doctrinal basis the actions and attitudes of Paul's rivals may have had, the actions and attitudes themselves are what Paul attacks, so the personal dimensions of the conflict are much more apparent than the doctrinal aspects of it (cf. Hickling 1975b:287). One of the merits of Theissen's analysis of the situation at Corinth (1982:40–54) is his recognition that *social* as well as *theological* differences separated Paul from his opponents, and that one of the key points at issue was the apostle's decision to remain financially independent of his congregation. Theissen himself argues that the conflict involved a clash between two understandings of apostolic legitimacy, with their corresponding styles of ministry: that of rural-oriented "itinerant charismatics" (typical of Palestinian Christianity) on the one hand—Paul's opponents; and that of urban-oriented "community organizers" on the other—the Pauline apostolate. An alternative possibility is offered in the work of P. Marshall (1980, especially 331–36, 525–26, 618), who also stresses the sociocultural aspects of the conflict. In his view, however, the controversy did not stem from social and cultural *differences,* but from the fact that Paul deliberately rejected the Hellenistic cultural conventions his critics valued and with which he himself felt most comfortable. This

position is especially attractive, not only because there is no clear evidence that
the opponents had Palestinian connections but also because it helps to explain
the concern—throughout 2 Cor—to show how suffering and weakness bear
witness to the gospel and are the true signs of apostleship.

On the basis of the primary sources alone (Letters D and E), little more than
this can be said about the identity of the "false apostles" (cf. the conclusions
of Machalet 1973:201–3, whose article is a model of careful and cautious
analysis). This picture of the opponents can be filled out with greater detail
only if one is willing to admit less direct and more problematic evidence, and
to proceed by hypothesis and even conjecture. It is probably better, however,
to operate with a general identification of Paul's rivals based on relatively clear
and unambiguous evidence—and which is therefore reasonably certain—than
with a more specific but essentially hypothetical identification which must
tease details out of difficult and ambiguous texts.

## IV. A CHRONOLOGICAL OVERVIEW

Paul's dealings with the Corinthian Christians, as these have been discussed
above in sections II and III, may now be recapitulated in the following chronological table. The reconstruction as a whole is hypothetical, and the dates must
remain quite tentative. But the overall course of the apostle's Corinthian
ministry could not have been radically different from the way it is presented
here.

50–51   founding of the congregation by Paul, Silvanus, and Timothy; dis-
        patch of a letter to the Thessalonians.

51      (summer): Paul's hearing before Gallio and subsequent departure
        from Corinth.

51–54   Letter A (lost) dispatched to Corinth sometime during these years,
        from some unknown place.

54      (perhaps summer or early fall): Timothy sent to Corinth by way of
        Macedonia.

54      (fall): Paul's receipt, subsequent to the departure of Timothy, of a
        letter from the Corinthian church, as well as independent oral
        reports of what is going on there.

54      (perhaps October): Letter B ( = 1 Cor) dispatched from Ephesus
        to Corinth by ship.

55      (early spring): Timothy's arrival in Corinth from Macedonia. Find-
        ing a difficult situation, he leaves quickly for Ephesus in order to
        report to Paul.

55      (spring): Paul's emergency ("sorrowful") visit to Corinth,
        prompted by Timothy's alarming report about the situation there.
        Paul himself has a traumatic confrontation of some kind with one

of the members of the congregation and returns to Ephesus after only a short stay, apparently determined to return en route to Macedonia.

55     (late spring): Letter C (a lost "tearful letter") dispatched from Ephesus.

55     (summer): Titus sent to Corinth from Ephesus; Paul arrested and jailed in the Asian capital; letters dispatched to the Philippians and to Philemon.

55     (late summer): Paul's release from prison and departure from Ephesus; inception of a mission to Troas, perhaps accompanied by Timothy.

55     (fall): Paul's departure from Troas for Macedonia, where (perhaps in Philippi) he is joined by Titus, just arrived from Corinth.

55     (fall): Letter D ( = 2 Cor 1–9) dispatched from Macedonia (Philippi?), carried by Titus and two other Christian brothers.

55–56  (winter): Paul in Macedonia (Philippi? Thessalonica? Beroea?).

56     (spring or summer): Paul receives new and profoundly disturbing reports about affairs in the Corinthian church and dispatches Letter E ( = 2 Cor 10–13), perhaps from Thessalonica or Beroea; dispatch of a letter to the churches of Galatia.

56     (summer or fall): Paul's arrival in Corinth for his third visit, en route to Jerusalem. In a letter dispatched from here to the Christians of Rome, the apostle indicates that the Achaians as well as the Macedonians have made a contribution to the collection for the Judean Christians.

57     (spring): Paul's departure from Corinth for Jerusalem.

## V. CHRISTIANITY IN CORINTH AFTER PAUL'S DEATH

After his departure from Corinth in the spring of 57, Paul traveled to Jerusalem, where presumably he delivered his collection to the leaders of the Judean church (although Acts is strangely silent on the matter of the collection; see, e.g., 21:17–20a). According to Acts 21–26, Paul was opposed by the Jews in Jerusalem and arrested there by the Romans. Following a long imprisonment in Caesarea, he was taken under guard to Rome (Acts 27–28), since he had appealed his case to the emperor, Nero (Acts 25:11). The apostle was eventually executed in Rome, perhaps sometime between 62 and 64 (see Jewett 1979:45–46, 102).

Nothing is known about the Corinthian congregation in the period from Paul's departure for Jerusalem in 57 until the last decade of the first century, when (about 96 or 97) the church at Rome sent a letter to the Christians of Corinth (1 Clem, on which see Koester 1982:287–92). The occasion of the letter from Rome was a schism in the church at Corinth, allegedly caused by "a few rash and self-willed individuals" (1:1, *AF* II:17; cf. 47:6). This schism had been either the cause or the result (it is unclear which) of the deposing of some of the leaders of the Corinthian congregation, referred to as "bishops" *(episkopoi)* in 44:1–6 (see vv. 1 and 4) and as "presbyters" *(presbyteroi)* in 47:1–7 (see v. 6); 54:2; 57:1; cf. 44:5. When the Corinthians are urged to be instructed by "the letter of blessed Paul the apostle" (47:1, *AF* II:77), it is certainly our 1 Cor to which they are being referred (note 47:3), but (as noted above, p. 30) there is no clear evidence that any portion of our 2 Cor was known to the Roman church. That the Christians of Rome saw fit to send a delegation to Corinth (Claudius Ephebus, Valerius Bito, and Fortunatus, named in 65:1), as well as a letter calling for peace and order in the congregation, suggests that there was regular contact between the churches of Rome and Corinth. This is not surprising, because Corinth, a Roman colony, had close political and commercial ties with the imperial city. There is no way to know whether the letter from Rome and the men who carried it were to any extent successful in bringing order to the Corinthian congregation.

By the second century Corinth was the seat of a bishopric, and Dionysius, bishop there about 170, attests that 1 Clem was still being read in the Corinthian congregation (Eusebius, *Ecclesiastical History* IV.xxiii.11, quoting from a letter of Dionysius to the Romans). Dionysius himself was in correspondence not only with the church in Rome but also with the churches in Lacedaemonia, Athens, Nicomedia, Gortyna, Amastris, Pontus, and Cnossus (ibid. IV.xxiii.2, 4–7). Letters to these churches, perhaps along with a letter to a certain Chrysophora (ibid. IV.xxiii.13), seem to have comprised a collection made by the bishop himself. This, plus the fact that Dionysius' letters had been edited by certain "apostles of the devil" in order to falsify his teaching (ibid. xxiii.12), suggests that he and the church over which he presided had considerable influence in Christian circles. Other second-century bishops in Corinth were Primus and Bacchyllus. The former is mentioned by Hegesippus as a bishop under whom false teaching became a problem (Eusebius, *Ecclesiastical History* IV.xxii.1–2), but his dates are not known. The latter was Corinth's episcopal leader at the time of the controversy about the date of Easter, ca. 190 (ibid. V.xxiii.4).

Of the various accounts of martyrdom suffered by Corinthian Christians (on which see Max 1919:51–55), the earliest datable cases come from the third century. Among these is Hippolytus' tale of a Christian virgin who was sold to a brothel for denouncing the empire and its gods (included in Palladius, *The Lausiac History;* R. T. Meyer 1965:146–47). According to the story, she was rescued from her fate by a young man who, when captured, was martyred for his deed. Frend (1967:241–42—who erroneously indicates that the woman herself was martyred) dates the incident to the early third century, during the reign of Septimius Severus (193–211). Other third-century martyrs identified with Corinth include Helikonis (of Thessalonica), under Gordion III (238–44) or Philip (244–49); Quadratus (whose mother had been martyred when he was a child), under Decius (249–51) or Valerian (253–57); Leonides and a large group who mourned him, under an unknown emperor; and a certain Alexandros, also under an unknown emperor (Scranton 1957:3–4).

As one might presume, archaeological evidence of Christianity in Corinth dates only from the time of Constantine in the fourth century. Virtually from the beginning of synodical organization, the church at Corinth had "metropolitan" status, meaning that it was recognized as the leading church of a large area, and eventually as many as forty-six suffragan districts came under its jurisdiction (Max 1919:60–64). No ecclesiastical building discovered so far in Corinth could have served as the metropolitan headquarters, but Scranton (1957:9–11) thinks it possible that the Julian Basilica (Figure 2, No. 36) was converted to this use in the fourth century C.E. The earliest specifically Christian remains, however, are gravestones which date from the second half of the fourth century (see Kent 1966:172–99). One of the earliest of these bears an inscription memorializing a certain Noumenios, whose name (inscribed on the stone in its familiar form, Noumenis) is thought to be of Jewish origin (ibid.:172–73, No. 522). The earliest Christian basilica excavated to date in Corinth proper was built toward the close of the fourth century in memory of the third-century martyr Quadratus (Wiseman 1978:85–86). However, it appears that the Isis sanctuary in nearby Cenchreae was converted to Christian use around the same time (Scranton, Shaw, and Ibrahim 1978:73–77). Two other church buildings, the basilica near Corinth's southeastern gate (Shelley 1943:166–89) and the large basilica at Lechaeum (Wiseman 1978:87), date only from the fifth century, while other churches and miscellaneous evidences of a Christian presence in Corinth are later still.

# SELECT BIBLIOGRAPHY

[*Note on citations in this commentary.* All references in the text to *commentaries* on 2 Corinthians cite the author's name and the page number(s), but no date. All references in the text to other books and to articles cite the author's name, the date, and, where appropriate, the page number(s).]

## 1. COMMENTARIES ON 2 CORINTHIANS: NINETEENTH AND TWENTIETH CENTURIES

Allo, Ernest Bernard
    1956    *Seconde épître aux Corinthiens.* 2nd ed. ÉBib.
Bachmann, Philipp
    1909    *Der zweite Brief des Paulus an die Korinther.* 1st and 2nd ed. Kommentar zum Neuen Testament, VIII. Ed. Th. Zahn. Leipzig: Deichert.
Baird, William
    1980    *1 Corinthians, 2 Corinthians.* Knox Preaching Guides. Atlanta: Knox.
Barclay, William
    1956    *The Letters to the Corinthians.* 2nd ed. The Daily Study Bible. Philadelphia: Westminster.
Barrett, Charles Kingsley
    1973    *The Second Epistle to the Corinthians.* HNTC.
Bernard, John Henry
    1903    "The Second Epistle to the Corinthians." Pages 1–119 in *The Expositor's Greek Testament,* III. Ed. W. Robertson Nicoll. New York and London: Hodder & Stoughton.
Boor, Werner de
    1978    *Der zweite Brief an die Korinther.* 4th ed. Wuppertaler Studienbibel. Wuppertal: Brockhaus.
Bousset, Wilhelm
    1917    "Der zweite Brief an die Korinther." Pages 167–223 in *Die Schriften des Neuen Testaments,* II. 3rd ed. Eds. J. Weiss, W. Bousset, and W. Heitmüller. Göttingen: Vandenhoeck & Ruprecht.
Bruce, Frederick F.
    1971    *1 and 2 Corinthians.* NCB.
Bultmann, Rudolf
    1976    *Der zweite Brief an die Korinther.* Ed. E. Dinkler. KEK Sonderband.
Collange, Jean-François
    1972    *Énigmes de la deuxième épître aux Corinthiens. Étude exégétique de 2 Cor. 2:14–7:4.* SNTSMS 18.

Denney, James
1894        *The Second Epistle to the Corinthians.* The Expositor's Bible. Lon-
            don: Hodder & Stoughton. [American ed. New York: Armstrong,
            1908.]
Fallon, Francis T.
1980        *2 Corinthians.* New Testament Message, 11. Wilmington, Del.: Mi-
            chael Glazier.
Filson, Floyd V.
1953        "Introduction and Exegesis." Pages 265–425 in *The Interpreter's
            Bible,* 10. Eds. G. Buttrick et al. Nashville, Tenn.: Abingdon.
Fisher, Fred L.
1975        *Commentary on 1 & 2 Corinthians.* Waco, Tex.: Word.
Godet, Georges Édouard
1914        *La Seconde Épître aux Corinthiens.* Neuchâtel: Attinger.
Goudge, Henry L.
1927        *The Second Epistle to the Corinthians.* Westminster Commentaries.
            London: Methuen.
Grosheide, Frederik Willem
1959        *Der tweede Brief aan de Kerk te Korinthe.* 2nd ed. Commentaar op het
            Nieuwe Testament. Kampen: Kok.
Hanson, Richard P. C.
1967        *The Second Epistle to the Corinthians: Christ and Controversy.* Torch
            Bible Commentaries. London: SCM.
Harris, Murray J.
1976        "2 Corinthians." Pages 301–406 in *The Expositor's Bible Commentary,*
            10. Ed. F. E. Gaebelein. Grand Rapids, Mich.: Zondervan.
Heinrici, C. F. Georg
1900        *Der zweite Brief an die Korinther.* 8th ed. KEK.
Héring, Jean
1967        *The Second Epistle of St. Paul to the Corinthians.* Trs. A. W. Heath-
            cote and P. J. Allcock. London: Epworth.
Hillyer, Norman
1970        "2 Corinthians." Pages 1075–88 in *The New Bible Commentary: Re-
            vised.* Eds. D. Guthrie et al. Grand Rapids, Mich.: Eerdmans.
Hughes, Philip E.
1962        *Paul's Second Epistle to the Corinthians.* NICNT.
Kümmel, Werner Georg
1949        Supplemental notes (pp. 165–214) to Lietzmann's *An die Korinther I,
            II.* HNT 9.
Kuss, Otto
1940        *Paulusbriefe.* I: *Die Briefe an die Römer, Korinther und Galater.*
            Regensburger N. T., 6/1. Regensburg: Pustet.
Lietzmann, Hans
1949        *An die Korinther I, II.* 4th ed. HNT 9.
Menzies, Allan
1912        *The Second Epistle of the Apostle Paul to the Corinthians.* CGNTC.

Meyer, Heinrich A. W.
1890    *Critical and Exegetical Handbook to the Epistles to the Corinthians.* Trs. D. Bannerman and W. P. Dickson. New York and London: Funk & Wagnalls.

Morgan, George Campbell
1946    *The Corinthian Letters of Paul.* New York: Revell.

Plummer, Alfred
1915    *A Critical and Exegetical Commentary on the Second Epistle of St. Paul to the Corinthians.* ICC.

Price, James L.
1971    "II Corinthians." Pages 813–23 in *The Interpreter's One-Volume Commentary on the Bible.* Ed. C. M. Laymon. Nashville, Tenn.: Abingdon.

Prümm, Karl
1960–67  *Diakonia Pneumatos. Der zweite Korintherbrief als Zugang zur apostolischen Botschaft. Auslegung und Theologie.* 2 vols. Rom-Freiburg-Wien: Herder.

Robertson, Edwin H.
1973    *Corinthians 1 and 2.* J. B. Phillips' New Testament Commentaries. New York: Macmillan.

Schelkle, Karl H.
1981    *The Second Epistle to the Corinthians.* Tr. K. Smyth. New York: Crossroad.

Schlatter, Adolf
1934    *Paulus, der Bote Jesu. Eine Deutung seiner Briefe an die Korinther.* 4th ed. Repr. 1969. Stuttgart: Calwer.

Sickenberger, Joseph
1921    *Die beiden Briefe des heiligen Paulus an die Korinther und sein Brief an die Römer.* 2nd ed. Die Heilige Schrift des Neuen Testaments V. Bonn: Hanstein.

Strachan, Robert H.
1935    *The Second Epistle of Paul to the Corinthians.* MNTC.

Tasker, Randolph V. G.
1958    *The Second Epistle of Paul to the Corinthians.* TNTC.

Thrall, Margaret E.
1965    *The First and Second Letters of Paul to the Corinthians.* CBC.

Walter, Eugen
1964    *Der zweite Brief an die Korinther.* Die Welt der Bible. Düsseldorf: Patmos.

Wendland, Heinz-Dietrich
1972    *Die Briefe an die Korinther.* Repr. of 13th ed. [1968]. NTD 7.

Williams, Charles S. C.
1962    "II Corinthians." Pages 966–72 in *Peake's Commentary on the Bible.* Eds. M. Black and H. H. Rowley. London: Nelson.

Windisch, Hans
1970    *Der zweite Korintherbrief.* Repr. of 9th ed. [1924]. Ed. G. Strecker. KEK.

Wordsworth, Christopher
   1877    *The New Testament . . . with Introductions and Notes.* II: *St. Paul's Epistles; The General Epistles; The Book of Revelation; and Indexes.* New ed. London: Rivington's.


## 2. COMMENTARIES ON 2 CORINTHIANS: SIXTEENTH, SEVENTEENTH, AND EIGHTEENTH CENTURIES

Bengel, Johann Albrecht (1687–1752)
   1742    *Gnomon of the New Testament.* Trs. C. T. Lewis and M. R. Vincent. Philadelphia/New York: Perkinpine & Higgins/Sheldon, 1860–62.
Calvin, John (1509–64)
   1547    *The Second Epistle of Paul the Apostle to the Corinthians and the Epistles to Timothy, Titus and Philemon.* Tr. T. A. Smail. Calvin's Commentaries. Grand Rapids, Mich.: Eerdmans, 1964.
Erasmus, Desiderius (ca. 1469–1536)
   1516    *Novvm Instrumentū omne.* Basel: Frobenius.
Grotius, Hugo (1583–1645)
   1646    *Hvgonis Grotii Annotationvm in Novvm Testamentvm Tomvs Secvndvs.* Paris: Pelé.
Locke, John (1632–1704)
   1707–18  *A Paraphrase and Notes on the Epistles of St. Paul to the Galatians, I & II Corinthians, Romans, Ephesians.* London: Awnsham and Churchill.
Semler, Johann Salomo (1725–91)
   1776    *Paraphrasis II epistolae ad Corinthios.* Halle.


## 3. BOOKS, ARTICLES, AND DISSERTATIONS

Ahern, Barnabas M.
   1960    "The Fellowship of His Sufferings (Phil 3, 10)." *CBQ* 22:1–32.
Allmen, Daniel von
   1968    "Réconciliation du monde et christologie cosmique." *RHPR* 48:32–45.
Amstutz, Joseph
   1968    *HAPLOTĒS. Eine begriffsgeschichtliche Studie zum jüdisch-christlichen Griechisch.* Theophaneia 19.
Andresen, Carl
   1965    "Zum Formular frühchristlicher Gemeindebriefe." *ZNW* 56:233–59.
Asting, Ragnar
   1925    "Kauchesis. Et bidrag til den religiose selvfoldese hos Paulus." *NTT* 26:129–203.

Attridge, Harold W.
1979        " 'Heard Because of His Reverence' (Heb 5:7)." *JBL* 98:90–93.
Bahr, Gordon J.
1968        "The Subscriptions in the Pauline Letters." *JBL* 87:27–41.
Baird, William R.
1961        "Letters of Recommendation: A Study of 2 Cor 3:1–3." *JBL* 80:
            166–72.
Balch, David L.
1972        "Backgrounds of I Cor VII: Sayings of the Lord in Q; Moses as an
            Ascetic *theios anēr* in II Cor III." *NTS* 18:351–64.
Baldwin, Charles Sears
1928        *Medieval Rhetoric and Poetic.* New York: Macmillan.
Barclay, William
1962        *Flesh and Spirit. An Examination of Galatians 5:19–23.* Nashville,
            Tenn.: Abingdon.
Barnett, Albert E.
1941        *Paul Becomes a Literary Influence.* Chicago: Univ. of Chicago Press.
Barré, Michael L.
1974        "To Marry or to Burn: *Pyrousthai* in 1 Cor 7:9." *CBQ* 36:193–202.
1975        "Paul as 'Eschatologic Person': A New Look at 2 Cor 11:29." *CBQ*
            37:500–26.
1980        "Qumran and the Weakness of Paul." *CBQ* 42:216–27.
Barrett, Charles Kingsley
1968        *A Commentary on the First Epistle to the Corinthians.* HNTC.
1969        "Titus." Pages 1–14 in *Neotestamentica et Semitica* (Black Fest-
            schrift). Eds. E. E. Ellis and M. Wilcox. Edinburgh: Clark.
1970a       *"HO ADIKĒSAS* (2 Cor 7.12)." Pages 149–57 in *Verborum Veritas*
            (Stählin Festschrift). Eds. O. Böcher and K. Haacker. Wuppertal:
            Theologischer Verlag-Brockhaus. (Repr. in *Essays on Paul* [Philadel-
            phia: Westminster, 1982], pp. 108–17.)
1970b       "PSEUDAPOSTOLOI (2 Cor 11.13)." Pages 377–96 in *Mélanges
            Bibliques* (Rigaux Festschrift). Eds. A. Descamps and A. de Halleux.
            Gembloux: Duculot. (Repr. in *Essays on Paul,* pp. 87–107.)
1971        "Paul's Opponents in II Corinthians." *NTS* 17:233–54. (Repr. in
            *Essays on Paul,* pp. 60–86.)
1978        "*Shaliaḥ* and Apostle." Pages 88–102 in *Donum Gentilicum* (Daube
            Festschrift). Eds. E. Bammel et al. Oxford: Clarendon.
Barth, Gerhard
1980        "Die Eignung des Verkündigers in 2 Kor 2, 14–3, 6." Pages 257–70
            in *Kirche* (Bornkamm Festschrift). Eds. D. Lührmann and G.
            Strecker. Tübingen: Mohr.
Barth, Markus
1974        *Ephesians.* AB 34, 34A.
Bartsch, Hans-Werner
1965        *Die Anfänge urchristlicher Rechtsbildungen: Studien zu den Pastoral-
            briefen.* Hamburg: Reich.

Bates, W. H.
1965        "The Integrity of II Corinthians." *NTS* 12:56–59.
Batey, Richard
1963        "Paul's Bride Image. A Symbol of Realistic Eschatology." *Int* 17:
            176–82.
1965        "Paul's Interaction with the Corinthians." *JBL* 84:139–46.
Baumert, Norbert
1973        *Täglich sterben und auferstehen. Der Literalsinn von 2 Kor 4, 12–5, 10.*
            SANT 34.
Baumgarten, Jörg
1975        *Paulus und die Apokalyptik. Die Auslegung apokalyptischer Über-*
            *lieferung in den echten Paulusbriefen.* WMANT 44.
Baur, Ferdinand Chr.
1875–76     *Paul: His Life and Work.* 2 vols. Rev. A. Menzies. London: Williams
            and Norgate.
Baus, Karl
1965        *From the Apostolic Community to Constantine.* Handbook of Church
            History, I. Montreal: Palm.
Beasley-Murray, George R.
1962        *Baptism in the New Testament.* London: Macmillan.
Benz, Ernst
1952        *Paulus als Visionär.* Abhandlungen der Geistes- und Sozialwissen-
            schaftlichen Klasse., No. 2. Wiesbaden: Verlag der Akademie der
            Wissenschaften und der Literatur in Mainz.
Berger, Klaus
1974        "Apostelbrief und apostolische Rede / Zum Formular frühchrist-
            licher Briefe." *ZNW* 65:190–231.
1977        "Almosen für Israel: Zum historischen Kontext der paulinischen Kol-
            lekte." *NTS* 23:180–204.
1980        "Die implizite Gegner. Zur Methode des Erschliessens von 'Gegnern'
            in neutestamentlichen Texten." Pages 373–400 in *Kirche* (Bornkamm
            Festschrift). Eds. D. Lührmann and G. Strecker. Tübingen: Mohr.
Best, Ernest
1972        *The First and Second Epistles to the Thessalonians.* HNTC.
Betz, Hans Dieter
1961        *Lukian von Samosata und das Neue Testament. Religionsgeschicht-*
            *liche und paränetische Parallelen. Ein Beitrag zum Corpus Hellenis-*
            *ticum Novi Testamenti.* TU 76.
1969        "Eine Christus-Aretalogie bei Paulus (2 Cor 12, 7–10)." *ZTK* 66:
            288–305.
1972        *Der Apostel Paulus und die sokratische Tradition. Eine exegetische*
            *Untersuchung zu einer "Apologie" 2 Korinther 10–13.* BHT 45.
1973        "2 Cor 6:14–7:1: An Anti-Pauline Fragment?" *JBL* 92:88–108.
1979        *Galatians.* Hermeneia.
———, and L. Schottroff, eds.
1973        *Neues Testament und christliche Existenz* (Braun Festschrift). Tü-
            bingen: Mohr.

Beyenka, Sister Mary Melchior, tr.

1954      *Saint Ambrose: Letters.* The Fathers of the Church. A New Translation. New York: Fathers of the Church, Inc.

Bieder, Werner

1961      "Paulus und seine Gegner in Korinth." *TZ* 17:319–33.

Bietenhard, Hans

1951      *Die himmlische Welt im Urchristentum und Spätjudentum.* WUNT 2.

1963      "Die Dekapolis von Pompeius bis Traian. Ein Kapitel aus der neutestamentlichen Zeitgeschichte." *ZDPV* 79:24–58.

Binder, Hermann

1973      "Versöhnung als die grosse Wende." *TZ* 29:305–12.

1976      "Die angebliche Krankheit des Paulus." *TZ* 32:1–13.

Bishop, Eric F. F.

1953      "Does Aretas Belong in 2 Corinthians or Galatians?" *ExpTim* 64: 188–89.

1966      " 'In Famine and Drought.' " *EvQ* 38:169–71.

Bjerkelund, Carl J.

1967      *Parakalô: Form, Funktion und Sinn der parakalô-Sätze in den paulinischen Briefen.* Bibliotheca Theologica Norvegica, 1. Oslo: Universitetsforlaget.

Black, Matthew

1976      "The New Creation in 1 Enoch." Pages 13–21 in *Creation, Christ and Culture* (Torrance Festschrift). Ed. R. W. A. McKinney. Edinburgh: Clark.

Blank, Josef

1968      *Paulus und Jesus. Eine theologische Grundlegung.* SANT 18.

Bonsirven, Joseph

1939      *Exégèse rabbinique et exégèse paulinienne.* Bibliothèque de théologie historique. Paris: Beauchesne.

Boobyer, George H.

1929      *"Thanksgiving" and the "Glory of God" in Paul.* Borna-Leipzig: Noske.

Bookidis, Nancy

1969      "The Sanctuary of Demeter and Kore on Acrocorinth. Preliminary Report III: 1968." *Hesp* 38:297–310.

1979      Personal conference, 16 June, in Athens.

1981      Letter, dated 23 August, from Ancient Corinth.

———, and Joan E. Fisher

1972      "The Sanctuary of Demeter and Kore on Acrocorinth." *Hesp* 41: 283–331.

———.

1974      "The Sanctuary of Demeter and Kore on Acrocorinth." *Hesp* 43: 267–307.

Bornkamm, Günther

1971      "Die Vorgeschichte des sogennanten Zweiten Korintherbriefes." Pages 162–94 in *Gesammelte Aufsätze,* IV. BEvT 53.

Borse, Udo
  1972        *Der Standort des Galaterbriefes.* BBB 41.
Bousset, Wilhelm
  1970        *Kyrios Christos: A History of the Belief in Christ from the Beginnings of Christianity to Irenaeus.* Tr. J. E. Steely. Nashville, Tenn.: Abingdon.
Bowersock, Glen W.
  1983        *Roman Arabia.* Cambridge: Harvard Univ. Press.
Bowker, John W.
  1971        " 'Merkabah' Visions and the Visions of Paul." *JSS* 16:157–73.
Braun, Herbert
  1966        *Qumran und das Neue Testament.* 2 vols. Tübingen: Mohr.
Bring, Ragnar
  1969        *Christus und das Gesetz: Die Bedeutung des Gesetzes des Alten Testaments nach Paulus und seine Glauben an Christus.* Leiden: Brill.
Broneer, Oscar
  1939        "An Official Rescript from Corinth." *Hesp* 8:181–90.
  1941        "Colonia Laus Iulia Corinthiensis." *Hesp* 10:388–90.
  1942        "Hero Cults in the Corinthian Agora." *Hesp* 11:128–61.
  1951        "Corinth: Center of St. Paul's Missionary Work in Greece." *BA* 14: 78–96.
  1954        *The South Stoa and Its Roman Successors.* Corinth I/4.
  1962        "The Apostle Paul and the Isthmian Games." *BA* 25:2–31.
  1971a       *The Temple of Poseidon.* Isthmia, I.
  1971b       "Paul and Pagan Cults at Isthmia." *HTR* 64:169–87.
  1973        *Topography and Architecture.* Isthmia, II.
  1977        *Terracotta Lamps.* Isthmia, III.
Broughton, Thomas R. S.
  1938        "Roman Asia." Pages 499–916 in *An Economic Survey of Ancient Rome,* IV. Ed. T. Frank. Baltimore: Johns Hopkins.
Brown, Raymond E.
  1966        *The Gospel According to John (i–xii).* AB 29.
Brun, Lyder
  1929        "Zur Auselegung von 2 Kor. 5:1–10." *ZNW* 28:207–29.
Buchanan, George W.
  1964        "Jesus and the Upper Class." *NovT* 7:195–209.
Buck, Charles H., Jr.
  1950        "The Collection for the Saints." *HTR* 43:1–29.
————, and Greer Taylor
  1969        *Saint Paul: A Study of the Development of His Thought.* New York: Scribner's.
Bultmann, Rudolf
  1947        *Exegetische Probleme des zweiten Korintherbriefes.* SEÅSup 9.
  1951        *Theology of the New Testament,* I. Tr. K. Grobel. New York: Scribner's.
  1960        *Existence and Faith: Shorter Writings of Rudolf Bultmann.* Selected, translated, and edited by S. M. Ogden. New York: Meridian.
  1964        "DIKAIOSYNĒ THEOU." *JBL* 83:12–16.

Burchard, Christoph
1970    *Der dreizehnte Zeuge. Traditions- und kompositionsgeschichtliche Untersuchungen zu Lukas' Darstellung der Frühzeit des Paulus.* FRLANT 103.

Burdick, Donald W.
1978    "With Paul in the Troad." *NEASB* 12:31–65.

Burton, Ernest DeWitt
1898    *Syntax of the Moods and Tenses in New Testament Greek.* 3rd ed. Repr. 1973. Edinburgh: Clark.

Cadbury, Henry J.
1955    *The Book of Acts in History.* New York: Harper.

Cambier, Jules
1960    "Connaissance charnelle et spirituelle du Christ dans 2 Cor 5:16." Pages 72–92 in *Littérature et théologie pauliniennes.* RechBib 5.
1962    "Le Critère paulinien de l'apostolat en 2 Cor. 12, 6s." *Bib* 43:481–518.
1963    "Une Lecture de 2 Cor 12, 6–7a: essai d'interprétation nouvelle." Pages 475–85 in *Studiorum Paulinorum Congressus Internationalis Catholicus, 1961.* AnBib 17–18.

Carmignac, Jean
1978    "II Corinthiens iii.6, 14 et le début de la formation du Nouveau Testament." *NTS* 24:384–86.

Carrez, Maurice
1980    "Le 'Nous' en 2 Corinthiens." *NTS* 26:474–86.

Casson, Lionel
1974    *Travel in the Ancient World.* London: Allen & Unwin.

Charlesworth, James Hamilton, ed. and tr.
1977    *The Odes of Solomon.* SBLTT 13.

Childs, Brevard S.
1974    *The Book of Exodus: A Critical Theological Commentary.* The Old Testament Library. Philadelphia: Westminster.

Clarke, William Kemp Lowther
1929    "Was St. Paul a Stammerer?" Pages 136–40 in *New Testament Problems: Essays—Reviews—Interpretations.* New York: Macmillan.

Clayton, Allen
1977    "II Corinthians and the Pauline Corpus." Unpublished seminar paper, Southern Methodist University.

Clements, Ronald E.
1965    *God and Temple.* Oxford: Blackwell.

Cohen, Boaz
1953    "Letter and Spirit in Jewish and Roman Law." Pages 109–35 in *Mordecai M. Kaplan Jubilee Volume.* New York: Jewish Theological Seminary.
1954    "Note on Letter and Spirit in the New Testament." *HTR* 47:197–203.

Collins, John J., ed.
1979    "Apocalypse: The Morphology of a Genre." *Semeia* 14.

Collins, John N.
1974    "Georgi's 'Envoys' in 2 Cor 11:23." *JBL* 93:88–96.

Conzelmann, Hans
1972    "Paul's Doctrine of Justification: Theology or Anthropology?" Pages 108–23 in *Theology of the Liberating Word.* Ed. F. Herzog. Nashville, Tenn.: Abingdon.
1974    "Korinth und die Mädchen der Aphrodite. Zur Religionsgeschichte der Stadt Korinth." Pages 152–66 in *Theologie als Schriftauslegung: Aufsätze zum Neuen Testament.* BEvT 65.
1975    *I Corinthians.* Tr. J. W. Leitch. Hermeneia.

Cook, John M.
1973    *The Troad. An Archaeological and Topographical Study.* Oxford: Clarendon.

Corriveau, Raymond
1970    *The Liturgy of Life. A Study of the Ethical Thought of St. Paul in His Letters to the Early Christian Communities.* Studia 25.

Couchoud, Paul-Louis
1923    "Reconstitution et classement des lettres de saint Paul." *RHR* 87: 8–31.

Craddock, Fred B.
1968    "The Poverty of Christ. An Investigation of II Corinthians 8:9." *Int* 22:158–70.

Cranfield, Charles E. B.
1975    *A Critical and Exegetical Commentary on the Epistle to the Romans,* I. 6th ed. ICC.
1982    "Changes of Person and Number in Paul's Epistles." Pages 280–89 in *Paul and Paulinism* (Barrett Festschrift). Eds. M. D. Hooker and S. G. Wilson. London: S.P.C.K.

Crownfield, David R.
1979    "The Self Beyond Itself: Hermeneutics and Transpersonal Experience." *JAAR* 47:245–67.

Cummer, W. Willson
1971    "A Roman Tomb at Corinthian Kenchreai." *Hesp* 40:205–31.

Dahl, Nils A.
1951    "Adresse und Proömium des Epheserbriefes." *TZ* 7:241–64.
1967    "Paul and the Church at Corinth according to I Corinthians 1–4." Pages 313–35 in Farmer et al.
1977    *Studies in Paul: Theology for the Early Christian Mission.* Minneapolis, Minn.: Augsburg.

Dahood, Mitchell J.
1955    "Two Pauline Quotations from the Old Testament." *CBQ* 17:19–24.
1970    *Psalms III.* AB 17A.

Dana, H. E., and Julius R. Mantey
1927    *A Manual Grammar of the Greek New Testament.* New York: Macmillan.

Daniel, Constantin
1966    "Une Mention paulinienne des Esséniens de Qumran." *RevQ* 5:553–67.

Daniel, Jerry L.
1979        "Anti-Semitism in the Hellenistic-Roman Period." *JBL* 98:45–65.
Danker, Frederick W.
1968        "Consolation in 2 Cor 5:1–10." *CTM* 39:552–56.
Davidson, Gladys R.
1952        *The Minor Objects.* Corinth XII.
Davies, William D.
1957        "Paul and the Dead Sea Scrolls: Flesh and Spirit." Pages 157–82 in
            *The Scrolls and the New Testament.* Ed. K. Stendahl. New York:
            Harper.
1980        *Paul and Rabbinic Judaism. Some Rabbinic Elements in Pauline The-
            ology.* 4th ed. Philadelphia: Fortress.
Dean, John T.
1947        *Saint Paul and Corinth.* London: Lutterworth.
Deichgräber, Reinhard
1967        *Gotteshymnus und Christushymnus in der frühen Christenheit. Unter-
            suchungen zu Form, Sprache und Stil der frühchristlichen Hymnen.*
            SUNT 5.
Deissmann, G. Adolf
1903        *Bible Studies.* 2nd ed. Tr. A. Grieve. Edinburgh: Clark.
1927        *Light from the Ancient East: The New Testament Illustrated by Re-
            cently Discovered Texts of the Graeco-Roman World.* Rev. ed. Tr.
            L. R. M. Strachan. New York: Doran.
Delcor, Mathias.
1968        "The Courts of the Church of Corinth and the Courts of Qumran."
            Pages 69–84 in Murphy-O'Connor (1968).
Delling, Gerhard
1962        *Worship in the New Testament.* Tr. P. Scott. Philadelphia: Westmin-
            ster.
1963        "Partizipiale Gottesprädikationen in den Briefen des Neuen Testa-
            ments." *ST* 17:1–59.
1970        *Studien zum Neuen Testament und zum hellenistischen Judentum.*
            Göttingen: Vandenhoeck & Ruprecht.
1975        "Die Bezeichnung 'Gott des Friedens' und ähnliche Wendungen in
            den Paulusbriefen." Pages 76–84 in *Jesus und Paulus* (Kümmel Fest-
            schrift). Eds. E. E. Ellis and E. Grässer. Göttingen: Vandenhoeck &
            Ruprecht.
Demke, Christoph
1969        "Zur Auslegung von 2. Korinther 5, 1–10." *EvT* 29:589–602.
Derrett, J. Duncan M.
1978        "2 Cor 6, 14ff. a Midrash on Dt 22, 10." *Bib* 59:231–50.
Dibelius, Martin
1909        *Die Geisterwelt im Glauben des Paulus.* Göttingen: Vandenhoeck &
            Ruprecht.
1956        *Botschaft und Geschichte: Gesammelte Aufsätze,* II. Ed. G. Born-
            kamm. Tübingen: Mohr.

1972      *The Pastoral Epistles.* Revised by H. Conzelmann. Trs. P. Buttolph and A. Yarbro. Hermeneia.

1976      *James.* Tr. M. A. Williams. Hermeneia.

Dick, Karl

1900      *Der schriftstellerische Plural bei Paulus.* Halle: Niemeyer.

Dinkler, Erich

1962      "Die Taufterminologie in 2 Kor. i 21f." Pages 173–91 in *Neotestamentica et Patristica* (Cullmann Festschrift). NovTSup 6.

1967      "Das Bema zu Korinth—Archäologische, lexikographische, rechtsgeschichtliche und ikonographische Bemerkungen zu Apostelgeschichte 18, 12–17." Pages 118–33 in *Signum Crucis: Aufsätze zum Neuen Testament und zu Christlichen Archäologie.* Tübingen: Mohr.

1970      "Die Verkündigung als eschatologisch-sakramentales Geschehen. Auslegung von 2 Kor 5, 14–6, 2." Pages 169–89 in *Die Zeit Jesu* (Schlier Festschrift). Eds. G. Bornkamm and K. Rahner. Freiburg: Herder.

Dodd, Charles Harold

1946      *The Johannine Epistles.* MNTC.

Doignon, Jean

1979      "Le Libellé singulier de II Corinthiens 3.18 chez Hilaire de Poitiers: Essai d'explication." *NTS* 26:118–26.

Donfried, Karl P.

1974      *The Setting of Second Clement in Early Christianity.* NovTSup 38.

Doskocil, Walter

1958      *Das Bann in der Urkirche, eine rechtsgeschichtliche Untersuchung.* MTS 3/11.

Drescher, Richard

1897      "Der zweite Korintherbrief und die Vorgänge in Korinth seit Abfassung des ersten Korintherbriefs." *TSK* 70:43–111.

Duff, Arnold M.

1928      *Freedmen in the Early Roman Empire.* Repr. 1957. Cambridge, Eng.: Heffer.

Dunand, Françoise

1973      *Le Culte d'Isis dans le bassin oriental de la Méditerranée,* II: *Le Culte d'Isis en Grèce.* ÉPRO 26.

Duncan, George S.

1930      *St. Paul's Ephesian Ministry. A Reconstruction with Special Reference to the Ephesian Origin of the Imprisonment Epistles.* New York: Scribner's.

Dunn, James D. G.

1970a      *Baptism in the Holy Spirit. A Re-Examination of the New Testament Teaching on the Gift of the Spirit in Relation to Pentecostalism Today.* SBT ser. 2, 15.

1970b      "2 Corinthians III.17—'The Lord is the Spirit.' " *JTS* 21:309–20.

1975      *Jesus and the Spirit. A Study of the Religious and Charismatic Experience of Jesus and the First Christians as Reflected in the New Testament.* Philadelphia: Westminster.

Dupont, Jacques
  1949    "Le Chrétien, miroir de la grâce divine, d'après 2 Cor. 3:18." *RB*
          56:392–411.
  1953    *La Réconciliation dans la théologie de saint Paul.* Louvain: Publ. univ.
          de Louvain.
Edelstein, Emma J., and Ludwig Edelstein
  1945    *Asclepius. A Collection and Interpretation of the Testimonies.* 2 vols.
          Baltimore: Johns Hopkins.
Edwards, Katharine M.
  1933    *Coins 1896–1929.* Corinth VI.
Egan, Rory B.
  1977    "Lexical Evidence on Two Pauline Passages." *NovT* 19:34–62.
Elliger, Winfried
  1978    *Paulus in Griechenland.* Stuttgarter Bibelstudien, 92/93. Stuttgart:
          Katholisches Bibelwerk.
Ellis, E. Earle
  1957    *Paul's Use of the Old Testament.* Edinburgh: Oliver and Boyd.
  1960    "II Cor v.1–10 in Pauline Eschatology." *NTS* 6:211–24.
  1971    "Paul and his Co-Workers." *NTS* 17:437–53.
Eltester, Friedrich-Wilhelm
  1958    *Eikon im Neuen Testament.* BZNW 23.
Enslin, Morton Scott
  1938    *Christian Beginnings.* New York and London: Harper.
  1972    *Reapproaching Paul.* Philadelphia: Westminster.
Everding, H. Edward, Jr.
  1968    "The Living God: A Study in the Function and Meaning of Biblical
          Terminology." Unpublished Th.D. dissertation, Harvard University.
Fahy, Thomas
  1964    "St. Paul's 'Boasting' and 'Weakness.' " *ITQ* 31:214–27.
Farmer, William R., C. F. D. Moule, and R. R. Niebuhr, eds.
  1967    *Christian History and Interpretation* (Knox Festschrift). Cambridge:
          Cambridge Univ. Press.
Fee, Gordon D.
  1977    "II Corinthians vi.14–vii.1 and Food Offered to Idols." *NTS* 23:
          140–61.
  1978    "CHARIS in II Corinthians i.15: Apostolic Parousia and Paul-
          Corinth Chronology." *NTS* 24:533–38.
Fenner, Friedrich
  1930    *Die Krankheit im Neuen Testament. Eine religions- und medizin-
          geschichtliche Untersuchung.* UNT 18.
Ferguson, John
  1958    *Moral Values in the Ancient World.* London: Methuen.
  1970    *The Religions of the Roman Empire.* AGRL.
Festugière, André-Jean
  1954    *Personal Religion Among the Greeks.* Berkeley and Los Angeles: Univ.
          of California Press.

Field, Frederick
1879      *Notes on the Translation of the New Testament.* Cambridge: Cambridge Univ. Press.

Fitzmyer, Joseph A.
1974a      *Essays on the Semitic Background of the New Testament.* SBLSBS 5.
1974b      "Some Notes on Aramaic Epistolography." *JBL* 93:201–25.
1975      "Reconciliation in Pauline Theology." Pages 155–77 in *No Famine in the Land* (McKenzie Festschrift). Eds. J. Flanagan and A. Robinson. Missoula, Mont.: Scholars Press.
1981      "Glory Reflected on the Face of Christ (2 Cor 3:7–4:6) and a Palestinian Jewish Motif." *TS* 42:630–44.

Forbes, Christopher
1978      " 'Strength' and 'Weakness' as Terminology of Status in St. Paul: The Historical and Literary Roots of a Metaphor, with Specific Reference to 1 and 2 Corinthians." Unpublished B.A. honors thesis, Macquarie University (Australia).
1982      "Comparison, Self-Praise and Irony: Paul's Boasting and the Conventions of Hellenistic Rhetoric." Unpublished paper read at a conference on "The Graeco-Roman Cultural Settings of the Conflict between Paul and the Corinthians" at Macquarie University (Australia) in July 1982.

Forkman, Goran
1972      *The Limits of the Religious Community.* ConB, NT ser. 5.

Fowler, Harold N., and Richard Stillwell
1932      *Introduction, Topography and Architecture.* Corinth, I/1.

Fraser, John W.
1974      *Jesus and Paul. Paul as Interpreter of Jesus from Harnack to Kümmel.* Abingdon, Eng.: Marcham Manor.

Frend, William H. C.
1967      *Martyrdom and Persecution in the Early Church. A Study of a Conflict from the Maccabees to Donatus.* Anchor Books. Garden City, N.Y.: Doubleday.

Fridrichsen, Anton
1928      "Zum Stil des paulinischen Peristasenkatalogs 2 Cor. 11:23ff." *SO* 7:25–29.
1929      "Peristasenkatalog und res gestae. Nachtrag zu 2 Cor. 11:23ff." *SO* 8:78–82.
1936      "Nachträge von Herausgeber." *ConNT* 2:45–48.
1944      "Zum Thema 'Paulus und die Stoa,' eine stoische Stilparallele zu 2 Kor. 4.8f." *ConNT* 9:27–31.

Friedrich, Gerhard
1956      "Lohmeyer's These über das paulinische Briefpräskript kritisch beleuchtet." *TLZ* 81:343–46.
1963a      *Amt und Lebensführung. Eine Auslegung von 2. Kor. 6, 1–10.* BibS(N) 39.

1963b     "Die Gegner des Paulus im 2. Korintherbrief." Pages 181–215 in *Abraham unser Vater: Juden und Christen im Gespräch über die Bibel* (Michel Festschrift). Eds. O. Betz, M. Hengel, and P. Schmidt. AGJU 5.

Fry, Euan
1976     "Translating 'glory' in the New Testament." *BT* 27:422–27.

Fuchs, Eric
1980     "La Faiblesse, gloire de l'apostolat selon Paul. Étude sur 2 Corinthiens 10–13." *ÉTR* 55:231–53.

Furnish, Victor Paul
1961     " 'Fellow Workers in God's Service.' " *JBL* 80:364–70.
1968     *Theology and Ethics in Paul.* Nashville, Tenn.: Abingdon.
1972     *The Love Command in the New Testament.* Nashville, Tenn.: Abingdon.
1977     "The Ministry of Reconciliation." *CurTM* 4:204–18.
1979     *The Moral Teaching of Paul: Selected Issues.* Nashville, Tenn.: Abingdon.
1981     "Theology and Ministry in the Pauline Letters." Pages 101–44 in *A Biblical Basis for Ministry.* Eds. E. E. Shelp and R. Sunderland. Philadelphia: Westminster.

Fürst, Walter
1968     "2 Korinther 5:11–21, Auslegung und Meditation." *EvT* 28:221–38.

Gärtner, Bertil
1965     *The Temple and the Community in Qumran and the New Testament. A Comparative Study in the Temple Symbolism of the Qumran Texts and the New Testament.* SNTSMS 1.

Geagan, Daniel J.
1968     "Notes on the Agonistic Institutions of Roman Corinth." *GRBS* 9: 69–80.

Gebhard, Elizabeth R.
1973     *The Theater at Isthmia.* Chicago: Univ. of Chicago Press.

Genths, P.
1927     "Der Begriff des *kauchēma* bei Paulus." *NKZ* 38:501–21.

George, A. Raymond
1953     *Communion with God in the New Testament.* London: Epworth.

Georgi, Dieter
1964     *Die Gegner des Paulus im 2. Korintherbrief. Studien zur religiösen Propaganda in der Spätantike.* WMANT 11.
1965     *Die Geschichte der Kollekte des Paulus für Jerusalem.* TF 38.

Gnilka, Joachim
1968a     "2 Cor 6:14–7:1 in the Light of the Qumran Texts and the Testaments of the Twelve Patriarchs." Pages 48–68 in Murphy-O'Connor (1968).
1968b     *Der Philipperbrief.* HTKNT X/3.

Goguel, Maurice
1926     *Introduction au Nouveau Testament. IV/2: Les Épîtres pauliniennes,* 2. Paris: Leroux.

Goodspeed, Edgar J.
1945　　Problems of New Testament Translation. Chicago: Univ. of Chicago Press.

Goppelt, Leonhard
1968　　" 'Versöhnung durch Christus.' " Pages 147–64 in Christologie und Ethik. Göttingen: Vandenhoeck & Ruprecht.
1978　　Der erste Petrusbrief. 8th ed. Ed. F. Hahn. KEK XII/1.

Gordon, Mary L.
1924　　"The Nationality of Slaves Under the Early Roman Empire." JRS 14:93–111.

Grabner-Haider, Anton
1968　　Paraklese und Eschatologie bei Paulus: Mensch und Welt im Anspruch der Zukunft Gottes. NTAbh n.F. 4.

Grant, Robert M.
1957　　The Letter and the Spirit. New York: Macmillan.
———, ed. and tr.
1970　　Theophilus of Antioch Ad Autolycum. Oxford: Clarendon.

Grayston, Kenneth
1964　　" 'Not ashamed of the Gospel.' Romans 1, 16a and the Structure of the Epistle." Pages 569–73 in Studia Evangelica, II/1: The New Testament Scriptures. Ed. F. L. Cross. TU 87.

Greenwood, David
1972　　"The Lord is the Spirit: Some Considerations of 2 Cor 3:17." CBQ 34:467–72.

Gregory, Caspar René
1907　　Canon and Text of the New Testament. New York: Scribner's.

Griffiths, J. Gwyn
1975　　Apuleius of Madauros: The Isis-Book (Metamorphoses, Book XI). ÉPRO 39.

Grobel, Kendrick
1960　　The Gospel of Truth. A Valentinian Meditation on the Gospel. Translation from the Coptic and Commentary. New York and Nashville: Abingdon.

Grossouw, Willem K. M.
1951　　"Over de echtheid van 2 Cor 6:14–7:1." StudCath 26:203–6.

Gulin, Eelis G.
1932　　Die Freude im Neuen Testament, I: Jesus, Urgemeinde, Paulus. Suomalaisen Tiedeaktemian, Toimituksia. Annales Academiae Scientarum Fennicae, ser. B, 26/2. Helsinki: Druckerei-A. G. der Finnischen Literatur-Gesellschaft.

Gundry, Robert H.
1976　　Sōma in Biblical Theology, with Emphasis on Pauline Anthropology. SNTSMS 29.

Gunther, John J.
1973　　St. Paul's Opponents and Their Background: A Study of Apocalyptic and Jewish Sectarian Teachings. NovTSup 35.

Güttgemanns, Erhardt
1966        *Der leidende Apostel und sein Herr. Studien zur paulinischen Christolo-gie.* FRLANT 90.

Haenchen, Ernst
1966        "The Book of Acts as Source Material for the History of Early Chris-tianity." Pages 258–78 in *Studies in Luke-Acts* (Schubert Festschrift). Eds. L. E. Keck and J. L. Martyn. Nashville, Tenn.: Abingdon.

Hagner, Donald A.
1973        *The Use of the Old and New Testaments in Clement of Rome.* NovTSup 34.

Hahn, Friedrich
1973a       "Das Ja des Paulus und das Ja Gottes. Bemerkungen zu 2 Kor 1, 12–2,1." Pages 229–39 in Betz and Schottroff.
1973b       " 'Siehe, jetzt ist der Tag des Heils.' Neuschöpfung und Versöhnung nach 2. Korinther 5,14–6,2." *EvT* 33:244–53.
1974        "Der Apostolat im Urchristentum." *KD* 20:54–77.

Halmel, Anton
1904        *Der zweite Korintherbrief des Apostels Paulus. Geschichte und literar-kritische Untersuchungen.* Halle: Niemeyer.

Halter, Hans
1977        *Taufe und Ethos: Paulinische Kriterion für das Proprium christlicher Moral.* FTS 106.

Hammond, Mason
1972        *The City in the Ancient World.* Cambridge: Harvard Univ. Press.

Hanhart, Karel
1969        "Paul's Hope in the Face of Death." *JBL* 88:445–57.

Hanson, Anthony Tyrrell
1965        *Jesus Christ in the Old Testament.* London: S.P.C.K.
1968        *Studies in the Pastoral Epistles.* London: S.P.C.K.
1974        *Studies in Paul's Technique and Theology.* Grand Rapids, Mich.: Eerdmans.
1980        "The Midrash in II Corinthians 3: A Reconsideration." *JSNT* 9:2–28.

Hardy, Ernest George, ed.
1923        *The Monumentum Ancyranum.* Oxford: Clarendon.

Harris, J. Rendel
1921–22     "Enoch and 2 Corinthians." *ExpTim* 33:423–24.

Harris, Murray J.
1974        "Paul's View of Death in 2 Corinthians 5:1–10." Pages 317–28 in *New Dimensions in New Testament Study.* Eds. R. N. Longenecker and M. C. Tenney. Grand Rapids, Mich.: Zondervan.

Harrison, Percy N.
1964        "Erastus and His Pavement." Pages 100–5 in *Paulines and Pastorals.* London: Villiers.

Hausrath, Adolf
1870        *Der Vier-Capitelbrief des Paulus an die Korinther.* Heidelberg: Basser-mann.

1875      *Neutestamentliche Zeitgeschichte,* 3: *Die Zeit der Apostel* II. 2nd ed. Heidelberg: Bassermann.

Heine, Susanne

1976      *Leibhafter Glaube: Ein Beitrag zum Verständnis der theologischen Konzeption des Paulus.* Wien-Freiburg-Basel: Herder.

Hemer, Colin J.

1972      "A Note on 2 Corinthians 1:9." *TyndB* 23:103–7.

1975      "Alexandria Troas." *TyndB* 26:79–112.

Hermann, Ingo

1961      *Kyrios und Pneuma. Studien zur Christologie der paulinischen Hauptbriefe.* SANT 2.

Herrmann, Léon

1976      "Apollos." *RevScRel* 50:330–36.

Heyob, Sharon Kelly

1975      *The Cult of Isis Among Women in the Graeco-Roman World.* ÉPRO 51.

Hickling, Colin J. A.

1975a      "The Sequence of Thought in II Corinthians, Chapter Three." *NTS* 21:380–95.

1975b      "Is the Second Epistle to the Corinthians a Source for Early Church History?" *ZNW* 66:284–87.

Hill, Andrew E.

1980      "The Temple of Asclepius: An Alternative Source for Paul's Body Theology?" *JBL* 99:437–39.

Hill, Edmund

1961      "The Construction of Three Passages from St. Paul." *CBQ* 23:296–301.

Hisey, Alan

1978      "A Paragnostic View of Paul the Apostle." *The Unitarian Universalist Christian* 33:12–19.

————, and James S. P. Beck

1961      "Paul's 'Thorn in the Flesh': A Paragnosis." *JBR* 29:125–29.

Hoad, John

1957      "Some New Testament References to Isaiah 53." *ExpTim* 68:254–55.

Hock, Ronald F.

1978      "Paul's Tentmaking and the Problem of His Social Class." *JBL* 97:555–64.

1980      *The Social Context of Paul's Ministry: Tentmaking and Apostleship.* Philadelphia: Fortress.

Hofius, Otfried

1980a      "Erwägungen zur Gestalt und Herkunft des paulinischen Versöhnungsgedankens." *ZTK* 77:186–99.

1980b      " 'Gott hat unter uns aufgerichtet das Wort von der Versöhnung' (2 Kor 5, 19)." *ZNW* 71:3–20.

Hofmann, Karl-Martin

1938      *Philema Hagion.* BFCT 2. Reihe 38.

Höistad, Ragnar
1944    "Eine hellenistische Parallele zu 2. Kor 6, 3ff." *ConNT* 9:22–27.
Holladay, Carl R.
1977    *Theios Aner in Hellenistic Judaism: A Critique of the Use of This Category in New Testament Christology.* SBLDS 40.
Holmberg, Bengt
1978    *Paul and Power: The Structure of Authority in the Primitive Church as Reflected in the Pauline Epistles.* Philadelphia: Fortress.
Holtzmann, Oskar
1926    *Das Neue Testament nach der Stuttgarter griechischer Text übersetzt und erklärt.* 2 vols. Giessen: Töpelmann.
Hooker, Morna D.
1981    "Beyond the Things That Are Written? St. Paul's Use of Scripture." *NTS* 27:295–309.
Hornbostel, Wilhelm
1973    *Sarapis. Studien zur Überlieferungsgeschichte, den Erscheinungsformen und Wandlungen der Gestalt eines Gottes.* ÉPRO 32.
Horsley, G. H. R.
1981    *New Documents Illustrating Early Christianity. A Review of the Greek Inscriptions and Papyri published in 1976.* North Ryde, N. S. W.: Macquarie University.
1982    *New Documents Illustrating Early Christianity. A Review of the Greek Inscriptions and Papyri published in 1977.* North Ryde, N. S. W.: Macquarie Univ.
Horst, Peter W. van der
1980    *Aelius Aristides and the New Testament.* SCHNT 6.
Hunzinger, Claus-Hunno
1963    "Beobachtungen zur Entwicklung der Disziplinarordnung der Gemeinde von Qumran." Pages 231–47 in *Qumran-Probleme.* Vorträge des Leipziger Symposions über Qumran-Probleme vom 9. bis 14. Oktober 1961. Ed. H. Bardtke. Deutsche Akademie der Wissenschaften zu Berlin, Schriften der Sektion für Altertumswissenschaft, 42. Berlin: Akademie-Verlag.
Hurd, John Coolidge, Jr.
1965    *The Origin of I Corinthians.* New York: Seabury.
Hyldahl, Niels
1973    "Die Frage nach der literarischen Einheit des Zweiten Korintherbriefes." *ZNW* 64:289–306.
Jervell, Jacob
1960    *Imago Dei. Gen 1, 26f. im Spätjudentum, in der Gnosis und in den paulinischen Briefen.* Göttingen: Vandenhoeck & Ruprecht.
1976    "Der schwache Charismatiker." Pages 185–98 in *Rechtfertigung* (Käsemann Festschrift). Eds. J. Friedrich, W. Pöhlmann, and P. Stuhlmacher. Tübingen/Göttingen: Mohr/Vandenhoeck & Ruprecht.
Jewett, Robert
1971    *Paul's Anthropological Terms. A Study of Their Use in Conflict Settings.* AGJU 10.

1978        "The Redaction of I Corinthians and the Trajectory of the Pauline School." *JAARSup* 44:389–444.

1979        *A Chronology of Paul's Life.* Philadelphia: Fortress.

Johnson, Franklin P.

1931        *Sculpture 1896–1923.* Corinth, IX/1.

Johnson, Sherman E.

1955        "Paul and the Manual of Discipline." *HTR* 48:157–65.

Jones, Arnold H. M.

1971        *The Cities of the Eastern Roman Provinces.* 2nd ed. Oxford: Clarendon.

Jourdan, George V.

1948        "*KOINŌNIA* in I Corinthians 10:16." *JBL* 67:111–24.

Judge, Edwin A.

1961        "The Literature of Roman Political Self-Advertisement." Page 24 in *Proceedings and Papers of the Seventh Congress of the Australasian Universities' Language and Literature Association* at Christchurch (Australia).

1964        "Roman Literary Memorials." Pages 28–30 in *Proceedings of the Ninth Congress of the Australasian Universities' Language and Literature Association* at Melbourne (Australia).

1966        "The Conflict of Educational Aims in New Testament Thought." *Journal of Christian Education* 9:32–45.

1968        "Paul's Boasting in Relation to Contemporary Professional Practice." *AusBR* 16:37–50.

1972        "St. Paul and Classical Society." *JAC* 15:19–36.

1973        "St Paul and Socrates." *Interchange* 14:106–16.

1980a       "Rank and Status in the Greek East Under the Romans." Unpublished seminar paper, Studiorum Novi Testamenti Societas Annual Meeting, Toronto.

1980b       "The Social Identity of the First Christians: A Question of Method in Religious History." *JRH* 11:201–17.

Kamlah, Ehrhard

1954        "Buchstabe und Geist. Die Bedeutung dieser Antithese für die alttestamentliche Exegese des Apostels Paulus." *EvT* 14:276–82.

1963        "Wie beurteilt Paulus sein Leiden? Ein Beitrag zur Untersuchung seiner Denkstruktur." *ZNW* 54:217–32.

Käsemann, Ernst

1942        "Die Legitimität des Apostels. Eine Untersuchung zu II Korinther 10–13." *ZNW* 41:33–71.

1969        *New Testament Questions of Today.* Tr. W. J. Montague. Philadelphia: Fortress.

1971a       "Some Thoughts on the Theme 'The Doctrine of Reconciliation in the New Testament.' " Pages 49–64 in *The Future of Our Religious Past* (Bultmann Festschrift). Ed. J. M. Robinson. New York: Harper & Row.

1971b       "The Spirit and the Letter." Pages 138–66 in *Perspectives on Paul.* Tr. M. Kohl. Philadelphia: Fortress.

1980     *Commentary on Romans.* Tr. and ed. G. W. Bromiley. Grand Rapids, Mich.: Eerdmans.

Kee, Doyle
1980     "Who Were the 'Super-Apostles' of 2 Corinthians 10–13?" *RestQ* 23:65–76.

Kennedy, George A.
1972     *The Art of Rhetoric in the Roman World.* Princeton: Princeton Univ. Press.
1980     *Classical Rhetoric and Its Christian and Secular Tradition from Ancient to Modern Times.* Chapel Hill: Univ. of North Carolina Press.

Kennedy, James H.
1900     *The Second and Third Epistles of St. Paul to the Corinthians.* London: Methuen.

Kent, John Harvey
1966     *The Inscriptions 1926–1950.* Corinth, VIII/3.

Ker, R. E.
1961     "Fear or Love? A Textual Note." *ExpTim* 72:195–96.

Kertelge, Karl
1967     *"Rechtfertigung" bei Paulus. Studien zur Struktur und zum Bedeutungsgehalt des paulinischen Rechtfertigungsbegriffs.* NTAbh n.F. 3.
1970     "Das Apostelamt des Paulus, sein Ursprung und seine Bedeutung." *BZ* 14:161–81.

Keyes, Clinton W.
1935     "The Greek Letter of Introduction." *AJP* 56:28–48.

Kierkegaard, Søren
1946     "The Thorn in the Flesh." Pages 49–73 in *Edifying Discourses,* IV. Trs. D. F. and L. M. Swenson. Minneapolis, Minn.: Augsburg.

Kijne, J. J.
1966     "We, Us and Our in I and II Corinthians." *NovT* 8:171–79.

Kim, Chan-Hie
1972     *The Familiar Letter of Recommendation.* SBLDS 4.

Kistner, Hilarion H.
1962     "The Meaning of 2 Cor. 8:9. A Historico-Exegetical Study." Unpublished doctoral dissertation, Catholic University of America.

Klein, Günter
1961     *Die zwölf Apostel. Ursprung und Gehalt einer Idee.* FRLANT n.F. 59.

Kleist, James A.
1944     "Emotion in the Gospels." *AER* 111:330–41.

Klinzing, Georg
1971     *Die Umdeutung des Kultus in der Qumrangemeinde und im Neuen Testament.* SUNT 7.

Knox, John
1942     *Marcion and the New Testament.* Chicago: Univ. of Chicago Press.
1950     *Chapters in a Life of Paul.* New York and Nashville: Abingdon-Cokesbury.

Knox, Wilfred L.
1939      *St. Paul and the Church of the Gentiles.* Cambridge: Cambridge Univ. Press.

Koester, Helmut
1982      *Introduction to the New Testament.* 2 vols. Hermeneia Foundations and Facets. Philadelphia: Fortress.

Kraft, Robert A., ed.
1974      *The Testament of Job.* SBLTT 5.

Kramer, Werner
1966      *Christ, Lord, Son of God.* Tr. B. Hardy. SBT 5.

Kremer, Jakob
1980      " 'Denn der Buchstabe tötet, der Geist aber macht lebendig.' Methodologische und hermeneutische Erwägungen zu 2 Kor 3, 6b." Pages 219–50 in *Begegnung mit dem Wort* (Zimmermann Festschrift). Eds. J. Zmijewski and E. Nellesen. BBB 53.

Krenkel, Max
1895      *Beiträge zur Aufhellung der Geschichte und der Briefe des Apostels Paulus.* 2nd ed. Braunschweig: Schwetschke.

Kuhn, Karl Georg
1951      "Die Schriftrollen vom Toten Meer." *EvT* 11:72–75.

Kümmel, Werner Georg
1967      *"Paresis* and *endeixis."* *JTC* 3:1–13.
1975      *Introduction to the New Testament.* Rev. ed. Tr. H. C. Kee. Nashville, Tenn.: Abingdon.

Lake, Kirsopp
1927      *The Earlier Epistles of St. Paul.* London: Rivington's.

Lambrecht, Jan
1976      " 'Om Samen te Sterven en Samen te Leven,' Uitleg van 2 Kor. 7, 3." *Bijdragen* 37:234–51.
1978      "The Fragment 2 Cor vi 14–vii 1. A Plea for Its Authenticity." Pages 143–61 in *Miscellanea Neotestamentica,* II. Eds. T. Baarda, A. F. J. Klijn, and W. C. van Unnik. NovTSup 47.

Lampe, Geoffrey W. H.
1951      *The Seal of the Spirit: A Study in the Doctrine of Baptism and Confirmation in the New Testament and the Fathers.* London: Longmans, Green.
1967      "Church Discipline and the Interpretation of the Epistles to the Corinthians." Pages 337–61 in Farmer et al.

Lang, Friedrich Gustav
1973      *2. Korinther 5, 1–10 in der neueren Forschung.* BGBE 16.

Larsen, J. A. O.
1938      "Roman Greece." Pages 259–498 in *An Economic Survey of Ancient Rome,* IV. Ed. F. Tenney. Baltimore: The Johns Hopkins Univ. Press.
1958      "The Policy of Augustus in Greece." *Acta Classica* I. Kaapstad: Balkema.

Larsson, Edvin
1962      *Christus als Vorbild. Eine Untersuchung zu den paulinischen Tauf und Eikontexten.* ASNU 23.

Lattey, Cuthbert
1943      *"lambanein* in 2 Cor. xi.20." *JTS* 44:148.

Laub, Franz
1973      *Eschatologische Verkündigung und Lebensgestaltung nach Paulus. Eine Untersuchung zum Wirken des Apostels beim Aufbau der Gemeinde in Thessalonike.* Münchener Universitäts-Schriften. Regensburg: Pustet.

Leivestad, Ragnar
1966      " 'The Meekness and Gentleness of Christ.' " *NTS* 12:156–64.

Leon, Harry J.
1960      *The Jews of Ancient Rome.* Philadelphia: Jewish Publication Society of America.

Lesky, Albin
1966      *A History of Greek Literature.* Trs. J. Willis and C. de Heer. New York: Crowell.

Lightfoot, Joseph B.
1884      *Saint Paul's Epistle to the Galatians.* 8th ed. London: Macmillan.

Lincoln, Andrew T.
1979      " 'Paul the Visionary': The Setting and Significance of the Rapture to Paradise in II Corinthians XII.1–10." *NTS* 25:204–20.

Lindars, Barnabas
1961      *New Testament Apologetic. The Doctrinal Significance of the Old Testament Quotations.* Philadelphia: Westminster.

Lofthouse, William F.
1947      "Singular and Plural in St. Paul's Letters." *ExpTim* 58:179–82.

Lohmeyer, Ernst
1927      "Probleme paulinischer Theologie. I. Briefliche Grussüberschriften." *ZNW* 26:158–73.

1954      *Der Brief an die Philipper.* 10th ed. KEK.

Lohse, Eduard
1953      "Ursprung und Prägung des christlichen Apostolates." *TZ* 9:259–75.

1971      *Colossians and Philemon.* Trs. W. R. Poehlmann and R. J. Karris. Hermeneia.

Lüdemann, Gerd
1980      *Paulus, der Heidenapostel.* I: *Studien zur Chronologie.* FRLANT 125.

Lührmann, Dieter
1965      *Das Offenbarungsverständnis bei Paulus und in paulinischen Gemeinden.* WMANT 16.

1970      "Rechtfertigung und Versöhnung." *ZTK* 67:437–52.

Lütgert, Wilhelm
1908      *Freiheitspredigt und Schwarmgeister in Korinth.* BFCT XII/3.

Luz, Ulrich
1967      "Der alte und der neue Bund bei Paulus und im Hebräerbrief." *EvT* 27:318–36.

McDermott, Michael
1975    "The Biblical Doctrine of *KOINONIA.*" *BZ* 19:64–77, 219–33.
Machalet, Christian
1973    "Paulus und seine Gegner. Eine Untersuchung zu den Korinther-
        briefen." Pages 183–203 in *Theokratia,* Jahrbuch des Inst. Judaicum
        Delitzschianum II, 1970–72 (Rengstorf Festgabe). Eds. W. Dietrich
        et al. Leiden: Brill.
McKenzie, John L.
1968    *Second Isaiah.* AB 20.
MacMullen, Ramsay
1966    *Enemies of the Roman Order; Treason, Unrest and Alienation in the
        Empire.* Cambridge: Harvard Univ. Press.
1974    *Roman Social Relations, 50 B.C. to A.D. 284.* New Haven: Yale Univ.
        Press.
MacRae, George W.
1968    "Anti-Dualist Polemic in 2 Cor 4:6?" Pages 420–31 in *Studia Evan-
        gelica,* IV/1: *The New Testament Scriptures.* Ed. F. L. Cross. TU 102.
Magie, David
1950    *Roman Rule in Asia Minor to the End of the Third Century after
        Christ.* 2 vols. Princeton: Princeton Univ. Press.
Malherbe, Abraham J.
1961    "Through the Eye of the Needle: Simplicity or Singleness?" *RestQ*
        5:119–29.
———, ed.
1977    *The Cynic Epistles: A Study Edition.* SBLSBS 12.
1983    "Antisthenes and Odysseus, and Paul at War." *HTR* 76:143–73.
Manchester, Paul T., and P. Thomas Manchester, Jr.
1972    "The Blindness of Saint Paul." *Archives of Ophthalmology* 88:316–21.
Manson, Thomas W.
1945    "HILASTĒRION." *JTS* 46:1–10.
1953    "2 Cor. 2:14–17: Suggestions Toward an Exegesis." Pages 155–62 in
        *Studia Paulina* (de Zwaan Festschrift). Haarlem: Bohn.
1962    "The Corinthian Correspondence." Pages 190–224 in *Studies in the
        Gospels and Epistles.* Ed. M. Black. Philadelphia: Westminster.
Marmorstein, Arthur
1927    *The Old Rabbinic Doctrine of God,* I. Jews' College Publications, 10.
        London: Oxford Univ. Press.
Marrow, Stanley B.
1982    "*Parrhēsia* and the New Testament." *CBQ* 44:431–46.
Marshall, I. Howard
1978    "The Meaning of 'Reconciliation.'" Pages 117–32 in *Unity and Diver-
        sity in New Testament Theology* (Ladd Festschrift). Ed. R. A. Guelich.
        Grand Rapids, Mich.: Eerdmans.
Marshall, Peter
1980    "Enmity and Other Social Conventions in Paul's Relations with the
        Corinthians." Unpublished Ph.D. dissertation, Macquarie University
        (forthcoming, Mohr, Tübingen).

1983 "A Metaphor of Social Shame: *THRIAMBEUEIN* in 2 Cor. 2:14." *NovT* 25:302–17.

Martin, Ralph P.
1976 *Philippians.* NCB.

Martyn, J. Louis
1967 "Epistemology at the Turn of the Ages: 2 Corinthians 5:16." Pages 269–87 in Farmer et al.

Marxsen, Willi
1968 *Introduction to the New Testament. An Approach to Its Problems.* Tr. G. Buswell. Philadelphia: Fortress.

Mason, H. J.
1971 "Lucius at Corinth." *Phoenix* 25:160–65.

Mattern, Liselotte
1966 *Das Verständnis des Gerichtes bei Paulus.* ATANT 47.

Mattusch, Carol C.
1977 "Bronze- and Ironworking in the Area of the Athenian Agora." *Hesp* 46:340–89.

Max, Herzog zu Sachsen
1919 *Das christliche Hellas.* Leipzig: Hiersemann.

Maxfield, Valerie A.
1981 *The Military Decorations of the Roman Army.* Berkeley and Los Angeles: Univ. of California Press.

Mazzeo, Joseph Anthony
1957 "Dante and the Pauline Modes of Vision." *HTR* 50:275–306.

Mealand, David L.
1976 " 'As having nothing and yet possessing everything,' 2 Cor 6:10c." *ZNW* 67:277–79.

Meeks, Wayne A.
1970 "Moses as God and King." Pages 354–71 in *Religions in Antiquity. Essays in Memory of Erwin Ramsdell Goodenough.* Ed. J. Neusner. NumenSup 14.

Meinardus, Otto F. A.
1973 *St. Paul in Greece.* 2nd ed. Athens: Lycabettus.

Menoud, Philippe H.
1978 "The Thorn in the Flesh and Satan's Angel (2 Cor. 12.7)." Pages 19–30 in *Jesus Christ and the Faith: A Collection of Studies.* Tr. E. M. Paul. PTMS 18.

Metzger, Bruce M.
1971 *A Textual Commentary on the Greek New Testament.* London and New York: United Bible Societies.

Meurer, Siegfried
1972 *Das Recht im Dienst der Versöhnung und des Friedens.* ATANT 63.

Meyer, Marvin W., ed. and tr.
1976 *The "Mithras Liturgy."* SBLTT 10.

Meyer, Paul W.
1979 "The Holy Spirit in the Pauline Letters: A Contextual Exploration." *Int* 33:3–18.

Meyer, Robert T., tr. and ed.
1965        *Palladius, The Lausiac History.* Ancient Christian Writers, 34. West-
            minster/London: Newman/Longmans, Green.
Michaelis, Wilhelm
1961        *Einleitung in das Neue Testament. Die Entstehung, Sammlung und
            Überlieferung der Schriften des Neuen Testaments.* 3rd ed. Bern:
            Haller.
Michel, Otto
1954        " 'Erkennen dem Fleisch nach' (II Kor. 5, 16)." *EvT* 14:22–29.
Minear, Paul S.
1960        *Images of the Church in the New Testament.* Philadelphia: Westmin-
            ster.
1979        "Some Pauline Thoughts on Dying: A Study of 2 Corinthians." Pages
            91–106 in *From Faith to Faith* (Miller Festschrift). Ed. D. Y.
            Hadidian. PTMS 23.
Moffatt, James
1918        *An Introduction to the Literature of the New Testament.* 3rd rev. ed.
            Edinburgh: Clark.
Momigliano, Arnaldo
1961        *Claudius: The Emperor and His Achievement.* Tr. W. Hogarth. Cam-
            bridge, Eng.: Heffer.
Moore, George Foot
1927, 1930  *Judaism in the First Centuries of the Christian Era. The Age of the
            Tannaim.* 3 vols. Cambridge: Harvard Univ. Press.
Morgan-Wynne, John E.
1979        "2 Corinthians VIII.18f. and the Question of a *Traditionsgrundlage*
            for Acts." *JTS* 30:172–73.
Morrice, William G.
1972        "The Imperatival *hina.*" *BT* 23:326–30.
Mott, Stephen C.
1975        "The Power of Giving and Receiving: Reciprocity in Hellenistic Be-
            nevolence." Pages 60–72 in *Current Issues in Biblical and Patristic
            Interpretation* (Tenney Festschrift). Ed. G. F. Hawthorne. Grand
            Rapids, Mich.: Eerdmans.
Moule, Charles F. D.
1953        *An Idiom Book of New Testament Greek.* Cambridge: Cambridge
            Univ. Press.
1972        "2 Cor 3, 18b." Pages 231–38 in *Neues Testament und Geschichte*
            (Cullmann Festschrift). Eds. H. Baltensweiler and B. Reicke. Zürich:
            Theologischer Verlag.
Müller-Bardoff, J.
1956        "Nächtlicher Gottesdienst im apostolischen Zeitalter." *TLZ* 81:347–
            52.
Mullins, Terence Y.
1957        "Paul's Thorn in the Flesh." *JBL* 76:299–303.
1962        "Petition as a Literary Form." *NovT* 5:46–54.
1964        "Disclosure: A Literary Form in the New Testament." *NovT* 7:44–50.

| | |
|---|---|
| 1968 | "Greeting as a New Testament Form." *JBL* 87:418–26. |
| 1972 | "Formulas in New Testament Epistles." *JBL* 91:380–90. |
| 1977 | "Benediction as a NT Form." *AUSS* 15:59–64. |

Munck, Johannes

| | |
|---|---|
| 1949 | "Paul, the Apostles, and the Twelve." *ST* 3:96–110. |
| 1959 | *Paul and the Salvation of Mankind.* Tr. F. Clarke. Richmond, Va.: Knox. |

Murphy-O'Connor, Jerome

| | |
|---|---|
| 1983 | *St. Paul's Corinth. Texts and Archaeology.* Good News Studies, 6. Wilmington, Del.: Glazier. |

———, ed.

| | |
|---|---|
| 1968 | *Paul and Qumran: Studies in New Testament Exegesis.* London: Chapman. |

Mussies, G.

| | |
|---|---|
| 1972 | *Dio Chrysostom and the New Testament.* SCHNT 2. |

Musurillo, Herbert

| | |
|---|---|
| 1972 | *The Acts of the Christian Martyrs. Introduction, Texts and Translations.* Oxford: Clarendon. |

Mylonas, George E.

| | |
|---|---|
| 1961 | *Eleusis and the Eleusinian Mysteries.* Princeton: Princeton Univ. Press. |

Nickle, Keith F.

| | |
|---|---|
| 1966 | *The Collection. A Study in Paul's Strategy.* SBT 48. |

Nielsen, Helge K.

| | |
|---|---|
| 1980 | "Paulus' Verwendung des Begriffes *Dynamis.* Eine Replik zur Kreuzestheologie." Pages 137–58 in *Die Paulinische Literatur und Theologie.* Teologiske Studier, 7. Ed. S. Pedersen. Aarhus/Göttingen: Aros/Vandenhoeck & Ruprecht. |

Nisbet, Patricia

| | |
|---|---|
| 1969 | "The Thorn in the Flesh." *ExpTim* 80:126. |

Noack, Bent

| | |
|---|---|
| 1948 | *Satanás und Sotería. Untersuchungen zur neutestamentliche Dämonologie.* København: Gads. |
| 1963 | "A Note on 2 Cor. 4:15." *ST* 17:129–32. |

Norden, Eduard

| | |
|---|---|
| 1913 | *Agnostos Theos. Untersuchungen zur Formengeschichte religiöser Rede.* Leipzig and Berlin: Teubner. |
| 1915 | *Die antike Kunstprosa vom VI. Jahrhundert v. Chr. bis in die Zeit der Renaissance.* 3rd ed. Repr. 1958. Stuttgart: Teubner. |

North, Helen

| | |
|---|---|
| 1966 | *Sophrosyne: Self-Knowledge and Self-Restraint in Greek Literature.* Ithaca: Cornell Univ. Press. |

O'Brien, Peter T.

| | |
|---|---|
| 1977 | *Introductory Thanksgivings in the Letters of Paul.* NovTSup 49. |

O'Collins, Gerald G.

| | |
|---|---|
| 1971 | "Power Made Perfect in Weakness: 2 Cor 12:9–10." *CBQ* 33:528–37. |

Olivier, Frank
1929        "SYNAPOTHNĒISKŌ; d'un article de lexique à Saint Paul, 2 Cor.
            7:3." *RTP* 17:103–33.
Olson, Stanley N.
1976        "Confidence Expressions in Paul: Epistolary Conventions and the
            Purpose of 2 Corinthians." Unpublished Ph.D. dissertation, Yale Uni-
            versity.
O'Neil, Edward, ed. and tr.
1977        *Teles (The Cynic Teacher).* SBLTT 11.
Oostendorp, Derk William
1967        *Another Jesus: A Gospel of Jewish-Christian Superiority in II Corinthi-
            ans.* Kampen: Kok.
Orr, William F., and James Arthur Walther
1976        *I Corinthians.* AB 32.
Osten-Sacken, Peter von der
1969        *Gott und Belial. Traditionsgeschichtliche Untersuchungen zum Dualis-
            mus in den Texten aus Qumran.* SUNT 6.
1975        *Römer 8 als Beispiel paulinischer Soteriologie.* FRLANT 112.
1981        "Geist im Buchstaben. Vom Glanz des Mose und des Paulus." *EvT*
            41:230–35.
Oxford Society of Historical Theology
1905        *The New Testament in the Apostolic Fathers by a Committee of the
            Oxford Society of Historical Theology.* Oxford: Clarendon.
Pagels, Elaine Hiesey
1975        *The Gnostic Paul: Gnostic Exegesis of the Pauline Letters.* Philadel-
            phia: Fortress.
Park, David M.
1980        "Paul's *skolops tē sarki:* Thorn or Stake? (2 Cor xii 7)." *NovT* 22:
            179–83.
Peabody, David
1974        "Boasting in the Lord. A Study of *KAUCHAOMAI* in Paul's Letters."
            Unpublished seminar paper, Southern Methodist University.
Pearson, Birger A.
1967        "Did the Gnostics Curse Jesus?" *JBL* 86:301–5.
Perrin, Norman
1974        *The New Testament: An Introduction.* New York: Harcourt Brace
            Jovanovich.
Peterson, Erik
1950        "Das Praescriptum des 1.Clemens-Briefes." Pages 351–57 in *Pro
            Regno Pro Sanctuario.* Eds. W. J. Kooiman and J. M. van Veen.
            Nijkerk: Callenbach.
Pfitzner, Victor C.
1967        *Paul and the Agon Motif: Traditional Athletic Imagery in the Pauline
            Letters.* NovTSup 16.
Pherigo, Lindsey P.
1949        "Paul and the Corinthian Church." *JBL* 68:341–50.

Philonenko, Marc
1968        *Joseph et Aséneth. Introduction, texte critique, traduction et notes.* SPB
            13.
Pierce, Claude A.
1955        *Conscience in the New Testament.* SBT 15.
Pope, R. Martin
1911        "Studies in Pauline Vocabulary: Of Indwelling Power." *ExpTim* 22:
            312–13.
Popkes, Wiard
1967        *Christus Traditus. Eine Untersuchung zum Begriff der Dahingabe im
            Neuen Testament.* ATANT 49.
Potterie, Ignace de la
1959        L'Onction du chrétien par la foi." *Bib* 40:12–69.
Pratscher, Wilhelm
1979        "Der Verzicht des Paulus auf finanziellen Unterhalt durch seine Ge-
            meinden: ein Aspekt seiner Missionsweise." *NTS* 25:284–98.
Preisker, Herbert
1926        "Zur Komposition des zweiten Korintherbriefes." *TBl* 5:154–57.
Price, James L.
1967        "Aspects of Paul's Theology and Their Bearing on Literary Problems
            of Second Corinthians." Pages 95–106 in *Studies in the History and
            Text of the New Testament.* Eds. B. L. Daniels and M. J. Suggs. SD
            29.
Price, Robert M.
1980        "Punished in Paradise (An Exegetical Theory on II Corinthians 12:
            1–10)." *JSNT* 7:33–40.
Proudfoot, C. Merrill
1963        "Imitation or Realistic Participation? A Study of Paul's Concept of
            'Suffering with Christ.' " *Int* 17:140–60.
Provence, Thomas E.
1982        " 'Who Is Sufficient for These Things?' An Exegesis of 2 Corinthians
            ii15–iii18." *NovT* 24:54–81.
Quinn, Jerome D.
1978        " 'Seven Times He Wore Chains' (1 Clem 5.6)." *JBL* 97:574–76.
Ramsay, William M.
1900        *A Historical Commentary on St. Paul's Epistle to the Galatians.* New
            York: Putnam's.
Reitzenstein, Richard
1978        *Hellenistic Mystery-Religions: Their Basic Ideas and Significance.* Tr.
            J. E. Steely. PTMS 15.
Rex, Helmut H.
1958        "Immortality of the Soul, or Resurrection of the Dead, or What?"
            *RefThRev* 17:73–82.
Richard, Earl
1981        "Polemics, Old Testament, and Theology. A Study of II Cor., III,
            1–IV,6." *RB* 88:340–67.

Riddle, Donald W.
   1940      *Paul, Man of Conflict: A Modern Biographical Sketch.* Nashville,
             Tenn.: Cokesbury.
Ridgway, Brunilde S.
   1981      "Sculpture from Corinth." *Hesp* 50:422–48.
Ringgren, Helmer
   1963      *The Faith of Qumran: Theology of the Dead Sea Scrolls.* Tr. E. T.
             Sander. Philadelphia: Fortress.
Rissi, Matthias
   1969      *Studien zum zweiten Korintherbrief. Der alte Bund—Der Predigt—Der
             Tod.* ATANT 56.
Rivkin, Ellis
   1978      *A Hidden Revolution: The Pharisees' Search for the Kingdom Within.*
             Nashville, Tenn.: Abingdon.
Robert, Louis
   1940      *Les Gladiateurs dans l'Orient grec.* Bibliothèque de l'École des Hautes
             Études 278. Paris: Champion.
Robertson, Archibald T.
   1923      *A Grammar of the Greek New Testament in the Light of Historical
             Research.* 4th ed. Repr. 1934. Nashville, Tenn.: Broadman.
Robinson, Henry S.
   1965      *The Urban Development of Ancient Corinth.* Athens: ASCSA.
Robinson, James M.
   1964      "Die Hodayot-Formel in Gebet und Hymnus des Frühchristen-
             tums." Pages 194–235 in *Apophoreta* (Haenchen Festschrift). BZNW
             30.
Robinson, John A. T.
   1952      *The Body. A Study in Pauline Theology.* SBT 5.
Roebuck, Carl
   1951      *The Asklepieion and Lerna.* Corinth XIV.
Roloff, Jürgen
   1965      *Apostolat—Verkündigung—Kirche.* Gütersloh: Mohn.
Rüger, Hans Peter
   1977      "Hieronymous, die Rabbinen und Paulus. Zur Vorgeschichte des Be-
             griffspaars 'innerer und äusserer Mensch.' " *ZNW* 68:132–37.
Saake, Helmut
   1973      "Paulus als Ekstatiker. Pneumatologische Beobachtungen zu 2 Kor.
             xii 1–10." *NovT* 15:153–60. (Also in *Bib* 53 [1972]:404–10.)
Sakellariou, Michael, and Nikolaos Faraklas
   1971      *Corinthia—Cleonaea.* Ancient Greek Cities, 3. Athens: Athens Center
             of Ekistics.
Salmon, Edward T.
   1969      *Roman Colonization Under the Republic.* AGRL.
Salom, A. P.
   1958      "The Imperatival Use of *hina* in the New Testament." *AusBR* 6:
             123–41.

Sánchez Bosch, Jorge
1970 *"Gloriarse" según San Pablo: Sentido y teología de kauchaomai.* AnBib 40.
Sand, Alexander
1967 *Der Begriff "Fleisch" in den paulinischen Hauptbriefen.* BU 2.
Sanders, Ed P.
1977 *Paul and Palestinian Judaism: A Comparison of Patterns of Religion.* Philadelphia: Fortress.
Sanders, Jack T.
1962 "The Transition from Opening Epistolary Thanksgiving to Body in the Letters of the Pauline Corpus." *JBL* 81:348–62.
Schildenberger, Johannes
1963 "2 Kor. 3:17a. 'Der Herr ist der Geist,' im Zusammenhang des Textes und der Theologie des hl. Paulus." Pages 451–60 in *Studiorum Paulinorum Congressus Internationalis Catholicus, 1961.* AnBib 17–18, I.
Schlier, Heinrich
1964 "Die Eigenart der christlichen Mahnung nach dem Apostel Paulus." Pages 340–57 in *Besinnung auf das Neue Testament: Exegetische Aufsätze und Vorträge,* II. Freiburg: Herder.
Schmidt, Karl Ludwig
1950 *"Iesous Christos kolaphizomenos* und die 'colaphisation' der Juden." Pages 218–27 in *Aux sources de la tradition chrétienne* (Goguel Festschrift). Bibliothèque Théologique. Paris: Delachaux et Niestlé.
Schmithals, Walter
1969 *The Office of Apostle in the Early Church.* Tr. J. E. Steely. Nashville, Tenn.: Abingdon.
1971 *Gnosticism in Corinth: An Investigation of the Letters to the Corinthians.* Tr. J. E. Steely. Nashville, Tenn.: Abingdon.
1972 *Paul and the Gnostics.* Tr. J. E. Steely. Nashville, Tenn.: Abingdon.
1973 "Die Korintherbriefe als Briefsammlung." *ZNW* 64:263–88.
Schnackenburg, Rudolf
1964 *Baptism in the Thought of St. Paul: A Study in Pauline Theology.* Tr. G. R. Beasley-Murray. New York: Herder.
Schneider, Bernardin
1953 "The Meaning of St. Paul's Antithesis 'the Letter and the Spirit.' " *CBQ* 15:163–207.
1976 "HE KOINONIA TOU HAGIOU PNEUMATOS (II Cor. 13, 13)." Pages 421–47 in *Studies Honoring Ignatius Charles Brady, Friar Minor.* Franciscan Institute Publications, Theology Series, 6. Eds. R. S. Almagno and C. L. Harkins. St. Bonaventure, N.Y.: Franciscan Institute.
Schneider, Norbert
1970 *Die rhetorische Eigenart der paulinischen Antithese.* HUT 11.
Scholem, Gershom G.
1965 *Jewish Gnosticism, Merkabah Mysticism, and Talmudic Tradition.* Rev. ed. New York: Jewish Theological Seminary.

Schrage, Wolfgang
  1974       "Leid, Kreuz und Eschaton: Die Peristasenkataloge als Merkmale
             paulinischer theologia crucis und Eschatologie." *EvT* 34:141–75.
Schreiner, Josef
  1974       "Jeremia 9, 22.23 als Hintergrund des paulinischen 'Sich-Rühmens.' "
             Pages 530–42 in *Neues Testament und Kirche* (Schnackenburg Fest-
             schrift). Ed. J. Gnilka. Freiburg-Basel-Wien: Herder.
Schubert, Paul
  1939       *Form and Function of the Pauline Thanksgivings*. BZNW 20.
Schulte, Hannelis
  1949       *Der Begriff der Offenbarung im Neuen Testament*. BEvT 13.
Schulz, Siegfried
  1958       "Die Decke des Moses. Untersuchungen zu einer vorpaulinischen
             Überlieferung in II Cor. 3.7–18." *ZNW* 49:1–30.
Schürer, Emil
  1973       *The History of the Jewish People in the Age of Jesus Christ (175 B.C.–
             A.D. 135)*, 1. Revised and edited by G. Vermes and F. Miller. Edin-
             burgh: Clark.
Schütz, John Howard
  1975       *Paul and the Anatomy of Apostolic Authority*. SNTSMS 26.
Schweizer, Eduard
  1959       "Zur Herkunft der Präexistenzvorstellung bei Paulus." *EvT* 19:65–
             70.
  1960       *Lordship and Discipleship*. SBT 28.
  1979       "Traditional Ethical Patterns in the Pauline and Post-Pauline Let-
             ters and Their Development (Lists of Vices and Household Ta-
             bles)." Pages 195–209 in *Text and Interpretation* (Black Festschrift).
             Eds. E. Best and R. McL. Wilson. Cambridge: Cambridge Univ.
             Press.
Scramuzza. Vincent M.
  1940       *The Emperor Claudius*. Cambridge: Harvard Univ. Press.
Scranton, Robert L.
  1949       "The Corinth of the Apostle Paul." *The Emory University Quarterly*
             5:72–83.
  1951       *Monuments in the Lower Agora and North of the Archaic Temple*.
             Corinth, I/3.
  1957       *Medieval Architecture in the Central Area of Corinth*. Corinth, XVI.
  ———, Joseph W. Shaw, and Leila Ibrahim
  1978       *Topography and Architecture*. Kenchreai, I.
Scroggs, Robin
  1976       "Paul as Rhetorician: Two Homilies in Romans 9–11." Pages 271–98
             in *Jews, Greeks and Christians: Religious Cultures in Late Antiquity*
             (Davies Festschrift). Eds. R. Hamerton-Kelly and R. Scroggs. SJLA
             21.
Seeberg, Alfred
  1903       *Der Katechismus der Urchristenheit*. Repr. 1966. TBü 26.

Seesemann, Heinrich
1933    *Der Begriff KOINŌNIA im Neuen Testament.* BZNW 14.

Segal, Alan F.
1980    "Heavenly Ascent in Hellenistic Judaism, Early Christianity and Their Environment." Pages 1333–94 in *ANRW* II, 23/2.

Seidensticker, Philipp
1977    "St. Paul and Poverty." Pages 81–120 in *Gospel Poverty: Essays in Biblical Theology.* Tr. M. Guinan. Chicago: Franciscan Herald.

Selwyn, Edward G.
1947    *The First Epistle of St. Peter.* 2nd ed. London: Macmillan.

Sevenster, Jan N.
1953    "Some Remarks on the *gumnos* in 2 Cor. 5:3." Pages 202–14 in *Studia Paulina* (de Zwaan Festschrift). Haarlem: Bohn.

Shelley, Joseph M.
1943    "The Christian Basilica Near the Cenchrean Gate at Corinth." *Hesp* 12:166–89.

Sherwin-White, Adrian N.
1963    *Roman Society and Roman Law in the New Testament.* Oxford: Clarendon.

Sjöberg, Erik
1951    "Wiedergeburt und Neuschöpfung im palästinischen Judentum." *ST* 4:44–85.
1955    "Neuschöpfung in den Toten-Meer-Rollen." *ST* 9:131–36.

Smith, Dennis E.
1977    "The Egyptian Cults at Corinth." *HTR* 70:201–31.

Souček, Josef B.
1959    "Wir erkennen Christus nicht mehr nach dem Fleisch." *EvT* 19: 300–14.

Speidel, Michael
1970    "The Captor of Decebalus. A New Inscription from Philippi." *JRS* 60:142–53.

Spencer, Aida Besançon
1981    "The Wise Fool (and the Foolish Wise): A Study of Irony in Paul." *NovT* 23:349–60.

Spicq, Ceslaus
1937    "L'Image sportive de II Cor 4:7–9." *ETL* 13:202–29.
1959    *Agapè dans le Nouveau Testament. Analyse des textes,* II. ÉBib.
1965    *Agape in the New Testament,* II. Trs. M. A. McNamara and M. H. Richter. St. Louis and London: Herder.

Spittler, Russell P.
1975    "The Limits of Ecstasy: An Exegesis of 2 Corinthians 12:1–10." Pages 259–66 in *Current Issues in Biblical and Patristic Interpretation* (Tenney Festschrift). Ed. G. F. Hawthorne. Grand Rapids, Mich.: Eerdmans.

Stachowiak, L. Remegius
1963    "Die Antithese Licht-Finsternis—ein Thema der paulinischen Paränese." *TQ* 143:385–421.

Stählin, Gustav
1962    "Zum Gebrauch von Beteurungsformeln." *NovT* 5:115–43.
1973    " 'Um mitzusterben und mitzuleben.' Bemerkungen zu 2 Kor 7.3."
        Pages 503–21 in Betz and Schottroff.
Starcky, Jean
1965    "Les Nabatéens dans la Bible." *BTS* 74:2–5.
Stephenson, Alan M. G.
1964    "Partition Theories on II Corinthians." Pages 639–46 in *Studia
        Evangelica, II/1: The New Testament Scriptures.* Ed. F. L. Cross. TU
        87.
1965    "A Defence of the Integrity of 2 Corinthians." Pages 82–97 in *The
        Authorship and Integrity of the New Testament.* S.P.C.K. Theological
        Collections, 4. London: S.P.C.K.
Stillwell, Richard
1952    *The Theatre.* Corinth, II.
———, Robert L. Scranton, and Sarah E. Freeman, with contributions by H. Ess
    Askew.
1941    *Architecture.* Corinth, I/2.
Stirewalt, Martin Luther, Jr.
1969    "Paul's Evaluation of Letter-Writing." Pages 186–90 in *Search the
        Scriptures* (Stamm Festschrift). Eds. J. M. Myers et al. GTS 3.
1972    "The Letters of Paul: The Letter-Setting." Privately circulated.
Stone, Michael E., tr.
1972    *The Testament of Abraham: The Greek Recensions.* SBLTT 2.
Strelan, John G.
1975    "Burden-Bearing and the Law of Christ." *JBL* 94:266–76.
Stroud, Ronald S.
1965    "The Sanctuary of Demeter and Kore on Acrocorinth." Preliminary
        Report I: 1961–62." *Hesp* 34:1–24.
1968    "The Sanctuary of Demeter and Kore on Acrocorinth. Preliminary
        Report II: 1964–65." *Hesp* 37:299–330.
Stuhlmacher, Peter
1965    *Gerechtigkeit Gottes bei Paulus.* FRLANT 87.
1967    "Erwägungen zum ontologischen Charakter der *kainē ktisis* bei
        Paulus." *EvT* 27:1–35.
Suhl, Alfred
1975    *Paulus und seine Briefe. Ein Beitrag zur paulinischen Chronologie.*
        SNT 11.
Sundberg, Albert C., Jr.
1973    "Canon Muratori: A Fourth-Century List." *HTR* 66:1–41.
Synofzik, Ernst
1977    *Die Gerichts- und Vergeltungsaussagen bei Paulus. Eine traditionsge-
        schichtliche Untersuchung.* GTA 8.
Tannehill, Robert C.
1967    *Dying and Rising with Christ: A Study in Pauline Theology.* BZNW
        32.

Tanner, R. G.
1980    "St. Paul's View of Militia and Contemporary Social Values." Pages 377–82 in *Studia Biblica 1978, III.* Ed. E. A. Livingstone. JSNTSup 3.

Thackeray, Henry St. John
1900    *The Relation of St. Paul to Contemporary Jewish Thought.* London: Macmillan.

Theissen, Gerd
1982    *The Social Setting of Pauline Christianity. Essays on Corinth.* Ed. and tr. with an introduction by J. H. Schütz. Philadelphia: Fortress.

Thierry, Jean J.
1962    "Der Dorn im Fleische (2 Kor. xii 7–9)." *NovT* 5:301–10.

Thompson, James
1982    "The Courage of the Apostle." An unpublished paper read at the Annual Meeting of the Society of Biblical Literature, Southwest Region, 12 March, in Dallas.

Thornton, Timothy
1972    "Satan—God's Agent for Punishing." *ExpTim* 83:151–52.

Thraede, Klaus
1970    *Grundzüge griechisch-römischer Brieftopik.* Zetemata, 48. München: Beck.

Thrall, Margaret E.
1962    *Greek Particles in the New Testament.* NTTS 3.
1967    "The Pauline Use of SYNEIDĒSIS." *NTS* 14:118–25.
1976    "2 Corinthians 1:12: *hagiotēti* or *haplotēti?*" Pages 366–72 in *Studies in New Testament Language and Text* (Kilpatrick Festschrift). Ed. J. K. Elliott. NovTSup 44.
1977    "The Problem of II Cor. vi.14–vii.1 in Some Recent Discussion." *NTS* 24:132–48.
1980    "Super-Apostles, Servants of Christ, and Servants of Satan." *JSNT* 6:42–57.
1982    "A Second Thanksgiving Period in II Corinthians." *JSNT* 16:101–24.

Thüsing, Wilhelm
1969    *Per Christum in Deum: Studien zum Verhältnis von Christozentrik und Theozentrik in den paulinischen Hauptbriefen.* 2nd ed. NTAbh n.F. 1.
1974    "Rechtfertigungsgedanke und Christologie in den Korintherbriefen." Pages 301–24 in *Neues Testament und Kirche* (Schnackenburg Festschrift). Ed. J. Gnilka. Freiburg-Wien: Herder.

Thyen, Hartwig
1970    *Studien zur Sündenvergebung im Neuen Testament und seinen alttestamentlichen und jüdischen Voraussetzungen.* FRLANT 96.

Travis, Stephen H.
1973    "Paul's Boasting in 2 Corinthians 10–12." Pages 527–32 in *Studia Evangelica,* VI. Ed. E. A. Livingstone. TU 112.

Ulonska, Herbert
1966    "Die Doxa des Mose." *EvT* 26:378–88.

Unnik, Willem C. van
1953    "Reisepläne und Amen-sagen, Zusammenhang und Gedankenfolge in 2. Korinther i 15–25." Pages 215–34 in *Studia Paulina* (de Zwaan Festschrift). Haarlem: Bohn. (Repr. in *Sparsa Collecta* I, NovTSup 29, pp. 144–59.)

1960    "La Conception paulinienne de la nouvelle alliance." Pages 109–26 in *Littérature et théologie pauliniennes.* RechBib 5. (Repr. in *Sparsa Collecta* I, NovTSup 29, pp. 174–93.)

1961    "*Hē Kainē Diathēkē*—A Problem in the Early History of the Canon." Pages 212–27 in *Studia Patristica,* IV, Pt. II. Ed. F. L. Cross. TU 79. (Repr. in *Sparsa Collecta* II, NovTSup 30, pp. 157–71.)

1964    " 'With Unveiled Face,' an Exegesis of 2 Corinthians iii 12–18." *NovT* 6:153–69. (Repr. in *Sparsa Collecta* I, NovTSup 29, pp. 194–210.)

1980    "The Semitic Background of *parrēsia* in the New Testament." Pages 290–306 in *Sparsa Collecta* II, NovTSup 30.

Vermes, Geza
1975    *The Dead Sea Scrolls in English.* 2nd ed. Pelican Books. Harmondsworth: Penguin.

Versnel, H. S.
1970    *Triumphus: An Inquiry into the Origin, Development, and Meaning of the Roman Triumph.* Leiden: Brill.

Vielhauer, Philipp
1969    "Paulus und das Alte Testament." Pages 33–62 in *Studien zur Geschichte und Theologie der Reformation* (Bizer Festschrift). Eds. L. Abramowski and J. F. G. Goeters. Neukirchen-Vluyn: Neukirchener Verlag.

1975    *Geschichte der urchristlichen Literatur.* Berlin and New York: de Gruyter.

1979    "Oikodome. Das Bild vom Bau in der christlichen Literatur vom Neuen Testament bis Clemens Alexandrinus." Pages 1–168 in *Oikodome. Aufsätze zum Neuen Testament,* 1. Ed. G. Klein. TBü 65.

Vittinghoff, Friedrich
1952    *Römische Kolonisation und Bürger-rechtspolitik unter Caesar und Augustus.* Akademie der Wissenschaften und Literatur Abhandlungen der Geistes- und Sozialwissenschaftlichen Klasse 1951/14. Wiesbaden: Steiner.

Vliet, Hendrik van
1958    *No Single Testimony. A Study on the Adoption of the Law of Deut. 19:15 Par. into the New Testament.* Studia Theologica Rheno-Traiectina, 4. Utrecht: Kemink & Zoon.

Vögtle, Anton
1936    *Die Tugend- und Lasterkataloge im Neuen Testament.* NTAbh 16, 4/5.

Wagner, Guy
1981    "The Tabernacle and Life 'in Christ,' Exegesis of 2 Corinthians 5.1–10." *IBS* 3:145–65.

Walter, Nikolaus
1979 "Christusglaube und Heidnische Religiosität." *NTS* 25:422–42.
Webber, Robert D.
1970 "The Concept of Rejoicing in Paul." Unpublished Ph.D. dissertation, Yale University.
Weber, Michael
1798 *De numero epistolarum ad Corinthios rectius constituendo.* Wittenberg.
Weinberg, Saul S.
1939 "On the Date of the Temple of Apollo at Corinth." *Hesp* 8:191–99.
1960a "Roman Twins: Basilicas at Corinth." *Arch* 13:137–43.
1960b *The Southeast Building, The Twin Basilicas, The Mosaic House.* Corinth, I/5.
Weiss, Johannes
1959 *Earliest Christianity.* 2 vols. Trs. F. C. Grant et al. New York: Harper.
Wengst, Klaus
1972 *Christologische Formeln und Lieder des Urchristentums.* SNT 7.
West, Allen Brown
1931 *Latin Inscriptions 1896–1927.* Corinth, VIII/2.
Westcott, Brooke Foss
1896 *A General Survey of the History of the Canon of the New Testament.* 7th ed. London: Macmillan.
Westermann, Claus
1969 *Isaiah 40–66: A Commentary.* Tr. D. M. G. Stalker. Philadelphia: Westminster.
White, John L.
1972 *The Body of the Greek Letter.* SBLDS 2.
Wiefel, Wolfgang
1977 "The Jewish Community in Ancient Rome and the Origins of Roman Christianity." Pages 100–19 in *The Romans Debate.* Ed. K. P. Donfried. Minneapolis, Minn.: Augsburg.
Wilckens, Ulrich
1982 "Zur Entwicklung des paulinischen Gesetzesverständnisses." *NTS* 28:154–90.
Wiles, Gordon P.
1974 *Paul's Intercessory Prayers.* SNTSMS 24.
Williams, Charles K., II
1978 "Corinth, 1977: Forum Southwest." *Hesp* 47:1–39.
1979 Personal conference, 14 June, at Ancient Corinth.
1982 "Zeus and Other Deities: Notes on Two Archaistic Piers." Pages 175–81 in *Studies in Athenian History, Sculpture, and Architecture.* HespSup XX.
———, and Joan E. Fisher
1975 "Corinth, 1974: Forum Southwest." *Hesp* 44:1–50.
———, and Orestes H. Zervos
1982 "Corinth, 1981: East of the Theater." *Hesp* 51:115–63.

Williams, Hector
1981       *The Lamps.* Kenchreai V.
Williamson, Lamar, Jr.
1968       "Led in Triumph. Paul's Use of *Thriambeuō.*" *Int* 22:317–32.
Winston, David
1979       *The Wisdom of Solomon.* AB 43.
Wiseman, James R.
1969a      "Ancient Corinth: The Gymnasium Area." *Arch* 22:216–25.
1969b      "Excavations in Corinth, The Gymnasium Area, 1967–1968." *Hesp*
           38:64–106.
1978       *The Land of the Ancient Corinthians.* Studies in Mediterranean Ar-
           chaeology, 50. Göteborg: Åströms.
1979       "Corinth and Rome I: 228 B.C.–A.D. 267." Pages 438–548 in *ANRW*
           II, 7/1.
Witt, Reginald E.
1971       *Isis in the Graeco-Roman World.* AGRL.
Wolter, Michael
1978       *Rechtfertigung und zukünftiges Heil. Untersuchungen zu Röm 5, 1–11.*
           BZNW 43.
Wright, Kathleen S.
1980       "A Tiberian Pottery Deposit from Corinth." *Hesp* 49:135–77.
Zmijewski, Josef
1977       "Kontextbezug und Deutung von 2 Kor 12, 7a." *BZ* 21:265–72.
1978       *Der Stil der paulinischen "Narrenrede." Analyse der Sprachgestaltung
           in 2 Kor 11, 1–12, 10 als Beitrag zur Methodik von Stiluntersuchungen
           neutestamentlicher Texte.* BBB 52.
Zuntz, Günther
1953       *The Text of the Epistles. A Disquisition upon the Corpus Paulinum.*
           London: Oxford Univ. Press.

# TRANSLATION
Notes and Commentary

## CHAPTERS 1-9 (LETTER D)

A letter sent from Macedonia, most likely Philippi, and perhaps in the fall of 55 c.e. Paul has received news about his Corinthian congregation from Titus, just returned from there, and now Titus is being sent back, accompanied by two other men and carrying this letter. It is the fourth known to have been sent to the Corinthians by Paul up to this time; thus "Letter D" in the whole body of Corinthian correspondence.

# I. LETTER OPENING, 1:1-11

# A. ADDRESS, 1:1-2

**1** ¹Paul, an apostle of Christ Jesus by the will of God, and brother Timothy; to the church of God which is in Corinth, including all the saints throughout Achaia. ²Grace to you and peace from God our Father and the Lord Jesus Christ.

### NOTES

1:1. The wording of v. 1a is reproduced exactly in Col 1:1. Apart from this salutation, Paul's name appears only once more in 2 Cor (10:1).

*an apostle of Christ Jesus.* A briefer form of the phrase "called to be an apostle . . ." in 1 Cor 1:1. The stereotyped nature of this shorter form is shown by its reappearance in Eph 1:1; Col 1:1; 1 Tim 1:1; 2 Tim 1:1. The probable original order in 1 Cor 1:1 is "apostle of Jesus Christ" (cf. Tit 1:1; 1 Pet 1:1; 2 Pet 1:1), but the order "Christ Jesus" would, at least in a brief and formalized salutation, carry no different meaning. See also "apostles of Christ" in 11:13; 1 Thess 2:6. The only Pauline salutations in which the designation "apostle" is lacking are 1 Thess 1:1; Phil 1:1; Phlm 1. The exact application of the term "apostle" in the earliest church and its background as a designation for specially commissioned persons within the church have often been investigated, but with varying results. In addition to the present letter (see COMMENT), the most important passages for assessing Paul's own conception of apostleship are Rom 1:1-6; 1 Cor 9; 15:7-11; Gal 1:1-2:10. Studies on the subject include those by Rengstorf (*TDNT* I:398-447); Klein (1961); Schmithals (1969); Roloff (1965); Güttgemanns (1966:53-198); Kertelge (1970); Hahn (1974); Schütz (1975); Barrett (1978) and, with specific attention to 2 Cor 10-13, Käsemann (1942).

*by the will of God.* Another phrase (also used in 1 Cor 1:1) which becomes part of the set formula exhibited in Eph 1:1; Col 1:1; 2 Tim 1:1.

*brother Timothy.* Timothy (on whom see COMMENT) is also named as a co-sender of a Pauline letter in Phil 1:1; 1 Thess 1:1; Phlm 1; cf. Col 1:1; 2 Thess 1:1. The only other persons ever so designated are Sosthenes (1 Cor 1:1) and Silvanus (1 Thess 1:1; cf. 2 Thess 1:1). "Brother" is a frequent Pauline designation for fellow Christians (see especially 1 Cor 5:11; 6:5–6; 7:12–15; 8:11, 13; Rom 14:10, 13, 15, 21; 1 Thess 4:6— and many instances of the plural). That it connotes a special relationship of respect, support, and care is illustrated by Paul's appeal to Philemon that Onesimus be regarded "no longer as a slave, but as more than a slave, a beloved brother . . ." (Phlm 16). Philemon himself is addressed as "brother" (vv. 7, 20). In 2 Cor 8:18, 22, Paul mentions two specific brothers. One or the other of these is presumably the brother referred to in 12:18. Elsewhere Sosthenes (2 Cor 1:1), Apollos (1 Cor 16:2), Titus (2 Cor 2:13), and Epaphroditus (Phil 2:25) are referred to as "brother," and "sister" is used of Phoebe (Rom 16:1) and Apphia (Phlm 2). Timothy is called "brother" again in the salutation of Phlm and in 1 Thess 3:2. In some instances Paul is clearly using the term with reference to the relationship the one so described bears to himself ("my brother Titus," 2 Cor 2:13; "Epaphroditus my brother," Phil 2:25) or to himself and others ("Timothy our brother," 1 Thess 3:2) as a co-worker (". . . and co-worker and fellow soldier," Phil 2:25). This is probably the primary reference, also, when the term is used in the salutations and elsewhere (1 Cor 16:12; 2 Cor 8:18 [cf. v. 22]; 12:18; Rom 16:23), although a reference to the brotherly relationship the one so designated bears to a wider circle of Christians cannot be excluded. See Ellis 1971:445–51. Rather than the literal translation, "Timothy the brother," or the paraphrase, "Timothy our brother" *(RSV),* it is perhaps best to render the phrase here as "brother Timothy" (Mof.).

*to the church of God which is in Corinth.* Exactly the same wording had been used in 1 Cor 1:2; cf. the salutation of 1 Clem. Peterson (1950) argues that the references to "the church of God" in these salutations had been modeled after Jewish letters directed to the Diaspora, and that the Christian letters were conceived as messages to believers in the "Gentile Diaspora." It remains to be explained, however, why only the three Corinthian letters (i.e., 1, 2 Cor and 1 Clem) actually exhibit the form in question. The salutations in Gal 1:2; 1 Thess 1:1; 2 Thess 1:1; Phlm 2 are substantially different, and the word "church" does not appear at all in the other Pauline or deutero-Pauline salutations. See COMMENT. Elsewhere in 2 Cor only the plural form *ekklēsiai* ("churches") is used (8:1, 18, 19, 23, 24; 11:8, 28; 12:13).

*including all the saints.* Literally "with all the saints." In 1 Cor 1:2 the members of the Corinthian church are themselves described as "saints," but here the term is used with reference to Christians elsewhere in the environs. The Christians in Corinth proper are also numbered among the "saints," just as it would not be precluded that Christians living outside of Corinth may belong to some local congregation (as Paul customarily uses the term *ekklēsia*). As used in Paul's salutations (in addition to 1, 2 Cor, see Rom 1:7; Phil 1:1; cf. Eph 1:1; Col 1:2), the word "saints" *(hagioi)* describes those who, by their commitment to Christ, are set apart for the service of God. The reference is to all the members of a congregation, not to some special group within it; all who have been baptized into Christ have been "made holy" (i.e., been sanctified, become saints) in that they have been summoned from the lord of this age to the God of Jesus Christ; see 1 Cor 6:11.

*throughout Achaia.* Literally "who are in the whole of Achaia." A formal parallel occurs in 1 Thess 4:10, "all the brothers throughout Macedonia." See also 2 Cor 11:10, "the districts of Achaia." The Roman province of Achaia included, in Paul's day, the whole Peloponnesus, plus the regions of Epirus, Akarnania, Aetolia, and perhaps also Thessaly. Corinth was its capital, the residence of the proconsul appointed by the Roman senate (see INTRODUCTION, pp. 9–10). According to Wiseman (1979:446), throughout most of antiquity residents of the other towns of the Corinthia (see Figure 1) regarded themselves as citizens of Corinth. Other Achaian cities mentioned by Paul are Cenchreae, Corinth's port on the Saronic Gulf (Rom 16:1; cf. Acts 18:18), and Athens, about fifty miles due east (1 Thess 3:1; cf. Acts 17:15–16, 22; 18:1). Most of Paul's references to this province mention it along with its northern neighbor, Macedonia (Rom 15:26; 1 Thess 1:7, 8; cf. 2 Cor 9:2; Acts 19:21; 20:2, where "Greece" is simply an alternate designation for Achaia—see Pausanias VII.xvi.10). This reflects not only their geographical proximity but perhaps also their combination—along with Moesia—into a single imperial province from 15 to 44 C.E. (see INTRODUCTION, p. 9).

2. *Grace to you and peace . . .* The whole blessing is identical with that in every other genuine Pauline letter except the one in 1 Thess 1:1*b*, which has only the invocation of grace and peace: see Rom 1:7*b;* 1 Cor 1:3; Gal 1:3; Phil 1:2; Phlm 3 (also Eph 1:2; but Col 1:2 and 2 Thess 1:2 are slightly different). Lohmeyer (1927) once argued that this blessing had its original *Sitz im Leben* in the liturgy, and that Paul includes it in his salutations out of consideration for the fact that the letters will be read aloud to congregations gathered for worship. He held that one mark of its liturgical background and style is the absence of articles before *Theou* and *Kyriou.* A serious difficulty with this view is that the initial blessings in later letters (1, 2 Tim; James; 1, 2 Pet; 2 John; Jude) show considerable variation from Paul's formula and from one another. Moreover, "peace" never has an article when used as a blessing in other contexts, and it is likely that this has influenced the omission of other articles in the epistolary blessing. See Friedrich 1956:345.

## COMMENT

If 2 Cor is actually a composite of two originally separate letters (see INTRODUCTION, pp. 30–41), it is impossible to say with certainty to which of those the present salutation was first attached. One may presume, however, that this is the salutation of the first of the two letters combined here (1:3–chap. 9), and that the salutation of the second was omitted when that letter (chaps. 10–13) was appended to the first. As it stands, this salutation is fairly formal, using several phrases and concepts which were, or were to become, familiar epistolary clichés (see NOTES). The theory has been advanced that this salutation was composed only after the middle of the second century by an editor who modeled it after the original Pauline salutation of 1 Cor (J. Knox 1942: 62–70). No firm evidence can be adduced for this, however. Moreover, the presuppositions on which the theory is based—namely, that the Pauline letters were arranged initially according to length, and that no formal distinction was made between two separate Corinthian letters in the original Pauline Corpus —are rendered especially questionable if the Muratorian Canon (to which appeal had been made) is to be dated to the fourth century rather than to the second (see Sundberg 1973, and in *IDBSup:* 609–10). Nor is it clear why, if 1 Cor 1:1–3 was an editor's model for 2 Cor 1:1–2, the name of Timothy was substituted for that of Sosthenes. Knox's explanation—that an "unfamiliar" name was replaced with "the usual" name of Timothy—is not convincing. An editor seeking to replace the name of Sosthenes would have more likely chosen the *two* names, "Timothy and Silvanus," because both of these are mentioned early in 2 Cor (1:19), and there was already a Pauline precedent for listing them both as co-senders of a letter (1 Thess; cf. 2 Thess). In summary, then, it seems likely that the salutation which opens our canonical 2 Cor stood originally with the first of the letters of which 2 Cor is a composite. 2 Cor 1:1–2 is perfectly intelligible as an original Pauline salutation and shows no marks of editorial alteration. Apparently Sosthenes, mentioned in the salutation of 1 Cor but not in this one, is no longer with Paul; perhaps he has stayed behind in Ephesus.

Although the term "apostle" appears in 2 Cor only five times apart from this salutation (8:23; 11:5, 13; 12:11, 12), the subject of Paul's apostolic standing and authority is present throughout. This includes, in a special way, the discussion which extends from 2:14 through 5:19, where, however, the word "apostle" never once appears. No hint of a special problem in Corinth concerning Paul's apostleship is present in this salutation, although the idea, repeated from 1 Cor 1:1, that Paul was (called to be) an apostle by the will of God gives a certain emphasis to the title. Paul uses the noun *thelēma* ("will") almost exclusively with reference to God's will (e.g., Rom 2:18; 12:2; 2 Cor 8:5; Gal 1:4; 1 Thess 4:3; 5:18), and he believes not only that he is an apostle by God's will but that his ministry is directed by God's will in certain specific ways (see Rom 1:10; 15:32). Ordinarily the verb *(thelein)* is used by Paul with reference to human willing or desiring, but sometimes it, too, is applied to the divine will (Rom 9:18, 22; 1 Cor 12:18; 15:38; Phil 2:13). In 1 Cor 4:19 the divine direction of his apostolic activity is again apparent where Paul writes of his coming soon to Corinth "if the Lord wills." The theme of obedience to the will of God of course pervades the religious traditions of Israel and of the synagogue to which Paul was heir (see Schrenk, *TDNT* III:44–62). But when he describes himself as "an apostle by the will of God," he is not emphasizing his own obedience or response to a divine call. He is, instead, emphasizing the call itself, God's sovereign initiative in establishing him in an office to which he was destined even before his birth (Gal 1:15) and for which, apart from the grace of God, he is in no way qualified (1 Cor 15:9–10). The apostolic authority about which he reminds his readers is based not in any personal merit of his own but solely in the grace of God which had been given to him (Rom 12:3). The question of what this means for Paul's relationship to the Corinthians in particular is present throughout 2 Cor.

Paul customarily associates another person (or persons) with himself in the salutations of his letters. Only Rom offers an exception to this (and, among the deutero-Paulines, Eph and the Pastorals). In the present instance Timothy is named, a co-worker known in Corinth by reason of his having assisted Paul in founding the church there (2 Cor 1:19; cf. Acts 18:5). According to Acts, Timothy was from the district of Lycaonia in Asia Minor, the son of a Jewish mother and a Gentile father (16:1). It is said that Paul enlisted him as an associate there and had him circumcised (16:2) before taking him along into Macedonia. We find Timothy with Silas (that is, Silvanus; see NOTES on 1:19) and Paul in Athens (17:13–15) as well as in Corinth (18:5), with Erastus in Macedonia (19:22), and then again with Paul en route from "Greece" (presumably Corinth) to Macedonia (20:4), from where he precedes Paul to Troas (20:5). Although Paul commends him in 1 Cor 4:17 as "my faithful and beloved child in the Lord," one should not interpret this to mean that Paul had been responsible for Timothy's conversion, as some do (Plummer, 2; Hughes, 3). Rather, the reference seems to be to the filial loyalty Timothy exhibited as one of Paul's most trusted associates; cf. Phil 2:22, "But you know [Timothy's] worth, that he has served with me in the gospel as a son with a father." According to Acts 16:1, both Timothy (a "disciple") and his mother (a "believer") were already Christians when Paul first met them. The close relationship which existed between Paul and Timothy, as well as the good reputation the latter continued to enjoy in the later church, is attested by the existence of the two "letters," supposedly from Paul to Timothy, which probably date from the second century.

For what purpose has Paul joined Timothy's name to his own in the salutation of 2 Cor? Nowhere in 2 Cor is there any indication that Timothy is to be the bearer of a letter, or that he is the one to whom a letter is being dictated. If he were to be the letter-carrier, it is doubtful whether he would be mentioned at all in the salutation (see Stirewalt 1969). And when the name of a secretary appears at all, it appears at the close of a letter, not in its salutation (e.g., Rom 16:22; 1 Pet 5:12. Lietzmann, 4, presumes that persons named in salutations could have functioned as scribes, but such a presumption is not warranted).

It is equally implausible to think that Timothy (or others) played any substantial role in the actual composition of Paul's letters. It is true that Paul often uses the first person plural in writing to his churches, and that this in fact predominates throughout 1 Thess, where Silvanus and Timothy are named in the salutation. However, in the other letters where Paul names associates who are with him, either he proceeds at once to use the first person singular (1 Cor 1:4ff.; Gal 1:6ff.; Phil 1:3ff.; Phlm 4ff.) or else, as here in 2 Cor, the plural is frequently interrupted by the first person singular (e.g., 1:13b, 15–17, 23). Even in 1 Thess, Timothy obviously cannot be included in the first person plural of 3:3–6. Thus, while the first person plural does in some instances seem deliberately to include one or more associates who are with Paul as he writes, one is conscious all the while that Paul is the writer. It is best, therefore, to describe those whom Paul names along with himself in his salutations as co-*senders,* not as co-*writers.* (The hypothesis that Timothy composed the first nine chapters and Paul chaps. 10–13 cannot be taken seriously; see INTRODUCTION, p. 34.)

In some or perhaps even most instances those named as co-senders were personally known to the churches being addressed, as Timothy was to the congregations in Philippi and Thessalonica (Phil 2:22; 1 Thess 3:2ff.) as well as to the church in Corinth. The identification of Timothy as a co-sender of a letter to these churches would serve to assure the recipients of Timothy's continuing concern for them, and that the apostle's letter was written in full cognizance of what Timothy could have reported about them (see 1 Thess 3:6; Phil 2:19). It is also possible that Paul's co-senders are meant to fulfill the legal requirement of Deut 19:15 that all testimony be sustained by at least two witnesses (Windisch, 33 n. 1; cf. Allo, 2; Schlatter, 462). Stirewalt (1972) assembles numerous examples of this practice from Jewish official letters and suggests that Paul also seems concerned for multiple testimony in 2 Cor 8:16, 22; 12:16b–18a; 13:1. If Stirewalt is correct, the co-senders would attest "both to the fact that a letter had been written and to the content of the message. Their witness served as a copy for the file" (ibid.:7–8).

Timothy's personal contacts with the Corinthian church are not easy to reconstruct, let alone assess. All that is really certain is that Timothy and Silvanus had been associated with Paul's initial missionary efforts among the Corinthians. Acts 18:5 reports that Silas (Silvanus) and Timothy came from Macedonia to Corinth, where they joined Paul in "preaching . . . to the Jews." Paul's own comment in 2 Cor 1:19 certifies at least the basic information that the three of them worked together during the apostle's initial visit to the city. From the references to Timothy in 1 Cor 4:17; 16:10, it is also clear that Paul had later sent him back to Corinth for the purpose of helping to straighten out the apparently deteriorating situation there. Whether he ever actually reached Corinth, however, has been seriously questioned by some scholars. There is no mention of any visit in 2 Cor. Moreover, it is possible to interpret 1 Cor 16:10 in such a way as to find Paul himself expressing uncertainty about the fulfillment of Timothy's mission to Corinth. Paul does not actually write *"When* [*hotan*] Timothy comes" *(RSV,* Mof.), but *"If* [*ean*] Timothy comes" *(NEB, TEV, JB).* If, as seems plausible, one identifies the mission of Timothy and Erastus mentioned in Acts 19:22 with the sending of Timothy reported in 1 Cor 4:17, then the reason for Paul's uncertainty could be conjectured: since in Acts only Macedonia is given as the destination of Timothy and Erastus, Paul evidently left it to Timothy's own discretion whether he should eventually go on to Corinth (so Barrett 1968:16, 390). This conjecture, however, overlooks the fact that *ean* ("if") can approach the meaning of *hotan* ("when") in certain instances *(GNTG* III:314–15; Conzelmann 1975:297), especially when expected but as yet unfulfilled travel plans are involved (see, e.g., Rom 15:24). Therefore, the use of *ean* in 1 Cor 16:10 does not necessarily reflect any serious doubt on Paul's part about Timothy's eventual arrival in Corinth. Moreover, the wording of 1 Cor 4:17 hardly leaves room for the possibility that Timothy could opt not to go; he has definitely been "sent." (The *epempsa*, "I sent," cannot, in view of the wording in 1 Cor 16:10, be interpreted as an epistolary aorist: "I am sending Timothy to you [with this letter]. . . ." Correctly Conzelmann 1975:92 n.19; Barrett 1968:116.) Had Timothy's mission to Corinth never been fulfilled, or had Timothy not been received in some reasonably hospitable way, one would expect to hear something further about the matter in 2 Cor. But there is no hint in 2 Cor that Paul needed to explain anything about Timothy's non-arrival or to plead any sort of a case for him. Paul's reference to Silvanus and Timothy in 1:19 actually presumes that the Corinthians will have a favorable memory of their preaching as well as of his own.

Timothy's identification as co-sender certainly does not indicate that he needs "rehabilitation" in the eyes of the Corinthians, as some have claimed (Strachan, 40–41; Filson, 277; cf. Kee, "Timothy," *IDB* R–Z:650–51). Simply identifying him as a co-sender would hardly suffice for this purpose. It indicates, on the contrary, that Timothy still has some sort of standing with the Corinthian Christians and that Timothy's association with Paul in sending this letter will help to certify what is being said. The silence in 2 Cor concerning Timothy's visit is well enough explained on the supposition that considerable time has elapsed since then, and that a different situation is now in view (Windisch, 33).

Timothy's designation here as "brother" rather than "apostle" accords with Paul's customary use of both terms. On the one hand, he specifically applies the term "apostle" to relatively few persons: the Twelve and himself (1 Cor 15:7–11), plus only Apollos (1 Cor 4:9 [cf. 3:5, 22]; 4:6), Andronicus, and Junia (Rom 16:7, *NEB* mg.). Epaphroditus is called an *apostolos* in Phil 2:25, but there the correct tr. is surely "messenger" *(RSV, TEV)* or "representative" *(JB),* for he was sent to Paul as an *apostolos* of the Philippians. It is uncertain whether Paul is thinking of Barnabas as an apostle when he refers to him in 1 Cor 9:6 (cf. v. 5). It is still less certain whether Silvanus and Timothy are meant to be included in the "we" of 1 Thess 2:7 ("though we might have made demands as apostles of Christ," *RSV* [v. 6]) just because they had been identified as co-senders of the letter (1:1). For the question in general, see Schmithals 1969:62–67; on 1 Thess 2:7 in particular, see Best 1972:100. On the other hand, the terms "brother," "brothers," and "sister" are often applied by Paul to specific individuals associated with him in the promulgation of the gospel (see NOTES). Therefore, when Timothy is called "brother," Paul's intent is not to emphasize Timothy's subordinate position but rather his status as co-worker. Cf. 1 Thess 1:1, where the names of Paul, Silvanus, and Timothy stand together with no distinguishing descriptions whatever; and Phil 1:1, where the phrase "slaves of Christ Jesus" describes both Paul and Timothy.

Since he addresses himself both to the "church of God in Corinth" and to "all the saints throughout Achaia," Paul evidently presumes that the contents of his letter will also be made known among Christians living in a wider area, at least in the immediately adjacent "districts of Achaia" (11:10) where, one may therefore presume, Paul had also preached. This could well include Corinth's eastern port, Cenchreae, where a Christian congregation also existed at an early date (see Rom 16:1, where, in commending "Sister Phoebe," Paul describes her as "a minister [*diakonos*] of the church in Cenchreae"). Corinth's western port, Lechaeum, had few residences (Strabo VIII.vi.22), but there may have been Christians in some of the other settlements which, according to Strabo, were close to Corinth: Cleonae, Crommyon, Tenea, and Schoenus (VIII.vi.19, 22). There is no knowledge of any organized congregations in Achaia at this date, however, except for those in Corinth and Cenchreae. It is hardly possible that any letter to Corinth would have been circulated literally throughout the *whole* province, because in Paul's day that included a vast geographical area, virtually the whole of Greece apart from Macedonia (see NOTES). It is also unlikely that Paul would have Athens in mind here (correctly Windisch, 34–38; Barrett, 56, as contrasted with the presumptions of Plummer, 4; Strachan, 43; Filson, 277), both because of the distance involved and because Athens was a completely distinct urban center (see, e.g., Baus 1965:379: "Athens . . . preserved even into the fourth century the character of a pagan city and a centre of secular learning").

The form of the address implies that some kind of regularized contact was maintained between the Corinthian congregation and Christians in the outlying communities, and that Paul regarded his letter as having some, if only secondary, meaning for them as well. In the relationship between the Corinthian church and neighboring groups of Christians presumed here, one catches a glimpse of the role the city congregation came increasingly to play as the leading church of Greece (see INTRODUCTION, pp. 55–57). It is not correct, however, to conclude that this salutation stands over a circular letter. In a circular letter the form of address would be substantially different, as one may judge from the actual case of Galatians ("To the churches of Galatia," 1:2). In 2 Cor, however, the Christian church in just one specific city is addressed, and the reference to other Christians in the vicinity is strictly secondary (correctly, Plummer, 4; contrast Windisch, 35). Throughout 2 Cor, Paul's concern is essentially for the church in Corinth and what is happening and ought to happen there.

The blessing which is pronounced upon the addressees as soon as they are named (v. 2) carries within itself an implicit claim for the writer's authority. He acts here already as an apostle of Christ, one who may impart "grace and peace" to the congregation. In this way the apostolic salutations certainly are more significant than the perfunctory "greeting" which characterizes the usual

Hellenistic letter (and, in the NT, Jas 1:1). Many commentators continue to hold the view that Paul deliberately replaced the usual Greek term *chairein* ("greeting") with the profounder and specifically Christian word *charis* ("grace") and then combined it with the Jewish blessing of "peace" *(eirēnē);* see, e.g., Hughes, 6 n.17; Orr and Walther 1976:143. It has become increasingly clear, however, that the two concepts of grace (or "mercy") and peace were already combined in ancient oriental (including Jewish) letters; see Lohmeyer (1927), on this point confirmed by Friedrich (1956:346). In addition to the one epistolary parallel originally provided by Lohmeyer (2 Apoc Bar 78:2, the opening of Baruch's letter to the tribes in exile, "Mercy and Peace"), Berger (1974) has assembled and assessed numerous passages where the same blessing form is used in non-epistolary settings (especially 191–207). Gal 6:16, "Peace and mercy be upon all who walk by this rule" *(RSV),* shows that Paul himself knew and applied it apart from epistolary salutations. Berger's findings suggest that the Pauline form of the blessing is not primarily influenced by ancient oriental epistolary conventions but more directly by the prophetic-apocalyptic-apostolic mode of oral discourse (ibid., especially 207–19). This possibility only serves to accentuate the special function and character of apostolic letters, of which Paul's are the earliest, and perhaps prototypical. Although, inevitably, they often show the influence of conventional style, vocabulary, and even ideas familiar to Paul, all of these are significantly qualified by the distinctive *apostolic* relationship which Paul knows to obtain, or believes should obtain, between himself and his Christian congregations.

# B. BLESSING, 1:3-11

1 ³Blessed is God, the Father of our Lord Jesus Christ, the Father of mercies and the God of all comfort, ⁴who comforts us in every one of our afflictions so that we are able, through the comfort with which we ourselves have been comforted by God, to comfort those who are in any kind of affliction. ⁵For just as the sufferings of Christ are overflowing to us, so also, through Christ, our comfort is overflowing. ⁶When we are being afflicted, it is for your comfort and salvation; when we are being comforted, it is for your comfort which expresses itself in your endurance of the same sufferings that we, too, are suffering. ⁷And our hope for you is certain because we know that you are partners in the comfort just as you are in the suffering.

⁸For we do not want you to be ignorant, brothers and sisters, concerning our affliction which took place in Asia, how we were so exceedingly burdened, beyond our strength, that we despaired even of survival. ⁹Indeed, it seemed to us that we had received the death sentence so that we would not rely upon ourselves but upon God who raises the dead. ¹⁰He who has rescued us from such severe threats of death, the one, indeed, on whom we firmly set our hope, will rescue us. And he will continue to rescue ¹¹as you also help with prayer for us, so that from many people thanks may be rendered on our behalf, through many, for the gracious benefit which shall have been bestowed on us.

## NOTES

1:3. *Blessed is God.* Most English trs. supply an optative form of the Greek verb, "Blessed *be* God," but the simple indicative is preferable (cf. especially 11:31, *ho ōn eulogētos,* "he who is blessed"); see Delling 1963:51 n. 2; O'Brien 1977:240; Kümmel 1975:196; Barrett, 58. Cf. the same formulation at the opening of Eph (1:3) and 1 Pet (1:3) and in Zechariah's prayer, Luke 1:68. See also the Mishnah tractate *Berakoth,* numerous passages in the texts from Qumran (e.g., 1QM xviii.6–7; 1QH xi.29; 1QS xi.15), and the many further examples in Delling 1963:2–11 and Deichgräber 1967: 40–43. The Greek form used here is often present in the LXX (e.g., Gen 14:20; 3 Kgdms [1 Kgs] 5:21; Pss 65:20; 67:36; 1 Esdr 4:40; 2 Mac 1:17). On the replacement of the *berakah* by the *hodayoth* formula in earliest Christianity, see J. M. Robinson 1964: 202–13. In Greek the definite article stands before *God.* This is not represented in the present English tr. because this initial phrase is taken to be essentially independent of the next phrase; see following note.

*the Father of our Lord Jesus Christ.* Interpreters are divided over the connection between this phrase and the opening blessing. Virtually all English trs. take the genitive "of our Lord Jesus Christ" with both "God" and "Father," as indeed the absence of a second definite article before "Father" might suggest. Thus, e.g., *RSV:* "Blessed be the God and Father of our Lord Jesus Christ. . . ." Moreover, in Eph 1:17 there is a clear reference to "the God of our Lord Jesus Christ." But in Paul's own letters there is no such unambiguous reference to "the God" of Jesus (Kümmel, 196), and it is probably better to take the initial blessing of God in our verse as an independent benediction (so, e.g., Windisch, 38, and Barrett, 58–59). In this case the intervening *kai* may be translated as in *KJV,* "*even* the Father of our Lord Jesus Christ," or else —perhaps preferably—omitted altogether. Either way, the *kai* introduces a Christian gloss on the synagogue formula (evident in 11:31; Rom 15:6 as well as in Eph 1:3; 1 Pet 1:3); the God who is blessed is none other than the one whom believers know as the Father of the Lord Jesus Christ.

*the Father of mercies.* Along with his loving-kindness, God's mercy is often stressed in the Hebrew Bible and by the rabbis. The plural *oiktirmoi* is regularly used in the LXX, as it is here, and in Rom 12:1; Phil 2:1; Heb 10:28. The singular appears in the NT only in Col 3:12. Here, again, the language of Jewish worship is doubtless present; the description of God as "Father of mercy" is also found in the *Seder Elijahu Rabbah,* and the related appellation "Lord of mercy" in *Pesiq. Rab Kah.* 65B; see Marmorstein 1927:56, 80–81. Cf. also 1QH x.14; xi.29; discussed by Delling 1963:11–12, and Braun 1966 I:197–98.

*and the God of all comfort.* This is another traditionally Jewish description of God (see "Lord of Consolations" in *Ketub.* 8B, 27, cited by Str-B III:494 and Marmorstein 1927:80), and like the preceding one it employs a genitive phrase. The adjective "all" represents a liturgical heightening (cf. 1 Pet 5:10, "the God of all grace . . ." and Rom 15:13, "the God of hope fill you with all joy and peace . . ."); see Bultmann, 26. In the benediction of Rom 15:5, where he is also indebted to the liturgical tradition, Paul once more writes of "the God of . . . comfort," and there comfort is linked with the concept of "steadfastness" *(ho . . . Theos tēs hypomonēs kai tēs paraklēseōs . . .).*

*comfort.* Greek *paraklēsis,* which with the verb *parakalein* (and its compound, *synparakalein*) is used more frequently by Paul than by any other NT writer. Moreover, of the combined fifty-nine instances of noun and verb in the seven Pauline letters, twenty-nine are in 2 Cor (the words are missing only in Gal). Within 2 Cor the words occur twenty-five times in chaps. 1–9 but only four times in chaps. 10–13. The word-group is capable of bearing a fairly broad range of meanings, principally (1) to comfort, (2) to beseech, and (3) to exhort. See Schmitz and Stählin in *TDNT* V:773–79; Schlier 1964; Bjerkelund 1967. For the special connotation of the verb in 2:7, see NOTES and COMMENT there. It should be noted that precise distinctions in the use of these terms are usually difficult to preserve; meanings often tend to overlap or to expand or contract in a given context (e.g., in 5:20, on which see the NOTES and COMMENT); cf. Grabner-Haider 1968:7–8. "Comfort" as a tr. for *paraklēsis* must not be confused with the more subjective notions of sympathy or pity. The meaning is, rather, to "comfort" in the strict sense, i.e., in the sense of the Latin *confortare,* "to strengthen much," to encourage; cf. the remarks of Proudfoot on the OT conception (1963:142–43).

4. *who comforts us.* This further description of God involves the use of an attributive participle *(ho parakalōn hēmas),* another liturgical convention—e.g., in the Psalms (LXX: 71:18; 134:21; 143:1). This liturgical usage is clear in the benedictions of 1 Pet 5:10; Heb 13:20–21; elsewhere in 2 Cor see 1:9; 4:6; 5:5. Note especially 7:6, "God, who comforts the downcast, comforted us." There is both a formal and a material parallel to the present passage in the Jewish prayer for mourners *(Ketub.* 8B, 27): "Our brethren, may the Lord of Consolations comfort you. Blessed be He, who comforts the mourners" (tr. Marmorstein 1927:80). In view of the liturgical cast of the language, the word *us* here, and *our* in the following phrase, should probably be understood inclusively, i.e., as embracing the recipients of the letter as well as the senders (against Cranfield 1982:287). On the problem, see Kijne 1966:176.

*in every one of our afflictions.* "Affliction" *(thlipsis;* Paul ordinarily uses the singular form, as here, but in 6:4 and in Rom 5:3; 1 Thess 3:3 he uses the plural), like "comfort," is more often mentioned by Paul than by any other NT writer, and more often in 2 Cor than in any other letter (noun and verb, twenty-four times in the seven letters, twelve times in 2 Cor). Not surprisingly, all of the occurrences in 2 Cor are in chaps. 1–9, where there is a corresponding emphasis upon comfort. *Thlipsis* can refer either to external, objective suffering (e.g., Rom 8:35; 1 Cor 7:28) or to mental anguish (e.g., Phil 1:17). In 2 Cor 4:8; 7:5 it is clear that both are involved. When, as in the first half of the present verse, the adjective *pas* is followed by a noun with the article *(epi pasē tē thlipsei hēmōn),* the reference is not indefinite and open-ended but is to something actually encountered. Here (and also in 7:4; 1 Thess 3:7, where the same usage is present) Paul has in mind specific instances of affliction in which God's comforting presence has been discerned. For the grammar see BDF § 275(3); *GNTG* III:200; and below.

*so that we are able.* This purpose-clause *(eis* with the articular infinitive) completes the blessing proper and at the same time begins to anticipate the theme which is developed in vv. 5–7. For this reason, while *we* and the following "we ourselves" in this part of the verse may still be regarded as inclusive of the recipients (see above), a certain contraction begins to take place until, clearly in vv. 6–7, the recipients are a distinct group. See COMMENT on vv. 5–7.

*those who are in any kind of affliction.* This tr. seeks to convey the meaning of the phrase *tous en pasē thlipsei,* where *pas* is followed by a noun without the article. The reference is thus to whatever kind of distress one may encounter, now or later. See preceding note.

5. *the sufferings of Christ.* Only here and at Phil 3:10 does Paul himself refer specifically to the sufferings *(pathēmata,* in both cases plural) of Christ, but the same or similar phrases are found also in 1 Pet 1:11; 4:13; 5:1; Col 1:24, "the tribulations of Christ," *tōn thlipseōn tou Christou;* cf. Heb 2:9, 10. The noun *pathēma* is nowhere present in the Gospels, although the verb *paschein* is employed throughout the Synoptics and Acts; see NOTES on v. 6 below.

6. *When we are being afflicted . . . ; when we are being comforted.* In this and the following verse "we" and "you" are distinguished, so the "we" is no longer inclusive; see NOTES on v. 4. Whether Paul is consciously including Timothy and/or other co-laborers cannot be determined. The reality of both affliction and comfort is presumed, and the *eite . . . eite* in this case is virtually equivalent to *kai . . . kai;* see BDF

§ 454 (3). The translation *"When . . . when"* seeks to avoid the more usual rendering "if . . . if" (which may be misunderstood as a reference to something hypothetical), and it also helps to bring out the force of the present-tense verbs *thlibometha* and *parakaloumetha.* Several textual witnesses for vv. 6–7 omit certain words, including parts of the second *eite*-clause, but this is doubtless the result of homeoteleuton—the eye of a copyist accidentally skipping from the *paraklēseōs* of v. 6*a* to the *paraklēseōs* of v. 6*b*. Other variants in the two verses result from attempts to correct the omission. See the discussion in Metzger 1971:573–74.

*for your comfort . . . ; for your comfort.* It is possible that the word *comfort* carries special and distinguishable connotations in the two instances (see COMMENT), but in order to exhibit the fact that in both cases Paul's word continues to be *paraklēsis,* no distinction has been made in the English tr. *For* translates *hyper,* which here means almost "for the sake of" (Moule 1953:65).

*salvation.* The noun is also used in 6:2 (twice) and 7:10 (never in 1 Cor), but the verb appears only in 2:15 (despite numerous instances in 1 Cor). Here, as in 7:10 (where the opposite is "death"), the noun seems to refer in a general way to that for which believers ultimately hope; see COMMENT.

*which expresses itself in your endurance.* The *RSV* tr. of *tēs energoumenēs* ("which you experience") does not accord well enough with the context, in which *comfort* is not so much a feeling experienced as a gift received; see COMMENT. The present tr. interprets the verb to be middle (BAG s.v. 1b), but a passive meaning might also fit here (e.g., "which is given expression"). *Your* is not represented in the Greek, but is necessary in English. *Endurance* translates *hypomonē,* which in 6:4 and then, schematically, in Rom 5:3 is associated with afflictions (*thlipseis,* in both instances plural); see also 1 Thess 1:3ff. The close connection in Paul's letters of the ideas of *hope* and *endurance* (Rom 5:3–5; 8:25; 15:4; 1 Thess 1:3) displays the essentially eschatological significance of the latter term. As Paul uses it, "endurance" refers not just to the human virtue of fortitude by which one bears up under adversity; it designates, rather, the obedient faith of those who can rejoice, precisely in the midst of adversity, in the confidence that God's love will not only perdure but will indeed prevail (Rom 5:1–5); see Hauck, *TDNT* IV: especially 586–87. Endurance and comfort are linked together in the benediction of Rom 15:5; see COMMENT.

*the same sufferings.* In 1 Thess 2:14 a comparison is made between the sufferings of two different groups of Christians: "and you suffered the same things . . . as they did . . ." *(ta auta epathete kai hymeis . . . kathōs kai autoi).* But here the reference is, in the first instance, to *the same sufferings* Christ suffered; see COMMENT.

*that we, too, are suffering.* Paul uses the verb "to suffer" *(paschein)* and the compounds *synpaschein* and *propaschein* only occasionally, and in different connections: 1 Cor 12:26, in a general sense of the suffering which any Christian may know; Gal 3:4, in the quite neutral sense of "experience"; 1 Thess 2:2, 14, in the sense of persecution; Rom 8:17; Phil 1:29; and here, quite explicitly in the sense of the suffering one shares with Christ. In the Synoptic traditions and Acts the verb is never used with reference to the suffering of believers; it is used principally of the suffering of Jesus himself; see COMMENT. Significantly, the only exception is Acts 9:16, where the risen Lord tells Ananias that Paul "will have to suffer for the sake of my name." The verb is never used in John.

7. On the textual problems see NOTES for v. 6.

*And our hope for you is certain.* That is, the hope of Paul (and Timothy) that the Corinthians will endure amidst affliction. That Paul is using the language of traditional Jewish piety is suggested by the parallel formulation of 4 Mac 17:4, where the mother of the seven martyrs is extolled as one who has "the hope of [her] endurance certain [*bebaios,* as here] at the hand of God" *(APOT).*

*because we know.* The grammatically errant form of the participle here, *eidotes,* must in any case be translated causally; on the grammar see Barrett, 63; Hughes, 15–16 n. 9.

*partners in the comfort . . . in the suffering.* Paul does not say, "in our [*hēmōn*] suffering and comfort," and the introduction of the possessive pronoun into many trs. (e.g., *RSV, JB, TEV*) is misleading; more is involved than the idea that all of God's people suffer together, e.g., 2 Apoc Bar 79:3, comparing the sufferings of the exiled Jews with the sufferings of those in Zion: "For what befell you we also suffer in a pre-eminent degree, for it befell us also" *(APOT).* Cf. the further Jewish materials collected in Str-B III:298, 448–49. *Partners* translates *koinōnoi,* which, with the compound *synkoinōnos,* the noun *koinōnia,* and the cognate verb *koinōnein* and its compound *synkoinōnein,* is used more often by Paul than by any other NT writer. The five terms occur in the NT a total of forty-three times, of which twenty-six instances—including 2 Cor 6:14 —are in the seven Pauline letters. For the background of the term see Hauck, *TDNT* III:797–803); the brief but useful discussion by Dodd 1946:6–8; and Seesemann 1933: 3–23. In 8:23 Paul describes Titus as his "partner and co-worker" for the Corinthians, and in Phil 4:14–15 the Philippian church as a whole is commended for its partnership with Paul in his ministry, including its hardships. Fundamental to such passages is the apostle's conception of the participation of all believers in Christ (1 Cor 1:9) or, alternately, in the Holy Spirit (2 Cor 13:13[14]; Phil 2:1), the gospel, etc. (Phil 1:5, 7; Phlm 5, 17; cf. Rom 11:17; 1 Cor 9:23). In Phil 3:10 as well as in the present passage, participation in Christ's sufferings is in view; see COMMENT on vv. 5–7.

8. *For we do not want you to be ignorant.* The phrase is an epistolary convention, well attested in ancient letters as a formula introducing information to be conveyed; see the examples of such "disclosure" formulas given by Mullins 1964:47–48 and White 1972: 12–13 (nos. 5–12) and 14 (nos. 28–31). Some (e.g., Bachmann, 35, and White 1972: 123–24) therefore regard the main body of Paul's letter to be opened with this verse, but it is better to take vv. 3–11 together and to regard v. 12 as the opening of the letter body; see COMMENT on vv. 3–11 and NOTES on vv. 12–14. Paul uses closely related formulas in Rom 1:13; 11:25; 1 Cor 10:1; 12:1; 1 Thess 4:13; cf. 1 Cor 11:3; Gal 1:11; Phil 1:12. Of all these Pauline examples, the first person plural is employed only in our passage (which accounts for the variant *thelō* in a few late mss.) and in 1 Thess 4:13, even though the apostle names co-senders in 1 Cor (Sosthenes) and Phil (Timothy), as well as in 2 Cor (Timothy) and 1 Thess (Silvanus and Timothy). Here, as well as in v. 13 ("we write you," *graphomen hymin*), Paul seems specifically conscious of Timothy's role as a co-sender of the letter.

*brothers and sisters.* Translates *adelphoi,* literally "brothers." But like the term "beloved" (with which it is linked in 1 Cor 15:58; Phil 4:1; cf. 1 Thess 1:4), *adelphoi* is used quite inclusively by Paul when he addresses a congregation; he is thinking of all those, female as well as male, who are in Christ. The same form of address occurs in 8:1 and 13:11 in 2 Cor, more frequently in the other Pauline letters (e.g., twenty times in 1 Cor).

*our affliction.* Whose? Does the *our* include Timothy (v. 1), and perhaps others as well? Since Paul offers little specific information about the nature of the affliction, this question must be left open. The first person plural continues through v. 11 and also opens the body of the letter in v. 12.

*which took place in Asia.* In Paul's day the Roman province of Asia, in western Asia Minor, extended from Bithynia on the north to Lycia on the south, as far east as Galatia, and included such islands in the Aegean as Rhodes and Patmos. The provincial capital and one of its chief cities was Ephesus, specifically named by Paul himself only in 1 Cor 15:32; 16:8 (cf. 1 Tim 1:3; 2 Tim 1:18; 4:12, and, in some mss., Eph 1:1). For the history and importance of the province, see Brandis in PW II:1538–63; Pellett in *IDB* A–D:258–59; and Jones 1971:28–94. Paul had previously written at least one letter to the Corinthians from Asia (1 Cor 15:19), from Ephesus specifically (1 Cor 16:8), but the present reference suggests that he is no longer there. It is possible that the affliction which took place in Asia was an imprisonment in Ephesus during which Paul wrote a letter to the Philippians and immediately after which he set out for Macedonia by way of Troas; see COMMENT.

*how we were so exceedingly burdened, beyond our strength.* For the sake of the English, *hoti* (literally "that") has been translated *how,* and *our* has been supplied. *So* helps to accent the intensity of Paul's language here and to prepare for the result-clause (see following note). The redundancy of the expression *(kath' hyperbolēn hyper dynamin)* underscores the severity of the affliction, as does the following clause. On Paul's fondness for superlatives, see NOTES on 3:10; 11:5.

*that we despaired.* Here the result of the affliction with which Paul was beset in Asia is introduced by a *hōste*-clause. The verb *aporein* connotes perplexity (cf. Gal 5:20), and the compound *exaporein,* used here, suggests an intensity of doubt best described as despair. The two words are contrasted by Paul himself in 4:8; see COMMENT.

*even of survival.* Literally "even [or: also] of living."

9. *Indeed.* Translates *alla,* which functions here to emphasize the reality of what is claimed.

*it seemed to us.* Or, more literally, "we in ourselves" *(autoi en heautois).* For *autos* with the reflexive pronoun, see BDF § 283 (4).

*we had received.* The perfect tense *eschēchamen* is variously interpreted. (a) It may be a true perfect, indicating a past event with present results (e.g., Allo, 10–19; Barrett, 64; Rissi 1969:9). This would be the more likely interpretation if it could be shown that Paul is thinking of the onset of some illness which continues to afflict him and threaten him with death. (b) Or it may be a "narrative perfect," used essentially like an aorist to refer to some past occurrence without any special thought of its continuing effect (so, e.g., Bultmann, 32; less certainly Windisch, 46). This is the more probable interpretation in view of 2:13, where the perfect tense of the same verb does seem to be used as an aorist (see NOTES there), and because there are indications that the reference is to a period of imprisonment (see following note and COMMENT).

*the death sentence.* The noun *apokrima (sentence)* stands nowhere else in biblical Greek, but it was used by other ancient writers as a technical term for any official decree which, coming in response to a petition or inquiry, settled a case (Büchsel, *TDNT*

III:945–46; Hemer 1972). The genitive *tou thanatou* is not subjective ("death's sentence") but appositional, describing the content of the decree. The apostle may well be thinking of an Ephesian imprisonment during which the threat of death was very real (see Phil 1:19ff. and COMMENT). It may be that he does not refer to the decree as a "condemnation" *(katakrima)* to death (note the use of the cognate verb in Matt 20:18; Mark 10:33) because he wants to interpret the experience theologically, and thus more positively.

*so that we would not rely upon ourselves.* Paul has employed the perfect participle of *peithein* to mean "have confidence in," as also in 2:3; 10:7; Phil 3:3. In 10:7 the context is polemical (cf. Phil 3:3) and the question concerns who is entitled to be truly confident.

*God who raises the dead.* An ancient Semitic description of God (parallels in Windisch, 47) which is used in the second petition as well as in the closing benediction of the "Eighteen Benedictions" of synagogue worship. Here, as well as in Rom 4:17, Paul's language echoes that of the Jewish liturgy (cf. also Heb 11:19); and in neither instance is there any explicit christianization of the formula (correctly, Windisch, 47, followed by Bultmann, 33).

10. *from such severe threats of death.* Translates the plural *ek tēlikoutōn thanatōn* attested by P⁴⁶ and most of the Old Latin mss. *GNT*-Nestle adopt the singular *ek tēlikoutou thanatou* (*RSV:* "from so deadly a peril"), which has the support of the great uncials (ℵ A B C Dᵍʳ), many minuscules, several ancient versions, and Clement. The *lectio difficilior* is clearly the first of these, used for the present tr., and it is hard to explain how it might have arisen had it not been original. It is also the reading of the earliest witness (P⁴⁶). These and other arguments in favor of its originality are set out capably by Zuntz 1953:104, who compares 2 Cor 6:4ff. and 11:23, concluding that the plural "bears the stamp of genuine Pauline diction." Turner suggests that the plural might imply various ways of dying or kinds of deadly perils (*GNTG* III:28); or perhaps, more likely, the plural represents a generalization about God's power to rescue from danger, based on the particular threat Paul had experienced in Asia. The arguments favoring the singular reading and the full evidence from the ancient witnesses are presented by Metzger 1971:574, to which A. Wikgren's comments in support of the plural are appended.

*the one, indeed, on whom we firmly set our hope.* In the Jewish tradition true believers are often described as those who hope in God, especially in the Pss, where the theme is pervasive; e.g., Ps 113:19 (LXX), "Those who fear the Lord have set their hope on the Lord" *(hoi phoboumenoi ton Kyrion ēlpisan epi Kyrion).* See also, in LXX, 4 Kgdms (2 Kgs) 18:5; 2 Chr 13:18; Isa 25:9. The confidence expressed by Paul in this verse is especially akin to that of Ps 21:5 (LXX): "Upon thee our fathers placed their hope; they hoped, and thou didst rescue them [*ēlpisan, kai errusō autous*]." The appearance here of the perfect tense, *ēlpikamen,* perhaps reflects a traditional usage within Hellenistic Judaism (although not found in the LXX, it is also used in the stylized expressions of 1 Tim 4:10; 5:5; 6:17). It may be interpreted as present in meaning, its effect being to intensify the thought. This is represented in the tr. by the adverb *firmly;* see BDF § 341; Burton 1898: § 77; Zuntz 1953:196 ("a general deep trust").

*will rescue us.* Some texts omit these words (*us* has been supplied for the English tr.), and yet other texts use the present tense, "rescues." The text translated has the best attestation, however ($P^{46}$ 𝕏 B C et al.), and the variants doubtless originated as attempts to deal with the fact that the *kai rysetai* appears twice, the second time as *kai eti rysetai* (see following note); see Metzger 1971:574. However, Zuntz (1953:197 n. 1) is doubtful enough about the words to place them in brackets.

*And he will continue to rescue.* The *hoti* read by many witnesses (including 𝕏 A) should probably be omitted (it is placed in brackets by *GNT*-Nestle). It is not found in $P^{46}$ or B, among others, and the perfect of *elpizein* is otherwise, in the NT, never followed by a specifying clause (Zuntz 1953:196–97). If this particle is omitted, then *kai eti rysetai* must begin a new sentence (Zuntz, ibid.; Metzger 1971:575).

11. The tr. of this verse seeks to be as clear as possible, while still conveying some of the extreme awkwardness of the Greek. The textual variants are readily explained as attempts by the early copyists to clarify the syntax; see Metzger 1971:575.

*as you also help with prayer.* A genitive-absolute construction, which is probably to be taken in a conditional sense (cf. Barrett, 57: "if you too cooperate . . ."; Wiles 1974:273 n. 6, who calls on Phil 1:19; Phlm 22 to support the conditional meaning here); the present tr., however, is designed to retain the indirectness of the original.

*for us.* At least for Paul, perhaps also for Timothy, who is in mind (v. 8) as the co-sender of this letter (v. 1), and conceivably for all of Paul's associates.

*from many people . . . through many.* The second phrase may be taken either as neuter, "through many prayers" (e.g., Hofmann, cited by Windisch, 50; Schlatter, 468; Wiles 1974:275, who incorrectly cites Windisch as also supporting this view, n. 5; *RSV*), or as masculine, "through many people" (e.g., Plummer, 21; Allo, 14; Barrett, 67; *NEB*). It is perhaps more likely to be the latter, and thus in effect to duplicate the first expression, *from many people (ek pollōn prosōpōn)*, thereby re-emphasizing the multitude of thanksgivings Paul has in mind; cf. Wiles 1974:275 and n. 6. It must be conceded, however, that there is no completely satisfactory way to unscramble the syntax of this verse.

*thanks may be rendered.* The passive form of *eucharistein* in a construction like this is extremely rare, and its active equivalent is "to thank for something" *(eucharistein epi tini);* see Schubert 1939:46–50, followed by Kümmel 1975:197.

Héring's attempt to construe the verb with *charisma* and to interpret it as meaning "to bestow a favor through prayer" not only fails to be supported by Jdt 8:25 (correctly, Barrett, 68) but also ascribes to a characteristic Pauline verb, *eucharistein,* a use present nowhere else in his letters. See also the following note.

*the gracious benefit.* Paul's word is *charisma,* which—whatever its precise connotation in a given context—invariably refers to a gift which comes from God (see the singular in Rom 5:15, 16; 6:23; 1 Cor 1:7; 7:7, and the plural in Rom 12:6; 1 Cor 12). Rom 1:11 is no exception, for there Paul is praying for a gift that he, as an apostle, might mediate to the Roman congregation. It is hardly conceivable that Paul could use the word, as Héring, 6, alleges to be the case here, with reference to the favor of their prayers accorded by the Corinthians to Paul. Does the word, however, refer to the divine rescue from which Paul has recently benefited (vv. 8, 10*a* [so, e.g., Plummer, 21; Windisch, 49; Dunn 1975:206]), or does it point to some future deliverance from danger (which could include deliverance from some present danger)? Bultmann, 35, is surely correct in holding the latter view, because the rescue and thanksgiving envisioned are to follow upon the petitions just now being urged.

*which shall have been bestowed on us.* The Greek is simply *to eis hēmas charisma,* so the verb has had to be supplied. The English future perfect tense is chosen to make it clear that the thanksgiving of the congregation will follow the bestowal of the gracious benefit which, however, is still to come; see preceding note.

## COMMENT: GENERAL

With the single exception of Gal, every Pauline letter (including the deutero-Pauline Eph, Col, 2 Thess, 2 Tim; also 1 Pet) opens with a formal introductory paragraph following the salutation. Most of these exhibit a high degree of structural similarity, dominated by thanksgiving (*eucharistein,* etc.) terminology; see Schubert 1939 and, in partial correction of Schubert's conclusions, Berger 1974:219–24. 2 Cor, however, offers one of the exceptions to this custom because it employs (as do Eph and 1 Pet) a different formal pattern in the introductory paragraph—namely, that of the Jewish blessing *(berakah),* vv. 3–4. This yields, in vv. 5–7, to an emphasis on the partnership in suffering and comfort which characterizes the life of the body of Christ and binds the apostle to the congregation. The blessing concludes with Paul's appeal for the prayers of the Corinthians (vv. 8–11) that he might continue to be rescued from danger by God's gracious favor, and also that their own thanksgivings to God might be multiplied. This introductory blessing represents, therefore, a curiously inverted form of the usual Pauline thanksgiving period: The *eucharistō-*clause concludes rather than opens the paragraph, and it has reference to the hoped-for thanksgivings of the addressees rather than the present thanksgiving of Paul himself; see Schubert 1939:50 and the further comments below.

## COMMENT: DETAILED

### The Blessing Proper, vv. 3–4

The language of this blessing has been heavily influenced by the Jewish liturgical tradition (see NOTES). Despite the similar blessings in the introduction of Huram's ( = Hiram, 3 Kgdms [1 Kgs] 5:21) letter to King Solomon (LXX 2 Chr 2:12) and in the introduction to the letter to Aristobulus (2 Mac 1:17) cited by Dahl (1951:250–54), it would appear that this blessing form was first taken over for use in epistolary introductions (see also Eph 1:3ff. and 1 Pet 1:3ff.) by the early Christians (Deichgräber 1967:64–65). Such introductions are inevitably more formal than the usual Pauline "thanksgivings," modeled after Greek forms. While the latter tend to stress the Christian faith and witness of the recipients (e.g., 1 Cor 1:5–7), these blessings necessarily emphasize the characteristics of God (Dahl 1951:252). Schubert suggests that "the particular epistolary situation" to which 2 Cor was responsive probably influenced Paul's use of the blessing formula rather than his customary thanksgiving (1939:50): Paul's relationship with the Corinthians has been sorely tried, and he cannot presume on their part nor exhibit on his own the kind of personal rapport reflected, for example, in the thanksgiving period of Phil 1:3–11 (cf. Dahl 1951:253). In addition, however, one must not overlook the fact that this particular epistolary introduction is dominated by Paul's immense relief at having recently been delivered by God from some mortal danger (vv. 8–11). In this case it is naturally the blessing form, an expression of praise to God for an act of deliverance from danger, that Paul chooses (cf. Dahl 1951:252).

Thus, the most striking feature of this blessing is not its form but its content. Here everything centers on the one theme of *comfort* in *affliction*. As *the God of comfort* (the phrase is not a description of God's "nature" but of what God bestows; Bultmann, *TDNT* V:161; Delling 1963:12; Käsemann 1980:383), God can be counted on to act with appropriate benevolence toward *those who are in any kind of affliction*. In the earlier reference to *every one of our afflictions*, however, there is already a hint that something specific may be in the apostle's mind (see NOTES for the grammatical indicators). This is confirmed in the verses which follow, above all in v. 8, where Paul writes of the mortal danger in Asia from which he has been saved. It is probably this, perhaps recent, deliverance from a situation Paul had himself considered hopeless that is chiefly responsible for the form as well as for the content of the opening verses.

The thanksgiving periods of Paul's letters usually give voice, at least indirectly, to the concerns which have prompted him to write (Phlm 4–9 is an especially striking example of this). In the present case, however, Paul's deliverance from the affliction in Asia is not mentioned again. The general theme of comfort in affliction does recur, however, and precisely in connection with Paul's narration of the events which have prompted him to write this letter (7:5–16). In that context, it must be noted, "affliction" will refer primarily to mental anguish, not to an external threat, and "comfort" will refer to the effect on Paul of Titus' coming from Corinth with good news about the congregation there (7:5–7, 13). Thus, Paul writes of being comforted "with the coming of Titus" (*en tē parousia*, vv. 6, 7) "about [the Corinthians]" (*eph' hymin*, v. 7).

Although there is this important distinction in the way the words are applied in these two passages, it is quite possible to understand how the two different applications could be joined in one letter, or even how they could be mutually reinforcing. This letter, which opens with a blessing of *the God of all comfort who comforts us in every one of our afflictions* (vv. 3–4), is being written by one who has been doubly comforted, indeed, in two different ways: by deliverance from a threat to his very life in Asia, and by the news Titus has brought from Corinth, which to some degree has alleviated his anxiety about the congregation there. Of the second of these, however, there is no direct hint in vv. 3–11.

*The Partnership of Suffering and Comfort, vv. 5–7*

In these verses the blessing form proper, but not the theme of comfort in affliction it has introduced, is left behind. Now Paul's relationship to the Corinthians comes into focus and remains so throughout vv. 8–11. There is also a significant development in the handling of Paul's main theme, however, as the idea of "afflictions" is specifically taken up into the idea of *the sufferings of Christ.* Apart from the Christian gloss in v. 3 (see NOTES), the introductory *berakah* does not depart from familiar Jewish texts, where the theme of God's comfort given to his people in the midst of their afflictions is frequent. See, for example, the epilogue of 2 Apoc Bar, formulated as Baruch's letter to the tribes exiled in Babylon. They will find comfort in their affliction, they are told, if they realize their suffering is a time of judgment *and* chastening, and if they will banish error from their lives. Then they can be accounted worthy of their fathers and "will receive eternal hope" (78:5–7; cf. Andresen 1965:246).

A significantly different kind of perspective, however, is introduced in v. 5, which is intended to clarify ("For," *hoti*) the way in which God's comfort is received (v. 4*a*); cf. Windisch, 39. Two fundamental affirmations are made here: (a) that "the sufferings of Christ are overflowing to us" (i.e., to the apostles, perhaps specifically to Paul), and (b) that "through Christ our comfort is overflowing." These two ideas have been conjoined in an arresting rhetorical pattern which has certain characteristics of a formal *chiasmus* without being, strictly speaking, chiastic (contrast Rissi 1969:54–55). The effect of the "just as . . . so also" *(kathōs . . . houtos)* structure is to accentuate the relationship Paul is intent on positing between the sufferings of Christ and the comfort of which Christ's apostles are agents. As various commentators have pointed out, one might have expected Paul to have written, "For just as the sufferings of Christ are overflowing to us, so also is his comfort overflowing to us." Instead, in the second clause attention is shifted to the abundance of comfort which has been received and its "spillover" effect for others. Paul's own recent experience of deliverance from a mortal danger (perhaps heightened by some good news from Corinth) apparently accounts for his present consciousness of having been comforted even beyond his own needs. Any reference to that, however, is momentarily delayed (see v. 8) in order to emphasize how comfort comes to Paul's readers.

*The "Sufferings of Christ"*

Commentators have not completely agreed about the meaning of the phrase *the sufferings of Christ* (v. 5). References in rabbinical texts to "the travail of the Messiah" *(ḥeblô šel māšîaḥ)* at first appear to correspond to it but are, in fact, references to the tribulations suffered by God's people, not by the Messiah himself, as the messianic age is opened. The Hebrew phrase is part of a metaphor in which Zion is the mother from whose womb the Messiah comes forth, and her sufferings are the labor pains; thus, "the travail of the Messiah." See Moore 1927 II:361–62, who also cites the pertinent texts. This conception undoubtedly lies behind the phrase Paul uses (Barrett, 61–62), but this is clearly evident only where the phrase appears in 1 Pet, especially in 4:13.

More important for understanding 2 Cor 1:5–7 is the development and use of the concept in the earliest church. The divine requirement that Jesus must suffer is embedded deep within the Son of Man traditions of the Synoptic Gospels (Matt 16:21, par. Mark 8:31 and Luke 9:22; Matt 17:12, par. Mark 9:12; Luke 17:25 [cf. 22:15]). Moreover, in Luke-Acts the title *Christos* is also used in connection with the suffering God requires of Jesus, and the scriptural prophecies of this are emphasized (Luke 24:26, 46; Acts 3:18; 17:3). Significant, too, is the appearance here of the more abstract notion of "the passion" *(to pathein)* of Christ (Acts 1:3), an expression which may suggest how the more concrete references to Jesus' suffering in the Passion Narrative (where only inflected forms of the verb are used) developed eventually into the use of the plural noun. The phrases found in 1 Pet 1:11 *(ta eis Christon pathēmata);* 4:13 and 5:1 *(tou Christou pathēmata);* and Col 1:24 *(ta thlipseis tou Christou)* are more likely to reflect a traditional usage on which Paul is also dependent (in Phil 3:10 [*ta pathēmata autou*], as well as in 2 Cor 1:5) than they are to derive specifically from Paul. In Heb 2:9, 10 this same tradition may be reflected, but it has been given a more restrictive reference (Jesus' "suffering of death," *to pathēma tou thanatou,* led to his exaltation) and has been linked with the idea of Jesus' perfection *(dia pathēmatōn teliōsai).*

One of the most important aspects of this tradition is the way in which Jesus' sufferings are coupled emphatically with his subsequent overcoming of them, through his resurrection (Matt 6:21 par.; Luke 24:46; Acts 17:3; Phil 3:10–11) or glorification (Luke 24:26; 1 Pet 1:11; 4:13; 5:1; perhaps a trace in Col 1:24, 27; also clear in Heb 2:9, 10). Another is the idea of Christians sharing in these with Christ (Phil 3:10–11, using the noun *koinōnia;* 1 Pet 4:13, using the verb *koinōnein;* 5:1, using the noun *koinōnos;* in Heb the idea seems to be reversed insofar as it is implied that Christ's suffering signals his condescension to human weakness [2:14–18]).

That this same tradition is at work in 2 Cor 1:5–7 cannot be doubted. Here, too, a reference to Christ's sufferings is coupled with a reference to his over-coming of them—implicit in the concept of *comfort*—and there is an emphasis upon Christians as partners *(koinōnoi,* v. 7) in suffering. One is surely justified, then, despite the objections of a few (e.g., Michaelis, *TDNT* V:931–32; Rissi 1969:55 n. 126), in interpreting what Paul has written here with the help of Phil 3:10–11, where the same tradition is reflected. Indeed, from Phil it becomes clear that in Paul's thinking this tradition is closely associated with the idea of the Christian's conformity to Christ's death; in 3:10 the participial phrase "being conformed to his death" *(symmorphidzomenos tō thanatō autou)* is appositional to "[knowing] the power of his resurrection and the partnership of his sufferings" *(hē koinōnia tōn pathēmatōn autou)*. One aspect of this compound formulation receives explication in Rom 6, where baptism is interpreted with the help of the bold metaphors of co-crucifixion and co-entombment with Christ (vv. 3–6). The other aspect is emphasized where Paul wants to identify the deeper significance of those trials and hardships which believers must undergo in the world (e.g., Phil 1:29; Rom 8:17; cf. 1 Thess 3:2–4). These, of course, are regarded as consequent upon baptism into Christ's death, and not requisite to or identical with it. Nevertheless, they may be described as the sufferings of Christ because they are the sufferings of Christ's body, the new community which is redeemed by his death and lives out of "the power of the resurrection" which is already present to faith. Cf. the discussions by Proudfoot (1963), Ahern (1960), and Tannehill (1967:90–98).

### The Partnership of Suffering and Comfort

These fundamental Pauline conceptions help to explain the present passage. In the first instance (v. 5) Paul probably makes reference to the abundance of sufferings he himself has experienced; *us* refers, first and certainly, to Paul, and perhaps secondarily to his associates. The same is true of the plural in the next phrase, where he writes that *also, through Christ, our comfort is overflowing.* Apostles know a special measure of suffering, but they also know a special measure of comfort. Paul makes this double affirmation, however, only in order to stress the suffering and comfort which embrace all within the body of Christ. Thus, in v. 6 a clear distinction is made between apostle(s) and congregation *(we . . . your)* as the afflictions endured by the apostles are said to be *for your comfort and salvation.* Significantly, Paul does not say here that the afflictions of the apostles serve to institute or increase afflictions for the congregation; rather, they lead to *comfort and salvation.* See McDermott 1975:222.

Elsewhere in Paul's letters "salvation" is used in a more or less traditional way with reference to the ultimate fulfillment of God's promises to his people. Insofar as it conveys something more specific, it is often the idea of deliverance from the wrath of God on the final judgment day (e.g., Rom 1:16; 1 Thess 5:8, 9; and many instances of the verb *sōzein,* e.g., Rom 5:9; 1 Cor 5:5). The word should probably be understood in this way here. As bearers of the gospel the apostles must inevitably encounter opposition and suffer many afflictions, but these are for the sake of the conversion and ultimate salvation of the unbelievers. Perhaps, therefore, the word *paraklēsis,* best understood as "comfort" in the rest of the passage (see NOTES on v. 3), connotes something more like "appeal," in the sense of a missionary appeal, when linked here with "salvation." Yet in the second part of this same verse the meaning is clearly "comfort." When the apostles are comforted in their afflictions, this enables others in the body of Christ to be comforted in theirs. The principle of 1 Cor 12:26 seems to be at work here.

Paul has already emphasized that one is comforted by God (*hypo tou Theou,* v. 4) and "through Christ" (*dia tou Christou,* v. 5). When he now specifies that the overflowing comfort granted to the apostles (v. 5) is imparted to the congregation for its comfort, he is conceiving of apostles not as the source of comfort but as agents of its transmission. What the Corinthians *see* in the apostles no less than what they *hear* from them becomes a proclamation to them of the power and love of God; cf. Proudfoot 1963:155; Rissi 1969:55–56 n. 127. The conception is the same as that which underlies 5:20 (see NOTES and COMMENT there), and it is also present in 4:10–11, where, as here, Paul portrays the apostles as bearers of Jesus' "death" ( = sufferings) and "life" ( = comfort). And there, as here, this enactment of the kerygma within the lives of the apostles is interpreted as a proclamation of the gospel for the sake of those to whom the apostles have been sent; see NOTES and COMMENT on 4:7–15.

That Paul does not just mean escape from calamity or an inward sense of tranquillity when he speaks of comfort is clear from what he says here about the way it expresses itself: *in your endurance of the same sufferings that we, too, are suffering.* What is promised is not immediate relief from afflictions, but that they can be endured. Specifically, they can be endured when they are understood as the sufferings of Christ—that is, *the same sufferings* which the apostles have known and through which the gospel has been proclaimed. These are *the same sufferings* shared by the whole body of Christ, as members of which believers are summoned to be conformed to Christ's life-giving death and to live in obedient expectation of the final glory (cf. 4:17). Formally considered, v. 7 is a sentence in the indicative mood which affirms Paul's confidence that the Corinthians are partners, along with the apostles and the whole body of Christ, in Christ's comfort as well as in his sufferings. Such Pauline affirmations of confidence, however, including those which occur in the opening thanksgivings, are often implicitly hortatory; see Furnish 1968: 94–95 and Schubert 1939:89. This is probably the case here, because Paul will subsequently appeal for his readers' full understanding, so that he can be proud of them "on the day of the Lord Jesus" (vv. 13–14). His hope for them on that day is certain, provided that, as "the church of God which is in Corinth" (v. 1), they are demonstrably "partners" in the whole body of Christ. The apostle is well aware that the Corinthians in particular have not always understood that sharing in the final glory is inseparable from sharing in Christ's sufferings (1 Cor 4:8–17; cf. de Boor, 30–31).

### An Appeal for Prayers, vv. 8–11

The theme of comfort in the midst of afflictions continues here as Paul presents an especially momentous, personal example of the overwhelming power of God to bring life from death. J. T. Sanders believes "Paul . . .

concludes the theme of the eulogiac [*sic*] period in v. 7" and formally opens the body of the letter in v. 8, only to be diverted ("under compulsion" of epistolary habit) to bring his introductory paragraph to a more suitable conclusion. Thus, after the false start in vv. 8–11 Paul must begin the body of the letter "anew" in v. 12 (1962:361). In fact, however, disclosure formulas like the one found in v. 8 may be used wherever specific information is introduced, and the presence of one does not invariably indicate the opening of the letter body (certainly not, e.g., in Rom 11:25). In the present case this form stands within another form (the introductory blessing) and serves not to open the body of the letter but to introduce information which helps to support and conclude the theme on which the whole blessing is centered.

A somewhat parallel case is found in the letter to Aristobulus in 2 Mac 1:10–2:18. The letter body clearly opens with 1:18 ("we thought it necessary to notify you," *RSV*), and the preceding paragraph is just as clearly the usual introductory paragraph praising God (1:11–17). Included within this introduction, however, is a block of informative material (vv. 12–16) which documents the greatness of what God has done.

### The Affliction in Asia

Paul does not say what the *affliction in Asia* was, beyond the indication that it posed a mortal threat from which, at the time, he saw no escape. (Against Dean 1947:44–47, the strong language used here, especially the reference to a *death sentence,* leaves no doubt that the threat Paul experienced was a physical one; see especially Duncan 1930:131–32.) Whether the use of the first person plural means that others with him were similarly imperiled is not clear. The intensity of feeling with which Paul refers to the incident suggests that it happened fairly recently, and the use of a disclosure formula *(For we do not want you to be ignorant)* suggests that the Corinthians are learning of it for the first time (so, e.g., Lietzmann, 100; Barrett, 63–64; against Schlatter, 466; Strachan, 51). This being the case, one would have expected Paul to convey some details about his experience, but he does not. Even the exact place is left unspecified, although *Asia* may (but need not necessarily) refer to the capital city of Ephesus (as in Acts 20:16). Rather, the apostle is primarily concerned to emphasize the *meaning* of the experience, perhaps assuming that the bearer(s) of this letter will provide the Corinthians with any details of the circumstances about which they may be curious.

It is not possible to identify this *affliction* with the Ephesian riot described in Acts 19:23–20:1 because—unless the severity of it has deliberately been minimized in the narration—the apostle's life seems not to have been threatened on that occasion. Similarly, when Paul subsequently avoids Ephesus en route to Jerusalem for Pentecost, the only threat seems to be one of delay (Acts 20:16). The hypothesis that Paul's *affliction in Asia* was the onset of some serious illness which continued to threaten his life (proposed, e.g., by Allo,

15–19; Barrett, 64) accords with certain other possible references to a physical infirmity (Gal 4:13; 2 Cor 12:7) but is not finally convincing. Is it not more likely that the onset of a disease would be identified with reference to its *symptoms*, to *how* it struck, rather than by a reference to *where* one was stricken? The near-fatal illness of Epaphroditus, for example, is described by Paul in quite another way: "he was ill to the point of death" (*ēsthenēsen paraplēsion thanatō*, Phil 2:27). This illness hypothesis is further weakened if, as seems likely, the verb *eschēchamen* in v. 9 is a narrative perfect (see NOTES on v. 9).

Although Acts says nothing about a Pauline imprisonment in Ephesus (or elsewhere in Asia), there are strong reasons to suppose that the apostle was in an Ephesian prison when he wrote to the Philippians about the prospect of his imminent execution (Phil 1:19–30; for detailed support of the hypothesis see Michaelis 1961:204–11 and cf. Duncan 1930, especially 59–123). According to Phil 2:19–23, Timothy was with Paul at this time but probably not in prison with him, since Paul seems to have no doubt that Timothy will soon be able to go to Philippi. If Phil was indeed written from Ephesus, then it is possible that Paul has the same imprisonment in mind as he writes now of the *affliction . . . in Asia* (2 Cor 1:8). The following points of correspondence between the present passage and Phil 1 and 2 may be noted: (a) Both passages refer to a life-threatening experience (2 Cor 1:8–9; Phil 1:20–23; 2:12–18; cf. Georgi 1965:46). (b) The presence of Timothy (Phil 2:19–23) could account for the use of the first person plural in 2 Cor 1:8ff., even though Timothy himself was probably not a prisoner. (c) Paul's remark in Phil 2:20 that no one else but Timothy is available to send to Philippi accords with the fact that Titus had been sent on a mission to Corinth (2 Cor 2:13; 7:7ff.). (d) Paul's intention to come to Philippi himself when (if) his life is spared (Phil 2:24) accords with the fact that the apostle did go to Macedonia shortly after his deliverance from the affliction in Asia (2 Cor 1:8ff.; 2:12–13; 7:5). (e) That Timothy is named as a co-sender of a letter from Macedonia (2 Cor 1:1) agrees with the plan of Phil 2:19–24 that Paul would follow his associate to Philippi as soon as he could.

This identification of Paul's *affliction . . . in Asia* with the Ephesian imprisonment during which he writes to the Philippians must remain hypothetical, and its cogency depends directly on the strength of the prior hypothesis that the Philippian letter was indeed written from Ephesus. But this hypothesis seems at least as likely as any other, given the scarcity of evidence our passage provides (so also Georgi 1965:46 and Gnilka 1968b:22–23).

Whether or not the Corinthians were as ignorant of the particulars of the affliction as the modern reader must be content to remain, the essential thing is what Paul wishes to say about its significance. The circumstances are beside the point, and their omission only accentuates Paul's real concern. How their inclusion would have detracted from this may be judged by comparing the opening paragraph of the letter to Aristobulus in 2 Mac. There, too, God is praised for having delivered the senders from "great dangers" (1:11), but the opening thanksgiving (1:11) and the closing blessing (1:17) are largely overshadowed by the narrative report of the circumstances of the deliverance which stands in between. That is not the case here, where Paul's single point is that the affliction had left him with no human options, utterly helpless so far as his own power was concerned. It had forced him to give up any pretense of being sufficient to overcome it, and had led him to rely solely on God. In vv. 8–10*a* the conviction that those who are partners in Christ's sufferings are also partners in the comfort which comes from God through Christ (vv. 5–7) is dramatized from Paul's own experience. The "God of all comfort" is powerful enough to overcome even the severest threats.

Paul's portrayal of the miserable state to which he had been reduced by the affliction in Asia, and of his reliance *upon God who raises the dead,* accords with one of the prominent themes in his letters to Corinth. While it may be too much to claim, with Rissi (1969:56), that "power" *(dynamis)* was one of the catchwords of Paul's opponents in Corinth, it does appear that one of the fundamental charges being brought against Paul there concerned his "weakness" *(astheneia).* There is evidence of this especially in chaps. 10–13 of 2 Cor (e.g., 10:10), but it is probable that the apostle's consciousness of such charges lies behind certain passages in 1 Cor as well (e.g., when Paul parodies the Corinthians in 4:8–13 and contrasts their "strength" with the "weakness" of the apostles; cf. 12:22). Instead of denying his weakness, Paul affirms it as a fact, and more than once catalogs the hardships he has experienced as an apostle (4:8–9; 6:4*c*–5; 11:23*b*–29; 12:10; cf. Rom 8:35; 1 Cor 4:9–13). In these various afflictions, he says, he will dare to "boast" (11:30; 12:5), because precisely in his endurance of them the divine power is revealed (12:9–10). See Käsemann 1942:53–56, and NOTES and COMMENT on the appropriate passages.

Superficially there may be some tension between Paul's acknowledgment of the despair to which he was reduced in Asia and the claim in 4:8 that despite profound uncertainty he has never despaired. In the present passage, however, no less than in chap. 4 and elsewhere, the point is that afflictions are overcome when one abandons reliance on one's own power and trusts solely in the power of God. (See Tannehill's comment, 1967:97: "Because suffering directs the believer away from himself to God and so prepares him to receive God's gift of comfort, Paul can assert the positive relation between suffering and comfort. . . .") This is a recurring emphasis in 2 Cor. The antithesis between "ourselves" and "God" *(heautoi/Theos)* occurs in 3:5 as well as here (N. Schneider 1970:22), and there is a similar one ("God . . . us") in 4:7. Moreover, this contrast between reliance upon God and reliance upon self (putting confidence in one's "flesh," Phil 3:3–4) is the same one Paul draws elsewhere between "boasting" in oneself and "boasting" in the Lord (see especially chaps.

10–12). The specific problems he has had in Corinth may well be on his mind as he expresses himself here.

The climax of this introductory blessing comes in vv. 10b–11. Despite numerous particular problems of translation and punctuation, it is clear enough that Paul is urging the Corinthians to join their prayers with his. They are to pray that the God who has already delivered him (and his associates) from mortal dangers will continue to do so. It is not unusual for Paul to ask for the prayers of his congregations, but this is the only letter in which such a request appears in the introductory paragraph. Customarily he mentions his prayers for them at the beginning of a letter (Rom 1:8–10; 1 Cor 1:4–8; Phil 1:3–5; 1 Thess 1:2–3; Phlm 4–6) and requests their prayers for him at its close (Rom 15:30–32; 1 Thess 5:25; Phlm 22). By standing where it does in the present letter, the request (expressed obliquely, to be sure [cf. Phil 1:19], and not directly as in Rom 15:30–32; 1 Thess 5:25) seeks to engage the readers immediately with Paul's own situation and to accentuate their need to be active participants in the partnership of suffering and comfort of which he has just written. It is in this respect a gesture of reconciliation (cf. Wiles 1974:276). The request is not so specific as when he asks the Romans to intercede for his deliverance from unbelievers in Judea (Rom 15:30–32), nor can the prayers of the Corinthians be so specific as those of the Philippians who, Paul knew, were praying for his release from prison (Phil 1:19). Here his concern seems to be as much for what the prayers will signify about them as for what the prayers will mean for him. They will signify the partnership of the congregation in the gospel and in the body of Christ.

The line between prayers of petition and prayers of thanksgiving is thin and indistinct; petition no less than thanksgiving is rooted in a profound trust in the power and goodness of God. This connection is presumed as the section draws to a close in the final, curiously inverted, and syntactically obscure clause (see NOTES). The prayers for Paul's continuing safety will be efficacious and will thereby be transformed into many thanksgivings to God. In this and similar passages (especially 4:15; 9:11–15) there is ground for concluding that thanksgiving had a special place in the liturgy of the Pauline churches and that it was directly related to the notion of increasing the glory of God; see Boobyer 1929, especially 80–81, followed by Schubert 1939, especially 89–91. It is this gathering together in worship of "the church of God in Corinth" which is probably in Paul's mind as he solicits their prayers of petition on his behalf and anticipates the thanksgivings which will follow (cf. Windisch, 49–50). By writing of this expectation, Paul has concluded his introductory paragraphs to the letter, just as he had opened them, with a reference to the praise due to God for help in the time of trouble.

# II. LETTER BODY, 1:12–9:15

## A. ASSURANCES OF CONCERN, 1:12–2:13

### 1. INTRODUCTION, 1:12–14

1  ¹²Now we can be proud of this, the testimony of our conscience that we have conducted ourselves in the world with candor and godly sincerity, not by any ordinary wisdom but by the grace of God—and all the more with you. ¹³For we write you nothing other than what you can read and also understand; and I hope that you will understand completely, ¹⁴as you have understood us partially, that we are your boast even as you are ours on the day of our Lord Jesus.

## NOTES

1:12. *Now.* Translates *gar,* "for," which in this instance, as elsewhere at the opening of the body of a letter (Rom 1:16, if this verse opens the body, but also v. 18 if it is opened there; Gal 1:11; 1 Thess 2:1), has no strictly causal force. Like the *de* used in Phil 1:12; 2 Thess 2:1, it is mainly an introductory word here and does not presuppose any specific continuation of the preceding thought; cf. BAG s.v. 4. Prof. D. N. Freedman has pointed out to me that in ancient Near Eastern letters, including those in Hebrew and Aramaic, the body of the letter after the salutation is almost always introduced by "Now" or "And now" (Hebrew: *wᵉᶜattâ* or the equivalent). It may be best simply to leave the word untranslated here (as in *NEB*).

*we can be proud of this.* Or "our boasting is this"; but *kauchēsis* should probably be interpreted in conjunction with the closely related term *kauchēma* in v. 14. There Paul is thinking of the verdict of blamelessness to be pronounced at the Parousia when "the Lord Jesus" will come to judge; cf. 1 Thess 2:19, where Paul asks (rhetorically) what his "hope or joy or crown of boasting [*stephanos kauchēseōs*]" will be on that day. The theme of "boasting" (in addition to the two different nouns in vv. 12 and 14, Paul uses the verbs *kauchasthai* and *katakauchasthai*) is more prominent in Paul's letters than elsewhere in the NT; otherwise the word group is present only in Jas (five times), and once each in Eph, 2 Thess, and Heb. The related noun "confidence" *(pepoithēsis)* should also be noted in this connection, especially since it appears primarily here in 2 Cor (for the verb *peithein* see NOTES on 1:9). In many places, as here, the various terms for boasting designate the confidence (whether legitimate or not) with which one will be prepared to stand trial before God (see, e.g., Rom 4:2; Phil 2:16). Paul uses *kauchasthai,* etc., more often in the Corinthian letters than elsewhere (thirty-eight of fifty-five instances), and most of these occur in 2 Cor (ten times in chaps. 1–9; eighteen times in chaps. 10–13); see also the discussion on 10:8, 17, as well as the studies by Bultmann, *TDNT* III:645–54; Asting (1925); Genths (1927); Sánchez Bosch (1970).

*conscience.* The word *(syneidēsis)* seems to have found a place in Paul's vocabulary because of the way it figured in the dispute in the Corinthian church itself about eating meat which had been offered in sacrifice to pagan gods (1 Cor 8:7–13; 10:25–29). Elsewhere (4:2, on which see the note; 5:11; Rom 2:15; 9:1; 13:5) Paul uses it more generally of the human faculty of critical self-evaluation, although with special nuances in each case. Here he enlists it in support of his expectation to be vindicated at the Parousia; the connection of conscience with the final judgment is quite explicit in Rom 2:15–16. Cf. also Rom 9:1, where, as here, the apostle invokes the witness of his conscience to certify what he is saying.

*conducted ourselves.* The verb *anastrephein* appears only here in Paul's letters. The noun, which is especially frequent in 1 Pet, is used by Paul only in Gal 1:13 and refers, like the verb, to one's "manner of life" *(NEB).*

*in the world.* Greek *en tō kosmō* as in 1 Pet 5:9; cf. "in the whole world" *(en holō tō kosmō),* Rom 1:8. Nothing specifically negative is connoted either in these expressions or, as happens more frequently in Paul's letters, where the phrase appears without the article simply as *en kosmō.* The reference is a neutral one to the everyday realities of people, places, and events. In Rom 5:13, Paul thinks of sin as invading the world, not as one of its inherent features, and in Rom 1:8; Phil 2:15 the world constitutes the sphere where the gospel is preached. See also 1 Cor 8:4; 14:10. The word appears only twice more in 2 Cor: in the theological slogan used in 5:19 and in an adjectival construction in 7:10.

*with candor and godly sincerity.* There is early and strong attestation for the alternate reading "with holiness and godly sincerity" (P[46] and most of the great uncials, etc.), and it is extremely difficult to make a choice between the two. Perhaps overriding the impressive external evidence for "holiness" *(hagiotēs),* however, are the following considerations: (a) *hagiotēs* is not used elsewhere by Paul; (b) the variant *haplotēs* is very close in meaning to the word *sincerity,* and Paul's use of two synonymous words dependent on one preposition can be otherwise attested; (c) the apostle's claim to *candor* has special appropriateness in view of charges which have been brought against him in Corinth (see 2:17, where he is defending his sincerity in similar terms). A full and balanced discussion of the evidence is presented by Thrall (1976), who believes the "more solid arguments" favor the reading *hagiotēs.* The arguments which led to the adoption of *haplotēs* in *GNT*-Nestle are summarized by Metzger 1971:575, and this reading is also adopted by Barrett, 71. The term connotes a frankness and openness in one's words and actions, holding nothing back (thus, in an extended sense, "generosity"; cf. 8:2; 9:11, 13; Rom 12:8); see Bauernfeind, *TDNT* I:386–87. The word *sincerity (eilikrineia)* denotes genuineness and truthfulness (cf. "the unleavened bread of sincerity and truth," 1 Cor 5:8, *RSV),* and is applied again by Paul to his conduct as an apostle in 2:17. *Tou Theou* is a genitive of quality, *godly,* and this description of sincerity is probably influenced by the same kind of eschatological perspective as lies behind other terms in this verse; see COMMENT.

*not by any ordinary wisdom.* Literally "not by fleshly wisdom" *(ouk en sophia sar-*

*kikē)*. Paul employs the adjective to contrast what is worldly, material, and human with what is spiritual and divine (10:4; Rom 15:27; 1 Cor 3:3; 9:11). The wisdom described here is therefore the same as that about which Paul had previously written to the Corinthians: "the wisdom of (this) world" (1 Cor 1:20; 3:19); "of this age" (1 Cor 2:6); "human" wisdom (1 Cor 2:5, 13). Here, where the *sophia sarkikē* is contrasted with the *grace of God,* Paul must be thinking of wisdom which, however perspicacious, is still only human and finite. The meaning of true wisdom is not a topic in 2 Cor, though, as it had been in his earlier letter (1 Cor 1–2).

*the grace of God.* In Greek no articles are used (simply *en chariti Theou*), perhaps because, as in the contrasting phrase *(en sophia sarkikē),* a mode of existence is in mind.

*and all the more with you.* Note the almost identical phrase in 2:4; 7:15; here *perissoterōs pros hymas,* there *perissoterōs eis hymas.* See COMMENT.

13. *we write.* The context (v. 12, how Paul and his associates have conducted themselves in the world) requires that this be taken as a general reference to Paul's apostolic letters, including but not restricted to the present one; cf. *NEB:* "There is nothing in our letters to you but what . . ."

*read and also understand.* The *ē kai* ("or indeed"; cf. BAG s.v. *ē,* 1aβ) effects the clearly intended intensification between the first *(anaginōskete)* and the second *(epiginōskete)* word; a similar pairing in order to intensify occurs in 3:2, "known and read" *(ginōskomenē kai anaginōskomenē).* Here the first verb is that which would normally be used for the reading out of a letter to the assembled congregation; cf. 1 Thess 5:27; Col 4:16. (J. H. Kennedy's arguments [1900:52–60] for the more ancient meaning "acknowledge," both here and in 3:2, are labored and unconvincing.) The second refers, as Paul uses it, to a mode of knowledge appropriated in such a way as to require that the one who "knows" in that fashion be properly responsive to it; hence, depending on the context, to "accept" (Rom 1:32) something; to "recognize" or "acknowledge" something or someone (13:5; 1 Cor 14:37; 16:18); or, as here and in 6:7, to come to a full cognizance of something or someone (see also 1 Cor 13:12).

*I hope.* This abrupt shift from the plural subject, which has appeared exclusively thus far in the letter, to the first person singular anticipates the sustained use of the singular in vv. 15–17, 23; 2:1–13. Its sudden surfacing in the present verse probably signals the special intensity with which Paul himself identifies with the thought expressed here— namely, that the Corinthians will understand in a certain way.

*completely.* The Greek *heōs telous* could mean "to the end" or "to the last" with a specifically eschatological referent (e.g., Plummer, 27; Windisch, 58; Barrett, 73); cf. the same phrase in 1 Cor 1:8; Herm Sim IX, 27:3; Dan 6:27 (Theod.), all in eschatological contexts. On the other hand, in Ps 37:7 (LXX) the meaning must be something like "fully" or "completely," and this meaning is perhaps the more likely in the present passage because of the contrasting phrase *apo merous* ("partially") in v. 14 (so also, among others, Lietzmann, 101; Allo, 21; Bultmann, 40 n. 11, and Delling, *TDNT* VIII:56). In fact, this second meaning could also apply in 1 Cor 1:8; Herm Sim IX, 27:3.

14. *that we are your boast.* Some commentators translate *hoti* "because," thus interpreting the phrase as giving the reason for Paul's hope (e.g., Windisch, 58). It is more likely, however, that this *hoti*-clause specifies what Paul hopes the Corinthians will understand completely; see Bultmann, 40, who calls attention to 5:12, where the readers are urged to find their "boast" in their apostle. This is not the basis but rather the *object* of Paul's appeal.

*on the day of our Lord Jesus.* It is uncertain whether *our* should be retained in the text, since the ms. evidence is about equally balanced; see Metzger 1971:575–76. Other comparable Pauline references to the eschatological day are found in 1 Cor 5:5; Phil 1:6, 10; 2:16; 1 Thess 5:2. Cf. also Acts 2:20 [Joel 3:4]; 2 Pet 3:10, 12; Rev 16:14.

## COMMENT

These verses open the body of the letter and introduce its first major topic —namely, the sincerity and constructive goodwill with which Paul has acted in relation to the Corinthian congregation. The argument suggesting that they are designed to show why the apostle deserves and may claim the recipients' prayers which had been requested in v. 11 (Windisch, 53) is not convincing. They introduce what follows (see NOTES on v. 12) and are related to the preceding blessing only insofar as that itself also anticipates the subject of Paul's relationship with the Corinthian Christians. Paul leaves an inadvertent clue to the function of these verses when he shifts quite unexpectedly to the first person singular in v. 13*b: I hope that you will understand completely.* Here is what is important to him, what concerns him most at present. These opening sentences constitute an appeal to the congregation to be attentive and receptive to what he will go on to write, in order that they can come to a full understanding of why he has conducted himself as he has toward them, as well as of the fact that his apostleship alone will be their boast on the day of Christ.

At the outset Paul invokes the testimony of his conscience in order to emphasize the validity of what he is writing about his past and present conduct; a comparable appeal to the testimony of conscience appears in Rom 9:1, where he seeks to emphasize the truth of what he is writing there. The "pride" of conscience which he mentions to the Corinthians should not be understood primarily as his confidence that they will be able to understand and affirm him when they examine his record. For Paul the judgment of ultimate significance comes from God *on the day of our Lord Jesus* (v. 14), and it is on that day that the testimony of his conscience will be proved true or false (see Rom 2:15–16). Thus, the pride of conscience referred to here must be interpreted eschatologically, first of all as the confidence Paul has *before God* that his conduct toward the Corinthians has been above reproach. This eschatological perspective also explains the expression *godly sincerity (eilikrineia tou Theou;* see NOTES); it is a reference to what is "sincere" in God's sight, to what will be judged as sincerity at the Parousia. Cf. Paul's prayer that the Philippians will be found "pure and blameless for the day of Christ" (Phil 1:10, *RSV*), where "pure" translates the adjective *eilikrinēs.* Functionally, these expressions of Paul's confidence before God are meant to evoke agreement from the Corinthians that their apostle's conduct does not warrant censure.

Why must Paul place so much emphasis upon the *candor and godly sincerity* with which he has acted? Apparently because there have been "some" in Corinth who have accused him of acting "according to worldly standards" (10:2; Bultmann, 38). In the present passage he has in mind, specifically, complaints that his actions belie his professed concern for them (see 1:15–2:2) and that his letters are overbearing and insensitive (see 2:3–11). Before responding to these two particular points, however, the apostle emphasizes in a more general way his conviction that his conduct has been governed by *the grace of God* and *not by any ordinary wisdom* (cf. "conducting ourselves according to worldly standards" [*kata sarka peripatountes*], 10:2). Paul is always conscious of being called to apostleship by God's "grace" (e.g., Gal 1:15; Rom 15:15–16), but here the word is used somewhat more particularly of the power of God by means of which the apostle is enabled to carry out the divine commission; 1 Cor 15:10*b* ("I have worked harder than any of the other apostles, although it was not really my own doing, but God's grace working with me," *TEV*) suggests this meaning for the present passage, and the parallelism of the references to God's "grace" and God's "power" in 12:9 (Bultmann, 38) helps to support it.

When Paul adds *and all the more with you* to his remark about the *candor and godly sincerity* of his conduct, his point is effectively particularized, and the remainder of the discussion pertains to his relationship to the Corinthians. Here, and again in 2:4, where a similar expression is used, he emphasizes that a special relationship has existed between himself and the Corinthian congregation, and in both instances the effect is to alert the Corinthians to their own responsibility to reciprocate.

Paul does not often show very much self-consciousness about the letters he writes to his congregations; in fact, specific indications about his concern for their effect are confined almost exclusively to the Corinthian correspondence. In v. 13*a* he is looking back over the whole course of that when he insists that he has written—and is now writing—them only what they can easily read and understand. He well knew that previous letters to Corinth had been misunderstood; in 1 Cor 5:9–11 he had had to clarify admonitions contained in a still earlier letter, and in 1 Cor 4:14 he had shown some apprehension that his words might again be misconstrued, and unnecessary offense taken, by the congregation. Yet again, in 1 Cor 9:15, he had tried to forestall the misunderstanding that his comments about not making use of his apostolic rights in Corinth were really designed to obtain them! When taken together, these passages in and of themselves already begin to suggest that someone or some group in Corinth was trying deliberately to turn Paul's letters to the apostle's own disadvantage. This is confirmed by 2 Cor 10:10–11, where Paul refers to certain persons in Corinth (for the wording see NOTES and COMMENT on the passage) who have charged that the letters are not truly representative of his real intentions and capabilities.

Apparently Paul's critics in Corinth have recently had new opportunities to use his letters as evidence against him, and he will proceed directly to clear up two special matters on which he believes he has been misunderstood: (a) the matter of his plans to visit Corinth (1:15–2:2) and (b) the matter of his instructions about disciplining one of the Corinthian brothers (2:3–11). In prospect of having to address himself to these two points, he is first of all making this general affirmation about all his letters; what he writes he means, nothing more and nothing less. The play on words which is achieved by using two different compounds of the Greek verb *ginōskein* ("For we write you nothing other than what you can *apprehend* and also *comprehend*" is a fair approximation; cf. Héring, 8) adds some emphasis to what is being said: if the Corinthians will but give Paul's letters a fair hearing, they will find them clear and straightforward. (Contrast the famous comment on Paul's letters made by a second-century writer, 2 Pet 3:16*b*.)

Paul hopes that the congregation *will understand completely* what it means for him to be their *boast* and for them to be his at the Parousia (vv. 13*b*, 14*b*). This hope goes beyond and is more general than the one implicit in the preceding remark that he writes only what they can understand, and the momentary use of the first person singular suggests that it is deeply felt. The idea that God himself is his people's "boast" (LXX: *kauchēma*) is present in Deut 10:21 and Jer 17:14, and once Judith is called the "great boast of [her] nation" (Jdt 15:9). This "old biblical formula" (Schlatter, 475 n. 1) has been used by Paul, however, in quite an exceptional way to apply to the ultimate interdependence of apostle and congregation. His apostleship has no meaning apart from the congregations which have been brought into existence by the gospel he has preached, and therefore their very existence confirms the authenticity of his apostolic commission (1 Cor 9:2; cf. 2 Cor 3:2–3). In line with this is the conviction that when he shall at last be called to account before God, his ground for "boasting" will not be in himself but in those who have been brought to faith through his gospel; 1 Thess 2:19–20; Phil 2:16; 4:1; cf. 1 Cor 15:31; 2 Cor 7:4. (The boasting about which he writes in 7:14; 8:24; 9:2–3 is of a different sort, however; see NOTES and COMMENT on those passages.)

The other side of this situation is that Paul's congregations may, for their part, look to him as their "boast" on that day. Because he views the matter less often from this angle (apart from the present passage, only in 5:12 and Phil 1:26), it is especially noteworthy that this is the side which is mentioned first, and therefore with some emphasis, here. His point would seem to be that there is more at stake than whether his congregation has a good or bad opinion of his manner of dealing with them. The Corinthians must understand that except for his apostleship—and that means, above all, except for the gospel with which he has been commissioned by God as an apostle—their congregation would not exist at all, and they could not hope to be found to belong to Christ on the day of his coming.

Paul yearns for the congregation's full understanding of the importance of his apostleship to them, even as he acknowledges that they have already understood in part (v. 14*a*). The clauses are not completely balanced, however, because in the secondary one the verb is given its own special object: "as you have understood *us,* " that is, Paul and his associates. Here the general hope that they will recognize the meaning of his apostleship for their salvation (vv. 13*b*, 14*b*) is related to the more specific confidence that now, finally, they have come to some understanding of why he acts as he does toward them. When he writes of his *hope* for their complete understanding of what their salvation involves, and at the same time of the *fact* of their partial understanding of his actions, the implication is that the hope cannot be fulfilled until the points at which they continue to misunderstand his actions and intentions are cleared up. This he sets out to do in the following paragraphs.

## 2. A CANCELED VISIT, 1:15–2:2

1   ¹⁵Since I was confident about this, I was wanting to come to you first so you could have a second benefit; ¹⁶that is, I was wanting to pass through en route to Macedonia and to come back to you again from Macedonia, and by your help to be sent on my way to Judea. ¹⁷Then did I really act irresponsibly when I wanted this? Or do I make such plans opportunistically, so it seems I am saying yes, yes and no, no?

¹⁸As God is faithful, our word to you is not both yes and no. ¹⁹For the Son of God, Jesus Christ, who was preached among you by us— by myself, and also by Silvanus and Timothy—was not "Yes" and "No." Rather, in him it has been an enduring "Yes." ²⁰All the promises of God have their Yes in him; hence, through him as well as through us the "Amen" glorifies God. ²¹The one who is confirming us along with you in Christ and anointed us is God, ²²who also sealed us and gave the Spirit as a down payment in our hearts.

²³I summon God as witness against me: I was sparing you when I did not come again to Corinth. ²⁴This is not to say that we are domineering over your faith; rather, we are co-workers for your joy, because you stand firm in faith. 2   ¹For I had made up my mind about this, not to pay you another sorrowful visit. ²For if I grieve you, then who is there to cheer me except the one who is grieved by me?

## NOTES

1:15. *I.* With the notable exception of vv. 18–22, an excursus on the faithfulness of God, the first person singular predominates from this point through 2:13.

*first . . . second.* Taken by itself, the word order of the Greek would favor associating *first* with *I was wanting* rather than with *to come to you (eboulomēn proteron pros hymas elthein);* thus, *TEV:* "I made plans at first to visit you. . . ." The context, however, seems to require the construction adopted here, as most commentators (as well as some early copyists who adjusted the word order to remove the ambiguity) have recognized. In the following verse Paul says explicitly that he was planning to visit Corinth on his way to Macedonia and then again on his way back from there. This virtually assures that, in v. 15, *first* is written in anticipation of *second;* he was planning to visit Corinth before going on to Macedonia in order that there could be another visit afterward.

*benefit.* Translates *charin,* a well-attested reading. There is also strong support, however, for *charan* ("joy"), which stands in ℵᶜ B and in a number of other mss. It is adopted by some commentators (e.g., Plummer, 32; Bruce, 180; also Webber 1970: 215–16; cf. the *RSV* tr., "pleasure"), but more often it is rejected as a scribal alteration designed to harmonize this verse with 1:24 and 2:3 (cf. Metzger 1971:576). Those who have accepted *charin* as the original reading have not been able to agree on its exact meaning in this context, however. There are at least four possibilities: (1) "Pleasure," thus in effect making the term synonymous with *charan* (Chrysostom, *NPNF,* 1st ser., 288: "By *charin* he here means *charan*"; Hughes, 30–31 n. 6; Héring, 9 and n. 34, who also cites the authority of Bleek for this interpretation). (2) "Kindness" (Barrett, 69 and n. 1), in which case Paul would be thinking of his coming to Corinth as a personal favor to the Christians there. (3) "Grace" (*NAB;* cf. *TEV:* "that you might be blessed twice"), thus virtually equating *charin* with the "spiritual gift" *(charisma pneumatikon)* Paul tells the Roman Christians he wants to share with them when he visits (Rom 1:11). A number of commentators believe this interpretation is the most likely (e.g., Windisch, 63; Lietzmann, 102; Wendland, 170–71; de Boor, 41 and n. 42). (4) "Opportunity for kindness," taking the *charis* to be not something Paul does, as in (2), or brings with him, as in (3), but something the Corinthians can do because Paul comes (Fee 1978, who argues that Paul wanted to give the Corinthians an opportunity to send him on his way, first to Macedonia and then to Judea). None of these possibilities can be ruled out entirely, but (2) and (3) seem the most likely (see COMMENT). The tr. *benefit* (also used by *KJV, RV, NEB, JB,* and *NIV, inter alia*) is itself, like the Greek *charis,* ambiguous enough to bear any one or even several of the suggested meanings.

16. *that is.* Translates *kai,* which is epexegetic here, introducing an explanation of the preceding reference to a "first" and "second" benefit.

*Macedonia.* A region on the Balkan Peninsula which became a Roman senatorial province in 44 C.E. Previously (from 15 C.E.) it had been joined with Moesia (farther to the north) and Achaia (to the south) into one large imperial province. (See Finegan, "Macedonia," *IDB* K–Q:216–17, and Thompson, *IDBSup:*561.) The famed Via Ignatia stretched from east to west across the province, giving it a special role in trade and commerce. Paul's letters to the Philippian and Thessalonian Christians (the latter situated in the administrative center of the province) testify to the importance of the congregations he had founded in Macedonia. According to Acts 17:10–14, the apostle had also found eager hearers in Beroea, and one may presume that a Christian congregation was established there as well. (In Acts 20:4 a certain "Sopater of Beroea" is named as one of Paul's traveling companions.)

*by your help to be sent on my way.* Literally "to be sent on by you," but the Greek verb had evidently become a technical missionary term (Acts 15:3; Rom 15:24; 1 Cor 16:6, 11; Tit 3:13; 3 John 6; Pol Phil 1:1). To help in sending persons on their way could include the provision not only of escorts (Acts 20:38; 21:5) but of everything else necessary for the journey (Tit 3:13; 3 John 6–8), perhaps including letters of recommendation (cf. 1 Esdr 4:47; 1 Mac 12:4; and NOTES and COMMENT on 2 Cor 3:1).

*Judea.* The old kingdom of Judah, that part of southern Palestine which lies roughly from the Mediterranean coast on the west to the Dead Sea on the east, and from slightly north of Jerusalem southward to Idumaea. In 6 C.E., Archelaus, Herod's eldest son, was deposed from his rule over this and the adjoining areas of Samaria and Idumaea. Although the Roman governors in the province of Syria had overseen affairs in Judea during Herod's time, Augustus decided against incorporating Judea into the older province and constituted it instead as an independent province. Whereas Syria was governed by a member of the senatorial order, an equestrian governor was appointed to Judea (a "prefect," from the time of Claudius called a "procurator"). Under the Romans the seat of government and the governor's normal residence became Caesarea (Maritima), although Jerusalem remained the province's largest city. Thus, Acts reports that Paul, after his arrest in Jerusalem, had to be taken to Caesarea in order to appear before Felix, then procurator over Judea (23:23–24). Paul's own references to "Judea," however, seem to have Jerusalem especially in view, as in the present verse (see also Rom 15:31; Gal 1:22; cf. 1 Thess 2:14). The same usage is sometimes evident in Acts (12:19; 15:1; 28:21). See Stern, "The Province of Judea," *CRINT* I/1:308–76.

17. *Then did I really.* The *mēti* in Greek shows that only a negative answer to Paul's question is appropriate, and the *ara,* translated here as "really," presupposes either a thought some may have harbored about Paul or a claim they have actually made about him which he now wishes to refute. Rhetorical questions like the two in this verse are a familiar part of Paul's epistolary style and invariably communicate a sense of the writer's special involvement with the point at hand. In chaps. 1–9 such questions are present only in the first two main sections (in addition to the present verse see 2:2, 16*b;* 3:1*a, b,* 7–8); in chaps. 10–13 they are more numerous (11:7, 11*a,* 22*a, c, e,* 23*a,* 29*a, b;* 12:13*a,* 15*b,* 18*b, c, d,* 19*a;* 13:5*c*).

*irresponsibly.* Translates *elaphria,* which describes action which is flippant and insincere. The noun occurs only here in the NT, but Paul uses the adjective *elaphros* in 4:17 (translated there as "trifling").

*opportunistically.* Literally "according to the flesh," which would mean "in a worldly manner," with a view only to what is personally expedient. See NOTES on 5:16.

*so it seems.* This interprets Paul's conjunction *(hina)* as consecutive rather than final, an instance of the substitution of *hina* for the infinitive of result in Hellenistic Greek; BDF § 391(5); Burton 1898: § 218; BAG s.v. II, 2. The reference is to an unintended consequence, not to a specific purpose.

*yes, yes and no, no.* P⁴⁶ (also the corrector of an eleventh-century minuscule, the Vulgate, and Pelagius) reads simply "yes and no." Some argue that the shorter reading is original and that the reading adopted here resulted from assimilation to the wording of Matt 5:37 and Jas 5:12 (e.g., Kümmel, 197). It is more likely, however, that the shorter reading is a secondary assimilation to v. 19 in this same context (e.g., Metzger 1971:576; Barrett, 69 n. 3). According to van Unnik (1953:219), this longer text could represent an Aramaism and have an iterative meaning: "constantly yes and constantly no." Hahn (1973a:234–37), however, would reject the longer text in favor of a conjectured "so that my 'yes' was 'yes and no,' " since he perceives this sort of a contrast in vv. 18–20. With the longer text, cf. especially Gnatho's self-description in Terence, *The Eunuch* 251–53. "Whatever they say I praise; if again they say the opposite, I praise that too. If one says no, I say no; if one says yes, I say yes. In fact I have given orders to myself to agree with them in everything." P. Marshall (1980:492–93) has noted that this passage from Terence is cited by Cicero (*On Friendship* xxv.93) when he is describing the kind of flattery that undermines true friendship.

18. *As God is faithful.* The same Greek phrase *(pistos de ho Theos)* occurs elsewhere as a simple description of God: "God is faithful" (1 Cor 1:9, 10:13; 1 Thess 5:24; 2 Thess 3:3). Plummer, 34, argues for the same meaning here; cf. Stählin 1962:131, who suggests it is "less an oath-formula than a confessional formula. . . ." In this case, however, the phrase is followed by a *hoti*-clause (as it is not in the other instances). It should be interpreted, then, as an oath formula (so also, e.g., Windisch, 66; Lietzmann, 103; Bultmann, 43). No two Pauline oaths are identical; in addition to the other one in this same passage (v. 23), see Rom 1:9; 9:1; 2 Cor 2:10; 11:10, 11, 31; Gal 1:20; Phil 1:8; 1 Thess 2:5, 10.

*our word to you.* In view of the verse that follows, the plural here must be a real one, referring to Paul and his associates, and the *word (logos)* must be their missionary preaching. The function of the solemn asseveration of this verse is to refute the idea that Paul had not been perfectly straightforward with the Corinthians about his plans. Thus, van Unnik is right in seeing here an instance of the familiar form of argument, "from the greater to the lesser," and in noting that *logos* can refer to the "word" about Paul's travel plans as well as to his missionary preaching (1953:218).

19. *the Son of God, Jesus Christ.* This combination of titles appears nowhere else in Paul's letters; in fact, Paul's references to Jesus as God's "Son" are relatively infrequent. In the other two places where the full title "Son of God" appears, he is quoting or adapting a traditional formulation (Rom 1:4; Gal 2:20); for the full statistics and a discussion of Paul's use of the title, see Kramer 1966:183–89. *Son of God* has perhaps been introduced by Paul into the present verse in order to emphasize Christ's relationship to the God by whose faithfulness he has just sworn (v. 18); ibid.:50 n. 110.

*was preached.* Paul uses a passive form of the verb *kēryssein* elsewhere only at 1 Cor 15:12.

*by myself, and also by.* This tr. seeks to reflect the subtle but significant nuance conveyed by the Greek. As Windisch, 67, points out, in identifying the preceding *us* by whom the gospel had been preached in Corinth, the apostle seems deliberately to have avoided the simple listing of names, "Paul, Silvanus, and Timothy." There is thus a special emphasis placed on Paul's role. See COMMENT.

*Silvanus.* A Latinized form of the name "Silas" and doubtless to be identified with the Silas of Acts. "Silas" is itself the Aramaic form of the Hebrew name "Saul." Silvanus was from Jerusalem (Acts 15:22, 27), was known as a "prophet" (Acts 15:32), and had been with Paul in Syria, several districts in Asia Minor and Macedonia (Acts 15:40–17:10), as well as in Corinth (Acts 17:15; 18:5). In 1 Thess 1:1 he is listed as one of the co-senders of that letter, probably written from Corinth (cf. 2 Thess 1:1). The reference to him in 1 Pet 5:12 as the amanuensis of that letter suggests that he was also known to have been associated in some way with Peter, but there is no hint of this either in Acts or in the Pauline letters. See Shroyer, "Silas," *IDB* R–Z:351–52.

*Timothy.* See COMMENT on 1:1. Although Silvanus and Timothy had not been with

Paul when he first arrived in Corinth, they soon joined him there (Acts 18:1–5; 1 Thess 1:1, from·Corinth). It is probably to their association with him in this initial period of work in the city that the present verse refers.

*it has been an enduring "Yes."* Literally "it has been 'Yes.'" This tr. seeks to bring out the force of the perfect tense *gegonen,* which, given the context, indicates the unchanging character of God's dealing with his people (vv. 18, 20).

20. *the promises of God.* The same phrase (according to the most likely reading) occurs in Gal 3:21, where Paul is thinking of God's promise to Abraham and his descendants. Compare Josephus, *Antiquities* III.i.5, who refers to "the promises from God" *(hai epangeliai hai para tou Theou)* which Moses received on the people's behalf. The singular, "promise," is more usual for Paul, and the reference is almost always to the story of Abraham and Sarah (Rom 4:13, 14, 16, 20; 9:7, 8; Gal 3:14, 16–18, 22, 29; 4:23, 28). In the present case, however, the reference is more general, as also in Rom 9:4 ("the promises" are among those things which belong uniquely to the Israelites) and 15:8 ("the promises given to the patriarchs"—*RSV*).

*through him as well as through us.* The whole second half of v. 20 is difficult to translate. This rendering seeks to do justice to the *di' autou . . . di' hēmōn (through him . . . through us)* and at the same time to make it clear that the topic is still *Jesus Christ* (v. 19). The plural *us* is broader in scope here than it had been in v. 19, where it had included only Paul and his associates (against Cranfield 1982:286). Now the Corinthian congregation is also included, as the "you . . . us" distinction of v. 19 is left behind (it will reappear momentarily in v. 21*a*).

*the "Amen."* See 1 Cor 14:16, where Paul also uses the substantive, and where it is clear that the reference is to a liturgical acclamation. In synagogue worship, from which the Christian practice derived, the "Amen" was spoken as the congregational assent to benedictions, the praise of God; it was not employed as the conclusion to prayers. See Delling 1962:71–75; Schlier, *TDNT* I:335–38. In Rev 3:14, Jesus is called "the Amen, the faithful and true witness" *(RSV)*—perhaps an echo of Isa 65:16.

*glorifies God.* The Greek is literally "to God for glory." This English tr. interprets the reference to be to a liturgical act of praise by which glory is ascribed to God and then confirmed with the "Amen." The practice seems to be reflected in several of the doxologies found in Paul's letters and elsewhere in the NT: Gal 1:5; Phil 4:20; 1 Tim 1:17; 2 Tim 4:18; Heb 13:21; 1 Pet 4:11; 2 Pet 3:18; Jude 25; Rev 1:6; 7:12. On the syntax and translation of the verse, see E. Hill 1961:298–99.

21. *is confirming.* The present tense of the participle is striking, since the three participles which follow in vv. 21–22 are all aorist (past tense). The cognate adjective had been used in v. 7 ("certain"), and Paul uses forms of the verb in Rom 15:8; 1 Cor 1:6, 8. The technical use of the word to refer to a seller's confirmation of a sale has been amply documented (see, e.g., Deissmann 1903:104–9; Schlier, *TDNT* I:600–3). The term had been used in a religious sense in oriental Gnosticism—e.g., Odes Sol 38:17, "For I was established and lived and was redeemed, And my foundations were laid on account of the Lord's hand" (Charlesworth 1977:132). Dinkler 1962:178 notes that the synonym "to establish" *(stērizein)* apparently had a fixed place in the baptismal liturgy of Valentinian Gnosticism (cf. Irenaeus, *Against Heresies* I.xxi.3).

*us along with you in Christ.* As in v. 19, Paul distinguishes himself and his associates *(us)* from the Corinthians *(you),* but now only in order to emphasize that God is confirming them all in Christ. The meaning is not that Paul and his colleagues are being certified *to* the Corinthians but that all of them together *(hēmas syn hymin)* are being incorporated *into* the body of Christ *(eis Christon)*. This affirmed, Paul reverts in the rest of v. 21 and in v. 22 to the fully inclusive "us" and "our." Contrast the view of Kijne (1966:176–77), who believes that *us* in vv. 21*b*–22 continues to refer only to Paul and his associates. Strachan, 59–60, follows Moffatt's tr., which renders the Greek plural as "me" and holds that the apostle is referring to himself in particular.

*and anointed us.* The Greek verb is *chriein,* and it is possible that Paul intends a play upon the name *Christos,* to which it is juxtaposed; in Luke 4:18; Acts 4:27; 10:38; Heb 1:9 the verb is used of the messianic anointing of Jesus. Paul himself uses the verb nowhere else. The noun *chrisma* appears in 1 John 2:20, 27 with reference to the anointing of believers with the Holy Spirit. The practice of an actual anointing with oil at the time of baptism is not certainly attested until the late second century; see, e.g., Tertullian, *On Baptism,* who not incidentally remarks on the etymological connection between "chrism" and "Christ." The connection between "chrism" and "Christians" is noted by Theophilus of Antioch: "Wherefore we are called Christians on this account, because we are anointed with the oil of God" (*To Autolycus* I.xii; tr. Grant 1970:17). See Dinkler 1962:180–83.

22. *who also.* In Greek *kai* introduces two further participles *(sealed . . . and gave)* which add to what has been said about God in v. 21; the phrase is thus appositional (Schlatter, 482).

*sealed us.* The verb *(sphragizein)* is also used by Paul in Rom 15:28, the noun *(sphragis)* in Rom 4:11; 1 Cor 9:2. The use of the verb in Eph 1:13; 4:30 is more important for understanding the present verse, however, because in Eph, as here, it is used metaphorically of the gift of the Spirit by which the believer is marked and claimed as God's own and "for the day of redemption" (Eph 4:30, *RSV*). See COMMENT. By the time of Hermas and 2 Clem (second century) the "seal" of the Christian was being identified specifically with Christian baptism (Herm Sim, IX 16:3–5; 2 Clem 7:6; 8:6, cf. 6:9); see Lampe 1951, especially 103–6, and Donfried 1974:124–28. Dinkler 1962: 183–88 discusses the possibility of an actual rite, known already in Paul's day, by which one was "sealed" at baptism.

*the Spirit.* The first of several references to the Holy Spirit in chaps. 1–9; see also 3:3, 6, 8, 17, 18; 4:13; 5:5; 6:6. In chaps. 10–13 the only two certain instances are in 11:4 and 13:13[14]; cf. 12:18 and NOTES.

*as a down payment.* The noun *(arrabōn),* a loanword from the Semitic, also appears in 5:5 and in Eph 1:13; in all three instances it is associated with the Spirit. The latter passage shows clearly that the genitive "of the Spirit" *(tou Pneumatos)* must be interpreted appositionally; the Spirit itself is given—thus the tr. provided here, *as a down payment* (Barrett, 80). In the LXX (Gen 38:17, 18, 20) *down payment* is used of a "pledge" *(RSV)* given as security and therefore due to be returned. Otherwise, however, it appears especially in the Greek commercial papyri as a technical term for the first installment of a total amount due (examples in MM s.v.). As such, it functions both to establish the contractual obligation and to guarantee its fulfillment. For further comments on the term, see M. Barth 1974:96–97. In Eph 1:13–14, as in the present passage, the idea of the Spirit as a *down payment* is linked with the idea of its being that by which the believer is *sealed.* See COMMENT.

*in our hearts.* The phrase is equivalent to *hēmin,* "to us," which is the term Paul actually uses in 5:5. Cf. Rom 5:5, where Paul writes of God's love "poured out into our hearts through the Holy Spirit which has been given to us," and Gal 4:6, where the reference is to "the Spirit of [God's] Son" sent "into our hearts, crying, 'Abba! Father!' " *(RSV).*

23. *I summon God as witness.* The first person singular of vv. 15–17 is now resumed in this oath formula. The emphatic *I (egō . . . epikaloumai),* as well as the solemnity of the oath itself, shows Paul's awareness of the criticisms which have been made of him—namely, that he has not been serious and considerate in his intentions with respect to the Corinthians. Paul also invokes God as his witness in Rom 1:9; Phil 1:8; 1 Thess 2:5, 10; cf. 2 Cor 11:31; 12:19; Gal 1:20. Such LXX passages as 1 Sam 12:5–6; 20:23; Jer 49(42):5 illustrate the general type of oath (on which see Pope, *IDB* K–Q:575–77, with bibliog.), but the name "Lord" is used in these instances—not *God,* as in the Pauline passages (in 1 Sam 12:5–6 also "the anointed one," *christos*). The formula used by Paul in the present verse is closer to Greek usage (examples from Polybius, Galen, Heliodorus, and Plato in Windisch, 74). There are some close parallels in Hellenistic-Jewish sources, notably the Jewish prayer of vengeance in the Rheneia inscriptions (Deissmann 1927:413–24) and Josephus' description of oath-taking in *Antiquities* I.xvi.1 ("they summon God as witness of their intentions," *epikalountai ton Theon martyra tōn esomenōn;* Schlatter, 484 n. 1, but with the wrong section of *Antiquities* I). Stählin (1962:132) notes the report of Josephus that oaths were strictly forbidden among the Essenes: "Any word of theirs has more force than an oath; swearing they avoid, regarding it as worse than perjury, for they say that one who is not believed without an appeal to God stands accused already" *(War* II.viii.6). See also Matt 5:33–37.

*against me.* The Greek *(epi tēn emēn psychēn)* could be rendered more literally "upon my own [taking *emēn* as reflexive, *GNTG* III:191] life." The use of *epi* following *epikaloumai* is also exhibited in the Rheneia inscriptions (see preceding note). The force of the *epi* is to call down the wrath of God upon oneself in the case of one's having spoken falsely. A similar self-imprecation from an inscription of the Augustan period (Asia Minor) is cited by Deissmann 1927:304: one who has taken an oath says, in case he violates it, "I pronounce a curse against myself [*kat' emou*], my body, soul, goods, children, etc."

*I was sparing you.* Compare 13:2, "If I come again, I will not be lenient," and NOTES and COMMENT there.

*when I did not come again.* The aorist verb *(ēlthon)* shows that Paul's reference is to a specific visit (see Barrett, 84), in this case a visit which had been planned but which had not taken place (vv. 15–16; 2:1). Manson (1962:213–14 n. 1) regards the word *ouketi* (translated here as *not . . . again*) as one of the "small indications" that the trip referred to is the return phase of the projected double visit referred to in vv. 15–16. It is more likely, however, that the double visit was canceled entirely; see COMMENT.

24. *This is not to say.* The Greek *(ouch hoti)* is elliptical, literally "Not that"; as elsewhere, it marks what follows as more or less parenthetical. It invariably introduces a clarification of what has preceded, designed to ward off a false inference from it. Other occurrences in the Pauline letters include 2 Cor 7:9; Phil 4:17 (both formulated *ouch hoti . . . alla,* as in the present verse) and 2 Cor 3:5; Phil 3:12; 4:11 (without a following

*alla*). Otherwise in the NT: John 7:22; 12:6; 2 Thess 3:9 (with *alla*) and John 6:46 (without *alla*). John 7:22 demonstrates effectively the parenthetical character of statements so introduced, and John 12:6 shows that the expression may usually be supplemented best with a verb of saying. See BDF § 480(5); Robertson 1923:1429.

*we are domineering.* In Rom 6:9, 14, Paul uses the same verb *(kyrieuein)* of the binding power of death and sin, respectively, which is broken and replaced by the liberating power of God. In Rom 7:1 the verb is used of the constraints of law. In the present verse it refers to the high-handed way a person may deal with others. Note the use of the first person plural again in this one clarifying (and therefore somewhat parenthetical) sentence.

*over your faith.* The verb *(kyrieuein)* requires the genitive *(hymōn;* see BDF § 177), to which Paul appends a reference to faith *(tēs pisteōs);* thus, perhaps, "over you in relation to your faith."

*we are co-workers.* One of Paul's most typical descriptions of his associates (of Timothy, Rom 16:21 [but not in 1 Thess 3:2; see note on "working together," 6:1]; of Titus, 2 Cor 8:23; of Prisca and Aquila, Rom 16:3; of Urbanus, Rom 16:9; of Epaphroditus, Phil 2:25; of Clement and others, Phil 4:3; of Philemon, Phlm 1; of Mark, Aristarchus, Demas, and Luke, Phlm 24; of Apollos, 1 Cor 3:9; otherwise only in Col 4:11; 3 John 8). If, in the present verse, Paul is referring to the whole congregation as his *co-workers,* the reference would be unique (see especially 1 Cor 3:9 and Phil 2:25, where Paul and his "co-worker" are clearly distinguished from the addressees; in Phlm 1 one of several addressees is called Paul's "co-worker"). It is more likely that the first person plural does not include the Corinthians, but only Paul, Silvanus, and Timothy (v. 19; so also Ellis 1971:440 n. 1). It would thereby correspond with the subject of *domineering* and with the references to *your faith* and *your joy.* See COMMENT.

*you stand firm.* The verb is in the perfect tense *(hestēkate),* "you have stood and continue to stand firm." Compare the use of the same form in 1 Cor 15:1, there with reference to the Corinthians' having received and stood firm in the gospel.

*in faith.* As almost all commentators agree, the dative *tē pistei* should be interpreted as local ("in the sphere of"), not as instrumental. On the latter view (adopted by Filson, 292; Barrett, 84–85), Paul would be affirming that it is "by faith" that the Corinthians continue to stand firm (see Rom 11:20), not by apostolic coercion. It is doubtful, however, whether this meaning should be assigned to the dative unless it is indicated by the context; where the dative is clearly instrumental (Rom 3:28; 5:2 [if *tē pistei* be the correct reading]; 11:20; Gal 2:20) the discussion is about the law and justification. This is not the topic here or anywhere else in 2 Cor. It is thus preferable to interpret the dative here as local. In 1 Cor 16:13 the Corinthians are exhorted to "stand firm" in their faith; in 1 Cor 8:7, as in the present passage, their faith is commended. For other instances of the dative with a local meaning, see 13:5; Rom 4:19–20; 14:1; Phil 1:27 (also Col 1:23; 2:7).

**2:1.** *For.* Translates *gar* (P⁴⁶ B, etc.), although the well-supported *de* (ℵ A C, etc.) cannot be ruled out. The reading adopted here (also by Plummer, 46; Kümmel, 198) is defended by Metzger 1971:576, because 2:1 neither supplements nor offers a contrast to 1:24, but gives Paul's reason for not having visited the Corinthians (1:23). Since 1:24 is parenthetical, the present verse does seem to be connected with 1:23, making the reading *gar* slightly preferable (see Barrett's comments, 72 n. 1; Windisch, 77 n. 2, writing before the availability of P⁴⁶, suggests that the substitution of *gar* for *de* in some mss. occurred under the influence of 1 Cor 2:2).

*1.* Paul returns now to the first person singular of 1:15–17, 23; his main thought is resumed.

*had made up my mind.* The verb *(ekrina)* is aorist tense and stands in contrast to the verb *(eboulomēn,* imperfect) Paul had used in 1:15. Paul *was wanting* to visit Corinth on his way to and from Macedonia (1:15–16); but after carefully weighing the pros and cons he decided that he ought not to make another troubling visit (2:1). Cf. the use of this verb in 5:14; 1 Cor 2:2; 7:37; 10:15; 11:13. On the use here of the *dativus commodi (ekrina . . . emautō),* see *GNTG* III:238, although Windisch, 78, allows that *emautō* may also be used here with the meaning *par' emautō.*

*about this.* Translates *touto,* used here as elsewhere to introduce something a writer regards as especially important. Other examples in Paul's letters include Rom 14:13; 1 Cor 7:37 (both with the verb *krinein,* as here); also, e.g., 1 Cor 15:50; 2 Cor 13:9, see BDF § 290(3).

*another sorrowful visit.* Literally, and adhering to the Greek word order, "not again in pain to you to come." Some (e.g., Heinrici, 86–87; Batey 1965:144–45) have argued that "again" is to be construed only with "to . . . come"; thus Paul's decision not to come again to Corinth, which would *this time* certainly result "in pain." The word order allows this construction, but it is not the most natural one. Moreover, the emphasis here, as Windisch, 78, has observed, is on a potentially sorrowful (literally "painful") visit, and it would be odd if the preceding word *(palin,* "again," represented by *another* in the present tr.) was not meant to be taken with it. Paul must have in mind at least one previous visit that was "painful." For the concept of "pain" (Greek *lypē*), see Bultmann, *TDNT* IV:313–24. In the present context the thought is not of physical pain but of emotional and spiritual distress; hence the tr. of *en lupē* as *sorrowful.* The Greek *en* is equivalent to the Semitic *be,* literally "with"—that is, "bringing distress" (Bultmann, 49; Héring, 14; Gulin 1932:264 n. 1 refers to Paul's use of this same idiom in 1 Cor 4:21; Rom 15:29). This meaning is confirmed by v. 2.

*2. if I grieve you.* The pronoun is emphasized *(egō lypō);* Meyer, 440; Plummer, 48. Meyer believes Paul contrasts himself with those who had a less intimate relationship with the Corinthians, but it is more likely that Paul has in mind his proper role of working for the *joy* of his congregation (1:24). Thus, "If *I,* who am one of the co-workers for your *joy,* grieve you . . ."

*then.* Represents the introductory *kai* which opens the apodosis by presuming the circumstances set forth in the protasis; see BDF § 442(8).

*who is there.* The Greek phrase is elliptical, and "is" must be supplied (as it was by some ancient copyists).

*to cheer me.* For the contrast between being "grieved" and "cheered" see, e.g., Philo, *On Abraham* 207. Héring would place a question mark after these words, but that does not seem to be justified. See following note.

*except.* Translates *ei mē.* Héring, 14, believes the usual tr. of v. 2 yields "a bizarre notion," and that it is more satisfactory to take this last phrase as Paul's response to the question, "For if I make you sad, who then will make me glad?" The answer would be: "Certainly not the one who has been plunged into sorrow by me." But this requires taking *ei mē* in an unusual sense ("Certainly not"); such a meaning is possible after a solemn vow (examples in BDF § 454[5]; cf. BAG s.v. *ei,* IV), but such is not present here. Moreover, the usual tr. produces a quite intelligible thought; see COMMENT.

*the one who is grieved.* No specific individual is in mind. The singular participles in this verse are used substantively to refer to "the representative Corinthian" (Barrett, 86) who gives joy *(ho euphrainōn)* or who is *grieved (ho lypoumenos).* So also Meyer, 441; Plummer, 48; Windisch, 79; Allo, 34.

## COMMENT: GENERAL

In 1:15–2:13, Paul is facing a matter which he knows to be of considerable concern to his readers. The report Titus had brought about affairs in the Corinthian congregation had been a generally encouraging one. Titus had been well received there and could speak favorably of the Corinthians' "obedience" and of their "longing" for Paul (e.g., 7:7, 15). At the same time, however, Paul had learned that at least some members of the congregation had taken affront at a letter he had sent them (7:8). For this reason the profession of concern and love for the Corinthian Christians with which the present letter opens (1:12–2:13) must also take account of the questions which have been raised about Paul's actions.

One learns from 1:15–2:2 that the letter in question was really only one part of the difficulty. To compound the matter, that letter had been sent in lieu of a personal visit the apostle had promised to make. The cancellation of the visit, plus the receipt of a letter which some had interpreted as overly severe, had occasioned the impression that Paul was both undependable and indifferent to the feelings of his congregation. For this reason, Paul is concerned to review the matter of the planned visit and to explain why it had been canceled. He is well aware that the broader issue is that of his own personal dependability, and that the most important issue is his credibility as an authentic apostle. The recognition of this prompts him to a somewhat ponderous excursus on the faithfulness of the God of Jesus Christ (1:18–22) in whose service he stands.

## COMMENT: DETAILED

### *The Planned Visit, 1:15–17*

The apostle's comments here presuppose what one actually learns only further on (v. 23b), namely, that a planned trip to Corinth had been called off. They also presuppose that Paul's failure to come as promised had resulted in some criticism of him. Because he is aware of this, and because it is his own integrity and credibility as an apostle that is at stake, beginning with these verses Paul switches from the first person plural to the first person singular. He alone has to answer for the change in plans which has displeased the

Corinthians. In responding to their displeasure, the apostle emphasizes why the visit had been projected at all. It had been predicated on the mutual respect and trust which he presumed—and presumes—to exist between them and him (see v. 15), and from it they were to have derived a double *benefit* (v. 15). In speaking of a twofold benefit, Paul is alluding to the projected form of the visit, as v. 16 shows. It was actually to have been a double visit, since he had planned to be in Corinth both going to and coming from Macedonia.

The word translated here as *benefit* is used often by Paul to refer to the "grace" (Greek *charis*) of God (e.g., 6:1; 8:1), especially as it is present for righteousness and life to those who have faith in Christ (e.g., Rom 5:15–17). Paul's own claim to apostolic status rests solely upon his conviction that he had been called to faith and sent out to preach the gospel of Christ by God's grace (12:9; 1 Cor 15:8–10; Gal 1:15; 2:9; Rom 1:5; 12:3; 15:15–16). This is the basis on which he has been able to tell his readers, just a few sentences earlier, that his conduct, especially toward them, has been governed "not by any ordinary wisdom but by the grace of God" (v. 12). It is likely that the *benefit* he had wanted the Corinthians to have would have included at least the spiritual advantages to be gained from any apostolic visit. It is legitimate, then, to compare Rom 1:11, where Paul hopes to take a "spiritual gift" to the Roman church, and Rom 15:29, where he says he will come to Rome with "the blessing of Christ," with the comment in v. 15.

Fee's objection that this view implies a "latent egotism and condescension" on Paul's part (1978:535) has force only if one forgets Paul's deep-seated conviction that he is an apostle only by God's grace. Fee has also objected to this view on the grounds that Paul had only planned to pass through Corinth, not to stay and minister there. But the distinction he makes between these two kinds of visit (ibid.:537) is quite artificial, as 1 Cor 16:5–7 (cf. 1 Cor 4:19) shows. Moreover, Fee's own interpretation of the present passage (see NOTES) undervalues the statement in v. 15 that Paul wanted to go *to* the Corinthians *(pros hymas elthein)* and overvalues the remark in v. 16 that he would be *pass[ing] through en route to Macedonia.* It is not impossible that Paul could also have been thinking of the opportunity the Corinthians would have to minister to his needs and send him on his way, but there is nothing in the text that requires this interpretation, and certainly nothing that suggests it is the apostle's main point. The other two interpretations which have been suggested for Paul's meaning here (see NOTES) may be similarly assessed. It is not impossible that he is thinking partly of the personal "kindness" he would have been doing the Corinthians or of the "pleasure" they would have derived from his visit. But Paul would have understood both of these as inseparably related to the grace of God operative in and through his apostolic ministry to them. Cf. Bultmann's comments on the point, 41–42, and also Phil 1:25–26, where Paul writes of his "coming" to the Philippians as his bringing them "joy *in the faith*" and enabling them "to glory *in Christ Jesus*" *(RSV)*.

When and under what conditions had this double visit been planned? Had the first part of it actually been carried out, so that only the second part of the visit, the one to have occurred on the way back from Macedonia, had been called off? And how does this plan for a double visit relate to the plan for a visit projected in 1 Cor 16:5–9? Any reconstruction of the course of Paul's ministry in, and letters to, the Corinthian congregation has to consider these questions, to which unfortunately there are no certain answers. The overall reconstruction of Paul's Corinthian ministry and correspondence adopted in this commentary is presented in the INTRODUCTION (pp. 54–55). The points which relate most directly to the present verses may be recapitulated as follows.

1. In the summer or early fall of 54, while he is resident in Ephesus, Paul dispatches Timothy to Macedonia and Corinth, intending to follow the same itinerary himself at a later date (1 Cor 16:5–9).

2. Later in the fall of 54, Paul writes to the Corinthians in response to a letter received from them (Letter B), and in the process asks them to receive Timothy cordially when he arrives from Macedonia (1 Cor 16:10–11). Paul now plans to remain in Ephesus at least until Pentecost, though he still intends to visit his congregations in Macedonia and Corinth, and anticipates the possibility that he will spend the next winter (of 55–56) with the Corinthians (1 Cor 16:5–6, 8). Whether from Corinth he will be going to Jerusalem, with the group that has been accredited to take a collection to the church there, is not yet clear to him; but he is prepared to if necessary (1 Cor 16:3–4).

3. Timothy reaches Corinth in the spring of 55, and upon his arrival finds a very difficult situation confronting him in the congregation. Presumably, all the problems to which Letter B had been directed are very much in evidence, rendering Timothy's original mission (which may have included promotion of the collection for Jerusalem) all but impossible to fulfill. Under these circumstances, Timothy takes his leave and hurries on to Ephesus.

4. Confronted by Timothy's alarming report, Paul decides that he himself must go at once to Corinth. The sea-lanes between the two cities are now busy with spring traffic, and passage is easily arranged. Within a few days he is in Corinth, on his second visit to the city. But this one, which he will later describe as "sorrowful" (2 Cor 2:1–2), accomplishes nothing, and he, too, returns quickly to Ephesus.

5. Before leaving Corinth, Paul decides that his original plan to go to Macedonia this coming summer, and from there to Corinth in the fall (1 Cor 16:5), needs to be revised. Unless conditions in the Corinthian congregation improve, there is little prospect of the Corinthians' completing the collection for Jerusalem he had expected them to have ready upon his arrival (1 Cor 16:1–4). It will be better if he returns to Corinth on his way to Macedonia, straightens things out there, and then comes back to Corinth from Macedonia as originally planned. This is the itinerary to which reference is made in 2 Cor 1:15–16, and which would have involved a "double visit" to the Corinthians.

Thus, the *first* in v. 15 may signify both "first, before Macedonia," and "a first visit before a second one." It is noteworthy, also, that the revised itinerary includes a trip to Judea (v. 16). This means that at some point after writing 1 Cor, Paul determined that he himself would have to make the trip to Jerusalem with the collection he had been raising among his congregations.

6. Back in Ephesus, pained and frustrated by his brief and inconclusive emergency visit to Corinth, Paul sends the congregation a letter which he later describes as having been written out of a bittersweet mixture of anguish and love (2 Cor 2:4). The salutary effects of this letter, now lost, are subsequently reported to Paul by Titus when the two later meet in Macedonia (see 2 Cor 7:8–13*a*). However, in that same letter the Corinthians learn that Paul's travel plans have once more been revised. He will not be coming to Corinth straight from Ephesus after all. This letter substitutes for that visit. He will go first to Macedonia, as he had originally planned. His arrival in Corinth will be some weeks or even months later than they have been expecting, and there will be no "double visit" at all. This news is not well received by the Corinthians, and their displeasure is evidently conveyed to Paul by Titus when the two meet in Macedonia, probably early in the fall of 55.

Judging from the rhetorical questions posed by the apostle in 2 Cor 1:17, Paul's change of plans has provoked the charge that he is trying to win friends by flattery: He agreed to the "double visit" when it seemed that the Corinthians wanted it, but he had no real intention of carrying out his promise. This is the kind of charge typically brought against "flatterers" by Greek and Roman writers (P. Marshall 1980:123–28, 491)—namely, that they are quite eager to second the opinions of those whose favor they seek, saying yes and no out of a concern to please and not because they mean it (see Terence, *The Eunuch* 251–53, quoted in NOTES).

It may be that Paul's change of plans was also interpreted in Corinth as one more indication of his partiality toward the churches of Macedonia. The lingering resentment in Corinth against the Macedonians could have dated from the founding of the Corinthian congregation. Paul had specifically declined to accept any financial support from the Corinthians (see 1 Cor 9:3–18), but he had gratefully received such support from the Macedonians (2 Cor 11:9), the Philippians in particular (Phil 4:15). From the beginning, then, some in Corinth might have taken umbrage at Paul's high praise of the Macedonian churches and interpreted that as an intentional belittling of their own church. Paul himself eventually becomes aware of the Corinthians' feelings in the matter and tries to counteract them (2 Cor 11:7–11). Earlier, however, he seems to have had no awareness of the problem. In the process of raising the collection for Jerusalem he had even sought to foster a spirit of friendly competition between the churches of Macedonia and those of Achaia, including Corinth (2 Cor 8:1–7; 9:1–5). Indeed, had Paul been alert to the Corinthians' feelings about the Macedonians, he might not have decided to cancel the first part of his promised double visit to their city. As it was, when the news came that he would be going to the Macedonians first after all, it could have been used by some in Corinth as proof that his yes's and no's were those of a flatterer, whose promises could not be trusted.

### The Faithfulness of God, 1:18–22

This paragraph is set apart both formally and materially from its immediate context in 1:15–2:2. It is formally distinct because of Paul's temporary reversion to the first person plural, and it is materially distinct because it momentarily leaves behind the specific issue of Paul's revised itinerary. Now the focus is on the faithfulness of God and the fulfillment of his promises in Jesus Christ. It is possible, then, to describe it as a kind of theological excursus. At the same time, however, this paragraph is an integral part of the larger discussion about Paul's canceled visit. Significantly, the apostle has chosen to use a theological argument to defend himself against charges of thoughtless and opportunistic behavior. His response is not to say, "Trust me! I know what I'm doing and it's for your good." Rather, he is saying, in effect, "Trust God! His promises have been fulfilled in Christ, and our faithfulness in dealing with you has been assured by our preaching of Christ to you."

The opening sentence of this paragraph (v. 18) effects a transition from Paul's outright dismissal of the criticisms of him (v. 17) to his appeal to the meaning of the gospel he has preached in Corinth (v. 19). In view of vv. 15–17, *our word to you* would most naturally be interpreted as a reference to Paul's promise that he would come to Corinth two more times, on the way to and from Macedonia. That was a promise he had fully intended to keep. Moreover, it had not been made casually or deceitfully. On the other hand, in view of v. 19, *our word to you* would most naturally be interpreted as a reference to the gospel which Paul and his associates had preached on their very first visit to Corinth. It was the gospel of Christ, and in Christ all the profoundest promises imaginable have already been fulfilled. In fact, then, the phrase *our word to you* has a twofold reference. Paul believes that his "word" about such practical matters as itineraries and visits is guaranteed by the dependability of the "word" of the gospel with which he has been entrusted. God himself stands behind that word; and as God's faithfulness is sure, so is that of those whom he has commissioned to preach Christ. Paul makes a similar point in 3:1–6. Thus, the appeal to God's faithfulness (v. 18*a*) is not a mere formality. It not only lends solemnity to what follows—it also identifies the theme of the entire paragraph.

In v. 19, Paul is making two points which, taken together, show how this apparent digression on the faithfulness of God is actually an integral part of his response to those who would question his reliability. In the first place, he reminds the Corinthians of that preaching by which faith had been established among them; it was the preaching of *the Son of God, Jesus Christ.* Paul had also summarized his missionary preaching in Corinth in an earlier letter to the congregation. In one place he had formulated it as "Jesus Christ and him crucified" (1 Cor 2:2), and in another he had relied on a traditional creedal statement in which the accent was, again, on Christ's death (1 Cor 15:3). Those passages are typical of many others in which the apostle identifies the center of his gospel as the cross and its meaning (e.g., Rom 5:6–11; Gal 3:1; 6:14; 2 Cor 5:14–15). The present summary, however, is formulated with reference to Jesus' divine sonship, a theme which has a relatively minor place in Paul's thought as a whole (see NOTES). It is probably used here because he wants to remind the Corinthians that Christ, as the Son of God, is the very embodiment of God's faithfulness. Christ is the one in whom the divine "Yes" has been spoken and in whom *all the promises of God* (v. 20*a*) have been fulfilled.

In the second place, Paul is concerned that the Corinthians remember the part he and his associates had in bringing Christ to them. The apostle was convinced, as he would write later to the Romans, that faith is possible only where Christ is preached, and that the *preacher* therefore plays a vital role in the establishment of the gospel (Rom 10:14–17). The Corinthians should remember that Paul had played that role in their case. He has emphasized to them all along that he alone is the founder (1 Cor 3:10) and father (1 Cor 4:15; cf. 2 Cor 11:2) of their congregation. (On the later tradition that Peter had been the co-founder of the congregation, see the INTRODUCTION, p. 22.) For this reason, and also because it was Paul's trustworthiness in particular that was being questioned in Corinth, the names of Silvanus and Timothy are mentioned here almost as an afterthought (see NOTES). Nevertheless, they are mentioned, perhaps because Paul wants the Corinthians to realize that the truth of the gospel had been verified among them by the testimony of the requisite "two or three witnesses" (see NOTES and COMMENT on 13:1). But the main point is Paul's own role in the evangelization of Corinth. In his preaching of the Christ in whom all the divine promises have been fulfilled, God's faithfulness has been assured, and along with that the faithfulness of those whom God had commissioned with the gospel.

When Paul writes that *all the promises of God have their Yes in [Christ]* (v. 20*a*), the thought is probably of Christ as the one in whom a new age has been inaugurated and salvation decisively established for God's people. This is in line with the concept of God's promise(s) found in many of the eschatologically oriented Jewish texts of Paul's day (e.g., 2 Apoc Bar 14:13; 21:25 [cf. 23:7]; 51:3; 57:2; 2 Esdr 4:27; 7:60, 119; Pss Sol 12:8 ["the promises of the Lord"]). In these, God's promises are associated specifically with the passing away of this world and the coming of the next, the final judgment, God's rewarding of the righteous and his gift of eternal life. (In rabbinic literature God's "promises" are associated especially with his faithfulness to the covenant with his people; see E. P. Sanders 1977:102–5.) In Christ, Paul is now saying, such promised blessings of God have been fulfilled. In the present context, however, it would not have served Paul's objective to enumerate and describe these. His one real concern here is to remind the Corinthians that Christ is the irrefutable proof of God's faithfulness (Rom 15:7–9 is an instructive parallel) and that the word of those who preach Christ is fully dependable.

The description of Christ as the one in whom the promises of God have their "Yes" seems to have reminded Paul of the traditional "Amen" of the Christian liturgy (v. 20b). In the Corinthian congregation, as elsewhere, this acclamation was a prominent part of the church's worship, associated in particular with praise and thanksgiving (1 Cor 14:16). Boobyer has argued plausibly that this liturgical "Amen" was regarded as actually increasing, in a certain material way, the "glory" of God (1929:79–84); see also 1:11; 4:15; 9:11–15. In Greek, *amēn* is a loanword, deriving from a Semitic root (ʾmn) for that which is firm, dependable, and faithful. Indeed, van Unnik (1953) believes that Paul's whole argument in the present passage is developed around this single verbal element. If so, Aramaic must have been Paul's first language, a conclusion van Unnik and some others have sought to defend but which has not been accepted by most scholars. In any case, the wordplay van Unnik finds here would have been lost on the Greek-speaking congregation in Corinth. It is enough that both Paul and his readers were acquainted with the "Amen" as a solemn liturgical response by which an act of praise was affirmed as one's own. (Most modern worshipers recognize quite as much without knowing anything at all about the linguistic origins or the root meaning of the word.) By alluding to this familiar liturgical act Paul is able to offer yet another kind of proof of the faithfulness of God and of those who preach the gospel. With the "Amen" of their own worship, he is suggesting, the Corinthians themselves are affirming Christ as the sign of God's faithfulness. They are thereby affirming as well the dependability of those who have brought Christ to them.

As Thüsing has pointed out (1968:179–80), Paul does not say that Christ *is* the "Yes." Rather, God's promises are said to have their "Yes" *in* Christ (note *in him* [*en autō*], vv. 19b, 20a). Paul's fundamental conception of the life of faith as a new life "in Christ" and "in the Spirit" is operating here and is vital to the argument. (This becomes fully apparent in vv. 21–22.) The fulfillment of God's promises is not conceived of in a static way but is presented as an ongoing event (*an enduring "Yes,"* v. 19b), as something experienced by believers as their lives are redeemed, renewed, and redirected through the agency of the Spirit. Promise and Spirit are closely associated in the apostle's mind, perhaps because he was familiar with a traditional formula linking the two (see Seeberg 1903:227, who refers to Luke 24:29; Acts 1:4; 2:33, [38–]39 as confirmation of this). This connection is evident in Gal 3:14, where Paul refers to "the promise of the Spirit"; and again in Gal 4:28–29, where, identifying believers with Isaac, he describes them as "children of promise . . . born according to the Spirit" *(RSV)*. It is also clear in the present passage when, in vv. 21–22, this excursus on the faithfulness of God is concluded.

The last two verses of the excursus speak of the community of faith which is formed as God establishes believers in the new life they share together *in Christ (eis Christon,* v. 21). Different interpretations have been offered, however, of the precise meaning of the four participles by which the central thought of this closing sentence is conveyed. A number of scholars believe that some or all of them derive from the church's baptismal liturgy (see, for example, Windisch, 70–74; Wendland, 172; Beasley-Murray 1962:171–77). Halter has even postulated Paul's adaptation here of an actual baptismal hymn, perhaps formulated under the influence of the apostle's own preaching (1977: 181 and 598 n. 30). A baptismal background is also seen by Dinkler, in whose view the first participle *(is confirming)* refers to the general effect of baptism, and the three subsequent participles refer, respectively, to the pouring of the water *(anointed),* the signing with the cross *(sealed),* and the gift of the Spirit *(gave . . . )* as the fulfillment of the anointing and sealing (1962, especially 190). Others, however, do not believe—or else seriously doubt—that Paul has the experience of Christian baptism specifically in mind (among these, Schnackenburg 1964:87–91; Hughes, 43–45; and especially Dunn 1970a:131–34).

It is well attested that both "anointing" and "sealing" were associated with the rite of Christian baptism from the second century on (see NOTES). Moreover, Eph 1:13–14, doubtless from the first century even though deutero-Pauline, may also offer an instance of the "sealing" image applied to baptism. There, a reference to being "sealed with the promised Holy Spirit" *(RSV)* is preceded by references to hearing the gospel and believing in Christ ( = conversion to Christianity). Paul himself, of course, associates the coming of the Spirit with baptism, as 1 Cor 12:13 shows especially well: "For by one Spirit we were all baptized into one body . . . and all were made to drink of one Spirit" *(RSV).* When, therefore, Paul refers in the passage before us to being *sealed* and given *the Spirit as a down payment in our hearts,* it seems likely that Christian baptism is in view. This does not mean, however, that all the terminology is in one way or another baptismal, or that successive steps in the baptismal rite are being identified (Dinkler). Even if there is an *allusion* to baptism here, baptism is not the subject of the discussion even in the last two verses.

The subject here continues to be God (note the emphatic position of *God* in v. 21) and his faithfulness. God is described first as the one who is forming believers into the body of Christ, establishing and *confirming* them *in Christ.* Paul's use of the present tense distinguishes this first of the four key participles from the others. The accent here plainly falls on the continuing action of God, by which those who have responded to the word of the gospel (v. 19*a*) are incorporated into Christ. This is the community whose "Amen" redounds to God's greater glory (v. 20*b*) and which by its very existence testifies to the fulfillment of the divine promises in Christ (vv. 19*b*, 20*a*). The second participle, *anointed,* is formulated as an aorist and thereby concretizes God's saving work with reference to a specific act. It may be, as de la Potterie has argued, that Paul is thinking of the "anointing of faith" which occurs when the gospel is heard and believed. Thus, the sequence here would match that in Eph 1:13–14, where conversion and the confession of one's faith are followed by the sealing with the Spirit in baptism (1959, especially 23–30). Given the context of the preceding verses (19–20), this reference is more probable than one to baptism in particular. Paul's choice of the metaphor of anointing could have been influenced well enough by the opportunity for a wordplay on the name "Christ" (see NOTES). In any case, the apostle's concern is to document and describe God's faithfulness, and not to detail the steps by which the Corinthians have come into the believing community.

This description is continued and further elaborated in v. 22, the whole of which stands in apposition to *God (who also sealed us and gave the Spirit . . . )*. Dinkler's contention that the three aorist participles explicate the first (present tense) participle by identifying three separate aspects of baptism must, in fact, disregard the syntactical structure of these two verses. The first two participles, despite the difference in tense, are closely joined together by the use of a single article for both (*ho de bebaiōn . . . kai chrisas*, v. 21), and the second two are similarly connected (*ho kai sphragizamenos . . . kai dous*, v. 22; see de la Potterie 1959:23). It is significant that Dinkler himself has to supply articles for the second and fourth participles when, in summarizing his interpretation of their meaning, he presents the Greek text (1962:176). This obscures the actual structure of Paul's own sentence in which *two distinguishable sets* of participles are used to describe God's faithfulness. The second set is added to the first not to explicate *it* but to emphasize further God's saving activity which the Corinthians themselves have experienced. This multiplication cf participles has resulted, then, from a rhetorical impulse, and not from an interest in specifying several discrete steps in Christian initiation (cf. Delling 1963:27 n. 5).

If there is an allusion to baptism anywhere in this passage, it is present when Paul describes God as the one *who . . . sealed us and gave us the Spirit . . .* (see NOTES, and the reference above to 1 Cor 12:13). Here, as elsewhere, Paul is considering the Spirit as a gift from God (see especially Rom 5:5) by which believers are drawn into the community of faith (the *koinōnia* of the Spirit, 13:13[14]; Phil 2:1) and adopted as his children and heirs (Rom 8: 14–17). For him the Spirit is above all an eschatological reality, the life-giving power of the New Age present and active already in this age (see Rom 8:2, 5–6, 11; 2 Cor 3:6—as love (Rom 5:1–5 [cf. vv. 6–11]; 15:30; Gal 5:22). It is thus appropriately described as the "first fruits" of the coming salvation (Rom 8:23) or, alternately, as in the present verse, as a *down payment* on that which is to come. This same metaphor is applied to the Spirit in 5:5, where it is called a down payment on the eternal life which God has laid up in the heavens for his people (cf. 5:1–4). The metaphor is also used in Eph 1:13–14, where, as in the present passage, it is combined with that of "sealing" and applied to the Spirit as the surety of the coming salvation (cf. Eph 4:30).

There is evidence that the Corinthians had not always understood God's giving of the Spirit as a guarantee of their future inheritance. Instead, it appears, they had regarded the various "spiritual gifts" *(charismata)* as signifying the present *fulfillment* of their salvation. Much of 1 Cor had been directed against such a misunderstanding of their possession of the Spirit (see especially chaps. 1–4 and 12–15). In the present passage, however, that problem is not on Paul's mind. He presumes that his reminder of their having been sealed by the Spirit will help him make his point that God's promises are sure. From this the Corinthians are to conclude that, since God is faithful in matters of ultimate significance, those who have brought them God's word can certainly be trusted in matters of substantially less importance.

The incipient "trinitarianism" of vv. 18–22 has frequently been noted, and it is especially visible in the last two verses. God's promises have been fulfilled in Christ, and the Spirit's presence with those who believe in him is the earnest of the life with him to which they are heirs. The same ideas are expressed in Rom 8:1–17, where, as here, the "raw materials" of a later "doctrine of the Trinity" are present. But the passage in Rom also shows how little Paul himself has reflected systematically on the interrelationship of God, Christ, and the Spirit. There he speaks alternately of "the Spirit of God" and "the Spirit of Christ" (Rom 8:9) and of "Christ . . . in you" (v. 10) and "the Spirit . . . in you" (v. 11). While the theologians of the later church were not wrong when they appealed to the Pauline letters in formulating their doctrine of the Trinity (see also, e.g., 1 Cor 12:4–6; 2 Cor 13:13[14]), Paul himself is neither dependent upon nor responsible for such a doctrine.

### The Cancellation of the Visit, 1:23–2:2

Here Paul reverts to the first person singular. This, plus the use of the resumptive particle *(de,* v. 23, where one might translate "Now, then, I summon God as witness . . ."), signals a return to the specific matter of the canceled visit which Paul had begun to raise in vv. 15–17. Having affirmed in the intervening paragraph the absolute faithfulness of God, and having reminded the Corinthians of how God's faithful word had been brought to them, he now proceeds with an explanation of why a projected visit had not been carried out. His pledge to tell the truth about this (v. 23*a;* see NOTES) is the pledge of an apostle, one who serves a faithful God and who is accountable to him in a special way (cf. Stählin 1962:134). The explanation itself is stated briefly and simply in v. 23*b:* it was in order to "spare" the Corinthians that he had not come as planned. After a parenthetical assurance about his overall intentions concerning them (v. 24; see below), he expands on his explanation only slightly (2:1–2): He wanted to avoid the kind of unpleasantness which had marred a previous visit in Corinth.

According to the reconstruction of events adopted in this commentary (see

INTRODUCTION, p. 54, and COMMENT on 1:15–17), the *sorrowful visit* to which Paul refers had been made after Timothy's return to Ephesus with a disturbing report about conditions in the Corinthian church. That had been an unplanned, emergency visit, and it had turned out to be an unpleasant one as well—so much so that Paul had cut it short. In the present letter there are only hints about the nature of the disturbance which led to the abrupt termination of that visit (see below on 2:5–11; 7:8–12). From a remark in another (probably later) letter one may infer that Paul could not bring himself to deal decisively with the situation and for that reason warned that he would be coming again, and that when he did he would not spare the troublemakers (see 13:2 and COMMENT). That would have been the promised visit to Corinth en route to Macedonia. Once back in Ephesus, however, Paul must have had second thoughts about his plans for dealing with the Corinthian problem in that way. Perhaps he realized that something had to be done about it much sooner (he would not be going to Macedonia for many months); or perhaps he decided that a strongly worded apostolic letter would carry more weight and be more effective than any single, risky visit (see 10:10 and COMMENT). Whatever the reason, Paul wrote a stern, admonitory letter to the Corinthians (2:3–4, 9; 7:8, 12) which seems to have had the desired effect (7:8–12). It is probable that in the same letter (which has not survived), or through its bearer personally, Paul had also informed the Corinthians of his change in travel plans: He would not be seeing them en route to Macedonia after all. Now, in 1:23 and 2:1, he is representing this as a thoughtful decision (on the force of *ekrina* in 2:1, see NOTES) which had taken into account the best interests of the Corinthians themselves. When he decided to cancel his projected visit it was in order to spare them what that would have involved.

The parenthetical remark of v. 24 (on the character of this aside, see NOTES) shows how sensitive Paul has become, during the course of his dealings with the Corinthians, to their criticism of his behavior toward them. He apparently fears that his comment about wanting to spare them (v. 23) could itself be misunderstood, or perhaps deliberately turned to his disfavor. Does he presume to exercise such control over their faith that every move on his part is somehow fateful for their salvation? He says that his comments should by no means be thus construed. He does not intend to tyrannize their faith (v. 24a), nor could he if he wished to, because he is confident that the faith in which they stand firm (v. 24b) rests solely "in the power of God," not "in the wisdom of men" (1 Cor 2:5, *RSV*). This is not the only place in the Corinthian letters where Paul shows an uneasiness about how his words will be taken. At the close of one series of admonitions in 1 Cor, he assures his readers that he is not trying to "keep [them] on a tight rein" *(NEB)*, but only to promote their good order and full commitment to the Lord (7:35). Similar concerns are expressed in what is probably his last letter to the Corinthian church; for instance, that it may seem he is flaunting his authority (2 Cor 10:8), or that he will have to use it for purposes of discipline when he visits (13:10; cf. 10:2). Compare also 8:8, 10 with NOTES and COMMENT.

In the parenthetical remark of v. 24, as in the excursus of vv. 18–22, Paul is employing the first person plural. In both cases the effect is to distinguish somewhat more general comments from those which are specifically and explicitly addressed to the matter of the canceled visit. In v. 24a, we obviously means Paul and his associates (Silvanus and Timothy specifically, as in v. 19), because there is at the same time a reference to your [i.e., the Corinthians'] faith. Most commentators—e.g., Plummer, 45; Lietzmann, 104; Barrett, 84— believe, however, that in the remainder of the verse the we includes the Corinthians. Thus Paul would be saying that, far from lording it over the Corinthians, he and his associates are co-workers with them for their joy. Windisch, 76, finds support for this interpretation in 1 Cor 4:14–21, where Paul assures the Corinthians that he does not want to shame them or come to them with a rod. He intends only to admonish them, with the gentleness of the loving father he actually is to them. But is the contrast in 1 Cor 4 between two kinds of fathers? And does not Paul's self-image as the father of the Corinthian congregation (see also 2 Cor 11:2) stand in some tension with the idea that the Corinthians are co-workers with Paul and his associates? It is better to interpret co-workers in accord with Paul's use of it everywhere else (see NOTES) as a reference to his own associates in ministry and not to the members of a congregation in general. Thus, in v. 24, Paul would not be contrasting two modes of ministerial service, the tyrannical and the co-operative. He would be contrasting two different objectives of the ministerial office: the enhancement of one's own position by the self-serving exercise of one's authority versus the enhancement of the joy of those who, by God's power, stand firm in faith.

In Paul's vocabulary, joy is one of the basic eschatological realities—a fruit of the Spirit (Gal 5:22) and one mark of God's sovereign rule (Rom 14:17). It is therefore closely allied with faith (as in v. 24b; see also Rom 15:13; Phil 1:25) and hope (Rom 12:12). It can exist even where there is worldly affliction (e.g., 6:10; 7:4; 1 Thess 1:6), and it is one of the ways in which apostle and congregation are bound together (Rom 16:19; Phil 1:4–5; 2:2, 17–18; 4:10). Thus, joy in the Pauline sense is above all joy before God (1 Thess 3:9), and the apostle can urge his congregations to "rejoice constantly" (1 Thess 5:16). See Gulin 1932, especially 168, 183–84.

The parenthetical reference to his concern for the Corinthians' joy (v. 24) leads Paul to expand on the reason for his not having come to them as promised. Specifically, he now says (2:1), he had wanted to spare them as well as himself the agony and frustration of another sorrowful visit. Elsewhere Paul expresses his conviction that his apostolic authority had been given him for "building up" and not for "tearing down" (10:8; 13:10). That same basic idea lies behind the present verses. As an apostle he is devoted to the joy of the

Corinthians, and he would hope to visit them "with joy," just as he will later write to the Romans that he wants to come to them "with joy" (*en chara,* Rom 15:32). But had he come to Corinth as he had proposed, it would have been "with sorrow" (*en lupē,* 2:1). Moreover, because his own joy is dependent on that of his congregations (see especially Phil 2:17–18), when they are brought to grief, so is he (2:2; cf. Rom 12:15, "Rejoice with those who rejoice, weep with those who weep," *RSV*). Paul writes subsequently about a grieving which is associated with contrition and is therefore itself a cause for rejoicing (7:8–11). But here he is thinking of the grief that is experienced where misunderstanding and distrust have driven a wedge between a father and his children. Paul had feared such a situation might develop between himself and the Corinthians (see 1 Cor 4:14–21), and his fears had been realized on the occasion of his short and painful emergency visit. Such an experience he had not wanted to repeat.

## 3. A TEARFUL LETTER, 2:3–11

2  ³And I wrote this very thing, so that I would not have to come and be grieved by those who ought to make me rejoice; because I remain convinced about all of you, that my joy belongs to you all. ⁴It was out of an exceedingly troubled, anguished heart that I wrote to you, through many tears—not that you should be grieved, but for the sake of love, that you might know how much of it I have for you.

⁵Now if some one has caused grief, he has caused it not to me but to some extent (I don't want to exaggerate) to all of you. ⁶This punishment by the majority is enough for such a person; ⁷so now you should forgive and deal kindly with him instead, that he not be overwhelmed by immoderate grief. ⁸Thus, I urge you to ratify your love for him. ⁹It was indeed for this purpose that I wrote, to know whether you would stand the test and whether you are in all respects obedient. ¹⁰To whomever you forgive something, I do, too; and whatever I, for my own part, have forgiven—if I have forgiven anything—has been for your sake, in the presence of Christ. ¹¹This was so we might not be cheated by Satan, for we are not oblivious to his designs.

### NOTES

2:3. *I wrote.* Paul continues to use the first person singular as he has, with the exception of 1:18–22, 24, since 1:15. The topic under consideration involves Paul in a way it does not involve Timothy, the co-sender of this letter (see NOTES on 1:1, 13). The reference here is to a previous letter, one subsequently described as having been written *through many tears* (v. 4) and in order to determine whether the Corinthians were *in all respects obedient* (v. 9). Since this is self-evidently the same letter whose salutary results are recounted in 7:8–12, *egrapsa* in 2:3, 4, 9 must be read as à true past-tense form, not as an epistolary aorist; the reference cannot be to what Paul is now writing in this letter.

*this very thing.* The Greek *(touto auto)* may be interpreted either adverbially ("for this very reason," BDF § 290(4); cf. *GNTG* III:4, and *RSV:* "I wrote as I did") or as the simple object of the verb, as in the present tr. (cf. *NEB:* "This is precisely the point I made in my letter"). Windisch, 80–81, notes that an adverbial interpretation is only possible where there is an intransitive verb like "come," or where, as in 2 Pet 1:5, a transitive verb is accompanied by its own object. The Greek construction is slightly different in v. 9 *(eis touto gar kai egrapsa),* where the purpose of the letter is stated more directly.

*and be grieved.* Translates *lypēn schō,* a well-attested reading. The variant *lypēn epi lypēn* (D, G, 1739 and some other witnesses), "grief on top of grief," is probably to be rejected as a scribal assimilation of this comment to the one in Phil 2:27, where the longer form is present. The contrary view—that the longer reading is original and that the shorter resulted from a copyist's accidental omission of the repeated *lypēn* (and thus of the preceding *epi*)—cannot be ruled out entirely. Thus, Manson (1962:213–14 n. 1) suggests that Paul is saying he wanted to avoid adding a second painful visit to the one he had already experienced. Cf. Phil 2:27, where the same phrase is used *(RSV:* "sorrow upon sorrow").

4. *through many tears.* Here *dia (through)* with the genitive expresses the circumstance which obtained as Paul wrote his letter, and thus the manner in which it was written; see BDF § 223(3), *GNTG* III:267.

*for the sake of love.* The words *for the sake of* do not stand in the Greek text, but they have been supplied in order to reproduce in English the emphasis on love which results from the unusual word order *(tēn agapēn hina gnōte);* see *GNTG* IV:94.

*that you might know.* Windisch, 83, suggests that the aorist tense used here *(gnōte)* indicates Paul's sense of the need for this knowledge to be re-established.

*how much.* Translates *perissoterōs,* here with an elative meaning (e.g., "the more," "the most," etc.). The word is often translated as if it were an adjective describing *love* (e.g., *RSV:* "the abundant love"; *NEB:* "the more than ordinary love"; Plummer, 52: "the exceptional love"). Barrett's tr., on the other hand ("the love that I have specially for you" [82, 88]), associates the adverb too closely with the following prepositional phrase, as if Paul were saying that he has "more" love for the Corinthians than for others (see the criticism of such an interpretation offered by Hughes, 54 n. 44). The present tr. (which supplies *of it,* referring to *love*) seeks to do justice to the adverbial form as well as to the elative meaning of the word in this sentence (cf. *JB, TEV*). The same construction appears in 7:15 with reference to the depth of Titus' affection for the Corinthians, but that in 1:12 is slightly different *(perissoterōs de pros hymas).*

5. *some one.* Subsequent comments (vv. 6–8; 7:12) make it clear that Paul has a specific individual in mind, although the person is never named.

*to some extent.* Translates *apo merous,* an expression Paul had also used in 1:14 *(partially)* and which he uses three times in Romans (11:25, "part"; 15:15, "on some points"; 15:24, "for a little"—*RSV*). The exact meaning in the present case is disputed. Some interpret Paul to be saying that not really *all* of the Corinthians have been grieved (e.g., Bultmann, 52, and Hughes, 65 n. 8; cf. Gdspd.: "at least . . . some of you" and

Mof.: "a section of you"). Others believe that Paul means not all the Corinthians have been equally grieved (e.g., Windisch, 85, and Barrett, 89; cf. *RSV, NAB:* "in some measure" and *JB:* "to some degree"). The tr. offered here (cf. *NEB, NIV*) permits either of these meanings, and Paul may indeed have intended to qualify his statement in both respects.

*(I don't want to exaggerate).* The same verb *(epibarein)* appears in 1 Thess 2:9 and 2 Thess 3:8, in both cases used transitively, "to lay a burden on" someone. If the verb is also used transitively here, its object could be either the offender or the Corinthians. Most modern commentators, however, are agreed that the verb should be interpreted as intransitive, expressing Paul's wish not *to exaggerate* the extent of the grief that has been caused.

*to all of you.* Some ancient versions (also Luther and Bengel) included these words *(pantas hymas)* in the preceding clause, as the object of the verb (thus, also, *KJV:* "that I may not overcharge you all"). But this destroys the clearly antithetical form of the sentence: *not to me but . . . to all of you.*

6. *punishment.* The Greek term used here *(epitimia)* usually described the condition of one (an *epitimos*) who enjoyed "all civil rights and privileges" (LSJ, 667). In this verse however, as also in Wis 3:10 and in an Egyptian papyrus of the first century A.D. *(OGI* 669.43, cited in LSJ, 667), it seems to have taken on the meaning of several cognate nouns *(epitimē, epitimēna, epitimēsis,* etc.) which denoted *punishment,* either in the form of a specific penalty laid upon an offender or in the form of a "reproof," "criticism," or "censure" (examples in LSJ, 667). Barrett's discussion of this term (90), although not without its merits, has been too much influenced by his wish to identify the offender as someone from outside of Corinth (see 212), and therefore as someone not subject to official punishment by the congregation there. Viewed as a whole, however, these verses (5–11) convey the impression of some formal disciplinary action decided on and carried out by the congregation. The tr. *punishment* is not unwarranted, therefore, and remains broad enough to cover various specific kinds of penalty, ranging from excommunication (Windisch, 86) to a "brotherly reprimand" (Doskocil 1958:80, who thinks, however, of a reprimand administered with a certain inflexibility and strictness [81]).

*the majority.* Translates *hoi pleiones,* a substantive derived from *pleiōn* ("more"), the comparative of the adjective *polys* ("much, many"). The same expression appears in 4:15; 9:2, as well as in 1 Cor 9:19; 10:5; 15:6; Phil 1:14. In most, if not all, of these instances, including the present passage, the use of the term seems to presume the existence of others, a "minority," not covered by it. This is not the case, however, when Paul refers to "the many" *(hoi polloi;* e.g., Rom 5:15, 19), and thus the two terms need to be distinguished (a distinction that Barrett, 91, and Forkman 1972:212–13 n. 319 have failed to make). The latter is probably a Hebraism and may be compared with the equivalent Hebrew phrase *ha-rabbim,* which appears often in the Qumran literature as a description of the community as a whole (e.g., 1QS vi.8ff., where the general membership assembled as a deliberating body is called the *Moshab ha-rabbim;* see Jeremias, *TDNT* VI:538). So, too, Paul can speak of "the many" who comprise the totality of the body of Christ (Rom 12:5; 1 Cor 10:17). In the present passage, however, his reference to *the majority* must be interpreted more narrowly (so also Braun 1966 I:198). The same term is used by Josephus in describing the way the Essenes governed themselves. "It is a point of honour with them to obey their elders *[tois presbyterois],* and a majority *[tois pleiosin];* for instance, if ten sit together, one will not speak if the nine desire silence" (*War* II.viii.9). It is possible, given the context in vv. 5–11 and the appearance here of other technical words (see discussion above on *punishment* and below on *enough* and *ratify*), that Paul has in mind a specific, deliberative session of the Corinthian congregation (see Windisch, 86–87; Delcor 1968:79–80).

*enough.* The adjective is neuter in Greek *(hikanon)* and does not agree with the feminine form of the subject, *punishment (hē epitimia hautē)*. This has been variously explained—for example, as a Latinism (Hughes, 66 n. 11) or as a reflection of classical usage (BDF § 131). Like other terms in this passage, it is probable that this one has a technical, forensic background (cf. Plummer, 57; Allo, 38). It is more likely that Paul has reference to the sufficiency of the duration of the punishment than to the sufficiency of its severity (so also Bultmann, 53; Windisch, 86, suggests that the degree of punishment may also be in mind), because he proceeds to counsel its termination (v. 7), not its alteration.

7. *now . . . instead.* Translates *tounantion mallon* (literally "on the contrary rather"); Paul wants the punishment to stop and a totally new course of action to be followed. For the use of *tounantion* see Gal 2:7, and especially 1 Pet 3:9, where, as here, an act of reconciliation is urged.

*forgive.* The verb is *charizesthai* (see also v. 10; 12:13), not *aphienai*. The latter is used regularly in the Synoptic Gospels (e.g., in the Lord's Prayer), but the only time it appears in a Pauline letter with reference to forgiveness it is in a quotation from scripture (Rom 4:7, quoting Ps 32). Paul ordinarily uses *charizesthai* to refer to the gracious benefits granted by God to his people (e.g., 1 Cor 2:12; Gal 3:18; Phil 1:29).

*deal kindly.* The verb *(parakalein)* is most often translated here as "comfort" (e.g., *RSV*), which is certainly possible, as are also "support" *(NAB)* and "encourage" *(TEV;* cf. *NEB, JB)*. In some contexts, however, it can approach the meaning "seek reconciliation," as perhaps in 2 Mac 13:23, where it is said that after military reversals Antiochus sought to reach an accord with the Jews: *tous Ioudaious parekalesen,* "[he] proposed peace to the Jews" *(APOT* [tr. J. Moffatt]). Similarly, in Luke 15:28 the father of the prodigal son, confronted by the anger and obstinacy of the elder brother, *parekalei auton* ("tried to appease him," Mof.); cf. Acts 16:39 and Goodspeed's tr., "conciliated." Paul himself had used the verb in this way in 1 Cor 4:13 in the third of a series of antithetical pairs describing how apostles respond to worldly adversity: to reviling— with blessing; to persecution—with forbearance (v. 12); and to slander—with *parakalein* (v. 13; *RSV:* "when slandered, we try to conciliate"). This same meaning accords well with the present context, and especially with the forgiveness which Paul asks the Corinthians to extend to the offender. If his offense had been a slander of Paul or others (see COMMENT), then the parallel between this passage and 1 Cor 4:13 would be even closer, and one could perhaps translate the word here specifically as "speak kindly." Note also 1 Thess 2:11–12, where Paul associates his own apostolic *parakalein* with the way a father handles his children (BAG s.v. 5, where 1 Tim 5:1 is also listed: one does not "rebuke" an elder but "exhorts" him as one would a father, i.e., in a respectful and kindly manner).

*overwhelmed.* A passive form of *katapinein,* "to swallow up." The image is of a person being drowned by (presumably his own) tearful grieving.

8. *I urge you.* The same verb *(parakalein)* translated in v. 9 as *deal kindly.* Here it is employed, as it often is by Paul, to introduce his apostolic counsel (see, e.g., Rom

12:1; 15:30, where, as here, it is followed by an aorist infinitive; in 2 Cor 6:1 the second person plural is followed by an aorist infinitive). Mullins 1972:380–81 identifies exhortations introduced with this verb as "personal petitions" and describes this instance as an example of a place where Paul's readers are addressed "in warm, friendly terms."

*to ratify your love for him.* The verb *(kyroun)* and its compounds *(akyroun, prokyrousthai)* are used by Paul in Gal 3:15, 17 in their technical, legal sense to refer to the ratification and annulment of a will. The technical sense is also present here, where the official actions of the Corinthians toward an offender are being reviewed (see also Spicq 1965:185–87). The aorist form of the infinitive here *(kyrōsai)* is appropriate, given Paul's appeal for action in a specific instance (see BDF § 338). One does not ordinarily think of *love* as something which can be "ratified," and the juxtaposition of these two apparently contradictory words forms an interesting example of a figure of speech known as oxymoron: "Paul desires a decision whose content is love. Right is to be replaced by right as pardoning love dictates and crowns the final legal decision" (Behm, *TDNT* III:1099).

9. *indeed for this purpose.* Here the *eis touto* (literally "for this") looks forward to and is specified in the following *hina*-clause, as in Rom 14:9 (cf. 1 Pet 4:6; 1 John 3:8); in v. 3 the construction is similar but not identical *(touto auto hina . . . ).* The comment here supplements Paul's earlier statement about why he had written (v. 3), not by adding a second reason but by formulating his earlier point in another way (this *kai* is translated here as *indeed*).

*to know whether you would stand the test.* Here, as in Phil 2:22 with reference to Timothy, Paul speaks of knowing someone's worth or quality *(hē dokimē ginōskein);* literally "that I might know your quality." The noun is rare, and Paul's letters apparently provide the earliest instances of it (Grundmann, *TDNT* II:255, citing Lohmeyer). It refers to that which has been tested *(dokimazein,* used often by Paul) and thereby "proved," found to be genuine *(dokimos,* in 13:5–7 contrasted with *adokimos,* that which has not been proved; in 1 Cor 11:19 used substantively of the members of the congregation who by their actions show themselves to be genuinely Christian).

*whether you are in all respects obedient.* This phrase explicates the preceding one; Paul had written to test specifically the obedience of his congregation. The concept of obedience plays a larger role in Rom than in any other Pauline letter. There it stands for the whole point and purpose of Paul's apostleship to the Gentiles: to win their obedience to the gospel (Rom 10:14), alternately described as "faith's obedience" (Rom 1:5; cf. 16:26) or simply "obedience" (Rom 15:18). See also Rom 6:12ff. and Rom 10, 11, where the disobedience *(apeitheia)* of Israel is considered. The adjective *(hypēkoos)* appears in Paul's letters only here and in the Christ-hymn of Phil 2:6–11 (v. 8). Elsewhere in 2 Cor the apostle refers explicitly to "obedience" only in 7:15; 10:5–6.

10. *I, for my own part.* This tr. seeks to bring out the force of the emphatic *I* *(egō).*

*in the presence of Christ.* The same phrase *(en prosōpō Christou)* occurs in 4:6, but with a different meaning. Here *en prosōpō* is the functional equivalent of such "prepositional adverbs" as *katenanti, emprosthen,* and *enōpion;* like most such terms, it can be a rendering of the Hebrew *lipnê* (e.g., Prov 4:3; 25:7; cf. BDF § 214). In both 5:10 *(before the judgment seat of Christ* [*emprosthen tou bēmatos tou Christou*]) and 8:21 *(in the Lord's sight* [*enōpion Kyrion*]) the references are to the final judgment. An eschatological reference is implicit in the present verse as well, making this phrase a kind of solemn oath (cf. Gal 1:20, "In what I am writing to you, before God [*enōpion tou Theou*], I do not lie!"—*RSV*) that whatever Paul has forgiven has indeed been for the sake of the Corinthians *(di' hymas;* cf. 1 Thess 3:9, "the joy which we feel for your sake before our God [*di' hymas emprosthen tou Theou hēmōn*]"—*RSV*). The formula that stands in 2:17; 12:19*b* ("in the sight of God [*katenanti Theou*] we are speaking in Christ") is only partially comparable (see NOTES there).

11. *cheated.* The verb *(pleonektein)* means to take advantage of someone with fraudulent intent. Elsewhere Paul uses the word when defending himself against charges of fraud being brought against him by some(one) in Corinth (7:2; 12:17–18), but in 1 Thess 4:6 it appears in a general parenetic context.

*Satan.* The Hebrew *śātān* means, literally, "accuser" or "prosecutor" (see *katēgōr* in Rev 12:10) and is a name which was applied, especially in Jewish literature of the Greco-Roman period, to God's archenemy, the personification of evil (LXX, *ho diabolos,* "the devil"). See Gaster, *IDB,* R–Z:224–28. The name *Satan* appears but rarely in the Gnostic texts from Nag Hammadi (Ap Jas [CG I, *2*] 4, 37–39 [*NHLE,* 31]; Melch [CG IX, *1*] 20, 15 [*NHLE,* 403]), where the most common name for the ruler of darkness and evil is Yaldabaoth. Paul also refers to *Satan* in 11:14; 12:7; Rom 16:20; 1 Cor 5:5; 7:5; 1 Thess 2:18; cf. 2 Thess 2:9; 1 Tim 1:20; 5:15. Elsewhere in 2 Cor there are references to *the god of this age* (4:4), *Beliar* (6:15), and *the serpent* (11:3), and in 1 Thess 3:5 this figure is described simply as "the tempter."

*designs.* In the NT only Paul uses this word, always in the plural (*ta noēmata,* here and in 3:14; 4:4; 11:3; Phil 4:7) or with a plural meaning (*every thought,* 10:5). In two of these instances the reference is to errant or potentially errant thoughts for which *the god of this age* is (4:4) or *the serpent* may be (11:3) responsible. Here, where Satan's own evil thoughts are mentioned, there is a subtle play on words in Greek: *ou gar autou ta noēmata agnooumen,* perhaps best paraphrased in English as "for we are not unmindful of his mind." This is a good example of litotes, or understatement for the sake of emphasis (Grayston 1964:569 n. 2). Héring's reference (16–17) to Rev 2:24, which alludes to the claim of some to have learned "the deep things of Satan," does not suffice as support for his suggestion that in the present passage Paul may be taking over a Gnostic slogan.

COMMENT: GENERAL

Having explained why a projected visit to the Corinthians had not taken place (1:15–2:2), Paul now proceeds to explain why, instead, he had written a letter which apparently seemed overly severe to some (see 7:8). The motivation and intent of the letter are set forth briefly and generally in vv. 3–4. The letter and the circumstances surrounding it are still the subject in vv. 5–11, as v. 9 shows clearly: *It was indeed for this purpose that I wrote. . . .* Thus, in vv. 5–11 one begins to learn something more specific about the *sorrowful visit* (vv. 1–2) which had led, first, to cancellation of another visit and, second, to the writing of a tearful letter (vv. 3–4). Someone had caused grief not to Paul alone but to the whole congregation (v. 5), and subsequently had been disciplined by the congregation (v. 6). This disciplinary act, whatever its specific form, had been in response to Paul's tearful letter, and thus a demonstration of the Corinthians' obedience (v. 9). It is clear that the same offense, the same letter, and the same Corinthian response to the letter are discussed also in 7:8–12, and that passage must be taken into account in any analysis of 2:3–11. It offers confirmation that the trouble which had occurred during Paul's unplanned, emergency visit to Corinth involved an injustice perpetrated by one person against another, and that Paul had interpreted this as a threat to the whole Christian community (7:12). Moreover, the apostle's comments in 7:8–12 suggest that the disciplinary action taken in Corinth was a sign of the congregation's acknowledgment of its own responsibility in the matter. Paul's letter had led them to be contrite, and their contrition had led them to punish the offender. Assured of this, Paul now urges that that person be forgiven and restored to fellowship (2:6–8).

## COMMENT: DETAILED

### The Tearful Letter, 2:3–4

Paul's unplanned, emergency visit to Corinth had been a disaster. He must have hurried back to Ephesus hurt, angered, and perplexed. Although he had evidently promised the Corinthians a return visit on the way to Macedonia, thus allowing him to see them yet again on his way from there (1:15–16), once back in Ephesus he seems to have thought better of the idea. His stated explanation for canceling the visit was that the Corinthians might be spared (1:23), presumably meaning that they might be spared his anger and censure. Other factors may also have entered into his decision—for example, his fear of being unable to cope with the situation; or, more positively, his unwillingness to delay or give up a mission to Troas (see 2:12), which lay along the route of his original itinerary (Ephesus-Troas-Macedonia-Corinth; cf. 1 Cor 16:5–9). Whatever the reason or reasons, the plan was changed, and in place of a visit Paul sent the letter which is described in these verses.

According to the traditional view, this tearful letter is to be identified with 1 Cor, and the offender referred to in 2 Cor 2:5–11 (and 7:12) is the man concerning whom Paul gives instructions in 1 Cor 5:1–5. However, there are decisive reasons (discussed below) why the person mentioned in 1 Cor cannot have been the offender mentioned here in 2 Cor, and if that identification falls through, so does the identification of 1 Cor with the tearful letter. There are also decisive arguments against the more recent and widespread view that 2 Cor 10–13 (and perhaps 2:14–7:4 as well) derive from that letter, one of which is that chaps. 10–13 were written in anticipation of a visit (12:14; 13:1), while the tearful letter was written in lieu of a visit (1:23). Indeed, the present passage shows that the cancellation of the visit and the dispatch of the tearful letter were very closely associated in the apostle's own mind. The visit had been canceled because he wanted to spare them and avoid further grief (1:23; 2:1–2), and the letter had been written out of his love for them and not to aggrieve them (vv. 3–4). In fact, then, it would appear that at least part of the impact of the letter on the congregation was the news it contained that the first phase of the "double visit" was being called off (see v. 3, *And I wrote this very thing,* referring to the canceled visit in vv. 1–2).

In 1:23 Paul had stressed the hurt another visit would have inflicted upon the congregation, and now he writes about the hurt it would have caused him (v. 3). Both points had been made in v. 2, consistent with the apostle's conviction that he and his congregations are bound so fully and closely together in the gospel that the joy of the one is the joy of the other (v. 3; cf. 1:5–7, 24 and Phil 1:25, and see Gulin 1932:265–66). Nowhere does Paul refer so directly and specifically to his love for the Corinthians as he does here (v. 4; cf. 1 Cor 4:21; 16:24). One could argue that the tearful letter had actually been written out of pique, not love, and that only Titus' report of its good effect (7:6–8) allows Paul to describe it now as he does. That may in part be the case. It is also true, however, that his "anxiety for all the churches" (11:28), and not least for the church in Corinth, is the type of anxiety a parent feels for a child, an anguish compounded of worry, fear, and hope, but rooted finally and decisively in love (see, notably, Gal 4:19–20; 1 Cor 4:21; cf. Gulin 1932:266).

### A Special Appeal, 2:5–11

The concern in these verses continues to be with the tearful letter and its effect (see v. 9), even though Paul is now writing somewhat more directly about the cause of the grief which had threatened his relationship to the Corinthians. One learns, for example, that some specific individual *(some one)* has caused grief which, Paul goes out of his way to emphasize, has touched the whole— or virtually the whole (see NOTES)—congregation (v. 5). Since he deems it important to say that the hurt was not to himself, one may infer that some could, and probably did, interpret the incident as purely a personal matter between the offender and the apostle. That interpretation Paul rejects. He insists that it was more than a private misunderstanding, dispute, or clash of personalities. Had it been only that, one might suppose that Paul would not have pursued the matter, thus following his own advice (in 1 Cor 6:7): "To have lawsuits at all with one another is defeat for you. Why not rather suffer wrong? Why not rather be defrauded?" *(RSV).* In this case, however, the integrity of the whole congregation is at stake (see Meurer 1972:134). See also v. 10 and 7:12.

It is further apparent that the offender had been disciplined in some way by the congregation, acting in the matter as a deliberative body guided by the judgment of *the majority* (v. 6). This reference to *the majority* does not require one to presume a formal "minority" with its own identifiable position, although the existence of such a group may well be implied. If so, did it favor greater or lesser leniency toward the offender? In view of the point Paul seems anxious to make in vv. 5, 10, it may be that the minority wanted to take no action at all on the premise that this was a strictly private affair between one individual and one particular apostolic leader.

What disciplinary action *the majority* had actually decided on is not disclosed here, since the Corinthians were certainly well aware of it and since Paul thinks it is *enough*. (On the range of meanings for the word *punishment*, see NOTES.) It could not have been a simple reprimand, because the wording here shows that it has some enduring aspect or consequences which can—and, Paul believes, ought to—be now discontinued. It is likely to have been some temporary exclusion from the Christian community, or at least from such central congregational activities as the eucharistic meal (in 1 Cor 5:11, for example, the prohibition of table fellowship with errant members would have required, at the very least, exclusion from the eucharist); cf. Hunzinger 1963:239; Meurer 1972:135–39. It is well known that the Jewish sectaries at Qumran had provided for various degrees of exclusion, some more and some less severe, depending on the offense. The provisions of 1QS vii.15–18 are of particular interest, not only because they give an idea of some types of disciplinary action a religious community might take but also because one or more of the offenses mentioned may have been involved at Corinth as well:

> Whoever has gone about slandering his companion shall be excluded from the pure Meal of the Congregation for one year and shall do penance. But whoever has slandered the Congregation shall be expelled from among them and shall return no more.
> Whoever has murmured against the authority of the Community shall be expelled and shall not return. But if he has murmured against his companion unjustly, he shall do penance for six months. (Tr. Vermes 1975:84)

Like this Qumran rule, Paul is concerned to distinguish an injury done to an individual from an injury done to the whole community; but, unlike the Qumran rule, Paul does not require permanent exclusion for those who commit the latter offense.

Whether the apostle had given exact directions or advice about the disciplinary action which had been taken at Corinth is uncertain. There is some likelihood that he had, or at least that his comments in the tearful letter had led the Corinthians to draw certain inferences in that regard, because now he counsels them to *forgive and deal kindly* with the offender instead (vv. 7–8). Paul's counsel to the Corinthians about this specific case is in accord with the rule he lays down for the Galatians in a more general hortatory context: "Should a person be overtaken in some trespass, you who are spiritual should restore such an individual with a spirit of gentleness" (Gal 6:1). If some reconciliation and support of the offending party does not occur in the present case, Paul fears, that person may *be overwhelmed by immoderate grief.* In 7:9–11 (where this same matter is being discussed) he will make a distinction between grief "that God wills" *(kata Theon)* and grief "of a worldly kind" *(tou kosmou).* The former, he will say, leads to "contrition" and "salvation," while the latter leads to "death." This distinction is in a sense anticipated in the present passage. Here the apostle seems to presume that the offending party has been grieved into repenting. Any further discipline would be strictly punitive and could only lead to grief of a worldly sort, unrelieved by any redemptive value.

This passage makes it apparent that the tearful letter had been prompted by Paul's concern about the original offense and about the congregation's attitude toward it (v. 9). This is confirmation of the close connection between the trauma of the emergency visit and the anguish with which he had written a subsequent letter (see earlier discussion on vv. 2–3). All things considered, it would appear that the offense in question had been some slander of Paul and his apostleship, an affront compounded by the congregation's unwillingness to discipline the individual responsible. It was clearly the congregation's involvement that bothered Paul the most. Thus, at least in retrospect, he insists that the tearful letter had been written to put the congregation to *the test* and to find out whether it was *obedient*—an obedience which now has been substantiated with news of the church's move, at last, to discipline the offender. In 7:7–12 the apostle writes rather effusively about the repentance and zeal of the congregation as a whole. It seems clear that, no matter how personally traumatic the offense itself had been for Paul, his chief concern had been the congregation's failure to deal with it forthrightly. It must not have realized that the injury done to Paul was an injury done to itself, for the authenticity of its existence as a church was indissolubly linked to the authenticity of Paul's apostleship.

In v. 9, as in 7:15, Paul stops short of identifying himself or his counsels as the object of the Corinthians' obedience. He shows a similar reticence in Phlm 21 ("Confident of your obedience, I write to you, knowing that you will do even more than I say"—*RSV*), even though he comes closer there than anywhere else to thinking of obedience as directed to himself. Rather, for Paul obedience is to God (Rom 10:30–32), Christ (10:5–6), and the gospel (Rom 10:16; cf. Rom 2:8; Gal 5:7, the "truth"). This concern to avoid leaving the impression that obedience is something owed to *him* is of course related to his insistence that apostles do not preach themselves "but Jesus Christ as Lord" (4:5). Finally, Paul knows, it is God alone who judges whether one has stood the test of Christian obedience (10:18; 1 Thess 2:4; cf. 1 Cor 3:13). Nevertheless, as an apostle he does not hesitate to serve as an instrument of that testing by which the authenticity and fiber of one's faith is brought to light.

Just as Paul had stressed in v. 5 that the wrong had not been an affront to himself (alone), so in v. 10 he emphasizes that he is as ready to forgive the wrongdoer as he wants the whole congregation to be. Moreover, he writes, whatever he may have forgiven was for the sake of the congregation. In this comment one sees again how reluctant Paul is to acknowledge that the injury had been to him as an individual. At every turn and in every way he is extraordinarily insistent that the real danger had been not to himself but to the whole Corinthian church. A plausible inference from this is that the opposite interpretation was being sponsored by someone else, very possibly the minority in Corinth who had not been in favor of the congregation's disciplinary action (see discussion above on v. 6).

The apostle's eagerness for an expeditious reconciliation of all involved parties is underscored in v. 11. Otherwise, he writes, Satan will take advantage of the situation. Elsewhere in his correspondence with the Corinthians Paul refers to certain "false apostles" as being Satan's servants in disguise (11: 12–15). In the same context he expresses his fear that the Corinthians may be seduced by such persons and espouse another kind of gospel, just as the serpent (viz., Satan) deceived Eve (11:2–5). It is reasonable to suppose that Paul has the same sort of opportunists in mind when, in the present passage, he remarks on the danger that Satan may take advantage of strife within the Christian community (see Dibelius 1909:51–54). If there is no reconciliation among the members of Christ's body, then the body falls prey to those who would possess it for their own purposes, and Satan has won the day. Whether the offending party had some connection with those whom Paul will later call "false apostles" or whether perhaps he was even their leader (so Barrett, 7–8 [cf. 89–93], and Kee 1980:73 n. 15) is far from certain. Unlike them, he seems to have been a member of the Corinthian congregation, although it is possible that the interlopers could have exploited his disaffection with Paul to their own advantage. The apostle's present worry, however, is not about the intentions of that one person but about the consequences of keeping him alienated from the Christian community. Perhaps Paul is mindful of a minority who had not wanted him disciplined at all. He wants to avoid any discord or injustice by which the body would be divided and its witness to the one true gospel placed in jeopardy.

### The Offense and the Offender

In 2:5–11 nothing is said directly about the character of the offense or the identity of the offender whom the congregation has disciplined. Who the person was and what he had done were well known to both Paul and his readers. The facts of the matter seem not to have been in question, only how the various parties involved were going to accommodate themselves to the consequences and to one another. Granting the general validity of the observations about the passage which have been made in the NOTES and in the comments above, it is perhaps most likely that the offense was some sort of slander perpetrated, whether by word or deed or both, against Paul and thus (at least according to Paul's interpretation) against the congregation as a whole. Even if the incident had occurred after Paul's departure from Corinth and had involved a slander against one of his associates (cf. Windisch on 7:12, 238–39, and Allo, 61–62)—for which there is no clear evidence—it was still, in effect, an injury to Paul and, more broadly, to the Corinthian church. It is also likely that the incident and its aftermath provide a glimpse, however fleeting, of the sort of jockeying for ecclesiastical position and religious leadership which, not much later, would seriously threaten Paul's apostolic role and gospel in Corinth.

The interpretation offered here has much in common with those found in other recent commentaries. Virtually all the ancient commentators, however (including Chrysostom, Ambrosiaster, Theodoret, and Theophylact), and most subsequent commentators until the twentieth century (e.g., Meyer, Denney, and Heinrici in the second half of the nineteenth century) identified the offense and the offender of 2:5–11 by referring to the case of the man who, according to 1 Cor 5:1–5, had become sexually involved with his stepmother. Among the earliest commentators only Tertullian disputed this (*On Modesty* XIII–XIV). His discussion of the matter dates from his Montanist period, however, and reflects his own ascetic presupposition that Paul would not have counseled leniency in the case of such a heinous sexual transgression. A few recent scholars have returned to the traditional view, notably Hughes, 59–65, and Lampe 1967:353–54. Stephenson (1965:96) and Hyldahl (1973:305–6) also want to connect the two passages, but neither offers arguments in favor of this or deals with the difficulties such an identification encounters.

At first glance there appear to be a number of similarities between the discussion in 2:5–11 and the one in 1 Cor 5:1–5. These are often used as evidence justifying an identification of the offender mentioned in 2 Cor 2 with the man in 1 Cor 5. Upon closer inspection, however, most of the arguments favoring this turn out to be ephemeral, and the differences emerge as far more basic and important.

1. It is true that both passages concern a specific wrong perpetrated by a specific individual, and that in each instance this person is left unnamed; one may compare *tis (some one)* and *ho toioutos (such a person)* in 2 Cor 2:5, 6, 7 with *tis* and *ho toioutos* in 1 Cor 5:1, 5 (Denney, 2; Hughes, 64 n. 6). At the same time, however, the name seems to have been omitted for a different reason in each instance; the effect of the anonymity in 1 Cor 5 is to emphasize the need to dissociate oneself from the individual, but in 2 Cor 2 the anonymity serves to help shield the person from further ostracism (see de Boor, 54).

2. In 1 Cor 5:2, Paul had urged the Corinthians to mourn the transgression, and in 2 Cor 7:7–8 one learns that a letter of Paul had indeed led to mourning. Two different Greek words are used, however: in 1 Cor 5 a form of the verb

*penthein,* and in 2 Cor 7 the adjective *odyrmos.* Moreover, in 2 Cor 7:7–8 it appears that Paul had been rather surprised to hear how his letter had saddened the congregation, whereas in 1 Cor 5:2 he had been surprised that the transgression itself had not prompted mourning.

3. In both instances, certainly, an act of congregational discipline is in view (1 Cor 5:4*b*–5; 2 Cor 2:6–8). It remains to ask, however, whether the same *kind* of disciplinary action is involved (see point 7 below). It may also be argued that the entirely democratic handling of the case presupposed in 2 Cor 2 does not accord well with the more authoritarian position taken by the apostle in 1 Cor 5 (cf. Allo, 59–60; Prümm I, 68). Also, Paul's comment in 2 Cor 2:9 that he had written to test the obedience of the congregation is not an apt description of what he had been doing in 1 Cor 5:1–5 (Allo, 58).

4. It has been alleged that the word *matter* (Greek *pragma*) in 2 Cor 7:11 *(you have demonstrated yourselves to be innocent in the matter)* is to be related to the word *immorality* (Greek *porneia*) in 1 Cor 5:1 (Denney, 2; Hughes, 64 n. 6). To carry any weight whatever, this point has to presume that Paul had used *pragma* in 1 Thess 4:6 with reference to sexual immorality; but a strong case can be made that his reference there is no longer to sexual transgression but to dishonesty in "business" (e.g., Laub 1973:55–56). The argument, then, is tenuous at best. The fact remains that there is no clear evidence in 2 Cor 2:5–11 or 7:5–12 that any *sexual* offense had been committed (cf. Schlatter, 488).

5. It has often been noted that *Satan* is mentioned in both 1 Cor 5:5 and 2 Cor 2:11 (e.g., Hughes, 64 n. 6; Lampe 1967:354). *Satan,* however, plays quite a different role in the two passages. In 1 Cor 5 he serves as the agent of punishment for the offender, but in 2 Cor 2 he is portrayed as a threat to Paul and the congregation unless the offending party is forgiven and reconciled (Windisch, 92; Allo, 57; Bruce, 186; cf. Dibelius 1909:52–53).

6. Christ, too, is mentioned in both passages (1 Cor 5:4; 2 Cor 2:10), but in very different connections. In 1 Cor 5 Christ is invoked as the authority by whom Paul pronounces judgment, but in 2 Cor 2 he is invoked as the eschatological Lord before whom both Paul and his readers are called to account (cf. Dibelius, ibid.; Tasker, 55).

7. Both passages have some specific punishment in view for the offender; Paul orders punishment in 1 Cor 5:4–5, and in 2 Cor 2:6 he refers to a punishment having been meted out. However, when one asks what *kind* of punishment is in view in each case, what seems to be a point of similarity becomes a point of fundamental difference. The punishment decreed in 1 Cor 5 is severe and permanent: that sexual offender is to be totally cut off from the community and left to the ultimately destructive powers of Satan—that is, physical death, the same order of judgment involved for those who profane Christ's body at the eucharist (1 Cor 11:29–30, illness and death). Paul's counsel in 2 Cor 2:6–8 to forgive and restore the offender is simply inexplicable

if the same case is in view (see Kümmel, 283; Bruce, 185; cf. Prümm I, 68). Tertullian saw this clearly and emphasized it (*On Modesty* XIV), and this much of his argument stands despite the ascetic biases with which he wrote.

8. One might argue that an interest in the offender's salvation is no less apparent in 1 Cor 5 than in 2 Cor 2, and in a general way this is so. But once again the interest in each case is of a rather different order. In 1 Cor 5:5 the reference is to the man's ultimate salvation, the salvation of his "spirit" *(psychē)* at the last day. In 2 Cor 2:5–11, however, the focus is on the offender's restoration to the life of the Christian community here and now. In 1 Cor 5:1–5 there is not the slightest intimation that the man might repent and thereby be reconciled to his Christian brothers and sisters; in fact, the character and permanence of the punishment had left no room for that. If, against all intentions and expectations, the man *had* repented, Paul would doubtless have expressed himself quite differently than he actually does in 2:5–11 (Windisch, 92).

9. In both passages Paul expresses his concern for the spiritual health of the congregation as a whole (1 Cor 5:1 [cf. vv. 6–8, 11]; 2 Cor 2:5, 9; 7:12). But this concern has such a different result in each case that two different situations must be in view. In 1 Cor 5 the concern is for the moral purity of the congregation, and the Corinthians are ordered to separate the immoral person from their midst. In 2 Cor 2 and 7, however, the concern is for unity and harmony within the congregation, and in this instance the appropriate action is to restore an errant member to fellowship.

In every case, then, the alleged similarities between 1 Cor 5:1–5 and 2 Cor 2:5–11 break down. It seems clear that Paul, in 2 Cor 2, is not asking forgiveness for the offender of 1 Cor 5; that matter has been settled long since by the man's permanent exclusion from the Christian community.

But can the alternative hypothesis, that the offense which lies behind 2 Cor 2 was a slander against Paul (or someone close to him), be defended against the objections which have been raised against it? Each of these objections deserves comment.

1. Does not Paul's insistence that the whole congregation had been injured (2 Cor 2:5) run counter to the view that the offense was some slander against the apostle (so Heinrici, 93; Hughes, 64)? This is by no means the case. One must not overlook 7:12, which mentions one specific wronged person. Other evidence—for instance, the wording of 2:10—makes it likely that that person was Paul himself. One is thus permitted to interpret *not to me* in 2:5 as "not only to me" (so Bruce, 185). The principle that is operating here had been expressed by Paul in an earlier letter to Corinth: "If one member suffers, all suffer together; if one member is honored, all rejoice together" (1 Cor 12:26, *RSV*); and it appears again in 2 Cor 11:29, in what is probably Paul's last letter to Corinth: "Who is weak and I am not weak? Who is made to stumble and I do not burn with indignation?"

2. If the offense was a slander against Paul, one is required to hypothesize not only an interim "emergency" visit, on which occasion the offense occurred, but also an intermediate letter which led the congregation to take disciplinary action, and some argue that neither hypothesis is warranted (e.g., even Tertullian identified the letter mentioned in 2 Cor 2:3ff. as 1 Cor; see Hughes, 61–63; cf. Meyer, 443, and Heinrici, 93). On the contrary, the evidence available is best satisfied on the hypothesis that both an emergency visit and a tearful letter intervened between the writing of 1 Cor and the writing of 2 Cor 2:5–11 (see COMMENT on 1:15–17 and 2:3–4). Moreover, the identification of 1 Cor 5 and 2 Cor 2 creates its own need for an elaborate hypothesis (de Boor, 54 n. 79; cf. Schlatter, 487–88): The Corinthians would have had to disregard Paul's order in 1 Cor 5:4–5; the man would have had to seek forgiveness, and the Corinthians would have had to arrange some other, less extreme punishment for him, so that now Paul needs to ask them to forgive the man and to be reconciled to him. The texts, however, give no basis for such a reconstruction. Again, if there had been no interim visit and no intermediate letter, then the visit on which Paul had founded the congregation would turn out to be the "painful visit" mentioned, for instance, in 2 Cor 2:1, and 1 Cor would have to be regarded as the "tearful letter" described in 2 Cor 2:3ff. Could Paul have described either one in the way this would require?

3. Lampe (1967:354) has argued that the forgiveness involved in 2 Cor 2:7–8 is too formal and ecclesiastical to be appropriate to a situation involving a personal insult to Paul or to one of his associates. It has been suggested earlier that perhaps some such point as this had been made by the minority in Corinth, who opposed any formal disciplinary action against the wrongdoer. Why should the congregation as a whole involve itself in a purely personal dispute? That is why Paul emphasizes it was *not* a purely personal affront but an injury to the whole community. Whatever involves the apostle involves the churches of his founding (see, e.g., 3:2–3; 1 Cor 9:1c–2).

4. The mild tone and lenient attitude of 2:5–11, it is observed, do not accord with the harsh and strident tone of chaps. 10–13, where Paul is clearly engaged in the defense of his apostolic status (Meyer, 443; Heinrici, 93). But if the reconstruction of events proposed in this commentary is correct, the difference in tone is well enough explained by the fact that chaps. 10–13 were written when the attack on Paul's apostleship had become more serious, or at least had come to be perceived by him as being more serious, than the affront experienced on the emergency visit. Furthermore, once the matter of "tone" has been raised, one must ask whether the leniency shown in 2:5–11 accords with the much stricter attitude toward sexual transgressions Paul normally assumed —for example, in 1 Cor 6:12ff.; 1 Thess 4:3ff.; Rom 13:12; and in 1 Cor 5:1–5 itself (Kümmel, 283; Prümm I, 68; cf. Tertullian, *On Modesty* XIII–XIV).

5. Hughes, 59, offers a different kind of objection when he asserts that, assuming Paul had followed up a traumatic interim visit with a scathing,

tearful letter, there would indeed be justification for the criticism of which he himself takes account in 10:10–11, namely, that he is bolder in his letters than in person. This is begging the question, for Paul's opponents may well have been correct in their assessment of the relative effectiveness of his disciplinary visits versus his disciplinary letters!

6. Finally, Hughes is also begging the question when he cites Gal 6:1 to show that Paul always wanted to keep open the possibility of repentance and restoration (63). This point has force only if one is willing to presume that the principle of Gal 6:1 was intended to apply in all instances, and that Paul himself was always and entirely consistent in his handling of every individual case.

None of these individual objections is sufficient, nor are they collectively sufficient, to require revision of the present-day consensus about 2:5–11. Paul had been slandered, probably to his face, by an unnamed individual. A majority of the Corinthian congregation had agreed to some sort of disciplinary action against him, but only after the seriousness and wider meaning of the offense had been brought home to it by Paul's tearful letter. Confident now of the church's obedience, he writes again about the matter, this time urging that the offending party be forgiven and brought back into the Christian community.

## 4. A TRIP TO MACEDONIA, 2:12–13

2 ¹²When I came to Troas on behalf of the gospel of Christ, a door having been opened for me in the Lord, ¹³my anxiety was unrelieved because I did not find my brother Titus there. So despite the opportunity I took my leave of them and came away to Macedonia.

### NOTES

2:12. *When I came.* The first person singular is still used in this and the following verse, as it has been fairly consistently since 1:15; see NOTES there.

*Troas.* The city of Alexandria, surnamed Troas *(Alexandreia hē Trōas)* to distinguish it as the important coastal city located in the Troad, a fifty-mile-wide promontory at the northwest corner of Asia Minor. (The use of the article here, *tēn Trōada,* does not require one to see a reference to the region instead of the city; the article is also used in Acts 20:6, where—as elsewhere in Acts [16:8, 11; 20:5]—the city is meant.) The city had been founded shortly after 311 B.C.E. by Antigonus, one of the successors of Alexander the Great, and was at first named Antigonia. After the death of Antigonus in 301 it was renamed (by Lysimachus) for Alexander himself, and prospered as a major seaport, probably until the sixth century C.E. In 133 B.C.E. the region was incorporated into the Roman province of Asia; under Augustus, Alexandria Troas itself became a

Roman colony, brought under the *ius Italicum* and designated henceforth on its coinage as either "Colonia Augusta Troadensium" or "Colonia Augusta Troas." Paul himself mentions the city nowhere else, but there is a reference to it in the deutero-Pauline 2 Tim 4:13, perhaps dependent on Acts 20:13; see Dibelius 1972:126. The city was an episcopal see during Byzantine times. For a general description of the region and of its history and exploration, see Cook 1973, especially 198–204. Hemer (1975) gives more attention to the history of the city itself and to the NT references. On Paul's mission in Troas, see COMMENT.

*on behalf of the gospel of Christ.* The Greek is simply *eis to euangelion tou Christou* (cf. Phil 2:22; Rom 1:1 [without the article]), literally "for the gospel of Christ." It is questionable whether the noun here should be taken as a pure *nomen actionis,* as Windisch, 94, and some others do (cf. *RSV:* "to preach the gospel of Christ"); see Schütz 1975:41 n. 1 (citing Molland). Rather, the phrase seems to be a functional equivalent of *dia to euangelion* ("on account of the gospel"), 1 Cor 9:23. Elsewhere in 2 Cor, Paul refers to *the gospel of Christ* in 9:13; 10:14; see also Rom 15:19; 1 Cor 9:12; Gal 1:7; Phil 1:27; 1 Thess 3:2. Cf. 2 Cor 4:4. In 2 Cor the verb *(euangelizein)* is employed only twice, at 10:16 and 11:7.

*a door having been opened.* Paul had used the same metaphor in 1 Cor 16:9, and it is also present in Col 4:3; Rev 3:8. The use of the perfect tense of the participle, which one might translate "stood open," suggests that Paul had thought of the opportunity in Troas as more than just a fleeting one. It is more important, however, that the tr. convey the sense of the passive voice: *having been opened,* presumably by God (as in Col 4:3). Thus the following phrase, *in the Lord,* might designate both the means by which the door was opened and the sphere wherein Paul's opportunity lay. It is doubtful whether Paul is thinking (also) of Troas itself as offering sea and land access to other places for evangelization, as Ramsay thought possible (*HDB* IV:814). The metaphor is used differently in Acts 14:27, where God is portrayed as having opened "a door of faith to the Gentiles" *(RSV).* See 1 Thess 1:9 for an alternate expression of the opportunity Paul found in a mission field (Plummer, 64).

13. *my anxiety was unrelieved.* KJV translates "I had no rest in my spirit," but *anesis* doesn't mean "rest" so much as release from some sort of burden (BAG s.v.); in 8:13 it is contrasted with *thlipsis* ("distress"). The phrase *tō pneumati mou* (*KJV:* "in my spirit") refers to Paul's whole being (cf. Rom 1:9; 1 Cor 16:18), and the relief the Corinthians had brought to Titus is expressed in similar terms (7:13*b*). Paul's statement in 7:5 is fully equivalent to the one in the present verse, even though the word used is *sarx* (literally "flesh") rather than *pneuma* (literally "spirit"); see Bultmann, 55; Schweizer, *TDNT* VI:435. For a different view see Jewett 1971:192–97, 451–53. The perfect tense *eschēka* (*KJV:* "I had") is probably used here in place of the aorist; BDF § 343(a); Moule 1953:14; *GNTG* I:145; III:148 ("narrative perfect"). Robertson suggests, however, that the present perfect was chosen to convey the *duration* of Paul's anxiety, Paul's *release* from that at the eventual arrival of Titus (see 7:5–16), and the *vividness* of the experience as Paul writes about it now (1923:900–1).

*because I did not find.* Only here in the NT does the articular infinitive with the dative have this causal sense. See BDF § 401; Robertson 1923:532; *GNTG* III:242.

*my brother Titus.* Paul only uses the expression *my brother* of a specific individual when he wishes to emphasize the importance of that person to him. The only other instances are in Phil 2:25, when Epaphroditus is commended to the Philippians, and in Phlm 16, when Onesimus is commended to Philemon ("a beloved brother, especially to me"); see, further, NOTES on 1:1. Windisch, 94, points out that Paul's description of Titus as his *brother* is an appropriate demonstration of the apostle's conviction that there is neither Jew nor Greek in Christ (Gal 3:28; 1 Cor 12:13, etc.), since Titus was a Gentile Christian. In 8:23 Paul describes Titus as "my partner and fellow worker on your behalf." There is no mention of Titus in Acts and none in 1 Cor, although he is mentioned more often in 2 Cor (see also 7:6, 13, 14; 8:6, 16, 23; 12:18) than anywhere else (Gal 2:1, 3). His association with Paul was memorialized by the writer who later composed the Pastoral Epistles, including the so-called letter of "Paul to Titus" (Tit 1:4; see also 2 Tim 4:10).

*despite the opportunity.* Translates *alla,* "but rather," which must have in mind the previous mention of the open door for missionary work Paul had found in Troas. "But rather" than take advantage of that, and because of his unrelieved anxiety, he left for Macedonia.

*I took my leave of them.* The verb is used similarly in Acts 18:18, 21 when Paul bids farewell to the Corinthian and Ephesian congregations, respectively. It remains unclear to whom, precisely, *them* refers: at least to whatever Christians and new converts there were in Troas, and perhaps also to one or more of Paul's associates left behind there.

*came away to Macedonia.* The present letter is written from somewhere in *Macedonia* (see INTRODUCTION, p. 41). On *Macedonia* in general, see NOTES at 1:16. What happened when Paul arrived there is disclosed in 7:5–16.

## COMMENT

Georgi (1965:51 n. 190) has suggested that these two verses essentially continue the matter of Paul's affliction in Asia, which had been introduced in 1:8. While it is very possible that Paul had experienced that affliction—whatever it was—not long before setting out on the mission to Troas mentioned here, the reference in 1:8 belongs to a stylistically and functionally different part of the letter. It is more satisfactory to read these verses in the context of 1:12ff., especially in connection with 1:15ff., where, as here, the first person singular predominates. Thus, vv. 12–13 conclude the first main section of this letter (Letter D = chaps. 1–9; see INTRODUCTION, pp. 41–44). In these several paragraphs Paul is intent on assuring his readers that, despite appearances to the contrary, he cares very deeply about their congregation. In 1:15–2:2 he has taken up the matter of a canceled visit, explaining that the cancellation was a sign of his caring for them, not of his indifference. In 2:3–11 he has dealt with the matter of a "tearful letter," written, he has insisted, for their own good. Now, in vv. 12–13 he further emphasizes how great his concern for them ‸has been: so great that he gave up a promising mission in Alexandria Troas in order to learn as soon as he could how Titus, who had been sent to Corinth earlier by Paul (7:5–16), had fared among them. Windisch, 93, believes that 'logically" vv. 12–13 should follow 2:1–4, and he even speaks of a "hiatus" between vv. 11 and 12 (225; rightly criticized by Thrall 1982:107–8). But when it is recognized that the matter of the "tearful letter" motivated Paul to comment as he does in 2:5–11 (see 2:9 and COMMENT on 2:3–11), and that the whole section (1:12–2:13) is addressed to Corinthian complaints that Paul is unconcerned about them, then the difficulty vanishes. The apostle is not *beginning* a narrative in vv. 12–13 (which would then be suddenly "broken off" and "continued" only in 7:5ff.); rather, vv. 12–13 conclude his initial effort to assure the Corinthians that he is by no means indifferent to them. On this point see the incisive comments of Rissi 1969:15–16, seconded by Thrall 1982:112.

Barrett, 94 (and 1969:9–10, 13), questions whether it was Paul's concern for the Corinthians that drove him on to meet Titus, and suggests that it was, rather, his anxiety about Titus' safety on the highways, since he had been collecting money for Jerusalem. Although Paul himself does not make the object of his anxiety explicit, given the context of 1:12ff. it seems clear that he wants his readers to interpret his eagerness to meet Titus as another sign of his concern (not necessarily "anxiety") for them. That his relationship to them was under some strain is quite apparent from 1:12ff.

While it may be that Paul left Ephesus shortly after his rescue from some mortal danger there (see NOTES and COMMENT on 1:8–10), it would be incorrect to say that he "fled" to Troas. Nor did he go there to meet Titus, even though he was disappointed when Titus was not there, and even though they may even have arranged to meet there. Rather, Paul himself says that he had gone there *on behalf of the gospel of Christ.* (Thus, Hughes's comment that Paul's "expectation had been, first, of finding Titus . . . and then of engaging in a period of missionary activity" [74] puts the matter backward.) He does not say whether he went by land or by sea. If the former, he would have traversed the important highway rebuilt under Augustus and recently (51 C.E.) repaired in the name of Claudius (see Magie 1950:41, 488, 547; for the stations, see 793–96), a journey of perhaps ten days (about 260 miles; Burdick 1978:41). As Pliny the Younger was to discover many years later (ca. 110 C.E.), the overland journey northward from Ephesus was intensely hot in the summer, but the coastal boats (to which he finally resorted at Pergamum) were often delayed by contrary winds (*Letters* X.xv; X.xvii A.1–2).

Troas had been described by Strabo as "one of the notable cities of the world" (XIII.i.26). Like Corinth, it had been colonized by Rome and had attained, by virtue of its strategic geographical location, the status of an important commercial center; see Hemer 1975 and Broughton 1938:708, 716, 859. Cook (1973:383) estimates its population at thirty thousand to forty thousand. According to Acts 16:6–10, Paul and Timothy had been in Troas when Paul, hindered from further missionary efforts in Asia, had a vision of a man from Macedonia saying, "Come over to Macedonia and help us" (16:10, *RSV*). The Acts account says nothing here about converts in Troas itself; rather, it was only a port of embarkation for Paul and Timothy (16:11). Later, however, Acts describes a week-long mission of Paul in Troas as he is on his way from Macedonia and Greece (Corinth) to Jerusalem (20:1–12; here is related the story of Eutychus' fall from a high window and the apostle's miraculous restoration of him). Neither of these accounts in Acts, however, matches exactly the visit to Troas of which Paul himself writes, and the history and development of Christianity in Troas remains as unclear—and as intriguing—as the still unexcavated ruins of the city itself. We do know that when Ignatius, bishop of Antioch, was being taken to Rome as a prisoner—sometime in the first decade of the second century—there was a well-established Christian congregation in Troas, because Ignatius conveys its greetings in letters written while resident there (Phld 11:2; Smyrn 12:1; cf. Pol 8:1). However, only two things are certain about Paul's missionary work in Troas: he thought he saw rich possibilities for the gospel there (did the door in Troas seem all the more "open" to him because of his recent troubles in Ephesus?), and Titus had not yet reached that city, prompting Paul, perhaps with some reluctance, to turn his back on the opportunities and to go on to Macedonia. It must have been arranged, then, that Titus would return from Corinth by way of the Pauline congregations in Macedonia. We are left in the dark, however, as to why Paul thought he could proceed on there—presumably by ship to the port of Neapolis (two to five days' sailing from Troas)—without missing Titus, sailing in the other direction.

These two verses are often regarded as the beginning of a travel narrative (Ephesus to Troas to Macedonia)—or, alternately, as the continuation of such a narrative, begun at 1:8, 15ff. (Georgi)—which is concluded only in 7:5–16, where the apostle's eventual meeting with Titus is recounted. Thus, the material from 2:14 through 7:4 has to be accounted for either as a long "digression" (e.g., Barrett, 97, who quotes with approval Bengel's description of 2:1ff., *nobilissima digressio*) or as an interpolation (e.g., Bornkamm 1971). The "problem" of 2:14–7:4 only exists, however, when one fails to observe that 2:12–13 belong, both formally and functionally, to 1:12–2:11. Formally, they continue to use the first person *singular,* adopted by Paul in 1:15 after the initial appeal for the Corinthians' understanding. Significantly, 7:5ff. opens with the first person *plural* and reverts to the singular only at the end of v. 7 (see NOTES there). Functionally, vv. 12–13 are quite satisfactorily understood as continuing the apostle's explanation of why he did not come to them as he had promised; he could, after all, have sailed directly from Troas when he was finished there. Instead, he now explains, his concern to meet Titus (he wants the Corinthians to understand this to mean "my concern for you") was so intense that he gave up a promising mission in order to learn how things were in Achaia. With this explanation and assurance, Paul hopes, the complaints that some in Corinth have registered about his indifference to them can be laid to rest. He will turn next to an even more fundamental issue which threatens his relationship to them.

# B. COMMENTS ON APOSTOLIC SERVICE, 2:14-5:19

## 5. INTRODUCTION, 2:14-3:6

2 <sup>14</sup>To God be thanks, who in Christ always puts us on display (as if we were prisoners in a triumphal procession), and who manifests through us the fragrance of the knowledge of him in every place. <sup>15</sup>For we are the aroma of Christ to God among those who are being saved and among those who are perishing; <sup>16</sup>to the latter the stench from death for death, to the former the fragrance from life for life. And for these things, who is adequate? <sup>17</sup>For we are not like so many, huckstering the word of God. Rather, we are acting from pure motives; from God in the sight of God we are speaking in Christ.
3 <sup>1</sup>Are we beginning once more to recommend ourselves? Surely, we do not need, as some do, letters of recommendation to you or from you, do we? <sup>2</sup>You yourselves are our letter, inscribed on our hearts, known and read by everyone. <sup>3</sup>You show that you are Christ's letter cared for by us, inscribed not with ink but with the Spirit of the living God; not on stone tablets but on tablets that are human hearts.

<sup>4</sup>Such confidence before God as this we have through Christ. <sup>5</sup>Not that we are of ourselves adequate, so that we evaluate anything as originating with ourselves. Rather, our adequacy is from God, <sup>6</sup>who has enabled us to be adequate as ministers of a new covenant, not written but spiritual. For the letter kills, but the Spirit gives life.

## NOTES

2:14. *To God be thanks.* There are similar expressions of praise elsewhere in the Corinthian letters and Rom, but nowhere else in the NT (1 Tim 1:12 is formulated differently and directed to "Christ Jesus our Lord"). 1 Cor 15:57 is exactly parallel to the present formulation. The usual word order, however, is "Thanks be to God" (Rom 6:17; 7:25; 2 Cor 8:16; 9:15). In 1 Cor 15:57 and 2 Cor 9:15 preceding discussions are being concluded on this triumphant note, whereas in 2 Cor 8:16 "Thanks be to God" introduces some comments about Titus (vv. 17ff). In Rom 6:17 the same expression occurs after a rhetorical question and right in the middle of Paul's discussion; cf. Rom 7:25, whose relation to the context is very often disputed. On the form in general, see Deichgräber 1967:43–44.

*who . . . puts us on display . . . and who manifests.* The grammatical form of this description of God and the influence of Jewish and early Christian liturgical forms on it are considered by J.M. Robinson 1964:230–31.

*puts us on display (as if we were prisoners in a triumphal procession).* Translates *thriambeuonti hēmas,* the meaning of which is difficult to determine. At issue, specifically, is Paul's use of the verb *thriambeuein* (elsewhere in the NT only in Col 2:15).

(1) *KJV*'s "causeth us to triumph" has no lexical support ("the accusative [after the verb] is never the triumphing subject, but always the object of the triumph"—Meyer, 451), and the passage often cited from Ctesias, *Persica* 13, to establish it cannot legitimately be translated in that way (despite BAG s.v. 2); see Williamson 1968:320; Egan 1977:36.

(2) Barrett, 97–98, follows Allo, 43–44, and Kümmel, 198, when he translates "in a triumphal progress," thus supposing that the image is of a victorious general leading his troops through the city streets in one of the famous Roman "triumphal" celebrations; the Roman custom is described in various ancient authors, including Josephus, *War* VII.v.4–6 (the triumph of Vespasian and Titus after the fall of Jerusalem), and Dio Cassius, *Roman History* VI. (On the Roman institution as such, see Versnel 1970.) *JB* clearly construes the meaning of the verb in this way ("makes us . . . partners of his triumph"); see also Calvin, 33; Héring, 18; Wendland, 176; Bruce, 187. However, as even Barrett, 98, acknowledges, there is also no lexical evidence that the verb was used in this way, and LSJ has no other text to cite for this meaning than 2 Cor 2:14; see Williamson 1968:319; Egan 1977:36 and 36–37 n. 11.

(3) A few of the older commentators followed the Vulgate *(triumphant nos)* in translating "triumphs over us" (e.g., Meyer, 452; cf. Denney, 86–89; Schlatter, 495), often with reference to Christian conversion as a being "conquered" by God, whereupon one is brought into God's triumphal procession. However, there is nothing in the context of 2 Cor 2:14 to support this meaning, it would be difficult to know what the adverb *always* could mean as applied to conversion, and the generalized meaning "triumph over" is not attested as early as Paul (Williamson 1968:322; Egan 1977:37).

(4) Many recent commentators and trs. apply to the present verse the meaning "to lead someone captive" (BAG s.v. 1), a well-attested use of the transitive verb in connection with the Roman triumph. Williamson (1968, especially 323–27) has argued for this interpretation; it is the one represented by *NEB* ("leads us about, captives in Christ's triumphal procession") and *TEV* ("led by God as prisoners in Christ's victory procession"), and it is adopted also by Filson, 299, Hughes, 77–78, and de Boor, 61; cf. Collange, 24–25. In its favor is the fact that it accords well with the apostle's conception of his own weakness as a means by which God's power is disclosed (e.g., 4:7–12; cf. 1:8–9; 6:4–10). However, Egan (1977:37–39) has raised several objections to this interpretation, the most important of which are that (a) there are no other known instances—at least, none as early as Paul—of the technical language for a Roman triumph being used metaphorically, and (b) the metaphor would in any case be inappropriate, since the triumphal procession was not endless (note Paul's use of the adverb *always*), since it always ended with the execution of the prisoners who had been paraded

in it, and since, by using the metaphor, Paul would be casting God as the oppressor to whom all of his sufferings are attributable.

(5) Egan (1977) rejects any association of the verb *thriambeuein* with the official Roman institution of the triumph, and would translate "to display," "manifest," or "make known." In support of this he can cite a papyrus text from Egypt dated 14 B.C.E. (BGU IV.1061, noted by Field 1879:181–82 and in MM s.v., but usually overlooked in discussions of 2 Cor 2:14 and Col 2:15). The text, which employs the compound *ekthriambizein,* reads: "For which crimes they were delivered up in Sinary itself and they were released in order that the matter not be noised abroad [*pros to mē ekthriambisthēnai to pragma*]" (tr. Egan 1977:41). This meaning is supported by other texts from the second century C.E., several ancient versions translate 2 Cor 2:14 in accord with it, and some of the remarks of the earliest Greek commentators, despite their allusions to the Roman triumph, seem also to point in this direction (Egan, ibid.:42–50).

(6) P. Marshall (1983)—responding to Egan's arguments, (5) above—returns to a position more nearly like that represented by (4), but with certain important modifications. In his view, Paul does intend that his readers should think of the celebration of a Roman triumph, which, he shows, was "a familiar institution to Greeks and Romans of all levels of society" (304). But the purpose of Paul's allusion, Marshall suggests, is really quite limited: namely, to identify himself with the shame and humiliation experienced by the prisoners who were put on parade. Marshall acknowledges that no metaphorical usage of the Greek term datable to the first century has come to light so far, but he is able to provide clear instances of the Latin metaphor (304–6). The most impressive of these is from Paul's contemporary, Seneca, who writes of the just complaints of a person whose benefactor will not allow him to forget who it is that has helped him (*On Benefits* II.xi.1): "I owe nothing to you if you saved me in order that you might have someone to exhibit [*ostenderes*]. How long will you parade [*circumducis*] me? How long will you refuse to let me forget my misfortune? In a triumph, I should have had to march but once [*semel in triumpho ductus essem*]!" The allusion to the Roman triumph celebration is clear, and so is the point of it: to be constantly reminded of one's dependence on a benefactor is an even more dreadful humiliation than being paraded as a prisoner of war in the streets of Rome. It is not impossible that Paul uses the Greek verb *thriambeuein* for a similar reason, and this has been taken into account in the present tr. Thus, the verb would not just mean "to display" (Egan) but would carry the additional connotation "as humiliated" (cf. 1 Cor 4:9*b*, "we have become a spectacle"); that is, *as if we were prisoners in a triumphal procession.* This last phrase has been placed in parentheses for two reasons. First, in itself the expression *thriambeuonti hēmas* need mean nothing more than *puts us on display,* and one cannot be completely certain that Paul intends an allusion to the Roman triumph. Second, even if there is such an allusion here, it is secondary to the main point in vv. 14–16*a*— namely, that the gospel of Christ is effectively proclaimed by means of Paul's ministry. There is no sustained application of the imagery of a Roman triumph to the Pauline apostolate, as some interpreters (and trs.) tend to suggest.

*manifests.* The verb (*phaneroun*) is used altogether nine times in 2 Cor, and all but one of these occurrences (11:6) fall in chaps. 1–9 (2:14; 3:3; 4:10–11; 5:10, 11 [twice]; 7:12); otherwise in the undisputed Pauline letters it occurs only in Rom 1:19; 3:21; 1 Cor 4:5 (and in the late doxology, Rom 16:26). On this basis some have surmised that

Paul has taken the term over from opponents in Corinth and that his use of it in contexts like the present one is polemically motivated (see, e.g., Schulte 1949:21; Güttgemanns 1966:107 n. 75; Lührmann 1965:60–66; Collange, 28–29, 40–41).

*fragrance.* The Greek word *osmē* may refer to either a pleasant (e.g., John 12:3) or an unpleasant (e.g., Tobit 8:3) odor. Here (and in v. 16*b*) the reference is clearly to the former—hence the tr. *fragrance;* contrast v. 16*b*.

*the knowledge of him.* The genitive is certainly objective, but whether the reference is to God (e.g., Windisch, 97; Manson 1953:157; Collange, 31) or to Christ (e.g., Plummer, 70; Hughes, 79 n. 11) is disputed. That the reference is to God is made probable by 4:6 *(the enlightenment coming from the knowledge of the splendor of God),* where the whole thought is closely parallel to that in the present verse. At the same time, it is also clear from 4:6 that Christ is the one through whom the knowledge of God is disclosed to the apostles.

*in every place.* The same phrase *(en panti topō)* appears in 1 Cor 1:2; 1 Thess 1:8; 1 Tim 2:8; Did 14:3 (citing Mal 1:11, "In every place and time offer me a pure sacrifice"). Various synagogue inscriptions, both Hebrew and Greek, attest to the idiomatic use of the word "place" by Jews to refer to a synagogue, and Manson (1962:208–9) suggests that the present phrase, as well as others in the NT, may represent an extension of that idiom to Christian places of worship. Barrett, 99, rightly rejects that interpretation of the phrase in the present verse, although he had accepted it for the same phrase in 1 Cor 1:2 (1968:33–34). The use of the phrase in 1 Tim 2:8; Did 14:3, and also in later texts dealing with cultic practice, suggests that it echoes an early Christian regulation that the eucharist shall be made everywhere, in fulfillment of the promise of Mal 1:11 (Bartsch 1965:47–59). This background would accord with the fact that Paul uses the expression "in the whole world" *(en holō tō kosmō,* Rom 1:8) in exactly the way he had used "in every place" in 1 Thess 1:8. This broader reference (and not a more limited reference to "all the churches," etc., as in 1 Cor 4:17; 7:17; 14:33) is also in accord with the description of God as one *who in Christ always puts us on display* (cf. Barrett, 99).

15. *aroma.* Greek *euōdia,* which, unlike *osmē* (v. 14), refers only to pleasant odors. The combination *osmē euodias* is frequent in the LXX to describe the scent of the burnt offerings presented to God (e.g., Lev 1:9, 13, 17; 2:2), and Paul himself has the sacrificial use of the words in mind when he employs them to describe the gifts the Philippians had sent to him in prison (Phil 4:18). Cf. Eph 5:2, where Christ is the fragrant *(osmē euōdias)* offering to God. In the present verse it is the apostles who are *the aroma,* but they are nonetheless *the aroma of Christ,* and in Greek *of Christ* is placed first, perhaps to make this clear (cf. Hughes, 79 n. 12). Here, however, in contrast to the passages in Phil and Eph, there is no specifically sacrificial imagery (see following note).

*to God.* Translates *tō Theō,* which Bultmann, 70 (following Weiss), would prefer to omit as a gloss. There is, however, very little textual support for omitting these words (only the ninth- or tenth-century Codex Mosquensis, K^ap [or K₂]), and they should probably be retained. Their presence has led some commentators (recently, e.g., Barrett) to think of the expression "a pleasing fragrance *to the Lord" (osmē euodias tō Kyriō),* which appears throughout the LXX as a description of a sacrificial offering made to God (see preceding note). Thus, Barrett, 99, would paraphrase the present verse to read "for we are the sweet savour of sacrifice that rises from Christ to God."

The idea of sacrifice, however, is really alien to this context (correctly Plummer, 71, who notes that the LXX phrase *osmē euodias* does not, in fact, occur here). Paul is not thinking about a scent which benefits God, but about one which is wafted over the world for the benefit of God's people (*among those who are being saved,* etc.). If the words in question are retained, Bultmann would interpret them to mean "to the honor of God" or perhaps "in God's service" (70; cf. Plummer, 71, who comments that the gospel "is always *euōdia* to God, but not always to men, to some of whom it breathes death"). If *Theō* in 5:13 (but without the article) is an analogous case, one might perhaps translate *"for* God." In any event, it is unwarranted to find sacrificial imagery here.

*those who are being saved . . . those who are perishing.* The same two classes are distinguished by Paul in 1 Cor 1:18; cf. 2 Thess 2:10. Only the latter group is mentioned in 4:3, where the context shows that those who belong to it may also be identified as "unbelievers" (see *tōn apistōn,* 4:4). Thus, *those who are being saved* are those who "believe" (note the parallelism of 1 Cor 1:18 and Rom 1:16—"to every one who believes"—and cf. 1 Cor 1:21).

16. *the latter . . . the former.* Translates *hois men . . . hois de,* a non-classical usage in which the relative pronoun has replaced the article *(ho men . . . ho de); GNTG* III:36. Note the chiastic structure of vv. 15–16: The two groups identified in v. 15 are dealt with in reverse order in v. 16.

*stench . . . fragrance.* In each instance the word is *osmē,* used in the first case for an unpleasant odor but in the second case for a pleasant one; see note on v. 14.

*from death for death . . . from life for life.* The majority of mss. omit the preposition *ek,* thus yielding the somewhat easier tr. "stench of death for death . . . fragrance of life for life. . . ." The preference in this case, however, must be for the more difficult text, which is attested by P⁴⁶ ℵ A B C et al. Parallel constructions in the LXX (Ps 83:8, "from strength to strength," *ek dynameōs eis dynamin;* Jer 9:3, "from evil to evil," *ek kakōn eis kaka*) suggest that a Semitic idiom is involved here (Hughes, 81 n. 18, cites Stanley, who calls these "Hebrew superlatives"), and Paul's own use of the same or similar constructions in Rom 1:17 ("from faith to faith," *ek pisteōs eis pistin*), 2 Cor 3:18 ("from splendor to splendor," *apo doxēs eis doxan*), and 2 Cor 4:17 ("incomparable to incomparable," *kath' hyperbolēn eis hyperbolēn*) helps to show that the present phrases should probably be interpreted as "the stench for ultimate death . . . the fragrance for ultimate life."

*for these things.* The words are emphasized by being placed first as the question is posed, and they refer to what has been said about apostolic responsibilities in vv. 14–16*a.*

*adequate.* The adjective is *hikanos,* which might also be translated "sufficient," "fit," or "competent." Its recurrence in 3:5 (along with the cognate noun [3:5] and verb [3:6]) shows that this is the key question being considered in the following section (see COMMENT).

17. *so many.* Translates *hoi polloi* (a substantive formed on the adjective *polys,* literally "the many"), probably preferable here to the alternative reading *hoi loipoi* ("the rest") which is attested by some witnesses, including P⁴⁶ and Marcion; see Metzger 1971:577. In 2:6, Paul had used a substantive formed of the comparative of the same adjective, warranting the tr. "the majority." That does not seem to be war-

ranted in the present case, however, despite Barrett, 103. On the other hand, "many other people" *(JB)* doesn't do justice to the use of the article: *"the* many." The context shows that the expression is being used with a certain degree of contempt for those to whom it is applied (see the following note). C. Daniel's attempt (1966) to find in this phrase a specific Pauline reference to the Jewish sectarians at Qumran, who often described themselves as "the many" *(ha rabbim;* cf. Josephus, *War* II.viii.9 [*hoi pleiōnes*]), is quite unconvincing, not least because it requires one to interpret *the word of God* in this verse as a reference to "the Old Testament and especially to the prophetic texts" (C. Daniel 1966:558); that would be quite un-Pauline (see below). Much nearer at hand, and much more in keeping with the present context, is the usage of the expression by Dio Chrysostom XXXII, 8 (where it is an equivalent for the general public [*plēthos*], the masses [*ochlos*]); Epictetus I.iii.4 (contrasted with "the few" [*hoi oligoi*]); II.i.22 (contrasted with "the philosophers" [*hoi philosophoi*]); and Philo, *Who Is the Heir* 42 (contrasted with "the praiseworthy" [*hoi asteioi*]). See also the quotation from Lucian, *Hermotimus* 59 (cited in the following note), where—as here—the expression is applied to those who offer their teachings for sale like unscrupulous merchants. The parallel *as some* in 3:1 suggests that one should not stress the *numerical* aspect of Paul's expression in the present verse. Note the mention of *many (polloi,* without the article) in 11:18.

huckstering. Cf. *NEB:* "hawking"; *JB:* "offering . . . for sale"; *TEV:* "handle . . . as if it were cheap merchandise." The verb *(kapēleuein)* appears only here in the NT and refers basically to the retailing of goods; the cognate noun *kapēlos* is virtually a synonym of *emporos,* "merchant" (the two are used interchangeably in Plato, *Sophist* 231 D and *Protagoras* 313 C; Sir 26:29). The ancient stereotype of the merchant was of a person concerned only for profit and quite willing to adulterate the product or give short measure for the sake of it. Thus, Dio Chrysostom mentions "tradesmen who cheat in their measures, men whose livelihood from the very nature of the business depends on base gain" (XXXI, 37; cf. 38), and *kapēlos* is used in the LXX version of Isa 1:22, "your [wine-]merchants mix the wine with water" (cf. Barrett, 103, who therefore translates the verb "watering down"). The passages cited from Plato show that the terms could be applied metaphorically to those who trade in ideas, and in Paul's day it was not uncommon for them to be used specifically by the opponents of itinerant teachers, who were charged with showing more concern for their own welfare than for the truth. We are told that Apollonius had criticized a certain Euphrates for "huckstering his wisdom" *(tēn sophian kapēleuein* [Philostratus, *Life of Apollonius* I.xiii]), and Lucian writes sharply of "philosophers [who] sell their wines—most of them [*hoi polloi*] adulterating and cheating and giving false measure" *(Hermotimus* 59; cf. Lucian's extended description of such cheats in *The Fisherman* 29–37). The huckstering of both wares and ideas at the time of the Isthmian Games (sponsored by Corinth) is described by Dio Chrysostom when he comments on "the wretched sophists" and Diogenes' presence among them (VIII, 9, quoted in the INTRODUCTION, p. 14). Paul must be thinking here of those who teach for their own gain and, in the process, adulterate the truth; see Windisch, *TDNT* III:603–5. (Additional texts are given by MacMullen 1974:139.) Hock (1978:562 n. 43) thinks Paul's use of it in this verse is further evidence of the apostle's "snobbish attitude toward work."

*the word of God.* The phrase is used again in 4:2, where it is to be understood as another expression for the "gospel" (4:3). This is also the meaning of the phrase in 1 Thess 2:13 (see 1:5–6, where "our gospel" is parallel to "the word"); Phil 1:14 ("the gospel," v. 12, is again parallel) and in the present verse (cf. *the gospel of Christ,* v. 12). See also Rom 9:6; 1 Cor 14:36 and "the word of the Lord" (1 Thess 1:8; 4:15); "the word of the cross" (1 Cor 1:18); "the word of reconciliation" (2 Cor 5:19); "the word of truth" (2 Cor 6:7); "the word of life" (Phil 2:16)—all virtual equivalents for "the gospel."

*we are acting.* These words are supplied because the Greek construction (*hōs ex eilikrineias*) is elliptical; see BDF § 425(4). One might also translate "we are speaking," thus picking up the verb Paul uses later in the sentence. The more inclusive word used here is perhaps preferable, however, because it is able to tie together the general reference of the preceding participle, "huckstering," with the later, more specific reference to "speaking."

*from pure motives.* Translates *ex eilikrineias,* "on the basis of [our] sincerity," in contrast to those who peddle the gospel out of self-interest; cf. 1:12.

*from God in the sight of God.* These two prepositional phrases go closely together, since the introductory *all' hōs* ("but as") is not repeated before the second. The first phrase anticipates 3:5, *our adequacy is from God* (but note also, in 1:12, that Paul describes his sincerity as *godly* [*tou Theou*] and associates it closely with *the grace of God*); the second indicates that apostles are held accountable by the God from whom their apostleship derives. According to Schütz (1975:211), "both stand parallel to and clarify *hōs ex eilikrineias* ["from pure motives"]." Some mss. replace *katenanti* with *katenōpion,* but the meaning remains the same, *in the sight of.* Cf. Rom 4:17 (said of Abraham).

*we are speaking in Christ.* The whole phrase, *in the sight of God we are speaking in Christ* is repeated verbatim in 12:19b. This is not simply an oath formula by which the apostle seeks to guarantee the truthfulness of what he is just now writing, and it is therefore misleading to compare it with the asseveration of Rom 9:1 ("I am speaking the truth in Christ, I am not lying [*alētheian legō en Christō, ou pseudomai*]"), as Schütz does (1975:212); there are similar attestations in 2 Cor 2:10; 11:10. Rather, the affirmations of this verse and of 12:19b concern Paul's total apostolic ministry, the authenticity of which is being questioned in Corinth (see 13:3). The reference here is not just to preaching in the narrow sense but to the whole apostolic witness to Christ (cf. Schütz 1975:211).

**3:1.** *once more.* Translates *palin* ("again"), which may be construed with either *archometha* ("Are we again beginning . . . ?") or with *synistanein* ("to recommend ourselves again?"). There is little difference in meaning, but the second interpretation is more likely in view of 5:12 (see COMMENT).

*to recommend.* The verb is *synistanein,* employed by Paul only four times outside of 2 Cor. In 2 Cor 1–9 alone, however, it occurs five times, and then four more times in chaps. 10–13. Used transitively it may mean "to demonstrate" or "to show" something, and this meaning is attested in the Pauline letters in Rom 3:5; 5:8; 2 Cor 7:11; Gal 2:18. In Rom 16:1, however, it is used with the meaning "to recommend," and specifically to recommend one person to another. This is clearly the meaning in the present verse as well (see below on *letters of recommendation*), and in all but one of the other occurrences in 2 Cor (4:2; 5:12; 6:4; 10:12, 18 [twice]; 12:11).

*Surely, we do not need . . . do we?* The question is introduced by *ē mē,* the *mē* signaling that a negative answer is presumed (thus, *we do not . . . do we?*). The word *surely* has been supplied in order to convey something of the force of the Greek word *ē* (literally "or," better attested than the phonetically identical *ei,* "if"). The question to which it provides the transition appears to have been prompted by the suggestion made by someone else that Paul *did* need commendatory letters.

*as some do.* The reference here *(hōs tines)* is clearly pejorative, the *some* referring to those whom Paul opposes, as in 10:2. The pronoun is used similarly in 1 Cor 4:18; 15:12, where the opponents are apparently members of the Corinthian congregation. In the present passage, however, as in Gal 1:7, *some* must refer to persons who have come to the congregation from elsewhere; otherwise the reference to their needing introductory letters makes no sense. Cf. *hōs hoi polloi* in 2:17, where it is likely that the same persons are in mind as here; their "huckstering" thus includes a concern for *letters of recommendation.*

*letters of recommendation.* A technical term has been used here. The "letter of recommendation" *(epistolē systatikē),* of which both Demetrius (second or first century B.C.E.) and Libanius (fourth century C.E.) provide models, was a well-established form in Paul's day (numerous Greek examples from the third century B.C.E. through the sixth century C.E. may be found in Kim 1972:Appendix III). Such letters were ordinarily carried by the person being recommended in order that he or she might be received hospitably and perhaps aided in some specified way; see Keyes 1935; P. Marshall 1980:141–202, 412–17. Acts 9:2; 22:5 attest to the use of letters of this kind also within Jewish circles, and Paul himself provides good examples of Christian *letters of recommendation* in Rom 16:1–2 (Phoebe of Cenchreae is commended to the Roman Christians—or to the Ephesians) and in his letter to Philemon on behalf of the runaway slave Onesimus. See also the commendatory passage in Phil 2:29–30 (Epaphroditus to the Philippians), and cf. 1 Cor 16:15–16, 17–18; Phil 4:2–3; 1 Thess 5:12–13a. Epictetus (II.iii) cites Diogenes as having criticized such letters in principle, holding that a good person, like a good coin, is easily recognized by intelligent, experienced people.

2. *yourselves.* This word is added to the English tr. to represent the emphasis which is present in Greek through the use of the second person (plural) pronoun. The juxtaposition in Greek of the first and second person pronouns is striking *(hē epistolē hēmōn hymeis este)* and cannot be reproduced adequately in English (only as "yourselves our").

*our letter.* In view of the context, this would not be in lieu of a letter written about Paul by others for the Corinthians (see *for you,* v. 1), but rather in lieu of a letter written about Paul by the Corinthians for others (see *from you,* v. 1). Plummer, 79, and Hughes, 87, find a possible allusion to Paul's description of the Corinthians as constituting a letter for their apostle(s) in Pol Phil 11:3 (early second century). The passage from Polycarp, however, is notoriously difficult, and the most likely tr. of the phrase in question is "in whose [i.e., the Philippians'] midst the blessed Paul labored and who are (mentioned) in the beginning of his letter"; see Schoedel in *AF* 5:32–34 for this tr. and a lengthy note on the problems involved.

*inscribed on . . . hearts.* Similar expressions are frequent in ancient Greek literature;

examples are given by Schrenk, *TDNT* I:770, and Windisch, 104 n. 5, and include, from the LXX, Jer 38(31):33 ("After those days I will certainly put my laws into their mind [*dianoian*], and I will write them upon their hearts [*kai epi kardias autōn grapsō autous*]"). Richard (1981:346) argues that Paul is actually quoting Jeremiah here. See NOTES on v. 3 below for other references. The compound *engraphein* ("to inscribe") was often used to emphasize the element of "documentation," as in some official list, petition, or credential (Schrenk, *TDNT* I:769), and that connotation (which the simple *graphein*, "to write," doesn't necessarily have) is fully appropriate to the present context.

*our.* This is the best-attested reading by far, and has been adopted by *GNT*-Nestle and by many modern commentators (e.g., Plummer, 80; Lietzmann, 110; Kümmel, 199; Allo, 80; Collange, 46). Virtually all of the modern English trs. have also adopted it (e.g., *JB, NEB, TEV, NIV*). The Sinaiticus reading "your" (also attested by a few other witnesses) has been followed by the *RSV* and *NAB*, however, and is preferred by several commentators (e.g., Bultmann, 74–75; Héring, 21 n. 2; Rissi 1969:20; Barrett, 96 n. 3). Barrett (ibid.) argues for this second, admittedly "weakly attested," reading on the basis of the context and the possibility that the strongly attested *our* represents an assimilation to 7:3. The latter text certainly cannot be used to confirm *our* in 3:2, as Lietzmann does (110), since the reference there to Paul's having spoken previously about the Corinthians being "in our hearts" could have been to some lost writing or oral comment (so Bultmann, 75; cf. Metzger 1971:577), or even to the remark of 6:11 (so Rissi, 1969:20 n. 30). On the other hand, it is inherently more probable that "your" originated in an attempt to assimilate the expression to the opening statement in v. 2 (*"You yourselves are our letter"*) than that *our* originated as an assimilation to the more remote text in 7:3. Moreover, Baird (1961) has shown that the better attested *our* makes perfectly good sense in this context; cf. Metzger 1971:577, and see COMMENT. Whether this is only a literary plural and thus refers to Paul alone ("my heart," as Gdspd. and Mof. have it; so Baird 1961:170 n. 11) must remain an open question.

*hearts.* Paul uses this term in the Semitic sense of one's inmost self and most authentic being, as contrasted with what is merely "present" in a more obvious way (e.g., 1 Thess 2:17). See further discussion on v. 3.

*known and read.* These present-tense participles, like the perfect participle *inscribed,* further identify the *letter* which the Corinthians are said to constitute for Paul. Commentators have often remarked on the surprising sequence of these terms (isn't a letter *read* before its contents are *known?*), and some have explained this by saying that one recognizes from whom the letter has *come* before one reads it (e.g., Plummer, 80; cf. *NEB*: "can see it for what it is and read it"). But Paul is fond of such wordplay as the one represented here (*ginōskomenē kai anaginōskomenē;* the same words are paired in Acts 8:30); and here, as in 1:13, where a similar one occurs (see NOTE there), the second (compound) word seems designed only to intensify the thought already expressed in the first word: what can be *known* can be known very well—that is, carefully *read.*

*by everyone.* The Greek (*hypo pantōn anthrōpōn*) is rendered "by all men" in *RSV* and *NAB* (cf. *NEB* and most older English versions), but *anthrōpos* is a generic term and requires some such tr. as the one provided here (cf. *JB, TEV, NIV*).

3. *You show.* This tr. (which follows Gdspd., *RSV, NIV,* and others) reads the

present participle *(phaneroumenoi)* as middle voice (so also, e.g., Windisch, 105; Héring, 21; Rissi 1969:21). But even if it is taken in a passive sense (Hughes, 88: "Being made manifest"; *GAGNT,* 539: "You are shown to be"), it is to be construed with the *hymeis (You . . . yourselves)* of v. 2. It carries forward Paul's affirmation that the Corinthians themselves constitute a letter for their apostle(s).

*Christ's letter.* Here, and in the context, there is less thought of what is "in" the *letter* represented by the Corinthian congregation than of the existence of the *letter* as an attestation of Paul's apostleship; the genitive *Christou* ("of Christ") is not, therefore, objective (a letter about Christ) but authorial, "a letter from Christ," a letter whose origin is Christ.

*cared for by us.* The same phrase, but with a present (instead of an aorist) passive participle, occurs in 8:19, 20, where Paul writes of the collection for Jerusalem. The verb *(diakonein)* is used by Paul elsewhere only in Phlm 13 and Rom 15:25, the latter again in relation to his collection for Jerusalem. The general meaning "care for" is appropriate to all four passages and leaves open the question whether, in the present case, Paul may be thinking of himself as the "amanuensis" of the letter "dictated" by Christ (e.g., Meyer, 461; Kümmel, 199; cf. *JB:* "drawn up by us") or as the courier (Lietzmann, 110; Windisch, 105; Baird 1961:169, with special reference to the use of the verb in Josephus, *Antiquities* VI.xiii.6; Collange, 50; cf. *RSV, NEB, TEV, NAB).* The aorist tense points back to the founding of the Corinthian congregation (Windisch, 105).

*inscribed.* The participle is repeated from v. 2, again to describe the "letter" which the Corinthian Christians represent for Paul. He has already indicated where the letter is *inscribed* (v. 2); now he proceeds to say by what means it has been *inscribed.*

*not with ink.* In Paul's day *ink* was compounded of a sooty carbon and a thin solution of gum; hence it is described in Greek as *melan* ("black") because of its black color. Used with a reed pen *(kalamos;* see 3 John 13), it was the usual means of inscribing papyrus *(chartēs;* see 2 John 12); see Williams, "Writing and Writing Materials," *IDB* R–Z:918–19.

*Spirit of the living God.* The phrase *living God (Theos zōn,* as here) is frequent in the LXX (e.g., Deut 5:26; Josh 3:10; 1 Kgdms [1 Sam] 17:26, 36; 4 Kgdms [2 Kgs] 19:4, 16; Ps 83[84]:3; Isa 37:4, 17), and in Rom 9:26 Paul directly quotes one of the passages in which it appears (Hos 2:1 [1:10]); see also 1 Thess 1:9 (where Hellenistic-Jewish motifs are prominent) and 2 Cor 6:16 (where Jewish concerns are again clear; see NOTES and COMMENT). Elsewhere in the NT: Acts 14:15; 1 Tim 3:15; 4:10; Heb 3:12; 9:14; 10:31; 12:22; Rev 7:2. The phrase with the articles is equivalent (see Ps 41[42]:3) and is found in this form in Matt 16:16; 26:63; Rev 15:7. Everding, who has provided a full study of the concept (1968), notes that it seems to have had no prominence at Qumran (ibid.:103–4). He classifies the present verse as an instance of its "rhetorical application" to emphasize "the superiority and correctness of the Spirit as that which is in keeping with the nature of God more than a code 'written in ink' " (ibid.:331; cf. 347). Commentators are divided on how the adjective should be construed in 1 Pet 1:23. The life-giving power of the *Spirit* is emphasized by Paul elsewhere (see especially Rom 8:1–11; Gal 5:25; 6:8), but only here does he combine a reference to the Spirit with the traditional description of God as *living.*

*stone tablets.* On Mount Sinai, according to the Pentateuch, Moses had received "the two tablets of testimony, tablets of stone [LXX: *plakas lithinas*] written with the finger of God" (Exod 24:12; 31:18; cf. 34:1 and Deut 9:10–11), and it is to this, certainly, that Paul alludes with his mention of *stone tablets (plaxin lithinais)*.

*tablets that are human hearts.* Translates *plaxin kardiais sarkinais,* substantially better attested than the variant *plaxin kardias sarkinais* ("in fleshy tables of the heart" —*KJV*), which is an attempt to improve the awkwardness of the preferred reading (Metzger 1971:577). There is no textual warrant for striking either *plaxin,* as WH and others (e.g., Bultmann, 77; Rissi 1969:22 n. 32) have suggested (thus the tr. "on human hearts"—*TEV;* cf. Gdspd.), or *kardiais,* as proposed by Wordsworth, 153 (noted by Hughes, 90) and Bachmann, 144 (thus the tr. "on fleshy tablets").

*human hearts.* Paul seems to have in mind not only the references in Exod and Deut to the stone tablets given to Moses (see above) but also the contrast drawn between "the heart of stone" *(hē kardia hē lithinē)* and "a heart of flesh" *(kardia sarkinē)* in Ezek 11:19; 36:26. In these passages, as in the present verse, the adjective *sarkinas* ("fleshy") is used for that which is a living substance, as opposed to that which is, as we say, "stone-cold"; thus the tr. *human* (see Schweizer, *TDNT* VII:143–44). In addition to Jer 38(31):33, mentioned in the NOTES on v. 2 above, the idea of something written inwardly on the heart is also present in the LXX in Prov 3:3A; 7:3; 22:20 (where the expression is *to platos tēs kardias sou,* "the breadth [ = the tablet] of your heart"). Paul certainly has the passage from Jer in mind by the time he writes about a *new covenant* in v. 6. The reference to "the tables of your heart" in 1 Clem 2:8 must allude directly to the expression as it occurs in Prov, because Clement uses the LXX term *platos* rather than Paul's term *plax* (J. H. Kennedy 1900:147–48; Hagner 1973:211–12).

4. *Such confidence . . . as this.* The emphasis in the sentence falls on this phrase, which stands first. When Paul uses the noun *pepoithēsis* in 1:15; 8:22, the Corinthians themselves are the objects of *confidence;* in 10:2, on the other hand, he uses the term in close association with the personal "boldness" *(parrēsia)* he hopes he will not have to demonstrate on his next visit. Closer to the thought of the present verse is the use of the perfect tense of the verb *peithein* in 1:9 (see NOTES), where Paul's confidence is *before God* (in God's power ultimately to save or vindicate).

*through Christ.* Compare the phrase "in the Lord," which Paul frequently uses to describe the basis or sphere of his (or others') confidence: Rom 14:14; Gal 5:10; Phil 1:14; 2:24 (in each case a perfect tense of the verb).

5. *Not . . . of ourselves adequate.* Here, as in 1:24 (see NOTES), the formula *ouch hoti* introduces the correction of a misunderstanding or criticism, actual or feared. The whole phrase forms the first part of a typically Pauline antithesis, this one contrasting reliance on self (cf. the following *ex heautōn*) with reliance on God (see below).

*so that we evaluate.* The infinitive *(logisasthai)* may have either final or consecutive force here. Héring, 22, opts for the former ("in order that"), but the latter is perhaps more likely. According to BAG s.v. 2, the verb is used here to mean "thinking out" or "considering" something; the context, however, would seem to require the more specific meaning of "estimate" or "evaluate" (BAG s.v. 1b). In this phrase Paul identifies the consequence of claiming sufficiency in oneself.

*anything as originating with ourselves.* In this context the *ti (anything)* has special reference to the gospel and the commission to preach it. Thus, as Georgi (1964:222 n. 9) observes, *regard anything as originating with ourselves (logisasthai ti hōs ex heautōn)* is placed over against that "speaking from God" *(lalein ex Theou)* to which Paul had referred in 2:17. It is what those do who peddle God's word as if it were a commodity at their own disposal.

*Rather, our adequacy is from God.* The second member of Paul's antithesis is now given; comparable antithetical formulations are present in 1:9; 4:5; 5:15; 10:18, and elsewhere in the Pauline letters (N. Schneider 1970:22). The noun *hikanotēs* appears nowhere else in the Greek Bible or early Christian literature (BAG s.v.; Windisch, 109).

6. *enabled us to be adequate.* This somewhat awkward tr. attempts to exhibit the fact that the verb *(hikanoun)* is cognate to the adjective *adequate* (2:16b; 3:5) and the noun *adequacy* (3:5). Outside the NT (see also Col 1:12) the verb is always passive (BAG s.v.). Here the aorist tense would seem to look back to a specific call and commissioning to apostolic service (Gal 1:15–16; cf. 1 Cor 15:8).

*ministers of a new covenant.* The expressions "ministers of God" (6:4), "ministers of righteousness" (11:15), and "ministers of Christ" (11:23) are parallel.

*ministers.* The term *(diakonos)* means, first of all, "one who serves," but it can also refer to one who has been dispatched on some kind of an errand for another. Georgi (1964:31–38) argues that Paul's opponents in Corinth used it of themselves (see 11:23) in the yet further extended sense of "envoy" or "ambassador," but J. N. Collins (1974) has shown that this conclusion cannot be supported from Epictetus III.xxiv, on which Georgi's case mainly rests.

*a new covenant.* The conception is first articulated in Jer 31:31–34 (LXX: 38:31–34), but it occurs as such nowhere else in the OT (cf., however, Ezek 36:26, where there is reference to "a new spirit" and to "a new heart" of flesh replacing the [old] heart of stone). At Qumran the term *(berit hadāsāh)* was used as a description of the community itself (CD vi.19; xviii.21 = xix.33–34; xx.12; 1QpHab ii.3 [conjectured]), but it is not found elsewhere in the intertestamental literature, even when the Jer passage is reflected (as in Bar 2:35; Jub 1:17–18, 23–25). In the NT the expression ([*hē kainē*] *diathēkē*) appears in the traditional eucharistic words, as handed on by Paul in 1 Cor 11:25 and as present in the Synoptic Gospels ([Matt 26:28; Mark 14:24]; Luke 22:20), but elsewhere only here and in Heb (8:8; 9:15; cf. 12:24, *diathēkēs neas*), where the concept is pervasive. On the concept in general see Holladay, "New Covenant," *IDBSup:* 623–25. On the Qumran concept specifically, see Braun 1966 I:198–99, 211–12; II:145–46. Neither here nor in v. 14 should *diathēkē* be translated "Testament," as if Paul presupposed an emerging body of Christian writings somehow parallel to Jewish scripture. The arguments of Carmignac (1978) to this effect are unconvincing. Nothing in the context supports this view, and the absence of any clear evidence for the formation of even a collection of Pauline letters before the end of the first century speaks decisively against it (see, e.g., Sundberg, "Canon of the NT," *IDBSup:* 136–40). A specific conception of Christian scripture as a "New Testament" is not documented before the end of the second century. Clement *(Miscellanies* V, 58.1; cf. IV, 134.2–3) and Origen (e.g., *On First Principles* IV, 1.1; *Commentary on John* V, 8) both distinguish between the "Old" and "New" Testaments, and in the Western church Tertullian employed the terms *Vetus* and *Novum Testamentum* in his refutation of Marcion's rejection of the former (see *Against Marcion* IV.i–ii, and his comments on 2 Cor 3 in V.xi; note also, from his Montanist period, *Against Praxeas* XV); see van Unnik 1961. See further discussion on v. 14 below. In addition to the passages already mentioned, the word *covenant* appears in Paul's letters only in Rom 9:4 (the covenants [plural] of Israel); Gal 3:15, 17 (with reference to God's covenant with Abraham), and—of most interest in connection with the present passage—in Gal 4:24 (where Hagar and Sarah are said to represent the "two covenants" of slavery and freedom, respectively).

*not written but spiritual.* The phrase *(ou grammatos, alla pneumatos)* might be translated, more literally, "not of the letter but of the Spirit." The singular, "letter," where one might expect the plural, is probably to be explained by the singular "Spirit" with which it is contrasted (see Kamlah 1954:277). As Käsemann notes (1971*b:* 143), it is likely that it is Paul himself who has coined the singular *(gramma)* in place of the original plural "holy writings" *(hiera grammata)* as a term for the law in its written form. The tr. "not literal" is to be avoided, because a similar distinction between "letter" and "Spirit" in Rom 2:29; 7:6 shows that Paul does not mean to contrast two levels of meaning in a text or two ways of reading, for example, the law. See COMMENT.

*the letter kills.* Now the article is used with *letter* as the destructive power of what is *written* is specifically accented (over against the enlivening power of *the Spirit*). The verb used here *(apoktennein;* see Kremer 1980:220–21) occurs only four times in Paul's letters; see also Rom 7:11; 11:3; 1 Thess 2:15.

*the Spirit gives life.* Here, too (see preceding note), the article is used, as the power of *the Spirit* is set over against that of *the letter*. The closest parallel to this thought elsewhere in the Pauline letters occurs in Rom 8:11; but see also 1 Cor 15:45 and cf. Rom 4:17; 1 Cor 15:22, 36. For various Jewish parallels to the life-giving work of the Spirit, see Windisch, 111, of which Ezek 37 is the most important.

## COMMENT: GENERAL

With these verses the second main section of the letter body (of chaps. 1–9 = Letter D) is opened. In the preceding section (1:12–2:13) Paul had assured his readers of his continuing concern for them despite certain things that might be interpreted to the contrary (viz., a canceled visit, a tearful letter, his present residence in Macedonia). He now proceeds to address an issue which, apparently, he perceives to be of the utmost importance if his newly strengthened but still precarious relationship to the Corinthians is going to be further improved. It is the issue of his apostleship itself, and specifically of its authenticity and meaning.

The present passage (2:14–3:6) is best regarded as introductory to the discussion proper, which takes place in 3:7–5:19. These introductory verses open with an affirmation (certainly, for the Corinthians, a reaffirmation), in doxological form (cf. Windisch, 96: "a little hymn"), of the apostolic vocation in general (2:14–16*a*). This is followed in 2:16*b*–3:6 by Paul's formulation and brief explication of the question he regards as fundamental: Who is adequate to fulfill the responsibilities of apostleship? Judging by the way Paul has formulated and addressed this question, it has special importance in his dealings with the Corinthian congregation. Others have evidently been making claims to apostolic authority there, and in the process Paul's own apostolic status has been questioned.

In marked contrast to the rather consistent use of the first person singular in 1:12–2:13, the first person plural is now reintroduced. This is, of course, part of the hymnic style of vv. 14–16a. More important, however, this return to the use of the plural helps to show that the discussion is now moving beyond the immediate and particular matters of the preceding section. There Paul had sought to put into perspective some of his actions, which had been misunderstood in Corinth. Now, in these verses, he is introducing for consideration the matter he believes to be absolutely fundamental: what true apostleship is and involves. His answer will be that it means (a) serving a *new* covenant, 3:7–4:6; (b) remaining confident despite adversity, 4:7–5:10; and (c) proclaiming the word of reconciliation, 5:11–19.

Scroggs is interested in classifying 2:14–6:10 as a homily after the fashion of Rom 5–9 (1976:295–96). The sub-sections he proposes, however (ibid.:296 n. 56), exhibit no clear rhetorical pattern and, in fact, obscure such important formal signals as the shift to an essentially hortatory mode in 5:20.

## COMMENT: DETAILED

### A Hymnic Affirmation, 2:14–16a

As pointed out in the COMMENT on 2:12–13, it is not the case that 2:14 "interrupts" a travel narrative "begun" in 2:12 and only "continued" in 7:5ff. Paul mentions Titus and Macedonia in 2:12–13 only in order to indicate why he must now write to the Corinthians from a faraway place, without any prospect of seeing them again very soon. In 7:5–16, on the other hand, Paul's Macedonian rendezvous with Titus is detailed in order to emphasize the apostle's confidence in the Corinthians, and to help support his appeal to them (5:19–7:16) to put away their lingering suspicions about his motives and objectives. It is unnecessary, therefore, to hypothesize the existence of 2:14ff. as part of an originally separate letter, placed here as the result of a later redactor's decision, or to view vv. 12–13 as misplaced from their original position between 7:4 and 5 (against Héring, 18). It is also unnecessary to explain 2:14ff. as a digression, however "noble" (Bengel, cited by Barrett, 97; Plummer, 67), or to explain the outburst of praise in 2:14 as evoked by Paul's "irrepressible gratitude" (Plummer, ibid.) that he had finally met Titus in Macedonia with encouraging news from Corinth. (In addition to Plummer and Barrett, ibid., see, e.g., Bruce, 187; Tasker, 56; however, Hughes, 77, and de Boor, 60–62, suggest that the praise was prompted by Paul's concern to correct the impression that his mission in Troas had been somehow thwarted or defeated.) After all, the meeting with Titus was not yet mentioned in 2:12–13 and will not be

until 7:6. Rather, Paul's thanksgiving is for what God accomplishes *always
. . . in every place* (v. 14) through his true apostles, and it does not look back
to anything said in the preceding verses, nor far ahead to what will be said in
chap. 7. It serves, instead, to help introduce the momentous issue of true
apostleship, an issue to which Paul is prompted not just by any one event or
piece of information but by the whole history of his dealings with the Corinthian Christians. (The same point, supported by the identification of certain
specific connections between 2:14–17 and chaps. 3–5, is made by Thrall 1982:
especially 112–16.)

With an exclamation of thanks to God (v. 14*a*), Paul introduces an affirmation of the universal scope and power of his apostolic mission (vv. 14*b*–16*a*).
Specifically, through the preaching of the gospel the salvation which God has
granted in Christ is made known—not just in the sense that people become
aware of it but in the sense that they experience its effects: *life* for *those who
are being saved* and *death* for *those who are perishing.* In 4:6 an optical
metaphor will be employed to describe the dissemination and reception of this
knowledge: "the enlightenment which comes from the knowledge of the splendor of God in the face of Jesus Christ." In the present verses, however, an
olfactory metaphor is used, as Paul identifies first the gospel and then the
apostles themselves with a sweet *fragrance* for salvation.

As indicated in the NOTES, one cannot be entirely certain about the meaning
of the phrase *thriambeuonti hēmas* in v. 14. It could simply mean *puts us on
display,* in which case Paul would be saying that apostles are authorized and
given visibility by God as they discharge their responsibility to disseminate the
gospel (cf. 3:4–6). It is possible, however, that Paul intends an allusion to the
"triumph" celebrated in Rome after great military victories. The central feature of these celebrations was a triumphal procession through the city streets,
including realistic tableaux of the decisive battles. In these, as Josephus reports
(*War* VII.v.5), the enemy generals themselves were compelled to take part,
showing how they had been captured. A passage from Seneca (quoted in
NOTES) shows how readily Paul's contemporaries could associate the public
exhibition of prisoners of war in the Roman triumph with the experience of
utter humiliation and shame. If the apostle himself is alluding to the triumph
in this passage, as many commentators have suggested, it is not to identify
himself with the conquering army, and probably not to identify himself as a
"prisoner of Christ." Rather, as P. Marshall (1983) has argued, it is more likely
that the allusion intends to call up the picture of public humiliation and shame
—*put on display (as if we were prisoners in a triumphal procession).* If so, the
meaning here is not unlike that in 1 Cor 4:9*b,* where, in an allusion to the
theater, Paul describes the weakness of apostles as "a spectacle [*theatron*] to
the world" *(RSV);* see also 2 Cor 4:7–12; 6:4–10, and especially chaps. 10–13.

It is improbable that Paul's description of the gospel as a *fragrance* (vv. 14,
16*a;* cf. v. 15) is intended to evoke the idea of a sacrificial offering. The smoke

of a sacrifice was meant to rise up to God, whereas here the apostle's point
is that the scent of the gospel is disseminated throughout the world. The same
objection applies to the suggestion, sometimes made, that here again Paul is
thinking of the Roman triumphal processions, during which incense was offered up (to the gods) in the streets of the city (Horace, *Odes* IV.ii.50–51;
Appian, *Punic Wars* 66, both cited by Windisch, 97, but overlooked by Field
1879:181–82 and Egan 1977:38). More likely, Paul is using the image of a
*fragrance* with reference to the presence and therefore the knowledge of God.
This not only fits the context but also conforms to the use of the same image
in other ancient religious texts, including Jewish texts. Thus, for example,
Wisdom speaks of herself in this way (Sir 24:15):

> Like cassia or camel-thorn I was redolent
> of spices [*osmēn:* Paul's word in vv. 14 and 16];
> I spread my fragrance [*euodian:* Paul's word in v. 15]
> like choice myrrh. *(NEB)*

Similarly, there is a reference in 2 Apoc Bar 67:6 to "the vapour of the smoke
of the incense of the righteousness which is by the law," and this is contrasted
with "the smoke of impiety" *(APOT);* cf. 1 Enoch 24–25, the fragrance from
the Tree of Life. (These and other texts are discussed by Bultmann, 68–70.)
This imagery is now applied by Paul to the gospel of Christ as it is spread
throughout the whole world by the preaching of the apostles (v. 14).

So closely does Paul identify the gospel with the apostolate that he can
proceed (in v. 15) to speak of the apostles themselves as *the aroma of Christ,*
serving God (see NOTES on the expression *to God*) as they bear testimony to
the gospel. The proclamation of God's word (see v. 17; 4:2, 5) is but one way
in which the apostolic testimony is conveyed. It is Paul's conviction that the
light of the knowledge of God's glory infuses the "hearts" of the apostles (4:6
= their entire being), so that they become in themselves living witnesses to the
gospel. In 4:7–12 he will take care to emphasize that apostles enjoy no immu-
nity from the pains and tribulations of mortality, and that their sufferings are
in fact a specific aspect of their witness to Christ's life and death. Paul's
conception of the apostle as one who is bound over in the totality of his being
to the service of the gospel surely lies behind this present image of the apostles
as themselves *the aroma of Christ* (see Collange, 33). A specifically Gnostic
development of this idea is present in Gos Thom (CG II, *2*) 33,34–34,34
*(NHLE,* 45), where "the children of the Father" are described as his "fragrance" whom he "loves . . . and manifests . . . in every place" (34, 1–5; see
Grobel 1960:149 nn. 418, 419, and cf. Pagels 1975:95).

In vv. 15b–16a, Paul distinguishes between those who receive the gospel and
those who do not—the believers and the unbelievers. In the one case the gospel
means life; in the other case, death. The perspective here is clearly eschatological, as it also is in Phil 1:28 and in 1 Cor 1:18. In the latter passage the same

two phrases are used as in the present verses: *those who are perishing* are identified as those who regard "the word of the cross" as foolishness, and *those who are being saved* are identified as those who receive the same word as "the power of God" (cf. Rom 1:16–17; 1 Cor 1:21). These two different ways of perceiving Christ's death are perhaps hinted at in Rom 8:34, where Paul speaks of "Christ Jesus, who died, or rather [*mallon*], who was raised to life . . ." *(TEV)*.

Citing this text, Barrett, 101, comments that the distinction between *those who are being saved* and *those who are perishing* is in effect the distinction between those who accept Jesus as the resurrected one and those who regard him only as "a dead Jew." Barrett himself admits that this is an oversimplification, but one must ask whether it is not so much so as to be useless and even misleading. Paul repeatedly emphasizes—and not least in his letters to Corinth —that Christ's death is itself the saving event by which life is bestowed; the "power" of the gospel (Rom 1:16) is the "power" of the cross (1 Cor 1:17–18, 24). Thus, Paul's statement that Christ "was crucified in weakness, but lives by the power of God" (2 Cor 13:4*a*) has to be interpreted in accord with the word the apostle reports having received from Christ—namely, that "power is made fully present in weakness" (12:9*a*). It is precisely in the death of Jesus, represented to the world in the mortality and suffering of Christian apostles, that "the life of Jesus" is manifested (4:11–12). The distinction between those who accept the gospel and those who reject it, therefore, is the distinction between those who perceive the meaning of Christ's death and identify themselves with that ( = faith; see Rom 5:1–11; 6:3–11) and those who do not perceive or receive the power of God there disclosed.

Further light is shed on v. 16*a* by the statement, in this same context, that *the letter kills, but the Spirit gives life* (3:6*b*). Here the power of the law to enslave and to kill is set over against the power of the Spirit to effect freedom from the law and to make alive (see below). Thus, 3:6*b* may be seen as establishing the point of 2:16*a*: the apostolic preaching means life for those who receive the liberating power of the gospel but death for those who persist in their reliance on the law and continue in their bondage to it (G. Barth 1980:269 n. 39).

The rabbinic texts often alleged as parallels to Paul's notion of the gospel meaning life for some but death for others are not completely convincing (see, e.g., Str-B III: 497; Lietzmann, 109; Manson 1953:157–60). The texts in question liken the Torah to a "drug" or "spice" *(sam)* which benefits those who obey it (Israel) but injures those who do not (the Gentiles). In all these texts, however, it is the medicinal working of the spice and not its aroma that is under consideration (see Kümmel, 198, 199, commenting on the parallels adduced by Lietzmann). While there are OT texts in which the Hebrew word is used with reference to an aroma (Barrett, 102, cites Exod 25:6; 30:7), these do not apply the idea to the Torah, much less to its twofold effect of life and death.

One must not, therefore, try to find here a more than general similarity between Paul's view of the gospel and the rabbinic view of the Torah: each could be regarded as the means of life for those who respond to it, but as judgment and death for those who do not. Paul's argument in Rom 9:31–33 (cited by Meyer, 453–54) is rendered the more significant when the rabbinic view is considered. There Paul insists that the Jews missed righteousness precisely because they sought it through the law rather than on the basis of faith. Because of their unbelief, he says (quoting Isa 28:6), Christ has become for them "a stone of stumbling." It is not likely that Paul is thinking only of Jewish unbelievers when he writes as he does in vv. 15–16a, because his vision here is of the worldwide mission of the apostolate (*in every place,* v. 14). But they are surely included in the reference, and it is of those who follow Moses that he is thinking specifically when, just a few paragraphs later, he writes again of *those who are perishing* (4:3).

### The Question of Adequacy, 2:16b–3:6

With the question of v. 16b the style abruptly changes from praise to dialogue (and subsequently to discourse). This change is neither so sudden nor so great, however, as to justify Völter's conjecture that v. 16a was originally followed by 4:6ff. (cited by Windisch, 99) or Windisch's suggestion that something has fallen out before v. 16b (99–100; rightly criticized by Bultmann, 72). The subject matter remains the same—the Christian apostolate; the formulation of the question in v. 16b has the effect only of shifting the focus from the generalized affirmation of vv. 14–16a to a specific—and, indeed, the fundamental—issue with which Paul is confronted in his dealings with the Corinthian Christians.

Granted the awesome responsibilities of those who have been called *the aroma of Christ* (v. 15), who is sufficient to take them up? Contrary to the opinion of some commentators (e.g., Meyer, 455; Plummer, 72–73; Lietzmann, 109), Paul does not pose this question in order to be able to answer "I am" (cf. also Rissi 1969:22). He poses it, as v. 17 shows, because there are *so many* who presume and probably have also claimed to be sufficient in themselves. Paul believes that is only because they have not perceived what is at stake *(these things,* v. 16b, with reference to vv. 14–16a) in preaching God's word. In fact, the question does not admit of either a "yes" or a "no" answer in Paul's view. In form and function it has the character of the question asked in Joel 2:11 with respect to the eschatological day of judgment: "And who will be adequate for it [*kai tis estai hikanos autē*]?" Both this question and Paul's are formulated only in order to emphasize the futility of aspiring or claiming to be *adequate,* in and of oneself, to meet the requirements of God. As Paul will affirm in 3:5–6, one's adequacy for apostleship comes only from God, and it is therefore of a fundamentally different kind from that presumed by those who are *huckstering the word of God* like so much cheap merchandise (correctly, Georgi 1964:223–24).

Verse 17 may be regarded as Paul's justification for having posed the question of v. 16*b* (note the introduction *for* [*gar*]): there are those who claim to be fit for apostleship in and of themselves, even as they peddle for their own profit an adulterated gospel. This is the first indication we have in this letter, indirect as it is, that Paul is aware of rival claimants to the apostolic office operating in Corinth; but it is enough to show that the question of v. 16*b*, as well as the discussion to follow in 3:7ff., has a polemical edge to it. From 4:2 it would appear that the *huckstering* to which Paul refers includes preaching a false gospel, and from 3:1–3; 4:5; 5:12, 16*a* it seems clear that it included some kind of pretentious claims made by these hucksters on their own behalf. Paul is concerned about these same points in chaps. 10–13 (e.g., in 10:7, 12; 11:3–5, 21*b*–23). There, however, one must speak not just of "a polemical edge" but of outright polemic, straightforward and sometimes harsh. Moreover, in those chapters—which are from a later letter to Corinth (Letter E), according to the hypothesis adopted in this commentary (see INTRODUCTION, pp. 44–48)—Paul insinuates that his rivals are hucksters also in the sense that they have sought financial gain at the expense of the Corinthians (see, e.g., 11:20; 12:14). In the present letter, however, the apostle is able to examine the underlying issue itself; the issue is there, and it is real, but it has not yet erupted in such a way as to require a full-scale defense of his own motives and actions.

In v. 17*b* (as in 1:12) Paul can speak of the sincerity *(pure motives)* from which he acts without any apparent sense of having been challenged in this respect. It is too much to say, with Georgi (1964:248), that "from 2, 16ff. Paul is engaged in massive polemic." Unquestionably, as noted above, this section has a polemical aspect to it, but throughout 2:14–5:19 the accent falls on affirmation, not denunciation. Here the fundamental affirmation is expressed already in the introductory verses: true apostles disseminate the knowledge of God through the gospel of Christ, whose aroma they are (vv. 14–15), and the Corinthians have observed this in Paul and his associates—who, unlike many others, have acted sincerely, *from God and in the sight of God . . . speaking in Christ* (v. 17). This is also the affirmation with which the next section opens: Paul and his associates "are serving as ambassadors for Christ, God appealing through us" (5:20*a*).

In an earlier letter Paul had already affirmed his conviction that his apostolic speaking *(lalein)* was not with "words . . . taught by human wisdom" but with words "taught by the Spirit" (1 Cor 2:13 [*RSV*]; cf. 1 Cor 7:40*b;* 12:3). The same point is made a bit later in this letter, when Paul cites the faith and speaking *(pisteuein* and *lalein)* of the psalmist and claims that he and his associates are moved to believe and speak by "the same Spirit of faith" (4:13). That this is not just a theme of Pauline polemics, articulated only in response to a specific challenge, is clear from 1 Thess, the earliest of the extant Pauline letters. There Paul reminds his readers how he had spoken (again: *lalein*) as one who has been approved by God and entrusted with the gospel (2:4), and he declares that this gospel is not "the word of men" but "the word of God" (2:13).

Nevertheless, the point receives special emphasis in the letters to Corinth, and by the time Letter E (represented in 2 Cor 10–13) is sent, Paul has been challenged on this very point. This is shown, above all, by the remark of 13:3a, "since you demand verification of the Christ who speaks through me [*tou en emoi lalountos Christou*]," and also by the almost verbatim repetition in 12:19b of the affirmation made here in v. 17b, *in the sight of God we are speaking in Christ.* When, during his last visit to Corinth, Paul writes to the Romans, the same conception is articulated, probably because the issue he has confronted in Corinth is fresh in his mind. Summarizing his sense of apostolic vocation, he vows: "I will not presume to speak of anything [*ti lalein*] other than those things Christ has wrought through me for the sake of the obedience of the Gentiles [*Christos di' emou eis hypakoēn ethnōn*]" (15:18).

Georgi (1964:225) believes that the Corinthian congregation had been "strongly influenced" by Gnosticism, and that numerous Gnostic motifs may be discerned in vv. 14–17. By identifying true apostles as agents of a divine revelation, he suggests, Paul wants to refute his opponents, whose claim to apostleship is based, rather, on their own special religious powers. However, specifically Gnostic elements are not all that clear in these verses (see Barrett, 104–5), and, as noted above, the conception of apostleship which underlies them is already present in 1 Thess. For the interpretation of these verses by the Gnostic Christians of the second century, see Pagels 1975:95–96.

*Letters of Recommendation*

The issue introduced by Paul in 2:16b–17 receives a preliminary response in 3:4–6, and that, in turn, becomes the point of departure for the whole discussion in 3:7–5:19. One must therefore regard 3:1–3 as a sort of parenthesis (as many commentators do), although it is by no means beside the point. Having contrasted his apostolate with the self-serving preaching of *so many* (2:17), Paul pauses to ask whether he seems thereby to be recommending himself again (3:1). The same concern is exhibited later in this letter when he asserts, using the same expression, "We are not recommending ourselves to you once more . . ." (5:12). Moreover, when in 4:2 and 6:4 he does venture to "recommend" his apostolate to the Corinthians, he chooses his words very carefully, and in such a way as to avoid being misunderstood (e.g., "in the sight of God," 4:2; "as ministers of God should," 6:4—see the NOTES and COMMENT on these passages and on 10:12, 18; 12:11). These passages, taken together, provide evidence that Paul has come in for criticism, from some quarter, for seeking to recommend himself in some inappropriate way. Perhaps something he had said in an earlier letter had been so construed (1 Cor

4:14–21? 9:1–26? 15:10? something in the tearful letter?). But the charge could have originated just as easily in something he had said or done on the occasion of his second—and spectacularly unsuccessful—visit to Corinth. In any case, the question of 3:1*a* shows that Paul is sensitive on the point, and that he does not want his present discussion of true apostleship to be in any way compromised by renewed complaints about his alleged self-recommendation.

Paul's response to the question is to pose a second one (v. 1*b*), by which means he is in effect extending the distinction he had made in 2:17 between true and false apostles. Are not the Corinthians themselves aware that he and his associates had not required, *as some* do, *letters of recommendation* either to or from them? Such letters of introduction, whether official (certifying someone as a duly commissioned representative or messenger of another) or unofficial (commending a relative, friend, or associate to others), played a larger role in the ancient world, when communications were poorer and hospitality in distant places more difficult, than they do today. Paul, unlike Diogenes (see NOTES), is not criticizing in principle the use of such letters, and he does not hesitate to supply his own associates with them on occasion (see NOTES). Rather, the rhetorical question of v. 1*b* (which presumes a negative answer; see NOTES) shows that Paul's concern is to distinguish his relationship to the Corinthian congregation from the relationship certain others have to it— others who did require letters of recommendation to the Corinthians, and who do require such letters from them whenever they go elsewhere.

Who had supplied Paul's rivals with their letters of recommendation? Some (e.g., Barrett, 40–41) believe they had been written by the leaders of the Jerusalem church. But in this case how could Paul presume, as he clearly does, that the holders of such letters would also require letters from the *Corinthian* church (*letters of recommendation to you or from you*, v. 1*b*)? It is therefore much more likely that the people in question bear letters from other Hellenistic congregations, perhaps including other congregations founded by Paul. The remark about letters *from* the Corinthians certainly need not mean that Paul's rivals have already departed (as Plummer, 78, and others have claimed). It means only that whenever they do leave Corinth for other places they will want to carry letters from Corinth with them.

As Theissen (1982:38–39) has observed, *letters of recommendation* are only advantageous to itinerant Christian teachers or preachers when there are already established congregations to whom to present them. Paul of course had brought no such letters to Corinth, because he had come as a missionary to a new field of evangelistic work. The Corinthians should know better than anyone that Paul alone was their "father" in the faith, even though others may serve them in other ways (1 Cor 4:15). Those who must bring introductory letters with them to Corinth show by that very fact that their ministry is not to be compared with that of Paul and his associates. That this is the distinction Paul wants to accentuate by asking the question he does in v. 1*b* is confirmed when, in a subsequent letter, he writes explicitly of those who boast and make claims as if his work had been theirs (10:13–18; 11:12–15).

The questions of v. 1 might have been left as a brief parenthetical aside, but they are not. Paul cannot resist the opportunity to make a point he has made before to this same congregation, but he makes it now by means of an image suggested by his own reference to commendatory letters. The Corinthians themselves, he suggests, constitute the only "letter" he and his associates need, and it is a letter they bear in their hearts, not just in their luggage. He had made essentially the same point in 1 Cor 9:1d–2 when he had declared that the very existence of a Christian congregation in Corinth was sufficient testimony to his apostleship: "Are not you my workmanship in the Lord? If to others I am not an apostle, at least I am to you; for you are the seal of my apostleship in the Lord" (RSV). It is unnecessary to worry about how a letter written on someone's heart, the most interior and secret dimension of one's being (certainly so for Paul; e.g., 2:4; Rom 8:27; 1 Cor 4:5a; 1 Thess 2:4), can at the same time be known and read by everyone. The phrase about the public visibility of the letter represents Paul's specific adaptation (or correction) of the metaphor for his present purposes. His remarks about the Thessalonians (1 Thess 2:17–20) offer an instructive parallel. Although physically separated from them, the apostle is still joined with them "in heart" (v. 17), where they reside as his "hope," "joy," and "crown of boasting before our Lord Jesus at his coming" (v. 19, RSV). Although Paul is thinking here of the existence of the Thessalonian congregation as attesting his work to Christ at his return (cf. Phil 4:1), elsewhere in 1 Thess the missionary effect of the attestation is also in view (1:7–10; note that Paul and his associates didn't have to say anything [v. 8], because the faith of the Thessalonians was itself the bearer of the gospel). It is not unusual, then, for Paul to speak of holding the members of his congregations in his heart, and by this he means, as Phil 1:7 shows particularly well, that they are shareholders with him in the gospel of Christ of which he is an apostle. He will again speak of the Corinthians in this way in 7:3, in the context of his appeal to them to be reconciled fully with those who have planted the gospel in their midst (see especially 6:11–13).

Some have argued (especially Georgi 1964:166, 246, 249–51) that Paul quickly leaves the metaphor of commendatory letters behind, and in v. 3 makes use of the notion, widespread in antiquity, of a letter sent down from heaven (see, e.g., Ezek 2:9–3:3; Odes Sol 23:5; Rev 2–3 [letters from Christ, specifically 1:10–13]; Herm Vis II.i–ii). If so, however, the possibilities of the new image are certainly not developed here. It is more likely that the description of the Corinthians as Christ's letter represents only an extension of the original metaphor, and that it is intended to avoid leaving the impression that the Corinthians themselves are the source of the recommendation Paul and his associates carry with them (correctly, Baird 1961:170; Rissi 1969:21). Paul is, at the same time, helping to avoid giving the impression that the existence of a Christian congregation is rooted, finally, in what apostles have achieved. Although he often compares his apostolic role to that of a parent—either a mother (1 Cor 3:1–2; Gal 4:19; 1 Thess 2:7–8) or a father (1 Cor 4:15; 2 Cor 11:2; 1 Thess 2:11–12)—he never claims for the apostolate more than a diaconal role in the propagation and nurture of the gospel; see especially 1 Cor 3:5–15: Jesus Christ is the one foundation of faith—not (as in the deutero-Pauline formulation of Eph 2:20) the apostles. When Paul adds that the Corinthians as *Christ's letter* were *cared for by us,* it is not important whether he is thinking of the scribal or courier function of the apostolate (see NOTES). It is important that here, as elsewhere, he conceives of apostles as those who serve not their own interests (as *so many* do, 2:17) but the gospel of Christ. This is the special theme of this whole section of the letter (see especially 2:17; 3:5; 4:2, 5, 7; 5:18).

The metaphor of commendatory letters is further extended when Paul describes by what agency and on what material they have been inscribed: *not with ink but with the Spirit of the living God; not on stone tablets but on tablets that are human hearts.* An oft-cited passage from Plato's *Phaedrus* provides a detailed exposition of the thesis that "written words" (*logous gegrammenous,* 275 D) are but the faint "image" *(eidōlon)* of "the living, breathing word" *(ton logon zōnta kai empsychon,* 276 A). Socrates argued (276 C–E) that truth is not effectively sown "in ink . . . through a pen" *(melani . . . dia kalamou),* in "gardens of letters" *(en grammasi kēpous),* but only by "the dialectic method," whereby truth is planted "in a fitting soul" *(psychēn prosēkousan).* In this connection, one may recall that Paul himself regards his own letters as but a poor substitute for his actual presence with those whom he addresses (see, e.g., 10:9–11; 1 Cor 4:14, 18–21; 5:3–5). This point of view corresponds to one frequently expressed by ancient letter writers (see Thraede 1970) and may also reflect, as Rivkin suggests (1978:275), Paul's background in Pharisaism, with its concern for the *un*written Torah and for traditions orally conveyed (cf. ibid.:241–43).

When Paul attributes to the Spirit the "writing" of the letter from Christ, this is in full accord with his conviction that his gospel has been able to take root in places like Corinth because of the powerful working of the Spirit (e.g., 1:22; 1 Cor 2:4; Gal 3:2–5; 1 Thess 1:5–6). It is also in accord with several of the scriptural passages he seems to have in mind as he continues to embellish his metaphor, most particularly Exod 31:18 (cf. Deut 9:10), where it is said that God's own finger had written the tablets given to Moses, and Ezek 11:19 (cf. 36:26), where God promises to give his people "another heart" and to put "a new spirit" within them.

The passages from the Pentateuch and Ezek are certainly among those that have influenced Paul to describe as he does the material on which God's Spirit writes. Those texts do not prepare us, however, for Paul's statement that the letter from Christ has *not* been written *on stone tablets.* On the contrary, the new "heart" and "spirit" mentioned in Ezek are clearly understood to be the vehicles by which God's commands (*prostagmata, dikaiōmata, krimata,* 11:20; 13:27) are inwardly established with his people for their obedience. The same is true in LXX Jer 38(31):31ff., to which Paul also alludes in these verses. There the promised "new covenant" (v. 31) is explicitly identified with the laws *(nomoi)* which God will cause to be placed upon the mind *(dianoia)* and written upon the hearts of his people (v. 33). Moreover, as Plummer, 82, has remarked, one would have expected Paul to contrast *human hearts* with *parchment,* thus staying within the bounds of his own developing metaphor: "You are Christ's letter, inscribed not with ink but with the Spirit, and not on parchment but on human hearts." When Paul here refers instead to *stone tablets,* it becomes evident that he is thinking of the tables of the law received by Moses on Mount Sinai, and that he specifically does not want to identify the law with the content of *Christ's letter* or his own apostleship.

### Apostolic Confidence

The apostle's parenthetical reflections in 3:1–3 will have served only to accentuate the question he himself has posed in 2:16b and to which he has not yet actually responded: How can anyone presume to be fit to take up the kind of responsibilities which have been envisioned in the grand affirmation of 2:14–16a, and which Paul believes he and his associates have fulfilled in Corinth specifically (3:1–3)? In vv. 4–6 Paul returns to that question, first of all, by asserting that true apostles do have just *such confidence before God* and *through Christ* (v. 3). A comparable declaration of apostolic confidence occurs in Rom 15:17 (noted by Windisch, 107), and it is significant that both there and here the declaration is followed immediately by an explanatory and, in a sense, qualifying statement. In Rom it takes the form of a resolve to speak confidently only of "what Christ has wrought through me . . ." (v. 18). Here it takes the form of a clarifying addendum (vv. 5–6): Paul and his associates make no claims to self-sufficiency; their sufficiency resides in God alone.

The title "Sufficient One" *(ho hikanos)* is applied to God several times in the LXX (see Ruth 1:20, 21; Job 21:15; 31:2 [40:2]), and Philo is fond of remarking that God is "sufficient unto himself" *(hikanos heautō, Allegorical Int.* I, 44; *Cherubim* 46; *Change of Names* 27, 46). It is altogether probable that Paul is familiar with this way of thinking about God in Hellenistic Judaism, so one must not conclude too quickly that his formulation of the question of 2:16b has been influenced by the fact that his rivals for leadership in Corinth are already using the term *adequate (hikanos)* to describe themselves, as Windisch, 108, and Georgi 1964:221 have suggested. Other passages from Philo adduced by Windisch, 108, to show that Paul is expressing his humility in a characteristically Hellenistic-Jewish way (e.g., *Confusion of Tongues* 127; *On Drunkenness* 166; *On Dreams* II, 25) are not true parallels. Quite absent from Philo's remarks about the insufficiency of human beings is the dialectic, so prominent in Paul's declaration (Bultmann, 79), that true apostles are only *adequate* because they have been enabled through an *adequacy* that comes from God. Moreover, Paul's comment does not function as an expression of religious humility but as an expression of his *confidence before God . . . through Christ* that his apostolic service is fit and proper (cf. Georgi 1964:223 n. 1). This dialectic of inadequacy/adequacy or unworthiness/ worthiness is present whenever, as here, Paul considers his call to apostleship and reflects on its meaning; see especially 1 Cor 15:9–10, "I am unfit [*ouk eimi hikanos*] to be called an apostle. . . . But by the grace of God I am what I am . . . ; not I, but the grace of God which is with me" *(RSV)*.

When Paul identifies himself and his associates as having been made *adequate as ministers of a new covenant* (v. 6), he is drawing a clear and significant connection between qualification for ministry and the content of the apostolic message—*a new covenant,* not the old; and, subsequently, *the Spirit,* not *the letter* (cf. G. Barth 1980:267, 269–70). Further elaboration of this ministry of a new covenant will come in 3:7–4:6.

The concept of "ministry" is especially prominent in 2 Cor, as even a glance at a Greek concordance will show: the nouns "minister" *(diakonos)* and "ministry" *(diakonia)* and the verb "to minister" *(diakonein)* occur a total of thirty-six times in the seven indisputably Pauline letters, and more than half of these occurrences (twenty) are in 2 Cor. The phrase "ministers of Christ" seems to have been a favorite of Paul's rivals in Corinth, and it is likely that they attached some kind of special meaning to it which had the effect of casting doubt on the validity of Paul's ministry (see 11:23 and NOTES and COMMENT there). Paul must later face that issue head on (see especially 11:12ff.), but for now he approaches it less polemically than didactically (so Luz 1967:324, although there is certainly a polemical dimension to Paul's discussion even here).

The title *ministers of a new covenant* occurs only here and is apparently an ad hoc formulation to which Paul has found himself led by the momentum of his own argument in the preceding verses. It does not provide any sure evidence that Paul's rivals were Judaizers of some kind. In v. 3 he had spoken of the ministry *(diakonein,* translated there as *cared for)* by which he and his associates had established the Corinthian congregation as *Christ's letter,* and he had described that "letter" as written with God's Spirit *on tablets that are human hearts.* Given that imagery, and the text from LXX Jer 38(31) which had helped to influence it, it is but a short step to the formulation of v. 6, where those who minister for Christ are identified further as *ministers of a new covenant.* The concept of a "new" covenant established in and with the redemptive work of Christ is part of Paul's Christian heritage (his citation of the words of eucharistic institution [1 Cor 11:25] is enough to prove that). The present verse, as well as Paul's discussion of the two covenants in Gal 4, shows that it is a fully compatible part of his theology, even though perhaps not as fundamental or determinative for it as van Unnik (1960) has sought to show.

First of all, the idea conveyed by the tradition that the new covenant was instituted in and with Christ's death (1 Cor 11:25 [Matt 26:28; Mark 14:24]; Luke 22:20; cf. Heb 8:15) is compatible with Paul's understanding of the gospel as "the word of the cross." God's eschatological power is made present and effective for salvation in Christ's death (1 Cor 1:18; cf. Rom 1:16–17). The promise of a "new creation" is bestowed upon those who by faith "glory" only in the cross of Christ (Gal 5:14–15; cf. Rom 5:1–11), and the reality of that new creation is manifested already in the "newness" which marks the present lives of those who live by faith (Rom 6:4; 7:6; 2 Cor 5:14–17).

In the second place, the new covenant idea is in accord with Paul's conviction that salvation must be understood essentially as promise, not as performance. Thus, God's covenant with Abraham, which has the character of a promise (Rom 4; Gal 3), is specifically distinguished from the covenant with Moses, based on law (Gal 3:17–18). To seek righteousness through the law is futile, Paul insists, because in seeking to establish one's "own righteousness" through works of the law one is turning aside from "the righteousness that comes from God," the promise that can only be received by faith (Rom 9:30–10:3). Therefore, Christ means "the end of the law" as the way of salvation (Rom 10:4). Because, as here in 2 Cor (1:22; 5:5), Paul can write of the Spirit as the "guarantee" of—or the "down payment" on—the promised inheritance of salvation, he finds it appropriate to contrast life according to the law (or "the flesh") with life lived according to the guidance of the Spirit (e.g., Gal 5:16–25; Rom 8:1–17); the law means "sin and death" (Rom 8:2, 6), but the Spirit means "life and peace" (Rom 8:6) and "righteousness" (Rom 8:10). The striking expression "the 'law' of the Spirit of life in Christ Jesus" (Rom 8:2), probably coined by Paul himself, presumes the antithesis between an "old" and a "new" way of understanding the law. This thought also lies behind Rom 7:6 ("We serve not under the old written code but in the new life of the Spirit" —RSV), as well as behind the distinction present here in 2 Cor between a "new covenant" and an old one (3:6, 14).

The discussion in Gal 4:21–31 presupposes the concept of a new covenant versus an old one, without either phrase actually being used. Paul allegorizes Abraham's two wives, Sarah and Hagar, to stand for "two covenants" (v. 24). Hagar, the slave wife, represents God's covenant with Moses on Mount Sinai (the law), and her children, born into slavery, belong to "the present Jerusalem" (vv. 24–25). Sarah, on the other hand, is associated with God's promise to Abraham and herself that she should bear a son, and with "the Jerusalem above," which is "free" (vv. 26–28). Paul specifically correlates the distinction between these two covenants with the distinction between "flesh" and "Spirit" (v. 29), and from all this he draws the lesson that believers are children "not . . . of the slave [of the law, of the flesh, of the old covenant] but of the free woman [of the promise (v. 28), of the Spirit, of the new covenant]" (v. 31).

In addition to demonstrating that the concept of a "new covenant" is fully at home in Paul's thought, even though the expression itself occurs only twice, the sampling of passages just presented should help to illumine what Paul has in mind when, in the present verses, he stipulates that the *new covenant* is *not written but spiritual*. (Some commentators would take these words as a description of *ministers*—e.g., Meyer, 465; Plummer, 88—but they are more suitably regarded as qualitative genitives referring to the *new covenant;* so Windisch, 110.) Paul applies the same distinction between "letter" and "Spirit" to circumcision in Rom 2:29. In that case it is clear that he wants to distinguish a circumcision that is external and therefore readily visible (see *en tō phanerō,* "in appearance," v. 28) from a "spiritual" circumcision, which is inward and therefore invisible except to God (see *en tō kryptō,* "in secret," and *peritomē kardias,* "a circumcision of the heart," v. 29). Moreover, in that same passage Paul asserts that having the law in its written form and being physically circumcised is no guarantee of fulfilling the law (v. 27). Indeed, later in Rom he writes of Christians as those who are "discharged from the law" which had held them in bondage, and thus free "to serve in the newness of the Spirit, and not under the old written code [*en kainotēti pneumatos kai ou palaiotēti grammatos*]" (7:6). It is thus clear that the distinction between "letter" and "Spirit" is fundamentally a distinction between two different powers, one which enslaves and one which liberates (see Käsemann 1971b, especially 146–48; G. Barth 1980:267).

In the present passage, then, one seems to be in touch with several of the ideas which Paul develops further in Gal and Rom (cf. Wilckens 1982:161–64). The distinction between what is visible and what is invisible is implicit in v. 3, where the apostle contrasts what is written on stone tablets with what is written on human hearts. The antithesis of law and Spirit is also implicit there; it becomes explicit now in v. 6, where the Spirit is identified with a *new covenant,* and what is *written* (the letter) is identified by implication with the old covenant (cf. Luz 1967:325). As Davies (1957:180–81) and Braun (1966 I:198) have both emphasized, it is precisely at this point that Paul's idea of the "new covenant" is fundamentally different from the conception of it which is found in the Dead Sea Scrolls. The Qumran sectarians regarded themselves as constituting a "household of the Spirit" devoted entirely to obeying the law; they seem to have had no sense whatever of any incompatibility between "life in the Spirit" and "life under the law." For Paul, on the other hand, these stand over against one another as two radically different and mutually exclusive modes of existence.

A survey of the history of the exegesis of this passage (see, e.g., B. Schneider 1953:165–87; Ebeling, "Geist und Buchstabe," *RGG* II:1292–94; Kremer 1980:236–39) shows that Paul has often been interpreted as sponsoring a "spiritual" as opposed to a "literal" approach to scripture. Even some recent scholars have taken this text as Paul's endorsement of the allegorical method of exegesis as it had long been practiced in the Greek world and as it was being practiced in the kind of Hellenistic Judaism represented by Philo of Alexandria (so Grant 1957:50–51). That a distinction between the "letter" and the "spirit" of a text was at home in the Greco-Roman world is certain (see Grant's survey, ibid.:1–40), although the usual way of expressing it in Greek was to contrast "what is stated" in a text *(to rēton)* with what the text intends *(hē dianoia)*. Cohen's elaborate attempt, nevertheless, to place Paul in that tradition (1953, 1954; cited with approval by Grant 1957:51) remains unconvincing. According to his view, Paul was arguing that the law must be read "spiritually," not "literally," and that the apostle's new way of expressing the distinction ("letter" versus "spirit") had been influenced, on the one hand, by the rabbinic emphasis on "the letter of the Torah" *(ōt min ha-Torah)* and, on the other hand, by the expression "spirit of judgment" *(ruaḥ mišpat)* found in Isa 4:4; 28:6 (LXX: *pneuma kriseōs)*. But this is not only to contrive an artificial context from two disparate sources; it is also to ignore the context Paul's own letters and thought provide for interpreting the distinction. Just as serious, it overlooks the important point that Paul nowhere disputes how the law should be *interpreted*. His concern is only with how the law is perceived to *function*, and, as Luz observes (1967:327), Paul himself continues to follow traditional rabbinic exegetical procedures. The description Paul gives of the *new covenant* does not so much reflect his hermeneutical perspective on the law or scripture in general as it does his eschatological perspective on God's redemptive work in history. That, he is convinced, is effected not through the law but through Christ, not through the old covenant delivered to Moses on stone tablets but through a new covenant of promise, established in the cross and sealed with the Spirit.

It must be emphasized that Paul does not reject the law as such, either in this passage or elsewhere; the "letter" mentioned in v. 6 is not fully synonymous with "the law" (correctly Kamlah 1954:277; cf. Käsemann 1971b:147; Kremer 1980:225–26). Paul can describe the law as "holy," "just," and "good" (Rom 7:12)—indeed, even as "spiritual" *(pneumatikos,* Rom 7:14)! What he does reject is that way of using the law which presumes that its "letter" provides a sure way to righteousness and life. (Cf. Provence 1982:62–68.)

That Paul's description of the new covenant as *not written but spiritual* reflects his fundamental distinction between life under the law and life in the Spirit is confirmed by the concluding statement in v. 6: *For the letter kills, but the Spirit gives life*. Kremer, who has closely analyzed the form, structure, and literary character of this succinct formulation (1980:229–33), has shown that the antithesis itself is probably "anchored" in the preaching of the early church (ibid.:233–35). It is, however, thoroughly Pauline in its present form and use, as a comparison of the thought with Rom 7–8 makes clear. There Paul contends that sin, using the commandment *(hē entolē),* "deceives" and "kills" the one who presumes to find life through the law (7:11). That is why he can say pointedly (Gal 3:21) that the law is unable to give life, and why he can write even more pointedly, here in 2 Cor, that *the letter kills.* Bruce, 190, quotes the contrasting Jewish view found in *Exod. Rab.* xli.1 on Exod 31:18: "While Israel stood below engraving idols to provoke their Creator to anger . . . God sat on high engraving tablets which would give them life." In Paul's view, however, *what is written kills* because it enslaves one to the presumption that righteousness inheres in one's doing of the law, when it is actually the case that true righteousness comes only as a gift from God (cf. "a righteousness of my own"/"the righteousness from God"—Phil 3:9, *RSV*). For Paul, as Käsemann has said, "everything which forces us back on our own strength, ability and piety kills because it snatches the creature out of his creatureliness and thus away from the almighty power of grace, of which we are in constant need" (1971b:150).

In Rom 8 the "law of sin and death" is contrasted with "the 'law' of the Spirit of life in Christ Jesus" (v. 2). Whereas sin (operating through the law) brings death, the Spirit is given for life (v. 10; P. W. Meyer [1979:8] shows that this verse should be translated "But if Christ is in you, the body is to be sure dead because of sin, but the Spirit is life for the sake of righteousness"). The Spirit "will give life" *(zōopoiēsei)* because it is "the Spirit of him who raised Jesus from the dead" (v. 11). Convinced of this, Paul is able to write as he does now to the Corinthians: *the Spirit gives life (zoopoiei).* (Paul may still have Ezek in mind, as he apparently had in v. 3. See especially 37:5–6, where the LXX has the expression *pneuma zōēs,* "Spirit of life"; cf. vv. 9–10, 14.) As *ministers of a new covenant,* he and his associates serve the gospel of Christ. Through Christ the old covenant (the law, embraced as the way of salvation) has come to an end, and through him a new covenant, inscribed on human hearts by the Spirit, has been given as the power and the promise of life.

## 6. THE MINISTRY OF THE NEW COVENANT, 3:7–4:6

3    ⁷Now if the ministry of death, chiseled in letters on stone, took place with such splendor that the Israelites could not bear to gaze at Moses' face—because the splendor of his face was being annulled—⁸will not the ministry of the Spirit be with greater splendor? ⁹For if there is splendor with the ministry of condemnation, how much more does the ministry of righteousness abound with splendor! ¹⁰Indeed, what has had splendor has not had splendor, in this case, because of the splendor which so far surpasses it. ¹¹For if what was being annulled was with such splendor, how much more the splendor of that which endures!

¹²Having, therefore, such a hope, we act with much boldness, ¹³and not like Moses when he used to put a veil over his face so the Israelites could not gaze at the end of what was being annulled.

¹⁴But their minds were hardened. Right up to the present day the same veil remains at the public reading of the old covenant—unlifted, because it is in Christ that it is being annulled. ¹⁵Indeed, to the present, whenever Moses is read a veil lies over their hearts. ¹⁶Whenever anyone turns to the Lord the veil is removed. ¹⁷Now "the Lord" is the Spirit, and where the Spirit of the Lord is, is freedom. ¹⁸And we all, with unveiled face, beholding as in a mirror the splendor of the Lord, are being transformed into the same image, from splendor to splendor, as from the Lord, the Spirit.

4 ¹Therefore, having this ministry, as recipients of mercy, we do not shrink back. ²Rather, we for our part have renounced the shameful things one hides, neither conducting ourselves craftily nor adulterating the word of God. Instead, by a full disclosure of the truth we are recommending ourselves to each and every human conscience, in the sight of God. ³And even if our gospel is veiled, it is veiled to those who are perishing. ⁴The god of this age has blinded the minds of those unbelievers, so that they do not see the enlightenment coming from the gospel of the splendor of Christ, who is the image of God. ⁵For it is not ourselves whom we preach, but Jesus Christ as Lord, and ourselves as your slaves for Jesus' sake. ⁶Because the God who said, "Light shall shine out of darkness," has caused a light to shine in our hearts, to provide the enlightenment which comes from the knowledge of the splendor of God, in the face of Jesus Christ.

## NOTES

3:7. *the ministry of death.* The word *diakonia* appears here for the first time in 2 Cor, and has been rendered *ministry* in keeping with the reference to "ministers of a new covenant" in v. 6 (see also 4:1). This noun recurs in vv. 8, 9 (twice); 4:1; 5:18; 6:3; and in 8:4; 9:1, 12, 13 it is applied more specifically to the collection for Jerusalem. It occurs but once in chaps. 10–13, however—namely, in 11:18. The genitive *of death (tou thanatou)* describes the kind of ministry: one that deals in death (cf. v. 9, "the ministry that deals in condemnation"). The reference here is first of all to the whole system of law (the "old covenant," v. 14), represented by the stone tablets (v. 3) with their death-dealing commandments (cf. v. 6), and only secondarily to the agents of that ministry.

*chiseled in letters on stone.* Literally "on stones" (*lithois;* the *en lithois* of some texts is certainly secondary), doubtless with reference to the two stone tables of the Mosaic law which Paul has already had in mind here (v. 3) and which also figure in the LXX passage now before him (Exod 34:29, *hai dyo plakes,* "the two tablets"). The verb *chiseled (entypoun)* appears in the Greek Bible only here and in the Alexandrinus text of LXX Exod 36:39.

*took place.* The Greek word here is *egenēthē,* an aorist (passive or deponent) form of the verb *ginesthai,* which can mean "to be made," "to be created," "to be established," etc. (BAG s.v. I, 2); hence the *NEB* and *NAB* tr. for this verse, "was inaugurated." That, however, probably attributes too much to the verb here, especially since the simple verb "to be" is used in the (antithetical) parallel in v. 8 (and no verb at all occurs in vv. 9 and 11). A more general meaning, then, is probably intended here (see BAG s.v. I, 3), without any special reference to a divine act of formal institution.

*with such splendor.* The adjective *such* has been supplied for the English tr. in view of the next part of the verse, which proceeds to emphasize how great the *splendor* was. The noun *doxa* (often best rendered "glory," as in 1:20), appears frequently in chaps. 1–9, primarily in 3:7–4:6, but never in chaps. 10–13; the verb *(doxazein)* is used only in 3:10 (twice) and 9:13. In the present passage (3:7–4:6) the word has been translated consistently as *splendor* (cf. *JB:* "brightness") because the thought is especially of the relative brilliance with which the ministries of the old and new covenants are endowed. For a summary of the range of meanings of this word in the Bible, see Fry 1976. Boobyer (1929, especially 7–14) has emphasized the concreteness and materialism of the concept of *doxa* as it is found in this and other Pauline passages.

*that.* Translates *hōste,* here followed by the infinitive and an accusative, expressing the actual result (see BAG s.v. $2\alpha\beta$).

*the Israelites.* Literally "the sons of Israel," as in the LXX passage Paul has in mind (Exod 34:32, 34, 35).

*could not bear to gaze.* Literally "were not able [*mē dynasthai*] to gaze." The verb *(atenisai)* means "[to] look intently [at something]." According to Exod 34:30, Moses' people were "afraid to come near him" (LXX: *ephobēthēsan engisai autou*).

*Moses' face.* This is the first explicit reference to Moses in the present letter, although his mediation of the law has been in view since v. 3. The name does not recur in 2 Cor after this passage (and vv. 13, 15). Elsewhere in Paul's letters: Rom 5:14; 9:15; 10:5, 19; 1 Cor 9:9; 10:2. The radiance emanating from *Moses' face* is central to the story in Exod 34:29–35.

*was being annulled.* Translates the attributive participle, *tēn katargoumenēn,* which describes the *splendor* of Moses' face. Most recent English versions render this as "fading" (e.g., *RSV, TEV, NIV*), but Paul, who uses the verb frequently (twenty-two out of the twenty-seven NT occurrences are in the undisputed letters), consistently employs it with reference to something in some way invalidated or replaced (see BAG s.v.). In v. 14 the form is certainly passive, and that is probably also the case in this and the other verses (11, 13) where it is used in this passage; see Hanson 1965:27, who notes that Paul could have used some such word as *aphanismos* (Heb 8:13) had he wanted to speak only of the "fading" splendor. The present-tense participle is translated *was being annulled* because it expresses action contemporary with that of the main verb, which in this case is the aorist *egenēthē, took place* (not taken into account by Osten-Sacken 1981:231).

8. *will not . . . with greater splendor?* An English tr. must paraphrase here in order to represent the effect of the Greek expression *pōs ouchi mallon.* Here and in vv. 9, 11 (note *pollō mallon*) Paul is following one well-established rabbinic exegetical procedure as he argues "from the lesser to the greater" *(qal wā-ḥômer).* The same model is apparent in Rom 5:9, 10, 15, 17; 11:12, 24; cf. Phil 2:12; Phlm 16.

*the ministry of the Spirit.* In contrast to the ministry that deals in death (v. 6) and condemnation (v. 9) is the one that deals in the Spirit, presently (v. 9) to be described as one that deals in righteousness, and later (5:18) as one that deals in reconciliation (the genitives are in every instance qualitative).

*will... be with... splendor.* The verb (*will be,* future tense) parallels *egenēthē* (aorist tense), used of the death-dealing ministry in v. 7. Should *estai* be read as a "real" (chronological) future tense (so Meyer, 468), as a "logical" future expressing result (most commentators), or as embracing both the present and future aspects of the *splendor* with which the ministry of the Spirit is attended (e.g., Windisch, 114–15; Collange, 77–78)? See COMMENT.

9. *with the ministry.* Translates the dative *tē diakonia,* attested by a number of excellent mss. (including P⁴⁶ ℵ A) and adopted by *GNT* and Nestle. Metzger (1971:578) remarks on the weight of the external evidence and the possibility that the nominative represents an assimilation to the nominative forms of the same word which immediately precede and follow. Barrett, 109 n. 1, adopts the nominative, however (as do most trs. and commentaries), on the basis that the dative represents a syntactical "improvement" of the text. There is little difference in meaning, whichever way it is taken.

*the ministry of condemnation.* This phrase is parallel to *the ministry of death* in v. 7; for the meaning of the genitive, see note there. The word *condemnation (katakrisis)* is rare, occurring only here and in 7:3 in the Greek Bible. For a few instances of the word in other literature (including 2 Clem 15:5) see BAG s.v. (cf. Deissmann 1927: 94–95). It is doubtless related closely in meaning to the noun *katakrima* (also rare) which Paul uses in Rom 5:16, 18; 8:1, even if this latter does refer more to the "punishment" and the former more to the "sentence" (so Deissmann 1903:264–65, followed by MM and BAG s.v.).

*how much more.* For the *qal wā-ḥômer* argument, see note on v. 8.

*the ministry of righteousness.* For parallel expressions, see note on v. 8. The noun *righteousness* also appears in 5:21; 6:7, 14; 9:9 (LXX), 10; and once in chaps. 10–13, in 11:15. The latter instance is of special importance for the present verse, because there Paul is accusing Satan's ministers of masquerading as "ministers of righteousness" *(diakonoi dikaiosynēs).* Neither the verb *(dikaioun)* nor the adjective *(dikaios)* is used in 2 Cor. In 1 Cor the noun occurs but once (1:30), the verb twice (4:4; 6:11), the adjective never (but the adverb, *dikaiōs,* is used in 15:34).

10. *Indeed.* Translates *kai gar,* "for even" (see BDF § 452[3]), which may be used to introduce a reason or to provide an example for something just mentioned (e.g., Rom 11:1; 15:3; 1 Cor 5:7; 12:13; 2 Cor 13:4), to explain a point just made (e.g., 2 Cor 7:5), to add a point (e.g., 5:2; 1 Cor 11:9), etc. In the present case, the expression introduces a comment intended to clarify and thus further support the argument to which it is added. This verse does not, therefore, seriously interrupt the argument (correctly Bultmann, 86; Collange, 80; contrast Windisch, 116); see following note.

*what has had splendor has not had splendor.* A second instance in this letter of oxymoron (see NOTES on 2:8), here yielding a paradox made even more pointed in Greek by the fact that both expressions (the substantive participle *to dedoxasmenon* and the verb *ou dedoxastai*) stand in the perfect tense. The neuter (substantive) participle *what has had splendor* stands for the ministry and the covenant of Moses. The influence of LXX Exod 34 continues to be apparent. According to that passage, when

Moses came down from Sinai he "did not know that the appearance of his countenance had been endowed with splendor [*dedoxastai*]," and when Aaron and the elders of Israel saw that Moses' face "had been endowed with splendor [*ēn dedoxasmenē*]" they were afraid to go near him (vv. 29–30).

*in this case.* Translates the phrase *en toutō tō merei* (literally "in this part"), the only other NT occurrence of which is in 9:3. Héring, 25, construes it closely with *to dedoxasmenon (what has had splendor),* thus yielding the idea of "that which has been glorified within limits" (so also *NAB:* "that limited glory"). E. Hill (1961:300) argues for the literal rendering of *meros* as "part" because Paul has been speaking of two "parts," the old and new covenants. Since Paul now refers to "*this* part" rather than "*that* part," the reference must be to the "part" mentioned last (in v. 9), specifically the new covenant (ibid.). Hill's overall argument is unconvincing, however, and it is doubtful whether this phrase should be construed very closely with any single element in the context. In this tr. it has therefore been set apart by commas. It relates in a general way to the whole preceding remark—that what was observed to have splendor no longer has it—and introduces the last part of the sentence in which that point is explained (cf. Plummer, 91–92; Collange, 81). There is no warrant, however, for striking it as a gloss, as Weiss does (cited by Windisch, 117).

*the splendor which so far surpasses it.* Translates *tēs hyperballousēs doxēs,* "the surpassing splendor." The attributive participle is formed from *hyperballein,* and this word-group is especially prominent in 2 Cor: the noun *(hyperbolē)* is used in 1:8; 4:7, 17 (twice); 12:7 (otherwise in the NT, only in Gal 1:13), the adverb *(hyperballontōs)* in 11:23 (and nowhere else in the NT), and the verb, again in the form of an attributive participle, in 9:14 (elsewhere in the NT, verbal forms are present only in Eph 1:19; 2:7; 3:19). See also 7:4 ("overcome with joy") and the NOTES on 11:5 for further remarks about Paul's use of superlatives in 2 Cor.

11. *For if.* As in v. 9, the *qal wā-ḥômer* argument (see note there) is introduced by *ei gar* (cf. *ei de, Now if,* in v. 7, but contrast the *kai gar, Indeed,* in v. 10—on which see the note).

*what was being annulled.* In v. 7 the attributive participle *tēn katargoumenēn* (feminine) described the *splendor of [Moses'] face* as *being annulled.* Here, however, the neuter participle must be interpreted more generally (and in accord with the neuter substantive participle in v. 10—see note) as applying to the entire ministry of the old covenant symbolized by Moses, a covenant previously described as dealing in *death* (v. 7) and *condemnation* (v. 9); see Windisch, 117 (who cites Godet). The participle is present tense but is nevertheless translated *was being annulled* because an aorist (past) tense of "to be" must be supplied as the main verb; see the following note and the NOTES on v. 7 above.

*was with such splendor.* The past-tense verb *was* is supplied for the tr., in accord with *egenēthē en doxē (took place with such splendor)* in v. 7. Also as in v. 7 (see note there), *such* is supplied for the purpose of tr. Some commentators believe it is significant that in the present verse the ministry of Moses is described as having been *dia doxēs* (literally "through glory") while that of the new covenant *(that which endures)* is *en doxē* (literally "in glory"); thus, e.g., Plummer, 92; Hughes, 105–6; Collange, 82–83, all of whom remark on the impermanence and permanence respectively connoted by these two expressions. However, *en doxē* is used of both dispensations in vv. 7–8, and Paul often changes his prepositions without any apparent reason (examples in Lietzmann, 112; Windisch, 117; so also Barrett, 118). Both phrases here describe the manner in which the covenants have operated (cf. Robertson 1923:11; *GNTG* III:267; Moule 1953:58—*dia doxēs* almost means "gloriously"), and do not in themselves imply anything about their respective impermanence or permanence.

*how much more.* As in v. 9; see the note on v. 8 about the *qal wā-ḥômer* argument.

*that which endures.* Greek *to menon,* a neuter participle formulated to contrast with *what is being annulled (to katargoumenon)* and thus parallel with *the ministry of the Spirit* (v. 8) and *the ministry of righteousness* (v. 9). The theme of the permanence of the new covenant is prominent in Heb (e.g., 7:3, 24; 10:34; 13:14; cf. 12:27).

12. *Having, therefore, such a hope.* The *therefore (oun;* ignored by·*NEB,* represented in other trs. by "Since" [*RSV*] or "Because" [*TEV*]) ties this verse closely to what has preceded (correctly van Unnik 1964:158), even as Paul moves on to apply the point made in vv. 7–11 to the topic of ministry. The term *hope* is introduced into the discussion under the influence of the reference to *that which endures* in v. 11, although it will not be used again in chaps. 1–9 (previously, only in 1:7, Paul's hope for the Corinthians; in Letter E at 10:15, Paul's hope for his ministry). In 2 Cor the verb is more frequent than the noun (1:10, 13; 5:11; 8:5; 13:6).

*we act.* It would not be impossible to take the verb here *(chrōmetha)* as a hortatory subjunctive, "let us act," especially because it has been preceded by the introductory *Having, therefore (echontes oun);* note Heb 4:14; 10:17, where *enchontes oun*—plus one or more hortatory subjunctives—is part of the homiletical style, and cf. Rom 12:6 *(echontes de),* plus the style of the closing admonition in the disputed material of 2 Cor 6:14–7:1 (7:1). However, the hortatory mode would be out of keeping with the present context (Windisch, 118), and the clear parallelism between the thought of this verse and that of 4:1 makes it certain that the former, like the latter, should be interpreted as a declaration rather than as an exhortation. Cf. 4:13. Paul had used this same verb *(chrasthai)* when defending himself against the charge of acting flippantly (1:17), and he will use it again when he expresses his desire not to have to be too severe with the Corinthians on his next visit (13:10; elsewhere in Paul's letters, only 1 Cor 7:21, 31; 9:12, 15).

*with much boldness.* The word *boldness (parrēsia)* was first used in the political sphere to designate a person's right to speak openly and publicly, then also in the private sphere with respect to the relationship between friends. Philo, *Special Laws* I, 321, illustrates how it came to be used by Hellenistic philosophers to describe the kind of openness which should characterize the genuinely moral person. (For this background see Schlier, *TDNT* V:871–79; Marrow 1982:431–40.) In the NT (Schlier, *TDNT* V:879–84; Marrow 1982:440–46), as at least once in the LXX (Job 27:10), it can refer specifically to the confidence of someone before God (e.g., 1 John 3:21, "we have confidence before God [*parrēsian echomen pros ton Theon*]"—*RSV*), and it is this religious meaning that Windisch, 118, finds in the present verse. In this case the term would be virtually synonymous with *confidence (pepoithēsis)* in v. 4, and the present verse would represent essentially a repetition of the whole thought there. However, Paul's concern for his relationship to the Corinthians, evident throughout chaps. 1 and 2 of this letter as well as in 3:1–6, is still alive in this passage (against the view of Windisch; see COMMENT), and it is surely his *boldness* with respect to *them* (as in 7:4) that he remarks on here. The other Pauline instances of this noun (Phil 1:20; Phlm 8) and of the verb (1 Thess 2:2) confirm this interpretation; see COMMENT.

13. *and not like Moses.* In comparisons, as here, it is not unusual for abbreviation to be used, and in this case one should probably fill out the truncated expression *(kai ou kathaper)* with something like "and we do not act [cf. v. 12] like Moses did"; BDF § 482.

*when he used to put.* Translates the one Greek word *etithei* which stands here in the imperfect, probably used in this instance as a narrative tense (Robertson 1923:883).

*a veil.* The word *(kalymma)* is drawn from the LXX text of Exod 34 (vv. 33–35), where it translates the Hebrew *mesĕh,* perhaps "mask," with which Moses is said to have covered his face. In the NT the word appears only in this passage.

*so the.* Here *pros to (mē),* followed by an infinitive, expresses a deliberate purpose *(GNTG* III:144) and is therefore to be distinguished from the use of *hōste* in v. 7 (see note there).

*gaze at.* As in v. 7, *atenisai.*

*the end.* Commentators differ on whether this expression *(to telos)* should be translated as a reference to (1) the "end" of something in the sense of its *terminus* (e.g., "until it was gone"—*NEB)* or (2) the "aim" and meaning of something (e.g., Héring, 25: "goal" or "ultimate significance"; so also Rissi 1969:32–33; Provence 1982:75–76)—hence, in a sense, its "fulfillment" (Hanson 1965:28). Larsson (1962:278) wants to interpret it as meaning both "end" and "goal." Proponents of the second view have in general not been persuasive in their explanations of *why* Paul thought Moses wanted to hide the aim of the old covenant—that is, Christ—from Israel (the most elaborate attempt at this is made by Hanson 1980; especially 15–17), or of *how* a veil could have done that (objections raised by Plummer, 97). The context here seems to require the first meaning (so also Collange, 96; Barrett, 120), and if the statement in Rom 10:4 about Christ being the *telos* of the law is at all pertinent here, then that supports the first view, not the second (despite, e.g., Bring 1969:1–72).

*what was being annulled.* A neuter substantive participle as in v. 11. Not just the radiant splendor of Moses' face was being annulled, which would require a feminine participle as in v. 7, nor the law specifically, which would require a masculine form; rather, and comprehensively, the entire ministry of the old covenant. So, e.g., Hooker 1981:299, 303–4.

14. *But.* The Greek *alla* should be regarded here as a true adversative. As such it introduces a clarification, and, in a sense, a correction of the preceding reference to Moses' veiling himself before *the Israelites:* "not that Moses sought to deceive; rather, their own minds were hardened"; Schildenberger (1963:455), Oostendorp (1967:40), and Barrett, 120, offer similar interpretations. See COMMENT.

*their minds.* The reference is to the *minds* (or "thoughts") of the Israelites (v. 13). The same expression *(ta noēmata)* appears in this context in 4:4, elsewhere in 2 Cor in 2:11 (see NOTES there); 11:3. It is not essentially different in meaning from *hearts* in the next verse; both terms describe, in this context, the overall perceptive, reasoning, and affective faculties of a human being.

*were hardened.* According to van Unnik (1964:162), the aorist tense here *(epōrōthē)* should be interpreted as ingressive, denoting the inception of the condition described. Paul uses the verb only once more, in Rom 11:7, as he introduces a scriptural citation

(v. 8) compounded of LXX Isa 29:10 and Deut 29:3(4). Both texts speak of God's causing the eyes of his people to be darkened and their ears stopped from perceiving the truth—a theme taken over by the earliest church, especially under the influence of yet a third passage, Isa 6:9–10. Neither the verb "harden" nor the noun "hardening" (*pōrōsis,* used by Paul, also of unbelieving Israelites, in Rom 11:25) appears in these LXX texts. Since, however, the verb is used in the citation of Isa 6:10 in John 12:40, it would appear that Paul is dependent here (and in Rom 11) on some familiar, Christian apologetic formulation; see Lindars 1961:159, 162–63.

*Right up to the present day.* This phrase *(achri . . . tēs sēmeron hēmeras)* and the similar one in v. 15 *(heōs sēmeron)* derive from LXX Deut 29:3(4): "And up to this day [*heōs tēs hēmeras tautēs*] the Lord God did not give you a heart to know and eyes to see and ears to hear"; see preceding note.

*the same veil.* The only *veil* mentioned so far is the one which, according to Paul (v. 13), Moses wore over his face when addressing the Israelites. Now Paul proceeds to apply the word metaphorically to describe another kind of veiling. (Cf. Fitzmyer 1981:637.)

*at the public reading.* The preposition *(epi)* is used here, as in 1:4; 7:4, with reference to "the occasion on which or circumstances in which something takes place" (Plummer, 99). The noun *(anagnōsis,* nowhere else in Paul's own letters, but compare his use of the verb in v. 15, and in 1:13 especially) is normally used of the reading out of something in public (BAG s.v. 1). Thus a Jerusalem synagogue inscription described the place as "for the public reading of the law" (cited, ibid.), and Acts 13:15 refers to "the public reading of the Law and the Prophets" in the synagogue at Pisidian Antioch (cf. 1 Tim 4:13, public reading in Christian worship). Barrett, 120, correctly points out that the preposition should not be read as if Paul were thinking of a veil lying "over the public reading," but in accord with v. 15, where the veil is said to lie over the hearts of the hearers. Although Hanson (1974:140–42) rightly emphasizes that Paul is not thinking here about readings from the "Old Testament" (see following note), his tr. of *epi tē anagnōsei* as "at the reading of the narrative of [the old covenant]" has little to commend it. The parallels he adduces from Mark 12:26; Luke 20:37 are not true parallels, for in the first of these the preposition *epi* and the verb *anaginōskein* ("to read aloud") are in different phrases ("have you not read in the book of Moses [*ouk anegnōte en tē biblō Mōüseōs*], in the passage about the bush [*epi tou batou*]"—*RSV*), and in the second, neither the noun nor the verb for "reading" appears at all.

*the old covenant.* This is the first known use of the phrase *hē palaia diathēkē,* and it is possible that Paul was the first to employ it (Windisch, 121). Although there is no specific elaboration of its meaning here, that is no reason to conclude, with Georgi (1964:252), that Paul's opponents must have been familiar with the concept. In this context, where the stone tablets of the Mosaic law (vv. 3, 7) have already been set over against the *new covenant* established by the Spirit (v. 6), the meaning of the expression *old covenant* should be at least generally clear, even if it is being coined here for the first time. Moreover, in v. 15 there is a parallel reference to "Moses" being read, and that confirms that the thought here is of the covenant made on Mount Sinai; cf. van Unnik 1961:220. The reference, then, is not to scripture in general (e.g., *NEB:* "the lesson . . . from the old covenant"; or *TEV:* "the books of the old covenant"), and it is certainly not a reference to the "Old Testament," as if the existence of a "New

Testament" were being presupposed (so Carmignac 1978:384–85). Melito, Bishop of Sardis (late second century), is the first writer known to have applied the phrase to the books of the Jewish scripture in general ("the books of the Old Covenant," cited in Eusebius, *Eccles. Hist.* IV.xxvi.13–14), but even then an equivalent list of Christian writings is not presumed (van Unnik 1961:219). The use of the designation "Old Testament" for Jewish scripture is in fact not traceable to Paul (ibid.). Even the later writer of Heb, who emphasizes the superiority of a new covenant, does not pick up the phrase "old covenant" but refers, rather, to "the first covenant" (*hē prōtē diathēkē*, 9:15; note 8:13, where "the first [covenant]" is further described as "growing old" [*RSV*], *to palaioumenon*). There are several references in the Jewish scriptures to "the book of the covenant" (Hebrew: *sēfer ha-běrît;* LXX: [*to*] biblion tēs diathēkēs), where either the Sinai covenant in particular (Exod 24:7) or the Torah as a whole ( = *nomos:* 4 Kgdms 23:2, 21; 2 Chr 34:30; Sir 24:23 [*biblos diathēkēs*]; 1 Mac 1:57) is in mind; see Bachmann, 166 n. 1; Windisch, 121.

*unlifted.* It is much disputed how the Greek phrase so translated here *(mē anakalyp- tomenon)* should be construed in the sentence. A number of trs. have interpreted it predicatively with the preceding verb, thus: "[the veil] remains unlifted" (e.g., Wey., Gdspd., *RSV, NAB*). This is almost universally rejected by the commentators, however, because that construction would normally require an *ou* rather than the *mē* which stands in the text (Bultmann, 89). It is not impossible that the phrase should be taken as an accusative absolute (cf. BDF § 424), in which case the following *hoti* would have to be regarded as declarative (which in itself poses no problem); thus Mof.: "Veiled from them the fact that the glory fades in Christ" (cf. Plummer, 100: "the revelation not having been made that it [the veil] is done away in Christ," although Barrett, 121, is wrong when he cites Plummer himself as preferring this view). Although Allo, 91, Schildenberger (1963:456), and Collange, 98–99, opt for this interpretation, it must be acknowledged that accusative absolute constructions are rare, that such a construction would be particularly clumsy in the present instance, and that this interpretation must give an unusual meaning to the verb *anakalyptein,* as Plummer's tentative rendering, "revelation not . . . made," and Moffatt's paraphrase, "veiled," clearly demonstrate (correctly Plummer, 100); in this case—as Bultmann, 90, observes—one would have expected, rather, *mē apokalyptomenon* ("it not having been revealed") instead of the *mē anakalyptomenon* ("it not having been lifted") which is actually present. In fact, this phrase goes most naturally with "veil," as v. 18 shows, and begins a new, indepen- dent thought (cf. Windisch, 122), the following *hoti* being accorded, as very commonly, a causal sense (thus, e.g., *NEB:* "and it [the veil] is never lifted, because . . ."); so also Barrett, 120–21.

*because.* This translates the Greek *hoti* as causal, in accord with the view adopted of the participial expression *mē anakalyptomenon.* The alternative would be to read *hoti* as declarative, "that." See preceding note.

*in Christ.* The present English tr., *it is in Christ that . . . ,* attempts to reproduce something of the emphasis the pregnant phrase *in Christ* receives by virtue of its placement in this clause. Cf. *RSV:* "only through Christ"; but the preposition *(en)* is not merely instrumental ("through")—it signifies that it is only "in relationship to" Christ that one is delivered from the bondage of the old covenant (cf. I. Hermann 1961:39–40).

*it is being annulled.* For the meaning of the verb, see note on v. 7. Commentators are divided on whether Paul is thinking here of the demise of the veil (e.g., Windisch, 122; Kümmel, 200; Hughes, 112–13; Rissi 1969:34 n. 60) or of the old covenant (e.g., Lietzmann, 113; Allo, 91; Bultmann, 89; Hanson 1965:29, 1974:139–40, and 1980:18). The chief points in favor of the first view are (1) that the subject of the preceding verb *remains* was *the·same veil,* and there is no explicit indication of a change in the subject (Kümmel), and (2) the verb is present tense rather than aorist or perfect, as one might expect were the reference to Christ's abrogation of the old covenant (Hughes). It is argued, on the other hand, (1) that elsewhere in this passage the verb refers to the annulment of the old covenant ( = the old splendor; vv. 7, 11, 13), and (2) that the proper word to use in referring to the "removal" of a veil is the one Paul actually employs in v. 16 (*perihairein;* see especially Hanson). On balance, it would seem that the overall context must be determinative of the meaning, and thus the second interpretation has been adopted here.

15. *Indeed.* Here, as in v. 14, the thought is introduced with the conjunction *alla,* which some wish to translate again as an adversative, "But" (e.g., *NEB*). In that case, it could be taken in relation either to *unlifted* in v. 14 ("not lifted up, but [so far from that] a veil lies over their heart" [Plummer, 101]) or to the very last words of that verse ("the law is done away in Christ, nevertheless . . ." [Barrett, 121]). The present tr., however, reads it as intensive (cf. *RSV* and *JB:* "Yes"), since the sentence essentially reiterates what has already been said in v. 14*b.* One is not justified in striking this as a gloss, as Heinrici does (131 n.), just because it is repetitive; in fact, the repetition serves the purpose of introducing the thought of v. 16; cf. Windisch, 122–23; Bultmann, 92.

*whenever.* The particle *hēnika* appears only here (and again in v. 16) in the NT (see BDG § 105); it has been drawn into this context from LXX Exod 34:34, which lies behind v. 16 (see NOTES there).

*Moses is read.* Here, as in Acts 15:21, which speaks of Moses "being read" every Sabbath in the synagogues, *Moses* stands for "the book of Moses" (2 Chr 25:4; Neh 13:1; Mark 12:26), which means his law ( = the Pentateuch). This includes but is more comprehensive than the more particular reference in the preceding verse to the Sinai covenant. Also, in Rom 10:5, Paul identifies Moses closely with the pentateuchal text ("Moses writes that . . ." [with reference to Lev 18:5]; cf. Rom 10:19 [introducing Deut 32:21], "First Moses says . . ."). The apostle uses the common OT phrase "law of Moses" only once, however (1 Cor 9:9). The opinion of Collange, 100, that "reading Moses" here means, specifically, interpreting the life and work of the person, Moses, in the way Paul's opponents are doing has no basis in the text itself or in general usage.

*their hearts.* A parallel to *their minds* in v. 14*a,* meaning those of the Israelites (see note there). In Phil 4:7 the use of both terms together in the benedictory form shows how closely related they are in meaning (". . . will keep your hearts and your minds in Christ Jesus").

16. *anyone.* This tr. presumes an unexpressed *tis* as the subject of the verb *turns* (so also Plummer, 101; Collange, 103), but others identify the subject as the Israelites (from v. 13; so, e.g., Bachmann, 170–71; Windisch, 123; Bultmann, 92; I. Hermann 1961: 38–39; cf. Mof. and *JB:* "they") or *their hearts* (literally "the heart of them," the noun being singular in Greek; so, e.g., Meyer, 476; Allo, 92; Rissi 1969:136 n. 66). The matter

remains uncertain because the LXX text which lies behind v. 16 (Exod 34:34) has been thoroughly altered (the changes are enumerated by Windisch, 123). In that text "Moses" was the subject of the verb: "And whenever Moses used to go before the Lord to speak with him, he would remove the veil until he went out." Trs. that represent Paul as actually quoting that text here (e.g., *NAB; NEB*—but see the footnote) naturally represent Moses as the subject still (e.g., Moule 1972:234–35). But the changes are too far-reaching to permit the conclusion that Paul is specifically citing (even if from a textual tradition unknown to us; contrast Dunn 1970b:312–13), and the fact that the subject is left unexpressed is probably a clue that Paul wishes to broaden the reference to include more than just Moses; cf. van Unnik 1964:166, who refers to v. 18.

*turns to the Lord.* The verb used in the LXX text of Exod 34:34 is "used to go in" (*eiseporeueto,* imperfect), whereas the verb used here (aorist subjunctive) is one commonly associated with Israel's penitent turning to their God; the exact expression "to turn to the Lord" (*epistrephein pros Kyrion,* as here) occurs in Deut 4:30; 2 Chr 24:19; 30:9; Ps 21(22):27; Sir 5:7; Isa 19:22. On the evidence of 1 Thess 1:9; Luke 1:16; Acts 9:35; 11:21; 14:15; 15:19; 26:20; 1 Pet 2:25; cf. Gal 4:9, it appears that this and similar expressions were often used in the church's missionary preaching, probably having been familiar already in the religious propaganda of Hellenistic Judaism. It is thus to be regarded as a technical expression for conversion (Bultmann, 92), although it is arbitrary to suggest that Paul here has his own conversion specifically in mind (Plummer, 102).

*the Lord.* In Paul's letters *Lord (Kyrios)* generally means Christ, except when the apostle is quoting scripture or working closely with a scriptural text (see Kramer 1966:151–82). The present occurrence (which in Greek is anarthrous, without the article) is difficult to interpret—partly because, while the text of Exod 34:34 obviously lies behind this verse, it has been so thoroughly altered by Paul that it can hardly be classified as an actual citation (despite *NEB, TEV* [though see the footnote in each], and various commentators, especially Dunn 1970b:312–17). Thus Windisch, 123, takes the reference here to be to Christ, and this view has been extensively defended by I. Hermann (1961, especially 39–43; cf. Hanson 1980:18–19). Others, however, argue that the reference must be to God (Yahweh), as in Exod 34 (e.g., Schildenberger 1963; Moule 1972:235, who points out that *Lord* is also anarthrous in Exod 34:34; Dunn 1970b, who is concerned to refute Hermann's views in particular; Collange, 103–4). The reference to Christ at the end of v. 14 cannot be used as an argument in favor of a christological interpretation, because there Christ is described as the one in whom the entire ministry of the old covenant is annulled, while in the present verse it is a matter simply of the removal of the veil in order to disclose that annulment. Therefore, these phrases in vv. 14 and 16 are not parallel, as Schmithals (1971:319), Ulonska (1966:387), and Hooker (1981:301) have claimed.

Four points in particular tell against a christological reference here: (1) Even though this is not an actual citation from scripture, not only has the text from Exod 34 been in Paul's mind since v. 7, but its language has in certain specific ways influenced his own throughout this whole passage. (2) While there are important christological aspects to the discussion in this part of the letter, these are nevertheless secondary to a specifically *theo*logical emphasis which has been present since 2:14 (see COMMENT). (3) When, in 1 Thess 1:9, Paul echoes the same missionary formulation which along with

Exod 34:34 has influenced the wording of the present verse (see preceding note), the reference is explicitly to God *(epestrepsate pros ton Theon)*. (4) When Paul proceeds in the following verse to identify *the Lord,* he does not do so with any specifically christological title.

*is removed.* In LXX Exod 34:34 the tense of this verb is imperfect, its voice is middle, and its subject is "Moses"; thus, "he would remove *[perihēreito]* the veil." Here, however, the tense has been changed to present (with a future reference, as in the case of the aorist subjunctive form *epistrepsē, turns to* ). Most commentators believe the voice has also been changed to passive, with *the veil* as its subject, and virtually all the English trs. presume this. It is not impossible, however, that the form should be interpreted as middle voice, in which case the subject could be either *the Lord* (so Barrett, 122) or, as in Exod 34:34, "Moses" (so Moule 1972:235). The LXX passage has been so far adapted here, however, that it is unlikely Moses is any longer thought of as the subject of the action (see note above on *one*), so if the verb is middle it is most likely that *the Lord* is the subject. Since even the usual interpretation of it as passive, retained here, implies that *the Lord* is the agent of the veil's removal, as Barrett acknowledges, a decision about the voice does not in itself affect the meaning. The compound form *peri-hairein* is more likely to connote a "complete" removal of the veil *(GNTG* II:321) than the removal of something that envelops (so Plummer, 102; Robertson 1923:617).

17. *Now.* Translates *de,* an unemphatic connective which sometimes introduces a gloss or comment on what has preceded. Note especially 1 Cor 10:4b; Gal 4:25, where —as here—a scriptural text is being explained (Dunn 1970b:313).

*"the Lord."* Quotation marks are used here in the tr. in order to show that the expression has been repeated from the preceding verse (the article *ho* is anaphoric; Barrett, 122, citing Turner and Kümmel); cf. *JB:* "this Lord" and Gdspd.: "the Lord here." *NEB* and *TEV* both insert a reference to "this passage," but that kind of paraphrase suggests more of a correspondence between v. 16 and Exod 34:34 than there actually is; see NOTES there. It is proper, however, to describe this as an "exegetical gloss" in a more general sense (e.g., Dibelius 1956:129–30; van Unnik 1964:165; Bultmann, 92). It is pure conjecture, based on his own re-punctuation of the second half of the verse, when Héring, 27, reads "there where the Lord is" *(hou de ho Kyrios).*

*is.* The verb here *(estin)* is not used with any metaphysical reference, as if there were a concern to define the "nature" of the Lord. As in other instances where a scriptural term is being explained (Kümmel, 200, notes Gal 3:16; 4:24 and Rom 10:6–8 [*tout' estin*]), one could translate "means" (so Gdspd.).

*the Spirit.* In vv. 3–6, Paul had introduced the antithesis of law and Spirit (old covenant, new covenant), and that antithesis was accentuated by his use of Exod 34:29–30 in vv. 7–11. The only other places where Paul associates *Lord* and *Spirit* (or "spirit") are 1 Cor 6:17 and 12:3. In both passages the "Lord" is Christ, but the association with the Spirit is very loose. There are two places where *the Spirit* is specifically associated with "(Jesus) Christ" (Rom 8:9–11; Phil 1:19), and one additional passage in which Paul refers to "the Spirit of [God's] Son" (Gal 4:6); but there is no direct identification of the two. Schmithals (1971:315–17) also emphasizes that Paul himself does not identify Christ and the Spirit, but he argues at the same time that such an identification is present here (ibid.:319). This becomes one of his arguments in support of the hypothesis that v. 17 in its entirety, together with v. 18b, constitutes a Gnostic gloss on v. 16. In contrast to these few passages in which *the Spirit* is (loosely) associated with Christ are the many passages in which Paul refers to "the Spirit of God," etc. (Rom 8:9, 11, 14; 1 Cor 2:10–14; 3:16; 6:11; 7:40; 12:3), including his mention of "the Spirit of the living God" in this same context, v. 3; cf. Collange, 113.

*the Spirit of the Lord.* This phrase (*[to] pneuma Kyriou*) is frequent in the LXX (e.g., Judg 3:10; 11:29; often in 1 Kgdms; 2 Kgdms 23:2; 3 Kgdms 19:11, etc.) and occurs elsewhere in the NT in Luke 4:18 (citing Isa 61:1) and Acts 8:39 (influenced by LXX 3 Kgdms 18:12 and 4 Kgdms 2:16). The genitive (*Kyriou*, "of the Lord") indicates origin and belonging, and it is clear that *Lord* and *Spirit* are not equated (cf. I. Hermann 1961:50–51; Kramer 1966:165); thus, "the Lord's Spirit." For this reason, Schildenberger (1963:458) argues that *Lord* is here a christological title (so also Hermann and Kramer)—because in vv. 16, 17*a*, where (he agrees) *the Lord* is Yahweh, an absolute identification with *the Spirit* is made with the use of the verb "is" (*estin*, v. 17*a*). That, however, reads too much into the verb (see note above on *is*); and both the LXX background of the phrase and its context here in chap. 3 support the view that Paul is thinking of the Spirit of God (see, e.g., Dunn 1970b:317–18; Collange, 111). Héring, 26–27, punctuates v. 17*b* so as to obtain the tr. "there where the Spirit is, is the liberty of the Lord," but this ignores the fact that *the Spirit of the Lord* is a biblical phrase firmly fixed in the Jewish-Christian tradition; it should not be broken up, as it is by Héring.

*is, is.* These verbs must be supplied, for none stands in the Greek text of v. 17*b*.

*freedom.* This is the only occurrence of this noun (*eleutheria*) in 2 Cor, and there are no instances of the cognate verb or adjective. Elsewhere in the Pauline letters the noun occurs in Rom 8:21; 1 Cor 10:29; Gal 2:4; 5:1, 13 (twice); the verb, in Rom 6:18, 22; 8:2, 21; Gal 5:1. The adjective is more frequent (mainly in 1 Cor and Gal). Some mss. read "there (is) freedom" (e.g., ℵ*c*), but the simple reading *freedom* is much better attested (P⁴⁶ ℵ A B C D et al.), and the variant construction (*hou . . . ekei*) does not accord with Paul's style as exhibited in Rom 4:15; 5:20 (Plummer, 104; Metzger 1971:578). On the meaning of *freedom* in this context, see COMMENT.

18. *And.* Translates *de* as a simple conjunction, carrying forward the idea of *freedom* (v. 17) in order to describe its meaning. It is less likely, but possible, that *de* is used here adversatively; thus, "but freedom means," which would imply that some false understanding of freedom needs to be corrected. Cf. Collange, 115.

*we all.* The Greek phrase *hēmeis pantes* (*pantes* is well attested despite its omission in P⁴⁶, Origen, and Augustine) is emphatic, and refers not just to "all of us apostles," but to "all of us who believe," all Christians. There are two references to "all the Israelites" in Exod 34 (vv. 32, 34), but since Paul himself has not repeated that adjective in referring to them in vv. 7, 13, one must hesitate to claim the influence of the Exod passage on this expression.

*with unveiled face.* It is disputed whether this description of Christian believers is meant to contrast with the previous description of Moses—who according to Paul (v. 13) veiled his face when talking with the Israelites—or with the previous description of unbelieving Israel, whose understanding has been veiled (v. 15). The use of the word *face* suggests the former (so, e.g., Plummer, 105), but the context favors the latter (so, e.g., Bultmann, 93–94). In this instance the context is that of vv. 14ff. in particular, in which the thought is not of the veil covering Moses' face but of the one that is present when the old covenant is read (v. 14*b*), and specifically the one that lies over the hearts of those who hear it read (v. 15). When, however, they turn *to the Lord,* the veil is taken away. Thus, *we all* who have turned to the Lord (as believers) stand before him *with unveiled face.* Here, then, *face* is equivalent to *hearts* in v. 15 (so also Bultmann, ibid.). Collange, 116, thinks Moses is in mind as an example of one who goes before the Lord with an *un*veiled face. But Paul has only alluded to Moses' unveiling of his face (in v. 16 "Moses" is the subject of the verb in only a secondary sense; see note), whereas he has strongly emphasized his veiling of it (v. 13).

*beholding as in a mirror.* Some (e.g., W. L. Knox 1939:131–33; Dupont 1949; Allo, 96; van Unnik 1964:167) argue that the middle participle *(katoptrizomenoi)* should be translated, rather, "reflecting as a mirror does" (thus *JB:* "reflecting like mirrors"; cf. *TEV* and *NIV*), but the linguistic evidence is clearly against this (see BAG s.v.). Note above all Philo, *Allegorical Int.* III, 101, where Moses addresses God: "for I would not that Thou shouldst be manifested to me by means of heaven or earth or water or air or any created thing at all, nor would I find the reflection *(katoptrisaimēn)* of Thy being in aught else than in Thee Who art God. . . ." The ancient versions also support this meaning (BAG s.v.), although the Vulgate's *speculantes* would involve no necessary reference to seeing "in a mirror" (cf. *RSV* and *NAB,* who take the verb in the weakened sense of "beholding" or "gazing"). The context, too, seems to require the tr. adopted here, because believers *(we all)* are not contrasted with Moses, whose countenance radiated (reflected) God's splendor, but with the Israelites, who could not look upon it (see preceding note). See also 1 Clem 36:2 (sometimes regarded as dependent on the present passage [e.g., Hughes, 119 n. 19]; but see Hagner 1973:211), where the related verb *enoptrizesthai* is clearly parallel to *atenizein* ("to gaze"); thus, "to see mirrored" (Graham's tr. in *AF* II:63).

*the splendor of the Lord.* The phrase is frequent in the LXX, often associated with Moses' ministry (e.g., Exod 16:7; 40:34–35; Lev 9:23) and even, specifically, with his ascent of Mount Sinai (Exod 24:17). Note in particular Num 12:8*a,* where the Lord says: "I will speak to [Moses] mouth to mouth, directly and not indistinctly [*en eidei kai ou di' ainigmatōn*]; and he has seen the splendor of the Lord [*tēn doxan Kyriou*]," and which Balch (1972:363) thinks Paul has in mind, along with Exod 34, in this verse. The expression occurs elsewhere in Paul's letters only in 8:19. The apostle's references to God's glory are much more numerous (e.g., Rom 3:23; 5:2; 1 Cor 11:7); when this fact is combined with the LXX background of the phrase *splendor of the Lord* and with the probability that *Lord* in vv. 17–18 is a reference to God, it would appear that here, as well, the reference is to Yahweh, not to Christ (so also Collange, 118–19).

*are being transformed.* The present tense here, *metamorphoumetha,* may be compared with the use of the present tense *katoptrizomenoi (beholding as in a mirror)* in this same verse and *perisseuei (does . . . abound)* in v. 9. Just as *the ministry of righteousness* "abounds" *in glory,* so believers are *beholding . . . the splendor of the Lord* and *are being transformed . . . from splendor to splendor.* Elsewhere in Pauline usage the eschatological aspects of the divine "splendor" or "glory" *(doxa)* are stressed (e.g., 4:17; Rom 5:2; 8:18; 1 Thess 2:12). The verb *(metamorphousthai)* is used elsewhere in the NT only of Jesus' transfiguration (Matt 17:2; Mark 9:2), and in Rom 12:2 in Paul's appeal that his readers not be "conformed to the pattern of this age," but that they should let themselves "be transformed in the renewal of their minds." Other Pauline passages pertinent to a discussion of the meaning of the verb in the present verse are those in which he uses the adjective *symmorphos,* "conformed" (Rom 8:29; Phil 3:21), and the verbs *symmorphizesthai,* "to be conformed" (Phil 3:10), *morphoun,* "to form" (Gal 4:19), and *allassein,* "to change" (1 Cor 15:51, 52). In the LXX, *metamorphous-thai* occurs only in Symmachus' text of Ps 33(34):1. Philo, *Moses* I, 57, uses it of Moses: "As he spoke he grew inspired and was transfigured into a prophet." For the meaning of the term in the present context, see COMMENT.

*the same image.* The Greek phrase is *tēn autēn eikona,* which is loosely construed with the passive participle *being transformed* to indicate both the manner and the goal of the transformation; see Robertson 1923:486; BDF § 159(4); Collange, 121. The preposition *into* has had to be supplied for purposes of tr. The word *image (eikōn)* is used again in 4:4, where Christ is described as *the image of God.* Jervell (1960:174–75) argues that Paul has in mind Gen 1:26–27, where the first man is said to have been created in God's image (LXX: *eikōn;* cf. also Gen 5:1; 9:6; Wis 2:23; Sir 17:3). That passage unquestionably lies behind 1 Cor 15:49, which portrays Christ as "the heavenly man" by whom the life forfeited by Adam, "the man of dust," has been regained, and whose "image" believers themselves can now bear, in place of the old (cf. Col 3:10; also Philo, *Allegorical Int.* I, 31; *Confusion of Tongues* 147). Indeed, a Samaritan midrash on Deut 34:7 (*M. Marqah* v. 4, quoted in another connection by Meeks 1970:363, using McDonald's tr.) shows that Moses' shining face could itself be associated with the image of God that Adam had lost: *"Nor his natural force abated* [Deut 34:7], for he was vested with the Form [*ṣalmā*] which Adam cast off in the Garden of Eden; and his face shone up to the day of his death." On the other hand, the reference to *beholding as in a mirror* might in itself be sufficient to explain the introduction of the word *image* into v. 18—as in Wis 7:26, where there is no allusion to Gen 1:26–27 (Barrett, 125). In any case, the question is wrongly posed when one asks (e.g., with Hanson 1980:22) whether the *image* mentioned here is "Christ's" or "God's." Since Paul is thinking of Christ as *the image of God* (4:4), the one in whom God's glory is disclosed (4:6), one must say that his concept of *image* has a christological and a theological dimension simultaneously. Christ is God's image because he is God's Son (see Rom 8:29) in whom God is beheld, and the image into which believers *are being transformed* is the *same* one they see mirrored there. (Contrast van Unnik [1964:167–68], who identifies *the same image* not with God's glory disclosed in Christ but with "that which we all have in common: we all with our different shapes are transformed into one *eikōn.*" Doignon [1979] discusses this and related matters as they come up in Hilary's interpretation of the verse.) On the background of the *eikōn* concept in Paul, see further below, on 4:4.

*from splendor to splendor.* The construction here *(apo doxēs eis doxan)* is similar but not identical to that in 2:16, "from death for death . . . from life for life" *(ek thanatou eis thanaton . . . ek zōēs eis zōēn),* on which see the NOTE. The context, as well as the idiom itself, makes it clear that the permanence (cf. *the splendor of that which endures,* v. 11) and even the increase of the *splendor* are being emphasized over against the diminishing *splendor* of Moses (e.g., Moule 1972:236; Larsson 1962:280; Hickling 1975a:393). A similar conception of being transformed into successively higher degrees of *splendor* is found in 2 Apoc Bar 51:1–10; see COMMENT. It is possible that the *apo (from)* should be given a causal sense (Schlatter, 521) and regarded as parallel to the following phrase, *from the Lord* (cf. Collange, 122–23; Robertson 1923:820 uses this verse as an example of *apo* occurring with a passive verb to express the agent, but does not specify whether he has reference to both occurrences of the preposition *from* or only to the second, *from the Lord,* which is certainly causal; cf. BDF § 210). Although *splendor* is closely identified with *image* here and elsewhere (see preceding note), Kittel (*TDNT* II:397 n. 103) goes too far when he suggests that Paul could have written just as well "from image to image."

*as.* The Greek word is *kathaper* (translated *like* in v. 13), but its exact meaning here is difficult to determine. Héring, 28, assigns it causal force, "for" (as also in Mof., Gdspd., *RSV*), and such a meaning may be illustrated by at least one other Pauline passage, 1 Thess 2:11. Others, however, give it a comparative meaning, "as" *(AT)* or "even as" (Wey.), certainly the most common use of the term by Paul (e.g., 1:14; 3:13; 8:11). Some recent English trs. apparently regard it as a simple conjunction and ignore it *(TEV, NAB),* while others take it in a restrictive sense ("this is," *JB;* "such," *NEB;* "which," *NIV*). The comparative meaning is the most likely, and it is at least indirectly attested by the variant reading of B, "just as" *(kathōsper).* Collange, 124, who reads the preposition *from* causally, both in the preceding phrase *(from splendor)* and in the one following *(from the Lord),* interprets this as "We are transformed by the glory as by the Lord . . . ," while Moule (1972:236) paraphrases to read "This is in keeping with —this is what we would expect from. . . ."

*from the Lord.* Here the preposition *(apo)* certainly has causal force—thus the paraphrase of *JB:* "this is the work of the Lord" (cf. *NAB:* "by the Lord"); see note on *from splendor to splendor* above.

*the Lord, the Spirit.* The tr. of the Greek *Kyriou Pneumatos* must remain problematic. There are at least six possibilities: (1) "The Lord of the Spirit" (e.g., Windisch, 129; Bultmann, 99), taking this as an instance of the general rule that the governing genitive precedes the dependent one. (2) "The Spirit of the Lord" (e.g., Héring, 28), taking this as one of the exceptions to the general rule about governing and dependent genitives; so *GNTG* III:218; BDF § 474(4). (3) "The Lord who is the Spirit" (e.g., Bachmann, 178; Lietzmann, 114–15; most recent English trs.), with reference to v. 17*a*. (4) "The Lord who is Spirit" (e.g., *JB, NEB*), a variation of (3), perhaps influenced by the fact that *Spirit* has no article here (contrast v. 17*a*). (5) "The Lord, the Spirit" (e.g., Wey., Mof.). (6) "The Spirit who is Lord" (Hort, cited by Collange, 123). Of these, (5) has the advantage of associating *Lord* and *Spirit*—as Paul clearly intends, both here and in v. 17—yet not identifying them absolutely. Such an identification is not present in v. 17*a* (see NOTES there, and Kümmel, 200), and is specifically precluded by v. 17*b*. Option (2) would also be possible. I. Hermann (1961:56) gives the interpretation "as from the Lord whom I experience as Spirit," but identifies *the Lord* as Christ. It is better to regard *the Lord* here, as in the preceding verses, as God (so Dunn 1970b:318); see COMMENT. J. R. Harris (1921–22) has argued that Tertullian's reading, "as from the Lord of Spirits" *(tanquam a domino, inquiti spiritum, Against Marcion V.xi),* derives from Marcion's own text and shows that Paul's thought here has been influenced by 1 Enoch 38:4: "And (the godless) shall not be able to behold the face of the holy, / For the Lord of Spirits has caused his light to appear / On the face of the holy, righteous, and elect" *(APOT).* The textual basis for this is tenuous, however, and the thought does violence to the context in 2 Cor 3, where *the Spirit* is a fundamental theme.

**4:1.** *Therefore.* The Greek is *dia touto* (as in 7:13; 13:10), which could be translated "For this reason [or: cause]"; cf. Plummer, 109. There is, however, no reason to distinguish it sharply from the *oun (therefore)* in 3:12 or from the *dio (Thus)* in 4:16. The present verse resumes the point initiated in 3:12, but now with the added support of 3:18 in particular: "since, therefore, we have an unhindered vision of the Lord's splendor. . . ." This corresponds to the reference implicit in 3:12 to the enduring splendor of the ministry of the Spirit (3:8, 11).

*having this ministry.* Cf. "Having . . . such a hope" in 3:12. The *ministry* is that *of the Spirit* (3:8), *of righteousness* (3:9), which is exercised by those who are *ministers of a new covenant* (3:6).

*as recipients of mercy.* Translates *eleēthēmen,* "as we have received mercy," an aorist passive form which here, as in 1 Cor 7:25; 1 Tim 1:13, 16, has in view the call to apostleship. The first person plural is probably meant to include not only himself and Timothy, but all true apostles, although his own experience of being called by God's grace (e.g., 1 Cor 15:10a; Gal 1:15) is doubtless foremost in his mind. Cf. 3:5. It is unclear whether *as (kathōs)* is meant to correlate the receipt of God's mercy with the preceding phrase ("seeing that, in full accordance with God's mercy, we have this ministry" [Plummer, 110]) or with what follows ("as we have received mercy, we do not shrink back"; cf. Grundmann, *TDNT* III:486). There would be no real difference in meaning, since even in the first case God's mercy (as the origin of ministry) would be the ground for one's confidence.

*we do not shrink back.* The verb *(enkakein)* may mean "to become weary," "to lose heart," or "to show fear" (BAG s.v.), depending on the context. Here, as in all other NT occurrences (v. 16; Luke 18:1; Gal 6:9; Eph 3:13; 2 Thess 3:13), it is preceded by a negative, and has as a variant reading—but weakly attested—*ekkakein* ("to lose heart"). In the present case the overall parallelism between 4:1 and 3:12 and the continuation of the sentence in 4:2 are decisive for the meaning. The *ouk enkakoumen* must be translated in such a way as to carry forward the thought of having *much boldness* (3:12), as well as in such a way as to accord with what will be said about apostles commending their actions to others, before God, without fear or trepidation (4:2). The same expression in 4:16 is parallel with the idea of "having confidence" in 5:6, 8 (cf. Bultmann, 102; and Collange, 128, who stresses as well the aspect of "perseverance" in the concept), and the tr. adopted for the present verse also fits well there. Bultmann (ibid.) also compares Rom 1:16a, "For I am not ashamed of the gospel" *(RSV).*

**2.** *Rather.* The adversative, *alla,* suggests that what follows is to be contrasted with the "shrinking back" which true apostles do not do (v. 1).

*we for our part have renounced.* The middle form *(apeipametha)* is given its full meaning here (cf. Robertson 1923:810: "for ourselves"; Barrett, 128: "As far as we are concerned"). The aorist corresponds formally with the aorist of v. 1 ("having received mercy") but need not for that reason be a reference specifically to the time of Paul's own conversion and call, as some (e.g., Hughes, 122; Collange, 128) suggest. It seems to mean that apostles have rejected entirely and in principle certain kinds of practices, but it does not necessarily imply that such were actually followed at one time (cf. Plummer, 111).

*the shameful things one hides.* Literally "the hidden things of shame" *(ta krypta tēs aischynēs).* The genitive here is probably qualitative, describing "the hidden things" as shameful acts. Whether Paul means to say that those who do them are themselves ashamed of them (e.g., *NEB:* "the deeds that men hide for very shame"; *JB:* "the reticence of those who are ashamed"), or whether he means they ought to be ashamed of them, is not clear. In 1 Cor 4:5; 14:25, *ta krypta* has a more neutral meaning than here: "the secret things (of the heart)," one's innermost thoughts and intentions. In the present verse, however, these are associated specifically with deceitfulness and chicanery (see the following phrases), and the furtiveness involved becomes an example of that "shrinking back" mentioned in the previous verse; thus it stands in sharp contrast to the *boldness* (3:12) of true apostles. Cf. Héring, 29: "shameful intrigues." Of special interest, in this connection, is a passage in which Philo also contrasts the furtiveness of one who practices evil with the boldness of one whose actions are honorable: "Let those who work mischief feel shame [*aischynesthōsan*] . . . and keep the multitude of their iniquities veiled out of the sight of all. But let those whose actions serve the common weal use freedom of speech [*parrēsia:* "boldness"] . . . and let the clear sunlight shine upon their own life . . ." (*Special Laws* I, 321).

*neither conducting ourselves craftily.* More literally, "not walking in deceitfulness" *(mē peripatountes en panourgia).* The verb *peripatein* occurs frequently in the Pauline letters with reference to the Christian's manner of life in the world (*en sarki,* ["in the flesh"], 10:3, in a neutral sense); *anastrephein* (used in 1:12) is a synonym. Elsewhere Paul criticizes those who "walk" (i.e., conduct themselves) "according to the flesh" (*kata sarka,* 10:2; Rom 8:4; cf. "[merely] human," *kata anthrōpon,* 1 Cor 3:3), "according to appearance" (*dia eidous,* 5:7), or "as enemies of the cross of Christ" (Phil 3:18). For positive characterizations of the Christian life, see NOTES and COMMENT on 5:7; 12:18. The noun *panourgia* (here translated by the English adverb *craftily*) appears again in 11:3, as well as in 1 Cor 3:19 ( = Job 5:13), and the adjective *(panourgos)* is present in 12:16. In the LXX, especially in Prov and Sir, the word generally has the positive meaning of "cleverness" or "shrewdness," but in the NT, as in the anti-sophistic polemic of the Greco-Roman world, it is usually pejorative: "craftiness," "cunning," etc. See Betz 1972:104–5.

*nor adulterating the word of God.* The reference in the following verse to *our gospel* confirms that here, as elsewhere in Paul's letters, *the word of God* means "the gospel"; see 2:17 and NOTES there. The verb *doloun* occurs only here in the NT (and as a variant reading in 1 Cor 5:6—D*, etc.), but its meaning, "to falsify" or "adulterate," is clear enough in the passage from Lucian (*Hermotimus* 59) quoted in the NOTES on 2:17. There the same word (parallel with "cheating and giving false measure") is used to describe fraudulent teachers of philosophy, out simply for their own gain. As here the verb *doloun* is associated with the noun *panourgia,* so in 12:16 the noun *dolos* ("deceit," used by Paul also in Rom 1:29; 1 Thess 2:3) is associated with the adjective *panourgos* ("crafty"). Plummer, 112, describes the meaning here as "using fallacious arguments and misinterpretations," but it is unlikely that this should be referred specifically—as it is by him—to the matter of "the relation of the old revelation to the new."

*Instead.* The Greek word is *alla,* as at the beginning of the verse, where it was translated *Rather.* Here it introduces a statement about the way true apostles act, in contrast to those practices they have renounced.

*by a full disclosure of the truth.* The word *phanerōsis (a full disclosure)* occurs only here and in 1 Cor 12:7 in the Greek Bible. In Rom 2:28 and 1 Cor 14:25 the cognate adjective *(phaneros)* is set over against what is kept secret, and the verb *phaneroun* is used similarly in 1 Cor 4:5.

*the truth.* Here, *the word of God* specifically (cf. "the truth of the gospel," Gal 2:5, 14), and not Paul's personal integrity in a more general sense (as, e.g., in 7:14; 11:10); see Windisch, 133; Bultmann, 104.

*we are recommending ourselves.* In the Greek sentence the present participle *synistanontes* (better attested than the variant *synistantes*) is still dependent on the main verb: *we . . . have renounced;* the positive side of repudiating deceitful practices is to present oneself openly as an exponent of the true gospel. The wording of 3:1 and 5:12 (on which see NOTES and COMMENT) suggests that Paul has been criticized for *recommending* himself. Here he takes care to specify what it means to do so (see the following phrases), so there is no real contradiction of the principle he lays down in 10:18.

*to each and every human conscience.* In the Greek phrase, *pasan* ("every") stands before *conscience,* probably for emphasis (Barrett, 129); thus the tr. *each and every.* The idea of *conscience* derives from the Greek world, not from Judaism, and in Hellenistic usage it ordinarily refers to the individual's capacity to experience guilt when considering his or her own past acts (cf. Pierce 1955:13–53; Maurer, *TDNT* VII:898–907). But Thrall (1967:123–25) shows (in refutation of Pierce 1955:87–88) that here, as well as in 5:11, Paul has expanded the idea to include the function of assessing the actions of others. In 1:12 the apostle had referred to his own *conscience* as a witness to his sincerity; now he appeals to the consciences of others as they evaluate and pass judgment on his actions.

*in the sight of God.* The identical phrase occurs in 7:12 and Gal 1:20 (the latter in an oath formula), and there is a similar one, with the same meaning, in 2:17 *(katenanti Theou).*

3. *And even if.* The Greek *(ei de kai)* suggests a concession (as in 4:16; 5:16; 7:8; 12:11); Plummer, 113; Hughes, 125 n. 28.

*our gospel.* Only here and in 1 Thess 1:5 does Paul use this expression, but one may also compare "my gospel" (Rom 2:16, as well as in the later doxology of Rom 16:25), "the gospel preached by me" (Gal 1:11), and "the gospel which I proclaim" (Gal 2:2). For a discussion of the meaning, see Schütz 1975:71–78, who shows that it indicates Paul's sense of involvement with the gospel as its bearer, and that it is not a reference to some particular Pauline content (77–78). Bultmann, 105, contrasts 2:12, "the gospel of Christ" (on which see the NOTES).

*is veiled.* A periphrastic construction in Greek, the participle being accompanied by a finite verb *(estin kekalymmenon).* The perfect tense should not be pressed to yield a reference to the inception of the veiling, because here, as elsewhere in periphrastic constructions, it may function as "virtually an adjective" (Moule 1953:18; Hughes, 125 n. 29). Plummer, 113, relates the emphatic position of the verb *estin (is)* to the concessive formulation *ei de kai (and even though).*

*to those who are perishing.* The Greek is the same as in 2:15 *(en tois apollumenois),* where with the presence of the dative "to God" *(tō Theō)* it seemed advisable to translate "among those. . . ." Here, where the *en* itself stands for the dative (cf. 1 Cor 1:18, simply *tois . . . apollumenois)* it is better translated "for" or *to;* see BDF § 220(1). For the idea involved, see COMMENT, as well as NOTES and COMMENT on 2:15.

4. Why this tr. omits the words "among whom" *(en hois),* which stand at the

beginning of the verse and tie it grammatically to v. 3, is explained in the note on *those unbelievers,* below.

*The god of this age.* Paul frequently refers to *this age* (*ho aiōn houtos:* cf. 1 Cor 1:20; 2:6, 8; 3:18; Rom 12:2), a concept which has both spatial and temporal dimensions (MacRae 1968:421) and which is not essentially different from his references to "this world" (*ho kosmos houtos:* 1 Cor 3:19; 5:10; 7:31 [twice]); see Dibelius 1909:66. Note, as well, Paul's references to "the present age" (*ho aiōn enestōs,* Gal 1:4) and to "the present time" (*ho nyn kairos,* Rom 3:26; 8:18; 11:5). The dualism apparent here is characteristic of Jewish apocalypticism—e.g., that of the Qumran sectarians; see 1QS iii.15–21, which describes "the spirits of truth and falsehood." These two spirits are also called "the Prince of Light" and "the Angel of Darkness," respectively, because they rule two different realms (Vermes 1975:75–76; the passage is cited by Lindars 1961:163 n. 1). For a summary of the dualism of Qumran and of similar themes in Jewish Christianity, see Fitzmyer 1974a:454–60. Elsewhere Paul speaks of "the rulers [*hai archontai*] of this age" (1 Cor 2:6, 8; cf. Eph 2:2, "the ruler [*ho archōn*] of the dominion of the air"), powers which he perhaps has in mind when he refers to "so-called gods, whether in heaven or on earth," and to the "many gods and many lords" (1 Cor 8:5). Compare, as well, the references in the Fourth Gospel to "the ruler [*ho archōn*] of this [or: the] world" (John 12:31; 14:30; 16:11), on which see Brown 1966:468. The dualism of Christian Gnosticism as known from the Nag Hammadi texts involves a view of the created order as inherently inferior and by nature evil—a view which is foreign to the thought-world of Jewish and early Christian apocalypticism; cf. MacRae 1968:429–30. The Gnostic concepts are nicely exhibited in Hyp Arch (CG II, *4*) and in Orig World (CG II, *5*); in the latter, note especially 97,24 (*NHLE,* 162), "the gods of the world." The Gnostic exegesis of 2 Cor 4:1–6 is summarized by Pagels 1975:97.

*has blinded the minds.* For the word *minds,* as well as for the pervasive biblical idea that it is God who has hardened the hearts, dulled the vision, and stopped up the ears of those who are disobedient, see NOTES on 3:14. It is not necessarily incongruous for Paul now to attribute the blindness of unbelievers to *the god of this age;* Philo, for example (*Confusion of Tongues* 171–82), argued that, while there is but one sovereign God, he has commissioned many lesser powers and ministering angels to serve his purposes, especially as regards the incitement to and punishment of evil, that the God of grace "should be kept free not only from all that is, but from all that is deemed to be, evil" (ibid.:182). Cf. T Judah 19:4 (cited by Bultmann, 106): "And the prince of deceit blinded me [*etyphlōse gar me ho archōn tēs planēs*], and I sinned as a man and as flesh, being corrupted through sins . . ." (*APOT*).

*those unbelievers.* Strictly construed, the grammar of this verse would require the tr. "among whom [i.e., those who are perishing, v. 3] the god of this age has blinded the minds of the unbelievers," in which case "the unbelievers" would be a subgroup within the more general category of "those who are perishing." However, nothing in this context or in the Pauline usage of the terms elsewhere suggests that the apostle actually intended any such distinction: *unbeliever(s)* is used in just as general a way (see 1 Cor 6:6; 7:12–16; 10:24; 14:22–25) as *those who are perishing* (see note on 2:15). The irregular construction here, in which "the minds of the unbelievers" stands where one might have had simply "their minds" (with reference to the *perishing*), is best attributed to Paul's "dictation style" (Windisch, 135); the grammatical structure is forgotten as a new but synonymous term is introduced. (It is unnecessary to strike *tōn apistōn* as a gloss, although Bultmann, 108, citing Schmiedel, is tempted to do so.) This tr. supplies the word *those*—not in the Greek—to make it clear that Paul still has in mind all *those who are perishing* (v. 3). Except for the problematic paragraph 6:14–7:1 (6:14, 15), this is the only reference in 2 Cor to *unbelievers,* and elsewhere Paul uses the term only in 1 Cor (passages cited above). There it always has reference to unconverted Gentiles; but here, given the reference to the Israelites who have been hindered from seeing the glory of the new covenant ( = the gospel; 3:14–15), unbelieving Jews may also be in mind (cf. Rom 11:20, 23, where "unbelief" [*apistia*] is used of unbelieving Jews). Contrast Oostendorp (1967:47), who thinks Paul is referring to errant Christians in Corinth.

*so that.* This ambiguous English tr. matches the ambiguity of the Greek *eis to,* which may be interpreted either as final ("in order that"), stressing the purpose of the blinding, or as consecutive ("with the result that"), stressing its consequence.

*they do not see.* All recent commentators agree that the infinitive [*mē*] *augazein* must be translated here as *(do not) see,* even though the original and more usual meaning is "shine forth" (BAG s.v.; Windisch, 136). The intransitive meaning would require an *autois* ("on them"), only poorly attested here. The overall context, as well as the specific reference in this same verse to being blinded, requires one to interpret the verb as a synonym of *gaze* in 3:13 and of *beholding* in 3:18. Cf. Philo, *Moses* II, 139: "behold . . . as in a mirror [*pros katoptron augazē*]" (cited by Windisch, 136).

*the enlightenment coming.* The noun *phōtismos* is used by Paul only here and in v. 6 (on which see the note), and it occurs nowhere else in the NT. Only later did it come to be applied to baptism (e.g., Justin Martyr; see Conzelmann in *TDNT* IX:357–58). In this verse the word probably has an active meaning—an enlightenment which itself enlightens—and is thus to be distinguished from the meaning in T Levi 14:4, where "the light of the law" is said to have come "for the enlightenment of every person [*eis phōtismon pantos anthropou*]" (see Windisch, 136). Compare the description of Wisdom as "a reflection of eternal light [*phōtos aidiou*], a spotless mirror of the working of God . . ." in Wis 7:26 *(RSV).*

*from the gospel of the splendor of Christ.* More literally, "of the gospel of the glory of Christ" *(tou euangeliou tēs doxēs tou Christou),* a succession of genitives which is not unusual in the Pauline letters (cf. v. 6, "of the knowledge of the glory of God"; 1 Thess 1:3, etc.) and which may be due to Semitic influence (so Barrett, 131, citing Schoeps). Héring, 30, believes the accumulation is so redundant that one of the genitives (probably "of the gospel," but perhaps "of Christ") should be struck out as a gloss, but that is too arbitrary. The pleonastic style is familiar from liturgical texts (e.g., the hymnic materials incorporated into Eph and Col), a fact which is not inconsistent with a possible Semitic background (through the prayers and liturgical forms of the Hellenistic synagogue); cf. Windisch, 136. Where genitives are thus accumulated, the governing genitive precedes and the dependent genitive follows; BDF § 168(a).

*from the gospel.* So translated, although the Greek preposition *apo* ("from") is not used, because *tou euangeliou* must be understood as a genitive of origin—that from which *the enlightenment* comes forth (so also Jervell 1960:195; MacRae 1968:421; Barrett, 131).

*of the splendor.* Here, as throughout this passage in which Exod 34 has been in view

(3:7–4:6), *doxa* ("glory") is translated as *splendor* (see note on 3:7). The genitive *tēs doxēs, of the splendor,* is dependent on *the gospel* (see the two preceding notes) and expresses its content. There is no clearly comparable description of the gospel elsewhere in the Pauline letters, but see *knowledge of the splendor* in v. 6.

*of Christ.* Paul frequently refers to "the gospel of Christ" (2:12; 9:13; Rom 15:19; 1 Cor 9:12; Gal 1:7; Phil 1:27; 1 Thess 3:2; cf. Rom 1:9), and it is not impossible that this genitive phrase should be taken more closely with *the gospel* than with what immediately precedes. In such a case, *of the splendor* and *of Christ* would be parallel descriptions of *the gospel.* The alternative and equally possible interpretation would be to regard *of Christ* as governed directly by *the splendor,* so that the content of the gospel would be identified as *the splendor of Christ* (with which phrase cf. 8:23 and 1 Cor 2:8 ["the Lord of glory"]).

*who is the image of God.* Cf. Col 1:15, "who is the image of the invisible God" *(hos estin eikōn tou Theou tou aoratou),* the opening phrase of a christological hymn (see Lohse 1971:41ff.; for *eikōn* see especially 47–49 and also the NOTES on 3:18, above). This christological use of the concept has close affinities with Philo's application of it to the Logos, described as "Himself the Image of God [*autos eikōn hyparchōn Theou*], chiefest of all Beings intellectually perceived, placed nearest, with no intervening distance, to the Alone truly existent One" *(On Flight and Finding* 101; see also *Confusion of Tongues* 97, 146; *Special Laws* I, 81). It is clear from this passage that Philo does not use the term "image" to emphasize the inferiority of the Logos, but rather to stress the intimacy of the Logos and God. Indeed, Philo understands Gen 1:26–27 to mean that God himself is an "image," so that the first-created man (Philo distinguishes the creation of Gen. 1:26–27 from that of Gen 2:7—the first man is an archetypal "idea" and incorruptible, the second has body and soul and is mortal [*Creation of the World* 134]) may be called "an image of an image" *(eikōn eikonos;* ibid.:25). An "image," then, according to Philo, is to be distinguished from a "copy" *(mimēma;* see *Who is the Heir* 230–31). Cf. further, Wis 7:25–26 (on which see Winston 1979:43, 185–87), where the divine Wisdom is described as "a breath of the power of God, and a pure emanation [*aporroia*] of the glory [*tēs doxēs*] of the Almighty," and further, where it is said to be "a reflection [*apaugasma*] of eternal light [*phōtos aidiou*], a spotless mirror of the working of God, an image of his goodness [*eikōn tēs agathotētos autou;* i.e., of God himself]" *(RSV).* As Eltester (1958) has demonstrated, the application of the concept "image of God," in Philo's case to the Logos, and in Paul's case to Christ, has its background in this kind of Wisdom speculation in Hellenistic Judaism (see especially 131–36). It is likely, however, that the christological application was not original with the apostle, but was present already in the pre-Pauline church. (Note its presence in the liturgical tradition, Col 1:15–20; Heb 1:2–3 shows the influence of the same background, especially of Wis 7:25–26, but without using the word "image.")

5. *For.* This connecting word *(gar)* ties the sentence to what has preceded, particularly in v. 4 (see Plummer, 118).

*it is not ourselves whom we preach.* This English tr. slightly reformulates the simpler Greek construction *(ou gar heautous kēryssomen:* "for we do not preach ourselves") in order to bring out the effect of the emphatic position of "ourselves" (Plummer, 118). Whether Paul is on the defensive here (so, e.g., Windisch, 138; Strachan, 92) or on the attack (so Collange, 136, following Bachmann) is difficult to determine, as it is throughout 3:7–4:6; see COMMENT. Similar allegations against self-proclaimed "philosophers" were a familiar part of the anti-sophistic polemic of Paul's day; see Dio Chrysostom XIII, 11: "Now the great majority [*hoi polloi;* cf. 2:17] of those styled philosophers proclaim themselves such [*hautous anakēryttousin*], just as the Olympian heralds proclaim the victors." This parallel helps to show that Paul's thought is not that apostles might themselves become the *content* of the gospel (although he had alluded to some such error in 1 Cor 1:13) but that apostles might be regarded as promoting themselves and their own interests. Cf. Phil 2:21, where—as here—the antithesis is between "selves" and "Christ" (N. Schneider 1970:22).

*but Jesus Christ as Lord.* Here the emphasis in the phrase *Iēsoun Christon Kyrion* falls on *Lord,* which is the new element in comparison with the end of v. 4 (so Windisch, 138). That *Lord* stands in the predicate position is indicated by the following phrase, which extends the thought (Bultmann, 109). The background of this christological formulation is in the confessional acclamation "Jesus is Lord" (Rom 10:9; 1 Cor 12:3; Phil 2:10–11; see Kramer 1966:200); cf. Phil 3:8, "Christ Jesus my Lord." In such traditional formulations as this the title accents Jesus' status as that of one who is lifted up on high to live and reign with God; cf. Collange, 136.

*ourselves as your slaves.* Given the sharp antithesis Paul has formulated *(not ourselves . . . but Jesus Christ as Lord),* it is impossible to believe that he now intends to include the apostles' role—even as servants of the congregation—as part of his gospel, although this phrase is grammatically dependent on the verb *we preach;* see Bultmann, 110. This striking present characterization of apostles has no parallel elsewhere in Paul's letters, but it is the positive counterpart of 1:24, where he disclaims any intention of trying to "lord it over" the Corinthians. Note also 12:15 (cited by Barrett, 134) and 11:20 (on which see the COMMENT).

*for Jesus' sake.* This reading *(dia Iēsoun)* is somewhat better attested (A\*vid B et al.) than "through Jesus" *(dia Iēsou;* P⁴⁶ ℵ\* Aᶜ et al.); see Metzger 1971:578; Windisch, 138 n. 1 (who regards the genitive as a change in imitation of Gal 1:1). Of the 17 occurrences of the name *Jesus* alone in Paul's letters, 8 occur in 2 Cor, and 7 of those in this chapter (in addition to the present verse, twice each in vv. 10, 11, 14; otherwise in 11:4).

6. *Because.* The *hoti* is here equivalent to *gar,* "for" (Robertson 1923:962) and introduces the grounding for v. 5 just as the introductory *For* in v. 5 had introduced the grounding for v. 4.

*the God who said.* It is possible that *God* should be treated as the predicate here, as in 1:21; 5:5 (so, e.g., Windisch, 139; Bultmann, 110); thus, "it is the God who said . . ." *(RSV).* On the other hand, the structure of this sentence seems to have been influenced by that of v. 4, over against which it has been set (cf. Plummer, 119): *the god of this age* brought blindness, the God of light has brought knowledge. The present phrase may be compared with the formula in 6:16 by which a series of scriptural quotations is introduced: "As God said" *(kathōs eipen ho Theos hoti).*

*"Light shall shine out of darkness."* The introductory formula (see preceding note) suggests that this is a scriptural quotation, and most commentators identify it with Gen 1:3, "And God said, 'Let there be light'; and there was light" (LXX: *kai eipen ho Theos, genēthētō phōs kai egeneto phōs).* In this case Paul would be quoting very freely, and perhaps with other LXX passages in mind—for example, Isa 9:2, where, as here, the

future tense "shall shine" appears ("You people who walk in darkness, behold, a great light; a light shall shine upon you who dwell in the region of the shadow of death"). Cf. also Ps 17(18):28(29); 111(112):4; 2 Kgdms 22:29; Job 37:15. Collange, 138–39, argues that such a celebrated text as Gen 1:3 would not be altered so radically, however, and prefers to view the allusion exclusively in terms of texts in Isa (in addition to 9:2, see 42:6–7, 16; 49:6; 60:1–2) which speak of God's bestowal of light on those who are in darkness, and of Israel's servant-ministry in bringing "light to the Gentiles." Cf. Oostendorp 1967:48; Richard 1981:360.

has caused a light to shine. In Greek a relative clause is opened here: "who has caused a light to shine . . ." (hōs elampsen), and some commentators (e.g., Meyer, 492; Plummer, 119) would supply the verb "is" (thus: "The God who said . . . is he who . . ."). Another possibility would be to supply "is" in the introductory formula (e.g., RSV). In the present tr. the relative clause is simply regarded as an anacoluthon, and the relative pronoun is rendered as if it resumed the subject, God (cf. Bachmann, 191). The verb here is more likely transitive ("to shine a light," thus bringing enlightenment [phōtismos]; see Meyer, 492–93; Bultmann, 110) than intransitive ("has gleamed"; cf. Plummer, 120) as earlier in this verse. Some (e.g., Hughes, 134) find in the aorist tense an indication that Paul has reference to his own conversion. See following note and COMMENT.

in our hearts. Whether this phrase refers more particularly to Paul and his co-workers (so, e.g., Bultmann, 111) or more generally to all believers (e.g., Plummer, 121) as contrasted with unbelievers (v. 4), depends partly on whether Paul is alluding here to his own conversion and, if he is, on how specific the reference is meant to be. See COMMENT.

to provide the enlightenment. The preposition pros ("for") here expresses purpose (BAG s.v. III, 3a) and is paraphrased here as to provide, in accord also with the active meaning of enlightenment (phōtismos). This noun should not be taken in a passive sense, as if knowledge were "lit up" (so Lietzmann, 115; Conzelmann, TDNT IX:346 n. 295), but, as in v. 4, in an active sense: the enlightenment coming from the knowledge . . . (so Bultmann, 110; Eltester 1958:132 n. 9; Jervell 1960:195). Cf. 2:14. For further comments on the word phōtismos, see note on v. 4, above, and on in the face of Jesus Christ, below.

which comes from the knowledge of the splendor of God. This accumulation of genitives (more literally, "of the knowledge," etc.) is parallel in form and in content to that in v. 4 ( on which see the note).

which comes from the knowledge. The noun (gnōsis) has been used previously in this letter only in 2:14. Both here and there it refers to the apostolic preaching (Bultmann, 110) and is therefore practically synonymous with the gospel in v. 4 (Jervell 1960: 219 n. 172; MacRae, 425). Paul's association of these two concepts may well have been influenced by his familiarity with Gnostic usage (in Corinth or elsewhere; Barrett, 135), whereby knowledge is the way to salvation. His own use of the term, however, is to be sharply distinguished from that in Gnosticism; see Bultmann, TDNT I: especially 708–11. The genitive here, tēs gnōseōs, expresses the origin of the enlightenment and is in this way, too, parallel with the gospel in v. 4 (Jervell 1960:195; MacRae 1968:421; contrast Barrett, 134, who describes it as appositional and translates as "illumination that consists in the knowledge").

*of the splendor.* See note on the same phrase in v. 4. Here the content of *the knowledge* is expressed, as there the content of *the gospel.*

*of God.* Not *of Christ,* as in v. 4 (but see the following phrase).

*in the face of Jesus Christ.* Contrast 2:10, where *prosōpon* is properly translated as "presence." Here it means *face,* and the whole phrase stands in sharp contrast to the reference in 3:7 (cf. 3:13) to *the splendor of [Moses'] face.* It is this contrast, and not the recollection of his own conversion experience (so Plummer, 121) that prompts Paul to the phrase here. Although the word *phōtismos (enlightenment)* occurs but rarely in the LXX (mainly in the Pss), there are two places in which "the light of your face" *(ho phōtismos [eis phōtismon] tou prosōpou sou)* refers to God's turning toward his people in mercy (Ps 43[44]:3) and in judgment (Ps 89[90]:8), respectively. Note also Ps 26(27):1, "The Lord is my light [*phōtismos*] and my saviour," which is quoted by Philo, along with Gen 1:3, in his essay *On Dreams* I, 75.

## COMMENT: GENERAL

Paul's affirmation about the scope and character of the apostolic vocation (2:14–16a) here begins to be spelled out, first of all with reference to the idea of the ministry of the *new covenant* which he had introduced in 3:6 (Hickling 1975a:384, characterizes 3:7–18 as "an extended . . . exegesis" of the phrase *ministers of a new covenant*). He has already associated that ministry, of which his own apostleship is exemplary, with the life-giving power of *the Spirit,* and in so doing he has specifically dissociated it from the death-dealing power of *the letter* (3:3, 6). In the present passage this contrast is further emphasized and illustrated.

It has already been noted (see COMMENT on 2:17) that the whole discussion here has a polemical dimension. Paul's elucidation of the apostolic commission under which he serves is being worked out in the light of and partly in response to the activities of others, of whose ministry in Corinth he clearly disapproves. It is often difficult to determine whether particular comments should be interpreted as more polemical in the strict sense (his attacks on others), or more apologetic (his rebuttal of charges others have brought against him). In most instances both functions are served, and the distinction becomes important only in trying to identify who Paul's rivals were and what they were doing and teaching.

This passage, 3:7–4:6, may be divided into two main parts.

1. In 3:7–11 the apostle is appealing to Exod 34:29–30 in support of his contention that the ministry of the new covenant is superior to that of the old. Using a familiar rabbinic form of argumentation, he argues that if Moses' service on behalf of the old covenant, *chiseled in letters on stone,* was accompanied with such splendor as indicated in scripture, then surely *the ministry of the Spirit* is accompanied by a far greater splendor.

2. Beginning in 3:12, Paul moves to apply this point to his own and his

colleagues' exercise of the apostolic office. In remarking on the difference between the way Moses acted and the way ministers of the new covenant conduct themselves, he mentions for the first time the veil Moses placed over his face (Exod 34:33–35). Subsequently, he turns the veil into a metaphor in order to comment on the situation of unbelieving Israel (3:14–15). The transition back to the main point of 3:12–13 is perceptible in 3:16–17, but that is not actually accomplished until 4:1, after the grand affirmation of 3:18 in which all the themes from 3:7–17 are impressively integrated. The climax of the passage as a whole is reached in 4:5–6. These two verses conclude the comments about apostolic boldness which had been introduced in 3:12–13 and then re-introduced in 4:1. At the same time they are a restatement of the point, established in 2:14–16a, that the apostolic task is to spread abroad the knowledge of God as it has been revealed in Jesus Christ.

## COMMENT: DETAILED

### A Surpassing Splendor, 3:7–11

These verses are bound together because they manifest a common theme and a common thesis, and because the form of argumentation is the same throughout. The theme is splendor (doxa: "glory"), a word that appears at least once in each of these verses. The thesis is that the ministry of the new covenant, to which Paul had made reference in 3:6 (identified here as the ministry of the Spirit [v. 8], the ministry of righteousness [v. 9], and that which endures [v. 11]), is attended with a far greater splendor than that of Moses (here termed the ministry of death [v. 7], the ministry of condemnation [v. 9], and what was being annulled [v. 11]). This thesis is supported by the use of a passage from scripture as the basis for an argument "from the lesser to the greater," in typically rabbinic fashion (see note on 3:8). The argument is presented first in vv. 7–8, and is subsequently restated in vv. 9 and 11.

The essence of the paragraph is present in vv. 7–8. To begin with, Paul adverts to Exod 34:29–30. There it is said that when Moses came down from Mount Sinai to deliver "the two tablets" of the law to the Israelites, his countenance was radiant (LXX: dedoxastai, had been "glorified" or "made splendid") from his talking with God. He himself, the story says, did not realize this; and when Aaron and the people of Israel saw it they were afraid to approach him. This is clearly the text Paul has in mind in v. 7 when he refers to the Israelites, who because of the splendor that came with the delivery of the law (chiseled in letters on stone) could not bear to gaze at Moses' face.

Already in v. 7, however, Paul intrudes his own comments into the account. First, he associates the letters chiseled . . . on stone with the ministry of death. It is clear that this characterization of the Mosaic law is Paul's own. It is fully compatible with his statement in 3:6 that *the letter kills.* One may also note his comments in Rom 7:10–11. There, explaining the deceitfulness of the law, he contrasts the "life" it promises (probably an allusion to Lev 18:5, as in Rom 10:5) with the "death" that actually comes to those who rely upon it. It is not so surprising, then, that Paul can here refer to the tablets of the law—indeed, rather matter-of-factly—as bringing *the ministry of death.* The phrase presupposes his overall teaching about works of the law and justification by faith, and it is essentially parallel to "the law of sin and death" in Rom 8:2.

In the second place, Paul glosses his reference to the story of Exod 34 with the comment that *the splendor* with which Moses' face shone was actually *being annulled.* Since there is no basis for this in the text of Exod 34, one must suppose either that Paul is imposing such an interpretation on it for the first time, or that he can presume his readers' familiarity with some such interpretation already current. Childs (1974:621) believes the former is unlikely, because the point is so fundamental in Paul's argument. Although contemporary rabbinic interpretations of the passage are not extant, Childs suggests the rabbis might well have spoken of the passing of the radiance from Moses' face. He points out (ibid.) that Moses' radiant face is not mentioned again after Exod 34, and that in Exod 40:35 Moses himself is hindered from entering the tent of meeting because of "the glory of the Lord" that filled it. However, one must reckon with evidence of well-developed traditions within Judaism which interpreted Moses' ascent of Sinai as an enthronement, at which time Adam's lost glory was bestowed on him. Meeks (1970:363–64) has quoted several midrashic passages in which the point is specifically made that the radiance of Moses' face continued "forever" (e.g., *Debarim R.* 11.3; *M. Marqah* v. 4, quoted above in the NOTES to 3:18). Note, as well, 2 Esdr 9:37: "the law . . . does not perish, but remains in its glory" *(RSV).*

So far, then, Paul has stressed two main points about Moses' descent from Mount Sinai with the tablets of the law. Only one of these two can be documented from the text itself—viz., the greatness of the splendor with which Moses' face was radiant. The second point—that this splendor was doomed to extinction, associated as it was with *the ministry of death*—is Paul's own interpretation. It is offered in the light of the contrast he has already drawn in vv. 3 and 6 between Spirit and letter. The concept of the Spirit's ministry introduced in those verses is now invoked again (v. 8), as the argument begun in v. 7 is completed: if *the ministry of death* was so radiant with splendor, then *the ministry of the Spirit* will surely be radiant with even greater splendor. Although a future-tense verb is used here in referring to the splendor of the Spirit's ministry *(will [it] not . . . be with greater splendor),* the present tense *(does . . . abound)* in the following verse suggests that *will (estai)* should be interpreted as a "logical" future: the splendor of the new covenant is already present. Since, however, it is a splendor that *endures* (v. 11), and since the Spirit, to whose ministry it adheres, is itself a "down payment" of that which is to come (1:22; 5:5; cf. Rom 8:23), Paul may also speak of this *splendor* as a *hope* (v. 12). For this reason the future tense in v. 8 probably has both a "logical" and a "real" meaning (see Windisch and Collange, cited in NOTES).

The argument of vv. 7–8 is repeated in v. 9, formulated more succinctly now because the basic terms of it have already been established. Here, however, two different phrases are used to describe what had been termed *the ministry of death* (v. 7) and *the ministry of the Spirit* (v. 8). First, what had just been called *the ministry of death* (v. 7) is now called *the ministry of condemnation.* This phrase, like the one to which it is parallel, is fully understandable in the light of Paul's teaching elsewhere about the commandments of the law. It is the law, he will write later, which brings "punishment" for sin (Rom 5:16, 18 compared with Rom 5:13; on the relationship of this word "punishment" [*katakrima*] to the word *condemnation* [*katakrisis*] used in the present passage, see NOTES), and it is exactly for that reason (Rom 8:1) that it may be called "the law of sin and death" (Rom 8:2). In an earlier letter, too, Paul had written of the law in this wày. After quoting the final and all-inclusive curse in a whole series directed against violators of the law ("Cursed be every one who does not abide by all things written in the book of the law, and do them," Gal 3:10, *RSV,* quoting Deut 27:26), he proceeds to affirm that "Christ redeemed us from the curse of the law" (3:13, *RSV*). Thus, when Paul now associates the law with *the ministry of condemnation,* it is apparent that he is referring to the judgment it decrees and delivers.

Also in v. 9, what had just been described as *the ministry of the Spirit* (v. 8) is now referred to as *the ministry of righteousness.* This follows naturally as a contrast to the law's *ministry of condemnation,* as a further examination of Rom 5:12–21 will show. There Paul contrasts the "judgment" *(krisis)* and "punishment" *(katakrima)* brought by Adam's trespass of the law with the "acquittal" *(dikaiōma, dikaiōsis)* and "free gift of righteousness" *(hē dōrea tēs dikaiosynēs)* brought by Christ's obedience. The terms of that contrast *(katakrima/dikaiōma)* are closely related, both linguistically and materially, to the terms of the contrast now drawn in v. 9 *(katakrisis/dikaiosynē).* Moreover, in Rom 5:17–18, as here, a further contrast is drawn between "life" and "death."

It is frequently noted that the Corinthian correspondence includes no exposition of Paul's thinking on justification by faith comparable to those in Gal and Rom; indeed, even the terminology of justification seldom occurs (see NOTES). This is readily explained, however, by the fact that the apostle is facing other kinds of issues in Corinth. It is clear that even in such passages as the present one, where the topic is the meaning of apostleship, Paul's commitment to the idea that justification comes as a gift is fundamental to the argument, and sometimes rises to the surface (e.g., 3:3, 6, 7, 9). In 11:15 he says that his rivals for leadership in Corinth are masquerading "as ministers of righteousness." That is but one of several indications that his conception of apostleship is closely tied to his conception of the gospel, at the center of which is Christ's death, interpreted as an act of justification. Significantly, this section of the present letter (chaps. 1–9, Letter D) will conclude with a reiteration of that central, saving event, using the word "reconciliation" in place of the word "righteousness" (but with little difference in meaning), and speaking, therefore, of "the ministry of reconciliation" (5:11–19).

In v. 10 the argument of vv. 7–8, 9 is supported by the reformulation of two points already made, or at least implicit. First, Paul repeats his earlier point about the temporary nature of the splendor that accompanied Moses' ministry (v. 7). It is formulated now as a paradox: *what has had splendor has not had splendor.* Given the context, this can only be a reference to the Mosaic covenant and ministry (against E. Hill 1961:299–301; see NOTES). Second, and in explanation of the paradox, Paul re-emphasizes the magnitude of the splendor with which the ministry of the new covenant is endowed. It is a splendor that *far surpasses* that of Moses. Neither in this verse nor in the argument as a whole is it denied that the ministry of Moses and of the old covenant was accompanied by splendor. Rather, the affirmation of its splendor becomes the basis for the claim that the ministry of the new covenant has an even greater splendor. At the same time, however, one must note that the effect of the surpassing splendor of the new covenant is to nullify the splendor of the old —*not*, as it were, to "supplement" it or to carry it forward to some kind of "fulfillment." The nullification of the law's splendor has already been emphasized once, at the end of v. 7, and it will be mentioned three times more as Paul's argument proceeds (vv. 11, 13, 14).

The first of these further references to the annulment of the old covenant comes in v. 11. This sentence is parallel to vv. 7–8 and 9, in that it is another formulation, even more succinct (and therefore memorable) than the one in v. 9, of Paul's argument "from the lesser to the greater." In his boldest move yet, Paul characterizes the whole Mosaic ministry as that which *was being annulled.* From its inception, not only the splendor of Moses' face (v. 7) but the whole of the Mosaic ministry, including the old covenant, was destined to pass away. Now its transiency is contrasted with the permanence of what has taken its place: the ministry of the new covenant (v. 6), of the Spirit (v. 8), of righteousness (v. 9). This is *that which endures,* an expression that is probably intended to be taken with the same kind of eschatological meaning as the declaration of 1 Cor 13:13 that faith, hope, and love "endure" (Bultmann, 86).

## The Boldness of True Apostles, 3:12–13

Windisch, 112, has characterized the whole of 3:7–18 as "a Christian midrash" on Exod 34:29–35 (so also Fitzmyer 1981:631–32), in which "the special apologetic motives" apparent in 2:16b–3:6 "completely recede," and where the contrast is in a quite general sense between "Christianity and Judaism." He believes that Paul resumes his apologetic only in 4:1ff., and that the whole of 3:7–18 could be removed without any injury to the context (ibid.). This passage certainly has several midrashic features, and the concentration on Exod 34 is undeniable. However, it is important to observe that, so far, Paul has picked up only one main point from the story in Exodus: the dazzling splendor radiating from Moses' face when he came down from Sinai with the law. Using this, Paul has built an argument for the surpassing splendor of the ministry of the new covenant. Thus, what has been exposited in vv. 7–11 is not Exod 34:29–35 as such but rather, with specific reference only to Exod 34:29–30, the meaning of the new covenant as a resplendent ministry of the Spirit and of righteousness. It is not the story in Exod 34 but his own remarks in 2:16b–3:6 that are the focus of Paul's attention in vv. 7–11. (So also Richard 1981: 352–59.)

This judgment is confirmed in vv. 12–13, where Paul begins to apply the argument developed in the preceding verses to the topic of the apostolic ministry. These verses are set apart by the phrase *Having, therefore,* which closely ties what follows to what has preceded, even as it distingushes what follows as the consequence of what has preceded. These two verses, then, are not themselves "midrashic," even if that is an apt description of vv. 7–11. They constitute an extension of the discussion opened in 2:16b about apostolic sufficiency, and of the declaration made in 3:5–6 that the apostles have been made sufficient for their task by God alone. Because their ministry has a splendor far greater than the ministry of Moses, they *act with much boldness* on behalf of the gospel (v. 12). The *hope* to which Paul refers as the basis for this bold action of apostles is that which is given by the present and enduring reality of the splendor of the new covenant, as affirmed in vv. 7–11. The argument for this from Exod 34 may perhaps be cited as an example of the operation of the Pauline principle: "whatever was written in former days was written for our instruction, that by steadfastness and by the encouragement of the scriptures we might have hope"—Rom 15:4 [*RSV*].

There is evidence that as Paul writes this letter he is aware that some in Corinth are criticizing him for canceling a promised "double visit" to their congregation (see NOTES and COMMENT on 1:15–2:2). He has sought to explain why this decision had not been thoughtless or motivated by self-interest (1:17); he was acting (*chrasthai*, 1:17), he has insisted, in order to spare them what would have had to be an unpleasant visit (1:23). This and other aspects of his conduct toward the Corinthian church may still be in the apostle's mind as he now characterizes the ministry in which he and his colleagues are engaged as an acting (*chrasthai*) *with much boldness*.

When Paul uses this noun, *boldness,* or the cognate verb "to be bold" elsewhere, it always refers to the courage with which he acts to fulfill his apostolic commission in relation to others. Thus, in this same letter, he will shortly be writing about the "much candor" (the same Greek phrase as in the present verse) he exercises toward the Corinthians (7:4), because he knows that he has acted honorably in his dealings with them (see 7:2). He had written to the Thessalonians about the boldness he and his associates had shown in preaching to them, despite great opposition (1 Thess 2:2); and he reminds Philemon that as an apostle he has "much boldness in Christ to command [him] what is proper" (Phlm 8), even though he will only "exhort" him now, "for love's sake" (v. 9). Similarly, in Phil. 1:20, Paul writes of his hope that even in his imprisonment his witness to the gospel (honoring Christ) can be clear and effective, "with all boldness as always, even now" ("all [*pasa*] boldness" is equivalent to "much [*pollē*] boldness" in 2 Cor 3:12; 7:4; Phlm 8).

There can be little doubt that Paul is using the word in the same way in all these passages. It describes the courage with which he is emboldened, as an apostle, to exercise his ministry openly and without fear. It means "not being ashamed," as Phil 1:20, where that phrase is parallel to *boldness*, makes clear. The meaning of the declaration in v. 12 is therefore equivalent to the declaration of Rom 1:16, "I am not ashamed of the gospel" (to preach it); cf. Bultmann, 88. In the present instance, however, given the circumstances in Corinth, the declaration has a more particular function than in Rom. For one thing, Paul is aware that he is being criticized for not meaning what he says or following through with what he has promised (1:15–2:2). He is also aware that the Corinthian congregation is being victimized by a number of persons who are simply "huckstering" the gospel, and thus really misrepresenting themselves (2:17). Hence, Paul's statement in v. 12 serves both to reaffirm the integrity of his own apostolate (cf. 1:12; 1:15–2:2; and later again, 6:11–13; 7:2, 4) and to distinguish the *boldness* with which it operates from the deceitful ways of others (correctly Collange, 87). That the second is involved along with the first is evident from 4:1–6, which resumes and carries forward the point begun here in v. 12 (see below).

Van Unnik (1964; 1980:292–306) has pointed out that the Aramaic expression for "confidence" (equivalent to the Greek word *parrēsia*, "boldness") means literally "to uncover the face [or: head]." He notes that Paul himself uses a similar Greek phrase in 3:18 *(with unveiled face)*, and that the literal meaning of the Aramaic expression must have been "lurking in his mind" even as he wrote of *boldness* in v. 12 (1964:161; cf. 1980:297). If so, this could account for Paul's return to the story in Exod 34 in order to pick up from there a point he had not exploited in vv. 7–11, i.e., the veiling of Moses' face. However, van Unnik's explanation is unnecessarily complicated and involves, as does his exegesis of 1:18ff. (see NOTES and COMMENT), the highly questionable view that Paul was as much at home in Aramaic as in Greek. There is no need to search for a special reason why Paul proceeds to contrast Moses' conduct with that of Christian apostles (v. 13); after all, a contrast between the two ministries has been implicit since v. 6, and vv. 12–13 only extend that, as the matter of apostolic behavior is now made explicit. Moreover, it should be noted that in Exod 34 the veiling of Moses' face is introduced only in v. 33, and only as a secondary motif (see Childs 1974:618–19 for a discussion of this). Thus, if Paul is following a midrashic tradition, as some hold (including Childs, ibid.:622–23; see further below), or even if he is consulting the text of Exod directly, as is also possible, it is not surprising that Moses' veil was not mentioned earlier. It has no place in the development of Paul's argument in vv. 7–11 because it had no place in Exod 34:29–30, on the basis of which his argument has been developed so far.

A more difficult question is what Paul intends by contrasting Moses' veiling of his face with the bold conduct of apostles. It is clear that Moses' veil is evaluated negatively by Paul, and in that respect he has already gone beyond the evidence of Exod 34. There, Moses' veiling of his face is simply stated as a fact (vv. 33–35). Moreover, the account in Exod provides no explanation whatever for Moses' use of the veil (for a discussion, see Childs 1974:618–19). In this respect, too, Paul goes beyond Exod, for in v. 13 he says explicitly that Moses veiled his face in order to keep the Israelites from seeing the end ( = the extinction; see NOTES) of the splendor that was being annulled. Indeed, this comment presumes what the Exod story in its present form specifically contradicts—namely, that Moses covered his face when addressing the Israelites. According to Exod, his face was uncovered when addressing them, just as it was when he spoke with God (see vv. 34–35).

Had Paul referred, like Exod 34, only to the fact of Moses' veil, one could suppose that he was simply contrasting Moses' timidity with the boldness of the apostles. Childs thinks this is indeed the case, noting that the rabbis sometimes connected the theophany to Moses in Exod 33, 34 with Num 12:8, and that in the context of the latter (v. 3) Moses is said to have been "very meek" (1974:623). Perhaps, then, Paul was acquainted with midrashic traditions (now lost) that interpreted Moses' veil as a sign of his meekness. But this is too conjectural, and leaves out of account the one explicit statement Paul gives on the matter—that Moses wanted to keep the Israelites from viewing the last of the splendor.

Here one must consider not only the contrast between Moses' veiled face and the open-faced boldness of the apostles, but also the contrast between two kinds of ministries which has been argued in vv. 7–11. The bold conduct of apostles is based on their assurance (*such a hope,* v. 12) that their ministry has a splendor that *endures* (v. 11). The Mosaic ministry, however, had a splendor that *was being annulled* (v. 11). Hence, Moses' veiling of his face was indeed an act of timidity, but that timidity, as Paul views it, was not merely a personal trait of character. It was a timidity born of Moses' knowledge that the splendor of his ministry was destined for extinction. It would be wrong to conclude that Paul here imputes a deceitful motive to Moses, for that idea seems to be excluded by the comment in v. 14a (see below). One might suppose that Paul viewed Moses as sparing his people the agony of seeing the last of the splendor, or that he sought to prevent them from profaning the last of it (cf. Windisch, 119; Hickling 1975a:390–91). But Paul himself offers no clarifying comment. His one and only specific point is that Moses could not act boldly because the splendor of his ministry, unlike that of the apostolic ministry, was destined to pass away.

### Unbelieving Israel, 3:14–15

There is a significant shift in focus between vv. 12–13 and v. 14. In the two preceding verses the subject had been the bold conduct of the Pauline apostolate as contrasted with the ministry of Moses. One would expect Paul to continue with this point, as he in fact does in 4:1ff. Instead, prompted by the mention of Moses' veiling his face *so the Israelites could not gaze at the end of what was being annulled* (v. 13), he interjects the comment that the Israelites' *minds were hardened* (v. 14a). The remark is best interpreted as Paul's clarification of what he has just said about Moses. Not Moses, but the Israelites themselves are responsible for their unbelief. This is in accord with Paul's remarks elsewhere about Israel's unbelief, and with early Christian teaching in general (references are given in the NOTES). This comment does not contribute directly to the overall discussion as it has proceeded through v. 13. It functions, rather, to correct any false inference which may be drawn from the reference to Moses in v. 13, to the effect that he had misled the Israelites concerning the covenant with which he had been entrusted. It is therefore difficult to agree with Ulonska (1966:386) when he says that Paul intended Moses' conduct to be a warning to the Corinthians: they should not allow themselves to be misled by Paul's opponents as the Israelites had been misled by Moses. *But,* writes Paul, Moses was dealing with those whose *minds were hardened.* The polemic of the passage does not hinge on Moses' character or intentions, but on the fact that his ministry, great and resplendent as it was, was destined to pass away, and that he confronted a people whose *minds were hardened.* This theme of Israel's *hardness* continues as the subject in vv. 14b–15.

In v. 14b Paul extends his previous reference to the Israelites ( = *their,* v. 14a) to include all unbelieving Jews up to his own time. Furthermore, he appropriates his own reference to Moses' veil (v. 13) in order to apply it now as a metaphor for the Jews' failure to perceive the splendor of the gospel. This sentence bristles with difficulties for the interpreter. However, granting the tr. and punctuation adopted here (for details, see the NOTES), and given the context supplied by vv. 14a and 15 especially, the main point seems fairly clear. In its synagogues unbelieving Israel hears the covenant of Moses read (perhaps the Torah in general) with veiled hearts (minds), not understanding that *in Christ* that *old covenant* and its ministry are *being annulled.* Here, in keeping with the argument of vv. 7–11, Paul describes the whole Mosaic ministry as destined for annulment. Elsewhere the apostle can write about the positive aspects of the law of Moses (e.g., Rom 3:21b; 7:12), but those are not taken into account by Paul in this passage (cf. Bultmann, 90). He is not, for example, thinking of the positive witness of the scripture to Christ. Here his point is that what is in the old covenant—to be revealed when the veil is taken away—is that it is really the *old* covenant, that in Christ the ministry of the law is nullified as the way of salvation (cf. Vielhauer 1969:48). A positive note is introduced in v. 16, but it does not pertain to the role and function of the old covenant as such.

### The Removal of the Veil, 3:16–18

The metaphor of the veil introduced in v. 14b still operates here, but now Paul seems deliberately to have broadened his perspective from unbelieving Israel to *anyone* (v. 16; see NOTES). Thus, neither Rom 11:25–26 (cited by Windisch, 124), which looks toward the ultimate (eschatological) conversion of Israel, nor Rom 11:14 (cited by Barrett, 122), which refers to Paul's preaching among the Jews, is a comparable text. Some commentators (e.g., Collange, 101–2) suggest that Paul now has his opponents in mind, but that involves presuming more about their teaching than is justified (see below, and the discussion in the INTRODUCTION of the opponents' identity). It is not unreasonable, however, to believe that Paul is thinking about the situation of his Corinthian converts themselves. Then he would be saying: Your conversion, for which we are responsible, should have meant the removal from your hearts of that veil which now seems to hinder you from seeing the true meaning of our ministry. This accords with the conversion terminology employed here (see NOTES) as well as with the overall context, which (from 2:14) has been concerned with the meaning of the Pauline apostolate.

Commentators are divided over whether *the Lord* in v. 16—and then in vv. 17 and 18 as well—is to be regarded as God or Christ. Several reasons have been given in the NOTES for believing the former is the more likely, and one of these in particular deserves further explication. Beginning in 2:14 and continuing through 4:6 at least, Paul is defining the role of Christian apostles first of all in relation to God, by whom they have been commissioned, from whom they have received their sufficiency, and before whom they stand ultimately accountable. Specifically, he opens this entire section by praising God (2:14) and by describing the apostolic task as spreading abroad the knowledge of God (2:14; 4:6) through the proclamation of God's word (2:17; 4:2). The whole apostolic ministry is thus oriented to God's service (cf. "the aroma of Christ to God," 2:15; "confidence before God," 3:4). Apostles speak "from God in the sight of God" (2:17), just as they have been made competent by God (3:5) and must finally be judged by God (4:2). Furthermore, and with special relevance for the meaning of *Lord* in vv. 16ff., the Corinthians have been reminded that precisely as believers in Christ their hearts have been "inscribed . . . with the Spirit of the living God" (3:3). The christological references in these same paragraphs should by no means be discounted, but they are nevertheless distinctly secondary to the fundamentally theological orientation of Paul's remarks. This is clearest precisely in 4:4–6, where Christ is presented as the image *of God* (v. 4) and where *the splendor . . . in the face of Jesus Christ* is identified as *the splendor of God* (v. 6).

To maintain that Paul is not referring specifically to Christ when he writes about turning *to the Lord* (v. 16) is not to say, however, that the expression should be isolated from Pauline christology. On the contrary, in Paul's view turning to the Lord means accepting the gospel of Christ, receiving by faith the saving love of God as it has been revealed and established in Christ's death (e.g., Rom 5:6–11). Yet Paul's christology stands ever in the service of his theology, if one may be permitted to phrase it so formally. Believers "belong to Christ," but "Christ belongs to God" (1 Cor 3:23). "When all things are subjected to him [sc., Christ], then the Son himself will also be subjected to him who put all things under him, that God may be everything to every one" (1 Cor 15:28, *RSV*). The formulation later in the present letter is thoroughly Pauline: the new creation is *from God,* who *through Christ* reconciles the world to himself (5:18–19). To turn *to the Lord* then would mean, in the context of Paul's preaching, to acknowledge and receive one's reconciliation with God through Christ. (Similar comments are made by Greenwood 1972 in discussing 3:17*a.*) The fact remains, however, that the role of Christ (christology) is not the subject in 2:14ff. and is not the point of vv. 16ff. The subject here is the meaning of the apostolic ministry, and the point in v. 16 specifically is that anyone who, like the Corinthian Christians, has truly turned to the Lord ( = been converted to Paul's gospel) should be able to perceive the surpassing splendor of that ministry.

In v. 17*a* Paul identifies *"the Lord,"* by whom the "veil" of misunderstanding is (or should have been) removed, as *the Spirit.* Here in particular many interpreters have found a christological statement, and indeed even the key to Pauline christology (e.g., Windisch, 125; Hermann 1961). Still others have sought to assess the implications of the statement for a doctrine of the Trinity, or for the "spiritual exegesis" of the OT, etc. (Five major approaches to the interpretation of v. 17 have been summarized by Collange, 107–10.) Here again, however, one's interpretation must be guided by the context. In this context *the Lord* (v. 16) is God (see NOTES), not only Yahweh of the Sinai theophany to Moses, to whom Moses spoke with his face uncovered, but also the God of Jesus Christ, to whom Paul's Corinthian readers have been converted. In this same passage Paul has contrasted the life-giving *Spirit* with the death-dealing *letter* (3:6), identifying the first with the ministry of the *new covenant* (3:6), "inscribed . . . with the Spirit of the living God . . . on tablets that are human hearts" (3:3), and the second with the ministry of the *old covenant* (3:14), *chiseled in letters on stone* (3:7).

When Paul now declares that *"the Lord" is the Spirit* (v. 17*a*), he is emphasizing that the Lord to whom the Corinthians turned at their conversion is the God of that new covenant which operates through *the Spirit* and not through *the letter*—thus for life and righteousness rather than for death and condemnation. It is not his purpose here to "define" the Spirit or to indicate anything very precise about the relationship of *the Spirit* to *"the Lord."* As Collange, 110, observes, this statement sheds very little light on Paul's view of the Spirit. It certainly sheds no light on his christology. In this context it serves, along with v. 16, a chiefly transitional function. The subject in 3:12–4:6 is the courage with which true apostles are emboldened by virtue of the surpassing splendor of the ministry with which they have been commissioned. Paul has been momentarily diverted from that subject as he has commented first on the "hardening" of Israel (v. 14*a*) and then on the veil that remains over the hearts of unbelieving Jews *to the present day* (vv. 14*b*–15). But in vv. 16ff. he is moving back toward his main theme, until it is specifically resumed in 4:1–6.

This transition continues in v. 17*b*, which again must be read in the light of the whole passage. Having asserted that God himself is the Spirit (by whom the resplendent ministry of the new covenant has been established), Paul goes on to emphasize that *where the Spirit of the Lord is, is freedom.* Freedom as such is not a special topic for discussion here, and the word appears nowhere else in 2 Cor (see NOTES). Elsewhere Paul writes of the believer's freedom from the law and for the true fulfilling of the law in love (Gal 4:21–5:14), of freedom from sin and for righteousness (Rom 6:15ff.), of the creation's longing for freedom from bondage to decay and for "the glorious freedom of the children of God" (Rom 8:21), etc. What he means by the word in the present passage is perhaps best understood with reference, first, to several other passages in which he associates *freedom* and *the Spirit,* and second, to the context of v. 17*b*.

There are three other passages in which Paul associates *the Spirit* with *freedom.* In Rom 7:6, concluding several paragraphs in which he has argued that slavery to righteousness is true freedom, Paul describes freedom from the law in its positive aspect as "the new life of the Spirit." The thought is repeated and elaborated in Rom 8, beginning with the statement that "the law of the Spirit of life in Christ Jesus has set me free from the law of sin and death" (v. 2 [*RSV*]). In what follows, "walking according to the Spirit" is contrasted with "walking according to the flesh" (vv. 3–8). When, further, God's "sons" and "heirs" are described as those who are "led by [his] Spirit" (vv. 14–16), it is evident why the apostle can presently refer to the believers' (creation's) ultimate hope of obtaining "the glorious freedom of the children of God" (v. 21). Finally, it is significant that Paul's discussion of freedom in Gal 4:21–5:25 moves at once into an appeal to "walk by the Spirit" (5:16ff.), and that here, as in Rom 7:6; 8:2ff., he enunciates the principle that under the Spirit's leading one is freed from the law (5:18). These passages show that Paul's association of the Spirit and Christian freedom can be very deliberate, at least where he is discussing the meaning of life apart from the law.

It is not freedom from the law as such that is the subject in 2 Cor 3:7–4:6, but rather the ministry of the new covenant—and in 3:12ff., more particularly, the boldness of those who serve in that ministry. The idea of *boldness*, however, is itself closely related to that *freedom*. The Greek word *parrēsia* (see NOTES on 3:12) means the freedom to speak and act without fear, openly and straightforwardly. It means not having to *shrink back* out of cowardice (4:1) or to act secretively and deceptively (4:2a). When, therefore, Paul introduces the word *freedom* into the discussion in 3:17b, it is proper to associate it first of all with the *boldness* he has just mentioned. But this does not mean that it is to be dissociated from Paul's conviction that believers are freed from the law. As pointed out in the COMMENT on 3:7–11, that conviction underlies the whole discussion here. Indeed, the boldness of the apostles springs from their assurance that their ministry is endowed with a great and enduring splendor (v. 12). That splendor, in turn, is understood to inhere in the fact that theirs is a ministry of *a new covenant*, imprinted by the Spirit on human hearts (3:3, 6), not *chiseled in letters on stone* (v. 7) like *the old covenant* of Moses.

Two passages from Philo may help to show how Paul's discussion of the boldness of apostles, rooted in their *ministry of the Spirit*, could have led him to introduce the idea of *freedom* into the context. In his essay *Every Good Man Is Free*, Philo contends that true freedom is not to be measured by one's outward circumstances. "Those in whom anger or desire or any other passion, or again any insidious vice holds sway, are entirely enslaved, while all whose life is regulated by law are free." This "law" is then defined as "right reason . . . engraved not by this mortal or that and, therefore, perishable as he, nor on parchment or slabs, and, therefore, soulless as they, but by immortal nature on the immortal mind, never to perish" (45–46, cited by Windisch, 126). Whereas for Paul the Spirit's covenant is inscribed on the heart, for Philo reason's law is engraved on the soul. And Philo is declaring, in effect, "Where reason is, is freedom."

A second passage in the same essay (148–55) is even more interesting, because in it Philo, too, connects the idea of freedom with that of boldness (*parrēsia*). Here the Jewish philosopher criticizes slaves who take refuge in sanctuaries, as the laws of his day indeed allowed. But if those are the only circumstances in which they dare to speak out and claim their equal rights, he says, then they are still enslaved (148–49). "Places," he argues, do not produce real "courage and free speaking [*parrēsia*, 'boldness']" (150). Rather, it is "those who take refuge in virtue" who are liberated from the bondage to "the passions which stalk them" (151), and who are able to claim with "boldness" (*parrēsia*) that they are in command of their own lives (152). Moreover, those who are "servile [*aneleutheros*, 'unfree']" and "slavish" are "double-faced and shifty" (154), while the one who is truly free and bold is possessed of a character (ēthos) "in which thoughts agree with words and words with thoughts" (155). In this passage, as in the other, a fundamental difference between Paul and Philo is evident. For Paul freedom comes as a gift and means, as it were, "taking refuge" in God's grace, thus being ruled by his love. For Philo freedom depends on "taking refuge in virtue," thus being ruled by reason. Nevertheless, Philo's linking of the ideas of "freedom" and "boldness" suggests what may be in Paul's mind when the same two ideas are joined in 2 Cor 3:12–17. Apostolic boldness derives from the freedom which is granted under the new covenant, written on the heart by the action of the Spirit of the Lord. Ministers of this covenant are emboldened to speak and act as their convictions direct, not deceitfully and not shrinking back (cf. 4:1–2).

The last verse in the paragraph (3:14–18) is distinguished formally by its almost confessional style. From 2:15 until this point the first person plural has included only Paul and his associates, the Pauline apostolate. Now the emphatic we all is certainly meant to include all believers—all, that is, who have turned to the Lord (v. 16). By thus identifying his Corinthian readers with the affirmation that follows, Paul is in effect enlisting their help in confirming the validity of his comments so far.

Materially, v. 18 is distinguished by the fact that its central affirmation introduces an entirely new idea into this context—the believers' transformation into the image of God. However, this is done in such a way that the themes of the preceding verses are both integrated and assimilated to the new affirmation. The related themes of splendor (vv. 7–11) and of veiling (vv. 14–16) are explicit here, and the related themes of boldness and freedom (vv. 12–13, 17) are implicit. Finally, as in v. 17 it had been said that freedom comes from the Spirit of the Lord, so here it is affirmed that the believer's transformation in splendor comes from the Lord, the Spirit.

More so than in most cases, one's judgment about the literary and situational contexts of this verse and about its conceptual background in the history of religion will determine one's conclusions about its meaning. What is its exact relationship to the discussion which has preceded? Is it a continuation of the themes of boldness and freedom in vv. 12–13, 17 (Windisch, 127)? Or does it expand the thought of v. 16 by showing what removal of the veil involves positively (Bultmann, 93)? Is the affirmation formulated with Paul's rivals in mind, who perhaps claimed that transformation into God's image was experienced only by a select few (e.g., Collange, 125)? And how is that transformation to be understood: against the background of the Hellenistic mystery religions, hence as apotheosis, or against the background of Jewish and early Christian apocalypticism, hence as an eschatological hope?

Interpretation of v. 18 is made more complex because of the many ideas crowded together here. These become more manageable, however, if the sentence is first broken down into its subject and predicate and the several dependent phrases arranged in relation to these. The subject is we all—that is, all believers. Two phrases describe them: *with unveiled face* and *beholding as in a mirror the splendor of the Lord*. The predicate is *are being transformed*. This central idea is expanded by three phrases: *into the same image, from splendor to splendor,* and *as from the Lord, the Spirit*. Each of these constituent parts of the sentence and their interrelatedness deserve comment.

First, believers are contrasted with those who have a veil lying over their understanding. One should not restrict this to a contrast between believing and unbelieving Jews, because, as noted above, Paul has moved in v. 16 *(anyone)* to broaden the scope of his remarks. It is probable, however, that the apostle continues to associate the removal of the veil with Christ's annulment of the old covenant (v. 14*b*). Believers in Christ have been freed from the impedimenta of the law. No longer do they need to be spared the sight of a splendor doomed to extinction. Now they are *beholding as in a mirror the splendor of the Lord*.

One should not try to assimilate the imagery here to that of 1 Cor 13:12. There one's present, partial understanding is said to be like seeing "in a mirror dimly" *(di' esoptrou en ainigmati)*. That is contrasted with the eschatological future, when one sees "face to face" and fully understands. In the present passage, however, nothing is said about the imperfect quality of a mirrored image, and one may not suppose that mirrors were generally associated with partial sight. Philo, indeed, thinks of a mirror as an instrument by which one "gains a lucid view of all that mind can perceive" (*Special Laws* I, 219; Corinth itself was long renowned for the unsurpassed brilliance of the bronze and bronze products—including mirrors—that it produced [see INTRODUCTION, p. 9]). As Collange, 116–17, points out, 1 Cor 13:12 shows that where the imperfection of a mirrored image is in mind, that must be expressly noted.

Why, then, is one's vision of *the splendor of the Lord* said to be a *beholding as in a mirror*? Is not this especially strange if, as some believe (see NOTES), Paul has Num 12:8*a* in mind, where Moses' vision of the Lord's splendor is described as direct? Part of the answer comes in one of the three phrases by which the predicate of this sentence is extended: believers *are being transformed into the same image*. Pauline usage generally (see references in the NOTES) and this context in particular show that Paul regards Christ as *the image of God* (4:4) in whose face *the splendor of God* is revealed (4:6). To behold that splendor *as in a mirror* is to behold it in Christ (although certainly not indistinctly or imperfectly; see above). Christ is himself the mirror of God for believers (Jervell [1960:185] compares Wis 7:26, where "mirror" and "image" are synonyms, and Odes Sol 13:1, "Behold, the Lord is our mirror" [Charlesworth 1977:64]). Moreover, the *beholding* and the attendant transformation into Christ's image are both going on in the present, and Paul characteristically reserves the believer's full and direct encounter with God for the eschatological future (5:6–8; 1 Cor 13:12).

The association made in this verse between one's *beholding . . . the splendor of the Lord* and one's *being transformed from splendor to splendor* is particularly noteworthy. A widespread idea in the Hellenistic age—for example, among the mystery religions—was that the beholding of a god or goddess could have a transformative effect on the worshiper. This is impressively attested in a famous passage from Apuleius' *Metamorphoses,* where Lucius ( = Apuleius) describes his initiation into the cult of Isis at Corinth. (This took place after he had pledged "to serve and honour the goddess," by which, he was assured, he would "feel the more the fruit of [his] liberty" [XI, 15, cited by Windisch, 126]. Cf. 2 Cor 3:17*b*!) The process reached its climax when, about midnight, Lucius saw the sun brightly shining, and with it all the gods, whom he fell down to worship (XI, 23). The next morning, symbolic of his rebirth, he was arrayed in brightly colored apparel "like unto the sun," and continued for several days "conceiving a marvellous pleasure and consolation in beholding ordinarily the image [*simulacri*] of the goddess" (XI, 24; the passage is discussed by Dibelius 1956:32–34, 53–54, 141–42).

Similarly, in the *Corpus Hermeticum* Hermes instructs his son, Tat, that if he will turn the eyes of his heart toward "the image of God" *(tou Theou eikōn)* Hermes has provided for him he will be drawn upward to God, "even as men say the loadstone draws the iron" (IV, 11*b*). More specifically, the mind of one who has thus seen God is bathed in light, God draws forth the soul from the body, and the whole person is transformed into a new substance *(kai holon auton eis ousian metaballei,* X, 6)—indeed, "into an immortal body" *(eis athanaton sōma,* XIII, 3).

There are obvious similarities between texts of the kind just cited and Paul's affirmation in 2 Cor 3:18. These similarities are not just superficially terminological; they extend also to the conception of a transformation in conformity to that which is beheld *(beholding . . . the splendor of the Lord,* [*we*] *are being transformed).* Yet there is a fundamental difference in the conception of transformation found in the Hellenistic mysteries and in Paul's letters, a difference not taken into account by Reitzenstein, for example, when he argues that Paul, too, spoke of a present, material transformation, "a kind of *apotheōsis . . .* through the [knowledge of God] and the reception of the [Spirit]" (1978:458, citing 1 Cor 2:7, 9, 10; cf. Bousset 1970:227 n. 68). In fact, the motif of transformation in glory was not restricted to the Hellenistic cults: it is also evident in the literature of Judaism. These texts, too, must be considered when assessing Paul's meaning in v. 18. For example, a prominent theme in *1 Enoch* is the transformation of God's elect when, in the eschatological day, the "light" and "glory" and "honour" of God will abide with them (50:1). This will be a transformation so profound that the godless and sinners will no longer be able to look upon the faces of the righteous (38:4; cf. 1:8; 5:7; 38:2; 45:4; 58:3–6). So, too, 2 Apoc Bar 51:3, 10, where it is said of the righteous that "their splendour shall be glorified in changes, and the form of their face shall be turned into the light of their beauty, that they may be able to acquire and receive the world which does not die, which is then promised to them. . . . And they shall be changed into every form they desire, / From beauty into loveliness, / And from light into the splendour of glory" *(APOT)*.

When one surveys all the Pauline passages which speak of the believer's transformation (for the various terms employed, see the NOTES), it quickly becomes evident that Paul shares to a great extent the eschatological perspective on transformation found in apocalyptic Judaism. The future tense predominates: "we shall (all) be changed" (1 Cor 15:51, 52); "predestined to be conformed to the image of his Son" (Rom 8:29, *RSV*), who "will change our lowly body to be like his glorious body" (Phil 3:21, *RSV*), etc. But these same passages show that the conception of transformation is closely tied to the apostle's christology. For him, transformation means conformity to the image of Christ (Rom 8:29), "to be like his glorious body" (Phil 3:21). Expressed otherwise, it means Christ's being "formed in" the believer (Gal 4:19), a transformative event which faith receives and affirms already in the present (Gal 2:20) as "a new creation" (2 Cor 5:17). It is clear that Hellenistic and apocalyptic Jewish notions have coalesced here, only to emerge as the distinctive Pauline view that the believer's transformation into a new being has both a present and a future aspect (cf. Bultmann, 101). The decisive point, however, is Paul's own conception of faith as a being conformed to the image of God in Christ. For him that means first of all sharing Christ's sufferings, "becoming like him in his death" (Phil 3:10) by being "crucified with him" (Rom 6:6). Although resurrection with Christ remains a hope (Rom 6:5, 8; Phil 3:11, etc.), God's power is operative for faith through the Spirit, by whom believers may even now "walk in newness of life" (Rom 6:4; cf. Rom 7:6, etc.). Although they remain in this age, they are not conformed to it. They are so far "transformed" by the renewal of their lives (Rom 12:2), of their "inward being" (2 Cor 4:16), that they may be said to be part of "a new creation" (Gal 6:15; 2 Cor 5:17).

These related Pauline passages provide the most important context for the interpretation of the affirmation in 2 Cor 3:18. The transformation of which Paul writes here is not attained through some ecstatic experience as believers are lifted out of their present mortal existence and joined to God. For Paul it is not an event through which one transcends history but an event in which one's transformation begins already in this age, and transforms all of one's relationships within history. It is a transformation inaugurated (though not yet completed) where by faith the believer is conformed to the image of God in God's Son, "who loved us and gave himself for us" (Gal 2:20). It is set in motion (though not yet finished) where by faith one dies to the old self and is raised up to new life through the renewing power of the Spirit. Nor is the *beholding* to which v. 18 refers that ultimate (eschatological) vision of God mentioned in Jewish apocalyptic works, and by Paul himself (for example, in 1 Cor 13:12). This is faith's present *beholding* of *the splendor of the Lord* as this is mirrored *in the face of Jesus Christ* (4:6), God's *image*. It is the free and unhindered participation in the splendor of the new covenant which is given with the gospel when the veil of unbelief is removed (v. 16). In this verse *beholding . . . the splendor of the Lord* comes very close in meaning to "hearing the gospel" (Jervell 1960:186, who notes Sir 17:13, "Their eyes saw [God's] glorious majesty, and their ears heard the glory of his voice"—*RSV*). It is that daily inward renewal of one's being (4:16) which occurs where one's life is put at God's disposal, and which thereby becomes the hallmark of the believer's existence while he or she is still in this world (Rom 12:1–2).

Although Paul's affirmation in v. 18 emphasizes faith's present *beholding,* here as elsewhere the apostle is concerned to indicate that faith is not itself the fulfillment of salvation. The Corinthians in particular have tended to think otherwise, as 1 Cor shows very well (e.g., 4:8ff.; chap. 15). In the immediate context of v. 18 he has described the surpassing splendor as *that which endures* (v. 11); it is thus a *hope* (v. 12), even while it is presently abounding (v. 9). This Pauline dialectic of present and future is clear in v. 18 itself when he affirms that the believer's transformation is *from splendor to splendor.* In this phrase the believer's transformation is described in dynamic, not static, terms. This is in accord with the use of the (durative) present tense, *beholding* and *are being transformed.* Furthermore, and in contrast to the splendor of the old covenant, that of the new generates more splendor. Its destiny is not extinction, and thus it does not need to be veiled like Moses'. Its destiny is to increase and to find fulfillment as that "eternal weight of glory" (4:17) that is going "to be revealed" (Rom 8:18) when God's people obtain their ultimate freedom in glory as his children (Rom 8:21; cf. 1 Cor 15:40ff., the glory of the resurrection body, and Phil 3:21, transformation into the likeness of Christ's "glorious body").

The final phrase of v. 18 draws into the affirmation still another point Paul has already made—that "the Lord" is "the Spirit" (v. 17a). It also returns us to the thought (in vv. 3, 6) that the ministry of the new covenant is instituted by the Spirit, and to the point (in vv. 7–11) that as *the ministry of the Spirit* (v. 8) it has a splendor far surpassing Moses' ministry of the letter. In the present phrase, *Lord* is not a christological title any more than it was earlier in the verse or than it was in vv. 16–17. Indeed, Paul's association here (and in v. 17a) of *the Lord* with *the Spirit* shows that he is still thinking of God himself (see especially "the Spirit of the living God," v. 3) as the ultimate source of that *splendor* with which not only the Pauline apostolate but also the life of every believer is being infused.

*Perspective and Intention in 3:7–18*

The foregoing discussion of this exceedingly complex passage has sought to follow as closely as possible the internal development of the argument, and to do that without resorting to any of the special hypotheses which have been proposed concerning its literary background or the teaching of Paul's opponents in Corinth.

On the one hand, and contrary to the views of Windisch, 112, this section has not been regarded as a "Christian midrash" on Exod 34, the removal of which from the context would make little difference. The NOTES and COMMENT have pointed out that the argument presented in 3:7–11 develops the point made in 3:3–6, that 3:12–13 directly resumes the topic of apostleship introduced in 2:14ff., and that vv. 16ff. supply a transition back to that topic (which is resumed once more in 4:1–6) after the momentary digression of vv. 14–15. Therefore, this passage is not to be regarded as an exposition of Exod 34:29ff. Much more, it is an exposition of Paul's own reference to the ministry of the new covenant in v. 6. As such, the passage must not be disengaged from its larger context in 2:14–5:19, throughout which Paul is elucidating the meaning of his apostolate in the light of questions which are being raised about it in Corinth.

On the other hand, and contrary to the views of some interpreters since Windisch, this section has not been interpreted as if its intention were *fundamentally* polemical. This much must be conceded to Windisch, that the polemical concerns which come to the surface particularly in 2:17; 3:1; 4:1–2 are somewhat less apparent (even though they are always just below the surface) in 3:7–18. These paragraphs are most accurately described as theological exposition with a polemical edge (cf. Olson 1976:162). For this reason, one must be extremely hesitant to use this section as a source for reconstructing some particular view that Paul is opposing.

One such attempt has been made by Schulz (1958), according to whom this passage incorporates a Jewish-Christian midrash on the veil of Moses which Paul is anxious to correct. As Schulz reconstructs it, that pre-Pauline tradition presented Moses as "the first 'Christian,' " and understood the new covenant established with Christ as the restitution of the old covenant, not as something totally new (ibid.:21). Thus the complexity of the passage is attributed to the fact that Paul is simultaneously presenting and refuting a Jewish-Christian interpretation of Moses.

Georgi (1964, especially 258–82) also believes that the key to the interpretation of 3:7–18 is its polemical intention. For him, this passage simultaneously provides evidence for and is illumined by the "divine man" theology of Paul's opponents in Corinth. On the basis of various comments by Philo and Josephus especially, Georgi argues that the missionary preaching of Hellenistic Judaism presented certain heroic figures like Moses as "divine men" *(theoi andres)* after Hellenistic models (1964:145–67). He holds, further, that Paul's rivals for leadership in Corinth have assimilated this view into their Christian preaching, and even present themselves as "divine men" (ibid.:220–34). In validating their claims, he believes, they must have appealed to the story of Moses' descent from Mount Sinai in Exod 34, interpreting it much as Philo does when he describes Moses' shining face: "a countenance far more beautiful than when he ascended, so that those who saw him were filled with awe and amazement; nor even could their eyes continue to stand the dazzling brightness that flashed from him like the rays of the sun" (*Moses* II, 70).

It is such an interpretation of Exod 34 that Georgi finds Paul attacking in 3:7–18. Indeed, he believes that the apostle has actually "cited" that interpretation, and that his rebuttal of it takes the form of his own interpolated "glosses" as he quotes (1964, especially 278–82). Georgi ventures a tentative reconstruction of this; and a re-presentation of that here, but without the alleged Pauline glosses, will show what he believes the apostle is intent on refuting. (Georgi's reconstruction is necessarily based on the Greek text [ibid.:282], but it is reproduced here in English, following as closely as possible the wording of the *RSV.*)

> The dispensation (of Moses [or: of the old covenant]) carved in letters on stone came with such splendor that the Israelites could not look at Moses' face because of its brightness. For what had splendor had a surpassing splendor. And Moses put a veil over his face so that the Israelites might not see the goal [Georgi interprets: of Moses' divinization; ibid.:270]. To this day, when they read the old covenant, that same veil remains. But to this day whenever Moses turns to the Lord the veil is removed. Now the Lord is the Spirit. (Therefore) we, beholding the glory of the Lord as in a mirror, are being changed from one degree of glory to another; for this comes from the Spirit.

This, according to Georgi, was the interpretation of Exod 34 being advanced by Paul's opponents. The remainder of what actually stands in 3:7–18 represents, on this view, the apostle's polemical glossing of that interpretation.

Both Schulz and Georgi have argued that the grammatical and syntactical peculiarities of this passage are best explained by hypothesizing Paul's actual incorporation of an interpretation of Exod 34 he wants to refute. Georgi has carried the analysis further than Schulz, and has linked it to his rather detailed reconstruction of the teaching of Paul's opponents. It is doubtful, however, that the difficulties in 3:7–18 are great enough to justify the complex and highly problematic literary analyses which have been offered to explain them. Collange, 68, shares this doubt, even while accepting Georgi's view that the passage is fundamentally polemical and directed against the "divine man" theology of Paul's opponents. But that, too, is a hypothetical construct, and it is based on a view of Hellenistic-Jewish missionary preaching which is itself hypothetical (see the critique by Holladay [1977]).

It is clear that there is a polemical aspect to the discussion in 3:7–18. In vv. 7–11, Paul is contrasting the surpassing splendor of the ministry of the new covenant with the passing splendor of Moses' ministry. Then, in vv. 12–13, he contrasts the boldness of apostles with the timidity of Moses. It is possible that Paul's rivals for leadership in Corinth have somehow linked their own claims to authority with the splendor of Moses as he descended from Sinai with the law. At any rate, we know that allusions to that story sometimes appear in the developing traditions about Moses as "god and king" (the phrase is used by Philo, *Moses* I, 158, on which see Holladay 1977:108–29), not only in Diaspora Judaism (e.g., Philo) but also in Palestinian Judaism and Samaritanism (see Meeks 1970). However, the evidence is insufficient to warrant moving from this possibility to a detailed reconstruction of the teaching of Paul's opponents, much less to the conclusion that their interpretation of Exod 34 is recoverable from 3:7–18. The passage as it stands, interpreted with reference to its own context—as an exposition of the ministry of the new covenant (v. 6)—and with reference to Paul's thought generally, yields a completely plausible meaning.

## Further Remarks on Apostolic Boldness, 4:1–6

Paul's elucidation of the apostolic commission had opened in 3:7–11 with an argument from scripture concerning the surpassing splendor of the ministry of the new covenant. In 3:12–13 he had pointed out that apostles who are commissioned to that ministry may act boldly because their hope is a ministry that endures, not a ministry like Moses' that is annulled. The subsequent comments, 3:14–18, may be said to interrupt the thought only in the sense that they extend it: first to the matter of Israel's unbelief (3:14–15), then to the subject of the freedom (from the law, for the gospel, for bold and forthright action) that is granted when the veil of unbelief has been removed from anyone's heart (3:16–17). The affirmation of 3:18 both completes this thought and supplies the basis for 4:1–6, in which the topic of apostolic boldness (3:12–13) is resumed.

What is invoked by the *Therefore* of 4:1 is not merely the *hope* enunciated in 3:7–11; it is also the present and ongoing event of *transformation* affirmed in 3:18. Paul's *ministry* (of the new covenant, of the Spirit, of righteousness) has a splendor that is not only unending but present with a transforming power in the lives of all (not just some) who, through its agency, have turned to the Lord. This is why Paul and his associates *do not shrink back* ( = act with boldness, 3:12) in their dealings with others. The Corinthians have accused Paul of recommending himself (3:1a), perhaps because of such expressions of apostolic confidence as those in 1 Cor 7:40b; 9:1–2; 15:10b, and perhaps, too, because of the way he boldly exercises his authority (or threatens to; cf. 1 Cor 4:21; 2 Cor 2:1, etc.). The Corinthians have been inclined—or have been led by Paul's rivals—to view the apostle as presumptuous and brazen in dealing with them. Paul himself describes this now as *boldness,* and attributes it not to self-interest but to the splendor of the ministry in which he serves. When he adds that he and his associates exercise this bold ministry *as recipients of mercy,* he is but reiterating a theme which had already been pervasive in an earlier letter to Corinth: the apostolic ministry is a gift and a task, not a personal accomplishment, and not, therefore, a reason for self-congratulation (e.g., 1 Cor 15:8–10*a;* 3:5–9; 4:1–2; and, with a reference—as here—to "mercy," 1 Cor 7:25*b*). Moreover, the boldness of which Paul now writes is not to be isolated from his emphasis in this very context on the point that apostles are inadequate of themselves, and that their adequacy is from God alone (3:5–6). Here Paul need not be thinking so specifically of the time of his call to apostleship as he is in 1 Cor 15:8–10*a.*

In v. 2 one learns what kind of things Paul has especially in mind when he writes about the forthrightness of apostles. Expressed negatively it means not hiding *shameful things,* not acting *craftily,* and *not adulterating the word of God.* Hiding *shameful things* would itself be deceitful, but in another sense craftiness and the adulteration of God's word could be regarded as two examples of *shameful things one hides.* In 12:16, Paul refers to charges of craftiness which have been brought against him in connection with his collection of an offering for Jerusalem. But if chaps. 10–13 are really from a later letter (Letter E), as seems probable (see INTRODUCTION, pp. 37–38), then one cannot be certain that those charges had already been made before the writing of chaps. 1–9 (Letter D). In this earlier letter (see also 6:8, "deceivers" [*planoi*]) he may be thinking of the criticism which arose after the cancellation of his promised "double visit" (e.g., 1:17). If so, the present verse would be functionally as well as materially parallel to 1:12, "we have conducted ourselves in the world with candor and godly sincerity, not by any ordinary wisdom." It is equally possible that 4:2 is written less in self-defense than in criticism of his opponents. Thus, P. Marshall (1980:592) suggests that the apostle alludes here to the "tricks of rhetoric" employed by his rivals. One may compare this to chap. 11, where he writes of their crafty ways both in preaching the gospel (11:3–4) and in representing themselves (11:13–15). And the reference to *adulterating the word of God* accords with 2:17, where Paul has already referred to those who are merely "huckstering the word of God" (see NOTES and COMMENT there).

The latter part of v. 2 expresses the positive side of apostolic boldness. While others may act craftily and preach a false gospel, the Pauline apostolate is devoted to *a full disclosure of the truth.* It is the gospel's disclosure that Paul here writes of, just as he had in 2:14–17. Here, as there, one meets an implicit contrast between true apostles and those who misrepresent both themselves and their message. Paul's use of the word *truth* to refer to the gospel is not unusual (see NOTES). Moreover, in this context he refers to the gospel as that *knowledge* which is spread abroad like a *fragrance . . . in every place* (2:14) and which provides *enlightenment* in place of unbelief (4:6; see Bultmann, 104). Here again Paul alludes to the criticism of those who have accused him of self-commendation (cf. 3:1*a*), and his response to the charge is essentially what it had been in 3:1*b*–3: the only recommendation he claims for himself and his associates is the gospel they preach. Paul presumes that all persons (even Gentiles who do not have the law [Rom 2:14–16]) are endowed with a *conscience* by which their own actions and those of others may be critically tested and evaluated. In the present case, at least, he seems to presume also that *each and every human conscience* will agree with the judgment of God, that his ministry is unflawed by deceitful and self-serving motives (cf. Thrall 1967:125). In 5:11, Paul will make the same double appeal to the consciences of his readers and to the ultimate validation of his apostolic service by the God who has commissioned him.

Most interpreters believe that the statement in v. 3 is written to counter the charge that Paul's own gospel, not the covenant of Moses, has been veiled. Georgi, however, argues that Paul's opponents view the veiling of their message in a positive way, and that Paul is responding to their introduction of this concept into the debate with him (1964:268–69). On this view, Paul—who himself evaluates the veiling of the gospel negatively—is saying that his gospel, too, is "veiled," but only to those who did not receive it and have not believed in it. The usual interpretation remains the most likely, however, since Georgi's must presuppose more knowledge about the opponents' teaching than the available evidence warrants. Collange, 132, 143, believes that Paul's rivals have charged that his gospel has been veiled by his own weaknesses. In that case the most direct response to the charge would come in 4:7ff., where Paul affirms that the splendor of the gospel treasure is manifested by his weaknesses, not masked by them (see also, e.g., 1:3–11). This interpretation is supported by 6:3ff. in particular—where, as in the present passage (v. 2), Paul is "commending" himself, and where, as in 4:7ff., he does it by enumerating the hardships he has endured as an apostle. Then he would be saying in v. 3 that *those who are perishing* (all unbelievers, as in v. 4; cf. 2:15) identify themselves as such when they do not perceive that the splendor of the gospel is disclosed in the sufferings of its ministers. (See further comment on 4:7–15.)

The reference in v. 4 to *the god of this age* may seem strange coming from one who will presently write of "a new creation" (5:17) and of the present time as "the day of salvation" (6:2*b*). But Paul is reflecting the dualism of apocalyptic Judaism (see NOTES), according to which the righteous are obliged to remain steadfast in hope, awaiting their eschatological deliverance from "the present evil age" (Gal 1:4). In the present passage, however, the point is not that the present age is "evil," or even that Satan's rule is exercised over it. The single point is that Satan, *the god of this age,* is the one who is responsible for the blindness of the *unbelievers.* Barrett, 131, interprets the comment as opposing the idea that some persons are "by nature incapable" of accepting the gospel. It certainly does preclude that deterministic view of *those who are perishing* (v. 3), but it may also be intended to preclude the mistaken notion that the cause of unbelief lies in Paul's gospel itself (cf. v. 3). No, says Paul, *the gospel* brings *enlightenment,* because it is about *the splendor of Christ, who is the image of God.*

Jervell (1960:197) believes that the conceptions employed in vv. 4–6 have been drawn largely from the baptismal liturgy of the Hellenistic congregations.

This is not impossible, but the word *enlightenment* cannot itself be used as evidence for it (see NOTES). The reference to *the splendor of Christ, who is the image of God* draws more directly on the affirmation of 3:18 (which could in turn have a liturgical origin), and by way of that on the argument of 3:7–11, 12–13. The Pauline apostolate has no need to veil the Lord's splendor because it is there to a surpassing degree in the gospel of Christ, present to faith, though not to unbelief. As Moses' face had once radiated the splendor of the old covenant, the splendor of the new covenant is now to be seen in Christ (cf. v. 6, *in the face of Jesus Christ*).

The christological hymn of Col 1:15–20 suggests that the concept of Christ as God's *image* already had a firm place in the church's liturgical tradition, and Paul is probably influenced by that tradition as he writes now to the Corinthians. In Hellenistic Judaism, God's "Word" and "Wisdom" were described in the same way (by Philo and Wis respectively; see NOTES); that background, too, must be taken into account here. In none of these contexts, including the present, is the word *image* employed to describe a "faint copy" of the original. Rather, it describes that by which and in which the original is truly represented; hence the frequent English tr. of the word as "likeness" (e.g., *RSV*). Although Paul's description of Christ as *the image of God* is in some respects comparable to what Philo says of the Logos (see NOTES) and to what is said about the divine Wisdom in Wis 7:25–26, there is also an important difference. In Hellenistic Judaism, God's image was regarded as an "emanation" or "reflection" from the divine being, and thus itself the mediating agency of the divine presence to men and women. This idea is still alive in earliest Christianity (see Heb 1:3), but here—and especially in the case of Paul—the concept of *the gospel* is a major additional factor (cf. Eltester 1958:135–36). The gospel is introduced as the fundamental re-presentative agency for the splendor of God. That splendor is present as Christ is proclaimed the crucified and resurrected one through the gospel. Furthermore, those who hear the gospel are challenged to respond in faith to its gift and claim. Thus, for Paul, God's splendor is understood primarily in terms of proclamation and decision, not primarily in terms of emanation and assimilation.

It should be noted further that there is no contradiction between Paul's reference in v. 4 to *the gospel of the splendor of Christ* and his more frequent identification of the gospel as "the word of the cross" (1 Cor 1:17–18), the proclamation of "Jesus Christ crucified" (1 Cor 2:2), etc. For Paul, it is precisely *as* the crucified one that Christ is "the Lord of glory" (1 Cor 2:8; see Bultmann, 108), and he reflects on this paradox more than once in his letters to Corinth (e.g., 4:7ff.; 12:9–10; 13:4). It is significant that in these passages he is articulating the implications of the paradox for his own apostolic role (see NOTES and COMMENT on 4:7ff.; 6:3ff.), and hence for the Corinthians' faith and life.

When Paul extends his reference to Christ in v. 4 by applying to him the traditional title *image of God,* the sentence has reached what Plummer, 117, calls its "supreme climax." This final relative clause has been motivated by Paul's concern to show that the splendor of the gospel and of Christ is finally the splendor of God (Bultmann, 109; Barrett, 132). It is true that the title employed here emphasizes Christ's equality with God and is therefore comparable to the description of Christ as having "the form of God" in the hymn of Phil 2 (v. 6, *RSV;* Eltester 1958:133). But Paul shows no interest here in how Christ is related to God as his *image,* or in Christ's cosmological role as God's *image* (contrast Col 1:15–20; Eltester ibid.). His point is only that those who have not seen *the splendor of Christ* in *the gospel* have not seen the splendor of God.

Even as Paul cannot think of God's spendor revealed in Christ without thinking of the proclamation of Christ in the gospel, so he cannot think of the proclamation of the gospel without thinking of its apostolic bearers. Indeed, that is why in this letter he is so intent on expounding the meaning of the apostolic commission, and why he consistently links the integrity of ministry to the integrity of the gospel that is served thereby. This close association of the gospel with those who preach it can lead to misunderstandings, however. It may be Paul's awareness that it has—or his fear that it may—in the case of the Corinthians that prompts him to affirm in v. 5: *it is not ourselves whom we preach, but Jesus Christ as Lord.*

In this particular formulation of the content of his preaching, Paul is probably alluding to the very early confession of faith, "Jesus is Lord" (see NOTES). But what accounts for the firm denial that he and his associates preach themselves? Have the Corinthians misunderstood Paul's appeals to imitate him, even as he imitates Christ (1 Cor 4:16; 11:1; cf. 7:7*a*)? Have they misinterpreted his claims to have the Spirit (1 Cor 2:12–13; 7:40*b*; cf. 2:4–5)? Is he concerned lest they misconstrue the close connection between apostleship and gospel that he has drawn in the present letter (Bultmann, 110, notes in particular 2:14–16)? Alternatively, it may be that Paul is accusing other claimants to apostolic authority of preaching *them*selves, in which case this affirmation would be more polemical than apologetic (so Oostendorp 1967:49) and would stand alongside the statement of 2:17*a.*

After the reference to *Jesus Christ as Lord* one might expect a description of the apostles as his *slaves.* Elsewhere Paul calls himself a "slave of (Jesus) Christ" (Rom 1:1; Gal 1:10*c*), and himself and Timothy "slaves of Christ Jesus" (Phil 1:1*a;* cf. 1 Cor 7:22, "a slave of Christ," and 1 Cor 4:1, "servants of Christ [*hypēretas Christou*] and stewards [*oikonomous*] of the mysteries of God" [*RSV*]). But in the present passage the apostles are called instead *your slaves,* meaning slaves of the Corinthians! Not only is this statement without an exact parallel elsewhere in the Pauline letters; on the face of it, it would appear to contradict the injunction of 1 Cor 7:23, "do not become slaves of men" *(RSV)*. That injunction, however, presumes that the one so "enslaved" is no longer under the dominion of Christ, and is therefore not truly free to be a servant of others (cf. Hughes, 132). In Paul's view, those whom Christ has "set free" are free to "be slaves of one another" through love (Gal 5:1, 13–14). This is the kind of "slavery" about which he writes in v. 5. It is the kind of apostolic service he will later describe as "spending and being expended" for the Corinthians (12:15, cited by Barrett, 134). It is the opposite of that tyrannizing of their faith he has disclaimed in 1:24. It is in fact the opposite of what he will later accuse the false apostles of doing—turning the Corinthian Christians into *their* slaves, by exploiting them for their own self-serving goals (11:20).

When Paul adds that apostolic service is *for Jesus' sake,* the phrase is equivalent to his saying that, above all, apostles remain the bond-servants of Christ (Bultmann, 109). That the simple name *Jesus* is used here is no indication that the historical career of Jesus is in mind, or even that his earthly humiliation is invoked particularly (so Hughes, 132). The background is still the confessional acclamation "Jesus is Lord" (Kramer 1966:200), and thus the reference is to Jesus the crucified, resurrected, and exalted one. Paul serves the Corinthians by nurturing among them the gospel of Christ which he first planted in their midst. His service to the congregation is motivated and guided by his commitment to a divine vocation. It is because he himself is a slave of Christ that he is free to be their slave *for Jesus' sake.*

The final and climactic sentence of the whole section, 3:7–4:6, does not actually recapitulate the argument as it has been developed. Rather, it provides a grounding for that argument, and more specifically for the statement in v. 5 that Paul and his co-workers preach *Jesus Christ as Lord.* Their whole ministry, Paul avers in v. 6, is verified by the illumination which *the knowledge of the splendor of God* brings to the hearts of those who have found that splendor *in the face of Jesus Christ.* In this sentence *the knowledge* stands in place of *the gospel* in v. 4, and may thus be compared with the use of the word *knowledge* in 2:14. In 2:14, however, Paul had been thinking of the dissemination of the gospel throughout the world *(in every place),* and for that purpose the imagery of a sweet odor penetrating the whole environment was appropriate. Now, in 4:6, the thought is of how the gospel is established in human hearts, and for this the imagery of light *(enlightenment)* is more suitable.

According to many interpreters, Paul is referring here to his own conversion experience, and specifically to its subjective aspect (e.g., Plummer, 122; Windisch, 140; Dunn 1975:106–7, 387 n. 45). It is true that the accounts in Acts all refer to a light which shone around Paul as he was on his way to Damascus (9:3; 22:6, 11; 26:13), but that is an external, blinding light, not an internal and illuminating one. (In Acts 26:18 the reference to turning from darkness to light with opened eyes concerns Paul's mission to the Gentiles, not his own conversion.) Moreover, Paul's own most specific comments about his conversion and call (Gal 1:15–16; 1 Cor 15:8) use the language of revelation, not the language of illumination. Therefore, the origin of the imagery of v. 6 is more apt to be Paul's earlier reference to the blindness of *unbelievers* in v. 4 than his personal experience of spiritual illumination at the time of his conversion. Even Mac-Rae, who believes (1968:423) that there is an allusion to Paul's own conversion here, must acknowledge that the language is "so imprecise that he seems to have wished to generalise to the level of the Christian experience of conversion."

As pointed out in the NOTES, there is a close structural relationship between v. 6 and v. 4. There are material relationships as well. Whereas *the god of this age* has darkened *the minds of . . . unbelievers,* the God who is the source of all light has illumined the *hearts* of those who have received the gospel. The scriptural passage used here must be Gen 1:3, even though Paul has let his application of that text shape the way he quotes it. MacRae (1968:420) points out that Tertullian used v. 6 against Marcion's view, based on v. 4, that the supreme God of the "other age" is to be distinguished from the creator God *of this age.* MacRae suggests that Paul himself may have thus formulated v. 6 precisely "to forestall any possible dualistic interpretation," such as Marcion's, of his own words in v. 4 (ibid.). This whole sentence, however, like the one in 3:18, is more confessional than polemical or didactic. For example, although Paul uses the term *knowledge* to describe his gospel, perhaps reflecting Gnostic usage with which the Corinthians are familiar (see NOTES), there is no more evidence here that he fears it may be misunderstood than there was when he used the same word in 2:14.

It is probable that Paul presumes here, as he had in 3:18, that his readers and all believers can join him in the affirmation that *God . . . has caused a light to shine in our hearts.* One may also compare 3:3, where he had been thinking especially of his converts in Corinth as those on whose hearts a letter of Christ had been inscribed by the Spirit. Nevertheless, in accord with the overall topic of apostleship in 2:14–5:19, it is likely that the affirmation in v. 6 is meant to be specifically applicable to the apostles. Paul does not say or imply that the light God *has caused . . . to shine* in the apostles' hearts has come in any extraordinary way or to any extraordinary extent. What he does say is that it has come for a special purpose: to enable them *to provide the enlightenment* (see NOTES for the active meaning of this word) that comes from the gospel they preach (cf. Bultmann, 110–11).

The unambiguous reference in v. 6 to *the splendor of God* confirms the judgment that the *Lord* mentioned in 3:18 (*the splendor of the Lord*) is God, not Christ (Collange, 141). The fact that God's *splendor* is manifested *in the face of Jesus Christ* explains Paul's use of the phrase *the splendor of Christ* in v. 4, as well as his description of Christ as *the image of God* in that same verse and in 3:18. There is no veil over the face of Christ hiding God's splendor, as

Moses' veil did (3:13). Rather, his face mirrors God's splendor, the gospel of Christ proclaims it, and the ministry of that gospel is endowed with it. Fitzmyer (1981) offers several passages from the Jewish sectarian texts of Qumran as evidence that the roots of this idea of illumination are Palestinian-Jewish rather than Greek. According to 1QH iv.5–6, 27–29, God has illumined the face of the Teacher of Righteousness (assuming he is the psalmist; otherwise, of the community's priests), and through him (or through the priests) the faces of all the members of the community are illumined (similarly, 1QSb iv.24–28; 1QS ii.2–4). The scriptural sources of the idea as it was developed at Qumran appear to be Num 6:24–26 and Pss 31:17; 67:2 (Fitzmyer 1981:641).

## 7. THE MINISTRY AND MORTALITY, 4:7–5:10

4 ⁷Now we have this treasure in earthen pots, in order that it might be seen that the power which is beyond any comparison belongs to God and not to us. ⁸In every way we are afflicted, but not crushed; despairing, but not utterly desperate; ⁹persecuted, but not forsaken; struck down, but not destroyed; ¹⁰always carrying about in the body the death of Jesus, in order that also the life of Jesus might be manifested in our bodies. ¹¹For we who are alive are constantly being given up to death on account of Jesus, in order that also the life of Jesus might be manifested in our mortal flesh. ¹²Accordingly, death is made active in us, but life in you. ¹³Because we have the same Spirit of faith as the one who wrote "I believed, and so I spoke," we also believe, and so we speak, ¹⁴knowing that the one who raised [the Lord] Jesus will raise us also with Jesus, and will present us with you. ¹⁵So everything is for your sake, that grace, extended through ever more people, may cause thanksgiving to overflow to the glory of God.

¹⁶Thus, we do not shrink back. Even though our outer person is being wasted away, our inner person is renewed daily. ¹⁷For our momentary, trifling affliction is bringing about for us an absolutely incomparable, eternal abundance of glory. ¹⁸We do not focus our attention on the things that are seen, but on the things that are not seen; for the things that are seen are temporary, whereas the things that are not seen are eternal. 5 ¹For we know that if our earthly, tent-like house should be destroyed, we have a building from God, a house not made with hands, eternal in the heavens. ²Also, indeed, in view of this we are sighing because we long to clothe ourselves over with our dwelling which comes from heaven—³presupposing, of course, that having once clothed our-

selves we shall not be found naked. ⁴Indeed, while we are in this tent we are sighing under a burden, because we do not wish to unclothe ourselves, but to clothe ourselves over, that mortality may be engulfed by life. ⁵The one who equipped us for this very thing is God, who gave to us the Spirit as a down payment.

⁶Therefore, having confidence always, and knowing that while we are at home in the body we are away from our home with the Lord—⁷for we conduct ourselves according to faith, not according to appearance —⁸we do have confidence, and we are resolved instead to get away from being at home in the body and to get on home to the Lord. ⁹Accordingly, whether we are at home or away from home, we make it our ambition to be acceptable to him. ¹⁰For we all must appear before the judicial bench of Christ, that each may receive back according to what each has done in the body, whether it be good or evil.

## NOTES

4:7. *treasure.* The term *(thēsauros)* occurs nowhere else in the indisputably Pauline letters, but the plural is used in Col 2:3 with reference to "all the treasures of wisdom and knowledge" hidden in Christ. In the LXX the word had already been used metaphorically of benefits deriving from the divine Wisdom (Wis 7:14, singular; Sir 1:25, plural). For the use of the metaphor here, see COMMENT.

*earthen pots.* Cf. Artemidorus V, 25. In LXX Lev 6:28; 14:50, the "earthen pot" *(skeuos ostrakinon)* is a vessel in which the temple priest offers certain kinds of sacrifice; see also Lev 11:33; 15:12, where such earthenware is regarded as readily expendable, to be broken when it becomes ritually unclean. The phrase *angeion ostrakinon* can be used in the same way (Lev 14:5; cf. 14:50; Num 5:17), or more generally (e.g., Isa 30:14; Jer 39[32]:14). See also *angos ostrakinon* (Jer 19:11; Ezek 4:9), *bikos ostrakinos* ("earthen jar," Jer 19:1, 10). In Lam 4:2 the inferiority of such earthenware is contrasted with the great value of vessels crafted of gold, and elsewhere the fragility and therefore expendability of (earthen) pots is particularly stressed (e.g., Jer 22:28, a pot *[skeuos]* that can be "cast out"; Ps 30[31]:12, *skeuos apolōlos,* a "broken pot"). The statement of Gen 2:7 that God "formed" man from the "dust" leads to the portrayal of God as a potter, both in God's act of creation (Isa 29:16; 45:9; 64:8) and in God's judgment of evil (Isa 30:14; Jer 18:1–11; 19:1–13). Cf. 1 Cor 15:42–48; Rom 9:21–23. There is similar imagery, emphasizing mainly the creatureliness, mortality, and sinfulness of human beings, in the Qumran scrolls (e.g., 1QS xi.22; 1QH i.21–22; iii.20–21; iv.29; x.5; xi.3; xii.24–31; xiii.15–16).

In Hellenistic and particularly in Stoic texts, one's physical body *(sarx* or *sōma)* is frequently described as a container (usually *angeion*) for the "mind" *(nous)* or "soul" *(psychē);* see Marcus Aurelius III, 3; VIII, 27; X, 38; XII, 1–3; *Corpus Hermeticum* X, 17; and among the Latin writers, Cicero, *Tusculan Disputations* I.xxii.52, "For the body is as it were a vessel *[vas]* or a sort of shelter for the soul *[anima]*." Also

Philo, *On Dreams* I, 26 ("the body . . . is the vessel of the soul [*to sōma . . . psychēs estin angeion*]," and it "comes to maturity, wears out, grows old, dies, is dissolved") and 2 Esdras 4:10–11; 7:88. Gos Phil (CG II, *3*) 63,5–11 (*NHLE*, 138) emphasizes the inferiority of earthenware to glass, for when glass is broken it can be melted down and a new vessel produced, but when a clay pot is broken it can only be thrown away.

*in order that it might be seen.* This English phrase interprets the more general Greek expression (*hina . . . ē*, "in order that . . . might be") in accord with *hina . . . phanerōthē (in order that . . . might be manifested)* in vv. 10, 11. Cf. Plummer, 127.

*the power which is beyond any comparison.* Here as elsewhere, and especially in 2 Cor, Paul uses a *hyper-*word (here, *hē hyperbolē tēs dynameōs*) to accentuate the overwhelming quality or extent of something. See NOTES on 3:10; 11:5. The apostle often emphasizes the power of God (e.g., 6:7; 10:4; 13:4; Rom 1:16, 20; 1 Cor 1:18, 24; 2:5); see Nielsen 1980.

8. *In every way.* This phrase should probably be taken as introductory to all four antitheses in vv. 8–9, even though the same phrase is linked particularly to *we are afflicted* in 7:5. The expression *en panti* is frequent in chaps. 1–9 (see also 6:4; 7:5, 11, 16; 8:7; 9:8, 11), but it also occurs in 11:6, 9. It is used here to indicate that the apostle has experienced all kinds of hardship, and it therefore functions, along with the adverbs *always* (v. 10) and *constantly* (v. 11), to accent the scope and intensity of what he endures.

*we are afflicted, but not crushed.* The first of four antitheses in vv. 8, 9. These are constructed of four sets of paired participles in which the first participle is affirmed and the second denied. That *ou* is used as the negative of the participles—and not *mē*, as would be normal—is perhaps to be explained by the fact that a single idea is being negated; see BDF § 430(3) and cf. Robertson 1923:1137–38. In this first pairing it is somewhat strange to find "affliction" and "distress" being contrasted, because the two nouns *(thlipsis* and *stenochōria)* are often virtually synonymous (e.g., in the LXX, Deut 28:53, 55, 57; Isa 8:22; 30:6; Esth 1:1g), even in this same letter, 6:4 (and in Rom 2:9; 8:35). As shown by a passage from Epictetus (I.xxv.26), both terms have to do basically with being pressed in, constricted, put under pressure (cf. 6:12, where the verb *stenochōreisthai* is used twice). In the present verse, then, one might translate this as "under pressure, but not crushed." The reference to affliction has been retained, however, to show that the verb used here *(thlibesthai)* is the same one that Paul has already used in 1:6 with reference to the affliction he had experienced in Asia (note the noun *thlipsis* in 1:4 [see NOTES there], 8; also in 6:4; 7:4; 8:2, 13). This verb is used again in 7:5. Spicq (1937:215) argues that the imagery of vv. 8–9 is "perfectly homogeneous" and is all based on the standard moves of the sport of wrestling, with which Paul's readers would have been familiar. However, Spicq himself must admit that there was no clearly fixed technical language for this sport (ibid.: n. 32), and the terms used here are quite understandable without recourse to the intricate explanations Spicq seeks to provide.

*despairing, but not utterly desperate.* No English tr. can successfully reproduce the wordplay *(paronomasia)* of the Greek phrase, *aporoumenoi all' ouk exaporoumenoi.* The verb *aporeuesthai,* from which both participles are formed, means "to be at a loss," uncertain of how to act—thus, "perplexed" (e.g., Gal 4:20). When the prefix *ex* is added to the verb, as in the second member of the present set, the meaning is intensified: "perplexed to the final degree" (cf. *GNTG* I:237; II:310). *NEB* is good: "bewildered, we are never at our wits' end." The compound form of the verb occurs also in 1:8, but nowhere else in the NT.

9. *persecuted, but not forsaken.* Some interpreters believe at least this and the following antithesis are drawn from the sports arena, even if those in v. 8 had not been (see NOTES on v. 8 for the view of Spicq 1937). Thus Héring, 31, renders this phrase as "pursued, but not overtaken" (cf. Plummer, 129; Fridrichsen 1944:30 n. 2). That is very unlikely, however, because the second term in particular *(enkataleipein)* is frequently associated, in the Greek Bible, with God's promise never to forsake his people: Gen 28:15; Deut 31:6, 8; Josh 5:1; 1 Chr 28:20; Pss 15(16):10; 36(37):25, 28; Sir 2:10; Acts 2:27, 31; Heb 13:5; cf. Ps 21(22):2 (cited in Matt 27:46; Mark 15:34) and 2 Tim 4:16–17. It is more likely, then, that Paul's reference here is to the steadfastness of God, and that one should interpret as "not forsaken by God." (Contrast Héring, 32, who interprets Paul to mean that, though pursued as in a footrace, "he never remained at the rear.") In this case the first term *(diōkein)* should be given its full (and frequent biblical) sense, "to persecute," as it clearly has in the comparable catalog of afflictions in 1 Cor 4:9–13 (see v. 12*b;* note also the hardship lists of Rom 8:35*b;* 2 Cor 12:10*a*).

*struck down, but not destroyed.* The first verb used here *(kataballein)* has a wide range of meanings, and in the passive voice (as here) could mean to be overthrown, laid low by a blow or a weapon, abused or bullied, cast off or rejected, stricken with an illness, or even slain (see LSJ s.v. I). Any of these would suit the present context, and since Paul uses this verb nowhere else there is little to commend one tr. over another. Naturally enough, the word had a technical use in the sport of boxing. Windisch, 144, is correct to reject the notion that such an image is invoked here, however. The second term *(apollunai,* "to destroy") has already been used twice in this letter (2:15; 4:3) with reference to the ultimate destruction of those who do not receive the gospel. It is possible but not certain that here, too, Paul is thinking of an ultimate destruction.

10. *always.* As in vv. 8 and 11, the adverbial expression here *(pantote)* stands first for emphasis (Meyer, 495). Whereas the one in v. 8 had more of a modal reference, this one has a temporal reference. Paul does not regard the hardships he faces as exceptions, but as what is usual in the work of apostles. See also 1 Cor 15:30, 31, where he had referred to being endangered "every hour" and to dying "daily," as well as his quotation of LXX Ps 43(44):23(22) in Rom 8:36: "For thy sake we are being killed all the day long" (*RSV;* Schrage 1974:144–45 compares 1 Enoch 103:8–11); cf. Phil 1:20. Windisch, 144, compares the thought with Philo's interpretation of Cain's punishment as a perpetual dying (*Rewards and Punishments* 72; cf. *The Worse Attacks the Better* 177–78; *Confusion of Tongues* 122; *Virtues* 200).

*carrying about.* The participle *(peripherontes)* may be an allusion to Paul's travels as a missionary; see, e.g., Plummer, 131; Schrage 1974:158 n. 44; Collange, 154 (who compares 2:14, where the same adverb, *always,* is used with it).

*the death of Jesus.* Commentators are divided on the significance of the word used here for *death (nekrōsis).* Most believe that it is to be distinguished from the word Paul ordinarily uses to refer to Jesus' death *(thanatos,* in Rom 5:10; 6:3–5; Phil 3:10; and in the traditional formulations quoted by Paul in 1 Cor 11:26; Phil 2:8). In this case it might refer to the process of Jesus' "being put to death"; so, e.g., Meyer, 495, 496; Plummer, 129; Windisch, 145; Strachan, 94; Hughes, 141 n. 12; Barrett, 139–40. Cf. Rissi 1969:49, who interprets it with reference to "weakness" in 13:4*a.* Others, how-

ever, argue that the word refers here to a condition, the "state of death," as in Rom
4:19, where it describes Sarah's womb ("barren" [*RSV*]; so Güttgemanns 1966:114–17
(following J. Schmid and others, 116), Ahern 1960:22, and Collange, 155.

*of Jesus.* Georgi (1964:286–89) believes that Paul's use of the simple name *Jesus* in
this passage (vv. 11, 14, as well as here) is due to his concern to combat the false
understanding of Jesus' earthly life held by opponents in Corinth (cf. 11:4). See COM-
MENT. It is true that usually a fuller christological title is used when Christ's sufferings
(e.g., 1:5) and death (e.g., Rom 6:3; 1 Cor 2:2; Gal 3:1) are in view, but the present
passage is not the only exception; see also 1 Thess 4:14 and cf. Gal 6:17. Kramer
(1966:200) believes *Jesus* here means nothing other than "Christ" elsewhere.

*the life of Jesus.* The phrase as used here (and in v. 11) does not refer to the course
of Jesus' earthly life and ministry, but to the power of his resurrection life (v. 14) as
that is manifested in the present (see following note).

*might be manifested in our bodies.* Cf. v. 11, *might be manifested in our mortal flesh.*
Thus, the words *sōma* ("body") in the present verse and *sarx (flesh)* in v. 11 are being
used interchangeably. Cf. Rissi 1969:48, 49. The power of Jesus' (resurrection) life is
disclosed already, precisely in Paul's sufferings. Collange, 157, believes that the apostle
is countering the claim of his adversaries that the power of that life is disclosed, rather,
"pneumatically"—through miraculous phenomena.

11. *For.* The use of this word *(gar)* shows that what follows is intended to support
the preceding statement (v. 10). Both the structure and the contents of the two verses
are parallel. Each opens with an adverb (see note on *constantly* below), followed by a
statement about the operation of Jesus' death in the life of the apostles, and each is
concluded with a *hina*-clause *(in order that)* about the manifestation of Jesus' life.

*we who are alive.* The reference here is not to the "resurrection" life of believers,
although Baumert (1973:78–81) argues for this, but to their physical life. It therefore
accentuates the point that life may be regarded as a constant dying. Plummer, 131,
paraphrases: "We are ever a living prey."

*constantly.* The adverb is *aei,* essentially synonymous with *always* in v. 10; cf. *in every
way,* v. 8. This word, like the two preceding adverbial expressions, has special emphasis
by reason of its place at the beginning of the phrase, but this cannot be reproduced in
English. In 6:10, the only other place where Paul himself has used this adverb, the
phrase is "constantly rejoicing." Some witnesses, including P[46], read *ei* (thus, "For if
we who are alive are being given up to death . . ."), and Barrett, 136 n. 1, suggests this
may be original. The reading *aei* would then be regarded as an assimilation to *pantote
(always)* in v. 10.

*given up to death.* This phrase is parallel to *carrying about in the body the death,* v.
10, and helps to explain that, even though the word for *death* is now *thanatos,* not
*nekrōsis* as in v. 10. The verb *(paradidonai)* is the same one used of Jesus' being
"handed over" or "delivered up" to the authorities, and thus to death (e.g., Matt 20:18;
Mark 10:33*a*). The eucharistic formula in 1 Cor 11:23 shows that Paul already knew
the technical use of the word as a reference to Jesus' being delivered up (by Judas?)
to death; see also Rom 4:25; 8:32; Gal 2:20. However, it is not necessary to suppose
that he has chosen the word here in order to accentuate the relationship of apostolic
hardships to Jesus' sufferings and death; the phrase "to deliver [be delivered] up to
death" is present in the LXX (2 Chr 32:11; Isa 53:12) and in secular Greek (POxy 471,

line 107, cited in BAG s.v. 1*b*) and can be used even in the Synoptic gospels quite generally (Matt 10:21, par. Mark 13:12). Cf. 1 Cor 13:3. For an overall study of the use of the term see Popkes (1967).

*on account of Jesus.* The prepositional phrase (*dia Iēsoun;* cf. 4:5) is not to be interpreted as "for Jesus' sake" (*RSV,* and virtually all recent English versions), as if for Jesus' benefit. Rather, the preposition has causal force here, as shown by Paul's citation of LXX Ps 43(44):23(22) in a similar context in Rom 8:36, where the preposition is *heneken.* Note also Phil 2:30 (Epaphroditus almost died "on account of" his work for Christ, *dia to ergon Christou*) and Gal 6:12 (Paul charges his opponents with seeking to avoid being persecuted "because of Christ's cross," *tō staurō tou Christou:* causal dative); see Schrage 1974:161–62.

*in our mortal flesh.* The paradox, implicit in v. 10*b*, that Jesus' life is disclosed *in our bodies* is now intensified as *our bodies (tō sōmati hēmōn)* is replaced by *our mortal flesh (tē thnētē sarki hēmōn).* The change emphasizes the vulnerability of the *sōma* ("body") to suffering and death (Bultmann, 121).

12. *Accordingly.* Translates the inferential particle *hōste: hōs te,* "and so"; see Moule 1953:144. It introduces the consequence of what has been stated in the preceding verses. Contrast Baumert 1973:74, 81–83, who argues that this whole verse goes more closely with vv. 13–15 than with vv. 7–11.

*death . . . life.* Most commentators and trs. have interpreted the Greek verb here (*energeitai,* middle voice) as an intransitive deponent, and thus active in meaning—e.g., "is at work" (Wey., *RSV,* and virtually every recent English version). Baumert, however, argues persuasively for a passive meaning here (1973:72–73 and Excursus A, 267–83). This would not only conform to the use of the middle form of this verb in Greek texts generally (ibid.:267–68), but would be in accord with the passive verbs used in vv. 10–11 (ibid.:72–73). The underlying subject of these three verses is God, or, more precisely, the incomparable "power" of God, which had been emphasized in v. 7. Elsewhere Paul associates God's power especially with Christ's resurrection (13:4 [cf. 12:9]; Phil 3:10; cf. 1 Cor 6:14; 15:43), and it is Christ's resurrection life above all that the apostle has reference to in the present passage (see v. 14).

*but life.* The Greek phrase here is *hē de zoē,* and given the form and content of the sentence one would have expected the *de* ("but") to have been preceded by a *men (ho men thanatos);* thus, "on the one hand, death . . . while on the other hand, life. . . ." As Plummer, 132, observes, the absence of a *men* in the first phrase makes the second phrase all the more unexpected.

13. *Because we have.* As in 3:4, 12; 4:1, 7, a form of the verb "to have" signals a transition to a new thought (Windisch, 148). Rissi (1969:58) believes that this is done in such a way as to pull the preceding thoughts together; contrast Baumert (1973:83), who argues that this verse goes closely with v. 12*a.* The participle here (*echontes*) is best construed with *we also believe* (Robertson 1923:1134; Barrett, 142) and is best interpreted causally (Plummer, 133). If—as Collange, 162, maintains—the *de* that goes with it is intended to have adversative force, one might translate this as "yet, because we have . . . ," etc.

*the same Spirit of faith.* Some commentators have argued that *to auto (the same)* means "the same as you Corinthians have" (e.g., Schlatter, 535; Strachan, 96; more recently Baumert [1973:83–84], who virtually equates *Spirit of faith* here with the *life* which, in 12*b*, Paul says the Corinthians have). Rissi (1969:59) ascribes a "demonstrative sense" to *to auto*, and believes it gathers up the ideas of vv. 7–12 into the concept of the *Spirit of faith*. It is more probable, however, that Paul means to identify the *Spirit of faith* he has experienced with *the same* one known to the psalmist from whom he proceeds to quote (so most commentators, including, e.g., Meyer, 499; Bultmann, 123; Collange, 162; Barrett, 142).

*Spirit of faith*. Hughes, 147 and n. 15, proposes that *pneuma* is used here as it is in the phrase "spirit of gentleness" in 1 Cor 4:21; Gal 6:1, and interprets it as a "disposition" or "impulse"; cf. Bultmann, 123. It is preferable, however, to read this as a reference to the (Holy) Spirit, in and with which faith comes, as in 1 Cor 12:9; Rom 8:14–16; Gal 3:2, 5, 14; 5:5; cf. 1 Cor 2:4–5; 1 Thess 1:5–7. See especially Collange, 162.

*as the one who wrote*. This is a paraphrase of the Greek, which is, more literally, "according to what is written" *(kata to gegrammenon)*. Paul uses this precise citation formula nowhere else (Deissmann 1903:250 compares it with a formula from an Egyptian legal papyrus, 52–53 C.E.), but it seems to be equivalent to his frequently employed "as it is written" *(kathōs* [or: *kathaper*] *gegraptai*: e.g., 8:15; 9:9; particularly frequent in Rom), as well as to "according to what was said" *(kata to eirēmenon)* in Rom 4:18. This is the first explicit citation of scripture in 2 Cor, not counting 4:6 (on which see the NOTES). Others occur in 6:2, 16–18; 8:15; 9:9; 10:17; 13:1.

*"I believed, and so I spoke."* Paul has followed exactly the wording of the LXX, Ps 115:1*a*. The Hebrew text which lies behind this actually stands in the middle of a Psalm (116:10) which in the Greek has been divided into two, Ps 114:1–9 ( = Hebrew 116: 1–9) and Ps 115:1–10 ( = Hebrew 116:10–19). The meaning of the Hebrew is problematic (for a discussion see Dahood 1955:23–24 and 1970:148), but it is certainly not given correctly in the LXX. Dahood (1970:144) renders the Hebrew as "I remained faithful though I was pursued."

*we also believe*. In this context the first person plural includes Paul's associates, not (first of all) the Corinthian congregation (note "us" and "you" in vv. 12 and 14). The *also* joins the faith of the apostles to the psalmist's.

*and so we speak*. Here, as in 2:17, "speaking" *(lalein)* means preaching the gospel, and this full phrase is used by Paul himself in 1 Thess 2:2. The comments about faith and preaching in Rom 10:14–17 show, from another angle, how seriously he takes the relationship between these.

14. *knowing that*. This phrase *(eidotes hoti)* frequently introduces a formulation that a writer may presume to be familiar to his readers, whether from a shared tradition (as here), from that writer's own previous teaching, or from the teaching of others; see, e.g., 1:7; 5:6; Rom 6:9; 1 Cor 15:58; Gal 2:16; Jas 3:1; 1 Pet 1:18; also "we know that" *(oidamen hoti)* in 5:1; Rom 7:14*a;* 8:28; 1 Cor 8:1, 4, etc.

*the one who raised* [*the Lord*] *Jesus will raise us also*. Both readings, *the Lord Jesus* and *Jesus*, are well attested, and it is difficult to decide between them; see Metzger 1971:579. The formula as a whole is clearly traditional, and occurs in closely similar forms in Rom 8:11 and 1 Cor 6:14; cf. 1 Cor 15:15, 22–23. For a discussion of the general formal category see Wengst (1972:27–48, especially 31, 35–36). The same formula is present in Ign Trall 9:2 and Pol Phil 2:2, and in neither case is there any reason to find "a loose quotation" of 2 Cor 4:14 (against Plummer, 133, who refers only to Pol Phil; also Schoedel, *AF* V:11).

*with Jesus.* This phrase *(syn Iēsou)* does not appear in the other versions of the traditional formula cited here (see preceding note; the "in Christ Jesus" of Ign Trall 9:2 has a different meaning). It is probably Paul's own addition (Collange, 164), but it is doubtful whether it should be compared too closely with Rom 6:5, 8; 8:17. See, rather, "with him" *(syn autō),* "with them" *(syn autois),* and "with the Lord" *(syn Kyriō)* in 1 Thess 4:14, 17.

*will present us.* The verb used here *(paristanai)* has a fairly broad range of possible meanings (e.g., to present a cultic offering, to appear before a king as his subject, to stand before a judge, to put something at someone's disposal) and there can be no certainty about its meaning in this verse. Some (e.g., Meyer, 500) believe it is used here with reference to a presentation before Christ for judgment (note 5:10; cf. Rom 14:10; Col 1:22). Others (e.g., Denney, 166; Lietzmann, 116) think rather of a triumphal presentation at court (cf. 11:2), the last and joyous act in the eschatological drama (cf. Windisch, 150). Bultmann, 124, cites the thought in Odes Sol 21:6–7: "And I was lifted up in the light, / And I passed before Him. / And I was constantly near Him, / While praising and confessing Him" (Charlesworth 1977:88). More recently, however, Baumert (1973:94–95 and Excursus B, 284–99) has argued that the verb has a "demonstrative" meaning in this passage: "to present in the open," "to manifest," "to show faith," etc. Such a meaning seems clear in Sir 23:22–23; Ps 49(50):21 (cf. 1 Clem 35:10); Acts 1:3; 9:41; Col 1:22; 2 Tim 2:15 (ibid.:297–98), but it is less certain in the present verse; see following note and COMMENT.

*with you.* Paul's sense of closeness to and interaction with the Corinthian congregation is often expressed in chaps. 1–9 (e.g., here in v. 12; 1:5–7, 21; 2:3, 5; 7:3), and the present phrase may certainly be added to these (cf. Baumert 1973:96). However, one should also take note of those passages in which the apostle is referring particularly to his being "with" his congregations at the eschatological day. See 1:14; Phil 2:14–18; 1 Thess 2:19–20. That this is the thought behind *with you* in this verse is rendered likely by the preceding reference to the believers' resurrection *with Jesus* (on which see note above). This would mean that the preposition *with* would have essentially the same force in the two phrases—*with Jesus* and *with you:* primarily, "in the company of." Cf. 1 Thess 4:17, where "with them" refers to the reunion of those who have been resurrected "with" those who have remained alive until Christ's return. Their joint ascension "to meet the Lord in the air" *(RSV)* will be in effect their "presentation" before him. See preceding note and COMMENT.

15a. *So.* Greek *gar,* "for."

*everything.* In this context the expression *(ta panta)* refers to the apostolic preaching (the "speaking" emphasized in v. 13) and all the hardships that attend it (vv. 8–11), as Bultmann, 125, has seen. Cf. 12:19c.

*for your sake.* The same expression *(di' hymas)* as in 2:10; cf. also 1:6 *(hyper . . . hymōn:* "for your comfort [and salvation]," twice); 5:13 *(hymin,* "for you"); 8:23 *(eis hymas,* "for you"). In this letter (chaps. 1–9) Paul often refers to the benefits he hopes the Corinthians will receive from his ministry (1:7, 15, 24; 3:2–3; 4:5, 12; 7:3; 8:16, etc.).

15b. This half-verse is a syntactical thicket, hardly less difficult than 1:11 (see NOTES there), in which a somewhat similar idea occurs.

(1) Most English versions, although they frequently resort to paraphrasing in this verse, presume that the verb *pleonazein* is intransitive (to "increase," "extend," etc.;

BAG s.v. 1a) and that the nearly synonymous *perisseuein* is transitive (to "cause something" to abound, be enriched, etc.; BAG s.v. 2a), with the accusative *tēn eucharistian (thanksgiving)* as its object. Plummer, 134–35, and Windisch, 150–51, provide arguments in support of this interpretation.

(2) On the other hand, Baumert (1973:105) reverses this, taking *pleonazein* as transitive (cf. 1 Thess 3:12, where both *pleonazein* and *perisseuein* are transitive: "cause you to increase and abound in love"), with *thanksgiving* as its object. Then *perisseuein* would be intransitive, as in 1:5; 8:2, 7; 9:12 (see ibid., Excursus C, 300–10 on *perisseuein*). The construction of the second verb would thus be the same here as in Rom 3:7: there, "God's truthfulness abounds to his glory [*eperisseusen eis tēn doxan autou*]" *(RSV)*, and here, "that grace may abound to God's glory [*perisseusē eis tēn doxan tou Theou*]."

(3) Noack (1963) argues that *pleonazein* and *perisseuein* are both intransitive in this verse. On his view the present text would represent either a conflation of two parallel clauses ("that grace may increase through more and more, and that thanksgiving may abound to the glory of God") or else the transformation of an intended subordinate clause into the subject of the main verb ("that grace . . . may abound" in place of "that as grace increases . . . thanksgiving may abound"; ibid.:131–32).

The construction here must remain problematic, although the proximity of the accusative *tēn eucharistian (thanksgiving)* to the verb *perisseusē (may increase)* is an important argument for (1); see Windisch, 150–51. The arguments for (3) are the least convincing.

*grace.* Paul often refers to the grace by which he has been summoned to apostleship and equipped for the task of preaching the gospel (Rom 1:5; 12:3; 15:15; 1 Cor 3:10; 15:10; Gal 1:15; 2:9). Earlier in this letter he has referred to God's grace as the norm of his apostolic conduct (1:12), and in the present context he has emphasized how, paradoxically, God's incomparable power is disclosed in his apostolic hardships (vv. 7–12). In 12:9 he will use both words, "grace" and "power," to characterize his ministry. It is probably this divine grace, which enables him to serve and suffer as an apostle, that is in Paul's mind here (so Bultmann, 126, and Rissi 1969:64 n. 154; contrast Barrett, 144, who interprets the term here on the basis of 8:9; 9:8).

*extended.* The participle *pleonasasa* is translated here as intransitive (see introductory notes to 15b, above); cf. the intransitive use of the same verb with the same subject in Rom 6:1b: "Are we to continue in sin that grace may abound?" *(RSV)*

*through ever more people.* Here the preposition *dia* with the genitive *(tōn pleionōn)* indicates the manner or medium (not the agency) in which *grace* is *extended;* see BDF § 223(3). Barrett, 144–45, interprets the substantive as referring either to "the main body" or to "the majority" of the congregation being addressed, as in 2:6 (see NOTES) and elsewhere. It is more likely, however, given the use of the verb *pleonazein,* that Paul is thinking of the "increasing number" of converts to the gospel; so, e.g., Lietzmann, 116; Moule 1953:108; Braun 1966 I:199–200.

*may cause thanksgiving to overflow.* The main verb is *perisseusē,* regarded here as transitive *(may cause . . . to overflow);* see preceding notes on v. 15b. The subject is *grace (charis)* and the object is *thanksgiving (tēn eucharistian).* Some commentators think Paul intends a play on these two words (e.g., Plummer, 134; Barrett, 144, who attempts to simulate it by rendering these as "grace" and "gratitude"). Collange, 167, notes that the same verb is also associated with *thanksgiving* in 9:12 and Col 2:7 (but intransitive in both cases). That Paul can use this verb (*perisseuein*) and *pleonazein* ("to increase," "extend," etc., earlier in this verse) interchangeably is demonstrated when, in Rom, first one (*perisseuein*, 5:15) and then the other (*pleonazein*, 6:1) is used (intransitively) with *grace* as its subject.

*to the glory of God.* For Paul, the ultimate aim of all apostolic service and the all-embracing responsibility of every believer is to glorify God; see, e.g., Rom 1:21; 3:7; 4:20; 15:6, 7, 9; 1 Cor 6:20; 10:31; Gal 1:24; Phil 1:11; in the present letter, also 1:20; cf. 8:19, 23. Boobyer (1929:77, 79) stresses the materialistic conception of *glory* lying behind this and other Pauline references.

*16a. Thus.* Translates *dio,* which ties this affirmation to what has preceded. Meyer, 501, relates it to v. 14; Windisch, 151, to vv. 7–12 (with special reference to vv. 8–9), and Bultmann, 126, to v. 15. There is no need to choose among these several possibilities, however, because this transitional particle in effect gathers up everything in vv. 7–15 and returns the readers to the point of v. 1; see following note.

*we do not shrink back.* This affirmation is repeated from 4:1. Hughes, 152, deals with this half-verse in association with vv. 7–15, and opens a new section with v. 16*b* (153). However, the doxological climax of v. 15 is thereby obscured. It is better to take v. 16*a* as introducing what follows rather than as concluding what has preceded.

*16b. Even though.* When, as here, an *ei kai* (the full Greek phrase is *all' ei kai,* "but even though") introduces a concessive clause, what follows is regarded as fulfilled, not just as contingent; Burton 1898: § 284.

*our outer person.* Paul uses this phrase *(ho exō hēmōn anthrōpos)* nowhere else, but cf. "the old person" *(ho palaios anthrōpos)* in Rom 6:6 (and subsequently in Col 3:9; Eph 4:22). He uses it here in contrast with *our inner person* (on which see below and COMMENT).

*is being wasted away.* The present tense points to an ongoing process, the passive voice to a sense of the inevitability of bodily deterioration. In this context, however, one should think first of all of the apostolic hardships to which Paul has just referred, vv. 8–9.

*our inner person.* The word *person* is left unexpressed in the Greek, to be supplied with reference to the earlier, contrasting phrase, *our outer person.* The present expression *(ho esō [anthrōpos])* is also used in Rom 7:22, where *RSV* translates as "my inmost self." The contrasting expressions are doubtless influenced by the widespread anthropological dualism of the Hellenistic world—e.g., Seneca, *Moral Epistles* LXXI, 27; CII, 23–27; Epictetus II.vii.3; viii.12–14; III.iii.13; Marcus Aurelius III, 3; X, 38; Philo, *Every Good Man Is Free* 111; *On Husbandry* 9; *On Noah's Work as Planter* 42; *The Worse Attacks the Better* 22–23; *Corpus Hermeticum* I, 18; XIII, 7–8. Rüger (1977) argues that Paul's distinction between the *inner* and *outer* person corresponds to the rabbinic distinction between the principles of good and evil *(yēṣer haṭṭôb* and *yēṣer hārāᶜ),* and that Paul has substituted the Hellenistic terms for the specific benefit of his Christian readers in Corinth (and Rome).

*is renewed.* Another present, passive verb (cf. *is being wasted away,* above); but in this case one should probably think of a repeated renewal (see following note) rather than of a progressive development. Elsewhere in the NT the verb occurs only in Col 3:10. Note, however, Paul's use of the noun "renewal" in Rom 12:2 (later, Tit 3:5). On the thought, compare 3:18.

*daily.* The Greek phrase *(hēmera kai hēmera)* is often described as a Hebraism (e.g., BDF § 200[1]; *GNTG* III:243; Windisch, 153), but the expression itself never occurs in the LXX, and both Plummer, 137, and Barrett, 145, question whether it really represents the Hebrew idiom *yôm yôm* (e.g., Gen 39:10; Ps 68:20; only once *yôm wāyôm*, Esth 3:4). In any case, Paul's phrase is equivalent to *kath' hekastēn hēmeran,* "every day," and suggests that the renewal he has in mind is not progressively accomplished but is repeated all over again each day. See COMMENT.

17. *For.* Against Plummer, 137, the *gar* here should probably not be interpreted as equivalent to "I mean that," and v. 17 is not simply restating the point of 16*b* in a new way. Rather, the thought of v. 16*a* is being further supported (correctly Bultmann, 129).

*our . . . affliction.* The possessive pronoun is missing from P[46], A, and the Peshitta text, but is adopted by *GNT*-Nestle. On the noun, *affliction (thlipsis),* see NOTES on 1:4.

*momentary.* This adverb *(parautika),* fairly rare, usually signifies something immediate, something "right now" in the present in contrast to something "later on" in the future, so it is sometimes paired with "thereafter" and "then" *(hysteron* and *epeita;* examples in Field 1879:183). In certain contexts the adverb connotes, as well, something of short duration (against Field [ibid.], who claims it means only "for the present" and never "for the moment"); that seems to be the case here, where it is closely associated though not fully identical with *proskaira (temporary)* in v. 18. The English word *momentary* (also used by *RSV*) captures both elements of the Greek adverb. Contrast "the present time" *(ho nyn kairos)* in Rom 8:18, where the temporary nature of the present sufferings is not stressed, even though the overall thought is parallel.

*trifling.* That is, "not heavy." For Paul's use of the neuter singular adjective for an abstract noun *(to elaphron)* see BDF § 263(2). Here it refers to the insignificance of the affliction when that is measured in relation to the incomparably weightier glory which shall be given.

*is bringing about.* This same verb *(katergazesthai)* occurs in two other places— where, as here, the topic is in effect "hope in the midst of suffering." Thus, in Rom 5:3, a "chain syllogism" is initiated with the affirmation that "suffering brings about endurance," and the same verb is to be supplied throughout v. 4, leading to the conclusion of v. 5. The point of Jas 1:2–3 is similar: believers may rejoice in their trials, knowing that the "testing" of their faith "brings about endurance." On the tradition lying behind Rom 5:3–5 and Jas 1:2–4, see Dibelius 1976:74–77. It is very likely the same tradition which has influenced Paul's choice of the verb here, and it is in the light of that tradition that it should be interpreted.

*an absolutely incomparable.* Paul's Greek expression *kath' hyperbolēn eis hyperbolēn* can only be paraphrased in English, and is roughly equivalent to the English idiom "to the nth degree." Hughes, 158 n. 10, believes it may derive from the Hebrew custom of intensifying by means of repetition. See the NOTES on 3:10 and 11:5 (with respect to Paul's use of hyperbolic expressions, especially in 2 Cor), and also on 1:8; 4:7.

*eternal abundance of glory.* Here *abundance* translates *baros* (*RSV:* "weight"); see LSJ s.v. VI. The "heaviness" of the coming glory is thus contrasted with the "lightness" of the present affliction. Some interpreters believe that Paul may have formulated the phrase under the influence of the etymological root of the Hebrew word for "glory" *(kābôd),* which is the verb *kābēd,* "to be heavy" (e.g., Moule 1953:186; Barrett, 148, tentatively), but that is not very likely (see the helpful remarks of Hughes, 157–58 n. 9). Reitzenstein (1978:451), followed by Bultmann, 130, thinks that *baros* derives, rather, from Mandaean (Gnostic) imagery, but the evidence for this suggestion is hardly stronger than for the other.

18. *We do not...* A new English sentence is begun here even though the Greek clause is dependent on what has preceded. The genitive absolute construction *(mē skopoun-tōn hēmōn)* is not strictly grammatical, however, since the subject has been given in the *us (hēmin)* of 17; see BDF § 423(5); *GNTG* IV:99. The effect of the genitive absolute here is to set the present clause somewhat apart from what has gone before, and thus to give it a certain emphasis; see especially Baumert 1973:136. This clause explicates what precedes, and it should not be interpreted as conditional ("if we do not . . ."), causal ("because we do not . . ."), or consecutive ("so that we do not . . ."); correctly Collange, 178; cf. Baumert 1973:136–37. One should not restrict the *we* to Paul, as Baumert (ibid.:138) does ("a literary plural of the author"); see COMMENT.

*focus our attention.* The verb *(skopein)* does not mean "[to] behold" or "[to] contemplate" as in a mystic vision, but "[to] direct one's attention toward" or "[to] be on the alert for." This meaning is clear in every other occurrence of the verb in the Pauline letters: to be on guard with respect to dissidents and troublemakers, Rom 16:17; to watch out lest one fall into temptation, Gal 6:1; to attend to the interests of others, Phil 2:4; to orient one's own conduct in accord with those who follow Paul's example, Phil 3:17. Paul's use of the verb *phronein* ("to set one's mind on") in Rom 8:5 (note the noun in vv. 6, 7) and Phil 3:19 is comparable. In Phil 3:14 the noun *skopos (RSV:* "goal") is used of "the upward call of God in Christ Jesus" *(RSV)* toward which the believer should press on, and Baumert, 137, notes correctly that the element of dedicated striving is also present when Paul uses the verb. See also Bultmann, 131; Hughes, 159 and n. 13.

*the things that are seen . . . that are not seen.* Lietzmann, 117, Windisch, 156, and others make reference to Seneca, *Moral Epistles* LVIII, 27, who echoes the Platonic distinction between things that are perceived by the senses and have only the appearance of reality and things "that really exist." Paul, however, is not questioning the "reality" of *the things that are seen,* but their ultimate significance. Cf. his reference to "earthly things" *(RSV; ta epigeia)* in Phil 3:19 and his contrast of "the things of the flesh" *(ta tēs sarkos)* with "the things of the Spirit" *(ta tou Pneumatos)* in Rom 8:5.

*temporary . . . eternal.* This contrast parallels the one in v. 17 between what is *momentary* and *light* and what is *eternal* and incomparably "heavy" with glory.

5:1. *For.* The introductory *gar* here ties vv. 1–5 closely to 4:17–18 (Meyer, 507; Bultmann, 132). See COMMENT.

*we know.* As in 4:18, the first person plural encompasses all Christians, not just the apostles (Plummer, 141 n.; Bultmann, 131 and 1947:4). Windisch, 158, believes that the expression introduces a teaching generally known and accepted among the Pauline congregations, and Osten-Sacken (1969:105) regards it as one of the indications that Paul is introducing a statement he then proceeds to correct. Collange, 187, thinks the reference is specifically to the saying of Jesus about the destruction of the old temple and the building of a new one "not made with hands" (Mark 14:58; John 2:19).

However, as Barrett, 151, points out, the expression does not require one to suppose that the teaching thus introduced was already familiar to the Corinthians; Paul could mean "We want you to know so and so." For a possible allusion to the temple saying (Mark 14:58, etc.) see below on *destroyed,* and COMMENT.

*if.* The construction here is *ean (if)* with the aorist subjunctive, and Windisch, 159, thinks that because the concessive form is not used (*ean kai,* "although") Paul has come to believe that most of his readers will indeed die before the return of Christ. This would be a change from the apostle's earlier expectation that most believers would be alive at the Parousia (1 Thess 4:13–17). But see the COMMENT.

*earthly.* The Greek adjective is *epigeios,* and in every instance where Paul uses it, it is contrasted with what is "heavenly"; cf. 1 Cor 15:40 (twice); Phil 2:10; 3:19(–20). It does not mean "made of earth" but "belonging to this earthly state" (Hughes, 163 n. 21).

*tent-like house.* Most commentators agree that the genitive *tou skēnous* ("tent") is appositional to *oikia* ("house"). The latter is therefore the dominant word, and that is described further in the appositional phrase; thus the present tr. (Cf. Baumert 1973:144; Lang 1973:183 n. 344.) Apart from this passage (see also v. 4) Paul does not use the word "tent," even though the author of Acts describes him as a *skēnopoios* ("tent maker") by trade (18:3). Since the time of Pythagoras and Plato, the Greek philosophers had often portrayed the physical body as a "tent" temporarily inhabited by the soul (references in Windisch, 158), and it is this kind of anthropological dualism that is reflected in Wis 9:15 (where *skēnos,* "tent," is parallel with "mortal body" [*phtharton sōma*] and is contrasted with the "soul" [*psychē*] and the "mind" [*nous*]; see note on *under a burden,* v. 3, for a further reference to Wis 9:16); cf. 2 Pet 1:13–14 (where the synonym *skēnōma* is used in place of *skēnos*). Some commentators (e.g. Windisch, 158–59) believe that Paul's words in the present passage must be interpreted against just such a Hellenistic background. Others, however, argue that a dualistic anthropology is foreign to Paul's thought, and that the tent imagery must derive in his case from Hebraic traditions—perhaps from Israel's nomadic life in the wilderness (cf. Hughes, 162) or from the Feast of Tabernacles specifically, since the LXX uses the term *skēnē* to translate the Hebrew *sukkāh,* "booth" (Davies 1980:313–14, following up a suggestion first made by Manson 1945:8–9). The quite distinctive view of Wagner (1981) is that Paul here uses the image of the *skēnos* to refer to "the presence of Christ" (150), and that "to be in the tent is to be under the sign of the Risen One" even as "the daily struggle of the earthly life" goes on (152). Hanhart (1969:454) thinks the whole expression here "probably reflects" the scriptural description of the Temple as the "house of the tent" (Tabernacle), which occurs in the LXX as *oikos tēs skēnēs* (1 Chr 9:23) or *skēnē oikou tou Theou* (1 Chr 6:33[48]); cf. Oostendorp 1967:69.

*destroyed.* This compound *(katalyein)* is used by Paul elsewhere only in Rom 14:20; Gal 2:18, in the latter passage as the opposite of *oikodomein,* "to build up" (cf. *oikodomē, building,* in the present verse). This is the first of three words in this verse (the others are *oikodomē* and *acheiropoiētos, not made with hands*) that have counterparts in the dominical saying transmitted in Mark 14:58: "I will destroy [*katalysō*] this temple that is made with hands, and in three days I will build [*oikodomēsō*] another, not made with hands [*acheiropoiēton*]" (*RSV;* cf. Matt 26:61 and John 2:19). Selwyn (1947:290) suggests that this saying was brought to Paul's mind here because of the equation of "temple" and "body" (see especially John 2:21) and "our Lord's reported promise that the destruction of the old temple (or body) would be the signal for His building of the new." Cf. Collange, 184–85.

*we have.* Present tense, *echomen,* although it is often interpreted as a reference to what will be given in the future. In this case the present tense is explained as expressing "religious certainty" about the future (Windisch, 160; cf. Robertson 1923:1019; Hughes, 163 n. 19; Barrett, 151). Bultmann, 134 (following Mundle), thinks that the present tense emphasizes the certainty of possession without referring to any specific time. This would seem to be substantiated by the observations of Lang 1973:182 n. 340: other Pauline examples of *ean* with the aorist subjunctive and the present indicative make what follows dependent on the fulfillment of the condition, and in these cases the present tense seems to be the sign of an axiomatic formulation (Rom 7:2–3; 1 Cor 7:39; 8:8; 14:23; 15:36). Thus, here the logical conclusion is emphasized: it is certain that if the *earthly, tent-like house should be destroyed,* a heavenly house is given.

*a building from God.* Collange, 191, construes *ek Theou* with *echomen* (thus, "we have from God a building . . ."), arguing that there is a polemical nuance here. But the word order is against this, and virtually all other commentators connect *ek Theou* with *oikodomē,* as in the present tr. (see, e.g., Bachmann, 217; Plummer, 143; Windisch, 159). As in 1 Cor 2:12 the Spirit which is *from God* is opposed to that which is "of the world" *(tou kosmou),* so here the *building* which is *from God* is distinguished from that *tent-like house* which is *earthly* (Windisch, 159). The biblical account, according to which human beings exist precisely as God's creation from the dust of the ground (Gen 2:7), is not within the apostle's purview here. His single point is to affirm the certainty that life is not restricted to one's mortal existence.

*building . . . house.* These two words *(oikodomē* and *oikia)* are used synonymously here, although it is true that the first usually connotes more the act or process of building *(oikodomein)* while the second refers more to the result (Plummer, 143), and thus to an inhabited building where a family dwells (see, e.g., 1 Cor 11:22; also 1 Cor 16:15; Phil 4:22, where the inhabitants themselves are in view—thus *RSV*'s tr., "household"; contrast Plummer, 145, who distinguishes *oikia* from *oikētērion,* v. 2, because the latter "implies . . . an inhabitant" while the former does not). In every other instance where Paul uses the noun *building* it has an ecclesiological reference (10:8; 12:19; 13:10; Rom 14:19; 15:12; 1 Cor 14:3, 5, 12, 26), and that is also the case with most instances of the verbal forms *(oikodomein,* e.g., 1 Cor 8:1; 14:4, 17; *epoikodomein,* 1 Cor 3:10, 12, 14). See especially 1 Cor 3:9, "You are a building of God" *(Theou oikodomē).* Thus, J. A. T. Robinson 1952:75–79, followed by Ellis 1960:217–19, interprets *building* here as a reference to the corporate Body of Christ and not, in the anthropological sense, to one's individual resurrection body. (Against this, Gundry 1976:149–51.)

Most interpreters believe that the imagery of the present passage is anthropological rather than ecclesiological, and the *building* (or *house) from God* is thus taken as a reference to the believer's resurrection body (e.g., Meyer, 507–8; Hughes, 165; Collange, 191). Vielhauer (1979:32–35) cites Mandaean texts which employ the building metaphor in describing one's earthly body, but there is no instance where it is used of the heavenly body of an individual (see Lang 1973:181). Qumran does supply at least one instance where the building metaphor is applied to an individual (as contrasted with its frequent use for the community), but there is no anthropological dualism of "body" and "soul" involved there (1QH vii.4–5, 8–9, cited by Rissi 1969:75; the "heart" as well as the "bones" of the human "edifice" are mentioned, Vermes 1975:172), and the image itself has an essentially collective, not individualistic reference (the "edifice" is planted within "the Council of Holiness," Vermes 1975:173); see Lang 1973:180.

*not made with hands.* The adjective *(acheiropoiētos)* appears elsewhere in the NT only in Mark 14:58 (see note above on *destroyed*) and Col 2:11 (with reference to Christian baptism as a "circumcision made without hands" [*RSV*]), but there are further instances of *cheiropoiētos* ("made with hands") used with the negative *ou* ("not") which convey the same idea: God does not dwell in temples "made with hands" (Acts 17:24; cf. 7:48 and 1 Kgs 8:27–30), and Christ does not enter into a sanctuary "made with hands," but (through a "tent not made with hands," Heb 9:11) he goes into heaven itself (Heb 9:24). The adjective, then, describes what is "supernatural, immaterial, spiritual" (Plummer, 144).

*eternal in the heavens.* A further description of the *building from God.* Cf. the use of the adjective *eternal* in 4:17, 18, the only other instances in 2 Cor.

2. *Also, indeed.* With this expression *(kai gar)* an additional point is being introduced. For a detailed justification of the tr. adopted here see Baumert 1973: Excursus G, 350–80, especially 379.

*in view of this.* The meaning of the Greek phrase here, *en toutō* (literally "in this"), is not altogether clear. A number of commentators (e.g., Plummer, 144–45; Windisch, 161; Barrett, 152) regard it as equivalent to *hoi ontes en tō skēnei (while we are in the tent)* in v. 4, in which case the antecedent of the pronoun would in effect be *tou skēnous (tent)* in v. 1; thus *NEB:* "in this present body." (Cf. *JB:* "in this present state.") Similarly, but with a more general reference to v. 1, other recent English versions render the phrase as "here" *(RSV)*, "now" *(TEV)*, or "while we are here" *(NAB)*. Hughes, 167 n. 27, argues that it should be treated independently of v. 1 and rendered "meanwhile" (so *NIV*). Yet a third possibility, and the one adopted here, is to regard *en toutō* as causal (cf. 1 Cor 4:4): "because of the knowledge we have about 'a building from God' " (v. 1). So Denney, 174–75; Bultmann, 136; Danker 1968:553; Lang 1973:196 and n. 377. (Cf. Gdspd. and Mof.: "This [It] makes me . . .")

*we are sighing.* The verb *(stenazein)* is used again in v. 4. In the present context it does not mean "groaning" with doubt or agony (e.g., because one continues to be burdened by the earthly body, as J. Schneider suggests, *TDNT* VII:601). Here it is the *sighing* which comes from a hopeful longing for something (thus *because we long . . . ;* see following note); correctly Barrett, 152; Lang 1973:197. The verb is used elsewhere by Paul only in Rom 8:23, in which context he also employs the compound form *systenazein* ("to sigh together with"), v. 22, and the noun *stenagmos* (a "sigh"), v. 26. Collange, 202, emphasizes the similarities between Rom 8:18–27 and the present passage, and notes in particular that it is not the sighing of unrelieved distress that Paul writes of there, but the sighing of a pain charged with hope (see Rom 8:23–25), like that of a woman in childbirth (Rom 8:22, *systenazei kai synōdinei* ["groaning in travail together," *RSV*]; cf. LXX Jer 4:31). So also Wagner 1981:157.

*because we long.* This tr. of the participle *epipothountes* interprets it causally (so Bultmann, 136; Baumert 1973:169), although it is also possible to regard it as expressing the content of the *sighing* (e.g., *NAB* ["even as we yearn"] and most recent English versions). In either case, the use of this verb here shows that the *sighing* Paul thinks of is not of despair, but of hope (see preceding note). The verb *(epipothein)* and its cognates *(epipothēsis* and *epipothia,* "longing"; *epipothētos,* "longed for") are found, in the NT, almost exclusively in the Pauline letters, and most often with reference to a longing to see (be with) someone (e.g., 7:7, 11; 9:14; Rom 1:11; 15:23; Phil 2:26; 1 Thess 3:6).

*to clothe ourselves over.* Translates the fairly rare (Windisch, 161 n. 1) compound form of the verb *endyesthai,* "to clothe oneself," "to put on [a garment]" (the latter is used in 1 Cor 15:53–54). The lexical evidence (summarized by Hughes, 168 n. 31) suggests that this compound form, *ep-endyesthai* (present here as an aorist infinitive), has the distinct meaning of "to put on over," to clothe oneself with some additional garment (BAG s.v.). Bultmann, 136 (and 1947:11), argues that *ependyesthai* is here equivalent to the simple form *endyesthai;* note the contrast between *ekdyesthai* ("to unclothe oneself") and *ependyesthai* in v. 4 (cf. Tasker, 79). This argument, however, really has no force (e.g., Hughes, 168 n. 31, and Barrett, 152 [cf. 156], argue to the contrary that v. 4 confirms an intended distinction between the simple and compound forms), especially if (to be sure, against Bultmann) one accepts the well-attested reading *endysamenoi* in v. 3 (see note below). In this case, Paul's use of the rarer compound form in vv. 2 and 4 and the more common simple form in v. 3 looks deliberate. In any event, it is important to note that Paul now makes a transition from the imagery of a heavenly house to that of a heavenly garment. The latter imagery is widespread in Jewish apocalyptic texts (e.g., 1 Enoch 62:15–16 ["garments of glory . . . of life"]; 1QS iv.7–8 ["eternal joy in life without end, a crown of glory and a garment of majesty in unending light," Vermes 1975:76]; cf. 2 Enoch 22:8), as well as in later Jewish and Christian (Gnostic) literature (e.g., Odes Sol 25:8; 2 Esdr 2:45; As Isa 7:22; 8:14, 26; 9:2, 9, 17, 24–26; 11:40; numerous Mandaean references are provided by Héring, 37 n. 4). See further Lietzmann, 119–20 (who also refers to Apuleius, *Metamorphoses* XI, 23–24), and Windisch, 164–65.

*our dwelling which comes from heaven.* This phrase continues the house imagery of v. 1, the word *oikētērion (dwelling;* cf. Jude 6; 2 Mac 11:2; 1 Enoch 27:2 [Greek version]) being used synonymously with *oikodomē (building)* and *oikia (house).* Thus the prepositional phrase *ex ouranou* (literally "from [out of] heaven") is parallel with *ek Theou* (from God) and *aiōniōn en tois ouranois (eternal in the heavens)* in the preceding verse.

3. *presupposing, of course.* The Greek phrase *ei ge* is followed by *kai,* as in Gal 3:4, but the three words should not be treated as one expression *(ei ge kai),* as they are by some; the *ge* strengthens the preceding conjunction, while the *kai* emphasizes what follows (see Baumert 1973:188). The meaning of Gal 3:4 is itself problematic (Baumert, ibid.:386), but even if Paul is there introducing a point he presumes, or at least hopes, is not true (that the Galatians have believed "in vain" [*RSV*]), that is not the case in the present passage. Here *ei ge* followed by *kai* introduces a point the apostle believes ought to be (even though it may not always be) presupposed (detailed support for this conclusion in Thrall 1962:86–91 and Baumert 1973: Excursus H, 380–85). Hughes (169 n. 32), Barrett (149 n. 1), and Baumert (1973:385–86) think the variant reading *eiper* (P⁴⁶ B D F G, etc.) may be original, which would imply even more strongly the validity of the presupposition.

*having once clothed ourselves.* GNT-Nestle adopt *ekdysamenoi* ("having once unclothed ourselves") as the original reading here (see also Reitzenstein 1978:452–53 and Weiss 1959:535 n. 19), even though the external attestation for that is extremely weak (only D*, Tertullian, and a few other texts). The editors themselves accord it a probability rating of only D (on their scale of A to D), but they adopt it, nonetheless, because they believe the better-attested *endysamenoi* yields a thought so banal as to be tautologous—"when we have been clothed we will not be naked" (see Metzger 1971:579–80). This is also the argument of Bultmann, 137 and 1947:11. But the external support for the reading adopted here (and by most recent commentators) is very strong (P⁴⁶ B C D², etc.), and the variant *ekdysamenoi* is well enough explained as "an early alteration to avoid apparent tautology" (Metzger 1971:580—his own view). Moreover, the thought—*having once clothed ourselves* [*once* is added to bring out the force of the aorist tense] *we shall not be found naked*—is not necessarily a tautology; see COMMENT.

*we shall not be found.* The verb *heuriskein* (here future passive) is often used to indicate "the result of a judicial investigation" (BAG s.v. 2): e.g., Acts 13:28; 23:9; 24:20; 2 Pet 3:10. This forensic connotation is also present in 1 Cor 4:2 (cf. v. 4); 15:15; Gal 2:17; 2 Pet 3:14—where, as here, the passive form is followed by a predicate adjective or nominative (here, "naked"; see Lang 1973:188). Collange, 210–11, following Bonnard, compares especially Phil 3:9, where the word has to do with what is "found" before God at the last judgment. In the present context, cf. v. 10.

*naked.* Paul uses the same adjective *(gymnos)* in 1 Cor 15:37, otherwise only the noun *gymnotēs* ("nakedness," 11:27; Rom 8:35, both in lists of his apostolic hardships) and the verb *gymniteuein* ("to be naked," 1 Cor 4:11, likewise in a list of hardships). In the Greek and Hellenistic philosophical tradition, as well as in various Hellenistic religious texts, the adjective was frequently applied to the soul, stripped of the physical body and thus free for a higher destiny; representative passages in Barrett, 153–54. The theme is present as well in Christian Gnostic texts of the second and third centuries: e.g., Gos Thom (CG II, 2) 39,27–36 (*NHLE*, 122)—cf. 36,34–37,19 (*NHLE*, 120) and POxy 655, lines 17–23—and Gos Phil (CG II, 3) 56,24–57,22 (*NHLE*, 134–35), in which Pagels 1975:98–99 finds an allusion to 2 Cor 5:3–4. Many interpreters believe that Paul himself is showing the influence of this Hellenistic dualism when he writes, in 1 Cor 15:37–38, of the *gymnos kokkos* ("naked kernel") which is sown at death and raised with a new "spiritual" body. On this basis, then, the apostle's reference to nakedness in the present passage is taken as a reflection of his fear that there could be a period of "bodilessness" between one's death and the resurrection of the dead at the Parousia (e.g., Sevenster 1953:207; Barrett, 154–55). Others (notably Ellis 1960; cf. Baumert 1973:175–79) argue that Paul is not using the term "naked" in an anthropological way here, but soteriologically, perhaps for a sense of moral shame and guilt at the last judgment (so Ellis 1960:219–21, citing numerous OT and Jewish texts in support of such a meaning, and Rissi 1969:92). Hanhart (1969:455–56) thinks that Paul is here using the adjective *naked* as a virtual synonym of the adjectives *kenos* ("vain") and *mataios* ("futile") which he uses elsewhere, and he compares with the present verse Gal 3:3–4 and 1 Cor 15:14–15 especially. One's decision in the matter requires an understanding of the passage as a whole, as well as clarity about the alleged parallel in 1 Cor 15:37; see COMMENT.

4. *Indeed.* The introductory words in Greek are *kai gar*, as in v. 2, but their function here is somewhat different. Rather than being used to introduce an additional point,

they essentially reiterate the point already made in v. 2; cf. Baumert 1973: Excursus G, 350–80, especially 379.

*in this tent.* Literally "in the tent," referring to the *tent-like house (oikia tou skēnous)* mentioned in v. 1; on the anaphoric use of the article here, see Robertson 1923:762.

*we are sighing.* As in v. 2, although Plummer, 148, disputes this, claiming that here the reference is to "groaning" in a more negative sense—i.e., caused by the fear of dying before Christ's return and thus being left "naked" in the interim. But see COMMENT. The first person plural continues to include all Christians; see NOTES on 4:18 and 5:1.

*under a burden.* This English tr. is a paraphrase of the present participle *baroumenoi,* which should be interpreted here as circumstantial, not causal (correctly M. Harris 1974:321 n. 21): thus, not "we are sighing because we are burdened." Cf. Paul's use of the same verb *(barein)* earlier in this letter to describe how he had been "exceedingly burdened" with an affliction in Asia (1:8). The meaning of the word is well illustrated by Epictetus I.xxv.17, where *baroumenos* ("being burdened") is closely associated with *thlibomenos* ("being afflicted"; cf. 1:6 and 4:8 in the present letter) and *hypolambanōn en kakois einai* ("supposing oneself to be in a bad way"). Some would punctuate between the preceding verb *(stenazomen)* and the participle, thus taking the latter with what follows ("we are oppressed because we do not want . . ." [NEB]; "we are weighed down because we do not wish . . ." [*NAB*]). However, it is more natural to associate the participle closely with the preceding verb as describing the condition under which the sighing takes place. The related verb *barynein* occurs in Wis 9:15, a text which, because of its general content, is sometimes thought to be in Paul's mind as he writes here (so, e.g., Plummer, 148): "a perishable body weighs down the soul [*barynei psychēn*], / and this tent of clay encumbers a mind full of cares" (Winston 1979:206). A number of other instances where this and similar words are so used are given by Winston (ibid.). But Paul's thought is moving along different lines, and one must not conclude too quickly that he shares the Platonic view reflected in Wis and other Hellenistic literature (see NOTES on v. 1 as well as COMMENT on 4:7, 17; 5:2–4).

*because.* Translates *eph' hō,* used in the NT only by Paul: here and in Rom 5:12; Phil 3:12; 4:10. Its meaning is disputed, although most commentators and grammarians believe it stands for *epi toutō hoti* and therefore should be translated causally, "for the reason that" or "because"; see BDF § 235(2) and § 294(4) and cf. Robertson 1923:604, 963; *GNTG* I:107 ("in view of the fact that"); III:272; Moule 1953:132 ("inasmuch as"). Thrall 1962:93–94 has dissented from this consensus, holding that the phrase means "on condition that," as in classical usage. The clause thus introduced would become "a caution against the kind of Gnosticism which regarded the disembodied state as the ideal, and so would misunderstand the preceding reference to physical weariness" (ibid.:94; followed by Danker 1968:552). But there are no instances of this meaning where, as here, *eph' hō* is followed by a verb in the present tense (here, *ou thelomen, we do not wish*), and it is doubtful that the use of a verb of wishing is equivalent to the future tense used invariably in the classical construction (as Thrall claims, 1962:94; against her view, Barrett, 155–56). Hanhart (1969:457) translates the phrase as "yet," but also without any clear lexical support. Baumert (1973:195 and Excursus I, 386–401) argues at length that the *eph' hō* must stand for *epi toutō hō,* the *hō* of Paul's phrase being an instance of the attraction of the case of the relative pronoun to that of an unexpressed antecedent. Then the meaning would be "on the basis of that which" (ibid.:195). But this amounts to the same thing as the usual view.

*to unclothe ourselves.* The verb is *ekdyesthai,* and except for the reading of a few texts in v. 3 (see NOTES there) it appears nowhere else in the Pauline letters. Here it is used as the opposite of *ependyesthai* (see following note), this being rather like the use of *gymnoi (naked)* as the opposite of *endyesthai* ("to clothe oneself") in v. 3; see Collange, 220.

*to clothe ourselves over.* As in v. 2, the compound form *ep-endyesthai* is used, so the meaning is not just "to clothe oneself" (*endyesthai,* v. 3) but to put something on "over" something that is already being worn; see note on the occurrence of this word in v. 2.

*mortality.* The adjective *(thnētos)* is used in the NT only by Paul, and always with reference to the mortal body (*sōma,* Rom 6:12; 8:11) or flesh (*sarx,* 2 Cor 4:11) subject to suffering (2 Cor 4:11), sin (Rom 6:12), and death (Rom 8:11). In 1 Cor 15:53, 54, as well as here, Paul uses the neuter substantive *to thnēton.* There (parallel with *to phtharton,* what is "perishable" [*RSV*]) it stands opposite *athanasia,* "immortality" (the same contrast as in Philo, *Eternity of the World* 46), just as here it stands opposite *life.* Elsewhere in the present passage *mortality* is described as *earthen pots* (4:7), *mortal flesh* (4:11; = *our bodies,* 4:10), *our outer person* (4:16), *our earthly tent-like house* (5:1), *this tent* (5:4). It clearly belongs among those *things that are seen* and *temporary* (4:18).

*engulfed.* The verb is *katapinein,* translated *overwhelmed* in 2:7, although to "drink down" or "swallow up" is the more literal meaning. The only other Pauline use of the verb comes in 1 Cor 15:54, where the apostle cites as scriptural the saying "Death has been swallowed up in victory." The biblical passage in question must be Isa 25:8, although it is unclear what text Paul is citing, or whether indeed he himself has altered the LXX text (where the verb *katapinein* also occurs, but in the active voice and with "death" as its subject); on the problems see Orr and Walther 1976:350–51. Cf. Rev 20:14, where it is said that the fate of Death and Hades will be to be "thrown into the lake of fire" at the End, there to be destroyed, although the word "drowned" is not actually used. In Treat Res (CG I, *3*) 45,14–46,2 (*NHLE,* 51) a Christian Gnostic develops the idea of death being "swallowed up" by life, and a similar metaphor (death "eaten up" by life) is involved in Gos Truth (CG II, *2*) 25,15–19 (*NHLE,* 41).

*by life.* The preposition used here is not *eis* as in 1 Cor 15:54 (*eis nikos,* "in [or: for] victory") but *hypo, by. Life* is here contrasted with *mortality,* and thus refers to "immortality" (cf. *athanasia = aphtharsia,* contrasted to mortality and perishability, respectively, in 1 Cor 15:53–54), that is, "eternal life" (the latter phrase, associated with "imperishability" [*aphtharsia*] in Rom 2:7, also occurs in Rom 5:21; 6:22; 6:23; Gal 6:8).

*5a. The one who equipped us.* Here *(ho de katergasamenos hēmas)* the *de* is merely "continuative" (Meyer, 516) and may be left untranslated. The Western reading *katergazomenos* (present tense) is certainly secondary, perhaps influenced by 4:17 and thus interpreting Paul to mean that present afflictions lead to eternal life; see Bertram, *TDNT* III:635. The reference is of course to *God,* but this does not appear to be a standard formula (Delling 1963:27 n. 5). The participle (*katergasamenos;* on the aorist tense see COMMENT) is formed from *katergazesthai,* used in 4:17 (see note) and in 7:10, 11; 9:11; 12:12 (also in 1 Cor 5:3; eleven times in Rom). Here it is used in the sense of "to prepare or equip [someone *(us)*]" for something (see following note). Bertram,

*TDNT* III:634, notes that the verb is used in some such sense in LXX Exod 15:17 and Ps 67(68):29(28). Windisch, 164, cites the use of the verb *kataskeuazein* (which can also mean "to prepare or equip," cf. BAG s.v. 3) by Epictetus III.xxiv.63: "But it is not becoming for us to be unhappy on any person's account, but to be happy because of all, and especially because of God, who equipped us for this [*dia ton Theon ton epi touto hēmas kataskeuasanta*]."

*for this very thing.* Translates *eis auto touto;* cf. *epi touto,* "for this," in the quotation from Epictetus given in the preceding note. As in Rom 13:6, the phrase refers to a point just mentioned: there, paying taxes; here, *mortality* being *engulfed by life* (v. 4). The expression is used in the same way in Eph 6:22, par. Col 4:8.

*God.* The predicate position and its placement at the end of the sentence gives special emphasis here to *God;* cf. 1:21. In Rom 5:3–5, as well as here (and finally also in 4:17; Phil 2:12–13), it is the working *(katergazesthai)* of *God* by which hope is fulfilled and salvation is accomplished (Bertram, *TDNT* III:635).

*5b. who gave to us.* The participle here, like those in vv. 3 and 5*a*, is aorist tense; see COMMENT. Cf. 1:22, *gave . . . in our hearts (dous . . . en tais kardiais hēmōn;* here, *dous hēmin).*

*the Spirit as a down payment.* The same phrase *(ton arrabōna tou Pneumatos)* and construction (the direct object of *dous, gave*) as in 1:22. See note there on *down payment (arrabōn).* In both places *tou Pneumatos* ("of the Spirit") is a genitive of apposition; *the Spirit* itself is the *down payment.*

*6. Therefore.* This connective particle *(oun)* seems to have a double function here. On the one hand, it introduces the resumption of the thought of 4:16*a* (see Lang 1973:198)—and thus of 4:1 (see following note); on the other, it also serves to introduce what follows from everything that has been affirmed since then, in 4:16*b*–5:5, and not just in 5:5 (e.g., Lang ibid.) or in 5:1–5 (e.g., Bultmann, 141). Cf. Collange, 228.

*having confidence.* The verb *(tharrein)* is used by Paul only in 2 Cor (also v. 8; 7:16; 10:1, 2), and elsewhere in the NT only in Heb 13:6. In Epictetus II.i, *confidence* is commended along with "caution" *(eulabeia),* and the two are also linked by Philo, *Who Is the Heir* 22, where *eulabeia* means "reverence" for the divine sovereignty and will (Attridge 1979:93). Note especially Epictetus II.i.38–39, where, after urging the importance of practicing "how to die, how to be enchanted, how to be racked, how to be exiled" (cf. 2 Cor 4:8–9), Epictetus continues: "Do all these things with confidence [*tharrountōs*], with trust [*pepoithotōs*] in Him who has called you to face them and deemed you worthy of this position, in which having once been placed you shall exhibit what can be achieved by a rational governing principle [*logikon hēgemonikon*] when arrayed against the forces that lie outside the province of the moral purpose." The word "confidence" is closely related in meaning to both *pepoithēsis,* "trust" (here in Letter D at 1:15; 3:4; 8:22; cf. the use of *peithein* in 1:9), and *parrēsia,* "boldness" (as in 3:12; in Philo, *Who Is the Heir* 19, both words occur). Cf. *ouk enkakoumen, we do not shrink back,* in 4:1, 16. Schmithals (1971:269) suggests that Paul has used the verb *tharrein* in the present verse in deliberate antithesis to the boasted "reigning" *(basileuein)* of the Corinthian "Gnostics" (1 Cor 4:8), while Rissi (1969:93–94) holds that he has taken the word over from his opponents, who have in fact accused him of lacking courage (cf. 10:1–2).

*always.* The word is *pantote,* as in 4:10. Plummer, 150, interprets thus: " 'in every event,' whether we die soon or live till the Lord returns, we have this confidence." But see the COMMENT.

*and knowing.* Barrett, 157, gives the participle *(eidotes)* a causal meaning and renders it as "since we know." But this ignores the conjunction *and (kai),* which seems to require one to take *knowing* as co-ordinate with *having confidence.* Schmithals (1971: 269) believes that this participle, like *oidamen (we know)* in v. 1, introduces a fact that the "Gnostics" in Corinth have disputed.

*at home.* The literal meaning of the verb *(endēmein)* is "to be at home with one's own people"; see Grundmann, *TDNT* II:63–64. Cf. the use of *menein* ("to remain") and its compounds *(epimenein* and *paramenein)* in Phil 1:24, 25.

*in the body.* This phrase *(en tō sōmati)* is equivalent to "in the tent" *(en tē skēnei),* v. 4 (cf. *our earthly, tent-like house,* v. 1), and *sōma (body)* here is parallel to *mortality* in v. 4 just as *sōma* in 4:10 was parallel to *our mortal flesh* in 4:11. Cf. also "in the flesh," Phil 1:22, 24.

*away from our home with the Lord.* The Greek phrase is *ekdēmoumen apo tou Kyriou,* which could also be rendered simply as "away from the Lord." The present tr., however, seeks to exhibit the antithetical use of *at home* and *away from home,* and in so doing must insert the English word *our* for the sake of clarity. *Ekdēmein* means literally "to leave one's own country," or "to go on a long journey," and is thus a synonym of the more frequent *apodēmein* (see Grundmann, *TDNT* II:63) used in the Synoptic Gospels (and in place of *ekdēmein* in a few mss. of the present verse). Cf. the use of *eis to analysai* ("to depart") in Phil 1:23. In *Special Laws* IV, 142, Philo also pairs the two words *endēmein/ekdēmein,* using them both in the literal sense: "to stay at home"/"to leave home." Note especially T Abr XV, 23–25[A], where Michael says to Abraham: "Make disposition concerning everything which you have for the day has come on which you are destined to depart from the body [*ek tou sōmatos ekdēmein*] and yet one more time to come to the Lord [*kai eti hapax pros ton Kyrion erchesthai*]" (Stone 1972:38, 39).

*the Lord.* Christ, as in Phil 1:23. With the phrase *apo tou Kyriou,* "(away) from the Lord," compare *apo tou Christou,* "(cut off) from Christ," in Rom 9:3.

7. *for.* In this instance *for (gar)* introduces a clarification of what has been said in v. 6*b.* In so doing, however, it also interrupts both the syntax and the thought; see NOTES on v. 8 and COMMENT.

*we conduct ourselves.* The verb is *peripatein,* as in 4:2. See the two following notes.

*according to.* The preposition *dia* ("through") can be variously interpreted: e.g., as designating the agency (thus virtually equivalent to *hypo,* "by"—*RSV, JB, NAB, NIV*), or the manner (thus equivalent to *en,* "in"—Mof.; Bultmann, 142, compares to this the use of *dia* in 2:4). Baumert 1973:230–31 argues for the meaning "in the realm of." This is the only place where Paul has used *dia* with the verb *peripatein;* elsewhere he uses *en* (4:2; 10:3; Rom 6:4) or *kata,* "according to" (10:2; Rom 8:4; 14:15; 1 Cor 3:3). The latter sense fits the context well, and so does Barrett's "on the basis of" (149, = *ek,* "out of"). (Elsewhere in Paul's letters, *dia* [*tēs*] *pisteōs,* "through faith," is found in Rom 3:22, 25, 30, 31; Gal 2:16; 3:14, 26; Phil 3:9.)

*faith.* The noun occurs only six other times in 2 Cor (1:24, twice; 4:13; 8:7; 10:15; 13:5), and the verb only twice (4:13). Here *faith* is contrasted with *eidos,* which must have the passive meaning *appearance* (see following note). Thus it is likely that faith, too, should be understood in a passive sense here, as *fides quae creditur,* that which is believed; so also Baumert 1973:230 (cf. Lang 1973:191 n. 362). The same meaning is present at least in Rom 10:8 and Gal 1:23; and Bultmann, *TDNT* VI:213, also lists Gal 3:2, 5. Various Pauline descriptions of the proper course of the believer's life *(peripatein)* occur elsewhere: "according to" *(kata)* love (Rom 14:15), in the Spirit (Rom 8:4; Gal 5:16; cf. 2 Cor 12:18), in newness of life (Rom 6:4), in accord with God's call (1 Cor 7:17; 1 Thess 2:12), circumspectly *(euschēmonōs;* Rom 13:13; 1 Thess 4:12), and with reference to the behavior of the apostle (Phil 3:17; 1 Thess 4:1). For the negative side see note at 4:2.

*appearance.* Translates *eidos,* which usually, if not always, has a passive meaning— that is, "form" or "outward appearance" (BAG s.v. 1), not the act of seeing. The instances of the latter given in BAG s.v. 3 are questionable; LSJ (s.v.) give no examples of an active meaning. Correctly, e.g., Hughes, 176 n. 52; Collange, 231–32; Barrett, 159; Baumert 1973:227–28; Lang 1973:190. LXX Num 12:8 may stand behind 1 Cor 13:12, but (against Windisch, 167) neither passage offers a true parallel to the present verse, and the LXX passage is not properly adduced (despite BAG s.v.; Rissi 1969:95) as an instance of *eidos* with an active meaning (correctly Lang 1973:190 n. 361). There is a certain correspondence between this verse and Rom 8:24–25, where Paul distinguishes between what is "seen" *(blepomenē,* cf. *eidos* in the present verse) and hope's true object, which is "not seen." Most of all, however, the contrast between *appearance* and *faith* is illuminated by the contrast earlier in this same passage between *the things that are seen* and those *that are not seen* (4:18); see COMMENT.

8. *we do have confidence.* Here *tharroumen de* repeats in a grammatically altered form the *tharrountes oun (Therefore, having confidence)* of v. 6a. Perhaps under the influence of the verb form in v. 7, Paul discards the participial construction of v. 6 and in effect begins all over again. The *de* is not adversative (against Bultmann, 143–44) but resumptive (Robertson 1923:1135)—thus the "I say" of *JB* and *NIV* and the "I repeat" of *NEB, NAB.* This is represented in the present tr. by the word *do,* which at the same time helps to convey the emphasis given to *confidence* by virtue of its position in v. 6 and its repetition here.

*we are resolved instead.* The Greek is *eudokoumen mallon,* which many commentators and most recent English versions regard as the expression of a preference ("would rather"—*RSV, NEB;* "would prefer"—*NIV*), perhaps a strong one ("would much rather"—*NAB;* "would much prefer"—*TEV*). Against this, however, one may note that *eudokein* with the infinitive (as in this verse) regularly means that one determines by deliberate choice to do something (Shrenk, *TDNT* II:738–42; Baumert 1973:233–34; Lang 1973:192–93). The construction in Sir 25:16 is different because the comparative particle *ē* is used; but even there a decision is involved, not just a subjective preference. The same is true in Polybius XXI, 23.8, where the construction is *eudokein,* plus a dative, plus *mallon ē;* see Lang 1973:193 n. 368. Here, preceded by the negative *not according to appearance* (v.7), the *mallon* is best regarded as having an adversative sense: "We do not conduct ourselves according to appearance; rather, we are determined to . . ." (cf. Lang ibid.).

*to get away from being at home.* The verb here is the same as the one in v. 6b, translated *away from our home;* but there Paul had used the present tense, while here he uses the aorist *(ekdēmēsai).* This should probably be interpreted as an ingressive aorist, thus focusing on the inception of the action (on the usage in general see Robertson 1923:834; BDF § 331). The English, somewhat awkwardly, seeks to exhibit this. The point here is not "being away" from home (as in v. 6b), but "leaving" home; cf. Grundmann, *TDNT* II:63; Lang 1973:192.

*in the body.* The Greek is actually "away from the body" *(ek tou sōmatos),* but the tr. adopted for *ekdēmēsai* (see preceding note) requires further paraphrase here. For the meaning of *sōma, body,* see note on v. 6.

*to get on home.* The present tense of v. 6b, *endēmountes (while we are at home),* has now been replaced by the aorist *(endēmēsai),* and this should be taken as ingressive. See note above on *to get away from being at home,* and also the following note.

*to the Lord.* Not "with the Lord," as in virtually all the English versions. In consideration of its use with the ingressive aorist *endēmēsai* (see preceding note), *pros* with the accusative *(ton Kyrion)* should here be given its frequent meaning (see BAG s.v. III, 1b, c) of "going" or "moving toward" something (against Moule 1953:52–53, who lists this occurrence as an instance of a "punctiliar" meaning, and Rex 1958:75, who thinks Paul is writing about "a union with the Lord at the hour of death which is complete in every respect"). Lang (1973:192 n. 366) contrasts "being with Christ" *(syn Christō einai)* in Phil 1:23, where the issue is different. See COMMENT.

9. *Accordingly.* Translates *dio kai.* Where, as here, the inferential conjunction is strengthened with the addition of *kai* (elsewhere in Paul at 1:20; 4:13 [but the construction is somewhat different]; Rom 4:22; 15:22; Phil 2:9), the inference is presented as self-evident; BAG s.v.; BDF § 442(12); 451(5). Contrary to the view of Bachmann, 240 (followed by Baumert 1973:243–44), a new section is not opened here. Nor is the thesis of vv. 6–8 ignored (Schmithals 1971:273; note Héring's erroneous tr. *mais* ["yet," 37]). Rather, the conjunctive phrase continues the preceding discussion by introducing its climax. See following note and COMMENT.

*whether . . . or.* Paul is fond of joining comparable ideas with *eite . . . eite,* "whether (this) or whether (that)" (10 times in the Corinthian letters alone). Note in addition the similar use of *ean te . . . ean te* twice in Rom 14:8. Apart from the Pauline and deutero-Pauline letters the usage occurs in the NT only in 1 Pet 2:13–14. The device serves well to sum up and conclude a point (e.g., 1 Cor 12:26; 15:11; Phil 1:18, 20; 1 Thess 5:10; also 1 Cor 10:31, a series of *eite*'s, and 10:31, triple *eite*). Against the view of Bachmann (see preceding note), it may be observed that the expression is used in only one instance to help introduce a new point (Phil 1:27).

*at home . . . away from home.* The terms *(endēmein/ekdēmein)* with which Paul has been working since v. 6 are repeated, and, as in that verse, in the present tense (see above for the significance of the aorist in v. 8). Whether in the present verse Paul is orienting his remark to life in/away from the body (so Plummer, 154–55; Windisch, 169, and most other commentators) or to life with/away from the Lord is unclear; see COMMENT.

*we make it our ambition.* The verb is *philotimeisthai,* elsewhere in the NT only at Rom 15:20; 1 Thess 4:11. Plummer, 154, compares it to Paul's use of *spoudazein,* "to be eager [or: zealous]" to do something (Gal 2:10; 1 Thess 2:17)—but that term places greater emphasis on the (subjective) resolve; this one, on the aim or goal. In this context it is, in a sense, the positive counterpart of "not focusing our attention on" *(mē skopountōn),* 4:18.

*acceptable.* Or "pleasing." This adjective *(euarestos)* and the verb *areskein,* "to be pleasing," are virtually synonymous when Paul writes of what is pleasing to God *(euarestos,* Rom 12:1–2; 14:18; Phil 4:18; *areskein,* Rom 8:8; 1 Thess 2:15; 4:1) or the Lord *(euarestos,* here; *areskein,* 1 Cor 7:32, 33). Philo *(On the Virtues* 67) remarks that one who is pleasing to God *(ho euarestos)* must be of good character.

10. *For.* The *gar* introduces what follows as further support for the ethical appeal implicit in the preceding statement (v. 9); cf. Synofzik 1977:74.

*we all.* The use of the article in the Greek phrase *tous pantas hēmas* indicates the "sum total" is contrasted with the part; BDF § 275(7); *GNTG* III:201. Thus "we the whole number of us" (Robertson 1923:773)—but meaning not all human beings universally but, in accord with the context, all Christians; cf., e.g., Bachmann, 242; Mattern 1966:155.

*must.* Translates *dei,* often used in solemn affirmations about what is divinely ordained, especially at the eschatological day; see also 1 Cor 15:25, 53. Elsewhere, e.g., LXX Dan 2:28, 29, 45; Matt 16:21 and par.; 24:6 and par.; Rev 1:1; 4:1; 22:6.

*appear.* A passive form (aorist) of the verb *phaneroun* (see note on *manifests,* 2:14), rendered here as intransitive, although it might also be understood transitively—e.g., "to be seen (for what we are)"; *GAGNT* 1979:544. In Rom 14:10 a middle form of *paristanein,* to "come" or "stand before," is used in a similar way; cf. Acts 27:24 (to stand before Caesar) and see the NOTES on 4:14. Collange, 240, believes that Paul's choice of *phaneroun* in the present verse is polemically motivated, as it had been in 2:14 (on which see the note). Paul uses an active form of the verb in 1 Cor 4:5 (there parallel with *phōtizein,* "to bring to light") to describe the Lord's disclosure of "the purposes of the heart" *(RSV)* at the last judgment. Cf. the use of the adjective in the similar eschatological statement of 1 Cor 3:13.

*judicial bench of Christ.* In Rom 14:10, "the judicial bench of God" *(tō bēmati tou Theou),* although there the reading "of Christ" is also attested, perhaps in assimilation to the present verse. Polycarp (Phil 6:2) is certainly quoting Rom, not 2 Cor (he draws from Rom 14:12 as well as from 14:10), despite the fact that he too reads "of Christ." While it may be that Polycarp also had 2 Cor 5:10 in mind (cf. Plummer, 156), it is misleading to suggest (so Windisch, 170) that he is actually citing 2 Cor. Paul could think either of Christ (as here and in 1 Cor 4:5; 1 Thess 2:19) or of God (as in Rom 14:10; 1 Thess 3:13) as the final judge; note especially Rom 2:16, where it is said that "God judges . . . through the agency of *[dia]* Christ Jesus" (cf. Rissi 1969:97–98 n. 263). On the various meanings of *bēma,* which in the NT refers generally to the "seat" or *bench* of the judge (thus also "throne," as in Matt 19:28; 25:31; Rev 20:11) rather than to a platform (as in the LXX), see BAG s.v. 2; Plummer, 156; Dinkler 1967:120–23.

*each.* Although *we all must appear before the judicial bench of Christ,* we are individually accountable; cf. Rom 14:12.

*receive back.* The middle forms of *komizein* (here the aorist subjunctive *komisētai)* mean to "receive, acquire, gain," etc. (e.g., what has been promised, Heb 10:36; 11:13, 39), often in contexts where what is received is understood to have been in some sense "recovered" (e.g., Matt 25:27; Heb 11:19) or received in respect of something else. It seems to be used in the latter sense here, indeed with a retributive force, as in other passages where the eschatological judgment is in view (especially Eph 6:8; Col 3:25; also 1 Pet 1:9; 5:4 [an eschatological sanction for the preceding admonitions]; 2 Pet 2:13, v.l. "receiving back," but "suffering" in the main textual tradition). Baumert's arguments against this meaning in the present passage are unconvincing (1973:Excursus L, 410–31, especially 429), and while Synofzik (1977:75) perhaps overstates the case when he claims the word is used here as a technical term for judgment, it should be noted that it occurs nowhere else in an indisputably authentic Pauline letter. Windisch, 171, summarizes the development of its use.

*according to . . . body.* The best-attested text reads, literally, "(may receive back) the things through the body in accordance with what each has done." The awkward pleonasm of this text is relieved when, as in P[46], one reads *ta dia tou sōmatos,* "the things through the body," and Hughes, 181 n. 57, takes this as the likely original reading. It is best regarded, however, as an early attempt to eliminate the awkwardness of the sentence. Another variant (D* F G) omits the article *ta* ("the [things]") and *pros* ("in accordance with") and transposes the relative pronoun *ha* ("what") to obtain "(may receive back) what each through the body has done." This is probably the meaning of the more awkward and evidently more original reading, but represents, again, an obvious attempt to improve the syntax. Most modern versions, including the present one, do essentially the same thing.

*according to.* Translates *pros:* as in Gal 2:14, a classical usage; BDF § 239(8); Moule 1953:53.

*what each has done.* The word *each* is not repeated in the Greek. The verb *prassein* (here aorist, *has done:* "looking back from Christ's tribunal, the whole life of the individual Christian is seen as a unity"—Hughes, 181 n. 58; also Plummer, 159) is used here in a neutral sense (as in Rom 9:11; cf. Rom 7:15; 1 Thess 4:11), although Paul, like other NT writers (Maurer, *TDNT* VI:636), ordinarily uses it of negative actions (e.g., 12:21; Rom 1:32; 2:1–3; Gal 5:21). He uses it in an unambiguously positive sense only in 1 Cor 9:17; Phil 4:9 (but cf. Rom 7:15; 1 Thess 4:11). With the present passage compare especially Rom 8:13, where Paul writes of putting to death "the deeds of the body" *(RSV; tas praxeis tou sōmatos).*

*in the body.* The Greek phrase involved here *(ta dia tou sōmatos)* is textually, syntactically (on these see note above on *according to . . . body*), and also grammatically problematic. The present tr. in effect ignores the article *(ta)* and includes the phrase in the relative clause, *what each has done.* Héring, 40 n. 15, is tempted to resort to the conjecture *dia tou stomatos,* thus: "he shall receive 'from the mouth' (of the judge) a reward in conformity with his works," but such a solution is surely too extreme. More plausibly, Synofzik 1977:76 suggests that *ta dia tou sōmatos* ("the things through the body") may be Paul's own addition to an otherwise traditional statement about eschatological retribution, an addition polemically motivated in view of the devaluation of *the body* by certain persons in Corinth. See COMMENT. Some take *dia tou sōmatos* as instrumental, "through the body" (e.g., Windisch, 172; Barrett, 160), while others interpret it temporally, "while in the body" (e.g., Bultmann, 145), as here; but the meaning is not greatly affected by one's choice.

*whether it be good or evil.* Here *whether . . . or* translates *eite . . . eite,* as in v. 9 (on which see the note). The phrase may be construed with *receive back* (thus BAG s.v. 2, with a reservation; *RSV, NAB*), with *has done* (thus Plummer, 160; M. Harris 1974:325 n. 51; *TEV*), or with both together (cf. *JB, NEB, NIV*). The latter is slightly preferable, and thus a subjunctive form of *einai* ("to be") has been understood in the present tr. (see *GNTG* III:302). The same two adjectives are similarly combined in Rom 9:11, the only other Pauline instance of *phaulos, evil.* Both Hughes, 181, and Héring, 40, think it significant that the apostle has used this word instead of *kakos* ("an evil intention such as could be attributed to the elect"—Héring, ibid.), and would translate this as "worthless." From a strictly lexical point of view, however, this distinction is difficult to support, as an examination of the contemporary use of the adjective *phaulos* shows (representative passages given in LSJ and BAG s.v.). Still, as Mattern (1966: 156–57) has pointed out, when vv. 9–10 are taken together as a reference to the accountability of all *Christians* (see note above on *we all*), then the distinction in v. 10 between *good* and *evil* must be read in association with the concept (v. 9) of the Christian's being *acceptable* to Christ at the last judgment. Therefore, the judgment in view here is not the same as the one Paul writes about in Rom 2:5–11, where the contrast is drawn between *agathos* ("good," vv. 7, 10) and *kakos* ("bad," v. 9), and on this basis one may indeed ascribe significance to Paul's choice of the word *phaulos* ("evil") in the present verse. See COMMENT.

### COMMENT: GENERAL

Paul's discussion of the meaning of apostleship continues, and with a certain concern (apparent also at various points in what has preceded) to counteract misunderstandings and complaints about his own apostolic service which he knows to be abroad in the Corinthian congregation. Thus, the judgment of Windisch, 141, that this section is simply a religious meditation designed to edify, with no apologetic or polemical dimensions, must be corrected. It is closely related to 4:1–6, where those concerns have been clear, and it is an integral part of the discussion of apostolic service opened in 2:14.

In one sense the subject of 4:7–5:10 is "apostolic confidence" (see 4:13, 16; 5:6, 8), and the section may thus be regarded as the direct continuation of a theme which has been implicit since 2:14 and which was already explicit in 3:4, 12; 4:1. Yet beginning in 4:7 another and special subject is present, initially formulated as the suffering of apostles (4:8–9), then enlarged to the topic of mortality (4:11), and thereafter further extended to include the situation of all believers (4:18ff.). Here Paul acknowledges that the sufferings and generally unglorious careers of himself and his apostolic associates might be (and evidently have been) taken by some as invalidating their claim to be ministers of a new covenant of surpassing glory (3:7–4:6). These mortal adversities he now interprets as an integral and appropriate part of true apostleship (4:7–15), and he follows this with a reiteration of the boldness of his apostolate and comments about the nature and meaning of Christian hope in general.

Paul's discussion and development of the interrelated themes of this passage are best exhibited if it is divided into three smaller units, as follows:

4:7–15, an acknowledgment and interpretation of the hardships and apparent defeats with which the Pauline apostolate has been beset;

4:16–5:5, a renewed affirmation of apostolic confidence, followed by comments on the hope with which all believers live out the course of their mortal existence;

5:6–10, a further affirmation of confidence, followed by a general, concluding statement of resolve.

### COMMENT: DETAILED

### *Treasure in Earthen Pots, 4:7–15*

The point of this paragraph is already given with the first sentence (v. 7), which postulates a necessary correlation between the mortality of apostles and their suitability as agents of the gospel. The following verses explain and elaborate this initial statement. This is done by the presentation of a catalog of apostolic hardships (vv. 8–9), followed by a series of interpretive statements designed to show how the sufferings of apostles *overflow to the glory of God* (v. 15). The interpretation begins already in v. 10, which is formally a part of the catalog, and continues through v. 15.

### *The Thesis, 4:7*

Paul's initial thetic statement (v. 7) employs an image *(earthen pots)* which had wide currency in the ancient world, not only in the Bible of the apostle's own Jewish tradition but in the literature of the broader Hellenistic society, both Greek and Roman (see references in the NOTES). Pottery vessels, unlike those made of glass or precious metal, have value only while they are whole and intact. Once damaged they cannot be repaired (stressed in a rabbinic saying, *Gen. Rab.* 14:7, quoted by Davies 1980:313) or melted down. They are cheap but fragile, and therefore they are of no enduring value. That means, also, that they are expendable. The context shows that Paul is using this image of an earthen pot to describe the mortal existence of himself and his apostolic associates, their humanity as it is subject to the ravages of time and adversity (vv. 8–9), their *outward person* that *is being wasted away* (v. 16). Because he contrasts these *earthen pots* with the *treasure* they contain, it seems clear that he has in mind the great value of the one and the trifling value of the other. But the frailty and vulnerability to breakage and destruction must be equally in view (Barrett, 137–38, thinks it is primarily the matter of value that is involved), because it is precisely the mortality of this earthly existence that is emphasized in the following verses. Respecting *our mortal flesh* (v. 11), Paul could have affirmed Seneca's description of the body as "a vessel that the slightest shaking, the slightest toss will break. . . . A body weak and fragile, naked, in its natural state defenceless . . . exposed to all the affronts of Fortune; . . . doomed to decay" (*To Marcia* xi.3).

However, as much as Paul could share the general Hellenistic view about human mortality, which was, after all, equally at home in the Jewish tradition, his intention in the present verses is certainly not to contrast *our mortal flesh* with "our immortal soul." Significantly, as many commentators have pointed out, the word "soul" *(psychē)* is not even used in this part of the letter (elsewhere in 2 Cor, only 1:23; 12:15), and the *treasure* which the *earthen pots* are said to contain is to be identified neither with that nor with the "mind" *(nous),* as in many Hellenistic sources (references in NOTES). In accord with his Jewish heritage, the apostle regards the body, mortal as it is, not as the receptacle of the soul but as a constituent part of the total human being (cf. Ahern 1960:19 n. 64, and see comment below on 4:16–5:5). Paul's reference to *this treasure* follows closely on the discussion of 4:1–6, and it is against that background that his metaphor must be understood. There he had written of the boldness which attends the apostolic ministry as *the enlightenment coming from the gospel of the splendor of Christ* (v. 4) is disclosed through it. Whether one identifies the *treasure* borne by apostles primarily with the gospel (vv. 3, 4; cf. v. 2*a*), as some do (e.g., Lietzmann, 115; Larsson 1962:388 n. 2), primarily with the ministry itself (v. 1; so Spicq 1937:210; Rissi 1969:45; Bultmann, 114), or especially with "the illumining power of the knowledge of Divine glory" (Plummer, 126; cf. Hughes, 135) makes little difference, finally, because these are all interconnected.

*This treasure* is not itself the point at issue in vv. 7–15, nor even in v. 7. What is at issue in these verses is how Paul and his associates, exhibiting all the frailties of mortal existence and, more than that, suffering various indignities and afflictions which attend their apostolic work, can yet claim to be agents for the gospel of the glory of God. It is likely that the Pauline apostolate has been challenged in this regard, and it is possible that Paul's rivals for leadership in Corinth had based their own apostolic claims on attestations of their special powers. In that case, vv. 7ff. would represent Paul's response to the challenge, beginning with the succinct statement of v. 7 and continuing with a summary listing of his own "credentials" in vv. 8–9 (so Georgi [1964:244], who notes that in this context, as in other passages where hardship lists occur, the subject is Paul's ministry, *diakonia,* 4:1). Paul's brief response, presented in v. 7, is that the frailty of the apostles is a demonstration of the essential point, *that the power which is beyond any comparison belongs to God and not to us.* Earlier in this same letter Paul has mentioned that the recent threat to his life experienced in Asia had taught him not to rely on self, but on God (1:9), and here one sees that realization now formulated as a principle applicable to apostolic service in general. The same principle is apparent in 12:9*b,* in another form in 3:5 ("Not . . . of ourselves adequate . . . our adequacy is from God"), and yet again in 13:4*b,* which Larsson (1962:289) believes is the best commentary on the present passage. There, as here (v. 7), Paul contrasts the weakness of apostles with the power of God, at the same time affirming an important relation between the two. And there, as here (vv. 10–11), the weakness of the apostles is related to the weakness of Christ seen in his crucifixion.

It is evident that Paul's interpretation of the meaning of the adversities by which apostles are beset is dependent upon his understanding of the gospel they preach. The gospel is God's "power for salvation" (Rom 1:16) present in "the word of the cross" (1 Cor 1:18, 24), and Paul is convinced that the manner in which the gospel is borne must be appropriate to its nature. Therefore, he had written in an earlier letter, the weakness, fear, and trembling with which he had brought the gospel to Corinth in the first place had allowed a full "demonstration of the Spirit and of power," that the Corinthians' faith "might not rest in the wisdom of men but in the power of God" (1 Cor 2:3–5 [*RSV*]). The same conviction underlies the present passage, even though the issue of the moment is not the skills and manner of an apostle but the sufferings and hardships to which apostles are subject.

### A Catalog of Hardships, 4:8–9

The list of hardships Paul introduces in vv. 8–9 should be compared with similar catalogs in 6:4c–5; 11:23b–29; 12:10; Rom 8:35; 1 Cor 4:9–13—all of which, like the present one, indicate the kind of adversities under which apostles labor. The present list has a special character, however, because it is more than a simple enumeration of hardships. Had it been just that, it would have explained well enough why the apostles, demeaned by the world and vulnerable, could be likened to *earthen pots* (v. 7). But here the list has been formulated into a series of antitheses, and these serve to illustrate not just the weakness of apostles but how that weakness discloses the incomparable power of God: they are afflicted, in despair, persecuted, and struck down, yet not crushed, desperate, forsaken, or destroyed. Many commentators have been puzzled by the apparent contradiction between v. 8b, *despairing, but not utterly desperate,* and Paul's comment earlier in this same letter that in Asia he had in fact "despaired even of survival" (1:8). The verb used in 1:8 is the same compound translated here as *(not) utterly desperate,* so it might appear that Paul has overstated himself in one case or the other. The contradiction is only a formal one, however, and not a material one, because the compound form of the verb in 1:8 is used there the way the simple form of the verb is used in 4:8b, with reference to a human judgment about the circumstances. Thus, apart from faith his situation in Asia had seemed hopeless (1:8), and so does the miserable existence of the apostles when it is measured by worldly standards. But faith's perspective is different. Where there is faith, despair becomes an occasion for the disclosure of God (1:9), and it is also from this standpoint that Paul now writes, in 4:8b, *despairing* (as the world judges things), *but not utterly desperate* (cf. Bultmann, 117). The antithesis of the present verse is thus present also in 1:8–9, although in another form, and the fundamental faith-conception which underlies the earlier passage underlies as well the whole series of antitheses in 4:8–9.

Similar lists of hardships are found in the philosophical and ethical treatises of many of Paul's contemporaries, especially those influenced by the Stoic ideal of the wise man as one who knows how to conquer adversity. Formally, at least, one of the most impressive parallels to the present list is a passage from Plutarch's *Conspectus of the Essay, "The Stoics Talk More Paradoxically than the Poets"* (first pointed out by Fridrichsen 1944). There it is said that the truly wise Stoic "is not impeded when confined, and under no compulsion when flung down a precipice, and not in torture when on the rack, and not injured when mutilated, and is invincible when thrown in wrestling, and is not blockaded under siege, and is uncaptured while his enemies are selling him into slavery" (1057 E). Another, also describing the ideal Stoic, is in Epictetus II.xix.24: "sick and (yet) happy, in danger and happy, dying and happy, condemned to exile and happy, in disrepute and happy."

These descriptions of the truly wise Stoic reflect the philosophical conviction that when the rational part of human nature is allowed to exercise its rightful supremacy over the irrational, life's hardships can be endured (Seneca, *Moral Epistles* LXXI, 26–27). The sage can remain "fearless," "undistressed," "invincible," and "unconstrained" in their midst (Plutarch, *Conspectus* 1057 D). While Seneca says that the courage of such a person may inspire "a certain religious sense" in others (*religionis suspicione, Moral Epistles* XLI, 3–4), it is nevertheless human reason ("philosophy") that "makes us joyful in the very sight of death, strong and brave no matter in what state the body may be, cheerful and never failing though the body fail us" (*Moral Epistles* XXX, 3). For the Stoic, then, the whole of one's mortal existence is seen as a struggle against adversity, as the wise person seeks to be liberated from external threats and circumstances in order to achieve an inner tranquillity. This requires moral discipline, courage, and stamina, and it is not surprising that Stoic writers turn to athletic and military metaphors in describing one's proper response to worldly afflictions (athletic: Epictetus I.xxiv.2; Dio Chrysostom VIII, 15–16; military: Epictetus III.xxiv.27–38). In Stoic thought generally, true happiness is gained as one learns to regard all difficult and unpleasant circumstances as unimportant. Thus, for the noble man "hunger, exile, loss of reputation, and the like have no terrors . . . ; nay, he regards them as altogether trifling" (Dio Chrysostom VIII, 16). Such things, says Epictetus, giving a very similar list ("exile and imprisonment and bonds and death and disrepute"), we must learn to call "indifferent," *adiaphora* (I.xxx.2).

It is clear that the presuppositions and intentions which underlie Paul's list of hardships in 4:8–9 are quite different. For one thing, the apostle does not hesitate to acknowledge the real impact outward circumstances have had on him. He does not share the Stoic ideal of training oneself to look upon afflictions as insignificant and inconsequential. He has already admitted to feelings of desperation in Asia (1:8), and he will write shortly about the afflictions which beset him when he first arrived in Macedonia (7:5ff.). Moreover, Paul does not speak of "happiness" in the midst of adversity (Epictetus) or of remaining "invincible" in the face of hardships (Plutarch), but rather of being comforted in his afflictions (1:4–7; 7:6–7, 13) and rescued from them (1:10; cf. Fridrichsen 1944:30; Schrage 1974:149). It is also significant that the Stoics, believing that external circumstances are oppressive only when one regards them as such, could refer to life's difficulties as self-imposed—thus Epictetus' comment that "we afflict ourselves, we distress ourselves" (*heautous thlibomen, heautous stenochōroumen,* I.xxv.28). Paul, on the other hand, who uses the same verbs in the first antithesis of 4:8 and the corresponding nouns in the hardship lists of chap. 6 (v. 4) and Rom 8:35 (*stenochōriais* ["pressures"] are also mentioned in 2 Cor 12:10), never doubts the external origin of the afflictions he catalogs (cf. Schrage 1974:149–50). Thus, Paul can by no means share the view of Epictetus that overcoming hardships involves finally persuading oneself that they do not exist (I.xxv.17, on which see Schrenk's comment, *TDNT* I:561).

The distinctiveness of the Pauline perspective on suffering is vividly exhibited when the opening sentence of Epictetus' discourse on struggling against difficulties *(peristaseis)* is put alongside 2 Cor 4:7–9. For Epictetus, "It is difficulties that show what men are" (I.xxiv.1), because difficulties must be met and overcome with the disciplined power of reason and with courage. For Paul, however, difficulties must be met and borne with faith, and thereby they disclose not "what men are" but *that the power which is beyond any comparison belongs to God and not to us.*

The literature of apocalyptic Judaism also offers various examples of hardship lists, as Schrage (1974:143–46) has shown. These are, in general, recitals of the present tribulations endured by the righteous as they wait in hope for eschatological deliverance from their suffering and for divine retribution against their oppressors (e.g., 1 Enoch 103:9–15, the wicked speaking derisively of the righteous; 1QH ix.6–7; 2 Enoch 66:6). The theological presuppositions, ethical concerns, and general eschatological perspective of these Jewish lists make them in these ways more comparable to Paul's than those of the Stoics. Thus, e.g., in 1QH ix.3ff. the psalmist praises God for the consolation which comes from the manifestation of God's divine grace and power in the midst of suffering. Indeed, elsewhere he is able to attribute the violence perpetrated against him to God's will, "that Thou mayest be glorified / by the judgement of the wicked, / and manifest Thy might through me" (1QH ii.23–25, Vermes 1975:155). There is a similar affirmation in 1QH v.15 (cf. also iv.22–23), leading Barré (1975:516–17) to compare Paul's statements in 2 Cor 4:7, 11. Once again, however, the distinctiveness of the Pauline conception must be noted, because the Qumran hymns do not actually speak of the manifestation of God's power in and through the suffering as such. Rather, they associate it closely with God's judgment of those who inflict suffering on the righteous (e.g., 1QH ii.23–25) and with God's protection, consolation, and assurances of ultimate deliverance from suffering (e.g., 1QH v.18–19; ix.13, 25–26; see also Schrage, 1974:146; Braun 1966 I:199).

### Death and Life, 4:10–12

Paul's interpretive comments on the catalog of adversities come in vv. 10–15, beginning in v. 10a with what amounts to a theological resumé of vv. 8–9. As the catalog itself had been introduced with an adverbial phrase, *In every way*, so the resumé is introduced with the adverb *always*. Taken together, these expressions show that Paul regards suffering not just as an occasional experience of apostles but as the essential and continuing characteristic of apostolic service. The theological summation of this in v. 10a reflects the same sense of apostolic vocation that is present when Paul identifies the gospel he bears as "the word of the cross" (1 Cor 1:18) or "Jesus Christ and him crucified" (1 Cor 2:2) and when he writes of his ministry as the public portrayal of Jesus Christ as crucified (Gal 3:1). There is no doubt but that the "full preaching" of Christ's gospel to which he refers in Rom 15:19 involves as an essential component this *carrying about in the body*, in his own sufferings, *the death of Jesus* (v. 10a). It is questionable whether one should place very much emphasis on the fact that Paul here uses the word *nekrōsis* for *death*, rather than his more usual *thanatos* (see NOTES). If the former has any special meaning here, that is probably shown by the phrase in v. 11, *given up to death*, where in fact the latter term is used. Thus in v. 10a Paul might be thinking of the whole course of Jesus' life as a "dying," a being given up to death, just as he is thinking of the whole of the apostolic life in that way.

The paradox of the gospel and of apostolic service which has been in view since v. 7—God's power disclosed through weakness—is sharpened in v. 10b, where Paul indicates that the *carrying about* of *the death of Jesus* is for the purpose of disclosing his *life*. The reference is not to Jesus' earthly life and ministry, as though Paul's apostleship were devoted to presenting Jesus' exemplary character. The context shows that Paul is thinking of the resurrection life of Jesus (on the title *Jesus*, see NOTES); the incomparable power of God (v. 7) is manifested above all and decisively in God's resurrection of Jesus from the dead (v. 14; cf. Rom 4:18–21, Abraham's faith in God's power to give life). Therefore, to be a bearer of Christ's death is to be a bearer as well of his resurrection, and that means to be an agent for the disclosure of God's power to save. Here Paul is referring specifically to apostles as participants in and bearers of the death and life of Jesus, because his subject here is the meaning and character of the apostolic ministry. But elsewhere he writes in the same way about all believers as participants in Christ's suffering and death (e.g., 1:5–7; 1 Thess 1:6–7), and thus bearers as well of his life—not only in their hope for resurrection with him (e.g., Rom 6:5, 8; 8:17; Phil 3:10–11) but in their present existence in faith (e.g., Rom 6:4; Gal 2:19). The manifestation, even now within the community of faith, of the resurrection power of God is seen in the present letter, where the apostle writes of the *down payment* proffered through the Spirit (1:22; 5:5), and of the transformation (3:18), renewal (4:16), and new creation (5:17) which signal the presence of the day of salvation (6:2).

The point of v. 10 is repeated and intensified in v. 11. When Paul writes that apostles *are constantly being given up to death* even as they live, he does not mean that they are only subject to mortal dangers. Those dangers he interprets here as an actual wasting away of the *outward person* (v. 16; cf. Bultmann, 118), just as in 1 Cor 15:30, 31 he had interpreted the hourly risks he faced as a real "dying every day." Moreover, one must distinguish Paul's meaning from that of his contemporary, Seneca, when the latter cites with approval the proverbial saying *cotidie morimur,* "we die every day" (*Moral Epistles* XXIV, 19). That is a general reference to the gradual deterioration of the mortal body, "For every day a little of our life is taken from us; even when we are growing, our life is on the wane" (ibid. XXIV, 20). Paul, however, is not thinking of the natural process of aging, but of the adversities which apostles must bear by reason of their serving the gospel, *on account of Jesus* (on this phrase, see the NOTES). The same point is stressed in 12:10: the apostle's sufferings are "because of Christ" (there *hyper Christou*) in the sense that they are the manifestation of his suffering and death and thus a proclamation of the gospel. The distinctiveness of Paul's thought is seen further in the purpose-clause of v. 11*b* which, like the one it parallels in v. 10*b,* refers to the manifestation of the resurrection life of Jesus (and thus of the incomparable power of God), precisely in and through the weakness, suffering, and death of Jesus borne by the apostles. A few sentences later Paul will write of an ultimate resurrection with Jesus (v. 14), but here the reference is first of all to the disclosure of God's power in the apostles' present, mortal existence *(in our mortal flesh);* note 6:9, "dying—yet see, we live."

The paradox of death and life is articulated in another way in v. 12, where Paul contrasts the *death . . . made active* in the apostles with the *life* made active in his congregation. Whereas the preceding verses have focused on the paradox of death and life as these operate within the apostles, this sentence identifies death exclusively with them, and life exclusively with those to whom they preach the gospel. (Tannehill [1967:87] points out that Paul had earlier written about the Corinthians sharing Christ's sufferings, 1:4–7.) The formulation of the paradox is altered here in order to bring out a point Paul stresses repeatedly in this letter (chaps. 1–9)—namely, that the exercise of his ministry is for the sake of those to whom he is an apostle (see NOTES on v. 15*a*). Now *death* and *life* are conceived as distinct entities, rather as in Rom 5:12–21 death's exercise of its power through sin (disobedience), vv. 14, 17, 21, is contrasted with the reign of grace, v. 21 (cf. v. 17, grace brings the reign of life). In 1 Cor 15:26, Paul had written of death as the last of all God's enemies to be destroyed, even though he understands that death's fatal grip has already been broken by Christ's resurrection from the dead (Rom 6:9). In the interim, between death's conquest and final destruction, death is forced to vent itself in *the death of Jesus* (v. 10), thereby serving the purpose of God (Tannehill 1967:85). "God," therefore, is the agent in v. 12, not *death* or *life*. These are *made active* to serve the gospel, as the disclosure of the saving *death* of Jesus through the apostles becomes *life* for those who respond in faith (cf. Kamlah 1963:226–29). Unlike Ignatius later (e.g., Ign Rom 6:3), Paul interprets the suffering of apostles (or believers generally) not as an imitation of the passion of their Lord but as the working out of Jesus' own sufferings in their ministry (service); see Bultmann 1960:277. Dunn (1975:328–29) compares our verse with Gal 4:19, where Paul suggests that his apostolic work involves the kind of travail experienced by a woman in labor, that new life might be generated for others ("until Christ be formed in you!" [*RSV*]). Calvin, 60, held that Paul was speaking ironically here, in which case *life* would have the weakened sense of "a prosperous and pleasant condition," and the apostle would be charging his readers with wanting the benefits of faith without the pain of it, much as he had in 1 Cor 4:8–13. But the present context is quite against this interpretation (so also Bultmann, 122; Hughes, 145), and the verse stands as a fully serious extension of what had preceded.

*Faith and Preaching, 4:13–15*

Paul is still thinking of the sufferings of apostles as death's operation within them when he introduces in v. 13 the first direct scriptural citation in this letter. This is drawn from Ps 115 (as that stands in the Greek Bible; see NOTES), and it is used to help support the statement of v. 12. Paul may or may not have the whole of the Psalm in mind ( = Hebrew Ps 116:10–19) when he cites its opening line (Plummer [133], Hughes [146–47], Rissi [1969:59], and Baumert [1973:87] all believe he does have; Barrett [143], that he hasn't), but it is certainly too much to describe vv. 13–15 as a "midrash" on Ps 116:8–19 (*sic* Hanson 1968:167). What has attracted him to the text, undoubtedly, is the relationship forged there between the two words "believe" *(pisteuein)* and "speak" *(lalein)*. Here the latter verb is employed with reference to preaching the gospel, as it also is in 1 Thess 2:2. Indeed, Paul's comment in the earlier letter about the conditions under which he had first preached to the Thessalonians matches in other ways as well the present context: "Though we had previously suffered and been abused in Philippi, as you know, we took courage in our God to speak to you the gospel of God in the face of substantial opposition." Courage to speak out despite adversity is also the point in 2 Cor 4:13, which (against Windisch, 147–48) does not sit loosely in its context but helps to support the statements about apostolic boldness Paul has already made (3:12; 4:1) and will make again (4:16; 5:6, 8). Here, as elsewhere, the apostle seems to be aware of the criticism that his weaknesses and sufferings invalidate his claims to apostolic status. On the contrary, he counters, these demonstrate that he speaks from faith.

The specific phrase *Spirit of faith* is used nowhere else by Paul, but the notion that faith comes with the power of the Spirit is common in his letters (references in the NOTES)—e.g., in 1 Cor 12:9, where "faith" is one of the gifts of the Spirit. In that passage, certainly, faith has a more restricted meaning than in the extended discussions of faith in Rom and Gal (see Orr and Walther 1976:32, 282), but Paul also links the Spirit's coming to the generation of faith, understood in the more fundamental sense of belief in and obedience to the gospel, as in Gal 3:2, 5, 14. The reference to the Spirit in the present verse is in accord with what Paul has written earlier about the Spirit's work (3:3, 6, 8, 17, 18) and with what he will shortly reiterate about the Spirit's presence (5:5; cf. 1:22).

Although the clear emphasis in v. 13 is on the affirmation *and so we speak* (Bultmann, 123), the extension of that comes only in v. 15. Before proceeding with that, Paul identifies the object of faith and thus the ultimate source of apostolic boldness as the God *who raised* [*the Lord*] *Jesus* and *will raise us also with Jesus,* v. 14a. This formulation is for the most part traditional (see NOTES), and nothing in the way Paul cites it here suggests that he is still concerned about the denial of a general resurrection which had elicited the lengthy discussion of 1 Cor 15. On the contrary, he expects that this restatement of faith's foundation in God's resurrection power will convincingly support his claim that apostles can speak with boldness even in the midst of adversity. If Paul is intending to correct any false notion here, it is not the denial of a final resurrection but the belief that afflictions are inconsistent with true apostleship. Further, the affirmation of this resurrection faith shows that for Paul the new *life* already disclosed and effective for believers in the present (cf. vv. 10–12) is not their own spiritual possession. It stands, as Bultmann, 125, puts it, both "outside of" and "ahead" of the believer, in Christ and in the future, and it is gospel now only by faith (v. 13; cf. 5:7).

To the resurrection credo (v. 14a) Paul has added a comment about God's presentation of *us with you* (v. 14b). The eschatological reference seems clear, and whether the "presentation" in mind is especially that before Christ the Judge, or, more probably, a presentation to be *with Jesus* (v. 14a; cf. 1 Thess 4:14, 17; see NOTES), the real emphasis falls on the being *with you* in that day (so also Bultmann, 124; Collange, 166). As Paul indicates more explicitly in other places (1:14; Phil 2:16; 1 Thess 2:19), this being together with his converts in the presence of the Lord will be the crowning evidence not only of the authenticity of their faith but also of the authenticity of those by whom they have come to faith. It is doubtful whether the preposition in the phrase *with you* should be interpreted to mean "reunited with you," although it could mean this if *will raise us* in the preceding formula presumes that Paul is now contemplating at least the possibility of his death before the Lord's return (so, e.g., Plummer, 134; Strachan, 96–97). In this case Paul's expectations about his own situation vis-à-vis the last day would be different here from those expressed in 1 Thess 4:17, where he had anticipated being among those "left alive" at the Lord's coming (apparently presupposed as well in 1 Cor 7:29; 10:11, and in a later letter, Rom 13:11*b*). But Paul's earlier expression of confidence in God's continuing deliverance of him from mortal danger (1:10) must be taken seriously, and the phrase *will raise us* need mean nothing else than "will raise us up 'to meet the Lord in the air' " (cf. 1 Thess 4:17).

The comment in v. 15 that *everything is for your sake* both expands on *with you* in v. 14 and introduces the conclusion of Paul's supporting argument (vv. 13ff.) for the statement of v. 12 (cf. Bultmann, 125). This is one of numerous instances in chaps. 1–9 (references in the NOTES) where Paul emphasizes that apostles are properly concerned only for the faith of those to whom they have delivered the gospel, and it is therefore part of his defense of the conduct of his apostolate in relation to the Corinthians. The style of the remainder of the verse is more emphatic than discursive, and the intention is doxological, not analytical (cf. Collange, 166). This has doubtless contributed to the jumbled syntax, for which there is no certain solution (details in the NOTES). The general meaning would seem to be that, as more people receive the gospel and respond to it, the thanksgivings of the expanding community of faith *overflow to the glory of God.* It is possible, then, that the *grace* mentioned here should be identified with that grace by which apostles are commissioned to the service of the gospel (so Rissi 1969:64 n. 154, citing Rom 1:5; 12:3; 15:15; 1 Cor 3:10). Barrett, 145, dismisses too quickly the possibility that Paul conceives of these thanksgivings as "objectively" increasing the glory of God, because that concept does seem to have been a part of the apostle's religious heritage (see reference to Boobyer's study in the NOTES on this verse and in the COMMENT on 1:20). In some instances the idea of "glorifying God" or "giving him glory" is closely associated with conversion, turning to God in faith (e.g., Abraham, Rom 4:20; the Gentiles, Rom 1:21 [cf. v. 23], 15:9), and that meaning would also fit the present verse.

In summary, Paul's concern in vv. 7–15 is to emphasize that the acknowledged weakness, vulnerability, and suffering which characterize his apostolate are an integral part of the ministry of the gospel. They are interpreted as the presentation (not as the imitation) of the passion and death of Christ, and therefore as fully appropriate to the apostolic vocation of preaching "Jesus Christ crucified." Georgi (1964:286–88) argues that the phrase "life of Jesus" was a slogan among Paul's opponents in Corinth, and that it referred to Jesus' sensational powers which they sought to imitate in their own ministry. Against this, Paul would be contending that God's power is disclosed in weakness and suffering (ibid.:288–89; cf. Rissi 1969:50). This is not impossible, but one ought to beware of hypothesizing too much about the Christology of Paul's opponents from Paul's own line of argument (see INTRODUCTION). His basic interest here is clear enough without that: it is to say that the legitimacy of apostles is not dependent upon a *curriculum vitae* filled with glorious accomplishments (cf. the earlier argument about *letters of recommendation,* 3:1–3). In fact, what is offered in 4:7–15 is an interpretation of the *curriculum vitae Pauli* as the *curriculum mortis et vitae Iesu.* Paul interprets the afflictions he knows as the operation in his ministry of the death and life of Jesus. This may be said to endow the lives of apostles with a sacramental character, but it is no more than what Paul writes elsewhere about the lives of all believers; their baptism into Christ joins them in his death and places them under the rule of grace where they "walk in newness of life" (Rom 6:3–14).

### The Unseen and Eternal, 4:16–5:5

The unfortunate placement of a chapter division after 4:18 has too often caused interpreters to overlook the close connection between the last verses of our present chap. 4 and the first verses of chap. 5. The overall theme of these eight verses is the contrast between what is of preliminary significance only and what is of absolute significance. This contrast is expressed in various interrelated ways in virtually every sentence of the paragraph: *outer/inner,* 4:16; *momentary/eternal,* 4:17; *trifling/abundance,* 4:17; *seen/not seen,* 4:18; *temporary/eternal,* 4:18; *earthly/heavenly,* 5:1–2; *tent-like house/building from God,* 5:1; *destroyed/eternal,* 5:1; *naked/clothed,* 5:2–4; *mortality/life,* 5:4. Furthermore, Paul's comments here continue to be directed to the subject of the apostolic ministry, and specifically to the question of how the hardships he and his associates experience are serving that ministry rather than invalidating it. This paragraph therefore should be viewed not as a detached theological soliloquy (the impression interpreters often leave when they handle 5:1–10 as a self-contained unit) but as a lively response to a real and current misunderstanding and criticism of the Pauline apostolate.

### A Reaffirmation of Confidence, 4:16–5:1

In 4:16*a* there is a verbatim resumption of the affirmation about apostolic boldness which had been made in 4:1 (and in other forms in 3:12; 4:13). The context here (see especially 4:2–6, 7, 10–12, 13, 15) makes it certain that Paul is not referring to boldness in facing death, but to boldness in preaching the gospel despite all manner of afflictions and despite the way some have falsely interpreted those. His own interpretation of those hardships (4:7–15) allows this restatement of confidence, but this leads in turn to some further supporting comments, 4:16*b*–5:5.

These supporting arguments emphasize first of all the preliminary nature of the earthly tribulations and of mortal existence in general (4:16*b*–5:1). This is expressed in 4:16*b* by the introduction of a distinction between the *inner* and *outer person*. The distinction is formally comparable to that between a physical body and the "mind" or "soul" that inhabits it, a distinction commonly made in the Hellenistic world (references in the NOTES). The one is visible and mortal, the other invisible but immortal, the "true" person (Philo) "hidden" within the "container" that overlies it (Marcus Aurelius; cf. 4:7). Yet Paul does not share the belief that life is gained only when, after the unrelenting application of one's efforts to let the rational rule over the irrational (see COMMENT on 4:7–15), the mortal body is shed at last, like a "foul and noisome womb" (Seneca, *Moral Epistles* CII, 27). The apostle's meaning here must be determined instead with reference to the immediate context of the passage and the wider context of his thought overall. The *outer person* being *wasted away* is to be identified, certainly, with the *mortal flesh* which is *constantly being given up to death* (4:11). The *outer person* is that aspect of one's humanity which is subject to the various assaults and hardships of historical existence (4:8–9) and which, because of its vulnerability to these, may be likened to *earthen pots* (4:7). Since the subjection of the "flesh" to sin is not the topic here, it would be wrong to associate this *outer person* with the fleshly existence of which Paul writes in Rom 7:14ff., or with the "old person" of Rom 6:6 (so Barrett, 146: "the man of this age").

What, then, is the *inner person*? In Rom 7:22 the same expression occurs —employed there, as Bultmann has argued (1960:151–52), for "man insofar as he knows about his authenticity and—consciously or unconsciously—is determined and driven in his entire existence by his concern for it." This formal description of Paul's use of the phrase is also applicable to the occurrence in the present verse. Here, as in Rom 7, *inner person* refers to that dimension of human existence which, though not visible, is yet of ultimate significance for it. But because the topic in the two passages is different, this formal concept is employed in two different ways: in Rom 7 for the "unredeemed person" still under the law, and here for the "new person" who lives by faith (Bultmann, 127). Therefore, while it is illegitimate to identify the *outer person* here with the "old person" of Rom 6:6 (see above), it is legitimate to identify the *inner person* here with the *new creation* in 2 Cor 5:17, and hence with the description in Rom 6 of those who have been set free from sin to be "alive to God in Christ Jesus" (v. 11). The *inner person* here is the one whose life, no matter how miserable and adverse the conditions of its mortal existence, has been transformed by the resurrection life of Jesus through which God's own incomparable power is present and manifest (4:7, 10–12). This *inner person* is, in short, the "I" of Gal 2:20 who by faith has grasped the reality of the new life in Christ.

It is a striking but thoroughly Pauline conviction that this *inner person* which has been made new is itself *renewed daily* (cf. Col 3:10, "the new which is being renewed"). The same idea is present in Rom 12:2, but in the imperative —"Be transformed by the renewal of your mind" *(RSV)*, where "mind" *(nous)* stands in place of *inner person* (note the parallelism of the two expressions in Rom 7:22, 23). The use of the passive voice in this passage *(is renewed)* and in Rom 12:2 ("Be transformed") accords with the passive voice of 3:18, where it is clear that *being transformed into [Christ's] image, from splendor to splendor* is God's doing. It is also clear that the transformation/renewal of which Paul conceives is neither instantaneous, to be held thereafter as a secure possession, nor something that is progressively deepened or increased. The use of the imperative in Rom 12:2 and the word *daily* in the present verse (see Notes) require us to associate this renewal with a repeated act of faith (despite Barrett's objection, 147) whereby *the life of Jesus* is received and appropriated in the believer's life over and over again. Paul's metaphor of the believer as a runner in a race (Phil 3:12–14, cited by Bultmann, 128) establishes the point well: having been made Christ's own (v. 12b) and set on course "for the prize of the upward call of God in Christ Jesus" (v. 14, *RSV*), the believer knows that faith's imperative requires a tireless pressing on to what lies ahead.

That Paul's interpretation of apostolic sufferings bears only a superficial resemblance to the teaching of his Stoic contemporaries (see Comment on 4:7–15) is illustrated in v. 17. The description here of earthly afflictions as *momentary* and *trifling* has a certain parallel in Seneca (*Moral Epistles* XLI, 4–5), who writes admiringly of the man who is able to be "unterrified in the midst of dangers" and "happy in adversity" because he "passes through every experience as if it were of small account" (cf. Epictetus I.ix.16–17). This is possible, says Seneca, because of the "peculiar property" *(proprium)* of man which is "the soul, and reason brought to perfection in the soul" (*Animus et ratio in animo perfecta*, ibid., 8). For Paul, however, it is not the inherent rationality of human nature that allows adversity to be endured, but only faith and hope, which in the midst of adversity point beyond and ahead of themselves to God. Verse 17 accents the hope when it describes the present afflictions as only preliminary to the coming glory. The same point is registered in Rom 5:2–5; 8:17–18, but it is by no means distinctively Pauline (cf., e.g., Mark 13:24–27; 1 Pet 4:12–13). Indeed, it was already a common theme of apocalyptic Judaism, as is plain from various passages in 2 Apoc Bar. Particularly comparable with the thought of 4:17 is 2 Apoc Bar 48:50, where Baruch, speaking of the "glory, which is reserved for [the righteous]" (48:49), says to them: "For assuredly as in a little time in this transitory world in which ye live, ye have endured much labour, / So in that world to which there is no end, ye shall receive great light" (*APOT;* note also 15:7–8; 21:22–23; 51:14). Paul does not appear to regard the hoped-for *glory* as a reward for enduring so much distress, or as a just "requital" (so Meyer, 503) for losses suffered, because he emphasizes the disproportionate *abundance of glory* in relation to the *trifling affliction* (cf. Wis 3:5, a "little" discipline will be followed by "a great good," and Rom 5:20, increased sin, but even more grace; Windisch, 155). Moreover, the subject of the verb *is bringing about* (on which see Notes) is not "apostles" (or "believers") but *affliction*. Thus, it is God who is at work (cf. Phil 2:12–13) in and through the present *affliction* to bring about an *eternal abundance of glory* as its eventual and lasting fruit.

The preliminary nature of the present affliction is still under consideration in 4:18 and 5:1, but the horizon is now broadened to include outward circumstances (4:18) and mortal existence (5:1) in general. Moreover, the first person plural now includes all believers, not just the apostles as it still had in 4:16*a* (4:16*b*, 17 are in this respect transitional to 4:18ff.). The emphasis placed on this *We* (see NOTES) suggests that Paul means to be contrasting the convictions shared by those who adhere to his gospel with the teachings of his rivals in Corinth who judge according to outward appearances (5:12, 16; 10:10; cf. Lang 1973:175–76). Hence, the declaration of 4:18 represents a sharpening of the expression of general confidence in the preceding verse. Paul now begins to emphasize the commitment which must attend one's hope for the coming glory. Since hope by definition attaches itself to what cannot be verified empirically ("Now hope that is seen is not hope. For who hopes for what he sees?" —Rom 8:24 [*RSV*]), hope requires the orientation of one's life away from *the things that are seen* to those *that are not seen*. The former are *temporary*, and among those are to be included not only "the sum of the tribulations . . . of which [one's] life is full" (Strachan, 98) but also the sum of all of one's seeking to secure and establish life on one's own terms, and thus all "earthly" and "fleshly" things insofar as these may rule one's willing and acting (Phil 3:19; Rom 8:5). *The things that are not seen* and *eternal*, which constitute the proper object of hope (Rom 8:25), would include above all the "life and peace" ( = "the things of the Spirit," Rom 8:5, 6) of which the Spirit is the *down payment* (1:22; 5:5), and hence the sum of that to which God has called those who belong to Christ. Those who *focus [their] attention (skopein)* on him, through their pressing forward to the "goal" *(skopos)* of God's call in Christ Jesus (Phil 3:14), are neither discouraged nor distracted by outward circumstances.

It is extremely important to recognize that this line of argument continues in 5:1. This verse has long been regarded as the *crux interpretum* for 5:1–10, and that cannot be disputed. But it is also true, though less often acknowledged, that this verse is an integral part—indeed, the climactic moment—of the paragraph which begins in 4:16. Now the argument that earthly tribulations belong to the realm of what is passing and preliminary (4:16*b*–18) is supported by an affirmation which is almost confessional in form *(For we know that . . . )*. Its function is not to introduce a new topic but to help undergird the renewed statement of apostolic confidence in 4:16*a*.

It must be conceded that most interpretations regard 5:1 as opening a new paragraph and introducing a new subject. (For a comprehensive survey and analysis of the history of the interpretation of 5:1–10, see Lang 1973.) Most commonly, Paul is understood to be turning now to a discussion of life after death, prompted to this by the dawning realization that he himself may not survive until the Lord's return. He had, of course, dealt with the question of the death of believers in an earlier letter (1 Thess 4:13–18). There he had assured his readers that those who die before the Parousia will be resurrected from the dead in order to be able to join with those who are still alive "to meet the Lord in the air" (v. 17, *RSV*). Clearly, however, Paul had presumed he would be among the living at the Lord's return ("we who are left," v. 17). Now, according to the usual interpretation of 2 Cor 5:1–10, Paul is not sure about surviving, perhaps because of his recent narrow escape in Asia (1:8–9). Thus, as he considers what hardships he has endured and continues to endure, he begins to think more closely about the "nature" and the "consequences" of death (so M. Harris [1974], who even speaks of Paul's development here of "a thanatology" [318]).

On this "classical view" of 5:1–10, the new issue for Paul—raised by his own brush with death—is the problem of bodily existence in the interim between the burial of the physical body and its resurrection as a new, "spiritual body." The latter he had described in 1 Cor 15:35–50, but he had said nothing there about the interim between the "sowing" of the old body and the "raising" of the new. There are many different opinions about the details of Paul's answer to this question, but those who follow the traditional approach to 5:1–10 are at least in agreement that the subject here is the fate of the body at death. Thus the images in 5:1 are interpreted anthropologically and individualistically: the *earthly, tent-like house* is the physical body which is *destroyed* when any given individual dies, and the *building from God . . . eternal in the heavens* is the new, immortal body which is given in its place—whether at the moment of death or later is disputed.

One difficulty with this general approach to the passage is that the question it alleges to be uppermost in Paul's mind is nowhere explicitly formulated within it, and certainly not clearly answered. This is especially puzzling if Paul means to be changing or supplementing the views he had expressed in 1 Cor 15:35–50, where both the issues and his responses to them are carefully stated. Many of the key terms of that discussion are missing here (e.g., "physical body," "spiritual body," "resurrection," "transformation," etc.), and so is any reference to Christ's role as the second Adam, or to his Parousia. The word "body" *(sōma)* itself does not even appear until v. 6.

Another difficulty is the fact that this interpretation must presuppose more about Paul's state of mind as he wrote than the available evidence warrants. It must presuppose that the threat of death he had experienced in Asia has left him doubtful and anxious about his own survival until the Lord's return. And it must presuppose that this personal agony leads him to address a matter which had not occurred to him before: What is the state of the dead between their burial and their resurrection at the last day? Or, at least, when do they receive the new spiritual bodies with which they shall be raised? However, we have Paul's own testimony that even as he wrote of the fate of the dead in 1

Cor he could think of himself as facing perils every hour and death "every day" (15:30–31); the mortal danger in Asia, then, was hardly a new experience for him (cf. Brun 1929:211, following Mundle). We also have Paul's own word that the whole experience in Asia had deepened his confidence in God and had enabled him to be hopeful that God would rescue him as well from future dangers (1:9b–10). That had turned out to be a renewing and uplifting experience for him, not a depressing one. When now he describes the experience of apostolic suffering in general as one of being *struck down, but not destroyed* (4:9b) and "receiving punishment—and yet not [being] put to death" (6:9c), he hardly sounds like a person suddenly distracted by thoughts of his own impending death. (Cf. Brun 1929:226, followed by Collange, 196–97.)

What is most important, however, is that interpretations which presume to find a "thanatology" in 5:1–10 fail to appreciate the way these verses fit into their context in 4:7ff. and, beyond that, into the whole discussion of apostolic service which began in 2:14. To illustrate this we may now return to 5:1 which, as already suggested, is the climactic supporting statement for the expression of apostolic confidence in 4:16a.

First, the context makes it clear that *our earthly, tent-like house* is to be identified with *our outer person* (4:16b), and thus with *our mortal flesh* (4:11) and *our bodies* (4:10). On this there is general agreement. It should be noted, however, that the house metaphor is primary here (it is carried forward in the second part of the verse, *a building . . . a house,* and in v. 2, *our dwelling*), and *our earthly . . . house* is described as *tent-like* only to emphasize that it is impermanent and collapsible. This is important because, in many other Hellenistic religious and philosophical texts, tent imagery is employed to describe the mortal body in distinction from the immortal soul which inhabits it until it "collapses" (references in the NOTES). Nothing in this verse indicates that Paul is making such a distinction, however, and the concept cannot be accommodated within his thought (see above on 4:7 and 4:16b especially). Rather, the image of the *tent-like house,* like that of the *earthen pots* (4:7), describes only the instability, and thus the vulnerability, of one's mortal existence (cf. Baumert 1973:151).

There is some disagreement about the meaning of Paul's reference to the destruction of this *earthly, tent-like house.* Does it refer (a) to the moment when an individual dies, (b) to the moment when, at the Parousia, this mortal body is "destroyed" through transformation into another kind of body, or (c) to the whole process of dying (Brun 1929:217–21) and therefore to the *being wasted away* of 4:16b? Barrett, 151, believes that (a) and (b) are both in Paul's mind. As for (b), *destroyed* is a poor word to use if "transformed" is what one means (see 1 Cor 15:51, 52, "we shall be changed"), and as for (c), *ean (if)* with the aorist subjunctive *katalythē (should be destroyed)* cannot mean "while . . . being destroyed" (cf. Bultmann, 134 n. 117). One must think, rather, of death itself, as in (a). However, one must beware of imposing on Paul's reference to death issues he has not raised—e.g., what happens to the body at death, and when is a new body given. Suffering and mortality are the issues here, not "embodiment." Death is understood here as the culmination of suffering and as constituting the most serious challenge to the boldness Paul has claimed for his apostolate. How can he say *we do not shrink back* (4:16a) in the face of death itself? That is the question behind 5:1.

Paul answers this question by affirming the certainty that we always have (see NOTES on the meaning of *we have*) *a building from God, a house not made with hands, eternal in the heavens.* The background and the meaning of this imagery have been debated extensively (see NOTES). (a) It is ordinarily interpreted anthropologically, as a reference to the new body which will be given to each individual believer. Whether this is thought to happen immediately at death, at the resurrection, or at the final transformation must then be further debated. (b) A few have opted for an ecclesiological interpretation, according to which the reference is to the incorporation of believers into the Body of Christ. (c) The interpretation most congenial to the context is the one that understands Paul's image against the background of Jewish and early Christian apocalyptic traditions (see Lang 1973, especially 182–85). There the *house* or *building* from God is associated, first, with the temple of the new eschatological Jerusalem (e.g., 2 Apoc Bar 4:3) and then, by extension, with the new Jerusalem itself, which awaits the righteous as their proper destiny (e.g., 2 Esdr 10:40–57; cf. also 1 Enoch 39:4; 41:2). Indeed, common indebtedness to this tradition would better explain the terminological coincidence between our verse and the saying of Mark 14:58 (see NOTES) than would the hypothesis that Paul is specifically alluding to some such saying.

In the passage just cited from 2 Esdr, not only the new Jerusalem but the whole of Zion's eschatological inheritance (see 10:44) is in prospect. There it is said that God, seeing the grief and distress which attends the destruction of the earthly Jerusalem, prepared to reveal to the seer "the brilliance of [the] glory" of the heavenly city (10:50). God told him "to go into the field where there was no foundation of any building, for no work of man's building could endure in a place where the city of the Most High was to be revealed. Therefore do not be afraid, and do not let your heart be terrified; but go in and see the splendor and vastness of the building, as far as it is possible for your eyes to see it . . ." (10:53–55, *RSV*). In this passage the "building" metaphor is used to describe the eschatological age, the glory and the vastness of what God has prepared for his people. If Paul is using the metaphor in a similar way in 2 Cor 5:1, it would be a further description of what he has referred to more generally as the *absolutely incomparable, eternal abundance of glory* which awaits those who endure the afflictions of this world (4:17). It would be another and more graphic reference to the realm of the unseen and eternal to which believers are oriented even as they exist in the present realm of the visible and the transitory (4:18).

The plausibility of this interpretation of the building metaphor is enhanced when one considers the parallels between the present passage and Phil 3:12–21. Lang (1973:184) has noted the verbal parallelism between the statement that *we have . . . a house . . . in the heavens (echomen oikian . . . en tois ouranois)* and that of Phil 3:20, "our commonwealth is in heaven" *(RSV; hēmōn . . . to politeuma en ouranois hyparchei)*. The contexts disclose material parallelism as well. In both passages Paul has written of believers as those whose lives are directed toward that which transcends the earthly—the latter described generally in Phil 3:19 as "earthly things" *(ta epigeia)* and more specifically in 2 Cor 5:1 as *our earthly [epigeios], tent-like house.* Conversely, whereas the focus of one's attention *(skopos)* is described generally in 2 Cor 4:18 as *the things that are not seen,* that is described more specifically in Phil 3:14 as "the upward call of God in Christ Jesus." But in both cases the fundamental conception is that believers are called to live out their lives in this age as those who ultimately, and thus in a decisive sense already, belong to another age (see also 1 Thess 5:8 and context; Rom 12:1–2 and context). Thus, the heavenly dwelling of 2 Cor 5:1, no less than the heavenly commonwealth of Phil 3:20, would be an image for that new age. Not even death, the final proof of mortality, need cause apostles to *shrink back* (4:16a), for they, like all believers, know that their true home is in heaven.

### The Sighing of the Spirit, 5:2–5

So far (4:16–5:1) Paul has been arguing that hardships and the wasting away of the *outer person* do not destroy the confidence of apostles, because they share the general Christian conviction that beyond the *earthly tent-like house* there is *a building from God . . . eternal in the heavens.* The argument is now extended in 5:2–5 by the addition (see note on *Also, indeed*) of a reference to the *sighing* which characterizes mortal existence, and a comment about its meaning. In the course of this, Paul subordinates the image of a heavenly dwelling to that of a heavenly garment (the two images are rather awkwardly combined in v. 2). The statement of v. 2 is repeated and explained in v. 4 (cf. Windisch, 160). Verse 3, albeit significant, is essentially a parenthetical remark, and v. 5 rounds off the thought of vv. 2–4 with references to God's work and the Spirit's presence.

The best commentary on vv. 2–5 comes in Rom 8:18–27, which seems to be a more developed statement of the view rather less fully expressed in this earlier letter (so Collange, 202). In Rom 8:23, 26 the sighing *(stenazein,* v. 23; *stenagmoi,* "sighs," v. 26), which characterizes mortal existence and its weakness, is specifically associated with the Spirit's presence as the "first fruits" of redemption. This interpretation of the sighing of mortal existence is fully applicable to the thought in 2 Cor 5:2–5 and is in accord with its broader context in 4:7–5:10. Here, too, Paul has argued that sufferings are preliminary to the eternal glory (4:17; cf. Rom 8:17), that faith is guided by what is not seen (4:18; cf. Rom 8:24–25), and that God's presence through the Spirit provides assurance of what is to come (5:5; cf. Rom 8:23). (The same ideas are expressed more compactly, yet following the same essential pattern—present sufferings/future glory/hope anchored in the Spirit's presence—in Rom 5: 2–5.) Given these parallels, one is surely warranted in concluding that the association of mortal *sighing* with the Spirit's presence, which is explicit in Rom 8, is implicit in 2 Cor 5. Here this sighing of the Spirit is mentioned as the consequence of one's having a heavenly dwelling (5:1) and thus as providing assurance about the unseen things toward which faith is oriented (4:18). If, in this passage, Paul has in mind the "groaning" under the burden of mortality mentioned in many Hellenistic texts, including Wis 9:15 (see note on *under a burden,* 5:4), it is not because he shares the dualistic anthropology that notion involves. Instead, he reinterprets that idea of mortal "groaning" in keeping with his conviction about the Spirit's presence helping us in the midst of our "weakness" (Rom 8:26). Unlike Epictetus, who promises that the person who learns how to deal with outward circumstances "will not groan [*ou stenaxeis*]" any longer under "this paltry body" made of clay (I.i.9–12, cited by Windisch, 163), Paul affirms the "groaning" as the *sighing* of the Spirit and as a confirmation that believers belong already to the coming age.

The clothing metaphor which first emerges in v. 2 must be interpreted in association with the metaphor of a *dwelling* with which it is rather inelegantly combined *(because we long to clothe ourselves over with our dwelling which comes from heaven).* If the heavenly *building/house* of v. 1 ( = *dwelling,* v. 2) has an anthropological reference, as many believe, then being clothed over in v. 2 would refer to putting on a glorious spiritual body, either at the moment of death (so, e.g., Windisch, 161, 163) or when the Lord returns (so, e.g., Héring, 37–38; Bultmann, 140; Barrett, 156). The most important argument for this view, especially in its second form (bodily transformation at the Parousia), is the use of the clothing image in 1 Cor 15:53, where the subject is the body (*sōma;* see 1 Cor 15:35*b*): "This corruptible shall be clothed with incorruptibility and this mortal shall be clothed with immortality" (cf. v. 54). But, as we have seen, the subject here in 2 Cor is not "embodiment" or the time and nature of bodily transformation. Here the issue is the meaning of mortality, and in particular the meaning of apostolic sufferings. In this context, as suggested above, the house metaphor of v. 1 is best interpreted in line with Paul's views about the eschatological existence of the believer between two ages. Therefore, the longing *to clothe ourselves over with our dwelling which comes from heaven* (v. 2) must have a more general sense, not restricted to the longing for a spiritual body. It must be the longing for the fulfillment of salvation, the longing for what Paul will describe in Rom 8:21 as "the glorious liberty of the children of God." Then the reference in v. 4 to the mortal being *engulfed by life* should also be understood more generally than the similar phrase in 1 Cor 15:54. In the latter, "death engulfed in victory" has the narrower meaning: the mortality (of the body) dissolved by immortality. But in v. 4, *mortality . . . engulfed by life* means "all that pertains to one's mortal existence . . . overcome when salvation shall be complete."

The broader eschatological (versus a narrowly anthropological) interpretation of 4:16–5:5 adopted here can also shed light on Paul's use of the compound verb ("to clothe oneself over") in 5:2, 4. In v. 3, by contrast, and also in 1 Cor 15:53, 54, the simple form is used ("to clothe oneself"). It is unlikely that the forms are used interchangeably (see NOTES), so one is left to inquire what special meaning the compound form may have. Although the simple form is used once as a metaphor for the eschatological transformation of the body (1 Cor 15:53, 54), it is used several times for "putting on" Christ (Gal 3:27; Rom 13:14) or Christ's armor (1 Thess 5:8; Rom 13:12; cf. Eph 6:11, 14ff.). In these passages, doubtless influenced by the language of the early Christian baptismal liturgy (see especially Gal 3:27), Paul is thinking of a moral transformation of the individual in his or her earthly existence, not of a future metaphysical transformation (cf. Col 3:9–10, 12ff. and Eph 4:22–24, where the "new nature" with which believers are clothed is also understood as a present moral transformation). This being "clothed" stands for the reception of the Spirit by faith (e.g., Gal 3:2, 5) and for the inception, through the Spirit's working, of the new life in Christ (e.g., Rom 7:6). Therefore, given the context of the present passage (2 Cor 4:16–5:5), it would appear that the longing *to clothe ourselves over with our dwelling which comes from heaven* (v. 2; = v. 4, that *mortality may be engulfed by life*) is the longing for the fulfillment of that salvation inaugurated at baptism (similarly, Lang 1973:187–88; Hanhart 1969:455).

Paul's comments on the sighing of the Spirit (v. 2) are momentarily broken off by the interjection of a parenthetical remark in v. 3. The way in which this is introduced (on which see the NOTES) suggests that the apostle is aware of some who do not share the presupposition he articulates, *that having once clothed ourselves, we shall not be found naked.* Here the aorist (past tense) participle *having once clothed ourselves* is formulated from the simple form "to clothe oneself," not from the compound form "to clothe oneself over" used in vv. 2 and 4. Interpretation of the participle is complicated by the fact that no specific object is given, and by the problems involved in trying to understand the precise meaning of the contrasting word *naked.* Nevertheless, it seems likely that the reference is to baptism, as in Gal 3:27 ("For as many as have been baptized into Christ have clothed themselves with Christ"). Thus, the aorist participle in v. 3 would match the two aorist participles of v. 5 which are associated with the coming of the Spirit (cf. Collange, 218; similarly, Thrall 1962:92–93; Lang 1973:188). Contrary to the view of Barrett, 153, this interpretation poses no difficulty for explaining the use of the compound verb "to clothe over" in v. 2. Indeed, the latter represents an extension of the primary metaphor: to "clothe oneself" with Christ at baptism is to receive the Spirit as *a down payment* on the fullness of salvation (v. 5; 1:22; cf. Rom 8:23), and to long to "clothe oneself over" with a heavenly dwelling is to long for the fulfillment of what has already been inaugurated.

Many different proposals have been made about the meaning of the word *naked* in v. 3 (see NOTES). It is very commonly interpreted on the presumption (a) that Paul had already written in 1 Cor 15:37–38 about the soul being stripped of its physical body at death in order to receive a new spiritual body at the resurrection; (b) that some in Corinth continued to hold to the contrary belief that there is no resurrection, because they thought the soul's destiny was to remain forever free of a body; and (c) that the reference to nakedness in 2 Cor 5:3 must be read against this background. However, it is doubtful that these presumptions can be validated. (a) The "naked kernel" mentioned in 1 Cor 15:37 is not the "soul" stripped of its body, but the present, death-ridden body, the person who dies and is buried without yet having received the body to come (see also Ellis 1960:221 n. 5; Baumert 1973:182–83). (b) The confessional statement of 2 Cor 4:14, affirming belief in God's resurrection of the dead, would have been pointless as a support for Paul's argument there had he thought the denial of the resurrection continued to be a problem in Corinth. (c) Since the subject in 2 Cor 4:7–5:10 is not "embodiment" as it had been in 1 Cor 15:35ff., one cannot assume that the same image (nakedness) has been applied in the same way in the two passages. The meaning of 2 Cor 5:3 must be determined primarily on the basis of the discussion of apostolic suffering within which it stands.

We have already determined that *having once clothed ourselves* (v. 3) probably refers to the baptismal "putting on" of Christ. In this context nakedness would most naturally refer not to the "nakedness of the soul" at death (which is not the subject here), nor to the nakedness of moral shame and guilt (which is also not the subject here), but to alienation from Christ, to having in some way denied one's baptism (cf. Collange, 215–18, 225). The image of nakedness is the logical counterpart to the clothing imagery familiar to Paul and his readers from the traditional baptismal liturgy. One need seek no further than this (be it in the traditions of Judaism, of Hellenistic anthropological speculation, or of Christian Gnosticism) for the origin and the significance of the metaphor as it is present in v. 3. Here Paul interrupts his comments about the longing to be "clothed over" with the fullness of salvation in order to interject a remark which is implicitly polemical. He warns that what has been affirmed about the coming salvation presupposes that those who have been once clothed with Christ will not be found alienated from him—"naked"—when they appear before their Judge (cf. v. 10 and remarks on *be found* in NOTES). Both the fact and the form (on which see NOTES) of this interjection suggest that Paul has reason to think there are some in Corinth who will not be able to meet this condition. It is likely that Paul has in mind specifically those who are vying with him for apostolic authority there—those whom he will characterize in a later letter as only "disguised" as apostles of Christ (11:12–15, cited by Lang

1973:188–89). They have been oriented only to *things that are seen* (4:18); but when their disguises are revealed, they themselves will be exposed for what they are *(found naked)*. On this interpretation of v. 3, the comment of v. 4 about not wishing *to unclothe ourselves, but to clothe ourselves over,* would be a statement of resolve—and thus an implicit appeal to the readers—to remain faithful to the gospel of Christ.

This paragraph, which opened with an affirmation of continuing confidence (4:16*a*), closes with an affirmation about God, the ultimate source of that confidence. God is *the one who equipped us* for the life which shall engulf our mortality (v. 4) by giving us *the Spirit as a down payment* on that life. The pattern of argument, as well as the content of the argument here, corresponds to Rom 5:1–5, which also opens with a statement of confidence ("we have peace with God," v. 1), proceeds with comments on suffering as preliminary to the coming glory (vv. 2–4), and concludes with an affirmation about God's gift of the Spirit as the ground of hope (v. 5). In the present verse, as in 1:22 earlier in the letter, the Spirit is described as *a down payment* on the promised inheritance (cf. "first fruits" in Rom 8:23), and the aorist participles *(equipped . . . gave,* corresponding to *having once clothed ourselves* in v. 3) point to a decisive moment in the past, doubtless the time of baptism into Christ (Bultmann, 141; Collange, 224; although Barrett, 157, cautions against restricting the reference only to conversion and baptism). This emphasis on the role of the Spirit in the Christian life generally, and for apostles specifically as they endure countless hardships for the sake of the gospel, accords fully with Paul's earlier description of the apostolic vocation as a *ministry of the Spirit* (3:8).

## A Note on the Polemic of 4:16–5:5

Bultmann, 132 (and 1947:3–5) has described 5:1–5 as a polemical "digression" aimed at "Gnostic" opponents in Corinth. On this view, vv. 3–4 in particular must be read as anti-Gnostic polemic: against the Gnostic longing for the "nakedness" which comes when one's mortal body is stripped away at death, Paul affirms the Christian desire to be clothed with a heavenly garment (Bultmann, 137–38). Since Gnostic teaching did in fact include a hope that, once stripped of the old body, one would "put on" a new, immortal body (for the evidence see, e.g., Lietzmann, 119–20; Windisch, 164–65), Bultmann, 139, must conjecture that Paul's knowledge of that teaching was incomplete. This same position is developed, more elaborately, by Schmithals (1971:259–75). He emphasizes "the polemical aim" of 5:1–10 (260), arguing that "in terminology and conception Paul follows his opposition as far as this is possible, in order better to be heard in his real concern" (261). That concern, according to Schmithals, was to defend belief in "a celestial corporeality in the consummation" (261) against the contrary ideal of disembodiment (nakedness) (264). Schmithals differs from Bultmann principally in his insistence that the longing for a heavenly garment played a role only in later Gnosticism, particularly in the circles associated closely with Judaism and the Mystery cults (266–67). The Gnostics of Corinth, he believes, despite their closeness to Judaism, were convinced that the soul ascended naked to heaven and would receive no new clothing (267). This is the view Paul would be attacking in the passage before us.

On the one hand, one may agree that Paul is aware of some opposing viewpoint(s) as he develops his thoughts in 4:16–5:5. The emphatic *We* of 4:18 is evidence of this, as is the pointed interjection of 5:3. Beyond these specific indicators in the passage itself, one may note that the whole discussion of which it is a part (2:14–5:19) has been prompted by contrary views of apostleship and by certain criticisms of his own performance as an apostle which Paul understands to be abroad in Corinth (see, e.g., 2:16b–3:6 and COMMENT). There can be no question but that polemical and apologetic considerations have influenced what—as well as how—Paul has written in 4:16–5:5.

On the other hand, the Bultmann-Schmithals hypothesis that the subject (in 5:1–5 or 5:1–10) is the body, that the section is essentially a polemical digression, and that the target of the polemic is Gnostic teaching is not convincing. Our exposition has sought to demonstrate that the subject here is the meaning of apostolic hardships and suffering, and that 5:1–5 is closely related to 4:16–18, just as the whole of 4:7–5:10 is an integral part of the commentary on apostolic service, 2:14–5:19. Here as elsewhere in this part of the letter the apologetic and polemical motifs have errant views of apostleship in view, not false notions about life after death. Moreover, the identification of the opposing views as "Gnostic" rests on precarious evidentiary foundations. Insofar as Paul himself is used as a source, one is relying on fragmentary, indirect, and partisan evidence—indeed, on evidence from one who, in the view of Schmithals, completely misunderstood his opposition in a most crucial matter. Insofar as the evidence is gleaned from other sources, these are in general later (e.g., the *Corpus Hermeticum,* cited often by both Bultmann and Schmithals), and on such an allegedly vital question as hope for a heavenly garment they yield data at variance with the proposed reconstruction.

Another polemical interpretation of the verses, but one which can be taken more seriously, is advanced by Osten-Sacken (1975:104–24). He argues that Paul is quoting a traditional affirmation in 5:1–2, one about life after death which the apostle seeks to correct. As reconstructed by Osten-Sacken (ibid.:121), this quoted material would include (following *RSV* as closely as possible): "If the earthly tent we live in is destroyed, we have a building from God, a house not made with hands, in the heavens. Here indeed we groan, longing for our heavenly dwelling." The remainder of vv. 1–2, and the verses following (save for vv. 6b, 8b, which are also judged to be quotations) are taken as Paul's glossing (vv. 1–2) and interpreting (vv. 3ff.) of the tradition. According to this view, the apostle's chief concern in 5:1ff. is to emphasize that, just as the life of Jesus is "manifested in our [mortal] bodies" (4:10, 11), and just as God has raised Jesus from the dead (4:14), so the Christian hope is for a somatic existence after death, not the putting off of the body (ibid.:118). The polemic, then, would be against the common Hellenistic conception of immortality, and Osten-Sacken is not required to reconstruct some special Corinthian form of "Gnosticism." A good case can be made for Paul's dependence on traditional ideas (e.g., the *we know* of 5:1 and several words which occur only here in the apostle's letters), at least in 5:1–2. But this view still requires one to believe that the main concern of the passage is with the fate of the body after death, and several of the objections which have been raised against the usual, "classical" interpretation can also be raised against this one.

In summary, 4:16–5:5 continues the discussion of apostolic service begun in 2:14 and the interpretation of the mortality of apostles (4:7–5:10) in particular. Although the style is essentially discursive, not polemical, polemical and apologetic concerns are evident. Paul is concerned to refute the false idea that hardships and suffering are proof that his apostolate is invalid. It is likely that his rivals were pointing to more generally acceptable evidence of apostleship in their own case. But Paul's argument is that those whose hope is in God are oriented to *the things that are not seen* (4:18), *eternal in the heavens* (5:1), not to *the things that are seen* and *temporary* (4:18). That is why true apostles need not be intimidated by the adversities or the adversaries they encounter in the course of their ministry (4:16a). With all believers, they share the conviction that their true home is not in this present age or in this *tent-like house* of mortal existence, but in the age to come, in a heavenly dwelling (5:1–4). Indeed, faith is able to perceive in our groaning under the burden of mortal existence (5:4) the sighing of the Spirit, given as *a down payment* on the coming eternal glory (5:5; cf. 4:17).

## Confidence and Commitment, 5:6–10

The expression of confidence with which this paragraph opens reformulates the declaration of apostolic boldness in 4:16a. The expanded sense of the first person plural, evident since 4:18 (not just "we apostles," 4:16–17, but "we believers"), is not relinquished here, although the primary reference is probably once more to the Pauline apostolate. Now the building and clothing images of 5:1, 2–4 have been left behind in favor of the image of one's "home place." Using this, Paul seeks to make a point about the commitment to the Lord with which one's confidence should be attended.

The two participial phrases of v. 6 *(having . . . and knowing . . .)* are grammatically incomplete as they stand. Most commentators believe that the thought is concluded in v. 8, but that is true only in the sense that v. 8 takes up again the theme of *confidence* and the image of being "at home/away from home." In fact, as Demke (1969:599) has observed, the first participle of v. 6

attaches most satisfactorily to v. 9. It would appear that Paul had started out to say, *Therefore, having confidence always . . . we make it our ambition to be acceptable to (the Lord)*. This thought is parallel to that in v. 8 (see below), but v. 8 cannot easily be explained as the completion of v. 6, because the imagery of the latter is significantly reformulated in the former.

The imagery of vv. 6 and 8, which is also present in v. 9, requires special consideration. It employs the contrasting terms *endēmein*, to be "at home," and *ekdēmein*, to be "away from home." Since neither term is used anywhere else by Paul (nor elsewhere in the NT or LXX), and since these words are used by him in three different ways in the present verses, it is likely that Paul is taking over a favorite image of his opponents in order to correct their use of it (cf. Schmithals 1971:269 n. 208; Lang 1973:192). If so, then the antithesis set out in v. 6b would have a polemical objective: to be *at home in the body* is not to be "at home with the Lord," as some must be claiming, but in fact to be *away from our home with the Lord*. This would be a restatement of the contrast already presented between life in the *earthly, tent-like house* and in God's *house . . . eternal in the heavens* (v.1), and it corresponds to Paul's concern about those who look to *the things that are seen* rather than to those *that are not seen* (4:18).

That Paul is not entirely pleased with the polemically formulated antithesis of v. 6b is suggested, first, by the fact that he interrupts his own sentence in order to shift over to more comfortable terrain. For Paul, the crucial point is not where one resides, although the formulation in v. 6b could lead one to that conclusion. For Paul, the crucial point is the orientation of one's life. This is what is conveyed by the fresh antithesis of v. 7, that believers are guided by what is believed, not by what is seen. This is simply a repetition of what has been emphasized already in 4:18. Here, as there, Paul's words are directed against those who have been guided by *appearance* rather than by *faith* when evaluating apostolic credentials. Therefore, the contrast in v. 7 is not between faith as the mode of one's present existence (in this age) and "seeing" as the mode of one's existence in the age to come. This common view (e.g., Windisch, 167; Bultmann, 142) is not supported by the context, and it is in fact contradicted both by the use of the passive term *appearance* (see NOTES) and by Paul's own statement in 1 Cor 13:13 that faith endures (cf. v. 12: even where there is a "seeing face to face"). Cf. Lang's discussion 1973:190. Paul's statement in Gal 2:20 may be compared, but not because both passages present faith as the preliminary or incomplete form of one's relating to the Lord (Windisch, 167, cf. Barrett, 158). Rather, in Gal 2:20 as in the present passage, Paul is contrasting two modes of existence in *this* age: "It is no longer I who live, but Christ who lives in me, and the life I now live in the flesh I live by faith [in him]" *(RSV)*.

Paul's uneasiness with the formulation of v. 6b becomes particularly apparent in v. 8. The syntax of v. 6 is abandoned in favor of a wholly new construction (see NOTES), and the image of v. 6*b* is now fundamentally reconceived. The original antithesis was directed against those who identify residence *in the body* and residence *with the Lord,* something Paul clearly does not want to do. But the interjection of a reference to faith in v. 7 and the declaration of Gal 2:20 ("in the flesh . . . by faith") make it equally clear that Paul does not believe life *in the body* is incompatible with life in Christ. Lest that false conclusion be drawn from the polemically formulated antithesis of v. 6*b,* he repeats the antithesis now in a radically altered form. Those who act with the boldness of apostles (and all true believers) resolve to orient themselves to the Lord, not to the body (v. 8). Here the apostle has transformed the image from one of location to one of direction (see NOTES on the shift from the present tense in v. 6*b* to the aorist tense in v. 8*b*). The issue is not one's present place of residence but what one gives as one's "home address," what place claims one's loyalty, where one longs to go. The alternatives presented in v. 8*b* are *body/ Lord,* and these correspond to the alternatives of 4:18, *things . . . seen/things . . . not seen,* and of 5:7, *appearance/faith.*

Because orientation (commitment) is involved here, not location, it is misleading to cite Phil 1:23, where Paul writes of departing this life to "be with Christ," or 1 Thess 4:17, where he writes of his hope "to meet the Lord in the air" at the Parousia, and so to "be with the Lord" forever. In such contexts being "in the flesh" (Phil 1:22; cf. "alive," 1 Thess 4:17) necessarily excludes being "with Christ [or: the Lord]." But the present context is different (cf. Kramer 1966:171–72), and despite the impression the polemically formulated antithesis of v. 6*b* might leave, Paul's subject here is the present life, not the future. Precisely for this reason he has reconceived the antithesis of v. 6*b,* in the process turning the more static conception of residency into the more dynamic conception of motion-toward. It is the same dynamic conception of "life toward Christ" which is expressed, perhaps more effectively, in the athletic imagery of Phil 3:13: "forgetting what lies behind and straining forward to what lies ahead" *(RSV).* As Lang notes (1973:199), both passages reflect the typically Pauline dialectic of "already but not yet." In the one case it is a matter of being "already on the course, but not yet at the goal," and in the other it is a matter of being "already on the road, but not yet home."

Bachmann, 240, separates vv. 9–10 from the preceding discussion and treats them as opening a section which extends through 6:10. He holds (1) that Paul in 5:8 had concluded one phase of his argument; (2) that a new theme— judgment and the necessity to please the Lord—is introduced in 5:9–10; (3) that this theme is then developed in 5:11ff.; and (4) that the judgment motif is still clear in 6:3, where the apostle expresses concern lest his ministry be criticized. These arguments are not convincing, however. (1) The "home place" imagery of vv. 6, 8 is still in play in v. 9, and vv. 9–10 together may be compared with the parenetic conclusions with which Paul typically closes discussions (see, e.g., 1 Cor 15:58; 1 Thess 4:18; 5:6–11). (2) When Paul writes in v. 9 of a commitment *to be acceptable to (the Lord),* this continues his insistence on the integrity and validity of his apostolate—a theme which, with an underlying polemical thrust, has been present throughout 4:7–5:8. The eschatological sanction in v. 10 buttresses the ethical concern (like similar ones in, e.g., Rom 13:11–14; 1 Cor 3:12–15; Gal 6:7–8). (3) The discussion in 5:11ff. is indeed closely related to what has preceded, but no more closely to 5:9–10 than to the whole of 2:14ff. In fact, beginning in 5:11, the first person plural —which in 4:18–5:10 generally includes all believers along with the apostles —again means, more narrowly, "we apostles," as it had most of the time in 2:14–4:17. (4) There is only the most general kind of relationship between the judgment theme of 5:9–10 and the remark in 6:3; and this proves nothing.

As noted earlier, it is really only in v. 9 that Paul completes the thought begun in v. 6*a:* since we have confidence always (guaranteed by the Spirit's presence as a down payment on the coming fulfillment of salvation, v. 5), our sole objective is to please the Lord. Following as it does on the general affirmations of 4:18ff., this one, too, is appropriate for all believers, and in that respect it may be said to contain an implicit appeal to the whole Corinthian congregation. At the same time, it is a further assurance to the Corinthians that the Pauline apostolate is committed only to the gospel, not to its own welfare (see, e.g., 2:17; 4:2, 5, 15; Collange, 237–38, also recognizes the relation of v. 9 to the theme of apostleship). The affirmation of v. 9 is essentially parallel to the resolve of v. 8 to be oriented to the Lord (cf. Baumert 1973:241), but with one significant difference. Now the "home place" imagery which Paul had adopted (in order to criticize) in v. 6*b,* and which he had substantially reconceived (in order to avoid misunderstanding) in v. 8*b,* is jettisoned entirely. In v. 9 the participles *(at home . . . away from home)* occur without any clarifying prepositional phrases, so that commentators over the years have been left to speculate whether one should supply "in the body" or "with the Lord" (see NOTES). But it would be misleading to supply either one, especially since in either case the thought of v. 9 would then conflict with that of v. 6*b.* It seems likely that Paul intends to leave the object of the participles unclarified, precisely in order to be done with the imagery entirely (cf. Lang 1973:193). The effect of his formulation here, *whether we are at home or away from home,* is to relativize the matter of "residency" so thoroughly as to dismiss it as an irrelevant issue. For him, what is alone important is whether one's service as an apostle (or as any ordinary believer) is finally adjudged *acceptable* to the Lord. Paul is constantly reminding himself and his congregations that whatever one says or does comes under God's surveillance and ultimate judgment (in this letter, e.g., 2:17*b;* 3:4; 4:2; 5:11; 7:12).

This point, and therefore the statements of resolve in vv. 8, 9, are reinforced and concluded in v. 10. Using language and concepts which have been drawn for the most part from the traditions of apocalyptic Judaism (see the NOTES and Synofzik 1977:75, as well as the excursus in Lietzmann, 122–23), Paul emphasizes that one's present actions will come at last under the scrutiny of Christ. It is the final judgment of all *believers* that is in view here, not a universal judgment (see NOTES), and the issue is not salvation or damnation (as in 2:14; Rom 2:5–11, etc.) but whether, as a Christian, one has been committed to the Lord (Mattern 1966:157).

As indicated in the NOTES, the syntax of this verse is extremely unclear. The troublesome phrase is the one that mentions the body. In addition to the syntactical problem, one should note that it is quite unique to have bodily existence mentioned at all when the topic is the last judgment, as it is here. Thus, the phrase calls attention to itself both grammatically and conceptually, leading Synofzik to argue plausibly that Paul intrudes it in order to make a point of some importance to him (1977:76–77). Synofzik suggests that Paul is countering enthusiasts in Corinth who act as though it will make no difference what one does *in the body*. The problem is documented in an earlier letter (e.g., 1 Cor 6:12–20), even if it is not very specifically reflected in the present one. Yet Paul could well be conscious of how his own negative remarks about the body in vv. 6, 8 might be misconstrued, and this may be enough to prompt the "body" reference in v. 10. In any case, what he says in this verse about the ultimate accountability of all believers is designed to support the appeal which is implicit in v. 9. The conviction underlying both verses is "We are the Lord's" (Rom 14:8 [*RSV*]). To belong to him means to be committed absolutely to him (v. 9), knowing that nothing one does *in the body* is a matter of indifference (v. 10). Just as in the discussion preceding (4:16–5:5; 5:6–9) the basic concern has been for the present (mortal) life, not for one's future (immortal) existence, so in the last verse the concern is really with the present. Nothing specific is said about rewards or punishments, or what those might entail. The emphasis falls on one's present accountability (cf. Mattern 1966: 158).

## 8. THE MINISTRY OF RECONCILIATION, 5:11–19

5 ¹¹Therefore, knowing the fear of the Lord, we are persuading people, but we have been made known to God—and I hope made known also to your consciences. ¹²We are not recommending ourselves to you once more, but rather providing you a suitable basis to be proud of us, that you may have something to say to those who are boasting of what is outward and not of what is within. ¹³For if we have ever been beside ourselves, it was for God; if we continue in our right mind, it is for you. ¹⁴For Christ's love lays claim to us, our decision having been this, that one has died for all; therefore, all have died. ¹⁵And he has died for all,

that those who live might live no longer to themselves, but to the one who for them died and was raised up.

¹⁶So from now on we regard no one according to worldly standards; if indeed we have regarded Christ according to worldly standards, now we no longer regard him in that way. ¹⁷So if anyone is in Christ, there is a new creation. Everything old has come to an end; behold, new things have come to be. ¹⁸All things are from God, who has reconciled us to himself through Christ, and has given to us the ministry of reconciliation. ¹⁹As it is said: God, in Christ, was reconciling the world to himself, not charging their trespasses to them. And he has established among us the word of reconciliation.

## NOTES

5:11. *Therefore.* The *oun* here connects what follows with what has preceded in v. 10 (on which see the following note), even as it opens a new phase of the discussion.

*knowing the fear of the Lord.* Here *knowing (eidotes)* is not just "knowing about" the final judgment before Christ, although it includes that, as the connection with v. 10 shows. More especially, *knowing* refers to an experience or sense of accountability. In addition, the phrase *fear of the Lord* must be understood primarily in relation to its background in the Jewish Bible and tradition (e.g., LXX 1 Chr 19:7, 9; Ps 18[19]:9; Isa 2:10, 19, 21; often in Prov, Sir, and T 12 Patr), not with reference to *the judicial bench of Christ* (v. 10). *The Lord* here is not Christ, but the *God* to whom the Pauline apostolate is fully known. Paul writes of *the fear of the Lord* nowhere else, and the equivalent phrase "fear of God" occurs only twice in his letters: once here in 2 Cor, in a section of uncertain origin (7:1), and once in a scriptural quotation in Rom (3:18, from LXX Ps 36:2[1]). Elsewhere in the NT, cf. "the fear of the Lord" in Acts 9:31 and "with reverence for Christ" *(en phobō Christou)* in Eph 5:21.

*we are persuading people.* The present tense here should perhaps be interpreted as conative, signifying the incompleteness of the action (not the attempt; see *GNTG* III:63; Barrett, 163). The same expression *(anthrōpous peithein)* occurs in Gal 1:10a, "For am I now persuading people [*anthrōpous peithō*] or God?"—where the verb *peithein* is used interchangeably with the verb *areskein* (v. 10bc, "Or am I seeking to please people [*anthrōpois areskein*]? If I were still trying to please people [*anthrōpois ēreskon*], I would not be a slave of Christ"); correctly Betz 1979:55, 56, against Bultmann, *TDNT* VI:2–3. The phrase had been used to define the objective of rhetoric and oratory (examples cited by Betz 1979:54 n. 103), and in Gal 1:10 the apostle is dissociating himself from the kind of artful deceptions with which the rhetoricians of his day were often identified (Betz ibid.:55, especially nn. 105–8). In the present verse Paul seems to be responding to those who have accused him of trying to "persuade people" in devious ways (cf. Plummer, 168–69; Bultmann, 148, 1947:13, and *TDNT* VI:2; Schmithals 1971:189); see COMMENT.

*but we have been made known to God.* The *de* has mild adversative force ( = *but*), following as it does Paul's qualified "concession" that he is *persuading people,* and introducing a further—indeed, the decisive—qualification. Héring, 41, interprets the perfect tense *(pephanerōmetha)* as a present, "we are visible just as we are," while Plummer, 168, and Hughes, 187, want to give it its full perfect sense, "to have been and to continue to be made known" (cf. Barrett, 164, to "stand open"). The verb is frequent in chaps. 1–9 (also 2:14; 3:3; 4:10, 11; 5:10; 7:12); elsewhere in Paul's letters only in 11:6 (Letter E); Rom 1:19; 3:21; 1 Cor 4:5 (and in the late doxology, Rom 16:26).

*and I hope.* Now the *de* is a simple connective ( = *and*) as a point is added. Momentarily Paul reverts to the first person singular as he expresses a deeply felt concern (similarly 1:13, where, however, a more sustained use of the singular, 1:12ff., is anticipated). Here the verb "to hope" moves in the direction of the meaning "to think" (BDF § 350) or "to believe" (Hughes, 187). Used with the following perfect-tense infinitive, it suggests that Paul entertains a certain optimism about registering his point with the Corinthians (cf. Bultmann, 148–49).

*made known also to your consciences.* For the meaning of "conscience," see the NOTES on 4:2. The plural, *consciences,* should perhaps be accorded the sense of the phrase *to each and every . . . conscience* in 4:2b (cf. Plummer, 169).

12. *We are not . . . once more.* Cf. 3:1 and NOTES and COMMENT there.

*providing.* Translates the participle *didontes,* literally "giving." Here, as often in Paul's letters, a participle stands where there should be another finite verb (e.g., "we are providing"); see BDF § 468(1); Robertson 1923:439; *GTNG* III:343. Similar instances of Paul's "free use of the participle" (Plummer, 170) in chaps. 1–9 are in 7:5, 7; 8:19, 20, 24; 9:11 (Lietzmann, 124).

*a suitable basis.* This word *(aphormē)* is used only by Paul (elsewhere, 11:12, twice; Rom 7:8, 11; Gal 5:13) and by the author of the Pastoral Epistles (1 Tim 5:14) in the NT. In 11:12, as well as here, the context is polemical, and the word could refer to any sort of data or arguments useful in impugning or defending someone's actions (cf. 1 Tim 5:14).

*to be proud.* More literally, "of [for] a boast." Here and in the other two places where Paul uses this noun in chaps. 1–9 (1:14 and 9:3), the word has a positive, not a negative meaning. The extraordinary frequency of the word-group in 2 Cor (see NOTES on 1:12) suggests that the matter of legitimate versus illegitimate boasting was an important part of the dispute between Paul and his Corinthian rivals *(those who are boasting of what is outward)* at this time. See further on 10:8.

*of us.* The reading "of you" *(hymōn* for *hēmōn)* has excellent attestation (the two great uncials, ℵ and B, and also P⁴⁶), and Collange, 248, adopts it. However, it is the conduct of the Pauline apostolate that is in question here, not the conduct of the Corinthians; had Paul meant to refer to their having something to be proud of, he almost certainly would have said "for yourselves" *(hyper hymōn autōn* or *hyper heautōn)* rather than just "for you" *(hyper hymōn);* see Barrett, 162 n. 1.

*that you may have something to say.* The Greek phrase *(hina echēte pros tous . . . ;* literally "that you may have to those who . . .") requires that something be understood, whether the preceding *aphormē* (thus, "that you may have this resource to use against those who . . ." [cf. Plummer, 170]) or *kauchēma* ("that you may have this boast . . ."), or simply *ti* ("that you may have something for those who . . ."). The present tr., like *NAB*, supplies *ti legein, something to say* (*to those who,* etc.); so also Bultmann, 150.

*those who are boasting.* The expression is formulated from the verb *kauchasthai,* used here in a negative sense (contrast the use of the same verb in 7:14; 9:2, and of the related noun *kauchēma* earlier in this verse). As in 11:12, the reference is to Paul's rivals for leadership in Corinth.

*of what is outward and not of what is within.* More literally, "in (the) face and not in (the) heart" *(en prosōpō . . . kai mē en kardia).* In 1 Thess 2:17 *prosōpō ou kardia* refers to Paul's absence from the Thessalonians "in person (but) not in spirit," as we might say. In the present context, however, the contrast is not between (physical) presence and absence but between appearance and reality. Paul's contrast in Rom 2:28–29 between false circumcision, which is "something external and physical" *(hē en tō phanerō en sarki),* and true circumcision, which is "a matter of the heart, spiritual and not literal" *(kardias en pneumati ou grammati; RSV* tr.), is similar. In the present passage Paul's expression seems to have been influenced, probably unconsciously, by 1 Kgdms (1 Sam) 16:7: "A person sees what is outward [*eis prosōpon*], but God sees what is within [*eis kardian*]." For this reason, the suggestion of Martyn (1967:283–84) that *prosōpon* should be taken here in its literal meaning of "face" is not persuasive. Boasting *en prosōpō (of what is outward)* may also be called boasting *kata sarka* (literally "according to the flesh"), as in 11:18; cf. Bultmann, 150.

13. *For.* Translates *gar,* which connects this verse closely to v. 12*b*.

*if. . . if.* Translates *eite . . . eite;* see note on 5:9, where the same words are translated *whether . . . or.*

*if we have ever been beside ourselves.* Used intransitively, as here, the verb *existanai* means "to lose one's mind," "to be beside oneself," etc. Paul employs this verb nowhere else, but in Mark 3:21 it is used in the same way with reference to allegations that Jesus was "beside himself" *(RSV),* that is, "possessed" (see v. 22). See also, e.g., LXX Isa 28:7, where it means "to be out of one's head because of strong drink"; Philo, *On Drunkenness* 146–47, where it is used of those whose religious ecstasy is mistaken for drunkenness; T Job 39:10, where the verb is linked with *mainesthai,* "to be mad." It is unclear whether the aorist tense of the verb in the present verse should be interpreted "historically" ("if we were once beside ourselves") or as "timeless" (so Hughes, 191), which it is in Mark 3:21 (cf. Burton 1898: § 47 and BDF § 342[1], who give it the force of a perfect—a present condition consequent upon a past action). The context (including the use of the present tense in the contrasting verb) suggests that Paul's meaning wavers somewhere between the two; thus the expression *have ever been* is employed in the present tr.

*for God.* Cf. 1 Cor 14:2, 28, where speaking in tongues has been characterized as a speaking "to God" ([*tō*] *Theō*).

*if we continue in our right mind.* Paul employs this verb *(sōphronein)* elsewhere only in Rom 12:3. There, in a play on words with *phronein* ("to think," "hold an opinion," etc.), it is contrasted with *hyperphronein* ("to think too highly of oneself"), and means "to think in a measured way." Here, however, where it is contrasted with *existanai,* the verb approaches more closely the meaning "to be possessed of one's senses." Cf. Plato, *Phaedrus* 244 A–D and *Republic* 331 C; Philo, *On the Cherubim* 69, where "sanity" *(sōphronein, sōphrosyne)* is contrasted with "madness" *(mainesthai, mania =* *existanai, ekstasis,* as the passages just cited from the *Phaedrus* and Philo—as well as T Job 39:10, cited above—clearly show). This contrast is frequent in Greek writers; see North 1966, especially 115 n. 90, 178–79, 317. (Contrast P. Marshall [1980:509–13], who suggests that v. 13 is Paul's response to those who have charged that his rhetorical style is "excessive" and "undisciplined.") The use of the word *continue* in the tr. is intended to help distinguish the present tense of this verb from the aorist tense of the preceding one (see above).

*for you.* Cf. 1 Cor 14:3, where prophesying—in contrast to speaking in tongues— is said to be a speaking "to people" *(anthrōpois)* for their good, that is, for the upbuilding of the church (v. 4).

14. *For.* As in v. 13, *gar,* which here introduces both v. 14 and v. 15. Whereas Bachmann, 251–52, speaks of "a thoroughly organic connection" between these verses and v. 13, Windisch, 180, insists that there is only a "very loose" connection between vv. 13 and 14. See COMMENT.

*Christ's love.* This tr. interprets the genitive *tou Christou* ("of Christ") as subjective (so also most commentators and grammarians), although Héring, 41–42, opts for the objective and translates this as "love for Christ." Spicq (1965:88) argues that the context here, especially v. 13, requires the conclusion that the genitive is at once objective and subjective (cf. Collange, 253; Moule 1953:41; Fürst 1968:224), and he suggests for it the name "comprehensive [or: simultaneous] genitive." But the evidence for the subjective (alone) is decisive: (a) Paul nowhere else writes about one's "love for Christ," and rarely about one's "love for God" (then using only the verb, Rom 8:28; 1 Cor 8:3; cf. 1 Cor 2:9, quoting Isa; 16:22, quoting a liturgical formulation [with *philein,* not *agapān* ]). (b) God's love for his people is an absolutely fundamental Pauline theme (e.g., Rom 5:5; 2 Cor 13:11, 13), and this is seen to have been established decisively through Christ (Rom 8:39), above all through his death (Rom 5:8). Thus, Paul writes specifically of *Christ's love,* Rom 8:35, 38; Gal 2:20. (c) It is precisely the redemptive power of Christ's death which is emphasized in vv. 14*b*–15*a,* and only a reference to *Christ's love* provides a suitable introduction for that (so also Bachmann, 252; Barrett, 167).

*lays claim to.* The verb used here *(synechein)* has a wide range of meanings, from "hold together" *(syn-echein)* to "hold fast," "hold shut," "hold in custody," "hold within bounds," etc. (see BAG s.v.; Köster in *TDNT* VII:877–87). In Phil 1:23 (the only other Pauline occurrence) it describes the apostle's situation of being "hard pressed" *(RSV;* BAG s.v. 5) to choose between life and death—that is, constrained to make a difficult choice. It is less clear which of the possible meanings or nuances the verb bears in the present verse: whether the idea of restraint (e.g., Plummer, 173), or of compulsion (e.g., *NIV:* "compels," and *NEB:* "leaves us no choice"), or of general control (e.g., Bultmann, 152; Barrett, 168; *RSV:* "controls"; *TEV:* "ruled by"), or of supplying an impulse to action (e.g., BAG s.v. 7; Bachmann, 252; Windisch, 181; Ahern 1960:24; Thüsing 1968:102–3; *NAB:* "impels"). Spicq (who himself translates the verb here as "étreint" [1959:127], "embraces" [not "impels," as in the English version of his book]), has noted that *synechein* commonly means "oblige" in the papyri, and soon became "the usual word for stating the executory force of a judicial decision" (1965: 192–93; cf. Collange, 253). In the present verse the English tr. "to lay claim to" (cf.

Köster, *TDNT* VII:883) seems the most satisfactory (despite my own earlier preference for "sustains," Furnish 1968:167–68 and 1972:92–93). Like Paul's own verb, it has a certain juridical connotation (see also following note), it satisfies the need for a tr. which can in fact cover a range of meanings (e.g., restraint, compulsion, impulsion), and it is in accord with what Paul writes elsewhere about the totality of love's claim over the life of the believer; see COMMENT.

*our decision having been this.* Translates *krinantas touto.* The participle should be interpreted as modal, not causal: the *decision* accompanies the receipt of *Christ's love,* it does not prompt it; see BDF § 418(5) and Furnish 1977:214 n. 29. Like *synechein* (see preceding note), the verb *krinein* often has a juridical connotation: to come to a firm and effective decision about something or someone; see BAG s.v. 4a. Spicq (1959: 135–36 n. 6) provides instances where it means specifically coming to a religious judgment ("conviction," Héring, 42 n. 20) about something. Cf. Paul's use of the verb in 2:1; Rom 15:5; 1 Cor 2:2. In the present verse it seems to be used much as the verb *logizesthai* is in Rom 3:28, to introduce a theological belief (cf. BAG s.v. *logizomai,* 3): "For we are of the opinion that . . ." (Bultmann, 152, who also cites Rom 6:11; 8:18; 14:14). On this, see also the following note. Windisch, 181, and Hughes, 193 n. 22, think the aorist tense points back to a judgment Paul formed at or shortly after his conversion. However, such an individualistic interpretation is hardly in keeping with the apostle's evident intent here to call upon a conviction held in common by all believers.

*that.* Translates *hoti,* which often introduces set theological formulations (Rom 6:3; 1 Cor 11:23; 15:3ff., etc.). Elsewhere in the present letter see especially *eidotes hoti* (*knowing that,* 4:14, on which see the note). As in the present verse *hoti* follows a participle and the demonstrative pronoun *(krinantas touto hoti),* so also in Rom 6:6 (*touto ginōskontes hoti,* "knowing this, that . . .").

*one has died for all.* Paul is citing, but with a significant alteration, a familiar creedal statement. The apostle had used it in its most complete form in 1 Cor 15:3, "Christ died for our sins," of which "Christ died for us" (Rom 5:8; 1 Thess 5:10; cf. 1 Cor 8:11; Rom 14:15) is but a slight variation; see also Rom 4:25; 1 Cor 11:24; Gal 2:20c; 3:13. In the present case, however, *one* stands for "Christ," and *all* stands for "us"; see COMMENT. The preposition *hyper* (translated here simply as *for*) cannot in and of itself bear the weight of any particular theory of the atonement. It may mean "for the sake [or: benefit] of" (so Binder 1973:306), or "instead of," thus overlapping in meaning with *anti,* as in Phlm 13 (see Robertson 1923:631 and Moule 1953:64; so, e.g., Hughes, 193; Bultmann, 152–53; Collange, 254).

*therefore.* Translates *ara,* which here introduces Paul's interpretation of the consequence of the preceding statement. Héring, 42, translates this as "yet" *(cependant),* and reads what follows as a sort of objection to what precedes; but there is no justification for such a rendering, and Héring does not say how he can adopt it.

*all have died.* Or "they all have died," since the use of the article with *pantes (hoi pantes)* must indicate that the *all* to whom reference has just been made *(one has died for all)* are still in view here; cf. BDF § 275(7).

15. *And.* This verse follows closely on the preceding one. Collange, 256 (following Godet), believes that the verse is still dependent on *krinantas (our decision having been,* v. 14), but it is preferable to interpret *kai (And)* here as epexegetical, introducing (in

he *hina*-clause; see below) an explication of the statement that *all have died* (v. 4c); so also Hahn 1973b:248; cf. BDF § 442(9).

*he has died for all.* Cf. *one has died for all,* v. 14 (and note).

*that.* The *hina* is to be read here in a strictly final sense, as expressing purpose (not n automatic result—e.g., *hōste,* "so that"); what follows it is implicitly imperatival. ee Bultmann, 153; Dinkler 1970:172; Minear 1979:101.

*those who live.* Plummer, 175, interprets this phrase *(hoi zōntes)* as "those who are live in the body and are still in this world," as if it were an abbreviation of Gal 2:20, 'the life I now live in the flesh. . . ." That seems to be the meaning of the same phrase n 4:11a (on which see the note), but not here. In this verse it probably refers to those ho, having died with Christ, have been raised to new life in him; see especially Rom :4, 11 and, in the present context, 4:10b, 11b. So also Bultmann, 154 (tentatively); Dinkler 1970:172; Fürst 1968:224-25; Thüsing 1969:103.

*might live no longer to themselves.* Here the dative *(heautois)* expresses that by which ne is possessed or claimed (see BDF § 188[2]), thus perhaps "might live no longer for heir own sake [or: under the direction of their own ambitions]"; cf. Gal 2:20, "it is o longer I who live" *(RSV).* Note also the Pauline notion of dying to the law (Rom :4; Gal 2:19), to sin (Rom 6:2, 10-11), and to the world (Gal 6:14)—on which see COMMENT.

*to the one who for them died.* On the force of the dative here, see preceding note and f. especially Rom 7:4, "to belong to another [Christ]"; 14:8, "we are the Lord's"; 1 Cor 6:19b, "You are not your own." Cf. also Paul's references to living "to God" (Rom :10-11; Gal 2:19).

*and was raised up.* Plummer, 175, and Hughes, 196 n. 33, believe that *egerthenti (was aised up)* belongs to *for them,* just as the preceding participle *apothanonti (who . . died)* does; thus, "might live . . . to the one who died and was raised up for them." Cf. Rom 4:25; 14:9; 1 Thess 4:14. See also Kramer (1966:28-29), who believes that here n v. 15c, in distinction to the preceding references to Christ's death alone, the full 'pistis formula" of the pre-Pauline church is echoed: that is, Christ died—was buried —was raised from the dead (1 Cor 15:3). On the other hand, Wengst (1972:47, 79) egards the reference to Christ's resurrection as Paul's own elaboration of the same eath formula he has already used in vv. 14b, 15a; cf. Rom 8:34a. The present tr., like he word order of the Greek text itself, allows either interpretation.

16a. *So.* The *hōste* is best interpreted as a true inferential particle (cf. Moule 1953: 44), introducing a consequence of what has been affirmed in vv. 14-15 (e.g., Kümmel, 05; Bultmann, 155, 156, and 1947:16; Tannehill 1967:67), and not as introducing a arenthesis (e.g., Plummer, 175; Lietzmann, 125; Strachan, 110; cf. Cambier 1960: 6-77, 79). Schmithals 1971:302-15 (followed by Güttgemanns 1966:284-98) argues hat this whole verse originated as a Gnostic gloss on v. 17. His argument (which lacks ny foundation in the textual tradition) must depend exclusively on the claim that there s no way to relate the verse meaningfully to its context. However, as shown in the COMMENT on vv. 16-17, this is not so: v. 16a, supported by v. 16b and then extended n v. 17, is not simply a plausible conclusion from v. 15; it also shows how the heological formula used in vv. 14, 15 is meant to serve the whole discussion in vv. 11ff. Cf. Collange, 262.

*from now on.* The same phrase is frequent in the papyri (examples in BAG s.v. *nyn,*

3b, and Deissmann 1903:253) and in the LXX: e.g., Isa 18:7; Ps 130(131):3; Sir 11:23–24; Tob 7:12; 1 Mac 10:41. Elsewhere in the NT it is found only in Luke-Acts: Luke 1:48; 5:10; 12:52; 22:18, 69; Acts 18:6 (but see also John 8:11, in an interpolated section). Of special interest for Paul's use of the phrase in the present passage is Isa 48:6, where there is a reference to "the new things from now on" *(ta kaina apo tou nyn);* cf. Stuhlmacher 1967:5–6. In 8:14; Rom 3:26; 8:18, 22; 11:5; Phil 1:5, the phrase "the present [time]" *(to nyn [kairos])* is used first of all to mean simply "now" ( = "the present age," 1 Tim 6:17; Tit 2:12), but from other passages it becomes clear that this "now" is also, for Paul, the time of faith and salvation: e.g., 6:2; Rom 3:21; 5:9, 11; 8:1; 11:30; 13:11; Gal 2:20; 4:9.

*we.* Emphatic, both because the pronoun *(hēmeis)* is used and because it is placed ahead of the adverbial phrase (see preceding note) in the Greek sentence; cf. Plummer, 176; Michel 1954:23. Interpreters are divided on whether the first person plural refers here only to Paul himself (so Windisch, 184; Cambier 1960:79–80; Stuhlmacher 1967: 5), to Paul and his apostolic colleagues (so Bachmann, 255; Plummer, 176), or to all Christians (so Bultmann, 155; Collange, 257–58; Dinkler 1970:174). This last, inclusive interpretation is supported by the fact that the statement follows directly upon the citation of the tradition about Christ's death *for all* (vv. 14, 15), and by the inclusive *anyone* in v. 17 (on which see the note).

*we regard.* Literally "we know" *(oidamen),* but here used in the sense of "to esteem" or "to value" someone. Plummer, 176, notes the same usage in 1 Thess 5:12, where the apostle urges his readers "to respect" *(RSV)* their leaders (cf. v. 13, "and to esteem *[hēgeisthai]* them very highly in love because of their work" *[RSV]*).

*no one.* Reitzenstein (1978:473–74) perceives a contrast "with the thrice strongly emphasized" *for all* and *all* in vv. 14–15.

*according to worldly standards.* This phrase *(kata sarka;* literally "according to the flesh") occurs a total of eighteen times in the genuine Pauline letters, twice in this verse. In some instances it is used in a positive (or at least neutral) way to describe simple "physicality" (Rom 1:3, a pre-Pauline formula; of Abraham, Rom 4:1; of the Jews [Israel], Rom 9:3; 1 Cor 10:18; of Christ, Rom 9:5). Ordinarily, however, it is used negatively, or with clear negative connotations—e.g., in Rom 8:4, 5, 12, 13, where life "according to the flesh" is set over against life "according to the Spirit"; cf. Gal 4:23, 29 (Esau contrasted to Isaac). Elsewhere in the Corinthian letters it refers to acting or making judgments in a purely secular manner (1 Cor 1:26; 2 Cor 1:17 [translated "opportunistically"]; 10:2, 3; 11:18 [translated "in a worldly way"]). Whether, in the present instance, the phrase is intended to qualify the substantive *(no one)* or the verb *(regard)* is subject to debate. Plummer (176), Bultmann (155–56) and Dinkler (1970: 174 n. 14) construe it with the former, although Bultmann and Dinkler minimize the importance of the question. Most interpreters, however, attach the phrase to the verb (e.g., Schlatter, 559; Hughes, 197; Collange, 258–59; Barrett, 170; Blank 1968:318; Sand 1967:177; Schweizer, *TDNT* VII:131; Fraser 1974:49). This is certainly correct; in no case where the phrase goes with a substantive does the verb intervene, as it does here, and although Paul usually places it before the verb with which it goes, in 11:18 the phrase does follow the verb with which it is certainly to be construed. See further discussion on v. 16*b*.

16*b. if indeed.* Translates *ei kai,* by far the best-attested reading. Collange, 262 n.

2, is tempted to opt for the variant *kai ei* (F G) only because he wishes to take *kai* as a comparative, "in the same way that, if we knew Christ according to the flesh," etc. Even so, the present case would not match any of the examples of comparative *kai* given in BDF § 453(1), to which Collange, 262, himself refers.

*if ... we have regarded.* Here *ei (if)* is used with the perfect indicative *(egnōkamen).* The change from the verb *eidenai* in v. 16a to *ginōskein* is significant only because Paul wishes to use the perfect tense, and there is none available for *eidenai* (Plummer, 176–77; Barrett, 170); the two words are virtually synonymous (cf. Souček 1959: 302–3). Grammatically, *ei* with the indicative must refer to "a real case" (BDF § 371), but here (and in Gal 5:11) one must think of something "hypothetically real" (so Lietzmann, 125; followed by, e.g., Bultmann, 157; Georgi 1964:256 n. 5, and 257; Dinkler 1970:174 n. 17). Nothing is thereby said about whether "in fact" Christ had been *regarded ... according to worldly standards.* Reitzenstein (1978:477) provides examples from other texts which show that "[Paul's] use of the indicative in the assumption only heightens the definiteness of the main affirmation" which follows. (Contrast Plummer, 177; Hughes, 198, both of whom believe that Paul concedes the reality of the fact as well as of the assumption.) The perfect tense enhances the distinction between what has (at least hypothetically) occurred and what the present fact is (cf. Blank 1968:320).

*Christ.* In Rom 9:5, with which the present verse is often compared (see following note), "the Christ" *(ho Christos)* is specifically identified with "the Messiah" expected by Israel (see Kramer 1966:210). That is not the case here, where the article is not used and where the context is different (see also Fraser 1974:50).

*according to worldly standards.* Translates *kata sarka,* as in v. 16a (on which see the note). As there, so here one must ask whether the phrase goes with the substantive (in this case *Christ*) or with the verb *(we have known).* The first argument for the latter is that the verbal connection seems assured in v. 16a; the list of scholars cited in support of the adverbial meaning there may simply be repeated for the same meaning here. In addition, one may note that whenever Paul does construe *kata sarka* with a noun or proper noun (Rom 1:3; 4:1; 9:3, 5; 1 Cor 1:26; 10:18), the phrase follows the noun (so also Souček 1959:304; Fraser 1974:49), whereas here *kata sarka* precedes the proper noun, *Christ* (and follows the verb directly, as in v. 16a; 11:18). By way of contrast, in Rom 9:5, where *kata sarka* is applied adjectivally to Christ, it not only follows the proper noun but is used with a "substantivizing" neuter article: *ho Christos to kata sarka,* "the Christ 'insofar as the physical is concerned'"; see BDF § 266(2). Finally, the adverbial sense accords best with the context here; Paul's concern is not, at least for the moment, with "christology" but with those who would assess other persons— apostles in particular—on the basis of appearance only (vv. 11–13; cf. Collange, 260). In this sense the issue is "epistemological" (cf. Martyn 1967). Contrast Georgi 1964: 290–92 (followed by, e.g., Schütz 1975:177), who nevertheless construes *kata sarka* with *Christ.*

*now ... no longer.* The *nyn ouketi* is preceded by the strongly adversative *alla* ("but rather"), here left untranslated. What follows stands in sharp contrast to what has just been conceded as a "hypothetically real" case.

*we ... regard.* The present tense is required again, as in v. 16a, but instead of returning to the verb *eidenai* used there, Paul employs the present form of *ginōskein,* to which he had switched for grammatical reasons only. The changes of tense (present–perfect–present) are significant here, but not the change of words (see note above on *if . . . we have regarded*). The object of this verb is left unexpressed, but it is still *Christ*, for which *him* has been supplied in the tr., as have also the words *in that way* (namely, *according to worldly standards*). There is no reason to think that the first person plural here is any less inclusive than that in v. 16*a*.

17. *So.* The inferential particle *hōste* as in v. 16*a*. A dispute arises as to whether this introduces a consequence drawn from v. 16 (e.g., Windisch, 189), whether it has absolutely no relation to v. 16 (so Schmithals 1971:303, who regards v. 16 as a gloss), or whether it is parallel with v. 16—like the latter drawing a consequence from vv. 14, 15 (e.g., Plummer, 179; Bultmann, 158–59; Allo, 167; Barrett, 173; Hahn 1973b:249). See COMMENT.

*if anyone.* In 2:5, where the context shows a particular individual is in mind, the same Greek phrase *(ei tis)* is properly translated *some one.* In the present case, however, it introduces one type of gnomic saying (cf. Stuhlmacher 1967:4) and has a general—indeed, "universal"—reference ( = "whoever," *hostis;* with the *hostis* of Luke 14:27 cf. the *ei tis* of Matt 16:24 par.). This particular gnomic form is used frequently by Paul, most often for warnings (Rom 8:9*b;* 1 Cor 3:12, 17*a;* 11:16; 14:37, 38; 16:22; Gal 1:9; 6:3—some of which are discussed by Käsemann 1969:66–81) and (closely related) challenges (see NOTES on 10:7), but also for ethical instructions (1 Cor 7:12, 13, 36; 10:27 [cf. *ean tis,* v. 28]). In the present verse, as in 1 Cor 8:3 ("If anyone loves God, that person is known by him"), one meets a general "theological" affirmation. The use of the gnomic form here helps to support the inclusive interpretation of the first person plural in v. 16*ab.* The *we (hēmeis)* there refers not just to Paul, or to Paul and his associates, but to all believers; see Bultmann, 158; Dinkler 1970:175; Hahn 1973b:249.

*in Christ.* Héring, 43, wishes to punctuate so as to obtain "if anyone is a new creature in Christ, then—for him—the old order has passed and a new world has arisen" (cf. Vulgate). However, the usual punctuation, which gives *a new creation* prominence in its own clause, accords better with the rest of the verse (which develops the idea of *a new creation*) and with Gal 6:15 (where the phrase is used quite independently). The phrase *in Christ* has been used previously in this letter (chaps. 1–9, Letter D) in 2:14, 17 and 3:14. It occurs again in 5:19, then twice more in chaps. 10–13 (Letter E), 12:2, 19. For its meaning here, see COMMENT.

*there is a new creation.* The Greek has only *kainē ktisis (a new creation),* so a subject and verb must be supplied; either "he is" (as in most English versions) or *there is* (as in Mof., *NEB, JB*). The latter is preferable because the context, as well as the background of the expression *kainē ktisis* in apocalyptic Judaism, suggests that something more inclusive than the new being of individual believers is in mind; see COMMENT. In Paul's letters *ktisis* virtually always refers to the creation in its entirety (Rom 1:20, 25; 8:19, 20, 21, 22; the one exception is Rom 8:39 [cf. Windisch, 189, n. 3]), and it is wrong to follow the Vulgate in translating it here as "creature" (so, e.g., *KJV, ASV,* Wey.; cf. Tannehill 1967:65). Paul uses the same phrase, *a new creation,* in Gal 6:15 (on which see Betz 1979:319–20), and he appears to have been the one who introduced it into the vocabulary of the Christian church (so Stuhlmacher 1967:3–4). For the concept, Paul is indebted to apocalyptic Judaism (e.g., 1 Enoch 72:1 [cf. 45:4–5; 90:28–29; 91:16]; 2 Apoc Bar 32:6 [cf. 44:12; 57:2]; Jub 4:26; 1QS iv.25; 1QH xi.10–14;

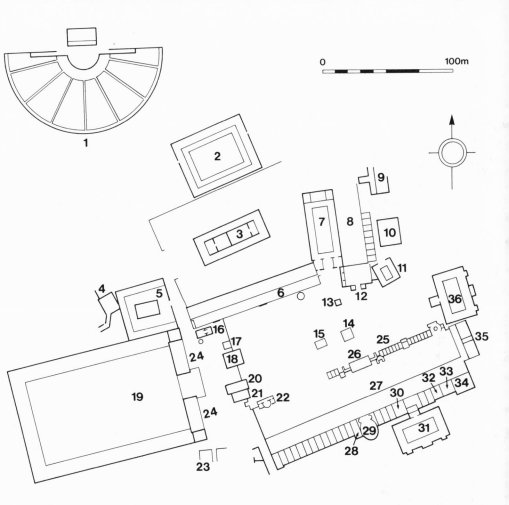

I. Corinth, central area, ca. 50 C.E.

1. Theater    2. North Market    3. Archaic Temple, sixth century B.C.E.    4. Fountain of Glauke, sixth century B.C.E.    5. Temple C (unidentified)    6. Northwest Stoa    7. North Basilica    8. Lechaeum Road (see Plate II)    9. Bath (of Eurycles?)    10. Peribolos of Apollo    11. Fountain of Peirene    12. Propylaea (see Plate II)    13. Tripod    14. Statue of Athena    15. Altar (unidentified)    16. Temple D (*Tychē;* see Plate VIII)    17. Babbius Monument    18. Fountain of Poseidon (Neptune)    19. Temple of the Imperial Cult    20. Temple G (Pantheon?)    21. Temple F (Aphrodite)    22. Unidentified Building (temple or civic structure)    23. "Cellar Building" (public restaurant or tavern)    24. West Shops    25. Central Shops    26. *Bēma*    27. South Stoa    28. Room XX (Sarapis shrine; see Plate VII)    29. *Bouleutērion* (see Plate III)    30. "Fountain House"    31. South Basilica    32. Room C (*Agonotheteion*)    33. Room B    34. Room A    35. Southeast Building (*Tabularium* and library?)    36. Julian Basilica

II. Lechaeum Road (Fig. 2, No. 8), looking south toward the monumental arch (Fig. 2, No. 12) and the Forum, with Acrocorinth in the background. *Photo: American School of Classical Studies, Corinth Excavations.*

III. Corinth, central area, looking north toward Lechaeum and the Gulf of Corinth. The *Bouleutērion* (council chamber) is in the foreground (see Fig. 2, No. 29), and the Archaic Temple (see Fig. 2, No. 3) is in the background. *Photo: American School of Classical Studies, Corinth Excavations.*

IV. Archaic Temple (sixth century B.C.E.), viewed from the southeast, with the Northwest Stoa in the foreground (Fig. 2, Nos. 3 and 6). *Photo: American School of Classical Studies, Corinth Excavations.*

V. Cenchreae (Kenchreai), the harbor viewed from the south mole (see Fig. 1), with remains of the Isis sanctuary/Christian basilica in the foreground. *Photo: Victor Paul Furnish.*

VIa. Erastus inscription ("Erastus in return for his aedileship laid [the pavement] at his own expense") in situ in the pavement east of the scene building of the theater (Fig. 2, No. 1); second half of the first century C.E. *Photo: American School of Classical Studies, Corinth Excavations.*

VIb. Synagogue inscription ("Synagogue of the Hebrews"), perhaps as late as the fourth century C.E. *Photo: American School of Classical Studies, Corinth Excavations.*

VII. Sarapis: life-size marble head, mid-first century C.E., found in Room XX of the South Stoa (Fig. 2, No. 28). *Photo: American School of Classical Studies, Corinth Excavations.*

VIII. *Tychē*, goddess of good fortune and protector of cities: a head of fine Pentelic marble, here adorned with the *corona muralis* ("crown for the wall"); late first or early second century C.E. *Photo: American School of Classical Studies, Corinth Excavations.*

IX. Archaic Temple (sixth century B.C.E.), viewed from the northwest. *Photo: American School of Classical Studies, Corinth Excavations.*

xiii.11–12); see especially Stuhlmacher (1967), who also notes the significance of the idea in Hellenistic Judaism (16ff.); see *Joseph and Asenath* 15:4, Joseph's words to his bride concerning her conversion: "Behold, from this day forth you shall be renewed and refashioned and revivified [*Idou apo tēs sēmeron anakainisthēsē kai anaplasthēsē kai anazōopoiēthēsē*], and you shall eat the bread of life and drink the cup of immortality; and you shall be anointed with the unction of incorruptibility" (Philonenko 1968: 182). The texts from 1 Enoch are discussed by Black (1976), and those from Qumran by Sjöberg (1955) and Ringgren (1963:164–66). The roots of the apocalyptic idea go back to Isa 65:17–25 (cf. Isa 42:9; 43:18–19; 48:6; 66:22), on which see, e.g., Westermann (1969:408) and McKenzie (1968:200). Elsewhere in the NT, see especially Rev 21:1–5a and 2 Pet 3:13. Although the expression *běrîyyāh ḥădāšāh* is also used by the rabbis (discussions in Moore 1927 I:533; Davies 1980:119–20; Sjöberg 1951), they seem to have employed it only to describe the new life of an individual—e.g., of the sinner who has repented or of the proselyte to Judaism ( = "new creature"). Paul's usage includes but is not restricted to this anthropological meaning. The broader, apocalyptic reference also attaches to the concept in Wis 19:6; 2 Esdras 7:75 (cf. 5:45).

*Everything old.* Literally, "the old things" *(ta archaia).* The substantive use of the adjective "old" occurs nowhere else in the NT, and Georgi (1964:257; cf. 138–39, 167ff.) has argued that this phrase may have been a slogan of Paul's opponents, for whom (according to Georgi's hypothesis) religious tradition played an important role. It is probable, however, that the apostle's use of the phrase derives from the general apocalyptic tradition and designates the totality of creation (note "all things," *ta panta,* v. 18, and cf. Barrett, 174, who translates *ta archaia* as "all old things"). See LXX Isa 43:18–19, where *ta archaia* is used in synonymous parallelism with *ta prōta,* "the first things" (cf. Rev 21:4) and is contrasted, as it is here, with *kaina,* "new things." Elsewhere in the LXX *ta archaia* is contrasted with *ta eschata,* "the last things" (Ps 138[139]:5), and with *ta mellonta,* "the things that are to be" (Wis 8:8).

*has come to an end.* The verb is *parerchesthai* (literally "to pass away"). Paul has again adopted a term which is used in the apocalyptic tradition. See especially 2 Pet 3:10: "But the day of the Lord will come like a thief, and then the heavens will come to an end [*pareleusontai*] with a 'whoosh,' the elements will be destroyed by fire, and the earth and everything in it will be exposed" (cf. Matt 24:35 par.). In Rev 21:4 *aperchesthai* (literally "to go away") is used in a similar apocalyptic context.

*behold.* One could also translate this demonstrative particle *(idou)* as "See!" or "Look!" The slightly archaic "Behold!" is appropriate in this particular instance, however. The expression occurs frequently in the LXX (e.g., for *hinnēh*) to preface an especially solemn pronouncement, not least in texts where divine promises are given (e.g., Isa 28:16, quoted by Paul in Rom 9:33). Its use is well established in the apocalyptic tradition, where it often introduces the description of heavenly visions (e.g., Rev 4:1, 2) and eschatological announcements concerning the End (e.g., Luke 23:29; cf. Matt. 24:23 par.). With the present instance compare especially Rev 21:5, "Behold, I make all things new," and (lying behind that) LXX Isa 42:9; 43:19; 65:17–18. See also *Joseph and Asenath* 15:4, quoted above in the note on *there is a new creation.* Paul's use of the expression in 6:2 (twice) and 1 Cor 15:51 reflects the same tradition, but the instances in 2 Cor 6:9; 7:11; Gal 1:20 are rather different. For some useful comments on translating this particle, see Kleist 1944:338–40. Here the expression not only calls attention to what follows but lends an almost triumphal note to the affirmation.

*new things.* Translates *kaina* (without the article), attested by the earliest and most important textual witnesses (P⁴⁶ ℵ B C D* et al.). The major variants have *ta panta* ("all things") as the subject, with *kaina* as the predicate adjective (either *kaina ta panta* or *ta panta kaina*); cf. *NAB:* "all is new." But the addition of *ta panta* may be explained as an assimilation either to the following verse (Metzger 1971:580) or to Rev 21:5 (Windisch, 189). Less probable is the suggestion that the expanded reading originated with Marcion, who "wanted to have done with everything old—including the God of the Old Testament" (Barrett, 162 n. 3); contrast Stuhlmacher (1967:22), who believes that the *ta panta,* though secondary, is a correct interpretation of Paul.

*have come to be.* Along with most English versions, this tr. presumes that the verb *ginesthai* is used here absolutely. Contrast Hughes, 201, who translates this as "they are become," with *kaina* ("new") as the predicate adjective. He is then able to remark on "a radical continuity" between the old and the new (203) and to refer to "a renewed cosmos" (204). However, the apocalyptic tradition to which Paul is clearly indebted in this passage conceives of a total replacement of the old by the new, not just a rehabilitation of the old. Moreover, it is unlikely that "the old things" (*ta archaia,* translated here as *everything old*) continues as the subject of the verb *gegonen,* as in Hughes's tr. ("*they* are become new"). It is more typical of the texts echoed here that "[the] new things" ([*ta*] *kaina*) are set over against "the old things" (*ta archaia, ta ap' archēs,* etc.); see, e.g., Isa 42:9; 43:18–19; 48:6; 65:17–18; and passages cited in the note on *Everything old.*

18. *All things are from God.* This verse is connected with what precedes it by the conjunction *de,* left untranslated here. The first phrase *(ta panta ek tou Theou)* echoes a doxological formula (see especially Rom 11:36, "For from him and through him and to him are all things" [*RSV; hoti ex autou kai di' autou kai eis auton ta panta*]), apparently adopted by the early church from the Hellenistic synagogue—which had, in turn, adapted it from a formula of Stoic pantheism. For the Stoic formula see especially Marcus Aurelius IV, 23 (speaking of Nature, *physis*): "All things are from Thee, all things (subsist) in Thee, all things are for Thee" *(ek sou panta, en soi panta, eis se panta).* In Judaism this doctrine was modified in accord with belief in a Creator who stands over creation; see, e.g., Sir 43, especially vv. 26, 27, 33, and cf. Philo, *Special Laws* I, 208; *Who Is the Heir* 36; *On Dreams* I, 241; *On the Cherubim* 125–26. The formula is also echoed in 1 Cor 8:6; 11:12*b;* Eph 3:9; 4:5; Col 1:16–17; Heb 1:3 [*RSV,* 1:2]; 2:10; Rev 4:11. The Hellenistic background of the formula is discussed by Norden 1913:240–50, 347–54; cf. Reicke, *TDNT* V:892–93.

*has reconciled.* The verb *katallassein* (here in the form of an aorist participle) and the related noun *katallagē* ("reconciliation") are used only by Paul in the NT (verb: also in vv. 19, 20; Rom 5:10, 11; 1 Cor 7:11; noun: also in v. 19; Rom 5:11; 11:15), although a compound form of the verb *(apokatallassein)* is used in Eph 2:16; Col 1:20, 22. A theological application of the terminology occurs in only a few texts of Hellenistic Judaism, most notably in 2 Mac 1:4–5; 5:20; 7:33; 8:29; see COMMENT. S. Johnson (1955:162) calls attention to a Qumran text which affirms that "(God) will draw me near by His grace" (1QS xi.13, Vermes 1975:94), but this offers an analogy to the Pauline idea of reconciliation only in the broadest sense (correctly Braun 1966 I:174, on Rom 5:11).

*us.* This *hēmas* is certainly not restricted to Paul and his associates, as Plummer, 182, holds. It must be interpreted in connection with *anyone . . . in Christ* (v. 17a) as inclusive of all believers (so, e.g., Lietzmann, 126; Windisch, 193; Bultmann, 159; Kijne 1966:178).

*us to himself.* Significantly, not "has been reconciled to us." Contrast 2 Mac 1:5, "May [God] hear your prayers and be reconciled to you [*katallageiē hymin . . .*" (*RSV;* see also 2 Mac 5:20; 7:33; 8:29) and 1 Clem 48:1, "And let us fall down before the Master, and beseech him with tears that he may have mercy upon us, and be reconciled to us [*epikatallagē hēmin*]. . . ." See COMMENT.

*through Christ.* The context (see vv. 14–15), as well as the parallel passage, Rom 5:10, shows that *dia Christou* is to be interpreted as *dia tou thanatou tou Christou,* "through the death of Christ" (Bultmann, 160; Dinkler, 176).

*has given.* Along with *has reconciled,* this participle *(dontos),* aorist like the first, identifies the saving work of God. See also *has established* in v. 19c.

*to us.* This first person plural *(hēmin)* is usually interpreted as if Paul were now thinking more narrowly—of apostles only, not of all Christians (e.g., Windisch, 194; Kijne 1966:178; Hofius 1980b:5 n. 8)—although Barrett, 176, must acknowledge that "the change from *us* Christians [in the first part of the verse] is abrupt and difficult." It is probable, therefore, that the first person plural here retains the inclusive sense it has had, clearly, since v. 16 (so Bultmann, 162; against my own previous opinion, Furnish 1977:211 n. 25).

*the ministry of reconciliation.* The phrase *(tēn diakonian tēs katallagēs)* parallels Paul's earlier references to "the ministry of the Spirit" (3:8) and "the ministry of righteousness" (3:9), which he had contrasted with "the ministry of death" (3:7) and "the ministry of condemnation" (3:9), respectively. The genitive *of reconciliation* is qualitative, as in the other instances: Paul refers to a ministry that deals with reconciliation. Cf. also 3:6, "ministers of a new covenant," and 4:1, "this ministry." In the earlier passages the thought is of apostles specifically as the agents of the ministry of the new covenant, but in the present verse the thought seems to be of all believers as recipients of *the ministry of reconciliation;* see preceding note, and COMMENT.

*19ab. As it is said.* This is a paraphrase of the Greek words *hōs hoti,* the meaning and function of which in this passage have been widely discussed. In 11:21 and 2 Thess 2:2, *hōs hoti* introduces the content of something said (11:21) or written (2 Thess 2:2). In these two passages the *hōs* functions to cast a certain doubt over the validity of what is reported, and the Vulgate translates, appropriately enough, *quasi,* "as though." This can hardly be the meaning in the present verse, however, since Paul is introducing something he unequivocally affirms (correctly Barrett, 176). The Vulgate, therefore, translates *hōs hoti* in this verse as if it were simply *hoti,* and gives it a causal sense, *quoniam quidem,* "since" or "because"; so also, e.g., Robertson 1923:964; Barrett, 176–77 (hesitantly); cf. Allo, 169–70; Héring, 43 n. 28. Others, interpreting *hōs hoti* = *hoti,* take *hoti* as epexegetical: "namely that," "that is," etc. (so, e.g., *GNTG* III:138; Bultmann, 163; Hughes, 206–7 n. 45; most English versions). BDF § 396, however, read the *hōs hoti* as if it were equivalent to *hōs* in v. 20, where, with a genitive absolute construction, it expresses "the subjective motivation" of the subject of the action described in the main clause (ibid. § 425[3]). Bachmann, 264–65, translates *hōs* in a comparative sense, and *hoti* as causal—thus: "as could and did happen, because. . . ."

Finally, Käsemann (1971a:53) takes the *hōs* as "transitional" and regards *hoti* as introducing a quotation. There are enough indications that Paul is indeed relying on a traditional formulation in v. 19*ab* to make this last suggestion the most plausible (so also Stuhlmacher 1965:77 n. 2; Fürst 1968:228; Lührmann 1970:444–45; Collange, 269–70), and it is the one adopted here. See also the following NOTES, and COMMENT.

*God, in Christ, was reconciling.* The tr. of this phrase is problematic, partly because of the Greek word order: "God was in Christ the world reconciling to himself." There are three main possibilities. (a) One may read the verb, *was (ēn)*, independently of the participle, *reconciling (katallassōn)*, thus obtaining "God was in Christ, reconciling . . ." (so, e.g., Bachmann, 265–66; Windisch, 193; Allo, 170; de Boor, 140–41; Hofius 1980a:187; cf. *NEB, RSV* mg., *TEV* mg.). The Greek word order may be cited in support of this (see above), but the idea of God's "being in" *(einai en)* Christ is not present elsewhere in Paul's letters, and an incarnational emphasis is not otherwise present in this context. (b) One may read *ēn . . . katallassōn* as an imperfect periphrastic construction (perhaps an Aramaism), thus obtaining "in Christ God was reconciling . . ." (*RSV;* so, e.g., Plummer, 183; Bultmann, 162; Héring, 44; Bruce, 209; cf. *TEV, NIV, NEB* mg.). This yields a meaning fully in accord with v. 18 (thus "in Christ" [v. 19*a*] would be equivalent to "through Christ" [v. 18]), although the periphrastic construction is not often used by Paul. (c) Barrett, 177, reads *God* as a predicate nominative rather than as the subject of the verb *ēn* (or of the periphrastic construction *ēn . . . katallassōn*), thus obtaining "it was God who in Christ was reconciling. . . ." So also Olson 1976:183. (Dinkler 1970:177 translates similarly, although he reads *was reconciling* as a periphrastic construction.) A further measure of difficulty is injected if, as seems probable, Paul is citing a traditional formulation in v. 19*ab* (see COMMENT). In this case one would have to be open to a distinction between the meaning of the tradition as such and Paul's interpretation of it. Although (a) cannot be ruled out as the meaning of the traditional formulation, it does seem to be ruled out as Paul's meaning, given the context supplied especially by v. 18. At the same time, the only real problem with (b) disappears if Paul is quoting, and Barrett's chief argument for (c), that v. 19 continues the thought of v. 18, loses some of its force. Since it is impossible to reproduce the ambiguity of the Greek in a good English sentence, the present tr. has opted for (b), which seems to be most in accord with Paul's understanding and use of the material he quotes.

*in Christ.* Set off by commas (as in *NAB*) to make it clear that "God-in-Christ" is not intended as an incarnational formula here (see preceding note). Nor does the phrase *in Christ* have the full eschatological meaning present in v. 17. Rather, as observed already by Chrysostom (*NPNF,* 1st ser. XII:333), it is equivalent to *through Christ* in v. 18.

*was reconciling.* For the periphrastic construction, see note above on *God, in Christ, was reconciling.* Büchsel, *TDNT* I:257 and Bruce, 209, are among those who believe the imperfect tense here expresses the continuing and uncompleted nature of God's reconciling action. According to von Allmen (1968:36–37), it is an "inchoative imperfect," accenting the inception of reconciliation (thus, "In Christ, God was beginning his work of reconciling the world"). Collange, 271, thinks the imperfect is best understood as expressing the duration and totality of the action (as, e.g., in Luke 2:51, "was obeying"; 4:20, "were gazing"; 5:18, "was paralyzed"). Paul himself, it would seem (presuming that v. 19*ab* is a citation), reads it as an aorist (cf. his own use of the aorist participle in v. 18; correctly Collange, ibid.).

*the world.* Here *world (kosmon)* stands in place of *us (hēmas),* v. 18, as the object of God's reconciling action. The absence of the article (in Greek) has no special significance (cf. *GNTG* III:174–75). *Kosmos* is also anarthrous, e.g., in Rom 4:13; Gal 6:14 (cf. Plummer, 183), as well as in Rom 11:15, where there is another reference to "the reconciliation of the world" *(katallagē kosmou).* In the latter passage, "world" means "the Gentiles" (cf. Rom 11:12, where "world" and "Gentiles" are parallel; Sasse, *TDNT* III:892), and doubtless reflects the familiar Jewish description of all who do not belong to Israel; cf. Luke 12:30, "all the nations of the world [*panta ta ethnē tou kosmou*]," i.e., the Gentiles (Sasse, ibid.). A cosmic reconciliation is also the theme in Col 1:20, although there the term *kosmos (world)* is not actually employed: God willed "to reconcile to himself all things [*ta panta*], whether on earth or in heaven . . ." *(RSV);* cf. Eph 2:16, specifically the reconciliation of Jews and Gentiles (within the *kosmos*). Bultmann, 163, believes that *world* in the present verse means "mankind," as in Rom 1:8; 5:12–13; 1 Cor 4:9 (cf. Hofius 1980a:191), and this would seem to be confirmed by the parallel *us* in vv. 18, 19*c,* and *their/them* in v. 19*b.* If, however, one reckons with a citation in v. 19*ab,* it becomes possible that *world* has a broader meaning, perhaps "the universe of creation," as Fitzmyer (1975:161) suggests; cf. Rom 8:19–23, where in Fitzmyer's view (ibid.:162) the concept of "freedom" is equivalent to that of "reconciliation" in the present passage. The only other references to "the world" in 2 Cor are in 1:12; 7:10.

*not charging their trespasses to them.* The phrase *(mē logizomenos autois ta paraptōmata autōn)* is doubtless an echo of Ps 31(32):2, "Blessed the man against whom the Lord will not charge (any) sin [*hou ou mē logisētai Kyrios hamartian*]" (Dupont 1953:281). See also T Zeb 9:7, and especially Rom 4:8, where Paul quotes the biblical text. The present participle (continuous action) matches the sense of the imperfect periphrastic construction in v. 19*a.*

*not charging . . . trespasses.* That a juristic concept is at work here is well illustrated by 2 Kgdms 19:20 (2 Sam 19:19; Shimei pleading with King David for clemency): "Let not my Lord now charge me with transgression [*mē dialogisasthō ho kyrios mou anomian*]." Note the use of a compound form of the verb in Rom 5:13, "Sin is not counted [*ouk ellogeitai*] where there is no law" *(RSV).* See also 1 Cor 13:5 (and cf. LXX Zech 8:17).

*trespasses.* The plural *(paraptōmata)* occurs in Paul's letters only here and in Rom 4:25; 5:16 (elsewhere, the singular: Rom 5:15, 17, 18, 20; 11:11, 12; Gal 6:1), although it is plural in every other NT passage (Matt 6:14, 15 par.; Eph 1:7; 2:1, 5; Col 2:13). In Rom 5:16 the plural is required to make the point. Here and in Rom 4:25 the non-Pauline plural is one of the marks of the apostle's dependence on a traditional formulation (cf. Stuhlmacher 1965:77 n. 2). The parallelism of Rom 4:25 (Christ died "on account of our trespasses") and 1 Cor 15:3 (Christ died "for our sins") shows that, in the tradition, "trespasses" and "sins" were interchangeable terms. Rom 5:12–13 ("sin"), 15–18, 20 ("trespass[es]") show that they were also interchangeable for Paul himself; see Bultmann, 163.

*their trespasses to them.* The use of the plural pronouns *their (autōn)* and *them (autois)* after *world (kosmon)* is an instance of a *constructio ad sensum;* see BDF §§ 272(3) and 282(3).

19c. *he has established.* The aorist participle *(themenos)* contrasts with the present-tense participle of v. 19b ([*not*] *charging,* [*mē*] *logizomenos)* and the imperfect-periphrastic construction of v. 19a. It accords, however, with the aorist participles of v. 18, *has reconciled* and *has given,* and thus offers further evidence for the suggestion that Paul has cited previously formulated material in v. 19ab (Stuhlmacher 1965:77–78 n. 2). In this case v. 19c would be neither a continuation of *was reconciling,* v. 19a (so Büchsel, *TDNT* I:257, 7.3), nor parallel to *not charging,* etc., v. 19b, and with it subordinate to v. 19a (so Bultmann, 163; cf. Plummer, 184). Rather, vv. 18, 19c together would constitute Paul's "gloss" on the citation of v. 19ab; see COMMENT. Although the nominative case of *themenos* has been determined by *Theos* in the citation (v. 19a), the participle is coordinate in meaning as well as in tense with the participles in v. 18 (cf. Barrett, 177–78). The verb itself *(tithenai)* is often used in the LXX with God as the subject (see Maurer, *TDNT* VIII:155–56); e.g., of the establishment of the covenant (Gen 17:2; Exod 34:10, etc.), of justice (Amos 5:7 [*dikaiosynē*]), of salvation (Isa 26:1), or of the appointment of someone to a special office (Jer 1:5, etc.). Paul uses the word in the latter way in 1 Cor 12:18, 28 (cf., elsewhere in the NT, Acts 13:47 [quoting Isa 49:6]; 20:28; 1 Tim 2:7; 2 Tim 1:11), but not here, where it is the whole community that is in view, and not special office holders (see following note).

Hofius (1980b:12–13) has shown (against Wolter 1978:82–83) that LXX Ps 104:27 cannot be adduced as a parallel to the thought here. A much closer parallel stands in LXX Ps 77:3–7, where it is said that "God established a law in Israel which he commanded to our fathers, to make it known to their sons" (v. 5), and Hofius argues that Paul's statement about God's establishment of *the word of reconciliation* is deliberately formulated in antithesis to this (1980b:13–16, comparing the antithesis of law and gospel implicit in 2 Cor 2:14–4:6). This is not impossible, but there is little in the context of 2 Cor 5:11–19(21) to support it. This section is primarily expository, not polemical or apologetic (see COMMENT: GENERAL).

*among us.* With this *en hēmin* the third-person pronouns of v. 19ab are replaced by the first-person pronoun, another indication that Paul is returning (after the citation in v. 19ab) to the discursive style of v. 18 (Stuhlmacher 1965:77 n. 2). In the opinion of most interpreters, *us* here means Paul and his colleagues, "us ministers." Kijne (1966:178) argues for this on the grounds that *Therefore* in v. 20 (where the first person plural certainly means the Pauline apostolate) refers back to the thought of v. 19. This is not persuasive, however, because v. 20 is better interpreted as opening a new section of the letter, in which case the introductory *Therefore* looks back on the whole of what has preceded (see NOTES and COMMENT on 5:20). It is better, with Windisch, 194, Bultmann, 164, and Hofius (1980b:5 n. 8), to interpret the *us* of v. 19c as including all believers. This is supported by the close connection between v. 19c and v. 18, where the plurals are also to be taken as inclusive (see above).

*the word of reconciliation.* P[46] has "the gospel of reconciliation" *(to euangelion tēs katallagēs),* which certainly interprets *word (logos)* correctly, even if it cannot be accepted as original. Elsewhere in this letter Paul refers to *the word of God* (2:17, see note; 4:2), again meaning the gospel. See COMMENT.

## COMMENT: GENERAL

With 5:11–19, the exposition of apostleship opened in 2:14 comes to a close. At the same time a transition is made to the last major section of Letter D (chaps. 1–9), the appeals of 5:20ff. Here (in 5:12) Paul alludes for the second time in this letter to persons whom he apparently regards as rivals for the leadership of the Corinthian congregation. However, Paul's style continues to be essentially expository (as it has been since 2:14), and not primarily polemical or apologetic. Now, after the long discussion of apostolic hardships in 4: 7–5:10, the apostle offers a kind of summation of the meaning of Christian ministry. This begins with some comments evidently prompted by a particular criticism which has been made of his own ministry (5:11–13), but it concludes with remarks about *the ministry of reconciliation* which apply to the whole believing community. For purposes of analysis, this section may be divided into four smaller units.

1. The actual situation in Corinth is most evident in 5:11–13, in fact more so than it has been since at least 3:1, where there was just a fleeting reference to "some" who used commendatory letters. Here Paul is mindful of the criticism that the authenticity of his apostolate has been supported by no "religious" evidence in the form of public displays of ecstasy. In response, he disallows the pertinence of ecstatic experiences for the question of apostleship (v. 13a), and emphasizes instead the commitment of his apostolate to the preaching of the gospel (v. 11a) and to the care of those who have received it (v. 13b).

2. The statements of vv. 14–15 constitute Paul's theological support for what has been said in vv. 11–13. Here he introduces the familiar creedal affirmation about Christ's redemptive death. Interpreting that as meaning the establishment of the rule of love, he indicates what a radical reorientation is involved for the lives of believers. With these verses, then, the perspective of the passage is broadened from the matter of apostolic credentials (vv. 11–13) to that of the Christian life in general.

3. In vv. 16–17, Paul emphasizes the radical newness of the situation brought about by Christ's death. Believers no longer operate *according to worldly standards* (v. 16) but within a creation which has been totally refashioned (v. 17).

4. The climax of this passage, and—in a sense—the climax of the whole discussion since 2:14, comes in vv. 18–19. Here the apostle employs a traditional formulation about reconciliation (v. 19ab) to interpret the tradition about Christ's death he has cited earlier (vv. 14b, 15a). The new theme provides, simultaneously, an especially appropriate transition to the series of direct appeals with which, in 5:20ff., chaps. 1–9 (Letter D) are concluded.

COMMENT: DETAILED

*Ecstasy and Apostleship, 5:11–13*

These verses are formally connected with what has preceded by the introductory *Therefore,* and there is also a certain material connection between the idea of the divine judgment in 5:10 and the reference to *knowing the fear of the Lord* in 5:11. At the same time, *Therefore* functions as a resumptive particle here. Now Paul is addressing once more, in a fairly direct way, the matter of his own ministerial practice (cf. 3:1–2; 4:2ff.). When he writes that *we are persuading people,* the word *persuading* should perhaps be placed in quotation marks, for elsewhere he has resisted the thought that he has engaged in "persuasion" (see especially Gal 1:10). Like many of his contemporaries he must associate it with the practice of artful but deceptive rhetoric (see NOTES).

How can Paul now admit to *persuading people,* and what does he mean by this? Some commentators think he was concerned to persuade people of his integrity as a person and of his authenticity as an apostle (e.g., Plummer, 169; Windisch, 176; Hughes, 186; Collange, 245). This is compatible with the context, but it is difficult to substantiate because of the technical meaning the term often had in Paul's day and the apostle's own use of it elsewhere in that sense. It is more satisfactory to understand Paul to be employing the term, as his critics have, with reference to his preaching of the gospel (see, e.g., Bultmann, 148; Schmithals 1971:189; Fürst 1968:222–23), but then qualifying it to such an extent that he is able to adopt it. This meaning, too, is compatible with the context, where Paul is clearly concerned with emphasizing the commitment of his apostolate to the preaching of the gospel (e.g., 2:14–17; 4:5, 7, 13–15; 5:20; 6:1).

In v. 11, Paul qualifies his remark about *persuading people* in several important ways. First, he says, this *persuading* is done *knowing the fear of the Lord.* He means by this, as a further comment shows, that everything is done in the sight of God *(but we have been made known to God).* A reference to "the fear of the Lord" in Sir 1:30 is instructive:

> Do not exalt yourself lest you fall,
>     and thus bring dishonor upon yourself.
> The Lord will reveal your secrets and cast
>     you down in the midst of the congregation,
> because you did not come in the fear of the Lord,
>     and your heart was full of deceit. *(RSV)*

But his ministry, Paul now insists, has been conducted in *the fear of the Lord,* and this should be for his readers assurance enough that when he writes of *persuading people* he does not mean "deceiving them." Since he is fully known to God, it should be clear that he has nothing to hide (Bultmann, 148, suggests this has been one of the charges against Paul). He seems confident that the Corinthians will acknowledge this. Reverting briefly to the use of the first person singular (v. 11b), the apostle urges his readers to consult their own consciences about his ministry. He has made this appeal earlier in the letter (4:2), and he repeats it now, anticipating that the judgment of their consciences will be congruent with the judgment of God (Thrall 1967:125). In a subsequent letter he will write of his reluctance to "boast" about himself: "so that no one can credit me with something beyond what one may see me doing or hear from me" (12:6b). That seems also to be his point here. His ministry has been open to their inspection, as to God's. If preaching the gospel must be called *persuading people,* then it must be acknowledged that it is persuasion of a special kind, and without deceitful intentions.

Why, then, has not Paul simply denied any interest in *persuading people,* as he does in Gal 1:10? The answer to this may be that he has already denied it, at least implicitly, in an earlier letter to this congregation. In 1 Cor 2:4 he protested that his preaching in Corinth had not been "with persuasive words of wisdom [*en peithois sophias logois*], but with a demonstration of the Spirit and of power." One may hypothesize that, subsequent to this denial, Paul's critics have charged him with offering no evidence for the power of the Spirit in his ministry equivalent to the evidence they present for that power in their own (see, e.g., Schmithals 1971:188–92; Georgi 1964:298–99). This hypothesis is supported by the description of the rivals in v. 12b as people who boast in externals, and also by v. 13a, where Paul specifically declines to use his own ecstatic experiences as proof of a special religious status (see below). Thus in the present passage the apostle is moved to abandon his earlier tactic of denying that his concern is only to "persuade people." Now he accepts that description of his apostolate, although in a highly qualified sense. By so doing he avoids what he clearly regards as the far less acceptable response—namely, boasting of worldly evidences of his own "spiritual" powers.

The comment in v. 12 is in a sense parenthetical (cf. Collange, 244), but it is nevertheless closely related to v. 11. Paul does not want anything he writes to be interpreted as a self-recommendation. His sensitivity on the matter, expressed in a nearly identical way in 3:1, shows that some previous words or actions have been misinterpreted in this way, and he does not want that to happen again. Rather, what he intends is to identify for his readers in what respect they may *be proud* of his apostolate. It is not entirely clear what Paul is offering them as the *suitable basis* for pride: it may be what he has just said in v. 11 and will reformulate in v. 13 (e.g., Schmithals 1971:192, 306); or it could be what he will shortly write in 6:4–10, which is specifically introduced as having an apologetic intent (6:3; so Windisch, 178). The suggestion that he is referring to what he is about to write (vv. 14–21) is less convincing (Blank

1968:313). Most likely, he is thinking of the whole discussion of apostleship (2:14ff.) which is now drawing to a close (cf. Bultmann 1947:14; Georgi 1964:296 n. 3).

Paul indicates that he also wishes to give his readers *something to say* to those who have criticized his ministry (v. 12*b*). This is the second place in the letter where Paul provides some fairly direct description of his rivals in Corinth. In 3:1 he had written of "some" who were presenting and soliciting letters of recommendation, and they were probably thought of as included in the "many" of the preceding verse (2:17) who were "huckstering the word of God." Now he describes them further as *those who are boasting of what is outward and not of what is within.* This conforms to what he writes about them in 11:18 (in a later and explicitly polemical letter; see INTRODUCTION), where they are described as boasting "in a worldly way" *(kata sarka).* Judging from the context there, Paul may be thinking of his rivals' boasting of their descent from Abraham (11:22), their apostolic accomplishments (e.g., 11:23ff.), and their ecstatic visions (12:1ff.). In the present passage it is perhaps the last of these which Paul has in mind particularly, since he proceeds at once (v. 13*a*) to disclaim any such boast on his own part (so Georgi 1964:296, cf. 298–99).

Behind v. 13*a* *(if we have ever been beside ourselves, it was for God)* Windisch, 179–80, sees the charge that Paul has used his ecstatic experiences to recommend himself (cf. Plummer, 172; Hughes, 191–92). It is far more likely, however, that the charge has been the opposite of this—i.e., that Paul has failed to produce as evidence of his apostleship the kind of ecstatic experience his rivals evaluate so highly. This would explain not only the claims of the present verses (11–13) but also Paul's lengthy attempt, in 4:7–5:10, to show that suffering and mortality are signs of apostleship because they allow the power of God and the resurrection life of Jesus to be revealed. He is writing to a congregation which is being tempted to think that only externals are important for estimating a person's authority (v. 12*b*). This problem will come into sharper focus in chaps. 10–13 (10:12*b;* 11:5–6, 13, 18, 20; 13:3*a,* etc.), where Paul finds himself resorting to his own kind of "boasting"—even of ecstatic visions (12:1ff.)—though much against his own best judgment (see, e.g., 12:11*a*). In this earlier letter, however, he declines to do anything like that. Whatever ecstatic experiences he may have had are a matter between himself and God. The point is similar to the one he had already made in 1 Cor 14, where, acknowledging that he himself has spoken in tongues (v. 18), he nevertheless insisted that "one who speaks in a tongue speaks not to people but to God" (v. 2) and cannot "build up the church" thereby (v. 4).

Exactly as in 1 Cor 14, so here in v. 13 it is Paul's concern to distinguish between the sphere of private religious experience, culminating in ecstasy, and the sphere of apostolic service to the community (Käsemann 1942:67–68; followed by Bultmann, 150–51). This is clear when, in v. 13*b,* Paul contrasts mental sobriety with the ecstatic state and affirms, *if we continue in our right* *mind, it is for you.* A similar contrast between the ecstatic *(ho mainetai)* and the sober-minded person *(ho sōphronei)* had been made by Plato in the *Phaedrus* 244 A–B. There the philosopher's main point had been that madness *(mania)* is not in itself evil, but—"when it is sent as a gift of the gods" *(theia mentoi dosei didomenēs)*—is capable of the greatest good. In substantiation of the point, he refers to "the prophetess at Delphi and the priestesses at Dodona," who "when they have been mad [*maneitai*] have conferred many splendid benefits upon Greece both in private and in public affairs, but few or none when they have been in their right minds [*sōphronousai*]." This was the prevailing view of religious ecstasy in the Hellenistic world and, evidently, the view of Paul's rivals in Corinth. It is, however, the view Paul specifically rejects in v. 13: ecstasy is not of benefit for others. His apostleship is not fulfilled by displays of religious frenzy, but by his sober-minded *persuading people* of the gospel and by his service to those who receive it (cf. Schmithals 1971:189–90, 192). Paul's concern in these verses—as it has been already a number of times in this letter—is to say that his apostolate is validated by nothing else but the congregation's own experience of having been established and nurtured by its preaching and its pastoral care (see especially 3:2–3; but also, e.g., 1:24; 4:2*b*, 5, 15).

## The Rule of Love, 5:14–15

In these verses Paul both supports and extends the point of vv. 11 and 13 by an appeal to one of the fundamental articles of the creed he and his congregation share: that "Christ died for our sins" (1 Cor 15:3; other references in NOTES). He cites this in v. 14*b*, *one has died for all,* and again in v. 15*a, he has died for all*—each of these followed by the apostle's own interpretive comment. Blank (1968:313) has made the interesting suggestion that Paul introduces in these verses a "reasoned speech" (Blank would extend this through v. 21 [ibid.]) which stands in marked contrast to the "fool's speech" the apostle finds himself beginning to deliver in chap. 11. The distinction is apt, so long as one recognizes that the "reasoned speech" of the present passage is essentially Paul's exposition of the creedal statement he cites in the opening verses.

The initial statement of v. 14, *For Christ's love lays claim to us,* follows closely on v. 13*b*, both explaining and supporting it (cf. Bultmann, 153). Being in one's *right mind* for others means being responsive to the claim of love under which one's life in faith always stands (cf. Gal 5:6, "faith enacted in love"). Paul's description of the life of faith as a being "under (the dominion of) grace" (Rom 6:14) reflects the same conviction about the nature of the life in Christ.

In this opening statement of v. 14, the pronoun *us* refers in the first instance to Paul and his colleagues (cf. Blank 1968:313), because it is the validity and character of their ministry which have been under consideration. Plummer, 173, understands Paul to be saying that *Christ's love* "restrains us from all self-seeking," not that it "urges us on to service." This, however, is too narrow a view of Paul's intent: while the first meaning is surely included in his statement, it is but one aspect of it. Paul has written earlier of his love for the Corinthians (2:4), and he will do so again, even when his relationship to them has badly deteriorated (11:11; 12:15, the later Letter E). The point in the present passage is that his apostleship operates in response to and out of the love God has bestowed in Christ. It stands totally under the claim of *Christ's love*. But this is nonetheless true of the life of every believer, for whom there is no such thing as separation from *Christ's love* (Rom 8:35–39) or release from the never-ending debt to manifest that love in the world (see, e.g., Rom 13:8–10, and my exposition of the whole topic, Furnish 1972:91–118). It is almost inevitable, then, that the *us* in this initial affirmation of v. 14 should begin to expand under the sheer weight of the affirmation itself, so that what Paul has applied in the first instance to apostles is seen immediately to be applicable to all believers (cf. Dinkler 1970:171).

The perspective is expanded even further in v. 14*b*, where Paul introduces for consideration the creedal statement, *one has died for all* (v. 14*b*). The association of *Christ's love* with Christ's death is thoroughly Pauline, and it is not surprising that the reference to the former (v. 14*a*) has prompted a reference to the latter (v. 14*b*). Paul understands faith itself to originate in God's love met in the cross. This is apparent when he writes elsewhere about his (i.e., every believer's) living "by faith in the Son of God who loved me and gave himself [ = died] for me" (Gal 2:20, *RSV*). Similarly, in Rom 8:31–39 "Christ's love" (vv. 35, 38) is identified with "God's love" (v. 39), expressed when he "did not spare his own Son but gave him up for us all" (v. 32, *RSV*; cf. v. 34*b*). This Pauline interpretation of the death of Christ is developed most extensively in Rom 5:6–11, where the apostle affirms that "God shows his love for us in that while we were yet sinners Christ died for us" (v. 8, *RSV*). From the present passage it becomes clear that the "demonstrating" (*synistanai,* Rom 5:8) of God's love in Christ's death means the establishment of God's rule of love in power (v. 14*a*), as well as the gift of reconciliation (vv. 18–19; Rom 5:10–11; Furnish 1977:214).

Paul's interpretation of the creedal formula about Christ's death begins with the way he quotes it in v. 14*b:* instead of the traditional "Christ died for our sins [or: for us]" (see NOTES), he has *one has died for all.* It is clearly the *all* that is meant to have the emphasis here (Windisch, 182), and that is achieved by the substitution of *one* for "Christ" in the usual formulation. The same notion has been accented in an earlier letter to this congregation, where Christ is presented as the second Adam: "For as in Adam all die, so also in Christ shall all be made alive" (1 Cor 15:22, *RSV*), and it will be spelled out more completely in Rom 5:12–21 (see especially vv. 12–14, 18). In these two passages, as in the present one, the eschatological and therefore universal significance of Christ's death is being stressed (see Dinkler 1970:186–87; Blank 1968:315–16). The same point is made in Rom 8:32 (God gave up his Son "for us all"), where it is clear that this characteristically Pauline emphasis is directly related to the apostle's conviction that God's love is sovereign (Rom 8:35–39). The universal significance of Christ's death ( = God's love) is still the subject in vv. 17, 18–19 of the present passage (on which see below).

More immediately, the emphasis on the universal significance of Christ's saving work continues in v. 14c, *therefore, all have died* (cf. Hahn 1973b:248). In this expansion of the creed the apostle draws out his understanding of the consequence of Christ's death. One cannot be certain, on the basis of the traditional formula alone, whether the statement that *one has died for all* presupposes a "substitutionary" interpretation of Christ's death (see NOTES). If it does, then the logical conclusion to be drawn would have been something like that in John 11:50 (cited by Tannehill 1967:66), where the Jewish high priest unwittingly articulates the Christian belief that the death of one man "for the people" can save them all from destruction. But that, perhaps surprisingly, is not the conclusion Paul draws in v. 14c. Nor does he draw the conclusion of Rom 5:18, "Therefore, all are acquitted and have life." Rather, in this instance the apostle wants to stress the death that *all have died*.

How inclusively should this *all* be read? It is tempting to restrict it to mean "all those who believe" (Rom 4:11) or "all who call upon him" (Rom 10:12), as does Tannehill (1967:65–69). But the grammar (on which see the NOTES) requires us to give the *all* in this statement the same universal scope as the *all* in the preceding one: just as Christ has died for all without exception, so all without exception have died. Some (e.g., Barrett, 168–69) would qualify this by understanding Paul to mean only that all have died "potentially," their actual death (with Christ) necessarily awaiting their act of faith. But this severely weakens a statement that is clearly intended to be emphatic and unqualified, and it does not take adequate account of an apparently deliberate narrowing of focus in the next verse, where *those who live* are a more restricted group. Minear (1979:97–101), who agrees that the reference here is unqualifiedly inclusive, interprets this universal death as a "death-in-sin," identifying it with the universal "disobedience" on which Paul remarks in Rom 11:32 (ibid.:100). But elsewhere Paul identifies this kind of death with Adam, not with Christ (Rom 5:12–21; 1 Cor 15:22). Moreover, the present context —as well as the creedal formula itself—would seem to require that *death* be interpreted here in a more directly positive way. It is perhaps better understood in relation to Paul's conviction that, with Christ, God has established *a new creation,* and that *everything old has come to an end* (v. 17). The perspective here, then, would be cosmic and eschatological: *all have died* in the sense that all without exception are the objects of God's love and as such have been drawn, quite apart from anything they have done (cf. Rom 5:6–11), into the sphere of God's saving purpose and power. On this reading one could say that the apostle has introduced his adaptation and expansion of the creedal statement in order to emphasize the sovereignty and universality of God's rule of love in Christ. No one stands beyond its reach and power.

This eschatological perspective is not abandoned in vv. 15ff., but Paul's special concern here is to indicate what Christ's death should mean for the individual. After repeating the creedal statement in a slightly altered form in v. 15a, he proceeds with a purpose-clause which is implicitly imperatival (see NOTES) in v. 15bc. Now the phrase *those who live* is substituted for the preceding *all,* and thereby attention is focused on those who would by a deliberate act of faith respond to Christ's love and identify with his death. Dying with Christ ought to mean dying to self (v. 15b). In Rom 6, Paul will describe this as the death of "our old person" (v. 6), which comes as one dies to sin (vv. 2, 10–11) and is freed from the tyranny of the law (v. 14). That is why he can also conceive of this dying to self as a dying to the law (Gal 2:19; Rom 7:4) and, more comprehensively, as a dying to the world and all its claims (Gal 6:14). Subsequent remarks in the present passage show he means that *those who live* in Christ must live no longer *according to worldly standards (kata sarka)* of judgment (v. 16) or according to "the old things" *(ta archaia)* which have *come to an end* (v. 17b).

The positive side of freedom from the law, sin, and death ( = from self), is indicated in v. 15c; it is freedom for Christ, freedom to live *to the one who for them died and was raised up.* For Paul, freedom means transfer from one dominion to another: from law to grace (Rom 6:14), from sin to righteousness (Rom 6:18), from death to life (Rom 6:21–23), from flesh to Spirit (Rom 8:4ff.); or, as he puts it here, from self to Christ (cf. "to God," Rom 6:10–11; Gal 2:19). Thus, faith is understood to be truly liberating precisely because it places one under the claim as well as under the gift of *Christ's love* (v. 14a), and gives the believer a wholly new identity as Christ's own. Paul brings this out elsewhere by writing of the death of the believer's old "ego" and its replacement by Christ's life (Gal 2:20), of the believer's life belonging to the one who has ransomed it from death (1 Cor 6:19–20; cf. 7:23), and of the believer belonging to Christ as a bride belongs to her husband (11:2; see NOTES there for other references).

What, concretely, does it mean to live no longer to oneself but to Christ? For Paul it means to live for others. For him, the new identity one has in Christ must be actualized in one's relationships with other people. Faith is "enacted" in love (Gal 5:6), and true freedom in Christ means serving the neighbor in love (Gal 5:13–15). A connection between serving Christ and serving others is made quite explicitly in Rom 14–15, where several themes of the present passage recur. First, whether one is alive or dead (in the physical sense), one belongs to the Lord (14:8). Second, Christ's death was the constituting event for the believing community (14:15; 15:3). Third, that community stands under the rule of love instituted in Christ's death (15:1–3). Finally, after urging his readers to be guided by love in dealing with one another (14:15*a*), Paul refers to the one who actually does so as "serving Christ" (*ho . . . douleuōn tō Christō,* 14:18). The same idea, expressed negatively, appears in 1 Cor 8:12: to sin against one's brethren is to sin against Christ. This association of living for Christ and living for others gives point to the present passage as well. Paul wants his readers to recognize that apostleship is not demonstrated by external characteristics of the apostles themselves (v. 12*b*), even should those be of an impressively "religious" sort, like ecstatic experiences (v. 13*a*). Rather, the apostle, like every believer, is called to serve Christ by serving others. That is one claim Paul can and does make for his apostolate. Thus, vv. 14–15 may be regarded as defining and supporting the remark of v. 13*b* that the Pauline ministry has been conducted sober-mindedly for the Corinthians. Paul and his associates are ruled by Christ's love, in that they have made the confession of faith common to all believers—that Christ *has died for all; therefore, all have died.*

## A New Creation, 5:16–17

The meaning of the creedal statement that *one has died for all* (v. 14*b*) is explicated further here. In v. 16*a, So from now on we regard no one according to worldly standards,* Paul indicates one practical consequence of being dead to self and alive to Christ (v. 15*bc*). The general point is seen best in Gal 3:28 (so, e.g., Blank 1968:318), where, using a formulation familiar to his readers from the baptismal liturgy (Gal 3:27; 1 Cor 12:13), Paul affirms that for believers all worldly distinctions (Jew/Gentile; slave/free; male/female) have become irrelevant, because now they "are all one in Christ Jesus." Thus, in accord also with the *anyone* of v. 17 (see NOTES), the emphatic *we* probably refers to the whole believing community. Similarly, the *now*—the point from which one abandons worldly ways of estimating others—must be the "eschato-logical now" of God's saving love effective in Christ's death (vv. 14–15), as that becomes actualized for each individual through the faith confessed and sealed at his or her baptism (cf., e.g., Tannehill 1967:67; Collange, 258). Set in the context of Paul's special concern in this letter, his point is that there is no place within the body of Christ for judging other people on the basis of externals, as his rivals do (v. 12*b*). Whether one is "wise" or "powerful" or "well-bred" *according to worldly standards* makes no difference to God, as the Corinthians should know (1 Cor 1:26–31), even if Paul's rivals do not. In a later letter Paul will refer more directly to the way his rivals attempt to commend themselves by belittling others (10:12*b*), and he will specifically disavow such tactics for himself (10:12*a*). One may also compare this to the apostle's comments in Gal 2:6 about the leaders of the Jerusalem church "who were reputed to be some-thing" *(RSV),* but whose status in the eyes of others, he says, makes no difference to him, since "God shows no partiality" (cf. Deut 10:17). In short, regarding others *according to worldly standards (kata sarka)* falls under the heading of that "ordinary wisdom" *(sophia sarkikē)* which Paul understands to have been overturned for those who live "by the grace of God" (1:12).

The meaning of the statement in v. 16*b*, *if indeed we have regarded Christ according to worldly standards, now we no longer regard him in that way*, has been long and widely debated. This tr. itself reflects the important judgment that *kata sarka* (literally "according to the flesh") is to be construed adverbially (with *we have regarded*) rather than adjectivally (with *Christ*). The justification for this decision is given in the NOTES. Beyond this, several other important points must be recognized if Paul's intention here is to be appreciated. (a) The *we* should not be read as if it referred to Paul alone, or to Paul and his closest associates. The context requires that it be taken as inclusive of all believers (see NOTES). (b) This is not a "christological" statement. The apostle is not concerned here to comment on his "doctrine of Christ," but only to support the point he has just made in v. 16*a*—that believers no longer judge other persons *according to worldly standards.* (c) Paul is arguing here "from the greater to the lesser" (the reverse of the argument he had employed in 3:7ff.). He cites the way in which believers now view Christ as the most extreme case of a transformed perception of others (Bultmann, 155–57 and 1947:17; Georgi 1964:256; Michel 1954:26; Dinkler 1970:174, 175; Barrett, 171, et al.).

Once these things have been determined, it becomes clear that some of the questions interpreters have sought to answer about this statement are beside the point of the text itself. Chief among these is the question whether the apostle had ever personally encountered Jesus during the course of his earthly ministry, a question Hughes, 200, believes can be answered affirmatively. Another of these secondary questions, although it is considerably more important than the first, is what it had meant to evaluate Christ *according to worldly standards.* Had it meant to regard him as a political Messiah (so, e.g., Denney, 205; Bruce, 208)? Or as a "heretical and turbulent teacher" who had been "justly condemned . . . and crucified" (Plummer, 177)? Or had it meant, perhaps, regarding him only in his human form, and not as the glorified and exalted one (e.g., Bultmann, 157)? The fact is that Paul's primary concern is not to identify any particular *worldly standards* of judgment with respect to Christ. His concern is to emphasize that for the Christian no *worldly standards* have any proper role in the evaluation of other persons (v. 16*a*), since they certainly play no role in one's evaluation of Christ (v. 16*b*).

It seems clear that Paul has been prompted to the statement of v. 16*a* by the fact that his readers are being tempted to judge him and his rivals *according to worldly standards*—that is, by *what is outward* rather than by *what is within* (v. 12*b*). Georgi (1964:254–57, 290–93) believes that the reference to Christ in v. 16*b* has also been prompted by polemical-apologetic considerations, and specifically by the Christology of Paul's opponents. According to Georgi's reconstruction, this involved no clear distinction between Jesus' earthly life and his exaltation, and therefore no appreciation of the decisive significance of Jesus' death and resurrection (1964:293). However, the evidence for the beliefs and particularly for the Christology of Paul's rivals is too indirect, fragmentary, and ambiguous to support Georgi's overall reconstruction (see INTRODUCTION, pp. 48–54). Moreover, v. 16b is better explained as the affirmation of something Paul's readers will readily acknowledge than as something with which they are predisposed to disagree (cf. Bultmann, 157). Were it the latter, it could hardly function in itself as support for v. 16a. Much the same can be said about the older view that Paul is responding to a charge by Jewish Christians who in some way are representative of the leaders of the Jerusalem church. According to this view, the validity of Paul's apostleship is being questioned on the grounds that he had not been personally acquainted with Jesus (see, e.g., Lietzmann, 125; Strachan, 110; Héring, 42; Hughes, 200–1—who mentions the "Christ party" of 1 Cor 1:12ff.). Although Paul's remarks in 10:7ff.; 11:23; 1 Cor 9:1 could have been prompted by some such complaint, neither the form nor the function of v. 16b supports such an interpretation of this statement. It is more confessional than polemical in form (this is also overlooked by Oostendorp 1967:52–55), and it functions in Paul's argument rather like his reference to Christ's resurrection in the argument of 1 Cor 15 (see v. 12): if this is true in the all-important instance of Christ, should it not also be true in the lesser instances of those who belong to him?

It is often remarked that the opposite of regarding Christ *kata sarka*, in a "fleshly" or "worldly" way, is regarding him *kata Pneuma*, "according to the Spirit," or in a "spiritual" way (e.g., Plummer, 176; Michel 1954:25). Martyn (1967:284) points out, however, that Paul does not actually employ this expression, nor the one he had used in 1 Cor 2:14, "to discern spiritually" *(anakrinein pneumatikōs)*. Perhaps, as Martyn suggests, this is because the Corinthian Christians, as well as Paul's rivals in Corinth, would have interpreted such a remark in ways Paul did not intend (ibid.:280–84). In any case, it is much more accurate to say that, for Paul, the opposite of knowing Christ "according to the flesh" is knowing Christ "according to the cross" *(kata stauron;* so Martyn [ibid.:285]). This would mean knowing him as he had been preached in Corinth from the very beginning, as "Jesus Christ and him crucified" (1 Cor 2:2), whose power is disclosed in what the world regards as weakness (1 Cor 1:17–18, 23–25; 2 Cor 13:4). That it is to this way of regarding Christ that Paul appeals in v. 16b is confirmed by the fact that the eschatological *now* (vv. 16a, 16b) of Christian existence is calculated from the institution of Christ's rule of love in the cross (vv. 14, 15). It is also confirmed by the wider context in which Paul has been discussing the meaning of apostleship. He has characterized his own apostolate as a "carrying about in the body the death of Jesus," and as a constant "being given up to death on account of Jesus" (4:10, 11).

He has been concerned to show that only this kind of apostleship is appropriate to "the word of the cross" (1 Cor 1:18). The argument of v. 16 "from the greater to the lesser" fits nicely into this overall discussion (against Schmithals, who regards v. 16 as a Gnostic gloss on v. 17; see NOTES): even as Christ himself is regarded *now* only as the crucified one, so *from now on* those who belong to Christ are to be evaluated not *according to worldly standards* but only "according to the cross" and according to what it requires.

In v. 17 the apostle emphasizes in a more comprehensive way the radical newness of the believer's eschatological existence. Like the preceding verse, this one also draws an inference from vv. 14, 15, and in this respect vv. 16 and 17 are parallel. At the same time, however, the point of v. 16 is being broadened in v. 17 (see, e.g., Bultmann, 158 and 1947:17; Tannehill 1967:68; Michel 1954:27). Those who are *in Christ* have not only abandoned *worldly standards* of judgment (v. 16); they have also become part of a wholly *new creation*. For this concept, which is also used in Gal 6:15 to describe the total newness of the life in Christ, Paul is indebted to apocalyptic Judaism (see NOTES). Plummer, 180, understands Paul to mean by it the re-creation and re-direction of "old feelings, desires and determinations of the will . . . into a new channel," but this is a far too limited definition. As Stuhlmacher (1967) has shown, the *new creation* of which Paul conceives has an ontic reality which transcends the new being of individual believers. It is the new age which stands over against this present evil age (see 4:4; Rom 12:2; 1 Cor 1:20; 2:6, 8; 3:18; Gal 1:4, cited by Stuhlmacher [ibid.:8]). It is not just a "re-creation," but the institution of a wholly new creation (cf. Betz 1979:320). The essence of this new reality is the power of God, which is made present and active in the preaching of "the word of the cross" (1 Cor 1:17–18, 23–24; = "the gospel," Rom 1:16) and in the accompanying gift of the Spirit (1 Cor 2:2–5; 1 Thess 1:5*a*). As the bearer of God's power, the Spirit can be described as the "down payment" of the future salvation (1:22, 5:5; cf. Rom 8:23, "first fruits"), the effective presence, already in this age which is "passing away" (cf. 1 Cor 7:29; 10:11), of the age which is yet to come.

Of all the places where Paul uses the phrase *in Christ (en Christō),* this verse is one of the most significant: *if anyone is in Christ, there is a new creation.* Here it is clear that he conceives of the life *in Christ* as involving a radical transformation of one's whole situation. The more "objective" side of this transformation is one's being drawn under the rule of *Christ's love,* which has been established through the cross (vv. 14–15) and is present in the powerful leading of the Spirit (see Rom 5:5; Gal 5:13–26). The more "subjective" side of it is the total re-orienting of one's values and priorities away from the world (self) and toward the cross (Christ, others), vv. 15*bc*, 16. It is no coincidence that Paul's other specific mention of the *new creation* (Gal 6:15) also occurs in a passage in which he has criticized those who boast of externals (Gal 6:12–13, "in the flesh"; cf. v. 12*b* in the present passage). But for believers, he says, the only boast is "in the cross of the Lord Jesus Christ, by which the world has been crucified to (them), and (they) to the world" (Gal 6:14). To be *in Christ,* and thus a participant in the *new creation,* means to be claimed by the rule of love instituted in the cross, and to be liberated from the powers of this present age.

The Pauline *in Christ* formula has an ecclesiological as well as an eschatological dimension. That is apparent from Rom 12:5, "we . . . are one body in Christ" *(RSV),* and also from Gal 3:27–28. In the latter passage (cf. 1 Cor 12:12–13) those who are "baptized into Christ" *(eis Christon)* are affirmed to be "all one in Christ Jesus" *(en Christō Iēsou),* whatever their ethnic origin, social status, or sex (cf. Gal 6:15, "neither circumcision nor uncircumcision means anything, but only a new creation"). Therefore, although Paul regards the *new creation* as an eschatological reality—and hence cosmic in scope, not narrowly ecclesiological—he understands it to be experienced concretely within the believing community (cf. Hahn 1973b:249), *in Christ.* Thus the affirmation of v. 17a helps to support the point of v. 16a, that *from now on no other person is judged according to worldly standards.*

The remainder of v. 17 does not describe the *new creation* so much as it celebrates its inauguration: *Everything old has come to an end; behold, new things have come to be.* The power of *the god of this age* (4:4), the *worldly standards* by which others have been assessed (v. 16a), and everything else which belongs to this world *has come to an end* for those who are in Christ. This must mean, not that *everything old* has been "destroyed," but that believers have been freed from "the rulers of this age" (1 Cor 2:6) and freed for the rule of Christ's love; the actual destruction of the old order is still in the future (1 Cor 15:24–28). But, in marked contrast with the views of Jewish apocalypticism, Paul can affirm that the new age has already broken in (see also 6:2), that the *new creation* is already a reality. One could imagine a baptismal setting for this exultant cry (cf. Michel 1954:28 n. 8), and yet it refers to more than the birth of a new "creature." For this reason, too, the "nice parallel" that Windisch, 190, cites, from *Sipre* 72a (to Deut 3:29), is a formal parallel only: "Behold, now you are new! What is past has already disappeared." Those words were addressed to Israel and pertained to its own life as the people of God. Paul's words here, more comprehensively, speak of the inauguration of a whole new order, *a new creation.* This exists by the power of God, decisively present in the cross as the rule of Christ's love, and continually active in the working of the Spirit as the word of the cross is proclaimed and received.

### Reconciliation, 5:18–19

Here Paul's long discourse on apostleship which had begun in 2:14 is drawn to a close. He had opened it with references to apostles as "ministers of a new covenant" (3:6) and to their "ministry of the Spirit" (3:8) and "of righteousness" (3:9). Now his comments are concluded with references to *the ministry of reconciliation* (v. 18) and *the word of reconciliation* (v. 19*c*) which God has established within the whole community of believers.

It is probable (against Hofius 1980a:187) that Paul is drawing upon another traditional theological formulation here, just as he had in vv. 14, 15, where he had cited the creedal affirmation about Christ's death. Käsemann (1971a:53) suggests that the citation is drawn in this instance from "a pre-Pauline hymnic fragment," and that it extends from v. 19 through v. 21. In his view, the earliest form of the tradition would be found in Rom 5:11; Col 1:20; Eph 2:16—where the emphasis is upon a reconciliation *within* the world *(kosmos)*. The notion (found in the present passage, v. 19) that the world itself is reconciled would then be a later development, and the idea of the reconciliation of humanity to God (v. 18) would be later still (ibid.:54–56). This reconstruction of the development of the tradition is not entirely convincing, however. For instance, the tradition appears to have included an anthropological aspect already in its pre-Pauline form (see, e.g., v. 19*b;* Dinkler 1970:180 n. 37; Lührmann 1970:445; I. H. Marshall 1978:129–30). Moreover, as Stuhlmacher (1965:77–78 n. 2) has shown (followed, e.g., by Lührmann 1970:444–45 and Collange, 268–69), Paul's citation from the tradition is probably confined to v. 19*ab: God, in Christ, was reconciling the world to himself, not charging their trespasses to them.*

There is convincing evidence that Paul is citing previously formulated material in v. 19*ab:* (a) the introductory *hōs hoti* is best explained as a citation formula, *As it is said;* (b) the imperfect-periphrastic construction, *was reconciling,* is rarely used by Paul himself; (c) Paul ordinarily uses the singular, "trespass," not the plural, as here; (d) the third-person pronouns *their* and *them* contrast with the first-person pronoun *(us)* employed in vv. 18, 19*c;* (e) the present participle *not charging* contrasts with the aorist participles of vv. 18 *(has reconciled, has given)* and 19*c (has established).* The NOTES may be consulted for details on these points. In addition, Collange, 269, notes a certain rhythmic pattern in v. 19*ab* which helps to set it apart. The question of the origin of this tradition should be left open. I. H. Marshall (1978:129–30) refers to this as kerygmatic (or creedal) language which Paul himself had previously formulated. Collange, 269, also allows for this possibility, or that it was a creation of the Pauline congregations under the influence of his preaching. Nevertheless, a pre-Pauline origin for the formulation (so, e.g., Käsemann 1971a; Stuhlmacher 1965:78 n. 2) cannot be ruled out and, given certain non-Pauline features in v. 19*ab,* may be the most likely.

In and of itself the tradition emphasizes three things: (a) that *God . . . was reconciling the world to himself;* (b) that *Christ* was the agent of this reconciliation; and (c) that reconciliation means *not charging* trespassers with *their trespasses.* The first of these points is especially important. Reconciliation seems to have become a significant religious theme first of all in the early Christian church (Büchsel, *TDNT* III:254), 2 Mac being one of the few places where the notion had been given a religious application in Hellenistic Judaism. In 2 Mac, however, God appears as the object of reconciliation, not as its originator. There the presupposition is that God has been justifiably angered by the evil ways of his people (7:33), but that because he is merciful (8:29) God can be prevailed upon to put his hostility aside and to be at peace with the supplicants (1:4–5; see Walter 1979:439; I. H. Marshall 1978:120–21). Against this background, the affirmation of v. 19a that *God . . . was reconciling the world to himself* is all the more arresting. Here the reconciliation is not of God but *from* and *to* God. Although the notion of God's being reconciled appears in later Christian writers (e.g., 1 Clem 48:1, quoted in the NOTES on v. 18), the tradition in its earliest Christian form (v. 19a) and in its earliest Christian applications (vv. 18, 19c, 20b; Rom 5:10–11; 11:15; Eph 2:16; Col 1:20, 22) emphasizes God's initiative in *reconciling the world to himself.* This was understood primarily as the remission of sins, God's *not charging their trespasses to them* (v. 19b: an echo of LXX Ps 31[32]:2; see NOTES). Hughes, 209, correctly notes that this presupposes a substitutionary view of Christ's death. The trespasses of others have been charged to him, and he has died in their place, paying the penalty for those sins.

Beyond this, however, one must consider how Paul himself interprets the tradition, and why he has chosen to quote it in the present passage. Respecting the second of these, two different answers have been proposed: Hahn (1973b:252) suggests that Paul cites the traditional statement about the reconciliation of *the world* in order to emphasize the cosmic scope and significance of the *new creation* (v. 17); but Collange, 268–69, thinks that Paul has been attracted by the concept of reconciliation itself, mindful as he is that his readers need to be reconciled not only with God but also with his own apostolate. These are not mutually exclusive suggestions, and it is possible that both concerns lie behind Paul's introduction of the quotation in v. 19ab. The second one, however, is particularly worth considering, because Paul uses the theme of reconciliation as a springboard for the series of appeals to the Corinthians which begins in 5:20.

Granting that a traditional formulation has been cited in v. 19ab, Paul's own understanding of that tradition would come in vv. 18 and 19c, within which the tradition has been embedded. Here it is apparent, first, that Paul identifies reconciliation closely with the *new creation.* The link between these two ideas is forged in v. 18ab, *All things are from God, who has reconciled us to himself.* . . . *All things* refers in the first instance to those *new things* which *have come to be* in the *new creation* (v. 17) and thus, in effect, to the whole new order in which *Christ's love* rules (v. 14). The radical theocentrism of Paul's thought is apparent here, as it has been throughout this discussion of apostleship (e.g., 2:14; 3:17–18; 4:1, 6, 7, 15; 5:1, 5) and as it is elsewhere in Paul's letters: God's power is the source and God's glory is the goal of *all things* (see especially Rom 11:36; 1 Cor 3:23; 8:6; 11:12b; 15:27–28).

In the second place, and in full agreement with the tradition, Paul understands reconciliation to be God's work. God is the author, not the object, of reconciliation: God *has reconciled us to himself through Christ* (v. 18*b*). Paul's use of the personal pronoun *us* in place of *world* (*kosmos,* v. 19*a*) represents an anthropological interpretation of the tradition, for which, however, the tradition itself had already supplied a precedent (v. 19*b, their* and *them*). As in the immediately preceding verses, all believers are in view—not just the apostles (see NOTES). Paul is also interpreting the tradition when, for the *in Christ* of the earlier formulation (v. 19*a*), he substitutes *through Christ,* meaning "through Christ's death," as in vv. 14, 15. The same connection is made in the other major passage where Paul writes of reconciliation, Rom 5:6–11. There, as Binder (1973:308) remarks, the reconciliation which comes through Christ's death means not only the overcoming of the enmity between God and his people but also the overcoming of their weakness, their ungodliness, and their sin. It is, in short, the transformation of their whole situation, *a new creation,* as in the present passage, v. 17 (ibid.:306). That this occurs through Christ's death means that it is rooted in God's love, which is present as both a gift and a claim (v. 14; Rom 5:8). Thus, the concept of reconciliation, rather more than that of justification to which it is closely related (see especially Rom 5:9, 10), emphasizes that God's saving power is essentially the power of his love (cf. Büchsel, *TDNT* I:258; on the connection in Paul's thought between reconciliation and justification see, e.g., Goppelt 1968:153–59; Lührmann 1970; Bultmann, 160; Dupont 1953:279–89; Furnish 1977:212–13).

Third, Paul significantly expands on the tradition cited in v. 19*ab* when he includes as an integral part of the act of reconciliation God's bestowal of a *ministry of reconciliation* (v. 18*c*). This ministry is not regarded merely as responsive to or a consequence of the eschatological event, but as a constituent part of the event itself (cf. Bultmann, 162; Dinkler 1970:177). This means that the ministry does not "bring" reconciliation, but exists only because reconciliation has already occurred. Moreover, if the *us* in v. 18*c* is really meant to be inclusive, as would appear (see NOTES), then Paul is affirming that *the ministry of reconciliation* has been given to the whole Christian community, not just to the apostles. Thus, Paul's perspective is broader—as he now closes his discussion of apostleship—than it had been when he first opened the discussion in 2:14ff. There his references to ministers of a new covenant (3:6), to *the ministry of the Spirit* (3:8), and to *the ministry of righteousness* (3:9) helped to define the character and responsibility of the Christian apostolate. But here his reference to *the ministry of reconciliation* helps to define the responsibility laid upon the whole community of faith as it is reconciled to God and drawn under the rule of Christ's love.

Finally, in v. 19*c,* following the citation about God's reconciling action in Christ, Paul adds that God *has established among us the word of reconciliation.* Most interpreters regard this as a restatement of the affirmation in v. 18*c* that

God has given the ministry of reconciliation (e.g., *RSV*: "entrusting to us the message of reconciliation"). It is quite true that the aorist participle in v. 19*c* continues the construction temporarily interrupted by the citation in v. 19*ab* (see NOTES). But it is more likely that the apostle intends his reference to *the word of reconciliation* to be a restatement, for the sake of emphasis, of the affirmation he has just cited in v. 19*ab*. In this case God's establishment of *the word of reconciliation* should be identified primarily with the reconciling event itself, as that is affirmed in the tradition Paul cites in v. 19*ab* and in the apostle's own words in v. 18*b*. This *word of reconciliation* is therefore God's word, the gospel, and it is not to be identified in the first instance with the church's "message about reconciliation." Like the prophet (Isa 55:10–11), Paul customarily associates God's word (see 2:17 and NOTES; 4:2, etc.) with God's eschatological, life-giving power (cf. Phil 2:16, "the word of life"), which accomplishes what God has purposed. The apostle sees this "power for salvation" (Rom 1:16) to be operative above all in Christ's death, an act of reconciling love (2 Cor 5:14; Rom 5:8–11), and for this reason one may say that *the word of reconciliation* is nothing else but "the word of the cross" (1 Cor 1:17–18). When Paul now writes of its establishment in the community of faith, he is writing once more of *Christ's love* by which that community is both constituted and governed (2 Cor 5:14*a*). (A similar conclusion is reached by Hofius [1980b], but on different grounds.)

# C. APPEALS, 5:20–9:15

## 9. RECONCILIATION WITH GOD, 5:20–6:10

5 <sup>20</sup>Therefore, we are serving as ambassadors for Christ, God appealing through us. We are entreating for Christ, be reconciled to God. <sup>21</sup>The one who knew no sin he made to be sin for us, that in him we might become the righteousness of God. 6 <sup>1</sup>So working together with him, we are also appealing to you not to receive the grace of God in vain. <sup>2</sup>For he says, "At the time of favor I heard you, and on the day of salvation I helped you." Behold, now is the time of favor! Behold, now is the day of salvation!

<sup>3</sup>We are giving no one cause to take offense at anything, lest the ministry be blamed. <sup>4</sup>Rather, we are recommending ourselves in every way, as ministers of God should:

with much endurance—in the course of afflictions, catastrophes, pressures; <sup>5</sup>in the course of beatings, imprisonments, riots; in the course of labors, sleepless nights, times without food;

<sup>6</sup>with probity, with knowledge, with forbearance, with kindness, with the Holy Spirit, with authentic love, <sup>7</sup>with the word of truth, with the power of God;

having the weapons of righteousness on the right hand and on the left, <sup>8</sup>being renowned and dishonored, being defamed and praised;

as deceivers—and yet true; <sup>9</sup>as unknowns—and yet fully known; as dying—and yet see, we live; as receiving punishment—and yet not put to death; <sup>10</sup>as sorrowing—but constantly rejoicing; as impoverished—but enriching many; as having nothing—and yet possessing everything.

## NOTES

5:20a. *Therefore.* This *oun* not only connects the preceding statement about reconciliation (vv. 18–19) to the following entreaty to *be reconciled,* but in a larger sense connects the whole discussion of apostleship since 2:14 with the appeals of 5:20–9:15. Cf. Rom 12:1.

*we are serving as ambassadors.* Translates the verb *presbeuein,* used of the work of a *presbeutēs,* one who carries a message for or in some other way represents another. Thus, e.g., the terms were used in the Greek-speaking part of the Roman Empire for an official representative of Caesar (Latin: *legatus*). See also, *inter alia,* 1 Mac 14:22; 2 Mac 11:34, "envoys" sent by the Jews on official business. Philo, *Who Is the Heir* 205–6, describes the Logos as God's ambassador to the world, sent on an embassy of peace *(epikērykeuesthai)* to creation. See Deissmann 1927:374; Bornkamm, *TDNT* VI:681–83. Here *we* means "we apostles"; see note on *through us.*

*for Christ.* Not just "on his behalf," nor, on the other hand, "in his place," as if he were not present. Rather, the phrase *(hyper Christou,* repeated in v. 20*b*) must be interpreted on the basis of the verb *presbeuein* (see preceding note): "with the full authority of Christ who has sent me." Note Paul's comment in 1 Cor 1:17 about having been sent by Christ to preach the gospel. Cf. also Rom 10:15 (preachers must be sent by another) and Epictetus III.xxii.23 (where the true Cynic is described as one who has been sent by Zeus as a messenger to humanity).

*God appealing.* A genitive absolute construction, *hōs tou Theou parakalountos.* The *hōs* (left untranslated here) expresses the motivation of the subject; thus, perhaps, "with the conviction that God is appealing . . ."; cf. BDF § 425(3); *GNTG* III:158; Plummer, 185. On Paul's use of the verb *parakalein,* "to appeal," etc., see NOTES on 2:7 (where it is translated "deal kindly"), on 2:8 (where it is translated "urge"), and COMMENT.

*through us.* Here the first-person-plural pronoun must refer to the Pauline apostolate, since the appeal subsequently formulated in v. 20*b* is addressed to the readers (second person plural); see Kijne 1966:178.

20*b. We are entreating.* The verb *deisthai* introduces earnest entreaties, as in Rom 1:10; 1 Thess 3:10 (where it is used of petitions addressed to God), and later in this letter, 8:4 (the Macedonians beseeching Paul). Here, as in 10:2; Gal 4:12, the apostle is exhorting his readers. Mullins (1972:381) identifies petitions which use this verb as more formal (even "forensic") than those which use, e.g., the verb *parakalein,* which appears in 6:1. One may justifiably supply *you* after the verb, even though *hymas* does not stand in the Greek, because an exhortation to the readers is being introduced (see, e.g., Barrett, 170). Plummer, 185, however, thinks it significant that Paul himself has not used an object either here or after the participle in v. 20*a*—as if he had "a wider field" than just Corinth in mind *(urbi et orbi).*

*for Christ.* Again *hyper Christou* as in v. 20*a;* the repetition emphasizes the official and authoritative capacity in which Paul writes (Plummer, 186). Mullins (1962:52) calls this a "divine authority phrase," and notes that it replaces the "courtesy phrase" of the usual formal petition.

*be reconciled to God.* The verb is passive (although I. H. Marshall [1978:123–24] suggests it could be deponent, referring "to human putting away of enmity"), and presupposes that God has already acted for reconciliation (vv. 18–19, on which see NOTES and COMMENT).

21. *The one who knew no sin.* That is, Christ. The expression "to know sin" *(hamartian ginōskein)* is Pauline (see Rom 3:20; 7:7), and the verb is to be interpreted as a reference to "practical knowledge" (in the Hebraic sense); thus, here, the actual experience of sin, involvement with it. See Bultmann, 166 and in *TDNT* I:703. Apart from this verse neither the word *sin (hamartia)* nor any cognate term occurs in chaps. 1–9 (Letter D); in chaps. 10–13, only in 11:7. Here, as almost always in the Pauline letters,

the singular is employed. Where Paul does use the plural, "sins," he is usually citing either scripture (Rom 4:7) or the church's tradition (1 Cor 15:3; Gal 1:4; Rom 3:25 [the synonym *hamartēmata*]); otherwise only in Rom 7:5; 1 Cor 15:17; 1 Thess 2:16 (perhaps a later interpolation). Hoad 1957:254 (cf. Hofius 1980a:196) compares this to Isa 53:9*b* (of the Suffering Servant): "he committed no lawless act, nor was deceit found in his mouth" (LXX: *anomian ouk epoiēsen, oude heurethē dolos en tō stomati autou*).

*he made to be sin for us.* The subject *(he)* is God. *Sin* here cannot mean "sin offering" (see Lev 4:25, 29), as some have held, for that would import an idea foreign to this context; see discussions in Bachmann, 272; Plummer, 187; Hughes, 214–15. Bultmann, 166, believes that *sin* here is an instance of the abstract standing for the concrete, "sinner" (*hamartōlos;* used by Paul only in Rom 3:7; 5:8, 19; 7:13; Gal 2:15, 17, and in no instance of Christ). It is more likely, however, that Paul is thinking in a general way of Christ's identification with sinful humanity; see Kertelge 1967:103 and COMMENT. Hoad 1957:254 compares the whole thought to Isa 53:10, but the comparison is not convincing. See especially Rom 8:3; Gal 3:13.

*for us.* Bjerkelund (1967:153) holds that the plural includes only Paul and his co-workers, as in the preceding verse. Here, however, the expression *(hyper hēmōn)* is surely drawn from the creedal tradition (cf. "for all" in 5:14, 15 and "for us" in Gal 3:13). This fact, plus the recapitulative function of v. 21 (see COMMENT), assures a more inclusive meaning for the pronoun (so also Kijne 1966:178; Hofius 1980b:5 n. 8, and most interpreters). *For us* could mean simply "for our benefit" (Kertelge 1967:105) or "in our place" (Dinkler 1970:181). The second includes the first, although the first need not involve the second.

*in him* This phrase *(en autō)* may be interpreted in either an instrumental (in that case: "by means of him") or local sense. Bultmann, 167, leaves the question open. Dinkler 1970:181 opts for the instrumental meaning, taking the phrase as a reference to Christ's death. It is better, however, to understand the phrase in accord with "in Christ" in v. 17, and to give it the full Pauline meaning of the latter (so the majority of commentators). Although the phrase stands at the end of the Greek sentence, it has been transposed to this point in order to make it clear that *him* refers to Christ, not God.

*the righteousness of God.* This phrase (or "his righteousness," referring to God) appears altogether ten times in the Pauline letters (Rom 1:17; 3:5, 21, 22, 25, 26; 10:3 *bis;* 2 Cor 5:21; Phil 3:9), elsewhere in the NT only in Matt 6:33; Jas 1:20; 2 Pet 1:1. Chronologically, the present verse represents the earliest known use of it by the apostle. Käsemann (1969:168–82) and Stuhlmacher (1965, especially 102–84) believe Paul is dependent on apocalyptic Judaism in his use of the phrase, and that it is to be associated primarily with the power by which God establishes the covenant and maintains his faithfulness to it. The genitive *Theou* is thus regarded as subjective, "*God's* righteousness." The opposing view is represented by Bultmann (1964) and Conzelmann (1972). They hold *Theou* to be a genitive of origin referring primarily to the righteousness God gives, his justifying action by which a possibility is opened up for salvation. For a brief review of the debate and further literature, see Klein, "Righteousness in the NT," *IDBSup:* 750–52, who himself assumes a somewhat mediating position. Hoad (1957: 254) cites Isa 53:11, where, according to the Hebrew text, the righteous Servant of God makes many righteous by bearing their iniquities (but the LXX refers to the justification of the Servant himself).

**6:1. So.** Translates *de,* which in this case functions as a resumptive particle connecting what follows to 5:20 after the semi-parenthetical affirmation of 5:21 (on which see COMMENT).

*working together with him.* The words *with him* have been supplied in the tr. on the basis of the close connection between this verse and 5:20. The two verses are tied together both by the particle *de* (see preceding note) and by the use of the word *parakalein,* "to appeal" (see following note). In 5:20 *God* is the subject of the *parakalein,* while in 6:1 the subject is Paul and his associates. Thus, the context strongly supports the position adopted here, and by most interpreters, that the present reference is to a *working together* of God *(him)* and the Pauline apostolate. In 1 Thess 3:2, Paul does not hesitate to describe Timothy as "a co-worker of God" (the textual variants are evident attempts to modify this striking expression; Metzger 1971:631), so the concept is not foreign to him. It is doubtful, however, whether 1 Cor 3:9 should also be invoked as support for this view (correctly Friedrich 1963a:25), since there the more probable meaning is that Paul and Apollos are "co-workers *for* God" (see Furnish 1961). Bachmann, 274, argues for the meaning "working together with you Corinthians," because their responsibility to *be reconciled* has been stressed in 5:20*b,* as it seems to be in this verse as well; so also Prümm I,361, who refers to 1:24 ("we are co-workers for your joy"), and Allo, 173. But the main subject here is the role of those who preach the gospel, not the role of those who hear it (correctly Plummer, 189), and everywhere else that Paul refers to "co-workers" (including 1:24, on which see NOTES and COMMENT) he has ministers of the gospel in mind, not the members of his congregations (so also in 1 Cor 16:16, where a participial form of the verb is used substantively).

*we are also appealing to you.* Cf. 5:20*a,* where the same verb *(parakalein)* had been used (in a participial form) of God's *appealing through* the apostles. Now the apostles themselves *(we)* are identified as the subjects of the action; cf. *we are serving as ambassadors,* 5:20*a,* and *We are entreating,* 5:20*b.* An acceptable English tr. requires that *to you* be placed after *appealing,* but *hymas (you)* actually stands at the very end of the Greek sentence, apparently for emphasis.

*not to receive.* The infinitive here *(dexasthai)* is a "timeless" aorist after a verb of exhortation *(parakalein,* "to appeal"); see Plummer, 190; Burton 1898: § 113.

*the grace of God.* The phrase appears elsewhere in this letter in 1:12; 8:1; 9:14, but in each instance the context determines the particular meaning. Here it gathers up the preceding references to reconciliation and righteousness (5:18–19, 20, 21); see Dinkler 1970:181; Bultmann, 168.

*in vain.* Or "without meaningful effect." Among the NT writers only Paul uses this phrase *(eis kenon),* but it appears in the LXX (especially in the prophetic books) and in other Greek sources. Elsewhere in the Pauline letters this precise phrase is applied to the apostle's own situation—i.e., his fear of having preached and labored to no effect (Gal 2:2; Phil 2:16 *bis;* 1 Thess 3:5). Here, however, he expresses anxiety about the Corinthians; cf. especially 1 Cor 15:14 ("Now if Christ has not been raised, then our preaching is in vain [*kenon*] and your faith is in vain [*kenē*]") and 15:58 ("knowing that your labor is not without effect [*kenos*] in the Lord"; cf. LXX Jer 28:58 [*RSV,* 51:58]).

2a. *For he says.* This phrase *(legei gar)* introduces a quotation from Isa (see following note), and probably reflects a rabbinic formula (Bonsirven 1939:30–31). Such formulas using the verb *legein,* "to say," appear fairly often in the Pauline letters, as elsewhere in the NT (collected in ibid.:340–42). In the Pauline examples the subject of the verb "says" is usually "scripture" (Rom 4:3; 10:11; 11:2; Gal 4:30; cf. "the law," Rom 7:7; 1 Cor 14:34 [in an interpolation?]) or an "author's" name: "Isaiah" (Rom 10:16, 20; 15:12), "Moses" (Rom 10:19), or "David" (Rom 4:6; 11:9). "God" (or "the Lord") is the understood subject of the verb in Rom 9:15, and again in Rom 9:17, where "the scripture" is a metonym. It is questionable whether the formula of 2 Cor 6:16 ("As God said") is directly attributable to the apostle. Since the words Paul quotes here are introduced in the LXX by the phrase "Thus says the Lord" *(houtōs legei Kyrios),* "the Lord" could be the understood subject of the same verb in the present verse; otherwise it would be "God" from 5:20; 6:1.

*"At the time of favor . . ."* This citation of Isa 49:8a follows the wording of the LXX exactly. The verse is quoted nowhere else in the NT. *Kairō dektō, At the time of favor,* renders the Hebrew *bĕ⁻ēt rāṣôn* ("a time of favor," *RSV*), which, in Second Isaiah, refers to the time of God's gracious turning toward his people; see Westermann 1969: 215.

2b. *Behold . . . Behold.* See note on the same expression in 5:17.

*now . . . now.* The same adverb *(nyn)* has also been used twice in 5:16 (see NOTES); its meaning here is similar. See COMMENT.

*the time of favor.* Instead of the adjective *dektos (of favor)* which stands in v. 2a in the quotation from Isa, Paul now uses the adjective *euprosdektos.* This is usually described as a strengthened form of *dektos* (e.g., Plummer, 191; Héring, 46; Bultmann, 169), so that Barrett, 183, and others translate the latter as "acceptable" (v. 2a) but the former as "welcome" (v. 2b). Although this is lexically defensible (see BDF § 117[1]), it is not certain that actual usage supports such a distinction in the present case. The so-called "strengthened form" was the one regularly used by Greek authors, and is the one preferred by Paul himself (Rom 15:16, 31; 2 Cor 6:2b; 8:12); the LXX form appears only where he is quoting (2 Cor 6:2a) or alluding to (Phil 4:18) a scriptural passage; see Field 1879:184. A comparison of Phil 4:18 *(dektos,* echoing Isa 56:7) and Rom 15:16 *(euprosdektos)* suggests that in this case Paul assimilated LXX usage to that of his own day.

*the day of salvation.* Paul has adopted the phrase from Isaiah *(hēmera sōtērias* for Hebrew *yôm yĕšû⁻āh),* but he uses it nowhere else. The noun *salvation* occurs elsewhere in 2 Cor only in 1:6 and 7:10. In general, Paul's references to the eschatological day ("the day of wrath," Rom 2:5; "the day of our Lord Jesus," 2 Cor 1:14, etc.) presume that it is yet to come; but note 1 Thess 5:5, 8, where those who hope for it (see 5:2) are said to belong to it already as "sons."

3. *We are giving.* Translates the present participle *didontes,* which most commentators describe as dependent on *we are . . . appealing,* v. 1, and therefore co-ordinate with *working together* in that verse. However, this may be simply another instance of Paul's use of a participle instead of a finite verb; see note on *providing* in 5:12, which translates the same participle.

*no one . . . at anything.* These expressions *(mēdemian en mēdeni)* stand together at the beginning of the Greek sentence. Their position, the alliteration, and the double negative (perfectly permissible in Greek) help to emphasize the apostle's point (literally: "no one in nothing . . .").

*cause to take offense.* The word used here is *proskopē,* a much less frequent form than *proskomma,* which Paul uses elsewhere with a similar meaning (Rom 14:13, 20; 1 Cor 8:9). Cf. also 1 Cor 10:32 (*aproskopoi,* "giving no cause for offense"), and the apostle's use of the terms *skandalon, skandalizein,* "stumbling block," "to cause to stumble" (11:29; Rom 14:13; 16:17; 1 Cor 8:13, twice), and *enkopē,* "hindrance" (1 Cor 9:12).

*the ministry.* Some texts (D F G 629, etc.) have "our ministry" *(hē diakonia hēmōn),* and most recent English versions also supply the pronoun (e.g., *RSV, NEB, JB, TEV*). This cannot be justified on textual grounds, however, and it is doubtful whether the word should be supplied here (despite Rom 11:13, "my ministry"). One might better supply "this" (cf. 4:1, "having this ministry"), which would mean "this ministry of reconciliation" (see 5:18).

*be blamed.* The same verb *(mōmasthai)* is used in 8:20, but with an active meaning. The verb and its cognates are not used with reference to the divine judgment, but always of censure coming from human agencies.

*4a. we are recommending ourselves.* See on 3:1; 4:2; 5:12.

*in every way.* Or "in everything" *(en panti);* the expression stands in direct contrast to *en mēdeni* (literally "in nothing"), v. 3.

*as ministers of God should.* This tr. supplies the word *should* to make it clear that Paul does not mean "We recommend ourselves as ministers of God." That would require the accusative *(hōs Theou diakonous),* but Paul uses the nominative *(hōs Theou diakonoi);* Robertson 1923:454 (cf. 481). In 1 Thess 3:2, according to some texts, Timothy is called "a minister of God," and the same term is applied to a civil authority in Rom 13:4. In 11:23, Paul will commend himself as "a minister of Christ"; cf. also the general reference to "ministers of a new covenant" (3:6, and note there). Pol Phil 5:2 has the phrase "ministers of God and of Christ."

*4b. with much endurance.* Here the dative *(en hypomonē)* is interpreted as instrumental; Paul recommends his apostolate, first, by means of its *much endurance.* As in 1:6 (on which see NOTES and COMMENT), the reference is to *endurance* in the midst of affliction. See also 12:12, where *endurance* is associated with "the apostolic signs."

*4c. in the course of afflictions, catastrophes, pressures.* These three terms are used more or less synonymously here, and with a general meaning. If there is any significance in the sequence, it is only that the longer Greek word (*stenochōriais,* five syllables, as compared to the first two words, *thlipsesin* and *anagkais,* three syllables each) comes last; see Fridrichsen 1944:28. The first and last terms are often paired, as in the similar lists in 4:8 (see note; verbal forms are used) and Rom 8:35. The first and second terms are paired in 1 Thess 3:7, but in reverse order (*RSV:* "distress and affliction"). The second and third terms are both again present in 12:10 in yet another list of apostolic hardships. The preposition *en* (literally "in") which precedes each of these three terms, as well as each of those that follow in v. 5, is best understood to mean "in the midst of"; it introduces the ways in which *endurance* is manifested in the Pauline ministry.

*5a. in the course of beatings, imprisonments, riots.* For the tr. of *en* as *in the course of,* see preceding note. These terms (again, the longest Greek word comes last; Fridrichsen 1944:28) are more specific than those in v. 4c. The first two appear again, but in reverse order, in 11:23b. See also Acts 16:23 (cf. 16:37), where it is said that Paul and Silas were beaten before being imprisoned. For the types of beatings Paul may have had to endure, see 11:24–25, with NOTES. Although the apostle here speaks of *imprisonments* (plural), Acts reports only one up to this point in Paul's ministry (in Philippi, Acts 16:23–40); see COMMENT. The third term *(akatastasiai)* is used in 12:20 with reference to general congregational disorder (cf. 1 Cor 14:33a, disorder in worship), and that could be the meaning here as well (cf. Bultmann, 172). However, because it is linked closely to *beatings* and *imprisonments,* it should probably be given a more specific meaning—if not "pogroms" (Windisch, 205), at least "mobbings" (cf. Barrett, 186) or *riots* (cf. Luke 21:9, "wars and riots"). According to Acts, Paul's ministry had precipitated such uprisings in numerous places, even in Corinth itself (Acts 18:12–17; also in Pisidian Antioch, 13:50; Iconium, 14:5–6; Lystra, 14:19; Philippi, 16:22; Thessalonica, 17:5–9; Beroea, 17:13; Ephesus, 19:23–41).

*5b. in the course of labors, sleepless nights, times without food.* Again, *en* is rendered as *in the course of* (see note on v. 4c), and precedes each of the Greek terms. Although the last is not the longest (as in vv. 4c, 5a), all three syllables are long *(nēsteiais),* so the effect is much the same (Fridrichsen 1944:28). These three hardships are also mentioned in the list in chap. 11 (v. 27). The first, *labors (kopois),* may describe the "wearisome toil" Paul endured as a craftsman (so Hock 1980:64), as the singular clearly does in 11:27—where it is coupled with *mochthos* ("our labor and toil")—and as the verb does in 1 Cor 4:9–13 ("and we labor, working with our own hands" [*RSV*]). However, it is also possible to interpret the plural here as a reference to "apostolic labors"—specifically, Christian missionary work (so Hughes, 225), as in 10:15 (and perhaps in 11:23). If the former, then the second and third terms in this series should probably be interpreted as deprivations associated with working at one's craft (so, e.g., Windisch, 205; Bultmann, 172; Friedrich 1963a:40; Barrett, 186); they almost certainly have this meaning in 11:27. Thus, Hock (1980:34–35) cites the difficult circumstances of Lucian's character Micyllus the Shoemaker, awakened before dawn to get to his workbench (*The Cock* 1), usually hungry and poorly clothed (ibid. 9, 22; *The Downward Journey* 20). But if the reference is to apostolic labors, then it would be possible to think of the *sleepless nights* and *times without food* as due to the exigencies of missionary service (so, e.g., Hughes, 225–26). Müller-Bardoff (1956) thinks that Paul refers here to religious vigils and fastings preceding prayer, but the context excludes this.

*6a. with probity, with knowledge.* As throughout the list of vv. 4c–5, each of the terms in vv. 6–7a is preceded by the preposition *en.* But now the sense is instrumental, *with* (as in v. 4b), not local, as in vv. 4c–5. This list is not continuous with the preceding one, then, but is co-ordinate with v. 4b, *with endurance* (correctly Plummer, 196; Héring, 47). *Probity* translates *hagnotēs,* attested by some witnesses also in 11:3. The related adjective *(hagnos)* is used in 7:11 with reference to moral "innocence," in 11:2 (metaphorically) of a "chaste" bride, and in Phil 4:8 of general moral integrity. This last meaning accords best with the overall point in the present letter; see especially 4:2, and cf. Phil 1:17, where the adverb *hagnōs* is used of sincere motives and purposes. The *knowledge (gnōsis)* of which Paul writes here is not the ultimate, "saving" knowledge mentioned in 2:14, 4:6 (contrast Hughes, 227), nor just a kind of practical Christian wisdom (cf. Barrett, 186, who cites 1 Pet 3:7 as the "closest parallel"). It is, rather, the divine gift of *knowledge* of which Paul has written in 1 Cor 12:8; cf. 1:5; 14:6 and, in the present letter, 8:7; 11:6 (Bultmann, 173; cf. Friedrich 1963a:43). 1 Cor 7:25 (cf. v. 40*b*) shows how Paul could think of his apostolic judgment (*gnōmē*) as informed by such charismatic *knowledge* (Bultmann, 173). The combination of *probity* and *knowledge* here may be compared with the combination of "goodness" (*agathōsynēs*) and "knowledge" in Rom 15:14.

6*b*. *with forbearance, with kindness.* These two also stand together (or in close proximity) in Rom 2:4 (of God); 1 Cor 13:4 (of love, using the cognate verbs); Gal 5:22 (among "the fruit of the Spirit"); Col 3:12. The first (*makrothymia*) relates more specifically to one's dealing with other people than does the general notion of *endurance* (v. 4*b*). The second word (*chrēstotēs*) has a somewhat more affirmative and active meaning than the first: not just being slow to criticize or punish (restrained), but extending goodness toward someone (cf. Friedrich 1963a:44).

6*c*. *with the Holy Spirit, with authentic love.* Some read the first phrase as a reference to the human spirit (thus Barrett, 186–87, who translates "in a holy spirit"; also Plummer, 196; *JB:* "by a spirit of holiness"). The chief argument for this anthropological interpretation is the position of the phrase in the midst of a list of moral attributes (*NEB* seeks to alleviate this with a paraphrase: "by gifts of the Holy Spirit"). However, the references to "the Spirit" and "the Lord" in the midst of Rom 12:9–13 (in 12:11) are somewhat comparable. Furthermore, the association of God's Spirit and *love* is thoroughly Pauline (e.g., Rom 5:5; 15:30; Gal 5:22; Phil 2:1–2), and the coupling of references to these in v. 6*c*, along with the references to God's *word* and *power* in v. 7*a*, forms a meaningful climax to the list begun in v. 6*a*. (See COMMENT.) The adjective in the phrase *authentic love* (*agapē anypokritos*) seems to have had a firm place in the parenetic traditions of Hellenistic Judaism and early Christianity. It means literally "non-hypocritical" (i.e., "unmasked," "frankly disclosed"; cf. Spicq 1965, II:197 n. 235). The word is first attested in the LXX (Wis 5:18; 18:16, on which see Winston 1979:150), and is found subsequently in Philo, *Questions and Answers on Genesis* III, 29 (Greek fragment from Procopius) and in Christian parenesis (e.g., describing wisdom, Jas 3:17, and faith, 1 Tim 1:5; 2 Tim 1:5). Paul uses it again to describe love (*agapē*) in Rom 12:9, and in 1 Pet 1:22 it describes "brotherly love" (*philadelphia*).

7*a*. *with the word of truth, with the power of God.* The first phrase in this set (*en logō alētheias*) could be translated "truthful speech" (*RSV, NIV*), thus being taken as a reference to the general trustworthiness of the Pauline apostolate: never dissembling, keeping promises, etc. (cf. 1:18; 7:14). However, the combination of this phrase with a reference to *the power of God* makes it almost certain that Paul is thinking of the gospel he preaches as *the word of truth* (so, e.g., Windisch, 206; Bultmann, 173; Friedrich 1963a:46–47): see 1 Cor 1:18, where "the word of the cross" is associated with God's power, and cf. 1 Cor 2:4; 1 Thess 1:5 (Paul's preaching of the gospel was with "word" and "power," etc.). In Eph 1:13; Col 1:5 "the word of truth" is specifically identified with "the gospel" (cf. 2 Tim 2:15). The absence of the articles in the present verse is no argument against the same meaning here, because the anarthrous phrase derives from the LXX, where "the word(s) of truth" refers to God's word delivered to his people (Ps 118[119]:43, 160); so also Jas 1:18. Cf. "the word of life" (*logon zoēs*) in Phil 2:16. See further Gal 2:5, 14 ("the truth of the gospel") and 2 Cor 4:2 (where "the truth" refers to "the word of God"). *The power of God* (here also anarthrous, *en dynamei Theou*) is a frequent and important Pauline topic, and the apostle emphasizes it particularly in this letter; see 4:7 with NOTES and COMMENT. In Rom 1:16 it is identified with the gospel, as here.

7b. *having.* In vv. 7b–8a the preposition used is no longer *en,* as in vv. 4c–5 *(in the course of)* and vv. 6–7a *(with),* but *dia* (with the genitive, literally "through"). It functions here to describe the manner in which apostles recommend themselves, or the attendant circumstances of that recommendation (*GNTG* III:267; Bultmann, 174; cf. BAG s.v. *dia,* III, 1b); thus, *having* or (v. 8a) *being.*

*the weapons of righteousness.* Cf. 10:4, "our weapons of war," and Rom 13:12, "the weapons [*RSV:* armor] of light." In Rom 6:13, Paul urges his readers to put themselves at God's disposal "as weapons of righteousness" rather than at sin's disposal "as weapons of wickedness." Paul is fond of military imagery (see Pfitzner 1967:157–64; Tanner 1980), perhaps because it enables him to emphasize that the resources for battle against the forces of this world come from God (Pfitzner 1967:163). That is surely the point when he refers to "the breastplate of faith and love" and the "helmet" of "the hope of salvation" in 1 Thess 5:8 *(RSV).* This is also probably the force of the genitive *(tēs dikaiosynēs, of righteousness)* here: not "having weapons to defend righteousness," but "having weapons that God's righteousness has provided" (*GNTG* III:207; Windisch, 207). According to Schoedel (*AF* V:16), Polycarp is probably quoting 2 Cor when he uses the same phrase in Phil 4:1. In Isa 59:17; Sir 5:18 righteousness forms the breastplate of God's own armor. Windisch, 207, notes Ps.-Crates, Epistle 16, where the Cynic philosopher's cloak and wallet are called "the weapons of the gods," and Epistle 23, where "the weapons of Diogenes" are contrasted with "the helmet of Hades" (Malherbe 1977:66–67, 72–73).

*on the right hand and on the left.* That is, fully equipped for battle, perhaps with specific reference to instruments designed for attack (the sword in the right hand) and for defense (the shield, held in the left). Tanner (1980:379) suggests that the reference may be "to a legionary soldier's role standing in a battle line."

8a. *being renowned and dishonored.* Here *being* translates the preposition *dia* (see note on *having,* v. 7b), while *renowned and dishonored* translates a phrase in which two nouns are employed in the Greek, *doxa* and *atimia.* The first (which in other contexts means "glory" or "splendor") is used here of "a good reputation" (cf. BAG, s.v. 3, and 1 Thess 2:20; Hughes, 231, suggests that it almost means "popularity"). It is contrasted with *atimia,* "dishonor," a contrast Paul also draws in 1 Cor 15:43 (the body "is sown in dishonor" but "raised in glory" [*RSV*]) and 1 Cor 4:10 (the Corinthians are "renowned" while their apostles are "dishonored"). Cf. Ps.-Crates, Epistle 16, where the philosopher's students are advised to pay no attention to criticism of the Cynics' style of life and teaching: "For all this is merely opinion [*doxa*], and to be enslaved to opinion and disgrace [*doxē kai adoxia*] . . . is most irksome of all" (Malherbe 1977:66–67).

*being defamed and praised.* These and the two preceding terms form a chiasm: renowned-dishonored-defamed-praised. Again, two nouns are used in the Greek, *dysphēmia* ("ill repute") and *euphēmia* ("good repute"). Neither is used elsewhere in the NT, but the adjective *euphēmos* stands in the list of commendable traits in Phil 4:8 (*RSV:* "worthy of praise"); and in 1 Cor 4:13, again describing his apostolate, Paul uses the verb *dysphēmein:* "when defamed, we try to conciliate."

8b. *as deceivers—and yet true.* Here and in the following two verses, *hōs (as)* introduces some ways in which the apostles are regarded by the world at large, "as seeming to be" (cf. *to dokein einai,* "to seem to be," Philo, *Migration of Abraham* 86, 88). Here and in vv. 9, 10c, *kai* introduces an unexpected fact—thus, *and yet* (cf. BAG, s.v. I, 2g). The word *deceives (planoi)* is used nowhere else by Paul, but he employs the adjective *dolios,* "deceitful," when charging his rivals in Corinth with being "false apostles" (11:13). In 12:16–18, Paul must defend himself against a similar charge.

9. *as unknowns—and yet fully known. Unknowns* either in the general sense of "obscure," "uncelebrated," as most believers are (1 Cor 1:26–28; so Windisch, 208), or in the more specific sense of those whose apostolic credentials have been questioned, thus "unrecognized" (Barrett, 189, who cites 1 Cor 9:1; 15:8–9; cf. Plummer, 199, "without proper credentials"; Collange, 298, without the evidence of ecstatic experiences offered by others). Standing in contrast to *agnooumenoi, unknowns,* the compound form *epiginōskomenoi* (not just *ginōskomenoi,* "known") should be accorded the more intensive meaning, *fully known.* Cf. 1 Cor 13:12b, "fully known" to God.

*as dying—and yet see, we live.* A reformulation of LXX Ps 117(118):17, "I shall not die, but I shall live [*ouk apothanoumai, alla zēsomai*], and I shall recount the works of the Lord." The future tenses of the LXX have been transformed into present tenses, and the text is thus accommodated to Paul's conviction that the mortality of the apostles is itself a means for the disclosure of "the life of Jesus" (see especially 4:7–12). (See also the following note.) *Idou,* translated "behold" in 5:17 and 6:2, is now rendered *see,* because it is used somewhat more spontaneously; cf. 7:11.

*as receiving punishment—and yet not put to death.* Here, as in the preceding antithesis, Paul has reformulated a statement from LXX Ps 117(118), now v. 18: "The Lord has punished me [*paideuōn epaideuse me ho Kyrios*], and yet [*kai*] he has not delivered me up to death." The apostle has changed the aorist tenses of his text to present tenses *(paidouomenoi . . . mē thanatoumenoi).* The first term (again passive) also appears in 1 Cor 11:32, where (with *krinein,* "to judge") it means "disciplined" or *(RSV)* "chastened."

10. *as sorrowing—but constantly rejoicing.* The conjunction *kai, and yet,* used in the antitheses of vv. 8b–9, is replaced in this one and the next by *de,* with a similarly adversative meaning, *but.* Paul writes more about *sorrowing (lypein, lypē)* in this letter than in any other; see 2:1–2, 3–7; 7:8–10. For the contrast between *sorrowing* and *rejoicing* see 2:3; 7:7, 9; cf. 9:7; Phil 2:27, 28 and Philo, *On the Change of Names* 163; *Allegorical Int.* III, 217–19. Paul frequently exhorts his congregations to let their lives be characterized by rejoicing (e.g., 13:11; Rom 12:12; Phil 2:18), by which he means a rejoicing "in the Lord" (e.g., Phil 3:1) which can take place even in the midst of adversity (Rom 5:3–5). With the remark here about *constantly rejoicing (aei chairontes)* compare especially the admonitions of 1 Thess 5:16; Phil 4:4, to "rejoice (in the Lord) always" *(chairete [en Kyriō] pantote);* see also Philo, *Allegorical Int.* III, 218: "Let sense-perception therefore be sorrowful, but let virtue constantly rejoice" *(lypeisthō toigaroun aisthēsis, aretē d' aiei chairetō).* Discussions of Paul's overall concept of rejoicing in Gulin 1932:139–276 and Webber 1970.

*as impoverished—but enriching many.* The idea of impoverishment here is to be understood literally. On Paul's poverty during the time of his ministry in Corinth see 11:7–10; and on apostolic poverty in general, Rom 8:35; 1 Cor 4:11–12a; 2 Cor 11:27; and especially Phil 4:11–12. The verb *ploutizein,* "to enrich," is used here metaphorically, however, as it is in 9:11; 1 Cor 1:5 (the Corinthians had been "enriched" in Christ "with all speech and all knowledge" [*RSV*]), and as the related verb *ploutein* is used in Rom 10:12; 1 Cor 4:8; 2 Cor 8:9. Cf. Philo's description of the Essenes as "exceedingly rich" *(plousiōtatoi)* by virtue of their being content with little in the way of material wealth *(Every Good Man Is Free* 77).

*as having nothing—and yet possessing everything.* The series begun in v. 4*b* concludes with a paradox made the more effective by its striking formulation *(hōs mēden echontes kai panta katechontes);* note *echontes . . . katechontes,* perhaps "having . . . really having." Cf. especially 1 Cor 3:21*b*–23, where Paul assures the Corinthians that all things belong to them ("all things are yours," *panta hymōn* [*estin*], vv. 21*b*, 22) because they belong to Christ, who belongs to God (v. 23). There are numerous Stoic and Cynic parallels to the general idea that *having nothing* in the way of material goods frees one to "have everything" in a higher sense; e.g., Seneca, *On Benefits* VII.ii.5, referring to the wise man, says that he doesn't need to be content with little because really "all things are his" *(omnia illius sunt;* cf. VII.iii.2; viii.1), and especially VII.x.6: "I possess all in the sense that all things belong to all!" Further, Cicero, *About the Ends* 75: "Rightly will he be said to own all things, who alone knows how to use all things"; Apollonius describing the Brahmans of India (Philostratus, *Life of Apollonius* III, 15): "living upon the earth and yet not on it . . . and possessing nothing, yet having the riches of all men [*kai ouden kektēmenous ē ta pantōn*]"; Ps.-Crates contrasting Cynics with the wealthy (Epistle 7): "But as for us, we observe complete peace since we have been freed from every evil by Diogenes of Sinope, and although we possess nothing, we have everything [*kai echontes mēden pant' echomen*], but you, though you have everything, really have nothing because of your rivalry, jealousy, fear and conceit" (Malherbe 1977:58–59, on which see Mealand 1976:278–79). The theme is present in Philo as well: "For God possesses all things, but needs nothing; while the good man, though he possesses nothing in the proper sense, not even himself [*kektētai men ouden kyriōs all' oud' heauton*], partakes of the precious things of God so far as he is capable" *(Moses* I, 157; cf. *Noah's Work as a Planter* 69).

## COMMENT: GENERAL

According to the hypothesis adopted in this commentary (see INTRODUCTION, pp. 54–55), Paul wrote at least five letters to the Corinthian church, and parts of at least two of these are preserved in our 2 Cor: Letter D in chaps. 1–9 and Letter E in chaps. 10–13. The major section of Letter D, insofar as this letter is still extant, consists of (1) Paul's assurances that he remains concerned about his Corinthian congregation, 1:12–2:13; (2) a long and theologically important discourse on the commission under which his apostolate operates, 2:14–5:19; and (3) a series of appeals to the Corinthians which opens here in 5:20 and extends at least through chap. 8, and perhaps through chap. 9. That the theme of reconciliation introduced in 5:18–19 is still present in 5:20 does not alter the fact that a major new section is opened in 5:20. With this verse the indicative mood gives way to the imperative, discourse to exhortation. See Olson 1976:185, 191.

The appeals of these closing chapters of Letter D are of three types, although they are closely related, the first preparing for the second and the second for the third. The initial appeal is for the Corinthian Christians to be reconciled to God (5:20–6:10). This is followed by an appeal to be reconciled to the Pauline apostolate (6:11–7:3). Finally, the Corinthians are urged to complete their congregational collection for Jerusalem (8:1ff.), an appeal to which 7: 4–16 is prefatory. As the NOTES and COMMENT indicate, one cannot be certain whether 6:14–7:1 and chap. 9 are integral to Letter D. Chap. 8 certainly is, however, despite the doubts of some. Indeed, the appeals which begin in 5:20 find their climax in those of chap. 8, and it may be that this whole letter has been prompted, more or less directly, by Paul's concern about the collection in Corinth.

The opening appeal to be reconciled to God, 5:20–6:10, consists of two parts. The appeal itself comes in 5:20–6:2. Here Paul builds on his immediately preceding comments about "the ministry of reconciliation," noting that the apostles are *working together with* [*God*] in urging the Corinthians to be faithful to the gospel they have received. Then, in order to support this appeal, he offers a brief resumé of the "credentials" with which his apostolate operates. These are introduced in 6:3–4a and enumerated in a rhetorically impressive way in 6:4b–10. There are four "strophes" within this list, each with a more or less coherent formal structure and theme. Here, in turn, Paul commends his apostolate (a) for its *endurance* through many adversities (vv. 4b–5), (b) for its working *with the power of God* (vv. 6–7a), (c) for its having *the weapons of righteousness* (vv. 7b–8a), and (d) by contrasting how the world perceives it with how it is seen by those who are "in Christ" (vv. 8b–10).

## COMMENT: DETAILED

### The Appeal Proper, 5:20–6:2

One may compare the appeal in these verses to that in Rom 12:1–2, where Paul in an equally fundamental way urges his readers to be conformed no longer to this present age, but to "be transformed" in the renewal of their whole being, as they give themselves over to God and to obedience of the divine will.

First, in both cases the introduction *Therefore* looks back over the whole preceding discussion—in the present instance, over the discussion since 2:14: since the knowledge of God has been entrusted to the apostles for the salvation of the world (2:14–16), since it is a knowledge which shines in the face of Christ (4:6) through whom God has reconciled the world to himself (5:18–19), and since Paul and his associates have shown themselves to be fit and faithful ministers of the new covenant God has established (e.g., 4:1–6; 4:7–5:10; 5:11–13), *therefore*, . . . *as ambassadors of Christ* and agents of

God's own appeal, they bring the summons to *be reconciled to God* (5:20).

This exhortation is also like that of Rom 12:1–2 in that each is what Goppelt (1968:160) has appropriately described as a "kerygmatic imperative." Each appeal presupposes and is an integral part of the reality of God's saving activity in Christ. Thus, "God has reconciled us to himself" (5:18), *therefore, . . . be reconciled to God* (5:20). In effect, this is an appeal to acknowledge the presence of "a new creation" (5:17), and to allow that new creation to "make a difference" in one's life (Furnish 1977:218; cf. Bultmann, 160, 165). There may be special significance in the fact that, twice in these verses (5:20; 6:1), Paul characterizes the gospel as an *appealing*. The verb *(parakalein)* can sometimes mean "to deal kindly" (see NOTES on 2:7) or "to try to conciliate" (Furnish 1977:216–17), and the related noun *(paraklēsis)* can refer to the gospel (note 1 Thess 2:2, 3, where "gospel" and "appeal" are closely associated) as both a comforting (see, e.g., 1:3–7) and a commanding (see, e.g., 8:17) reality. This twofold reference may well be intended in the present verses: the "word of reconciliation" is both a gift and a summons to receive the gift; the apostles' role is at once to proclaim the good news of God's reconciling love in Christ and to make clear the scope and the character of the claim inherent in that love (see 5:14–15). The concept of reconciliation employed here expresses particularly well the radical priority of God's grace to which faith is a response (cf. Walter 1979:440 n. 84, 441).

Dupont (1953:278), remarking on the ambassadorial role which the apostles assume here, comments that Christ's death has made it necessary for them to carry the word of God's reconciling action. Paul, however, does not seem to mean that the apostles come in Christ's absence, but that they come at his behest and therefore with his authority and in his service. The image of diplomatic service evoked here (cf. also 3:3) may be compared with the image of priestly service evoked in Rom 15:16. In both cases the emphasis lies upon apostleship as the agency of Christ's being present to his people and of his calling them to obedience. This is of course the heart of Paul's "missionary preaching" (see Rom 15:18), but it is no less the heart of the appeals he directs repeatedly to those who have already professed belief in the gospel. The call of 5:20 to *be reconciled to God* is not just a "missionary" call (Windisch, 196) addressed to "the world at large" (Hughes, 211). It is also a call to believers —to be renewed in their faith and life as individuals and as a believing community. The distinction Windisch, 199, makes between the "official message" of 5:20 and the "personal parenesis" of the messenger in 6:1ff. is unfounded; the appeal in 6:1 is but a variation of that in 5:20 (see below), and is uttered with the same high sense of apostolic vocation. Moreover, these appeals are foundational for the more specific and concrete exhortations which follow in 6:11ff. and 7:4ff. (cf. the relation of Rom 12:1–2 to the concrete exhortations of 12:3ff.). In all of these Paul is thinking of the Corinthians, of his ministry to them, and of their mutual responsibilities in the service of the gospel.

The appeal of 5:20 is supported in 5:21 by what Dahl (1977:66 n. 10) has described very well as "a delayed conclusion to 5:17–19." That is, as Paul moves on to the next phase of his discussion (the appeals of 5:20ff.) he pauses to recapitulate a point in the preceding discussion. Exactly the same thing occurs in Rom 3:22*b*–23 (also cited by Dahl, ibid., along with Rom 7:25*b;* 10:17), where the argument of Rom 1:18–3:20 is concluded only after a new section has opened (3:21ff.). There the conclusion, "all have sinned and fall short of the glory of God" *(RSV)*, functions effectively to support the new point that righteousness comes only from God, as a gift (*"since* all have sinned," etc.). In the present case, the "delayed conclusion" in v. 21 recapitulates the kerygma on which the imperatives of 5:20ff. are based, and the emphasis falls on the purpose-clause: *that in (Christ) we might become the righteousness of God* (cf. Kertelge 1967:105–6).

It is likely that the summary affirmation in 5:21 represents a Pauline reworking of traditional, probably Jewish-Christian theological notions (so Stuhlmacher 1965:74–77), and not a citation as such (against Käsemann 1971a:53; Collange, 275, who thinks specifically of a formula current among the Christians of Corinth). The doctrine of the sinlessness of Christ stems from that tradition (e.g., Heb 4:15; 5:7–9; 1 Pet 1:19; 3:18), and is perhaps dependent ultimately on the description of the Suffering Servant in Isa 53:9 (note 1 Pet 2:22; cf. Thyen 1970:188 n. 5, and especially Hofius 1980a:196–99). The idea that Christ was *made to be sin for us* is also clarified against the background of Isa 53, whether one has reference to the Hebrew or to the Greek text. According to the former, "the Lord has laid on him [sc., the Servant] the iniquity of us all" (v. 6, *RSV*); according to the latter, the Servant "bears our sins" (v. 4). The same verses are echoed in 1 Pet 2:24: "He himself bore our sins in his body on the tree, that we might die to sin and live to righteousness. By his wounds you have been healed" *(RSV)*. See also Diogn 9:5. Christ, then, was *made sin*—not "a sinner"—in the sense that he was made to bear the burden of sin (Thyen 1970:188), an idea which Paul expresses in similar ways in Gal 3:13 (in his death on the cross Christ "redeemed us from the curse of the law, having become a curse for us" [*RSV*]) and in Rom 8:3 (God sent his Son "in the likeness of sinful flesh and for sin" to condemn sin). In these passages as in the present one, Paul is dependent upon traditional ideas of atonement, and is not concerned either to harmonize them or to elaborate one of his own. In 2 Cor 5:21, Paul is drawing on the tradition in order to reaffirm and re-emphasize that God has acted in and through Christ *for us.*

That the "delayed conclusion" respecting reconciliation in 5:17–19 is formulated as a statement about righteousness in 5:21 shows how closely associated these two ideas are in Paul's thinking. The two concepts are not identical (I. H. Marshall 1978:124 rightly observes that Paul could not have spoken of God's "justifying the world"), but they are complementary (see, e.g., Bultmann 1951:286; Lührmann 1970:445–46; Thüsing 1974:312). "Justification" identifies primarily the source and means of salvation: God's righteousness established on the basis of faith. "Reconciliation" accents especially the result of that work, Rom 5:1 being the classical statement of the relationship: "Therefore, since we are justified by faith, we have peace with God [ = we have been reconciled to God] through our Lord Jesus Christ" (*RSV;* Blank 1968:287; cf. Héring, 44).

In 1 Cor 1:30 (also in reliance on traditional ideas) Paul had written that Christ "was made . . . righteousness" for us *(hēmin),* a statement which may seem at first to conflict with the idea that God *made (him) to be sin for us.* But the relationship is clarified by Rom 6:10–11 (Thüsing 1968:108), where Paul writes of Christ's dying to sin and living to God, and of the believers' sharing in the benefits of his death and life. For Paul, Christ becomes "righteousness for us" (1 Cor 1:30) precisely in that, identifying with sin *for us* (2 Cor 5:21), he "dies to sin" and breaks its power, freeing those who are *in him* to *become the righteousness of God* (cf. Rom 6:11, to be "alive to God in Christ Jesus" [*RSV*]). The present verse, then, does not contradict the identification of Christ with righteousness in 1 Cor 1:30; it presupposes that identification (cf. Kertelge 1967:103–4) as it emphasizes the reality of the new life opened up for believers through the gift of righteousness (cf. Phil 3:9, and Thyen 1970:189). In this way the points about the redemptive effect of Christ's death (5:14–15), the presence of "a new creation" (5:17), and the reality of reconciliation (5:18–19) are effectively summarized and applied to the situation of the individual believer (cf. Lührmann 1970:445).

The appeal to *be reconciled to God,* 5:20, is re-emphasized in 6:1–2, where (against Windisch, 199) it is no less emphatically stated that the apostles are serving God in extending it. Indeed, they are *working together with him*—a striking expression (for possible parallels, see NOTES), but not an inappropriate description of the apostolic role as it has been presented in 5:20, and earlier in 2:14–15; 3:3. There is no thought here of the apostles as God's equals. On the contrary, Paul has been emphasizing all along that the apostles are in themselves inadequate for their task (e.g., 2:16*b;* 3:5). It is in fact through their weakness and suffering that the power for salvation is shown to belong to God alone (4:7–12; cf. 6:4–10).

The warning of 6:1 *not to receive the grace of God in vain* is less severe, but similar in other ways to the one in Gal 3:1–4. Here God's *grace* is a reference to the gospel and everything for which it stands, but particularly the reconciling love of God established through Christ's death (for this use of the term see Gal 2:20–21; Rom 5:2 in the context of 5:1–11), Paul's topic in 5:14–15, 17–19. As in 5:20, the appeal is to conform one's life to the reality of the new creation, to let one's conduct be "worthy of the gospel of Christ" (Phil 1:27) lest one "become alienated from Christ" and fall away from grace (Gal 5:4). It is possible that the appeal of 5:20 now takes the form of a warning because, as in 5:12, the apostle is mindful of those in Corinth who by their teaching and behavior would subvert the faith he has sought to nurture among them.

Paul's second explicit quotation of scripture in this letter (the first was in 4:13) occurs in 6:2. It is drawn from Second Isaiah (Isa 49:8a), in the context of which *the time of favor* is the time when God speaks the comforting words of pardon to Jerusalem concerning her sins (40:1–2). Westermann (1969:215) ventures the opinion that Paul has given the prophet's words "the exact sense" they had originally. One may say, at least, that the text is generally appropriate to what Paul has been emphasizing about *the grace of God* (6:1), through which believers *become . . . righteousness* in Christ (5:21) and are reconciled (5:18–19). More important than the quotation itself, however, is Paul's application of it: *Behold, now is the time of favor! Behold, now is the day of salvation!* This *now* is in the first instance the eschatological *now* of life "in Christ" and of the "new creation" (5:17), as in 5:16. But it is not to be restricted to this, as it is by Kümmel, 205. It is also the *now* of the present appeal to the Corinthians to *be reconciled to God* and to allow *the grace of God* to manifest itself in appropriate ways in their lives (correctly, e.g., Bultmann, 169; Friedrich 1963a:29–30; Collange, 289). For Paul, *the day of salvation* heralded by the gospel is also the day of decision for those who are addressed by it, and the claim, as well as the gift, is renewed every day that the believer continues to live in the world (cf. Gal 2:20).

## The Appeal Supported, 6:3–10

Windisch, 202 (cf. 220), argues that there is a significant material discrepancy between 6:1–2, where Paul had spoken with authority, and these verses, where he seems to be reckoning with criticism. Therefore, according to Windisch, one must suppose that the text is out of order, and that something has fallen out that stood originally between vv. 2 and 3. This, he suggests, could have been some transitional statement like that of 4:1–2, but more probably it was the material that stands now in 6:14–7:1. One must grant that 6:14–7:1 is difficult where it stands, but it would be hardly less problematic between 6:2 and 3, even if there were textual warrant for it there. Most especially, however, there is no reason to separate 6:3–10 from 5:20–6:2; the two passages are in fact organically related (Bultmann, 169). Paul's comments on his apostolate and his listing of its "credentials" in 6:3–10 are altogether appropriate in view of the significant relationship between the gospel and the apostolate presumed in 5:20–6:2. Even more so is this the case in a letter written with the awareness that some are disputing the authenticity of his ministry and thereby—in Paul's view—subverting the gospel. These same points can be made against the proposal of Schmithals that 6:3–13 (+ 7:2–4) belonged to a letter which had been sent to Corinth some time after the letter to which 6:1–2 originally belonged (1973:275–79).

The words of vv. 3–4a are introductory only. The comment of v. 3 about *giving no one cause to take offense at anything, lest the ministry be blamed,* complements the comment in 5:12 that Paul wants the Corinthians to be able to be proud of his apostolate. Similarly, the mention of self-recommendation in v. 4a seems to pick up the rejection of that in 5:12. What was rejected was the pretentious boasting in externals (ecstatic experiences and the like) of his rivals. What he and his associates now offer in place of that are "credentials" of a markedly different order, appropriate to *ministers of God.* These follow in vv. 4b–10, and may be what Paul had in mind when he said he was giving the Corinthians "something to say" to the rival apostles (5:12). They could, in any case, readily serve that purpose. Collange, 290–91, suggests that Paul may be using a previously formulated text here, one that he himself could have composed as a "brief" for his own and his associates' use. This is possible, but it cannot be proved. It is equally possible that it is an ad hoc composition which simply follows the general pattern of similar lists in vogue in other Hellenistic circles, and especially in apocalyptic Judaism.

(a) Vv. 4b–5. In this first of four distinct strophes Paul stresses the *much endurance* which characterizes his apostolate and which should help to certify the sincerity and commitment of himself and his associates (v. 4b). Various afflictions and deprivations through which this endurance has been demonstrated are listed in vv. 4c–5, arranged in three groups of three terms each, all plural and all prefaced (like the word *endurance* in v. 4b) by the Greek preposition *en.* Of the nine items listed, only one of them, *riots* (v. 5a), does not appear in at least one of the other Pauline catalogs of adversities to which this one is parallel (4:8–9; 11:23b–29; 12:10; Rom 8:35; 1 Cor 4:9–13); see NOTES for details, and NOTES and COMMENT on 4:8–9 for a discussion of the general character and background of these catalogs. In the present list the first three terms are quite general characterizations of apostolic hardships, the next three specify hardships endured at the hands of others, and the last three all seem to be associated with the plying of one's trade.

Specific instances of most of these trials and deprivations may be found elsewhere in Paul's letters, in Acts, or in both sources (see NOTES). Thus, Paul's Philippian imprisonment, described in Acts 16:23–40, seems to be confirmed by his own comments in 1 Thess 2:2. Since this is the only imprisonment up to the time of the writing of this letter for which direct evidence exists, it is interesting that Paul uses the plural, *imprisonments,* both here and in 11: 23b. This may be hyperbole, or it may be a way of indicating that various members of Paul's company have suffered incarceration. However, it is also possible that this, along with the mention of severe troubles in Asia (1:8–10), is indirect evidence of a recent imprisonment, perhaps in Ephesus. An Ephesian imprisonment—although nowhere reported in Acts—has long been hypothesized by some scholars as the place and occasion of the (or a) letter to the Philippians (on which see the commentaries). If Quinn (1978) is correct that 1 Clem 5:5–7 refers to seven Pauline imprisonments because seven different sources mention at least one of these (2 Cor, Phil, Phlm, Eph, Col, 2 Tim, Acts), then this would be evidence that 2 Cor was known in Rome by the last decade of the first century.

There is ample evidence that, simultaneously with his ministry in Corinth, Paul worked at his own craft (of tent-making) in order not to be a financial burden on the newly founded congregation there, just as he had earlier in Thessalonica (1 Thess 2:9). Not only the *labors,* but also the *sleepless nights* and the *times without food* listed in v. 5c are perhaps to be explained as references to this practice (see NOTES). On the one hand, it was his resolve not to depend on the Corinthians for even his basic needs (1 Cor 9:4–18; 2 Cor 11:7–11; 12:14–18) that caused him often to be in want. On the other hand, he was unable to earn enough from his own labor to meet those needs, and in Corinth (2 Cor 11:8–9), as well as earlier in Thessalonica (Phil 4:14–18), he had had to rely on help from congregations in other cities. It is likely that he frequently had no time for meals because of his labor, and no money for food despite his labor (cf. 1 Cor 4:11–12). The *sleepless nights* would be due to his need to use some nighttime hours either to work at his trade or—because others, too, would be work-bound from dawn to dusk—to preach and to teach (on the latter see Friedrich 1963a:41; and note the Sunday night meeting in Troas, Acts 20:7–12).

Höistad (1944) emphasizes the parallelism between the adversities listed here and those mentioned by Dio Chrysostom in his discourse on virtue ("hunger and cold," "thirst," "the lash," etc.—VIII, 15–16). But Paul does not treat these trials lightly (as the Stoics do, suggesting that they should be approached "in a spirit of contempt" and even "cheerfully"—ibid. VIII, 18). For him they are real adversities, to be endured. (See also COMMENT on 4:8–9.)

(b) Vv. 6–7a. The use of the preposition *en* continues in this second strophe, but now there are eight expressions arranged in pairs, of which the last, *the power of God,* provides an apt summary. The characteristics of apostolic service enumerated here do not continue the list of hardships in vv. 4c–5, but rather the main list of "credentials" which begins in v. 4b, *with much endurance.* Now, in the second place, the Pauline apostolate is commended as an agency through which God's power is made manifest and in which the Holy Spirit is at work (cf. Nielsen 1980:148–50). Three of the first four terms (v. 6ab) are closely identified by Paul with the Spirit: *knowledge* is one of the gifts of the Spirit (e.g., 1 Cor 12:8), while *forbearance* and *kindness* are included among the fruit of the Spirit (Gal 5:22). Barrett, 186, describes these as "moral characteristics," but they are more than that. They represent the special gifts and powers which are present where the community of faith and individual believers are open to the guidance of the Holy Spirit. It is not so strange, then, that Paul next refers (v. 6c) to the *Holy Spirit* itself, and to the *authentic love* which is the first and all-inclusive fruit of the Spirit's working (Gal 5:22; it is, perhaps, this divine origin of *love* that Paul emphasizes by using the adjective *authentic*—cf. Spicq 1965:195). The preaching of the apostles is also a sign of the Spirit's presence, so Paul mentions that, too *(the word of truth,* v. 7a), even as he sums up everything listed in vv. 6–7a with a reference to *the power of God.* It is not only their endurance in the midst of hardships that authenticates Paul and his associates as bearers of the Spirit and true ministers of God, but also their honesty, their insight, their treatment of others, and their preaching of the word.

Certain of the gifts and powers listed in vv. 6–7a may owe their inclusion to apologetic and polemical considerations. The mention of moral *probity* is understandable in the light of Paul's insistence that his ministry has been conducted openly, with no intention to deceive (4:2). The listing of *knowledge* may reflect the criticism that Paul lacks this spiritual gift (cf. 11:6). Earlier in this letter he has tried to explain, using other words, that his cancellation of an anticipated visit to Corinth was really a sign of his *forbearance* (1:23), not of his indifference. Similarly, his mention of *kindness* and *authentic love* accords with his concern that his work in Corinth will not have to be disciplinary ("with a rod") but can be done "with love and a gentle spirit" (1 Cor 4:21, *NAB;* cf. 2 Cor 13:10 and Paul's emphasis on his love for the Corinthians in 2:4). Furthermore, the specific mention of the operation of *the Holy Spirit* should perhaps be associated with the emphasis on the Spirit in 3:7–18 (Collange, 296), and it is quite likely that the description of the Pauline gospel as *the word of truth* is intended to cut polemically against Paul's rivals, whom he views as "huckstering" and "adulterating" God's word (2:17 and 4:2; cf. Collange, 296 n. 4, who notes how often the word *truth* appears in polemical contexts in 2 Cor, and Barrett, 187). For Paul, *the word of truth* is nothing else than "the word of reconciliation" (5:19), and thus "the word of the cross" (1 Cor 1:18) through which God's power is present as redeeming and renewing love (2 Cor 5:14ff.). Finally, Paul's specific reference here to *the power of God* corresponds with his concern to refute the claims of his rivals in Corinth that their apostleship is validated by their miraculous powers and ecstatic experiences (Collange, 296). Over against this, Paul has described God's power as disclosed only through the weakness and suffering of apostles (4:7ff.), and through their dedication to the service of others (5:12–15).

(c) Vv. 7b–8a. This third strophe is the least coherent of the four in its structure, and the most difficult to characterize as to content. It consists of three prepositional phrases beginning with *dia* (literally "through"), but the first strings together a series of genitives, while the second and third present two sets of contrasting words.

In the first phrase, v. 7b, apostles are commended as warriors for the kingdom of God, fully armed with *the weapons of righteousness.* It is worth noting that *righteousness,* too, is closely associated with the Spirit by Paul, as in 3:8, 9, where he refers successively to "the ministry of the Spirit" and "the ministry of righteousness." See also Rom 14:17, "For the kingdom of God is righteousness and peace and joy in the Holy Spirit" *(RSV)*, and cf. Gal 5:5. Thus, Friedrich (1963a:48) is correct in his judgment that in terms of content v. 7*b* could be said to belong with vv. 6–7*a*. Their *weapons of righteousness* are another sign that Paul and his co-workers have been fully equipped by God to do battle for the gospel in the world.

The two short phrases in v. 8*a* form a chiasm when they are taken together: the first and last terms describe positive responses to the apostles (they are *renowned* and *praised* in some quarters), while the two middle terms describe negative responses to them (by some they are *dishonored* and *defamed*). Perhaps in these phrases Paul intends to emphasize how God's warriors must be prepared for defeats as well as for victories as they wage the battle of righteousness, and how quickly apparent victories may turn into serious defeats. Thus, Paul himself had been highly honored in Galatia—received there, he says, "as an angel of God, as Christ Jesus" (Gal 4:14, *RSV*). But such fame had proved fleeting, and too soon the Galatian Christians had been bewitched by "a different gospel" (Gal 1:6–9; 3:1–5, etc.), so that Paul was no longer certain whether his ministry had been successful or not (e.g., Gal 4:19–20). Similarly in Corinth itself: even as Paul was honored by some he was dishonored by others, and those who praised him no less than those who defamed him showed how seriously they had departed from the gospel (1 Cor 1:10–17). Now in this letter (chaps. 1–9), and later in another (chaps. 10–13), he must do battle against those who continue to dishonor and to defame his ministry (e.g., 2:17; 4:2; 10:2; 12:16; cf. Windisch, 207). But this battle is waged with *the weapons of righteousness on the right hand and on the left*.

(d) Vv. 8*b*–10. In this last strophe there are seven pairs of contrasting terms, each set introduced by *hōs, as.* Throughout the list the first terms characterize how Paul and his associates have been treated by many: *as deceivers . . . unknowns . . . dying,* etc. But these are false estimates, formed by those who, like many in Corinth, judge others "according to worldly standards" (5:16). For those who are "in Christ," however, "worldly standards" are part of that old order which "has come to an end" (5:17), and they recognize Paul and his associates for what they really are: *true . . . fully known,* etc. Thus, the description of a true Stoic as one who is "happy" even though he is "sick . . . in danger . . . dying," etc. (Epictetus II.xix.24), often compared with these verses (e.g., Windisch, 207–8, "a full parallel"), is really no parallel at all. Paul's statements here are not formulated as paradoxes, but as antitheses: we are perceived in one way according to the false judgment of the world, but in quite another way by the true judgment of those who are in Christ.

The apologetic function of this whole apostolic resumé is especially clear in these final antitheses. Here Paul seems to be aware of certain charges being made by those who are contesting the validity of his apostleship (so, also, P. Marshall 1980:497, who finds in vv. 8*b*–9*a* "poignant reference to [the Corinthians'] mistrust and suspicion"). In the first antithesis *(as deceivers—and yet* *true*) the issue of his canceled visit may be in mind (see 1:15–2:2; and cf. in particular the protestation of complete integrity in 1:12), or, less certainly, charges of fraud in connection with his attempts to take up a collection for the Jerusalem church (as in 12:16–18; see COMMENT on 4:2). In the second antithesis (*as unknowns—and yet fully known*) Paul acknowledges that his apostolate has no worldly status (cf. 1 Cor 4:13, "we have become, and are now, as the refuse of the world, the offscouring of all things" [*RSV*]). The lack of worldly fame was frequently a topic for reflection by the Stoics (Windisch, 208, cites examples from Seneca, *Moral Epistles* XXXI, 10: Epictetus IV. viii.35; Marcus Aurelius VII, 67), but Paul's thought here is not, like Seneca's (*Moral Epistles* XXXIX, 14), that one's virtue will ultimately be known to the world, even if it be after one's death. Here the point is that Paul and his colleagues are already *fully known*, even though not to the world at large. This is probably to be interpreted, as in 5:11, in the sense that their honesty and integrity as apostles have been "made known also to your [sc., the Corinthians'] consciences" as they "have been made known to God" (cf. 1:12, 4:2).

The third and fourth antitheses seem to have been constructed on the basis of LXX Ps 117(118):17–18 (see the NOTES). The third one in particular (*as dying—and yet see, we live*), epitomizes very well the theme of the central section of Paul's discussion of apostleship (4:7–5:10), if not—as Collange, 298, remarks—the entire discussion from 2:14. In 1 Cor 4:9 (cf. 1 Cor 15:32), Paul had likened apostles to men sentenced to death in the arena. That imagery (on which see Pfitzner 1967:189–90) may also lie behind the present reference to the world's perception of apostles *as dying*. Or, the recent actual threat to his life in Asia (1:8–9) may be in Paul's mind here. However, since the theme is present in virtually all the catalogs of apostolic hardships (4:8–9; 11:23*b*; Rom 8:36, citing LXX Ps 43[44]:23[22], as well as here and in 1 Cor 4:9), the main point is certainly not that God has delivered his apostles from death. It is, rather, that the apostles are bearers of "the death of Jesus" in order that in their mortal bodies "the life of Jesus," the resurrection power of God, may be disclosed (see 4:7–11). The fourth antithesis (*as receiving punishment—and yet not put to death*) should be interpreted in the same way, even though the text on which it is based reflects the widespread view that suffering is a form of divine discipline (e.g., Prov 3:11–12). This is not Paul's view, however (see Schrage 1974:166–67); for him, the suffering of the apostles is a means of God's self-disclosure (see discussion on 4:7ff.). It is not a sign that the Pauline apostolate is invalid, as some are evidently charging, but that it is true to its divine commission.

It is quite clear that Paul could admit to the appearance of being unknown, dying, and punished, in a way that he could not admit to the charge of deceit. This is also true of the *sorrowing* mentioned in the fifth antithesis. In the present letter especially, he acknowledges the sorrow he has felt—for example, over the Corinthians themselves (2:1). But here he is thinking in more general terms, probably of the *sorrowing* which the world usually associates with the fear of death and the pain of punishment. Despite what the world may suppose, Paul says, the apostles are *constantly rejoicing,* as all believers should (references in the NOTES). That they are also "constantly being given up to death on account of Jesus" (4:11) does not contradict but actually explains their constant rejoicing; it is a rejoicing "in the Lord" (cf. Phil 3:1; 4:4) as the gospel is served through their ministry.

Also in the sixth antithesis the world's perception of the apostles can in one sense be affirmed. With respect to material goods the apostles are indeed *impoverished.* This theme, too, is often present where Paul describes the apostolic life, just as it is in contemporary descriptions of the lives of the Cynic and Stoic philosophers (references in the NOTES). It may be that Paul's rivals in Corinth have sought to interpret his poverty and his unwillingness to ask help from the church there as a tacit admission that he lacks apostolic authority (see 1 Cor 9:1–18; 2 Cor 11:7–11). Paul's response to this is to have the Corinthian Christians consider what his apostleship has meant to them: how their existence as a Christian community is due to his preaching of the gospel (1 Cor 9:2), how their own faith attests that he is an apostle for Christ (2 Cor 3:2–3). These may be the points Paul has in mind when he counters here that his apostolate, though materially *impoverished,* is active in *enriching many.* To this one point, at least, there are no clear parallels in the descriptions of the Cynic and Stoic philosophers (Seidensticker 1977:96). It is frequently said that they have moral and spiritual riches despite their lack of worldly goods (see the quotations in the NOTES), but their enrichment of others is not a special theme. For Paul, however, this is the essence of apostleship, its bringing of the "riches" of salvation (see Rom 10:12; 11:12) to the world (2 Cor 2:14–16; 4:6; 5:13*b;* cf. Rom 1:11; 1 Cor 1:5, etc.).

The final antithesis is closely related in meaning: the apostles are perceived by the world *as having nothing,* but by those who are in Christ as *possessing everything.* Once more, Paul can affirm that the apostles have *nothing* in the way of worldly goods. He could indeed go farther and say that believers do not even "own" themselves (1 Cor 6:19*b;* cf. the quotation from Philo, *Moses* I, 157, given in the NOTES), because they belong to Christ (e.g., 1 Cor 3:23; Phil 3:12*b;* cf. Plummer, 201; Barrett, 191). Because they belong to him, *everything* belongs to them (cf. 1 Cor 3:21*b,* 22) in the sense that they are no longer held in bondage to the standards or to the claims of the present age.

## 10. RECONCILIATION WITH THE PAULINE APOSTOLATE, 6:11–7:3

6  ¹¹Our mouths are open to you, Corinthians, our hearts are wide. ¹²You are not cramped by us; you are cramped, rather, in your feelings.

¹³As a response in kind—I am speaking to children—widen your hearts, too.

¹⁴Do not get misyoked with unbelievers. For what have righteousness and lawlessness in common, or what partnership has light with darkness? ¹⁵What concord has Christ with Beliar, or what share has a believer with an unbeliever? ¹⁶And what agreement has God's temple with idols?

For we are the temple of the living God. As God said: "I will dwell in them and walk about among them; and I will be their God and they shall be my people." ¹⁷Therefore, "Come out from their midst and be separate," says the Lord. "Do not touch what is unclean. And I will receive you, ¹⁸and I will be a father to you, and you shall be sons and daughters to me," says the Lord Almighty.

7 ¹Therefore, having these promises, beloved, let us cleanse ourselves from every defilement of flesh and spirit, making holiness perfect in the fear of God.

²Provide us room! No one did we wrong, no one did we corrupt, no one did we defraud. ³I do not say this in condemnation, because I have stated before that you are in our hearts to die together and to live together.

## NOTES

6:11. *Our mouths are open to you.* To "open one's mouth" (here the perfect tense of the verb has a present meaning; Robertson 1923:895) conforms to a common Hebraic circumlocution for "speaking" (*GNTG* IV:92; see, e.g., LXX Job 3:1; Sir 51:25). Here it describes in particular the free and candid expression of one's thoughts and feelings (cf. LXX Judg 11:35–36).

*Corinthians.* Only here, in Gal 3:1, and in Phil 4:15 does Paul address a congregation by using the name of their city or province. In each case the effect is both to personalize and to emphasize what is being said: in Gal, a reprimand; in Phil, an expression of gratitude; here, an assurance of complete candor.

*our hearts are wide.* The verb is perfect in tense but present in meaning. In LXX Deut 11:16 the wide heart represents conceit, but in LXX Ps 118(119):32 it represents understanding. Here the broadened heart is a sign of affection; see 7:3, *you are in our hearts.*

12. *cramped.* The verb is *stenochōreisthai,* translated as "crushed" in 4:8 (on which see the note).

*rather.* Translates *de,* which has adversative force here.

*feelings.* The Greek word (*ta splanchna,* here plural, as usual) refers literally to the organs contained in the thoracic cavity (heart, lungs) and upper abdomen (kidneys, liver). Used figuratively it may refer, as here and in 7:15, to the seat of emotion, just as "heart" often does.

13. *As a response in kind.* Interpreters differ on how the accusative phrase *tēn autēn antimisthian* (literally "the same recompense") should be construed, but the general meaning is fairly clear. Here it is taken as meaning "with the same widening as recompense" (BDF § 154; for other discussions and possibilities see Moule 1953:34, 36, 160–61; *GNTG* III:245; Plummer, 204; Hughes, 240 n. 3).

*I am speaking to children.* Paul not infrequently thinks of himself as a spiritual parent to his churches, and the imagery is especially prominent in the letters to Corinth. See also 11:2; 12:14b–15a; 1 Cor 3:1–2; 4:14–15 (elsewhere, Gal 4:19; 1 Thess 2:7–8). No special point is made here about the Corinthians' immaturity in the faith (as in 1 Cor 3:1–2). Rather, *children* is a term of endearment, as in 1 Cor 4:14; Gal 4:19; 1 Thess 2:7–8.

*widen your hearts, too.* The words *your hearts* do not appear in the Greek, but are to be understood from v. 11.

14a. *Do not get misyoked.* Here the present imperative ([*mē*] *ginesthe*) is combined with a present participle *(heterozygountes)* in a periphrastic construction; see BDF § 354 (cf. 98); *GNTG* III:89; Robertson 1923:330, 375, 890. The presumption is not that those addressed have already gotten *misyoked;* they are simply warned against that (Plummer, 206). It is true that Paul uses the prohibition *mē ginesthe (Do not be)* several other times in his letters (Fee 1977:147, who cites Rom 12:16; 1 Cor 7:23; 10:7; 14:20 [and Eph 5:7, 17]), but in none of these does it occur in a periphrastic construction, as it does here.

*misyoked.* The verb *(heterozygein)* occurs nowhere else in the NT, but Paul uses the adjective *syzygos* when he refers to an otherwise unnamed "yokefellow" *(RSV)* in Phil 4:3. The adjective *heterozygos* is used in LXX Lev 19:19 ("You shall not let your cattle breed with one of a different kind [*heterozygō*]"), but it is not used in LXX Deut 22:10, where one might expect it to be ("You shall not plow with an ox and an ass together [*epi to auto*]"). In *Special Laws* III, 46, Philo invokes Lev 19:19 against adultery and other forms of sexual vice. In the same work (IV, 203–18) he applies the text to the topic of justice *(dikaiosynē),* and employs the prohibition of Deut 22:10 as an example (205).

*unbelievers.* Most interpreters take this as a reference to non-Christians, as in 4:4 (on which see NOTES) and in 1 Cor. A decision on the point depends at least in part on whether one attributes the reference to Paul himself or to someone else. See COMMENT.

14b. *righteousness and lawlessness.* These two words *(dikaiosynē* and *anomia)* are also presented as opposites in Rom 6:19, where *RSV* translates the second word as "iniquity." The noun *lawlessness* appears elsewhere in Paul's letters only in a scriptural quotation in Rom 4:7. Cf. the cognate adverb in Rom 2:12, and adjective in 1 Cor 9:21. *Righteousness* and *lawlessness* ( = iniquity) often stand as opposites in the texts from Qumran—e.g., 1QH i.26–27: "For thine, O God of knowledge, / are all righteous deeds / and the counsel of truth; / but to the sons of men is the work of iniquity / and deeds of deceit" (Vermes 1975:152); xvi.10–11: "I know that Thou hast marked the spirit of the just, / and therefore I have chosen to keep my hands clean / in accordance with [Thy] will; / the soul of Thy servant [has loathed] / every work of iniquity" (ibid.:196). See also 1QH xiv.16; 1QS i.4–5; v.1–4, etc.

*in common.* Translates the noun *metochē,* which occurs nowhere else in the Greek Bible. It is hardly distinguishable in meaning from the two nouns *partnership* and *share* which follow in vv. 14c and 15b respectively. Paul uses the cognate verb in 1 Cor 9:10, 12; 10:17, 21, 30.

*partnership.* The word here is *koinōnia,* used in 8:4; 9:13 of the collection for Jerusalem. The cognate adjective *koinōnos* is used substantively in 1:7 ("partners," on which see the note). Here the noun is a virtual synonym for *metochē* in v. 14b (see preceding note) and *meris (share)* in v. 15b. Fitzmyer (1974a:209 n. 8) observes that the construction with *pros (partnership . . . with)* is also found in Sir 13:2 (with the verb *koinōnein:* "How can the clay pot associate with the iron kettle?" [*RSV*]), and may be a Hebraism. In Sir 13:17 the verb is followed by a dative. McDermott (1975:222) describes the use of the noun in 2 Cor 6:14 as "unique" in Paul's letters.

*light . . . darkness.* The imagery is often found in parenetic texts, including the Pauline letters (see Rom 2:19; 13:12; 1 Cor 4:5; 1 Thess 5:4–5). Thrall (1977:145) calls attention to 2 Cor 4:3–6, which builds on the same contrast. The imagery is especially frequent in the Qumran texts, where "the sons of darkness" stand over against "the sons of light" (e.g., 1QS i.9–11; ii.16–17; iii.3, 13, 19–20, 24–25; 1QM i.1, 3, 9, 11, 13; xiii.5–6, 9; 4QFlor i.9). For a full discussion of the imagery in Paul's letters see Stachowiak (1963), who also discusses in particular the similarities between the imagery of 6:14–7:1 and that of the Qumran literature (ibid.:399–407).

15. *concord.* This word *(symphōnēsis)* appears only here in the Greek Bible, although Paul uses the adjective *symphonos* in 1 Cor 7:5 (*RSV:* "by agreement").

*Christ . . . Beliar.* The name *Beliar* is also found in certain intertestamental literature, and is one of the variant forms of the name "Belial." The latter derives from the Hebrew word which means "worthlessness," "evil," "perversion," etc., but which is never personified in the OT. Belial plays a prominent role in the "War Scroll" from Qumran (e.g., 1QM i.1, 5, 13). Note especially xiii.2, 4: "Blessed be the God of Israel . . . , but cursed be Belial with his hostile purpose . . . !" (tr. Fitzmyer 1974a:211), in which context, as throughout 1QM, Belial is associated with the forces of darkness, and God with the forces of light (xiii.5). This accords with various passages in T 12 Patr, where *Beliar* (the same form as in 2 Cor 6:15) stands over against God—e.g., T Levi 19:1: "Choose . . . for yourselves either the light or the darkness, either the law of the Lord or the works of Beliar" *(APOT);* so also T Naph 2:6–7; T Jos 20:2. For discussions and further references see Osten-Sacken 1969, especially 73–78; Fitzmyer 1974a:211–13; Gnilka 1968a:54–56. The name "Belias" is applied to the devil in Ap John [CG II, 1] 11,3 [*NHLE,* 104], and perhaps in Gos Eg [III, 2] 58,21 [*NHLE,* 201], where it is restored. The name *Beliar* (or "Belial") occurs nowhere else in the NT; for Paul's terminology see the note on "Satan" in 2:11.

*share.* This word *(meris)* is also used in Col 1:12 (literally: "for the share of the lot of the saints in light"), but nowhere else in the unquestionably authentic letters of Paul. It is a synonym for *metochē (have . . . in common)* and *koinōnia (partnership)* in v. 14. Fitzmyer (1974a:209–11) believes the word reflects the Qumranian idea that the members of the sect are the "lot of light" and the "lot of God" (e.g., 1QM xiii.9; 1QS ii.2).

*a believer . . . an unbeliever.* Elsewhere in the letters of certain Pauline authorship the adjective *pistos* means "worthy of belief" or "faithful," but here, where it is contrasted with *apistos (unbeliever),* it must mean "one who believes." Because the contrast between *a believer* and *an unbeliever* is closely linked to the preceding one between *Christ* and *Beliar*, one must understand the reference to be to those who "believe in Christ," as in 1 Tim 4:10, 12; 5:16 (and perhaps Eph 1:1). See Gnilka 1968a:57.

*16a. agreement.* This noun *(synkatathesis)*, which Stoic philosophers used technically for the mind's assent to perceptions (references in LSJ s.v.), occurs only here in the Greek Bible, although the cognate verb is used twice in the LXX (Exod 23:1, 32) and once in the NT (Luke 23:51).

*God's temple . . . idols.* The call to turn from *idols* to serve God was a fundamental part of Paul's missionary preaching; see especially 1 Thess 1:9 and the vice lists in 1 Cor 5:10, 11; 6:9; Gal 5:20. The apostle has more to say about idolatry in 1 Cor than in any other letter, especially in chap. 8 and in 10:7, 14ff. See also Rom 2:22 and cf. Rom 1:22–25. The reference here to *idols* should perhaps be interpreted metaphorically, like that to *God's temple.* See Gärtner (1965:50–52), who cites in particular 1QS ii.11, " 'Cursed be the man who enters this Covenant while walking among the idols of his heart' " (Vermes 1975:73); cf. 1QS ii.16–17; iv.5; 1QH iv.19; CD xx.9, and Fitzmyer 1974a:213. But contrast Klinzing 1971:176. For Pauline and Qumranian references to *God's temple,* see note on v. 16*b.*

*16b. we are.* P⁴⁶ and some other witnesses read "you are" *(hymeis . . . este)* instead of *we are (hēmeis . . . esmen),* but the latter is strongly attested, while the former is readily explained as an assimilation to the second person of vv. 14, 17 and to 1 Cor 3:16; Metzger 1971:580. The *we* is "very emphatic" here (Plummer, 208).

*the temple of the living God.* The definite article is supplied before *temple;* it does not stand in the Greek. Everding (1968:324 n. 2) notes the formal parallel in LXX Dan 5:23, where "the house of the living God" *(tou oikou tou Theou tou zōntos)* describes the actual temple in Jerusalem whose holy vessels have been profaned. (For the phrase *living God,* see NOTES on 3:3.) Here, however, the word *temple (naos)* is used metaphorically for the whole people of God, the Christian community, as in 1 Cor 3:16; Eph 2:21 (1 Cor 6:19 refers to the body of each individual believer as a "temple" of God); for this and related NT imagery see Minear 1960:96–98. Although God's dwelling with and among the people of Israel is a pervasive OT theme, Israel is never identified there with God's temple as such; see Clements 1965. Gärtner believes such an identification was made at Qumran, especially in 4QFlor (1965:22–42; cf. Fitzmyer 1974a:214), but Klinzing (1971:85ff., 175) has strongly contested Gärtner's arguments for this.

*16c. As God said.* This formula introduces a series of scriptural citations. Cf. 4:6, "the God who said," which introduces what is more an allusion to than a citation from scripture; but there are no other parallels to the formula in Paul's letters (elsewhere in the NT, cf. Matt 15:4; Acts 7:6, 7). A virtually identical formula occurs twice in the so-called "Damascus Document," which is closely associated with the texts from Qumran: CD vi.13 and viii.9 (ᵓšr ᵓmr ᵓl [ᶜlyhm], "as for what [about whom] God said"); see Fitzmyer 1974a:11, 216.

*"I will dwell in them."* This statement is not found in the OT; and in the LXX, God is never the subject of the verb *enoikein,* "to dwell in." See COMMENT.

*"walk about among them."* In the Greek text *en autois* (which must be translated *in them* following the verb *enoikein;* see preceding note) stands between the two verbs *dwell* and *walk about,* and is doubtless to be taken with the second as well as with the

first. After the second, however, it is best translated *among them.* LXX Lev 26:12, one of the two texts drawn on in v. 16c, has *emperipatēsō en hymin,* "I will walk about among you."

*"and I will be their God,"* etc. The principal text would seem to be Lev 26:12 (see preceding note), "And I shall be your God, and you shall be my people"; but, as in Ezek 37:27, the third person is used instead of the second person: *their God . . . they shall be.* Cf. Rev 21:3.

17a. *Therefore.* Translates *dio,* used to connect the preceding citations (v. 16c) with those that follow.

*"Come out from their midst and be separate."* Quotes LXX Isa 52:11b, changing only the possessive pronoun ("her midst" to *their midst*).

*says the Lord.* A second citation formula (see *As God said,* v. 16c), this one joining the preceding citation of Isa 52:11b with the following citation of Isa 52:11a. The phrase *(legei Kyrios)* appears often in the LXX—e.g., Isa 49:18 (quoted in Rom 14:11); 52:4, 5—and is present elsewhere in the Pauline letters in Rom 12:19; 1 Cor 14:21.

17b. *"Do not touch what is unclean."* A quotation of LXX Isa 52:11a, without variation.

17c. *"And I will receive you."* This could be an allusion to Ezek 20:34, God's promise to return the scattered people of Israel from their various places of residence among the Gentiles (LXX: "And I will lead you out from the people, and I will receive you from the lands where you have been dispersed"); cf. Zeph 3:19–20; Zech 10:8, 10. Gnilka (1968a:60) notes that Ezek 20:34–35 seems to be echoed in 1QM i.2–3. On the other hand, Betz (1973:96–97) thinks it unlikely that this phrase is drawn from scripture, and regards it as an interpretive gloss on the following text from 2 Kgdms (2 Sam).

18. *"and I will be a father to you . . . ,"* etc. A free adaptation of 2 Kgdms (2 Sam) 7:14, God's promise to David about Solomon: "I will be a father to him, and he shall be a son to me" (cf. 1 Chr 22:10; 28:6). The same text is incorporated into 4QFlor i.11, where it is interpreted with reference to one of the two anointed ones (messiahs) expected by the Qumran sectarians. Elsewhere in the NT see Heb 1:5b; Rev 21:7.

*sons and daughters.* Here the original text, a promise to David (see preceding note), is altered not only by the use of the plural, *sons,* but also by the addition, *and daughters.* The addition may have been influenced by LXX Isa 43:6, God's command with respect to Israel: "Bring my sons from afar, and my daughters from the ends of the earth."

*says the Lord Almighty.* The third citation formula in this passage (see also vv. 16c, 17) concludes the chain of scriptural allusions and quotations. The description of God as *Almighty (pantokratōr)* is frequent in the LXX, but apart from this passage its occurrence in the NT is confined to Rev (1:8; 4:8; 11:17; 15:3; 16:7, 14; 19:6, 15; 21:22), on which see Delling 1970:442–48. Its use here is perhaps to be attributed to its presence in the context from which the last citation has been drawn, 2 Kgdms (2 Sam) 7:8 (see also v. 27), but Gnilka (1968a:53) believes it could just as easily be "a spontaneous creation on the part of the author."

7:1. *Therefore, having . . . let us.* The style is homiletical, as in Heb 4:14; 10:19 (cf. 12:1), where *echontes oun* (here, *oun echontes, Therefore, having*) is followed by a hortatory subjunctive ( = *let us*). This precise construction is not present elsewhere in Paul's letters, although Gal 6:10 comes close (only "we have" instead of "having"). Neither 3:12 nor 4:1, often cited as parallels in the present letter (e.g., Fee 1977:147), employs a hortatory subjunctive form.

*these promises.* That is, the *promises* cited from scripture in vv. 16c, 17c–18. Paul ordinarily speaks of "the promise" (singular), but the plural also occurs in 1:20 (on which see the note); Rom 9:4; 15:8; Gal 3:16, 21. Cf. the description of Abraham in Heb 7:6 as one "who had the promises" *(ton echonta tas epangelias).*

*beloved.* This form of address occurs elsewhere in Paul's letters (Rom 12:19; 1 Cor 10:14; 15:58; 2 Cor 12:19; Phil 2:12; 4:1 [twice]), but is not a special characteristic of Pauline style. It is a feature of homiletical-hortatory style in general, and in fact occurs more often in the later NT letters than in Paul's (Heb 6:9; Jas 1:16, 19; 2:5; 1 Pet 2:11; 4:12; 2 Pet 3:1, 8, 14, 17; 1 John 2:7; 3:2, 21; 4:1, 7, 11; Jude 3, 17, 20). It does, however, seem to be a specifically Christian form of address (so Goppelt 1978:157).

*let us cleanse ourselves.* The verb *katharizein* ("to cleanse") occurs nowhere else in the unquestioned Pauline letters, and nowhere else in the NT does it refer to believers' cleansing themselves (see Eph 5:26; Tit 2:14; Heb 9:14, 22, 23; 10:2). But see 1QS iii.8–9 (cited by Gnilka 1968a:59), where the Qumran sectary is described: "And when his flesh is sprinkled with purifying water and sanctified by cleansing water, it shall be made clean by the humble submission of his soul to all the precepts of God" (Vermes 1975:75). Paul uses the cognate adjective (which is frequent in the Pastoral Epistles) only in Rom 14:20 ("Everything is indeed clean" [*RSV*]).

*from every defilement.* The noun *molysmos, defilement,* occurs only here in the NT, although Paul uses the cognate verb in 1 Cor 8:7 (elsewhere in the NT, Rev 3:4; 14:4). The two instances in which the noun is used in the LXX (1 Esdr 8:80[83]; 2 Mac 5:27; the verb is frequent) show how closely it could be associated with the pollution of pagan idolatries; see also Ep Arist 166. The noun could also be translated "uncleanness" or "impurity," and is thus virtually synonymous with *akatharsia,* a word that does appear elsewhere in Paul's letters, principally in vice lists (12:21; Rom 1:24; 6:19; Gal 5:19), but not only there (1 Thess 2:3; 4:7). Note the adjective "unclean" in the quotation from Isa in this passage (v. 17), and in 1 Cor 7:14.

*of flesh and spirit.* These two *(sarx* and *pneuma)* are not set over against each other —as, e.g., in Gal 5:16ff., where *pneuma* is a reference to the Holy Spirit and where *sarx* stands for everything which opposes the will of God. Here *spirit* is used anthropologically, and the combination *flesh and spirit* refers either to the totality of human existence or to its outward and inward aspects. In anthropological references (1 Cor 7:34; 1 Thess 5:23) Paul links "spirit," respectively, with "body" *(sōma)* and with "soul" *(psychē)* and "body" *(sōma).* The apostle refers nowhere else to the *defilement* of either the flesh or the spirit, only to the subjection of the flesh to sin (e.g., Rom 7:25; 8:3; 13:14), to the "works" of the flesh (Gal 5:19–21), etc. See, however, 1QM vii.4–6, where it is said that no man "afflicted with a lasting bodily blemish, or smitten with a bodily impurity" can be enlisted for the war against the forces of darkness, but only those who are "perfect in spirit and body" (Vermes 1975:132–33). Marcion's reading, "flesh and blood," makes the text compatible with the dualistic anthropology of Gnosticism.

*making holiness perfect.* Apart from this verse, the noun *holiness (hagiōsynē)* occurs in Paul's letters only in Rom 1:4 (in what is generally regarded as a pre-Pauline formulation) and 1 Thess 3:13 (in a prayer that "the Lord" will establish the hearts of the Thessalonians "unblamable in holiness" before God). The verb *epitelein* (here as a present participle, perhaps "advance constantly in holiness" [Hughes, 258]) is used by Paul in six other places, usually with its common meaning: "to complete" or "fulfill" an obligation—notably, the collection of a fund for the believers in Jerusalem (8:6, 11 [twice]; Rom 15:28). Neither this usage, nor that in Gal 3:3 ("Having begun with the Spirit, are you now ending with the flesh?" [*RSV*]), nor that in Phil 1:6 (a reference to God's bringing his work to completion) accords with the usage in the present verse. However, Philo's reference to those who "fulfil the laws by their deeds [*tous nomous ergois epitelountōn*]" (*On Rewards and Punishments* 126) is comparable (cited by Windisch, 219), and the notion of "perfect holiness" was in vogue among the sectarians of Qumran (1QS viii.20; CD vii.5, cited by Gnilka 1968a:59).

*the fear of God.* Cf. "the fear of the Lord" (5:11, with note). The variant "in the love of God" is attested by P⁴⁶ (Héring, 52 n. 3: a Marcionite reading?), but by no other witnesses, though Ker (1961) is tempted to adopt it.

2. *Provide us room!* Allo, 188, followed by Héring, 53, takes the verb here *(chōrein)* to mean "understand," which is possible (BAG s.v. 3b). It is better, however, to interpret it in the light of the imagery of v. 3 *(you are in our hearts)* and 6:13 *(widen your hearts, too).* Thus, "to make room for" (ibid., 3a); specifically, "in your hearts." Such trs. as *RSV,* "Open your hearts to us," are misleading; Paul's plea is not that the Corinthians disclose their feelings but that they take their apostle into their affections as he has taken them into his (correctly Field 1879:184).

*No one.* The emphasis falls on this *oudena,* the object of the verbs (used with each in turn), and not on the subject of the verbs *(we).*

*did we.* Each of the verbs is aorist, looking back to Paul's previous visits in Corinth (cf. Hughes, 260 n. 26).

*wrong.* The verb is *adikein* as in 7:12, where it is used twice (substantive participles), with reference, respectively, to someone who perpetrated a wrong in Corinth and to the party who had been wronged thereby. It is unlikely that the same incident is in mind here, because Paul was in that case the victim of the wrong, not the one accused of it (see NOTES and COMMENT on 7:8–12).

*corrupt.* In 11:3 the same verb *(phtheirein),* used in connection with the bride metaphor, refers to an act of seduction. Here, however, it has a more general meaning, or refers in a general way to what is specified in the following verb.

*defraud.* The same verb *(pleonektein)* is used of Satan in 2:11, but 12:17–18 is the more important parallel to the present verse. See COMMENT.

3. *I.* The first person singular, last used extensively in 1:23–2:13 (only briefly in 5:11b; 6:13), recurs here and is retained through much of the remainder of chap. 7.

*not . . . in condemnation.* As a clarification of v. 2b, this remark is in accord with the apologetic (not polemical) stance assumed there (see note on *No one*).

*I have stated before.* In 13:2 the same expression *(proeirēka)* refers to a previous warning. Here the reference is to a previous word of assurance. This could have been given on a visit (cf. 13:2) or in an earlier letter (the one mentioned in 7:8, 12; 2:4, 9; nothing in 1 Cor seems to fit), or earlier in the present letter (so most commentators). Whether, in the latter case, the reference is to 6:11–12 (e.g., Kümmel, 206; Bultmann, 179; Barrett, 204), to 6:9 (Stählin 1973:518), to 1:4–7 (Tannehill 1967:94) or 1:6 (Windisch, 222; cf. Lietzmann, 131; Barrett, 204), to 3:2 (Lietzmann, 131), to 4:10ff. (de Boor, 165) or 4:12 (cf. Lietzmann, 131; Windisch, 222; Barrett, 204), or to 5:14 (Bachmann, 294–95; cf. de Boor, 165) is debated.

*in our hearts.* The plural *hearts* (the Greek would allow "in our heart," as in 6:11) makes it clear that Paul includes his associates in the reference (cf. Plummer, 214). Note 3:2–3; 1 Thess 2:17.

*to die together and to live together.* Many (e.g., Plummer, 214; Windisch, 222–23; Héring, 53; Bultmann, 179–80; Bruce, 217; Barrett, 204; cf. Olivier 1929) interpret this as a formula of abiding friendship, Paul's pledge to his readers that he is bound to them, whether in death or in life. See Athenaeus, *Deipnosophistae* VI, 249b, quoting Nicolas of Damascus about the vows taken by the bodyguards of the Celtic kings: "to live and to die with them" *(syzōntas kai synapothnēskontas);* also Euripides (cited by Bultmann, 179–80), *Orestes* 307–8; *Ion* 852–53, 857–58; Horace, *Odes* III.ix.24; and in the LXX (Ittai to David): "In whatever place my lord shall be, whether for death or for life, there your servant shall be" (2 Kgdms [2 Sam] 15:21). Note, too, Peter's pledge of loyalty to Jesus, Mark 14:31, " 'If I must die with you *[ean deē me synapothanein soi]*, I will not deny you' " *(RSV).* Some (e.g., Bachmann, 294–95; Tannehill 1967:93; de Boor, 165), arguing principally from the word order *(to die . . . to live),* think Paul is referring to the death and life he and his readers share in Christ. Stählin (1973:508–21) interprets the phrase as a confessional formula, and regards its principal reference to be to dying and living together "with Christ" (see 2 Tim 2:11; cf. Rom 6:8). Finally, Lambrecht (1976), arguing (principally against Stählin) that the traditional friendship formula does lie behind this expression, holds nonetheless that Paul has significantly re-written that formula in order to give it a specifically Christian meaning. See COMMENT.

## COMMENT: GENERAL

In 5:20–6:10, Paul had urged the Corinthian Christians to be reconciled to God. Now, although he does not use the language of reconciliation, he follows that up with an appeal to be reconciled, as well, with those who have brought them "the word of reconciliation," namely, with Paul and his associates (6: 11–13; 7:2–3). This concern for an improvement in relations with the church in Corinth has been present throughout the letter—indeed, as early as 1:12–14. There Paul had asked for the complete understanding of his readers. Here he implores them, *Widen your hearts* (6:13), *Provide us room!* (7:2). And here, as earlier, the appeal is coupled with assurances of his own concern and affection for the Corinthians (6:11; 7:3; cf. 1:14–15, 23; 2:4, etc.). One might also mention the confidence Paul expresses in them in 7:4, a verse most commentators (and versions) take with what precedes. There are sound reasons, however, for regarding 7:4 as the opening, summary statement for the rest of chap. 7 (see, e.g., the parallel statement in 7:16), and the verse is dealt with in this commentary as part of the third section of appeals, 7:4–9:15.

The material in 6:14–7:1 is also fundamentally hortatory. An introductory exhortation to stay away from *unbelievers* (6:14*a*) is supported by a series of rhetorical questions (6:14*b*–16*a*) and an affirmation about *the temple of the living God* (6:16*b*). The latter is in turn supported by a series of scriptural quotations (6:16c–18), one of which (Isa 52:11) is itself admonitory (v. 17). Finally, the appeals of 6:14a, 17 are summed up in the exhortation to "perfect holiness" in 7:1.

It is uncertain how the appeals of 6:14–7:1 relate to the clearly primary appeal expressed in 6:11–13, and then again in 7:2–3. Most commentators agree that the intervening material is at least to some extent disruptive. Beyond this, however, there is little agreement. Some hold that 6:14–7:1 is a fragment of another Pauline letter, placed here when the apostle's Corinthian correspondence was edited for circulation. Some argue that it is in fact an interpolation of non-Pauline or even anti-Pauline origin. Some believe it is previously formulated material the apostle is himself quoting. Finally, some regard it as both Pauline in origin and integral to the context in chaps. 6–7. The arguments and evidence for these various positions are examined below.

## COMMENT: DETAILED

### The Primary Appeal, 6:11–13; 7:2–3

The appeal contained in these verses is marked by a warmth and a tenderness which distinguish it from the more formal entreaty of 5:20ff., as well as from the more general admonitions of 6:14–7:1. This is appropriate, given that the Corinthians are being urged to be as accepting of Paul and his associates as they have been of the Corinthians. The style and the tone here are thoroughly pastoral. The apostle begins by addressing his readers by name (6:11). Then as he continues he lapses momentarily into the use of the first person singular (6:13), in order to emphasize that he is calling upon them as his spiritual *children* (see 1 Cor 4:14–15). The appeal itself (6:13; 7:2a) is prefaced in 6:11 by the assurance that Paul's ministry has been conducted with full candor *(our mouths are open to you)* and with genuine concern and understanding for the Corinthians *(our hearts are wide).* It is significant that Paul follows this (6:12) with the comment that any limitation of candor or concern they may have experienced has been due to their own *feelings,* not to the conduct of his ministry. Here, as in 1:12–2:13, the apostle seems to be aware of certain criticisms of his ministry which are abroad in Corinth, perhaps to the effect that he has been neglectful of the believers there (e.g., 1:17–18), insensitive to their feelings (e.g., 1:24), unloving in the way he has acted toward them (e.g., 2:4). (Cf. Windisch, 210–11.) Earlier in the letter he had sought to assure them his actions had been wrongly interpreted. Now he counters that if there has been any lack of concern and understanding it has been on their part, not his.

The appeal proper is first expressed in 6:13, where Paul urges that the love which has been exhibited toward his readers be returned in kind: *Widen your hearts, too.* The exhortation of 7:2a *(Provide us room!)* is but a variation of this. If, as some believe, 6:14–7:1 is to be regarded as an interpolation added to Paul's original letter, then the apostle himself would have written, without a break, *Widen your hearts, too. Provide us room!*—which would make good sense. If there has been no interpolation, then the appeal of 7:2a would be interpreted as a resumption of the one in 6:13 after a digression in 6:14–7:1. A third possibility, that 6:11–13 and 7:2–4 are parallel and belonged originally to two different editions of a letter (Collange, 300), has little to commend it (see below on 6:14–7:1).

The appeal to be accepting of Paul and his apostolate is supported in 7: 2b–3. The emphatic profession of innocence *(No one did we wrong . . . corrupt . . . defraud,* 7:2b) can only have been prompted by charges or at least by insinuations to the contrary. Since the apostle seems to presume that a simple denial will suffice, one learns very little from this passage about the nature of those charges. The third denial, however, *no one did we defraud,* provides an important clue. The same verb ("to defraud") is used in 12:17–18. From that passage and its context it would appear that the apostle has been suspected of duplicity and fraud in the matter of the collection for Jerusalem (see NOTES and COMMENT on 12:14–18). That the nature of the suspicions is clearer in chap. 12 than in chap. 7 does not prove that chaps. 10–13 were written before chaps. 1–9. Indeed, for other reasons it is probable that chaps. 10–13 were part of a letter written a little after the letter represented by chaps. 1–9 (see INTRODUCTION, p. 38). If so, then the present, simple denial of having defrauded anyone would suggest either (a) that so far there were only vague rumors in circulation about possible fraud, or (b) that Paul was not yet aware of how serious and widespread suspicions about him were. Cf. Windisch, 221; Barrett, 203.

Lest his profession of innocence be construed to suggest that others have been guilty of wrongful behavior, Paul adds a clarifying comment: *I do not say this in condemnation* (7:3a). The reference is to what has just been said (7:2b) and is compatible with the fact that the emphasis there was on the object, not the subject of the verbs: not *"we* [implying: unlike others] have wronged no one," etc., but rather, *"no one at all* have we wronged," etc. (see NOTES). Thus, Paul's stance here is apologetic, not polemical; he is on the defensive, but not on the attack. This cannot be said of chaps. 10–13 (see, e.g., 10:12; 11:13–15, 19; 12:20–21; 13:2), and is also one of the reasons it is probable that chaps. 1–9 and 10–13 are parts of two different letters. The abrupt return to the use of the first person singular here has the effect of shortening the distance between Paul and his readers and thus intensifying what he writes.

In order to support his contention that he does not wish to condemn the Corinthians, Paul assures them once more of how close he and his associates (note again *our hearts*) feel to them (v. 7b). Where or when Paul has *stated* this *before* is disputed. The reference is probably to something in the present letter, for if it were to something in an earlier letter one would have expected Paul to be more specific (cf. 2:3, 4, 9; 1 Cor 5:9). The same would be true about a reference to something said orally during a visit (de Boor, 165). Some, focusing on the statement that *you are in our hearts,* naturally think either of 6:11–12, *Our hearts are wide. You are not cramped by us,* or of 3:2, "You yourselves are our letter, inscribed on our hearts." Others, however, believe Paul's most important point is contained in the phrase *to die together and to live together,* and that he is consciously repeating what he has said about the fellowship of suffering and comfort in 1:4–7, or the bearing of Jesus' death and life in 4:10–12, or dying with and living for Christ in 5:14–15. (See NOTES for proponents of these different views.) A reference to what has been said in 6:11–12 is the most likely, whether or not the material of 6:14–7:1 has intervened. (*I have stated before* implies nothing about how much before; correctly Bultmann, 179.) Tannehill's objections to this (1967:94) are not persuasive. (a) The comments about broadening and narrowing in 6:11–13 do not overshadow the reference to "hearts," but are a vital part of that imagery. (b) There is no need to suppose that it is "the most striking part of 7:3" (the reference to death and life) that Paul is conscious of repeating; it would more likely be something he has just (6:11–12) or repeatedly (also 3:2) written.

The phrase *to die together and to live together* is highly problematic. (a) It could mean simply that, whether they die or live, Paul and his associates will continue to bear the Corinthians in their hearts. (b) It could be regarded as a summary-reference to what Paul has said earlier in 1:4–7 and (or) in 5:14–15. In 1:4–7 he has emphasized the common bonds of suffering and comfort which tie the readers to those who serve them in the gospel, and in 5:14–15 he has interpreted the death "all" die with Christ as freeing them to live for him. References to 4:10–12 and 6:9 are less appropriate. The present statement actually contradicts the comment in 4:12 ("Death is made active in us, but life in you"), and in 6:9 only the experience of apostles is in mind. (c) It could be interpreted as a confessional formula, referring primarily to the death and life which believers share with Christ. This would include the point of (b), but as secondary to and dependent upon the main point—that believers die and live together with Christ. See the NOTES for proponents of each of these views.

In support of (a) one may cite the immediate context (6:11–13; 7:2–3a), which stresses the reality of pastoral affection, not sharing in Christ's death and life, and the numerous ancient examples of friendship vows similarly formulated (see NOTES). The word order, *to die . . . to live,* permits but does not require (b) or (c). A number of the friendship formulas have the same order —not only 2 Kgdms (2 Sam) 15:21 quoted in the NOTES but also the passages cited there from Euripides ("With thee I will make choice of death or life"; "Let me die or live"; ". . . or death, or honourable life"). One need not suppose that Paul himself is responsible for reversing the order (against Lambrecht 1976:249–50, 251). Perhaps the strongest argument for (c) is the formally similar statement in the christological confession of 2 Tim 2:11–13, where the "dying-with" *(synapethanomen)* and "living-with" *(syzēsomen)* are properly translated "we have died with him" and "we shall live with him," referring to Christ. But the immediate context of the statement in 2 Cor 7:3*b* is pastoral and personal, not confessional, and (a) remains the most likely meaning. Chrysostom *(NPNF,* 1st ser. XII:347) presumes it as the undisputed interpretation. In this context, of course, the expression has more than its traditional, "profane" meaning (correctly Lambrecht 1976:248–50, 251), but it is less clear whether one can find here a reference to "eternal life" specifically (so Lambrecht ibid.:250, 251).

## A Secondary Appeal, 6:14–7:1

Whether this passage actually belongs where it is located in our canonical 2 Cor has been discussed since early in the nineteenth century, and whether it can be attributed to Paul himself has been discussed almost as long. (For references to early critical investigations see Moffatt 1918:125–26.) Any consideration of these questions, however, must be preceded by an examination of the structure and content of the passage, conducted without prejudice as to its origin or its relationship to the letter in which it stands.

### Structure and Content

The structure of this passage is fairly clear. Formally it consists of (a) an opening exhortation formulated as a direct, second-person-plural imperative (6:14*a*); (b) a series of rhetorical questions (6:14*b*–16*a*); (c) an affirmation (6:16*b*); (d) a series of scriptural allusions and quotations consisting of promises and admonitions (6:16*c*–18); and (e) a closing appeal using a hortatory subjunctive construction (7:1). The opening exhortation is supported by the rhetorical questions and the affirmation. The affirmation itself is supported by a set of scriptural promises (6:16*c*). The opening exhortation is renewed by the quotation of two scriptural admonitions (6:17*ab*), and these are supported by a second set of scriptural promises (6:17*c*–18). All of this is summarized in the final appeal. To facilitate commentary, this material may be divided into three sections: 6:14–16*a,* 6:16*b*–18, and 7:1.

1. *The initial admonition, 6:14–16a.* The introductory admonition, *Do not get misyoked with unbelievers,* is illustrated and thereby supported in the series of rhetorical questions which follows. That this paragraph is of Christian origin, at least in its present form, is clear from the reference to *Christ* in v. 15*a,* where he is set over against *Beliar,* the devil. Similarly, the contrast between *a believer* and *an unbeliever,* which is closely linked to the Christ-reference (v. 15*b*), is probably a contrast between those who believe in him and those who do not. If so, then the *unbelievers* mentioned in v. 14*a* should also be identified as non-Christians, and not as Paul's Christian opponents in

Corinth (as they are by Collange, 305–6, who believes Paul is responsible for this passage) or as Gentile Christians who do not follow the Jewish law (so Betz 1973:89–90, who argues that this passage is anti-Pauline). The former view is also undercut by the observation that, if Paul is somehow responsible for this material (even as its redactor), the application of the term *unbelievers* to other Christians would be against his usage everywhere else (see NOTES). Two additional points cause difficulties for the latter view. (a) Although one may point to the Ignatian letters for instances where the word *unbelievers* is used of Christians who sponsor false doctrines (Magn 5:2; Trall 10:1; Smyrn 2:1; 5:3), neither there nor anywhere else (e.g., in Paul's letters or Acts) is there any hint that *Gentile* Christians had ever been charged with "unbelief" because of their "lawlessness" (cf. Thrall 1977:148 n. 1). (b) Even in the Pastoral Epistles, where those who hold fast to "sound doctrine" are called "believers" (1 Tim 4:10, 12; 5:16) and there is sharp criticism of those who espouse false teaching, the latter are not called "unbelievers"; that term is still used for those who do not profess the gospel at all (1 Tim 5:8; cf. Tit 1:15).

How, then, shall the admonition of v. 14a be understood? Some (e.g., Windisch, 213; Hughes, 246; Barrett, 195–97) interpret it in general terms, as a prohibition of any relationship with non-Christians which would seriously involve a believer with "idolatry and moral defilement" (Barrett, 196). Others, however, think in more specific terms of a prohibition of marriages between Christians and non-Christians (e.g., Héring, 49; Hurd 1965:237; also Cyprian, *Treatises* III, 62 [*ANF* V:551]) or of a participation with pagans in their cultic meals (Fee 1977:158–59, with reference to 1 Cor 10:16–17). But nothing in this passage itself, or even in the wider context of 2 Cor 1–9, warrants particularizing the admonition in these ways. Those who do so must invoke the yet wider context of Paul's Corinthian ministry as a whole, and the teachings of 1 Cor —and so must presume Paul's own responsibility for this passage, at least in its present form. It is better, pending a convincing judgment on this point, to regard the appeal as a very general one, hardly more specific than the concern expressed in Jas 1:26, "to keep oneself unstained from the world."

It is not unusual for rhetorical questions to be used to reinforce moral instruction or an exhortation, as they are in vv. 14b–16a. The literature of Hellenistic moral philosophy and of Hellenistic Judaism offers many parallels (e.g., Epictetus III.xxiii.16; Philo, *On Drunkenness* 57, the latter cited by Windisch, 213). Of these, the one in Sir 13 is certainly the most impressive, because it exhibits both formal and material similarities to the present verses. The topic in Sir 13 is the dangers inherent in associating with the proud and the rich, regarded as evil men (see vv. 1–2). In support of the admonitions to stay away from them, several rhetorical questions are asked: "What fellowship has a wolf with a lamb? No more has a sinner with a godly man. What peace is there between a hyena and a dog? And what peace between a rich man and a poor man?" (vv. 17–18, *RSV*). Paul, too, makes frequent use of the pointed rhetorical question. Perhaps the best examples of his use of such in the service of moral instruction come from Rom 2:3–4 (a series of three questions), 21–23 (a series of five questions).

There are parallels elsewhere in Paul's letters to some, but not all, of the contrasts drawn in vv. 14b–16a. In Rom 6:19, as here, *righteousness* is contrasted with *lawlessness* (*RSV*: "iniquity"), and the light/darkness imagery is also used by Paul (see NOTES). The description of the Christian community as *God's temple* is present in 1 Cor 3:16, and in 1 Cor 6:19 the "body" of the individual Christian is so described, but this imagery is not present where Paul specifically warns against idolatry (references in NOTES). There are no clear equivalents elsewhere in the Pauline letters for the contrasts formulated in v. 15. Paul's usual name for the devil is "Satan" (e.g., 2:11, on which see the note), and this is the only NT passage in which he is called *Beliar*, as well as the only place in Paul's letters where unbelievers are presented as his followers. Indeed, the contrast between *a believer* and *an unbeliever* is also without parallel elsewhere in the apostle's letters, because *believer* is not a Pauline term (see NOTES).

2. *An affirmation, promises, and further admonitions, 6:16b–18.* The affirmation of v. 16b, *For we are the temple of the living God,* follows closely on the question which has contrasted *God's temple* with *idols* (v. 16a), and in the first instance it functions to show why that question is pertinent. Beyond this, however, the statement provides added support for the admonitions, stated (v. 14a) and implied (vv. 14b–16a), in the preceding paragraph. Those imperatives are here grounded in the indicative: believers are to avoid any alliance with the world that would be unworthy of a community which understands itself as *the temple of the living God.* This identification of the community as God's temple is in accord with 1 Cor 3:16–17, and so is its use to support an ethical appeal.

Formally, vv. 16c–18 are best described as a collection of "testimonia," a patchwork of excerpts from and allusions to various biblical texts chosen and adapted in order to make them useful for instruction, edification, etc. There are good examples of this genre among the scrolls from Qumran (see Fitzmyer 1974a:59–89). Other examples of testimonia in the Pauline letters include Rom 3:10–18; 9:25–29; 10:15–21; 11:8–10, 26, 34–35; 15:9–12 (ibid.:66–67), although none of these offers an exact parallel to the kind of collection present in 2 Cor 6:14–7:1. In these verses three or four principal texts have been used, and there are others which seem to have been influential. It is altogether possible, although not susceptible to proof, that this particular collection already existed prior to its use in 6:14–7:1, whether this passage as a whole be attributable to Paul or to someone else.

The testimonia are introduced by the formula *As God said,* v. 16c (on which see the note). The first two are promises: that God will be present to his people, and that he will be their God. The first text used here is Lev 26:12, but with the original second-person references ("among you . . . your God . . . you shall be") changed to the third person, apparently under the influence of Ezek 37:27. A more important alteration, however, is the addition of the phrase *I will dwell in them*. This phrase appears nowhere in the OT, and it must be considered an interpretive comment on Lev 26:12: God's "walking about" among his people (a common OT theme) is understood as his actual dwelling *in them*, as in a temple. However, because it has been placed after the introductory citation formula, this interpretive phrase is presented as if it were part of the text itself. See Betz 1973:93–94; Gärtner 1965:52–54. In his essay *On Dreams* (I, 148–49; II, 248), Philo also interprets Lev 26:12 as a promise of the divine indwelling, but he is thinking of the divine presence within the individual, and in his essay *On Rewards and Punishments* 123, where there is an allusion to Lev 26:12, he identifies "the wise man's mind" as "a house of God" *(oikos Theou)*. Here, as in 1 Cor 3:16–17 and perhaps in the texts from Qumran (see NOTES), it is the community as a whole which is regarded as the place of God's dwelling. That the scriptural promises conveyed in v. 16c are understood to be fulfilled in the community's present life is shown by the fact that the text is used to support the affirmation in v. 16b (cf. Betz 1973:94–95).

The second primary text employed in this collection is Isa 52:11, which consists of a pair of admonitions. These are quoted in v. 17ab, being joined to the preceding set of promises by *Therefore* and thus represented as following from those. In effect, then, these scriptural admonitions renew the one of v. 14a to avoid *unbelievers: "Come out from their midst and be separate. . . . Do not touch what is unclean."* These appear in the reverse order in the text being quoted, and in the process of repositioning them they have been joined by a second citation formula, *says the Lord*. It is doubtful whether one should attribute this formula to some particular OT text, as Plummer, 209, tries to do. It is common in the LXX, and Paul himself adds the same phrase when he quotes Isa 28:11–12 in 1 Cor 14:21 (Fee 1977:147).

The admonitions are followed in vv. 17c–18 by two more promises. Unlike those of v. 16c, these seem to be offered as promises for the future, contingent upon the community's obedience to the preceding ordinances (see Betz 1973: 96). The first promise, v. 17c, is either drawn from Ezek 20:34 or is a comment on the following text which, like the comment in v. 16c, has been melded with that (see NOTES for details). The second promise, v. 18, is based on 2 Kgdms (2 Sam) 7:14, God's promise that he will be a father to Solomon and that Solomon will be a son to him. Elsewhere this same text is interpreted messianically (at Qumran [see NOTES]; and in Heb 1:5b), but here and in Rev 21:7 it is cited as a promise that those who are faithful to God's will shall know him as their father. This use of the text obviously required changing the original reference to "a son." It could have been changed simply to "sons," or else to "children." In fact, it has been changed to *sons and daughters*, perhaps recalling Isa 43:6 (quoted in the NOTES). Barrett, 201, who regards Paul as the compiler of these texts, attributes this change to the apostle's emphasis on the inclusive church, a community in which there is no longer either male or female (Gal 3:28). It is significant, however, that even in the context of Gal 3:28, Paul refers to believers as "sons of God" (Gal 3:26; cf. 4:5–7), though to be sure with the inclusive meaning of "children" (Gal 4:3). This leads Betz to argue that the phrase *sons and daughters* (found nowhere else in the Pauline letters) is in fact un-Pauline and would not have been used by anyone who, like the apostle, believed that the distinction between male and female had been abolished in Christ (1973:106). The point carries a certain weight, but is hardly sufficient for precluding a Pauline origin for this passage.

The testimonia are concluded with a third citation formula (cf. those in vv. 16c, 17a), which serves to emphasize the seriousness with which the preceding promises and admonitions must be taken.

3. *The concluding appeal,* 7:1. While it may be too much to say that this last appeal is "the only concern" of the whole passage, 6:14–7:1 (Betz 1973:98), it is at least close to the truth. Here, in a firm but also warmly pastoral way, the opening admonition (6:14–16a) is reformulated, apparently under the influence of the intervening promises and exhortations cited from scripture (6:16b–18). Specifically, *these promises* would be those of v. 16c (already fulfilled) and vv. 17c–18 (yet to be fulfilled), and the entreaty to strive for a cleansing *of flesh and spirit* and for the perfecting of *holiness* reflects the admonitions of v. 17ab. It is not clear how Fee can argue that the cultic language of this verse derives from the temple imagery of v. 16ab, and that the *defilement* mentioned here is neither "ritualistic" (as in Qumran) nor "simply ethical and moral" (1977:160). The word *defilement* is in no way related to temple imagery when it is used in the LXX or in Ep Arist (references in NOTES). Moreover, it is significant that it is the cultic language of Isa 52:11 and not the temple metaphor of v. 16ab that has been employed in this concluding summary-appeal. *Let us cleanse ourselves from every defilement of flesh and spirit* is a positive and hortatory reformulation of the prohibition cited in v. 17b, *"Do not touch what is unclean."* The subsequent words, *making holiness perfect in the fear of God* ( = *the Lord Almighty,* from whom the preceding promises and ordinances derive, v. 18), likewise refer back to the fulfillment of that command (cf. Betz 1973:98 n. 76). Windisch, 218, thinks *defilement of flesh* would refer chiefly to sexual vices (cf. Rev 14:4), and *defilement of . . . spirit* to pride, but it is more likely that the appeal is intended as a quite comprehensive one.

## Origin

The preceding analysis of the structure and content of 6:14–7:1 has left open two questions—whether Paul himself is responsible for the content of the passage and whether it has always been in its present location between 2 Cor 6:13 and 7:2. These questions are at least partly separable, for some interpreters uphold the authenticity of the passage but deny that it originally stood where it now stands. For this reason a consideration of its origin must precede consideration of its place in the present context.

1. *Non-Pauline features.* Quite apart from the question whether or not this passage disrupts the clearly related appeals of 6:11–13; 7:2–3 (or 4), many interpreters have been struck by certain non-Pauline features within the passage itself. Because of these, they hold, the passage is not attributable to Paul. (a) The passage contains a number of words found nowhere else in the certainly Pauline letters. Even if one excludes consideration of the testimonia (6:16c–18), the list is impressive: *misyoked* and *have . . . in common,* 6:14; *concord, Beliar,* and *share,* 6:15; *agreement,* 6:16a; *cleanse* and *defilement,* 7:1. (b) Certain terms that do appear elsewhere in the apostle's letters are used differently here (for the details, see NOTES): *partnership,* 6:14; *believer,* 6:15; *promises* and *making . . . perfect,* 7:1. (c) Paul nowhere else cites or even alludes to any of the scriptural passages reflected in 6:16c–18, and the opening and closing citation formulas are not found elsewhere in his letters. (d) Finally, several of the most fundamental ideas in the passage seem to be non-Pauline. Nowhere else does the apostle counsel the kind of separation from *unbelievers* envisioned here (6:14–16a, 17a). In fact, the admonition to avoid any association with unbelievers is at least in tension with two passages in 1 Cor 5:10, where Paul concedes the impossibility of "going out" of pagan society, and 7:12–16, where he urges the maintenance of marriages between believers and unbelievers (though 7:39b would preclude believers' entering newly into such alliances). Furthermore, nowhere else does the apostle suggest that the fulfillment of God's promises is contingent upon one's obedience to God's commands (6:17–18). Nowhere else does he hold that believers are morally defiled in both *flesh and spirit* (7:1). And nowhere else does he presume that cleansing from this defilement lies within the power and responsibility of believers themselves (7:1).

2. *Anti-Pauline features.* The points just mentioned under 1(d) are sometimes regarded not only as un-Pauline but as standing in direct contradiction to the apostle's own teaching. It has even been suggested that the implicit loyalty to the law, the tendencies toward perfectionism and asceticism, the underlying dualism, and the conception of God's people as God's temple which are found in the passage are in no way incompatible with the views of Paul's opponents (Gunther 1973:308–13). Indeed, Betz argues specifically and in detail that the point of view in 2 Cor 6:14–7:1 is precisely that of Paul's Galatian opponents (1973; cf. 1979:5–9 and 329–30). According to Betz, this passage is directed against just that kind of association between Jewish and Gentile Christians for which Paul had pleaded at Antioch (Gal 2:11–21) and again in his letter to the Galatians. Further, the scriptural testimonia in 6:16c–18 summarize the Sinai covenant as the divine *promises* (7:1), while Paul himself identifies that covenant with the law and slavery, and sets over against

it the one "promise" made to Abraham (e.g., Gal 4:21–31). Betz also contrasts the emphasis on purity in the present passage with Paul's comment in Rom 14:20 that nothing is in itself unclean, with Pauline parenesis generally (e.g., Gal 5:1–6:10) where there is no special concern for "ritual purity," and with Paul's view that the church has already been "washed . . . sanctified . . . justified" (1 Cor 6:11, *RSV*). Although this sampling of evidence for Betz's hypothesis is all that can be given here, it should be noted that some of it has been drawn from the pseudo-Clementine literature and other relatively late sources (see especially 1979:329 nn. 4, 10, 11, and 330 nn. 16, 18).

3. *Affinities with Qumran sectarianism.* From very early on in the study of the Dead Sea Scrolls, scholars have noted similarities between the form and content of 2 Cor 6:14–7:1 and forms, themes, concerns, and imagery that were current at Qumran in the first two centuries B.C.E. (For a conspectus of early research see Braun 1966 I:201–3.) As already noted, the catena of scriptural passages in 6:16c–18 resembles the scriptural testimonia in use by the sect. Moreover, at least one of the passages reflected in the present collection, 2 Sam 7:14, also played a role in the thinking of the Qumran sectarians (6:18; cf. 4QFlor i.11; and also Ezek 20:34 [6:17c] if one suggested reading of the text of 1QM i.2–3 is correct). Of greatest significance is the fact that the fundamental concern of 2 Cor 6:14–7:1 for a separation of what is clean from what is unclean also pervades the literature from Qumran; see especially 1QS v.13–14; ix.8–9; CD vi.14–18; cii.19–20, and other references provided by Fitzmyer 1974a:215. Beyond this, one may note that here—as at Qumran—the faithful community is understood to be God's "lot" (see NOTES, 6:15); that *righteousness* is above all an ethical concept set over against *lawlessness* (see NOTES, 6:14b); that "Belial" (here spelled "Beliar") is a proper name for the devil (see NOTES, 6:15); and that the dualism of good and evil is portrayed as the opposition of *light* and *darkness* (see NOTES, 6:14b). Finally, even Gärtner, who regards 6:14–7:1 as Pauline, acknowledges that in the closing appeal (7:1) "the distance dividing Paul from the Qumran texts is minimal" (1965:56). Here, as at Qumran, God's people are urged to cleanse themselves from every defiling pollution *of flesh and spirit* in order to perfect their *holiness* and to obtain the *promises* of salvation (see NOTES, 7:1).

How are these similarities between 6:14–7:1 and Qumran sectarianism to be assessed? Some interpreters, dismissing them as more apparent than real (e.g., Fee 1977:146–47) or explaining them as due to the fact that the OT influenced Paul just as it did the Jewish community at Qumran (e.g., Barrett, 197), deny that they preclude Pauline authorship of the passage. Others, impressed with the cumulative force of the evidence, think they do (e.g., Grossouw 1951, Gnilka 1968a, Fitzmyer 1974a:205–17), and describe the passage variously as "a Christian exhortation in the Essene [i.e., Qumran] tradition" (Gnilka 1968a:66) or as "a Christian reworking of an Essene paragraph" (Fitzmyer 1974a:217). Still others suggest that the passage represents Paul's own citation of previously formulated material, perhaps taken over directly from Qumran (e.g., Kuhn 1951:74–75) but in any case adapted by Paul for use in the present context of a letter to the Corinthians (e.g., Dahl [tentatively] 1977:68–69).

4. *Pauline features*. Many interpreters believe that certain features in 6: 14–7:1 are genuinely Pauline, and that these guarantee that the apostle is in some way responsible for its content. Fee (1977:147) provides a list of thirteen of these, most of which are words and phrases *(Do not get, unbelievers, living God, says the Lord, Therefore, having these, promises, beloved, making . . . perfect, holiness, in the fear of God)* or rhetorical devices (rhetorical questions, composite OT quotations) found elsewhere, and in a few cases exclusively or mainly in the Pauline letters. Fee also notes that the idea of the church as *God's temple* is Pauline, and that the contrasts *righteousness/lawlessness* and *light/ darkness* are present elsewhere in the apostle's letters. Lambrecht, too, believes the non-Pauline elements in the passage have been overemphasized and some genuinely Pauline features overlooked. Among the latter he notes in particular "the very Pauline 'already–not yet' tension, the presence of both the indicative and imperative" (1978:159). Moreover, Lambrecht (ibid.:159–60) thinks it is unfair to contrast the concern for moral righteousness evident in 6:14–7:1 with Paul's teaching about justification by faith. On the one hand, Paul, too, was concerned for doing good works (e.g., Gal 6:10); on the other hand, one must not expect theological reflection in "a piece of 'common' parenesis" like that in the present passage.

The Pauline authorship of 6:14–7:1 is also defended on the grounds that the content of the passage is integrally related to the situation Paul faced in Corinth. Some (e.g., Strachan, xv, 3–6; Schmithals 1971:94–95 and 1973: 283–84; Hurd 1965:235–37) find its teaching in accord with what, by Paul's own testimony in 1 Cor 5:9–11, had once been written to Corinth about not consorting with immoral people. Fee believes the concerns expressed in 6: 14–7:1 are congruent with those of 1 Cor 10:14ff., where Paul prohibits believers from eating in pagan temples (1977, especially 148–61), and he finds that prohibition restated here. Barrett, 196–97, who interprets 6:14–7:1 in more general terms, cites both 1 Cor 6:18 and 1 Cor 10:14 in defense of its authenticity, while Thrall (1977:144–48) concentrates on points which seem to join the passage closely to its context and thus to guarantee its Pauline origin (e.g., the concern for involvement with *unbelievers*, Satan, and *darkness*, cf. 4:3–6).

*Place in the Context*

Moffatt (1918:125) refers to 6:14–7:1 as standing "like an erratic boulder" in its present location, and all interpreters are agreed that its relationship to the context in 2 Cor is problematic. For one thing, the appeal to the Corinthians in 6:11–13 to open their hearts is specifically continued only in 7:2–3 (or 4), making 6:14–7:1 seem like a digression. For another, while the topic in the context—indeed in the whole letter—is the relationship of the Corinthian

Christians to the Pauline apostolate, the topic of 6:14–7:1 is clearly and emphatically the relationship of believers to unbelievers. To some, therefore, the passage is best explained as an interpolation, even though there is no textual evidence that 2 Cor ever existed without it. Others, however, think this hypothesis is unwarranted, and believe there are enough points of contact between these verses and their context to permit the conclusion that they are in their original position. A third view, that they belong to this context but have been dislocated from their original position following 6:2 (so Windisch, 220, who thinks there was probably an intervening transitional phrase), has had few supporters; 6:3–10 is closely related to 6:1–2, and the theory requires the conjecture that yet a second transitional phrase has fallen out between 7:1 and 6:3 (ibid., 202–3). Collange, 302–17, also believes that 6:14–7:1 once followed 6:2, but only as an alternate ending (with 7:2–4) in the "second edition" of a letter which in its "first edition" ended with 6:3–13 (plus, perhaps, chap. 8; ibid., 300). But this hypothesis is built on another, and highly unlikely, hypothesis—that 2:14–7:14 represents a letter distinct from that in 1:1–2:13; 7:5–16, and it raises many more questions than it answers.

1. *Interpolation theories.* These theories are of two types: (a) those which attribute the fragment to Paul, and (b) those which do not.

(a) A Pauline fragment. In 1 Cor 5:9–11, Paul refers to a previous letter of his to the Corinthians in which he had charged them "not to associate with immoral people" (v. 9). The Corinthians had understood Paul to mean that they should separate themselves from pagans in general, but in 1 Cor the apostle calls that a misunderstanding. He had meant, rather, that believers should separate themselves from any members of their own Christian community who are found guilty of immorality, etc. (v. 11). Otherwise, he acknowledges, the Corinthians would indeed have "to go out of the world" (v. 10, *RSV*), as some of the Corinthians must have been protesting. Over the years, many scholars have argued that 2 Cor 6:14–7:1 is part of that "previous letter" to which Paul refers (e.g., among the commentators, Strachan, xv, 3–6). In the view of Schmithals (who draws on various passages from both 1 and 2 Cor to reconstruct a series of letters to Corinth), not only 2 Cor 6:14–7:1, but also 1 Cor 6:1–20; 9:24–10:22; 15:1–58, and 16:13–24 belonged to that letter (1973: 282–86). Hurd, too, believes 2 Cor 6:14–7:1 was part of the previous letter, and that what had been said there about separating from unbelievers and avoiding any kind of idolatry would explain why Paul must deal with the kind of misunderstandings addressed in 1 Cor—e.g., in 5:9–11; 7:12–16; chap. 8 (1965:235–39). However, if 2 Cor 6:14–7:1 is of Pauline composition, as this theory holds, it is difficult to believe that the references to *unbeliever(s)* were meant to be references to immoral Christians, as this theory must presume. Everywhere else in the Pauline letters, "unbelievers" means non-Christians. Furthermore, the one thing certainly known about the "previous letter" is that it prohibited association with sexually immoral people (*pornoi,* 1 Cor

5:9, 10), whereas sexual vices are not specifically mentioned in 2 Cor 6:14–7:1.

(b) A non-Pauline fragment. Under this heading one may include Betz's view that the passage is specifically anti-Pauline (1973), as well as the more common view that it reflects un-Pauline concerns and concepts (e.g., Wendland, 212–14; Bultmann, 169; Bornkamm 1971:187; and Grossouw 1951, Gnilka 1968a, and Fitzmyer 1974a:204–17). Proponents of this theory believe that it alone is sufficient to explain the many non-Pauline features of the passage. Their chief problem is to explain how and why this un- or even anti-Pauline material came to be incorporated in a letter circulated under the apostle's name. Proponents of these theories have generally despaired of finding an explanation, and respond only with such comments as "difficult to answer" (Bornkamm 1971:193 n. 3), "not clear" (Gnilka 1968a:67), "remains unsolved" (Fitzmyer 1974a:217), and "for reasons unknown" (Betz 1973:108). A possible motive for the interpolation at this point has been suggested by Jewett, who nevertheless thinks the authenticity of the passage is still an open question (1978:433 n. 4, in contrast to his earlier view that 2 Cor 6:14–7:1 was part of Paul's first letter to Corinth, 1971:184–86). He suggests that, since Paul's letters were presumably edited when competing Christian groups were trading charges of heresy, the insertion of 6:14–7:1 (whether Pauline or not) would have served to limit the scope of the tolerance apparently called for in 6:11–13 (1978:395; cf. Schmithals 1971:95). This is a plausible suggestion, but one must still ask why a redactor would have placed the material before the point at which the appeal of 6:13 was actually concluded. If the motive was to qualify or clarify the appeal, would not the interpolation have been effected after 7:3, or at least after 7:2a?

2. *Defenses of integrity.* As in the case of interpolation theories, defenses of the integrity of 6:14–7:1 within 2 Cor are of two kinds: (a) those which argue that the fragment is essentially Pauline, and (b) those which treat it as essentially non-Pauline traditional material used by the apostle.

(a) Pauline, and in place. Most recent commentators believe that 6:14–7:1 is a fully integral part of 2 Cor 6–7 and may be regarded as essentially Pauline in origin (e.g., Héring, 49–52; Allo, 189–93; Hughes, 241–44; Prümm I, 379–81; Bruce, 213–16; de Boor, 157–63; Barrett, 192–203). Having argued that the evidence against Pauline authorship is at best inconclusive, these commentators proceed to point out ways in which the material seems to be related to its context, and to offer explanations for Paul's writing just this way at this point in his letter. Two explanations are fairly typical: (1) Paul must repeatedly warn the Corinthians about compromising with the world, and this seems to be a good place for that, since it is "cushioned" by expressions of his love in 6:11–13; 7:2–4 (Hughes, 244); (2) Paul interposes the admonitions here to warn his readers that his affection for them does not mean he will be tolerant of their consorting with those who would turn them to a different gospel (e.g., Barrett, 194). Derrett's view is distinctive, for he regards 6:14ff. as more of a positive reinforcement of Paul's plea that the Corinthians become his trusting partners: when others "are clearly of your faith," Paul means, "they both should be and must be partners" (1978:247). Derrett also offers the distinctive suggestion that Paul "has simply adapted to his present purpose a 'purple passage' which could conceivably have originated as a sermon—perhaps his own—on a theme which *is* much to his present purpose" (ibid.:233).

Others are less hesitant to call 6:14–7:1 an "interruption" of the thought in chaps. 6–7, even though they attribute this to the apostle himself. Thus, Lambrecht cautions that the possibility of a logical connection between 6:14–7:1 and its context is not sufficient evidence for integrity (1978:152). He finds better evidence for it in 7:2–4, where, in his opinion, Paul himself seems to be aware of his digression and self-consciously resumes the thought of 6:11–13 (ibid.). Fee also describes 6:14–7:1 as an interruption of the appeal in 6:13 (1977:155), and 7:2a as a resumption of that appeal (ibid.:161). According to him, the intervening passage is better explained by the argument in 1 Cor 10 than by anything in 2 Cor. He argues that the apostle's prohibition of Christian participation in pagan temple meals (1 Cor 10:14–22) has been rejected by some Corinthians as Paul's attempt to impose himself upon them (ibid.:143–44, 155). Now, in 2 Cor 6:1–3, 11–13, Paul addresses himself to that matter by affirming his love and asking for theirs in return (ibid.:155). Then in 6:14 "he interrupts the appeal, not simply to reiterate the prohibition but to reinforce the reasons for it in a more positive way" (ibid.).

Finally, in the opinion of Thrall, the real digression comes not in 6:14–7:1 but in the preceding passage, 6:3–13 (1977:144). She argues that 6:14 resumes 6:1–2 by supplying the kind of concrete exhortation "which logically should have followed immediately" (ibid.). Beyond this, in her view, there are a number of specific "points of connection" between 6:14–7:1 and earlier sections of the letter (ibid.:144–47)—even though, in 6:16c–18, Paul seems to have made use of "an existing catena of scriptural allusions" (ibid.:148).

(b) Non-Pauline, but in place. Some hold that, while the material in 6:14–7:1 is non-Pauline in origin, the apostle himself is responsible for having taken it over and used it in this context. This theory must be distinguished from those which, like Thrall's above-mentioned, regard the passage as essentially Pauline, even though it makes use of a previously formulated collection of scriptural citations. Proponents of this view think only of Pauline redaction, not of Pauline composition, and they stress the un-Pauline features which are present throughout the passage. Collange (316–17) may perhaps be regarded as one representative of this viewpoint, because he refers to Paul's use of a "pre-existing Jewish-Christian document" employed by the apostle in the hypothetical "second edition" of his letter, 2:14–6:2 + 6:14–7:4. But the possibility of Paul's use of traditional material has been discussed most fully by Dahl (1977), who on the one hand is impressed by the many affinities between 2 Cor 6:14–7:1 and the Qumran texts, and, on the other, is impressed by the way in which the verses in question seem to serve Paul's concerns in the context of 2 Cor. Dahl agrees that the outlook of 6:14–7:1 is in itself un-Pauline, but he also believes that when it is read as part of Paul's argument in 2 Cor it can be understood well enough as supporting the apostle's concerns: *Do not get misyoked with unbelievers* (6:14a) becomes a call to the Corinthians to resist involvement with Paul's opponents (1977:65), and the entreaty to cleanse themselves from every *defilement* and to seek perfect *holiness* (7:1) becomes an appeal to show the same kind of "integrity and sincerity" toward Paul that he has shown toward them (ibid.:67). This interpretation has been adopted by Olson (1976:190), but Dahl himself regards it more tentatively. Commenting on the lack of specific links between this passage and its context, and on the absence of "any full analogy" to the testimonia collection elsewhere in Paul's letters, he declines to rule out the possibility that 6:14–7:1 is a post-Pauline interpolation (1977:69).

### Concluding Observations

The origin of 6:14–7:1, its place in the context, and therefore its meaning remain unclear. There is distressingly little hard evidence pertinent to the critical questions of authenticity and integrity, and a great deal of the scholarly discussion has been in effect a sharing of opinions and a trading of conjectures. This is especially true of attempts to trace logical connections between the content of the passage and its context in 2 Cor, all of which must necessarily fall short of actually "proving" the case for integrity. On the one hand, the context exhibits nothing resembling the concern for avoiding pagan idolatries and impurities present in 6:14–7:1. And, on the other hand, the *unbeliever(s)* mentioned in 6:14a, 15 can hardly be Paul's rivals, about whom there is a manifest concern in the context. Elsewhere in Paul's letters, even in this one, *unbelievers* are non-Christians, and it is just as unlikely that Paul would have left the term unaltered in some cited material as that he himself would have used it just this once for errant Christians. The attempt to interpret this passage in the light of the prohibition against dining in a pagan temple (1 Cor 10) is also unpersuasive. The evidence is at best circumstantial, and again there is nothing in the context of 2 Cor which suggests that kind of concern here.

At the same time, one must acknowledge that there are important reasons for questioning the Pauline origin of 6:14–7:1. It is not just a matter of several non-Pauline words, or the form and content of the citations from scripture. In themselves, these things are not decisive. What must be taken seriously is the clustering of so many non-Pauline features in these few verses, the fact that so many of the ideas, including the most fundamental appeals, of the passage are not easily attributable to the apostle, and the many general and specific affinities between these verses and the Jewish sectarian texts from Qumran. Moreover, many of the elements cited in support of the authenticity of the passage are only superficially Pauline. For example, Paul does indeed use the plural "promises" elsewhere, but only five times (the singular, thirteen times), and ordinarily with specific reference to the promises given the patriarchs (certainly in Rom 15:8; Gal 3:16, probably in Rom 9:4; 3:21, perhaps in 2 Cor 1:20). Again, Paul does use the word *holiness* elsewhere, but only in two instances—one of them being a creedal formula (Rom 1:4). In the other, the word is used in a benedictory form (1 Thess 3:13); there, in contrast with 2 Cor 7:1, holiness is not a human achievement but God's gift. To cite just one more example, it is also misleading to claim that the expression *making . . . perfect* is a good Pauline concept. The word is indeed Pauline, but nowhere else is it used as it is here (see NOTES on 7:1).

The hypothesis which views 6:14–7:1 as part of the letter to Corinth mentioned in 1 Cor 5:9–11 is no longer as popular as it once was. In addition to the problems encountered by any hypothesis which attributes the passage to Paul, this one is encumbered by the fact that 1 Cor 5:9 is not a very good description of what actually stands in 2 Cor 6:14–7:1. Indeed, since an accidental intrusion of 6:14–7:1 into its present location is highly unlikely, and since there is no textual evidence that 2 Cor ever existed without the passage, all interpolation theories must suppose that the material was added deliberately to this position at the time the Corinthian correspondence was assembled for general circulation. But then the question becomes why the passage was placed just here, even if it was a genuine Pauline fragment. For those who regard the fragment as non-Pauline in origin, the question is rather more difficult; for those who describe it as anti-Pauline, the problem is almost insurmountable.

What evidence there is would seem to be best satisfied by the hypothesis that the passage is of non-Pauline composition, but was incorporated by the apostle himself as he wrote this letter. One might speak of a Pauline interpolation of non-Pauline material, perhaps drawn from Christian baptismal parenesis (Klinzing 1971:179–82). But if this were the case, could not one expect more adaptation and specific application of the material than seems to have taken place? (The few "Pauline traces" suggested by Klinzing [ibid.:182 n. 82] are not very convincing: *for we are,* v. 16*b* [cf. Phil 3:3; Gal 4:28; 5:5—but also 1 Pet 2:9; and for the change to the first person plural within a parenetic section, Rom 14:13; 15:1; 1 Cor 5:8; Gal 6:9], and *Therefore, having these promises,* 7:1.) For example, the Christ hymn of Phil 2:6–11 is not just inserted into the letter but carefully integrated into the argument and very specifically applied to the appeal the apostle is making (see Phil 1:27–2:5 and 2:12–18).

This passage therefore, remains an enigma within 2 Cor, neither its origin nor its place in the context being entirely clear. It may be integral to the context, but—if it has only been cited by Paul and not actually composed by him—it remains only marginally Pauline. And even if it is both integral to the context and of Pauline composition, it remains a secondary appeal, subordinate to the primary one which is introduced in 6:11–13 and then resumed and concluded in 7:2–3.

## 11. THE COLLECTION FOR JERUSALEM,
### 7:4–9:15

### a. PRELIMINARY ASSURANCES OF CONFIDENCE,
### 7:4–16

7 ⁴I feel I can speak quite candidly to you; I have much pride in you. I am filled with comfort, I am overcome with joy in every one of our afflictions. ⁵Indeed, when we came into Macedonia there was no relief for us. Instead, we were afflicted in every way, disputes without and fears within. ⁶But God, who comforts the downcast, comforted us with the coming of Titus; ⁷yet not only with his coming, but also with the comfort with which he was comforted about you, as he reported to us your longing, your sorrowing, your zeal for me, so that I rejoiced even more.

⁸Because even though I grieved you with that letter, I have no regrets. Even though I did have regrets (for I see that that letter grieved you, even if temporarily), ⁹now I rejoice—not because you were grieved, but because you were grieved to contrition. For you were grieved as God willed, that you might not sustain a loss in any way because of us. ¹⁰The grief that God wills brings about contrition that leads to salvation, unregretted; but grief of a worldly kind brings about death. ¹¹For see how much earnestness this grieving that God wills has brought about for you: such a concern to defend yourselves, such indignation, such alarm, such longing, such zeal, such reprisal! On every point you showed yourselves to be innocent in the matter. ¹²Thus, even though I wrote to you, it was neither because of the one who did the wrong, nor because of the one wronged, but in order that your earnestness for us might be disclosed to you in the sight of God. ¹³This is why we are comforted.

In addition to our own comfort, we rejoiced very much more at the joy of Titus, because his mind has been set at ease by all of you. ¹⁴For if I have been boasting some to him about you, I was not disgraced. On the contrary, just as everything we said to you was true, so too what we boasted to Titus has turned out to be true. ¹⁵And his feelings toward you are the more enlarged as he remembers the obedience of all of you, how with fear and trembling you received him. ¹⁶I rejoice, because I have every confidence in you.

## NOTES

7:4. *I feel I can speak quite candidly to you.* Or, more literally, "I have much candor toward you," where "candor" would stand for *parrēsia*, the freedom of speech one has when addressing those whom one trusts. Cf. 6:11, "Our mouths are open to you, Corinthians." In 3:12, where Paul was speaking of his apostolic service more generally, the same word is more properly translated as "boldness" (see note there). To illustrate the present usage, Windisch, 223, cites Philo, *Who Is the Heir* 6: "When, then, is it that the servant speaks frankly [*agei parrēsian*] to his master? Surely it is when his heart tells him that he has not wronged his owner, but that his words and deeds are all for that owner's benefit." See also Marrow 1982:445.

*I have much pride in you.* The same noun, *kauchēsis*, is also used of Paul's *pride* in the Corinthians in 1:12 (see note); 7:14; 8:24.

*I am filled with comfort.* The theme of *comfort* is prominent in 1:3–7 (see NOTES and COMMENT), where it is connected with a threat to his life Paul had experienced in Asia (1:8). Now the theme is prominent again as Paul writes of the *comfort* which attended his meeting with Titus in Macedonia; see also vv. 6, 7, 13.

*I am overcome with joy.* Elsewhere in this letter, in 2:3; 6:10, Paul writes of his *joy* (or rejoicing), but there is special emphasis on this in the present passage; see also vv. 7, 9, 13*b*.

*in every one of our afflictions.* The same phrase exactly as in 1:4, on which see the note. Here the first person plural (*our*) represents a break with the first person singular to which Paul had returned in v. 3.

5. *Indeed.* Here, as in 3:10 (on which see the note), *kai gar* introduces an explanation of what has just been said; in this case, an explanation of the reference to *our afflictions*, v. 4.

*when we came into Macedonia.* The first person plural is resumed (with few exceptions, it is predominant in 2:14–7:2) as the preceding reference to *our afflictions* is explained. One may presume (despite the first person singular in 2:13) that Paul was accompanied by others (e.g., Timothy, 1:1*a*) on his trip from Troas to *Macedonia* (cf. Windisch, 226). For *Macedonia* see note on 1:16.

*there was no relief for us.* Literally "Our flesh has had no relief," reading *eschēken* (perfect tense = "has had") with most witnesses. The comment has a close parallel in 2:13, but here the first person plural is used, and it is the "flesh" rather than the "spirit" that is said to have no relief. See note on the corresponding phrase in 2:13. As there, the perfect tense here should probably be interpreted as an aorist (so, e.g., Moule 1953:14), and some witnesses do in fact read the aorist form (P⁴⁶ B G K). Contrast Robertson (1923:897), who thinks the perfect is used to make the point more vividly.

*we were afflicted.* Translates the participle *thlibomenoi*. There is a kind of anacoluthon in the Greek sentence, since the participle is in the wrong case to continue the preceding construction. Paul's meaning is not in doubt, however. See BDF § 468(1); Moule 1953:179 (who calls this a Semitism); Robertson 1923:415, 439.

*in every way.* The sense of the phrase *(en panti)* is determined by what follows, in which two kinds of affliction are mentioned.

*disputes without.* The noun *machē* appears nowhere else in Paul's own letters, but elsewhere in the NT (2 Tim 2:23; Tit 3:9; Jas 4:1) it refers to "fighting" in the figurative sense ("quarrels") rather than to armed conflict (thus, not "persecution"—e.g., Denney, 252). The same is true in the LXX, the papyri, and the literature of Hellenistic Judaism in general (BAG s.v.). Cf. LXX Deut 32:25, quoted in the following note.

*fears within.* For the plural *fears,* unattested elsewhere in the NT, see LXX Job 20:25; Wis 18:17 (classical examples in BAG s.v.). Windisch, 226, suggests that this and the preceding phrase—*disputes without, fears within*—could be a play on LXX Deut 32:25, "Without, the sword shall make them childless [*exōthen ateknōsei autous machaira*], and from the inner chambers shall come fear [*kai ek tōn tamieiōn, phobos*]."

6. *God, who comforts the downcast.* Perhaps an allusion to LXX Isa 49:13, "God has had mercy on his people, and has comforted the lowly among his people [*kai tous tapeinous tou laou autou parekalesen*]"; cf. also Ps 118(119):50 (cited by Windisch, 227). There is a similar description of God in 1:3–4, on which see the NOTES. The *downcast* here are to be understood as those who, like Paul and his associates when they came into Macedonia, are beset by all kinds of difficulties and anxieties (v. 5); cf. Grundmann *TDNT* VIII:19.

*comforted us with the coming of Titus.* Paul writes much the same about the comfort which came to him with the arrival of Timothy (in Corinth), bearing good news about the congregation in Thessalonica (1 Thess 3:6–7). *Titus* has been mentioned once already in this letter, 2:13 (on which see NOTES and COMMENT).

7. *yet.* Translates *de,* which has a slightly adversative force here; what has just been written is now to be clarified lest it be misunderstood. The idiom, "(yet) not only . . . but also" *(ou monon [de] . . . alla kai)* is used frequently by Paul (elsewhere in 2 Cor: 8:10, 19, 21; 9:12).

*the comfort.* For Paul's use of this term *(paraklēsis),* and its special frequency in 2 Cor 1–9, see NOTES and COMMENT on 1:3–4.

*about you.* Translates *eph' hymin,* used (as in 1 Thess 3:7a) following *parakalein,* "to comfort," a verb of intense feeling (see BAG s.v. *epi,* II, by—although there the present instance is translated "among you," II, aδ).

*as he reported.* The present participle *(anangellōn)* describes what Titus did to convey his *comfort* to Paul, and the nominative case is thus to be explained as following an understood "and with which he comforted me" (Windisch, 228). Apart from its appearance in a quotation from Isa (Rom 15:21), the verb *anangellein* occurs nowhere else in the Pauline letters; note the use of *euangelizesthai,* "to bring good news," in 1 Thess 3:6.

*your . . . your . . . your.* Repeated for emphasis, perhaps to stress that previously the *longing,* etc., had all been on Paul's part (Denney, 252; Hughes, 267).

*longing.* The noun *(epipothēsis)* appears again in v. 11; for the word-group, of which Paul is fond, see the note on the verb in 5:2. The *hyper emou,* which stands only after *zeal* (see below), should also be understood here: *your longing for me;* here, probably (cf. 1 Thess 3:6) "to see me."

*sorrowing.* Understand, again, *for me* (see preceding note). *Odyrmos* occurs else-where in the NT only in Matt 2:18, in a quotation from Jer; one may also translate it as "lamentation."

*zeal for me.* Here Paul lapses back (see vv. 3–4) into the use of the first person singular, and this continues through v. 12. He mentions the Corinthians' *zeal* (for him) again in v. 11. Cf. 11:2, Paul's zeal for the Corinthians. The word is used interchange-ably with *spoudē (earnestness)* in this passage; for the latter see vv. 11, 12.

*even more.* For this use of the comparative, *mallon,* see BDF § 244(2). Cf. v. 13*b.*

8. *grieved.* The same verb *(lypein)* has been used earlier in the letter, but with different shades of meaning: in 6:10, of "sorrowing" in a quite general sense; in 2:2, of the shame the Corinthian Christians would have experienced had Paul not canceled a projected visit (see 2:1); in 2:5, of the grief caused to Paul and the whole congregation by someone in Corinth. Here it refers to the shame the Corinthian Christians had actually felt upon receipt of the tearful letter—which, Paul has said earlier (2:4), had not been sent in order to grieve them in that way.

*with that letter.* Literally "with the letter," but the reference is clearly to the one mentioned in 2:3–4, 9; cf. *hē epistolē ekeinē, that letter,* which stands in the parenthesis of the present verse.

*Even though I did have regrets.* RSV places this phrase in a parenthesis, but it is better to regard it as opening a new sentence, as most recent English versions do. The verb tense is imperfect *(metamelomēn);* Paul had had *regrets* over a period of time.

*(for I see . . .).* This tr. presumes the reading *blepō gar* favored by the majority of the editors of *GNT-*Nestle, although no great degree of certainty can be attached to it; see Metzger 1971:581. Hughes (269 n. 6) and *NEB* prefer the reading of P⁴⁶* (reflected also in several versions, including the Vulgate), *blepōn,* "seeing." Even before the discovery of P⁴⁶ this had been conjectured by Hort on the basis of the Vulgate, and adopted in Mof. (see Strachan, 126–27). Whichever of these readings is original, how-ever, the syntax of the verse remains difficult, whether because of Paul's own lapse as he dictated (Barrett, 208, attributes it to Paul's embarrassment about the earlier tearful letter) or because of some later disturbance of the text. The problems are best solved by regarding the phrase—from *for I see* through the end of the verse—as parenthetical (so, e.g., WH, *GNT-*Nestle, *ASV, NAB;* also Plummer, 220; Héring, 54; Hughes, 269 n. 6; cf. *NIV*). For a good analysis of Paul's evident intentions here, see Barrett, 209, who paraphrases accordingly.

*temporarily.* Literally "for an hour" *(pros hōran),* which can envision a period of either shorter (Gal 2:5) or longer (Phlm 15) duration (Plummer, 220).

9. *grieved.* As in v. 8.

*contrition.* Translates *metanoia,* which could also be rendered as "repentance." Paul uses the noun only here, in v. 10 and in Rom 2:4, and the cognate verb only in 12:21 (cf. the adjective, *ametanoētos,* "unrepentant," Rom 2:5). What the OT and Judaism mean by "repentance" is included in Paul's concept of "faith," a term he finds much more congenial to his theological point of view. In the present case *metanoia* refers to a genuine acknowledgment of wrongdoing, coupled with the humble resolve to change one's behavior.

*as God willed.* This tr. is an interpretation of the abbreviated Greek expression *kata Theon* ("according to God"), also used in vv. 10, 11 and in Rom 8:27 (elsewhere in the NT: Eph 4:24; 1 Pet 4:6; 5:2 [some witnesses]). The meaning suggested here also applies in 1 Pet 4:6; 4 Mac 15:3 and Philo, *On Flight and Finding* 76.

*that you might not sustain a loss in any way.* Héring, 55, suggests that the loss envisioned may be Paul's refusal to return to Corinth ever again, but *en mēdeni* (literally "in nothing"; here translated *in any way*) makes a more general reference probable.

*because of us.* Note the first-person-plural pronoun, despite the first-person-singular orientation of this section as a whole (vv. 8ff.).

10a. *that God wills. Kata Theon,* translated *as God willed* in v. 9 (on which see the note).

*brings about.* Translates *ergazetai,* much better attested than the alternative reading, *katergazetai,* which is easily enough explained as assimilation to the form used in vv. 10b, 11.

*contrition.* See note on the same word in v. 9.

*that leads to.* Translates *eis,* literally "for," "to," or "unto."

*salvation.* Elsewhere in this letter the word *sōtēria* appears only in 1:6; 6:2. Here, as in 1:6, it is used quite generally for the fullness of life (contrast *death,* v. 10b) promised to those who believe.

*unregretted.* Translates the adjective *ametamelētos,* cognate to the verb used twice in v. 8. Here, with the word *contrition,* it forms a striking oxymoron, a coupling of words which ordinarily do not go together (so Lietzmann, 132; Windisch, 232). Thus, as it were, "regrets with no regrets," which makes sense only because the "regrets" ( = *contrition*) lead on to *salvation* (cf. Hughes, 271–72 n. 11; Barrett, 211).

10b. *grief of a worldly kind.* Literally "of the world," as opposed to *the grief that God wills,* v. 10a..

*brings about.* In this case the verb is the compound *katergazetai* (contrast *ergazetai,* v. 10b), but no distinction in tr. is warranted—e.g., as if the compound form had a negative connotation; it is retained in v. 11 in a positive sense. The two forms are also used interchangeably by Paul in Rom 2:9–10.

11. *earnestness.* Members of this word-group (here the noun *spoudē;* Paul also uses the cognate verb, adverb, and adjective) occur eight times in chaps. 7–8 of this letter, more often than in all the other Pauline letters combined (five times; never in chaps. 10–13 or 1 Cor). In 8:8 the reference is to the *earnestness* of the Macedonians for the collection, and in 8:16–17, 22 it is to the *earnestness* that Titus and an unnamed brother manifest for the Corinthians. However, here and in v. 12 (and probably in 8:7) Paul is writing of the *earnestness* the Corinthians demonstrated to Titus during his recent visit, and specifically their concern to amend the wrong which had been committed. This word is very close in meaning to the word *zeal* which is also used in this verse.

*such.* In each instance this English word renders *alla,* which introduces additional points with special emphasis; see BDF § 448(6); *GNTG* III:330. Cf. 1 Cor 6:11 (cited by Hughes, 274 n. 14).

*a concern to defend yourselves.* The Greek is simply *apologian,* meaning a reasoned statement in defense of oneself (as, e.g., in 1 Cor 9:3; Phil 1:7, 16). Cf. the use of the cognate verb in 12:19.

*indignation.* This word *(aganaktēsis)* appears in the NT only here.

*alarm.* The word is *phobos,* "fear," which could be taken to mean either (a) dread of what Paul might do to discipline the congregation (so, e.g., Windisch, 235; Hughes, 274)—cf. 13:2; 1 Cor 4:21—or (b), less likely, the fear of God's judgment (so Héring, 55). However, Paul's reference, perhaps less specific than either of these, is rather to a general state of apprehension (cf. *NEB*) and nervous concern.

*longing . . . zeal.* Both these words had been used in v. 7, and here, as there, they seem to refer to the *longing* and *zeal* of the Corinthians for Paul; here, perhaps, to please him by being responsive to his concerns. (P⁴⁶ and ℵ* read *epipothian* instead of *epipothēsin,* but this does not affect the tr. *longing.*)

*reprisal.* In the scriptural quotation presented in Rom 12:19 the same word *(ekdikēsis)* is used of the "vengeance" *(RSV)* with which God "repays" evil doers, and "retribution" is often its meaning in legal texts. Here it is used, like *epitimia* ("punishment") in 2:6 (on which see the note), of the action taken by the Corinthian congregation against a specific offender.

*On every point.* Or "in every way" *(en panti).*

*you showed.* The same verb is properly translated "to recommend" in 3:1; 4:2; 5:12; 6:4 (as well as in 10:12, 18; 12:11), but here it is used with reference to what has been convincingly demonstrated (*RSV:* "proved"). The aorist is used because this demonstration took place on the occasion of Titus' recent visit to Corinth (Barrett 1970a:153, 154).

*innocent.* In the context of 11:2 this same adjective *(hagnos)* describes the chastity of a bride, but here it has a more general (and probably legal) meaning: *innocent* of alleged wrong.

*in the matter.* The best-attested reading has only *tō pragmati* (omitting *en,* "in"), "with respect to the matter." This very non-specific reference to *the matter* in question perhaps reflects Paul's own eagerness to put it behind him (cf. Plummer, 223). In 1 Cor 6:1, *pragma* has a clearly technical meaning (a "legal case"). In the present verse it is more general, though less so than in Rom 16:2 ("undertaking"), for it still has a quasi-legal connotation. The exact reference of the word in 1 Thess 4:6 is disputed.

12. *Thus.* Translates *ara,* which Webber (1970:231) would connect more with vv. 5–7 than with vv. 8–11. But see COMMENT.

*even though I wrote to you.* Cf. v. 8, *even though I grieved you with that letter,* and 2:3, 4, 9.

*neither because of . . . nor because of.* Here *heneken* followed by the genitive is equivalent to *dia* with the accusative ("on account of"). Plummer, 224, rightly observes that one should interpret the negatives according to Hebraic modes of expression— thus, "*less* because of" rather than "*not* because of."

*the one who did the wrong.* Clearly the same person mentioned in 2:5–8, but still left unnamed. The use of the masculine gender here *(ho adikēsas)* and in chap. 2 indicates only that the wrongdoer was male. See COMMENT for remarks on his identity and the offense.

*the one wronged.* In 2:5, Paul had stressed that the whole Corinthian congregation had been harmed by the offense in question, but here he acknowledges that one specific individual was the focus of it. Most commentators have identified this chief victim as the apostle himself, although some (e.g., Kümmel, 206, against Lietzmann, 133) believe that the wording of 2:5 ("not to me") excludes that. The sense of 2:5, however, is probably "not *only* to me" (see NOTES and COMMENT there), and the main point is that the whole congregation has been affected by the injury, whether the offense had been directed against Paul or against one of his associates.

*in order that.* This meaning is already conveyed by the genitive of the articular infinitive, *tou phanerōthēnai (in order that . . . might be revealed),* and the preceding *heneken* is really superfluous, although there are other instances of this redundant usage (e.g., 1 Esdr 8:21); see BDF §§ 216(1) and 403; Moule 1953:83, 140.

*earnestness for us.* Paul drifts from the first person singular to the first person plural. Cf. the shift in the opposite direction in v. 7, *your zeal for me. Zeal* (see NOTES for v. 7) and *earnestness* (see NOTES for v. 11) are used interchangeably in this passage.

*disclosed to you.* The same verb *(phaneroun)* is translated as "show" in 3:3. Here as there it is used with reference to what the Corinthian congregation manifests about itself (and also, here, to itself) in its behavior and attitude (especially toward the Pauline apostolate).

*in the sight of God.* See note on the same phrase in 4:2. It reminds the readers that they are accountable to God for all their actions and attitudes.

13a. *we are comforted.* The first person plural carries forward the *for us* in v. 12 (on which see the note), and is sustained through chap. 8 with only a few exceptions (in 7:14, 16; 8:3, 8, 10, 23).

13b. *our own comfort.* Cf. v. 4, *I am filled with comfort.*

*very much more.* Translates *perissoterōs mallon,* a strengthened comparative; BDF §§ 60(3) and 246. Cf. v. 7, *so that I rejoiced even more.*

*the joy of Titus.* Cf. the reference to Titus' *comfort,* v. 7.

*his mind.* Literally "his spirit" *(to pneuma autou).* Cf. 2:13, where, however, the word *pneuma* has been left untranslated (see note there).

*has been set at ease.* Cf. 1 Cor 16:18, where Paul testifies that his own mind had been *set at ease (RSV:* his "spirit" had been "refreshed") by a delegation from the Corinthian church. In Phlm 7, as here, the "refreshing" of someone by another (or others) is mentioned as the basis for joy and comfort.

*by all of you.* Paul could have written simply "by you" *(apo hymōn),* so the *all (apo pantōn hymōn)* seems deliberate. Cf. v. 15 and COMMENT.

14. *I have been boasting . . . about you.* Note the temporary reversion to the use of the first person singular. The verb is perfect tense *(kechauchēmai);* Paul continues to boast about the Corinthian Christians. Cf. v. 4, with the note there about Paul's *pride* in the Corinthians, and see 8:1-5 for an example of how Paul boasts about his congregations (there, the churches in Macedonia).

*some.* Literally "something" *(ti).*

*I was not disgraced.* Or, "I was not caused to be ashamed" *(ou kateschynthēn);* that is, Paul's *boasting* to Titus had not been unwarranted.

*everything we said to you was true.* Paul returns to the first person plural. Does the aorist *(elalēsamen, we said)* mean that Paul is thinking of some special occasion, a past letter or visit? The problem would be solved by reading "always" *(pantote)* instead of *everything (panta),* but only late witnesses attest the former (C F G et al.), and it is certainly an attempt to make sense of the aorist. Could this be an "epistolary aorist," referring to what is said in this letter (cf. 1:12-14; 4:2)?

*what we boasted.* Or "our boast(ing)" *(hē kauchēsis hemōn);* the same noun is translated *pride* in v. 4.

*has turned out to be true.* That is, Titus himself experienced the truth of it on his recent visit in Corinth; it "became true" *(alētheia egenēthē)* for him.

15. *his feelings.* As in 6:12, *feelings (ta splanchna)* of affection.

*the more enlarged.* Translates *perissoterōs,* which has an elative meaning here, as in 1:12; 2:4 (see NOTES for each). *Enlarged* is supplied in English to convey the sense required by the context.

*the obedience of all of you.* Paul's tearful letter had been written out of a concern for the *obedience* of the congregation (2:9, and NOTES). As in v. 13, *all of you* indicates that Titus had perceived the congregation as a whole to be obedient, with no notable exceptions (cf. Barrett, 215).

*with fear and trembling.* Paul uses the same phrase *(meta phobou kai tromou)* to describe his own "nervous anxiety to do his duty" (Plummer, 228) on the occasion of his original mission to Corinth (1 Cor 2:3). In Phil 2:12 he applies it to the Philippians as he admonishes them to work for their salvation with knowledge that it is God's gift (Phil 2:13). See also Eph 6:5, describing the way in which slaves should devote themselves to the service of their masters. The phrase derives from the LXX, where it usually refers to the "terror and dread" which is felt when an opponent threatens hostile action (Exod 15:16; Deut 2:25; 11:25; Jdt 2:28; 15:2; Isa 19:16; 4 Mac 4:10), hence (as in Ps 54[55]:5) to anxiety about one's death.

16. *I have every confidence.* Translates *en panti tharrō;* for the verb, see note on 5:6.


## COMMENT: GENERAL

The virtually unanimous opinion of interpreters is that 7:4 should be read as the concluding sentence of the preceding section, 2:14ff., whether that be regarded as Paul's own long digression (e.g., Plummer, 217; Barrett, 206) or as part of a different Pauline letter later interpolated there (e.g., Bornkamm 1971; Bultmann, 180). On this view, 7:5 is regarded as either the resumption or a continuation of the "travel narrative" broken off after 2:13. Thus Windisch, 224, lists six points at which 7:5–16 provides the necessary completion of what had been started in 2:12–13: how Paul and Titus met, what news Titus brought, how the congregation in Corinth had responded to Paul's tearful letter, etc. It is perfectly true that 7:5–16 helps to provide the modern reader with additional important information about such matters; but for the original readers, already aware of the essential points, 7:5–16 would have had a different function. For them the most significant "information" in these verses would not have been—what they already knew well—the effect of the tearful letter and how they had received Paul's emissary, Titus. It would have been Titus' interpretation of what he had found in Corinth and Paul's response to that. Thus, just as 2:12–13 has its own function in the section 1:12–2:13, so 7:5–16 has its own function in the section of appeals which opens in 5:20. In 2:12–13, Paul has concluded his assurances of concern for the Corinthians by indicating why the present letter is being written from Macedonia, when the Corinthians had been led to expect he would be visiting them again soon (see COMMENT on 2:12–13). In 7:5–16 he is supporting his present appeals by writing of his joy and of the confidence he has in his Corinthian congregation.

If, then, 7:5ff. is not to be regarded as either continuing or resuming a "travel narrative" broken off with 2:13, one is free to reassess the relationship between 7:4 and 7:5ff. As shown below, 7:4 reads almost like the topic sentence of what follows, for there—as v. 4 suggests—Paul will indeed *speak quite candidly* to his congregation, even as he explains why he is proud, comforted, and joyful at the news of them he has received from Titus (see also Thrall 1982:109–10). These are the main themes in 7:5ff., and they are summed up in v. 16: *I rejoice, because I have every confidence in you.* For this reason, it is better to begin a new paragraph with v. 4 rather than with v. 5. (So also Olson [1976:191–200], who nevertheless continues to think of v. 5 as returning to a narrative broken off in 2:13.)

This passage, 7:4–16, stands within the long section of appeals, 5:20–9:15, and directly follows those of 6:11–7:3, which urge the Corinthians to be reconciled with Paul and his associates. In part, these paragraphs reinforce the preceding ones by continuing the emphasis on the affection Paul feels for his congregation. More significantly, however, they look ahead to and prepare for the appeals of chaps. 8–9, in particular the appeal to complete the collection for Jerusalem (8:6–7). Olson has made an impressive case for the view that chaps. 1–7 are in their entirety an "apologetic introduction" to the collection appeal (1976:207); but, even if one is not prepared to go that far, 7:4–16 does seem to have an introductory function (cf. also Webber 1970:233). In conformity with a familiar Hellenistic literary pattern, Paul emphasizes his confidence in those of whom he is about to make a substantial request. Dio Chrysostom's appeal to the Apamaeans is typical of this style (*Discourses* XLI), and so is the appeal of Nicocles to the Cyprians (as composed by Isocrates, *Nicocles*). In the latter the movement from the introductory statements to the appeal proper is particularly well marked: "But the reason why I have spoken at some length both about myself and the other subjects which I have discussed is that I might leave you no excuse for not doing willingly and zealously whatever I counsel and command" (*Nicocles* 47).

The material framed by the opening and closing expressions of confidence (vv. 4 and 16) may be divided into three sub-sections, in each of which Paul writes of the great joy he has as he thinks of his congregation in Corinth. In vv. 5–7, focusing on Titus' arrival from Corinth, the apostle writes of the joy generated by the news Titus brought from there. In vv. 8–13*a*, Paul returns to the subject of the tearful letter (see NOTES and COMMENT on 2:3–11) and remarks on the joy he has in the knowledge that this letter has prompted the congregation to an act of contrition. And in vv. 13*b*–15 the apostle explains why the joy of Titus is itself a ground for his own rejoicing.

## COMMENT: DETAILED

### The Topic Sentence, v. 4

There are numerous and substantial verbal links between this verse and the remainder of the passage, and the juxtaposition of 7:4 with 7:5ff. can hardly be explained as due solely to the observations of a later redactor (so, e.g., Bultmann, 181). Paul's *pride* in the Corinthians is stressed again in v. 14 (his "boasting" to Titus), *comfort* is mentioned also in vv. 6, 7, 13, *joy* in vv. 7, 9, 13, 16, and the *afflictions* alluded to at the end of v. 4 are specified in v. 5 (see Lietzmann, 131; Webber 1970:228). Moreover, the *candor* with which Paul feels he can speak to the congregation (v. 4) is exhibited when in vv. 8ff. he takes up the touchy subject of the tearful letter. The apostle has been emboldened to such candor, doubtless, because of his confidence in the complete integrity of his ministry in Corinth. He has expressed this repeatedly in the letter (e.g., 1:18; 2:17; 4:2), most recently in 7:2*b;* his conscience is clear toward those whom he addresses (Windisch, 223). Cf. the quotation from Philo given in the NOTES. Therefore, while this sentence also follows meaningfully on vv. 2*b*–3, where Paul has stressed the closeness he feels to his congregation, it expresses that closeness in terms which are only explained in vv. 5ff.: *pride, comfort,* and *joy in . . . afflictions.*

### Joy at the News from Titus, vv. 5–7

The subject of these verses is not Paul's coming into Macedonia or his meeting there with Titus after the latter's arrival. The subject is, rather, the generally comforting news Titus brought from Corinth and Paul's rejoicing in that. This emphasis is obscured when v. 5 is interpreted as resuming (or continuing, if 2:14–7:4 be regarded as an interpolation) the "travel narrative" of 2:12–13. In fact, v. 5 does not attach particularly well to 2:12–13, as various interpreters have noted. (a) In 2:12–13, Paul is using the first person singular; here, the first person plural. (b) In 2:12–13, Paul remarks that his "spirit" (*RSV:* "mind") had no rest, but here he uses the word "flesh" (see NOTES). (c) In 2:12–13, Troas is the site of the restlessness, but here it is Macedonia. (d) In 2:12–13, Macedonia is the place where Paul goes to look for Titus, but here it is mentioned first of all as the place where the apostle encountered further afflictions (cf. Webber 1970: 228; Olson 1976:194).

To which Macedonian city Paul came he does not say. There were certainly Pauline congregations in Philippi and Thessalonica, and probably one in Beroea as well (see NOTES on 1:16). En route from Troas he would have come first to Philippi, and it may well have been there that his meeting with Titus took place. If so, Philippi would be the city in which the present letter is being written, for this account of that meeting reads as if the reunion has just occurred. If the place of writing is Philippi—and the point must remain conjectural—then the *disputes* Paul says he encountered in Macedonia could be quarrels with those to whom he contemptuously refers in Phil 3 as "dogs" and "evil-workers" (v. 2, *RSV*). This possiblity is enhanced if, with many scholars, Phil (or this part of the present canonical letter) is dated to an Ephesian imprisonment prior to the writing of 2 Cor 7:5 (see COMMENT on 1:8–11). However, the possibility that the *disputes* mentioned had been with non-Christian adversaries cannot be ruled out. Nor can the nature of Paul's inward *fears* be identified with confidence: that they were "states of depression, perhaps caused by illness" (Héring, 54) is much too conjectural; that they were *fears* about Titus' reception in Corinth (and perhaps his safety on the return journey) is very likely, given the remainder of this chapter (cf. Barrett, 207).

The apostle writes about his meeting with Titus (vv. 6–7) in much the same way he had written to the Thessalonians about Timothy's return with good news about their congregation (1 Thess 3:6–10; cf. also 1 Cor 16:17). In the present passage, however, something more specific is in view than the general "faith and love" for which the Thessalonian Christians had been commended (1 Thess 3:6; cf. vv. 7, 10). In the case of Titus' report, the apostle had hoped for news that the tearful letter (see comments on 2:3–11), written after his own "sorrowful visit" to Corinth (see comments on 1:15–2:2), had led to the disciplining of the individual who had "caused grief" both to Paul and to the congregation as a whole (2:5–6). This, apparently, is exactly what Titus has reported; in addition to the *longing* of the Corinthians to see Paul again, Titus has spoken of their *sorrowing* over what had happened previously and their *zeal* to make amends. The matter becomes clearer in the next paragraph as Paul refers directly to the letter which had brought this about.

### Joy at the Effect of an Earlier Letter, vv. 8–13a

In 2:3–11 (on which see NOTES and COMMENT) Paul has already mentioned an earlier letter written "out of an exceedingly troubled, anguished heart . . . , through many tears" (2:4). In the present verses that letter, as well as its occasion and effect, are referred to again. It had been occasioned by some grievous injury perpetrated, evidently against Paul himself, on the occasion of a visit the apostle subsequently described as "sorrowful" (see comments on 2:1). Unable or unwilling to return for another such visit, Paul wrote a letter instead (now lost), in which he apparently urged the congregation to consider the incident a blow to its own integrity, and to take appropriate action against the individual who had been at fault. One now learns (v. 8) that Paul was so uncertain about the effect his letter would have that he at first regretted having sent it. But with Titus' return Paul receives the good news that the letter has been successful: although it had initially grieved the congregation, their grief became *contrition* and their contrition found expression in decisive action against the wrongdoer (vv. 9–11).

The apostle's concern in chap. 2 (see especially 2:6–8, 10) had been to counsel the Corinthians that their punishment of the offending party must now be tempered with love and forgiveness. Paul's intention in the present passage, however, is not to give further advice about the handling of that case. His single purpose here is to emphasize how much he rejoices to learn that his letter has achieved its purpose. That purpose, evidently, had been to test the Corinthians' commitment to Paul's gospel and ministry by challenging them to take some appropriate action against the one who had injured him (see especially 2:9). They must have failed to do this at the time, thereby contributing to the injury and raising doubts in Paul's mind about their loyalty. It is probable that he had expressed these doubts in his tearful letter, even as he urged the Corinthians to demonstrate their support for him by punishing the offender. Paul is now relieved to hear that, as a result of his letter, the congregation experienced a divine grief, not *grief of a worldly kind* (v. 10; the distinction was perhaps proverbial: cf. 4 Mac 15:3; T Gad 5:7, and Windisch, 231–32), and was moved to action in support of its apostle.

Further comments on the congregation's response to Paul's tearful letter are provided in v. 11a. Their former indifference gave way to an *earnestness* to clear themselves of all charges, whether specific or implied, that the letter had contained. Paul seems to accept this eagerness as a sign that the congregation, however negligent it had been in punishing the offender, was not as such guilty of the offense. The *indignation* the letter had aroused was probably directed against the offender, although Hughes, 274 (following Chrysostom and others), suggests that it was with themselves for having permitted the offense to go unpunished. What Paul means in referring to their *alarm* is less clear—perhaps their well-founded fear of the consequences of continued indifference. He remarks also on their *longing* (to assure him in person of their concern?) and of their *zeal* (to carry out his instructions?), both terms repeated from v. 7. And finally (but hardly to minimize its significance; against Plummer, 223), he lists their *reprisal,* the "punishment" (2:6) they had laid upon the offender after receipt of the tearful letter. In all these ways, Paul concludes (v. 11b), the Corinthians have proved themselves to be *innocent in the matter.* He is satisfied with the evidence, all charges are dropped, and the case is now closed.

Paul's comments in vv. 8–11 have been in explanation of the great comfort and joy he experienced when Titus arrived with good news from Corinth (v. 7). Until then the apostle had been worried that his tearful letter might have offended his congregation to the point of alienating it from him. But now, having received a generally encouraging report from Titus, he knows that the letter has moved its recipients to an *earnestness* (v. 11) to right the wrong in which, if only by their initial indifference to it, they had become involved. This newly reported *earnestness* of the Corinthians is still the subject in v. 12, where the apostle explains that this was exactly the intention of his letter; it was written less for the benefit of either of the two individuals involved than for the benefit of the congregation. This is consistent with his earlier comments on the subject—in which he had expressed concern for the harm sustained by the Corinthian church as a whole (2:5) and had contended that his letter had been written to test the church's obedience (2:9). It is therefore quite understandable why v. 12 provides only passing references to the two individuals who had been involved in some kind of serious confrontation, describing them only as the *one who did the wrong* and *the one wronged.* It is probable that the latter is Paul himself, and that the confrontation had occurred during the brief emergency visit to Corinth which the apostle refers to as "sorrowful" in 2:1 (see, e.g., Barrett, 213–14 and 1970a); but it is just possible that it was Timothy, for whose reception in Corinth Paul had once expressed some anxiety (1 Cor 16:10–11).

Who the offending party was is much less clear. That it was the errant brother whose case was discussed in 1 Cor 5:1–5 (so, e.g., Hughes, 277) can be ruled out for the reasons already detailed (above, pp. 164–66), and because the present reference to *the one wronged* would then have to be to the man's father, who in fact is never mentioned in 1 Cor 5 (probably because he was already separated from his wife, or else deceased). What evidence there is points to someone who "had challenged the apostle's position, belittled his authority, and had thus both injured and insulted his person" (Barrett 1970a:155). Was this a member of the congregation itself, or someone from outside but closely enough associated with it to be subject to its discipline? Barrett, 212 and 1970a:155, believes the latter, arguing that this alone explains how the Corinthians could be at the same time *innocent in the matter* (v. 11; they themselves had not done the wrong) and contrite (vv. 9, 10; they had not, at first, taken up Paul's cause with enough zeal). But one could just as readily explain the simultaneous innocence and contrition of the congregation by its delay in taking disciplinary action against one of its own resident members, and the wording of Paul's counsels in 2:6–10 could even be interpreted as favoring this view. Moreover, Barrett's identification of the offender as the leader of Paul's opponents in Corinth rests to a considerable degree on his interpretation of several places in chaps. 10–13, where he believes Paul has one specific individual in mind but where it is more probable that the references are to his critics in general (see NOTES on 10:7, 10, 11; 11:4).

It is important to recall that earlier paragraphs in the present letter suggest that not all of the news Titus brought from Corinth was encouraging. At least some of the Christians there, upset that Paul had canceled a promised visit, perceive him as an opportunist and unconcerned about his congregation (see comments on 1:15–2:2), and must be raising questions about the propriety of his writing as he did in the so-called tearful letter (see comments on 2:3–11). Paul himself betrays a certain lingering self-consciousness about the letter, even as he writes here in vv. 8–12—perhaps too emphatically—about his motives for sending it and its beneficial results. This self-consciousness is apparent when Paul says that he no longer regrets the letter—although he once did; and that it had grieved the Corinthians—but only for a while. It is also apparent in how he says this: haltingly, repetitiously, and—not least remarkable—in the first person singular (vv. 8–12), as if to exempt his associates from any involvement. Only when he leaves the matter of the tearful letter behind in order to re-emphaize the comfort Titus' report has brought (v. 13*a*) does he return to the use of the first person plural.

### Joy at the Joy of Titus, vv. 13b–15

The first sentence in this paragraph (v. 13*b*) re-introduces a thought that is implicit but left undeveloped in v. 7: that Paul was comforted by the fact that Titus himself had been comforted in Corinth. Now this is put in terms of Titus' *joy,* and how that has caused Paul to rejoice, too. Significantly, the apostle uses the phrase *all of you* to describe the source of Titus' joy (see also v. 15); whatever questions and complaints continue to be raised about Paul in Corinth are not deemed to be serious, or representative even of a significant minority in the church there. Subsequent events (as reflected in Letter E, chaps. 10–13) will show that this was probably a false perception, whether due to Titus' overly optimistic report or to Paul's overly optimistic interpretation of that report.

In v. 14 (note the momentary lapse into the first person singular in v. 14*a*) Paul explains why he rejoices so in Titus' joy. Paul acknowledges that he had done some *boasting . . . to him* about the Corinthian church, and the apostle is relieved to learn now that he had not misled his emissary about what he would find there. From this comment one may deduce that (a) Titus had not been on any previous mission to Corinth for Paul, and (b) whatever the problems Paul knew about in the church there, he did not consider his own apostolic authority to be seriously threatened. Both these points are important arguments against the hypothesis that chaps. 10–13 antedate the present letter (see INTRODUCTION, p. 38), and the second point makes it extremely unlikely that Titus himself had been the bearer of the tearful letter. He had probably been sent with the hope—yet without full certainty—that the tearful letter had been well received, for it would appear from 8:6 that one or perhaps even "the main purpose" (Barrett, 215) of Titus' trip to Corinth was to organize the collection for Jerusalem, about which Paul had already given directions in an earlier letter (1 Cor 16:1–4; see Barrett 1969, especially 8–11). In any case, Paul's remarks in v. 14 certainly preclude the notion that Titus had been sent to deal with a church in open rebellion against its apostle.

Paul extends his point about Titus' joy when in v. 15 he mentions particularly *the obedience* which his emissary had found in Corinth. As in v. 13*b*, Paul presumes no significant exceptions; his reference is to *the obedience of all of* *you.* It is likely that Paul is referring primarily to Titus' discovery that the congregation had responded to the tearful letter by punishing the wrongdoer. This would have been just the proof of obedience Paul had sought in sending that letter (2:9); they have passed the test. But the *fear and trembling* with which they had *received* Titus would be further evidence of their obedience; newly sensitized to their responsibilities as a Pauline congregation, they had welcomed the apostle's emissary as one who came with authority.

### A Summary Statement, v. 16

In this final verse of the section, Paul reverts once again to the use of the first person singular, perhaps a sign of the intensity of his feeling: *I rejoice, because I have every confidence in you.*

On the one hand, this is an apt summary of the preceding verses. It sounds again the note of joy which has reverberated throughout the passage (vv. 4, 7, 9, 13*b*), and it reiterates Paul's pride and confidence in the Corinthian congregation, which has been the subject since v. 4. The Corinthians have proved their concern for Paul (vv. 7, 12), their innocence in the unpleasant business of Paul's confrontation with one particular detractor (v. 11*b*), and their continuing obedience to the apostle's instructions (v. 15). All of this is summarized in the simple but sweeping expression of confidence presented in v. 16—a statement, one may note, which could hardly have stood in the same letter with the worried polemic of chaps. 10–13 (contrast, e.g., 10:6, 9–10; 11:2–3; 12:11, 16, 20–21).

On the other hand, the statement of v. 16 serves as much more than a summary of vv. 4–15. It sharpens and focuses the point of those verses in such a way as to form a transition from those fervent expressions of pride and joy to the equally fervent appeal in chap. 8 (cf. Olson 1976:196). Titus is returning to Corinth (he is presumably the bearer of this letter) to complete the collection for Jerusalem which he had begun on his first visit (8:6), and Paul has *every confidence* that the same *earnestness* the Corinthians showed before (7:11, 12) will be in evidence again (see 8:7, where the excellence of their "earnestness" is specifically invoked to support the appeal). Here as elsewhere in his letters the apostle praises what his readers have already done only in order to encourage them to do still more (see, e.g., Phil 2:12–13; 1 Thess 4:9–12; Phlm 7, 20–21).

### b. THE APPEAL PROPER, 8:1–15

**8** ¹We would like to inform you, brothers and sisters, about the grace of God which has been granted to the churches of Macedonia, ²for during a severe testing by affliction their abundance of joy and their profound poverty have overflowed into the wealth of their generosity. ³For as they were able—I swear, even beyond what they were able—of their own accord, ⁴imploring us most urgently for the benefit of participation in the relief work for the saints, ⁵and not merely as we had expected, they gave themselves first to the Lord, also to us, by the will of God. ⁶In consideration of this, we have urged Titus that, as he had previously made a beginning, so he should complete among you this benevolence as well.

⁷Now as you excel in everything—in faith, in speech, in knowledge, in utmost earnestness, and in the love that we have for you—excel also in this benevolence. ⁸I do not say this as an order. Rather, by mentioning the earnestness of others, I intend to verify the reality of your love also. ⁹For you know the grace of our Lord Jesus Christ, that for your sake he became poor though he was rich, so that you, by means of his poverty, might become rich. ¹⁰And so I am giving my counsel in this matter; for this is in your interest, you who already made a beginning last year, not only in taking action but also in wanting to. ¹¹But now complete the task as well, so that your goodwill in wanting to may be matched by your completing it from what you have. ¹²For if goodwill is present, that is acceptable according to what one has, not according to what one has not.

¹³It is not that others should have relief and you a hard time; but rather, it is a matter of equality. ¹⁴Your surplus at the present time is for their need, that their surplus may be for your need, that there may be equality. ¹⁵As it is written, "He who gathered much had nothing extra, and he who gathered little had no shortage."

## NOTES

8:1. *We would like to inform you, brothers and sisters.* Similar expressions (but with the first person singular) occur in 1 Cor 15:1; Gal 1:11 (cf. 1 Cor 12:3), and an equivalent disclosure formula stands in the present letter in 1:8 (see NOTES there).

*brothers and sisters.* As in 1:8, on which see the note.

*the grace of God.* In 1:12, God's *grace* is associated with Paul's apostolic labors, and in 6:1 with the gospel generally. Here and in 9:14 it is associated with the willingness of his congregations (here, in Macedonia; 9:14, in Corinth) to contribute to a collection for Christians in Jerusalem. Note the other uses of the word *charis (grace)* in 8:4, 6, 7, 9, 16, 19; 9:8, 15.

*to the churches.* The Greek phrase *(en tais ekklēsiais)* could also be translated "among the churches" (Robertson 1923:587) or "within the churches" (*GNTG* III:264). However, it is sufficient to regard the preposition *en* as standing for the usual dative, as in 4:3; see BDF § 220(1).

*of Macedonia.* Elsewhere Paul refers to "the churches of Galatia" (1 Cor 16:1; Gal 1:2), "of Asia" (1 Cor 16:19), and "of [or: in] Judea" (Gal 1:22; 1 Thess 2:14). It is immaterial whether Paul is using the name *Macedonia* with reference to the Roman province (on which see NOTES for 1:16) or with reference to the original kingdom of Macedonia (so Plummer, 233; Strachan, 133). In either case, he must be thinking of the congregations he had established in Philippi, Thessalonica, and (probably) Beroea.

2. *during a severe testing by affliction.* More literally, "in a severe test of affliction." For the noun *dokimē (testing)* see NOTES on 2:9; it is used again in 9:13; 13:3. *Affliction* is often mentioned in chaps. 1–9 (see also v. 13 [*a hard time*]; 1:4–6, 8; 2:4; 4:8, 17; 6:4), but not in chaps. 10–13. Here the reference is to afflictions experienced by the Macedonian Christians (cf. Phil 1:29–30; 1 Thess 1:6; 2:14; 3:3–4).

*joy.* The theme has been prominent in this letter (e.g., 1:24; 2:3; 6:10), especially in chap. 7, vv. 4 (as here, joy in the midst of affliction), 7, 9, 13, 16.

*profound poverty.* More literally, "down-to-the-depth poverty" *(hē kata bathous ptōcheia).*

*poverty . . . wealth.* The idea of *poverty* overflowing into *wealth* yields an effective oxymoron (the combination of apparently contradictory words).

*of their generosity.* The genitive, *tēs haplotētos,* is epexegetical, describing the Macedonians' wealth as their generosity. The noun (*haplotēs;* translated as *candor* in 1:12) connotes a simplicity of purpose and action, absolute guilelessness; see Amstutz 1968:103–11, who argues for the tr. "sincerity" here and in the two occurrences in chap. 9 (vv. 11, 13). At the same time, one must acknowledge that in the context of chaps. 8 and 9 the word is tending toward the extended meaning of *generosity* (BAG s.v. 2; so *JB, NIV, NAB;* cf. *RSV:* "liberality"): an open-hearted—and open-handed—concern to do what is right.

3. *as they were able . . . even beyond what they were able.* The Greek is *kata dynamin . . . kai para dynamin,* with which Hughes, 290 n. 10, compares Rom 11:24, *kata physin . . . para physin,* "naturally . . . unnaturally," to illustrate the antithetical force. On the use of *para* here see BDF § 236(2).

*I swear.* Paul interrupts himself to attest the truth of what he is reporting, and for this the momentary reversion to the first person singular *(martyrō)* is appropriate. (The first person singular appears elsewhere in chap. 8 only in vv. 8, 10; cf. v. 23.)

*of their own accord.* In Greek just one word, *authairetoi,* which *GNT*-Nestle would associate with what follows in v. 4; thus, e.g., *TEV* and *NIV* begin a new sentence here (*TEV:* "Of their own free will they begged us . . ."). This is possible, but it is better to regard the word, with most recent English versions, as an independent element of the long, admittedly unwieldy sentence which runs from 8:3 through 8:6 (see NOTES below on *they gave,* 8:5, and *As a result,* 8:6). The adjective *authairetos* occurs again in 8:17 (of Titus), but nowhere else in the Greek Bible. (Examples from the papyri in MM s.v.) The adverb, *authairetōs,* is used in 2 Mac 6:19; 3 Mac 6:6; 7:10 to mean "voluntarily," and the adjective is used in a similar way. It is unclear how Héring, 59, can say that 8:3–4 "remind us that the collection had been made at Paul's request." The point is, rather, that in the case of the Macedonians a contribution had been made at their own initiative. There is thus no reason, either lexical or contextual, to interpret *authairetoi* here as meaning only "in good heart" *(de bon coeur)* or "without restraint" *(sans contrainte)* as Héring does.

4. *imploring us most urgently.* Literally "with much appealing, imploring us" *(meta pollēs paraklēseōs deomenoi hēmōn).* Moule (1953:179) mentions this as an instance where a participle *(deomenoi, imploring)* has been used in place of the more correct finite verb (thus, perhaps, "with much appealing they implored us"). But the participle can be understood just as well as dependent on the finite verb, *edōkan,* in 8:5 (see note there on *they gave).* There is an interesting parallel in T Job 11:2–3: "And there were certain others at that time without resources and unable to spend a thing. And they came urging me [*parakalountes*] and saying: We beg you [*deometha sou*], since we could also engage in this service [*diakonian*], but own nothing, show mercy on us and furnish us money so we may depart for distant cities and by engaging in trade we can do the poor a service [*tois penēsin dynēthōmen poiēsasthai diakonian*]" (Kraft 1974:32, 33).

*the benefit of participation.* The Greek construction involves hendiadys, the combining of two different nouns by a conjunction in order to express one complex thought: here *(tēn charin kai tēn koinōnian),* in order to avoid a piling-up of genitives *(tēn charin tēs koinōnias tēs diakonias tēs eis tous hagious).* See BDF § 442(16) for hendiadys in general, and Lietzmann, 133; Allo, 214; Hughes, 291–92 n. 11 for this particular instance.

*the benefit.* The same word *(charis)* used in 8:1 with reference to God's *grace.* But here (as in 1:15) it refers to something regarded as a "favor" *(RSV* and other versions) by those who seek it, almost in the sense of a "pleasure" (see LSJ s.v., III, IV, VI).

*participation.* Here and in 9:13 the word *koinōnia* is used in connection with the collection for Jerusalem. Elsewhere in Paul's letters (see note on "partners in the comfort," 1:7) it is used of the partnership of believers as they share together in the gospel, in Christ's sufferings, etc. In Rom 15:26, where Paul is also referring to the collection, it is properly translated as "contribution," though it retains there the connotation of something done out of a sense of partnership. Cf. the use of the cognate verb in Rom 15:27: the Gentiles are to "make some contribution" for the saints in Jerusalem because of the spiritual blessings the Jerusalem Christians have "shared" with them. In the present passage *koinōnia* has not yet become a technical term for the collection, as the addition of the phrase *in the ministry* shows; see McDermott 1975:222, and following note.

*the relief work.* The Greek word is *diakonia,* which in 3:7–9; 4:1; 5:18; 6:3 is best translated "ministry" (see NOTES for 3:7). But here and in 9:1, 12, 13; Rom 15:31; less certainly, 1 Cor 16:15, it is used specifically of Paul's collection for the church in Jerusalem; see also 8:19, 20; Rom 15:25, where the verb *(diakonein)* is employed in the same way. That Greek-speaking Judaism had come to use these words in a technical sense for supplying the needs of the poor is shown particularly well by T Job 11:1–3 (quoted in part, above, in the note on *imploring us most urgently);* 12:2; 15:1, 4, 8 (discussed by Berger 1977:189, 199–200). So also Acts 6:1.

*the saints.* Paul sometimes uses this term (literally "holy ones," *hoi hagioi)* of believers in general (e.g., Rom 8:27), more frequently of specific groups of believers, especially the members of the congregations to which he writes (e.g., Rom 1:7; 1 Cor

1:2; 2 Cor 1:1; Phil 1:1). But here and in 9:1, 12; Rom 15:25, 26, 31; 1 Cor 16:1 (perhaps in 1 Cor 16:15; cf. Rom 12:13), Paul means specifically the believers who are in Jerusalem. Note especially Rom 15:26, "For Macedonia and Achaia have been pleased to make some contribution for the poor among the saints [*eis tous ptōchous tōn hagiōn*] in Jerusalem." As Windisch, 246, notes, it is striking that in the present letter (in contrast to 1 Cor 16:1–4 and Rom 15:26–31) Paul does not once specifically name "Jerusalem" as the destination of the collection.

5. *not merely as we had expected.* More literally, "not as we had hoped," but the context shows that the Macedonians had done *more* than Paul could have hoped for. Here *elpizein* ("to hope") is equivalent to *prosdokan* ("to look for," "expect," etc.), as in Acts 3:5 (Windisch, 247).

*they gave themselves.* The verb has been anticipated since the beginning of the sentence, 8:3, but delayed until now as Paul's thoughts have piled up during the course of his dictation (cf. Plummer, 234; Hughes, 290). *Themselves* is emphatic *(heautous edōkan);* Plummer, 236.

*first to the Lord, also to us.* Here *the Lord* is Christ. P⁴⁶ and a few other texts read "God," perhaps in assimilation to the reference to God later in the verse. The Greek *(prōton tō Kyriō kai hēmin)* translates literally as "first to the Lord and to us." But the *prōton (first)* is to be construed only with *to the Lord,* distinguishing the self-giving to him as more important than the self-giving *to us* (there is no *epeita,* "then," following *first,* so sequence is not in mind). The ambiguity is avoided by reading *kai* as *also* rather than "and," or by changing the order of the words (e.g., *RSV*).

6. *In consideration of this.* For Paul's full use of *eis to* with an infinitive here, see BDF § 402(2); *GNTG* III:143.

*we have urged Titus.* The verb *parakalein* is used here, as in 2:8; 5:20; 6:1, for an earnest request. See also 8:17 (the cognate noun is used) and 12:18 (again the verb), the former certainly and the latter probably with reference to this same appeal. The mention of *Titus* (on whom see NOTES for 2:13) follows naturally on the discussion in 7:4–16 (see especially 7:6–7, 13*b*–15).

*he had previously made a beginning.* The verb (aorist of *proenarchesthai*) is found only here and in 8:10 (therefore the variant reading *enērxato,* "he had started it," in B and a few other texts). The use of it here clearly presumes that Titus has already been active in Corinth for the collection (not just in general); but it need not presume that Titus had been in Corinth on some occasion previous to the visit reported in 7:5–6. The contrast in Paul's mind is not between the visit from which Titus has just returned and a still earlier one (which seems precluded by 7:14; see NOTES and COMMENT), but between the visit from which Titus has just returned and the one he is making even as the Corinthians read this letter.

*so.* Translates *houtōs kai,* "thus also," but this would be slightly redundant (pleonastic) in English.

*complete.* This same verb *(epitelein)* is used with respect to the completion of the collection in 8:11 (twice) and Rom 15:28.

*among you.* One could translate *eis autous* as "for you" (Barrett, 216, 221).

*benevolence.* Greek *charis,* as in 8:1 (God's *grace*) and 8:4 *(benefit).* But here and in 8:7, 19; 1 Cor 16:3 it refers to an "act of grace" (*NIV* [v. 6]; cf. *RSV*: "gracious work")—specifically, the collection Paul is taking up for *the saints* in Jerusalem.

*as well.* Translates *kai,* which stands before *tēn charin tautēn* (literally "also this grace") in Paul's Greek sentence. It implies that Titus had done something in Corinth besides starting up the collection (so Barrett, 221, who thinks Titus had probably carried the tearful letter [2:3ff.; 7:8ff.]; but see COMMENT on 7:13*b*–15).

7. *Now.* Translates *alla,* which is not an adversative particle here, but functions to strengthen the command. See BAG s.v. 6.

*you excel in everything.* Cf. this phrase *(en panti perisseuete)* with 1 Cor 1:5, "in everything you were enriched in him [Christ]" *(en panti eploutisthēte en autō),* and 1 Cor 1:7, "you are not lacking in any spiritual gift [*charismati*]" *(RSV).* See also the following note.

*faith . . . speech . . . knowledge.* Cf. 1 Cor 12:8, 9, "the utterance [speaking] of knowledge . . . faith," in which context *faith (pistis)* is the gift to heal and to work miracles (1 Cor 12:9, 10; cf. 1 Cor 13:2 and Barrett 1968:285–86), *speech (logos)* is associated with religious discourse in general ("the utterance of wisdom and . . . the utterance of knowledge," 1 Cor 12:8 [*RSV*]), and *knowledge (gnōsis)* means special spiritual insight (e.g., 1 Cor 8:1, 7, 10; 13:2, 8).

*in utmost earnestness.* For the translation of *pas* (literally "all") as *utmost* see BAG s.v. 1aδ. On *earnestness,* see NOTES for 7:11, 12.

*the love. Agapē,* as in 8:8, 24; 2:4, 8; 5:14; 6:6; 13:11, 13 (the verbal form in 9:7; 11:11; 12:15 [twice]). Here the article is used, as it had not been with the four preceding nouns in the series, and *love* is thereby given a certain emphasis.

*that we have for you.* Translates *ex hēmōn en hymin,* adopted by GNT-Nestle as the more difficult reading (after *earnestness* one naturally expects that *love* would refer to an attribute of the Corinthians) and because it has impressive early attestation in P⁴⁶ and B (cf. Metzger 1971:581); see also Hughes, 297; Barrett, 216 n. 1. The reading *ex hymōn en hēmin,* "that you have for us," is more widely attested (ℵ D G et al.) and has been adopted by *RSV* (also by *NEB, TEV, NIV,* but with footnote references to the important alternative reading). Fee (1978:536 n. 1) calls "that you have for us" the more difficult reading, because it suggests (against 6:12, which Fee might have cited) that the Corinthians had great love for their apostle. But in this immediate context there are two references to the Corinthians' *love,* 8:8, 24 (though not specifically for Paul), so Fee's argument is not convincing. Cf. Spicq (1965:211)—according to whom, moreover, the reading that speaks of the Corinthians' love for Paul could have been prompted by the mention of their *earnestness,* which in 7:11 refers to their concern to be responsive to Paul's direction (1959:158 n. 3).

*excel also.* This tr. regards the subjunctive clause *hina . . . perisseuēte* as imperatival in function; see BDF § 387(3); *GNTG* III:95. Contrast Georgi (1965:60), who wishes to interpret it as a normal consecutive clause ("so that you may excel"), even though he admits that the sentence is implicitly admonitory (ibid.: n. 224). But the imperatival usage of *hina* with the subjunctive is not as rare as Georgi implies when he refers to its "occasional use in popular Greek"; for a sampling of Hellenistic instances from outside the NT, see Salom 1958:127–31. Other possible Pauline examples of this imperatival use occur in 10:9; 1 Cor 5:2; 7:29; 16:15–16; Gal 2:10; Phlm 19 (some of these cited by Morrice 1972:328–29).

*this benevolence. This* is emphatic by reason of its position in the Greek (Plummer, 238). For *benevolence,* see discussion on 8:6.

8. *I.* Although the first person plural has been predominant in 8:1–7 (as in chaps. 1–7), apart from v. 9 (a special case; see below) it does not appear in 8:8–15. In this paragraph the first-person references are both singular (8:8, 10); see also *my partner* (8:23) and 9:1–5.

*not . . . as an order.* The same expression *(ou kat' epitagēn)* is used in 1 Cor 7:6 where the reference is probably to a divine command (from the Lord; cf. 1 Cor 7:25). A similar reference is possible here (so Horsley 1982:86, no. 49, commenting on a second-century C.E. papyrus text). But such a reference does not seem to be present in Phlm 8, 9 where Paul uses the verb, "to order" *(epitassein).*

*by mentioning the earnestness.* Literally "by [or: through] the earnestness" *(dia tēs . . . spoudēs).* For *earnestness* (as in 8:7), see NOTES on 7:11–12.

*of others.* That is, of the Macedonians, 8:1–5.

*I intend to verify.* The word *intend* has been supplied for clarity, since this English tr. does not follow exactly the grammatical form of Paul's Greek. In the latter there is a participle, *dokimazōn* ("verifying"): thus, literally "by the earnestness of others verifying," etc. The verb *dokimazein* can mean "to put to the test" or "to prove, approve" (having put to the test); here and in 8:22 it means the latter (hence, "to verify").

*the reality.* Translates *to . . . gnēsion,* a neuter singular adjective used for a noun; see BDF § 263(2). The adjective *(gnēsios)* means literally "true-born," and, when applied figuratively, "legitimate," "genuine," "regular," etc. Cf. Sir 7:18, "Do not exchange a friend for money, or a real brother [*adelphon gnēsion*] for the gold of Ophir" *(RSV).* See Büchsel, *TDNT* I:727; Spicq 1965:197 (and 1959:140 n. 3, for evidence from the papyri). Note Paul's description of love as "authentic" *(anypokritos)* in 6:6; Rom 12:9.

*love.* As in 8:7, etc. Both here and in 8:24 the apostle writes simply of *your love,* without specifying any particular recipient(s). It is by no means clear that he is thinking particularly of their love for him, especially if the correct reading in 8:7 (see note) is *the love that we have for you.* See COMMENT.

9. *For.* This introductory *gar* probably attaches what follows to both parts of the preceding verse: it offers an explanation of why it is unnecessary for Paul to issue *an order* (8:8*a*) and why Paul is concerned *to verify the reality of* [*the Corinthians'*] *love* (8:8*b*).

*you know.* Paul is stating something with which he presumes his readers are very well acquainted.

*the grace of our Lord Jesus Christ.* A liturgical phrase which appears regularly (with some slight variations) in the closing benedictions of Paul's letters (Rom 16:20; 1 Cor 16:23; 2 Cor 13:13; Gal 6:18; Phil 4:23; 1 Thess 5:28; Phlm 25, and also in 2 Thess 3:18). This explains the plural *our,* despite the first person singular of 8:7, 10.

*that.* Greek *hoti,* which sometimes marks the citation of a traditional formulation; cf. *knowing that* in 4:14, and the note there.

*for your sake.* Or simply "for you" *(di' hymas).* Its position at the beginning of this clause gives it emphasis.

*he became poor.* An ingressive aorist *(eptōcheusen),* pointing to the inception of the poverty. Cf. especially Phil 2:7–8 and Rom 15:3. For the meaning of this assertion see COMMENT.

*though he was rich.* More literally, "being rich" *(plousios ōn),* which has a material as well as formal parallel in Phil 2:6, "though he was in the form of God" *(RSV; en morphē Theou hyparchōn,* "being in the form of God"). See COMMENT.

*so that you, by means of his . . .* Both pronouns are emphatic.

*might become rich.* The riches Christ gave up accrue to those who believe in him. The thought here is not of the spiritual gifts with which the Corinthians are proud to be enriched (1 Cor 1:5; 4:8; cf. 2 Cor 8:7) but of the riches of salvation (see especially Rom 10:12; 11:12) to which Paul's ministry is devoted (cf. 6:10 and COMMENT there).

10. *And so.* Translates *kai* ("and"), which here seems to introduce the result of Paul's decision not to give an *order* (8:8); for this usage see BAG s.v. I, 2f.

*I am giving my counsel.* Here, as in 1 Cor 7:25, Paul employs the expression *gnō-mēn didonai,* and in both instances it is contrasted with the conveyance of an *order* (*epitagē;* in the present context, 8:8). By *gnōmē* he does not mean simply his own present "notion," but his "considered opinion" *(NEB)* as one who is guided by God's Spirit (1 Cor 7:40). This is serious, apostolic counsel. See Bultmann, *TDNT* I:717–18.

*in this matter.* In Pauline usage the phrase *(en toutō)* normally looks back to some point already introduced (see 3:10, Rom 14:18; 1 Cor 11:22; Phil 1:18). Here *this matter* is *the reality of [the Corinthians'] love,* 8:8.

*for this.* That is, this *giving . . . counsel* (cf. Héring, 60), as shown by *for (gar),* which connects what follows with what has preceded (cf. Windisch, 254).

*is in your interest.* Translates *hymin sympherei.* The verb *(sympherein),* also used by Paul in 12:1; 1 Cor 6:12; 10:23; 12:7 (in the latter as a participial substantive), is frequent in Stoic texts (see Weiss, *TDNT* IX:72–73), and is also found in the LXX. In describing the "deliberative" speech as either "hortatory" or "dissuasive," Aristotle explains exhortation as the recommending of some action that will be "expedient" or "beneficial" *(to sympheron), Rhetoric* I.iii.3–5. Olson (1976:214) cites Paul's use of the word here as one indication that the apostle has been influenced by the formal patterns of Hellenistic rhetoric. However, it is more important to observe that the apostle identifies what is "beneficial" with what "builds up" Christian community; note 1 Cor 10:23, where "not everything is beneficial" *(ou panta sympherei;* cf. Sir 37:28, *ou gar panta pasi sympherei,* "for not everything is beneficial for every one") is parallel to "not everything builds up" *(ou panta oikodomei).* Paul's concern for what is in the best interest of the Christian community is also apparent in 1 Cor 12:7 and when he uses the related adjective in 1 Cor 10:33. See Weiss, *TDNT* IX:78–80.

*already made a beginning.* As in 8:6 (see note there on *he had previously made a beginning*), the verb is *proenarchesthai,* and again there is the expected variant *(enērxasthe,* D* F G 629*). Here the *already* is further explained as *last year* (following note).

*last year.* Or "from last year" *(apo perusi),* referring to the previous calendar year. Hence, the time which has elapsed since then could be very short (a month or two) or as much as twenty-three months, depending on when in the current calendar year this letter is being written. The tr. "a year ago" (e.g., *RSV*) is in error because it suggests a definite span of (about) twelve months. There is no way of knowing whether Paul is thinking in terms of (a) the Roman calendar, according to which the year begins on 1 January, (b) the Jewish ecclesiastical calendar, according to which the year begins in the spring, or (c) those calendars according to which the year begins in the autumn (the Jewish civil calendar, the Macedonian calendar, etc.). Windisch, 255–56, and Hughes, 303, prefer (a), and in favor of that one may cite not only the apostle's alleged Roman citizenship (see especially Acts 22:25–29) but also the possibility that he is writing this letter (chaps. 1–9) from Philippi, a Roman colony. Barrett, 225 (without giving reasons), prefers (c). A decision in the matter turns out to be unnecessary, however. Since 1 Cor 16:1–4 presupposes that the Corinthians had agreed to contribute to the collection, and since it is likely that the present letter (Letter D) was written some ten or eleven months after 1 Cor (Letter B; see INTRODUCTION, pp. 41–42), one may suppose that some such interval is involved here, no matter what calendar Paul is following (cf. Lüdemann [1980:133–34], who reckons sixteen months).

*not only . . . but also.* The idiom (see note on *yet,* 7:7) compares something important with something still more important (here, the *wanting to*).

*in taking action . . . in wanting to.* Translates two articular infinitives, *to poiēsai* (literally "to do" or "the doing") and *to thelein* (literally "to will" or "the willing"), the emphasis falling on the second (see preceding note). The second infinitive is not an aorist, like the first, but present tense, and thereby gains yet further emphasis; the Corinthians' *wanting to* take action is something Paul is still able to presuppose, although they may no longer actually be *taking action* (cf. Plummer, 242).

11. *But now.* The particle *de (but)* here emphasizes the contrast between *now* and *last year,* which in the Greek are the final words in 8:10.

*complete the task as well. Complete* (as in 8:6, on which see the note) is the only formal imperative in chaps. 8, 9, although everything Paul says in these two chapters is implicitly hortatory. *The task* translates *to poiēsai,* rendered as *taking action* in 8:10, and in Greek the *kai (as well)* immediately precedes it: the willingness is still there, so the Corinthians should "also finish the work" they have let drop.

*your goodwill in wanting to.* The Greek here is difficult to translate satisfactorily. The noun ordinarily connotes a certain "eagerness" to do something (cf. *NAB:* "ready resolve"), a genuine disposition to act. (See Rengstorf, *TDNT* VI:697–700.) Considering that Paul uses it only in this immediate context, and mainly of the Corinthians' readiness to contribute to the fund for Jerusalem (8:11, 12; 9:2; of Paul and his associates in 8:19; the adjective only once, Rom 1:15), it may be a word they themselves have used in that connection, or that Titus has used of them. It is combined here with the genitive articular infinitive *tou thelein,* to which BDF § 400(2) would assign a consecutive (final) meaning: "zeal in willing so that one really wills." Cf. Plato, *Laws* III, 697 E, *meta prothymias tou ethelein,* "with [no] ready willingness" (to endanger themselves in battle).

*may be matched by.* Translates *kathaper . . . houtōs kai,* "just as [there is goodwill in wanting to], so also there is. . . ."

*your completing it.* Literally "the completing" *(to epitelesai);* it refers to *the task* ( = of contributing to the collection for Jerusalem).

*from what you have.* One may compare this phrase *(ek tou echein)* with *as they were able (kata dynamin)* in 8:3, and Hughes, 305 n. 30, argues for a virtually identical tr. Cf. LXX Prov 3:27, 28 where "what your hand may have" *(echē hē cheir sou)* and "when you are able" *(dynatou sou ontos)* are parallel.

12. *goodwill.* As in 8:11.

*that is acceptable. That* (referring to the *goodwill* which is the subject of the sentence) is supplied for the tr. Here and in Rom 15:16; 1 Pet 2:5 the thought is of something *acceptable* to God. However, in Rom 15:3, again with reference to the collection, Paul hopes that his "relief work" (*diakonia;* see note on 8:4, above) will be "acceptable to the saints" *(euprosdektos tois hagiois)* in Jerusalem. (In Rom 15:16 "the offering [*prosphora*] of the Gentiles" is not their contribution to the collection but their offering of themselves to God, their "obedience" to the gospel, v. 18.)

*according to what one has.* Translates *katho ean eche;* see note above on *from what you have,* 8:11. What *one has* may be much or little; cf. Tob 4:8: one is to give alms in relation to *(kata)* one's means, whether those be great *(to plēthos)* or restricted *(to oligon).* See also Philo, *Who Is the Heir* 145, quoted in the note on *equality,* 8:13.

13, 14. These verses are numbered in different ways by modern editors and translators. *GNT-*Nestle begin v. 14 with *en tō nyn kairō (at the present time),* and this numbering is followed here (as also, e.g., by *JB, NIV, NAB*), although others (e.g., *RSV, NEB*) would begin v. 14 with *all' ex isotētos (but it is a matter of equality).*

13. *relief.* Greek *anesis,* as in 2:13; 7:5.

*a hard time.* More literally, "affliction" *(thlipsis),* as in 8:2.

*but rather, it is a matter of equality.* Translates *all' ex isotētos,* supplying *it is.* This tr. interprets the phrase as completing what has preceded, though departing from the grammatical construction (not uncommon in the Pauline letters). Instead of "It is not that . . . ; but rather that there may be equality," we have: *It is not that . . . ; but rather, it is a matter of equality* (in Greek, a prepositional phrase in place of a second *hina* [final]-clause). So also *NIV.* Some, however, regard this phrase as beginning a thought which runs on into v. 14 (so, e.g., *GNT-*Nestle; *RSV*). Barrett, 226, argues that the lack of a connecting particle at the beginning of v. 14 favors the latter view. On the other hand, the double reference to *equality* which his punctuation involves (one at the beginning and one at the end of the sentence) favors the punctuation adopted here.

*equality.* Paul uses this term *(isotēs)* only here and in 8:14; elsewhere in the NT it occurs only in Col 4:1, where (with *to dikaion,* "what is just") it means "what is fair" (in relation to one's slaves). It is found but twice in the LXX (Job 36:29; Zech 4:7), there being no exact Hebrew equivalent. The concept of *equality* was developed by the Greeks (see Stählin, *TDNT* III:343–55) and commended as a moral principle by such Hellenistic writers as Dio Chrysostom—who, quoting Euripides ("Equality . . . knitteth friends to friends, / Cities to cities, allies to allies," etc.), contrasts its merits with the dire consequences of greed (XVII, 9–10; cited by Mussies 1972:178). Philo once praises *equality* as the highest good (*Special Laws* IV, 165–66, developing the thought of Deut 17:20), and elsewhere devotes a long essay to the subject (*Who Is the Heir* 141–206). Georgi (1965:62–65) argues that *equality* is nothing less than a divine power of cosmic dimensions in Philo's thought, and that he and Paul are indebted to the same Wisdom tradition for this concept. In Georgi's view, *equality* is closely related to "grace" and "righteousness" in this tradition, and Paul's phrase *ex isotētos* ("from equality") almost means *ek Theou* ("from God"). This proposal, however, moves quite beyond the plain sense of what is said in vv. 13–14 (correctly Barrett, 226–27). Here the apostle's reference to *equality* parallels Philo's own example of it (*Who Is the Heir* 145): "One essential form of equality is the proportional [*hē dia analogias*], in which the few are regarded as equal to the many, and the small to the greater. This is often employed by states on special occasions when they order each citizen to make an equal contribution from his property, not of course numerically equal, but equal in the sense that it is proportionate to the valuation of his estate. . . ."

14. *surplus.* Translates *to perisseuma,* used only here (twice) by Paul, but virtually synonymous with *hē perisseia (abundance),* used of the Macedonians' *joy* in 8:2.

*the present time.* This same phrase *(ho nyn kairos)* has a pregnant theological sense when Paul uses it in Rom 3:26 (the time of the disclosure of God's righteousness) and Rom 8:18 (this time of suffering before God's glory is revealed). However, in Rom 11:5 it probably means only "in our day," in contrast to "back then when God spoke to Elijah" (see vv. 2b–4), and here it probably means only "now when the saints in Jerusalem have need and you have some extra."

*is for their need.* The tr. supplies *is* on the basis of *may be (genētai)* in the following clause. *Their need (to ekeinōn hysterēma)* here contrasts with *Your surplus* (cf. Phil 4: 12b, where the related verbs are contrasted) and refers to the situation of the Christians in Jerusalem (see 9:12, *the needs* [plural] *of the saints*). The same noun (but plural) and the related verb are used in 11:9 of Paul's own needs, as is the synonymous noun *hysterēsis* in Phil 4:11.

*that their surplus,* etc. Philo, *Special Laws* II, 71, supports the law about the cancellation of debts every seventh year (Deut 15:1–3) by commenting that the rich "by giving some share of their own to the needy . . . may expect to receive the same kindness themselves, if any disaster befall them."

*equality.* See note on 8:13, above.

15. *As it is written.* Paul frequently uses this formula *(kathōs gegraptai [hoti])* to introduce (once, Rom 2:24, to conclude) a citation from scripture; see also 9:9; Rom 1:17; 3:10; 4:17; 8:36; 9:33; 11:26; 15:3, 9, 21; 1 Cor 1:31; 2:9.

*"He who gathered much . . ."* Paul quotes from Exod 16:18 with only slight variation from the Greek text. Here as in the LXX itself a verb must be supplied, and the context in Exod suggests that it should be *gathered* (cf. also Num 11:32); see BDF § 263(1).

## COMMENT: GENERAL

Paul's expressions of confidence in the Corinthians, 7:4–16, are followed here by his appeal to them to complete the collection "for the saints" in Jerusalem. The Christians of Corinth have previously committed themselves to this project, and their apostle is anxious that they now follow through on that commitment. Two points of special contact between 7:4–16 and 8:1–15 may be noted. First, just as Paul has remarked on the *earnestness* of the Corinthians (7:11)—specifically their *earnestness* for his ministry (7:12)—so now he remarks on the *earnestness* of the Christians in Macedonia, describing it in 8:2–5, and specifically identifying it as *earnestness* in 8:8. So, too, the *earnestness* of the Corinthians is again noted, precisely to help support the appeal to complete the collection (8:7). Second, the notice in 8:6 that Paul is now dispatching Titus on a return mission to Corinth reads like an altogether logical consequence of the emphasis placed earlier (7:6–7, 13b–15) on the confidence and affection Titus has toward the congregation there.

The whole of chap. 8 is devoted to the collection project, and so is the whole of chap. 9 (on the relation of these chapters to one another see below, pp. 429–33). The appeal itself is most sharply focused in 8:1–15, particularly in 8:7–12. But even here Paul is careful to explain that the appeal (vv. 7, 11–12) is to be regarded as his *counsel,* not as *an order* (8:8–10). Elsewhere in these paragraphs the appeal is only—but nonetheless clearly—implicit, as Paul describes the *earnestness* of the Macedonians (8:1–15), the purpose of Titus' return to Corinth (8:6), and the importance of observing the principle of *equality* (8:13–15).

These paragraphs resist the imposition of any rigid outline. Indeed, the paragraphing itself is problematic, so closely does one thought attach to the preceding one and lead on to the next. For the purposes of commentary, however, one may subdivide this material into half a dozen smaller units. In the first paragraph Paul invokes the example of the Macedonian Christians who have contributed more than generously to the collection (8:1–5) and gives notice of Titus' present mission to Corinth (8:6). In the second paragraph he draws out the consequence for his readers (8:7), clarifies the nature of his appeal (8:8–10), and emphasizes the importance of actually doing what one has professed a willingness to do (8:11–12). Then, in the third paragraph, he supports his appeal with some comments on the principle of *equality* (8: 13–15).

Before these points are examined in detail, it will be useful to summarize what can be known about the background of Paul's collection project and why he regarded it as such an important undertaking.

## The Collection Project in Paul's Ministry

In addition to chaps. 8 and 9 of 2 Cor, three other Pauline letters attest to the importance the apostle placed on a collection for the Christians in Jerusalem. These are:

a. *1 Cor 16:1–4.* The way Paul introduces the topic of the "collection" *(logeia)* here shows that he is responding to a question about it which has been put to him by the Corinthians themselves. Either in a previous letter or through a representative, Paul had apparently urged the congregation to contribute to the fund (see Lüdemann 1980:112–14). One may assume that Paul had also indicated why their participation was important, because the Corinthians' question seems to have pertained only to the *way* they should raise the money, not to the reasons for doing so. In the course of the response one learns that Paul has also solicited contributions from the churches in Galatia (v. 1), that he expects the Corinthian share to be ready when he comes (v. 2), that he wants the congregation to select representatives to carry it to Jerusalem (v. 3), and that if he decides to go to Jerusalem himself, those persons will accompany him (v. 4).

b. *Rom 15:25–32.* Sometime between the writing of 1 Cor and Rom, Paul decided that it was indeed "appropriate" (1 Cor 16:4) that he himself should convey the collection to Jerusalem. His letter to the Roman Christians is almost certainly being written from Corinth, and he indicates that he is about to set out on the journey to Jerusalem (v. 25). He mentions specifically only the contributions which have been made by Macedonia and Achaia (vv. 26–27); one misses any reference to contributions from Paul's churches in Asia and (most particularly, 1 Cor 16:1) Galatia. Paul's Roman readers are told that the Gentile churches are sharing their "material blessings" with the poor in Jerusalem because the Jerusalem Christians have shared their "spiritual blessings" with them (v. 27, *RSV*). And finally, he asks for prayers that his "relief work for Jerusalem may be acceptable to the saints" (v. 31).

c. *Gal 2:9–10.* In these two verses Paul is summarizing the outcome of a crucial meeting he and Barnabas had had in Jerusalem with Peter and the other leaders of the church there (see Gal 2:1–8). Titus, a representative of the uncircumcised Gentile Christians to whom Paul's gospel was increasingly appealing, had also been present at this meeting. It was precisely Paul's gospel that was at issue in Jerusalem, at least according to the apostle's recounting here. Must Gentile converts to the gospel submit to the Mosaic Law as well, including the requirement of circumcision (the position of the Jerusalem leaders)? Or does the gospel of Christ free one from the law and accept the Gentiles as they are, without their having to submit to circumcision and similar requirements (Paul's view)? The decision, Paul explains, was that he would conduct the mission to the Gentiles, preaching the gospel he had been preaching without amendment or addition (cf. vv. 6–7), while James, Cephas, and John would continue to superintend the mission to the Jews (v. 9). In recognition of this agreement Paul was committed (or re-committed, as he would have it) "to remember the poor" (v. 10). Although the point has been disputed by Georgi (1965, especially 13–41), it seems clear that Paul's work on behalf of the collection in Galatia, Macedonia, and Achaia was directly related to this agreement reached earlier in Jerusalem (Lüdemann's discussion of this includes an effective critique of Georgi's objections [1980:105–10]; cf. Nickle 1966: e.g., 59–62). It is true that Paul does not mention the Jerusalem accords in his letters to Corinth and Rome, not even when appealing for contributions in 2 Cor 8, 9. But the reasons for the collection Paul gives in 2 Cor and Rom are formulated primarily in the light of his present convictions about the significance of the collection, and secondarily with a concern for what can win the assent and response of his readers (cf. Berger 1977:201). His silence about the Jerusalem agreement by no means precludes that agreement being viewed as the historical origin of Paul's present efforts on behalf of the collection.

Given the evident importance of the collection project in Paul's ministry, it is surprising that one hears almost nothing about it in Acts. It is often suggested that the relief fund carried to Jerusalem by Barnabas and Paul on behalf of the Christians of Antioch (Acts 11:29–30) was the prototype of Paul's later collection in the churches of Asia Minor and Greece (e.g., Nickle 1966: 28), but nothing about the latter is reported in Acts except the remark in Paul's defense before Felix (24:17): "Now after some years I came to bring my nation alms and offerings" *(RSV)*. It is also possible to refer to Acts 20:4, which gives a list of seven men—representatives of churches in Macedonia, Galatia (Lycaonia), and Asia—who are to accompany Paul from "Greece" (presumably Corinth) to Judea. It may be that these men are among those who are to help convey the collection to Jerusalem (cf. 1 Cor 16:3—although no Corinthian is named in Acts 20:4!), but this is not specifically indicated. Various explanations have been offered for the silence of Acts on this topic, all of them more or less conjectural and none of them entirely convincing. The fact remains that our knowledge of the collection comes almost exclusively from the apostle's own letters.

Why was Paul so concerned that his churches contribute to this fund for Jerusalem, and even send their delegates to accompany it? What was its importance for him, that he should finally decide to take it to Jerusalem himself, thus further postponing a long-delayed trip to Rome and mission to Spain? Several factors seem to have been operative.

First, Paul was undoubtedly concerned to provide needed economic assistance to "the poor among the saints in Jerusalem" (Rom 15:26, *RSV*). In this respect the so-called "famine-relief" mission he and Barnabas had carried out for the Christians at Antioch could well have been prototypical. Thus, in 2 Cor 8, 9, Paul does not hesitate to commend the collection as a genuinely charitable act, those who have much sharing with those who have little (8:13–15), assisting those who are in need of material support (9:12). It is hardly surprising, then, that one of the terms the apostle uses to identify the collection is the word *diakonia* (Rom 15:31; 2 Cor 8:4; 9:1, 12, 13; the corresponding verb in Rom 15:25; 2 Cor 8:19, 20), in these instances used by him in the technical sense of "relief work" (see note on 2 Cor 8:4).

However, several of Paul's other terms for the collection show that it also had important theological significance for him. In fact, he refers to it as a "collection" *(logeia)* only in 1 Cor 16:1, 2 (*RSV:* "contribution[s]"). More frequently he uses words which have rich theological associations; these include *eulogia* (2 Cor 9:5; sometimes "blessing"), *charis* (1 Cor 16:3; 2 Cor 8:6, 7, 9; sometimes "grace," as in 2 Cor 8:1, 9; 9:14), *leitourgia* (2 Cor 9:12, and the verb in Rom 15:27; sometimes "priestly service"), and *koinōnia* (Rom 15:26; 2 Cor 8:4; 9:13, and the verb in Rom 15:27; sometimes used to mean "partnership" in Christ, the Spirit, the gospel, faith, etc.). (For a more complete list see Dahl 1977:37–38.) The last term is especially important. Above all, Paul seems to have promoted the collection among his largely Gentile congregations as a tangible expression of the unity of Jew and Gentile in the gospel. It was to be further evidence, now offered by his congregations themselves, of that "partnership" *(koinōnia)* he and Peter had once celebrated with a handshake in Jerusalem (Gal 2:9). The "relief work" is at the same time a work of "grace" and an act of Christian "partnership," and it is described as such in 2 Cor 8:4, where all three terms are used (literally: "the grace and the partnership of the relief work for the saints"). Paul can also think of it as an expression of love (2 Cor 8:8, 24), and he compares one's participation in it with the utter self-giving of Christ for others (2 Cor 8:9). For he is convinced that participation in the sufferings, death, and resurrection of Christ (e.g., Phil 3:10–11; cf. 2 Cor 1:5–7) both bestows and requires a community of caring and concern. That partnership in Christ transcends even such apparently un-breachable barriers as those between Jew and Greek, slave and free, male and female (Gal 3:27–28). Paul's collection, then, was also an ecumenical act, an act of Christian fellowship, an enactment of the partnership of Jew and Gentile in the gospel of Christ.

It seems likely that still another factor lies behind the seriousness with which Paul applied himself to the collection project. Munck in particular (1959: 272–308) has argued that the collection was also an enactment of the apostle's missionary theology as that is expressed in Rom 11. There the apostle antici-pates that Israel will be saved only after "the full number of the Gentiles come in" (Rom 11:25–26, *RSV*). By leading a large representative delegation of believing Gentiles to Jerusalem, then, Paul would be demonstrating the success of the gospel among the Gentiles in order to make the Jews jealous, and thus win them to the gospel (Munck 1959, especially 302–3). The trip to the Holy City could be viewed at the same time as the fulfillment of OT prophecies about the pilgrimage of the Gentiles to Mt. Zion, bringing their gifts in the last days (see Isa 2:2–3; Mic 4:1–2; Isa 60:5–6, cited by Munck [ibid.:303–4]). This view has been widely influential (see especially Nickle 1966:134–42; also Georgi 1965:84–86), and it undoubtedly helps to explain two special features of Paul's letter to the Romans, written just before he sets out for Jerusalem with the collection: (1) the apostle's lengthy discussion of the problem of Israel's un-belief, and the role of the Gentiles in winning the Jews to Christ (chaps. 9–11), and (2) his request for prayers that he "be delivered from the unbelievers in Judea" and that the Christians of Jerusalem (those who by previous agreement [Gal 2:9] have been in charge of the mission to the Jews) will find his service "acceptable" (15:31).

Holmberg (1978, especially 35–56) argues that the theological interpretation given to the collection by Paul is more or less beside the point. In his view, the apostle had been compelled to take over this project by the Jerusalem church, who sought thereby to exercise and demonstrate its power, authority, and superior status, as well as the dependence of the Gentile congregations and their apostles. However, as Holmberg acknowledges, the most important evi-dence in the matter comes from Paul's letters, where his own interpretation is set forth—so it is very difficult to know how the collection was viewed from the other side. Indeed, Holmberg's supposition that an exchange of money typically demonstrates the inferior status of the giver and the superior status of the recipient is invalid when applied to social relations in the ancient world. In that setting, it is more likely that Paul's churches would have understood their gifts to Jerusalem to be an act of patronage, placing the Judean churches under obligation to them as client congregations (cf. Judge 1980b:210–11; and for patronal relationships in general, P. Marshall 1980:224–30; Mott 1975). That the collection had been requested by the Jerusalem church conforms to the fact that it was usually the weaker party (the client) who initiated the patron-client relationship (P. Marshall 1980:225).

## COMMENT: DETAILED

### The Example of the Macedonians, 8:1–5

Here Paul eases himself into the subject of his collection for the poor among the Christians of Jerusalem by describing the enthusiastic participation of the Macedonian churches in the project. But it is significant that he describes their participation first of all as an act of divine grace (v. 1). He attributes it neither to his own successful ministry (correctly Georgi 1965:53) nor to their own selfless action. It is God's grace working in them, just as it will be when the Corinthians have completed their contribution to the fund (see 9:14). That the Macedonian Christians acted by God's grace is underscored as the apostle points out that they contributed despite their *severe testing by affliction* and their *profound poverty* (v. 2). In 7:5, Paul has referred to the affliction he himself experienced when he came into Macedonia from Troas (see COMMENT on 7:5–7), and it is likely that the *affliction* now mentioned as experienced by the Macedonians themselves (especially in Philippi and Thessalonica; references in NOTES) was somehow related to that. The apostle's comment about the extreme poverty of the churches in Macedonia shows that he perceives the Corinthian Christians to be relatively well off (see also 8:14). There is no need to look for a special cause of the Macedonians' poverty, least of all in Livy's report about the effects of Roman occupation (cited by Plummer, 233). Livy reports not only that the Romans took charge of certain natural resources and restricted trade in the area, but also that the Macedonian cities were granted their freedom and that taxes were reduced by half (XLV.xxix–xxx). Moreover, it should be noted that Livy's comments pertain in the first instance to the second century B.C.E., almost two centuries before the time of Paul's ministry there.

In the long and somewhat awkward sentence of vv. 3–5, Paul interprets the Macedonians' *participation in the relief work for the saints* (v. 4) as "an act of Christian devotion" (Barrett, 221), *first to the Lord,* but then also to the

Pauline apostolate (v. 5). It may be that Paul is already thinking of the example of the Lord's (Christ's) own self-giving, to which he will appeal in 8:9 (so Windisch, 247, who compares what is said of Christ's self-giving in Gal 1:4); but it is equally possible that the present remark leads to the later reference. In a subsequent letter (Letter E, chaps. 10–13) the apostle finds it necessary to assure the Corinthians that his appeal has been for themselves, not for their possessions (12:14, cited by Windisch, 247). This point is implicit in the present sentence, where the main statement is not that the Macedonians gave their money but that *they gave themselves* (v. 5). At the same time, Paul emphasizes that the Macedonians contributed generously—even beyond what seems right and reasonable, considering their limited resources—and voluntarily (vv. 3–4). From a remark in 9:2 it would appear that the Macedonians had been prompted to their magnanimous action upon hearing of the commitment made by the Christians of Corinth. That Paul now holds up the Macedonian churches as an example to the Corinthians suggests that the latter had been negligent in following through on their original commitment. And it may be significant that when Paul later writes to the Romans about the completed project, he mentions first the contributions from Macedonia, and only secondly those from Achaia ( = Corinth; Rom 15:26, cited by Lüdemann 1980:132).

## The Mission of Titus, 8:6

According to this verse, Titus had *previously made a beginning* in taking up an offering from the Corinthians for the Christian poor in Jerusalem. Since 1 Cor 16:1–4 presumes that the congregation had already committed itself to participation by that date, it is often suggested that Titus must have been active in Corinth sometime before the writing of 1 Cor (e.g., Hughes, 293). There is no solid evidence for this, however, and the wording of 2 Cor 7:14 (see NOTES and COMMENT) seems to require the conclusion that the Corinthian visit from which he has just returned (see 7:6) was Titus' very first one to the Achaian capital. Paul therefore cannot mean that Titus introduced the collection project to the Corinthians, or even that he secured their initial commitment to it.

Those who are willing to identify 1 Cor with Paul's tearful letter and believe that Titus was the bearer of it could hold that Titus had initiated the program of "planned giving" laid out there (1 Cor 16:2); but this view presents difficulties as well. First, it is unlikely that Titus carried the tearful letter to Corinth: it seems to have gotten results before Titus' arrival (see 2 Cor 7:15). Moreover, the arguments advanced for identifying 1 Cor with the tearful letter are simply not persuasive (see COMMENT on 2:3–4, and INTRODUCTION, pp. 37–38). However, even if Titus had not carried 1 Cor with its instructions about the collection, it could still have fallen to him to begin the effective implementation of the plan sketched out there. Indeed, this fits very well into the reconstruction of Paul's dealings with the Corinthians proposed in this commentary (INTRO-

DUCTION, pp. 54–55). Subsequent to the writing of 1 Cor, Paul had found it necessary to make a brief "emergency visit" to the Corinthian church to try to straighten out affairs. The visit failed to accomplish this, in part at least because of a gross injury sustained by Paul on that occasion (and alluded to in the present letter, 2:5–10; 7:11–12). There could hardly have been any effective implementation of the collection plan of 1 Cor 16:2 during these troubled months—and it is not inconceivable that the collection project was at least one of the points in dispute between Paul and his congregation. In any case, it is quite possible that the *beginning* Titus succeeded in making for the collection was the *re*-commitment of the Corinthians to the project, and their pledge to implement the instructions Paul had already given them.

As Paul writes the present letter he is in receipt of Titus' report, and is encouraged to believe that now at last there is a real possibility that the Corinthians will fulfill their commitment to the collection. Significantly, although the apostle has praised the Macedonians for their participation, he does not directly commend their action as a model for the Corinthians. Instead, he refers to what the Corinthians have already accomplished (cf. Windisch, 248), even though he must be disappointed that it is still only *a beginning*. Here, too, however, Paul approaches a delicate matter very circumspectly, referring to the beginning and the completion of the collection in Corinth as if it were Titus' responsibility. Nevertheless, this notice about the purpose of Titus' return to Corinth conveys in itself an unmistakable appeal to the church. The persuasiveness of this is directly dependent on what Paul has said in chap. 7 about Titus' confidence in the *obedience* of the Corinthian Christians (cf. Webber 1970:234).

### The Responsibility of the Corinthians, 8:7

The preceding verses have been formulated as information for the Corinthians, first about the Macedonians (8:1–5) and then about Titus (8:6), even though Paul's clear intention there is exhortation: the Corinthians should follow through on their commitment to contribute to the fund for Jerusalem. Now in this verse Paul's appeal is explicit, although even here he avoids a direct, second-person-imperative form (see NOTES).

This appeal is introduced with an acknowledgment that the Corinthians *excel* in many things, and first of all in *faith, speech,* and *knowledge.* These are probably to be identified with the spiritual gifts *(charismata)* mentioned in 1 Cor 1:5; 12:8–9 (cited in the NOTES). Thus, *faith (pistis)* here is not faith in Christ, shared by every Christian without exception or distinction (as, e.g., in 1:24). Here it is rather the wonder-working faith with which some but not all Christians are understood to be gifted. Similarly, *speech (logos)* here does not refer specifically to preaching God's "word" (as in 1:18; 2:17; 4:2; cf. 5:19; 6:7), but to such religious discourse as speaking in tongues and prophecy (1 Cor

12:10, 28), and perhaps also to "the interpretation of tongues" (1 Cor 12:10, *RSV*). Nor should this *knowledge* be identified as the saving knowledge to which Paul has referred in 2:14 and 4:6. In this passage it is more probably a reference to the kind of special spiritual insight on which the Corinthians had been so keen. (See NOTES for further details and references.)

The *earnestness* which Paul mentions next is not, however, one of the spiritual gifts. It is almost certainly to be identified with the *earnestness* which the Corinthians had exhibited to Titus on his recent visit and about which Titus has now reported to Paul—specifically their concern to follow the pastoral direction of Paul and to take responsible action in the case of the offending brother (7:11–12). This is a reminder that the Corinthians have already shown their desire to do what is right, and as such it becomes an important part of Paul's case that they should now do what is right in the matter of the collection for Jerusalem.

But before the appeal is made the apostle adds one final item to his list of things in which his congregation excels: his *love* for them. One might have expected him, rather, to mention their love for him (see NOTES); but that is something he cannot presuppose (see 6:12). What he can do is to reaffirm his love for them, and to insist as he has once before in this letter (2:4) that it is very great. Now with these two key points established—that they excel in earnestness to do what is right and in the love their apostle has for them—Paul issues his challenge to *excel also* in fulfilling their pledge to the collection. Here, as in 8:6, he refers to the collection as a *benevolence,* using the same Greek word *(charis)* which in 8:1 refers to God's *grace* and in 8:4 refers to the *benefit* of taking part in the collection project. The Corinthians are to understand that for them, as for the Macedonians (8:1–5), contributing to the collection will be a sign that God's grace is active among them.

### The Nature of the Appeal, 8:8–10

In these verses Paul is explaining the intention of his preceding appeal to *excel* in contributing to the collection for Jerusalem (8:7), and he is thereby substantially reinforcing that appeal. In saying he does not want to be interpreted as giving *an order* about the collection he is perhaps showing the same sensitivity to criticism he has shown earlier in this letter, where he protests that he does not intend to be "domineering" over the faith of his congregation (1:24). Alternatively, he could be suggesting that his appeal is based on no specific command from the Lord (see NOTES). In any event, Paul assures the Corinthians that his remarks about the *earnestness* of the Macedonians (8:1–5) have been directed only at the verification of their own *love.* It would be wrong to assume that Paul is referring here to the Corinthians' love for him. Had he meant that, he could have said it (note the appeal of 2:8 to show their love "for [the offending brother]"). It is probable that he is thinking of that love which "lays claim" to all who by faith share in Christ's death and life and therefore live no longer for themselves (5:14–15). His collection for Jerusalem provides them an opportunity to demonstrate *the reality of (their) love,* for the collection itself is a practical expression of the oneness of Christ's body. (See the general discussion of the collection, above, pp. 409–13.)

The plausibility of this interpretation is enhanced when one considers the following sentence, v. 9. Here Paul emphasizes that the Corinthians are beneficiaries of *the grace of . . . Christ,* thereby explaining why his readers need no *order* from him, but also why they must *verify the reality of (their) love* (see NOTES). Georgi (1965:61 and n. 227) seems to believe that Paul is actually citing a church tradition here, but it is more probably the apostle's own very free adaptation of a traditional theological statement (as at 5:21). It seems to be based on the kind of christological affirmation present in the creedal fragment of 1 Tim 3:16 and in the hymn of Phil 2:6–11. All three texts presume that Christ enjoyed a heavenly existence with God before his incarnation (for the background of this doctrine see Schweizer 1960:101–3, and 1959, especially 67–68). Thus, according to the hymn of Phil 2, Christ divested himself of the outward signs of his deity as he assumed human form and gave himself up to death (vv. 6–8; cf. Rom 15:3). Similarly, in the present verse Paul characterizes *the grace of our Lord Jesus Christ* (a phrase familiar from the Christian liturgy; see NOTES) as his divesting himself of riches and becoming *poor.* There can be no question here of a reference to the literal poverty of the historical Jesus (correctly, e.g., Craddock 1968:164–65; Seidensticker 1977:95; against Buchanan 1964, who—contrary to his own intention—succeeds in showing only how futile it is to argue for a literal interpretation). Paul is not speaking about the manner of Jesus' earthly life, but about his incarnation and death as an act of *grace.*

It is not surprising that the christological presuppositions and implications of this sentence have stirred the interest of the church's theologians from the time of the Church Fathers. (Kistner 1962:10–58 provides a survey of patristic interpretations of the verse.) But Paul's own interest is in its implications for the Corinthians. Thus, while he often leaves the "for us" of familiar confessional statements intact (e.g., Rom 5:8), here he applies the affirmation directly to his readers: *for your sake (Christ) became poor . . . so that you . . . might become rich.* The principle enunciated here is the same as that set forth in 5:21, where Paul affirms that Christ gave up his righteousness (becoming "sin") in order that believers might become "the righteousness of God." Now, employing metaphors appropriate to the context, he affirms that Christ gave up his riches (becoming *poor*) in order that believers might *become rich.* This is the good news of salvation, the basis of existence as "a new creation" (cf. 5:14–19). It is also the indicative upon which all the specific imperatives of the Christian life are ultimately based, including the apostle's present appeal on behalf of the collection.

Paul is not presenting Christ's act of grace as an example for the Corinthians to emulate. If that were the case he ought to urge them to become "poor" for the sake of others as Christ did, but this he specifically does not ask them to do (see 8:13). Elsewhere, it is true, the apostle presents Christ's self-giving love for others as a kind of prototype for believers (see especially Rom 15:2–3, often compared with 2 Cor 8:9; also 1 Cor 10:24, 33–11:1 [perhaps, too, Phil 2:6–13] and the discussion in Larsson 1962:231–35). But here the emphasis falls much more on the salvation (the riches) with which the Corinthians have been enriched by Christ (references in the NOTES). The admonition implicit in this statement is not "Do what Christ did," or even "Do for others what Christ has done for you." It is, rather, "Do what is appropriate to your status as those who have been enriched by the grace of Christ."

In v. 10 Paul returns to the thought of v. 8, now formulating that in a somewhat more positive way. He wishes to give them not an order (v. 8a) but his serious apostolic *counsel* about *this matter* of their Christian love (v. 8b), and it will be in their own best *interest*. (Cf. 10:8 and 13:10, where Paul emphasizes that his apostolic authority has been granted to him for "upbuilding," and see the NOTES to the present verse for comments on this phrase.) The direct *counsel* is postponed, however (that will come in 8:11), while the Corinthians are reminded (again; see 8:6) that they have *already made a beginning* in regard to the collection for Jerusalem. This beginning was some time before (on *last year,* see NOTES), even before the Macedonians had joined in, for the latter had been prompted to contribute by the example of the Corinthians, of whose *goodwill* Paul has been boasting (9:2). It is this same long-standing *goodwill* of the Corinthians toward the collection project that the apostle wishes to emphasize in the present appeal to them (see 8:11–12). *Goodwill,* at least, they have, even though their goodwill has so far borne little or no fruit. This is why Paul describes the beginning they have made as *not only . . . taking action but also . . . wanting to,* where one might have expected "not only wanting to, but actually taking action." He wishes to avoid direct criticism of their failure to make good on their commitment to the project and at the same time to praise their professed desire to take part in it. What he is able now to praise becomes the basis for urging them to take action where they are now at fault (8:11–12).

### On Goodwill, 8:11–12

The only direct imperative form in the whole of chaps. 8 and 9 occurs here in v. 11, and in it the essence of Paul's appeal is disclosed: *complete the task as well.* There is *goodwill* in Corinth toward the collection project—Paul has probably learned this from Titus—but little or no serious effort on its behalf. Here Paul is saying, first, that *goodwill* must be matched by action.

There is also a second point made in these verses, and it may help to explain why the Corinthian church has been slow to follow through on its commitment. They are to contribute, Paul says, *from what (they) have* (v. 11). It is not the size of their gift that makes it *acceptable,* but their *goodwill* in giving as their resources allow (v. 12). From this one may reasonably infer that the Corinthians have so far declined the actual taking up of a collection on the grounds that they could not expect to raise a very large sum. Yes, they want to take part—but later, when they are in a position to do more. If this was the situation Titus reported to Paul, it is quite understandable why the apostle responds as he does. The example of the Macedonians can show them that even the poorest of the Pauline congregations have made contributions of great value, indeed beyond their means (8:1–5). If in their case poverty has been no excuse for postponing action, then surely the better-off Corinthians have no excuse. Yet the Corinthians are not expected to give more than they are able, only *as* they are able, be that much or little.

In making this point about proportionate giving (v. 12) the apostle is drawing freely on Jewish teaching, found especially in the Wisdom tradition, about aiding the needy. Paul may have the teaching of Prov 3:27–28 specifically in mind, and one may also compare Tob 4:8 (both cited in the NOTES). The point of the saying in Mark 12:43–44 is different (correctly Bultmann, 256–57), although it is sometimes cited as comparable (e.g., by Tasker, 117; Bruce, 223). There the poor widow's small gift to the temple treasury is praised as greater than the gifts of those who contribute more from their abundance, because she gave everything she had. But here the principle is that one should give prudently, in relation to one's means. The saying of Luke 12:48 is somewhat more comparable: "Every one to whom much is given, of him will much be required" *(RSV).*

### On Equality, 8:13–15

Evidently prompted by his remark on giving in proportion to what one has (8:12), Paul extends and supports the point by offering some comments on the subject of *equality.* This ideal is frequently explained and commended in Hellenistic literature (examples in the NOTES), and here it is applied to relationships within the Christian community. The needs of the poor are to be met out of the *surplus* of others, not that they themselves should become needy but that all might share equally in what is available. It is not the ascetic ideal that is involved here. It is the ideal of Christian partnership *(koinōnia)* as that is presented, for example, in Acts 2:44–45, where the earliest believers are described as having had "everything in common," selling their possessions whenever money was needed to support the poor (cf. Acts 4:36–37).

Despite the way the principle of equality is expressed in v. 14, it is unlikely that Paul supposes the saints in Jerusalem may one day be called on to assist the poor in Corinth. Nor is it likely that he means the Jerusalem Christians will continue to exchange "spiritual blessings" with the Gentiles who, in turn, assist them materially (so Nickle 1966:121). While this kind of exchange is mentioned in Rom 15:27, written later, there is no indication it is in Paul's mind here. Verse 14 is a formal statement of the principle of equality, with no special thought for what its operation might involve in the future (cf. Héring, 61). The Corinthians will understand well enough what it involves for them *at the present time.*

Paul illustrates this principle of equality by drawing a text from the story of Israel's experience in the wilderness, v. 15. He quotes almost verbatim the Greek version of Exod 16:18, the fourth explicit citation of scripture so far in this letter (previous ones occur in 4:13; 6:2; 6:16–18). According to the biblical story, along with the miraculous gift of bread from heaven the Lord issued instructions that "an omer apiece," one day's supply, was to be gathered for each person in the camp (Exod 16:16). Although in fact the people gathered it up in varying amounts (v. 17), when measured by the omer each had enough, and no more than enough, to meet the daily ration (v. 18). This is the text Paul quotes: *"He who gathered much had nothing extra, and he who gathered little had no shortage."*

For him the sole point of interest in the text is the notion of *equality* (so, too, for Philo, *Who Is the Heir* 191, who quotes the same verse with regard to the equal distribution of wisdom by the divine Word); in the church as in Israel there should be an equal sharing of the resources at hand.

### c. COMMENDATION OF THE REPRESENTATIVES, 8:16–9:5

8   [16]Thanks be to God, who has placed the same earnestness for you into the heart of Titus. [17]For he received our urging, and being extremely earnest he is going out to you of his own accord. [18]And we are sending with him that brother who is renowned in all the churches because of his work for the gospel—[19]who, moreover, has been appointed by the churches to accompany us with this benevolence being administered by us, to show the glory of the Lord himself and our goodwill. [20]We are taking this action lest anyone blame us about this large sum being administered by us; [21]for we pay attention to what is honorable, not only "in the sight of the Lord" but also "in the sight of human beings." [22]And we are sending with them our brother whose earnestness we have verified in many ways and often, who is now the more earnest by reason of his great confidence in you. [23]As for Titus, he is my partner and co-worker in toiling for you; as for our brothers,

they are representatives of the churches, the glory of Christ. [24]So you should clearly demonstrate to them your love and our boasting about you, as in the presence of the churches.

**9** [1]So it is superfluous for me to be writing to you concerning the relief work for the saints [2]because I know your goodwill, which is the subject of my boasting about you to the Macedonians—telling them that Achaia has been ready since last year. And your zeal has been a spur to most of them. [3]But I am sending the brothers in order that our boasting about you may not be in vain in this matter, and in order that you may be ready, just as I was saying, [4]lest if Macedonians should come with me and find you are unready, we be disgraced—to say nothing of yourselves—in this undertaking. [5]Therefore, I considered it necessary to urge the brothers to go on ahead to you and to organize in advance the gift you had already pledged, that it may be ready as a gift and not as an extortion.

## NOTES

8:16. *Thanks be to God.* In this phrase *(charis de tō Theō)* Paul uses the word *charis* (translated as *grace* in 8:1, 9; as *benefit* in 8:4; as *benevolence* in 8:6, 7) in yet another way, to give *thanks* to God (see BAG s.v. 5). See also 2:14 (with note) and 9:15.

*has placed.* Reading the aorist participle *donti* (literally "gave") with P[46] D F G L et al. (adopted by *GNT*-Nestle and followed also by, e.g., *NIV, NAB*). Others (e.g., *RSV, JB, TEV*) follow ℵ B C et al. in reading the present participle *didonti* (literally "gives"). The aorist would be expected after 7:7, and therefore Barrett, 217 n. 1, tends to favor "the less obvious present."

*the same earnestness for you.* It is unclear how *the same (tēn autēn)* should be understood here. Most interpret it with reference to Paul's own earnestness for the Corinthians (e.g., Lietzmann, 135; Hughes, 311; Barrett, 227; cf. *JB, NEB, TEV, NIV*). Paul has not spoken directly of his *earnestness* for the Corinthians, however, but of that of the Corinthians themselves (8:7; cf. 7:11, 12) and of the Macedonians (8:8). One could therefore understand this as "the same earnestness for you that you have for us" or (so Windisch, 261) "the same earnestness (to organize the collection) for you that the Macedonians have shown for the collection." The usual interpretation is preferable, however, given 8:17.

*Titus.* See NOTES on 2:13.

17. *received.* If Paul is meaning to specify the act of receiving as "past" in relation to the time when the Corinthians will be reading this, then *edexato* should be regarded as an epistolary aorist (so, e.g., Plummer, 247; Moule 1953:12) and translated (according to the English idiom) "is receiving." However, even if the next two verbs (*is going,* 8:17b; *we are sending,* 8:18) are epistolary aorists (see below), *edexato* can be treated as a real aorist; Titus' "receiving" is already past for the writer.

*urging.* Translates *paraklēsis* which could also be rendered as "appeal" (see note on *imploring us,* 8:4) or as "encouragement." The related verb is translated *urged* in 8:6 (on which see the note). *Our* is supplied for the tr., although it does not occur in the Greek and despite the use of the first person singular in 8:8–15; in the present paragraph (8:16–24) Paul has returned to the use of the first person plural (see 8:18; 8:23*a* provides an exception).

*extremely earnest.* Here the comparative form *(spoudaioteros)* has an elative meaning; see BDF § 244(2) and *GNTG* III:30.

*is going out.* Translates *exēlthen,* which, like *we are sending* (8:18, 22), should be regarded as an epistolary aorist: something in the present is described as past because it will be concluded by the time this letter is received. Pherigo's argument for this interpretation in 8:18, 22 (1949:350) also applies here: the appeal in 8:24 presumes that the three men commended in 8:16–23 have just arrived.

*of his own accord.* Cf. *of their own accord,* 8:3, and see the note there.

18. *we are sending.* An epistolary aorist; see note on *is going out,* 8:17.

*that brother.* Literally, "the brother" *(ton adelphon),* but the definite article anticipates the relative clause to follow; BDF § 258(1).

*who is renowned.* Paul uses a noun here, "whose fame (is)" *(hou ho epainos).*

*all the churches.* Paul uses the same phrase without any further qualification in 11:28; 1 Cor 7:17 (elsewhere in the NT it occurs only in Rev 2:23). When in Rom 16 he writes about "all the churches of the Gentiles" (v. 4) and "all the churches of Christ" (v. 16), it is clear that he is thinking quite generally of the churches (at least his churches) in Asia Minor and Greece; cf. "all the churches of the saints" (1 Cor 14:33*b,* part of an interpolation?). (In Rom 16:23 and 1 Cor 14:23, however, "the whole church" [*hē holē ekklēsia*] means the entirety of a particular congregation, probably inclusive of several separate house-churches [on which see Murphy-O'Connor 1983:158].) It is not certain whether Paul is thinking here of *the churches of Macedonia* (as in 8:1) or of the churches in some larger area, perhaps his whole mission field, as most commentators (and also Morgan-Wynne 1979) seem to presuppose. (Hughes, 311–12, and de Boor, 184–85, are among the few who even raise the question.) Nickle (1966:18–22) argues that this and the subsequent references, simply to *the churches* (8:19, 23, 24), are to the churches of Judea; but see COMMENT.

*because of his work for the gospel.* The Greek *(en tō euangeliō)* has to be paraphrased, and it might mean "because of his preaching of the gospel" (e.g., *RSV, TEV, NAB;* cf. *JB*). It is preferable, however, lacking any clear indication that "preaching" is specifically in mind, to interpret the expression more generally (so also, e.g., *NEB, NIV*). Cf. Phil 4:3, cited by Windisch, 262.

19. *moreover.* Literally "not only (this), but also" (as in 8:10, on which see the note).

*has been appointed.* Or "has been elected" *(JB).* The word used here *(cheirotonein)* originally meant "to elect by a show of hands," then simply "to elect" in any manner or "to appoint." In the only other NT occurrence, Acts 14:23, Paul and Barnabas appoint elders for some churches without any congregational elections being involved. But here the appointment is *by the churches;* cf. Did 15:1; Ign Phld 10:1; Pol 7:2; Smyrn. 11:2–3, and Philo, *Special Laws* I, 78, quoted in the COMMENT. Only later did the word come to be used for "ordination" (an example from about 600 C.E. in Deissmann 1927:221–24). Paul uses a participial form here—where the rules of grammar would call for a finite verb—and the result is anacoluthon; see BDF § 468(1) and Robertson 1923:433, 1134.

*by the churches.* Most commentators believe the reference is to *the churches of Macedonia,* 8:1 (e.g., Lietzmann, 137; Windisch, 263; Barrett, 228–29). But others think this is unlikely because of the remark in 9:4; thus Hughes, 316 ("no doubt the churches of Asia Minor") and Nickle 1966:18–22 ( = the churches of Judea). See COMMENT.

*to accompany us.* Literally "as our traveling companion" *(synekdēmos hēmōn);* in Acts 19:29 two Macedonians, Gaius and Aristarchus, are called Paul's "traveling companions." Note *us,* which seems to indicate that this *brother* is also to travel with Paul, perhaps clear to Jerusalem, as the apostle takes up and delivers the collection (de Boor, 185).

*with this benevolence.* The textual variation here *(syn* is slightly more probable than *en;* see Metzger 1971:581–82) has no effect on the meaning. For *benevolence,* see note on 8:6.

*being administered by us.* See note on the similar phrase "cared for by us" in 3:3. The verb *(diakonein)* corresponds to one of the terms *(diakonia)* Paul uses for the collection itself (see note on *the relief work,* 8:4).

*to show the glory of the Lord.* Perhaps even "to increase the glory of the Lord" (cf. Boobyer 1929:79–84, and COMMENT on 1:20). More literally, "for the glory of the Lord" *(pros tēn . . . tou Kyriou doxan).* The phrase is dependent on *has been appointed* (so, e.g., Plummer, 248–49; Windisch, 264), and not on *being administered.* In 8:5 *the Lord* was Christ, but here the reference is probably to God, as in 3:18 (on which see the note). Cf. "to the glory of God" in 4:15; Rom 15:7; 1 Cor 10:31; Phil 1:11; 2:11 —all of which, however, use the preposition *eis,* rather than *pros* as here (and in 1:20 [literally "for glory"]; cf. 3 Mac 2:9).

*himself.* This *(autou)* is omitted by B C D* F G L et al., and is retained only in square brackets by the editors of *GNT*-Nestle. See Barrett, 217 n. 2, for a plausible explanation of its presence in the original text.

*and our goodwill.* For the word translated *goodwill,* see note on 8:11 ("impatience" *[JB]* is inaccurate). These words conclude the prepositional phrase begun with *pros* (translated here as *to show*), but Lietzmann, 137 (followed by Barrett, 229) believes that the preposition has two different meanings here: "for" the Lord's glory, but "in accord with" ( = *kata*) the intention of Paul (Barrett even translates "at our suggestion"). However, it is likely that Paul would have expressed himself differently were this his meaning. How the appointment of the brother shows Paul's *goodwill* is clarified in 8:20 (cf. Kümmel, 207).

20. *We are taking this action lest anyone.* Translates the participle *stellomenoi,* which may be construed with either *we are sending,* 8:18 (so, e.g., Windisch, 264), or (involving anacoluthon) *to accompany us,* 8:19 (so BDF § 468[1]), but more probably the former. One could also translate as "We are trying to avoid anyone's (blaming us)," etc. See Rengstorf's discussion of the word, *TDNT* VII:588–90. Although it was occasionally used with respect to steering ships, there is no reason to think Paul is using "a nautical metaphor" here (against Hughes, 318, n. 46, who cites Wettstein). Philo employs the word for the annual "dispatching" of envoys with the offerings of Diaspora Jews for the Temple treasury *(Embassy to Gaius* 216).

*blame us.* For the verb "to blame," see the note on 6:3.

*large sum.* Greek *hadrotēs,* only here in the Greek Bible, although the adjective from which it derives *(hadros)* occurs several times in the LXX, always substantively and with reference to men who are "great," "mighty," etc. See especially LXX Jer 5:5, "the rich men."

*being administered by us.* As in 8:19.

21. *we pay attention to . . .* etc. Here Paul is alluding to LXX Prov 3:4, which has the (singular) imperative form, "pay attention to" (more literally: "take thought for").

*what is honorable.* Or "what is good" *(kala,* as in Prov 3:4).

*not only . . . but also.* As in 8:10 (see note) and 8:19. Here Paul employs the idiom in order to emphasize one part of his text from Prov (see following note).

*"in the sight of the Lord" . . . "in the sight of human beings."* Both phrases are drawn from LXX Prov 3:4, and *the Lord* here is God, as in 8:19 (cf. "in the sight of God," 4:2; 7:12; P⁴⁶ reads "of God" in the present verse as well). It is the second phrase that Paul wishes to emphasize; cf. Rom 12:17, where echoing the same text he omits any reference to *the Lord:* "Pay attention to what is honorable in the sight of all human beings [*anthrōpōn;* "men" used generically, as in Prov 3:4 and 2 Cor 8:21]."

22. *we are sending.* As in 8:18 (see note).

*with them.* That is, with Titus (8:6, 16–17) and *that brother . . . renowned in all the churches* (8:18).

*our brother.* Contrast *that brother,* 8:18. (*NAB* is misleading here.)

*whose earnestness we have verified.* More literally, "whom we have verified . . . (he) being earnest." For the verb see NOTES on 8:8. Paul has previously remarked on the *earnestness* of the Corinthians (8:7; 7:11–12), of the Macedonians (8:8), and of Titus (8:16, 17).

*in many ways and often.* There is paronomasia in Greek (*en pollois pollakis*—the juxtaposition of two words with a common stem), but this cannot be reproduced in English.

*confidence.* Translates *pepoithēsis* (as in 1:15; 3:4; 10:2). Paul's own confidence in the Corinthians has been emphasized in 7:4–16 (see especially v. 16, where "confidence" translates the verb *tharrein* [on which see the note, 5:6]).

23a. *Titus.* See 8:6, 16–17.

*my partner.* Paul earlier remarked that the Corinthians themselves are "partners" with him in comfort as well as in suffering (1:7; see the note), and elsewhere he appeals to Philemon as his *partner* (Phlm 17; cf. v. 6, which refers to their "partnership in faith"). Note the use here of the first-person-singular pronoun, *my,* although the first-person plural is present elsewhere in this paragraph (8:16–24).

*co-worker.* Paul's favorite description of his associates in ministry; see NOTES for 1:24 ("co-workers") and 6:1 ("working together").

*in toiling for you.* The Greek has simply *for you* (*eis hymas;* cf. 13:3, 4). The present tr. is suggested by Rom 16:6; Gal 4:11—where, using a missionary term, Paul writes of "working hard for you" *(kopian eis hymas).* *NIV*'s "among you" is misleading, for Paul and Titus have not (at least so far) labored in Corinth at the same time.

23b. *our brothers.* Paul again uses the first-person-plural pronoun (contrast *my partner,* 8:23a), and now includes both of the unnamed brothers as his own, not just the one mentioned in 8:22.

*representatives of the churches.* "Apostles of the churches" *(NAB)* is misleading, because Paul is not using *apostoloi* here (as he does, for example, in 1 Cor 15:9) of himself and certain others who have seen the risen Lord and have been commissioned to preach the gospel. Here the reference is to brothers who have been chosen by a group of local congregations for a specific task. Cf. the description of Epaphroditus in Phil 2:25 as "your representative [*apostolos*] and a minister [*leitourgos*] to my need." The *hieropompoi* ("escorts of the sacred tribute") who conveyed an offering to Jerusalem each year (see Philo, *Special Laws* I, 78 [quoted in the COMMENT] and *Embassy to Gaius* 216) served a similar function for Diaspora Judaism.

*the churches.* As in 8:19 (see note there).

*the glory of Christ.* Like *representatives of the churches,* this is an honorific title applied to the brothers (not to *the churches*). Cf. 2:15, "we are the aroma of Christ" (referring to his apostolate), and 3:3, "you are Christ's letter" (referring to the Corinthians themselves); further references in Kramer 1966:138.

24. *you should clearly demonstrate.* The adverb is supplied for the tr. in order to convey some of the effect of the Greek, which more literally would be something like "demonstrating what is to be demonstrated" *(tēn endeixin . . . endeiknymenoi).* The Greek participle has imperatival force here. The imperative form *endeixasthe* (■ C D²  et al.) probably originated with copyists who were not acquainted with the Semitic idiom (participles used as imperatives); Metzger 1971:582. For the thought, cf. 8:8.

*to them.* Principally, to the *brothers* (8:23b), for Titus has already seen evidence and brought word of the Corinthians' earnestness and love (see 7:6–16).

*your love.* See the note on *love* in 8:8.

*our boasting about you.* Paul has been boasting about the Corinthians not only to Titus (7:14) but also to the Macedonians (9:3). The phrase here is probably to be understood as "why we have been boasting about you" or "what our boasting of you has been all about."

*as in the presence of the churches.* Translates *eis prosōpon tōn ekklēsiōn,* "in the face of [ = before] the churches"; thus, "in such a way as to be seen by them." *As* is added in the tr. since this phrase stands in apposition to *eis autous (to them).* Because the brothers represent *the churches* (8:23b), what is demonstrated *to them* is demonstrated to the churches.

9:1. *So . . . concerning.* The Greek phrase *(peri men gar)* is often compared with one which Paul uses elsewhere to introduce a new topic *(peri de,* "now concerning"; 1 Cor 7:1, 25; 8:1; 12:1; 16:1; 1 Thess 4:9; 5:1). Thus, some commentators (e.g., Windisch, 269; Wendland, 222; Héring, 65; Bultmann, 258) believe the present phrase completely overlooks the discussion in chap. 8, and is one indication that chap. 9 did not originally stand in the same letter. It must be observed, however, that the introductory formula of 1 Cor 7:1, etc., is not exactly reproduced here. Instead of *de* ("Now") there is *gar* *(So;* or "For"), which some believe presumes a reference to what has preceded. In this case the phrase should be called "resumptive" (so Bruce, 225) rather than introductory. Plummer, 253, believes it connects in particular with the reference to the sending of the *brothers* (Paul is recommending them rather than giving a direct command about the collection [8:8], because the Corinthians have no need of the latter), whereas Barrett, 232, thinks it connects with the reference to *boasting* (8:24). Dahl (1977:39) agrees that the phrase could just as well be resumptive of a previous topic (after the recommendation of Titus and the two brothers in 8:16–24) as introductory of a new one. (The Greek particle *men,* left untranslated here, may anticipate the *de* of v. 3: "while on the one hand there is no need to be writing this to you . . . yet, on the other hand, I am sending the brothers. . . ." Cf. Plummer, 253, 254; Barrett, 233, and the note on *But,* 9:3.)

*it is superfluous for me.* Cf. "you have no need," 1 Thess 4:9; 5:1. Note *me;* the first person singular predominates in 9:1–5, but the plural surfaces in 9:3 and 4.

*to be writing to you.* Translates *to graphein hymin.* Plummer, 253, notes that the infinitive is present tense rather than aorist, although this is also true of the corresponding infinitives (one active, as here; the other passive) in 1 Thess 4:9; 5:1. More significantly, the infinitive here has the article—as those in 1 Thess do not—and it is possible to interpret it as anaphoric (BDF § 399[2]). It would then denote something already known, and one could translate with Denney, 280 (followed by Barrett, 233): "to be writing to you as I do."

*the relief work for the saints.* As in 8:4, on which see the NOTES. Bultmann, 258, finds in the repetition of this full description of the collection another reason for concluding that chaps. 8 and 9 belonged to different letters. But see COMMENT.

2. *because.* Greek *gar* ["for"], which introduces a reason why it is really needless for Paul to be writing about the collection.

*I know your goodwill.* Their *goodwill* is referred to in 8:11, 12.

*my boasting about you.* Cf. 7:4, 14; 8:24; 9:3.

*the Macedonians.* That is, the members of the Christian congregations in Macedonia; see 8:1.

*telling them that.* The Greek *hoti (that)* introduces something which has been said.

*Achaia.* See 1:1, "the saints throughout Achaia" (and note there). Some believe that chap. 9 was originally sent as a circular letter to Christians in the whole province of Achaia, while chap. 8 was sent specifically to Corinth, the capital city (e.g., Windisch, 286–88, followed by Georgi 1965:57). In the NT, *Achaia* usually has the article, but that is missing both here and in Rom 15:26 (see *GNTG* III:170).

*since last year.* Not "for a year"; see note on the same phrase in 8:10.

*zeal.* In 7:7, 11, Paul refers to the Corinthians' *zeal* to please him. Here it is more specifically their *zeal* for the collection; cf. the earlier reference in this verse (and in 8:11, 12) to their *goodwill.*

*has been a spur.* This tr. follows *JB.* The verb *(erethizein)* usually means to "irritate" or "provoke," as in Col 3:21 (the only other NT instance). But here it means to "stir up" in a good sense, to rouse to action.

*most of them.* The same expression is translated "the majority" in 2:6 (see note there).

3. *But.* Translates *de,* which should perhaps be regarded as answering the *men* in 9:1 (see note there on *So . . . concerning*). What is introduced here limits the whole thought of 9:1–2 (one need not choose between these two verses, as Windisch, 271, suggests): because Paul knows the *goodwill* of the Corinthians it is really needless for him to be writing as he is; nevertheless, there is some reason for him to be sending the brothers to them in advance of his own coming.

*I am sending.* This tr. of *epempsa* as an epistolary aorist (as in 8:18, 22) presumes that chaps. 8 and 9 belong to the same letter. If, as some hold, chap. 9 was composed and sent after the brothers had left for Corinth (therefore after chap. 8), one should probably translate this as a true aorist, "I have sent." See also following note.

*the brothers.* Presumably those mentioned in chap. 8, whether Titus and both of the unnamed brothers who are accompanying him to Corinth, or just the two specifically called *brothers* (8:18–22 and 8:23*b*). Héring, 65, who argues that chap. 9 was dispatched earlier than chap. 8, believes some other brothers are meant—men whom Paul has previously sent ("I have sent") to Corinth.

*our boasting about you.* Paul slips into the use of the plural, *our,* despite *my boasting about you* (literally "I am boasting about you") in 9:2. In Greek the noun has the article, and this is repeated for emphasis (more literally: "the boasting we do, the [boasting] about you"); see BDF § 269(2). Here *boasting* translates *kauchēma* (rendered as "boast" in 1:14 and "pride" in 5:12); in 8:24 *kauchēsis* is used in the same way.

*may not be in vain.* Here a passive form of the verb *kenoun.* Paul often uses the corresponding adjective to express the concern that his apostolic labors on behalf of his congregations shall not have been "in vain" (1 Cor 15:14; Gal 2:2; Phil 2:16; 1 Thess 2:1; 3:5). In all these cases, as in the present passage, he means that he wants the faith of his congregations to bear fruit (see 6:1; 1 Cor 15:14, 58).

*and in order that.* The second *hina* [*in order that*]-clause in this verse is, like the first, dependent on *I am sending;* the *and* is supplied in English to make this clear.

*I was saying.* The verb is imperfect tense; the action extended over a period of time.

4. *lest if Macedonians should come with me.* Paul himself will be visiting Corinth, perhaps accompanied by some Macedonian Christians. Héring, 66 n. 4, believes this remark confirms that chap. 9 predated chap. 8: Paul's original plan had been to accompany Titus and some Macedonians to Corinth, but by the time he wrote chap. 8 he had decided to send Titus and the two brothers instead. But this hypothesis is unnecessarily complex. Paul also refers to an impending visit to Corinth in 12:14; 13:1.

*we be disgraced.* Paul lapses again (see note on 9:3) into the use of the first person plural.

*to say nothing of yourselves.* Literally "lest I say you," a good example of paralipsis, where a point is made by indicating that the writer or speaker is not making it; see BDF § 495(1) and Robertson 1923:1199. The variant *legōmen* ("we say" for "I say" in אֵ B C² et al.) is secondary, an apparent assimilation to *we be disgraced* (Metzger 1971: 582).

*in this undertaking.* Translates *en tē hypostasei tautē.* The addition *tēs kauchēseōs* ("of boasting") in a few texts is a clear assimilation to 11:17. The noun *hypostasis* (in the NT only here and 11:17 and Heb 1:3; 3:14; 11:1) has a wide range of meanings, depending on the context in which it appears (medical, astrological, philosophical, etc.). There is no evidence, however, that it can mean "confidence" or "assurance," as most recent English versions of the present verse (as well as of 11:17; Heb 3:14; 11:1) assume; see Köster, *TDNT* VIII:571–89. The meaning adopted here (following Köster, ibid.:584–85, who suggests "project" or "plan") is also suitable for 11:17, and corresponds to one frequent use of the word elsewhere (e.g., in LXX Jer 23:22; Ezek 19:5; Wis 16:21, discussed by Köster, ibid.:581–82). The *undertaking* referred to would be the collection project itself. Thus, Paul's disgrace would not be (as it is in 7:14) that his boasting has been unwarranted (this point has been made in 9:3) but, more than that, that his whole project has been damaged—and the Corinthians themselves would also experience this disgrace. See COMMENT.

5. *to urge.* The same verb used with reference to Titus in 8:6. See also 8:17, *our urging.*

*the brothers.* As in 9:3.

*to go on ahead to you.* As in 9:4, the presumption is that Paul (and others) will come later.

*to organize in advance.* Again, *in advance* of Paul's own coming (see preceding note).

*the gift.* Translates *eulogia* (in other contexts, e.g., 1 Cor 10:16; Gal 3:14, "blessing"), which here, as in LXX Josh 15:19; 4 Kgdms 5:15, refers to something bestowed on one person by another, especially in token of their relationship (cf. Georgi 1965:67–68). There may be an intentional wordplay on *logeia* (or *logia*), "collection," a term which Paul had in fact used in 1 Cor 16:1. (Deissmann [1903:144] thinks it "not impossible" that Paul himself had written *logeia* here, in anticipation of *eu-logia* in the next phrase.)

*already pledged.* Or "already promised," in either case the emphasis being on the fact that the Corinthians have previously made a commitment to participate in the collection project.

*that it may be ready.* The Greek accusative-plus-infinitive *(tautēn . . . einai)* is interpreted here in a final sense (so also, e.g., Barrett, *RSV*), although it could be regarded as consecutive: "Then it will be" *(TEV, NIV;* cf. *NEB).*

*an extortion.* The same noun *(pleonexia)* occurs frequently in vice lists with reference to "covetousness" or "greed" (in Paul's letters, Rom 1:29; cf. the related noun, "greedy person[s]," in 1 Cor 5:10, 11; 6:10). The corresponding verb has already been used in this letter with the meaning "to cheat" or "defraud" (2:11; 7:5—see note on each), and that is also the meaning of the verb in 12:17–18. The latter passage, as Barrett, 235, emphasizes, is especially important because it shows that Paul has been accused of acting with fraudulent intent in the matter of the collection for Jerusalem; see COMMENT. The present tr. follows *NEB* (cf. *RSV, NAB, JB*). Others take the word as referring to something given only grudgingly, out of a desire to keep everything for oneself (e.g., *NIV*); for this interpretation see Plummer, 256; Windisch, 275; Hughes, 328 n. 60.

## COMMENT: GENERAL

The discussion of the collection for Jerusalem continues here. As in 8:1–15, Paul refers to his pride in the Corinthians (8:24; 9:2), to the Corinthians' eagerness to be responsive to him (9:2), and to Titus' confidence in the Corinthians (8:16–17)—three points which also had been stressed in 7:4–16. But now in these paragraphs special attention is given to Titus and the brothers Paul is sending with him to Corinth to work there on behalf of the collection in advance of the apostle's own arrival. (There is no compelling reason for believing with Windisch [260, 268] that 8:16–24 originally stood between 8:1–6 and 8:7–15.)

In 8:16–24, Paul commends his representatives by indicating their credentials for the mission: Titus, just back from Corinth, is eager to return (8:16–17);

one of the brothers accompanying him is well known among the churches and has actually been chosen by them for this task (8:18–21); and a second brother coming with Titus has served Paul well and is himself eager to be going to Corinth because of his confidence in the Corinthian church (8:22). The commendation of these three is summarized in 8:23 and concluded with an appeal in 8:24. Then, after commending the Corinthians themselves for their goodwill toward his project (9:1–2), Paul indicates why, nevertheless, he considers it important that these men precede him to Corinth to arrange for the collection (9:3–5).

This commentary treats chap. 9 as an integral part of the letter referred to in the INTRODUCTION as Letter D (pp. 41–44), and therefore as intended by Paul himself to follow directly on chap. 8, just as it does in our canonical 2 Cor. An alternative possibility is to regard these chapters as "doublets"—that is, two independent discussions of the same topic which belonged originally to different letters. Before proceeding with detailed comments on chap. 9, the arguments for this alternative view need to be considered.

## The Relation Between Chapters 8 and 9

To many interpreters the discussion of the collection in chap. 9 seems partly repetitive of and partly inconsistent with the discussion of the same topic in the preceding chapter. This has led to the hypothesis that these chapters did not originally stand in the same letter, and the points mentioned in favor of this are important enough that the hypothesis must be taken very seriously.

a. Arguments advanced to support the view that chap. 9 is or belongs to a separate letter. Three of these are especially important.

First, two features of 9:1 can be regarded as signs that a new topic is being introduced. One of these is the phrase *So . . . concerning (peri men gar),* similar to a phrase with which Paul introduces new topics in other places—for example, in 1 Cor 16:1, where the collection is mentioned for the first time. However, as indicated in the NOTES on this phrase, this is not the exact formula Paul uses elsewhere to introduce something new, and in the present instance the *gar* ("for"; translated here as *So*) could be regarded as joining chap. 9 to what has preceded. The other feature of 9:1 that could be called introductory (so Bultmann, 258) is the reappearance of the full description of the collection, already used in 8:4: *the relief work for the saints.* One must admit that, with chap. 8 preceding, some shorter or alternate description would have been quite adequate (for instance, "the relief work" or "this benevolence"). Yet the repetition of the full phrase need not be considered unusual after the amount of material that separates the two references, and it is always possible (Bruce, 225) that the apostle had paused in his dictation between 8:24 and 9:1. The repetition of the full phrase, then, could be explained as signaling Paul's resumption of his discussion. Or it could be explained as re-emphasizing the subject at hand, as the preceding discussion is now extended or reinforced.

Second, Paul says in 9:2 that he boasts to the Macedonians about the response to the collection in Achaia, and that the Macedonians have been prompted thereby to make their own contribution. To many (e.g., Windisch, 270; Bultmann, 258) this seems inconsistent with 8:1–5, where Paul presents the Macedonians as an example to the Corinthians, and 8:10–12, where Paul's remarks about the *goodwill* of the Corinthians (also mentioned in 9:2) suggest that it was not much to brag about (it had not yet borne fruit). In Bultmann's opinion, if chap. 9 be regarded as a separate and earlier letter the apparent inconsistency is resolved: earlier, Paul had boasted to the Macedonians about the Corinthians, and this had prompted the Macedonians to join in the project (9:2); subsequently, Paul was able to use the zeal of the Macedonians as an example for the Corinthians, whose *goodwill* had not yet produced results (Bultmann, 258). But this same explanation can be (and is) used by those who believe chaps. 8 and 9 belong to the same letter (e.g., Hughes, 324–25; Barrett, 233). After all, the remarks in 9:2, no less than those in 8:1–5, 10–12, are addressed to the Corinthians as part of Paul's present appeal to them (cf. Lüdemann 1980:120 n. 150), and it is characteristic of Paul to use whatever arguments he can to support his exhortations (see, for example, 1 Cor 11: 2–16). Here these include the example of the Macedonians (8:1–5), as well as the argument (1) that *goodwill* is not enough (8:10–12), and (2) that the Corinthians should live up to the reputation they have among the Macedonians (9:2).

Third, it is frequently alleged (Windisch, 271, and Bultmann, 258, are again exemplary) that the reason offered in 8:20 for the coming of the brothers differs from the one presented in 9:3–5. In the former passage Paul mentions his concern that no one suspect him of taking up a collection under false pretenses, perhaps to further his own missionary work rather than to help the poor Christians of Jerusalem. Yet in chap. 9 he emphasizes the responsibility of *the brothers* to get some Corinthian money together before his own arrival, so that his previous boasting about the Corinthians' commitment will not seem unwarranted to any Macedonians who may accompany him. It is worth noting, however, that the remark in 8:20 pertains only to the role of the first brother, while the remarks in chap. 9 have both brothers (perhaps including Titus) in view. Also, unless one is willing to argue that *the brothers* in chap. 9 are different from those in chap. 8 (e.g. Héring, 65), this alleged inconsistency is not greatly eased by assigning the two chapters to different letters. Furthermore, the two reasons for the mission are certainly not incompatible: it should not be overlooked that in chap. 8, too, Paul expresses a concern that what he has been boasting about may be demonstrated to those who are coming (v. 24). And finally, the concern expressed in 8:20 is also present in chap. 9. The coming of the brothers will not only assure that Paul's boasting turns out to have been warranted (9:3); it will also assure that the Corinthians' contributions have been freely given, not extorted from them by a devious apostle (9:5).

In addition to these three principal arguments for chaps. 8 and 9 to be regarded as independent discussions, two other points are sometimes noted. (1) *Achaia* is mentioned in chap. 9 but not in chap. 8, which could mean that chap. 9 was not directed to the Christians in Corinth, but to Christians in the outlying districts of the province (e.g., Windisch, 288, followed by Georgi 1965:57). But there are other plausible explanations for Paul's use of the name of the province here; for example, a concern to include all those to whom this letter is addressed (see 1:1; cf. Plummer, 254), or to use a designation that would correspond to his reference to "Macedonians" (which had to be used to include the Philippians, Thessalonians, and others). (2) The first person plural predominates in chap. 8, but the first person singular is used in chap. 9 (cited by Georgi 1965:57 n. 212). Actually, however, the whole of 8:8–15 is dominated by the first person singular of 8:8, 10 (see NOTES), and the first person singular also appears (incidentally) in 8:3, 24. Moreover, the first person singular appears only in the first five verses of chap. 9, and even there the plural surfaces momentarily in vv. 3, 4. In 9:6–15 there is only one first-person form, and that is plural (9:11).

b. If chap. 8 and chap. 9 are independent discussions, what is the occasion of each? This question receives different answers.

Some (e.g., Bultmann, 258; Héring, 65) regard chap. 9 as earlier than chap. 8. Thus, Héring, xiii, describes it as a note carried to Corinth by Titus when he was sent to organize the collection for the first time—the visit on which the "beginning" mentioned in 8:6 took place. On this view chap. 8 is one part of a later, so-called "conciliatory letter" (ibid., and Bultmann, 258). Windisch, 287, who does not himself subscribe to this view, concedes one point in its favor: that 8:1–5 presumes the collection has already been concluded among the Macedonians, while Paul uses the present tense in 9:2 as he writes of his *boasting* (literally "I am boasting") to the Macedonians about Achaia. The latter may be—although it certainly need not be—interpreted as an indication that the collection is still being taken up in Macedonia.

Most scholars who separate the two chapters believe, however, that chap. 9 must be dated slightly later than chap. 8. The grounds for this (as given by Windisch, 287, followed by Georgi 1965:57) are that (1) chap. 9 presumes the collection is near completion, while chap. 8 urges that it be completed; (2) chap. 9 presumes that the brothers introduced in chap. 8 are already known; and (3) chap. 9 alludes to an impending visit of Paul (v. 4), while chap. 8 does not. Windisch (ibid.) suggests that chap. 9 may have been a circular letter to the churches of Achaia (see 9:2), and to this Georgi adds the suggestion that the differences between chaps. 8 and 9 are further clarified if chap. 8 was written from Philippi and chap. 9 from Thessalonica (1965:58).

Whether chap. 8 or chap. 9 be dated earlier, no great span of time could have separated their composition. Most scholars think in terms of a few weeks only. Indeed, Vielhauer (1975:153) tentatively favors the idea that chap. 9 was an integral part of that so-called "conciliatory letter" (1:1–2:13 + 7:5–16 + chap. 9), and that chap. 8 was a separate letter of recommendation for Titus and the brothers with whom the longer letter was being sent. If so, while the two chapters belonged to two separate letters they were in fact written on the same occasion and sent out at the same time. This proposal has the advantage of explaining the wording of 9:1 and the varying emphases in chaps. 8 and 9, and yet not requiring that fundamentally distinct occasions, different points of origin, or different addresses be posited for the two chapters. On the other hand, those who believe there are serious points of conflict between the two chapters can hardly find this hypothesis more satisfying than the traditional presumption that the chapters have always stood in the same letter.

c. Can chap. 9 be understood as a meaningful extension of the discussion in chap. 8?

The majority of commentators and other interpreters answer this question affirmatively. The possibility that chaps. 8 and 9 represent two independent discussions of the collection cannot be ruled out, yet the arguments for that are not fully convincing. No one of the points discussed under a. above is in itself decisive, for the reasons given there. Nor are all of them put together decisive, for on the other side it may be remarked:

(1) The alleged redundancy of the two chapters is more apparent than real. As pointed out in the NOTES, the anaphoric article with the present infinitive in 9:1 permits the tr. *So it is superfluous for me to be writing to you concerning the relief work for the saints . . . ,* and the sentence as a whole need not be interpreted as introducing a new topic. What may appear redundant (e.g., the full description of Paul's project, 9:1; references to the *goodwill* of the Corinthians and to Paul's *boasting* about them, 9:2; mention of *the brothers,* 9:3–5) is easily enough explained as repetition for the sake of emphasis. Furthermore, the affirmations of 9:6–15, which constitute two thirds of chap. 9, present no real problem at all. They could stand as well with chap. 8 as with 9:1–5.

(2) In at least two respects what is said in chap. 9 seems to require chap. 8 in order to be understandable (cf. Kümmel 1975:291). The mention of *the brothers,* 9:3, presumes that the readers already know who these men are (8:18ff.), and the emphasis on their completing the collection before Paul's arrival, 9:4–5, presumes the readers already know that its completion is an important obligation (8:7–15).

(3) The first paragraph of chap. 9 (vv. 1–5) may be interpreted as a meaningful extension of 8:16–24. In 9:1–2, Paul acknowledges that it might seem unnecessary to be writing the Corinthians about the collection because he has indeed been *boasting* about their commitment to it (cf. 8:24). But that commitment does not preclude his dispatch of *the brothers,* he says (9:3–5; cf. 8:18ff.), because they are to make sure that contributions to the fund are forthcoming before Paul's own arrival in order to avoid jeopardizing the whole project by even the appearance of fraudulent behavior on Paul's part (cf. 9:5 with 8:20).

(4) The second paragraph of chap. 9 (vv. 6–15) may be readily seen as a general conclusion to the whole discussion since 7:4, invoking several types of reasons for being generous with one's aid for the poor.

d. Conclusions.

The arguments in favor of the hypothesis that chaps. 8 and 9 were not originally in the same letter are important, and the hypothesis itself is not implausible. If they were indeed originally separate, it is understandable why the later redactor of the Corinthian correspondence would have seen fit to combine them where they stand in our 2 Cor. On the other hand, no serious problem stands in the way of reading these two chapters as a single, integrated discussion of the collection project, preceded by the preliminary assurances of confidence in 7:4–16. Following the appeal proper, 8:1–15, Paul commends the representatives he is sending, 8:16–9:5, identifying their credentials (8:16–24) and indicating why their mission is warranted (9:1–5). The entire discussion is then concluded in 9:6–15 with some general remarks on the values of generous giving.

## COMMENT: DETAILED

### Titus and the Two Brothers, 8:16–24

a. Titus, vv. 16–17. Since Titus is probably the bearer of this letter to Corinth (chaps. 1–9) it is appropriate that he should be commended to the recipients. (See note on *letters of recommendation,* 3:1.) Indeed, one can imagine that the members of the Corinthian congregation would be surprised to see him again, since he had already spent some considerable time with them and had only recently (measured by travel times in the ancient world) left their city with a report for Paul. It is extraordinary that he has so soon retraced his steps for the long return journey to them. Perhaps to explain this, Paul assures his readers that Titus has been motivated to come back to them primarily because of his *earnestness.* This is equal to Paul's own, v. 16, so while it is true that the apostle has urged him to return (8:6), that *urging,* v. 17, was not really necessary.

Significantly, Paul says that the *earnestness* of Titus was for the Corinthians (*for you,* v. 16). He does not specifically say that it was for the collection, or even for the completion of the collection in Corinth, although this thought is certainly implicit (see 8:6). Paul has chosen a more tactful way to express this. Yet more than simple tact is involved here. Paul regards participation in the collection as a *benefit* to those who give as well as to those who receive (8:4), as a genuine "work of grace" (see note on *benevolence,* 8:6). In his efforts for the collection, as in every aspect of his apostolic work, Paul's concern is for what he can give to others, not for what they can give to him (see 12:14*b*–15).

b. The renowned brother, vv. 18–21. Along with Titus, Paul is sending *that brother who is renowned in all the churches,* v. 18. (The use of the first person plural, *we are sending,* is more likely due to the predominating style of chaps. 1–9 than to Paul's specific interest to associate Timothy, 1:1, with the decision to send this brother. It certainly should not be interpreted as "I, Paul, and all the churches," because the role of the churches is indicated in v. 19.) Only three things are known about the brother mentioned here.

For one thing, he is *renowned in all the churches* because of his activities for the gospel, v. 18. How he has been serving the gospel is not said, but his fame indicates that he is more than a local congregational leader. Nor is it clear how far his fame has spread, since *all the churches* could mean, following 8:1, "all the churches of Macedonia," or it could mean "all the churches" in some more inclusive sense, as it does in Rom 16:4, 16 (see NOTES). There is nothing in the context to indicate that Paul means "all the churches in Judea," as Nickle (1966:18–22) holds. Moreover, the two references to Judean churches which occur in other letters suggest that had he meant them here he would have left no uncertainty about the matter (Gal 1:22, "the churches of Christ in Judea"; 1 Thess 2:14, "the churches of God in Christ Jesus which are in Judea" [*RSV*]).

In the second place, this *renowned brother* has been *appointed by the churches* to travel with Paul's entourage as it completes the collection of the fund for Jerusalem and, apparently, as it conveys that gift to the Judean Christians, v. 19. It is reasonable to suppose that the churches who have chosen this man are those referred to in v. 18, but again there is no indication of just which churches these are. The comment in 9:4 that Macedonians may come to Corinth with Paul later on does not preclude identifying this brother as a Macedonian (against Hughes and Nickle, cited in NOTES). It is only if the Corinthian collection is still not complete when Paul arrives that he will be disgraced (9:4).

The third and most important thing that Paul says about this brother is that his service for the collection project is *to show the glory of the Lord himself and our goodwill,* v. 19. The point becomes clearer in the two following verses, where the apostle explains that the presence of this *renowned brother* will certify the integrity of the enterprise. As the administrator of what he expects to be a fairly sizable fund, v. 20, Paul wants to take (or at least is willing to endorse) any step that can be taken to assure that no impropriety occurs or is even suspected. He is clearly sensitive to the kind of sentiment expressed by Cicero: "But the chief thing in all public administration and public service is to avoid even the slightest suspicion of self-seeking" (*On Moral Obligation* II.xxi.75). This is also the point of Paul's allusion to Prov 3:4 in v. 21. It is of ultimate importance that one act in accord with *what is honorable* before God, but it is also important that those actions be accepted as *honorable* by other people. Were it to be otherwise, the integrity of the ministry itself would be compromised and its effectiveness substantially reduced (cf. 6:3). Polycarp, writing more than half a century later about the duties of presbyters (Phil 6:1), uses the same text to make a very similar point.

Commenting on the collection for the Temple organized annually among Diaspora Jews, Philo remarks on the magnitude of the funds involved and the logistics of getting them to Jerusalem (*Special Laws* I, 78). Whether or not the collection from the Pauline congregations was modeled on this Temple tax, the Jewish custom of entrusting the money to men especially appointed for the task sheds some light on the appointment of this *renowned brother*. According to Philo, "at stated times there are appointed to carry the sacred tribute envoys selected on their merits, from every city those of the highest repute. . . ." The Christian brother *appointed by the churches* to travel with Paul in the interests of the collection for Jerusalem must have had a similar function. He was an official delegate of the churches he represented, and probably one of a number of delegates representing the same (or other) congregations (cf. Acts 20:4, and the comments below about the identity of this brother). He was at the same time, however, subordinate to Paul, because he was in fact sent on ahead of Paul to Corinth at the apostle's specific direction (vv. 18, 20; cf. Windisch, 263).

Why this *renowned brother* and a second brother mentioned in 8:22 are not specifically named must remain a mystery. Many interpreters believe that Paul himself did name them, but that the names were subsequently deleted by some editor (e.g., Windisch, 262; Georgi 1965:54; Dahl 1977:39), perhaps because the two had left "a bad memory" in Corinth (Lietzmann, 134) or had lost credibility in the church (Héring, 62). But Plummer, 248, disputes this, suggesting that if the two were unknown in Corinth anyway it would have been useless to give their names, for Titus would be introducing them. This is not very convincing. Does one commend a famous person (the *renowned brother* of 8:18–21) anonymously? And would a long-time associate of Paul (the earnest brother of 8:22) have been utterly unknown in Corinth?

Attempts to identify the *renowned brother* are little more than conjecture. (There is an extensive discussion of a number of candidates in Hughes, 312–16; see also Windisch, 264.) Traditionally he has been identified as Luke, whom Paul mentions in Phlm 24 as one of his "co-workers" and who is described as "the beloved physician" in Col 4:14 (so, e.g., Plummer, 248; Strachan, 140; Hughes, 312–13; see also 2 Tim 4:11). But against this is the fact that, in distinction from the man described in 8:22 as *our brother,* this *renowned brother* seems not to have been associated closely with Paul, apart from the present collection project. Because he is described, rather, as a representative of *the churches* (v. 19), it is preferable to think of one of the men listed among Paul's entourage in Acts 20:4. There, the apostle is setting out from "Greece" (Acts 20:2, presumably Corinth) for Syria, and among his traveling companions are three Macedonians (Sopater of Beroea and Aristarchus and Secundus of Thessalonica), two Asians (Tychicus and Trophimus), and Gaius of Derbe (in Lycaonia, southern Galatia). This is doubtless to be identified with Paul's journey to Jerusalem to convey the collection (cf. Rom 14:25–31). If the *renowned brother* was a representative specifically of the Macedonian churches, then one might suppose that he was Sopater, Aristarchus, or Secundus (so Windisch, 264). Nickle would identify him with the Judas Barabbas of Acts 15:22 (1966:18–22, especially 21–22), but this is only conceivable if Nickle is right about the reference in 2 Cor 8:19 being to the churches of Judea (on which see above).

Paul's remarks in 12:18b–d seem to be prompted by his awareness that some people in Corinth suspect that his collection for Jerusalem is being raised under false pretenses, that some if not all of the money may be going to support the apostle himself. In the present passage, however, there is no hint that the *renowned brother* has been appointed in response to such concerns. This is strange if chaps. 8 and 12 belong to the same letter, or if chap. 12 belongs to a letter written and sent prior to chap. 8 (correctly Windisch, 265). However, if chap. 12 belongs to a letter written and sent subsequent to chap. 8 ( = Letter E, as identified in the INTRODUCTION, pp. 44–48), the situation is clearer: despite the fact that a representative of the churches accompanied Titus in order to guarantee the integrity of the collection as such, suspicions arose that Paul was somehow benefiting personally from it. When the apostle is alerted to that, then he can appeal, as he does in 12:18, to the acknowledged integrity of Titus, his representative.

c. A very earnest brother, v. 22. Not only the *renowned brother,* 8:18–19, but also a second person is being sent to Corinth with Titus. As in the case of the first individual, no name identifies the man, although it is possible that originally a name did stand in the text (see discussion above). In distinction from *the renowned brother,* Paul refers to this man as *our brother* and says nothing about his having been appointed by the churches. He is commended specifically for his *earnestness,* which has been *verified in many ways and often* by Paul (and his associates). Paul must be referring in particular to his *earnestness* for the Corinthians (note what is said of Titus in 8:16, 17), his eager concern to come to them. He observes that this earnestness has become the more intense because of the brother's confidence in them, perhaps gained like the apostle's own from the report Titus has brought from Corinth (Windisch, 266).

Because the earnest brother is mentioned second and no specific function is assigned to him, one may presume that his role in Titus' mission to Corinth was regarded as of less importance than that of *the renowned brother.* However, this lesser-known brother is probably the one mentioned along with Titus in 12:18a (on which see COMMENT), but again with no indication of who he is or what exactly his role may have been.

It is no easier to pin a name on this earnest brother than on *the renowned brother.* He seems to have been more closely identified with Paul's ministry than the other, and in this instance Windisch, 266, thinks Luke could be meant. But there are numerous other associates of Paul who could be meant, including some of the others listed in Acts 20:4. Timothy, of course, is to be excluded since he is a co-sender of the present letter (1:1). Apollos is also to be ruled out since he was so well known in Corinth (see 1 Cor 1:12; 3:5, 6; 16:12) as to make the comments of 8:22 seem quite patronizing as well as unnecessary (cf. Windisch, 266; Hughes, 319). For the same reason this earnest brother cannot have been Silvanus (see 1:19). Nickle, presuming that this brother—like the first—must have been a representative of the Judean churches (see COMMENT on 8:18–21), identifies him with "Silas" (Acts 15:22), expressing some reservation about whether the "Silas" of Acts should be identified with the "Silvanus" of Paul's letters (1966:21–22).

d. Summation and appeal, vv. 23–24. Paul's summary commendation of Titus and the two brothers, v. 23, functions primarily as an introduction to the appeal in v. 24. Thus, one is reminded that chap. 8 is not, as such, a letter of recommendation for these three men but an appeal on behalf of the collection for Jerusalem; the commendations in 8:16–22 return us finally to the appeal of 8:1–15. (Windisch, 268, conjectures that in the original letter 8:16–24 preceded 8:7–15, so that 8:24 actually introduced the exhortations of 8:7–15. But this requires Windisch to postulate a lost connecting link between 8:24 and 8:7, as well as an accidental misplacement of "pages." The hypothesis is unnecessary as well as conjectural.)

Titus, v. 23*a,* is now commended as Paul's *partner* and *co-worker,* a commendation comparable to those of two other associates, Timothy (1 Cor 16:10; Phil 2:19–22; cf. 1 Thess 3:2) and Apollos (1 Cor 16:12). It may also be compared to the commendations of Phoebe (Rom 16:1–2) and Epaphroditus (Phil 2:25–29); but each of these persons is identified with the leadership of a specific congregation (Cenchreae and Philippi, respectively), and not principally with Paul's itinerant ministry. Paul's use here of the singular pronoun, *my (partner and co-worker),* stands in marked contrast with his use of the plural, *our (brothers),* in the very next phrase. Like Paul's references to Titus in 2:13 ("my brother Titus") and 7:6–7, 13*b*–15, it suggests that Titus was especially esteemed by Paul, and regarded as a particularly valuable associate.

The distinctive positions of the two accompanying brothers, articulated so clearly in 8:18–21, are completely ignored in v. 23*b.* There is no hint that one has been *appointed by the churches* while the other is more closely associated with Paul's ministry, or that the association of the former with the collection campaign is intended to attest its absolute integrity. The men are linked together as *our brothers,* as *representatives of the churches,* and as *the glory of Christ.* Against Windisch, 267, it is not likely that the names of these men ever stood in the text at this point, because Paul is only summarizing. This also explains why the two men are no longer distinguished as to their status and function. What is important now is to praise them both, and in the process they both become *our brothers* and *representatives of the churches*. The former phrase is parallel to *Titus* in the first part of the verse, so that *representatives of the churches* and *the glory of Christ* parallel the two honorific titles bestowed on Titus there *(my partner and co-worker . . . for you)*. (Consult the NOTES for details on these four phrases.)

The purpose of the summary commendations in v. 23 is to prepare for and support the appeal in v. 24. The Corinthians are to *demonstrate* their *love* to these men, showing in the process that Paul's *boasting* about them has not been ill-founded. This is not an admonition to love Titus and the two brothers (cf. 1 Thess 5:13, "to esteem [those who labor among you] very highly in love" [*RSV*]), although of course Paul desires that they should. Nor is it a general admonition concerning love, like the one in 1 Cor 16:14 ("Let all that you do be done in love" [*RSV*]). It is a renewal of the appeal of 8:7–15 to make their promised contribution to the fund for Jerusalem. Paul has already referred to this action as a sign of genuine love (8:8). Now he urges his readers to make sure that this love is embodied in action, specifically in their participation in the relief work for the needy Christians of Jerusalem. It is toward the concrete, public expression of their love that this appeal is aimed (see especially Spicq 1965:212–14, and Kümmel 1967:4–5). If they will now follow through on their promise to give, they shall have demonstrated their love not only before Titus and the brothers, but before the churches they represent.

### The Importance of Their Mission, 9:1–5

It is possible but not necessary to interpret the wording of 9:1–2 as introducing the topic of the collection for the first time (see NOTES and the general comments above on the relation between chaps. 8 and 9). There is no serious difficulty, however, in reading the verses as a continuation of the preceding discussion. Paul acknowledges that because he has been *boasting* to the Macedonians about the commitment of the Achaian churches (including Corinth) to the fund for Jerusalem (v. 2a) it is *superfluous* for him *to be writing* them about contributing (v. 1). Indeed, when the Macedonians heard of that commitment they, too, were inspired to join in (v. 2b). They have now given generously despite their own abject poverty (see 8:2), while those whose commitment has inspired them to do so have not yet followed through on that commitment.

Thus, while it really is superfluous for Paul to write about Corinthian *goodwill* toward the collection, it is necessary for him to write about the present mission of Titus and the two accompanying brothers (vv. 3–5). They are coming to make sure that the congregation's good intentions are followed by action. Since it is clear that Paul himself is anticipating another trip to Corinth (v. 4), why does he regard it as important to send these men *on ahead*

(v. 5)? Could not Paul take care of this, perhaps more effectively, when he comes? It may be that the apostle, being anxious to finish with the collection so he can get on to Rome and launch a mission to Spain (see Rom 15:24), does not want to spend the time in Corinth that this would require. The advance party could save him time. But Paul—perhaps sensitive to criticism that he has spent too little time in Corinth as it is (see 1:15–2:2)—does not mention this as a reason. He says, first, that he does not want his *boasting* about them to have been *in vain* (v. 3a). As once before Titus had found Paul's pride in the church fully warranted (7:14), so now *in this matter* of the collection he wants his boasting before the Macedonians to be verified. If their goodwill is still only latent when he himself arrives, that will endanger both his credibility as an apostle and theirs as believers (see note on the phrase *in vain*).

A second reason for sending Titus and the brothers on ahead is given here. It is closely related to but also distinguishable from the first. Should Paul arrive to find that the Corinthians still have made no contribution to the Jerusalem fund, not only he but they will be *disgraced* in respect of *this undertaking* (vv. 3b–4). One should not assume that Paul is thinking only about the disgrace which will come if he has been boasting about something that was not true (v. 3a). Something else concerns him, too. What if he should come, perhaps with some Macedonians (this is being written from somewhere in Macedonia, 7:5), and should have to plead with the Corinthians to contribute? How could any contribution coaxed from them under such conditions possibly be made as an expression of their *love* (see 8:8, 24)? That kind of contribution could hardly serve as an affirmation of the partnership in Christ which Paul wants the collection project to attest. This entire effort may be damaged if the Macedonians should now find the Corinthians still unready to fulfill their pledge. After all, the Macedonians would be representing poorer churches who have already given spontaneously and generously under the impression that the Corinthians have done the same.

This is the point emphasized in v. 5. If the Corinthians are ready with their contribution by the time Paul arrives, whatever Macedonians may be with him will see the Corinthian gift, like their own, as *a gift* of love. But if Paul himself must beg for the money to be given, it might appear to be *an extortion*—money obtained from reluctant donors by inappropriate means, and perhaps even under false pretenses. To avoid such an unhappy situation, Paul is now sending on ahead a small delegation—one of its members a brother renowned in the churches and specifically appointed by them to guarantee the integrity of the project. If, as seems likely, chaps. 10–13 are from a subsequent letter, we have evidence that despite his precautions Paul is being criticized—even before his own arrival in Corinth—of acting deviously in the matter of the collection (see 12:14–18). But in the present letter he seems reasonably confident that those who are being sent *to organize in advance the gift . . . already pledged* will encounter no great difficulty.

### d. CLOSING REMARKS ON GENEROUS GIVING, 9:6–15

9 ⁶I am saying this: one who sows sparingly will also reap sparingly and one who sows liberally will also reap liberally. ⁷Let each person contribute as each has decided, not grudgingly or by compulsion; for God loves a cheerful giver. ⁸And God has the power to provide for you every benefit in abundance, that in every way ever having everything you need, you may abound in every good work. ⁹As it is written:

"He has scattered abroad, he has given to the needy;
his righteousness endures forever."

¹⁰And he who supplies seed to the sower and bread for food will supply and multiply the seed for your sowing and will increase the yield of your righteousness. ¹¹You are enriched in every way for the greatest generosity, which through us brings about thanksgiving to God; ¹²for the ministration of this service not only supplies the needs of the saints but also overflows with many thanksgivings to God. ¹³Because of the verification which this ministration provides, they glorify God for the obedience of your confession of the gospel of Christ and the generosity of your sharing with them and with all; ¹⁴while they too, with prayer on your behalf, are longing for you because of the surpassing grace of God among you. ¹⁵Thanks be to God for his indescribable gift!

### NOTES

9:6. *I am saying this.* Translates *touto de,* which involves ellipsis (the omission of one or more words necessary to the meaning). Cf. especially *touto de phēmi* ("This is what I mean") in 1 Cor 7:29; 15:50, and see BDF § 481.

*one who sows sparingly . . . ,* etc. The idea that one must reap whatever one has sown is widespread in ancient literature, including the literature of the Jewish Wisdom tradition. See especially LXX Prov 11:21, 24, 26, 30; 22:8; Job 4:8; Sir 7:3. Georgi (1965:68 n. 266) also notes T Levi 13:6 and several passages from Philo, while Barrett, 236, quotes Aristotle, Cicero, and 3 Apoc Bar 15:2–3. Paul himself employs the metaphor again in Gal 6:7–9 (on which see Betz 1979:306–10). In both Pauline examples there is chiasmus; here (literally), "one who sows sparingly sparingly will reap," etc.; cf. Gal 6:8 (sow–flesh/flesh–reap; sow–Spirit/Spirit–reap). The formulation here bears some of the marks of what Käsemann has described as "sentences of holy law" (1969:73; cf. Mattern 1966:163).

*liberally.* More literally, "in blessings" *(ep' eulogiais),* the preposition *(ep')* having adverbial force here, where the phrase stands opposite *sparingly;* see BAG s.v. *epi,* II, 1b*ζ.*

7. *Let each person contribute.* As in the preceding verse, there is an ellipsis here; the Greek has only *hekastos, each person* (see BDF § 481).

*as each has decided.* More literally, "as each has chosen in the heart [ = mind]." Cf. LXX Deut 15:10, quoted in the following note.

*not grudgingly.* Or "not sorrowfully," "not with pain" *(ek lypēs).* Cf. LXX Deut 15:10: "You shall most certainly give to him [the poor man] and lend him as much as he lacks, according to his need; and you shall not be grudging in your heart [*ou lypēthēsē tē kardia sou*] as you are giving to him, because on account of this the Lord your God will bless you in all your works. . . ."

*God loves a cheerful giver.* Almost a quotation of LXX Prov 22:8*a* (a Greek addition to the Hebrew text), "God blesses a cheerful and giving man" *(andra hilaron kai dotēn eulogei ho Theos).* The general idea is also found in Sir 35:9, "With every gift show a cheerful face, / and dedicate your tithe with gladness" *(RSV;* 35:8 in LXX); LXX Deut 15:10, quoted in the preceding note; *Lev. Rab.* xxxiv.9 (131 *b*), quoted by Barrett, 236; Philo, *Special Laws* IV, 74: "So then let not the rich man collect great store of gold and silver . . . , but bring it out for general use that he may soften the hard lot of the needy with the unction of his cheerfully given liberality" (cited by Georgi 1965:69; Philo goes on to say the rich man should "honor equality" [cf. 2 Cor 8:13–15]); cf. T Job 12:1; *ᵓAbot R. Nat.* 13. After emphasizing that one should give to the needy as promptly as possible, Seneca says: "One who acts thus readily leaves no doubt that he acts willingly; and so he acts gladly, and his face is clothed with the joy he feels" *(On Benefits* II.ii.2). There is also Paul's own counsel in Rom 12:8 about contributing "generously" *(en haplotēti),* giving aid "with zeal" *(en spoudē),* and doing acts of mercy "with cheerfulness" *(en hilarotēti).*

*loves.* Hughes, 331 n. 65, suggests that this is the LXX reading Paul knew, but Georgi 1965:68 thinks Paul has deliberately replaced *eulogei* ("blesses") with *agapa (loves,* a gnomic present [*GNTG* III:63]). Georgi, then, believes that here as elsewhere Paul is referring to the basis on which one acts (God's love) rather than to the reward for one's actions (ibid.:70). However, it is doubtful whether *loves* here means any more than "approves" or "values" (correctly Barrett, 236) as elsewhere in the Wisdom tradition, where it occurs in formally similar affirmations (e.g., Wis 7:28, "For God loves nothing so much as the man who lives with wisdom"; Sir 4:14, "the Lord loves those who love [wisdom]"; LXX Prov 22:11, "The Lord loves holy hearts . . .").

8. *God has the power.* Or simply "God is able" *(dynatei ho Theos),* but the specific idea of God's power should probably be expressed; cf. Rom 14:4 *(dynatei ho Kyrios,* "the Lord has the power") and Rom 4:21; 11:23 *(dynatos estin [ho Theos],* "God is powerful").

*every benefit.* Paul again uses the word *charis,* which is used in different ways in chaps. 8, 9; here *benefit* is an appropriate tr. (as in 8:4), although it could also be rendered as "grace" (as in 8:1, 9; 9:14).

*in every way ever having everything you need.* An attempt has been made to reproduce the striking paronomasia of the Greek sentence (the recurrence of the stem *pas [pasa, pan]).* When *every benefit* (preceding note) and *every good work* (see below) are included, one has *pasan . . . panti pantote pasan . . . pan;* see BDF § 488(1*a*) and Robertson 1923:1201.

*everything you need.* Translates *pasan autarkeian,* perhaps "complete sufficiency." The noun *(autarkeia)* was used in a technical sense by various Greek and Hellenistic philosophers. Among the Cynics and the Stoics, especially, "self-sufficiency" or "contentment"—gained by freedom from external circumstances and other people—became an important ideal. (Discussions in Ferguson 1958:133–58 and Kittel, *TDNT* I:466–67.) The noun occurs nowhere else in the Greek Bible, but the adjective appears a few times in the LXX and is used by Paul in Phil 4:11. Paul's conception of "having enough" is quite different, however, from the Cynic-Stoic view; see COMMENT, and NOTES and COMMENT on 12:9.

*every good work.* The same expression *(pan ergon agathon)* is a favorite of the author of the Pastoral Epistles (1 Tim 2:21; 3:17; Tit 1:16; 3:1) and it recurs in 1 Clem 2:7 (drawing on Tit 3:1; see Hagner 1973:211); 33:1; 34:4. However, the plural "good works" *(erga agatha* or *erga kala),* found often in the Pastorals and elsewhere (1 Tim 2:10; 5:10, 25; 6:18; Tit 2:7, 14; 3:8; also in Eph 2:10, etc.) is never used by Paul. (The singular also appears in Rom 2:7; 13:3 and—with God as the subject—in Phil 1:6.)

9. *As it is written.* The same formula as in 8:15, on which see the note.

*"He has scattered abroad . . . ,"* etc. Paul is quoting without alteration from LXX Ps 111(112):9. This psalm, a description of the pious man, seems to be paired with the preceding psalm (110[111]), in which God is described in a comparable way. Dahood (1970:129) regards the two verbs in the Hebrew text as an instance of hendiadys (two words expressing just one thought), and translates: "He gives lavishly." One might interpret the Greek version similarly—e.g., "He has given generously to the needy."

*his righteousness.* Paul himself refers to *righteousness* only infrequently in the present letter (so far only in 3:9; 5:21; 6:7, 14, although 6:14–7:1 may not be Pauline). Exactly what he understands it to mean in the text he is quoting (and in the text in Hos to which he alludes in the following verse) is unclear; see COMMENT.

10. *he who supplies . . . ,* etc. The reference here is to God (see 9:8*a*), and Paul himself is probably responsible for the formulation of this ad hoc description; see following note.

*seed to the sower and bread for food.* This phrase *(sporon tō speironti kai arton eis brōsin)* is drawn from LXX Isa 55:10 *(sporon* replacing *sperma* for seed). Despite the fact that the prophet is speaking of what the rain brings, this text has become the basis for Paul's description of the beneficence of God. See Delling 1963:28 n. 1.

*will supply and multiply.* The verbs are read as future indicative in this tr., following ℵ* B C D* D² et al., and including P⁴⁶ (Barrett, 232 n. 1, needs to be corrected). Some other texts have optative forms for these two verbs and the following one, thus reading the sentence as a kind of benediction: "May he [God] . . . supply and multiply . . . and increase. . . ."

*the seed for your sowing.* The Greek is simply "your seed" *(ton sporon hymōn),* to be understood here metaphorically: your "resources" *(RSV)* for giving.

*will increase.* Translates *auxēsei,* future indicative, which is read by ℵ* B C D* P et al. However, in contrast to their readings for the two preceding verbs (future indicative), P⁴⁶ D² 104 have an optative here (with ℵ² et al.), "may he increase," a reading adopted by Kümmel, 206, and Amstutz 1968:106 n. 62 (cf. BDF § 474[4]), but rejected by Barrett, 232 n. 1.

*the yield of your righteousness.* This phrase *(ta genēmata tēs dikaiosynēs hymōn)* is drawn from LXX Hos 10:12, "Sow to yourselves for righteousness, gather in for the fruit of life . . . ; seek the Lord until the yield of righteousness comes to you."

11. *You are enriched.* Although the context would lead one to expect the future tense here (see 9:10), Paul lapses into the present tense and continues with that through the remainder of the paragraph; see COMMENT. This tr. treats the participle *ploutizomenoi* as standing in place of a finite verb (so BDF § 468[2]). Alternatively, one could regard the participle as involving anacoluthon—the nominative being used, whereas the preceding *hymōn (your)* requires a genitive (see *GNTG* III:343); or (less likely) as parallel with *echontes (having)* in 9:8, in which case 9:9–10 would be regarded as a long parenthesis (so *KJV*). Héring, 67, thinks it not impossible that the participle should be taken as middle voice rather than passive: "enriching (others)."

*in every way.* Or "always" *(NEB, TEV).* But this same phrase *(en panti)* must mean *in every way* in 9:8 (where *pantote* stands for "always" [in this tr., *ever*]).

*for the greatest generosity.* For the word *generosity (haplotēs)* see note on 8:2. *The greatest* translates *pasan,* in accord with one common usage of the adjective (see BAG s.v. *pas,* 1aδ).

*through us.* Note the plural, *us,* despite the predominating first person singular of 9:1–5. Paul is probably thinking of the journey he and his entourage will be making to Jerusalem to deliver the collection (see 9:12 and Georgi 1965:74 n. 288).

12. *the ministration of this service.* Translates *hē diakonia tēs leitourgias tautēs.* Elsewhere in chaps. 8, 9 *diakonia* has been translated as *relief work* (8:4, see the note; 9:1); but here, where *leitourgia* is used to describe the collection, *diakonia* seems to refer to its "performance" (cf. *TEV, NIV*), "rendering" *(RSV),* or "execution" (Barrett, 239), perhaps specifically to its delivery to Jerusalem (Georgi 1965:74 and n. 288). In 3:7–9; 4:1; 5:18; 6:3 the same word is translated "ministry."

*this service.* A *leitourgia* was any act of public service, whether of wealthy citizens who supported civil events and institutions, of civil magistrates (e.g., Rom 13:6), or of priestly officials who conducted the ceremonies of religious cults. For the latter meaning see, e.g., LXX Num 8:22 ("the Levites went in to perform their service [*leitourgein tēn leitourgian*] in the tent of witness"). In the present verse the word describes Paul's collection for Jerusalem (cf. the use of the corresponding verb in Rom 15:27), and Strathmann (*TDNT* IV:227) argues that it has a strictly profane meaning here, as also in Phil 2:30 (Epaphroditus had risked his life in order to make up for the "service" the Philippians had otherwise been unable to render Paul [*anaplērōsē to hymōn hysterēma tēs pros me leitourgias*]). However, as in the case of other Pauline terms for the collection (e.g., *charis,* "grace," translated as *benefit* in 8:4; 9:8 and as *benevolence* in 8:6, 7, 19; *eulogia,* "blessing," translated as *gift* in 9:5), the apostle probably intends the theological connotations this word often has (so, e.g., Bachmann, 330–31; Georgi 1965:75–76 n. 298; and especially Corriveau 1970:97–109). Cf. Phil 2:17, where the same word has a certainly cultic sense, and Rom 15:16, where Paul writes of himself as "a minister [*leitourgos*] of Christ Jesus . . . in the priestly service of the gospel of God" *(RSV).*

*the needs of the saints.* The *saints* are, as in 8:4; 9:1, the Christians in Jerusalem who are in *need* (see 8:14) of financial help (Rom 15:26; cf. vv. 25, 31).

*with many thanksgivings to God.* The plural *thanksgivings* occurs only here and in 1 Tim 2:1 in the NT. Textual evidence strongly supports the genitive form (rather than the accusative; see Metzger 1971:582–83) following *dia*—which here seems to describe attendant circumstance (cf. 2:4): the collection for the saints "overflows" in that it produces *many thanksgivings to God*. Cf. what has been said of "grace" in 4:15. Plummer, 266, would render: "thanksgivings of many people."

13. *Because of the verification.* Here *dia* with the genitive *(dia tēs dokimēs)* is used causally (BAG s.v. *dia,* A, IV). In 8:2 *dokimē* is translated as *testing,* but here it refers to what has been "tested and approved" (cf. the use of the related verb, *dokimazein,* in 8:8, 22).

*which this ministration provides.* Translates *tēs diakonias tautēs,* interpreting the genitive as indicating what *the verification* is. As in the preceding verse (see note), *diakonia* is rendered as *ministration.*

*they glorify.* Literally "glorifying," a nominative plural participle *(doxazontes);* essentially the same problems and options obtain as in the case of the participle *ploutizomenoi* in v. 11 (see note there on *You are enriched*).

*for the obedience of your confession.* This phrase, *epi tē hypotagē tēs homologias hymōn,* is difficult because (1) Paul nowhere else uses the noun *homologia* ("confession [of faith]"); (2) he uses the noun *hypotagē* only once more (Gal 2:5, of the "subjection" of one person to another); (3) the genitive ("of the confession") may be interpreted in different ways (as "subjective," Seeberg 1903:182; "objective," Hughes, 339 n. 75; "epexegetical," Georgi 1965:76 n. 302; etc.).

Seeberg, who argues that the genitive must be taken as subjective (1903:182), believes that *hypotagē* cannot mean "obedience" as many claim, but only "submission," and that the notion of one's confession of faith meaning submission to the gospel is so un-Pauline that one may suspect some early disturbance of the text, the original word perhaps being *hyperochē* ("superiority") rather than *hypotagē* ("submission") (ibid.:182–84 n. 2). Jewett (1978:394) suggests that 9:13*b–c* (everything from *for the obedience* through *with all*) may have been interpolated by the late first century redactor of 2 Cor who (in Jewett's view) added 9:1–15 to chap. 8. The intention would have been "to place apostolic authority behind the effort to institutionalize charity and the support of ordained clergy, shifting both 'gospel' and 'service' in the direction of submission to ecclesiastical norms."

The textual tradition offers no evidence to support either one of the conjectures just noted. Moreover, Jewett's remark that "the conceptual pattern [of 9:13] is considerably closer to the Pastorals than to Paul" (1978:394) is misleading in two respects. On the one hand, while it is true that both nouns, "submission" and "confession," do occur in the Pastorals (*hypotagē,* 1 Tim 2:11; 3:4; *homologia,* 1 Tim 6:12, 13), they do not occur together as in 2 Cor, and the idea of "submission" (the verb as well as the noun) is present only where the topic is the subjection of one person to another. And, on the other hand, in certain instances Paul himself seems to have identified *the gospel* with a message which is to be confessed, just as, on occasion, he thinks of "faith" as that which is believed *(fides quae creditur;* see the note on "faith" at 5:7). For instance, in Rom 10:9, 10, where Paul writes about "confessing" *(homologein)* and "believing" *(pisteuein),* both verbs are related to "the content of faith fixed in the confession," the "faith which is believed" (Käsemann 1980:290). Moreover, in the same context (Rom

10:3), Paul uses the verb "to submit" *(hypotassein)* when he remarks that the Jews, by "seeking to establish their own" righteousness, have failed "to submit" to God's *(RSV)*. This conception may be compared with "the obedience of faith" *(hypakoē pisteōs)* mentioned in Rom 1:5, for in both places the reference is to accepting the call to place oneself under the jurisdiction of God's redemptive power, accepting "the word of faith" about Jesus Christ which comes in the gospel (Rom 10:8, 14–17).

Thus, with respect to the three points mentioned at the beginning of this note, the following may be said: (1) the idea of making a "confession" of one's faith is not un-Pauline (see Rom 10:9, 10); (2) there is adequate warrant for taking the noun *hypotagē* in the sense of *obedience* (see Rom 10:3; cf. Rom 1:5); and (3) the genitive *tēs homologias* may be quite satisfactorily understood as identifying that of which the obedience consists—namely, one's confession of the faith contained in *the gospel of Christ* by and to which one has been converted (see Rom 10:14–17).

*the gospel of Christ.* This phrase has also been used in 2:12, on which see the note. Here *the gospel* is thought of primarily in terms of what is preached, believed, and confessed; cf. Rom 10:16–17 and see the preceding note.

*the generosity.* As in 8:2 (see the note) and 9:11.

*of your sharing.* Translates *tēs koinōnias;* for the noun see the note at 8:4, where it is rendered *participation,* and for the present tr. see especially McDermott 1975:223. The *your* is supplied in English for clarity.

*with them.* The poor Christians in Jerusalem, *the saints* of the preceding verse.

*with all.* That is, "all Christians." When Paul admonishes the Galatians and Thessalonians to do "good" (Gal 6:10; 1 Thess 5:13), "all" clearly means "also non-Christians"; but here, following the reference to *koinōnia (sharing), all* must mean "the household of faith" (Gal 6:10), "one another" (1 Thess 5:13).

14. *while they too . . . are longing.* The *kai autōn . . . epipothountōn* is best regarded as a genitive-absolute construction (e.g., Plummer, 267; Windisch, 285). The alternative would be to take *deēsei (with prayer)* as a "suspended dative" *(GAGNT* 1979:553) after *they will glorify* (cf. *KJV).* The *too* presumes that someone else is longing for the Corinthians, and the readers are doubtless meant to think of Paul (see Windisch, 285; Filson, 379; Wiles 1974:251 n. 8). The verb is *epipothein,* as in 5:2 (on which see the note; in 7:7, 11, the corresponding noun has been used of the Corinthians' longing to see Paul).

*with prayer on your behalf.* The dative *(deēsei)* indicates the circumstance which attends the *longing.* In 1:11, Paul has referred to the Corinthians' *prayer* for him (and Timothy).

*the surpassing grace of God among you.* Cf. what is said about the *grace of God* among the Macedonians, 8:1.

15. *Thanks be to God.* As in 2:14 (see note) and 8:16. But here (as in 1 Cor 15:57) the expression concludes rather than opens a discussion. Georgi (1965:77) believes there is a deliberate play on the word *charis,* which refers to God's *grace* in the preceding verse but which must be translated *Thanks* in this one.

*indescribable gift.* The adjective *(anekdiēgētos)* occurs only here in the NT, never in the LXX. Elsewhere Paul uses the noun *(dōrea, gift)* of the righteousness which comes as an act of grace through Christ (Rom 5:15, 17; cf. the use of *dōrean* in Rom 3:24). For its use here see COMMENT.

## COMMENT: GENERAL

If, indeed, chap. 9 as a whole continues the discussion of chap. 8 (see above, pp. 429–33), then 9:6–15 contains Paul's closing remarks on the subject of the collection for Jerusalem. Along with the introductory assurances of confidence (7:4–16), 9:6–15 serves to support the appeal to the Corinthians to complete their collection for the needy Judean Christians (8:1–15) following the guidance of Titus and the two brothers (8:16–9:6). Moreover, if chaps. 10–13 are to be distinguished from chaps. 1–9 as part of a separate letter to Corinth, then the present verses constitute the last surviving paragraph of the appeals and thus of the main subject matter of the letter Paul wrote from Macedonia after Titus had arrived there with a report about the Corinthian church. It is unlikely that any other major appeals followed this one on behalf of the collection, for this seems to have been the practical point Paul wanted most to emphasize in this letter. One may suppose that this appeal was followed almost at once by some final words of encouragement and greeting, and by the customary apostolic benediction. This closing salutation would have had to be removed, of course, when the person responsible for combining materials from separate letters into our 2 Cor decided to append chaps. 10–13 (Letter E) to chap. 9. It is possible but not likely that the original conclusion of chaps. 1–9 (Letter D) was transferred to the end of chap. 13 to conclude the composite letter (see COMMENT on 13:11–13).

In his closing remarks about the collection Paul strengthens and extends the appeal by emphasizing the importance of generous giving. He makes two fundamental points here, although they may also be understood as two aspects of a single point: God provides the means to be generous (9:6–10) and (therefore) generosity redounds to the glory of God (9:11–15).

## COMMENT: DETAILED

### God Enables Generosity, 9:6–10

Paul makes only one further appeal before his discussion of the collection is concluded, and that comes in v. 7a (even so, expressed elliptically; see NOTES): each person is to contribute to the collection for the saints according to his or her own best judgment, and *not grudgingly or by compulsion*. Although Paul continues to refrain from holding the Macedonians up as a model for the Corinthian action, it is probable that he has the Macedonian example in mind as he writes this (see 8:3–5). His admonition is explicitly supported from scripture, v. 7b, as he alludes to the teaching of Prov 22:8a (only in the

LXX) that God blesses *a cheerful giver*. It is also supported by his use of the metaphor of sowing and reaping (v. 6; cf. v. 9), with which he clearly wishes to inform the judgment of his readers in order to encourage them to be generous in their contributions.

The apostle's argument is, first, that sparse sowing yields only a skimpy harvest, while one who gives generously will reap a generous harvest (v. 6). Here the issue is not "what" one should sow, as it is in Gal 6:7–8, but "how much" one should sow—that is, "contribute" to the collection for Jerusalem. Taken by itself, this saying (a bit of agricultural folk wisdom; references in the NOTES) would be an expression of the hedonistic principle that those who give generously to others are rewarded by the multiplication of their own resources (cf. Windisch, 276). But in this context Paul wants to say something else—perhaps, as in 8:13–15 (see COMMENT), being mindful especially of Corinthian concerns that it would work a hardship upon them to give very much just now. His point is that God will provide the means to be generous, that one can sow *liberally* (which also means freely and cheerfully, v. 7a) in the confidence that God will bestow a liberal harvest.

That this is Paul's meaning is shown first of all in v. 8, where the abundant harvest which comes to the generous and cheerful giver is described as a *benefit* or "grace" *(charis)* given by God. It is important to notice that the apostle does not think of this as "payment for services rendered." Elsewhere he specifically contrasts what is received as a divine act of "grace" with what is earned as a "reward" (Rom 4:4; cf. a similar contrast between a "free gift" [*to charisma*] and "wages" [*ta opsōnia*] in Rom 6:23). Moreover, this *benefit* which is provided by God's grace is bestowed not for the enjoyment of those who have given generously but in order that they *may abound in every good work*. Paul is thinking quite concretely here of specific acts of Christian service, like the collection he is now taking up for the needy Christians of Jerusalem. Yet it is characteristic that here, as elsewhere, he avoids using the plural "good works" (see NOTES). Rather, every specific instance of Christian charity is part of a larger whole (cf. Kümmel, 207), an instance of faith's "working in love" (Gal 5:6). Thus, to *abound in every good work* is the same as to be "always abounding in the work of the Lord" (1 Cor 15:58 [*RSV*]).

When in this same connection Paul assures his readers that God will provide them *everything (they) need* (v. 8), he uses a word that some of them might recognize as a technical term of Hellenistic philosophy—*autarkeia*, "self-sufficiency" or "contentment" (see NOTES). The word does not bear its full technical meaning here, however. In this case it has a more restricted reference, specifically to having enough of what one needs in an economic sense (Windisch, 278; Dahl 1977:23). But Paul does not mean having enough resources to be independent of other people. Paul means having enough resources to be able to help other people, to be able to affirm one's community with others by contributing to those in need (cf. Georgi 1965:71; Barrett, 237). There are, then, two fundamental ways in which Paul (or the church before him) has transformed the Hellenistic ideal of "sufficiency" or "contentment." First, it is affirmed to be a gift of God, not something gained by earnest self-discipline. This same point is evident in Phil 4:11–13, where the apostle declares that it is by God's strength (not his own) that he is enabled to "be content" *(RSV)* whatever the outward conditions of his existence (cf. 2 Cor 12:9). Then, in the second place, the "sufficiency" Paul is talking about enables one to relate more effectively to other people, not to withdraw from them. The case in point is his collection for Jerusalem, participation in which is itself a *benefit* or "grace" (see 8:3), effected through the sharing of those who "have enough to share" with those who are in need (cf. 8:13–15).

The quotation of LXX Ps 111(112):9 in v. 9 is the last explicit citation of scripture in chaps. 1–9, Letter D (others have been in 4:13; 6:2; 6:16–18; 8:15). It is drawn from a psalm in which the godly man is described, but it is not altogether clear how Paul himself has understood the text or what he intends by quoting it here. The references to scattering abroad and giving to the needy obviously conform to the apostle's present appeal to the Corinthians (see vv. 6–7), but interpreters disagree about two other points: who, in Paul's judgment, is the agent of this scattering, and how Paul understands the phrase *his righteousness*. One may identify at least four possibilities.

(1) Paul regards the subject of the sentence to be the pious man, and takes *his righteousness* to mean the general moral uprightness in which he is forever established by reason of his giving generously to the needy (cf. Barrett, 238, who thinks in the first place of a "general moral sense" here). This would conform in at least a general way to the meaning presumably intended by the psalmist.

(2) Paul regards the subject of the sentence to be the pious man, but he understands *his righteousness* almost in the sense of "his alms" or "his almsgiving" (e.g., Windisch, 278–79; Bultmann, 259; Berger 1977:200; cf. Chrysostom [*NPNF*, 1st ser. XII:369], who interpreted it here as *philanthrōpia*). This would conform to late rabbinic usage (references in Str-B III:525) and to certain other NT passages where *dikaiosynē* is closely associated with the performance of specific righteous acts (note the idea of "doing righteousness" in 1 John 3:7, 10; Rev 22:11; cf. Tit 3:5; perhaps also Matt 6:1, cited by Lietzmann, 138).

(3) Paul intentionally avoids specifying any subject when quoting the text, although he knows full well that in the psalm from which it comes it is a description of the pious man. This is the view of Georgi (1965:71–72), who notes that Paul inserts his text into a discussion where God is the subject (9: 8a, explicitly; 9:10, implicitly). He would thereby be making the point implied also by the juxtaposition of Pss 110(111), 111(112) in the Psalter (see NOTES), that all human righteousness has its origin in God's. Thus, *his righteousness* could be a reference to that divine righteousness by which one is held fast in God's covenant and held accountable to God's will.

(4) Paul may have interpreted Ps 111(112) christologically, especially if he was acquainted with the rabbinic tradition that regarded the psalm as Abraham's and that interpreted "his seed" *(to sperma autou)* in v. 2 as Isaac. This is the suggestion of Hanson (1974:179–80), who in any event wants to read *his righteousness* as a reference to "Christ's righteousness in Christians" (ibid.:180), doubtless a characteristic Pauline theme. (Note in the present letter 5:21; also Rom 5:17–21, etc.)

Of the four views, (4) is the least plausible, since it must presuppose an idea which, however Pauline, is not even hinted at in the present context. On the other hand, (2) accords exceptionally well with Paul's concern to assure his readers that they themselves will be supported by God when they give generously to the needy (see especially vv. 6, 8): their "act of righteousness" will be established forever. But insofar as this means established forever "with God," one cannot exclude the more specifically theological meaning of righteousness proposed in (3). Then Paul's citation of LXX Ps 111(112):9 in v. 9 could be regarded as his way of drawing together the affirmations of vv. 6, 7*b*, and 8, all in support of the appeal in v. 7*a*: each person should contribute to the collection gladly and freely (v. 7*a*), knowing that liberal sowing brings a large harvest (v. 6), that God approves the cheerful giver (v. 7*b*), and that because God provides abundantly for everything they need, God's people *may abound in every good work* such as this one (v. 8). In summary (quoting scripture), those who give generously to the needy should know that their charitable act is a part of that larger righteousness of God by which they themselves live and in which they shall remain forever (v. 9).

The point Paul has been driving at in vv. 6–9 is given its clearest expression in v. 10, which (against Amstutz 1968:105) is better taken as concluding what had preceded than as introducing what is to follow. Here Paul draws on two further scriptural texts, but without citing either one of them specifically. From LXX Isa 55:10 he extracts a phrase about *seed to the sower and bread for food* and fashions it into a description of God. The resulting formulation both continues the metaphor of sowing and reaping with which he has been working (v. 6; cf. v. 9) and enables him to emphasize that everything needful is given by God. Indeed, because liberal sowing leads to a liberal harvest (cf. v. 6), one may expect progressively larger harvests as there is ever more seed available for sowing in the next season. If the Corinthians will contribute generously to the collection, they will see how God can multiply their resources for yet more generous giving.

In the latter part of v. 10, Paul employs a phrase from LXX Hos 10:12, a text in which "righteousness" and "life" are identified as the content of the harvest reaped by those who repent and "seek the Lord." Now Paul joins this reference to the content of the harvest to his point about its magnitude: *God will increase the yield of your righteousness.* In this way the apostle is also able to integrate his earlier reference to *righteousness* (quoted from Isa in v. 9) into the sowing/reaping imagery. Georgi (1965:72–73) argues that Paul is thinking of his impending delivery of the collection to Jerusalem as the inaugural event in the pilgrimage of the Gentiles to Mt. Zion, and that the increasing *yield of . . . righteousness* would be the consequent demonstration of the truth of the gospel to the unbelieving Jews (cf. Nickle 1966:137). There are grounds (mainly from Rom) for believing that Paul did regard the collection as having some such eschatological significance as this (see above, p. 412). However, it is unlikely that Paul would allude so obliquely to so important a point when it is not made elsewhere in the same context. It seems clear that *your righteousness* is parallel to *your sowing* in this same sentence (v. 10), and in this case *the yield of your righteousness* would most naturally be the "produce" of that sowing, the amount of the Corinthians' contributions for Jerusalem (cf. Windisch, 280; Amstutz 1968:106 n. 62).

### Generosity Glorifies God, 9:11–15

The first half of v. 11 effectively summarizes the main point in the preceding five verses: the Corinthians can afford to be generous contributors to the fund for Jerusalem because God provides the means for them to be (cf. especially 9:8). It is noteworthy that Paul now begins to write in the present tense (contrast the future tense in 9:10) and continues in this way through the rest of the paragraph. Although the Corinthians have yet to make any substantial contribution to the collection, Paul's confidence in God's power to supply everything needful for that (cf. 9:8) is so strong that he can write as if this is already being accomplished, and as if the Corinthians are already showing *the greatest generosity.*

In v. 11*b* the apostle introduces the theme of *thanksgiving,* and with it the second major point in the present passage. Now Paul observes that the God who makes it possible for the Corinthians to be generous in their contributions for the needy Christians of Jerusalem will be praised by those to whom the gifts are delivered. Just as he has written in theological terms about the giving of this aid (it is an act of grace), so now he writes in theological terms about its receipt: those who are helped by it properly direct their thanks to God, the real source of the benefit, not to the Corinthians or to other human agents.

This idea emerges even more prominently in v. 12, which (as noted by Georgi 1965:74), supports v. 11*b*. Here Paul emphasizes that the conveyance of the collection *not only supplies the needs of the saints but also overflows with many thanksgivings to God.* The theological conviction which lies behind this statement is the same as that which has prompted Paul to express himself in similar ways in two earlier passages. In 1:11 he has written of the "thanks" given to God by "many people" as they recognize the "gracious benefit" *(to charisma)*—rescue from mortal danger—which God bestows on Paul and his colleagues. And in 4:15 he has written of his intention that "grace [*charis*], extended through ever more people, may cause thanksgiving to overflow to the glory of God." In the present passage Paul is thinking specifically of the "grace" ( = *benefit,* 8:4; 9:8) which finds concrete expression in the relief fund. That is not only a *service* for the saints but also *service* to God, administered by Paul as a vital part of his "priestly service" to God on behalf of the Gentiles (see NOTES and cf. especially Rom 15:16). God, too, is served by it, because when the collection has been delivered to the saints they will praise God for the gift. As he also does elsewhere, Paul operates here with the notion that praise and thanksgiving actually strengthen the divine glory (Boobyer 1929:79; cf. NOTES and COMMENT on 1:11; 4:15).

There may be an echo of v. 12 in 1 Clem 38:2, written to the Corinthian church as it existed at the end of the first century: "Let the rich man bestow help on the poor and let the poor give thanks to God, that he gave him one to supply his needs." The phrase about "supplying needs" (Paul: *prosana-plērousa ta hysterēmata;* Clement: *anaplērōthē . . . to hysterēma*), as well as the notion that thanksgiving is directed *to God* for providing human benefactors, is common to both. Hagner (1973:210) does not think that this parallel should be used as evidence of Clement's acquaintance with this passage because, he suggests, 1 Clem 38:2 could just as well be an echo of 1 Cor 16:17 as of 2 Cor 9:12. But while the phrase *to . . . hysterēma anaplērōsan* does occur in 1 Cor 16:17, it is used differently there (*RSV* translates "made up for . . . absence") and Paul speaks of "rejoicing" in that, not of "giving thanks" for it. The present verse undoubtedly offers a much closer parallel (cf. Windisch, 281).

Paul's strong confidence that God will direct and enable the Corinthians to contribute generously to the collection is still evident in v. 13. Now, continuing to use the present tense as he has since v. 11, he specifies two reasons why the recipients will most certainly *glorify God.* For one thing there is the *generosity* of those who graciously share their resources *with them and* (so the saints may presume) *with all* Christian brothers and sisters who are in need. But another, and indeed the first reason Paul mentions is the Corinthians' faith: the *obedience* shown in their *confession of the gospel of Christ.* Their participation in the collection project is a concrete manifestation of that faith and therefore, not incidentally, of the progress of Paul's gospel among the Gentiles. This point is consistent with Paul's concern that the Corinthians should *clearly demonstrate (their) love* by making a contribution (8:24; cf. 8:8). It also corresponds with what he has said about the Macedonians—that their contribution was subsequent to their giving of *themselves* (8:5). And finally, it explains why, faced with severe criticism of his efforts in Corinth on behalf of the collection, he can write as he does in 12:14b: "I am not after what is yours, but you." This point is more precisely made in Phil 4:17, where the apostle is expressing his gratitude for the aid he himself had been sent by the Philippians (cited by Bultmann, 260): "Not that I am after the principal; rather, I am after the interest that accrues to your account." So it is with the Corinthians. Their participation in the collection is solicited not only for what it will do but also for what it will be—a sign of their faith and a signal, especially to the Jewish Christians of Jerusalem, that the Gentiles have become full partners in *the gospel of Christ* (cf. Georgi 1965:76–77).

In v. 14, Paul anticipates that those who have been aided by the collection will also respond with intercessory prayers on behalf of their benefactors. The belief that the prayers of the poor were especially efficacious was present in the early church (see especially Herm Sim II, 5, 7) as well as in Judaism (e.g., Ꜣ*Abot R. Nat.* 38), and is doubtless reflected here, too. But the most important point is that the poor of Jerusalem will be stirred to this intercession *because of the surpassing grace of God* they shall have perceived to be at work in the Corinthian congregation. At the beginning of his appeal Paul has pointed to God's grace operative among the Macedonian churches as they eagerly joined the collection project. Now at the close of his appeal the apostle expresses his confidence that *the . . . grace of God* will move the Corinthians to the same kind of action.

Given Paul's conviction that this collection prospers because of the operation of divine grace in his Gentile congregations, it is appropriate that the last line of his discussion of it should be an exclamation of praise: *Thanks be to God for his indescribable gift!* (v. 15). The outburst is characteristically Pauline (see NOTES). Here he undoubtedly has something more specific in mind than salvation in general. Some (e.g., Strachan, 145; Hughes, 342) believe the reference is to God's *gift* of his Son, but—despite 8:9—this has not been a special theme in the preceding discussion. In every other instance where Paul breaks forth with such an exclamation, he is giving thanks for something very clearly indicated in the immediate context: in 2:14 for being sent forth "in Christ" (cf. vv. 15, 17; 3:3); in 8:16 for *earnestness* (cf. vv. 7, 8, 18, 22); in Rom 6:17 (cf. Rom 7:25) for freedom from sin (cf. vv. 16, 18); and in 1 Cor 15:57 for "the victory" (cf. vv. 54, 55). In the present case the subject is God's *grace,* v. 14, and in a sense that has been the principal emphasis since 8:1 (although the Greek word *charis* must be translated in other ways in 8:4, 6, 7, 16, 19; 9:8). Paul is giving thanks for the *indescribable gift* of God's grace, which he has seen at work as the Macedonians unexpectedly contributed to the collection and which he is confident will be operative among the Corinthians, too.

Throughout this entire appeal on behalf of the collection, beginning with the preliminary expressions of confidence in the Corinthians (7:4–16) and concluding with these comments on generosity, the apostle seems to be unreservedly optimistic about the whole venture. He seems to be confident that the Corinthians will fulfill their commitment to contribute, that they will do so generously, and that the Christians of Jerusalem will receive these gifts as genuine tokens of the faith and love of the Pauline congregations. Even if Paul does have some reservations at one or more of these points, one could understand that he would not want to voice them here lest his appeal to the Corinthians be weakened. Unfortunately, there is relatively little firm evidence available concerning (1) the actual outcome of Paul's collection efforts in Corinth and (2) the circumstances surrounding the delivery of the entire fund to the church in Jerusalem.

(1) There is no reason to think that Paul is excluding the capital city of Corinth when he tells the Roman Christians that "Achaia" as well as Macedonia has contributed to the relief fund for Jerusalem (Rom 15:26). It is clear that the Corinthians have responded in some degree to the apostle's appeal. However, Clement's remark that the Corinthians are known for "giving more gladly than receiving" (1 Clem 2:1, alluding to Acts 20:35; cited by Plummer, 267 n.) should not be pressed as evidence that the Corinthians had responded enthusiastically. In fact, if the hypothesis is correct that 2 Cor 10–13 come from Paul's last (surviving) letter to Corinth (see INTRODUCTION, pp. 44–48), then there is solid evidence that whatever amount was raised there was raised with some difficulty (see especially 12:14b–18).

(2) On the eve of his departure for Jerusalem to deliver the money he has collected, Paul seems apprehensive about his reception there. After explaining to the Romans why he must go to Jerusalem before coming to them, he asks that they pray for him to be "rescued from the unbelievers in Judea" and that his "relief work for Jerusalem may be acceptable to the saints" (Rom 15:31). Where now is the optimism of 2 Cor 9:11–15? Where now is the confidence that the generosity of his churches will redound to the glory of God as the Christians of Jerusalem give thanks to God for the faith and the gifts of the Gentile congregations? It is difficult to correlate the details of Rom 15:31 with the narrative of Paul's arrival in Jerusalem given in Acts 21:17ff. Nothing in the Acts account suggests that Paul had any kind of relief fund with him when he arrived; it is only said that the Christians of the city received his party "gladly" (v. 17). Acts also reports a favorable reception of Paul by the elders of the church. Indeed, after a full recital of all the things that "God had done among the Gentiles" through his ministry, the elders "glorified God" for it (vv. 19–20), as if in fulfillment of 2 Cor 9:13. But again, there is no mention of the relief fund, though this would doubtless have been the time and place for its presentation. Subsequently, of course, "the Jews from Asia" stir up the crowds against Paul (Acts 21:27–30) and only the intervention of the Romans saves him from a mob-lynching (vv. 31–36). Therefore, if one is to judge from the narrative in Acts, Paul had nothing to fear from the leaders of the Jerusalem church, who "glorified God" for the faith of the Gentiles even without any concrete evidence of its reality. But he rightly feared "the unbelievers," whose charges against him led eventually to his arrest and finally to his execution in Rome.

A letter sent from Macedonia, more likely from Thessalonica or Beroea than from Philippi, perhaps in the spring or summer of 56 C.E. Since his dispatch of a letter to Corinth in the fall of the previous year, Paul has learned—or has come to realize—that certain rival apostles are succeeding in their attempt to demean and discredit him in the eyes of the Corinthian Christians. Now, writing in advance of an impending third visit, Paul responds to several charges and suspicions which they have raised, and warns that he will exercise strict discipline, should that still be necessary, when he arrives. This is the last of the five letters Paul is known to have written to the Corinthians—thus, "Letter E."

# I. LETTER BODY, 10:1–13:10

## A. AN APPEAL FOR OBEDIENCE, 10:1–18

### 1. THE APPEAL PROPER, 10:1–6

**10** ¹I myself, Paul, appeal to you by the gentleness and kindness of Christ—I who am demeaned when with you in person, but make bold toward you when I am away. ²I ask that when I am present I will not need to be bold with that confidence with which I have it in mind to summon up courage against certain persons who reason that we are conducting ourselves according to worldly standards. ³For though it is in the world that we conduct ourselves, we do not wage war according to worldly standards—⁴for the weapons of our campaign are not ordinary ones, but are mightily effective for God in the demolition of strongholds. We demolish reasonings ⁵and every great height raised up in opposition to the knowledge of God; we take every mind captive for obedience to Christ; ⁶and we stand at the ready to punish every disobedience when your obedience is complete.

## Notes

10:1. *I myself, Paul.* Cf. "I myself" in 12:13; Rom 7:25; 9:3; 15:14, where the apostle emphasizes his own personal involvement. When he writes "I Paul" in 1 Thess 2:18 he is singling himself out from the preceding "we," which includes Silvanus and Timothy (see 1 Thess 1:1), but such formulas do not automatically presume that others have just been mentioned (against de Boor, 196). The closest parallel to the present phrase, in both form and function, is Gal 5:2, "Now I, Paul, say to you . . ." *(RSV);* there—as here—the apostle wishes to give emphasis and authority to what follows. See also Phlm 9–10, where—as here—Paul's use of his name is followed by an appeal *(parakalō,* etc.). This formula does not indicate that everything which follows has been written by Paul's own hand (against Deissmann 1927:167 n. 7; more recently, Bahr 1968:37), because the apostle invariably introduces such "subscriptions" with a direct reference to his "own hand" (1 Cor 16:21; Gal 6:11; Phlm 19; cf. Col 4:18; 2 Thess 3:17; correctly Meyer, 616–17).

*appeal to you.* Or, "entreat you," "beseech you," "urge you" *(parakalō hymas),* as in 2:8; Rom 12:1; 15:30; 16:17; 1 Cor 1:10; 4:16; 16:15, and cf. 1 Thess 4:1, 10; 5:14; Phlm 9, 10. Bjerkelund (1967), who provides a full study of the use of the verb in the Pauline letters, holds to the integrity of our 2 Cor and suggests that in the present verse it is used to effect a transition from the milder to the sharper portion of the letter (ibid.:154–55). If, however, chaps. 10–13 represent a separate letter, as seems most probable, *parakalō* can be regarded equally well as opening the letter body, as in 1 Cor 1:10 and Phlm 8–9; see INTRODUCTION, pp. 35–41.

*by the gentleness and kindness of Christ.* As in other instances where Paul is issuing a strong appeal, the verb of entreaty *(parakalō)* is here followed by a prepositional phrase *(dia . . .);* see Rom 12:1; 15:30; 1 Cor 1:10, and cf. Phlm 9. Bjerkelund (1967:164–67) has shown that such phrases function as oath formulas.

*gentleness and kindness.* These two terms *(praytētos kai epieikeias)* were frequently paired in ancient texts (e.g., Philo, *Creation of the World* 103; Plutarch, *Pericles* XXXIX, 1; *Sertorius* XXV, 4; cf. *Caesar* LVII, 3; Lucian, *The Dream* 10), including other early Christian texts (1 Clem 30:8; Diogn 7:4), though customarily in the reverse order. They overlap in meaning, and here form almost a hendiadys describing a "gentle, humble and modest attitude" (Leivestad 1966:159–60).

*gentleness (praytēs)* is used nowhere else of Christ in the NT, but in LXX Ps 44(45):4 it describes the messianic king (cf. the use of the adjective in LXX Zech 9:9, quoted in Matt 21:5). See also Matt 11:29, where Jesus calls his hearers to take his yoke upon them and learn of him because he is "gentle and lowly in heart [*prays kai tapeinos en kardia*]" *(RSV).* This saying, which has a parallel in Gos Thom [CG II, 2] 48,16–20 [*NHLE,* 127], has clear affinities with the Jewish Wisdom tradition—one of these being the identification of the wise man as "gentle." Note especially the references to the *gentleness* of David (LXX Ps 131[132]:1) and of Moses (Sir 45:4). Aristotle defines this virtue as a slowness to anger (*Nichomachean Ethics* IV.v.1–12).

*kindness (epieikeia)* is used elsewhere in the NT only in Acts 24:4 (Paul to Felix): "I beg you in your kindness to hear us briefly" *(RSV).* The adjective tends to connote "forbearance" as contrasted with vindictiveness (e.g., Phil 4:5; 1 Tim 3:3; Jas 3:17; 1 Pet 2:18), and the noun is often used this way in the LXX (e.g., Wis 2:19; 3 Mac 7:6). In Wis 12:18; 2 Mac 2:22; 10:4, God is so described.

*demeaned.* Translates *tapeinos,* which here has its usual meaning: to be stripped of one's dignity and personal sense of worth. See Philo, *Who Is the Heir* 29, where it is associated with a sense of "nothingness" and being "reduced to such an elemental state, as seems not even to exist." Hellenistic writers often employed this word and its cognates to denigrate flatterers (P. Marshall 1980:118, 499). Paul uses the same word with a less negative meaning in 7:6 ("the downcast") and Rom 12:16 ("the lowly" [*RSV*]). The cognate verb is used in 11:7; 12:21.

*when with you in person.* Or, "when encountering you face to face" *(kata prosōpon . . . en hymin),* as in Gal 2:11 (Paul's confrontation with Peter in Antioch). Cf. "face to face" *(prosōpon pros prosōpon)* in 1 Cor 13:12.

*make bold toward you.* In 5:6, 8; 7:16 the same verb *(tharrein)* means to "have confidence in" something or someone. But here, in specific contrast with *demeaned,* it means to act with courage and self-assurance in one's dealings with others *(eis hymas);* cf. Philo, *Who Is the Heir* 29, where the same contrast *(tapeinos/tharrein)* is drawn (Windisch, 292). A similar antithesis in 11:7 is formed with two verbs: "demeaning myself [*emauton tapeinōn*] that you might be exalted [*hymeis hypsōthēte*]" (cf. Phil 2:8, 9).

*when I am away.* Translates *apōn,* which contrasts not only with the preceding *when with you in person* (cf. Pol Phil 3:2) but also with *parōn (when I am present)* in v. 2. The same contrast *(apōn/parōn)* is drawn in v. 10, and then later in 13:2, 10. Ancient letter-writers frequently gave assurances that they were in a sense "present" to their readers even while they were "absent" from them, and this conventional topic is taken up by Paul in 1 Thess 2:17 and 1 Cor 5:3 especially (discussed by Thraede 1970:95–102).

2. *I ask.* Bachmann, 338–39, argues that this verb *(deomai)* should be interpreted as a beseeching of God in prayer, and one may cite the use of the same verb in Rom 1:10 and 1 Thess 3:10 in support of this. It is more likely, however, that Paul is resuming the appeal inaugurated in v. 1, and that here (as in 5:20) he is entreating the Corinthians. The *de,* regarded as emphatic by some (e.g., Dana and Mantey 1927:244; *ASV:* "yea"), is probably merely resumptive, and is best left untranslated; it is certainly not adversative (*KJV:* "But").

*that . . . not.* Translates *to mē,* which is here equivalent to *hina mē;* BDF § 399(1).

*when I am present.* Contrasts with *when I am away,* v. 1 (see note there). On the nominative form of *parōn* see BDF §§ 405(1); 409(5), and *GNTG* I:212.

*to be bold.* For the verb, see note on *make bold toward you* in v. 1.

*that confidence.* Literally "the confidence" *(tē pepoithēsei).* In 1:15; 3:4; 8:22 (Letter D) this word refers to confidence in the Corinthians. Here it refers to Paul's sense of self-confidence in facing down his critics.

*I have it in mind.* Or, "I reckon on, count on, consider," etc. The same verb *(logizesthai)* later in the sentence is used of those who are criticizing the Pauline apostolate (translated *reason*), and yet again in vv. 7 (translated *be aware*), 11 *(count on),* and 11:5 ("consider"). This repetition of the word, plus the use of a related nominative form in v. 4 (translated there as *reasonings*), suggests that it is a term being used by Paul's critics which he now wishes to redirect against them. This juxtaposition of what Paul "has in mind" in relation to what they "reason" about his ministry is typical of the sense of confrontation which pervades chaps. 10–13.

*to summon up courage.* Paul uses this verb *(tolman)* three more times in this letter (v. 12; twice in 11:21), as often as in all of his other letters combined. Betz (1972:67–69) has shown that it was regularly used in a pejorative sense by the philosophers in their anti-sophistic polemic; almost, "be audacious."

*against certain persons.* Translates *epi tinas,* with which one may compare *tines,* "some," in 3:1 (see NOTES).

*who reason that we.* Or, "who charge us with" *(tous logizomenous hēmas);* see note above on *I have it in mind.* With this phrase Paul abandons the first person singular with which his appeal began (v. 1). The first person plural continues through v. 7.

*are conducting ourselves.* As in 4:2 (see NOTES); 5:7 and elsewhere, the verb *peripatein* (literally "to walk") is used metaphorically of one's behavior.

*according to worldly standards.* For this phrase *(kata sarka)* see NOTES on 1:17 (where it is translated "opportunistically") and 5:16a.

3. *For though it is in the world.* The connective *gar (For)* introduces a correction of the preceding thought (cf. Plummer, 275). The phrase *in the world (en sarki;* literally "in the flesh") is formulated to contrast with *according to worldly standards (kata sarka;* literally "according to the flesh"), which is used at the end of v. 2 and once more later in the present verse. In both formulations *sarx* ("flesh") stands for what is finite, worldly, limited, and limiting. What distinguishes the two phrases is the use of two different prepositions, whereby *en sarki* takes on the neutral sense of *en tō kosmō* ("in the world," 1:12), as also in Gal 2:20 (cf. Phil 1:22, 24; Phlm 16). One might also translate: "For though we are subject to all human limitations" (Pfitzner 1967:160; cf. *NEB*).

*conduct ourselves.* The verb, as in v. 2, is *peripatein.*

*wage war.* With the introduction of this verb *(strateuesthai;* also used in 1 Cor 9:7) Paul begins a portrayal of his apostolic service as a military campaign. The metaphor continues through v. 6 (see Malherbe 1983), making this by far the most elaborate instance of the use of military imagery in the Pauline letters. Cf. his reference to "the weapons of righteousness" in 6:7b (see note), and Phil 2:25; 1 Thess 5:8; Phlm 2.

*according to worldly standards.* As in v. 2 (see note).

4. *the weapons of our campaign.* Or, "the weapons of our warfare" *(RSV),* the word *strateia* (spelled *stratia* in many mss.; see Deissmann 1903:181–82) denoting in particular a military campaign.

*not ordinary ones.* Literally "not fleshly" *(ou sarkika);* thus, "not of this world," not subject to the limitations of created objects. See the note on "not by any ordinary wisdom" in 1:12, where—as here—the adjective has the sense of "inadequate." In the present instance, contrasted with *dynatos (mightily effective),* it also connotes "weakness" (Jewett 1971:127–28; Schütz 1975:241). Cf. *NEB:* "not merely human."

*mightily effective for God.* Or, "powerful for God," the adjective *dynata* being the opposite of *sarkika* (see preceding note). Most English trs. regard the dative *tō Theō* as a Semitism and translate it as a Hebrew intensive (e.g., *NEB:* "divinely potent"; cf. Hughes, 351 n. 6; Moule 1953:184); but it is better to regard it as a dative of subjective judgment ("in the eyes of God") or, better yet, as a dative of advantage (cf. *JB:* "in God's cause"). See BDF § 192; *GNTG* II:4; III:238; Bultmann, 186–87; Barrett, 251.

*the demolition of strongholds.* Translates *kathairesin ochyrōmatōn.* Cf. Prov 21:22
and Philo, *Confusion of Tongues* 128–31. It is more likely that Paul and Philo have been
influenced in their choice of this imagery by its widespread use in the Hellenistic
philosophical tradition than that they have drawn it from Proverbs (Malherbe 1983).
Behind the metaphor stands the tactics of siege warfare as practiced in the Greco-
Roman world—e.g., at Hebron in the second century B.C.E. ("Judas . . . demolished
its strongholds [*katheilen ta ochyrōmata autēs*] and burned its towers all around," 1
Mac 5:65; cf. 8:10, the Romans "demolished the strongholds" of the Greeks), and by
the Romans at Jerusalem in 70 C.E. (cf. Luke 19:43–44, cited by Windisch, 297).
Malherbe (1983, especially 148–56) cites numerous passages in which philosophers
commended "moral" fortification and armament. Paul uses the noun *demolition* only
here and in the statement of v. 8 (repeated in 13:10). It is specifically a part of the
military metaphor employed against his critics in Corinth.

*We demolish reasonings.* This tr. takes the participle *(kathairountes)* as a nominative
absolute (e.g., Bultmann, 187; Hughes, 354 n. 10), although it may also be regarded
as dependent on *strateuometha (we . . . wage war)* in v. 3. In either case, it both
continues and clarifies the military imagery of the first part of the verse: the *strongholds*
which are "demolished" are the *reasonings* of those who would subvert the work of
the Pauline apostolate. By using the word *logismoi* here, Paul leaves no doubt that he
is still thinking of those *certain persons who reason (tinas tous logizomenous)* against
his ministry in Corinth (v. 2).

5. *every great height raised up in opposition to.* The military imagery continues. A
*hypsōma* may be any kind of a *great height* (see Rom 8:39), and here it would seem
to be an allusion to the high bulwarks from which the defenders of a city may oppose
a besieging army (against Tanner 1980:379, who thinks of the "conquest and pacifica-
tion of a frontier district"). The verbal form, too *(epairomenon, raised up),* can be used
of military operations; e.g., of the rebellion of a city against a king (LXX Ezra 4:19),
or of the attack of one army upon another (1 Mac 8:5; 10:70).

*the knowledge of God.* The genitive is objective, as in 2:14 (see note), "knowledge
about God"; and here—as there—the reference is probably to the gospel. Paul knows
very well how important *knowledge* is to the Corinthian Christians (note, e.g., 1 Cor
8:1, 10; 13:2), but this is not at issue in 2 Cor as it had been in 1 Cor; apart from this
verse the word *(gnōsis)* appears in chaps. 10–13 only in 11:6, and the verb only in 13:6.

*take . . . captive.* As in the case of *demolish* (v. 4), the participle (here *aichmalōtiz-
ontes*) is a nominative absolute. The image of siege warfare is continued; once the
battlements of a city have been destroyed the defenders are taken into captivity (see
1 Mac 8:10; Luke 21:24; cf. Windisch, 297–98). The term is also used metaphorically
in Jdt 16:9, and by Paul himself in Rom 7:23. Cf. Odes Sol 29:8–9 (cited by Bultmann,
187).

*every mind.* Translates *pan noēma,* which could also be rendered as "every thought"
*(RSV)* or even "all thoughts" (Héring, 70 n. 3); elsewhere Paul uses only the plural
*noēmata* (see note on *designs* in 2:11). In the present instance, as in 3:14; 4:4; 11:3; Phil
4:7, the reference is probably to the *mind* as representative of the whole "intellective
centre" of one's being (Hughes, 353–54 n. 10; cf. Jewett 1971:381–82).

*for obedience to Christ.* The genitive *tou Christou* must, in view of *your obedience,*
v. 6, be objective, not subjective.

6. *we stand at the ready.* This phrase (*en hetoimō echontes;* the participle is nominative absolute [see NOTES on vv. 4, 5]) continues the military imagery of vv. 3–5; see Polybius II, 34.2 ("When they had these troops they kept them in readiness [*eichon en hetoimō*] and awaited the attack of the enemy") and Philo, *Embassy to Gaius* 259 (Gaius feared the governors who "had resources ready for an uprising [*aphormas herōn echontas en hetoimō*], particularly those who had large provinces and commanded large armies . . ."). Cf. 1 Mac 7:29; 12:50.

*to punish.* This verb, *ekdikein,* is used elsewhere by Paul only in Rom 12:19; the cognate noun is translated as "reprisal" in 2 Cor 7:11.

*every disobedience.* Paul uses the word *parakoē (disobedience)* only here and in Rom 5:19, in both cases set over against *hypakoē (obedience).* His usual terms for disobedience/disobeying are *apeitheia/apeithein* (Rom 2:8; 10:21; 11:30–32; cf. 1:30), presumably following LXX usage (where *parakoē* is never used and where the related verb is infrequent).

*when your obedience is complete.* The *your (hymōn)* is very emphatic; see COMMENT. The apostle is probably still thinking of *obedience to Christ,* as in v. 5, and not of some specific act of obedience to himself. The attitude expressed here corresponds to Paul's concern in writing the tearful letter (see 2:9), but contrasts with his commendation of the Corinthians' obedience after their receipt of that letter (7:15).

## COMMENT: GENERAL

For the reasons indicated in the INTRODUCTION (pp. 35–48), it is probable that 2 Cor 10–13 did not originally belong to the letter represented by chaps. 1–9 (Letter D). Chaps. 10–13 appear to be part, perhaps nearly the whole, of a later letter to Corinth—the fifth and last of Paul's letters sent to the congregation in that city (thus, Letter E). This letter seems to have been sent (a) in response to Paul's receipt of news about the growing intensity of attacks on his apostolate in Corinth, and (b) in anticipation of his third visit to the congregation.

It is likely that 10:1–6 opened the body of Letter E (see INTRODUCTION, pp. 47–48), and it is significant that this first paragraph is in the form of an appeal issued in prospect of Paul's impending visit. In an important sense Paul's plans for this visit, and his hope that it might be a constructive one, dominate the whole of chaps. 10–13. This appeal is supported by a discussion of his conduct as an apostle (10:7–18), and then—after a long section of reluctant self-praise and sharp polemic (11:1–12:13)—the appeal is renewed and concluded in 12:14–13:10. The specific appeal of 10:1–6 is that the Corinthians give their full obedience to Christ (vv. 1, 2, 6). In pleading for this, Paul acknowledges that certain serious charges have been made against him in Corinth (e.g., v. 2); but he assures his readers that these charges are specious. He portrays his apostolate as operating with the mighty power of a conquering army, an army which is, indeed, quite able to overcome every opposing force (vv. 3–5, 6)

## COMMENT: DETAILED

In vv. 1–2, Paul emphasizes the authority, the integrity, and the urgency of his present appeal to the Christians of Corinth. Its authority is assured by the fact that it comes from Paul himself, their apostle; its integrity is assured by the fact that it is issued by one who is claimed *by the gentleness and kindness of Christ* (cf. 5:14); and its urgency results from the fact that Paul does not want to have to be harsh with them when he arrives for his third visit in their city (cf. 12:21).

It is not impossible that the reference to Christ's *gentleness and kindness* echoes the dominical saying present in Matt 11:29, as many commentators have claimed. It is likely, however, that that saying was attributed to Jesus by the church under the influence of the Jewish Wisdom tradition, according to which the truly wise man is always "gentle" (see NOTES). Moreover, in the LXX *gentleness* and *kindness* are, respectively, attributes of the Messiah and of God (see NOTES). For these reasons the frequent suggestion that Paul is here revealing his knowledge of the "character" of the earthly Jesus (e.g., Plummer, 273; Kümmel, 208; de Boor, 198 n. 297) cannot be taken seriously. It is much more likely that Paul is thinking of the pre-existent Lord who, in the gracious condescension of his incarnate life, became lowly, weak, and poor (Leivestad 1966:163–64; cf. Bultmann, 184). This same "kenotic" tradition finds expression in 8:9 (see COMMENT); Rom 15:3; Phil 2:6–8 and (Leivestad 1966:161) in several Christian interpolations in T 12 Patr (T Dan 5:13; T Benj 9:5; 10:7).

The relative clause in the second half of v. 1 momentarily interrupts the appeal, and as usual in the Pauline letters the interruption reveals something important. In this case Paul breaks off the formulation of his appeal in order to point out the irony in a criticism that has been made of him, apparently by some people in Corinth. It is said that when he is with them *in person* he cuts a sorry figure, weak and undignified *(demeaned);* and that he dares to *make bold* only when he is far *away* from them, safely removed from the possibility of challenge or rebuttal. A bit later Paul will specifically quote the charge brought against him (v. 10), but for the moment he only alludes to it, that the irony of the complaint not be missed (Betz 1972:46, 51; Bultmann, 185). Has Paul appeared to be cowardly, servile, and weak when present with them? If so, they have not perceived that in reality he has been acting with *the gentleness and kindness of Christ.* If Paul seems to have been *demeaned* among them, that is not evidence that he lacks the credentials of an apostle; rather, it is evidence that he is a true apostle of the one who "demeaned himself and became obedient" even unto death on the cross (Phil 2:8). Paul has already written to the Corinthians about the correspondence between his weakness and that of the Christ he serves (4:10, "always carrying about in the body the death of Jesus"), and he will do so again, very explicitly, later in this letter (13:3–4; cf. Leivestad 1966:161–64).

It is only in v. 6 that Paul identifies that for which he is appealing—the *obedience* of the Corinthians; but this is implicit in v. 2, where the reason for the urgency of the appeal is given. The apostle will soon be in Corinth, and he does not want to have to *be bold* with his congregation there. What he means is shown more explicitly in 13:10—he does not want to have to exercise his apostolic authority to punish them (cf. 12:21; 13:2; 1 Cor 4:21). At the same time, Paul acknowledges that there are *certain persons* against whom he does expect to have to *summon up courage* when he comes. Paul may be thinking of "a malignant coterie" of disobedient persons in the congregation itself (Plummer, 274), but it is much more likely that he has in mind outsiders who have come into Corinth preaching "a different gospel" from his and thereby posing a serious threat to the faith of the congregation (see 11:4).

Whoever these *persons* are (for a discussion of their identity see INTRODUCTION, pp. 48–54), they have suggested (whether by innuendo or more directly) that Paul's ministry has been conducted *according to worldly standards* (literally "according to the flesh"). Paul had already taken a similar complaint into account in an earlier letter (see 1:12, 17 with NOTES and COMMENT), the criticism in that instance being his apparent disregard of a promise he had made to the Corinthians about visiting them. Since then, either the criticism itself has been broadened and sharpened or else Paul's awareness of the full extent and seriousness of the original criticism has been enlarged. Now he knows that he is dealing with those who would deny the authenticity of his apostleship and even his relationship to Christ (e.g., v. 7; 11:5; 13:3a), at least partly on the grounds that he has been weak and cowardly in his personal dealings with the Corinthian church (vv. 1, 10). This they seem to have taken as evidence of his bondage to the flesh and of his lack of charismatic power and authority (see, e.g., 12:12; 13:3–4, and cf. Bultmann, 185–86; Schmithals 1971:164–66). Paul's refusal to give up working at his craft during his residence among them (see NOTES and COMMENT on 11:7–9, and cf. 1 Cor 9:3–18; Acts 18:1–3) was perhaps also used against him. To Paul's rivals, as well as to the Corinthian citizenry in general, his work as a craftsman could well have seemed to be an indication of his worldliness, another specific way in which he had humiliated himself in Corinth (v. 1; cf. 11:7–9) and had demeaned the apostolic office (Theissen 1982:45; Hock 1980:64).

In vv. 3–5 the appeal is again interrupted, this time for an extended "apologetic aside" (Olson 1976:216) in response to the charge to which Paul has just alluded (v. 2). That his ministry is "worldly" insofar as "the world" is the place of his apostolic service, Paul concedes, v. 3a. At the same time, however, he wishes to emphasize that life *in the world* does not have to involve living *according to worldly standards;* the latter he completely disavows, v. 3b, as in 5:16a. This general distinction is characteristic of Paul, although it is variously formulated (see Rom 12:1–2; 1 Cor 7:29–31; Phil 3:19–20, and Furnish 1979: 115–16), and nowhere else precisely as it is here.

Paul has introduced a military term into the discussion when, in v. 3*b*, he writes of "waging war" in this world. Whether he does this in order to move beyond a merely defensive stance (Windisch, 296) or because he wants to counter his critics' picture of him as weak and cowardly (cf. Plummer, 275), he proceeds to elaborate on the metaphor in vv. 4–5. Now Paul describes his apostolate as if it were Christ's army engaged in battle, its *weapons* powerful enough to overwhelm any defensive work raised up against it and thus invincible in carrying out the divine strategy for salvation (v. 4*a*). Perhaps Paul wishes his readers to think of these as "the weapons of righteousness" of which he has written earlier (6:7*b*). In any case they *are not ordinary ones,* not the empty claims and sly deceits often associated with the itinerant teachers and propagandists of the time (cf. 2:17; 4:2; Bultmann, 186). They are instead *mightily effective* in destroying whatever stands in the way of the gospel.

When Philo refers to a "stronghold" as a structure built "through persuasiveness of argument [*dia tēs tōn logōn pithanotētos*]" in order to divert the mind from honoring God (in *Confusion of Tongues* 129), he is attacking the Sophists, orators, and teachers who were sometimes more concerned for the form and style of an argument than for its substance, often more devoted to rhetorical ornamentation than to the truth (on the sophistic tradition see G. A. Kennedy 1972:553–613; 1980:25–40; Koester 1982 I:351–53; Lesky 1966:340–60, 829–45, 870–74). Paul is standing in this same anti-sophistic tradition (Windisch, 298; Betz 1972:68–69) when he, too, writes of *reasonings* as *strongholds* which must be demolished before *the knowledge of God* can be spread abroad (vv. 4*b*–5*a*). It is probable that Paul is thinking in particular of the half-truths and specious reasoning of those who are trying to turn the Corinthians to another gospel. However superficially impregnable their arguments, they consist of nothing but empty words and bombast. Against them the apostle brings the power of the gospel (see Rom 1:16) as that is present in "the word of the cross" (1 Cor 1:18, 23) and proclaimed through his apostolic witness (2 Cor 2:14–17). Some would see in Paul's reference to *every great height raised up in opposition* to this gospel an allusion to his critics' claims of their own superiority (so Friedrich 1963b:215; Barrett, 252). That Paul is concerned about this is clear from 10:12–13 and 11:5, but it is more likely that Paul's reference is to whatever high bulwarks are thrown up against his gospel (see NOTES, and cf. Bultmann, 187). That he here describes this gospel as *the knowledge of God* (cf. 2:14) may well be due, however, to his awareness of the Corinthians' special fondness for the concept of "knowledge" (references in the NOTES)—a knowledge which his critics, moreover, may have accused him of lacking (11:6; cf. Bultmann, 187, and Barrett, 252–53).

When Paul writes of taking *every mind captive* (v. 5*b*) he is extending his notion of apostleship as a military campaign against a fortified city. After the city's defenses have been demolished, the defenders themselves are taken prisoner. Thus *every mind* is virtually equivalent to *every great height* in v. 5*a* (Windisch, 298), and it should not be pressed to mean "the intellectual culture of the time" (Héring, 70). The gospel conquers unbelief (cf. Odes Sol 10:4, where Christ speaks of capturing the world [10:3 is not a parallel, as frequently alleged; see Charlesworth 1977:48 n. 5]) and the believer is won over *for obedience to Christ.* Elsewhere Paul writes of this victory as a conquest of sin and death (1 Cor 15:54–57), or as release from the dominion of the law and transferral to the dominion of grace (Rom 6:14), a being freed from slavery to the law in order to "serve . . . in the new life of the Spirit" (Rom 7:6, *RSV*; cited by Kittel, *TDNT* I:196). What Paul here refers to above all is "faith's obedience" (Rom 1:5), the obedience to the gospel (Rom 10:16) which he seeks to win from the Gentiles by his apostolic efforts (Rom 15:18). That it is *his* gospel his hearers are urged to obey means that they are summoned to accept his authority as a preacher of the gospel, but their *obedience* as such is to be directed to Christ ( = the gospel, Rom 10:16; the truth, Rom 2:8; Gal 5:7; God, Rom 11:30–32; cf. 6:22; righteousness, Rom 6:16–19).

The appeal begun in vv. 1–2 is finally concluded in v. 6 (cf. Olson 1976:216), where Paul looks forward to the completion of *obedience* in the Corinthian congregation. Now, as in vv. 1–2, the apostle is urging his readers to be ready for his impending visit to them (12:14; 13:1; cf. Bultmann, 188). However, Paul's image of himself as a military field commander (perhaps in a messianic war; cf. Windisch, 298) is continued from vv. 3–5. He assures the Corinthians that his forces *stand at the ready* [for the military use of this phrase see NOTES] *to punish every disobedience.*

Interpreters are confronted with two significant difficulties in this verse. The first is that the comment about being ready to punish is followed by the remark *when your obedience is complete.* One might have expected, rather, "while your obedience is still incomplete," but that is not what Paul says. The other difficulty is that elsewhere in 2 Cor the apostle has written as if the readers' obedience had already been tested (2:9) and had been found adequate (7:15). How, then, can he now imply that it is not yet really *complete?*

The second of these problems may be taken up first. While it is true that the apostle expresses a certain confidence about the Corinthians' obedience even here in v. 6, one must not forget that this verse is part of an urgent appeal (vv. 1–2), indeed a warning to the Corinthians; Paul has real doubts about their obedience (cf. 12:21; 13:2). The measured confidence in v. 6, therefore, is not really comparable to the relatively unreserved confidence of chap. 7 (against Hughes, 354–55). This difficulty can be resolved, however, if chaps. 10–13 are regarded as belonging to a separate letter, perhaps earlier than the one of which chap. 7 was a part, but more probably later (see INTRODUCTION, p. 38). In this case, then, one must suppose that something has happened since the writing of chap. 7 to make Paul wonder whether the Corinthians are really so obedient after all. Perhaps Titus' report (7:7–16) had been overly optimistic, or Paul had read into it what he himself wanted to hear (note 7:14). Or perhaps Paul's critics in the city have mounted new and more persuasive attacks on his apostleship. Whatever the case, Paul needs to appeal to his congregation to fulfill their obedience to the gospel.

The other difficulty involves an apparent tension within v. 6 itself. How can the apostle say that his forces stand *at the ready to punish every disobedience* precisely when *obedience* shall have been fulfilled? Oostendorp (1967:18) proposes that Paul's opponents have charged him with neglecting moral discipline at Corinth, and that the apostle is now responding to that: once the congregation is generally obedient and willing to cooperate he will begin to exercise the needed discipline. Apart from the fact that Oostendorp's identification of the opponents as Judaizing Christians (therefore particularly concerned about moral discipline) is not convincing (see INTRODUCTION, p. 53), it must be objected that the term *punish* seems to have something more specific in mind than general congregational discipline. An easier explanation is suggested by the emphatic *your* before *obedience,* as if the *obedience* of Paul's readers were being specifically distinguished from the *disobedience* of others (Barrett, 239). There are various indicators throughout 2 Cor (Letters D and E) that Paul's rivals for leadership of the Christian community in Corinth (the *certain persons* of v. 2) are not themselves members of the congregation (see especially 11:4, and note the use of the third person in 10:10–12, etc.; see INTRODUCTION, pp. 52–54). The present verse is readily understood when this fact is considered. Paul is promising that whenever the obedience of the congregation itself has been completed, whenever their commitment to his gospel—and thus to his apostolate—is firm, then he will punish *every disobedience* of those who now seek to turn them to "another gospel" (11:4; so also Barrett, 239, 253–54). Here, as in v. 5, *obedience* must refer above all to the obedience of faith, *obedience to Christ,* and the "completion" of this obedience may perhaps be interpreted in accord with the remark in v. 15 about the "increase" of faith in Corinth (cf. Bultmann, 188). When Paul is certain enough of the basic Christian commitments of the congregation, then his own hand will have been strengthened to deal with *every disobedience* of the interlopers. What particular forms the disobedience of these latter may have taken is not disclosed here, but certain clues do emerge as this letter proceeds (see especially 10:13–18; 11:4, 12–15).

## 2. THE APPEAL SUPPORTED, 10:7–18

10 ⁷Be alert to what is right in front of you! If someone is confident of being Christ's, let that person be aware of this, that we, too, are

Christ's. ⁸Now even if I boast a little more about our authority which the Lord has given for your upbuilding and not for your destruction, I shall not be ashamed—⁹lest I should seem as if I wanted to be scaring you with my letters. ¹⁰For it is said, "His letters are demanding and impressive, but when he is actually present he is weak, and his speech is contemptible." ¹¹Let such a person count on this, that what we are in the words of our letters when we are away, we also are in action when we are present.

¹²For we do not have the audacity to class or compare ourselves with certain persons who recommend themselves. Indeed, when they measure themselves by themselves and compare themselves with themselves they have no understanding. ¹³Yet we will not boast beyond the proper limits, but only in accord with the measure of the jurisdiction which God has apportioned to us as our measure, to reach out even as far as you. ¹⁴For we are not overextending ourselves, as if we do not reach to you; we came even as far as you with the gospel of Christ. ¹⁵We are not boasting beyond the proper limits, in the labors of others; and our hope is that as your faith grows we may be abundantly praised among you —in accord with our jurisdiction—¹⁶and that we may preach the gospel in places beyond you, not boasting about what has been done already in another's jurisdiction. ¹⁷"Let the one who boasts boast in the Lord." ¹⁸For it is not the one who engages in self-recommendation who is approved, but the one whom the Lord recommends.

## NOTES

10:7. *Be alert to.* Translates *blepete* as imperative (so also *RSV, NEB, JB*), but it could also be regarded as indicative (*ASV, TEV, NIV, NEB* mg., *JB* mg.) or interrogative (*KJV, ASV* mg.). The interpretation adopted here is supported by the fact that *blepete* is virtually always used in the imperative sense in the Pauline (1 Cor 8:9; 10:18; 16:10; Gal 5:15; Phil 3:2) and deutero-Pauline (Eph 5:15; Col 2:8; 4:17) letters (only 1 Cor 1:26 is unclear), and that one would expect an introductory *but* before the exhortation in the latter part of the verse if *blepete* were to be read as indicative or interrogative (Héring, 71). It is no objection to this that the verb usually stands first, not last as here, for the object of the verb may come first for emphasis (Windisch, 300; cf. Plummer, 279). As in 1 Cor 8:9; Gal 5:15; Phil 3:2 (and Col 2:8), *blepete* is probably used here to warn about a present danger.

*what is right in front of you.* More literally, "the things right in front of you" *(ta kata prosōpon);* see *GNTG* III:15, 268. There is no reason to believe that *kata prosōpon* has the meaning here that it has in 5:12, where—contrasted with what is "within" the heart —it refers to what is merely "outward" (against Bultmann, 189, who would also take *blepete* as interrogative [see preceding note]: "Do you look at what is external?"). Here the implicit contrast is with what is "not visible" because it is not present (cf. v. 1, where *kata prosōpon* has a similar meaning).

*If someone.* In 2:5 the same phrase *(ei tis)* refers to one particular individual, "some one" (see NOTES and COMMENT on 2:3–11), and this could also be true here; so Barrett, 256. On the other hand, the phrase usually has a generalized meaning in Paul's letters ("If anyone at all," "Whoever"; cf. Rom 8:9b; 1 Cor 3:12; Phil 3:4, etc.), and the apostle seems to be aware of a group of critics as he writes now to his Corinthian church (see "certain persons" in vv. 2, 12); so Bultmann, 190.

*being Christ's.* Whether this phrase *(Christou einai)* is to be associated with 1 Cor 1:12 *(egō de Christou)* is debated. Schmithals, who believes it is (1971:197–206), regards the genitive as partitive, and the slogan as Gnostic in origin. Theissen, however, citing Mark 9:41 *(hoti Christou este,* "because you are Christ's"), associates it with the viewpoint of itinerant charismatics who took no thought for their own material needs (1982:46–47, 66–67 n. 59); see COMMENT. Whatever its origin, Paul has made it his own; see 1 Cor 3:23 and Gal 3:29 *(hymeis [de] Christou);* 1 Cor 15:23 and Gal 5:24 *(hoi [de] tou Christou),* and cf. Rom 8:9b; 14:8.

*let that person be aware of this.* Literally: "let him consider this again in [or: by] himself." As in the formulation of similar warnings, challenges, or instructions, Paul follows an introductory *ei tis (If someone)* with a third-person-singular imperative (cf. 1 Cor 3:18b; 7:12, 13, 36; 11:34a; 16:22; Gal 1:9). Here *be aware* translates *logizesthai.* This repeats a term which the apostle's critics have apparently been using in mounting their attacks on his ministry, and which he has already turned back on them in vv. 2 and 4 (on which see the NOTES).

*that.* Translates *hoti,* which (as in v. 11) specifies the demonstrative pronoun by introducing what is to be taken into consideration *(touto logizesthō . . . hoti;* cf. Rom 2:3, *logizē de touto . . . , hoti).*

*we, too, are Christ's.* Literally: "just as he is Christ's, so are we." Here, as in the preceding verses (since the end of v. 2), the first person plural includes Paul and his associates in ministry.

8. *Now even if.* Translates *ean te gar,* in which *gar* (literally "For") is merely introductory. The *te* is not copulative here, but (unless it is to be omitted, as in P⁴⁶ B G H et al.) seems to strengthen *ean* (thus *even if* rather than just "if"); see Windisch, 303 n. 1, and Bultmann, 190, and cf. BDG § 443(3); *GNTG* III:339.

*I boast.* Note the first person singular, rather unexpected after the first person plural which has been in force since the end of v. 2. This is the first of many occurrences of the verb *kauchasthai* in chaps. 10–13 (it also appears in vv. 8, 13, 15, 16, 17; 11:12, 16, 18, 30; 12:1, 5, 6, 9, and the noun *kauchēsis* is used in 11:10, 17). See the note on "we can be proud of this" in 1:12 for remarks on the prominence of this word-group in the Pauline letters. Two of the three instances of the verb in chaps. 1–9 pertain to Paul's justifiable pride in the Corinthians (7:14; 9:2). In the third passage Paul refers to those who wrongly boast "of what is outward and not of what is within" (5:12), and there the apostle's rivals were certainly in mind; cf. 11:12. See COMMENT.

*a little more.* Or "somewhat more" *(perissoteron ti),* meaning probably "somewhat more than I already have in claiming to be Christ's."

*about our authority.* This is the subject of what Paul might well boast about further.

Apart from this verse and the close parallel in 13:10, Paul uses the word *exousia* of apostolic *authority* only in 1 Cor 9 (vv. 4, 5, 6, 12, 18). Note the use of the first person plural, *our,* which contrasts with the first person singular in the rest of the verse and in vv. 9–11a; and contrast 13:10, "the authority which the Lord has given to me. . . ."

*the Lord.* Here (and in 13:10) the reference is certainly to Christ (cf. 12:19). It is through him that Paul has received his apostolic authority (e.g., 1 Cor 9:1–2; Gal 1:1).

*for your upbuilding and not for your destruction.* The imagery *(eis oikodomein kai ouk eis kathairesin hymōn)* probably derives from Jeremiah; see especially LXX Jer 1:10; 24:6, but also 38(31):28; 49(42):10; 51(45):4 (and Vielhauer 1979:73; Schütz 1975:224).

*your upbuilding.* In Greek the possessive pronoun occurs only after *destruction,* but it should doubtless be construed with *upbuilding* as well. (Like *our* with *authority,* which it seems intended to balance, it is omitted altogether in the parallel in 13:10.) In the Pauline letters the noun *oikodomē, upbuilding,* usually refers to the building up of the Christian community (cf. 12:19; 1 Cor 3:9; 14:3, 5, 12, 26, and the use of *[ep]oikodomein* in Rom 15:20; 1 Cor 3:10, 12, 14), effected as others are served in love (Rom 14:19; 15:2; 1 Cor 8:1; 1 Thess 5:11, etc.). While this thought is doubtless present here as well (and in 13:10), Paul seems to be thinking, in addition, of the authority he had to come to Corinth with the gospel on which the congregation there had been founded in the first place (vv. 13–14).

*not for your destruction.* The same noun *(kathairesis)* is translated "demolition" in 10:4, the only other occurrence in Paul's letters apart from the present statement and its parallel in 13:10.

*I shall not be ashamed.* Note the change from the aorist subjunctive in the first part of the verse *(if I [should] boast)* to the future indicative here, and cf. the same kind of formulation in 12:6; in both places Paul is confident that whatever boasting he may be prompted to do will be fully warranted (cf. Plummer, 281; Barrett, 259). The verb *aischynesthai* is used similarly in Phil 1:20 and (in composition with *ep-*) in Rom 1:16.

9. *lest I should seem.* This is to be preferred as the most straightforward translation of *hina mē doxō,* even though the exact connection between vv. 8 and 9 must remain a matter of uncertainty. Chrysostom *(NPNF,* 1st ser. XII:380), as well as some modern commentators (e.g., Heinrici, 328–29; cf. BDF § 483), would read v. 9 as the protasis of v. 11 (v. 10 would then be parenthetical), but the form of v. 11 is against this (correctly Windisch, 305). A better alternative would be to regard the *hina* as imperatival (see NOTES on 8:7), thus opening a new sentence (as in *NEB:* "So you must not think of me . . ."; also Wey.). Still another possibility, proposed already by Grotius (cited by Meyer, 625), would be to supply before the *hina*-clause something like "But I will say no more about this authority . . ." (so also Denney, 304 n. 2; Lietzmann, 142; Barrett, 259). However, it is difficult to see how a thought like this could have remained unexpressed (correctly Windisch, 305, who would prefer to supply here a phrase like "what I emphasize"). It is simpler to supply something within the clause itself (see following note).

*as if I wanted.* This tr. presumes that *hōs an* is equivalent to *hos ean* (e.g., Robertson 1923:959, 1095) and that the verb *boulōmai* should be supplied (thus, *hina mē doxō hōs ean . . . boulōmai;* so Moule 1953:152); cf. *JB, TEV, NIV.* In contrast to other suggestions about what should be supplied (see preceding note), this adds relatively little to the thought, while helping to show how vv. 8 and 9 are connected; see COMMENT.

*to be scaring you.* This tr. presupposes that the infinitive *ekphobein* (the compound form of the verb, frequent in the LXX but used only here in the NT, intensifies the meaning—not just "frighten" but "scare to death") depends on an understood *boulōmai* (see preceding note). Alternatively, one could take it directly with *doxō* and translate: "lest I should seem (as it were) to be scaring you. . . ." Bachmann, 350, followed by Héring, 72–73, would understand an "only" (or "merely") before the infinitive.

*with my letters.* Literally "through [i.e., by means of] the letters," meaning letters previously sent to Corinth by Paul, on which his critics have commented (see v. 10).

10. *For it is said.* Or, "For one says," *phēsin* being far better attested than *phasin* ("they say"). Here, as in vv. 7 *(someone)* and 11 *(such a person)*, the singular is probably used with reference to "anyone" of the group of Paul's critics and rivals in Corinth (cf. "certain persons," vv. 2, 12). This usage of *phēsin* is frequent in Hellenistic Greek; see, e.g., Epictetus III.ix.15; IV.i.11, 151, 158; ix.6, 7 and cf. BDF § 130(3); *GNTG* III:293; BAG s.v. *phēmi,* 1c; Bultmann, 192; Plummer, 282. Barrett, 260, who believes Paul is thinking of the criticism as having originated with one particular person, translates: "he says." While there are also examples of this usage, it is usual for the person to be named in the immediate context (e.g., Epictetus IV.viii.17 [Euphrates]; IV.viii.25 [Socrates]).

*His letters.* In Greek, *Hai epistolai,* "the letters."

*demanding and impressive.* More literally, "weighty and strong" *(RSV).* Here the adjective *barys* seems to be used (as, e.g., in Matt 23:4) of heavy, even burdensome obligations (cf. 1 John 5:3), while *ischyros* suggests something that is forceful and effective. Cf. v. 1, "I who . . . make bold toward you when I am away." In this citation Paul himself has provided us with the earliest documented assessment of his letters. For other, later comments on them see Pol Phil 3:2 and 2 Pet 3:15–16. Judge (1968:41) notes also Epistle 13 in the apocryphal correspondence between "Paul" and "Seneca" (third century) and from the fourth and early fifth centuries, Gregory of Nyssa, *Against Eunomius* I, 253 B *(NPNF,* 2nd ser. V:37); Jerome's commentary on Gal 2:4; Chrysostom, *On the Priesthood* IV, 5–6 *(NPNF,* 1st ser. IX:66–67), and especially Augustine, *On Christian Doctrine* IV.vii (discussed by Judge 1968:38–40). To these may be added Ambrose, Epistle 47 (see Beyenka 1954:129), discussed by Thraede (1970:185–87).

*when he is actually present.* Translates *hē parousia tou sōmatos,* "[his] bodily presence"; cf. "with you in person" *(kata prosōpon . . . en hymin)* in v. 1.

*weak.* Cf. 1 Cor 2:3, Paul's own reference to the "weakness" he manifested on the occasion of his first visit to Corinth, and 2 Cor 2:2–3, 5, where there are references to a second, unpleasant visit. In the present instance *weak (asthenēs)* stands in direct contrast to *impressive (ischyros,* literally "strong"), so that the criticism would seem to be that the apostle cuts a sorry figure in person. Cf. Epictetus' emphasis on the importance of the physical appearance of the true Cynic, III.xxii.86–89, and Lucian, *The Lover of Lies* 34 (discussed by Betz 1972:53–54) and *The Dream* 13 (cited by Hock 1980:99 n. 95); also Dio Chrysostom VIII, 2 (cited by Mussies 1972:178).

*his speech is contemptible.* Here *logos* refers more to the manner and style of Paul's speaking than to what he says (cf. 11:6), and *exouthenēmenos (contemptible)* may be compared with *tapeinos* ("demeaned") in v. 1.

11. *such a person.* That is, whoever would criticize Paul for writing one thing in his letters and acting quite differently in person (vv. 1, 10); cf. vv. 7 and 10, where the singular is also used to mean "whoever," and vv. 2 and 12, which show that Paul has a group of critics in mind.

*count on.* Paul again employs the verb *(logizesthai)* which his rivals have used in criticizing him; see NOTES on vv. 2 ("have it in mind"), 4 ("reasonings"), and 7 *(be aware),* and cf. Bultmann, 192.

*this.* The *touto* is emphatic by reason of its position as the first word in the Greek sentence (Plummer, 283).

*what we are.* Paul reverts to the first person plural, as in vv. 2*b*–7 and 8 *(our authority),* then further and at length in vv. 12–18.

*in the words of our letters.* Literally: "by word in [or: through] letters" *(tō logō di' epistolōn).* In contrast with v. 10, *logos* refers here to the written word (which has been called *demanding and impressive*), whereas the *logos* of v. 10 refers to the apostle's oral address (which has been called *contemptible*).

*when we are away.* Cf. v. 1, "when I am away."

*we also are.* The Greek has only *toioutos kai* ("such also"), but the *esmen (we are)* of the phrase to which it refers *(what we are)* is surely to be understood (cf. Plummer, 284).

*in action.* Translates *tō ergō* (more literally, "by deed") which here, as often in ancient Greek texts, is paired with *tō logō* (see note above on *in the words of our letters*); see, e.g., Rom 15:18; Col 3:17; 2 Thess 2:17; Luke 24:19; Acts 7:22; Polybius III, 3.10; Philo, *Against Flaccus* 40; and the examples from Aelius Aristides cited by van der Horst (1980:26).

*when we are present.* Cf. "in person," v. 1, and *when he is actually present,* v. 10.

12. *For we do not have the audacity.* The verb is *tolman,* translated *to summon up courage* in v. 2 (see NOTES). The introductory *gar (For)* helps to show that Paul is writing ironically here (Georgi 1964:230 n. 2; cf. Bultmann, 194); in vv. 2–6 he had made it clear that he is quite ready to stand up boldly against his critics if need be, and this is also the point in v. 11 (he can be as strong in person as he is in his letters). See also 11:21*b*. It is therefore misleading to speak of a "hiatus" between vv. 11 and 12 due to "a pause in dictation" (so Windisch, 308). From here through the end of the chapter the apostle continues the use of the first person plural to which he had reverted at the end of v. 11.

*to class or compare ourselves.* There is a play on words here in Greek, *enkrinai ē synkrinai,* for which Plummer, 286, suggests the English "to pair . . . or compare."

*to class.* The Greek word, used only here in the NT, means "to place together with as an equal," and it therefore sometimes refers to enlistment or enrollment—e.g., among the ephebes (*CIG* II.2715a, 11), among the Essenes (Josephus, *War* II.viii.7), or along with other competitors in an athletic context (Xenophon, *Hellenica* IV.i.40; Aristides, *Panathenaicus* 109, cited by Hughes, 364 n. 21). Against Hughes, however (ibid.), there is no reason to suppose that Paul is using specifically athletic imagery here.

*compare.* Paul employs the same word in 1 Cor 2:13, where it probably means "to interpret." MM (s.v.) note that in non-literary sources it usually means "to decide," normally in a judicial sense. But here it must have the meaning *compare,* as in many other writers contemporary with Paul (BAG s.v. 2a). Betz (1972:119–21) calls attention to the ancient rhetorical form of *synkrisis*, whereby, in encomiums and later in the writing of history, persons were praised by being compared with others of acknowledged superiority (see, e.g., Lucian, *Essays in Portraiture Defended* 19). See especially Forbes 1982:2–10, and P. Marshall 1980:503–25, 538–46. Particularly illuminating for the present passage is the letter (first century C.E.) of Neilus to Theon (POxy 2190; first called to my attention by Edwin A. Judge); see COMMENT.

*with certain persons who.* Or "with some of those who" (*RSV* et al.); but the context suggests that Paul is thinking of all those who recommend themselves (cf. Bultmann, 194). Note *epi tinas,* "against certain persons," in v. 2.

*recommend themselves.* There is a similar negative appraisal of self-recommendation in v. 18 (cf. 3:1; 5:12).

*Indeed.* Translates *alla,* which here both introduces and emphasizes the point that must be registered in opposition to those *who recommend themselves.*

*they measure . . . and compare.* Here *they* translates *autoi* which—with the participles (literally "measuring . . . and comparing")—refers to Paul's opponents. But if the shorter text of vv. 12–13 is read (discussed below), *autoi* would be translated as "we" and would be, along with the following participles, a reference to the Pauline apostolate.

*by themselves . . . with themselves.* Translates *en heautois . . . heautois,* although this may be an instance where the reflexive pronoun is used in place of the reciprocal pronoun (cf. BDF § 287; MM s.v.; Robertson 1923:690); thus, *RSV:* "by one another . . . with one another." Usually, however, where this is the intended meaning one has *pros heautous.*

*they have no understanding.* These words, *ou syniasin,* along with the first words of v. 13 *(hēmeis de, Yet we),* are missing from the Western text (D* F G et al.). According to the Western reading, Paul would be saying: "On the contrary we measure ourselves by ourselves, by our own standard of comparison" (*NEB* mg.). This shorter reading is preferred by Windisch, 309, followed, e.g., by Lietzmann, 143; Mof.; Bultmann, 194–95 and in *TDNT* III:651 n. 44; Käsemann 1942:56–57; Héring, 73; Georgi 1964: 230, and Fuchs 1980:249 n. 40. In favor of this it has been argued (1) that *alla autoi* after *ou gar tolmōmen,* etc., requires a positive complement and that the *autoi* must therefore refer to the Pauline apostolate ("we") and not (still) to Paul's critics ("they"); (2) that the charge *they have no understanding* is much too feeble to have been original in this context; and (3) that the idea of self-measurement makes more sense if it is meant to be applied to Paul himself and thus taken as something good: it is as a Spirit-directed person that Paul measures himself by himself (1 Cor 2:15–16).

There are, however, decisive reasons for favoring the longer text, which is read by *GNT*-Nestle (cf. Metzger 1971:583) and which is followed here—as well as in most recent English versions and by many interpreters (e.g., Bachmann, 353 n. 1; Strachan, 16; Kümmel, 208–9, followed by Barrett, 263–64; Tasker, 140; Hughes, 365 n. 22; Schmithals 1971:186; Oostendorp 1967:22–23 n. 13; Betz 1972:119 n. 558): (1) The longer reading has superior attestation, including P⁴⁶ and **א**ᵃ. (2) The *autoi* in v. 12*b* must introduce a new subject *(they,* whereas the subject of vv. 12*a* and 13 is *we* [. . . *do not have the courage; . . . will not boast*]); if, as on the shorter reading, *autoi* still refers to Paul and his associates ("we measure ourselves by ourselves") it becomes superfluous. (3) In view of v. 12*a,* where Paul writes negatively of those *who recommend themselves,* it is difficult to interpret the idea of measuring and comparing oneself with oneself (v. 12*b*) as anything but a criticism, and the connection some seek to draw between this statement and 1 Cor 2:15–16 is forced. (4) The accidental omission of the problematic words is more easily explained than the intentional addition of them. Thus, the eyes of a copyist might have confused the *ouk* which follows the four Greek words in question with the *ou* which is the first of those words, the result being the shorter text as we have it in the Western tradition; see Metzger 1971:583, who also deals with the other but less important variations in the textual witnesses. This is a simpler and therefore somewhat more plausible explanation than the one offered by Barrett, 264, who conjectures that a Latin translator's mistake is responsible for the shorter reading —yet that, too, is conceivable. However, the *interpolation* of the four Greek words (so, e.g., BDF § 416[2], in addition to those already cited) is extremely hard to explain; if the intention was to "improve" the text, that would have been a poor way to do it.

13. *Yet we.* These words *(hēmeis de)* are missing in some textual witnesses; see the preceding note. The *we* is emphatic, contrasting with *they* in v. 12: perhaps, "Yet we, for our part. . . ."

*beyond the proper limits.* Translates *eis ta ametra,* which could be taken in a general adverbial sense to mean "excessively" or "inappropriately." Cf. the use of the adverb in Epictetus, *Encheiridion* 33.14 ("In your conversation avoid making mention at great length and excessively [*ametrōs*] of your own deeds or dangers"), and see also Ign Trall 4:1, where "I take my own measure" *(emauton metrō)* is an expression of resolve not to boast at all. However, given the context and the use of the identical phrase in v. 15, it would appear that in this passage Paul is also thinking of *the proper limits* in a more specific sense, with reference to the areas where he has labored as an apostle planting the gospel (cf. Bultmann, 196); see COMMENT.

*but only.* For this sense of the *alla* here, see Barrett, 265, and the references given there.

*the measure of the jurisdiction.* An exceedingly difficult phrase to translate. The idea of measurement introduced in v. 12 *(metrountes)* is carried forward now with a reference to *to metron,* that which has been measured (a word also used by Paul in Rom 12:3, "the measure of faith" [*RSV*]). This *measure* is then qualified with the genitive *tou kanonos,* a *kanōn* being the standard by which something is measured (see BAG s.v.; Beyer, *TDNT* III:596–602); thus, "yardstick" in *JB* and "norm" in Beyer, ibid.:599 n. 12. Apart from these verses Paul employs the word *kanōn* only in Gal 6:16, where it certainly does mean something like "rule," "norm," or "standard." This meaning is doubtless present here in 2 Cor as well. But the word *kanōn* may also connote, like the word *metron,* the extent or area which has been measured or which is governed by the rule or norm. In the present context both meanings seem to be operative: on the one hand it is a reference to the apostolic authority given to Paul (v. 8); on the other, a reference to the authority *to reach out even as far as* Corinth (vv. 13–15) and beyond (v. 16). The English word *jurisdiction* adopted in the present tr. is capable of bearing both of these meanings: not only the "right" or "authority" to do something, but also the "sphere" within which that authority is to be exercised. This interpretation would seem to be supported by the way *kanōn* is used in a first-century text from Pisidia in Asia Minor, where it translates the Latin *formula* and is used of a "schedule" of what is required in a particular region (text, translation, and commentary in Horsley 1981:36–45). Barrett, 264–65 (and 1971:239), believes that Paul is thinking specifically of the division of missionary responsibilities agreed on at his meeting with the Jerusalem apostles (Gal 2:9), in which case he would be using the word *kanōn* here to mean not just the exercise of his apostolic authority in Corinth and beyond, but his assignment "to the Gentiles" generally. The key word *kanōn*, however, does not appear in Paul's account of the Jerusalem agreement (Gal 2:1–10), nor does anything here in 2 Cor 10 require us to think that Paul has that meeting specifically in mind.

*which God has apportioned to us as our measure.* The antecedent of the relative pronoun *(hou, which)* is probably *to metron* (the measure), and it stands in the genitive case only by virtue of its attraction to the case of the immediately preceding phrase, *tou kanonos (the jurisdiction).* The subsequent *metrou, as our measure,* was likely added to clarify this; see BDF § 294(5); *GNTG* III:324; Robertson 1923:719. Several English versions omit *metrou* as redundant *(RSV, NEB, TEV, NIV). NAB's* "[the God] of moderation" is hardly defensible.

*apportioned.* As in Rom 12:3 (with reference to a "measure of faith") and in 1 Cor 7:17 (with reference to one's situation in society), the verb is used of what God has "dealt out" or "assigned."

*to reach out even as far as you.* The infinitive *(ephikesthai;* a participial form of the verb is used in v. 14) is loosely dependent on *apportioned,* and may be regarded as an infinitive of result (Bultmann, 196, with reference to BDF § 391[4]). The emphatic *even as far as you (achri kai hymōn)* is repeated in the following verse.

14. *as if we do not reach to you.* The participle is present tense *(ephiknoumenoi),* which may indicate that Paul has in mind his present and continuing pastoral responsibility and concern for the Corinthian congregation (cf. 11:28) as well as his founding of it.

*we came.* Translates *ephthasamen,* which some would render as "came first," etc. (e.g. *RSV; NEB;* Tasker, 141; Barrett, 267). Although Paul does use the verb once with the meaning "to precede" or "to come in advance of" (1 Thess 4:15; in the LXX see Wis 6:13; 16:28, cited by Windisch, 311), in the other three places where, as here, he uses it with a preposition (Rom 9:31; Phil 3:16; 1 Thess 2:16) it means simply "to come to" or "to arrive." This is also a fully sufficient meaning here (so too, e.g., Fitzer, *TDNT* IX:90; Windisch, 311; Plummer, 289, tentatively), where the idea of Paul's having preceded the rival apostles to Corinth is well enough conveyed by his reference to having taken the gospel there (Bultmann, 197). Although Barrett, 267, argues that Paul deliberately replaces *ephikeisthai* ("to reach [out] to") in vv. 13, 14*a* with *phthanein* in order to inject the idea of his having "come first" to Corinth, one could just as well argue that *phthanein* is used only for the sake of variety, and is therefore synonymous with *ephikeisthai* in this context.

*even as far as you.* Repeats *achri kai hymōn* from v. 13.

*the gospel of Christ.* See NOTES on 2:12 for other occurrences of this phrase in Paul's letters; cf. especially Rom 15:19, where—as here—the apostle is thinking of the gospel he has been sent to preach to the Gentiles.

15. *We are not boasting.* The participle ([*ou*] *kauchōmenoi*) is here interpreted as absolute (Plummer, 289), a frequent Pauline usage.

*beyond the proper limits.* As in v. 13.

*in the labors of others.* Paul often uses the noun *kopos* (singular or plural) and the related verb *kopian* in reference to his own missionary or pastoral work (e.g., 1 Cor 3:8; 15:10*b;* Gal 4:11; Phil 2:16) or that of others, as here and in Rom 16:6, 12; 1 Cor 15:58; 16:16; 1 Thess 5:12. In the present context the *labors* must be specifically missionary efforts, carrying the gospel to un-evangelized places.

*and.* Translates *de,* which serves to connect an additional point with the preceding one.

*our hope is.* Another absolute use of the participle is involved here (*elpida echontes,* literally "[we] having hope"). Paul's hope for his congregation in Corinth is expressed  ·
elsewhere in 2 Cor in 1:7, 10, 13; 5:11; 13:6.

*as your faith grows.* A genitive-absolute construction. Among the other references to the Corinthians' *faith* in 2 Cor, note especially 1:24; 8:7; 13:5; and see COMMENT. The idea of a "growing faith" is also present in 2 Thess 1:3. Cf. 1 Cor 3:1–4.

*that . . . we may be abundantly praised.* Translates *megalynthēnai . . . eis perisseian,* the aorist passive infinitive being dependent upon *elpida echontes (our hope is)* and gaining its subject from that ( = *we*). The meaning is "we in our labors," thus "our work." Cf. Rom 11:13, where Paul writes of "glorifying [*doxazein*]" his "ministry [*diakonia*]" as he expands it to the whole Gentile world.

*among you.* In the Greek, this *en hymin* stands between the genitive-absolute construction and the infinitive, and is occasionally attached to what precedes—thus, "as your faith grows among you" (so, e.g., Bultmann, 198). But this is almost tautologous, as most commentators and trs. have recognized, so it is probably intended to go with the infinitive—thus, *praised among you.*

*in accord with our jurisdiction.* Cf. v. 13, *in accord with the measure of the jurisdiction which God has apportioned to us.* The repetition of part of the phrase in the present verse serves to qualify the mention of being "praised" with the principle laid down in the earlier verse.

16. *and that we may preach the gospel.* It is tempting, with Windisch, 313–14, to emend the *eis ta* to *eis to,* thus yielding the familiar construction of *eis* with an articular infinitive (in this case *eis to . . . euangelisasthai, to preach the gospel*), expressing purpose or result. There is no textual warrant for this, however, and it is best to retain the reading *ta,* which then goes with *hyperekeina* (see following note). The infinitive *euangelisasthai* should probably be regarded, like *megalynthēnai* in v. 15, as dependent upon *elpida echontes (our hope is,* v. 15). To express this the present English tr. supplies *and that we may.* Cf. *NAB.*

*in places beyond you.* Translates *eis ta hyperekeina hymōn.* Here *eis* with the accusative, replacing *en* with the dative, has a local sense (cf. BAG s.v. 9; BDF § 205); for the use of the genitive see BDF § 184. The substantive is formed from the adverb which means simply "beyond." Instead of "places" (also used in *JB*), one could supply "lands" *(RSV, NEB),* "countries" *(TEV),* "regions" *(NIV),* or "areas" (Barrett, 255, 267), but when one is required to supply a word the least specific term is usually to be preferred. Paul is presumably thinking of *places* to the west, perhaps Spain (see Rom 15:24, 28), and some have argued that the expression *beyond you* could not have been written in Macedonia (the evident place of origin of chaps. 1–9; see 7:5; 8:1ff., etc.), but only from somewhere to the east of Corinth, presumably Ephesus (e.g., Strachan, 16). However, even discounting the fact that Paul did not have the advantage of a modern cartographer's map, there is no necessity to interpret *beyond you* in a strictly geometric sense (correctly Tasker, 143; Barrett, 268). This expression, then, indicates nothing about the place of writing of chaps. 10–13 (Letter E).

*not boasting.* Windisch, 314, would supply *thelontes* with the infinitive *kauchēsasthai* ("to boast"), thus yielding "not wanting to boast" (cf. *NIV*). But, like the two preceding infinitives (*megalynthēnai,* v. 15; *euangelisasthai,* v. 16), this one too may be regarded as (loosely) dependent on *elpida echontes* (*our hope is,* v. 15).

*about what has been done already.* Translates *eis ta hetoima,* the *eis* indicating that in respect of which the boasting might be done (see BAG s.v. 5).

*in another's jurisdiction.* The phrase is *en allotriō kanoni,* with which one may compare *en allotriois kopois (in the labors of others)* in v. 15. In the present phrase *kanōn (jurisdiction)* refers to the sphere within which authority is exercised rather than to the authority in and of itself.

17. *"Let the one who boasts boast in the Lord."* A free adaptation of a LXX text, probably of Jer 9:24 ("Let the one who boasts boast rather in this, the understanding and knowing that I am the Lord . . ."), although the LXX expansion of the Hebrew text in 1 Kgdms (1 Sam) 2:10 is almost identical. The same text is cited by Paul, and with the same wording, in 1 Cor 1:31, but there with a fuller introductory formula ("As it is written"; here, only *de,* "And" or "But"). While the context of 1 Cor 1:31 (the theme of strength and weakness) shows more similarities to the context in 1 Kgdms 2 than to that in Jer 9 (Peabody 1974:9–10), the point of Jer 9:23–24, that "mercy," "judgment," and "righteousness" are God's doing, is more compatible with the Pauline emphasis upon God's gift of righteousness in Christ (1 Cor 1:30) than is the point of 1 Kgdms 2:10, that God's people are to execute "judgment and righteousness in the midst of the earth" (Schreiner 1974:541–42). Moreover, the allusion to Jer 9:25–26 in Rom 2:29 shows that the passage was important to Paul.

*in the Lord.* Boasting specifically *in the Lord* (*en Kyriō*) is not mentioned in either Jer 9 or 1 Kgdms 2 (see preceding note). Schreiner (1974:540) thinks it possible that Paul was acquainted with the rendering of certain passages in the Psalms—as attested by Aquila—which speak of boasting "in God" (43[44]:9; 55[56]:11) or "in the Lord" (33[34]:3). Cf. also LXX Deut 10:21 and the notion of boasting "in the fear of the Lord" in Sir 9:16; 10:22; 25:6. When Paul cites the same text in 1 Cor 1:31 it is probable that he is thinking of *the Lord* as Christ (see 1 Cor 1:30); and it is probably also of Christ that he would have his readers think in the present instance (so Bousset 1970:149; Kramer 1966:156 n. 570; against Plummer, 290; Windisch, 314); for the idea of "boasting in Christ" see 1 Cor 15:31; Phil 1:26; 3:3, and cf. Rom 15:17; Gal 6:14.

18. *For it is not the one who engages in self-recommendation.* More literally, "For it is not the one who recommends himself [*ho heauton synistanōn*]"; for a similar critique of self-recommendation see v. 12 (and cf. 3:1; 5:12).

*approved.* Translates *dokimos,* "tested and found acceptable." This adjective, as well as its opposite, *adokimos,* and the related noun (*dokimē*) and verb (*dokimazein*) are prominent in 13:3, 5–7, a passage which suggests that Paul's own apostleship is being put to the test by his critics in Corinth (Windisch, 315; Bultmann, 199).

*the Lord.* Here, as in Rom 14:7–8, *ho Kyrios* stands in rhetorical antithesis to *heautos,* "oneself" (N. Schneider 1970:22). In Rom 14:6–9 "the Lord" is certainly Christ; and if indeed Paul intends a christological reference even with the scriptural citation in v. 17 (see NOTES above), then the reference in the present verse is also certainly to Christ.

## COMMENT: GENERAL

Having opened this letter (chaps. 10–13) with an appeal to the Corinthians to be obedient (10:1–6), Paul now proceeds to support that appeal by writing of the authority he has exercised as an apostle in Corinth. In v. 8 he identifies this as the authority expressed in his *upbuilding* of the Corinthian church, by which he evidently means his evangelization of Corinth and his founding of a church there (vv. 13–14) as well as his subsequent nurturing of that church's faith (vv. 15–16). Underlying the discussion here is an argument for his apostolic authority which Paul has used in previous letters to the Corinthians: there is no surer evidence for the validity of his claim to be an apostle of Christ than their own faith in Christ and the very existence of their congregation. These have come to be through his preaching (see 1 Cor 9:1–2; 15:14; 2 Cor 3:1–3; 13:5b–6).

This matter of Paul's apostolic authority has been rendered urgent by the fact that there are some in Corinth who in the process of making claims about their own status have called Paul's authority, perhaps even his faith, into question (vv. 7, 10). It is evident, then, that Paul's appeal for obedience includes as an essential aspect an appeal that the Corinthian congregation continue to recognize his status as their apostle and continue to be responsive to his pastoral direction. One also senses in these paragraphs some uncertainty on Paul's part about how his critics should be answered. In vv. 7–11 he is tempted to answer them point by point: he belongs to Christ as much as they do (v. 7) and his authority is expressed not only in absentia (vv. 10–11). But in vv. 12–18 he goes more clearly on the offensive against his critics: he uses irony (v. 12a); he charges them with not understanding the true source of authority (vv. 12b, 17–18); and by insisting that he himself does not boast *beyond the proper limits, in the labors of others* (v. 15a) he insinuates that his critics have done exactly that.

## COMMENT: DETAILED

### On the Matter of Authority, vv. 7–11

Paul's appeal for his readers' obedience (10:1–6) is followed, first, by a sharp warning to *be alert* to the present danger *right in front* of them, v. 7a. Just as the foregoing appeal had been issued with the keen awareness that some serious charges about him are circulating among the Corinthians, so now his comments in support of that appeal disclose his knowledge of those charges. One of them has been that he does not have the same relationship to Christ as that claimed by his critics, rivals for leadership of the congregation who have proudly commended themselves as "ministers of Christ" (11:23). In the present instance, at least, Paul does not deny what his critics are claiming for themselves; he declares only that his relationship to Christ is equal to theirs (cf. 11:5; 12:11c). Paul is here supporting his own status by comparing it to the status of others, a device which the ancient rhetoricians called *synkrisis* (Latin: *comparatio;* cf. Olson 1976:216 n. 2, and NOTES on v. 12), and a practice about which Paul himself will have second thoughts very shortly (v. 12a). (In 11:12 Paul suggests his rivals may be trying to compare themselves with *him.*)

What precisely were Paul's opponents claiming about their relationship to Christ? It is improbable that their claims are to be associated with the claims of those he had described in 1 Cor 1:12 as boasting of "being Christ's" (against, e.g., Hughes, 356; de Boor, 203; Schmithals 1971:197–206; cf. Kee 1980: 73–74). There the apostle was referring to a group within the congregation itself, while the critics he has in view here in chaps. 10–13 (e.g., 11:4) are persons who have come in from elsewhere (Kümmel, 208; Barrett, 257). Such an identification is also precluded by the fact that here Paul is willing to claim for himself what his critics are also claiming *(we, too, are Christ's),* whereas in 1 Cor 1:12ff. he had regarded all the factional claims as inappropriate (so most commentators). One possibility is that Paul is responding to those who have claimed some distinctive spiritual relationship to Christ (so Bultmann, 189; Héring, 72, and Schmithals 1971:197–98, who identify Paul's opponents as Gnostic Christians; but also Georgi 1964:227–28, 228 n. 1, who identifies them as Hellenistic-Jewish Christians). Or it could be that Paul's credibility as an apostle has been challenged by those who claim to have been personally acquainted with Jesus during his ministry, or at least to have been authorized by those who were (e.g., Hughes, 356), a claim which Paul seems to have had in mind when he wrote 1 Cor (see 9:1; 15:5–8, and cf. 1 Cor 7:40b).

It is not impossible that both claims—to have been authorized to ministry directly by Jesus or his original disciples, and (therefore) to stand in a special relationship to Jesus as the Christ—were being made by Paul's rivals (cf. Windisch, 302–3; Barrett, 257). Theissen (1982:46) not implausibly connects the slogan *being Christ's (Christou einai),* to which Paul responds here, with the formula in Mark 9:41: "Whoever gives you a cup of water to drink in [my] name because you are Christ's [*Christou este*] will certainly not lose his reward." These words seem to have been addressed to "itinerant charismatics," who are promised that since they belong to Christ their material needs will be supplied wherever they go. If Paul's opponents in Corinth are claiming to have been sent out with some such promise as this, and to preach and teach with the kind of charismatic status this implies, then their criticism of Paul may include the objection that he cares too much about his material needs, failing to trust solely in Christ as one who belongs to him (Theissen ibid. and 66–67

n. 59). In support of this hypothesis one may appeal to 11:7ff., where there is evidence that Paul's refusal to accept financial aid from the Corinthians had been criticized by them (cf. 12:13, 15), and to 13:3, where Paul refers to the Corinthians' desire for proof that he really speaks for Christ.

In v. 8 the apostle begins to betray a certain self-consciousness about appearing to boast about himself. This uneasiness continues through most of the rest of the letter (see vv. 13, 15; 11:16, 18, 30; 12:1, 5, 6), doubtless because of Paul's firm conviction that one's only proper boast is in the Lord (see v. 17), and also because he does not want to do what he criticizes others for doing ("boasting of what is outward and not of what is within," 5:12; cf. 11:12). Yet nothing less than the legitimacy of Paul's apostleship, and therefore of his gospel, is at stake, and though he may appear to be boasting he will take the risk.

He proceeds to write, first, of the *authority* granted to him by the Lord— that is, Christ (as in 1 Cor 9:1ff.; cf. 1 Cor 15:8–10; Gal 1:1, 11–12). Theissen (1982:45) observes that in the only other place where Paul uses the word *exousia* of his apostolic authority it refers specifically to his "right" to be materially supported by his congregations (1 Cor 9:4ff.), and that a similar thought may be in his mind here. It is difficult to see, however, how boasting about this right would "scare" his readers (v. 9); it is more likely that the reference is to Paul's authority to preach the gospel and to command and discipline the members of the congregation. This authority, he insists, has been given him for their *upbuilding*, for planting the gospel in Corinth as the founding apostle, and for nurturing the gospel there (see NOTES). Some idea of what is meant by a constructive use of authority may be gained from 13:10, where a parallel statement envisions Paul's coming to Corinth without having to take any punitive action. The remarks in 1:24–2:2 are similarly instructive: Paul does not wish to use his authority to strengthen his hold over the Corinthians, but only to strengthen their grip on the gospel, their faith. Even Paul's admonitions are tempered with this concern, as the remarks of 8:8–10 specifically indicate (see NOTES and COMMENT there).

It is unclear why Paul adds that this authority is *not for your destruction.* Perhaps the imagery of Jeremiah, by whose sense of prophetic vocation Paul's self-understanding as an apostle seems to have been influenced (see Jer 1: 9b–10, and cf. Gal 1:15 with Jer 1:5), is explanation enough (see also, and in particular, LXX Jer 24:6; 49[42]:10; and Schütz 1975:224). It is also possible, however, that the remark is motivated by a concern to counter some charge that the apostle's critics have brought against him in Corinth: that his teaching is actually destructive of faith (Friedrich 1963b:215 suggests attention may have been called to Paul's pre-conversion persecution of the church [Gal 1:13, etc.]), or that he abuses his authority. Conversely, Paul may be insinuating that his opponents are engaged in a destructive ministry insofar as they intrude on his jurisdiction (see discussion below on vv. 15–16), undermining his work and thereby the faith of those who have received his gospel (cf. Héring, 72 n. 10). Or it could be only that Paul wishes to contrast the destructive action he may be forced to take against some with the fundamentally constructive objectives of his overall ministry in Corinth (thus, *not for "your" destruction*).

When Paul emphasizes that now he will *not be ashamed* to boast a little (v. 8), he is indicating both that he would be ashamed to boast under normal circumstances and that the present circumstances are not normal: they require some boasting. If the tr. given here of v. 9 is approximately correct (for the syntactical difficulties in this verse see NOTES), then Paul is stating one particular way in which he proposes not to be shamed by his boasting. His authority is not something about which he can only write to them, as if he wanted to frighten them into accepting his apostleship (v. 9); it is a real authority which he can and does also demonstrate when he is with them (v. 11).

From v. 10 it is evident that Paul has been criticized for exactly this: flaunting his authority in writing but not delivering on it when he is present. Clearly, Paul had not been aware of any such criticism when, in 1 Cor 5:1ff., he had given directions about the disciplining of an immoral brother. There he had presumed that the congregation would find his presence strong and persuasive—"as if present, I have already pronounced judgment in the name of the Lord Jesus . . ." *(RSV)*. Now it is otherwise. While there is a certain element of admiration in the comment that the apostle's letters are *demanding and impressive*, the point of it is not to praise Paul (against Oostendorp 1967:20) but to criticize him. That this is so is confirmed by vv. 1*b*, 9, and 11, where there are allusions to a complaint that the apostle's letters are full of empty threats. It is clear from 7:8–11 that an earlier, severe letter to Corinth had evoked the desired action in Paul's congregation there. But it may well be that the combination of that letter with (a) the apostle's ineffectiveness on the occasion of a brief visit that preceded it (see comment on 1:23–2:2), and (b) his unexpected cancellation of a return visit (see comment on 1:15–17), led his critics to make the charge that is quoted in this verse: in his letters he claims more authority than he is able to demonstrate when he is present.

There are various points in the letters to Corinth at which Paul himself seems to be concerned that his words, especially his advice and admonitions, could be misunderstood. In 1 Cor (Letter B) one may note 4:14; 7:35; 9:15; in 2 Cor 1–9 (Letter D) see 1:13, 24; 8:8, 10 (with COMMENT); and in 2 Cor 10–13 (Letter E) see especially 13:10. Then, in a later letter still—written *from* Corinth to Rome—the same sort of concern is disclosed in the rather self-conscious remark that "on some points" he has had to write "very boldly" (Rom 15:15, *RSV*). Clearly, Paul's opponents in Corinth had tried to portray him as being too bold in his letters, perhaps even overbearing (2 Cor 1:24).

The evidence regarding Paul's mien and manner when *actually present* in Corinth is necessarily less direct. Although some physical malady may have plagued the apostle (see comment on 12:7) and threatened on occasion to hinder his ministry (Gal 4:13–14), the charge against him which he quotes in v. 10 is inclusive of more than his state of health: it is his entire "presence" (not just his body) that has been perceived as "weak" (cf. Lietzmann, 142; Barrett, 261), and this is associated in the first place with his unmannered style of speaking. The same association of "weakness" and unadorned speech occurs in 1 Cor 2:3–4, where the apostle is recalling the impression he made on the occasion of his original mission to Corinth. His failure to convey his message with the kind of rhetorical display so favored by the sophistic teachers of his day (see 10:4 and 11:6, with COMMENT) had apparently been a disappointment to many of his hearers. But his physical appearance, including his general state of health, could well have contributed to the impression of weakness. Epictetus insists that the true Cynic, to be a persuasive teacher, must not be "a consumptive . . . , thin and pale," for then "his testimony no longer carries the same weight"; his "body" *(sōma)* as well as his "soul" *(psychē)* must be altogether admirable (III.xxii.86–87). It is probable that Paul's critics saw yet a further sign of weakness in the apostle's insistence on continuing to work at his craft during the periods of his Corinthian ministry (so Windisch, 306; cf. Hock 1980:50–65). In 11:7–11 he specifically defends this, even as he tacitly acknowledges that it is demeaning (cf. 10:1). It is significant that these remarks follow immediately on the apostle's reference to his lack of rhetorical skills (11:6). There is a similar association of ideas in Lucian's contrast between the "sublime words [*logous semnous*]" and "dignified appearance [*schēma euprepes*]" of truly great teachers, and the filthy clothes and unkempt appearance of the craftsman who does not pursue eloquence or learning, but who clutches his tools, "back bent over his work; . . . altogether demeaned [*tapeinos;* cf. 10:1; 11:7]" (*The Dream* 13).

Some interpreters, rejecting the idea that Paul was perceived as weak because of his lack of rhetorical skill, general appearance, or work as a craftsman, argue that the complaint against him was exclusively that his preaching lacked the kind of power *(dynamis)* by which a true bearer of the Spirit is always supported (e.g., Reitzenstein 1978:460–61; Käsemann 1942:35; Schmithals 1971:176–79). There is ample evidence in 2 Cor that Paul is being required to defend himself as one who speaks with the power of God as bestowed through the Spirit or through Christ (in Letter D see especially 2:17; 3:3–4:6, 7; 5:20; 6:6–7; in Letter E see especially 10:4, 7; 12:9, 12; 13:3–4). But this does not mean that the charge quoted here in v. 10 pertains only to the apparent lack of spiritual power, and not to the way Paul speaks and comports himself in general. It is a mistake to assume with Reitzenstein (1978:461) that only "free and improvised discourse" could have been regarded as proof of a speaker's possession of the Spirit. Rhetorical skill itself could be so regarded (Betz 1972:58–59), and it is likely that Paul's lack of such skill was one of the things his critics invoked to try to prove that his ministry was not endowed with divine power.

*On the Matter of Jurisdiction, vv. 12–18*

From the question of apostolic authority (vv. 7–11) Paul turns to the closely related issue of apostolic jurisdiction. In this paragraph he is directly and specifically critical of his opponents for having overstepped the limits of their commission, and he pledges that he will in no way exceed the limits of his own. His rivals are referred to now as *persons who recommend themselves,* even as they had been characterized in 5:12 as "boasting of what is outward and not of what is within." There is intentional irony in Paul's statement that he and his associates lack *the audacity to class or compare* themselves with those people (v. 12*a*), since the apostle has just written that he is prepared to be firm in dealing with them (vv. 2–6, 11) and since he has already ventured to compare his relationship to Christ with theirs (v. 7). Later in this letter he will dare to make further comparisons, even though reluctantly and as "a fool" (11:21*b*ff.; cf. 11:1, 17, 19; 12:6, 11).

In Paul's day each of the cities of the Roman Empire had its complement of teachers vying with one another for students who would pay for instruction in rhetoric and philosophy. A late first century letter from Neilus to his father, Theon, nicely illustrates this. In this letter, probably written from Alexandria, Neilus complains about a particularly bad teacher he has had to put up with, one Didymus, who though he "used to be a mere provincial teacher sees fit to compete with the rest" (POxy 2190, lines 28–29). In this criticism of Didymus for presuming to "compete" with the better-credentialed teachers of the big city ("compete" translates *eis synkrisin,* "to make a comparison" as in v. 12*a*) we may catch a glimpse of the sort of criticism Paul was having to face in Corinth. Now, with mock deference to the boasted superiority of his rivals, he disclaims any ability to compete with them on their grounds (cf. Judge 1972:35). Behind this disclaimer lies the apostle's conviction that it is not self-praise but only the commendation which comes from God that finally matters (v. 18).

The criticism, thinly veiled in v. 12*a,* is fully exposed in v. 12*b.* Here Paul charges that his rivals *have no understanding* when they seek to *recommend themselves.* Here, it seems, Paul is accusing his competitors of having so far exceeded the boundaries of what is true and proper as to expose their lack of self-knowledge, their failure to understand their own limitations (P. Marshall 1980:311, 575). In 3:11; 5:12, Paul's reference to self-recommendation suggests that he himself had been criticized for it, but here the charge is turned around and flung at his critics. Their self-recommendation is now described as a measuring and comparing *themselves by (with) themselves,* by which Paul may mean a concern with the visible "signs" of apostleship (12:12; Käsemann 1942:50) and the other supposedly authenticating characteristics of a truly "apostolic life" (cf. Theissen 1982:52, who refers to the duty of charismatic asceticism set forth in Did 11:3, 4–6). The "measure" according to which Paul conducts his own ministry is something quite different, as the following verses show.

There is a sense in which the thought of vv. 13ff. resumes that of v. 8, where Paul had indicated that he was willing to boast about his authority and could do so without being shamed in the process. Now he emphasizes that he and his associates will boast only in a strictly measured way, v. 13, thus adhering to one of the basic principles of Greek humanistic ethics, "Nothing too much" (*mēden agan,* the Delphic maxim cited by Betz 1972:131 and n. 644, along with several references to Epictetus). In the present context, however, the principle must be understood in relation to Paul's sense of apostolic vocation: *the proper limits* of boasting are defined by *the measure of the jurisdiction* he has been granted by God. This is a reference, first of all, to the "authority" given to him as an apostle (vv. 8–11), his divine commission to take the gospel to the Gentiles (e.g. Rom 15:15–16; Gal 1:15–16). Nothing here suggests that Paul is thinking of the agreement reached with the Jerusalem apostles, as if his *jurisdiction* had been determined at that meeting; and even in Gal 2:9, Paul refers to that agreement as founded upon an acknowledgment of "the grace" that had been given to him (cf. Georgi 1964:229–30 n. 3). In the present context, however, the term *jurisdiction* (on which see the NOTES) also has a more particular reference—i.e., to the divine commission by which Paul had been impelled to carry the gospel to Corinth specifically: *to reach out even as far as you,* v. 13 (cf. Beyer, *TDNT* III:599).

It is this second point, the exercise of his apostolic commission in Corinth, that Paul develops in vv. 14–15a. The *gospel of Christ* had been planted there by his labors and he has every right to boast of that (v. 14); he is the "father" of the Corinthian church, a claim no one else can make (1 Cor 4:15). But others have been claiming authority in Corinth, and it is doubtless with them in mind that Paul repeats the assertion of v. 13a in v. 15a: his boasting is within *the proper limits,* to which he now adds that it is not, like theirs, *in the labors of others* (cf. v. 16, *in another's jurisdiction*). The principle by which Paul has operated and to which he intends to adhere is subsequently formulated in Rom 15:20: his objective is to preach the gospel where it has not yet been taken and where no one else has yet laid a foundation. It is obvious that his opponents in Corinth do not operate by any such principle, that they in fact claim to have an authority equal to his even in this congregation which he has founded (see 11:12). In the face of this, Paul wants the Corinthians to know that he will not be deprived of the boast which is rightfully his as their father in the faith.

Paul's determination to preach only where the gospel has not yet been heard is emphasized in vv. 15b–16. His *hope* that the faith of the Corinthians will grow should probably be identified with his concern, already expressed (v. 6), that their "obedience" to the gospel—and thus to his apostolate—should be "complete" (cf. Bultmann, 198). It is less the content of their belief than their commitment to what they believe that seems to be in view here. How this strengthening of their faith-commitment is related to the praise of the Pauline apostolate is suggested by some remarks near the close of the present letter (13:5–6): if the Corinthians are strong in their faith, then both they and their apostle will be shown to have "passed the test." The Pauline apostolate is *abundantly praised* as its legitimacy is attested by the faith of those to whom it has brought the gospel. But here, just as when Paul writes of "glorifying" his ministry (Rom 11:13), the thought is primarily of the expansion of that ministry in keeping with "the cosmic range of the mission" (Käsemann 1980: 306) with which he has been entrusted. The praise for which Paul hopes is in effect the empowerment for yet greater tasks, perhaps specifically for the mission to Spain about which he will write to the Romans (Rom 15:24, 28; cf. Bultmann, 198; Barrett, 268). He will not be content, as his opponents are, to boast of what has been accomplished so far; his eye is always on a farther goal (cf. Phil 3:13–14).

The appeal to the Corinthians to be obedient is supported, finally, by a citation from scripture, v. 17, and the succinct formulation in v. 18 of a conviction which has been implicit throughout the preceding discussion. The scriptural citation, the first of only two in chaps. 10–13 (the other will come in 13:1), seems to be a free adaptation of LXX Jer 9:24 (see NOTES; Schreiner 1974 discusses the idea of boasting as it runs throughout the OT). It is a fundamental tenet of Paul's preaching that faith excludes all boasting (Rom 3:27) because it is one's acceptance of the righteousness which God has bestowed in Christ as a gift of grace (Rom 3:24ff., 28–29; 1 Cor 4:7, etc.). This gift of righteousness in Christ is what the apostle has in mind when he quotes the same text from Jer in an earlier letter to Corinth (1 Cor 1:31; see v. 30), and when he writes elsewhere of boasting only "in Christ Jesus" (Phil 3:3; see v. 9) or "in the cross of our Lord Jesus Christ" (Gal 6:14). It is probable, therefore, that Paul's introduction of the text from Jer into the present discussion is meant as a reminder that faith's only true boast is in Christ.

The apostle's text is of course not applied as it had been in 1 Cor 1:31, because the topic here is not—as such—God's justifying grace bestowed in Christ. Nevertheless, this basic Pauline idea is certainly operative even here as, in v. 18, he gives his text a polemical application. Both his readers and his opponents should know that it is not *self-recommendation* but only Christ's commendation that really counts. Behind this lies the familiar Pauline distinction between one's own righteousness, based on personal achievements and credentials, and the righteousness from God "which is through faith in Christ" (Phil 3:9, *RSV*). The present formulation of this (into a gnomic saying: Windisch, 314) is clearly aimed at Paul's rivals in Corinth who have been seeking to recommend themselves by calling attention to achievements and characteristics the apostle considers quite irrelevant (5:12). They have thereby shown themselves to *have no understanding* (v. 12b). Their foolishness consists finally in this, that they presume to be able to commend themselves when it is only the Lord's commendation that has any meaning. Moreover, they have apparently sought from Paul some proof of his apostleship comparable to the proofs they offer of theirs (13:3). But insofar as Paul responds to this with any kind of self-recommendation, he does so hesitantly and with important qualifications, as in 4:2 and 6:4 (on which see NOTES and COMMENT). There he seems to be mindful of the principle that only the Lord's commendation really counts, just as he is guided by that principle in the present passage, where he confines himself to a strictly measured boasting, a boasting only of what God has granted (vv. 13ff.).

That one's true "praise" *(epainos)* comes from God and not from other people is also emphasized by Paul in Rom 2:29b, with which may be compared the Stoic ideal as expressed by Marcus Aurelius: "What a capacity a person has to do only what God will praise and to accept all that God assigns!" (XII, 11, cited by Käsemann 1980:77). Unlike the Stoics, however, Paul conceives of one's praise from God in a primarily eschatological way: it is the praise which shall come to the faithful when at Christ's return they shall stand before the one "who will bring to light the things now hidden in darkness and will disclose the purposes of the heart" (1 Cor 4:5, *RSV;* see also 2 Cor 1:14).

# B. A FOOL'S SPEECH, 11:1–12:13

## 3. PROLOGUE, 11:1–21a

**11** ¹If only you would put up with me in a little bit of foolishness. Indeed, do put up with me! ²I care deeply for you with God's own jealousy, for I betrothed you to one man in order to present you as a pure bride to Christ, ³but I fear that as the serpent quite deceived Eve with his craftiness, your minds may be lured away from a total and a pure commitment to Christ. ⁴For if a person comes and preaches some other Jesus than the one we have preached, or if you receive another Spirit than the one you did receive, or another gospel than the one you did accept, you put up with it well enough.

⁵I consider myself in no way inferior to the super-apostles. ⁶Even though I am an amateur in public speaking, I am certainly not in knowledge. Certainly, in every way we have made this clear to you in all things. ⁷Or did I commit a sin by demeaning myself that you might be exalted, because I preached the gospel of God to you free of charge? ⁸I plundered other churches by taking pay from them in order to serve you, ⁹so when I was present with you and was in need I did not burden anybody—for the brothers who came from Macedonia supplied my need. Thus, I have kept and I shall keep myself from being a burden to you in any way. ¹⁰As Christ's truth is in me, this boasting of mine shall not be silenced in the districts of Achaia. ¹¹Why? Because I do not love you? God knows that I do!

¹²What I am doing I shall also keep on doing, in order to cut off the opportunity of those who want an opportunity to be recognized as our equals in what they boast about. ¹³For such people are false apostles, deceitful workers, disguising themselves as apostles of Christ. ¹⁴And no wonder! For Satan himself is disguised as an angel of light. ¹⁵It is therefore no great surprise if also his ministers disguise themselves as ministers of righteousness; their end shall be in accord with their deeds.

¹⁶I repeat, let no one think I am a fool. But should it be otherwise, at least accept me as a fool so I too can boast a little bit. ¹⁷(What I am

saying I say not as one in the Lord, but—when it comes to this business of boasting—with a certain foolishness. [18]Since many are boasting in a worldly way, I too will boast.) [19]For you gladly put up with fools, being wise yourselves! [20]You put up with it when someone enslaves you, when someone eats you up, when someone takes you in, when someone acts presumptuously, when someone slaps you in the face. [21a]I am ashamed to say that we seem to have been weaklings in comparison.

## NOTES

11:1. *If only.* Translates *ophelon,* which introduces a wish presumed to be unattainable, as at 1 Cor 4:8; Gal 5:12. In Rev 3:15b, as here, it is followed by an imperfect (also, e.g., Epictetus II.xxii.12).

*you would put up with me.* Paul has used the same verb *(anechesthai)* in a hardship list in 1 Cor 4:12 ("we endure" [*RSV*]), but nowhere else apart from the present passage, in which it is prominent (twice in this verse, and also in vv. 4, 19, 20). The following pronoun *(mou)* should probably be construed with this verb (thus, *with me*) as it must be in the latter part of the verse (so also *RSV, TEV;* and, among the commentators, Bachmann, 358; Lietzmann, 144; Plummer, 293; Windisch, 318; Barrett, 271). Others, however (e.g., *NEB, JB, NIV, NAB,* and, among the commentators, Bultmann, 201, and Héring, 78), attach it to the noun *foolishness* ("put up with a little foolishness from me"), which is also possible. The first person singular predominates throughout the rest of this letter (the plural recurs only in 11:4, 6, 12, 21a; 12:18c–19; 13:4b, 6b–9).

*in a little bit of foolishness.* Here *mikron ti (a little* [*bit of*]) is taken as an "accusative of reference" (Plummer, 293), indicating the respect in which Paul would hope his readers could bear with him. The alternative would be to read it as the direct object of the verb (see preceding note).

*foolishness.* Eight of the twelve Pauline instances of this and related terms *(aphrosynē, aphrōn, aphronos)* occur here in Letter E (see also vv. 16, 17, 19, 21; 12:6, 11), and three of the remainder in Letter B (1 Cor 12:2; 14:10; 15:36); elsewhere in Paul's letters, only Rom 2:20. The Greek terms used in 1 Cor 1–3 are different *(mōria* [*RSV:* "folly"] in 1:18, 21, 23; 2:14; 3:19, and *to mōron* [*RSV:* "foolishness"] in 1:25; so also in 4:10); there foolishness is contrasted with "wisdom" *(sophia).* But in the present context the contrasting term would be "moderation" *(sōphrosynē),* a sober estimate of oneself (as in Rom 12:3); cf. Bultmann, 202.

*Indeed.* The *alla kai* is best taken as introducing and emphasizing the following imperative (*GNTG* III:330; Héring, 78 n. 4; cf. BDF § 448[6]). The alternative is to take it as adversative (e.g., Lietzmann, 144; Windisch, 318; Zmijewski 1978:78), followed by an indicative (see following note).

*do put up with me!* The context, especially vv. 2–3, makes it more likely that *anechesthe* is intended here as an imperative than as an indicative (so also, e.g., Bachmann, 358; Héring, 78 n. 4; Barrett, 271; *RSV, NEB, TEV, NAB*). The contrary view is held by those commentators who take *alla kai* as strongly adversative (in addition to those mentioned in the preceding note, see Hughes, 373 n. 31; Bultmann, 201; also *JB* and *NIV*).

2. *I care deeply.* The Greek *gar* ("For") which connects this verse closely with the preceding one has been left untranslated. The verb *(zēlō)* could also be rendered as "I have zeal" (cf. 7:7) or, in accord with the subsequent reference to *God's own jealousy,* "I am jealous" (cf. *RSV* and most English versions). For the meaning of the word see Betz's comments on Gal 4:17*a* (1979:229–30), where Paul remarks on how his opponents have been "paying court" *(zēlousin)* to the Galatian congregations.

*with God's own jealousy.* Here *Theou* may be taken as a genitive of quality (e.g., "a divine jealousy," *RSV, NEB*) or, perhaps better, as a genitive of origin (e.g., "with the jealousy of God himself," *NAB*). Bultmann, 202, suggests that it may be equivalent to *kata Theon,* i.e., "with a jealousy corresponding to God's will" (cf. 7:10). God's *zēlos* is associated with God's wrath in LXX Ezek 5:13; 16:38, 42; 23:25, but more generally with God's concern to act on behalf of Israel in LXX Isa 9:7(6); 37:32. See especially Isa 63:15–16, where it is closely related to God's "might," "abundance of mercy," and "compassion" as "Father."

*for.* Greek *gar* introduces the reason Paul is so concerned about the Corinthians.

*I betrothed you.* In classical Greek the middle voice of the verb *harmozein* means "to betroth oneself," but here (as in Philo, *Allegorical Int.* II, 67 and *On Abraham* 100) the middle is used in place of the active (BDF § 316[1]), perhaps because of Paul's sense of personal involvement in the matter (*GNTG* I:160; Plummer, 294; Barrett, 272). For the imagery involved see COMMENT.

*one man.* Cf. 1 Cor 7:2, where Paul writes that each woman should have "her own husband" *(ton idion andra),* and Eph 5:22, where the "household code" provides that women should be subject "to their own husbands" *(tois idiois andrasin).* Here, as in Rom 7:4, the bride is the Christian community and the *one man* to whom she is betrothed is *Christ.*

*in order to present you.* The aorist infinitive *(parastēsai)* has a "final" sense here (Zmijewski 1978:81) and the word has a clearly eschatological reference, as in 4:14 (on which see NOTES and COMMENT); Rom 14:10; 1 Cor 8:8, etc. Cf. especially Eph 5:27, where the conception of the church's presentation to Christ as his bride recurs.

*a pure bride.* Or "a pure [chaste] virgin," as in 4 Mac 18:7; Philo, *Special Laws* I, 107 ("a virgin . . . innocent of marriage"); II, 30; *On Joseph* 43; *On Rewards and Punishments* 159. Note particularly Paul's use of the noun in 1 Cor 7:36–38.

*to Christ.* This phrase, like the comparable one at the end of the following verse, has special emphasis by virtue of its placement in the sentence (Zmijewski 1978:83).

3. *but.* The *de* is adversative, and what follows stands in some contrast to what has preceded (Zmijewski 1978:86).

*I fear that.* For the same construction *(phoboumai . . . mē pōs* with an aorist subjunctive) see 12:20*a,* and cf. the variation of this in Gal 4:11. Borse (1972:89) compares *thaumazō* ("I am astonished" [*RSV*]) in Gal 1:6.

*the serpent.* In Wis 2:24 (on which see Winston 1979:121–22) and in certain later Jewish literature (e.g., Apoc Mos 16) *the serpent* of Gen 3 is identified with "the devil" or "Satan"; see also Rev 12:9; 20:2; Testim Truth [CG IX, *3*] 47, 5; 48, 17 [*NHLE,* 412]. This identification seems to be presumed by Paul here (so most interpreters; but a few disagree—e.g., Allo, 277; Amstutz 1968:113–14). The work of Satan in Corinth is of special concern to him (see also 2:11; 11:14; 1 Cor 7:5, and cf. 1 Cor 5:5; 2 Cor 12:7).

*quite deceived Eve.* The allusion is to Gen 3:13, which reads in the LXX: "And the woman said, 'The serpent deceived me [*ēpatēsen me*], and I ate.' " Here Paul uses a compound form of the verb *(exēpatēsen)* which intensifies the meaning, *quite deceived* (cf. Plummer, 295; Hughes, 375 n. 33). Cf. 1 Tim 2:14 (the only other NT occurrence of the name *Eve* comes in 1 Tim 2:13), where the simple form of the verb is used of Adam ("Adam was not deceived") while the intensive form is used of the woman ("but the woman, having been quite deceived, became a transgressor"). In Rom 7:11, Paul uses the intensive form for sin, which, "finding opportunity in the commandment, quite deceived me and by it killed me." Various rabbinic texts interpret the serpent's deception of Eve as her seduction and the infusion of lust (*ᶜAbod. Zar.* 22b; *b. Šabb.* 145b–146a; *Yebam.* 103b; cf. *Soṭa* 9b), and there are indications such an interpretation was current in Paul's day (1 Enoch 69:6; 2 Enoch 31:6; Apoc Abr 23; perhaps also 1 Mac 18:7–8); see especially the discussions by Thackeray (1900:50–55) and Dibelius (1909:50–51). Cf. also 1 Tim 2:13–15, which Hanson (1968:71–72) characterizes as "the earliest attestation for 2 Corinthians" because, in his estimation, its author must have been acquainted with 2 Cor 11:1–3.

*craftiness.* For the meaning of the word *(panourgia)* see NOTES on 4:2. The adjectival form is used with reference to the serpent in the Greek translations of Gen 3:1 by Aquila and Symmachus; and Philo, too, employing the same text, refers to the "craftiness" of the serpent, which he identifies with "pleasure" (*Allegorical Int.* II, 105–8).

*minds.* See NOTES on the same word in 3:14, and cf. especially 10:5.

*lured away.* Translates a form of *phtheirein* which is often used of moral "ruin" or "corruption" (e.g., 1 Cor 15:33; LXX Gen 6:11; Hos 9:9). It can also be used specifically of the seduction of a woman; in addition to the references given in BAG s.v. 1c, note Euripides, Fragment 485 and Dio Chrysostom XI, 153 (both cited in LSJ s.v. I, 3b). See especially Diogn 12:8, where the seduction of "the virgin" Eve is in view, as it seems to be here as well.

*from a total and a pure.* A number of good ancient witnesses, including ℵ² (D²), attest a shorter text here which omits the words "and a pure" *(kai tēs hagnotētas)*. The suspect phrase is retained but placed in brackets in *GNT*-Nestle. A number of commentators (e.g., Bachmann, 361–62 n. 1; Windisch, 324–25; Strachan, 18; Héring, 77; Barrett, 270 n. 1) and trs. (e.g., Mof., Gdspd., *JB, NEB*) have adopted the shorter reading—primarily because its position in the sentence varies in those texts which do include it, and because its presence can be explained as a gloss prompted by the reference in v. 2 to *a pure bride.* Others, however (e.g., Allo, 275–76; Malherbe 1961:120–21; Hughes, 276 n. 37; Prümm I, 594; *RSV, TEV, NIV, NAB*), adopt the longer text, principally on the basis of its somewhat better attestation (P⁴⁶ ℵ* B G et al.) and because its absence can be explained as a case of scribal oversight (the last six letters of *hagnotētos* [*pure*] and *haplotētos* [*total*] are the same). For a discussion see Metzger 1971:583–84.

*total.* In Greek a noun *(haplotēs),* translated as "candor" in 1:12 (see NOTES there) and as "generosity" in 8:2; 9:11, 13. Here it has the "specifically Jewish meaning" of "wholeness" (Amstutz 1968:114) and "singleness of purpose" (Malherbe 1961:124, with special reference to its use in T 12 Patr).

*pure*. In Greek a noun *(hagnotēs)*, translated as "probity" in 6:6. Here, whether the reference be ascribed to Paul himself or to a later glossator (see above), the image of *a pure bride* (v. 2) is in mind.

*commitment to Christ*. The word *commitment* has been supplied for purposes of translation. Although the Greek has only *tēs eis ton Christon* (thus, literally: "the wholeness and the purity which is toward Christ"), it is clear that Paul is thinking of the relationship his congregation is to maintain with Christ. The phrase is parallel with *to Christ* in v. 2, and stands—as it does there—in an emphatic position (Zmijewski 1978:87).

4. *For*. The Greek *gar* connects this verse with the appeal of v. 1 and introduces a support for it: since the Corinthians have "put up" with the false teaching of Paul's rivals, they ought to be able to "put up" with a little foolishness from their own apostle. There is also a certain connection with v. 3 (Paul fears for the Corinthians, v. 3, because of their tolerance for a false gospel, v. 4), but this connection is distinctly secondary; contrast Munck (1959:176–77), who connects v. 4 only with v. 3.

*if*. Here, as most commentators recognize (but not Munck 1959:177), *ei (If)* with the present indicative *(you put up with it)* expresses a real condition (see BDF § 372), not just a hypothetical possibility. This is suggested by vv. 1–3 and confirmed by vv. 19–20, which are parallel to v. 4 and clearly refer to an actual situation in Corinth (Windisch, 326; Bultmann, 203).

*a person comes*. More literally, "the one who comes" *(ho erchomenos)*. Barrett, 275, interprets this along with 10:7, 10, 11 as a reference to one particular individual, identifying him specifically with the offending brother of 2:5–11; 7:12 and thinking of him as the leader of the rival apostles in Corinth (see also ibid.:7–8, 89–93, 212–14, 256, 260–61). It is much more probable, however, that the singular in the present verse is to be interpreted generically (so most commentators) because (a) Gal 5:10 shows that Paul can use the singular article generically (cf. also 2 Cor 10:11; Col 2:8); (b) the references in 10:7, 10, 11 are not likely to be to a particular individual (see NOTES); (c) in this chapter (certainly in v. 13 and probably also in v. 5), as in chapter 10 (vv. 2, 12), Paul refers to his rivals as a group; and (d) Paul's use of the singular in v. 4 is well enough explained by his reference to *the serpent* in v. 3 (Zmijewski 1978:99) as a symbol for the deceitful opponents in Corinth. Moreover, even in the unlikely event that Paul does have an individual in mind here, that could hardly be the offender mentioned in Letter D, for he was a resident member of the congregation in Corinth (see NOTES and COMMENT in 2:5–11), while the present reference is to someone who *comes* from elsewhere with an alien gospel (cf. Betz 1972:13).

*some other Jesus . . . another Spirit . . . another gospel*. Nowhere else in Paul's letters are *Jesus*, the *Spirit*, and the *gospel* drawn together as they are here; Borse, however (1972:84–85), points out that there are certain formal similarities between this verse and Gal 1:6–9. The material correspondence with Gal 1:6–9 is also noteworthy, for there as here the apostle refers to "another gospel" which is being preached in a congregation of his founding (Gal 1:6). There is probably no significance in the variation of the adjective from *allos (some other)* with *Jesus* to *heteros (another)* with *Spirit* and *gospel* (against Schmithals 1971:128–29); the two can be used quite interchangeably, as they are in Gal 1:6–7; 1 Cor 12:9–10; Rev 4:12, etc. (other examples in BAG s.v. *heteros*, 1bγ; cf. BDF § 30[4]; *GNTG* III:197).

*we have preached.* It is possible that the unexpected use of the first person plural here (however, cf. Gal 1:8) is meant to include Silvanus and Timothy, as in 1:19 (cf. Windisch, 327). However, the plural intrudes itself elsewhere in this "fool's speech" (vv. 6, 12, 21), and it is more likely that in all four instances it simply replaces the singular, for rhetorical effect only. Zmijewski (1978:96 and n. 162) describes them as "epistolary" plurals.

*if you receive.* Translates *lambanete*, which some commentators are inclined to strike as an interpolation (so, e.g., Windisch, 327; Héring, 79 n. 10). This would yield a better-balanced sentence ("If a person comes and preaches some other Jesus than the one we have preached, or another Spirit than the one you did receive, or another gospel than the one you did accept"), but that is hardly warrant enough to omit it. On the other hand, there is also insufficient evidence to support the suggestion of Schmithals that Paul himself has emphasized "receiving" the Spirit (1971:169 n. 79) in order to counteract the Gnostic idea that the Spirit is one's "inalienable possession" (ibid.:167–68).

*another Spirit than the one you did receive.* In the language of the earliest church the Spirit is characteristically something one "receives" (John 7:39; 14:17; 20:22; Acts 2:38; 8:15–17; 10:47; 19:2; Rom 8:15; 1 Cor 2:12; Gal 3:2—all cited by Schmithals 1971:167).

*another gospel than the one you did accept.* Whether the content of the alien gospel Paul refers to here can be identified with that of the alien gospel to which he makes reference in Gal 1:6–7 is disputed; see COMMENT. The verb "to accept" *(dechesthai)* is used nowhere else in the NT with "the gospel" as its object, but its use with "the word" (Luke 8:13; Acts 17:11; 1 Thess 1:6; Jas 1:21) or "the word of God" (Acts 8:14; 11:1; 1 Thess 2:13) is fairly common and certainly comparable. Elsewhere Paul writes of "receiving" *(paralambanein)* the gospel (1 Cor 15:1, cf. v. 3; Gal 1:9, 11–12), and it is clear from the parallel use of the two words in 1 Thess 2:13 that Paul perceives no essential difference in meaning between "accepting" and "receiving" his preaching.

*you put up with it well enough.* Translates *kalōs anechesthe,* although there is substantial ms. support for the imperfect form of the verb, *aneichesthe* ("you would put up with it well enough"). Zmijewski (1978:93) adopts the latter because, given the preceding present-tense verbs, it is the *lectio difficilior,* and because the present-tense form can be regarded as a "correction" based on v. 20. But the context, including v. 20, shows that Paul is dealing with a real situation, not a hypothetical one (Barrett, 270 n. 2), and the "correction" to an imperfect form can be explained as an attempt to free the Corinthians from the stigma of having actually given in to the rival apostles (cf. Windisch, 326). In either case the expression is ironic, and *kalōs (well enough)* is echoed by *hēdeōs (gladly)* in v. 19.

5. *I consider.* Translates *logizomai,* as in 10:2 (on which see the NOTES). The Greek *gar* ("for") is left untranslated because in this verse it has no clear causal force and seems to function merely as a connective ( = *de,* as in 1:12); see BAG s.v. 4 and cf. Zmijewski 1978:115.

*in no way inferior.* The *mēden, in no way* (not *ouden* as in 12:11c, since verbs of thinking are followed by *mē;* BDF § 429), is emphatic (Barrett, 277). The perfect tense here *(hysterēkenai,* literally "to have been inferior") has the sense of a present (cf. BDF § 341).

*the super-apostles.* The same expression *(tōn hyperlian apostolōn)* occurs in 12:11c in the epilogue to this "fool's speech." Whether Paul is applying the description ironically to his rivals in Corinth or—perhaps more straightforwardly—to the leaders of the church in Jerusalem is widely debated; see COMMENT. Compounds with the preposition *hyper-* are particularly frequent in 2 Cor; fifteen of the thirty-four occurrences of such words in the seven indisputably Pauline letters occur in 2 Cor: seven times in chaps. 1–9 (see NOTES on 3:10, "the splendor which so far surpasses it") and eight times in chaps. 10–13 (in addition to this verse and 12:11, see 10:14—"overextending," 16—"places beyond"; 11:23b—"far worse beatings"; 12:7—"the extraordinary character"; "exalted" [twice]). See also "I am more of one" in 11:23a and "beyond what one sees me doing" in 12:6b. Georgi (1964:299) suggests that Paul's use of these expressions has been prompted by the claims of his opponents—who, far from espousing a world-fleeing or world-denying position, are intent on exalting themselves within the world. P. Marshall (1980:574), who describes Paul's rivals as "hybrists," speaks of the apostle's "vocabulary of *hybris*" which he employs against them.

6. *Even though I am.* Translates *ei de kai,* the pronoun and the verb having to be supplied; see BDF § 128(2).

*an amateur in public speaking.* Cf. 10:10. Betz (1972:66) has emphasized that Paul's conceding his lack of oratorical eloquence corresponds to the way philosophers in the Socratic tradition typically attacked the pretentiousness of the Sophists. See, e.g., *Dio Chrysostom* XLII, 3, who modestly refers to his "inexperience [*apeirian*] in simply everything, but especially in speaking [*tous logous*], recognizing that I am only a layman [*idiōtēs*]" (cited by Betz 1972:66 and n. 154; Mussies 1972:179); cf. XII, 16; XXV. The word *idiōtēs (amateur)* is used here of one who is "unskilled," "untrained," hence "not an expert" (Schlier, *TDNT* III:216–17; BAG s.v. 1). Norden (1915:506–7; followed by Judge 1968:41) points out that the rhetoric which Paul disavows would not have been that of the great Attic orators, but the rhetoric of the artificial, undisciplined, and highly flamboyant style known as "Asianism," immensely popular among the Sophists of Paul's day, and precisely in the areas where Paul was active. For later assessments of Paul's amateurish style see Epistle 7 in the apocryphal correspondence between the apostle and Seneca, and the Latin recension of the *Acts of Phileas* 3:1 (Musurillo 1972:347). According to Acts 4:13, Peter and John were "uneducated, common men [*agrammatoi . . . kai idiōtai*]" *(RSV).*

*public speaking.* Here, as in 10:10, *logos* refers to the manner of the apostle's speech, and specifically to the style of his public discourse (so most commentators). Some (e.g., Friedrich 1963b:182; Georgi 1964:228) associate it rather with the gift of free, Spirit-endowed speech allegedly being touted by Gnostic opponents. But in contrast with *gnōsis (knowledge),* and in view of the overall context, *logos* must refer to the form of speech, and *gnosis* to the content (cf. Betz 1972:59).

*certainly not.* Translates *all' ou.* In an apodosis after *ei,* as here, *alla* can mean "yet," "certainly," or "at least"; BDF § 448(5).

*knowledge.* This noun *(gnōsis)* appears elsewhere in chaps. 10–13 only in 10:5 ("the knowledge of God"), where it probably refers to the gospel as such (cf. 2:14; 4:6). But here it is best understood as a reference to the divine gift of spiritual insight (cf. 6:6; 8:7; 1 Cor 12:8; 1:5—also coupled with *logos*).

*Certainly.* Again *all';* see note above on *certainly not.*

*in every way.* As in 4:8, on which see the NOTES.

*we have made this clear.* As elsewhere, Paul uses a participle (*phanerōsantes;* the verb, variously translated as "manifest," "disclose," "show," is frequent in chaps. 1–9) in place of a finite verb. For the use of the first person plural see the note on *we have preached* in v. 4. The sentence in its present form contains no object, however; this doubtless explains the appearance of a passive form of the participle in some ancient texts (thus, "we have disclosed ourselves"), and the addition of *heautous* ("ourselves") in a few others. Most commentators think the original object has somehow dropped out of the text, although Bachmann, 367–68 (followed by Zmijewski 1978:119), suggests that Paul intentionally omitted the object, thereby diminishing the verbal element and accentuating the *en panti . . . en pasin* (see following note). Many commentators would understand *knowledge* or "it" (referring to *knowledge*) as the object (e.g., Barrett, 280–81), but it is best, with most English trs., to introduce only the pronoun *this*, which can have a broader reference—i.e., perhaps, "that I am no amateur when it comes to knowledge" (cf. Hughes, 382–83 n. 44).

*in all things.* It is possible that *en pasin* is masculine here; thus Hughes, 382 n. 44, would translate "among all men" (cf. Plummer, 300; Windisch, 332). But it is more apt to be neuter, thereby strengthening the point that the depth of Paul's spiritual insight should have been clear to the Corinthians in every dimension and detail of his ministry among them. Cf. Phil 4:12, *en panti kai en pasin,* "in any and all circumstances" *(RSV).*

7. *Or.* Here *ē* functions to introduce a rhetorical question to which a negative response is anticipated (Zmijewski 1978:123); cf. especially Rom 3:29.

*commit a sin.* This expression *(hamartia poiein)* occurs nowhere else in the Pauline letters (5:21 is different), but it is found in John 8:34; 1 John 3:4, 8, 9 (all but the last have the article before *hamartia*). See also Jas 5:15 (plural, "sins") and 1 Pet 2:22 ("[Christ] committed no sin"). The last passage echoes LXX Isa 53:9, where, however, *anomia* ("a lawless deed") is used, not *hamartia.* In the present passage *hamartia* apparently refers to a specific wrongful act (cf. *adikia,* "offense," in 12:13b), so the phrase is hardly different in meaning from [*to*] *kakon poiein* ("to commit evil"), 13:7; Rom 13:4. Elsewhere in Paul's letters "sin" is a power which enslaves and causes one to "commit" evil (Rom 7:20); only in Rom 4:8, quoted from LXX Ps 31(32):2, is it used as in the present verse of a concrete wrong. Here the aorist *(did . . . commit)* is probably complexive, looking back over the apostle's past conduct as a whole (Zmijewski 1978:125).

*by demeaning myself.* See NOTES and COMMENT on 10:1 (where the adjective, "demeaned" [*tapeinos*], occurs); the verb (*tapeinoun,* "to demean") also appears in 12:21 ("humiliate"). Cf. Phil 4:12, "I know how to be abased [*tapeinousthai*]" *(RSV).*

*that you might be exalted.* The OT theme of God's exaltation of the lowly (e.g., 1 Sam 2:7; Job 5:11; Ezek 17:24; 21:26) is found also in the NT: e.g., Matt 23:12; Luke 14:11; 18:14; Jas 4:10; 1 Pet 5:6. See especially Phil 2:8, 9, Jesus' voluntary humiliation and his subsequent exaltation. In the present case, however, one party (Paul) demeaned himself that others (the Corinthian Christians) *might be exalted;* cf. 6:10; 8:9.

*because.* Translates *hoti,* which could also be understood here as explicative, "in that" (so Lietzmann, 146; Bultmann, 207; criticized by Zmijewski 1978:123 n. 80). In either case the word introduces the nature of Paul's alleged "sin."

*the gospel of God.* As in Rom 1:1; 15:16; 1 Thess 2:2, 8, 9. Contrast *another gospel,*

v. 4. Elsewhere in 2 Cor: "the gospel of Christ" (2:12; 9:13; 10:14; cf. 4:4), "our gospel" (4:3), and "the gospel" (8:18).

*free of charge.* Here the adverb *dōrean* means "without money," as in LXX Exod 21:11 (*dōrean aneu argyriou,* "free, without money"). See also 2 Thess 3:8; Rev 21:6; 22:17, and especially Matt 10:8. In 1 Cor 9:18, Paul uses the adjective *adapanos* in the same way.

8. *I plundered.* The verb *(sylan)* is often used in the military sense of stripping an enemy's arms or pillaging a captured city (cf. Col 2:8, where the compound *sylagōgein* means "to carry off as booty"); LSJ s.v. 1, 2.

*other churches.* Presumably certain congregations in Macedonia, v. 9.

*by taking . . . from them.* Or "receiving . . . from them"; but the reference to plundering suggests the tr. given here. The words *from them* do not stand in the Greek, but this is the meaning required by the context.

*pay.* Translates *opsōnion,* which may simply mean "salary" or "wages" in a general sense (e.g., Rom 6:23). But here, used in connection with a reference to "plundering," it should be allowed its more particular sense of a soldier's *pay.* Cf. 1 Cor 9:7*b* (where the plural is used; *RSV:* "expense"), and see Deissmann 1903:266; MM s.v.

*in order to serve you.* Or "with a view toward the serving of you" *(pros tēn hymōn diakonian).* The noun *diakonia* ("service") occurs only here in chaps. 10–13, although it is frequent in chaps. 1–9 (see note on "ministry" in 3:7). In the present instance one should perhaps think of a soldier's dutiful "service" (Zmijewski 1978:134). The whole phrase (ibid.:130), but especially the *you* (Plummer, 303), is emphatic.

9. *so.* Here *kai* ("and") is used to introduce a result (BAG s.v. I, 2f).

*present with you.* The idiom *(pareinai pros hymas)* also appears in Gal 4:18, 20.

*in need.* As in Phil 4:12 (*RSV:* "want"), the reference is to the lack of physical necessities like food, clothing, and shelter. Zmijewski (1978:133) understands the aorist participle here as ingressive, suggesting the sudden inception of want during Paul's residence in Corinth, but there is nothing to require this interpretation.

*I did not burden.* The verb *(katanarkan),* also used in 12:13, 14, was originally a medical term ("to make numb," "to stupefy," etc.; see Windisch, 336, and Plummer, 304), but several ancient commentators and versions understand it here to mean "weigh down," "be a burden to" (BAG s.v.).

*for.* This *gar* introduces the reason Paul did not have to burden the Corinthians during his residence with them (Zmijewski 1978:130). As such, it clarifies the statement of v. 8.

*the brothers.* Either representatives of the congregations in question or, as many commentators suggest, Paul's own co-workers, Silvanus (Silas) and Timothy (1:19), who, according to Acts 18:5, "came down from Macedonia" after Paul had inaugurated his mission in Corinth.

*Macedonia.* See NOTES on 1:16.

*supplied my need.* Some would interpret the double compound here to mean "supplemented" (e.g., Tasker, 151; Hughes, 387–88 n. 52; Hock 1980:64, 93 n. 2), but it is doubtful whether it means more than *supplied* (cf. 9:12; Wis 19:4; Philo, *On Rewards and Punishments* 103; Windisch, 336).

*Thus.* Translates *kai* ("and"), in this case introducing a clause which both sums up and extends the thought of vv. 8–9 (Zmijewski 1978:132).

*I have kept and I shall keep.* Cf. v. 12, *What I am doing I shall also keep on doing,* and 12:13, 14, "I myself did not burden you . . . I will not be a burden" (Betz 1972:102).

*from being a burden.* Translates the adjective *abarēs,* "not burdensome." On this and the cognate terms used in 12:16 *(katabarein);* 1 Thess 2:7 *(en barei),* 9 *(epibarein),* see Strelan 1975:267–70.

10. *As Christ's truth is in me.* This oath formula is closely comparable to that in Rom 9:1 ("I speak the truth in Christ, I do not lie"). Other oath formulas in 2 Cor occur in 1:18 (see NOTES), 23; 2:10; 11:11, 31. The formula of 2:17; 12:19*b* is more general, as is the remark of 13:3, and these are more comparable with 1 Cor 2:16 ("But we have the mind of Christ" [*RSV*]; cf. 1 Cor 7:40) than with the oath formulas as such. Here, then, *truth* does not refer to the gospel, as it does in 4:2; 6:7; 13:8; Gal 2:5, 14, etc., but simply to "truth-telling," as in 7:14; 12:6.

*this boasting.* Or "this boast," if *kauchēsis* here has the sense of *kauchēma* which normally (e.g., 1:14) refers to the object of one's boasting. Although *kauchēsis* bears this sense in 1:12 ("we can be proud"), in the present context (see v. 17) it is better understood as a reference to the act of boasting. (See also following note.)

*of mine.* Paraphrases *eis eme,* more literally "to me" or "in me." Bachmann, 371 (followed by Zmijewski 1978:139) interprets it as "toward me," and thus regards the *kauchēsis* to be the objective "pride" the Achaian Christians have in Paul. But in the context of this letter (chaps. 10–13) it is primarily Paul's own boasting that is in view (see NOTES and COMMENT on 10:8), as it certainly is in vv. 16, 17, 18, 30, etc.

*the districts of Achaia.* The word *districts (klima)* is not a political but a geographical term, ordinarily referring to a fairly small "area" or "region" (see Ramsay 1900: 278–80). Here the plural (also used in Rom 15:23; Gal 1:21; cf. Polybius V, 44.6) is probably intended to include the entire province (BAG s.v.), so the expression may be understood as equivalent to "throughout Achaia" in 1:1 (on which see NOTES and COMMENT).

11. *Why?* The question looks back primarily to v. 9*b,* and only secondarily to v. 10. Again in Rom 9:32 this expression *(dia ti)* appears as a freestanding question, there with reference to vv. 30*b*–31.

*Because I do not love you?* Paul emphasizes his love for the Corinthians in 2:4; 8:7; 12:15*b.* Spicq (1965:32) interprets *I do not love you* as an example of litotes, meaning "I detest [or: despise] you."

*God knows that I do!* The exclamation *God knows* (the words *that I do* have been supplied for the tr.) is used here to emphasize Paul's veracity, and therefore it may be characterized as an abbreviated oath formula, the fuller form of which stands at 11:31 (Stählin 1962:132–33). Cf. Athenaeus *Deipnosophistae* XV, 673d: "The gods know [*isasin hoi theoi*] that I was the first to discover all this. . . ." In 12:2, 3 the statement "God knows" functions differently, to emphasize Paul's ignorance.

12. *What I am doing I shall also keep on doing.* The *doing (poiein)* here refers to the action referred to in v. 7 as "committing a sin" *(hamartia poiein).* Cf. also v. 9*b, I have kept and I shall keep* (with note). In all three instances the reference is to Paul's refusal to accept financial support from the Corinthians.

*to cut off.* On the use of the word *(ekkoptein)* see Stählin, *TDNT* III:857–60.

*opportunity.* Cf. 5:12, where the same word *(aphormē)* is translated "basis."

*to be recognized.* More literally, "that they should be found" *(hina . . . heurethōsin),* taking the clause (with most commentators) as dependent on *those who want an opportunity.* Contrast Hock (1980:101 n. 118), who regards it as dependent on *What I am doing,* etc. In that case it would be parallel with *in order to cut off (hina ekkopsō)* and would represent what Paul intends for his rivals—that they *should* change their ways and decline support from the Corinthians. Thus (paraphrasing), "What I am doing I shall continue to do in order to cut off the opportunity of those who seek one, and in order to enable them to boast along with us [of not accepting support from you]." But the context is against this; see COMMENT.

*as our equals.* Translates *kathōs kai hēmeis,* "just as we are." The momentary intrusion of the first person plural is appropriate where Paul is referring to *those who want* (plural) their ministry to be compared with his apostolate.

*in what they boast about.* As in 5:12, the illegitimate boasting of Paul's opponents is in view.

13. *For.* The introductory *gar* presents what follows as the ground of what has preceded.

*such people.* Greek, *hoi toioutoi.* Here—as in 10:11, where the singular had been used (*ho toioutos,* "such a person")—Paul is referring specifically to his rivals (v. 12).

*false apostles.* The term *(pseudapostoloi)* occurs nowhere else (Rengstorf, *TDNT* I:445), and it may have been coined by Paul himself (Kümmel, 211) in the heat of his argument with his rivals in Corinth. It is perhaps patterned after the term "false prophets" (Windisch, 341), which occurs in the LXX (once in Zech, otherwise in Jer), in later Jewish literature (e.g., Philo and Josephus), and elsewhere in the NT (the Synoptic Gospels and Acts, 2 Pet, 1 John, Rev—but not in any of the Pauline letters). These and other related terms are discussed in detail by Barrett 1970b. Cf. especially the references to "false brothers" in 11:26; Gal 2:4 and to "false witnesses" in 1 Cor 15:15.

*deceitful workers.* "Worker" *(ergatēs)* seems to have been used in the early church as a technical term for a missionary (e.g., Matt 9:37–38 par.; 10:10 par. [cited in 1 Tim 5:18; Did 13:2]; 2 Tim 2:15). One may presume that the rival leaders in Corinth applied it to themselves (Georgi 1964:49–50; Theissen 1982:48), but here, as in Phil 3:2 ("evil workers," the only other Pauline occurrence of the term), the apostle applies it in a negative sense to his opponents. Given the idea of "disguising oneself," the adjective *dolios* is best rendered as *deceitful,* but it may also mean "treacherous" or "dishonest"; cf. the cognate noun *dolos* in 12:16, where Paul acknowledges that he himself has been charged with acting deceitfully.

*disguising themselves.* As in 4 Mac 9:22; T Reub 5:6, the middle voice *(metaschēmatizesthai)* is used to describe the alteration of one's outward appearance; here, with deceitful intent. The word is repeated in vv. 14, 15.

*apostles of Christ.* This term, like "ministers of Christ" (11:23*a*), must have been used by the opponents in reference to themselves. Cf. *ministers of righteousness* in v. 15.

14. *And no wonder!* With this exclamation (*kai ou thauma;* on the omission of *estin,* "it is," see BDF § 127[4]) one may compare *kai thaumaston ouden* ("and it is no wonder") in Philo, *On Husbandry* 71 and *Moses* I, 156 (cited by Windisch, 342).

*Satan.* As in 2:11, on which see NOTES.

*disguised as an angel of light.* This description of Satan clearly derives from Jewish legends about the deception of Eve by the devil (cf. 11:3) in Paradise (against Allo,

286–87, and Hughes, 393–94 n. 57). According to Apoc Moses 17:1–2, "Satan appeared in the form of an angel and sang hymns like the angels" *(APOT)*, and in the Latin version of *Adam and Eve*, 9:1, it is said that "Satan was wroth and transformed himself into the brightness of angels, and went away to the river Tigris to Eve, and found her weeping, and the devil himself pretended to grieve with her . . ." (ibid.); cf. the Slavonic version, 38:1, "The devil came . . . wearing the form and brightness of an angel . . ." (ibid.). In 1QS iii.21 the "Spirit of Falsehood" who is set over against the "Spirit of Truth" (the "Prince of Light") is also described as "the Angel of Darkness" (Vermes 1975:75–76). Borse (1972:102–3) suggests that the present passage reads like a later clarification and correction of the nearly blasphemous idea in Gal 1:8 that "an angel from heaven" might come preaching a false gospel. Note also Gal 4:14, where the apostle recalls that the Galatians had received him "as an angel of God." Only in 2 Cor 11:14; 12:7; Gal 1:8; 4:14 does Paul refer to "an angel" (singular); elsewhere (Rom 8:38; 1 Cor 4:9; 6:3; 11:10; 13:1; Gal 3:19; cf. Col 2:18; 2 Thess 1:7) he uses the plural (Borse 1972:101).

*an angel of light.* Or, if the genitive *phōtos (of light)* is used in a Semitic way ( = *phōteinon;* Moule 1953:175), "a shining angel." Given the Jewish background of the idea of Satan's disguise (preceding note), it is unlikely that this phrase is Paul's own ad hoc creation (against Zmijewski 1978:161).

15. *no great surprise.* Translates *ou mega;* more literally: "nothing so great," a form of litotes (understatement for the sake of emphasis; so Grayston 1964:569 n. 2). Cf. *And no wonder* in v. 14 and, for this specific idiom *(ouden mega)*, Plato, *Menexenus* 235 D, and Diogenes Laertius VI, 44 (the latter cited by Fridrichsen 1936:46). Note also LXX Gen 45:28 *(mega moi estin,* "It is no great thing for me").

*ministers of righteousness.* Cf. *apostles of Christ*, v. 13, and "ministers of Christ," 11:23, both probably self-designations of Paul's rivals in Corinth; and "ministers of a new covenant" (3:6) and "the ministry of righteousness" (3:9), the two latter expressions applied by Paul himself to the authentic servants and service of Christ. In the present verse *righteousness* is to be understood generally (Plummer, 310) and positively (Georgi 1964:249) as a term for true "ministers of God" (as in 6:4; contrast "minister of sin," Gal 2:17); nothing should be concluded from it about the content of the preaching of Paul's rivals (correctly Bultmann, 211; Barrett, 287).

*their end shall be in accord with their deeds.* For the form of this threat *(hōn to telos . . . ,* literally "whose end . . .")* see Phil 3:19 *(hon to telos apōleia,* "whose end is destruction"). The traditionally Jewish idea that one is ultimately accountable before God for one's deeds is common in the NT (e.g., Matt 16:27; John 5:28–29; Eph 6:8; Col 3:24–25; 2 Tim 4:14; 1 Pet 1:17; Rev 2:23; 20:12–13; 22:12) and is by no means foreign to Paul (e.g., Rom 2:6, citing LXX Ps 61:13[62:12], Prov 24:12; 1 Cor 3:13–15; 2 Cor 5:10; Gal 6:7–9).

16. *I repeat.* More literally, "I say again" *(palin legō)*, referring back to v. 1. For the same expression see Gal 1:9 (with reference to v. 8); and cf. Phil 4:4*b*, "I will repeat" *(palin erō,* with reference to v. 4*a*).

*a fool.* The adjective *(aphrōn)* occurs twice in this verse, then again in v. 19 and in 12:6, 11. It is perhaps best to translate it as a substantive in each instance. Neither in this verse nor in 12:6 is Paul willing to concede that he is really *a fool*, but in 12:11 he does confess that his boasting has made him one.

*at least accept me as a fool.* On the ellipsis in Greek see Moule 1953:151. The verb *accept (dechesthai)* goes a bit further than the verb *put up with (anechesthai)* used in v. 1 (Zmijewski 1978:194).

*I too.* That is, as well as his rivals in Corinth, v. 12. Cf. v. 18.

*a little bit.* Translates *mikron ti,* as in v. 1. Paul feels constrained to boast, but he wants to do as little of that as possible.

17. *I say not as one in the Lord.* Literally: "I say not according to the Lord [*ou kata Kyrion lalō*]," with which one may compare Paul's references to speaking *(lalein)* "in Christ" in 2:17; 12:19b. The point is not that he has no specific command from the Lord on the present subject, as in 1 Cor 7:12, 25, but that the subject itself is a "worldly" one—*according to the flesh (kata sarka,* v. 18). Cf. *kata Theon* ("as God wills") in 7:9, with note.

*when it comes to this business of boasting.* This phrase *(en tautē tē hypostasei tēs kaucheseōs)* stands at the end of the Greek sentence, apparently to qualify the point made in the preceding phrase beginning with *but.* The simple preposition *en* ("in") has been freely rendered here as *when it comes to* (cf. *NEB*). Many versions and commentators take the meaning of the noun *hypostasis* to be "confidence" or the like (e.g., *RSV, JB;* Allo, 289–90; Barrett, 290), but it is best to take it in the sense of "matter" or "project" (as, e.g., *TEV;* Bachmann, 375; Bultmann, 212; Zmijewski 1978:199–200); see note on the same word in 9:4, where it has been rendered as "undertaking."

*this . . . boasting.* As in v. 10.

*with a certain foolishness.* More literally, "as in foolishness" *(hōs en aphrosynē).* The *hōs* ("as") somewhat qualifies Paul's judgment about his present boasting; ordinarily it would be pure *foolishness,* but under the present circumstances he must boast in order to serve the gospel. Cf. Plutarch, *On Praising Oneself Inoffensively,* especially 2–3, 15–16, and also (cited by Mussies 1972:179) Dio Chrysostom, LVII, 4–5. The noun *aphrosynē* occurs also in vv. 1 (see note) and 21b.

18. *many.* The word *(polloi)* is used contemptuously; cf. *so many (hoi polloi)* in 2:17, with note.

*boasting in a worldly way.* Paul's rivals are similarly described in 5:12 ("boasting of what is outward [*en prosōpō*]"). For the phrase *kata sarka (in a worldly way)* see the note on *opportunistically* in 1:17; in 5:16; 10:2, 3 it is translated "according to worldly standards." Here *kata sarka* stands over against *kata Kyrion* (literally "according to the Lord") in v. 17.

*I too.* As in v. 16.

19. *For.* The introductory *gar* links this verse with v. 16, making clear the parenthetical nature of vv. 17–18.

*gladly.* Cf. *well enough* in v. 4. The emphatic position of this word *(hēdeōs)* in the sentence (Plummer, 315) heightens the irony. (The superlative form of the word occurs in 12:9, 15.)

*put up with.* In 11:1 the same form *(anechesthe)* is properly translated as an imperative, and it is taken in the same way here by Bachmann, 275–76. However, the word order and the context require an indicative, even though indirectly the apostle is summoning his readers to *put up with* his own foolishness as well, v. 16 (Zmijewski 1978:205–6).

*fools, being wise yourselves.* Here the *fools* are Paul's rivals for leadership in Corinth.

In Greek the terms *fools* and *wise* stand side by side, this juxtaposition heightening the sarcasm. Cf. 1 Cor 4:10, where—as here—Paul has referred to the Corinthians as *wise* *(phronimoi)* only in a highly ironic sense. The word *yourselves* is supplied in the tr.

20. *You put up with it.* The introductory *gar* ("for"), omitted in this tr., shows that what follows is intended to elaborate v. 19. The verb *(anechesthe)* is used ironically, as in vv. 4 and 19. Plummer, 315, cites a nice parallel from the speech of Ananus as re-created by Josephus *(War* IV.iii.10): "When plundered you put up with it [*aneches-the*], when beaten you are silent . . . ," etc.

*when someone.* The phrase *(ei tis)* is repeated five times in this verse for rhetorical effect. The Greek *ei* ("if") has been translated as *when* because the reality of what follows is taken for granted; the *tis* means "anyone at all" (see note on 10:7), but Paul's rivals (as a group) are clearly in view.

*enslaves.* The verb *(katadouloun)* is used elsewhere by Paul only in Gal 2:4, where he is thinking of bondage to the law. Here Paul thinks of the enslavement of a congregation under domineering pastoral leadership, something he seeks to avoid in his own apostolic work (1:24; 12:14; cf. 4:5).

*eats you up.* In Gal 5:15 the same verb *(katesthiein)* is used metaphorically (with *daknein,* "to bite"), as it also is in Matt 23:14 par.; Luke 15:30; John 2:17; Rev 11:5; 20:9. This could also be true here, in which case the reference would be to exploitation rather generally (e.g., *NEB, NIV:* "exploits you"); similar instances of the metaphor in Hellenistic literature are noted in BAG s.v. 2 and Betz 1979:276–77. Or, one may take the word here—in a more literal sense—as equivalent to "plunder" in v. 8 (so Windisch, 347), and thus as a further reference to the opponents' dependence on the Corinthian congregation for their livelihood (e.g., Barrett, 291: "eats you out of house and home" [citing 1 Cor 9:4ff.]; *JB:* "makes you feed him").

*takes you in.* Lattey 1943:148, on the basis of LXX Gen 37:24; 2 Kgdms (2 Sam) 21:8; 4 Kgdms (2 Kgs) 10:7; Jer 52:24, 26, would interpret the verb here *(lambanein)* as "lay hands upon you," to take by violence or to seize. But the use of the same verb in 12:16 is more pertinent, and suggests the meaning "to bring under one's control" (cf. Barrett, 291 ["gets you in his power"]; Zmijewski 1978:211).

*acts presumptuously.* Or, "puts on airs." In Sir 11:4 the verb *(epairesthai)* is parallel with *kauchasthai,* "to boast," and it is therefore appropriate that Paul should use the verb here of his rivals, whom he has already charged with boasting that their standing is equal with his.

*slaps you in the face.* The expression is probably to be taken figuratively: to "insult" or otherwise demean someone (so, e.g., Plummer, 316–17; Windisch, 347; Zmijewski 1978:212—although Hughes, 400, understands it literally).

21a. *I am ashamed to say.* More literally, "I speak with respect to shame" *(kata atimian legō),* without any explicit indication of who is shamed, Paul (so most commentators) or his congregation (so Lietzmann, 149; Schlatter, 651). The context, however, requires the former (see especially Plummer, 317; Kümmel, 211).

*that.* Translates *hōs hoti,* the same expression which seems to introduce a quotation in 5:19 (see NOTES there). Some (e.g., Schmithals 1971:178 n. 93) suggest the same usage in this passage, but that would require one to understand a *legousin* ("they say") after *hōs* ("as"). It is more likely that *hoti* is dependent directly on *legō (I . . . say)* and that the *hōs* qualifies what follows as Paul's subjective judgment—in this case an ironic concession to the claims of his opponents (see BAG s.v. *hoti,* 1d$\beta$; Zmijewski 1978: 214–15).

*we seem to have been weaklings.* The English phrase *seem to have been* attempts to convey the force of the Greek *hōs* (see preceding note). The pronoun is emphatic in Greek *(hēmeis, we)* because Paul is contrasting his apostolate with the conduct of his rivals (v. 20). The first person plural, used here momentarily, is less forceful than the first person singular would have been, and thus goes better with the ironic confession of weakness (cf. Zmijewski 1978:215). Paul has been called "weak" by his critics (10:10). "Weakness" *(astheneia)* is also associated with "shame" or "dishonor" *(atimia)* in 1 Cor 4:10; 15:43. This and related terms are frequent in chaps. 10–13 (see also 11:29, 30; 12:5, 9, 10; 13:3, 4, 9), but none of them is present in chaps. 1–9.

*in comparison.* There is no corresponding phrase in Greek, but the context warrants supplying it since Paul is contrasting his "weakness" with the brute force exercised by his rivals (v. 20).

## COMMENT: GENERAL

In the final paragraph of chap. 10 (vv. 12–18) Paul is critical of those who, by recommending themselves to and claiming a certain authority over the Corinthian congregation, have encroached upon his apostolic jurisdiction. This criticism is continued, indeed sharpened, in 11:1–12:13, which by reason of the way it is introduced and concluded (see especially 11:1 and 12:11) is aptly described as "a fool's speech." Here the apostle deliberately—but nonetheless reluctantly—adopts the procedure of his rivals and boasts of his own credentials. This is a dangerous tactic, for Paul has just quoted scripture against boasting of this sort (10:17–18); but he clearly feels constrained to it in order to regain the confidence of the congregation. Plutarch's essay *On Praising Oneself Inoffensively* helps to show how the pros and cons of this practice could be evaluated in the Hellenistic era (see P. Marshall 1980:546–49; Forbes 1982:10–13).

The passage before us stands as an extended prologue to the speech proper, which commences only with 11:21*b*. In fact, the prologue could have been much briefer, consisting of no more than what is said in v. 16: *Let no one think I am a fool. But should it be otherwise, at least accept me as a fool so I too can boast a little bit.* Similarly, the epilogue (12:11–13) could have been restricted to the short, retrospective comments of 12:11. But in both cases Paul's uneasiness about this whole *business of boasting* (v. 17) leads him into a nervous prolixity. This is especially true here in the prologue, where he argues that despite his refusal to accept financial assistance from the congregation he is in no way inferior to others who have received its support (vv. 5–15). These remarks are not a diversion from the issue facing Paul in Corinth; they are a diversion from the appeal of v. 1, which must then be renewed in v. 16. The prologue is therefore best subdivided into three major sections: vv. 1–4, 5–15 and 16–21*a*.

## COMMENT: DETAILED

### An Awkward Appeal, vv. 1–4

Because Paul anticipates that he may offend his readers with the boasting which is to follow, he begs their indulgence in advance, v. 1. (The technical rhetorical term for this is prodiorthosis; BDF § 495[3].) It is an awkward appeal, however, because he has just criticized his opponents for their boasting (10:12–18), and now he finds himself resorting to a similar kind of self-display. The foolishness of this is affirmed again in the epilogue to his speech (12:11), but it is significantly qualified in 11:16, 17. It is apparent that the apostle is uneasy in this role.

Paul supports his appeal, first, by portraying himself as a father who has pledged his virgin daughter to her future husband and is therefore responsible that she be presented to him pure and undefiled, vv. 2–3. The imagery here conforms to Jewish marriage customs, according to which the father of the bride-to-be is responsible for safeguarding his daughter's virginity between the time of her betrothal and the time when he actually leads her into the bride-groom's house (see Gen 29:23; Deut 22:13–21; Windisch, 320; Batey 1963: 178–79). In the OT, Israel is frequently depicted as betrothed to Yahweh (e.g., Isa 54:5–6; 62:5; Ezek 16:8; Hos 2:19–20), and in later rabbinic traditions Moses is sometimes thought of as the one who presents Israel to Yahweh as his bride (Bruce, 234, provides the references). Paul now thinks of the Christian community (specifically, his Corinthian congregation) as the *pure bride*, of *Christ* as the bridegroom, and of himself as the one who is *to present* the bride to her husband. This application of the OT imagery to a marriage between Christ and his church is also seen in Eph 5:23–32; Rev 19:7–9; 21:2, 9, and may be presumed in certain other NT passages as well. In Eph 5:27 it is clearly an eschatological "presentation" of the church to Christ that is in view, and this is also the case in the present passage. The pastoral affection (v. 2) and anxiety (v. 3) which Paul discloses here is for his congregation during the interval between their conversion to Christ and their ultimate presentation to him at his return (the Parousia). Note, however, that in Eph there is no conception of an apostolic mediator for that presentation (Windisch, 321–33), whereas here Paul thinks of himself as serving that function.

In v. 3 the apostle expresses his fear that his readers may not be able to keep their "virginity" intact for the coming of the one to whom they are betrothed. Although Paul has not abandoned hope for the congregation, he is aware of the reality of a present threat to its faith (Käsemann 1942:38), and he is clearly worried (Barrett, 273, compares this to the general statement of pastoral concern in 11:28) that his objective of capturing "every mind . . . for obedience to Christ" (10:5) may not be fulfilled in Corinth—that their *minds may be lured away from a total and a pure commitment to Christ.* His concern is not specifically with the Corinthians' moral behavior, but more fundamentally with the congregation's understanding of the gospel (Kümmel, 210; Barrett, 274) and its loyalty to Christ alone (Amstutz 1968:113; according to Jewish law the violation of a betrothed virgin is no less serious than if the marriage has been physically consummated—e.g., Deut 22:23–27; Philo, *Special Laws* I, 107; III, 72). Here, as in Gal 1:6–9 (discussed by Borse 1972:89–91) and Rom 16:17–20 (which Malherbe 1961:129 regards as the closest parallel), the apostle is aware of specific persons who would subvert the true gospel. The later, more direct attack upon them as *false apostles* and Satan's ministers in disguise (see vv. 13–15) is anticipated as Paul uses imagery evidently drawn from Jewish interpretations of Eve's seduction by the serpent in the garden. According to these legends the serpent was actually Satan and his designs on Eve were specifically sexual (see NOTES for details). It is the apostle's fear that in some similar way his readers may be lured away from Christ by the attention of seducers posing as ardent suitors (cf. Gal 4:17, cited by Windisch, 319). But as their "father" in Christ he is pledged to save them from this, and thus he begs for their patience as he prepares to do a little foolish boasting.

The appeal for patience (v. 1) is further supported in v. 4. Now it becomes evident that the congregation's defection to a false gospel is already under way. Since the Corinthians have been quite able to *put up with* those who preach a false gospel, they should certainly be able to indulge their own apostle in a little bit of foolish boasting. The irony here is gentle in comparison with that in vv. 19–21a, but the criticism of the Corinthians it contains is clear enough. They are in the process of succumbing to the teachings of certain persons who have come to Corinth (some sense an intended contrast here with Paul, who had been "sent" to Corinth as Christ's "apostle") bringing a different kind of gospel.

At first glance v. 4 would seem to offer valuable information about the identity of Paul's opponents, but upon closer inspection it is apparent that only three points can be established with certainty from it: (a) they are not themselves members of the congregation in Corinth, but are itinerant missionaries who have "come" from elsewhere (cf. the reference in Did 12:1–2 to "everyone who comes" as a traveling teacher); (b) not just their conduct and their attitude toward Paul are defective, but their preaching is, too; and (c) they have achieved a certain measure of success in the congregation. Who these people are, where they have come from, and why they have come are not indicated. Moreover, what is said about their teaching is so general as to have led interpreters to quite different conclusions about their theological point of view.

*Some other Jesus.* Does the use of the name *Jesus* (rather than "Christ" or "Jesus Christ") provide a clue to the identity of the rival preachers? A number of interpreters think so, but at least three different conclusions have been reached on the basis of it. (1) Some (e.g., Windisch, 328; Héring, 79; Tasker,

148; Bieder 1961:324; cf. Friedrich 1963b:189–91) believe it marks Paul's opponents as persons who view Jesus in an essentially Jewish way, as "purely human," declining to identify him with the risen Lord (cf. 4:10–14). (2) Schmithals argues, to the contrary, that the use of this simple name points to Gnostic preachers who regard the earthly Jesus as "the execrable dwelling of the heavenly spiritual being," although not as an integral part of the divine revelation itself (1971:134). (3) Georgi finds support here for his hypothesis that Paul's rivals were Hellenistic Jews who, contrary to the apostle, evaluated Jesus' earthly life as that of a "divine man" (1964:286).

It is doubtful whether 1 Cor 12:3 can be used to reject Schmithals' interpretation (2), as it has by some (e.g., Friedrich 1963b:189; Georgi 1964:285 and n. 6) who claim that Gnostics did not "preach Jesus" but cursed him, because it is by no means clear that 1 Cor 12:3 has Gnostics in view (see, e.g., Conzelmann 1975:204–6). Moreover, there is good evidence, at least for certain second-century Gnostics, that the earthly Jesus was highly esteemed as the *vas mundum* ("pure vessel") which had received the descending Christ (Irenaeus, *Against Heresies* I.xxx.12, cited by Pearson 1967:305; see also Gos Phil [CG II, *3*] 56, 4–15 [*NHLE,* 134]; 62, 7–17 [*NHLE,* 137]; Acts Pet 12 Apost [CG VI, *1*] 6, 14–19 [*NHLE,* 268]; Ep Pet Phil [CG VIII, *2*] 133, 6–8 [*NHLE,* 395]). Indeed, the claims of Paul's opponents to be "Hebrews . . . Israelites . . . descendants of Abraham" (2 Cor 11:22) are not those one would expect from Gnostics. Furthermore, to the extent that Paul had faced any "Gnostic" problem in Corinth, it must have been essentially indigenous there (see 1 Cor) and not the result of outsiders coming in (cf. Windisch, 328). Georgi's view (3) is also questionable, since there is no clear evidence that a "divine man" concept was current in Hellenistic Judaism in the first century (see especially Holladay 1977). And against the conclusion that *Jesus* indicates interlopers who preached a "merely human Jesus" (1), it must be noted that elsewhere Paul alludes to the claims of his opponents that they belong in a special way to "Christ" (10:7; 11:23).

The fact is that Paul, upon occasion, can use the simple name *Jesus* as a full equivalent for "Jesus Christ" (4:5; Rom 3:26 [cf. v. 22], cited by Barrett 1971:241) or "the Lord Jesus" (4:14, cf. vv. 10–11). It is therefore quite possible that here, along with references to *another Spirit* and *another gospel,* this characterization of his rivals as preaching *some other Jesus* is intended only as a general condemnation of their teaching—and, if so, it would not be any more precise than the criticism Paul directs against his opponents in Galatia, Gal 1:6–9 (against Georgi 1964:284–85). It is not even clear that this verse warrants the identification of "Christology" as the basic difference between Paul and his opponents in Corinth (so Georgi ibid.), since nowhere else in 2 Cor is Christology taken up as a topic in and for itself—not even in 3:7–18; 4:4–6, 9–14; 5:14–19, where the real theme is the nature of Paul's apostolic service.

*Another Spirit . . . another gospel.* These phrases provide even fewer possibilities for identifying the opponents and characterizing their teaching than the reference to *some other Jesus*. No other references to the Spirit occur in the course of Paul's argument here in chaps. 10–13. And insofar as he has the preaching of his rivals in view when he writes of the Spirit in chaps. 1–9, it would appear that the opponents leave little or no room for the Spirit, not that they teach *another Spirit* (3:3, 6, 7–18; cf. 1:22; 4:13; 5:5; 6:6; cf. Windisch, 328). Similarly, to identify this different Spirit with the "spirit of slavery" (Rom 8:15), which Paul associates with "the law of sin and death" in Rom 8:2ff. (so, e.g., Plummer, 297), is to connect it with a topic (the law versus the gospel) which is nowhere specifically addressed in chaps. 10–13 and which is only indirectly present in chaps. 1–9 (3:7–4:6). For this same reason it is wrong to think that the reference to *another gospel*, simply because it is parallel to Gal 1:6–9, indicates that the opponents are preaching a "gospel of works" (so, e.g., Windisch, 328). From the context here it is evident that Paul understands the primary threat to be to his apostolic authority and jurisdiction (10:7–18; 11:12–15, etc.), and this in itself would be a sufficient reason (quite apart from any specific errant teaching about Jesus, the Spirit, the law, etc.) for him to refer to his rivals as bringing *another gospel* (cf. Bultmann, 204).

### Some Remarks on the Question of Status, vv. 5–15

In vv. 2–3, 4 the apostle, intent on supporting the appeal of v. 1, has alluded to certain persons who have brought alien teachings to Corinth and who are subverting his work there. Although v. 5, taken by itself, constitutes additional support for the initial appeal (since Paul is not of inferior status, he too should be allowed to boast), it actually becomes the topic sentence (cf. Zmijewski 1978:114) for a somewhat more direct and specific discussion of the objectives and tactics of the rival preachers themselves.

As Paul in 10:7 has affirmed his equality with those who claim to be Christ's in some special way, so now in v. 5 he claims equal status with those he calls *super-apostles*. It would appear that we are in touch here with the fundamental theme of the entire fool's speech, because this same claim is repeated in the epilogue (12:11c), and the speech proper opens on a similar note (11:21b–22). But then what of 11:12–15, where instead of pleading the equality of his apostolic status Paul denounces his rivals as *false apostles* and *deceitful workers*? This raises the important question of whether the *super-apostles* of 11:5 and 12:11c are to be identified with the *false apostles* of 11:13, and thus with the outsiders who have been preaching *another gospel* to the Corinthians (11:4), or whether they are to be distinguished from these intruders.

### The Super-Apostles, vv. 5–6

Most of the patristic commentators seem to have distinguished the *super-apostles* from Paul's Corinthian rivals. Thus, Chrysostom remarked that, in

11:5, Paul is "no longer making comparison" with the intruders mentioned in v. 4, but rather, now, with the leaders of the Jerusalem church, "Peter and James and John," who are therefore lauded (*met' enkomiōn*, "with encomiums") as *the super-apostles* (*NPNF*, 1st ser. XII:385). The same interpretation is defended by Baur (1875–76, I:285), who does not, however, regard the phrase *super-apostles* as unambiguously laudatory, but describes it as "admirably chosen . . . to show that [Paul] had no fault to find with themselves, but only with the exaggerated view of them held by others" (cf. Heinrici, 354; Schlatter, 636–40).

More recently, this general interpretation has been expounded by Käsemann (1942:41–48) and Barrett (1971, especially 242–44, 249–53), who provide the most important arguments in defense of it. Foremost among these are: (1) Paul could hardly be expected to claim equal standing with those he regards as *false apostles* (11:13) and ministers of Satan (11:14–15), whereas he does draw a similar comparison between himself and the original apostles in 1 Cor 15:9 (cf. especially 2 Cor 12:11c); (2) the dispute about apostolic jurisdiction (10:12–18) makes sense against the background of Paul's agreement with the Jerusalem leaders about the division of missionary responsibilities (Gal 2:9), and the mild irony of the phrase *super-apostles* conforms to that of the reference in Gal 2:9 to James and Cephas and John as men "reputed to be pillars" (*RSV*); (3) after each of his references to *the super-apostles* (2 Cor 11:5; 12:11c) Paul proceeds to address the matter of financial support for apostles (11:7–11, 12; 12:13, 14–15), and this conforms to 1 Cor 9, where he compares his standing with that of "the other apostles and the brothers of the Lord and Cephas" (v. 5, *RSV*) when it comes to eligibility for such support. If, then, the *super-apostles* are to be identified with Peter and his colleagues in Jerusalem, one may suppose that Paul mentions them here because the *false apostles* who are actually present in Corinth claim to have been sent out by them, or at least to have their backing (so, e.g., Käsemann 1942:46–47).

Although this hypothesis explains the alleged discrepancy between the comparison made in 11:5 and the denunciation leveled in 11:12–15, it presents its own difficulties, as most interpreters have recognized (admirably summarized by Windisch, 330; see also, e.g., Meyer, 644; Plummer, 298; Kümmel, 210; Munck 1959:177–78; Hughes, 378–80; Schmithals 1971:133; Georgi 1964:39, 48–49; Oostendorp 1967:11 n. 16).

(1) Immediately preceding his first reference to *super-apostles* in 11:5, Paul's attention has been focused on the outsiders who are now in Corinth preaching an alien gospel (v. 4). These are unquestionably the same as the *false apostles* and *deceitful workers* of v. 13. It is difficult to believe that the reference to *super-apostles* in the very next sentence could have different persons in mind. Barrett thinks this argument has no real force because the comparison in v. 5 functions to support the appeal in v. 1 and is not directly linked to v. 4 (1971:243). But the appeal of v. 1 itself springs from Paul's concern to match

the boasting of the intruders with his own, as shown not only by vv. 2–3 but especially by the remarks in vv. 16–21a, where the appeal is renewed.

(2) Since the comparison made in v. 5 is explained in v. 6, and the two verses constitute "one integrated statement" (Thrall 1980:45, who offers solid grammatical reasons for this conclusion), one must presume that the *super-apostles* are still in mind in v. 6. But Paul's concession in v. 6a that he is *an amateur in public speaking* would hardly be necessary if he were comparing himself with the Jerusalem apostles. They could not have qualified as more polished orators than he—certainly not in Greek (note Acts 4:13)—and there is no unambiguous evidence, besides, that they had ever been in Corinth. Thrall's attempt to answer these two points (ibid.:46, 47) is not convincing. Her own conclusion is that Paul is not fully informed about the claims his opponents were making, so he has to allow that some may actually be "original apostles" from Jerusalem: "hence his duality of approach" (i.e., comparison and denunciation; ibid.:55).

(3) The mention of the *super-apostles* in 12:11c occurs in the epilogue to the fool's speech which looks back over the speech proper (11:21b–12:10), in which Paul is comparing himself not with the Jerusalem apostles but with those who have intruded themselves into the Corinthian congregation (the self-styled "ministers of Christ," 11:23, are certainly those whom Paul characterizes as Satan's ministers in 11:14–15). Here again the context makes it probable that Paul is using the term *super-apostles* in a highly ironic way to refer to his opponents, who are making pretentious claims in order to win the allegiance of the Corinthian Christians (cf. P. Marshall 1980:574).

Although the points which have been registered against this identification and in favor of the identification of the *super-apostles* with Peter and his colleagues need to be taken seriously, they are by no means decisive. (1) It may be, as some have argued, that Paul is willing to compare himself with the false apostles—even as he denounces them—in order to get his readers to take him seriously (Bultmann 1947:26; Schmithals 1971:133 n. 24; Oostendorp 1967:11 n. 16). Be that as it may, he certainly does compare himself with them (e.g., 11:22), even though it violates his own best judgment to do so (cf. 10:12, 17–18). This is one reason why he must admit he is talking like a fool. (2) It is doubtful whether Paul's comments about apostolic jurisdiction in 10:12–18 have the "Jerusalem agreement" of Gal 2:9 in view (see NOTES and COMMENT on 10:13); thus, while the ironic use of the term *super-apostles* is analogous to the use of the term "pillars" in Gal 2:9, one need not conclude that the former, like the latter, refers to James and Cephas and John. (3) Although "the brothers of the Lord and Cephas" are mentioned in 1 Cor 9:5, where Paul is concerned to explain why he has not accepted financial support from the Corinthians, he also writes there about "the other apostles," meaning probably not the Twelve but "other missionaries" (so, e.g., Munck 1949:104; Lohse 1953:267; even Barrett 1968:203). It is therefore no argument for identifying

Peter and his colleagues as the *super-apostles* just because the latter, too, are mentioned in a context where apostolic support is the issue.

It is probable, therefore, that the term *super-apostles,* whether or not Paul himself coined it (Tasker, 149, thinks this likely; Hughes, 379 n. 40, thinks it unlikely), is used of his missionary rivals in Corinth, who are thus described because of the exaggerated claims they are making about themselves. Whether or not they have or claim to have the support of the Jerusalem leaders, it is apparent from 11:22 that they are proud of their Jewish heritage. It is equally certain, however, that their background is Hellenistic-Jewish, since Paul's concession in v. 6a makes it clear that they, unlike himself, were recognized by the Gentile Christians of Corinth as skilled in the rhetorical arts. It is possible that Paul's critics had themselves charged him with being only *an amateur in public speaking* (so Windisch, 331; Zmijewski 1978:121; cf. 10:10); or this concession may be part of his own attack on the sophistry of his opponents (Betz 1972:59, 60–66), in which case it should perhaps be taken with a grain of salt, as when similar anti-sophistic statements are made by the skilled Dio Chrysostom (e.g., XII, 13ff.; XXXV, 1, cited by Windisch, 332). Indeed, P. Marshall (1980:527–607) has shown how many traditional rhetorical techniques Paul himself uses in responding to the accusations of the rival apostles. In any case, Paul's concession in v. 6 accords with a number of instances in which he is critical of rhetorical ornamentation (2:17; 4:2, 7; 10: 4b–5 [with NOTES and COMMENT]; 1 Cor 1:17; 2:1, 4, 13; 1 Thess 2:4–5, 13 [cf. Gal 1:10]). Apparently he believes that unadorned speech is more appropriate for conveying the "folly" of the cross, in the very weakness of which God's power is disclosed (see especially 1 Cor 1:17, and cf. 2 Cor 4:7; 13:3–4; similarly Zmijewski 1978:122).

It seems that Paul's rivals have also accused him of lacking the kind of deep spiritual insight so emphasized in the Corinthian congregation (see NOTES and COMMENT on 10:5), probably contending that his plain speech was itself evidence for that lack (see COMMENT on 10:10). But the apostle is unwilling to concede any deficiency in *knowledge,* v. 6b. Instead, he protests that the way he has conducted his ministry in Corinth should be evidence enough of his stature as a spiritual leader, v. 6c. The form and, in part, the content of Paul's argument in this verse have parallels in Dio Chrysostom XXXII, 39 ("I am quite ordinary and prosaic in my public speaking, though not ordinary in my theme," cited by Mussies 1972:179) and in Josephus, who points out that Jews "do not favour those persons who have mastered the speech of many nations, or who adorn their style with smoothness of diction," but rather those who show their true wisdom by having "an exact knowledge of the law" (*Antiquities* XX.xii.1, cited by Windisch, 332, who also notes *Antiquities* XIV.i.1 and *Against Apion* 27). Similarly, Paul is firmly denying that rhetorical skill can be used as an index of a preacher's true knowledge, something the Corinthians were apparently being encouraged to believe.

*On Refusing Financial Support, vv. 7–11*

The very general statement of v. 6c is followed in vv. 7–11 by an example of one specific way in which Paul has demonstrated his spiritual insight (Bachmann, 368; Zmijewski 1978:124), although this involves the apostle in a defensive maneuver at the same time. With ironic exaggeration (a convention of Hellenistic polemical discourse; Betz 1972:100–1), Paul asks rhetorically whether by declining to accept financial support from the Corinthian congregation he has in fact committed some *sin,* v. 7. Criticism of him for declining such assistance is something Paul had tried to deal with in an earlier letter (1 Cor 9:3–18), but apparently not too successfully; or else the rival missionaries have revived the issue as part of their campaign to discredit his apostleship.

In the earlier letter Paul had staunchly defended his right as a legitimate apostle to be supported by those to whom he had been sent to preach (1 Cor 9:3–12a, 13–14), using scripture (Deut 25:4 in v. 9; Deut 18:1 in v. 13), the command of the Lord (v. 14, evidently alluding to the principle of Matt 10:10; cf. Luke 10:7), and common sense (vv. 7, 11) to establish the point. The same right is articulated in 1 Tim 5:18 and Did 13:1–2, which suggests that we are dealing here with an early Christian "missionary rule." It is significant, however, that in 1 Cor 9 the apostle defends with equal firmness his refusal to invoke his right to be supported, not only on the practical grounds that this might impede his missionary work (v. 12b), but also on the theological grounds that it would be inconsistent with the nature of his apostolic commission (vv. 16–18). Here another kind of "missionary rule" seems to be at work—namely, that the gospel must be given without cost to the hearers (note Matt 10:8; Acts 8:20; Rev 21:6; 22:17; Did 11:3–6, 8b–9, 12; Herm Man XI, 12).

The two principles are not necessarily incompatible if the one be regarded as a rule for the congregations (to establish their responsibility to support Christian leaders), and the other as a rule for the leaders themselves (to warn them that they should keep their motives pure and their priorities clear). But something has gone wrong in Corinth. Although Paul needed assistance when he was there, and even accepted help from elsewhere (2 Cor 11:8–9a), he declined it from the Corinthians themselves. His rivals, on the other hand, seem to have accepted—in Paul's view actually demanded—support from the congregation (v. 20), and it is perhaps they who have encouraged the Corinthians to think that Paul's remaining financially independent of them shows that he does not love them (v. 11).

It is probably no one factor, but a combination of factors that has put the apostle on the defensive in this regard. First, he had continued to work as a tent-maker (on this see Acts 18:3 and Hock 1980:20–25) during the time of his Corinthian ministry (Acts 18:1–3; 1 Cor 4:12; see Hock 1980:40–65). Among the philosophers and itinerant teachers of Paul's day, continuing to work at a craft was regarded as the least acceptable way of providing for life's necessities

(Hock 1980:56–59). This accords with the generally low estimate of craftsmen in the ancient world, reflected for example in Lucian's remark that they are "altogether demeaned" (*The Dream* 13, quoted more fully in the COMMENT on 10:11; many other examples are provided by MacMullen 1974:114–15). In 10:1, and now again in 11:7, Paul uses exactly the same word in speaking of the appearance he presented in Corinth—as one who "demeaned" himself—and his activity there as a craftsman no doubt contributed substantially to this (so also, e.g., Windisch, 334; Bultmann, 207; Hock 1978:561 and 1980:64).

It is probable, in the second place, that the Corinthians were distressed with Paul's refusal of support from them because it seemed inconsistent with his accepting support from other congregations. In Thessalonica, for example, Paul had received contributions from the Philippians at least twice (Phil 4:16) in order to supplement what he was able to earn from his craft (see 1 Thess 2:9), and the Philippians continued their support of his ministry even after he left Macedonia (Phil 4:15). Indeed, it is likely that the aid which was brought to him in Corinth by certain *brothers who came from Macedonia* (2 Cor 11:9) had been sent by the Philippians. It may have been Paul's custom to decline aid from every congregation while he was still present (see 1 Thess 2:9) and to accept aid only in the form of "missionary" support after he had moved on to a new field of service (see, e.g., Pratscher 1975:290–92). If so, that policy did not operate in the case of Corinth, for Paul declares emphatically not only that he never has accepted aid from the congregation there, but also that he has no immediate plans to do so (11:9*b;* 12:13). This would be further evidence for his critics of the inconstancy and inconsistency of which they have long suspected him (e.g., 1:17; cf. P. Marshall 1980:275–76, 502).

A third factor at work here involves something more serious than the appearance of procedural inconsistency. In the ancient world, giving and receiving, placing someone under and being oneself placed under financial obligation were extremely important components of the social structure. Thus, within Roman society specifically—and the Corinth Paul knew was a Roman colony—the wealthy expressed and enhanced their power by becoming patrons of the needy. The extent of one's philanthropies and the number of one's clients were important measures of a person's social standing and influence (see, e.g., MacMullen 1974, especially 106–7). To be the recipient of a benefaction was to be placed immediately under an obligation of gratitude to the benefactor, and the gratitude of the beneficiary in turn placed the benefactor under further obligation (see Mott 1975, especially 61–63, and Judge 1980b:211). Therefore, to accept a gift was to become a client of and dependent upon the more privileged person, even though the patron, too, assumed the obligation of further benefaction. At base, the relationship sprang not from friendship, although the conventions of friendship were there, but from the patron's quest for power and prestige and from the client's need to be helped. "One made friends by money" (Judge 1980b:214), and since friendship was based on benefaction, not the reverse, to refuse a benefaction was an act of social enmity, for which in Paul's day an elaborate protocol had been developed (fully described by P. Marshall 1980:12–202). If this social context is taken into account, it is understandable why the Corinthians were upset by Paul's refusal to accept their financial support: it was a renunciation of their status as a patron congregation (cf. 2 Cor 12:13) and therefore a repudiation of their friendship (cf. 11:11), as well as a regrettable act of self-humiliation (cf. 11:7 and Judge 1973:115; 1980b:214; P. Marshall 1980:260–397).

A final complicating factor was undoubtedly Paul's eagerness to have the Corinthians complete their contribution to his collection for the church in Jerusalem (see especially 2 Cor 8 and 9). His promotion of this project at the same time that he was declining to let the congregation become his own patron evidently aroused the suspicion, or allowed his rivals to plant the suspicion, that the collection was but a subterfuge, a way of gaining support from the Corinthians without obligating himself to them as their client (see 12:16). This, too, seems to lie behind Paul's remarks in 11:5–15.

It is apparent, then, that the point at issue is not only Paul's status as an apostle compared with the status of the so-called "super-apostles." The status of the congregation is also involved, for Paul's rivals seem to have encouraged the belief that by demeaning himself he has demeaned the Corinthians, and perhaps even defrauded them. On this reading of the situation, the remarks of 11:5–15 are readily understandable. Because Paul's acceptance of aid from the impoverished Macedonians (on their poverty see 8:2) must have been perceived by the relatively well-off Corinthians (see 8:14) as a special affront to themselves, he refers to it as "plunder" (11:8, 9a), the exact opposite of a benefaction. The point is that he was not a "client" of the Macedonians either. Moreover, he stresses that his concern was to serve the Corinthians, v. 8, and to avoid burdening them, v. 9 (cf. 12:14b). Here he may have in mind the false apostles, whom he will subsequently accuse of exploiting the congregation (v. 20; cf. Zmijewski 1978:135–36). More important, he is asserting his desire to be independent of anyone's patronage. This is consistent with his appeal to the Thessalonians that they should "work with [their] own hands" in order to "command the respect of outsiders, and be dependent on nobody" (1 Thess 4:11, 12). It also accords with Lucian's opinion that teachers who attach themselves to wealthy patrons—from whose standpoint the client represents a certain "burden" (*On Salaried Posts* 20)—have thereby been taken in like a fish on a baited hook (ibid. 3; Lucian's whole essay, cited and discussed by Hock 1980:30 and 55, is instructive). A similar concern for a philosopher's independence is expressed by Musonius (Fragment 11, quoted by Hock ibid.: 48). Whether the resolve in v. 9b means that Paul will never in the future accept aid from the Corinthians (so, e.g., Windisch, 337) or only that he will decline it so long as the present climate of distrust prevails (so, e.g., Pratscher 1979:293–94, 298) is unclear. In either case, the vow which follows in v. 10

makes the same point in another way: at least in the foreseeable future Paul intends that the congregation shall not be burdened with responsibility for his maintenance.

The questions Paul interposes in v. 11 *(Why? Because I do not love you?)* indicate his awareness of the criticism that his refusal of support from the Corinthians (v. 9b) stems from his lack of affection for them, perhaps from a breakdown of their partnership in the gospel (cf. Phil 4:15, cited by Hock 1980:63). His response is not to offer arguments to the contrary (see, e.g., 11:2; 12:14–15; also 6:11–13; 7:2–3) but to invoke God as his witness that the reasons he has just been giving for his behavior constitute a sure sign of his love. It comes down finally to two points—Paul's concern that the Corinthians *be exalted* (v. 7), and that they not be burdened with having to care for his personal needs (vv. 8–10). Although these two concerns are related, it is doubtful whether they should be equated (against Bultmann, 207). In the context of v. 7 the exaltation of the Corinthians would most naturally be their conversion to the gospel that Paul preached *free of charge* (cf. Windisch, 334; Zmijewski 1978:123–24). It is therefore parallel to the idea of being graced with the riches of salvation which appears in 6:10 and 8:9. Indeed, there is also a parallel between the way Paul depicts himself in 6:10 and 11:7—in the former as "impoverished—but enriching many," and in the latter as *demeaning* himself that others *might be exalted.* Because he serves the Christ who himself "became poor though he was rich" that others "might become rich" (8:9), his self-humiliation is not a sign of his inferior status, but of the authenticity of his apostleship (cf. 10:1, with COMMENT, and Zmijewski 1978:127). Paul has refused aid from the Corinthians not because he despises them but because he regards himself as responsible for them, as their father in the faith (11:2; 12:14–15).

### Satan's Ministers, vv. 12–15

Paul's remarks on status reach their climax here as he goes directly on the attack against his rivals. Previously in this letter he has argued that he is their equal (v. 5; 10:7b), and he will do so again, both in the fool's speech proper (11:21b–12:10) and in the epilogue to it (12:11–13). But in this passage he portrays them as the ones on the defensive and as wanting to be his equals, v. 12. That, however, Paul regards as impossible, since he has no immediate intention of reversing his policy of declining all financial aid from the Corinthian congregation (cf. v. 9b). The implication is that his rivals have accepted such aid (note also v. 20), that they will continue to do so, and that this proves they are not Paul's equals—that they are not in fact true apostles of the Christ who became poor that others might be enriched (see above on vv. 7–11).

In vv. 13–15, Paul is both supporting and broadening the criticism of his rivals begun in v. 12. Now the polemic becomes sharp and uncompromising as he labels his opponents *false apostles* and *deceitful workers,* v. 13. Given the portrait of these people which emerges from the letter (chaps. 10–13) as a whole, it is understandable why Paul regards them as *false apostles*. In his view they have presumptuously intruded into a congregation of his founding, thereby challenging his apostolic authority (10:7–11) and violating his apostolic jurisdiction (10:12–18); they have boasted in their own accomplishments (10:12; 11:12, 18, 21*b*) rather than in the Lord (10:17–18); they have preached another gospel with the intent of luring his converts away from the commitment to which he had led them (11:2–4); and, taking advantage of their boasted superiority, they have cruelly exploited the Corinthian congregation (11:20). That by *false* Paul does not just mean they are "errant" is made clear when he adds that they are *deceitful*. Although they present themselves as true *workers* (a technical term for missionaries; see NOTES) and *apostles of Christ*, they are guilty of a deliberate deception (cf. Barrett 1970b:383). It may be that Paul himself has been accused of deception by them (ibid.:390–91, cf. 385), but if so there is no trace of that here, where he is strictly on the offensive.

Paul's attack is intensified in vv. 14–15, where—without ever formulating the phrase as such—he accuses his opponents of being ministers of Satan, only masquerading as *ministers of righteousness* (that is, of God; see NOTES). According to certain Jewish traditions Satan *disguised* himself *as an angel of light* in order to seduce Eve (references in the NOTES; cf. v. 3, which echoes other legends that Satan came in the guise of the serpent). Although not many of the Gentile Christians in Corinth may have been familiar with these stories, Paul draws on them now to argue that the deception perpetrated by his opponents should come as no surprise, since they are ministers of Satan, the master deceiver (vv. 14*b*–15*a*). Formally, the argument here is similar to the typically rabbinic procedure of arguing "from the lesser to the greater" (as in 3:8 [with note], 9, 11), and Zmijewski has pointed out that semantically it resembles the proposition of Matt 10:25 that "the slave is like his master" (1978:164). No more serious charge can be brought against the false apostles; for if they are really Satan's ministers, and not Christ's (as they claim to be, v. 23*a*), they are not merely opponents of Paul, but of God, of Christ, and of the gospel. This is hardly less severe than the condemnation in 1 John 4:1–3 (noted by Strachan, 24) of certain "false prophets" who are said to be representatives of the Antichrist. Indeed, the severity of Paul's charge would seem to preclude what is in any case the rather far-fetched suggestion that his rivals are identified with Satan because they claim to represent Peter, who according to tradition (Matt 16:23 par.) had once been rebuked by Jesus with the words "Get behind me, Satan!" (Thrall 1980, especially 50–56). The apostle's reference to the judgment which awaits these deceivers, v. 15*b*, is the more impressive for being so abrupt (Héring, 82), and it stands not as a general remark about the accountability of all believers (as in 5:10) but as a specific warning to a particular group (as in Phil 3:19, against "enemies of the cross of Christ," v. 18).

*Renewal of the Appeal, vv. 16–21a*

Here Paul restates the appeal with which he had started out in v. 1. He proposes to engage in *a little bit* of boasting, and even though his readers may think that is foolish, as he himself believes, he hopes that they will give him a hearing, if only *as a fool* (v. 16). Although vv. 17–18 are properly regarded as parenthetical (so also *RSV;* Zmijewski 1978:195), they have an important function in the context (cf. Zmijewski ibid.:219). On the one hand, they support the appeal of v. 16 by explaining that Paul has been forced into boasting by the rival apostles (v. 18; cf. v. 12). The boasting to which he has been forced would include, although subsequent paragraphs will show that it is not restricted to, his boast that he has not been dependent on the Corinthians for his livelihood (vv. 9–10). On the other hand, vv. 17–18 also explain why Paul must regard all boasting as essentially foolish—because it is not a speaking *in the Lord* (v. 17) but a speaking *in a worldly way* (v. 18). Therefore, *when it comes to this business of boasting* he will not be addressing them as an apostle, but as a worldly man driven to self-praise by the exigencies of the situation. This position is all the more awkward for him since he has been sharply critical of the worldly boasting of his opponents (5:12; 10:12–18). As elsewhere, these opponents are referred to in veiled language, here simply as *many* (cf. 2:17), and this oblique manner of reference (see also *a person,* v. 4; *such people,* v. 13, *someone,* vv. 20, 21*b,* etc.) is a further way of seeking to diminish their stature in the eyes of the Corinthians (cf. Zmijewski 1978:202; P. Marshall 1980:528–38, who discusses the non-naming of one's enemies as a Hellenistic rhetorical convention).

Although the parenthetical comments of vv. 17–18 serve in their own way as support for the renewed appeal in v. 16, the main support for that is presented in vv. 19–21*a.* Verses 19–20 are parallel to v. 4, which had supported the original formulation of the appeal by noting that the Corinthians were indeed tolerating preachers who had come with an alien gospel. That point is now repeated in v. 19, although here the apostle is far less restrained in his use of irony. In v. 4 the rival preachers had been referred to by the neutral, generic term *a person;* here they are called *fools.* Here the adverb *gladly* intensifies the less emphatic *well enough* in v. 4. And here, to heighten the irony further, Paul refers to the Corinthians sarcastically as *wise* (cf. 1 Cor 4:10). It was a commonplace of ancient oratorical style to intermingle praise of one's audience with one's appeals to them (see, e.g., Plutarch, *On Praising Oneself Inoffensively* 9), but the irony of the apostle's "praise" in v. 19 turns it into the sharpest criticism. This is extended and intensified in v. 20, which is aptly characterized as "a grotesque parody" of the behavior of Paul's opponents (Zmijewski 1978:230). One should not press the series of terms used here *(enslaves you . . . eats you up . . . takes you in . . . acts presumptuously . . . slaps* *you in the face)* too closely for the particulars of what the intruders have been doing to the Corinthians (see NOTES for certain suggestions). The general point is clear enough—that Paul believes his rivals have tyrannized and exploited the congregation. Given the context (especially vv. 7–11), their dependence upon the congregation for financial support is probably uppermost in the apostle's mind (so Friedrich 1963b:188), but it is likely that he also wishes to characterize them as domineering over the Corinthians in a more general sense, not least with their pretentious self-praise.

The picture drawn of the opponents in v. 20 contrasts sharply with the concept of pastoral leadership to which Paul is committed. He and his coworkers do not want the Corinthians to think of them as their "lords" ("domineering over [their] faith," 1:24), but as their "slaves" ("for Jesus' sake," 4:5); or—using a different metaphor—as their parents upon whom they are dependent, not for whom they must provide (12:14b–15a). Indeed, in the final, ironic statement of this prologue, Paul caricatures his own ministry as one of *weaklings* when compared with that of his opponents, v. 21a. Here, as, e.g., in 1 Cor 4:10, he appears to accept the judgment of his critics (cf. 10:1, 10) that his social standing is very low (see Forbes 1978). But this concession itself is ironic, since Paul will go on to insist that his "weakness" is his greatest boast (see COMMENT on v. 30).

### 4. THE SPEECH PROPER, 11:21b–12:10

11    ²¹ᵇIn whatever respect someone is audacious (I am speaking foolishly), in that respect I, too, am audacious. ²²Are they Hebrews? I am, too. Are they Israelites? I am, too. Are they descendants of Abraham? I am, too. ²³ᵃAre they ministers of Christ? (I am out of my mind to speak this way.) I am more of one:

²³ᵇwith many more labors, many more imprisonments, far worse beatings, often at the point of death;

²⁴from the Jews on five occasions I received the forty lashes minus one; ²⁵three times I have been beaten with the rod; once I was stoned; three times shipwrecked; a night and a day I spent out in the water;

²⁶on many journeys, risking dangers from rivers, dangers from bandits, dangers from my people, dangers from the Gentiles, dangers in the city, dangers in the open country, dangers at sea, dangers among false brothers and sisters;

²⁷with labor and toil, many sleepless nights, hunger and thirst, many times without food, cold and ill-clothed.

²⁸Not to mention other things, there is the pressure I am under every

day, my anxiety for all the churches. [29]Who is weak and I am not weak? Who is made to stumble and I do not burn with indignation? [30]If boasting is necessary, I will boast about my weaknesses. [31]God, the Father of the Lord Jesus, who is blessed forever, knows I am not lying. [32]At Damascus, the ethnarch under King Aretas was guarding the city of the Damascenes in order to seize me, [33]and I was lowered in a basket through a window in the wall and escaped his hands.

**12** [1]Boasting is necessary. Although it is not beneficial, I shall move on to visions and revelations granted by the Lord. [2]I know a person in Christ who fourteen years ago was caught up (whether it was in the body or outside the body I do not know; God knows) clear to the third heaven. [3]Indeed, I know such a person (whether in the body or apart from the body I do not know; God knows)—[4]that he was caught up into Paradise and heard things that must not be divulged, which it is forbidden a human being to repeat. [5]I will boast on behalf of such a person, but on my own behalf I will not boast, except of weaknesses. [6]For should I wish to boast, I will not be a fool, for I shall be telling the truth. But I am declining to do this, so that no one can credit me with something beyond what one may see me doing or hear from me, [7]specifically, because of the extraordinary character of the revelations. For this reason, that I not be overly exalted, there was given to me a thorn in the flesh, an angel of Satan to abuse me, that I not be overly exalted. [8]Three times I appealed to the Lord about this, that it should go away from me. [9]And he said to me: "My grace is enough for you; for power is made fully present in weakness." Rather, then, I will very gladly boast of my weaknesses, that the power of Christ may reside with me. [10]So because of Christ I am pleased with weaknesses, with insults, with catastrophes, with persecutions and pressures. For when I am weak, then I am powerful.

## NOTES

11:21*b*. *someone.* As in 10:7; 11:20, *tis* has Paul's rivals especially in view. When Barrett, 292, translates this as "anyone else" he is taking unwarranted liberty with the text, all the more serious because he proceeds to identify this word as indicating Paul's shift of focus from his competitors in Corinth to the Jerusalem leaders whose authority they claim (ibid.).

*is audacious.* The verb is *tolman,* as in 10:2, 12. See the note on "to summon up courage" in 10:2.

*foolishly.* Literally "in [or: with] foolishness," as in 11:17; cf. 11:1 (with NOTES and

COMMENT). Here (and again in v. 23a) Paul excuses himself in advance for what he is about to say (prodiorthosis; see BDF § 495[3]).

*I, too.* This expression *(kagō)* is repeated three times in the next verse.

22. *Hebrews.* A title of honor, used primarily of one's ethnic descent. It may also suggest the Palestinian origin of one's family (or of oneself) and one's command of Hebrew or Aramaic; see Gutbrod, *TDNT* III:388–91. Cf. especially Phil 3:5, "a Hebrew of Hebrews"; also Eusebius, *Ecclesiastical History* II.iv.2, where Philo, the Alexandrian philosopher, is described as "descended from Hebrew stock," and IV.iv.2, where Trypho of Ephesus is called "a most distinguished Hebrew" (both passages cited by Friedrich 1963b:181–82). Elsewhere in the NT the name is used only in Acts 6:1, where the "Hebrews" are distinguished from the "Hellenists" in the Christian community of Jerusalem.

*I am, too.* As in v. 21b, and twice more in this verse, *kagō.*

*Israelites.* The Greek expression is *Israēlitai,* not *huioi Israēl* ("sons of Israel") as in 3:7, 13. As Paul uses the term, an "Israelite" is one who belongs to the "stock" *(to genos)* of Israel (note Phil 3:5, "of the people [*ek genous*] of Israel" [*RSV*]; cf. 4 Mac 18:1, quoted in following note), and especially one who shares in Israel's religious heritage and traditions (Rom 9:4; 11:1). It thus includes the ethnic aspect of "Hebrew," but focuses more particularly on the religious meaning of being a Jew; cf. Georgi 1964:60–63.

*descendants of Abraham.* Literally "the seed [*sperma*] of Abraham." The expression is hardly to be distinguished from *Israelites* (preceding note), as is suggested by the same juxtaposition of the two titles in Rom 11:1 ("I myself am an Israelite, a descendant of Abraham" [*RSV*]; cf. 4 Mac 18:1, "O Israelites, children born of the seed of Abraham, obey this Law" [*APOT*]). If anything were added here, it would be an allusion to the promise given to Abraham, which Paul identifies with the gospel; see especially Rom 4:13–18; 9:6–8; Gal 3:16–18.

23a. *ministers of Christ.* Only here and in Col 1:7 in the NT, but one may compare 1 Tim 4:6 ("a minister of Christ Jesus") and Pol Phil 5:2 ("ministers of God and of Christ"). Cf. also 2 Cor 6:4 ("ministers of God") and 3:6 (with note); 11:15.

*out of my mind.* Translates the participle *paraphronōn,* which is somewhat stronger than the idea of "foolishness" present in v. 21b.

*I am more of one.* This expression *(hyper egō)* represents a rhetorical heightening of *I am, too* in vv. 21b–22, and also of the claim in 11:5; 12:11c (Bultmann 1947:26). Paul does not say that he is something "more than" a servant of Christ; here *hyper* is used adverbially in approximately the same way as *mallon* is in Phil 3:4: "to a higher degree" or "better" (BDF § 230). Zmijewski (1978:241–43) prefers to understand the expression in a superlative sense, perhaps something like "I am the very best" (cf. *hyperlian* ["super-"] in 11:5). But the *hyper* in v. 21a seems to be specified in the twofold *perissoterōs* of v. 21b (Fridrichsen 1928:26), and this points rather to a comparative meaning. The words *of one* have been supplied for the sake of tr. into English. In Greek, as Spencer (1981:353) observes, there is an ellipsis—where one would expect "I [am] even more [a minister of Christ]"—the effect of which is to emphasize the omitted phrase.

23b. *with . . . labors . . . imprisonments . . . beatings . . . death.* All four nouns are plural, including (in Greek) the last one; each is preceded by the preposition *en* (here translated *with*), and each is represented in at least one of the other hardship lists in the Pauline letters (details below).

*many more labors.* In v. 27, *labor* certainly refers to Paul's work as a craftsman, and that may be the meaning here as well, even though the plural is used; see also 1 Cor 4:12 (the cognate verb). If so, then one could regard the further listing in v. 27 as an elaboration. One might also argue, however, that the plural should be interpreted in accord with 10:15, where it clearly refers to Paul's missionary activities; see NOTES on 6:5*b*, where the plural is used in a similar list of hardships. It seems probable that the adverb *perissoterōs* should be taken here as indicating greater frequency (thus, *many more*), since it most naturally has that meaning when it is used with *imprisonments* in the very next phrase. But it could mean *labors* of greater difficulty or, perhaps, of greater extent.

*many more imprisonments.* As in the hardship list at 5:4*c*–5, Paul refers here to imprisonments (plural), even though Acts recounts but one brief incarceration up to this point in his career (in Philippi, Acts 17:23–40); for possible explanations see NOTES and COMMENT on 6:5*a*.

*far worse beatings.* Paul varies the adverb, *hyperballontōs (far worse)* now replacing *perissoterōs,* which had been used with the two preceding terms in the list. *Beatings* are also mentioned in 6:5*a*, but immediately preceding *imprisonments* rather than immediately following. Two different types of beatings are mentioned in 11:24–25.

*often at the point of death.* In Greek the word *death,* like the three preceding terms, is actually plural here, leading some to interpret this as "mortal dangers" (e.g., Héring, 83; Bultmann, 217). However, the specification of these in vv. 24–25 suggests that the apostle is thinking not just generally of threats to his life, but of particular experiences which brought him close to death. Cf. 4:12, "death is made active in us," referring back to the hardships listed in 4:8–9 as well as to Jesus' death in 4:10, and the quotation of LXX Ps 43[44]:22 in Rom 8:36, which supports the hardship list in the preceding verse.

24. *from the Jews.* The preposition *(hypo)* could also be rendered "at the hands of" (Plummer, 323); for the whole expression cf. 1 Thess 2:14. A certain emphasis attaches to the phrase here, not only because it stands first (see following note) but also because no agent is specified for either of the similar experiences which follow immediately in the list (v. 25).

*on five occasions.* The numerical reference is somewhat less prominent in this first example of death-dealing experiences than in those which follow in v. 25, simply because this first one has been introduced with reference to the agents. But here, too, the number is important, for it adds to the overall impressiveness of the list. Cf. the patterned enumeration of Augustus' honors on the *Monumentum Ancyranum:* e.g., "Twice I received triumphal ovations. Three times I celebrated curule triumphs. Twenty times and one did I receive the appellation of imperator" (Hardy 1923:37). Similarly, the tabulated exploits of Pompey (Pliny, *Natural History* VII.xxvi.98), Lucius Siccius Dentatus (ibid.101–3), M. Manlius Capitolinus (ibid.103–4), and Julius Caesar (*Civil Wars* II, 32).

*the forty lashes minus one.* Deut 25:1–3 provides that one convicted in a court of law may be punished with whipping, the number of blows to be proportionate to the seriousness of the offense but in no case to exceed forty. The present list is the earliest evidence for the practice of stopping one short of the maximum allowed, probably to avoid going over the maximum due to a miscount. See also Josephus, *Antiquities* IV.viii.21 (a "most disgraceful penalty"), 23. The later rabbinic tractate *Makkot* indicates some of the crimes for which this punishment was administered (3.1–9), and explains that the administrator was liable if more than forty blows had been given (3.10–14).

25. *three times . . . beaten with the rod.* A specifically Roman punishment, as Paul's readers in the Roman colony of Corinth would have known very well. Roman officials entitled to mete out punishments were customarily accompanied by "lictors," who bore wooden rods with which beatings such as those referred to here could be administered. Although a law promulgated under M. Porcius Cato, probably in 198 B.C.E., prohibited the scourging of Roman citizens (see, e.g., Livy X.ix.4–5), the law was frequently ignored. Thus, Josephus (*War* II.xiv.9) refers to Florus—who scourged and even crucified Jews of Roman equestrian rank; Plutarch (*Caesar* XXIX, 2) writes of Marcellus—who, "while he was consul, beat with rods a senator of Novum Comum who had come to Rome"; and Cicero (*Against Verres* II.v.139) accuses the governor of Sicily of beating Roman citizens. The case of Gaius Servilius (described by Cicero, ibid. 140–42) illustrates how severe a beating with rods could be. According to Acts 16:22, Paul and Silas had been stripped and beaten with rods at the order of the Roman magistrates (Greek: *stratēgoi*) in Philippi, despite Paul's right, as a Roman citizen, to appeal (Acts 16:37). This is doubtless the occasion Paul has in mind in 1 Thess 2:2. Apparently he experienced such beatings on other occasions as well. For general discussions of Paul and the Roman law, see Cadbury in *BC* V:297–338 and Sherwin-White 1963:48–119.

*once I was stoned.* In Lystra, according to Acts 14:19, Paul had been stoned by a mob stirred up by hostile Jews from Antioch and Iconium. This is presumably the incident to which Paul refers here. One is not to think of the specifically Jewish punishment (provided for, e.g., in the Mishna, *Sanh.* 61ff.), but of mob action in which Gentiles as well may have participated (see Acts 14:5–6). A stoning of Paul is also listed in 1 Clem 5:6.

*three times shipwrecked.* Acts reports no experiences of shipwreck endured by Paul up to this point in his ministry (that of Acts 27 is later), but the apostle was frequently on the sea: Acts 13:4 (from Seleucia to Cyprus), 13 (Paphos to Perga); 14:25–26 (Attalia to Antioch); 16:11 (Troas to Neapolis via Samothrace); 17:14–15 (Macedonia to Athens); 18:18–22 (Corinth to Caesarea via Ephesus), 27 (Ephesus to Achaia [probably Corinth]). To these one may add the emergency visit Paul had made to Corinth from Ephesus (2 Cor 2:1, with NOTES and COMMENT) and, probably, his journey from Troas to Macedonia in order to meet Titus (2 Cor 2:13; 7:5). Despite the ever-present danger of shipwreck (see Seneca, *On Leisure* VIII, 4), ancient sailing vessels carried no lifeboats (Casson 1974:157). The Romans, especially, were nervous about sea travel (ibid.:149–50, 346–47). It was regarded as a life-threatening experience (e.g., Epictetus II.vi.20, cited by Hock 1980:79 n. 19). Dio Chrysostom recounts a shipwreck on the eastern coast of Euboea which he survived (VII, 2–10; cited by Mussies 1972:179), and Synesius, later the Christian bishop of Ptolemais, tells of his terrifying voyage from Alexandria to Cyrene in 404 C.E. (Epistle 4, quoted at length by Casson 1974:161–62).

*a night and a day.* In Greek the one copulative compound *nuchthēmeron*, referring to a full twenty-four-hour period; see BDF § 121. Cf. 1 Thess 2:9; 3:10 (where, however, the compound is not used). The emphasis, even in 1 Thess 3:10 ("praying . . . night and day"), is on the duration of the hardship. Contrast the contemporary inscription from Magnesia on the Maeander in which a certain Claudius is praised for many benefactions to his city, including the provision of oil "continuously . . . by day and by night" during the year he was gymnasiarch (text in Robert 1940:168, No. 152, lines 6–8).

*I spent.* Here the verb *poiein* is used in the sense of "spending time" (BAG s.v. I, 1e*y*). Although the preceding verbs in vv. 24–25 have been aorists, this one is perfect tense, perhaps without any difference in meaning (so, e.g., BDF § 343[2]; *GNTG* III:70; Moule 1953:14). Many, however, take the form as an indication that Paul has a particularly vivid memory of these events (e.g., *GNTG* I:144; Plummer, 325; Robertson 1923:897; Windisch, 357). Or it may mark the rhetorical climax of the instances given in vv. 24–25 (Zmijewski 1978:250–51).

*out in the water.* Translates *en tō bythō,* literally "in the depth," referring to the sea. Despite the fanciful views of some of the ancient exegetes, Paul does not mean that he was literally under the water for a full day. Rather, he was at the mercy of the rolling sea, presumably tossed about on some piece of wreckage.

26. *on many journeys.* The noun *(hodoiporia),* which also occurs in John 4:6, refers particularly to travels over land (e.g., Wis 13:18). The phrase stands as a heading for the list of *dangers* which follows (cf. Windisch, 357; Zmijewski 1978:255).

*risking dangers.* The Greek has simply *dangers (kindynois),* but the probably modal sense of the dative is best suggested by some such word as *risking* or "experiencing."

*from rivers.* This genitive *(potamōn)* and the three which follow *(bandits . . . people . . . Gentiles)* designate the origin of the dangers (BDF § 166), not the place of them (so *GNTG* III:212). Presumably, rivers would be dangerous whenever the crossing was treacherous or when they suddenly overflowed their banks.

*from bandits.* Although the main highways were well policed and relatively free of *bandits* during the early centuries C.E. (Casson 1974:122, 149; note Epictetus III.xiii.9, "no brigandage on a large scale"), banditry still posed a threat, especially to small groups of unarmed travelers (cf. Seneca, *On Benefits* IV.xvii.4, cited by Hock 1980:78 n. 19). For a general discussion of brigandage during Roman imperial times, see MacMullen 1966:255–68. Marauding bands of outlaws were still a threat to travelers toward the middle of the first century, especially in the mountainous regions of Cilicia (ibid.:261–62, citing Tacitus, *Annals* VI.xli; XII.lv).

*from my people.* In Greek, simply *ek genous,* "from [the] people," but Paul clearly means his own people (Gal 1:14), "the people of Israel" (Phil 3:5). Numerous instances of Jewish hostility toward Paul are mentioned in Acts, including the opposition of some Jews in Corinth which had resulted in the apostle's being brought before Gallio (Acts 18:5–17).

*from the Gentiles.* In Acts, specifically Gentile opposition to Paul is mentioned somewhat less frequently than Jewish hostility to him, but one may note especially the uprising among the silversmiths of Ephesus (Acts 19:23–41; see also 14:15; 16:16–24).

*in the city . . . in the open country . . . at sea.* The three phrases together include the whole world, wherever Paul's apostolic commission might require him to go (Plummer, 326–27; Windisch, 358). The cities were the primary places of Paul's preaching and the places where he encountered the hostility of unreceptive Jews and Gentiles and suspicious Roman magistrates. The dangers he faced in the *open country* (in contrast to cities; "uninhabited places") and *at sea* were those which any traveler faced, including the *dangers from rivers, bandits,* and (v. 25) shipwrecks he has just listed.

*among false brothers and sisters* (see note on "brothers and sisters" in 1:8). Windisch, 358, conjectures that this phrase stood originally after the reference to *Gentiles,* since it is more logically listed with dangers from groups of people. Barré (1975:505) thinks, rather, that its placement here is part of the style of the passage, in which there is an intricate chiasm involving places and people: *rivers–bandits–my people, Gentiles/city, open country–sea–false brothers and sisters.* Thus, in the larger pattern, *rivers* (places) and *false brothers and sisters* (people) would frame the whole list. It is simpler, however, to regard the mention of *false brothers and sisters* as coming at the end for the sake of emphasis (so Zmijewski 1978:258–59); see COMMENT. The expression occurs also in Gal 2:4, but nowhere else in the NT (though later in Pol Phil 6:3), and it was perhaps coined by Paul himself (Héring, 86 n. 37). Cf. "false apostles" in 2 Cor 11:13.

27. *with labor and toil.* The two Greek nouns *(kopō . . . mochthō)* are phonetically similar and seem to have become a set phrase, rather like "toil and moil" in English (references in BAG s.v. *mochthos*). Paul uses the same phrase in 1 Thess 2:9 (cf. 2 Thess 3:8) to describe his hard work as a craftsman during the time of his ministry in Thessalonica. Here, too, his work as a craftsman must be in view (cf. v. 23*b;* 6:5*b,* with NOTES). The phrase becomes a kind of heading for the remainder of the verse, in which some particular deprivations associated with a craftsman's lot are listed (cf. Zmijewski 1978:264).

*many sleepless nights.* As in 6:5*b,* a reference to going without sleep follows mention of Paul's labor(s). Here Paul is probably alluding to the many hours of sleep given up, either to work at his tent-making craft (note Sir 38:27, and cf. the case of Micyllus cited in the NOTES to 6:5*b*) so that his days could be free for preaching, or to preach when others were free from their own labors to hear (e.g., Acts 20:7–11, 31).

*hunger and thirst.* The hardship list of Rom 8:35 also includes *hunger (limos),* but not *thirst (dipsos).* However, the phrase *peinōmen kai dipsōmen* ("we hunger and thirst" [*RSV*]) in the list at 1 Cor 4:8–9 is equivalent. See also Dio Chrysostom's list of the hardships a "noble man" challenges, where "hunger," "cold" (see below), and "thirst" are all mentioned, and in that order (VIII, 16). Voluntary abstention from food and drink is certainly not involved here, nor do the more general notions of "famine and drought" match the context (against Bishop 1966:169–70).

*many times without food.* For the list at 6:4*c*–5, *nēsteiais (times without food)* follows directly after *sleepless nights.* Since in the present list it follows directly after *hunger and thirst,* a number of commentators believe it must refer to something different— namely, a "voluntary" giving up of food (so, e.g., Plummer, 328; Barrett, 300). If so, however, one should not think of this as "fasting" (cf. *KJV*) in commitment to some ascetic discipline, since that would be inappropriately listed as one of numerous troubles encountered in the course of ministry. If something voluntary is meant, it would be in the nature of going without eating in order to work or preach (Plummer, 328). Still, there is no insuperable difficulty in taking the present phrase, like the one that precedes, as a reference to an experience Paul underwent involuntarily. In this case the phrase *many times without food* could be interpreted as added in order to emphasize the external condition that caused the *hunger and thirst* and, in particular, the frequency of it.

*cold and ill-clothed.* The word *psychos (cold)* appears in none of the other Pauline hardship lists, but it does appear in Dio Chrysostom's (VIII, 16), between "hunger" and "thirst." Here, however, it is associated closely with being *ill-clothed.* That *gymnotēs* need not mean "stark naked" is shown by Epictetus III.xxii.45–47 (cited by Hock 1980:84 n. 94), where the ideal Cynic who has "one rough cloak" is described as *gymnos,* "naked." Hock (ibid.) suggests that one could interpret the term here as "stripped for work," but that would make little sense in a list of hardships, especially when it is associated with being *cold.* It is better to follow Hock's other suggestion, that the lack of adequate clothing goes with trying to make a living as a craftsman (e.g., Lucian, *The Cock* 9, and *The Downward Journey* 20, where Micyllus speaks of being "half-naked" [*hēmigymnos*]). In 1 Cor 4:11 being *ill-clothed* is listed after the mention of being hungry and thirsty (cf. LXX Deut 28:48), and in Rom 8:35 it follows the mention of hunger.

28. *Not to mention other things* translates *chōris tōn parektos,* which some interpreters and translators take to mean "Apart from these external things" (*NEB;* Barrett, 300). There seems to be no other instance of *parektos* having this meaning, however (BAG and LSJ can cite only this passage as a possible instance), and the word normally refers to what is additional or exceptional. Thus *NEB* mg.: "Apart from things which I omit" (cf. *NAB:* "Leaving other sufferings unmentioned"; supported by, e.g., Plummer, 329; Windisch, 360). The present tr., which follows closely *TEV,* interprets the expression as an instance of paralipsis (so also Zmijewski 1978:269)—Paul indicating that something will be omitted when actually he proceeds to include it.

*the pressure.* The best-attested reading here is *epistasis* (not *episystasis,* which would be "uprising" or "disturbance"). Although *epistasis* itself can have various meanings (identified and discussed by Hughes, 415–16 n. 79), most interpreters and translators have adopted *pressure* as the most satisfactory one in this context; cf. the use of the same word in Acts 24:12; 2 Mac 6:3.

*I am under.* More literally, "on me" *(moi).*

*my anxiety.* The possessive pronoun is not present in Greek, but may be understood from the foregoing *moi* (see preceding note). Paul uses the noun *(merimna)* only here, but the cognate verb occurs in 1 Cor and Phil. Twice it has the positive sense, "to care for" (1 Cor 12:25, the Corinthians for one another; Phil 2:20, Timothy for the Philippians), but elsewhere it is used more negatively, referring to a kind of anxiety it is better to be free of (1 Cor 7:32–34; Phil 4:6). In the present context the latter meaning is more probable than the former, since Paul is enumerating the hardships he must endure as an apostle.

*all the churches.* As in 8:18, on which see the note. Paul is probably thinking specifically only of those congregations he has founded and for which, therefore, he feels responsible.

29. *Who is weak and I am not weak?* Barré (1975:507–8) argues that this and the following question are the interrogative equivalent of vv. 21*b*–23*a,* and in fact represent the climax of a "crescendo" pattern which begins in a fully declarative mode (v. 21*b*) and passes through the mixed mode of v. 22*ab* and vv. 22*c*–23*a* to the fully interrogative mode of v. 29. On this basis he suggests that the *tis (who)* of the present verse refers, like the *tis (someone)* in v. 21*b,* to Paul's opponents (ibid.:508). However, it is at best precarious to suppose that the referent of the indefinite pronoun *tis* (v. 21*b*) will also

be the referent of the interrogative pronoun *tis* (v. 29), even when they occur in the same context. Interrogative *tis* is frequently employed by Paul in rhetorical questions of a quite general kind (e.g., 2:2, 16; 5:7). This may reflect a widespread oriental hymnic style (so Fridrichsen 1929:82), or scriptural precedent more specifically (see, e.g., Isa 40:13–14, quoted in Rom 11:34:35; 1 Cor 2:16 and Isa 53:1, quoted in Rom 10:16). Especially noteworthy is the rhetorical question of Rom 8:35a, which like the ones in 2 Cor 11:29 is closely associated with a list of hardships (Rom 8:35b; see also Rom 8: 31b, 33a, 34a). In view of Paul's fondness for posing questions of this sort, it is doubtful whether the apostle has any specific person or persons in mind in v. 29. Rather, the questions seem to have an almost "universal" scope.

*weak.* For the occurrences of this and related words in 2 Cor, see NOTES on 11: 21a. In 12:10a and 1 Cor 4:10b, as well as here, Paul includes a reference to his weakness in a list of hardships. Whatever the nature of this weakness (see COMMENT) it is clear that he means to boast about it, as about his other hardships (v. 30; 12:5, 9, 10b), despite the fact that a certain shame attaches to it (v. 21a). Barré's arguments for translating the verb used here *(asthenein)* as "to stumble" (1975:509–13) require assent to too many dubious hypotheses: for instance, that Paul's vocabulary was influenced by Semitic usage and—most significantly—that the interrogative pronoun in v. 29, like the indefinite pronoun in v. 21b, refers to Paul's rivals in Corinth (see preceding note).

*made to stumble.* A passive form of *skandalizein,* a verb which Paul uses elsewhere only in 1 Cor 8:13. The related noun "stumbling-stone" occurs in Rom 14:13; 16:17; 1 Cor 1:23; Gal 5:11 and, in scriptural quotations, in Rom 9:33; 11:9. Barré (1975: 513–14), citing Matt 18:7 par.; 24:10; Did 16:5 and various LXX passages, argues that the verb had become "an apocalyptic convention" in certain Christian circles, and that it has this meaning here: to be "ensnared [by the agents of Satan in the eschatological struggle that characterizes true apostolic ministry]" (ibid.:518). But Paul's own use of the verb and of the related noun must be given the major consideration, especially since, as in 1 Cor 8 and Rom 14, the apostle has the welfare of his congregations in mind here (v. 28). Being *made to stumble* is, in this context, closely related to being *weak* (Windisch, 361), and yet seems to be a more intensive expression of that (Zmijewski 1978:273).

*burn with indignation.* Literally: simply "burning," "ablaze," or "inflamed" *(pyrou-mai)*. The words *with indignation* interpret the verb in accord with its use in, e.g., 2 Mac 4:38; 10:35; 14:45, where the passive form is followed by *tois thymois,* "with anger"; so, also, most interpreters. However, Plummer, 331, thinks of Paul's shame and distress on behalf of those who have been injured rather than of his wrath at those who have made them stumble. Zmijewski (1978:273–74) would include both ideas. The distinctive view of Barré is that the verb "to burn" has a specifically eschatological reference in every NT occurrence, including the two in Paul's own letters, 1 Cor 7:9 and 2 Cor 11:29 (1974, especially 194–201; 1975:515–18). If so, in the present verse "to burn" would mean "to undergo the fiery trial of the eschatological ordeal" (1975:515; cf. 518). But the case for this depends on the correctness of Barré's conclusions about the meaning of *skandalizein* in this verse and about the function of v. 29 in the passage. On the former see the preceding note, and on the latter see COMMENT.

30. *If.* Here the *ei* is virtually equivalent to *epei* ("Since") in 11:18, where Paul has

already conceded that some boasting is indeed required in the present circumstances.

*boasting.* Here, as in 12:1a, the infinitive *(kauchasthai)* with *dei:* "It is necessary to boast." Other instances of the verb in 2 Cor are listed in the NOTES to 10:8.

*I will boast about my weaknesses.* The future tense is used, not because Paul will only now begin to boast, but because his statement here is a summary of his reason for carrying on as he must in this "fool's speech." This statement is therefore a repetition of the one in 11:18, but with the subject of the boasting specified. Cf. 12:1, where *kauchasthai dei* (see preceding note) is again followed by a verb in the future tense (Betz 1972:73 n. 201).

*weaknesses.* The plural also appears in 12:5, 9b, where—as here—Paul says that he boasts in his weaknesses, and in 12:10a, where they are listed among the hardships accepted *because of Christ.* The plural suggests that in each case the apostle is thinking of concrete experiences of weakness (cf. Barré 1975:513 and 1980:217–18, who identifies these specifically with instances where Paul was the object of hostile actions). The *asthenēmata (RSV:* "failings") of those whose faith is not strong (Rom 15:1) are something else.

31. *God, the Father of the Lord Jesus.* Or (less likely), "The God and Father of the Lord Jesus"; see note on the similar phrase in 1:3.

*who is blessed forever.* The grammar here requires that the reference is to *God,* not to *the Lord Jesus.* This traditionally Jewish description of God is also present in Rom 1:25; 9:5 (see Deichgräber 1967:31, 42 for a brief discussion).

*God . . . knows I am not lying.* The closest parallel to this oath formula is the one in Gal 1:20, which also stands in the midst of certain autobiographical remarks (Stählin 1962:133; cf. Borse 1972:96). See also Rom 9:1 (where, however, there is no specific appeal to God) and 2 Cor 11:10 (with note).

32. *At Damascus.* These words serve as a heading for the vignette which follows in vv. 32–33. The Syrian city of Damascus, continuously inhabited since at least 2000 B.C.E., is located on the fertile plain watered by the Abana and Pharpar rivers, to the north and east of Mt. Hermon in the Anti-Lebanon Range. In 85 B.C.E. it became the capital of an independent Nabatean kingdom under the Romans, but in 65 B.C.E. Roman forces under Pompey conquered Syria, and the city of Damascus was placed under a Nabatean governor. (General discussions and bibliographies are provided by Haldar, *IDB* A–D:757–58, and Unger, *ISBE* One:852–55; see also Cohen on "Nabateans," *IDB* K–Q:491–93.) According to Acts 9:1ff.; 22:2ff.; 26:12ff., Paul's conversion had occurred near Damascus while he was en route there to purge the synagogue of any Christians he might find, and this location seems to be confirmed by Gal 1:17, the one other instance where Paul himself mentions the city. The incident he records here is also narrated in Acts 9:23–25, but with certain differences (see COMMENT). What the exact political status of Damascus was at the time of Paul's flight from the city is uncertain; see the following note.

*the ethnarch under King Aretas.* Who the *ethnarch* in Damascus at this time was is unknown, and it is also unclear what his exact responsibilities would have been. In some cases an ethnarch served as the "governor" of a whole city, but there are also instances of ethnarchs whose jurisdiction was limited to a particular ethnic group within a city. (Examples of each are provided by Sandmel, *IDB* E–J:178–79.) Windisch, 366, believes the former is probably meant here, but Hughes, 424, and Bruce, 245, think the latter is more likely. Yet a third possibility is that this ethnarch was the potentate of an ethnic group living outside Damascus, but in the vicinity. A closely related question is what kind of jurisdiction *King Aretas* had over Damascus at this time. It is known that Aretas IV reigned over the Arab kingdom of Nabatea from 9 B.C.E. until his death about 40 C.E. His daughter (perhaps the *Sha^cudat* named in an inscription from the twenty-ninth year of his reign; Starcky 1965:5) was the first wife of Herod Antipas—who, however, divorced her to marry Herodias, the wife of his half-brother, Herod Philip. It was this second marriage which John the Baptizer denounced, and which cost John his life (see Matt 14:3–12 par.). Subsequently, in 36 C.E., Aretas IV attacked and defeated the army of Herod Antipas (Josephus, *Antiquities* XVIII.v.1–2; see Schürer 1973:350). The only direct evidence that Aretas IV ever exercised political control over Damascus is Paul's reference (here in 2 Cor 11:32) to his having an ethnarch there. It is known, however, that the emperor Caligula (reigned 37–41 C.E.) reinstituted a policy of client kingdoms in the eastern provinces, and granted territorial control to certain eastern rulers. If, indeed, such an arrangement had been made with Aretas IV, giving him supervisory control over Damascus (so, e.g., Bietenhard 1963:56; Jones 1971:290–91; Cohen in *IDB* K–Q:492; Jewett 1979:30–33), then the incident to which Paul refers here must have occurred sometime between 37 and 40 C.E. (Jewett ibid.:99 dates it more precisely in the period August–October of the year 37). For some, however, this evidence seems insufficient. Thus, e.g., Burchard (1970:158–59 n. 100) believes that Damascus itself could not have been under the control of Aretas, and that his ethnarch functioned only as the sheik of a Nabatean tribe which controlled certain neighboring territory; but see Bowersock 1983:68–69, and the following note.

*was guarding the city.* The imperfect tense suggests a watch had been kept over a substantial period of time (cf. Acts 9:24, "day and night"), presumably by posting watchmen at the gates (cf. Athenaeus, *Deipnosophistae* V, 214a, where Athenion is reported to have "set guards at the gates of Athens"). The verb *(phrourein)* may mean to stand guard either outside or inside a walled city (Field 1879:186–87; BAG s.v.). Some interpreters (e.g., Lake in *BC* V:193; Haenchen 1966:268–69) believe that here it must mean the former (thus, e.g., *JB:* "put guards round the city") since there is no direct evidence that Aretas IV had any jurisdiction over the city itself. In this case Paul's flight from Damascus could be more appropriately described as a "safe departure" from the city than as an "escape" (so Burchard 1970:158–59 n. 100). But it is in principle unlikely that the Romans would have tolerated Nabatean control of the territory around a city under direct Roman administration. Moreover, a Nabatean watch over the city from outside would have had to be little short of a siege. Finally, Paul narrates the event in such a way as to leave the clear impression that the danger was from within, not outside the city. See Bietenhard 1963:57, and especially Jewett 1979:30–31.

*in order to seize me.* Translates *piasai me,* the infinitive expressing purpose. A number of texts read "wanting [*thelōn*] to seize me," but the addition of *thelōn* is more understandable (as a clarification) than its omission would be; see Metzger 1971:584.

33. *I was lowered.* The verb *chalan* is often used technically of the lowering of fishing nets (e.g., Luke 5:4, 5) or of ship's gear (e.g., Acts 27:17) into the water, but it has wider applications as well (BAG s.v.). The passive voice here indicates that Paul had assistance, and this is in accord with Acts 9:25, which says that "his disciples" lowered him (Zmijewski 1978:285).

*in a basket.* The Greek word used here is *sarganē,* and it occurs nowhere else in the

NT; it probably refers to a braided, flexible *basket* (BAG s.v.). In Acts 9:25, too, Paul is said to have used a basket for his escape, but the Greek word there is *spyris,* found elsewhere in the NT.

*through a window in the wall.* More literally, "through a window through the wall" *(dia thyridos . . . dia tou teichous).* The *wall,* which would be the city wall—but not the *window*—is mentioned in Acts 9:25. One might perhaps translate *dia tou teichous* in both passages as "along the wall" (so *NAB* at Acts 9:25; see BDF § 223[5]); if so, the phrase in the present verse would attach more closely to *I was lowered* than to *through a window.* The Greek word order could in fact be taken as support for this, and Josephus seems to employ the phrase in a similar way (*Antiquities* V.i.2). How an escape could be made "through a wall" is explained in Josh 2:15 (in the Hebrew [ = English] version, but not in the LXX), which tells how Rahab helped Joshua's spies escape from Jericho "through the window" in her house—the house itself being "built into the city wall" *(RSV).* Josephus' recounting of the incident (*Antiquities* V.i.2) mentions no window (simply, "letting themselves down along [*dia*] the wall by means of a rope"), while a similar escape by David from Saul mentions only a window ("down through the window," 1 Sam 19:12 [*RSV*]). Notable among such escapes, as recorded in secular literature, are those of the Athenians from the tyrant Athenion ("Many Athenians . . . let themselves down over the walls [*kata*—or, in two mss., *dia—tōn teichōn*] with ropes by night and fled," Athenaeus, *Deipnosophistae* V, 214a; cited by Cadbury 1955:21), and of Perseus from a Samothracian prison ("letting himself down through a narrow window in the wall [*para to teichos*]," Plutarch, *Aemilius Paulus* XXVI, 2; cited in BAG s.v. *chalaō*).

*escaped his hands.* Or "his clutches" (*NEB;* cf. Mof. and Gdspd.); for a similar metaphorical use see, e.g., Sus 22; Tob 13:2 (cited in BAG s.v. *ekpheugō,* 2b*β*).

12:1. *Boasting is necessary.* Cf. 11:30, to which the expression here is assimilated in some texts (e.g., אּ²) by the addition of *ei* ("If"). Paul may be alluding to a view held by the rival apostles in Corinth and accepted by certain members of the congregation there (so Barrett, 306); see COMMENT. In some witnesses (e.g., אD*) *dei (is necessary)* has been replaced by *de* (a simple connective; thus, "Boasting is of no benefit, yet I shall move on . . . ," etc.), probably in order to resolve a perceived contradiction between the thought that boasting is required and the comment that it is not beneficial (cf. Metzger 1971:584).

*Although it is not beneficial.* Translates *ou sympheron men,* as in P⁴⁶ אּ B, etc. The variant readings seek to improve the awkward style and syntax (Metzger 1971:584). At 8:10 the same verb has been translated "in your interest" (see the note there). The particle *men* in the present phrase seems to point ahead to the connective *de* in the one which follows, thus joining the two closely together (so also Barrett, 306). This results in giving the present phrase a concessive sense (see BAG s.v. *men,* 1a); thus, *Although . . .*

*I shall move on to.* The connective *de* (left untranslated) joins the phrase with the one preceding. The use of the verb *erchesthai* (literally "to come") to indicate movement to a new point, topic, or incident in a narrative account appears to have been a literary convention. Windisch, 369, cites examples from Herodotus (e.g., II, 35, 40, 99; III, 6), who uses the present tense; Paul's future tense only makes the sense of the present explicit.

*visions and revelations.* Cf. 2 Apoc Bar 76:1, "the revelation of this vision" *(APOT),* cited by Baumgarten (1975:138). In Paul's defense before Agrippa in Acts 26:19 there is a reference to the "heavenly vision" he had had at his conversion, but the apostle himself uses the word (Greek: *optasia*) only here (elsewhere in the NT, only Luke 1:22; 24:23). The plural *revelations (apokalypseis)* occurs only here and in v. 7 in the NT, but Paul uses the singular elsewhere: of events at the eschaton (Rom 2:5; 8:19; 1 Cor 1:7), of his call to apostleship (Gal 1:12), of a divine instruction (Gal 2:2), and of a divine communication during public worship (1 Cor 14:6, 26). In the present verse, the absence of articles and the use of the plural indicate only that Paul is taking up a general topic, not that he has numerous specific *visions and revelations* in mind (against Windisch, 369; Bietenhard 1951:165; correctly Bultmann, 220; Georgi 1964:297). At least in this context, the terms may be regarded as synonymous (Windisch, 368).

*granted by the Lord.* The reference here is certainly to Christ, as in vv. 7–8, not to God (against Strachan, 30). The English paraphrase, *granted by,* interprets *Kyriou* ("of the Lord") as a genitive of origin. Schlatter (658, 662, 663) presumes it to be an objective genitive (as in 1 Cor 1:7, referring to the Parousia), and Lincoln (1979: 205–6) suggests that the Lord was not only the originator but also the content of the visions. However, the experience to be recounted in vv. 2–4 seems to have involved no appearing of Christ to Paul.

2. *I know a person.* This phrase introduces an instance of someone who has had the kind of ecstatic experience mentioned in the preceding verse. It is clear from vv. 6b– 7a that the *person (anthrōpos)* to whom Paul refers here is himself; the convoluted argument of L. Herrmann (1976) that it was Apollos cannot be taken seriously. Similar impersonal forms of self-reference are found, for example, in Sophocles (examples in Bultmann, 221–22), but this is the only passage (see also vv. 3–4, 5) where Paul has employed it. For its probable significance in this instance, see COMMENT.

*in Christ.* There is no reason to suppose, with Schmithals (1971:214), that *a person in Christ* is "a technical designation for the person in ecstasy." The phrase *in Christ* may simply mean "a Christian" (see, e.g., Rom 16:7); or, more probably, it is used to identify this *person* (Paul) as one whose life has been transformed and made new through faith in Christ (cf. Rom 6:11; 8:1; 1 Cor 1:30 and especially 2 Cor 5:17).

*fourteen years ago.* In the prophetic and apocalyptic traditions it is usual for the time of a vision or revelation to be indicated in some way. See especially Ezek 1:1–3; also Amos 1:1; Hos 1:1; Isa 6:1; Jer 1:1–3; 26:1; 42:7; Ezek 3:16; 8:1; Zech 1:1; 7:1; 2 Esdr 3:1; 2 Apoc Bar 1:1, etc. But similar chronological notices often accompany narratives of unusual or important events, as in Lucian, *The Lover of Lies* 11 (Ion: "I was still a young lad, about fourteen years old, when . . .") and 22 (Eucrates: "Let me tell you . . . what I saw five years ago [*pro etōn pente*]"). It is doubtless "a mere coincidence" (J. Knox 1950:78 n. 3) that Paul refers, both here and in Gal 2:1, to an interval of *fourteen years.* In Gal the reference might be to the time elapsed since Paul's vision of Christ, by which he had been called to apostleship (Gal 1:15); but it is more likely a reference to the time elapsed since he went into Syria and Cilicia (Gal 1:21; so Betz 1979:83). If, as seems probable, the present letter (chaps. 10–13) was written in the summer of 56 C.E. (see INTRODUCTION, pp. 44–46), then the experience referred to here would have occurred sometime around the year 42. By most reckonings this would have been almost a decade before Paul's first visit to Corinth, but also substantially after his call to apostleship.

*caught up.* Here, as in Acts 8:39 and Rev 12:5, a passive form of the verb *harpazein* is used to describe the experience of someone's being lifted up, at least temporarily, to a supramundane realm. In Wis 4:11 the reference is probably to Enoch's translation into heaven (so Winston 1979:140; cf. 1 Enoch 39:3–4; 52:1–2; 2 Enoch 7:1[B]; 8:1[B], etc.). Philo uses the verb in a similar way (*Special Laws* III, 1–2; *On the Contemplative Life* 12; cited by Barrett, 310, and Reitzenstein 1978:469 respectively). Note also Lucian, *The Lover of Lies* 3 and *The Judgement of the Goddesses* 6 (cited by Betz 1961:169). In Apoc Mos 37:3, it is Adam who is "carried off" to be in the presence of God, and in 2 Esdr 14:49 (Syriac version) it is Ezra. Paul himself uses the same expression to describe how believers will be taken up into the clouds to meet their Lord when he returns at the last day, 1 Thess 4:17. For a general discussion of "rapture" in ancient religions, see Strecker in *RAC* 5:461–76.

*in the body or outside the body.* Jewish traditions about the translation of famous people ordinarily presume that they were enraptured *in the body:* thus Enoch (see 1 Enoch 12:1; 14:8; 39:3–4; 2 Enoch 38:1–2), Abraham (see T Abr VIII[B], where Abraham's ascent to the clouds is described as *en somati,* the same as Paul's phrase here), Seth and his mother (*Adam and Eve* 37:1, cited by Lietzmann, 154), and Baruch (see, e.g., 3 Apoc Bar 11:1–2). The rabbinic story of R. Akiba's journey to Paradise, accompanied by three friends, of course presumes the same (*b. Ḥag* 14b, etc.; see, e.g., Scholem 1965:14–19; Bowker 1971). In Greek thought, on the other hand, translation into another realm is almost always a flight of the soul from the body, as in the Myth of Er in Book X of Plato's *Republic* (see 614 B). A bodiless rapture is also presumed by Philo, *Dreams* I, 36, and Josephus, *War* VII.viii.7 (cited by Barrett, 308), and even in 1 Enoch 71:1, 5 (cited by Lincoln 1979:216).

*I do not know.* The Greek phrase actually appears twice in this verse, thus accentuating Paul's uncertainty or—more likely (see COMMENT)—his indifference to the matter. A more literal tr. might run: "whether in the body I do not know; whether outside the body I do not know."

*God knows.* In 11:11 the same phrase functions as an abbreviated oath formula; see NOTES there. Here the apostle uses it only to emphasize his own ignorance—and indifference.

*clear to.* The preposition here is *heos,* which specifies how far Paul had been transported ("all the way to")—not *eis,* which would indicate, as in v. 4, "entry into." Cf. Matt 11:23 par., *heos ouranou* [*hypsothēnai*]: "[to be exalted] clear up to heaven."

*the third heaven.* The original text ( = *a*) of T Levi 2:7–10; 3:1–4 seems to have conceived of the heavenly spheres as three in number, in the third of which Levi found himself standing in the presence of the Lord and his glory. Later, however, this material was re-worked to refer to a set of four additional heavens, conforming the narrative to the common Jewish and Christian tradition about seven heavens, as in Apoc Mos 35:2; 2 Enoch 3–20; *b. Ḥag* 12b; *Ascension of Isaiah;* Apoc Paul 29, etc. For a review of Jewish speculation on the number of heavens see Lincoln 1979:212–13. According to 2 Enoch 22[A] and the Gnostic Apoc Paul (CG V, *2*) 24,8 (*NHLE,* 241) there are ten heavens, while in 1 Apoc Jas (CG V, *3*) 26,2–19 (*NHLE,* 243) there are seventy-two. The otherworldly journey is a common feature in ancient apocalyptic literature, and numerous examples are surveyed in J. J. Collins, ed., 1979:36–43 (Jewish), 84–95 (early Christian), 136–39 (Gnostic), 161–65 (Greek and Latin), 190–95 (Rabbinic), 213 (Persian). For a more general discussion of the topic see Segal 1980. Paul's brief remarks in these verses about his own journey became the basis for later, more elaborate tales about his experience. From the second century there is the Gnostic Apoc Paul (CG V, 2); see especially 18,21–24,9 (*NHLE,* 240–41). Another Apoc Paul is from the late fourth or early fifth century (in HSW II:759–98); and one may also note the passage in Pseudo-Lucian, *The Patriot* 12 (tenth century), where Triepho reports to Critias that he had recently been met "by a Galilean with receding hair and a long nose, who had walked on air into the third heaven [*es triton ouranon*] and acquired the most glorious knowledge. . . ." For a survey of Patristic and medieval fascination with and commentary upon Paul's account, see Mazzeo 1957.

3. *Indeed, I know such a person.* Some commentators regard this phrase as introducing the description of a second experience (so, e.g., Plummer, 344; de Boor, 231). But it is better to regard the *kai* as ascensive (see BAG s.v. I, 3), not as a simple conjunction (thus, *Indeed,* not "And"), for what follows in v. 4 explicates v. 2.

*whether in the body or apart from the body.* The point made in the parenthesis in v. 2 is repeated. This tr. follows the text of P⁴⁶ B D* in reading *chōris (apart),* since *ektos (outside),* found in many witnesses, is probably an assimilation to v. 2 (Metzger 1971: 585).

*I do not know.* Barrett, 310, omits this as a further assimilation to v. 2, but the textual evidence for the omission is not strong.

*God knows.* As in v. 2.

4. *that he was caught up.* The parenthesis in v. 3 has interrupted the syntax, for Paul should have continued with a participial construction, "who was caught up." For the verb, see note on v. 2.

*into Paradise.* Parallel with *clear to the third heaven* in v. 2 (see also following note). Here, however, the preposition *eis* indicates an actual entry *into* Paradise (Zmijewski 1978:339).

*Paradise.* From the Persian word for "enclosure," often a "park" or "garden." In the Greek text of Gen (chaps. 2, 3) it refers to the earthly garden (Hebrew: *gan*) where Adam and Eve first resided (so also, e.g., LXX Ezek 28:13; 31:8–9; cf. 2 Enoch 3:1–3[A]; 8:6–8[A]). However, in Jewish apocalyptic literature Paradise appears most often as a heavenly realm (e.g., 2 Esdr 4:7–8), sometimes described as the place of judgment (as in *Adam and Eve* 25:3, where it is called "the Paradise of Righteousness"; 2 Enoch 10:1–6; T Abr 10[B]), but usually identified with the place which those who have been found righteous will inherit as their reward (either at their death or at the final resurrection); see, e.g., 2 Esdr 3:5–11; 7:36,123; 8:52; Apoc Abr 21; 2 Enoch 9:1; T Abr 20[A]; 2 Apoc Bar 51:11; T Levi 18:10–11; and the other two NT occurrences of the term, Luke 23:43 and Rev 2:7. Aelius Aristides also uses the term with reference to a place of eternal bliss (*Romans* 26, 99; cited by van der Horst 1980:26). In 2 Enoch 8:1–8[B] and Apoc Moses 37:5; 40:2, *Paradise* is located specifically in "the third heaven," thus supporting what the parallelism of v. 2 and vv. 3–4 also suggests—i.e., that Paul is referring to one and the same experience here. Of four rabbis who according to rabbinic tradition made a similar journey into *Paradise,* only one (R. Akiba) came back unharmed; see *b. Ḥag* 14b, discussed by Scholem (1965:14–19) and Bowker (1971). For general discussions of *Paradise* see Jeremias, *TDNT* V:765–73 and McArthur, *IDB* K–Q:655–56; also Lincoln 1979:213–14.

*things that must not be divulged.* In Greek *(arrēta rēmata)* an oxymoron, the combination of two apparently incompatible ideas: "unutterable words." The following phrase shows that they are unutterable not because they cannot be repeated, but because they may not be. The adjective *(arrētos)* was often used of things disclosed in Mystery rites which the initiates were charged to keep secret—e.g., Euripides, *Bacchanals* 472; Herodotus V, 83; Plutarch, *Isis and Osiris* 360 F (all cited in BAG s.v.); cf. Apuleius, *Metamorphoses* XI, 23. Philo uses it in a broader sense of certain kinds of religious knowledge (e.g., *The Worse Attacks the Better* 102, 175; *Dreams* I, 191; *Change of Names* 14–15; *Allegorical Int.* II, 57–58; *Sacrifices of Abel and Cain* 60). Whether 2 Enoch 17[A] offers a similar instance is unclear. It may be that the seer found it "impossible to describe" the singing of the heavenly angels simply because he was unable to express its beauty in words. Or it may be that he had been instructed not to describe it. Among Jewish and Christian examples of the latter see Dan 12:4; Rev 10:4; 13:2–3.

*a human being.* The noun *(anthrōpos,* as in v. 2, where it is translated *person)* is anarthrous (without an article) and refers to humankind in general. There is an implied contrast here between a "mere" *human being* and the heavenly things disclosed, so the meaning is not so general as "anyone" *(tis);* see Bachmann, 388; Bultmann, 224; Zmijewski 1978:340.

5. *I will boast.* For the probable significance of the future tense, see NOTES on 11:30.

*of such a person.* It would be possible to regard the expression *(tou toioutou)* as neuter, and to translate: "of such an experience" (cf. Mof.). But the context requires the masculine (i.e., personal) sense (arguments in Hughes, 441 n. 120).

*of weaknesses.* The preposition *(en;* literally "in") may be interpreted as both causal and instrumental; it is both because of and by means of weaknesses that Paul can boast (Zmijewski 1978:348). For the plural, *weaknesses,* see 11:30 (with note); 12:9, 10.

6a. *For should I wish to boast.* See v. 5b for the only kind of boasting Paul will allow himself.

*I will not be a fool.* The reference here, as in v. 16a, is to being an actual *fool,* not just to playing a fool's role as in v. 16b; 12:11. Cf. Zmijewski 1978:361–62.

*for I shall be telling the truth.* The apostle makes similar claims about his veracity in 6:8; 7:14; 11:10.

6b. *I am declining to do this.* More literally, because here the verb *(pheidomai)* is used absolutely, "I forbear" (see BAG s.v.). What Paul refrains from is the sort of boasting to which he has referred in v. 6a, about things like his journey to Paradise (vv. 2–4). Barrett, 312, interprets the word according to the usage of 1:23, where Paul writes about "sparing" the Corinthians, but there is every indication that they would welcome some boasting from him just now; it is nothing he would have to "spare" them (correctly Bultmann, 225).

*no one.* Against Barrett (1971:244–45), there is no indication that a particular individual is in mind here.

*credit.* A commercial term *(logisetai);* see BAG s.v. 1a; BDF § 145(2).

*may see . . . or hear.* Cambier (1962:499–504) notes that the Hebrew prophets often referred to what could (or could not) be "seen and heard" (e.g., Isa 6:9; 29:18; Jer 5:21; Ezek 12:2), and that this theme is also prominent in the NT (e.g., Matt 11:4; 13:14–15; Mark 8:18; Acts 8:6; 28:26–27), including the letters of Paul (e.g., Rom 11:8; 15:21; 1 Cor 2:9). With the present passage cf. especially Phil 4:9 (ibid.:502).

*see me doing.* This tr. follows the suggestion of Zmijewski (1978:360) that the participle *poiounta* be supplied; the Greek itself has only *blepei me,* "see me."

*7a. specifically.* Translates *kai,* interpreting it as explicative (BDF § 442[9]) over against many commentators (e.g., Barrett, 313–14) and virtually all English trs., following the punctuation of *GNT*-Nestle, whereby v. 7a is read as the conclusion of v. 6b. Other proposed interpretations are surveyed by Cambier (1963:475–79) and Zmijewski (1977:266–68; 1978:352–54), both of whom argue for the punctuation adopted here. Zmijewski's arguments are particularly compelling (1977:268–71; 1978:354–55):

(a) a new sentence more likely begins with the *dio (For this reason,* v. 7b) than with the *kai;*

(b) if vv. 7a and 7b formed one sentence there would be an awkward multiplication of dative forms and the verb *was given* would be too long delayed;

(c) if v. 7b is taken as a separate sentence, then the repetition of the phrase *that I not be overly exalted* is readily understood as comprising the "framework" for what intervenes;

(d) syntactically, v. 7a goes well with v. 6b, explicating the preceding phrase (*so that no one,* etc.), just as the last phrase of v. 6a (*for I shall be telling the truth*) extends what precedes it. Thus a protasis (*For should I wish to boast*), followed by two explanatory phrases (the remainder of v. 6a), is matched by an apodosis (*But I am declining to do this*), followed by two explanatory phrases (the remainder of v. 6b and v. 7a).

*because of the extraordinary character of the revelations.* Translates *tē hyperbolē tōn apokalypseōn,* taking the dative as causal (BDF § 196). The word *hyperbolē (extraordinary character)* is applied here, as in 4:7, 17 (translated, respectively, "beyond any comparison" and "absolutely incomparable"), to something which cannot be surpassed. On Paul's use of superlatives in 2 Cor, see NOTES on 3:10 and 11:5. The *revelations* in mind would be like the one Paul has just described as having been granted to him in Paradise (v. 4; correctly R. M. Price 1980:35).

*7b. For this reason.* Although the introductory *dio* which this phrase translates is omitted in some witnesses (including P⁴⁶ and D), there are important witnesses which include it (e.g., ℵ A B). It may be accepted not only as the *lectio difficilior,* but also because its omission can be explained as deriving from copyists who mistakenly began a new sentence with v. 7a, and then found the *dio* awkward (see Metzger 1971:585). Retained as itself the beginning of a new sentence, it serves to link v. 7b with vv. 6b–7a.

*that I not be overly exalted.* This phrase *(hina mē hyperairōmai)* occurs twice, framing the statement of v. 7b (Zmijewski 1978:366, who detects a chiastic structure). There are some good witnesses that omit the second occurrence (including ℵ*), but the evidence for retaining it is strong and the repetition makes sense in the context (Metzger 1971:585).

*there was given.* That is, by God. This is a conventional use of the passive voice to avoid mentioning the divine name; see BDF § 130(1) and note especially Luke 6:38, "Give, and there shall be given to you."

*a thorn in the flesh.* Both the tr. and the meaning of this phrase have been widely debated. The noun *skolops* can refer to a pointed stake, especially the kind used for defense, for execution, or for impalement (Delling, *TDNT* VII:409–10; Park 1980: 179–82), and some interpreters argue for that meaning here (e.g., Schlatter, 666;

Hughes, 447; Bieder 1961:332; Park 1980:182–83). In this case *tē sarki* would certainly have to be translated as a "dative of disadvantage" (see BDF § 188), "for the flesh." (1 Cor 7:28 would then offer a formal parallel: those who marry will have "affliction for the flesh" [*tē sarki*].) But *skolops* can also mean "thorn" or "splinter," as it always does in the LXX (Num 33:55; Ezek 28:24; Hos 2:6; Sir 43:19). In this case *tē sarki* is most suitably translated *in the flesh*, even though *en* ("in") is not used (as it is, e.g., in LXX Num 33:55, where Israel's enemies are described as "thorns in [their] eyes," *skolopes en tois ophthalmois* [*autōn*]). Since the apostle's subsequent reference to being "abused" suggests an affliction which, however aggravating, need not have involved any intense pain or mortal threat, this second meaning has been adopted here. For the question of whether this affliction was some physical ailment, see COMMENT.

*an angel of Satan.* See NOTES on 2:11 and 11:14, where the name of *Satan* also appears. Although Satan himself is sometimes referred to as *an angel* in Jewish and Christian texts (e.g., 1QS iii.21–24, an "angel of darkness"; Herm Man VI, 2:1, an "angel of evil"), he is also said to have "angels" who serve as his agents, e.g., T Asher 6:4; Matt 25:41; Rev 12:7, 9; Barn 18:1. Cf. Paul's own reference to Satan's "ministers" *(diakonoi)* in 11:15. Elsewhere the apostle indicates that he himself had been received as "an angel of God" by the Galatians (Gal 4:14).

*to abuse me.* More literally, "that he should abuse me," or—to bring out the apparently durative force of the present tense (Hughes, 447; Zmijewski 1978:368, 369)— "that he should constantly abuse me." The verb *(kolaphizein)* is relatively rare (never in the LXX), although the noun *kolaphos* ("a box on the ear") is rather frequent (Schmidt, *TDNT* III:818).

For the literal meaning of the verb see Matt 26:67 par., of blows inflicted on Jesus after his arrest; and (perhaps) 1 Pet 2:20, of the suffering of Christians. Here, however, as in 1 Cor 4:11, the verb may well have its broader meaning: "to revile" or "ill-treat" (see Schmidt, *TDNT* III:819; Noack 1948:95).

*that I not be overly exalted.* As above, on which see the note.

8. *Three times I appealed to the Lord.* Paul often uses the verb *parakalein* in appeals to his congregations (e.g., 10:1) or with reference to appeals to his fellow-workers (e.g., 9:5, "to urge"), but only here has he used it of a petitionary prayer. There are, however, numerous examples of this usage in other Hellenistic texts (see BAG s.v. 1c), e.g., in a letter in which Zoilus says that he "appealed" to his god, Sarapis, to be relieved of the responsibility of building him a temple (line 8, as reconstructed; in Deissmann 1927:153). See also POxy 1078, line 8 (cited ibid.:308 n. 2). In particular, the word is used in ancient accounts of how some god has answered a petitioner's prayer for healing —as in the case of M. Julius Apellas, who was cured by Asclepius at Epidauros: "And concerning this I appealed to the god" *(kai gar peri toutou parekalesa ton Theon;* cited by Deissmann 1927:308, from Dittenberger, *Sylloge).* Paul's reference to praying *three times* for relief may possibly reflect the Jewish practice of morning, afternoon, and evening prayers (Ps 55:16–17; Dan 6:10, 13; 1QS x.1–7; 1QH xii.3–9; on which see Windisch, 389–90; Moore 1927, II:219–20; Ringgren 1963:222–23), adopted as well by the Christian church (e.g., Did 8:3). It is, however, at least equally possible that Paul was familiar with the threefold petition for assistance sometimes found in Hellenistic accounts of divine healings (examples in Windisch, 389–90, and Betz 1969:292–93).

*the Lord.* Here, undoubtedly, Christ (see v. 9). Congregational prayers were customarily offered not "to" Christ but "through" him to God (see, e.g., 1:20), and so were many personal prayers (e.g., 1:5; Rom 1:8; 7:25). In this instance, however, as perhaps in others where more personal requests were involved, prayer is directed to Christ (see Bultmann 1951:127–28). Cf. 1 Cor 1:2; 1 Thess 3:12–13.

*about this.* As in 1 Cor 16:12; 2 Thess 2:1, the preposition *hyper* is used in place of *peri;* see BDF § 231(1); Bjerkelund 1967:120, 137. The pronoun could be neuter ( = "this thing," i.e., "this circumstance"), but it is more probably masculine, referring to the *thorn in the flesh,* personified as Satan's *angel.*

9a. *And he said to me.* The use of the perfect tense *(eirēken),* conventional in reporting solemn (especially divine) decrees (e.g., Acts 13:34), indicates that what had been once said is understood to have lasting significance (Moule 1953:15; Zmijewski 1978:378).

*grace.* Apart from the benediction (13:14), this is the only mention of *grace* in chaps. 10–13 (Letter E). As in 8:9; Gal 1:6 and the closing benedictions of Paul's letters, it is the *grace* that Christ imparts, for he is speaking. Here it is understood primarily as that power by which Paul has been commissioned to and is constantly supported in his apostolic ministry (see NOTES on 4:15); so also, e.g., Windisch, 391; Käsemann 1942: 53; Bultmann, 229; Güttgemanns 1966:166.

*is enough for you.* The verb *(arkei,* present tense: "continues to be enough") is used only here by Paul, but occurs elsewhere in the NT in Matt 25:9; Luke 3:14; John 6:7; 14:8; 1 Tim 6:8; Heb 13:5; 3 John 10. One may also compare the use of the related adjective in Matt 6:34; 10:25; 1 Pet 4:3. The Cynic and Stoic philosophers of Paul's day taught that one should be "content" with whatever one has *(arkeisthai tois parousi,* as in Teles II, line 84; IVA, lines 84–85, 130 [O'Neil 1977:10, 38, 42]; in the NT, Heb 13:5), and thus they promoted the ideal of "self-sufficiency" *(autarkeia;* see NOTES and COMMENT on 9:8). This, however, is not the point of the oracle that Paul now reports he has received from the Lord. Rather more comparable is the Midrash Tannaim on Deut 3:26, interpreting God's refusal to let Moses cross over the Jordan: "Be content that the evil impulse has no power over thee, yea rather that I will not deliver thee into the hand of the angel of death, but will Myself be with thee" (cited by Kittel in *TDNT* I:466). Cf. Betz 1969:301.

*power.* Some ancient witnesses (e.g., ℵ² A D²) and a number of English trs. (e.g., *RSV, JB, TEV, NIV*) have "my power," which in this context would mean Christ's. But the textual evidence (including P⁴⁶ ℵ* B D*) strongly favors omitting it (see Metzger 1971:585–86). In this case, one might argue that the present reference is to the power of God (so, e.g., Barré 1980:220), not to the power of Christ. It is, indeed, more common for Paul to write of God's power (see especially 4:7; 6:7; 13:4; Rom 1:16, 20; 1 Cor 1:18, 24; 2:5; 6:14) than of Christ's (v. 9*b;* 13:3; 1 Cor 5:4; cf. Phil 3:10), and one could understand the explicit mention of *the power of Christ* in v. 9*b* as a particularization of the more general reference to God's power here in v. 9*a* (cf. Zmijewski 1978:383). But too fine a distinction is unwarranted, for the power of Christ and the power of God are inseparably linked in the apostle's thinking, as 13:3–4 and 1 Cor 1:17–18, 24 show especially well (also 1 Cor 6:14 compared with Phil 3:10). It is not surprising that the efficacy of divine power is a motif of ancient stories of miraculous cures (Betz 1969:300 n. 69 cites, e.g., POxy 1381, lines 215–18: "For every place has been penetrated by the saving power of the god [Asclepius]").

*is made fully present.* Translates *teleitai,* which might also be rendered "is brought to completion" or ". . . to its goal" (see Delling, *TDNT* VIII:59). For the idea of completion, however, Paul seems to prefer the compound *epitelein* (e.g., 8:6, 11; Phil 1:6), and elsewhere he uses *telein* to mean something like "actualize" (Rom 2:27; 13:6; Gal 5:16). See Bultmann, 229–30.

*weakness.* So far in this letter Paul has used the plural, referring to his own weaknesses (11:30; 12:5; again in 12:10). Where he juxtaposes the idea with that of *power,* however, the singular is ordinarily used, as it is here (also in 13:4; 1 Cor 2:3–4; 15:43); v. 9*b* is the exception.

*9b. Rather.* Translates *mallon,* which must go with the verb *(I will boast)* and not with the adverb (see following note) which, in the Greek, precedes it (BDF § 246; BAG s.v. *mallon,* 3a). In view of the word he has received from the Lord (v. 9*a*), Paul will now boast of his weaknesses *rather* than pray that they be taken away.

*very gladly.* A superlative form *(hēdista)* used as an elative, to intensify the meaning. See Robertson 1923:670; BDF § 60(2).

*boast of my weaknesses.* Repeats v. 5*b* (see NOTES), but now using the possessive pronoun (omitted in B and a few other witnesses, but otherwise very well attested).

*the power of Christ.* See the note on *power* in v. 9*a*.

*may reside with me.* One should probably understand "may be seen to reside with me," for the apostle surely does not mean that his boasting has caused Christ's power to take up residence with him. (Cf. Zmijewski 1978:392–93.) The compound verb *(episkēnoun)* is found only here in the NT, and is otherwise very rare. Some interpreters (e.g., Hughes, 452; 453 n. 141; Güttgemanns 1966:169) read it against the background of the Jewish notion of God's sheltering presence, rooted in such OT passages as Exod 25:8–9 and Ezek 37:27 (the LXX employs the noun *skēnē* ["tent"] and related words in these passages), developed in the "shekinah" theology of the rabbis, and echoed not infrequently in the NT (e.g., John 1:14, on which see Brown 1966:32–34; Rev 7:12; 21:3). Note Gdspd., "may shelter me." One should exercise due caution about this, however, for in all other known instances the verb *episkēnoun* means "to take up residence with" (see Pope 1911; Michaelis, *TDNT* VII:386–87). Before Paul it is found only in Polybius IV, 18.8 (as here: *episkēnoun epi*); 72.1, with reference to the billeting of soldiers. Betz (1969:303 n. 89) suggests that Paul has taken the word over from his rivals in Corinth.

*10a. because of Christ.* Translates *hyper Christou.* The phrase, although it stands (in the Greek text) at the end of the list of hardships, is not to be construed with them, but with the verb (Bultmann, 230; Zmijewski 1978:389 n. 477). A causal interpretation is required by the context (Schrage 1974:161–62; Zmijewski 1978:391); Paul does not accept hardships "for the sake of" (in order to benefit) Christ, but because Christ's power is made present in weakness (v. 9). Cf. "on account of Jesus" in 4:11 (with note).

*I am pleased.* In this context the verb *(eudokein)* must mean something less than "take delight in" (e.g., Wey., *NIV*), but something more than "be content with" (*RSV* and most other English trs.).

*weaknesses.* As in vv. 5, 9*b,* but now the first item in a list of difficulties with which Paul has had to cope as an apostle. Similar lists are found in 4:8–9 (see COMMENT there for a general discussion); 6:4*c*–5; 11:23–29; Rom 8:35; 1 Cor 4:9–13. Two of these others, like the present list, mention Paul's weakness (1 Cor 4:10*b;* 2 Cor 11:29*a*).

*insults.* Or perhaps, more generally, "difficulties" (Bertram, *TDNT* VIII:305). The noun (*hybris,* on which see P. Marshall 1980:283–302) rarely occurs in the plural form used here, and neither the singular nor the plural is used elsewhere by Paul. In Rom, however, the adjective is used substantively in a list of vices (1:30, *RSV:* "insolent"); and Paul in 1 Thess 2:2 uses a verbal form to describe how he and his associates had been "mistreated" in Philippi. Something like the latter is probably in mind here.

*catastrophes.* As in an earlier list, 6:4 (see NOTES).

*persecutions and pressures.* The same two words appear in the list of hardships in Rom 8:35, although in the singular and not in the plural. The *kai (and)* that links them is probably original, since it breaks the pattern of a noun preceded by *en (with);* see Metzger 1971:586. With *persecutions (diōgmois)* cf. also the use of the verb "persecute" *(diōkein)* in 4:9 and 1 Cor 4:12. The list in 2 Cor 6:4c–5 also mentions *pressures,* and the related verbal form appears in the list of 4:8–9 (v. 8, translated "crushed").

10b. *For when I am weak, then I am powerful.* The form of the statement *(when . . . then)* accentuates the paradox it involves (Zmijewski 1978:389). This form has a certain parallel in Philo, *Moses* I, 69: "When the enemy is surest of ravaging you, then your fame will shine forth most gloriously." Even more striking is the apparently material parallel in the same passage, where Philo is commenting on what Moses learned at the burning bush (Exod 3): "Your weakness is your power" *(to asthenes hymōn dynamis estin);* but see COMMENT.

## COMMENT: GENERAL

After a lengthy prologue (11:1–21a), Paul launches at last into the "foolish" boasting with which he has been so reluctant to become involved. Even as he begins, however, his self-consciousness about it is apparent: *I am speaking foolishly* (v. 21b); *I am out of my mind to speak this way* (v. 23a). He obviously feels that he has been forced to this tactic by his rivals in Corinth, who have made extravagant claims for themselves while at the same time impugning, at least indirectly, the authority of the Pauline apostolate (see 11:18, 21b–23; 12: 1a). From Paul's response to those claims, one may infer that the rival apostles (1) took special pride in their Jewish heritage, (2) pointed to various specific accomplishments as evidence that they were Christ's true *ministers,* and (3) boasted of being the recipients of extraordinary *visions and revelations.* Following a brief introductory remark (11:21b), Paul counters each of his rivals' claims with claims of his own: (1) he, too, is of Jewish stock (11:22); (2) his career as an apostle distinguishes him as a better minister of Christ than his rivals are (11:23–29); and (3) he himself is no stranger to extraordinary religious experiences (12:1–4). At the same time, however, Paul's uneasiness about responding in this way to the claims of others leads him to include two special comments about the kind of boasting he is permitting himself to do here: he would boast only about his weaknesses (11:30–33; 12:5–10).

Thus, Paul is not really matching the claims of his rivals, although he appears to start out this way (11:22), following the Hellenistic conventions of rhetorical self-display and comparison (*synkrisis;* see, e.g., Fridrichsen 1929: 81; P. Marshall 1980:543–46; Forbes 1982:2–10). Rather, as both Betz (e.g., 1969, with specific reference to 12:7–10) and Judge (e.g., 1972:35 and 1973: 114, with specific reference to 11:22–33) have recognized, Paul ends up parodying the claims of his rivals, much as he had in 10:12 (on which see the COMMENT). Over against the pretentious boasts of those who claim for themselves special apostolic powers and religious insights, Paul offers a long list of sufferings (11:23*b*–29) and the curious account of a journey to heaven which yielded no useful religious knowledge (12:1–4). This, as the apostle explicitly says in 11:30–33 and 12:5–10, is a boasting *of weaknesses.* The Corinthians themselves should know, on the basis of an earlier letter (Letter D, chaps. 1–9; see especially 4:7–15; 5:11–12; 6:4–10), that such weaknesses, not worldly achievements or otherworldly experiences, are the distinguishing marks of the true apostle.

## COMMENT: DETAILED

### Introduction, 11:21b

This remark serves as the functional introduction to everything that follows through 12:10 (not just through 11:29, as Barré [1975:506] suggests), even as it reiterates the point of 11:18—namely, that Paul feels compelled by his rivals to boast of his apostolic credentials. Windisch, 350, notes a similar comment in Phil 3:4*b,* but the list which follows in Phil 3:5–6 is summarily rejected (Phil 3:7) as no longer valid. Here, however, Paul offers his first credential (11:22) without specifically qualifying its validity, even though his subsequent boasts turn out to be about things which show his weakness. The parenthetical remark that he is *speaking foolishly* by attempting this (cf. 11:1, 16–17, 19) shows that he would rather not be doing it, and is at the same time an implicit request that his readers excuse him for it. Barrett, 292, believes that Paul here sets out to compare himself, not directly with persons in Corinth whom he considers intruders and competitors, but with the leaders of the Jerusalem church by whose authority they claim to operate. The context is against this, however. The Corinthian rivals themselves have been under attack in the preceding verses (11:12–21*a*) and, despite Barrett's claim (on which see NOTES), Paul gives no indication that he is now shifting his attention to some other group. (See also the COMMENT on 11:5–6.)

### On Being of Jewish Stock, 11:22

Paul is never hesitant to identify himself as "a Jew" (Rom 3:9; 11:14; Gal 2:15; cf. 1 Cor 9:20), but here—whether intentionally (Windisch, 350) or not

—he avoids that term. Rather, as in Rom 11:1 and Phil 3:5–6 (cf. Rom 9:3–5), he employs terms that emphasize the ethnic, social, and religious (rather than political) meaning of being a Jew. They were, perhaps, the terms his rivals were using to boast about their religious origins and heritage. In any case, Paul declares without qualification or hesitation that he is no less a Hebrew, an Israelite, and a descendant of Abraham than they (for particulars, see NOTES). The matter of one's "good breeding" *(eugeneia)* was a standard topic of Hellenistic rhetoric (Betz 1972:97), whether taken up in order to praise another or in order to commend oneself. As an example of the first, Judge (1972:36 n. 85) cites the inscription (mid-first century C.E.) dedicated by Tiberius Claudius Zopas to his father, honored as a "son of his city, lover of his country, both on account of the gravity of his manners and of the good breeding (he inherits) from his ancestors" (Greek text in Robert 1940:168, No. 152; tr. by Judge 1980a:9). An example of an appeal to "good breeding" in the course of self-praise is the boast of Paul's rivals that they were of good Jewish stock. When Paul now claims the same for himself *(I am, too),* he is following the rhetorical convention of *synkrisis* ("comparison"; see NOTES and COMMENT on 10:12) as it is characterized, e.g., in the school exercises *(Progymnasmata)* attributed to Hermogenes of Tarsus (second century C.E.): "for we compare city with city . . . , race with race, nurture with nurture, pursuits, affairs, external relations . . ." (tr. Baldwin 1928:33; cited by Forbes 1982:7–8).

However much must remain uncertain about the identity of those whom Paul regards as his rivals for apostolic leadership in Corinth, it is clear from this series of rhetorical questions that they, like Paul, were Jewish by birth, and proud of it. Their concern to present themselves as *Hebrews* could, but does not necessarily mean that they themselves were Palestinians (see NOTES on *Hebrews;* Friedrich 1963b:182), perhaps even sent out from the Jerusalem church. Moreover, that they were proud of their Jewish heritage certainly does not mean, in itself, that they were "Judaizers," Jewish-Christian legalists bent on imposing selected points of the Mosaic law on Paul's Corinthian converts. There is in fact no direct polemic against the law in 2 Cor. Furthermore, had Paul viewed his rivals as Judaizers, it is likely that the argument in the present passage would have run more or less as it does in Phil 3, where the validity of the law clearly is an issue (Bultmann, 216). There, also speaking of his Jewishness, Paul stresses in particular how completely devoted he had been to the law (Phil 3:5–6). But then he proceeds to discard his alleged gains under the law as absolutely worthless (Phil 3:7).

Indeed, if the rival apostles in Corinth were making it a special point to call themselves *descendants of Abraham,* that would help to support the view that they were Hellenistic-Jewish Christians, for Abraham played an important role in Hellenistic-Jewish apologetic (e.g., Philo, *On the Virtues* 212–19; see Georgi 1964:63–81). Paul's own appeals to the example of Abraham's faith doubtless owe something to this particular theme of Hellenistic-Jewish propaganda. In effect, Paul identifies the promise given to Abraham and to his descendants ("that they should inherit the world," Rom 4:13) with the gospel, and declares that it has been fulfilled in Christ (Gal 3:16–18; other references in the NOTES). Identification of Paul's competitors as Hellenistic-Jewish Christians would also accord with the special importance they seem to have attached to ecstatic experiences (e.g., 2 Cor 5:12–13; 12:1–10) and to other extraordinary powers (e.g., 2 Cor 12:12; 13:3) as signs of true apostleship.

## On Being a Minister of Christ, 11:23–29

### A Claim to Superiority, 11:23a

Here a fourth and climactic rhetorical question is added to those of the preceding verse. The three previous ones all pertained to the Jewish heritage of Paul's rivals in Corinth, and in that respect Paul has claimed absolute equality with them. This fourth question now pertains to their present role and status as agents for the gospel, and in this decisive respect Paul claims that he is superior to them. The phrase *ministers of Christ* is used nowhere else by Paul himself, but it is fully compatible with his descriptions of apostles as *ministers* "of a new covenant" (3:6), "of God" (6:4), and "of righteousness" (11:15). Schmithals (1971:207–8) believes that the present phrase, as well, is Paul's own formulation; but, given the way it is introduced here, that can hardly be the case. Along with the phrase "apostles of Christ" (11:13), it must be one of the ways Paul's competitors are representing themselves to the Corinthians. It may be that they had charged Paul with not having this status (Theissen 1982:48–49). For his part, however, and in contrast to his earlier denial of apostolic status to his competitors (11:13–15), Paul now chooses to leave their claim uncontested. Instead, he proposes to show how he is more than their equal as Christ's minister.

### A Catalog of Hardships, 11:23b–29

In these verses Paul supports his claim to superiority as a minister of Christ (11:23a) by cataloging various things he has had to endure in the course of his apostolic labors. This list should be compared with similar ones in 4:8–9; 6:4c–5; 12:10; Rom 8:35; 1 Cor 4:9–13. Parallel lists known from Cynic and Stoic sources emphasize the relative insignificance of such tribulations and how, by courage and insight, the wise person may overcome them (see COMMENT on 4:8–9). It is possible that Paul's rivals in Corinth made this sort of claim about themselves (note the use of comparative terms in 11:23b). It is more likely, however, that they boasted of their personal boldness (see comments on 10:1–11), their missionary achievements (10:12–16), their eloquent speech (11:5–6), their ecstatic experiences (5:12–13; 12:1–4), and their ability to perform miraculous deeds (12:11–12), claiming these as evidence of the spiritual power with which their ministry was endowed. So, in the present passage, Paul is not saying that he has "suffered more" than his rivals, but rather that he will boast only of his weaknesses (Georgi 1964:295).

Paul's Corinthian readers would have been familiar not only with Cynic and Stoic lists of hardships that the truly wise person can readily dismiss as trifling (cf. Betz 1972:99), but also with lists of impressive achievements compiled by and on behalf of such notable public figures as Julius Caesar, Pompey, and Augustus (cf. Fridrichsen 1928:28; Judge 1961 and 1964; and see NOTES on 11:23b). What Paul is doing here constitutes a parody of both of these familiar forms of (self-)praise: the first is parodied in that the apostle presents the adversities he has faced as humiliating experiences rather than as ennobling ones; the second, in that he is chronicling examples of apparent failure rather than instances of obvious achievement. While self-derision was one conventional rhetorical device in Paul's day (P. Marshall 1980:553–63), the sustained cataloging of adversities found here seems to be quite unique among Greek and Roman writers (ibid.:558). There is a long and strikingly parallel listing of the misfortunes of Augustus in Pliny's *Natural History* VII.xlv.147–50 (cited in ibid.:558–60); these misfortunes, however, are not listed by the victim himself, as in Paul's case, but by one who wishes to counterbalance the deceased emperor's own famous catalog of accomplishments (cited in the NOTES on 11:24) with a sobering recital of his failures.

In the present passage the catalog proper runs through v. 27 and comprises four patterned sets of adversities in v. 23b, vv. 24–25, v. 26, and v. 27 respectively. To this more or less straightforward listing of difficulties vv. 27–29 constitute an addendum, formally but not materially distinct from the catalog itself. Along with certain formal characteristics (identified by Zmijewski 1978: 322–23), this catalog of hardships is distinguished from those in 4:8–9 and 6:4c–5 by its greater length and specificity, giving it special value as an autobiographical statement.

To be sure, the four items which head the list in v. 23b are not specific instances of adversity, but serve, rather, to typify the kinds of adversities to be cataloged. Three of these four types, *labors, imprisonments,* and *beatings,* also appear in the list of 6:4c–5. By *labors* Paul means either his work as a craftsman, regarded by the Corinthians (and probably by himself) as in one sense demeaning (see comments on 11:7–11), or else his missionary work (see NOTES for details). He is perhaps more likely to mean the former, for then v. 27 could be regarded as a further description of the hardships his *labors* involved, just as two other items in v. 23b are further described in vv. 24–25. Although the apostle's *imprisonments* remain unspecified in this list, as they do in 6:4c–5 (on which see the NOTES and COMMENT), he has more to say about his *beatings* and about his having been *often at the point of death.*

The numerical specification which characterizes the second set of adversities, vv. 24–25, is typical of other ancient lists of exploits of notable personages (examples in NOTES; see Judge 1966:44 and nn. 113, 114). Paul first specifies the *beatings* (v. 23*b*) he has received as an apostle, five times by Jews (v. 24) and three times by Romans. (Details on the typically Jewish and Roman forms of beating are given in the NOTES.) In Acts there is no actual portrayal of Paul being flogged by Jews, although it does portray several occasions, prior to the writing of the present letter, when that could have occurred (e.g., Acts 13:45, 50; 14:5), including one in Corinth itself (Acts 18:12). Note also 1 Thess 2:14–16. There is specific documentation of one beating Paul received from the Romans in Acts 16:22 (with Silas, in Philippi), and Paul alludes to this in 1 Thess 2:2. The experiences listed in vv. 24*b*–25 (one stoning, three shipwrecks, and twenty-four hours adrift at sea; see NOTES for details) provide instances of the fourth general item in v. 23*b*, that Paul had been *often at the point of death.*

The opening phrase of v. 26 supplies the heading under which all the more specific adversities in the third set may be grouped. How, in particular, Paul could have been endangered by each of the places and groups mentioned is indicated in the NOTES. The *dangers from [his] own people* would include the floggings mentioned in v. 24, and those *from the Gentiles* would include the beatings with a rod mentioned in v. 25*a*. The last and climactic dangers listed in this particular set are those *among false brothers and sisters.* In Gal 2:4, Paul's only other use of the expression, the reference is to Jewish Christians who seek to impose certain requirements of the law of Moses upon Gentile converts. It is possible that here, too, Paul is thinking of the difficulties he has had with "Judaizers" (so Barrett 1970b:378–79) in such places as Galatia (e.g., Gal 1:6–7) and Philippi (e.g., Phil 3:2–3). But it is also possible that he is using the term more broadly, to include Christians whom he regards as in any way unfaithful to the gospel as he himself has preached it. In this case, Paul could be thinking as well, or even in particular, of his rivals in Corinth—those whom he has described elsewhere in this letter as "false apostles" (11:13).

All of the adversities in the fourth set, v. 27, fall under the heading of *labor and toil* and pertain to hardships commonly faced by those who, like Paul, must earn their living by working at some craft or trade (see NOTES for details). Similar difficulties appear in the lists in 6:4*c*–5 and Rom 8:35. If the *labors* mentioned in v. 23*b* also refer to Paul's work as a craftsman (see note there), then the present set of deprivations specifies the kinds of hardships involved.

With the fourth set, the formal cataloging of adversities has been concluded. From what follows, however, it is clear that Paul wants his readers to know that the list could go on and on. But instead of merely stating that (see, e.g., John 20:30; 21:25), he finds himself actually adding another sort of problem with which he has been burdened (vv. 28–29)—that is, the daily *pressure* and *anxiety* he feels for the congregations he has founded, including the one in Corinth, v. 28. The *pressure* might be, in particular, the weight of his responsibility for exercising pastoral leadership in those congregations, such as responding to questions of faith and conduct on which his advice has been sought (e.g., 1 Thess 4:13–5:11; 1 Cor 7, 8, 11, 12) and carrying out specific projects like the raising of a collection for Jerusalem (1 Cor 16:1–4; 2 Cor 8, 9; Rom 15:25–28). The *anxiety* would refer, somewhat less concretely (Zmijewski 1978:269–70), to Paul's constant worrying, especially with regard to those congregations from which he is separated, that his converts will compromise or even abandon the gospel he has delivered to them (see, e.g., Gal 1:6–9; 3:1–5; 4:15–20). The church in Corinth has caused him special anxiety almost from the first—as his letters directed to that congregation, including the present one (2 Cor 10–13), amply demonstrate—and he may well have the Corinthians especially in mind as he adds this point to his list of woes.

The rhetorical questions of v. 29 do not conclude and summarize the whole catalog, as Barré (1975:517) maintains. Rather, they are to be taken closely with v. 28, as both reiterating and emphasizing how the constant pressure of pastoral responsibilities and the persisting anxiety about the welfare of his churches constitute for Paul yet another kind of adversity (cf. Plummer, 331; Windisch, 361).

To what sort of weakness does Paul refer in v. 29a when he asks, *Who is weak and I am not weak?* It is certainly not the weakness of unbelief, as in 1 Cor 9:22, for in the present verses it is believers—not unbelievers—that must be in mind (see v. 28). Four possibilities remain: (1) Some (e.g., Windisch, 361; Bruce, 244; apparently *JB*) suggest that Paul is thinking of those in Corinth whom he had once described as weak in conscience, burdened by inappropriate moral scruples (1 Cor 8:7–13; cf. 10:24–11:1). While this is not impossible, there is nothing in the present context (or anywhere in 2 Cor) to support it. (2) Somewhat more plausible, because it would conform to the general concerns expressed in v. 28, is the suggestion that Paul is referring to those who are in any way weak in faith (Zmijewski 1978:273; cf. Fuchs 1980:245). Or (3), more general still, he could be thinking here, as he is in 1 Cor 12:20–26, of Christians who, for whatever reason, are less honored within the body of Christ. Then, what the apostle suggests about himself in 2 Cor 11:29 could be read as a specific example of the operation of the principle enunciated in 1 Cor 12:26a: "If one member suffers, all suffer together" *(RSV)*. Finally (4), Paul might be thinking in particular about his physical weakness (so, e.g., Barrett, 301–2; Jervell 1976:191–92, 193), particularly if the *thorn in the flesh* mentioned in 12:7b is to be identified with some bodily infirmity. Whichever of these may come the closest to Paul's thought, the main point is that he so far identifies himself with those whom he serves as an apostle that their weaknesses are also his.

The second rhetorical question, v. 29b, is closely associated with the first, so the precise meaning of the "stumbling" referred to is to a certain extent dependent on the meaning of the weakness in v. 29a. In general, however, it must refer to some sort of "falling away" from one's faith (see Stählin, *TDNT* VII:355–56). In this second question, therefore, Paul does not allude to his identification with those who are *made to stumble,* but rather to his *indignation.* It is unclear whether he means that he is indignant in general, with those who stumble, or with others known to have caused the stumbling (cf. 1 Cor 8:13; Rom 14:13). It is clear, however, that he regards any sort of stumbling as a weakening of the fabric of Christian community and, in that sense, a destruction of "the work of God" (Rom 15:20; cf. 1 Cor 8:11, 12; Rom 14:12 and Stählin, ibid.:356).

### On Boasting, 11:30–33

Opinions vary on the place and function of these four verses within the overall context of this "fool's speech" (11:1–12:13). Some regard vv. 30–31, or v. 30 alone, as concluding what has gone before (e.g., Windisch, 362; Wendland, 242, 243; Tasker, 166–67), while others read them, or at least v. 31, as introducing what follows (e.g., Denney, 343, 344; Hughes, 418; Bruce, 244; Travis 1973:531). They are perhaps best interpreted, however, as a comment on the "fool's speech" as a whole. As it turns out, they also—along with vv. 32–33, which attach closely to them (see below)—effect a transition from the first, declaratory part of the speech (11:22–29) to the closing, narrative part (12:1ff.).

### Boasting About Weaknesses, 11:30–31

*Boasting* is the subject of v. 30, where the apostle admits with some reluctance that it *is necessary.* He has said as much in 11:18, where he refers to the boasting of others (cf. 11:12), and he says it again, explicitly, in 12:1a. The necessity of boasting makes it no less foolish, however, as Paul reminds his readers several times (11:16, 17; cf. 11:1; 12:11). Moreover, he wants them to realize that the boasting in which he is now engaged concerns only his *weaknesses.* This is how they are to understand the long recital of adversities with which he has just concluded (11:23b–29): as documentation of how much he has suffered, and therefore of his vulnerability. In this sense the present comment looks back over what has gone before; but, more fundamentally, it also articulates the principle according to which the apostle wants his whole speech to be interpreted (Zmijewski 1978:278–79). It is a principle to which he will subsequently allude in 12:5, 9b, 10a, and which is in full accord with his conviction that it is the weakness of his apostolate through which God's mighty power is disclosed (4:7; cf. 13:3–4). It is probable, therefore, that the reference to *weaknesses* is meant to be broadly inclusive of the various kinds of afflictions with which Paul has been beset as an apostle. These would certainly include the adversities cataloged in 11:23b–29 and elsewhere, showing his vulnerability, but also the personal characteristics (appearance, manner, and speech, 10:1, 10; 11:6) and behavior (see discussion on 1:17; 11:7) which at least some in Corinth have regarded as further signs of weakness.

The oath of v. 31 (see NOTES for Paul's use of similar formulas elsewhere) should be seen primarily in relation to v. 30, and only secondarily in relation to vv. 32–33. God is invoked as a witness that the apostle is *not lying* when he claims to boast only about his weaknesses. This serves to distance Paul still further from his rivals in Corinth, whom Paul has accused not only of unwarranted boasting (see discussion on 10:12–18) but of outright deceits (11:13–15; cf. Zmijewski 1978:282).

### An Escape from Damascus, 11:32–33

To many interpreters this little narrative of Paul's flight from Damascus seems out of place here (e.g., Bishop 1953:189, "out of context, out of style, quite out of connection"). One's first impression is that it might better have been included among the adversities listed in 11:23*b*–29, perhaps to illustrate the *dangers in the city* (v. 26), just as the *beatings* mentioned in v. 23*b* are illustrated in vv. 24–25*a*. A number of scholars, in fact, regard it as an interpolation, perhaps having originated as a scribal gloss on the earlier catalog of hardships. This conjecture dates back at least to the nineteenth century (see Moffatt 1918:126 and Windisch, 364 n. 1 for the literature), and it has a number of more recent advocates (e.g., Couchoud 1923:12; Windisch, 363–64; Goudge, 110; Betz 1972:73 n. 201). A more radical conjecture is that this narrative has been misplaced from its original location between Gal 1:17 and 1:18, where, after Paul's mention of his return from Arabia to Damascus, it could be seen to fit in quite well with other personal reminiscences (Bishop 1953:189, following J. R. Harris). However, in the absence of any textual evidence to support these interpolation theories, one needs to make an effort to see how the verses may in fact make sense where they stand.

Some commentators believe that the story was included here as an "afterthought," another instance of a hardship like those already listed, which occurred to Paul as he proceeded to dictate the letter (e.g., Wendland, 243; Héring, 87; Tasker, 167). But in Paul's narration of the incident it is the escape itself that is highlighted, not the seriousness of the threat, and certainly not any suffering he experienced while engineering the escape (see further, below). The same objection applies to the suggestion of Plummer, 335, that the apostle intended to record several such incidents as illustrations of dangers he had faced in cities, and then (inexplicably) stops after mentioning only this one. Somewhat more plausible is the suggestion by Hughes, 422, that Paul relates this story just here in order to counter-balance the "ineffable 'ascent' " to heaven to be described in 12:2–4 with "the undistinguished 'descent' " from a window in the Damascus wall (cf. Zmijewski 1978:289). Had that been the apostle's intention, however, one would expect a transitional comment substantially different from the one provided by 12:1.

Any conclusions about the function of vv. 32–33 must proceed from a consideration of their form and content. Formally, they constitute a brief narrative account of a notable experience. Judge (1966:45 n. 116) compares it to the anthology of such incidents compiled by Valerius Maximus in his *Facta ac dicta memorabilia*. Closer at hand is the cycle of stories told about Paul himself in Acts 9:1–30, including a slightly different version of this same incident (vv. 23–25). A close analysis and comparison of the two versions leads Burchard (1970:150–59) to the conclusion that the author of Acts has drawn his account from a tradition which was itself dependent on 2 Cor (ibid.:158–59). In the context of Acts 9, the story helps to show how Paul, having been converted and "filled with the Holy Spirit" (v. 17), was empowered by God as an agent for the gospel (see, e.g., vv. 22, 28–29, 31). According to Acts, the threat to Paul in Damascus was from the Jews, who were intent on killing him (vv. 23, 24). His escape from them illustrates how effectively Paul (Saul) had been strengthened (v. 22) for carrying on his ministry (cf. Lietzmann, 152; Barrett, 304).

For all of the similarities, there are several substantial differences between the account in Acts and Paul's own narrative. The most important of these are that (1) Paul indicates the threat was from the ethnarch of the Nabatean king, Aretas IV (on whom see NOTES), not from the Jews, and (2) by Paul's account the threat was only of arrest, not of being killed. Why he was sought by the Nabatean official is not indicated, although it could have been because of some incident during Paul's time in Arabia (Bruce, 245, with reference to Gal 1:17). In any event, when Paul's account is compared with the one in Acts, it becomes evident that Acts gives more attention to the threat and to its seriousness (Acts 9:23–24). Here in 2 Cor the escape as such receives proportionately more attention, v. 33, and the picture of Paul's ignominious descent in a basket is not blurred by mention of who assisted him, as in Acts 9:25 ("his disciples").

The straightforwardness of the narration here makes it unlikely that the apostle's aim is to reinterpret the incident as "a crowning act of God's mercy" in the face of charges by his detractors that Paul's flight had been an act of cowardice (so Strachan, 28; correctly Bultmann, 220).

In the context of Acts the story does help to illustrate God's mercy and provident care of Paul. But its context in 2 Cor is quite different. Here the apostle has just provided a long list of his hardships (11:23*b*–29), not to suggest how well he has overcome them or how much he has suffered, but to illustrate his vulnerability. Indeed, the story of the flight from Damascus is told immediately following his emphatic declaration that these adversities are to be viewed as *weaknesses* and that he will boast of them only as such (11:30–31). It is in connection with these preceding verses, and as a part of the "comment on boasting" they provide, that this narrative is to be interpreted. Although the same story is presented in Acts as a sign of strength, Paul himself offers it here as further proof of his weakness (correctly Barrett, 303; Zmijewski 1978:287, 288–89). He places no special emphasis on the seriousness of the threat (contrast Acts), and he makes no mention of his own suffering (contrast Plutarch's account of Perseus [cited in NOTES], who "suffered pitifully in letting himself down through a narrow window in the wall"). Here in 2 Cor it is a story about Paul's humiliation, not about his heroism.

The narrative's function is described in the same way by Judge, who offers a further intriguing suggestion about it. There is no doubt that the recipients of this letter, residents of an important Roman colony, would have been well acquainted with the *corona muralis,* or "wall crown" (Greek: *stephanos teichikos*), one of the highest Roman military awards (general discussions in Haebler, PW IV:1640–41, and Maxfield 1981:76–77). From the time of the Republic, it was given to the first soldier up and over the wall into an enemy city (e.g., Polybius VI, 39.5; Livy VI.xx.8; X.xlvi.3; XXVI.xlviii.5). It was an actual crown, fashioned to resemble the turreted wall of a fortified city, and made of gold. A head of the Roman goddess Fortuna (Greek: Tyche), found in Corinth and dated to the late first or early second century C.E., is adorned with one (see Plate VIII). Under the empire it was still being awarded as a military honor, but to no one under the rank of centurion. Its original significance was not forgotten, however, as the second-century description of it by Aulus Gellius attests: "The 'mural crown' is that which is awarded by a commander to the man who is first to mount the wall and force his way into an enemy town; therefore it is ornamented with representations of the battlements of a wall" (*Attic Nights* V.vi.16). Similar feats of military courage were often recorded and depicted on the tombstones of Roman soldiers; e.g., that of T. Claudius Maximus (Speidel 1970), to which Professor Judge has called my attention. Judge's suggestion is that Paul has followed the conventional form of such accounts in telling of his flight from Damascus, and that he intends for the Corinthians to contrast his frightened descent of the wall with the daring ascent of a wall for which a courageous soldier would be honored (1966:44–45; 1968:47; followed by Travis 1973:530 and Lincoln 1979:208 n. 2). This would be a curious reversal of the military imagery Paul had applied to his apostolate earlier in the letter (10:3–6), but it is just such reversals as this that are characteristic of his "fool's speech." Earlier he assured the Corinthians of his courage (10:2) and boasted of his authority (10:8). Now he is writing to them of his humiliations and boasting of his weaknesses.

### On "Visions and Revelations," 12:1–10

#### A Journey to Paradise, 12:1–4

It is now generally agreed that Paul is describing one experience in these verses, not two (so, e.g., Bietenhard 1951:164; Betz 1972:89–90; Baumgarten 1975:140 n. 59; Zmijewski 1978:332–35). Any tr. of v. 1 must remain problematic because of various textual and syntactical difficulties (detailed in NOTES), but it is clear enough that the function of the verse is to effect a transition between the preceding comment about boasting (11:30–33) and the following description of a journey to Paradise (vv. 2–4).

Paul's reiteration that *boasting is necessary,* v. 1 (cf. 11:30), is perhaps a concession to his competitors in Corinth, who may be faulting him for not having displayed the kinds of apostolic credentials of which they themselves boast. Among these, apparently, are accounts of ecstatic experiences they claim to have had (see comments on 5:12–13). Here one sees Paul agreeing to *move on* to meet them on that point, although he observes more or less parenthetically (Zmijewski 1978:325) that *it is not beneficial.* What he believes is not helpful, either as a proof of apostleship or for the welfare of the congregation as a whole (Barrett, 306–7; Schütz 1975:236–37), is the recounting of one's extraordinary *visions and revelations* (a phrase probably taken over from his rivals; Spittler 1975:260; Zmijewski 1978:329). But if Paul really believes this, why does he propose now to tell about one of his own? Ostensibly, to give his readers what they have been wanting to hear about him—or what his rivals have prompted them to require of him. In fact, however, Paul describes his experience in a way that only accentuates how useless it is as a proof for anything (see below), and he specifically declines to boast about it (see comments on vv. 5–10). Thus its very recounting constitutes a sort of parody of the practice of his rivals (cf. Betz 1972:89–90, who, however, overemphasizes this aspect). His move here is generally similar to one he had made in an earlier letter to Corinth. On the one hand he had claimed more experience with ecstatic speech than anyone in the congregation, but on the other hand he had dismissed that as far less important than speaking "with [one's] mind" (1 Cor 14:18–19). For Paul, as Käsemann has emphasized (1942, especially 67–69), true apostleship is demonstrated as one serves the church for its upbuilding (e.g., 5:13; 1 Cor 14:3–5, 26*c*), not by how many ecstatic gifts and experiences one can claim (see also below on 12:6*b*–7*a*).

Various explanations have been offered for the fact that Paul uses the third person, not the first person, in describing his experience, vv. 2–4. Some have proposed that the apostle is distinguishing between his "natural" self and his "pneumatic" self, and that it was the latter, not the former, that journeyed to Paradise (so, e.g., Reitzenstein 1978:468; Lietzmann, 153). But, since Paul holds open the possibility that the ascent was *in the body* (vv. 2, 3), that explanation does not suffice. The text offers somewhat more support for the suggestion (Windisch, 369–70) that Paul is distancing himself from the experience as a matter of discretion, so that not too much of it will be revealed (note v. 4). But that is hardly a major concern in the context. It is more likely that Paul's style, like that of other ancient accounts of heavenly journeys, reflects the sense of self-transcendence which such experiences seem to entail. Thus, having returned to earth, Baruch can say, "And having come to myself, I gave glory to God . . ." (3 Apoc Bar 17:3; cf. the Mithras Liturgy, "You will see yourself being lifted up and ascending to the height" [M. W. Meyer 1976:7]). Or, it is possible (so Betz 1972:95; Lincoln 1979:208–9) that Paul has been moved to adopt this form because he shares the conventional wisdom that it is better to praise another with whom one can expect to be compared (see 12:5) than to praise oneself directly (e.g., Plutarch, *On Praising Oneself Inoffensively* 10; cf. Quintilian XI, 21). The context, however, probably supplies the best explanation. Paul will support his apostleship only by boasting of his weaknesses (11:30; 12:5, 9*b*–10): while he is willing to record this one instance of a private religious experience, he is quite unwilling to claim it as an apostolic credential (cf. Käsemann 1942:67; Georgi 1964:298 n. 4; Zmijewski 1978:336). Paul does not want to be known as a "visionary," but only as a weak and suffering apostle (see Crownfield 1979:254; Jervell 1976:195 and n. 56), through whom God's incomparable power is disclosed (4:7–15).

Paul indicates that he experienced the journey *fourteen years ago,* which would have been considerably before his first visit to Corinth. Since he has not mentioned it to the Corinthians before now, he has probably never regarded it as an event of any great significance, at least for them (contrast the judgments of Benz 1952:109; Saake 1973:154; Lincoln 1979:211). At the same time, however, it must have been an unusual, perhaps unique experience for him, since otherwise he surely would have chosen a more recent instance to describe (Barrett, 308; Dunn 1975:215). That Paul bothers to date it at all is not to be attributed to any special autobiographical or historical interests, but—as in other ancient accounts of extraordinary events or religious visions (see NOTES) —to an interest in emphasizing that it really happened (Windisch, 373). If the present letter was written in the year 56 (see INTRODUCTION, pp. 44–46), then the experience of which Paul now writes would have occurred in about the year 42, not long after his escape from Damascus (see NOTES on 11:32) and during a part of his apostolic career about which he himself is otherwise silent. Attempts to date it earlier, in order to identify it with the experience Acts describes as his conversion (Acts 9:1–19; 22:4–16; 26:9–18), are far from convincing (see, e.g., Riddle 1940:63; Buck and Taylor 1969:220–26; Enslin 1972:53–55). Moreover, that experience—interpreted by Paul himself as a call to apostleship (Gal 1:11–17)—involved no journey to heaven, and neither of the essential aspects of the experience, the revelation of Christ or the charge to preach the gospel to the Gentiles (Gal 1:16), is mentioned as part of the heavenly journey described here.

In marked contrast to other ancient accounts of heavenly journeys (references in NOTES), Paul has surprisingly little to say about the experience itself. Only two points are clear:

1. The apostle had been *caught up into Paradise* (v. 4), which—as in certain Jewish apocalyptic literature (see NOTES)—he locates in *the third heaven* (v. 2). Paul is operating here quite within the categories of the Jewish cosmology of his day (references in the NOTES; see especially Bietenhard 1951:165–66). It is impossible to say whether he thinks of his experience more as a journey into another realm or as a journey into the future; in fact, the spatial and temporal aspects of Jewish cosmology are closely related. Nor can one be

certain whether the ecstatic experiences of which Paul's rivals were boasting were specifically of this type, although that could well have been the case.

2. In Paradise, Paul had *heard things that must not be divulged* (v. 4). Significantly, and in striking contrast to other ancient accounts of such journeys, the apostle has nothing to say about what he saw in Paradise. He focuses exclusively on the "word character" of the event (Baumgarten 1975:144; Zmijewski 1978:343ff.). But, quite unlike the oracles granted to Israel's prophets and Paul's own encounter with Christ, by whom he was called to preach to the Gentiles, this audition received in Paradise was for his ears alone. Even the secret words that constituted the high point of initiation into a Hellenistic Mystery cult were shared with all the cult members. But about the words he heard in Paradise, Paul can say only—that he is allowed to say nothing. It is doubtful that he would have expressed himself this way if, as Käsemann suggests (1942:64–65, 68), he had heard only ecstatic speech, the language of the New Age (cf. 1 Cor 14). Had he heard the divine name pronounced (Bowker 1971:168 n. 1)? Or, perhaps more likely, had he been told about certain "deep things of God" (see Windisch, 379, and Dunn 1975:215, who refer to 1 Cor 2:9–10)? Paul offers no clue and, more important, expresses no regrets that he was *forbidden . . . to repeat* what he had heard.

On a third point, whether he had been taken up to Paradise *in the body or outside the body,* he not only acknowledges but actually emphasizes his own complete ignorance (vv. 2, 3). One would suppose, on the basis of 1 Cor 15:35–50, that a bodiless journey would have been inconceivable to Paul—just as it was, theoretically, to anyone whose anthropology was essentially Jewish (see NOTES; cf. Baumgarten 1975:142). If the apostle has Gnostic opponents in mind here, as Schmithals believes, then by tacitly allowing the possibility of a bodiless experience he would, to that extent, have become "a Gnostic to the Gnostics" (cf. 1 Cor 9:19–23) in order to make a point (Schmithals 1971: 216–17; followed by Baumgarten 1975:142–43). His point, considering the context (especially 12:9*a*), would be that the Gnostics are mistaken to presume their own perfection and that they do not need the grace of God (Schmithals ibid.). However, nothing about Paul's narration of his journey to Paradise requires one to think that he has Gnostic experiences specifically in mind, for there is nothing here which cannot be found as well in non-Gnostic forms of Hellenistic mysticism (see Georgi 1964:179ff., 298). It is enough to observe that, by emphasizing his uncertainty about the mode of his rapture, Paul seems to be saying that he does not really care; and this suggests that there are some in Corinth who really do.

In summary, the apostle has provided his readers with very little information about this extraordinary journey, and he has had nothing to say about its possible religious significance. How, precisely, he was taken up to Paradise he does not know, what he saw there he does not say, and what he heard there he must not repeat.

*A Further Comment About Boasting, 12:5-10*

As in 11:30-33, but now with special reference to the preceding account of a journey to Paradise, Paul insists that he will boast only of his weaknesses. The centerpiece of the present comment is the apostle's report of an oracle that the Lord has given to him in response to his plea for relief from a certain personal affliction (vv. 7*b*-9*a*). With Paul's application of this oracle to his own situation (vv. 9*b*-10), the main part of his "fool's speech" (11:21*b*-12:10) has been concluded.

In v. 5, Paul continues to maintain the distance he had established in vv. 2-4 between himself as narrator and the *person* whose journey to Paradise he has been describing. It is evident now why he makes the distinction. Because religious experiences, no matter how extraordinary, cannot legitimate one's apostleship, but only weakness and suffering, Paul will boast solely of the latter. Therefore, while he is able to claim for his private self the kind of experience of which his rivals boast, he does not register that as an apostolic claim. For his "public" self—that is, in order to demonstrate his apostolic status—he boasts only *of weaknesses* (as in 11:30, on which see the COMMENT). These would include, doubtless, the weakness he had demonstrated by his craven flight from Damascus (see COMMENT on 11:32-33) and the personal affliction to which he will refer in 12:7*b*.

It is clear from v. 6*a* that, in the present comment (vv. 5-10), Paul has abandoned the mask of the fool worn through most of 11:1ff. He means that if he really wanted to boast of things other than his weaknesses, he could do so truthfully. Does he want the Corinthians to infer from this that his rivals have boasted of experiences they have never actually had (so Barrett, 312)? Perhaps, but that is probably not the main point. Nor should the comment be read as an attestation of the reality of his own journey to Paradise (so, e.g., Lincoln 1979:209), although it serves that function indirectly. Rather, by declaring that he could truthfully boast about other things, he is supporting what he wants most to get across—namely, that he has deliberately chosen to boast about his weaknesses (cf. Bultmann, 225).

This point is explicit in vv. 6*b*-7*a*, where the apostle says why he refrains from boasting about the experience he has just described (vv. 2-4). (See NOTES for a justification of the text, punctuation, and tr. adopted here.) Elsewhere in this letter Paul alludes to the Corinthians' desire for proof that Christ is speaking through him (13:3), probably in the form of evidence of special religious experiences and spiritual powers. Here, however, Paul declares that he does not want anyone to *credit* him with *extraordinary . . . revelations,* but only with what they can *see* him doing and *hear* from him: that is, his apostleship cannot be demonstrated by a recitation of his otherworldly experiences, but only by the effectiveness of his this-worldly service as an apostle (cf. Windisch, 382; Käsemann 1942:69). The effectiveness of this service, and thus the legitimacy of Paul's apostleship, is confirmed by what the Corinthians can *see* and *hear* of his human frailties (the point of this "fool's speech") and of his apostolic work in establishing their own congregation (see comments on 13:5–6 and 3:2–3; cf. Cambier 1962:503–4; Lincoln 1979:210). For his only proper work as an apostle is to let the death, and therefore the life, of Jesus be disclosed through his weaknesses (4:7–15), and to build up the churches (10:8; 13:10).

For decisive authorization of his resolution not to boast of things like private religious experiences, Paul reports in vv. 7*b*–9*a* on an oracle he has received from Christ (cf. Cambier 1962:513). His intention here is not to boast of having received this oracle, but to convey its content and to explain its meaning. Thus, while one may agree with Betz (1969:290–303) that the report follows in general the conventional form of healing narratives (aretalogies), one cannot agree with him that Paul offers one of his own because he knows his opponents especially value them (ibid:304) and because he wants to parody them (ibid., e.g., 289; 1972:85–86, 93). In this section, 12:5–10, the apostle is not mocking the boasts of his rivals but explaining why his own boasting consists of what it does.

Paul begins by describing an affliction from which he needed relief, v. 7*b*, although he emphasizes that God has given it to him for a purpose—that he not be *overly exalted* by such things as his journey to Paradise. (Thompson 1982:10 notes that Paul in 11:20 has accused his rivals of just that kind of presumptuousness.) One may compare Philo's interpretation of the affliction visited upon Jacob (see Gen 32:25)—that when the soul attains power and perfection it must be saved from conceit by a certain disablement (*Dreams* I, 130–31; cited by Windisch, 385). Or, again, there is Plutarch's advice that self-praise is rendered more palatable if one includes a reference to some personal flaw (*On Praising Oneself Inoffensively* 13). Paul describes the affliction given to him for this purpose as, first, *a thorn in the flesh* (see NOTES for this tr.). Whatever else this image may suggest (see below), one may infer from it, at least, that the apostle regards the affliction as affecting him continuously and in a very direct way.

In the second place, Paul personalizes the affliction by calling it *an angel of Satan*. This does not really contradict the point that God had given it to him for a reason, because Satan is often portrayed in Jewish and Christian literature as an agent of God's purposes (cf. Job 2:6–7; Noack 1948:96). Indeed, Paul himself can think of him as inflicting appropriate punishment (1 Cor 5:5; see Delling, *TDNT* VII:412 n. 28; Thornton 1972). Here, however, Satan's angel is not described as having been sent to punish Paul, but to "abuse" him. If by using this word (on which see NOTES) he is alluding to the physical abuse suffered by Jesus after his arrest (Schmidt 1950:221; Bieder 1961:332), then here as elsewhere (e.g., 1:5; 4:7–15) he would be associating his sufferings with those of the Lord whom he serves as an apostle.

Can the affliction Paul is describing be identified any more specifically? Many have thought so, and the literature on the subject is enormous. Indeed, as Kierkegaard observed more than a century ago, "This passage . . . seems

to have afforded an uncommonly favorable opportunity for everyone to become an interpreter of the Bible" (1946:52). A survey of what has been presumed and proposed about Paul's *thorn in the flesh* across the centuries amply
confirms this. While such a survey cannot be undertaken here, and need not
be (see, e.g., Lightfoot 1884:186–91; Fenner 1930:30–37; Allo, 313–23;
Hughes, 443–46; Güttgemanns 1966:162–64; Prümm I, 660–64; Schmidt,
*TDNT* III:820–21), a general review of the major options may be useful.

1. A number of interpreters have identified Paul's affliction as some type of
personal anxiety or spiritual torment. A favorite view in the Middle Ages,
perhaps encouraged by the Latin rendering of *a thorn in the flesh* as *stimulus
carnis* (Lightfoot 1884:188 credits Luther with this observation), was that Paul
suffered the torment of sexual temptations. This view in a somewhat modified
form is still endorsed by certain scholars, who prefer, however, to speak rather
more generally of spiritual weakness and the temptation to sin (e.g., Fahy
1964:218–19; de Boor, 234). But this interpretation, at least in its original form,
is contradicted by the fact that Paul regarded himself as gifted with the
strength to remain celibate (1 Cor 7:7); and even in its modified form there is
nothing in the context to support it (Plummer, 350). One may also list here
the view of Schlatter, 667, that Paul's thorn was the judgment of a guilty
conscience, his sense of unworthiness. But this presumes an un-Pauline, moralistic view of sin, and it reduces the meaning of *grace* in v. 9a to simple
forgiveness, whereas the context requires something more (Binder 1976:10). A
more distinctive proposal is that of Menoud, who argues that Paul's affliction
is his agony over the unbelief of the Jews (1978:24–27). But this requires a very
specialized interpretation of *in the flesh,* based especially on Rom 9:2, 3
(Binder 1976:10), and it is difficult to know how this agony could be classified
among the kinds of *weaknesses* listed in v. 10 of our passage (cf. Delling, *TDNT*
VII:412). Finally, one might include here the view of R. M. Price (1980:36–37)
who identifies the affliction as Paul's harassment by "a demon or malevolent
angel" sent to him while he was still on his heavenward journey to keep him
from being too elated by it. Price finds parallels to this in the more elaborate
versions of Jewish Merkabah visions (ibid.) and in later Christian literature
from the second into the eighth century (ibid.:38–39). But, while this permits
taking the reference to Satan's angel in a very straightforward way, it requires
that the apostle's prayers for relief and the Lord's answer (vv. 8–9a) also took
place on the journey to Paradise, a view which is untenable on other grounds
(see below).

2. The most widely accepted view, at least in modern times, identifies Paul's
thorn in the flesh as some kind of physical or perhaps mental illness. Indeed,
this was also one of the earliest interpretations, presumed by Tertullian,
Jerome, Pelagius, and Primasius—who, along with still others, identified
Paul's affliction as headache. In support of the view that Paul's thorn was some
kind of bodily ailment, one may point to (a) the metaphor he has chosen to

describe it (a thorn in the flesh causes physical discomfort); (b) the widespread ancient belief that illnesses were caused by demons, and especially by Satan (Schmidt, *TDNT* III:819); (c) Paul's own reference to a serious physical malady by which he had been burdened during his mission in Galatia (Gal 4:13–14, on which see Betz 1979:224–26); and (d) the general formal similarity between the account here in 2 Cor 12:7b–9a and Hellenistic stories of miraculous cures (Betz 1969:290–303). While many interpreters are content to leave the illness undiagnosed for want of sufficient data (e.g., Betz 1979:224–26; Plummer, 351; Güttgemanns 1966:163, 164–65; Bruce, 248), many others have been tempted to speculate, often arriving at very precise conclusions: malarial fever (most recently, Prümm I, 664–65); some form of epilepsy (e.g., Dibelius 1909:46–47; Hisey and Beck 1961:125–29; Hisey 1978:12–19); solar retinitis (Manchester and Manchester 1972; cf. Nisbet 1969:126); a speech impediment (e.g., Clarke 1929; Barrett, 315) or—expanding the category to include psychosomatic disorders—hysteria (e.g., Fenner 1930:37–40; Windisch, 387) or states of depression (Lietzmann, 157).

3. Finally, there are those who argue that the thorn in the flesh is to be associated with the persecution which Paul often experienced. This idea, too, was held by certain of the Church Fathers, among them Chrysostom (see *NPNF,* 1st ser. XII:400), Augustine, Theodoret, and Theophylact. Modern proponents of this view (e.g., Mullins 1957; Bieder 1961; Thierry 1962; Binder 1976; Barré 1980) have marshaled a number of serious arguments to support it, these being the most important ones: (a) Paul's reference to the agent of the affliction as *an angel of Satan* requires that one think of a person or group of persons as its cause (Mullins 1957:301), and it corresponds with Paul's earlier reference to his opponents in Corinth as "ministers" of Satan (11:15; Mullins ibid.:301–2; Bieder 1961:332; Thierry 1962:309); (b) the only other time Paul uses the term here translated *to abuse (kolaphizein)* is in the hardship list of 1 Cor 4 (v. 11c), where it refers to hostility he has suffered from those who oppose him (Barré 1980:221); (c) in LXX Num 33:55; Ezek 28:24 the word "thorn" is employed metaphorically with reference to Israel's enemies (Mullins 1957:302; Barré 1980:226); (d) the phrase *in the flesh* may be understood as a reference to one's whole earthly existence—as, e.g., in Phil 1:24 (Delling, *TDNT* VII:411; Thierry 1962:304); and (e) the hardship lists which closely precede and follow this mention of a thorn in the flesh (11:23b–29; 12:10a) both include references to persecution (Barré 1980:225).

The weight of the evidence would seem to favor (2) or (3), and perhaps (2) more than (3). Against the hypothesis that Paul is referring to opponents from whom he must endure hostile words and/or actions, it may be objected (a) that the reference to *an angel of Satan* does not sound like a reference to a group of persons (Güttgemanns 1966:164); (b) that in 2 Cor 11:14–15, Satan himself is the angel and his minions are called "ministers," not "angels" (ibid.); and (c) that the imagery of a *thorn in the flesh* requires us to think of some affliction more directly personal than persecution, which Paul shared with the whole church (Plummer, 350; Menoud 1978:24; cf. Noack 1948:96). The most serious objection to intepreting the affliction as an illness, on the other hand, is that Paul could not have endured and achieved what he did as a missionary had he been burdened by some debilitating physical (or psychosomatic) condition. But a chronic ailment need not have been debilitating, only aggravating, to have prompted his plea to the Lord that it be removed from him.

In v. 8, Paul reports that he had besought the Lord *three times* for relief from the affliction. Taken by itself, this remark suggests that the apostle's account will follow the standard pattern for Hellenistic narratives about divine healings (see NOTES). In this context, however—where no healing is recorded—the comment shows, on the one hand, how intent he once was on being helped and, on the other hand, that this is a request he no longer makes (Zmijewski 1978:377–78, 379). It is surely unwarranted to fuse this account with the preceding report of a heavenward journey, and to suppose that these petitions were addressed to the enthroned Lord as Paul stood before him in Paradise (so R. M. Price 1980:37), for the apostle has already said that what he heard there he was forbidden to repeat (v. 4). The two accounts are formally and functionally distinct. Neither the setting in which the apostle's prayers were offered nor the span of time over which he sought relief are indicated.

What was the Lord's response? This stands in v. 9a, formulated in the style typical of divine oracles (see NOTES and Betz 1969:294–300). These are, of course, not the words of the earthly Jesus, drawn from the church's tradition, but a proclamation addressed to Paul by the risen and exalted Christ. The striking thing is that the Lord neither effects nor promises removal of Paul's thorn in the flesh. In this respect, the apostle's prayers go unanswered. Rather —and this is what Paul himself now wants to impress on his readers (see vv. 9b–10)—the apostle is directed to understand his affliction as part of that *weakness* in and through which God's powerful grace is operative. It is clear that, from Paul's point of view, the decisive demonstration of the truth of this oracular pronouncement is Christ himself, "crucified in weakness," but alive "by the power of God" (13:4a; cf. 1 Cor 1:17–18, 22–24). This is why weakness is the hallmark of his apostleship, because he has been commissioned to the service of the gospel through the grace of this Christ—a grace whose power is made present in the cross. Paul therefore does not, like the Cynic and Stoic philosophers of his day, strive to transcend his weaknesses by dismissing them as trifling (see COMMENT on 4:8–9). Nor does he, like them, hold to the ideal of self-sufficiency (see NOTES), striving to limit his needs and therefore his dependency on others. Rather, precisely by accepting his tribulations as real weaknesses he is led by them to acknowledge his ultimate dependence on God (cf. 1:8–9). Thereby his weaknesses—not just the frailty which inevitably characterizes his creaturely status, but the adversities and afflictions he has had to bear as an apostle—have become a means by which the incomparable power of God is revealed (4:7–15; cf. Bultmann, 228; Betz 1969:302; Jervell 1976:195, 197; Fuchs 1980:245–46). The oracle he now quotes is therefore but a special formulation of the gospel itself: salvation, one's only true sufficiency, is by God's grace and in God's power (cf. 3:5; 8:9; Rom 1:16; and the midrash on Deut 3:26 cited in the NOTES).

Having cited the oracle (v. 9*a*), Paul goes on in vv. 9*b*–10 to show how it applies to him, and therefore how it supports what he has been doing in this "fool's speech." Three sentences express essentially the same point in three different ways (cf. Windisch, 392). In the first, v. 9*b*, the apostle says that he has now stopped praying for relief from the thorn in the flesh which he had formerly considered an angel of Satan sent to bedevil him. Now, instead, he boasts of his weaknesses, including that specific affliction, because now he understands them not as Satan's work but as the operation of the grace of the crucified Christ (cf. Güttgemanns 1966:168–69; Betz 1969:303). It is this grace that Paul here speaks of: the grace that constitutes *the power of Christ,* just as it is constitutive of the gospel itself. Since power is actualized in weakness (v. 9*a*), he calls attention to his weaknesses in order that Christ's power can become effective (not just recognized; see O'Collins 1971:536–37) in his apostolic presence and service (see especially 2:14–17; 4:7–11; cf. 1 Cor 5:4).

In v. 10*a* one sees Paul actually boasting in his weaknesses. By pointing out that he is doing this *because of Christ,* as an apostolic agent of Christ's power, he is able to keep inviolate the principle about boasting he had cited in 10:17 (Zmijewski 1978:394 and n. 517). Here Paul offers, for the second time in this "fool's speech," a catalog of the hardships he has endured. It is much shorter than the one in 11:23*b*–29 (and those in 4:8–9; 6:4*c*–5), and the adversities listed are much more general (for details, see NOTES). The only item that does not appear in any other of Paul's hardship lists is *insults,* which is possibly inserted here because of the slanders he has had to put up with from the rival apostles, and perhaps from certain members of his congregation, in Corinth (Zmijewski 1978:393; P. Marshall 1980:314).

The hardship list is followed in v. 10*b* by a reiteration of the point of the oracle Paul had received (v. 9*a*). Now, however, it is formulated as an expression of the apostle's own deep conviction. Moreover, it is formulated in such a way as to accentuate the paradox which was less directly stated in the oracle itself. The power Paul says he has when he is weak is surely not to be identified only with the "patience" he can show when confronted with adversities (against Windisch, 394). It must refer primarily to *the power of Christ* which his weaknesses disclose to be operative in his ministry. The paradox with which Paul is working here is profound, and it must not be misunderstood. He is not saying that "weakness is power" (correctly Jervell 1976:197), as Philo is when he refers to Moses and the people of Israel who because of their weakness were sheltered from harm by the providence of God (*Moses* I, 69, quoted in NOTES; cf. 67, 68: by God's power the victims of aggression overcome the aggressors).

Nor does Paul mean that he lives in the confidence that the weak will them-selves be clothed with power, displacing the mighty from their seats (as, e.g., in Hannah's song, 1 Sam 2:1–10; cf. Luke 1:46–55). He is saying, rather, that the weaknesses which continue to characterize his life as an apostle—of which the Corinthians are very much aware and from which he neither seeks nor expects relief—represent the effective working of the power of the crucified Christ in his ministry.

## 5. EPILOGUE, 12:11–13

12 ¹¹I have been a fool! You have forced me to be, since I ought to have been recommended by you. For I was in no way inferior to the super-apostles, even though I am nothing. ¹²The apostolic signs were performed among you with utmost endurance, by signs and wonders and deeds of power. ¹³In what respect were you treated worse than the other churches, except that I myself did not burden you? Pardon me for this offense!

## NOTES

12:11. *a fool.* Cf. 11:16, 19; 12:6.

*You have forced me to be.* The *you (hymeis)* is emphatic. The words *to be* have been supplied for the tr., since one must understand some infinitive after the verb *anakazein* ("to force"). Cf. Plutarch's reference to "those who are forced to speak in their own praise [*tous anagkasthentas epainein autous*]" (*On Praising Oneself Inoffensively* 11, cited by Windisch, 395).

*since I.* Again (see preceding note), the pronoun *(egō)* is emphatic.

*ought.* Here the imperfect tense *(opheilon)* is used of an obligation which has not been fulfilled; BDF § 358.

*recommended by you.* The *you (hymōn)* is emphatic. Earlier in this letter (10:12, 18) Paul has criticized his rivals for recommending themselves.

*I was in no way inferior.* An equivalent statement stands in 11:5, except that here the verb is aorist *(hysterēsa)*. Thus it corresponds in tense with the verb in v. 12 and, like it, must refer back to the time of Paul's residence in Corinth (Plummer, 358; Windisch, 395; Bultmann, 233 and 1947:48); contrast Barrett, 320, whose view that Paul is comparing himself with the Jerusalem apostles, not his rivals in Corinth, constrains him to interpret the aorist as "constative," without specific reference to a past occasion.

*the super-apostles.* As in 11:5.

*I am nothing.* This formula *(ouden eimi*—for the use of a neuter predicate with a personal subject see BDF § 131) derives from the dispute between the Socratic philo-sophical tradition and ancient rhetoric. See Betz 1972:122–28, who cites, among others,

Plato's *Phaedrus* 234 C–D and Epictetus III.ix; IV.viii.22ff., and suggests that the roots of the idea go back to the Delphic teaching that human beings are nothing in comparison with the divine power. The formula is also present in 1 Cor 13:2, and it seems to be reflected as well in 1 Cor 3:7 (perhaps also in Gal 2:6, cited by de Boor, 239). Cf. also 1 Cor 15:9–10; 2 Cor 3:5.

12. *The apostolic signs.* More literally, "The signs of the apostle" *(ta men sēmeia tou apostolou)*, leaving the *men* (which has no matching *de*) untranslated (although it sometimes has "concessive or restrictive force" in such cases; Robertson 1923:1151). The articles with "signs" and "apostle" mark these as generic terms here (Plummer, 359; Windisch, 396, with reference to the generic articles in Matt 18:17), so that no specific signs are in view, and "the apostle" is representative of the class (Robertson 1923:408, cf. 757). According to Matt 10:1, 8 par., Jesus had commissioned his disciples to cast out demons, and such activity is mentioned in Mark 16:17–18 as one of the "signs" by which their preaching was confirmed (cf. Mark 16:20). In Acts there are frequent references to the "signs" performed by apostles (e.g., 2:43; 5:12). Apart from the present passage, Paul uses the word *signs* in this sense only in Rom 15:19.

*were performed.* The verb *(katergazesthai)* is used similarly in Rom 15:18, but here it is passive. The tense is aorist because Paul is thinking of a specific time in the past when he was in Corinth.

*with utmost endurance.* Here the dative *(en pasē hypomonē)* indicates the manner in which (not the means by which) the apostolic signs were done in Corinth (cf. BDF § 198[4]; Cambier 1962:512 n. 1). As in 8:7 (on which see the NOTES), *utmost* translates *pas.* The noun *endurance* involves much more than simple "patience" (Hughes, 457) or "constancy" (Héring, 95); see NOTES and COMMENT on 1:6 and 6:4, where (as also in Rom 5:3–4) it means enduring with hope in the face of afflictions.

*by signs and wonders and deeds of power.* These same three terms *(sēmeia, terata, dynameis)* are also combined in Acts 2:22; 2 Thess 2:9; Heb 2:4. Cf. Rom 15:19, "by the power of signs and wonders" *(RSV).* Here all three words stand in the dative case, expressing the means by which the apostolic signs had been exhibited in Corinth (Windisch, 397, rightly cites Rom 15:18–19, where *en* with the dative has this meaning; contrast Barrett, 321). Thus, *signs* here has a rather more specific meaning than in the earlier part of the verse. "Signs and wonders" is a stock phrase in the Hebrew Bible and in the LXX (e.g., Exod 7:3; Deut 34:11; Isa 8:18; Jer 32 [LXX:39]:20, 21; Wis 8:8; 10:16), but also in secular literature (e.g., Polybius III, 112.8; cited along with other instances in BAG s.v. *sēmeion,* 2a). Elsewhere in the NT it is found in Matt 24:24 par.; John 4:48; Acts 2:43; 4:30; 5:12; 6:8; 7:36; 14:3; cf. Acts 2:19. In Acts 8:13 "signs and deeds of power" are joined. Paul refers to *deeds of power* also in 1 Cor 12:10, 28, 29; Gal 3:5 (in all these cases rendered as "miracles" by *RSV*).

13. *In what respect.* Following Barrett, 322, the *gar* ("for") is left untranslated. The neuter *ho* ("which") is taken as an accusative of respect (Moule 1953:131).

*treated worse.* The word *(hēssothēte,* as in P⁴⁶ and the other best witnesses) occurs only here in the NT.

*the other churches.* Possibly, following on 11:28, an inclusive reference to all the other congregations Paul has founded (cf. Rom 16:4, 16 and the NOTES and COMMENT on 8:18–19, 23–24). Probably, however, Paul's Macedonian congregations are specifically in mind, as in 11:8–9 (and 8:1).

*I myself.* Cf. 10:1. The emphasis *(autos egō)* suggests that Paul will not presume to speak for others. Does he have in mind associates who may have been a burden to the Corinthians in some way? Or the rival apostles (e.g., 11:20)?

*did not burden you.* As in 11:9.

*Pardon me.* The same verb is translated "forgive" in 2:7 (see NOTES), 10. Here it is used with great irony.

*this offense.* The noun is often used by Paul to describe the moral wickedness of unbelievers (e.g., Rom 1:18, 29). Here, as in Rom 3:5; 9:14, it is more nearly a juridical than a moral term. Cf. the use of the cognate verb *(adikein)* in 7:2, 12 (translated "to wrong").

## COMMENT

These verses constitute an epilogue to the "fool's speech" (11:21*b*–12:10), because in them Paul is looking back over that speech and offering a justification for the foolish boasting he allowed himself to do in it. Thus, particularly in v. 11 we have an epidiorthosis (subsequent justification; BDF § 495[3]) which corresponds to the prodiorthosis (advance justification) contained in the much lengthier prologue to the speech (11:1–21*a,* especially vv. 1–4, 16–20). At the same time, a transition is made to the last major section of the Letter Body (12:14–13:10).

In v. 11*ab* the apostle justifies his foolish boasting on the grounds that he has been forced to defend himself because others have not. Two rhetorical rules set forth by Plutarch are in play here. One is that those who praise themselves are blameless because they are doing what others should do *(On Praising Oneself Inoffensively* 1). The other is that self-praise is justified when the truth must be told, not only in self-defense, but also—by winning the confidence of others—to do them good (ibid. 2,3; note as well the speech attributed to Manlius by Livy XXXVIII.xlix.6, where the speaker asks that he be excused for his lengthy, boastful address because he needs to defend himself against certain untrue accusations). Since the Corinthian Christians, whom Paul regards as his best "letter of recommendation" (3:1–3), have not defended him against the slanders directed at him by the rival apostles, he has had to boast on his own behalf, doing what he has criticized those others for doing (note 10:12, 18).

The essence of his boast is summarized in v. 11*c.* Here Paul reasserts the point—made in other words as early as 10:7, and in almost identical words in 11:5—that he is *in no way inferior to the super-apostles.* As in 11:5 (on which see NOTES and COMMENT), the term *super-apostles* is used ironically of those who have intruded into Paul's Corinthian congregation, making extravagant claims about themselves and challenging Paul's apostolic legitimacy. If, as Schmithals argues (1971:187; cf. Héring, 95), the opponents in view are Gnostics who have accused Paul of being "a 'nothing,' " (that is, a "sarkic" [person of the flesh] devoid of real life), then one would have to interpret the closing remark of v. 11 as a tongue-in-cheek concession to them: "even though they say I am 'nothing.' " But the rivals should probably not be identified as Gnostics (see INTRODUCTION, pp. 48–54), and the apostle's reference to his "nothingness" here, as elsewhere (1 Cor 3:7; 13:2), is more readily understood against the background of the Socratic tradition (Betz, cited in NOTES). Especially when he is tempted or, as here, forced to boast, he takes care to remind himself and his readers that he is an apostle only by the grace of God (1 Cor 15:9–10; cf. 2 Cor 3:5).

It is apparent that Paul's rivals have alleged several different kinds of deficiencies in trying to prove his "inferiority" as an apostle. In 11:5–6, Paul had in mind specifically their charge that his plain speech shows his lack of deep spiritual wisdom. Here, the remark in v. 12 suggests that he has also been denounced for having accomplished none (or few) of *the apostolic signs* (a phrase perhaps used by his opponents) people have a right to expect. Paul concedes nothing to his challengers on this point (contrast 11:6), but states (with a certain matter-of-factness) that *the apostolic signs were* indeed *performed* in Corinth. He clearly shares the widespread ancient belief, at home as well in the earliest church, that certain manifestations of divine power will accompany the propagation of any valid religious truth (see the references to the Synoptic Gospels and Acts given in the NOTES). Not only here, but also in Rom 15:18–19 and Gal 3:5 (perhaps also in 1 Cor 2:4; 1 Thess 1:5) he readily associates such signs with his work as an apostle.

Paul is nonetheless guarded as he writes about these signs. For one thing, he uses the passive voice, *were performed,* attributing them ultimately to God, just as he attributes to God everything that makes him adequate as an apostle (see 3:5). By making no direct claim about his own miraculous powers he is perhaps intending to distinguish himself from his rivals (see, e.g., 5:12). Moreover, when he indicates that the signs had been performed *with utmost endurance* he is saying that they were performed in the context of a ministry distinguished, first of all, by the kinds of hardships and afflictions he has cataloged in 11:23b–29 and 12:10. At this point, too, one may detect a difference between Paul and his rivals. He does not refer to these signs in order to emphasize his own possession of unique, supernatural powers. He associates them, rather, with the power of the Holy Spirit (Rom 15:18–19; Gal 3:1–5; see Käsemann 1942:61–62), and thus regards them as signs of the New Age—present, however, in a world where weakness and suffering continue to exist (Nielsen 1980:153–54). Finally, and in marked contrast to the detail he gives about his hardships in 11:23b–29 and his weaknesses in 11:32–12:10, his reference to *apostolic signs* is left quite vague. Even the specification of them as *signs and wonders and deeds of power* does not change this, because he is simply relying on traditional phrases (see NOTES) which are themselves very general.

To what, then, is the apostle referring in v. 12? Acts portrays him as performing miraculous deeds on a number of occasions: in Lystra he heals a man crippled since birth (14:8–10); in Philippi he exorcizes an unclean spirit from a slave girl (16:16–18); in Ephesus he does "mighty deeds'" of various sorts (19:11–12); in Troas he revives Eutychus after the young man's fall from a third-floor window (20:7–12); on the island of Malta he survives a snake bite (28:1–6), cures Publius' father of dysentery (28:7–8), and cures other islanders of their diseases (28:9). Indeed, he and Barnabas could report to the Jerusalem conference on "what signs and wonders God had done through them among the Gentiles" (15:12, *RSV*). As it turns out, none of these wondrous deeds described in Acts is located in Corinth, and none of them is mentioned or even alluded to by Paul in his letters. Moreover, in the list of charismatic gifts in 1 Cor 12:28–30, those who work miracles and do healings are distinguished from apostles, which shows clearly that, for Paul, these activities do not as such constitute one an apostle.

Failing any indication to the contrary, Paul must be using the phrase *signs and wonders and deeds of power* in the way his readers would naturally take it—namely, with reference to some kind of miraculous occurrences, perhaps healings, which took place (despite the silence of Acts 18) when he was preaching the gospel to them. For this reason, the suggestion of Schmithals that the reference is to "the wondrous effect of the Word" itself (1969:37; cf. 1971:281; 1972:29–30 n. 42) is not persuasive. It is important to notice, however, that when Paul mentions such phenomena in Rom 15:18–19 and Gal 3:1–5 (cf. 1 Cor 2:4; 1 Thess 1:5, possible allusions), he is clearly subordinating them to the primary and distinguishing task of the apostle, which is to proclaim the word of the gospel.

The subject of apostolic signs is abruptly dropped, however, as Paul turns in v. 13 to another matter. Actually, he is only returning to a subject he had already broached in 11:7–11—his refusal to accept financial support from his Corinthian congregation, even though he was accepting it from his congregations in Macedonia (probably *the other churches* mentioned here). See the discussion of this in the COMMENT on 11:7–11. There is splendid irony in the way he poses the question here, and it is double-edged. On the one hand, how strange they should object that he has burdened other churches with his support, and not theirs. On the other hand, how strange they should object that he has not tried to exploit his relationship to them, as his rivals have (11:20). Consistent with the remark in 11:9*b*, he does not indicate that his practice is going to change, at least in the near future, but he only begs their pardon (the irony continues!) for this alleged injustice. Perhaps he fears that any alteration in his practice now could be interpreted by people in Corinth as confirmation of what his rivals have been saying about his practice until now (cf. Pratscher 1979:293–94, 298). At any rate, Paul is not finished with this matter, and he will continue with it even as he proceeds, in the next paragraph, to write of his impending visit to Corinth (see 12:14*b*–18).

# C. RENEWAL AND CONCLUSION OF THE APPEAL, 12:14–13:10

## 6. EXPRESSIONS OF CONCERN, 12:14–21

12 <sup>14</sup>Look here, I am ready to come to you for this third time, and I will not be a burden. I am not after what is yours, but you, for it is not the duty of children to save up for parents, but rather parents for children. <sup>15</sup>But for my part, I will very gladly spend and be expended for you. If I love you more, am I to be loved less? <sup>16</sup>Now, it is agreed that I did not burden you; nevertheless (you say), since I am crafty I have taken you in by deceit. <sup>17</sup>Did anyone whom I have sent to you— did I defraud you through him? <sup>18</sup>I urged Titus and I sent the brother along with him. Did Titus defraud you? Did we not conduct ourselves with the same spirit? Did we not take the same steps?

<sup>19</sup>You suppose all along that we are defending ourselves before you. In the sight of God we are speaking in Christ. Everything, beloved, is for your upbuilding. <sup>20</sup>For I fear that when I come I may find you not as I would wish and that you may find me not as you would wish: that there may be discord, jealousy, explosive tempers, cases of self-seeking, slanders, gossiping, cases of arrogance, general disorder; <sup>21</sup>that my God may again humiliate me in your presence when I come, and that I may have to mourn over many who have continued in their former sinning and did not repent of the impurity and sexual immorality and licentiousness they practiced.

## NOTES

12:14. *I am ready.* The Greek verb is *echō* (literally "I have"), but this can often mean "to be" in some particular condition (*GNTG* III:52; Moule 1953:161), and the present idiom is attested elsewhere (see Acts 21:13; 1 Pet 4:5 and Deissmann 1903:252).

*for this third time.* This phrase is to be taken with *to come,* not with *I am ready.* The grammar permits this interpretation (Plummer, 361, with reference to Acts 21:13) and the wording in 13:1 requires it. The arguments of Hyldahl (1973:303) to the contrary are not persuasive, although he is constrained to them by his desire to maintain the unity of 2 Cor 1–13. Thus, in his view, Paul twice before was "ready" to go to Corinth but then changed his plans (the visits in view in 1 Cor 1:15–16 and 1 Cor 16:5–9, respectively).

*I will not be a burden.* For the verb, see 11:9; 12:13.

*I am not after what is yours, but you.* Paul uses the verb (*zētein,* to "seek," "desire," etc.) in a rather similar way in 1 Cor 10:24 (cf. 1 Cor 13:5). With the whole thought here cf. Cicero, *About the Ends* II.xxvi.85: "So you must love me myself, not my possessions, if we are to be genuine friends." See also 1 Cor 8:5.

*not the duty.* Translated *ou opheilei,* which could also be rendered "ought not." It is probable, however, that Paul has in mind duties which derive from a "natural law"; see following note.

*to save up.* The verb is *thēsaurizein,* which means "to set aside," as for an inheritance. Cf. Plutarch, *On Love of Wealth* 526 A: "Someone will say, 'But they preserve and lay up [*thēsaurizousin*] their goods for children and heirs' "; and especially Philo, *Moses* II, 245: "But since, in the natural order of things [*nomos physeōs esti*] children are the heirs of their fathers and not fathers of their children . . ." (both passages cited by Windisch, 399). Aristotle (*Nichomachean Ethics* VIII.vii.1–2; cited by P. Marshall 1980:381–87) offers the parent-child relationship as an instance of a friendship between a superior and an inferior, and comments on the duties incumbent upon each of the parties.

15. *But for my part, I.* This paraphrase is meant to bring out the emphatic *egō* (*I;* see Plummer, 362; Barrett, 324), and interprets the *de* as mildly adversative (Plummer, 363).

*spend and be expended.* Paul is fond of using pairs of words like this, where the second form intensifies the first. Cf., e.g., "read and also understand" (1:13, with note); "despairing, but not utterly desperate" (4:8).

*for you.* Literally "for your souls" *(hyper tōn psychōn hymōn),* but that would be an over-translation since in this case (cf. Rom 16:14; 1 Thess 2:8) the word *psychē* means simply one's whole "natural" life (Schweizer, *TDNT* IX:648).

*If.* Following the best witnesses, which read *ei* (P⁴⁶ ℵ* et al.), although there is some support for "Even though" (*ei kai,* ℵ² D² et al.). Both words are omitted in D* et al. See Metzger 1971:586.

*I love.* Translates *agapō* (found in ■* A and some other witnesses). There is substantial support, however, for the participle, "loving" *(agapōn,* in P⁴⁶ ℵ² B D G et al.). The participle is undoubtedly better attested, and it is also the more difficult reading, since one must then supply *eimi* ("I am"). But this would be the only Pauline instance of this particular construction (Metzger 1971:586), so the finite verb may in fact be the correct reading. The sense, however, is the same in either case. Elsewhere in 1 Cor, Paul has referred to his love for the congregation in 2:4; 8:7; 11:11.

16. *Now, it is agreed.* Translates *estō de,* taking *de* as a transitional particle, not as adversative (thus, *Now,* not "But" as in *RSV*). Windisch, 402, offers examples from Philo, *Embassy to Gaius* 357, and Epictetus I.xxix.22; II.iv.5 to illustrate Paul's use of *estō* (translated here as *it is agreed;* more literally, "let it be"). Of these, the last provides the closest parallel to the present passage: "For, assuming that [*estō gar*] you cannot hold the place of a friend. . . ." The idiom here introduces a point on which the speaker (writer) and those addressed can at least provisionally agree.

*I.* The *I (egō)* is emphatic.

*did not burden.* The verb *(katabarein),* different from the one used in 11:9; 12:13, 14 (on which see NOTES), is used nowhere else by Paul; but cf. his use of *barein* in 1:8 and of *abarēs* in 11:9.

*nevertheless.* Here *alla* introduces a statement which stands in contrast with the preceding one; see BAG s.v.

*(you say).* These words are supplied in the tr. for the sake of clarity. In this part of the sentence Paul is citing a charge being made against him in Corinth.

*since I am crafty.* Translates *hyparchōn panourgos,* the participle having a causal sense here *(GNTG* III:157; Barrett, 324). The adjective *crafty* is used only here in the NT; but cf. Paul's use of the noun *panourgia* in 4:2 (with note) and 11:3.

*I have taken you in.* As in 11:20 (see NOTES), *lambanein* is used to mean taking advantage of someone for one's own gain.

*deceit.* Paul uses the term *(dolos)* elsewhere in Rom 1:29, in a list of vices, and in 1 Thess 2:3. Cf. also his use of the cognate verb, *doloun* (to falsify or adulterate), in 2 Cor 4:2, and of the adjective *dolios* in 2 Cor 11:13.

17. *Did anyone.* The accusative case of *tina* is variously explained as (a) due to attraction (BDF § 466[1]), (b) an accusative of respect (Hughes, 465–66 n. 153), or (c) perhaps a Semitism (Moule 1953:176). That the question is introduced by *mē* shows that Paul presumes it must be answered negatively ("No one . . . did they?").

*whom.* Translates *hōn,* which is to be interpreted as *toutōn hous,* "of those whom"; see BDF § 466(1).

*I have sent.* The perfect tense *(apestalka)* could be aoristic here, referring to one specific occasion on which someone had been sent to Corinth by Paul (so, e.g., BDF § 343[2]; *GNTG* I:144; Bultmann, 237). Otherwise it would be interpreted as "a perfect of broken continuity" *(GNTG* I:144), indicating that Paul has "from time to time" sent persons to Corinth (so also Barrett, 325). In view of v. 18*a,* the former is the more probable.

*did I defraud you.* After *anyone* there should be a third-person-singular verb, but the construction of the sentence is broken *(anacoluthon).* It seems clear that Paul does not have just *anyone* in mind, but a specific person (Titus), who is named in v. 18. The verb *pleonektein* ("to defraud") is used in 2:11 (translated there as "cheated") and 7:2, as well as here in 12:17, 18. It means, basically, the greedy acquisition and protection of more than one's proper share (Delling, *TDNT* VI:266–67), and this was often a topic of ethical discourses in the Greco-Roman world (surveyed by Delling, ibid.:268–70). See, e.g., Dio Chrysostom XVII *(Peri Pleonexias,* "On Covetousness"). Betz (1972: 116–17) emphasizes the use of the word in the humanistic tradition to describe the Sophists as "cheats."

*through him.* The reference must be to Titus, specifically; see preceding note and v. 18.

18. *I urged Titus.* On Titus, see NOTES for 2:13. Here, as in 8:6, the verb *parakalein* ("to urge") is used with reference to a mission of Titus to Corinth. See also 8:17, where the cognate noun is used in the same way. If chap. 8 indeed belongs to an earlier letter (see INTRODUCTION, pp. 35–41), then it is probable that the aorist tense used here *(urged)* looks back on the mission which was undertaken by Titus as he was sent off with the letter represented by chaps. 1–9. Thus the visit would have been Titus' second one to the congregation (so also, e.g., Windisch, 405), not his first (as, e.g., Lietzmann, 159, and Plummer, 364–65, maintain).

*the brother.* In chap. 8, two "brothers" are mentioned as accompanying Titus to Corinth. *The brother* referred to here is probably the "earnest" brother of 8:22; see COMMENT.

*Did Titus defraud you?* As with the question in v. 17, Paul presumes that the only appropriate answer is "No" *(mēti).* For the verb, see NOTES on v. 17.

*Did we not . . . ?* The second and third questions in v. 18, unlike the preceding ones in vv. 17, 18, are introduced with *ou* and presume that only an affirmative response is appropriate. In these two questions the first person plural probably stands for "Titus and I."

*conduct ourselves.* The verb is *peripatein* (literally "to walk"), as in 4:2; 5:7; 10:2, 3.

*with the same spirit.* A few (e.g., Windisch, 404; Heine 1976:102) interpret *pneuma* here as the Holy Spirit, and in support of this one might cite Rom 8:4; Gal 5:16 and Paul's references to "the same Spirit" *(to auto Pneuma),* meaning God's Spirit, in 1 Cor 12:8, 9, 11; 2 Cor 4:13. But the parallelism of the present question with the one that follows suggests that Paul is here using *pneuma* in an anthropological sense (as, e.g., in 7:13, where it has been translated as "mind") rather than in a theological sense (as, e.g., in 3:6–18; 11:4; 13:14). Cf. Phil 1:27, where, again, most commentators interpret *pneuma* anthropologically.

*take the same steps.* Since the verb must be supplied, this could be translated "walk in the same steps," and one may understand the verb to be *peripatein* ("to walk"), used in the preceding question (but translated there as "to conduct oneself"). Paul uses a similar metaphor in Rom 4:12 when he refers to "those who are not only circumcised, but also follow in the steps of the faith of our father Abraham while he was uncircumcised." Cf. also 1 Pet 2:21.

19. *You suppose.* Or, "Do you suppose," etc. Among the editors and trs. who read this as a question are WH, *GNT,* Beza and Calvin (but not Luther, as Plummer, 367, erroneously reports), *KJV, RSV, NIV, NAB.* It is read as a statement, however, by Nestle, Luther, *ASV, JB, NEB, TEV,* and others. The latter is slightly preferable, not only because "Paul knew his Corinthians" (Barrett, 328) but also because, taken as a question, it would blunt the effect of the preceding series of questions (vv. 17, 18) to which it does not belong.

*all along.* Reading *palai,* which is better attested than *palin* ("again") as well as the more difficult reading (Metzger 1971:587; against Héring, 97). The position of *palai* in the Greek sentence gives it a certain emphasis: "All along you suppose," etc.

*we are defending ourselves.* The first person plural, introduced at the end of v. 18 as Paul associated his behavior and that of Titus, continues in this verse—where, however, the reference is just to Paul himself; cf. v. 20. The verb "to defend" *(apologein)* is used elsewhere by Paul only in Rom 2:15, but the cognate noun appears also in 1 Cor 9:3; 2 Cor 7:11; Phil 1:7, 16. Note, too, the adjective *anapologētos* ("without excuse") in Rom 2:15.

*In the sight of God we are speaking in Christ.* As in 2:17, on which see the NOTES.

*Everything.* Is the reference to be restricted to *everything* Paul has written up to this point in his letter (cf. Plummer, 368), or is it to be taken as a reference to the whole of Paul's ministry to the Corinthians (cf. Barrett, 328)? Probably to anything Paul has said, written, or done which the Corinthians might regard as merely self-serving, but in particular to what he is writing in the present letter.

*beloved.* As in 7:1, on which see the note. If 6:14–7:1 is not to be attributed to Paul (see COMMENT there), then the present passage is the only one in 2 Cor where the Corinthians are addressed in this way.

*for your upbuilding.* Translates *tēs hymōn oikodomēs,* in which the *hymōn (your)* is emphatic by reason of its attributive position (*GNTG* III:190). Cf. 4:15a, "So everything is for your sake [*di' hymas*]." Paul's concern for exercising his authority in order to "build up" the Corinthian congregation is stated as a firm principle of his apostolic work in 10:8 (on which see NOTES) and 13:10.

20a. *For I fear that.* Paul expresses his anxiety about the Corinthians similarly in 11:3; see also Gal 4:11. Note that the use of the first person singular resumes after vv. 18c–19.

*when I come.* That is, for the third time, v. 14; 13:1a.

*I may find you not as I would wish . . . ,* etc. The English is a slight paraphrase of the Greek, which exhibits a nice chiastic pattern: [*ou*] *thelō heurō . . . heurethō . . . ou thelete* ("What I do not wish I find . . . I am found what you do not wish"); see Windisch, 408.

20b. *that there may be.* The *mē pōs (that)* depends on *For I fear* in v. 20a, but the verb has to be supplied. The present tr. presumes *ōsin (there may be);* see *GNTG* III:302.

*discord.* Translates *eris,* a term which occurs in several of the other vice lists in the NT (Rom 1:29; 13:13; Gal 5:20; 1 Tim 6:4; cf. Tit 3:9). See also 1 Cor 1:11; 3:3. "Quarreling" and "strife" are other possible trs. The plural *(ereis)* which is read by some witnesses is doubtless secondary, to agree with the other plural forms in the list (Metzger 1971:587).

*jealousy.* Or, "envy." Elsewhere in 2 Cor the word *(zēlos)* is used in a good sense, of "zeal" (7:7, 11; 9:2) or of the divine jealousy (11:2). Paul also lists it among the vices cataloged in Rom 13:13; Gal 5:20. See also 1 Cor 3:3. As in the case of *discord,* some witnesses read the plural (see preceding note).

*explosive tempers.* Translates *thymoi,* which might also be rendered as "angry outbursts." The vice lists in Gal 5:20 and 1 Clem 46:5 also use the plural (cf. Philo, *Who Is the Heir* 64; Josephus, *War* IV.v.2, cited in BAG s.v. 2), but the singular stands in Eph 4:31; Col 3:8. For the meaning of the word see Barclay 1962:49–53.

*cases of self-seeking.* The exact meaning of this term *(eritheia),* rarely found outside the NT, is not certain. See the discussions of it by Büchsel, *TDNT* II:660–61; Cranfield 1975:148–49, and in BAG s.v. 2. In Aristotle it is a term for the intrigues by which ambitious men seek to attain political office (*Politics* 1302b, 4; 1303a, 14), although Paul may understand it more as factiousness than as selfishness (cf. Windisch, 408). The plural form also appears in the vice list of Gal 5:20, but elsewhere in the NT one finds only the singular (Rom 2:8; Phil 1:17; 2:3; Jas 3:14, 16).

*slanders.* The noun (*katalalia;* literally "evil speech") occurs elsewhere in the NT only in 1 Pet 2:1, but Paul employs the adjective substantively in the list of vices in Rom 1:30. Note the verb in Jas 4:11; 1 Pet 2:12; 3:16.

*gossiping.* Translates the plural *psithyrismoi,* which must refer to multiple instances of secret tale-bearing. In Rom 1:29, Paul refers to "gossips," but the terms appear nowhere else in the NT.

*cases of arrogance.* The word (here plural, *physiōseis*) occurs only here in the NT.

But note Paul's frequent use of the cognate verb in 1 Cor (4:6, 18, 19; 5:2; 8:1; 13:4; elsewhere in the NT, only Col 2:18).

*general disorder.* This tr. follows *NEB* in attempting to represent the force of the Greek plural, *akatastasiai.* The same noun is translated as *riots* in 6:5, where it probably refers to specific civil commotions and not to *general* congregational *disorder.* The word also occurs in a vice list of sorts in Jas 3:16; elsewhere in 1 Cor 14:33; Luke 21:9. Note the related adjective in Jas 1:8; 3:8.

21. *that.* What follows is still dependent on *For I fear* in v. 20.

*again humiliate.* It is better to take *palin (again)* with *tapeinōsē (humiliate)* than with *elthontos mou (when I come),* for otherwise one would have expected *palin* to be used in v. 20 (Hughes, 472 n. 166; see also Plummer, 369; Barrett, 330; and for the contrary opinion Windisch, 409). In 11:7 the verb *tapeinoun* is translated "to demean"; see NOTES there and at 10:1, where the adjective "demeaned" appears. The suggestion of Bultmann, 241; 1947:30–31 (the latter translated by Barrett, 331) that an *ou* ("not") has dropped out before *humiliate* (thus, "that my God may not humiliate me") is unsupported by any textual evidence; moreover, it is quite unnecessary, since the text makes good sense as it stands (see COMMENT, and cf. Barrett, 331).

*in your presence.* Translates *pros hymas,* which frequently has this meaning; see especially 11:9; Gal 4:18, 20, where it is used with *pareinai* ("to be [present]").

*when I come.* The Greek *elthontos mou* (genitive case) is grammatically wrong, and has been corrected to *elthonta me* (accusative case) in some witnesses; see *GNTG* III:322; IV:99.

*to mourn.* Here the verb *(penthein)* refers to the apostle's own grief (cf. 2:3) over the failure of believers to live up to their Christian commitment (cf. Windisch, 410). In 1 Cor 5:2, the only other place where Paul uses the word, it also refers to distress over moral failure.

*many who.* This tr. understands the Greek, *pollous tōn prohēmartēkotōn* (strictly: "many of the ones who have continued in their former sinning"), to be an inexact expression for *pollous tous prohēmartēkotas* (Windisch, 410; cf. Bultmann, 241).

*have continued in their former sinning.* The perfect tense of the verb suggests persistence in sinning (Plummer, 370). The compound verb *prohamartanein* occurs nowhere else in the LXX or NT except in 13:2.

*and did not repent.* The verb *(metanoein)* is used by Paul only here, and the cognate noun only in 7:9, 10 (where it is translated "contrition"; see NOTES) and in Rom 2:4.

*impurity.* The same word *(akatharsia)* is used in the vice lists of Rom 1:24; Gal 5:19; Eph 5:3; Col 3:5, and is often associated, as it is here, with *sexual immorality* in particular. Paul uses the noun apart from lists in Rom 6:19; 1 Thess 2:3; 4:7, and the adjective appears in 1 Cor 7:14 (cf. 2 Cor 6:17).

*sexual immorality.* The Greek word *(porneia)* refers to any kind of illicit sexual activity, but not specifically to adultery, for which *moicheia* and its cognates are ordinarily employed (see, e.g., Rom 2:22; 1 Cor 6:9). The vice lists of 1 Cor 5:11; 6:9; Gal 5:19; Eph 5:3, 5; Col 3:5; 1 Tim 1:10, as well as Matt 15:19 par. Mark 7:21, also include this (or a cognate) term. Apart from such lists, note in particular Paul's discussion in 1 Cor 6:13*b*–18, and cf. 1 Cor 5:1, 9–10; 7:2; 10:8; 1 Thess 4:3.

*licentiousness.* In Paul's letters this word *(aselgeia),* which connotes flagrant public immorality and debauchery, is found only in vice lists (Rom 13:13; Gal 5:19, in addition to the present verse). It is also present in lists in Mark 7:22; Eph 4:19; 1 Pet 4:3. Elsewhere in the NT: 2 Pet 2:1, 7, 18; Jude 4. Like *impurity*, it is often associated specifically with illicit sexual behavior.

*practiced*. For Paul's use of the verb *(prassein)* see NOTES on 5:10, where it is translated "has done."

## COMMENT: GENERAL

Some commentators, alert to the thematic continuity, especially between 12:13 and 12:14–18, prefer to treat 12:11–18 (e.g., Plummer, 356–65; Barrett, 318–26), or at least 12:13–18 (Bultmann, 232–33), together. It is perhaps more helpful, however, to make the break between 12:13 and 12:14 (e.g., Windisch, 398), since the mention of a planned third visit to Corinth in 12:14, repeated in 13:1, constitutes a resumption of the concern with which Paul had begun in chap. 10. The so-called "fool's speech" of 11:21*b*–12:10 is meant to support the appeal, first expressed in 10:1–18 and now renewed and concluded in 12:14–13:10, that the obedience of the Corinthians be "complete" by the time of their apostle's arrival (see especially 10:1, 6 and COMMENT). Therefore the "prologue" and "epilogue" of that speech (identified above as 11:1–21*a* and 12:11–13, respectively) also serve a certain transitional function, and remind us that any division of the argument in chaps. 10–13 is to some extent artificial. It is not surprising, then, to find that certain topics which had arisen in the course of the speech are echoed in 12:14–13:10, notably Paul's refusal to let the Corinthian church support him financially (12:14–15; cf. 11:7–11; 12:13) and the theme of power in weakness (13:3*b*–4, 9*a*; cf. 12:9–10). But it is still his impending visit to Corinth (12:14, 20, 21; 13:1, 2, 10; cf. 10:1, 2, 10, 11) that moves Paul to write as he does here. (Jewett [1978:402–3] has suggested that 1 Cor 9:1–18 originally stood between 2 Cor 12:13 and 12:14. This is, of course, purely conjectural, since nothing in the textual tradition supports it. Even if one were convinced, as some have been, that 9:1–18 cannot have stood where it does now in 1 Cor, it is difficult to think of those paragraphs as coming after 2 Cor 12:13. Although Paul's apostleship and his refusal of financial support from Corinth are themes common to 1 Cor 9 and 2 Cor 10–13, the form and style of argument are quite different in the two. Moreover, the placement of 1 Cor 9:1–18 between 2 Cor 12:13 and 12:14 would seriously disrupt the close connection between the two verses, both of which use the unusual verb *katanarkan* ["to be a burden to"], not found in 1 Cor 9:1–18.)

In 12:14–21 specifically, the apostle expresses the two major concerns he has as he plans his forthcoming visit. First, he is worried because his refusal of financial support from the Corinthian congregation still seems to be misunderstood, and because there may even be some people in Corinth who suspect him of duplicitous behavior, vv. 14–18. Second, he is fearful that some members of the congregation still persist in a way of life that is incompatible with the gospel he has proclaimed to them, vv. 19–21. To the extent that these conditions do exist, the contention by Paul's rivals that he is not a fit apostle will be strengthened, and when Paul arrives in Corinth he may find it more difficult to reassert his leadership over the congregation.

## COMMENT: DETAILED

### About the Suspicion of Fraud, vv. 14–18

What was implicit in 10:1–18 (see 10:1, 2, 10, 11) is now made explicit: Paul will soon be coming to Corinth for the third time, v. 14a. It is conceivable that he means he will be coming for the third time since his founding of a congregation there, but it is more probable that he is thinking of the "founding visit" as one of the first two. His second visit, according to the most likely reconstruction of events, would have been the "sorrowful" one to which he alludes in 2:1 (see INTRODUCTION, pp. 41–42, 54). That visit, notably unsuccessful (see COMMENT on 1:23–2:2), had been abruptly terminated when one particular member of the congregation did something to Paul which seriously offended him (see COMMENT on 2:5–11; 7:8–12). Clearly, he does not want his forthcoming visit to turn out as badly as that earlier one, and so he writes now (chaps. 10–13, Letter E) in order to try to prevent that (see especially 10:2; 12:20–21; 13:2).

To begin with, he wants the Corinthian Christians to understand what he does and does not seek from them. He has never before allowed them to support his apostolic work financially (11:7–11; 1 Cor 9:3–18), and he is not going to change that policy when he comes this time (*I will not be a burden*, v. 14a; cf. 11:9b). Paul is persisting in this policy even though his rivals seem to have encouraged the congregation to believe it is evidence for their claim that he is not a true apostle (see especially 11:7, with COMMENT). Indeed, he may be deliberately setting his policy over against that of his opponents when he emphasizes *I am not after what is yours, but you*, v. 14b (contrast the practices he ascribes to his competitors in 11:20). Paul makes a similar point to the Philippians (4:17), from whom he had accepted financial aid; and when he writes of the collection for Jerusalem he makes it clear that the obedience to the gospel represented by one's contribution is as important as the contribution itself (2 Cor 8:5; 9:13a). In the present instance Paul wants his readers to know that it is the gift of their lives to Christ, not of their money to himself, that he covets. Because his apostleship is devoted exclusively to building them up in Christ (note v. 19c; 10:8; 13:10), its legitimacy is demonstrated only as their obedience and faith are demonstrated (cf. 10:6; 12:20–21; 13:5, 7, 9b), not by his ability to extract material favors from them. When he supports his point by appealing to the commonly recognized duty of parents to *save up* an inheritance for their children (see NOTES), he is presuming that, despite the questions which have been raised in Corinth about his authority, the congregation there still recognizes him as its "father in Christ Jesus" (1 Cor 4:15; cf. 2 Cor 6:13; 11:2, and see Furnish 1981:111, 112 for general remarks on parental imagery in the Pauline letters).

The point of v. 14*b* is intensified in v. 15*a* (Windisch, 400) as Paul emphasizes that he will not only *save up* for his children in the faith, but *will very gladly spend and be expended* on their behalf. The point is the same one he makes in Phil 2:17, using different imagery (he is "poured as a libation on the sacrificial offering of [the Philippians'] faith" [*RSV*]), and is consistent with his remark in 2 Cor 11:28–29 about the constant pressure he is under because of his "anxiety for all the churches" (Bultmann, 236). He had written in the same vein to the Thessalonians (1 Thess 2:8) when, as in the present case, he was concerned to emphasize his apostolic authority and personal integrity (see 1 Thess 2:5–7, 9–11). But if the apostle is so utterly devoted to the welfare of the Corinthian Christians, why have they taken so seriously the allegations of his rivals? That is the question, cloaked in a feigned naïveté and reminiscent of the irony of 12:13*a*, that is posed in v. 15*b*. The point of it is less to reaffirm Paul's love for the Corinthians (Lietzmann, 158, and Windisch, 401, both regard it as answering the question of 11:11) than to accuse the Corinthians of not loving Paul as they should (Betz 1972:117).

The apostle's point in v. 16*a*—that he and his readers can agree he has not burdened them by taking their money for his personal needs—is only partly correct. His readers will certainly agree that he has never requested material support for himself from them (1 Cor 9:12*b*, 15, 18; 2 Cor 11:7, 9; 12:13*a*), but they disagree with him about the significance of this. Paul wants the Corinthians to regard it as an indication of his concern for them, that he does not wish to be "a burden" (see 11:9; 12:13*a*, 14*b*). But the Corinthians are inclined to regard it as an affront, a sign of social enmity, and thus an indication that Paul is, indeed, an unfit apostle (see 11:7–11, with COMMENT). Moreover, the suspicion seems to be abroad among them, perhaps encouraged by Paul's rivals, that he has perpetrated a certain *deceit* in this regard, v. 16*b*. Verses 16*b*–18 are addressed to this matter.

It is not entirely clear, and it may not have been entirely clear to Paul himself, what the specific deceit was of which he was suspected. Perhaps some of his associates—Silvanus? Timothy? (1:19)—had accepted financial aid from the Corinthians, and the suspicion is that Paul secretly benefits from that while boasting about his financial independence (cf. Plummer, 364); this could explain the emphatic *I (egō)* in v. 16*a*. It is rather more likely, however, given the reference to Titus in v. 18, that the suspicions centered on Paul's efforts to raise a collection for Jerusalem. Since 1 Cor 16:1–4 responds to a question from Corinth about the collection, one may presume that Paul had solicited the congregation on behalf of it sometime previously, perhaps even on the occasion of his first, "founding" visit. Subsequently, Titus has been active in securing the church's recommitment to the project and, most recently, in seeking to get the Corinthians to fulfill their commitment (see 8:6, with COMMENT). This latest dispatch of Titus to Corinth seems to be in view in vv. 17–18*ab* (see NOTES), where Paul's questions challenge the Corinthians to produce even one shred of evidence of fraud. He knows that they cannot (the questions presume negative replies). It would appear that the apostle is responding to charges, or at least to the suspicion, that he himself is benefiting in some way from the collection for Jerusalem. In an earlier letter, written after Titus' first trip to Corinth, Paul had shown some awareness of rumors about fraud (see 7:2, with COMMENT), but now he takes them more seriously, perhaps because they have indeed become more serious and specific in the meantime. On the streets of Corinth, as of other large cities, charlatans and cheats passing themselves off as philosophers were a familiar sight (cf. Hock 1980:49; Betz 1972:116–17), and the apostle will not allow himself to be classified with them (cf. 2:17; 4:2).

*The brother* mentioned in v. 18*a* as having been *sent . . . along with* Titus must be one of the two brothers who accompanied him to Corinth on the occasion of his second visit there and who are commended to the Corinthians in 8:18–22. Which one of them does Paul have in mind here, and why has he made no reference to the other? One is probably to think of the "earnest" brother of 8:22 (so also, e.g., Bruce, 251; Barrett, 325) since he, and not the "renowned" brother of 8:18–19, would have been directly responsible, along with Titus, for completing the collection in Corinth. The renowned brother had been appointed to the delegation by other contributing churches, not to raise money but to help guarantee the honest administration of the collection and its safe conveyance to Jerusalem (see COMMENT on 8:18–19). Indeed, the two questions of 12:18*cd* (both of which presume an affirmative reply) have more point if both Titus and the other man of whom the Corinthians have been reminded were Paul's own associates. The apostle is confident that no one in Corinth will be able to produce any evidence of a fraud perpetrated by his representatives or by himself.

### About Improper Behavior, vv. 19–21

This paragraph, like the preceding one, is written in anticipation of Paul's impending third visit to Corinth. He begins by insisting that, despite what his readers may be thinking, he is not writing just in order to defend himself, v. 19. In 1 Cor 9:3, Paul does not hesitate to identify his apologetic intentions (cf. Phil 1:7, 16), and in 2 Cor 7:11 he cites the Corinthians' eagerness to defend themselves as evidence of their sense of guilt and contrition. But here, in common with the anti-sophistic tradition (Betz 1972:14–15), he will not allow his remarks to be interpreted as apologetic, perhaps for two reasons (Windisch, 406): because that would give too much credibility to the charges being brought against him by his opponents, and because it would suggest that he writes more out of self-interest than out of concern for his readers. Thus (v. 19*bc*) he emphasizes that in what he now writes, as in everything he says and does, he is exercising his apostolic authority and fulfilling his apostolic responsibility to work for the *upbuilding* of his congregation. If, as it seems, the Corinthians are looking for evidence that Paul is *speaking in Christ* (note 13:3 and COMMENT on 2:17), they would do well to pay close attention to this present letter (chaps. 10–13): he writes as their apostle to admonish them to amend their lives in advance of his arrival, that when he is present he may use his authority—as any proper apostle should—not to punish them, but to enlarge and enrich their life as a community of faith (cf. 10:8; 13:10).

The affirmations of v. 19*bc* introduce vv. 20–21, where the apostle expresses his concern that he may find some members of the Corinthian congregation in need of being disciplined when he comes. In that case, the Corinthians will be just as disappointed with him as he with them, v. 20*a*. The conviction that lies behind this comment is undoubtedly the same one that is reflected, more clearly, in 13:5–6—that the legitimacy of his apostleship is demonstrated by the Christian faith and life of the congregations he has founded and over which he exercises pastoral care (see also 3:2–3; 1 Cor 9:1–2). The Corinthians, if they really want proof of his apostleship, will therefore have to do their part. If, on his arrival, he finds a general lack of moral discipline in the congregation, he will be just as humiliated as he was on his second, "sorrowful visit" (2:1; see Windisch, 410; Héring, 98). But this time Paul's humiliation will come from God, not from some specific member of the congregation (see 2:5–11, with COMMENT), because he will be reduced to mourning over the situation and to using his authority for punitive rather than constructive action. One may see here the same concern with which this letter (Letter E, chaps. 10–13) opened: when the congregation's "obedience is complete," then Paul's hand will be strengthened "to punish every disobedience" of the rival apostles, in comparison with whom he has previously appeared to be so weak and ineffective (10:1–11).

One should be careful not to over-interpret the catalog of vices that stands in v. 20. These are all quite traditional, and many of them are found in other vice lists in the NT, as well as in Hellenistic catalogs generally (see NOTES for details). The first four also appear in Gal 5:20, and in the same order; the first three occur (with the first and third reversed) in Sir 40:4[5] (cited by Vögtle 1936:218 n. 86); and the first two are also found together in Rom 13:13 and 1 Cor 3:3 (although in the latter the order is reversed). It is worth observing, however, that all eight terms (which seem to be arranged in four pairs; Plummer, 369; Windisch, 408) refer to conditions which are symptomatic of the breakdown of co-operation, trust, and mutual support in a community (cf. Schweizer 1979:197). It is understandable how the erosion of these qualities could occur precisely under the conditions Paul knows to exist in the Corinthian church, where intruders have challenged his leadership by making ex-

travagant claims for themselves and planting doubts about his apostolic credentials and personal integrity (cf. Georgi 1964:232–33). Indeed, Paul must
realize that the boasts and innuendos of the rival apostles could well have
revived the *discord, jealousy, arrogance,* and *disorder* for which he has criticized the Corinthians in an earlier letter (see 1 Cor 1:11; 3:3; 4:6, 18, 19; 5:2;
8:1; 13:4; 14:33, and Vögtle 1936:32–33).

Although the three vices named in v. 21 all pertain especially to gross sexual
misbehavior, one should not make too much of the contrast between these and
the "social vices" listed in v. 20, for both types are traditionally present in
Hellenistic ethical lists. Indeed, the three vices named in v. 21 head Paul's list
of the "works of the flesh" in Gal 5:19 (although the order of the first two is
reversed). Nevertheless, one must acknowledge that, apart from the problematic admonitions in 6:14–7:1 (on which see COMMENT), this is the only
place in 2 Cor where the apostle betrays any fear that *sexual immorality* is a
current problem in his congregation. It is possible that he has learned (or
suspects) that the sexual libertinism about which he had been so concerned as
he wrote 1 Cor (see 1 Cor 5:1–13; 6:9, 13b–18; 7:2, 14; 10:8) lingers on (cf.
Windisch, 412; Barrett, 332, and 1971:247–48). But it is also possible that he
fears the recurrence of the problem in the wake of the activity of his rivals,
especially if they were Hellenistic-Jewish Christians who, in the interest of
making their missionary preaching more attractive to Gentile hearers, did not
emphasize the moral implications of conversion to the gospel (cf. Georgi
1964:233–34). In either case, Paul is probably thinking of his own converts,
since he goes on to say that he had warned them about their immorality on
his previous visit (13:2).

## 7. WARNING AND ADMONITION, 13:1–10

**13** ¹This is the third time I am coming to you. "By the testimony of
two or three witnesses must every point be substantiated." ²I gave
warning and I give warning, as when I was present the second time, so
now while I am absent, to those who have continued in their former
sinning and to all the rest: if I come again, I will not be lenient ³—since
you demand proof of the Christ who speaks through me, who is not
weak toward you, but powerful among you. ⁴Indeed, he was crucified
in weakness, but lives by the power of God. Indeed, we are weak in him,
but toward you we shall live with him by the power of God.

⁵It is yourselves you must test to find out whether you are in the faith;
it is yourselves you must put to the proof. Or do you not recognize
about yourselves, that Jesus Christ is in you? Unless, of course, you are
unproved! ⁶I hope you will come to know that we are not unproved.

⁷Yet we pray to God you do nothing evil—not that we may appear to be proved, but that you may do what is good, even though we should seem to be unproved. ⁸For we can do nothing against the truth, but only in support of the truth. ⁹For we rejoice when we are weak and you are powerful; this is what we pray for, your restoration.

¹⁰This is why I am writing these things while I am absent, so that when I am present I shall not have to deal harshly, according to the authority which the Lord has given to me for upbuilding and not for destruction.

## NOTES

13:1. *the third time.* See note on *this third time* in 12:14.

*"By the testimony . . . ,"* etc. The regulation given here is a slight abbreviation of the requirement laid down in LXX Deut 19:15. In Matt 18:16 it is presented as a commandment of Jesus to his disciples. See also 1 Tim 5:19, and cf. Mark 15:56; John 8:17; Heb 10:28; 1 John 5:8. The rule is cited often in the Talmud, and it also played a role in the disciplinary procedures of the Jewish sectarians at Qumran (note 1QS v.25–vi.1 [Vermes 1975:80]; CD ix.16–23 [Vermes 1975:111]). For a discussion of the use of Deut 19:15 in Judaism and the NT, see van Vliet 1958. In the whole of chaps. 10–13, Paul quotes scripture only here and in 10:17, and in neither case with any kind of introductory formula.

*testimony.* Literally "mouth" *(stoma)*, which often, by metonymy, stands for what is spoken.

*of two or three witnesses.* Literally "by the testimony of two witnesses and of three," but doubtless to be understood as it is translated here (and as it stands in Matt 18:16, where *ē* ["or"] is used). Both the Pauline and Matthean versions abbreviate LXX Deut 19:15, which has "by the testimony of two witnesses or [and] by the testimony of three witnesses."

*must . . . be substantiated.* Literally "shall be substantiated [or: established]," but here, as often, the future indicative *(stathēsetai)* is used to express a categorical imperative; see BDF § 362.

*every point.* Literally "every word" *(pan rēma)*, but it is often the case that the specific meaning of *rēma* derives from the context. Here one could also translate as "every charge" *(RSV)*, "every matter" *(NIV)*, or even "everything."

2. *I gave warning and I give warning.* There are similar expressions in Gal 1:9; 5:21b (on which see Betz 1979:284) and 1 Thess 4:6. The verb *(prolegein)* means literally "to say beforehand," as, e.g., in 7:3. In particular contexts it can mean, more specifically, "to predict" (e.g., Rom 9:29) or, as here and in Gal 1:9; 5:21b; 1 Thess 4:6, "to warn." Note the perfect tense *(gave* translates *proeirēka)*, appropriate with reference to a warning which, though given on one specific occasion, had been meant to remain in effect over a period of time.

*as when I was present . . . so now while I am absent.* Translates *hōs parōn . . . kai apo nyn.* For the *hōs . . . kai (as . . . so)* see BAG s.v. *hōs,* II, 1, who cite Gal 1:9; Phil

1:20 and other passages to exemplify this construction. Therefore *hōs* need not mean "as if" here, and the interpretation of Hyldahl 1973:304, "as (already) present . . . and (yet actually) now absent," is indefensible; see also following note. On the "presence/absence" theme see 10:1–2 (with NOTES), 11; further, 13:10.

*the second time.* Not "a second time" (against Hyldahl 1973:304), for the use of the article *(to deuteron)* shows that a specific time is meant (Allo, 336; Hughes 475 n. 168).

*those who have continued in their former sinning.* As in 12:21. From the present verse it becomes clear that the apostle is thinking of those who had sinned before his previous visit to Corinth and whom he had warned on that occasion.

*all the rest.* Most probably, "all the rest of the congregation" who by their indifference to or leniency toward immoral conduct on the part of church members have tacitly condoned it (so, e.g., Windisch, 415; Bultmann, 244; de Boor, 248); less likely, those who have sinned since Paul's last visit (so Plummer, 373; Hughes, 476).

*if I come.* An introductory *hoti* ("that") is left untranslated, since it is to be understood as a *hoti-recitativum*, functioning like quotation marks to identify what follows as something someone has said; cf. BDF § 470(1). In this case, it introduces the warning which Paul had delivered on the occasion of his second visit, and wishes now to repeat. See Hughes, 476 n. 170, and cf. the remarks of Betz (1979:284) on Gal 5:21*b. If (ean)* need not, and does not here express any particular uncertainty about Paul's coming. As in 1 Cor 16:10, it almost means "when."

*again.* The Greek is *eis to palin,* where *eis* has a temporal sense; see BDF § 206(1); Moule 1953:69. (Windisch, 415, thinks it more probable that the expression goes with what follows; thus, "I will not spare you again.")

*I will not be lenient.* Here *ou pheisomai* is used absolutely. Cf. 1:23, where a participial form, followed by *hymōn* ("you"), is translated "to spare [one]." In the earlier passage Paul insists that he had canceled a visit to Corinth only because he had wanted to spare the congregation the scolding he would have had to give them. Here, however, the apostle leaves no doubt that the visit now planned will take place, and that he is prepared to be stern with them if he must. Cf. 10:2–6; 12:10–21; 13:10.

3. *since.* This *(epei)* introduces the reason Paul will not be lenient on his forthcoming visit.

*you demand.* Here, as in 1 Cor 1:22; 4:2, the verb *zētein* means more than just "to desire" (so *RSV*). See BAG s.v. 2c.

*proof.* Elsewhere the same word *(dokimē)* has been translated *test* (2:9, on which see the note), *testing* (8:2), and *verification* (9:13). In the present context it is followed by the related verb *dokimazein* *(put to the proof,* v. 5; translated "to verify" in 8:8, 22) and by the related adjectives *adokimos* *(unproved,* vv. 5, 6, 7) and *dokimos* *(proved,* v. 7; as in 10:18).

*the Christ who speaks through me.* More literally, "the Christ who speaks in me," but here the *en* ("in") is surely instrumental, "by means of" or "through." Cf. especially 2:17; 5:20*a,* and COMMENT on each of these.

*who.* That is, Christ. In Greek, the formulation that follows is chiastic: *toward you–not weak/powerful–among you.*

*not weak.* The charge of 10:10 (cf. 11:21*a*) is in mind.

*but powerful.* As in 9:8, the verb is *dynatein,* found elsewhere in the NT only in Rom 14:4. The theme of power in weakness, specifically introduced in 12:9–10, is especially prominent in the present passage (see also vv. 4, 8–10).

*among you.* Or "in you" *(en hymin),* as it is translated in v. 5.

4. *Indeed.* As in 3:10 (on which see the note), *kai gar.*

*he was crucified.* The verb *(stauroun)* appears only here in 2 Cor; elsewhere in Paul's letters: 1 Cor 1:13, 23; 2:2, 8; Gal 3:1; 5:24; 6:14.

*in weakness.* Literally "out of weakness" *(ex astheneias),* which some interpret as causal (e.g., Robertson 1923:598; *GNTG* III:160; Barrett, 336, with qualifications). It is doubtful, however, whether Paul could think of Christ's death as the result of his weakness. He seems to view it, rather, as a demonstration of that weakness in and through which God's power is operative for salvation (e.g., 1 Cor 1:17–31, especially vv. 25, 27); cf. Käsemann 1942:55. Thus, one may perhaps interpret *ek* here as "in accordance with" the apparent "weakness" of God (cf. BAG s.v. *ek,* 3i). Or, if the Greek has been formulated this way only in order to provide a rhetorical parallel for the following *ek dynameōs Theou (by the power of God),* one could interpret it more loosely, "as a weakling" (so Bultmann, 245).

*lives.* The word encompasses Christ's resurrection from the dead and his continuing life "to God"; cf. Rom 6:9–10 (Windisch, 418). Windisch, 418, thinks that a traditional christological formulation lies behind the reference here to Christ's crucifixion and subsequent resurrection to life (he compares 1 Cor 1:23–24, 30; Heb 2:9–10; Ign Eph 7:2), but that is doubted by Käsemann 1942:55 n. 134 and Georgi 1964:294 n. 1.

*by the power of God.* Here *by* translates *ek* (literally "from" or "out of"), used in this instance causally (cf. BAG s.v. 3e, f). For other references to God's power in 2 Cor, see 4:17; 6:7; 12:9a, with NOTES and COMMENT. For God's power as the agency of Christ's resurrection, specifically, see Rom 1:4; 6:4 (where "glory" = "power"); 1 Cor 6:14; cf. Phil 3:10.

*Indeed, we.* The *we (hēmeis)* is emphatic. Note the first person plural, which tends to broaden the statement to include Paul's associates, even though the apostle's own life and work are primarily in view. Cf. 1 Cor 4:10 (of the Pauline apostolate): "we are weak." Instead of "so that we, too" *(hōste kai hēmeis,* Rom 6:4), as one might expect, the *kai gar (Indeed)* of the preceding statement is repeated to indicate that here, too, the comment is offered in support of v. 3 (Bultmann, 246).

*in him.* This text *(en autō)* is well attested (Metzger 1971:588), although some witnesses (ℵ A F et al.) have "with him" *(syn autō),* assimilating this to the next prepositional phrase.

*toward you.* In the Greek sentence this phrase *(eis hymas)* stands in an emphatic position at the very end. The emphasis is best retained in English by transposing it. Although the phrase, also found in v. 3, is omitted in B D², it is undoubtedly original.

*we shall live.* Fuchs (1980:246) regards this as a reference to life in the eschatological future; but that disregards the *eis hymas* (see preceding note), which requires a reference to a present life *with Christ.* Thus, the tense is to be interpreted either as a "logical future" (so Windisch, 419) or, preferably, as referring to Paul's impending visit (so, e.g., Bultmann, 246; Tannehill 1967:99; Schütz 1975:215).

5. *It is yourselves you must test.* Translates *heautous peirazesthe,* in which *yourselves* stands first with emphasis. The verb occurs only here in 2 Cor, and elsewhere Paul usually employs it with the meaning "to tempt" (1 Cor 7:5; 10:13; Gal 6:1; 1 Thess 3:5). In 1 Cor 10:9, however, it means "to put to the test," as it does here, where it is virtually synonymous with *dokimazein (put to the proof;* see below).

*to find out.* These words have to be supplied in translating, since the Greek has only "[test] if you are" *(ei este).* Cf. 1 Thess 3:5: Paul sent Timothy in order to "know" the faith of the Thessalonians.

*are in the faith.* One may properly understand "are standing firm in the faith"; cf. 1:24; 1 Cor 16:13 (and 1 Cor 10:12; Gal 5:1; Phil 1:27). The only other reference to faith (or believing) in chaps. 10–13 is in 10:15b, on which see NOTES and COMMENT.

*it is yourselves you must put to the proof.* As in the preceding admonition, *yourselves* is emphatic. The verb *dokimazein* (translated "to verify" in 8:8, 22) is cognate with the word *proof* in v. 3, and regularly means "to test in order to prove genuine." In 1 Cor 11:28; Gal 6:4, as well as here, Paul employs the verb in urging critical self-evaluation. The importance of this was stressed in the Greek philosophical tradition. To the numerous passages cited by Betz (1979:302 nn. 90–94) one may add, e.g., Marcus Aurelius X, 37 (cited by Windisch, 420 n. 1). In accord with this tradition, Dio Chrysostom commends the famous Delphic oracle "Know yourself" as the foremost of Apollo's commandments (IV, 57, noted by Mussies 1972:181); cf. Betz 1979:302.

*Or do you not recognize about yourselves.* The question, introduced by the particle *ē* (cf. 1:17; 3:1b, note; 11:7), expects that the Corinthians will want to answer in the affirmative *(ou).* The formulation here is but a variation of Paul's more usual "[or] do you not know" ([*ē*] *ouk oidate*), found in Rom 6:16; 11:2; 1 Cor 3:16; 5:6; 6:2, 3, 9, 15, 16, 19; 9:13, 24. Cf. "Or are you ignorant" (*ē agnoeite*) in Rom 6:3; 7:1.

*recognize about yourselves.* The verb *(epiginōskein)* suggests knowledge complete enough to warrant appropriate action. See NOTES on 1:13, 14, where it is translated "to understand," and on 6:9, where it is translated "to know fully." In the present case the subsequent *heautous (about yourselves)* is not strictly necessary, and is left untranslated in many English versions; but see Bultmann, 248.

*that Jesus Christ is in you.* Or "among you" *(en hymin)*, as the same expression has been translated in v. 3. But in the present case the preceding *heautous (yourselves)* would seem to require *in* rather than "among."

*Unless, of course.* Translates *ei mēti,* on which see BAG s.v. *ei,* VI, 9.

*unproved.* The adjective *adokimos* describes that which has been tested and found "counterfeit" (Bruce, 254), unfit, etc. In v. 7 it is contrasted with what is *dokimos (proved).* Apart from this passage, Paul uses it in Rom 1:28 (*RSV:* "base") and 1 Cor 9:27 (*RSV:* "disqualified"). Note the cognate verb, *to put to the proof,* in v. 5a.

6. *I hope.* Whereas the same expression in 1:3; 5:11 indicates a certain optimism about the Corinthians (cf. 1:7), in the present context it is less an expression of confidence in them (against Olson 1976:231, 232) than a charge to them to amend their ways before Paul's arrival (cf. v. 2b, and Windisch, 421).

*you will come to know.* Translates *gnōsesthe;* cf. v. 5a, *do you not recognize (epiginōskete).*

*that we are not unproved.* The *we (hēmeis)* is emphatic. Here Paul lapses once more (cf. v. 4b) into the use of the first person plural, which continues through v. 9.

*unproved.* As in v. 5.

7. *Yet we pray.* The *de (Yet)* has mildly adversative force here. The verb *(euchesthai)* is used by Paul only here in vv. 7, 9 and in Rom 9:3. More often, *proseuchesthai:* Rom 8:26; 1 Cor 11:4, 5, 13; 14:13–15; Phil 1:9; 1 Thess 5:17, 25.

*you do.* Taking *hymas (you)* as the subject of the infinitive *poiēsai (do)*, with most commentators (e.g., Windisch, 422; Bultmann, 249; Barrett, 339).

*evil.* One might have expected *to kakon* ("what is evil," as in Rom 2:9; 7:21; 13:4; 16:19; 1 Cor 13:5), since the contrast is with *to kalon (what is good).* Paul also speaks of "doing evil" (using *poiein,* as here, or *prassein* ["practicing"] or *katergazesthai* ["performing"]) in Rom 3:8; 7:19; 9:11; 13:10; 2 Cor 5:10.

*not that we.* The pronoun is emphasized, as at the end of v. 6 *(hēmeis).*

*may appear to be proved.* Cf. 1 Cor 11:19. In the present case the verb *(phainesthai)* is used to mean, in effect, "only appear superficially." Cf. Betz 1972:134. The word translated *proved* is *dokimos* (rendered as "approved" in 10:18); see note on *proof* in v. 3.

*that you may do what is good.* Like the preceding *we,* the *you* here is emphatic *(hymeis).* *To kalon,* what is good (or "noble," or "right," etc.), was a cardinal theme of Hellenistic ethics. Elsewhere in Paul's letters: Rom 7:18, 21 (in the latter contrasted with *to kakon,* "what is evil"); Gal 6:9; 1 Thess 5:21. Cf. Rom 2:10; 12:9, 21; 13:3; 16:19; Gal 6:10; 1 Thess 5:15, where *to agathon* is used in the same way. In Rom 7:18 the reference is to "performing [*katergazesthai*] the good"; elsewhere, as here, to "doing" *(poiein)* it.

*even though.* Paraphrases *de,* which here introduces a kind of concession.

*we should seem to be unproved.* The pronoun *(hēmeis)* is once more emphatic. *Seem to be* represents the *hōs* ("as," "as if") before *adokimos* (*unproved,* as in vv. 5, 6).

8. *we can do.* The use of the first person plural continues (cf. end of v. 6, v. 7). As often with *dynasthai* ("to be able"), the helping verb *poiein* ("to do") must be supplied; see BAG s.v. *dynamai,* 3.

*nothing against the truth.* Here, as in 4:2; 6:7 (on which see NOTES), *the truth* is probably to be identified with "the gospel" (not, e.g., with "righteousness"—cf. v. 7— as it is in Rom 2:8; 1 Cor 13:6 [*RSV:* "the right"]). See especially Bultmann, 250, and in *TDNT* I:244. Cf. 1 Esdr 4:35, 38 (wrongly cited as 1 Esdr 3:35, 38 in Bruce, 254): "The truth is great, and stronger than all things," v. 35; "The truth endures and is strong for ever, and lives and rules for ever and ever," v. 38. Also, Sir 4:25, 28 (cited by Windisch, 423): "Never speak against the truth, but be mindful of your ignorance," v. 25 *(RSV);* "Strive even to death for the truth and the Lord God will fight for you," v. 28 *(RSV).*

9. *we rejoice.* The verb *(chairein)* is used in this sense only here in chaps. 10–13 (it probably has a different meaning in 13:11), but more often in chaps. 1–9 (2:3; 6:10; 7:7, 9, 13, 16), where "joy" *(chara)* is also a theme (1:24; 2:3; 7:4, 13; 8:2; never in chaps. 10–13).

*when we are weak and you are powerful.* The pronouns are emphasized *(hēmeis . . . hymeis).* This statement could be an allusion to what the Corinthians themselves have claimed (cf. 1 Cor 4:10, where the contrasting terms are *astheneis,* "weak," and *ischyroi,* "strong"). In this part of the letter Paul has the theme of weakness/power *(astheneia/dynamis)* very much in mind; see also 12:9, 10; 13:3, 4; cf. 10:10 *(ischyrai* instead of *dynatai).*

*pray.* As in v. 7.

*restoration.* The noun *(katartisis)* appears only here in the NT (and never in the LXX), although the more common *katartismos* ("preparation," etc.) is used in Eph 4:12. The latter was a technical term in medicine for the setting of a bone, and the related verb *(katartizein)* usually bears a similar meaning: to put right, mend, set in place, etc. (so, e.g., Epictetus III.xx.10, cited by Betz 1979:297 n. 43; in Paul's letters see especially 1 Cor 1:10; 2 Cor 13:11; Gal 6:1). In the present context *katartisis* is closely related in meaning to the idea of *upbuilding,* v. 10; 12:19 (Windisch, 424).

10. *I am writing.* Here, after adhering to the first person plural since the end of v. 6, Paul reverts to the first person singular. He does not use an epistolary aorist here ("I wrote," looking at the time of writing from the standpoint of the letter's recipients, as, e.g., in Gal 6:11). The use of the present tense *(graphō, I am writing)* is, in fact, more usual in the NT (Robertson 1923:845); cf. 1 Cor 4:14; 14:37; 2 Cor 1:13 ("we write"), etc.

*these things.* The reference is to everything in chaps. 10–13. What is said here about the purpose of writing does not readily apply to chaps. 1–9, however.

*absent . . . present.* Cf. 10:1–2 (with NOTES), 11; 13:1.

*deal harshly.* For the verb *(chrasthai)* see NOTES to 3:17, where it is translated "act." The adverb *(apotomōs)* occurs only here and in Tit 1:13 in the NT; cf. *apotomia* ("severity") in Rom 11:22.

*according to the authority,* etc. A phrase from 10:8 is here repeated almost verbatim. For the imagery and specific terms see NOTES and COMMENT there. The major differences here are: *the authority,* instead of "our authority"; *gave to me,* instead of "gave"; *for upbuilding and not for destruction,* instead of "for your upbuilding," etc. Cf. also the reference to "upbuilding" in 12:19 and to "restoration" in 13:9.


## COMMENT: GENERAL

The appeal initiated in 10:1–18, supported by the lengthy "fool's speech" of 11:1–12:13 and then resumed in 12:14–21, is now concluded with a stern warning and an earnest admonition. Paul's warning is that when he comes to Corinth this time he will show no leniency toward those members of the congregation whose practical conduct continues to belie their professed commitment to Christ (vv. 2–4). His admonition is that, in advance of his arrival, the Corinthian Christians critically examine their own life as a community of faith, and then effect the needed changes (vv. 5–9). The matter is summed up in v. 10, where Paul indicates why he is writing the present letter: to warn them of his determination to exercise his authority when he comes, and to ensure that it need not be used to punish wrongdoers, but only to build up the congregation.


## COMMENT: DETAILED

### A Warning, vv. 1–4

As Paul proceeds to issue a warning to his readers in advance of his forthcoming visit, he reminds them that this will be *the third time* he has come to them, v. 1a. Since he has already pointed this out once (12:14), he must believe that repeating it will somehow support the warning he is about to give. Of course, the simple fact that he will soon be coming in itself supports that, for he will have an opportunity to deal with the Corinthians in person. Beyond this, however, Paul seems to want his readers to associate this, his *third* visit, with the traditional rule of evidence that requires three, or at least two, witnesses to establish the facts in a case. The words of v. 1*b* essentially reproduce the regulation of LXX Deut 19:15, but Paul does not identify them as such —nor as a commandment of Jesus, although they are attributed to him in the Synoptic tradition (Matt 18:16). Rather, Paul seems to quote the rule only as "a sort of proverb" (van Vliet 1958:88). But what is the point of it just here?

According to some interpreters, the apostle intends to hold a formal hearing in Corinth, and he quotes the rule about evidence to assure his readers that he will follow due process in evaluating whatever charges of misconduct may be brought against any member of the congregation (so, e.g., Schlatter, 675; Allo, 335; Filson, 417; Hughes, 475; Delcor 1968:76; cf. Tasker, 186, who, however, believes Paul will hear charges being brought against himself—but the context [note 12:10–21; 13:1] is against this). This is unlikely, because there is no specific reference to a formal court of inquiry anywhere in this letter— not even after v. 2, where one would most expect it (cf. Hyldahl 1973:304). Moreover, it can hardly be coincidental that Paul quotes this rule immediately after emphasizing that he is about to come for *the third time.* It would appear that he is thinking of his impending visit as potentially the third and decisive witness against wrongdoers in the Corinthian church. In this case the first two "witnesses" could be his first two visits (e.g., Chrysostom [*NPNF*, 1st ser. XII:411–12]; Calvin, 169; Lietzmann, 160; Windisch, 413; Bruce, 253; de Boor, 248; Barrett, 333—following van Vliet 1958:96 n. 8). However, in view of v. 2, and because it is difficult to understand how the first ("founding") visit could have constituted a witness against them, it may be that Paul is thinking of the first two witnesses as, respectively, his second, "sorrowful visit" (2:1) and the present letter (so Bultmann, 243).

It is true that Paul's three visits, or his two visits and one letter, do not, strictly speaking, satisfy the requirement he himself quotes. They still represent the testimony of just one witness, Paul. But this does not mean that the rule is being applied loosely, "to clothe his own thoughts" (Ellis 1957:10), or "with a certain whimsy" (Bousset, 222; also Strachan, 38). As van Vliet has shown (1958:53–62), in Palestinian Judaism the Deuteronomic rule was widely used to support the requirement that persons suspected of wrongdoing should be carefully forewarned about the possibility of punitive action against them. In this context, Paul's quotation of the rule makes good sense: he will have given the requisite *two or three* warnings, so he will not hesitate to exercise discipline when he comes to Corinth. This is, in fact, precisely what he says in v. 2.

Paul's brief characterization of his second visit to Corinth, v. 2, supplements his other reference to that visit in 2:1ff. On the basis of the evidence of these two passages, it is safe to conclude that it had been unplanned, that its purpose had been essentially disciplinary, and that it had been unsuccessful and therefore abruptly terminated. In the present passage, the apostle presumes that the wrongdoers he had warned on that occasion have not reformed (see also

12:21), and so he warns them again. Perhaps he has learned (or fears) that the activity of his rivals, particularly their challenging of his authority, has caused his previous warning to go unheeded. In the face of this, he assures the Corinthians that he means what he has said about taking strong action when he comes; he *will not be lenient* in administering discipline. Not only those who are guilty of actual misconduct but also *the rest* of the congregation, who have tolerated it, should know that he is prepared to act decisively—presumably, to excommunicate the errant members (cf. 1 Cor 5:1–13).

In vv. 3–4 one learns how Paul related his concern about misconduct among the Christians of Corinth (12:20–13:2) to the broader and fundamental concern of this letter. That concern, evident throughout chaps. 10–13, but especially in 11:1–12:13, is with the challenge to his apostleship represented by the appearance in Corinth of certain persons who have sought, with some success, to take over the leadership of the congregation there. Those intruders not only have assailed Paul's apostolic credentials and conduct (e.g., 10:10; 11:6, 7–11) but have made extravagant claims about themselves (e.g., 10:7*b*, 12; 11:12, 21*b*–23). Encouraged by this, and in accord with their own belief that spiritual authority must be manifested in certain spiritual gifts (e.g., 1 Cor 12–14), the Corinthians have demanded *proof* from Paul that Christ really speaks through him. Indeed, Paul himself claims that, as an "ambassador for Christ," he is Christ's spokesman (5:20), or—an alternative formulation—that, as an apostle, he speaks "in Christ" (2:17; 12:19*b*). It is of this that the Corinthians want some specific evidence, perhaps in the form of ecstatic speech (Schmithals 1971:194; Fuchs 1980:247) or of miraculous deeds (see discussion on 12:12), since on his previous visits he has given the impression of lacking spiritual boldness and power (see especially 10:1, 10). Now, says Paul, he is prepared to give them proof of Christ's power working through him—although it will not be the kind of proof they have wanted. It will come on his next visit when he refuses to show leniency to any who may remain impenitent sinners.

When the apostle writes that *Christ . . . is not weak toward you, but powerful among you* (v. 3), he may be alluding (as he probably does again in v. 9; see below) to the Corinthians' own triumphalist boast that they are "strong" (1 Cor 4:10; cf. Windisch, 418). In claiming this, they think of themselves as possessing Christ's power in such a way as to reign with him (1 Cor 4:8). For Paul, however, believers do not rule with Christ's power (the point of the irony in 1 Cor 4:8–13) but are to be ruled by it (cf. 2 Cor 5:14); and so he writes here of Christ being powerful *toward* or *among* (not "in") them (cf. Bultmann, 244–45). It is of this power that Paul will be an agent when, on his arrival in Corinth, he boldly disciplines the errant members of the congregation.

Whether the christological affirmation of v. 4*a* is traditional or, as is more likely, Paul's own, it supports the preceding statement about Christ's powerful presence with the congregation. Christ *lives* (and rules) *by the power of God* who raised him from the dead, which means that he lives and rules, also, as the Crucified One (cf. Bultmann, 245). This affirmation is also used to support Paul's promise that his next visit to Corinth will provide proof of Christ's speaking through him, v. 4b. If Paul has appeared "weak" in the past (cf. 10:1, 10; 11:21a, etc.), the Corinthians must realize that his is the weakness of one who has been crucified with Christ (*in him;* cf. Rom 6:6; Gal 6:14, etc.) and who carries about "the death of Jesus" in his own body (2 Cor 4:10–12). But it is also the case that Christ now lives in him (Gal 2:20), so that when Paul comes he will be able to exhibit, as well, that resurrection life, and thus *the power of God.*

### An Admonition, vv. 5–9

There are actually two admonitions in this paragraph, although one is presented only indirectly. The primary and explicit one is that the Corinthians should *test* themselves (v. 5a), and the other, implicit one is that they should *do nothing wrong* (v. 7a).

In the first of these, v. 5a, Paul directs his readers to examine critically their own situation as believers, to learn whether they are really standing firm *in the faith* to which they are ostensibly committed. They have been demanding from him some evidence that he belongs to Christ in a special way (e.g., v. 3; 10:7). Now he insists that it is about their own Christian existence that they should be concerned: *it is yourselves you must put to the proof.* Here, as in the only other place in chaps. 10–13 where Paul mentions *faith* (10:15), he is thinking of it as primarily obedience (cf. 10:6—and not in a moralistic sense (correctly de Boor, 250), but in the sense that one's whole life, placed under the rule of Christ's love (5:14), is to be conducted according to the guidance of the Spirit (e.g., Rom 7:6; 8:4, 12–13; Gal 5:16, 25; see Bultmann, 247, and in *TDNT* VI:212, 218). Thus the "testing of faith" of which the apostle now writes is really no different from the "testing of obedience" of which he has written in an earlier letter (2:9). In each instance, the question is whether the congregation's life is conformed to the gospel by which it was called into being.

Clearly, the confidence Paul once expressed in the Corinthians' faith (1:24) has now been shaken. While he is certain of their affirmative response to the question whether *Jesus Christ is in* them, v. 5b, he cannot be certain (*Unless, of course you are unproved!*—v. 5c) that they really understand what this means (Bultmann, 247): that Christ is with them as their Lord, whose presence both graces them with new life and calls them to obedience. The rhetorical question here is therefore not only formally, but also materially and functionally parallel with the one in 1 Cor 3:16 about the indwelling presence of God's Spirit. In each case the intent is to secure the Corinthians' acknowledgment that they belong (as a community of faith, and individually) to Another, in whom they have their life and by whom their lives are to be guided. The interrogation, then, conveys an "indicative" which incorporates an "imperative."

Following v. 5c, in which Paul expresses some concern that the Corinthian Christians, upon examination, may be found *unproved* in their faith, one would expect v. 6 to read: "I hope you will come to know that you are not unproved" (Lietzmann, 161). Instead, Paul writes: *I hope you will come to know that we are not unproved.* The *we,* which is emphatic, is probably used here in order to include those who were associated with Paul in the founding of the Corinthian church (specifically, Silvanus and Timothy, 1:19). Thus, Paul would be taking the challenge to himself (v. 3) as a challenge to the authenticity of his whole apostolate. But even if the *we* stands simply for "I," it is clear that Paul wants his readers to understand the inseparable relationship that exists between their faith and his ministry. If their faith is authentic, that in itself is evidence of the authenticity of the ministry of the one(s) through whom they have come to believe (cf., e.g., 11:2; 12:14; 1 Cor 4:15). He has made this point to them in earlier letters (1 Cor 9:1–2; cf. 15:14; 2 Cor 3:1–3), and it probably explains a remark earlier in the present letter (10:15b) which correlates the Corinthians' growth in faith and their praise of Paul's ministry. However much they may boast of spiritual achievements and powers, Paul's rivals in Corinth can never usurp his position as the one who first brought the gospel to that city (cf. 10:12–18). Paul's hope that his ministry will not go *unproved* in Corinth is thus, simultaneously, the hope that the Corinthians' faith will not remain unproved either.

Indeed, Paul goes on to emphasize that the authenticity of the Corinthians' faith is his first concern, vv. 7–9. He does not just "hope" (v. 6), but "prays" (*we pray,* vv. 7, 9; the first person plural continues under the influence of *we are not unproved,* v. 6) that the congregation's life may be conformed to the requirements of the gospel. Here, as elsewhere (e.g., Phil 1:9–11; Phlm 6), Paul's disclosure of his prayers becomes in effect an exhortation to his readers (Furnish 1968:95; cf. Wiles 1974:247): they are to *do nothing evil;* rather, they are to *do what is good,* v. 7. This continues the concerns expressed less directly in 10:6, that the congregation's "obedience" should be "complete," and in 12:20–21, that certain specific types of behavior should no longer be tolerated. To *do what is good* (*to kalon,* as here, or *to agathon* in other passages; see NOTES) means, quite generally, to do the will of God (see especially Rom 7:21–22; 12:9, 21 and 13:3, following on 12:1–2; 1 Thess 5:15, 21, in connection with 5:18). If the Corinthians will apply themselves to this, that is quite enough for Paul, since he believes that their obedience constitutes the only valid proof both of the genuineness of their faith and of the legitimacy of his apostolate. Whether this will satisfy the Corinthians' demand for some authenticating sign of Paul's apostolic status is doubtful. He himself recognizes this, and expresses his indifference: *not that we may appear to be proved . . . even though we should seem to be unproved.* What the Corinthians would require does not, in any case, constitute real "proof" (cf. Bultmann, 250).

Looking back over vv. 5–7, it is apparent that Paul is challenging his readers to reconsider what constitutes the real "proof" of apostleship. Do they want some evidence that Christ's power is operative through Paul? Then they must allow Paul's gospel to have scope in their midst, shaping, judging, and nurturing their life as a community of faith. For Paul, apostles are legitimated only by the word they bear—and not by the form in which it is conveyed or by the amazing feats which may accompany it, but by the way it takes effect in the lives of those to whom it is addressed (e.g., 2:14–3:3; 5:13, 20; 1 Cor 9:1–2; cf. Bultmann, 244).

There is widespread agreement that v. 8 sounds like a general maxim affirming the sovereign power of *the truth* (cf. 1 Esdr 4:35, 38; Sir 4:25, 28, quoted in the NOTES), but it is difficult to know exactly why Paul includes such a statement just here. If, as seems probable (see NOTES), Paul's reference is to the gospel, his point may be that, even though he remains "unproved" in the eyes of the Corinthians, the gospel is still being served through his ministry (cf. Fuchs 1980:251). All that matters is whether the Corinthians are doing *what is good* (v. 7). If they are, then *the truth* is being supported (note that "the truth" and "the good" are used interchangeably in Rom 2:8, 10), even while Paul's apostolic status is still being challenged.

The declaration of v. 9a does not support v. 8 (against Plummer, 378); rather, it extends the point made at the end of v. 7 (Bultmann, 251). Paul is not only indifferent to whether the Corinthians get the kind of "proof" they want of his apostleship; he can actually *rejoice* when they perceive him as *weak* (cf. 10:10; 11:21a) if, in fact, this means that they are *powerful*. In an earlier letter the apostle had been sharply critical of the Corinthians' claim that he is "weak" and they are "strong" (1 Cor 4:10), and it is remarkable that now, in an apparent allusion to that same slogan (see also comments on v. 3 above), he seems to accept it. But he does so on his own terms. In accord with the principle enunciated in 12:9—that "power is made fully present in weakness" —Paul does not just endure weakness, but accepts it as a mark of his apostolic office. In this important respect the sentiment he expresses in this passage (vv. 7, 9a) is different from the declaration of Rom 9:3 to which commentators often refer. In Rom 9, it is true, Paul expresses his willingness to sacrifice his own salvation if that would promote the faith of others (Israel). But here in 2 Cor he writes with the fundamental conviction that it is precisely through his weakness that God's power is disclosed and is mightily effective for others (4:7; 12:9–10; 13:3–4; cf. 10:3–4). That is now the special point in v. 9a, which in effect extends the principle of 12:9. "The power of Christ" which is given to Paul in his weakness is present as well to those who have come to the gospel through his ministry; so he can rejoice when he is weak and they, through his weakness, have experienced the power of Christ.

From the context it is clear that Paul is willing to identify the Corinthians as *powerful*, not according to external measurements such as their possession of spiritual gifts, but only according to their faith: insofar as they stand firm in their faith-commitment (v. 5), insofar as they are completely devoted to the will of God (v. 7), and therefore insofar as they are constantly prepared to deal with those whose behavior threatens the integrity of the community's witness (12:20–21). If Paul finds them thus when he arrives, with the consequence that he does not have to exercise his disciplinary power, the Corinthians may again perceive him as weak. But in that "weakness" he will rejoice, because he has found them strong in their faith. That is, in fact, what he prays for, as he says again in v. 9b: their *restoration* (see NOTES), the amendment of their lives as individuals, and their corporate upbuilding as a community of faith.

### The Purpose of the Letter, v. 10

By this statement, which looks back over the whole of chaps. 10–13, the apostle shows that he is thinking of his present letter as essentially hortatory (see also 10:1, "I . . . appeal to you," and 13:11, "be attentive to my exhortations"). Throughout, Paul has been thinking of his impending visit to Corinth (10:1–2, 10–11; 12:14; 13:1). Specifically, he has been warning and admonishing the Corinthians in advance of that, so that when he arrives he will *not have to deal harshly* with them. These warnings (10:11; 12:10–21; 13:2) and admonitions (explicitly, only in 13:5, but implicitly throughout, especially in 13:7, 9) have been prompted by the apostle's fear that the faith of the Corinthians is being seriously threatened by outsiders who seem to have claimed his mission field as their own (see especially 10:12–18; 11:1–4). In the process, these competitors have been increasingly successful in raising doubts about the authenticity of Paul's apostleship (e.g., 10:2, 7, 10; 11:5–11; 12:11, 16), and the bulk of the letter has been a response to those charges (11:1–12:13). Significantly, however, the present statement of purpose makes no mention of that. As he has already emphasized in 12:19, his readers are not to think that he is writing in self-defense. He writes only to urge their re-commitment and their obedience to the gospel they have received from him (cf. 13:5–9). If they are not responsive to his appeal, then they will see him exercise his power (neither as they would wish, 12:20, nor as he would wish, 10:8, repeated here) to punish their disobedience (cf. 10:2, 11; 12:10–21; 13:2–4).

While this statement of purpose is admirably suited to the material found in chaps. 10–13, it is ill-suited as a description of the purpose of chaps. 1–9. Nothing in chaps. 1–9 suggests that Paul is planning a visit to Corinth in the near future, and nothing there suggests that he would find it necessary to *deal harshly* with the congregation if he were to come. Moreover, it is unthinkable that Paul would sum up the purpose of any letter which included the kind of appeal found in chaps. 8, 9 (on behalf of the collection for Jerusalem) without the slightest further reference to that request. But these problems are solved if, as seems probable for a variety of reasons, chaps. 10–13 constitute a separate letter (see INTRODUCTION, pp. 35–41).

# II. LETTER CLOSING, 13:11–13[14]

13 ⁱⁱFinally, brothers and sisters, rejoice; be restored; pay attention to my appeals; be of one mind; be at peace—and the God of love and of peace will be with you.

¹²Greet one another with a holy kiss. [¹³]All the saints greet you.

¹³[¹⁴]The grace of the Lord Jesus Christ, and the love of God, and participation in the Holy Spirit be with all of you.

## NOTES

13:11. *Finally.* Translates *loipon,* as in 1 Thess 4:1, which is perhaps "more colloquial" (Plummer, 380) than *to loipon* in, e.g., Phil 3:1; 4:8.

*brothers and sisters.* Literally: "brothers"; but see NOTES on 1:8. The appellation occurs nowhere else in chaps. 10–13, although "beloved" in 12:19 is comparable. Here, as elsewhere, it functions to accentuate the following admonitions by stressing the writer's solidarity with his readers; note, e.g., how often Paul uses it in association with the verb *parakalein,* "to exhort," especially toward the close of a letter: Rom 16:17; 1 Cor 16:15; 1 Thess 4:10; 5:14. In Phil 4:8 and 1 Thess 4:1 as well as here, it follows *(to) loipon,* "Finally"; cf. 1 Cor 15:58; Phil 4:1, following *hōste* ("So," "So that").

*rejoice.* Some would translate the imperative form here *(chairete)* as a greeting; thus, "farewell" *(RSV)* or "good-bye" (Barrett, 342), and it is true that the verb *chairein* may be used as a salutation (e.g., at the beginning of letters, Acts 15:23; 23:26; Jas 1:1). In favor of the tr. adopted here, see, among others, Hughes, 486, and Webber 1970: 184–86. To support this, one may note (a) that here the term stands as the first in a series of imperatives, and is most naturally given an imperative sense along with those that follow (Bultmann, 252); (b) that the same verb has just been used in v. 9 to mean "rejoice"; and (c)—perhaps decisively—that in 1 Thess 5:16, where the imperative form also heads a list of brief admonitions at the end of a letter, it can only mean "to rejoice" *(pantote chairete,* "Always rejoice"). A similar question of tr. occurs in Phil 3:1; 4:4, where some interpret the verb as "farewell" (e.g., Goodspeed 1945:174–75), and others as "rejoice" (e.g., Lohmeyer 1954:123, 167–68). For the theme of rejoicing in Paul's letters, see NOTES on 6:10.

*be restored.* If *katartizesthe* is middle voice, one could translate "Mend your ways" *(RSV, NEB)* or, with Barrett, 342, "Pull yourselves together." However, given the use of the cognate noun in v. 9, where Paul has indicated that he prays that God may restore the Corinthians to a firm faith, it is slightly preferable to treat the verb as a passive (thus

Chrysostom, *NPNF,* 1st ser. XII:418; Windisch, 426; Allo, 342). Less likely, "set one another right" (Héring, 101, 103).

*pay attention to my appeals.* This interprets *parakaleisthe* as passive voice (so also, e.g., *RSV;* Plummer, 380; Hughes, 487; Windisch, 426—tentatively), and as a reference to exhortation (note 10:1) rather than to "comfort" or "encouragement." The expression thus would seem to function like the appeal in Heb 13:22, cited by Windisch, ibid.: "Bear with my word of exhortation" *(RSV).* Another possibility is to take it as equivalent to *parakaleite allēlous* in 1 Thess 4:18; 5:5, "exhort one another" (thus, e.g., Bultmann, 252; Barrett, 342).

*be of one mind.* The expression *(to auto phronein)* is also found in Rom 12:16; 15:5; Phil 2:2; 4:2, and derives from political discourse (many examples from Aelius Aristides are assembled by van der Horst 1980:49–50).

*be at peace.* Cf. Rom 12:18, "Be at peace with all people," and 1 Thess 5:13, "Be at peace among yourselves" *(RSV);* also Mark 9:50, "Be at peace with one another" *(RSV).* Similar exhortations appear as closing formulas in some Aramaic letters (Fitzmyer 1974b:217).

*the God of love and of peace.* The phrase *the God of love* appears only here in the NT, and never in the LXX (or Hebrew Bible). On the other hand, Paul also refers to *the God of peace* in Rom 15:33; 16:20; Phil 4:9; 1 Thess 5:23; cf. 1 Cor 14:33. Jewish sources have yielded only one example of this predicate used of God, T Dan 5:2 ("But ye shall be in peace, having the God of peace" [*APOT*]), so it seems not to have been a fixed formula (Deichgräber 1967:94–95; Delling 1975:80). There are, however, frequent references to an "angel of peace" (1 Enoch 40:8–60:24; T Dan 6:2, 5; T Benj 6:1; T Asher 6:5–6; cited by Delling, ibid.:78). Cf. also 2 Thess 3:16; Heb 13:20.

*will be with you.* For the overall form of this blessing, in which the naming of the divine source is followed by the wish and then the identification of the recipient(s), see Mullins (1977:62, 63), who believes it bears the marks of the LXX and of the synagogue (ibid.:64). For the promise of God's presence, which is also the content of the blessing in Phil 4:9, see 1 Kgs 11:38; Amos 5:14; and LXX Isa 58:11 (cited by Delling, ibid.:80).

12a. *Greet one another.* The aorist tense *(aspasasthe)* is striking after the string of present-tense imperatives in v. 11 (noted in *GNTG* III:75 and by Moule 1953:21), but it is always used when Paul asks his readers to "greet" someone (Rom 16:3–16; 1 Cor 16:20; Phil 4:21; 1 Thess 5:16; cf. Col 4:15).

*a holy kiss.* In Rom 16:16a; 1 Cor 16:20b; 1 Thess 5:26 there are virtually identical instructions to *greet one another with a holy kiss* (but in 1 Thess 5:26, "all of the brothers [and sisters]" instead of "one another"). Cf. 1 Pet 5:14a, "Greet one another with a kiss of love [*agapēs*]." In Phil 4:21, where Paul closes a letter with the instruction to "greet every saint in Christ Jesus," there is no mention of a kiss. Stählin (*TDNT* IX:119–24) provides an excellent survey of the meaning and forms of kissing in the ancient world apart from the Bible. This was practiced first of all within the family and among relatives. There was also the kiss which betokened friendship (e.g., Ps.-Lucian, *The Ass* 17: "they greeted one another with kisses," cited by Conzelmann 1975:299 n. 23), the erotic kiss, and others which signified reception into a closed group (e.g., Apuleius, *Metamorphoses* VII, 9), reconciliation, respect, or subservience. Upon initiation into a Mystery cult, one kissed the mystagogue (ibid. XI, 25), and members of such groups were known as "those within the kiss" *(hoi entos tou philēmatos;* misunderstood as an erotic gesture by Lucian, *Alexander the False Prophet* 41 [Betz 1961:115 n. 1]).

A kiss could take many forms: it could be placed on the foot, the knee, the hand, the breast, the cheek, the forehead, the mouth (the erotic kiss, specifically); or it could be placed on some object (e.g., certain kinds of cultic kisses) or even "blown" with the hand. It may be that the *holy kiss* to which Paul refers was no more than a kiss of greeting bestowed upon another member of one's particular religious association (so Thraede, *RAC* VIII:508), but it is also possible (so, e.g., Stählin, *TDNT* IX:139–40; Goppelt 1978:354–55; Käsemann 1980:416) that the kiss had already become a feature of the Christian liturgy, associated perhaps with the eucharist (see especially 1 Cor 16:20, followed closely in v. 22 by the formulas "Anathema" and "Maranatha"). And —it may be noted in support of the latter—in the mid-second century Justin can attest that those gathered for the eucharist "salute one another with a kiss" following the prayers and immediately preceding the offertory of bread and wine (*Apology* I, 65). For this liturgical usage in the later church, see especially Hofmann 1938:94–144 and Stählin, *TDNT* IX:142–46. There seems to have been no precedent in the synagogue liturgy for this practice (Stählin, ibid.:125–28).

12*b*[13]. Many English versions (e.g., *KJV, ASV, RSV, NEB, NIV*) number this sentence v. 13, and the closing benediction v. 14; but others (e.g., *TEV* and all Roman Catholic trs. into English) retain the versification first introduced into the Greek and Latin texts by Robert Estienne (in 1551 and 1555, respectively), whereby this sentence is still part of v. 12. The re-numbering to obtain fourteen verses, which is peculiar to the English versional tradition, appears to have originated with the second folio edition of the so-called "Bishops' Bible," published in 1572, for the first edition of 1568 has the older division of 2 Cor 13 into thirteen verses.

*All the saints greet you.* As in Rom 16:16, the instruction to the readers to greet one another with a holy kiss (v. 12*a*) is followed by the communication of greetings to them from someone presently with Paul; in Rom 16, from "all the churches of Christ." See also 1 Cor 16:20, where the conveyance of greetings from "all the brothers and sisters" precedes the instruction about the holy kiss; and cf. 1 Pet 5:13, which precedes the reference to the "kiss of love" in v. 14. But then again, in Phil 4:21*b*–22, Paul conveys greetings from others only after he has instructed the Philippians to greet one another (v. 21*a*). Other third-person greetings occur in Rom 16:21, 23, and Phlm 23–24, leaving Gal and 1 Thess as the only certainly Pauline letters which do not have them. Mullins (1968:421) cites POxy 530 as an example of such greetings in a secular letter.

*the saints.* For the term in general, see NOTES on 1:1, where it is used of all the believers in the province of Achaia (around Corinth). In 8:4; 9:1, 12 it designates the Christians of Jerusalem. On the identity of *the saints* to whom reference is made in the present verse, see COMMENT.

13[14]. On the matter of verse division and numbering, see note on v. 12*b* above.

*The grace of the Lord Jesus Christ.* Note the benedictions in Rom 16:20*b;* 1 Cor 16:23; Gal 6:18; Phil 4:23; 1 Thess 5:28; Phlm 25. Similar blessings customarily open Paul's letters, as in 2 Cor 1:2 (on which see NOTES). Apart from 12:9, this is the only occurrence of the word *grace* in chaps. 10–13. In chaps. 1–9 see especially 8:9, where the readers are reminded of "the grace of our Lord Jesus Christ." In all these cases the genitive is certainly subjective, referring to the grace bestowed in Christ.

*the love of God.* As in Rom 5:5 and 8:39, the genitive *tou Theou* is subjective; God is the one who loves (e.g., Rom 5:8; 1 Thess 1:4). Cf. v. 11, *the God of love,* and 9:7, with note. Christ's love is spoken of in 5:14 (as in Rom 8:35, 37; Gal 2:20), and is to be closely identified with God's (e.g., Rom 5:8; 8:39). See also Rom 15:30, "the Spirit's love"; 1 Cor 16:24, "My love be with you all in Christ Jesus" *(RSV);* and 2 Thess 3:5.

*participation in the Holy Spirit.* To this phrase *(hē koinōnia tou Hagiou Pneumatos)* Phil 2:1 offers the closest parallel: "If there is any participation in the Spirit" *(koinōnia Pneumatos).* Some have argued that the genitive *tou Hagiou Pneumatos* (literally "of the Holy Spirit") should be interpreted as subjective, like the two preceding genitives referring to the source of a divine gift (so, e.g., Plummer, 383–84; Bruce, 255; Jourdan 1948:118; Spicq 1965:217); thus, "the fellowship given by the Holy Spirit." Others, however, interpret the genitive as objective, designating the Spirit as that which is shared by believers (so, e.g., Windisch, 428; Kümmel, 214; Barrett, 344; Hauck, *TDNT* III:807; George 1953:180–81); thus the tr. given here (and in *RSV* mg.). Decisive reasons for espousing the latter view are given by Seesemann 1933:62–72, who argues for the same meaning in Phil 2:1 (ibid.:56–62). In fact, even scholars who hold to the former position acknowledge that "the fellowship given by the Holy Spirit" would have to mean, also, a *participation in the Holy Spirit* (thus Schweizer, *TDNT* VI:434; McDermott 1975:223–24; B. Schneider 1976:422, 436–47). Cf. the remarks by Martin (1976:86–87) on Phil 2:1. Elsewhere in 2 Cor the word *koinōnia* and its cognate *koinōnos* are found only in chaps. 1–9 (1:7, "partners," on which see the note; 6:14, "partnership"; 8:4, "participation"; 8:23, "partner"; 9:13, "sharing"). The only other certain reference to God's Spirit in chaps. 10–13 is in 11:4 (but see 12:18, with NOTES); for the occurrences in chaps. 1–9, see NOTES on 1:22. The only other Pauline benediction which refers to God's Spirit is the one in Rom 15:33 ("that by the power of the Holy Spirit you may abound in hope" [*RSV*]).

*with all of you.* The benedictions which conclude Paul's other letters have either "with you" (Rom 16:20*b;* 1 Cor 16:23; 1 Thess 5:28) or "with your spirit" (Gal 6:18; Phil 4:23; Phlm 25).

## COMMENT: GENERAL

Paul devotes the last lines of his letter to (a) final, succinct admonitions (v. 11), (b) the matter of greetings (v. 12[–13]) and (c) a concluding benediction (v. 13[14]). If our canonical 2 Cor is indeed a composite of two or more originally separate letters to Corinth, as many hold (INTRODUCTION, pp. 35–41), one must ask to which of them these last verses most likely belonged. Bornkamm, who discerns parts of at least three different letters in 2 Cor, suggests that 13:11–13[14] is perhaps best taken with the so-called "conciliatory letter" which he finds in 1:1–2:13; 7:5–16 (perhaps including chap. 8), although he acknowledges the possibility that it may belong with the letter of chaps. 10–13 (1971:187; cf. Marxsen 1968:90; Bultmann, 252). Strachan, 145, who divides 2 Cor into two letters only, takes the verses as the conclusion to chaps. 1–9, because he believes the "tone" of this ending better fits that letter. However, Plummer, 379–80, and Windisch, 426, who divide 2 Cor in the same way, believe that vv. 11–13[14] are in their original place following chaps.

10–13. (Cf. Borse 1972:111; Barrett, 341. Windisch, however, thinks it conceivable that chap. 9 originally stood between 13:10 and 13:11 [ibid.].)

Two points may be mentioned in support of the view that 13:11–13[14] originally concluded the letter of chaps. 10–13. First, it is a priori probable that when two or more letters are combined into one the editor would retain the opening of the one placed first and the closing of the one placed last—unless there were some compelling reason to do otherwise. Second, there are several significant links between v. 11 and the letter of chaps. 10–13. (a) The admonition to *rejoice* may well echo "For we rejoice" in 13:9. As Paul rejoices in the prospect of his readers' being strengthened in their faith, so he would have them rejoice that his prayers are directed to that end. Just as there is no real difficulty in understanding how Paul can write "we rejoice" in 13:9, so there is no problem with taking the call to *rejoice* in 13:11 as part of the letter of chaps. 10–13. (b) The admonition to *be restored* seems clearly to echo the apostle's statement in 13:9 that he prays for the *restoration* of the Corinthians. (c) The admonition to *pay attention to my appeals* is in accord with Paul's stated intention in chaps. 10–13 to "appeal" to the Corinthians (10:1) in advance of his forthcoming visit (13:10).

## COMMENT: DETAILED

The brief, summary-like admonitions of v. 11*a* are an apt conclusion to the appeal being made in chaps. 10–13: that the Corinthians renew their commitment to the gospel and bring their behavior into conformity with the latter before Paul's arrival (see especially 10:1–6; 12:19–13:10). The succinct admonitions which stand near the close of Rom (12:9–13), 1 Cor (16:13–14), and 1 Thess (5:12–22) are comparable. The exhortation to *rejoice* follows on 13:9, where Paul has written of his own rejoicing in the anticipation that his prayers will be answered and that the Corinthians will become truly strong in their faith (cf. Phil 2:17–18, "I am glad and rejoice with you all. Likewise you also should be glad and rejoice with me" [*RSV*]). It is therefore a "rejoicing in the Lord" that he has in mind (Phil 3:1; 4:4), a rejoicing which is an integral part of the life of faith. It is not surprising that this appeal heads the list (as in 1 Thess 5:16). The remaining four admonitions also have special meaning in this context. Just as Paul's prayer is that God may "restore" the Corinthian congregation as a community of faith, so he now urges his readers to allow that to happen, to *be restored* (cf. the passive-voice imperative of Rom 12:2, to "be transformed"). The exhortation to *pay attention to my appeals* looks back especially to 10:1–6 and 12:19–13:10. And the two final admonitions in this series, *be of one mind* and *be at peace,* are fully appropriate in view of Paul's fear that he may find "discord, jealousy, explosive tempers," etc., when he gets to Corinth (12:20).

The admonitions of v. 11a are supported by the promise of v. 11b, which functions here exactly as the parallel promise of Phil 4:9b does after the appeals of Phil 4:8–9a (Deichgräber 1967:95). The point is not that God's presence will come as a reward for obedience (against Windisch, 426), but that God's presence will (a "logical" future) enable the Corinthians to be restored, etc. (Barrett, 343). Formally, this promise represents Paul's adaptation of the type of peace-blessing which stands near the close of 1 Thess (5:23) and Rom (15:33; 16:20; cf. Bultmann, 252; Wiles 1974:107 n. 2; Delling 1975:83). First, the usual connective, de (ho de Theos), has been replaced with kai ("and"), which ties the promise more effectively to the preceding admonitions (the same thing has happened in Phil 4:9b). Second, the usual reference to "the God of peace" is expanded into a reference to the God of love and of peace. This expansion serves to emphasize that aspect of God's presence which is most pertinent to and therefore most supportive of the preceding admonitions: as God's love and peace are with them, the Corinthians can be of one mind and at peace. Thus, the peace-blessing has been accommodated to this particular context (Delling 1975:80, 84; cf. Spicq 1965:215).

In v. 12a, as in Rom 16:16a; 1 Cor 16:20b; 1 Thess 5:26 (cf. 1 Pet 5:14a), Paul asks that his readers greet one another with a holy kiss. Whether the exchange of such a kiss among the congregants already had a stated place in the liturgy of Paul's churches must remain an open question (see NOTES). Even if it did, the presence of this instruction in a few of his surviving letters is not sufficient warrant for concluding that the apostle's letters were always read out in the service just before that liturgical act. Clearly, Paul is not simply giving a direction to proceed with the liturgy. Rather, by asking the members of his congregation to exchange this recognized Christian greeting he is asking them to affirm and demonstrate their existence as Christ's body. The "holiness" of the kiss inheres in its being the sign exchanged among "the saints" ( = "holy ones") who, as a people called to the service of God, constitute an eschatological congregation (cf. Käsemann 1980:415). It probably would not have been a kiss on the lips, since that kind of a kiss always had erotic connotations. Although by the latter part of the fourth century it was deemed prudent that male and female worshipers not exchange the kiss with one another (Apostolic Constitutions II.vii.57)—and that the clergy should kiss only the bishop (ibid. VIII.ii.11)—in Paul's churches the kiss seems to have been a fully communal and inclusive act.

It is characteristic that Paul either precedes or, as here, follows the instruction to his readers to greet one another with the transmittal of greetings on behalf of others (see NOTES). Thus, in v. 12b (for the numbering of this as v. 13 in some English versions, see NOTES) he conveys greetings from all the saints. Who are these saints? The reference is certainly more inclusive than is the case when, in other letters, the apostle conveys greetings from particular individuals (Rom 16:21; Phlm 23–24) or from his entourage (Phil 4:21b;

perhaps also 1 Cor 16:20). But it does not seem to be as inclusive as when, to the Romans, Paul conveys greetings from "all the churches of Christ" (16:16). Since this letter is probably being written from Macedonia (see INTRODUCTION, pp. 44–46), he could mean "all the Macedonian Christians"; or, more specifically, it could be a reference to "all the Christians" in the city from which the letter is being sent (more likely Beroea or Thessalonica than Philippi; see INTRODUCTION, p. 46).

No other Pauline letter concludes with a benediction so theologically imposing as the one in v. 13 (v. 14 in some English versions; see NOTES on v. 12b). The present benediction refers not only to Christ's *grace* (as in Rom 16:20b; 1 Cor 16:23; Gal 6:18; Phil 4:23; 1 Thess 5:28; Phlm 25; cf. 2 Thess 3:18; 1 Tim 6:21; 2 Tim 4:22b; Tit 3:15b), but also to God's *love* and to *participation in the Holy Spirit*. In the NT, only the benedictory form of Eph 5:23 is comparable. It is evident that the triadic benediction here in 2 Cor represents an expansion of the shorter form found elsewhere in Paul's letters, and it is at least conceivable that this expansion was effected not by the apostle himself but by the person(s) responsible for the final redaction of 2 Cor (or of the Pauline Corpus; so Goodspeed 1945:57; cf. Barrett 341, 343). There is, however, no reason why Paul himself could not have expanded his own more usual form, just as he expanded the peace-blessing in v. 11b.

Spicq (1965:216) calls this benediction "the most explicitly Trinitarian formula in the entire Pauline corpus," and believes that it "establishes clearly both the equality of the three Persons and their separateness" (cf. B. Schneider 1976:437, 438). However, the sequence *Christ . . . God . . . Holy Spirit* should in itself be a warning about too quickly reading the church's later Trinitarian theology into this benediction. Unlike the clearly Trinitarian baptismal formula of Matt 28:19, this benediction does not refer to Christ as "the Son" nor to God as "the Father." It neither presupposes nor teaches anything specific about the relationship of Christ, God, and the Holy Spirit. Rather, it focuses attention only on the *grace* and the *love* which characterize God's dealings with humanity, and on the believers' joint *participation in the Holy Spirit*. All three themes are at home in Paul's theology, and the three are always closely related. It is specifically through Christ that one is gifted with God's saving grace (e.g., Rom 5:1–2; cf. Gal 1:15–16; 2:12; 2 Cor 8:9). God's love, because it is decisively present to faith in Christ's death (Rom 5:8), can also be referred to as "Christ's love" (e.g., 2 Cor 5:14); and, because it is also known through the presence of the Spirit (Rom 5:5), it can even be called "the Spirit's love" (Rom 15:30). Moreover, just as Paul can characterize the life of faith as a *participation in the (Holy) Spirit* (here, and in Phil 2:1), he can also characterize it as a participation in Christ (1 Cor 1:9), especially in his sufferings (2 Cor 1:7; Phil 3:10).

One could cite many further examples of the great freedom and flexibility which characterize Paul's references to Christ, God, and the Holy Spirit. In one sentence he can refer to "the Spirit of God," and in the very next one to "the Spirit of Christ" (Rom 8:9). Is it Christ (so, e.g., Gal 2:20) or is it the Spirit (so, e.g., Rom 8:11) who "dwells" within believers? And though, at first glance, it may seem that different roles have been assigned to "the Spirit," "the Lord," and "God" in 1 Cor 12:4–6, a closer inspection will show that the distinction is simply for rhetorical effect. The triadic formulation of 2 Cor 13:13[14], however, is not merely rhetorical, even though it is also not "Trinitarian" in the more technical sense. Whether or not this benediction in its present form be attributed to Paul himself, it is a fully appropriate summation of the history of salvation as he understands it (e.g., in Gal 4:4–7, where Father, Son, and Spirit are in fact all mentioned; cf. Kümmel, 214). In and through Christ, God's love is present and active as a gracious redeeming, reconciling, and renewing gift (cf. 2 Cor 5:14, 17–19). As believers accept the rule of Christ's love, they are turned from self to him, and thus to one another (2 Cor 5:15), quickened by the life-giving Spirit (e.g., Rom 8:1–17; 2 Cor 3:3, 6) into a community of faith devoted to the service of God and of God's people (Gal 5:25–6:10).

# INDICES

# MODERN AUTHORS

# SUBJECT INDEX

Achaean League, 4, 6
Achaia, Achaians, 9, 10, 101, 106, 426, 431, 493
Achaicus, 27
Acrocorinth, 12, 19, 20, Plate II
Affliction. *See* Suffering
Alexandria Troas. *See* Troas
"Amen," 136, 147, 148
  *See also* Prayers
Anonymous brothers. *See* Brothers, unnamed
Aphrodite, 16, 17
Apollo, 15–16, 19
Apollos, 28, 100, 437, 524
Apostleship, 99, 102, 105, 106–7, 120–21, 130, 131–32, 142, 152–53, 185–337, 350, 352, 359, 462–63, 475–83, 506–9, 544, 546, 556, 564, 567, 578–79
  *See also* Ministers, ministry; Signs (of apostleship)
Aquila, 21, 24, 25–26
Aretas IV, King, 521–22, 541
Asclepius, 17, 20, 529, 530
Asia (Roman province), 113
Athena, 15–16, 17
Athens [Figure 3, p. 23] 106
Augustus, emperor, 16, 17–18, 171, 515, 536

Babbius. *See* Philenus
Baptism, 137, 148–49, 288, 297–99
Boasting, 124, 126–27, 131, 307, 308, 323–24, 466, 474, 477–78, 481, 482, 493, 496, 499, 511, 521, 523, 539–42, 543, 546–52, 554
  *See also* Foolishness; "Fool's Speech"; Weakness(es)
Boldness, 206–7, 229–33, 237–38, 245–52, 286, 288, 301
Brothers, unnamed, 422–23, 424–25, 434–38

Cenchreae (Kenchreai) [Figure 1, p. 5; Figure 3, p. 23] 8–9, 12, 13, 16, 19, 24, 57, 101, 106, Plate V
Chloe, 24, 28
Christ, death of, 119–20, 121, 189, 198, 229, 248, 255–56, 283–85, 287, 309, 310–11, 325–29, 331–32, 336, 417, 571, 576–77

gospel of, 169, 179, 187–90, 191–92, 219, 222, 235, 248–49, 250, 279–80, 445
Parousia of, 126–27, 129, 131, 157–58, 259, 264, 286–87, 292, 483, 499
resurrection of, 189, 256, 257, 283–85, 286, 311, 571, 576–77
sufferings of, 110, 112, 118–20
and Wisdom, 222
  *See also* Love, Christ's
Claudius, emperor, 10, 15, 19, 21, 25, 171
Collection for the saints. *See* Jerusalem, collection for
Comfort, 109–10, 111, 112, 117, 118, 120–21, 385
Comparison. *See* Synkrisis
Conscience, 127, 129, 219, 246–47
Corinth [Figure 1, p. 5; Figure 2, p. 11] Plates I–IV, IX
  church buildings in, 57
  church in, 22–28, 55–57, 106, 481
  Greek city, 4–6
  Roman colony of, 6–22
  *See also* Achaia; Isthmia; Isthmian Games
Corinthians, Second, date(s) of, 42, 46, 55
  editing of, 40–41, 43, 47, 585, 587
  external attestation of, 29–30, 40
  integrity of, 30–35
  place(s) of writing, 41, 46, 393–94, 473–74
  purpose(s) of, 41–43, 44–46, 459, 574, 580
  structure of, 43, 47, 455, 459
  style of, 43–44, 47–48
Crispus, 21, 24, 26

Damascus, 521–22, 540–42
Demeter and Kore, 17–18
Diaeus, 6
Dionysius of Corinth, 22, 56
"Divine man" theology, 243–44, 501

Endurance, 111, 121
Ephesus, Paul's imprisonment in (?), 42, 55, 113–15, 122–25, 292–93, 354, 394.
Erastus, 24, 25, Plate VIa

Faith, 139, 189, 272–73, 280–81, 283–88, 289–90, 326, 328, 577, 578
  *See also* Justification by faith; Love; Obedience

Paul, apostle, arrest and execution, 55
  conversion of, 250–51, 544
  in Corinth, 22–26, 41, 46, 52, 54–55, 564,
    567, 574
  as craftsman, 24, 25–26, 52, 264, 344, 355,
    461, 476, 506–7, 518, 536, 537
  illness of (?), 123, 478–79, 538, 547–50
  letters to Corinth, 26–29, 35–48, 54–55
  as speaker, 479, 490, 505
  sufferings of, 113–14, 117, 118, 122–25,
    247, 256, 278–88, 343–44, 354–59,
    514–23, 535–39, 544, 546, 550–51
  See also Apostleship; Ephesus, Paul's
    imprisonment in (?); Hardship lists;
    Jerusalem, collection for
Peristasenkataloge. See Hardship lists
Peter, apostle, 22
Philenus, Gnaeus Babbius, 10, 12
Philippi, city of, 393–94
Phoebe, 9, 24, 100, 106
Plural, first person (in 2 Cor), 32, 43–44, 47,
    103–4, 123, 141, 152, 172, 186, 238,
    304, 320, 325–26, 385, 390, 397, 404,
    422, 431, 434, 485, 489
Pompey, 20, 515, 536
Poseidon, 17, 18
Power. See God, power of
Prayers, 125, 452, 578
  See also "Amen"
Preaching, 285–88
  See also Apostleship
Prisca, 21, 24, 25–26
Priscilla. See Prisca

Quartus, 24

Reconciliation, 229, 316–20, 333–37, 350–53
  See also God, grace of; Love
Rejoicing. See Joy
Righteousness, 201, 204, 228, 340–41, 346,
    351–52, 356–57, 448–50, 482–83
  See also Justification by faith

Salvation, 111, 120, 177, 187, 198, 296–97,
    342, 353, 388, 418
  See also Reconciliation; Righteousness)
Sarapis, 19, 20, 529, Plate VII
Satan, 158, 163, 165, 247, 485–87, 494–95,
    500, 510, 529, 547
Signs (of apostleship), 51, 52, 54, 555–56
  See also Apostleship

Silas. See Silvanus
Silvanus, 22, 100, 135, 146, 437, 565, 578
Sin, 200–1, 228, 339–40, 351, 491, 562,
    567–68
Sophists, 14, 462, 490, 559
"Sorrowful visit," 41, 42, 52, 54–55, 140,
    143, 151, 152–53, 159–60, 167, 394, 396,
    564, 567, 575
  See also Offending brother; Paul, apostle,
    in Corinth
Sosthenes, 21, 43, 100, 102
Spirit, Holy, 137–38, 147–50, 182, 185, 189,
    195–96, 198–201, 204, 212–13, 227,
    235–37, 242, 286, 295–96, 297, 299, 345,
    355–56, 555, 577, 584, 587–88
Stephanus, 24, 27
Suffering, 110, 111, 112, 113, 117, 118, 121,
    285
  See also Christ, sufferings of; Hardship
    lists; Paul, sufferings of
"Super-apostles," 49, 489–90, 502–5, 554–55
  See also Opponents in 2 Cor
Synkrisis, 469–70, 476, 480, 534

"Tearful letter," 32, 33, 35, 36, 37–38, 39,
    41, 42, 44, 55, 144, 151, 154, 159–60,
    162, 167, 387, 394–97, 398
  See also Offending brother; Paul, letters to
    Corinth; "Sorrowful visit"
Tertius, 24
Theodosius, emperor, 13
Tiberius, emperor, 10, 13, 21
Timothy, 22–23, 27, 28, 34, 42, 43, 100,
    103–6, 112, 121, 143, 146, 396, 437,
    565, 578
Titius Justus, 24–25
Titus, 31, 36, 38, 41–42, 44, 45, 46, 100,
    144, 169–70, 172, 393–94, 397–98, 402,
    414–15, 433, 437, 559, 565–66
Transformation, 239–42, 245, 296–97, 332
Troas, 42, 46, 159, 168–69, 170, 171–72
Tyche. See Fortuna

Venus. See Aphrodite

Weakness(es), 124, 189, 247, 278–83, 479,
    498, 512, 521, 538, 539–40, 541–42, 544,
    546–47, 550–52, 571, 573, 577, 579–80
  See also Boasting; Paul, sufferings of;
    Suffering

# SCRIPTURAL AND OTHER PASSAGES

*Old Testament and Apocrypha

*References in the Notes have not been indexed.

## Old Testament Pseudepigrapha and Other Jewish Literature

*New Testament

*References in the Notes have not been indexed.

*Only references in the Introduction have been indexed.

## Other Christian Literature

## Greek and Latin Authors and Inscriptions

# KEY TO THE TEXT

## I. Letter D, Chapters 1–9

| Chapter | Verses | Section |
|---------|--------|---------|
| 1 | 1–2 | I A |
| 1 | 3–11 | I B |
| 1 | 12–14 | II A1 |
| 1 | 15–24 | II A2 |
| 2 | 1–2 | II A2 |
| 2 | 3–11 | II A3 |
| 2 | 12–13 | II A4 |
| 2 | 14–17 | II B5 |
| 3 | 1–6 | II B5 |
| 3 | 7–18 | II B6 |
| 4 | 1–6 | II B6 |
| 4 | 7–18 | II B7 |
| 5 | 1–10 | II B7 |
| 5 | 11–19 | II B8 |
| 5 | 20–21 | II C9 |
| 6 | 1–10 | II C9 |
| 6 | 11–18 | II C10 |
| 7 | 1–3 | II C10 |
| 7 | 4–16 | II C11a |
| 8 | 1–15 | II C11b |
| 8 | 16–24 | II C11c |
| 9 | 1–5 | II C11c |
| 9 | 6–15 | II C11d |

## II. Letter E, Chapters 10–13

| Chapter | Verses | Section |
|---------|--------|---------|
| 10 | 1–6 | I A1 |
| 10 | 7–18 | I A2 |
| 11 | 1–21a | I B3 |
| 11 | 21b–33 | I B4 |
| 12 | 1–10 | I B4 |
| 12 | 11–13 | I B5 |
| 12 | 14–21 | I C6 |
| 13 | 1–10 | I C7 |
| 13 | 11–13[14] | II |

69673

R
227.307

F989

c. 2

3 4711 00150 6098